THE CAMBRIDGE HISTORY OF JAPAN

General editors
JOHN W. HALL, MARIUS B. JANSEN, MADOKA KANAI, AND DENIS TWITCHETT

Volume 5
The Nineteenth Century

THE CAMBRIDGE HISTORY OF JAPAN

Volume 5
The Nineteenth Century

Edited by
MARIUS B. JANSEN

CAMBRIDGE UNIVERSITY PRESS
CAMBRIDGE
NEW YORK   NEW ROCHELLE   MELBOURNE   SYDNEY

Published by the Press Syndicate of the University of Cambridge
The Pitt Building, Trumpington Street, Cambridge CB2 1RP
32 East 57th Street, New York, NY 10022, USA
10 Stamford Road, Oakleigh, Melbourne 3166, Australia

© Cambridge University Press 1989

First published 1989

Printed in the United States of America

Library of Congress Cataloging-in-Publication Data
(Revised for volume 5)
The Cambridge history of Japan.
Includes index.
Contents: – v. 5. The nineteenth century /
edited by Marius B. Jansen – v. 6. The twentieth
century / edited by Peter Duus.
1. Japan – History. I. Hall, John Whitney, 1916–
DS835.C36   1989   952   88-2877
ISBN 0 521 22356 3 (V. 5)

British Library Cataloguing in Publication Data
The Cambridge history of Japan.
Vol. 5 : The nineteenth century
1. Japan to 1912
I. Jansen, Marius B. (Marius Berthus)
952

ISBN 0 521 22356 3

GENERAL EDITORS' PREFACE

Since the beginning of this century the Cambridge histories have set a pattern in the English-reading world for multivolume series containing chapters written by specialists under the guidance of volume editors. Plans for a Cambridge history of Japan were begun in the 1970s and completed in 1978. The task was not to be easy. The details of Japanese history are not matters of common knowledge among Western historians. The cultural mode of Japan differs greatly from that of the West, and above all there are the daunting problems of terminology and language. In compensation, however, foreign scholars have been assisted by the remarkable achievements of Japanese scholars during the last century in recasting their history in modern conceptual and methodological terms.

History has played a major role in Japanese culture and thought, and the Japanese record is long and full. Japan's rulers from ancient times have found legitimacy in tradition, both mythic and historic, and Japan's thinkers have probed for a national morality and system of values in their country's past. The importance of history was also emphasized in the continental cultural influences that entered Japan from early times. Its expression changed as the Japanese consciousness turned to concerns over questions of dynastic origin, as it came to reflect Buddhist views of time and reality, and as it sought justification for rule by the samurai estate. By the eighteenth century the successive need to explain the divinity of government, justify the ruler's place through his virtue and compassion, and interpret the flux of political change had resulted in the fashioning of a highly subjective fusion of Shinto, Buddhist, and Confucian norms.

In the nineteenth century, the Japanese became familiar with Western forms of historical expression and felt the need to fit their national history into patterns of a larger world history. As the modern Japanese state took its place among other nations, Japanese history faced the task of reconciling a parochial past with a more catholic present. Historians familiarized themselves with European accounts of the course of civilization and described Japan's nineteenth-century turn from military to civilian bureaucratic rule under monarchical guidance as part of a larger, worldwide pattern. Buckle, Guizot, Spencer, and then Marx successively provided interpretative schema.

The twentieth-century ideology of the imperial nation-state, however, operated to inhibit full play of universalism in historical interpretation. The growth and ideology of the imperial realm required caution on the part of historians, particularly with reference to Japanese origins.

Japan's defeat in World War II brought release from these inhibitions and for a time replaced them with compulsive denunciation of the pretensions of the imperial state. Soon the expansion of higher education brought changes in the size and variety of the Japanese scholarly world. Historical inquiry was now free to range widely. A new opening to the West brought lively interest in historical expressions in the West, and a historical profession that had become cautiously and expertly positivist began to rethink its material in terms of larger patterns.

At just this juncture the serious study of Japanese history began in the West. Before World War II the only distinguished general survey of Japanese history in English was G. B. Sansom's *Japan: A Short Cultural History*, first published in 1931 and still in print. English and American students of Japan, many trained in wartime language programs, were soon able to travel to Japan for study and participation with Japanese scholars in cooperative projects. International conferences and symposia produced volumes of essays that served as benchmarks of intellectual focus and technical advance. Within Japan itself an outpouring of historical scholarship, popular publishing, and historical romance heightened the historical consciousness of a nation aware of the dramatic changes to which it was witness.

In 1978, plans were adopted to produce this series on Japanese history as a way of taking stock of what has been learned. The present generation of Western historians can draw on the solid foundations of the modern Japanese historical profession. The decision to limit the enterprise to six volumes meant that topics such as the history of art and literature, aspects of economics and technology and science, and the riches of local history would have to be left out. They too have been the beneficiaries of vigorous study and publication in Japan and in the Western world.

Multivolume series have appeared many times in Japanese since the beginning of the century, but until the 1960s the number of professionally trained historians of Japan in the Western world was too small to sustain such an enterprise. Although that number has grown, the general editors have thought it best to draw on Japanese specialists for contributions in areas where they retain a clear authority. In such cases the act of translation itself involves a form of editorial cooperation that requires the skills of a trained historian whose name deserves acknowledgment.

The primary objective of the present series is to put before the English-reading audience as complete a record of Japanese history as possible. But the Japanese case attracts our attention for other reasons as well. To some it has seemed that the more we have come to know about Japan, the more we are drawn to the apparent similarities with Western history. The long continuous course of Japan's historical record has tempted historians to look for resemblances between its patterns of political and social organization and those of the West. The rapid emergence of Japan's modern nation-state has occupied the attention of comparative historians, both Japanese and Western. On the other hand, specialists are inclined to point out the dangers of being misled by seeming parallels.

The striking advances in our knowledge of Japan's past will continue and accelerate. Western historians of this great and complex subject will continue to grapple with it, and they must as Japan's world role becomes more prominent. The need for greater and deeper understanding of Japan will continue to be evident. Japanese history belongs to the world, not only as a right and necessity but also as a subject of compelling interest.

JOHN W. HALL
MARIUS B. JANSEN
MADOKA KANAI
DENIS TWITCHETT

CONTENTS

General editors' preface	page v
Preface to Volume 5	xiii
Map	xiv

Introduction   1
by MARIUS B. JANSEN, *Princeton University*

    An end, a beginning, and a transition   7
    The stages of transition   12
    Historians and nineteenth-century Japan   34

1   Japan in the early nineteenth century   50
by MARIUS B. JANSEN

    Shogun and regent   51
    The Kansei reforms   52
    Towns, travel, and urban culture   62
    The countryside: growth, surplus, and the problem of control   71
    The image of the Western world   87
    Probings toward synthesis   111

2   The Tempō crisis   116
by HAROLD BOLITHO, *Harvard University*

    The Tempō famine   117
    Civil disorder   120
    The foreign threat   124
    Critics and criticism   126
    Domain reforms   133
    Bakufu reforms   139
    Mizuno Tadakuni   155

	The aftermath	158
	The implications	164
3	Late Tokugawa culture and thought by H. D. HAROOTUNIAN, *University of Chicago*	168
	The culture of play	168
	The play of culture	178
	Good doctrine and governance	182
	The restoration of worship and work	198
	Religions of relief	215
	Defense and wealth	231
	Cultural practice and the triumph of political centralization	252
4	The foreign threat and the opening of the ports by W. G. BEASLEY, *University of London*	259
	The challenge to national isolation	261
	The commercial treaties of 1857–1858	271
	Problems of implementation	284
	Settlement	297
	Trade relations under the treaty port system	304
5	The Meiji Restoration by MARIUS B. JANSEN	308
	Troubles within, disaster from without	308
	The Harris treaty and its aftermath	314
	The loyalists	320
	Court and camp, daimyo style	325
	The treaty ports and foreign influence	335
	Bakufu rally	342
	Regional reform	345
	Restoration	353
	The Restoration in history and historiography	360
6	Opposition movements in early Meiji, 1868–1885 by STEPHEN VLASTOS, *University of Iowa*	367
	Early rural protests	368
	The Meiji land tax and village protests	372

	Shizoku revolts	382
	The popular rights movement	402
	Conclusion	426
7	Japan's turn to the West by HIRAKAWA SUKEHIRO, *University of Tokyo* Translated by BOB TADASHI WAKABAYASHI	432
	The medium of books: first awareness of modern Western civilization	435
	From books to experience: late Tokugawa and early Meiji travelers	448
	Teachers of "arts and sciences": foreigners in Meiji government employ	466
	The Japanization of Western thought and institutions	472
	The spirit of capitalism: first translations from Western literature	477
	The return to Japan: a consciousness of self in Meiji youth	487
8	Social change by GILBERT ROZMAN, *Princeton University*	499
	Assumptions reexamined	501
	Social stratification	505
	Urban transformation	533
	Household decisions	548
	Conclusions and comparisons	562
9	Economic change in the nineteenth century by E. SYDNEY CRAWCOUR, *Australian National University*	569
	The economy at the beginning of the nineteenth century	571
	The Tempō reforms	587
	The opening of foreign trade	600
	The Meiji Restoration: continuity and change	605
	Economic development, 1868–1885	610
	The transition and its nature	614

10	Meiji political institutions by W. G. BEASLEY	618
	Initial decisions	620
	The abolition of the domains	628
	Central and local government	641
	The Meiji constitution	651
	Political society after 1890	665
11	Meiji conservatism by KENNETH B. PYLE, *University of Washington*	674
	The challenge of the Japanese enlightenment	676
	Early Meiji conservatives: the moral imperative	679
	Conservatives and the problem of foreign relations	688
	The emergence of bureaucratic conservatism	696
	The conservative approach to industrial society	704
	The social program of the conservatives	710
	The legacy of Meiji conservatism	716
12	Japan's drive to great-power status by AKIRA IRIYE, *University of Chicago*	721
	The foreign policy of a modern state	721
	The Meiji polity and society	728
	Consolidation of domestic and foreign affairs, 1868–1880	733
	Domestic politics and overseas expansion, 1880–1895	747
	Imperialism and militarism, 1895–1912	765
	Works cited	783
	Glossary-index	813

PREFACE TO VOLUME 5

Japanese is romanized according to the Hepburn system, and Chinese names according to the Wade–Giles system. Japanese and Chinese personal names follow their native form, with surname preceding given name, except in citations of Japanese authors writing in English. Where alternative readings of personal names exist, they are given in both forms in the Glossary-Index, as are technical terms. References cited in the footnotes are listed in alphabetical order by author in the list of Works Cited at the end of the volume. As to dates, Japanese and Western years do not exactly coincide before 1872, when Japan adopted the Western calendar. Years prior to that date are normally given in the Japanese lunar days and months, together with the Western year most closely coinciding with the Japanese (e.g., fourth month, 1848). Where day and month have been converted to the Western date they are given in that form (e.g., April 6, 1868).

We wish to thank the Japan Foundation for grants that covered costs of manuscript fees, translation of chapters by Japanese contributors, and editorial expenses and meetings. During the years that this volume has been in preparation, a number of young scholars have been of assistance in the editorial process by helping to put the manuscript on the word processor, standardizing usage, and assembling the bibliography and the Glossary-Index. Bob Tadashi Wakabayashi's editorial help was particularly important. Luke Roberts and Lee Butler assembled the list of Works Cited and David Howell and Thomas Schalow compiled the Glossary-Index. To them, to Scott Miller and Constantine Vaporis, and especially to the contributors, go my thanks for their patience and forbearance.

MARIUS B. JANSEN

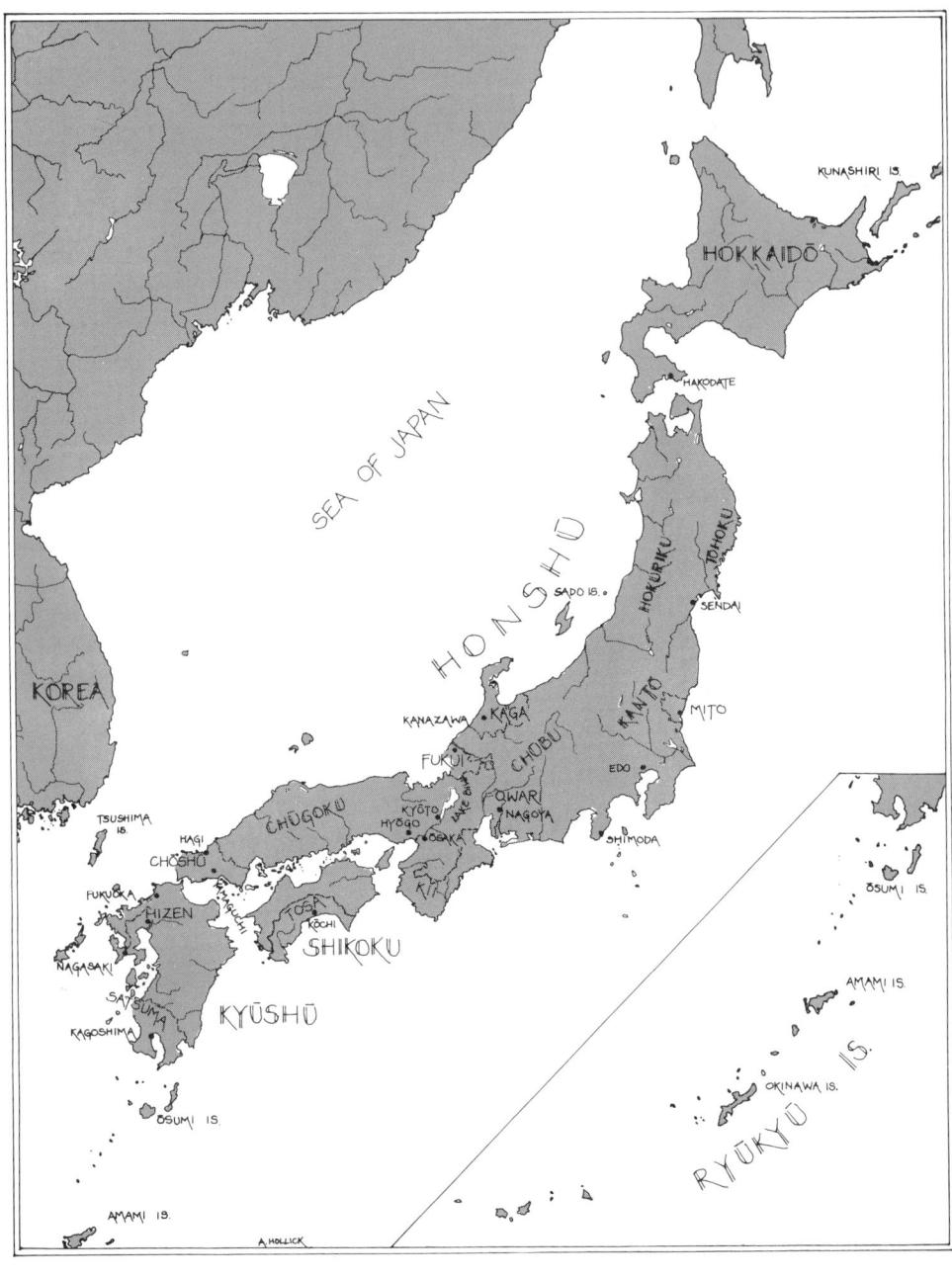

INTRODUCTION

This volume deals with nineteenth-century Japan. The century is usually broken in its third quarter by historians who treat the Meiji Restoration as a watershed in Japanese history, but we shall treat it as a whole. The Restoration surely marked an important divide in Japanese social history, but it is impossible to analyze its elements without a perspective of what preceded and what followed it.

The nineteenth century saw Japan transformed from a society that was divided territorially, politically, socially, and internationally. Japan's borders were still unclear, for its sovereignty over Okinawa, the Kurils, and Hokkaido was not established. Politically, Japan was still structured in the territorial divisions that had been worked out in the early seventeenth century. The Tokugawa shogun held dominion over lands that produced about one-quarter of the national agricultural yield of rice, which was the sole measure of productivity, but although he retained about half of that for his own house as *tenryō*, the rest he allocated to his vassals. The balance of the country was divided among some 260 feudal lords, who in turn allocated part of their holdings to their retainers. The domains were substantially autonomous in internal administration; each had its own army, its own administrative system, and its own capital city, which had grown, in the larger domains, around the daimyo's castle. The lords and their domains were not taxed by the shogun, who, as primus inter pares, was restricted to the revenue of his own holdings.

The daimyo were, however, expected to perform acts of fealty to their overlord, and in the absence of warfare, that service had become ritualized in the procedures of alternate attendance whereby they spent half their time in residence at the shogunal capital of Edo. In that city, large estates, usually three each, were set aside for the lords, and these they built up as residences and garrisons for their retainers during their duty stay. The lords' families, and their principal retainers' families, were expected to remain in Edo as hostages during the daimyo's sojourn at home. The lords thus contributed to the shogun's wealth through their expenditures during their stays in his territory, and they were substantially autonomous at home and even enjoyed a sort of extraterritoriality during their residence in Edo. But the fact that their families remained there meant that after the first generation, the ruling elite was born and brought up in Edo, knew its own lands only after acceding to rule, and oriented itself more to the luxury and ritual of the capital than to the problems and realities of its territories. The daimyo, in turn, expected their own retainers to reside in the domain castle towns, in most cases permanently. As a result the ruling military estate had become a circulating and highly urbanized status group. The polity was premised on a disarmed and compliant countryside, one that had been restrained by the legislative measures of the late sixteenth century when Hideyoshi and his peers separated the warriors from the agriculturists, disarmed the countryside, and carried out cadastral registers to provide a sure base for future consideration of rural governance and productivity.

Japan was no less divided socially. The four status groups of samurai, agriculturalist, artisan, and merchant that had been established in the early seventeenth century continued to maintain distinct patterns of status, shown in clothing, appearance, manner and behavior, and residence despite considerable changes in relative well-being that developed during the Tokugawa centuries. The samurai, in particular, whose fiefs had for the most part given way to stipends paid from their lord's granaries as rationalized administration replaced the extremes of early territorial fragmentation, existed on fixed incomes during periods of economic growth and changing standards in which their lords' needs for additional revenue found those stipends inviting targets of retrenchment. Lords and vassals alike were constantly in debt to the merchant brokers who changed their rice income into spendable coinage through the mechanisms of the commodity markets that had developed. Years of peace had dulled the samurai's martial proclivities, and years of service had changed the warriors from an unlettered and unruly fighting force to educated bureaucrats who competed eagerly for the positions available to them. The samurai had become an underemployed and unproductive elite. Despite this and the accelerated movement in and out of lower ranks and even sale of status membership, the perquisites of samurai standing in 1800 remained substantially what they had been two centuries earlier.

In 1800 most Japanese were agriculturalists living in the seventy-thousand-odd villages that bound isolated hamlets into administrative units. The Tokugawa authorities desired a countryside populated by hardworking peasants responsive to the directives of their own elite, the landowning farmers with membership rights to water and representation in village assemblies that ruled on matters of common interest. The village was taxed as a unit, and that burden was allocated by the same landed families under the leadership of an appointed or elected headman. Village families were arranged in groups of five for purposes of surveillance and mutual responsibility. Heavily burdened by a tax that initially averaged 50 percent of its product, the village was still fairly autonomous, thanks to the absence of the samurai administrators who lived in the castle towns and dealt only with the village head. Reclamation of new fields, agricultural improvement, and underreporting combined to make the countryside more prosperous and less responsive to the expectations of those who taxed it. By 1800 the presumed uniformity of status for peasants had given way to a far more varied scene in which managerial farmers were profiting from commercial agriculture that grew in areas able to ship to the great metropolitan centers of Osaka and Edo. The spread of literacy among the village leaders made for a lively trade in and distribution of agricultural texts as well as other products of urban printing establishments throughout the countryside. More and more a single culture was informing all status groups throughout Japan, even though the status divisions of the past continued to divide the population. Economic change had created change in social realities, but not yet in formal social relations.

In the early nineteenth century, Japan's isolation from the outside world also continued the patterns that had been instituted in the 1630s. State-to-state relations existed only with Korea, which sent twelve embassies to Japan in Tokugawa times, and yet even those relations were attenuated and camouflaged by being implemented through the daimyo of Tsushima, who maintained a trading station at Pusan under circumstances of inequality and some indignity. At Nagasaki a trading station maintained by the Dutch East India Company until its abolition in 1799 was continued by the Java colonial administration, which sent ships from Batavia and agents who lived under strict surveillance on the manmade islet of Deshima. A Chinese station was also maintained at Nagasaki for private traders who brought goods for sale to authorized guild representatives. The southern domain of Satsuma also had access to Chinese goods through its control of the Okinawan kingdom. Yet over the years the exhaustion of Japan's silver and copper mines combined with the development of Japanese handicrafts, which substituted for the Chinese silk and embroidered textiles that had been the heart of the trade, to reduce the number of Chinese and of Dutch vessels to a trickle; the trade had become more ritual than real.

At the end of the nineteenth century, where this volume ends, Japan was a highly centralized state whose government had little tolerance for local variety and divergence. A powerful Home Ministry appointed governors and mayors. A national police system had replaced the myriad forms of local control with a network of police stations and boxes that were the marvel of Japan's neighbors. The Education Ministry prescribed texts for a school system whose uniformity was such that pupils all over the country could be expected to be going over the same lessons out of the same textbooks at the same time. Precise distinctions of class and status had given way to a homogenized nation of commoners. The substatus groups of feudal times had been assimilated by law but continued to suffer from discrimination; the highest of the old elite had been declared a new aristocracy so as to provide a conservative counterweight to possible radicalism in the newly established Imperial Diet. The nation was being schooled in gratitude and veneration for a uniformed sovereign whose picture was beginning to appear on the walls of even the humblest homes.

On every hand the variety of local precedent and personal government had given way to firmly established codes of law for commercial, civil, and criminal procedures. Feudal variety in landholding obligations had given way to individual ownership with firm legal rights and equally firm tax obligations. The samurai class had been disestablished and pensioned off, its military functions assumed by a conscripted army of commoners and its administrative role transferred to a meritocracy trained in the imperial university. The imperial court, which had survived the Tokugawa years on the fringe of public notice with attenuated ceremonies and posts, had been "restored" to rule. Press, school, armed services, and police competed in affirmations of loyalty and fealty to the sovereign. The last Tokugawa shogun had so far outlived his displacement and disgrace that his house ranked with the few in the new aristocracy that were qualified to provide imperial consorts, and his successor presided over the deliberations of the House of Peers. Japan was no longer feudal, decentralized, and status bound, but unified, homogenized, and capitalist. A century that encompassed such changes needs to be treated as a whole for historical analysis.

By the end of the nineteenth century Japan's relations with the outside world had changed no less profoundly. The tenuous relations with outside powers and the shadowy outlines of Japanese sovereignty were replaced by firmly differentiated ties and boundaries. To the south, the Ryūkyū chain had been incorporated as a prefecture. To the north, an exchange of disputed territories with Russia had resulted in full Japanese sovereignty over the Kurils. More important, the island of Hokkaido had been fully occupied and its development begun. Relations with China were formalized, and in 1894–5 Japan bested its larger neighbor in a contest centered on the future control of Korea. The treaties that had been worked out with the Western powers in the 1860s, with their humiliating provisions for limitations on tariff autonomy, extraterritoriality, and most-favored-nation clause, were revised in 1894 after a quarter-century of effort. Japan's electrifying victory over China brought with it possession of Taiwan and full membership in the imperialist club, with opportunities for further exploitation of China and further competition with Russia for Korea and Manchuria.

Thus the Japan of 1900 was no longer the Japan of 1800. The secluded island nation of the past had become an active and aggressive participant in world politics, proud of its achievement and insistent upon its place, ready to enter the European alliance system, and eager for a foothold on the Asian continent.

Yet it would be foolish to claim particular significance for the century mark and to claim too much for the years at the century's beginning and close. In some ways, better arguments are at hand for a periodization beginning in 1790 and ending in 1890: 1790 brought the Kansei reforms directed by the bakufu official Matsudaira Sadanobu. Those reforms stand as the last major effort to shore up the Tokugawa order after the relaxation of its policies under the administration of Tanuma Okitsugu. As had been the case under Sadanobu's ancestor, Yoshimune, who led the Kyōhō reforms in the 1720s, a determined effort was made to return to the martial simplicity of earlier times. In fact, however, the measures that Sadanobu introduced served to illustrate how far commercialization had proceeded since the first quarter of the century. Bakufu steps were designed to bolster the economy of the Kantō plain and liberate it from the dominance of Osaka merchant capital. Edicts were issued to provide for the urban poor and needy debtors, and stringent measures were introduced to control economic activity in the great eastern metropolis of Edo. More striking still was the attention paid to warrior education and training to prepare government officials for the new complexity of bureaucratic life. Ideological orthodoxy in Confucian teachings was decreed for the bakufu acaemy, a step that was quickly followed by the administrators of domain schools. Sadanobu also showed an awareness of the rising importance of Western studies and began the steps toward official patronage that led to the creation of a center of Western studies soon after the coming of Commodore Matthew Perry in the 1850s. In the aftermath of Sadanobu's measures, the bakufu insisted for the first time that its forthright refusal to deal with foreign countries was the legacy of the original Tokugawa founders. A new rigidity in such matters, emphasized by the punishment meted out to scholars of Western learning who presumed to publish their views on the possible dangers that Japan faced, and the insistent and archaic moral absolutism of government pronouncements all combined to make the Kansei reforms of 1790 the true beginning of the nineteenth century in Japan. The same was true in international affairs: Japanese responses to Russian probings in the north signaled a new awareness of the need to prepare for a possible military confrontation.

By 1890, a century later, the Meiji institutional structure had been completed by the implementation of the Meiji constitution and the formulation of the Imperial Rescript on Education. Once again the government defined what was expected and moral while insisting that what it was doing was fully in touch with Japanese tradition. Civic morality was a public duty and not a private matter. The Imperial Oath made in the palace upon the promulgation of the constitution explained that document as "merely a reiteration in Our own day of the grand precepts of government that have been handed down by the Imperial Founder of Our House and by Our other Imperial Ancestors to their descendants." In much the same way, Matsudaira Sadanobu had argued that his measures conformed with the will of the founder of the bakufu (shogunate).

Between these confident assertions of orthodoxy and continuity lay an interval of openness and questioning. For this, too, it had been possible to find justification in Japan's past. The "turn to the West," as Professor Hirakawa terms the Charter Oath's promise of 1868 to seek "wisdom throughout the world," could cite as precedent the turn to the Chinese continent for political and cultural institutions a millennium before. The willingness of the bakufu minister Abe Masahiro to seek daimyo counsel when confronted by Commodore Perry's demands for treaty relations in 1853 reflected consensual patterns of decision making, a tradition that was echoed in the same Charter Oath's affirmation that deliberative councils would be "broadly convened." That promise led to two decades of intense discussion about the way "people's rights" (*minken*) might best be institutionalized. By the century's end, however, Japan's leadership was largely satisfied that proper "wisdom" and institutions had been found and had decided that councils should be used to assist, and not to lead, imperial rule.

Of course, 1890 did not bring an end to change, for implementation of the new institutions required continuous adaptation and experimentation. During the decade of 1890 to 1900 the leaders of the "People's Rights" movement were co-opted, step by step, into the governing system and gradually incorporated into the cabinet structure. At the century's end, Itō Hirobumi, the principal architect of the new institutions, found it desirable to form his own political party, in order, as he put it, to free himself from mercenaries by mobilizing his own army.

The consolidation of parliamentary government made it possible to concentrate on international equality and to develop new and larger goals abroad. In 1894 the revision of the unequal treaties after a quarter-century of effort brought diplomatic equality and dignity and provided the prospect of tariff autonomy for 1911. Japan's success in the Sino-Japanese War of 1894–5 brought a seat at the imperialist banquet table in China, and the acquisition of Taiwan and the indemnity that accompanied it made for rapid strides in heavy industry with the establishment of the iron–steel complex of Yawata. Further steps pointed toward the domination of Korea. That final decade of the century and the first decade of the twentieth century loom large in Professor Iriye's discussion of Japan's rise to great-power status with which this volume ends. The same years signaled the beginning of large-scale industrial developments and social discontents, described in Volume 6, problems that preoccupied bureaucratic leaders in the twentieth century. A lowering of the tax qualification for electoral franchise in 1900 represented a first effort to co-opt and guide the bourgeoisie and the labor movement, and brought Japan into the twentieth century.

AN END, A BEGINNING, AND A TRANSITION

A beginning is also an ending. The changes in early modern Europe that Jakob Burckhardt interpreted as heralding the Renaissance had more meaning for Johan Huizinga as the waning of the Middle Ages, and in the same way the closing decades of Tokugawa rule can as well be seen as a waning of military governance, or *bakumatsu*, as they can as a prelude to the modern state. The Tokugawa system was clearly spiraling downward. Matsudaira Sadanobu's efforts to shore up the polity in the Kansei reforms enjoyed some success, particularly where education and the economy and administration of the Kantō were concerned, but the same cannot be said for the reform attempt under Mizuno Tadakuni, the subject of Professor Bolitho's discussion of the Tempō (1830–1844) period in Chapter 2. Mizuno's attempt to rationalize and concentrate landholdings around the major metropolitan centers succeeded only in alienating lords whose fiefs would be affected and brought him quick dismissal from office. His efforts to attack urban poverty by ordering recent migrants to return to their villages, and his legislation against displays of luxury brought such unpopularity that Edo townsmen stoned his residence in a show of contempt. Ideology-motivated revivalism, in the 1837 revolt of Ōshio Heihachirō, succeeded only in burning a large part of Osaka and increasing the distress that Ōshio was trying to alleviate.

The late Tempō years were in fact notable for evidence of waning effectiveness on the part of Japan's rulers. Famine stalked the land. Bureaucratic jealousy combined with ideological rigidity to bring about a purge of scholars concerned with Western studies. In 1844, a year after Tempō came to an end, the Dutch king wrote to warn the shogun of the West's growing power and Japan's inability to withstand the new currents. The bakufu explained its inability to respond by the fact that there were no precedents for such communications. On the contrary: Policies adopted in 1825 had specified that foreign ships be turned back without hesitation, no matter what their purpose. These, and other rigidities described in Professor Beasley's discussion of the coming of the West in Chapter 4, suggest that the Tokugawa system was indeed coming to the end of its resources and unlikely to respond with imagination or effectiveness to future challenges.

A reflective article by Hayashiya Tatsusaburō draws some interesting comparisons between the Tokugawa bakumatsu and those of the earlier Kamakura and Ashikaga shogunates. Both of the earlier bakufu, Hayashiya points out, lost control over their vassals after they were unable to deliver rewards and impose sanctions. Both declines were accompanied by succession disputes, and both took place in the presence of growing entanglement in foreign trade. In each case a growing impatience with the invocation of stern standards ascribed to the founders' wisdom indicated changing social values and a preoccupation with new, untraditional, and antiestablishment sentiments.[1]

---

[1] Hayashiya Tatsusaburō, ed., "Bakumatsuki no bunka shihyō," in *Bakumatsu bunka no kenkyū* (Tokyo: Iwanami shoten, 1978), pp 3–39. See also Professor Harootunian's reference in Chapter 3.

In the Kamakura case the intensity of the effort to ward off the Mongol invasions of 1274 and 1281 was followed by a long period of mobilization in the expectation of a possible third invasion, without any increase of territory with which to reward bakufu vassals. Before that, the increase of trade with Sung China had accompanied a commercialization that made difficult for the bakufu the interruption of the China trade after the Mongol conquest of the mainland. The Hōjō regency in Kamakura found itself isolated. Rising discontent was accompanied by changing social values within the elite, a trend symbolized by the vogue for a new ostentation and unstructured unconventionality. *Basara,* the contemporary term coined for this aberration, was warned against in the Jōei formulary with which the bakufu tried to restrain its vassals, but in vain.

In late Muromachi times the Ashikaga bakufu was even more obviously involved with continental trade, commercialization, and, at the last, arms brought by Westerners. Yoshimitsu's acceptance of a title as vassal of the Ming emperor, and his successors' efforts to attract larger supplies of Ming coinage, set the stage for disorderly competition by his vassals for those goods in the operation of the "tally trade" with the continent. At its last the Muromachi bakufu was further buffeted by the trade and technology that arrived on Western ships. This time the term for the irregular and unconventional that symbolized the cultural shift was *kabuki,* a term redolent of emotion and hedonism that became enshrined in the stage genre of the age that followed. The Ashikaga inability to control their vassals, and the accompanying popular disorders of those *bakumatsu* times, led directly into the violence of the sixteenth century.

The Tokugawa parallels to these phenomena are evident. Commercialization and social change had grown throughout the Tokugawa period, not, to be sure, as a result of increasing contract with the continent, but through internal economic growth and change. But the opening of the ports for the West in 1859 brought a flood of foreign goods and coinage as well as a large new market for Japanese tea and silk. Discrepancies in the relative values of gold to silver between Japan and the outside world resulted in a currency flow that quickly drained Japan of precious metal. The trade produced a wild inflation that sent prices skyrocketing out of the reach of samurai on fixed incomes and denied domestic craftsmen access to materials essential to them. Bakufu efforts to monopolize the profits from the trade drew sharp opposition from powerful vassals who were able to draw on foreign protests and speeded the erosion of confidence and control.

The Edo bakufu was even more sensitive to the alarm created by the Western victories in China. Instability on the continent brought a quick response from an elite fully informed about those matters. To some it seemed that Japan's security had in fact depended on a stable China. Transfer of the treaty port system to Japan, with foreign missions and foreign troops on Japanese soil, became a standing reproach to the pretensions of the "barbarian-subduing generalissimo."

This in turn was accompanied by a fascination with the new and with what had been irregular and unconventional. In late Tokugawa times, violations of the accepted code became expected of activists, who proliferated in the new political atmosphere. The growing importance of an underworld of gamblers and adventurers provided a context in which the politically motivated could operate. Theater and literature were fascinated by evil and the grotesque. All this served to help and hide "grass-roots" (*sōmō*) idealists who fled their normal obligations to family, group, and lord to taste the heady wine of political involvement. Glorification of the "chivalrous adventurer" (*kyōkaku*) represented praise for what had been illegal and deplorable in more structured times, and the tradition survived to be claimed by China adventurers and right-wing extremists later in the Meiji period.

Yet surely the power and self-confidence of the modern West made the Tokugawa *bakumatsu* more extreme than earlier periods. Thinkers moved beyond the bakufu to consider new forms of political organization. As early as the 1860s, loyalist activists like Kusaka Genzui of Chōshū and Takechi Zuizan of Tosa were proposing court-centered polities with institutions drawn from the classical past of Nara–Heian times. The activists who beheaded the statues of Ashikaga shoguns in Kyoto were the predecessors of others who would rewrite all of earlier Japanese history to decry the substitution of military for imperial rule.

In a larger sense however, the nineteenth century is more customarily treated as a beginning, and the Restoration years are best described as a transition between late-feudal and modern Japan. The transition from warrior to civil rule, albeit one directed by former members of the warrior estate, is particularly noteworthy and calls to mind Hayashiya's comparison with the transition from civil to warrior rule centuries earlier. It is equally possible to compare the process with the transition from the Yamato state to the *ritsuryō* order modeled on that of China a full millennium earlier. A third transition to which attention might be called is the Tokugawa stabilization of the status structure and vassal system in the early seventeenth century.[2]

Each of these transitions was preceded by a lengthy period of preparation. The formal assumption of rule by the military houses came in the twelfth century, but the remarkably pacific order of the Heian days had undergone steady change as Japan's aristocratic leaders turned to military specialists for support and protection. Military rule knew three shogunates and three *bakumatsu* declines before being exchanged once more for civil and bureaucratic institutions. They too, however, had been anticipated by the bureaucraticization of the samurai in the Tokugawa years of peace; the educational consequences of measures taken after the Kansei reform were an important step toward the maturation of that system. The desperate efforts of the Tempō reforms to restore solvency found the bakufu and important domains taking stronger steps to direct economic growth and develop mercantilist policies of regional autarchy, on the one hand, while also promoting exports to other domains. These steps brought to the fore a new type of samurai bureaucrat, and the experience and expectations they provided has led some historians to see in the Tempō reforms a starting point for the modern bureaucratic state.

Each major transition, that from civil to warrior and from warrior to civil rule, was also accompanied by archaicization and revivalist rhetoric and action as new governments tried to establish their legitimacy. Hayashiya points to the early Kamakura restorationist emphases in the projects to refurbish the great Nara temples. The self-professed return to antiquity of the nineteenth century produced more recent and striking examples: the building of the Heian Shrine in Kyoto, the institution of the Meiji Shrine in central Tokyo – complete with a forest of trees from all parts of the country – and the exhuming of ancient cultural forms at the court. This had been anticipated in late Tokugawa times by the bakufu's increasing demonstrations of respect for the ancient court and its restoration of the great "imperial" tumuli of the Yamato state, but in Meiji cultural policy these efforts were far outdone. The reign title *Meiji* was selected from the *Book of Changes,* and the characters used to designate *ishin,* or "restoration," changed from a straightforward "renewal" to the now-standard *ishin,* were taken from the *Book of Songs'* reference to the renewal of the mandate of the Chou. First used in the conscription rescript, this orthography

---

[2] See, on these comparisons, Marius B. Jansen and Gilbert Rozman, eds., *Japan in Transition: From Tokugawa to Meiji* (Princeton, N.J.: Princeton University Press, 1986), pp. 13ff.

brought with it the implication that an imperial order had brought light into darkness. Other Meiji revivalist attempts in culture and religion are too numerous to require mention; the attack on feudal culture and with it Buddhism was in fact so fierce as to bring from one student the description of that campaign as a "Great Cultural Revolution."[3]

THE STAGES OF TRANSITION

The century proper opened with the Bunka (1804–18) and Bunsei (1818–30) eras. They seem, in retrospect, relatively untroubled decades with good weather and harvests, political stability in the aftermath of the vigorous reforms of Matsudaira Sadanobu; there was a lag in the frequency of the peasant demonstrations and rebellions that had peaked during the 1780s. There were, however, portents of trouble from without, for the Russian envoy Rezanov came to Nagasaki in expectation of a permit to trade there in 1804, and the rebuff he received was followed by raids on northern coasts by his young lieutenants. At Nagasaki the isolation of the Dutch trading station during the Napoleonic era led the Dutch to hire American ships to supply their needs, and that in turn led to bakufu inquiries that brought word of far-ranging changes in the European state system. A few years later an English ship, the *Phaeton*, boldly entered Nagasaki harbor and seized supplies that the startled Japanese authorities had tried to withhold. In 1824 a party of English sailors came ashore in Mito and alternately puzzled and alarmed the local negotiators sent out to deal with them, who thought they were probably Russian. The bakufu responded with measures to increase the study of European languages and to strengthen Hokkaido. In 1826 Fujita Tōko saw five Dutchmen in Edo, where they had come for the quadrennial visit to the shogun's court. Alarmed because they seemed dressed like the Russians in the Rezanov party two decades earlier, he concluded that Russia must have conquered Holland and that Japan was being surrounded, north and south, by the same malevolent foreign power. His associate Aizawa Yasushi (Seishisai), involved in the Mito interrogation of the English sailors, began to put together the threads of ethnic, religious, and nationalist thought that became the influential *New Theses* of 1825. The Mito daimyo, Tokugawa Nariaki,

---

[3] Alan Grappard, "Japan's Neglected Cultural Revolution: The Separation of Shinto and Buddhist Deities in Meiji (*Shinbutsu bunri*) and a Case Study: Tonomine," *History of Religions* 23 (1984): 240–65.

was stirred by these warnings. Within a decade he requested the bakufu to allow him to take over Ezo (Hokkaido), and after that request was denied, he became and remained the most troublesome advocate of rigorous exclusion among the feudal lords until his death in 1860.

The 1820s were a period of growing interest in Western learning. The German doctor Philip Franz von Siebold was attached to the Nagasaki Dutch station from 1823 to 1828. His stay marked both the height of interest in things Western, as a variety of able young scholars attended the academy he was permitted to set up in Nagasaki, and the beginning of officials' fears that such studies could lead to subversion and ideological contamination; his departure was marred by the discovery of a map he had received from a friend in the Bureau of Astronomy. That friend, Takahashi Kageyasu, whose life was forfeit to this incident, was, however, himself the author of the rigorous "don't think twice" order of 1825 that called for the immediate expulsion of foreigners incautious enough to try to enter Japan.

Although there was evidence of future problems in international affairs during this era, however, the growth of public and private interest in things foreign testified to the relative liberality and confidence of the times. Urban culture was never more prosperous, the reading public never larger, and publishers never more numerous than during these decades. It might well be characterized as an "era of good feelings" in comparison with the political intensity that lay ahead.

Behind the outward show of prosperity and confidence there were also portents of the economic crises ahead. After a prolonged period of price stability, a creeping inflation began to be apparent around 1820, one that continued for more than half a century. Its causes were many. Most conspicuous was the growth of bakufu expenditures during the long and luxurious shogunate of Tokugawa Ienari (shogun from 1787 to 1837 but unchallenged until his death in 1841). This was a factor in a twenty-year program of currency deflation that began in 1818, a procedure in which the precious metal content of some specie was reduced by as much as 50 percent. Prices lagged somewhat behind these moves, but they were clearly moving up by the time the bad harvests of the 1830s sent them skyrocketing. Another factor in this rise was the growth of population that accompanied economic growth in the less developed parts of Japan. Population and economic growth, which had seemed stationary in the wake of the disastrous decades at the close of the eighteenth century, began an upward turn that continued throughout the rest of the decade, with the exception of the disaster years of Tempō.[4]

The chief element in – or result of – this, however, was the inexorable growth of commercialization in central and northern Japan. In the Kantō region the centrality of Edo in economic life resulted in commercial farming, increased access to commercially produced goods, growing variety in consumption, and higher labor costs. The village was beginning to lose its long-maintained self-sufficiency. Its inhabitants were able to respond to this according to their endowments and ability; commercialization was less an option than a fact, and even though some profited from trends, others suffered from them. Vagrancy, flight, migration, and abandoned fields gave evidence of a social and economic differentation that was brought home by intravillage disputes and violence. In its "Bunsei" reforms of 1827, the bakufu tried to respond to this by instituting a new design of control by setting up a new inspectorate for the Kantō (Edo) plain that was designed to rationalize administration by grouping villages into economic and geographic units without reference to their nominal feudal overlords. Village officials were required to report on peasant side employments, and efforts were made to reduce the less necessary and less desirable aspects of commercialization such as pawn shops, drinking establishments, gambling, and related "lawless" and "luxurious" life-styles. More troubled waters lay ahead.

Chronology, Bunka–Bunsei eras

1804	Rezanov appears at Nagasaki and is denied permit to trade.
1805	Bakufu warns lords to be vigilant about Russian ships.
1806	Bakufu takes western Hokkaido as bakufu territory.
	Russian ships attack points in north.
1808	Bakufu orders six men to study French at Nagasaki, six to study English, and all interpreters to study Russian.
1811	Translation office is established in Astronomy Bureau.
1813	The ten major guilds are issued 1,195 permits, in sixty-five groups.
1815	Doeff ("Halma") Dictionary is completed; many other works in Dutch studies are published.
1822	Cholera breaks out at Nagasaki and spreads to central Japan.
1824	English whaling ship lands in Mito.
1825	Bakufu orders foreign ships to be driven off (*ninen naku* decree).
1828	On his departure, Siebold is discovered to have map and is expelled in 1829.

Source: Selected from Hayashiya Tatsusaburō, ed., *Kasei bunka no kenkyū* (Tokyo: Iwanami shoten, 1976).

4 Discussions of those trends are conveniently summarized by Nishikawa Shunsaku, *Nihon keizai no seichōshi* (Tokyo: Tōyō keizai shimpōsha, 1985), pp. 30ff.

The crisis years: Tempō (1830–1844), Kōka (1844–1848), and Kaei (1848–1854)

The next two decades saw these problems intensify. The agricultural disasters and the famine that followed, which are described by Professor Bolitho, were formative in the life experience of the leaders of midcentury Japan. Many individual domains were able to inaugurate reforms in the first years of the 1830s, but the bakufu itself was so immobilized by the prolonged influence of the former shogun Ienari that its own program could begin only at his death in 1841. Tokugawa Nariaki of Mito, who petitioned the bakufu for the resources and responsibility of Ezo in 1834 and continued to request this throughout most of the decade, surely realized that his attendants arranged his processions through his domain with the greatest care to avoid having him see the bodies of famine victims along the roads. In the instructions he left for his successor he grouped the evils of his time as "barbarians, thieves, and famine." Neither the reforms he called for in Mito nor the advice he proffered the bakufu was successful. Nariaki himself was first told to stay in Mito for more than five years and then was recalled to domiciliary confinement in Edo.

Some other domains, particularly several in the southwest, were more successful with the economic reforms they instituted during the Tempō years. The famine was most severe in central and northern Japan; even there, however, after a temporary decline in population, growth and commercialization resumed. What was particularly important about the "Tempō reform" period, in the eyes of economic historians, was the way that it impelled daimyo governments to take on a planning function. Domain monopolies were set up to centralize and exploit the growing commercialization of the economy; in turn they speeded the process. This was usually to the disadvantage of local producers, who correctly saw the moves as a device whereby the domain governments tried to be the chief gainers of such enterprises. Not surprisingly, the "reforms" were frequently accompanied by protests from those whose livelihoods were being reformed; protests and petitions marked the process. The protests tended to be more successful in the central area essential to bakufu finance than they were in the more remote and more highly militarized domains of the "outside" lords. Those domains tried to profit from, monopolize, and simultaneously repress the commercialization of their economies. They could profit from the nationwide inflation: Satsuma, which set out to reduce domain indebtedness and market its products through domain-established agencies, was helped by the inflation. The bakufu, with reforms that came later and that had to be carried out in areas that were far more heavily commercialized and less responsive to official control, was more hobbled by resistance and protest. The unhappy tenure of its counselor Mizuno Tadakuni, who found himself resisted by Tokugawa vassals and his residence stoned by Edo townsmen after his dismissal, can stand as a symbol of the larger forces at work.

The most striking evidence of bakufu difficulty came in the 1837 revolt of the Osaka samurai official Ōshio Heihachirō. Located as it was in the great commercial city of central Japan, the incident had reverberations throughout the entire country. Because the participants were for the most part products of Ōshio's own school and following, it illustrated some of the possibilities that might be expected from politically motivated teachers and academies and stood as a portent of additional insurrections to come in future decades.[5]

Chronology, Tempō–Kaei

1830	Kumamoto forbids import and use of products of other domains.
	Satsuma institutes priority program for sugar.
1831	Tokuyama domain forbids sale of domestically made paper.
1832	Tokugawa Nariaki urges bakufu to build cannon.
	Mito establishes bureau to sell domestic goods in Edo.
1837	Ōshio Heihachirō stages revolt in Osaka.
	Morrison enters Uraga bay and is shelled.
1839	Watanabe Kazan held in "Bansha no goku" (d. 1841, suicide).
1840	Bakufu orders Dutch to provide full account of Opium War.
	Bakufu decrees that astronomy office alone may translate Dutch works on medicine, astronomy, and science.
1841	Bakufu Tempō reforms call for revival of Kyōhō, Kansei spirit.
1842	Bakufu forbids domain monopolies.
1843	Bakufu rescinds order rationalizing domains; Mizuno Tadakuni is dismissed.
	Sugita Seikei is ordered to translate Dutch constitution.
1846	Bakufu informs court of foreign ships and is told to be vigilant.
1850	Court orders services at seven shrines and temples to guard against foreign ships.
	Penalty for unauthorized publication about Opium War.

Source: Selected from Hayashiya Tatsusaburō, ed., *Kasei bunka no kenkyū* (Tokyo: Iwanami shoten, 1976), and *Bakumatsu bunka no kenkyū* (Tokyo: Iwanami shoten, 1978).

The foreign crisis (1854–1860)

The arrival of Commodore Matthew Perry in 1853 is discussed by William Beasley in Chapter 4. The sense of crisis that came to charac-

---

5 Okubo Akihiro, "Bakumatsu ni okeru seijiteki hanran to shijuku," in Kano Masanao and Takagi Shunsuke, eds., *Ishin henkaku ni okeru zaisonteki shochōryū* (Tokyo: San'ichi shobō, 1972), pp. 110–33.

terize the Ansei (1854–60) era was intense but not entirely new. The *Morrison* event of 1837, in which an American ship trying to establish contact by returning Japanese castaways had been driven away by coastal batteries, produced expressions of alarm from scholars of Western learning as well as official directives for position papers on Japan's impending problems. Some of those involved in the preparation of these became targets for charges of subversion: The trial and conviction of Watanabe Kazan in 1839 was followed by his suicide two years later. In 1844 the Dutch king unsuccessfully attempted to advise the shogun on the impossibility of maintaining policies of seclusion and expulsion, and two years later Commodore James Biddle came to Japan in a futile effort to establish formal United States–Japan relations. In addition to these direct approaches to Japan, word of China's defeat in the Opium War spread rapidly among educated Japanese. Interrogation of the Dutch at Nagasaki confirmed the superiority of Western military technology, and Japanese editions of Wei Yüan's *Hai-kuo t'u-chih* served as a preface to the near-hysterical denunciations of the West from the brush of Shionoya Tōin, a Confucian scholar who edited the Japanese editions of Wei Yüan.[6]

Perry's report to his president predicted a promising future for a Japan he described as "the youngest sister in the circle of commercial nations." If only, he wrote, the powers would "kindly take her by the hand, and aid the tottering steps, until she has reached a vigor that will enable her to walk firmly in her own strength," commercial and diplomatic relations would soon be firm. Unfortunately Townsend Harris, who followed in 1856, found that hand more often clenched than open, and the commercial treaty he negotiated in 1858 stirred such intense opposition that its enactment shook the very foundations of Tokugawa rule. Much scholarship relating foreign affairs to internal politics has centered on the events in Kyoto that led to court opposition to the Harris treaty – discussed in the Beasley and Jansen chapters that follow – and relates the bakufu decline to the inability of the "barbarian-subduing generalissimo" to control the intrusive West.

Discussions by Bitō Masahide have provided an additional context for facts that have become familiar. The bakufu leader Abe Masahiro circulated Perry's letter among the daimyo and at court in an effort to build consensus for a decision he knew to be inevitable.

6 Marius B. Jansen, *Changing Japanese Attitudes Toward Modernization* (Princeton, N.J.: Princeton University Press, 1965), p. 57; and Ōba Osamu, "Ahen sensō to *Kaikoku zushi*," in *Edo jidai no Ni-Chū hiwa* (Tokyo: Tōhō shoten, 1980), pp. 242ff.

By this act he helped activate a politics that had long seemed dormant, and succeeding years saw the ripples of participation move outward from the heads of the military families to their retainers and among sectors of the commoners as well. As Bitō pointed out, this sequence too was foreshadowed in the 1840s, when the same Abe Masahiro was serving a term as bakufu *rōjū*. Abe had discussed the bakufu response to the Dutch king's letter of 1844 with daimyo Tokugawa Nariaki of Mito, who criticized its wording and urged that future matters be brought before the leading daimyo, *tozama* as well as *gosanke* and *fudai*, in a survey of "public opinion" (*shūhyō*). This, Nariaki urged, would "be to the benefit of Japan and will help ensure that no disgrace befalls the nation." So too with political participation by the imperial court. In 1846 the court had directed the bakufu to strengthen the coastal defenses, and so it was natural for Abe to include Kyoto in his distribution of the United States's request for treaty relations.

These same steps proved disastrous a few years later when Hotta Masayoshi tried to repeat them in presenting the Harris Commercial Treaty of 1858. By now the disagreement was clear, for Harris's provision for genuine trade went well beyond Perry's original demands. Worse, the awareness of weakness at the very center of the bakufu led some of the great lords to try to influence the Tokugawa succession by tying approval of the treaty to the selection of Hitotsubashi Keiki, Nariaki's son, as the shogunal successor. A strong backlash of authoritarianism within the bakufu came with the leadership of Ii Naosuke, who resorted to force in the "Ansei purge" of 1858–60. Ii's assassination in the spring of 1860 brought on a decade of increasing violence that ended with the (Boshin) civil war of 1868–9. The opening of Japan thus reactivated politics at all levels of Japanese society.

In Bitō's treatment, the moves taken by Abe Masahiro helped establish a polarity between referral to broader opinion (*kōron*) and the authoritarian centralism pursued by Ii Naosuke. The bakufu, despite its experimentation with wider referral and its professions of respect for the court, found itself condemned by partisans who now linked those themes and attached to them the issue of expulsion of unwelcome foreigners. The higher morality of *kōron*, buffeted by the political disputes of the 1860s, reemerged with the promise of the infant Meiji government (in the Charter Oath of 1868), which in turn became the demand of the "People's Rights" movement of the Meiji period.

These were themes whose changing interpretation helped unify and illuminate the transition decades of the nineteenth century.[7]

The assassins' bill of complaint against Ii Naosuke in 1860 illustrated the way in which a cluster of complaints had formed. They charged that Ii had wielded his power willfully and in disregard of "public opinion and morality" (*kōron seigi*). He had abandoned standards of religion as well as those of public policy; it was contrary to the national interest to conclude treaties with the foreigners and to give up the established practice of requiring foreigners to trample on pictures of Christ; in short, "too much compromise has been made at the sacrifice of national honor." Political decisions judged in terms of moral absolutes would have little room for discussion or for compromise.

The Tokugawa fall

The Meiji Restoration of 1868, discussed in Chapter 5, was the result of the turbulent politics of the 1860s. Ii Naosuke's Ansei purge had turned doubts into conviction for many, and his successors' uncertain course produced a zigzag trail that left even Tokugawa vassals uncertain as to what their course should be. Efforts to work out new relationships with a more important imperial court involved all parties. For most of the decade the bakufu was able to maintain close relations with Kyoto, but professions of loyalty were no substitute for the active support of the most able courtiers around the sovereign. The bakufu began with the selection of an imperial princess as consort for the young Tokugawa Iemochi (shogun from 1858 to 1866). The domain of Chōshū followed with a scheme for court participation in politics, one that was quickly strengthened by proposals put forward by Satsuma and Tosa. Political reorganization in the Bunkyū (1861–64) era brought members of Tokugawa collateral houses into new positions and tried to enlist the cooperation of highly placed lords from outside domains. These steps succeeded in weakening the control of Edo-centered traditionalists, but without securing the support of the domains they were designed to co-opt. Requirements of alternate attendance were relaxed, never to be

---

[7] Bitō Masahide, "*Bushi* and the Meiji Restoration," *Acta Asiatica* 49 (Tokyo: Tōhō gakkai, 1985), pp. 78–99; and in expanded form, Bitō Masahide, "Meiji ishin to bushi: 'kōron' no rinen ni yoru ishinzō saikōsei no kokoromi," *Shisō* 735 (September 1985). Harold Bolitho, however, stands this appraisal of Abe on its head to argue that Abe misjudged the situation to pursue an essentially debilitating course of consultations and that Ii Naosuke and his purge, and the concept of authoritarian government behind it, represented the wave of the future. See Harold Bolitho, "Abe Masahiro and the New Japan," in Jeffrey P. Mass and William B. Hauser, eds., *The Bakufu in Japanese History* (Stanford, Calif.: Stanford University Press, 1985).

restored, and politics centered on the Kyoto court began to make the ancient imperial capital a national center at the expense of Edo, where the bakufu began to resemble a more regional, though still immensely important, power.

The opening of the ports in 1859 brought additional problems into play. Foreign relations provided opportunities for self-strengthening and rearmament for the bakufu, but the same contacts soon made it possible for vassal dissidents to import modern weaponry. The domain monopolies that had been set up in the Tempō years brought resistance to Tokugawa efforts to control and monopolize foreign trade, and domains began to treat directly with outside suppliers and customers through the treaty ports. They also began to trade with one another in defiance of bans on lateral contact; Chōshū with Fukui, Kokura, and Gotō (1862) and Tsushima (1864), and Satsuma with Okayama, Hiroshima, Wakayama, Toba, and Tosa. Additional lateral arrangements developed in the years that followed.[8] More serious for the bakufu was a rampaging inflation that broke out in metropolitan areas. Divergence in gold–silver ratios between Japan and the China coast brought a run on Japanese precious metals. The sudden growth in outside markets for Japanese goods, particularly raw silk and tea, raised prices and brought hardships to domestic processors and samurai on fixed incomes. Some of the larger domains began experimenting with modern technology and production in armaments, shipbuilding, and textiles.

The political process was continually exacerbated by the foreign presence and pressure. Outraged samurai generated antiforeign incidents for which the bakufu had to make amends at cost to its prestige and treasury. The foreign response to these incidents chastened antiforeign radicals in Chōshū and Satsuma, but without producing unity in either domain. In Satsuma, bureaucratic regulars defeated ambitious radicals, and in Chōshū, by a much more complex process, those radicals gained leadership of domain policy. The bakufu first succeeded and then failed to mobilize opinion against Chōshū radicals: When its effort to punish Chōshū a second time failed badly in 1866, the end was in sight.

Tokugawa Yoshinobu (Keiki), son of Nariaki and the successor proposed and rejected in 1858, became the fifteenth and last Tokugawa shogun upon the death of Iemochi in 1866. He was never once free to leave Kyoto to return to Edo and his real power base, and he was never

8 Nishikawa, *Nihon keizai no seichōshi*, p. 137.

fully in tune with the *fudai* at that center. His conviction of foreign danger and the attraction of an apparent opportunity to emerge as first in a new alignment of equals led him to agree to a proposal put forward by Tosa in 1867 that he resign his powers. Outmaneuvered by the Satsuma leaders and their allies at court who secured an imperial demand that he surrender his lands as well as his offices, the shogun then tried to march on Kyoto from Osaka. This ended in disaster, a retreat to Edo, and there surrender to a newly constituted "imperial army" led by Saigō Takamori of Satsuma. The new government's forces moved on to the north, fighting where necessary in a war that came to a close in the late spring of 1869.

These tumultuous political events produced the leaders of the modern state and the heroes of modern Japanese nationalism, but they have overshadowed equally interesting and important developments that were taking place. Abundant signs of popular disaffection were shown in a new rebellious mood that often took on millenarian overtones. Crop failures in the latter 1860s produced hardship conditions that complicated the tasks of government everywhere in Japan. The disruption of life caused by the military mobilization and campaigns brought resentment and opposition from commoners who were tired of providing ever-greater amounts of service labor and produce. The long stay of the bakufu forces in the Osaka area while preparations were under way for the second expedition against Chōshū produced resistance shown by desperate burnings and riots. The new "imperial" armies were able to utilize this discontent and disillusion by offers of tax reduction and benevolence in the virtuous era that they announced was at hand.

Bakufu attempts to acquaint the strategic elite with the requirements of the times also produced a much-improved communication system. The previously sheltered reports from Dutch and Chinese merchants now gave way to officially sponsored news of foreign events in early newspapers. One unexpected product of this was a consensus, common to late-Tokugawa political pronouncements, that because no other country had the divided administration that characterized Japan, political reconsolidation was needed to produce a single and effective national decision center. There was substantial agreement between the bakufu and its opponents as to what was needed in terms of political change, and disagreements over who should lead were resolved by eliminating the Tokugawa bakufu.

Although a number of merchant sympathizers helped support and, when necessary, hide the Restoration activists and although local notables in many areas contributed sons to the Restoration fighting, for the most part ordinary Japanese played little or no part in the events that have been described. This is not to say that they were ignorant of or out of sympathy with what took place, but they were unarmed and not involved. English who participated in the shelling of Shimonoseki in 1864 remarked on the objectivity of the commoners, who watched from a safe distance and helped landing parties load or destroy the Chōshū batteries after the danger was past. When "imperial" forces reduced the Aizu castle town of Wakamatsu in 1868, commoners came forward with summer fruits to sell during lulls in the fighting. As the Restoration forces approached Edo, foreigners wrote of the unearthly calm and quiet that came over that normally bustling city, maintained in perfect order despite the sudden absence of its usual police forces. Nor did this change quickly. After the ill-fated Hagi rebellion of the Chōshū leader Maebara Issei in 1876, Kido Takayoshi noted in his diary that the townsmen were so angered by the destruction that "in the event Maebara is treated leniently, the people in Hagi castletown are saying that they want to behead him themselves" and that "they will not sell the *shizoku* a sheet of paper or a single towel unless they are paid in cash."9 The enthusiastic ebullience of a millenarian frenzy in 1867 served the Restoration activists' purposes in the complications it made for public order, but at no time did commoners contribute to the process by politically motivated disorder. They left for others a struggle that did not seem to concern them directly.

Selected chronology of foreign relations, 1860s

1858   Ii Naosuke forces approval of American treaty, Ansei purge.
1859   Dutch terminate Deshima station at Nagasaki and establish consulate at Edo.
       Yokohama, Nagasaki, and Hakodate are opened as treaty ports.
       Bakufu permits import of military materials.
1860   Mission is sent to Washington to ratify commercial treaty.
       Ii Naosuke is assassinated.
1861   Russians occupy Tsushima.
       Chōshū proposes first of *kōbu-gattai* plans.
       Officially sponsored *Batavia News* begins publication.
1862   Institute of Barbarian Books is renamed Institute of Western Books.
       Bunkyū reforms are announced.
       Richardson (Namamugi) incident takes place.
       Sankin kōtai regulations are eased; hostages are released.
       Bakufu sends fifteen students to Europe.
1863   Chōshū shells foreign ships in Shimonoseki Straits.
       Chōshū forces are driven from Kyoto.
       Institute for Western Books is renamed the Development Office.

9 Sidney D. Brown and Akiko Hirota, trans., *The Diary of Kido Takayoshi, vol. 3: 1874–1877* (Tokyo: University of Tokyo Press, 1986), pp. 395, 402.

English shell Kagoshima.
Group of outside domain lords is named court counselors.
1864 Chōshū units try to seize palace in Kyoto and are driven off.
Bakufu orders thirty-five domains to contribute to campaign against Chōshū.
English, French, American, and Dutch ships shell Chōshū batteries at Shimonoseki.
1865 Satsuma sends fifteen students to England.
Bakufu orders second Chōshū expedition.
1866 Satsuma–Chōshū alliance is formed.
Second Chōshū expedition begins.
Shogun and Emperor Kōmei die.
1867 Shogun Tokugawa Yoshinobu (Keiki) resigns office.

Political centralization

The great task of the 1870s was to end the political and social separatism so that Japan could become an effective political unit. For several years, "Restoration" left the domains intact. The regime, dominated by Satsuma and Chōshū, soon co-opted Tosa and Saga as allies and masked its efforts as the will of the boy emperor Mutsuhito with proclamations of a new era of "enlightened rule" (*Meiji*). Yet it was effectively restricted to that part of the Tokugawa domain that it kept. The only certainty was that the Tokugawa bakufu had been eliminated.

Many feared the development of a new hegemon in accordance with the patterns of previous *bakumatsu* periods, and chaos in a struggle between Satsuma and Chōshū for such hegemony seemed equally possible. Tosa leaders organized other Shikoku domains in a regional alliance, with contingency plans to snatch and "protect" the boy emperor in the event of such violence. In the north a league of domains that had slowed the "imperial" advance in the closing months of the civil war had been animated more by suspicion of the southern fiefs than by loyalty to the Tokugawa cause, for they professed themselves no less "loyal" than their opponents. Indeed, even within the Tokugawa camp, there had been no dispute about imperial sovereignty, for the last shogun assured foreign representatives even after the outbreak of violence that no one disputed the imperial preeminence.

The problems that existed were thus inherent in the existence of a "government" dependent for its force and much of its resources on two domains of the southwest while aspiring to national hegemony. Worse, the leaders of those two domains had until recently distrusted each other as thoroughly as they had disliked the Tokugawa bakufu. Those who worked at the political center in Kyoto and Tokyo, as Edo was renamed in 1868, were quickly criticized by their peers at home as deficient in loyalty to their domain lords in the expectation of national prominence for themselves. Several factors helped offset this. In both Satsuma and Chōshū, effective leadership lay with samurai counselors who had the prestige of successful leadership in the maneuvering of the 1860s. Perhaps more important still, they had control of the domain's armed forces and thus of samurai loyalties that came with military command. Nevertheless it was a situation that could not be long continued, and quick action was necessary.

The political experimentation of the early months, described in William Beasley's discussion of political institutions, saw the leaders maneuver behind a pattern of apparently "open" institutions, in which they held second-rank status themselves in deference to the court aristocrats and feudal lords who were in the top positions. Early pronouncements, like the emperor's "Charter Oath" of April 6, 1868, promised all that decisions would be reached on the basis of "general opinion," that "councils" would be established to work that out, and that "all classes" would enjoy equal opportunities to work out their reasonable desires. Then, as the warfare drew to a close, institutions were reshuffled to reduce the incubus of the old elite, and responsibility was narrowed to reflect the role of the Satsuma–Chōshū middle samurai more accurately. It was a fascinating moment of changing status. Just as the imperial court provided the focus for changing loyalties from bakufu and domain to nation, imperial office and court attire provided the blind for a shift from hierarchic samurai loyalties to a new and more nearly egalitarian (in samurai terms) world of imperial service. It was not immediately successful. When the lord of Tosa slighted a retainer who presumed to stand his ground, he drew a retort that, samurai though he had been, he was now an imperial official. As late as 1876, on the other hand, Kido Takyoshi expressed his anger that the lord of Satsuma denied equality to an imperial messenger; "the General was treated exactly as if he were still a retainer, and could not sit on the same level with [Lord] Shimazu, [who] waited for him in a haughty manner."[10]

There were two principal steps in the process of political unification. In 1869 the samurai leaders of Satsuma, Chōshū, and Tosa persuaded their lords to petition the imperial court to accept the return of their registers. "The abode wherein we the undersigned dwell is the Sovereign's land," their petition read, "the people over whom we rule

10 See Albert M. Craig, "The Central Government," and Michio Umegaki, "From Domain to Prefecture," in Jansen and Rozman, eds., *Japan in Transition*, pp. 36–67 and 91–110; and Kido, *Diary*, p. 480.

are his people. Why should we privately own them?" They went on to ask that

an Imperial command be issued that the domains of all the *han* be reorganized; and also that all the regulations, from the ordering of laws, institutions, and military affairs, even until the fashioning of uniforms and instruments, issue from the Imperial Government, and the conduct of all the affairs of the realm, whether great or small be placed under unified control.

Significantly, it was only then that Japan would "stand beside the foreign Powers." The court hesitated some months before accepting this petition. During that period, other domains, anxious not to seem less loyal than the Restoration leaders, came flooding in with comparable petitions, and so when the acceptance was made public, it was no longer a chiefly Satsuma–Chōshū idea.

With authority came responsibility, and the court responded by appointing the former lords as governors of their domains. Uniform procedures were prescribed for all domains, and one of these stipulated that the lords reserve one-tenth of their revenue for their own needs. Thus an embryo distinction between public and private was worked into the system. Next came the regularization and simplification of samurai ranks from the complexity they had known. Lords and court nobles were to be distinguished as *kazoku*, samurai as *shizoku*, and the lower ranks as *sotsu*. The national government was now in theory responsible for samurai stipends, and it soon found that burden impossible to combine with effective administration. Meanwhile, a number of domains petitioned to be absorbed into the imperial land. These requests were held at arm's length for a time, but they indicated that many were aware of the necessity for a rationalization of administrative units.

There were good reasons for the Satsuma and Chōshū leaders to plan more effective centralization. Suspicion of their desires would continue so long as their domains existed. Military costs would be heavy for them as long as they alone had effective armies. Therefore it was not long before Satsuma, Chōshū, and Tosa pooled their troops to establish a ten-thousand-man "imperial guard" and, with that as a prelude, worked out the ordinance that abolished the domains and established seventy-five (later reduced to forty-seven) units for administration. The lords-become-governors were recalled to Tokyo "for consultation," and the central government appointed real governors to administer the newly designated prefectures. This took place in 1871.

The government had now taken full responsibility upon itself, and it would require drastic new measures to make a success of the new system. Plans were immediately begun for a single and rational system of landholding and taxation, for a conscription system to replace the samurai as a national army, and for a school system to replace with a single educational grid over the land the mix of status-group schools that had proliferated in the last half-century of Tokugawa rule.

These measures were announced in the waning months of 1872 and 1873. Before that, however, forty-eight of the new government's leaders sailed from Yokohama, in implementation of another of the Charter Oath's promises, to "seek wisdom throughout the world in order to strengthen the foundations of imperial rule." An eighteen-month tour followed that was of tremendous importance for the future policies of selective modernization. The United States brought home the importance of public schooling; "I have resolved," Kido wrote from America, "to devote myself entirely to military and educational matters." And again, "We clearly must have schools if we are to encourage our country's development as a civilized country, improve ordinary people's knowledge, establish the power of the state, and maintain our independence and sovereignty." "Our people," he went on, "are no different from the Americans or Europeans of today; it is all a matter of education or lack of education."[11] His Satsuma counterpart, Ōkubo Toshimichi, wrote equally enthusiastically about the industrial developments he witnessed in Great Britain, and the embassy scribe, Kume Kunitake, concluded that Japan was only thirty or forty years behind the "advanced" West, which had known neither railroads nor modern weapons at the turn of the century.

The Iwakura mission thus persuaded its members of the need to adopt Western institutions as appropriate to their needs, to educate and elevate their people into military, industrial, and political participation, and to maintain those priorities upon their return. Kido Takayoshi, for example, was inclined to favor continental military moves before his departure but returned firmly convinced that it was much too early to do so. Before seeing the rest of the world, others were inclined to doubt the morality or wisdom of a decline in samurai support but returned convinced of the need to devise a system to convert that unproductive class into one that could contribute to national wealth and strength. When the ambassadors returned home to

---

11 Quoted in Irokawa Daikichi, *The Culture of the Meiji Period*, translation edited by Marius B. Jansen (Princeton, N.J.: Princeton University Press, 1985), pp. 54–5.

find that their colleagues were far advanced with plans for a show of strength with Korea, which had rejected overtures for modern international relations, they canceled those plans. Ōkubo soon concocted substitute plans for a more modestly sized force against Taiwan, but by then Kido, earlier belligerent with regard to Korea, objected strongly, though unsuccessfully, to that as well.

The ambassadors' reversal of their colleagues' decision divided the ruling group. Some petitioned for an elective council that would reach decisions more democratically, whereas others retired in anger. The opposition movements of the decade are taken up by Stephen Vlastos in Chapter 6. They can be divided, as he shows, into agricultural, samurai, and liberal movements of protest. Farmers were alarmed by change, alienated by the tax reassessment that brought them hard and fast requirements after a more precedent-based and flexible village survey, and frightened by a new kind of state that had access to effective police enforcement of its requirements. When the countryside was faced with the realities of the new order, the optimistic expectations of a utopian future that millenarian religious leaders had held out faded, though some of those expectations survived into the democratic movements of the 1880s. The new regime proved to have ideological expectations of its own that conflicted with those of many folk cults.[12]

Samurai movements posed a sterner test for the new regime. They were centered in the same areas whose domains had led in the Restoration, for the civil war of 1868–9 had extinguished samurai expectations in the north. The great Satsuma Rebellion led by the Restoration hero Saigō Takamori in 1877 presented the regime with its most difficult test and required the expenditure of great financial and military resources. With its failure the Restoration decade can be said to have come to its end. Thereafter regional and class separatism had no future, for if Satsuma failed, no other domain could succeed. The nature of the samurai class helps explain the failure of these insurrections. Indignant as they might be over issues of personal disadvantage inherent in the decision to pension them off, a decision that culminated in compulsory commutations of stipends for interest-bearing bonds in 1876 and the simultaneous prohibition of wearing swords, the warrior code of service and contempt for gain ruled out appeals to self-interest. Feudal barriers and jealousies also made it impossible to secure effec-

---

12 Kano Masanao, "Yonaoshi no shisō to bummei kaika," in Kanao Masanao and Takagi Shunsuke, eds., *Ishin henkaku ni okeru zaisonteki shochōryū* (Tokyo: San'ichi shobō, 1972), pp. 288–324.

tive cooperation between different domains, so that the insurrections came, and were repressed, piecemeal. The rebellions were proclaimed over issues of honor – policy on Korea, use of swords, real or imagined disrespect for local custom and leaders – and, with the exception of the case in Satsuma, involved relatively small numbers of men, usually too proud to seek assistance and too parochial to inspire wide support.

Selected chronology for the 1870s

1868	Edo is renamed Tokyo; era is changed to Meiji, one era per sovereign.
1869	Satsuma, Chōshū, and Tosa ask the court to accept the return of their registers.
	Yasukuni Shrine is established as memorial to those killed in Restoration.
1870	Commoners are permitted to take family names.
1871	Ten-thousand-man unit established from Satsuma, Chōshū, and Tosa troops.
	Court calls in all daimyo-governors and announces the abolition of domains.
	Iwakura mission leaves.
1872	Permanent sale of land is permitted.
	Conscription ordinance and education ordinance are enacted.
1873	Signs forbidding Christianity are taken down.
	Emperor's picture distributed to prefectures to build affection for him.
	Land taxes are revised.
	Itagaki, Soejima, Etō, and Saigō leave government and petition for constitution.
1875	Japan exchanges with Russia Sakhalin for Kurils.
1876	Medical system revision finds 14,807 Chinese-style, 5,097 Western-style, and 2,524 eclectic-style doctors.
1877	Satsuma Rebellion takes place.
1878	Laws for local government are enacted.
1879	Ryūkyū kingdom is renamed prefecture.
	Army is revised with general staff, directly reporting to emperor.

Source: Hayashiya Tatsusaburō, ed., *Bummei kaika no kenkyū* (Tokyo: Iwanami shoten, 1979), pp. 3–42.

The 1880s: fashioning political institutions

The three principal leaders of the Restoration government died within a year of one another a decade after the political overturn of 1868: Kido Takayoshi from illness, Saigō Takamori by his own hand upon the failure of the Satsuma Rebellion, and Ōkubo Toshimichi by assassination in May 1878. The government leaders had used as structure the Council of State (Dajōkan) of an earlier age, but the decision center was with the imperial councilors and not with titular ministers. The loss of the early triumvirate and the suppression of localism made it necessary to think about more enduring forms that would better serve a modern national state.

The Charter Oath of 1868 had spoken of a "council chamber," and in 1876 the experimental but powerless "senate" (*genrōin*) had, as William Beasley's discussion of institutions shows, begun deliberation on a more enduring form of state structure. The decision of the samurai leaders who left the government in 1874 to petition for an elective council was soon followed by a surge of activity in support of such goals. The government tried to co-opt some of this enthusiasm by drawing the Tosa leader, Itagaki Taisuke, back into its ranks in 1875, and a council of prefectural governors was set up to provide a forum for the discussion of problems, but those meetings proved unproductive. Prefectural assemblies did provide elective experience and parliamentary practice for a constituency chosen on the basis of a tax qualification, but more was needed.

The samurai leaders of the "People's Rights" movement worked with a series of organizations. Initially they were based on the needs of their samurai peers, but before long the movement had found echo in the interests of a local elite, ranging from village notables to rural brewers and informed farmers. National meetings were held in Osaka in March and October 1880, and the Liberal Party was formed at the second of those meetings to emerge as a national political movement at Osaka a year later in 1881. By that time the government was finding itself in trouble on several scores. The revelation of plans to sell off government assets developed for the colonization of Hokkaido stirred widespread discontent. This reached high quarters with petitions and resignations from high-ranking members of the armed forces. Non–Satsuma–Chōshū officials in the central government were discussing ways to checkmate their more powerful colleagues, and unease extended to court officials with ready access to the young emperor. As the fever of discontent mounted, Ōkuma Shigenobu, the minister of finance, submitted directly to the court a proposal for early adoption of an English-style constitutional system.

In the fall of 1881, the Satsuma–Chōshū leaders utilized the person of the young emperor to co-opt the popular movement and curb its leaders. Plans to sell the Hokkaido assets were canceled. Ōkuma was forced out of government to be replaced by Matsukata Masayoshi, who headed the Ministry of Finance for the rest of the decade. An imperial rescript, perhaps the most important of the era, announced that a national assembly would meet in 1890 and commissioned "the officials of Our Court" to take charge of all the preparations. With regard to the assembly and its constitution, the rescript said, "We shall personally make an impartial decision and in due time issue a proclamation." The statement ended with warnings of punishment for those who, by trying to speed the timetable, might harm "Our great and farsighted plans." Soon Itō Hirobumi was appointed head of a commission that journeyed to Europe to study other state charters. The product of its labors, the Meiji constitution of 1889, was cast in the mold of Prussian and Austrian institutions. It was to channel Japanese political life until the defeat of 1945.

In the meantime, the People's Rights movement that had begun as samurai centered had made deep inroads into Japanese popular consciousness, particularly in central and northern Japan. Hundreds of organizations of local notables met in eager discussion of alternative formulations for electoral restraint on arbitrary government. The Meiji leaders saw themselves in a race against time to head off what they saw as anarchy and what their opponents saw as liberalism. Between 1882 and 1884 a number of outbreaks of violence confirmed the leaders' fears and dismayed the Liberal Party leaders. They were harshly suppressed, and political activity went into decline during the final steps of constitutional preparation. When the document was completed, the party leaders returned to political activity as candidates for elective office. In the twentieth century, party representatives went on to hold the highest cabinet posts; fully absorbed into the government structure, they vied with their former opponents to praise the enlightened statecraft of the monarch who had granted the constitution.

The economic policies of the decade affected the modern Japanese state as profoundly as did the political institutions that were worked out. The centralization and pacification of the 1870s had been expensive. Assuming samurai debts, funding samurai pensions and bonds, suppressing rebellion, and launching experimental industries and pilot plants had forced the government to issue an ever-increasing volume of paper money, and the result was a strong inflationary tide. This benefited the landowners whose produce grew in value, but it hurt agricultural and urban workers, former samurai, and especially the government, which soon found itself overextended. Debates within the government polarized around two positions. Ōkuma Shigenobu, a Saga councilor who favored a policy of rapid growth, advocated a foreign loan to bolster the currency and the continuation of easy money. His opponents argued the case for deflationary policies that would lower the price level and increase the real value of the land tax. After Ōkuma's ouster from the government in 1881, he entered the party movement as a rival of Itagaki Taisuke. In his place as finance minister came Matsukata Masayoshi of Satsuma. Matsukata pursued orthodox financial policies to provide a basis for future capitalist growth by curbing the money supply and, in so doing, brought on a drastic deflation. This contributed to rural hardship and helped bring about the participation of villagers in the political party movement. At several points it combined with insensitive and arrogant administrative tactics to produce flash points of violence in the period between 1882 and 1884. Matsukata's policies also established the infrastructure for capitalist development by building the Bank of Japan and other financial institutions on a sound basis and prepared the way for Japan's adoption of the gold standard in 1898. In the process many of the provisional, pilot plants that the government had launched in the 1870s were sold to private interests to get them off the government treasury. The opportunities that this provided for investors in many fields helped lead to the phenomenon of large combines which came to be known by the derogatory term of *zaibatsu*. These developments are treated at length in E. Sydney Crawcour's discussion of economic innovation in Chapter 9.

The 1880s also saw the development of institutions of local government. These were under the direction of the military leader Yamagata Aritomo, who served as home minister. On the local, as on the national, level, models were found in Prussian and Austrian examples. Just as the drafters of the constitution used the German legal specialist Herman Roessler, Yamagata took as his guide Albert Mosse. Together they devised a series of measures to structure local participation under the direction of an appointed governor, in the expectation that this would provide a grass-roots defense against the spread of "people's rights" radicalism. Governors could block local initiatives when they seemed undesirable; they could dissolve prefectural assemblies; and they could order local taxes without the approval of the assembly. Like the Meiji constitution, this set of laws for the organization of villages, towns, districts, and prefectures remained basically unchanged until 1945.

Internal reform dominated the priorities of the 1880s, but issues in foreign affairs were by no means lacking. The galling inequality of Japan's treaties with the Western powers affected the leaders' priorities. A series of unsuccessful efforts to secure reform ran afoul of the powers' refusal to consider abolition of extraterritoriality in the absence of the completion of modern codes of law. Government leaders' willingness to compromise on these points by suggestions to share jurisdiction with foreign judges inflamed nationalist opinion, costing one foreign minister his post and another, very nearly, his life. Efforts to work out a psychologically satisfactory relationship with Korea stirred Korean conservatives' resentment of Japanese interference. In

1882 and 1884, disorder in Korea brought on confrontations with Ch'ing China, which tried to maintain primacy in Korea under the tributary tradition. By a treaty worked out at Tientsin between Itō Hirobumi and Li Hung-chang, Japan and China agreed to mutual disengagement in Korea, with promises not to introduce military strength without formal notification to the other. In this lay the seeds of conflict a decade later once Japan's modern political institutions were in place.

Selected chronology, 1880s

1881   Government announces sale of Development Office assets in Hokkaido; Ōkuma leaves office.
       Imperial rescript promising constitution in nine years.
1882   Itō Hirobumi leaves for Europe to study constitutional systems.
       Bank of Japan is established.
       Fukushima incident involves Liberal Party leader Kōno Hironaka.
1884   Peerage is created for former lords and court nobles.
       Chichibu incident leads to suppression of thousands of dissenters; Liberal Party disbands.
1885   Cabinet system is established; Council of State is dissolved.
1886   Police station network is developed for entire country.
1887   Itō and commission work in seclusion to prepare constitution.
       Government bans 570 opposition leaders from having residences within three miles of imperial palace.
       Local government system is completed.
       Privy Council is established to rule on constitution, with Itō as its head.
1888   Army and navy general staff systems separated.
1889   Constitution is promulgated.
1890   First national election is held.
       Imperial Diet convenes.

Constitutional government

The Meiji state was completed in the 1890s. In that year the constitution went into effect with the first election, which found the political parties besting a jerry-built coalition that conservatives had designed in hopes that it would checkmate them. In the House of Peers sat members of the new nobility, created in 1884 from former court aristocrats and feudal lords, together with a scattering of new peers named from among government leaders. Provision was also made for representation of the growing plutocracy by setting aside a number of seats for the highest taxpayers in the land; term imperial appointees completed the body. Out of respect for the imperial sovereignty, however, the constitution made little explicit provision for executive power, and cabinets were selected behind the scenes. For the decade an alternation between Satsuma and Chōshū, and to some degree between civil and military leaders, characterized the central government. At the end of the decade, however, the designer of the new institutions, Itō Hirobumi, concluded that it would be desirable to form his own political party in order to avoid relying on coalitions with party leaders. This represented an admission that the new institutions, which had been designed to "assist" and not to direct affairs, had provided genuine opportunity for participation, if only to hinder.

Much of the Western world viewed Japan's experimentation with limited popular participation with profound doubt, uncertain that the product of centuries of Western institutional growth could be transplanted to an Asian country. The Meiji leaders were well aware of this and were determined to show the outsiders to be wrong. Once they had done so, they knew, their prospects for abolition of the unequal treaties would be much improved. Events proved them correct. In 1894 the existence of "Western" political and legal institutions made it possible to persuade England, and then the other powers, to implement the treaty revision that had been sought at intervals since the 1870s. Akira Iriye's discussion of Japan's rise to great-power status in Chapter 12 documents the course of Meiji diplomacy. It begins with the early Meiji delineation of national borders and culminates with Japan's victories over China in 1895 and Russia in 1905, making possible the annexation of Korea that brought Japan into the club of imperialist powers.

A focus on cultural and intellectual trends would, of course, produce a different periodization, and for those areas, a division of the Meiji period into decades is no more satisfactory than the division of Japan's longer history into centuries is for general history. Kenneth Pyle's discussion of the emergence of Meiji conservatism in the late 1880s in Chapter 11 illustrates this. His account reminds us that in the 1880s there was much more than institution building going on. For a time, government leaders tried to promote a "crash" program of cultural Westernization in their program to speed change and win foreign favor. Their failure to achieve treaty reform combined with widespread charges of toadying to the powers to produce a strong backlash of nationalist emphasis. The more interesting aspect of this came when Shiga Shigetaka and other writers tried to articulate a cultural identity and role for Japanese tradition. The vigorous battle of words and books that followed enriched Meiji cultural life. This development is best seen as one of a number of cycles of popular and official enthusiasm. Some of the Meiji figures who promoted "Western" outlooks in the early 1880s were concerned a decade later that the tides of change were running too fast, and they feared that they might soon be too strong to control. The popular enthusiasm for people's rights made it seem urgent to harness Japanese tradition in the cause of conservatism. According to Carol Gluck, the panoply of emperor-centered ideology was unfurled at the end, and not the beginning, of the Meiji period.[13] The sovereign whose statements exhorted his subjects to reform and modernization in the early years of his reign sounded a good deal more traditional by the end of his rule.

A focus on economic development, as Sydney Crawcour's discussion shows, might provide yet another chronology. The 1880s would be a period of preparation for the building of the infrastructure of modern capitalism, and genuine industrial development would become quantifiable only in the first decade of the twentieth century. Nevertheless, the stated aims and priorities of the Meiji leadership were focused on building central government strength through modern political institutions, and for those efforts the periodization that has been adopted, distinguishing periods of unification, preparation, and implementation retains coherence and validity.

Select chronology for the 1890s

1889	Yamagata Aritomo heads first cabinet under the Meiji constitution.
	Civil code is announced, stirs opposition as too Western, and is deferred.
1893	Imperial rescript required to get Diet to support costs of navy.
1894	Treaty reform succeeds with England.
	War is fought with China over Korea.
1895	Treaty of Shimonoseki is signed.
	Liberal Party joins Itō cabinet.
1896	Commercial treaty with China adds new concessions for all powers.
1898	Revised civil code is adopted with strong powers for family head.
1899	Bureaucracy is sheltered from political appointments.
	Itō Hirobumi begins formation of political party with lecture tour.
1900	Service ministers are restricted to generals and admirals on the active list.
	Rikken seiyūkai is formed under Itō.
	Japan joins Western intervention against Boxer disturbance in China.
	Electorate tax qualification lowered form ¥15 to ¥10.

HISTORIANS AND NINETEENTH-CENTURY JAPAN

History, politics, and values have intersected in interpretations of the development of modern Japan. It could hardly have been otherwise.

---

13 Carol Gluck, *Japan's Modern Myths: Ideology in the Late Meiji Period* (Princeton, N.J.: Princeton University Press, 1985).

The state that emerged from the nineteenth-century transition veered so sharply from parliamentary constitutionalism to militarism and then to pacifism, from the pursuit of national strength through arms to that pursuit through commerce, that no responsible historian could fail to ask why that was so. Contemporary Japanese are only two generations away from their Restoration forebears. The Shōwa emperor, Hirohito (1901–), grandson of the Meiji founder of the modern state, has frequently traced the postwar democratic and "peace" constitution to promises made in the Charter Oath of 1868. The Tokugawa–Meiji transition is inevitably seen through contemporary attitudes and problems, and it has been explained and evaluated differently, first from the euphoria of military success and more recently from the trauma of political failure. In history-conscious Japan, the understanding of the Meiji Restoration has seemed central to the needs and hopes of each successive present.

The official view, the way that the government leaders wanted things to be seen, was cast along the lines of a morality play of heroic dimensions. The "great work" (*taigyō*) of the Meiji Restoration consisted of the return of power to the throne and represented the culmination of a long process of growing public affection for and loyalty to a long-neglected sovereign. Once in power he had shaped the policies of his ministers. His rescripts encouraged and praised his people and his ministers.[14] All successes were ascribed to his wisdom, and difficulties were eased by his compassion. The leaders felt themselves ennobled by having had the privilege of acting as his servants. In conversations and recorded discussions they usually checked themselves at the point of self-congratulation to emphasize their dependence on the imperial favor and charisma.

The Meiji government was not long in following, in its own fashion, Chinese traditions of official historiography. An office for this was established as early as 1869, when the boy emperor prepared for Sanjō Sanetomi, then the chief minister, authorization to initiate a historiographical office charged with the proper preservation and compilation of Japanese history, presumably to free it from the shogunal bias that had slanted historical writing in the samurai world that was now passing. The *Fukko ki* (Chronicle of the return to antiquity) was the product of a directive to "establish the merit of lords and subjects, make clear the speech of the civilized at home and the barbarian without,

---

14 For the rescripts and their role, see Marius B. Jansen, "Monarchy and Modernization in Japan," *Journal of Asian Studies* 36 (August 1977): 611–22.

and thereby contribute to virtue in the realm."[15] The editorial board of this project represented leaders from the principal Restoration centers, and it was clear that interests of those groups would not be slighted. In 1911 an imperial edict established the Society for the Compilation of Records of the Restoration and established it within the Ministry of Education. When the bill authorizing this was introduced in the Imperial Diet, representatives of the political parties expressed their misgivings about the probable political nature of a historical project sponsored by the Satsuma–Chōshū men who ran the government. In response, the government spokesmen assured them that it was not the intent to write history so much as it was to compile the documentary record. Even so, the nature of the advisory board (Yamagata Aritomo of Chōshū, Ōyama Iwao and Matsukata Masayoshi of Satsuma, Hijikata Hisamoto, Tanaka Mitsuaki, and Itagaki Taisuke of Tosa), showed how vigilant the authorities were to protect their interests. The presence of representatives of the principal lords and court aristocrats as counselors gave additional evidence of such concern. Baron Kaneko Kentarō, who chaired the commission together with Inoue Kaoru of Chōshū, personally checked and at points intervened in the summary narrative account of the Restoration, *Ishin shi*, that was issued in six volumes in 1938.[16]

For the most part, however, these institutions were true to their promise to compile sources and eschew interpretive narratives. The society's staff came to number nearly fifty specialists who gathered and checked relevant documents, many of them in family record collections, to assemble one of the world's most massive collections of documents.[17] The project continued under the Ministry of Education and was located on the campus of the Imperial University of Tokyo (after 1946, the University of Tokyo) until 1949, after which it was placed under the University of Tokyo as the Historiographical Institute. Actual direction was in the hands of the university's professoriate of historians, who exercised strict standards for documentary authentic-

15 *Fukko ki*, 16 vols. (Tokyo: Naigai shoseki, 1929–31). This is a printed edition of the original manuscript, begun in 1872 and completed in 1889, and thereafter housed in the collection of Tokyo Imperial University. Editorial responsibility lay with the Teikoku daigaku rinji hennenshi hensan gakari, the forerunner of the Historiographical Institute of the University of Tokyo.
16 Some have gone so far as to relate the establishment of the society to the concern over the anarchist movement that led to the execution of Kōtoku Shūsui and other anarchists in 1911, for participation in an abortive plot on the emperor's life, and the publication of *Ishin shi* to the time of the outbreak of full-scale war with China. See Tōyama Shigeki, *Meiji ishin to gendai* (Tokyo: Iwanami shoten, 1968), pp. 16–17.
17 For a brief description of the product, too vast for publication, see Conrad Totman, *The Collapse of the Tokugawa Bakufu, 1862–1868* (Honolulu: University of Hawaii Press, 1980), pp. 549–52, who describes it as "one of the great historiographical triumphs of humankind."

ity. Until the opening of private collections to research scholars in the years after Japan's surrender in 1945, these records, to which access was restricted, furnished the chief sources for Japan's mid-nineteenth-century history.

Narrative and interpretive accounts on a more popular level did not become important until the latter part of the Meiji period. When the entire education system was in place, the preparation of standard textbooks for the lower schools required officially approved versions of past Japanese history, in which imperial loyalty was identified with morality. The textbook accounts represented a conscious effort to educate young Japanese in a heroic myth of nation foundation. Inevitably, the government leaders were important beneficiaries of this effort. Men are rarely heroes to their contemporaries, and it was some time before a hierarchical structure of prestige developed in the Meiji period. There are accounts of sharp disagreements between the Iwakura ambassadors and the young chargé at the Japanese legation in Washington in 1872, and as late as 1898, well into the era of parliamentary government, Hoshi Tōru, minister to Washington, refused to follow the orders of his foreign minister.

The elevation of the emperor by the institutions that were completed in 1890 – the constitution, imperial house law, and education rescript – had as their corollary the elevation of his ministers. By the time the general-circulation magazine *Taiyō* appeared in 1895 with the capability of glossy illustrations, they were frequently photographs of ministers of state resplendent in their imperial decorations. The memoirs of Kozaki Hiromichi, a pioneer Christian pastor whose Kumamoto peers shared his early distaste for the Meiji leaders, could note with gratification the inclusion of a high official's lady, "Princess Katsura," among his congregation.

By the late Meiji years, however, the struggles of the 1860s were no longer divisive but inclusive in character. Tokugawa culture and the shogunal capital of Edo had become part of a romantic and nostalgic past. Yoshinobu (Keiki), the last shogun, was honored with the restoration of his court rank in 1880, was appointed to the highest rank in the new peerage in 1884, and was received in private audience by the sovereign in 1898. Saigō Takamori, a Restoration military hero whose exploits had begun with the surrender of Edo in 1868 and had ended with his suicide in rebellion in 1877, received a posthumous imperial pardon and court rank in 1889. An era of good feeling surrounded the events of the Restoration days with something like the nostalgic haze that gradually obscured Civil War antagonisms in the United States.

The Restoration violence gradually became a national epic that had been essential to the creation of a state structure capable of resisting the foreign threat. Its figures, losers as well as winners, had been activated by pure, though in some cases mistaken, concepts of imperial loyalty. Yoshinobu's memoirs, *Sekimukai hikki*, recorded between 1907 and 1911, stressed the consistency of his loyalist motivations. The full elaboration of the myth of the creation of the emperor-centered state structure, the *kokutai*, was a product of the late Meiji state, essentially of the twentieth century. In the words of a recent study, "Whatever was completed in the years before 1890, ideology in national earnest had more truly just begun."[18]

In one sense, the emphasis on national ideology in late Meiji times was created to offset an earlier and pervasive view that had been more concerned with fitting Japan's experience into that of world, Western history than with emphasizing its uniqueness. Fukuzawa Yukichi's *Outline of a Theory of Civilization*, published in 1875, spoke of imperial loyalism as having value chiefly because it could stir the national effort to improve the country. He argued that "we should venerate this union between the empire and our national polity not because it goes back to the origins of Japanese history, but because its preservation will help us maintain modern Japanese sovereignty and advance our civilization. A thing is not to be valued for itself, but for its function." And again, "Every country has its political legitimization; Japanese legitimation has frequently undergone change, and in this it is no different from other countries; thus there is no reason for boasting on this score." What mattered was the state of a country's civilization and the capacity of its inhabitants to respond to the spirit of the times. This had been a factor in the history of every country in the world: "Even had the American people been defeated and temporarily set back, they would have produced 480 great leaders [as successors to the original 48] and ten George Washingtons."[19] For Fukuzawa and the writers of the 1880s, the problem was to fit Japan's experience into the larger patterns of Western history. Fukuzawa found his models in Buckle and Guizot. He used the word *revolution* for the Meiji change, but his view, though it included public dissatisfaction as an element of that overthrow, was closer to the classical Confucian view of a change-over resulting from a changed spirit of the times in which a government loses its mandate. "In the end," he wrote, "public opinion

---

18 Gluck, *Japan's Modern Myths*, p. 26.
19 Fukuzawa Yukichi, *An Outline of a Theory of Civilization*, trans. David A. Dilworth and G. Cameron Hurst (Tokyo: Sophia University Press, 1973), pp. 33, 24, 27, 60.

coalesced around the one slogan of 'overthrow the Bakufu,' the intellectual powers of the whole nation were directed toward this single goal, and the end result was the successful revolution of 1867."[20]

A decade later a group of writers saw the Restoration somewhat differently. Intent on the People's Rights movement of their day, they saw the events of the 1860s and 1870s as preliminary to a new stage of political change, and the Restoration as the first step in a process that had still to be completed. Political theorists like Nakae Chōmin spoke of this with confidence, but the most thorough treatment of the theme came at the hands of generalists who wrote for a mass audience: Tokutomi Sohō, Taguchi Ukichi, Ukita Kazutami, Yamaji Aizan, and Takekoshi Yosaburō.[21]

These writers had been stirred by Macaulay and Carlyle, and they looked for indications that the change in Japan would go on to produce the betterment of life that had followed the English revolution. The emergence of the popular democratic movement seemed to suggest that Japan might in fact be following the path of Western liberalism and enlightenment. Unfortunately, the promise had remained unfulfilled. No social revolution had followed the political overturn, and the government was still dominated by a restrictive regional clique. These writers of "Whig" history, as Peter Duus called it, saw it as their task to build sentiment for the work of a "second restoration" to complete the first, so that a commoner society would replace the one in which they lived. Tokutomi, for instance, relied on the work of Herbert Spencer to argue the inevitability of Japan's becoming an "industrial society" in which popular sentiment and ability would lay the foundation for a mighty "floating wharf in the Pacific," its sky black with the "smoke rising from thousands of smokestacks. . . . And all this will come just because there is this precious freedom."[22] Tokutomi felt his society was ready for this because of the material and social developments that had prepared the way for truly significant progress. Inexorable laws of social progress had brought down the bakufu; the causes of the Restoration were to be found in the development of basic discontents within Tokugawa society, and its course had been determined less by the brilliance of its leaders than by the social disorder generated by an oppressed people that could suffer no longer. These writers

---

20 Fukuzawa, *An Outline*, p. 15. See also the recent commentary by Maruyama Masao, "*Bummeiron no gairyaku*" *o yonde*, 3 vols. (Tokyo: Iwanami shoten, 1986).
21 See Peter Duus, "Whig History, Japanese Style: The Min'yūsha Historians and the Meiji Restoration," *Journal of Asian Studies* 33 (May 1974): 415–36.
22 John D. Pierson, *Tokutomi Sohō 1863–1957: A Journalist for Modern Japan* (Princeton University Press, 1980), p. 114; and Irokawa Daikichi, *Meiji seishinshi* (Tokyo: Chikuma shobō, 1964).

wrote with approval of the strength of a rural squirarchy (a class from which many of them sprang) which had developed resentments against urban samurai bureaucrats. These "country gentlemen" (*inaka shinshi*) had dominated society in Kumamoto, where Tokutomi and Ukita had had their youthful schooling under the tutelage of the American Civil War artillery captain L. L. Janes, whose school had produced the "Kumamoto band" of Christian Westernizers.[23]

Tokutomi, Takekoshi, Ukita, Taguchi, Yamaji, and other "Whig" historians thus produced a "progressive" view of Meiji changes in which the accomplishments were possible because of social developments and not because of the achievements of a leadership for which they had only limited respect. They were in fact suspicious that the leadership was reactionary and determined to retain its grip on power in the face of rising popular demand for participation, and they designed their histories as political statements. In turn, as Professor Pyle's discussion of Meiji conservatism shows, they had the effect of stimulating a more conservative opposition, one that valorized Japanese tradition more highly than they did themselves. Out of that crucible of contending views came the official textbook accounts of modern Japanese history. It was a struggle that went beyond the Meiji changes themselves, for loyalty rendered absolute made it necessary to rewrite much of the past to select the virtuous for praise. Political considerations in the first decade of the twentieth century made it advisable to rearrange accounts of fourteenth-century political history and resulted in rewording course titles at the imperial universities.[24]

In a setting that politicized any matter related to the imperial court, academic historians were usually content to leave the events of the nineteenth century for other scholars. At the pinnacle of the educational structure the state universities had no chairs in modern history, and students seeking topics for graduation theses were usually advised that the events of the Restoration were still too close to the present and better suited to politics and journalism.[25] For the most part, the field was left to specialists in legal history and institutional history like Yoshino Sakuzō and Osatake Takeki, who led in the collection and publication of sources neglected by the official institute,[26] and eco-

---

23 F. G. Notehelfer, *American Samurai: Captain L. L. Janes and Japan* (Princeton, N.J.: Princeton University Press, 1985).
24 See H. Paul Varley, *Imperial Restoration in Medieval Japan* (New York: Columbia University Press, 1971).
25 Tōyama, *Meiji ishin to gendai*, p. 17.
26 Yoshino Sakuzō, *Meiji bunka zenshū*, 24 vols. (Tokyo: Nihon hyōronsha, 1927–30).

nomic historians who focused on social and economic changes rather than political events.²⁷

In the 1920s and 1930s a new group of writers was drawn to nineteenth-century themes precisely because they were political. World War I and its aftermath brought a new stage of industrial development to Japan as manufacturers seized the opportunities that resulted from the West's preoccupation with the conflict. Its aftermath brought new social problems; the postwar slump produced unprecedented numbers and sizes of labor disputes. Meanwhile, the Bolshevik revolution in Russia, together with its reverberations in postwar Europe, gave Marxist economic theory a new theoretical relevance. It now became possible to relate the foreign ("capitalist") threat to Japan to the development of modern ("capitalist") Japan, thereby combining what had been discrete fields of inquiry. These concerns centered in economic history, a field that had already led in the examination of late Tokugawa developments. Out of this context came two schools of interpretation whose propositions divided and dominated most writing for the decades to come. Their arguments centered on the nature of the late Tokugawa economy, but they had relevance to Japan's political present and future.

One group held that the Meiji Restoration, because of the leadership of members of the ruling class and the lack of popular participation, had resulted in an emperor-centered absolutism and that the step required for further social change was a move toward a bourgeois revolution. The classical collection in which this position was argued, the *Lectures on the History of the Development of Japanese Capitalism*,²⁸ gave its adherents the name of the "Lectures" (*kōza*) faction. A second group held that the changes of the nineteenth century, though incomplete, had nevertheless constituted a bourgeois movement and that it was consequently possible to work for further social progress through the existing political system. Its adherents worked with labor and farm groups, in publications and political organizations, to earn the "Labor–Farmer" (*rōnō*) label. Growing political pressure in the late 1920s and 1930s gradually made difficult a more explicit pursuit of these Marxist themes, and so practitioners had to cope with censorship and persecution by masking their arguments in prose that was increasingly opaque and convoluted. The controversy had direct relevance to the pro-

---

27 For example, Honjō Eijirō, *Nihon keizai shi gaisetsu* and *Kinsei hōken shakai no kenkyū*, both published in 1928. Osatake Takeki was also the author of a standard narrative of the Restoration struggle, published after World War II: *Meiji ishin*, 4 vols. (Tokyo: Hakuyosha, 1946–9).
28 *Nihon shihonshugi hattatsushi kōza* (Tokyo: Iwanami shoten, 1932).

grams of the Japanese left. The term *tennōsei* ("emperor system") focused on the imperial institution as the keystone in the arch of complementary interest groups – the "feudal" landed class, the military, and the great combines or zaibatsu – which combined to block democratic developments. Fear of impending militarism and continental war gave new relevance and urgency to scholarly analysis. In 1932, shortly after the invasion of Manchuria and the renewed suppression of the Japanese left, new theses of the Japan Communist Party called for an attack on the *tennōsei* as the central problem facing the country. This coincided closely in time with the appearance of the first volume of the *Lectures*. *Tennōsei* as a term had been used earlier, but from this point on it had a more specific definition. In terms of historical discussion, the importance of this debate lay in the way that it forced its participants to go beyond and behind the political history that had been the chief focus for earlier scholars and to trace social currents and relationships on both sides of the Restoration so as to stress continuities. Wartime repression and solidarity provided little encouragement for the development of these themes, but it helped prepare for the explosion of scholarly activity that followed the lifting of the taboos that had surrounded discussions of the imperial state before the surrender of 1945.

In postsurrender Japan, disillusion and derogation of the military-imperial state combined with respect for the Marxists who had tried to resist that order and had predicted its disastrous end. Marxism was in fact almost unchallenged for a time, as real or apparent supporters of the old order were silenced by dismissal and purge. The sudden lifting of taboos on discussions of recent history produced an emphatic rejection of the values of prewar Japanese orthodoxy and especially of the affirmation of loyalism that had been its center. A new and vehement denunciation of the "emperor system" led to efforts to find its origin. It was, wrote the literary critic Takeuchi Yoshimi, "a total mental and spiritual structure" and part of every Japanese who had grown up under its sway. "Seeing it as a part of our consciousness," he argued, "is the precondition for freeing ourselves from it."[29]

The postsurrender turn to social history, most of it phrased in Marxist categories, had many aspects. In the early postsurrender years of hardship, little research of substance was possible, and Marxist categories offered an inviting framework for the facts that lay at hand. With economic and social recovery, however, a prodigious effort was poured into documentary, local, and regional study in an effort to

---

29 Quoted in Irokawa, *The Culture of the Meiji Period*, p. 13.

provide a better base for understanding what had gone wrong in modern Japan. The "Lectures"–"Labor–Farmer" dispute of the 1930s revived in vigor amid an explosion of effort and produced a literature so voluminous that several histories of the debate were written.[30] In the course of this dispute, positions came to be refined, merged, and even reversed, until their genealogy became tedious for all but the most committed participants. Some of the contentions were once again related to contemporary politics. Writers saw in the anticommunist measures that were taken during the Korean War of 1950–53, and in the debates about revision of the postwar constitution and about rearmament, a revival of militarism and ultranationalism, and made it their task to criticize the past. The Meiji Restoration and the Meiji state remained contemporary and relevant, and they contained portents of a future that could seem alarming.

In the 1960s many American and some Japanese historians tried to extricate the discourse from categories that seemed to have become sterile by discussing nineteenth-century Japan in terms of "modernization" instead of "capitalism" and "absolutism." Japan's economic recovery and its stability under its revised constitutional order seemed to place it much closer to the developed or modernized polities of the West and to make of it a contrast with the turbulence being experienced by the so-called Third World countries, especially mainland China. *Modernization* was in origin a neutral term, designed to describe the maturation of scientific knowledge, bureaucratic organization of life in school, workplace, and politics, mass education, urbanization, industrialization, and internationalization. For most of those who used it, the term represented an effort to avoid politics and to substitute one generalization for others, in the hope that it would prove more objective and more inclusive.

Seen through the categories of modernization, nineteenth-century Japan became more nearly a unit, with a steady increase in education, urbanization, internationalization, and bureaucratization; the late Tokugawa efforts for self-strengthening by leading domains demonstrated a mode of rational planning that was centralized and intensified in the Meiji unification, and the commercialization of late Tokugawa society prepared the way for the capitalist institutions of Meiji Japan. That these could and did lead to unfortunate consequences as Japan

---

30 For a recent discussions, see Yasukichi Yasuba, "Anatomy of the Debate on Japanese Capitalism," *Journal of Japanese Studies* 2 (Autumn 1975): 63–82; and Germaine A. Hoston, *Marxism and the Crisis of Development in Prewar Japan* (Princeton, N.J.: Princeton University Press, 1986).

turned to the construction of an empire in the twentieth century was not at issue, but that they were nevertheless of critical importance in the construction of the advanced democracy of contemporary Japan seemed no less important. A series of conference volumes in which Western specialists explored these themes exercised considerable influence as they reoriented thought along these lines.[31]

Meanwhile, economic historians in Japan, with new access to primary materials and new instruments of statistical and demographic analysis at hand, took up quantitative studies that revised long-held postulates about immiseration in late Tokugawa Japan and in turn stimulated sweeping new hypotheses from Western scholars.[32]

As could have been anticipated, these developments were contested by many Japanese scholars, especially those committed to the left-of-center political positions. They were offended by what seemed the substitution of a "positive" for a previously "negative" view of nineteenth-century developments. Although those who wrote of modernization saw the term as neutral – Hitler's Third Reich, after all, was the product of a "modernized" society – their critics charged them with having a hidden agenda of support for contemporary capitalist Japan and denied the possibility or, indeed, the desirability of value-free analysis. For many Japanese the term *modern* was, furthermore, one that brought with it the opprobrium of prewar cultural and literary struggles in which ideologists of Japanism had called for efforts to "transcend" modernity and Western materialism. Most directly, perhaps, they were alarmed by the possible political utility of the theme for Japan's governing conservatives who seemed to be restructuring the postwar polity by urging revision of the constitution of 1947, restoration of nationalist holidays, and especially rearmament. As the centennial of the Meiji Restoration approached in 1968, the influential historian Tōyama Shigeki pointed to areas of agreement between modernization analysis and prewar nationalist writing (a high evaluation of industrialization, the indiscriminate listing of criteria instead of valori-

---

[31] The conference volumes, all issued by Princeton University Press, are *Changing Japanese Attitudes Toward Modernization*, ed. Marius B. Jansen (1965); *The State and Economic Enterprise in Japan*, ed. William W. Lockwood (1965); *Aspects of Social Change in Modern Japan*, ed. R. P. Dore (1967); *Political Development in Modern Japan*, ed. Robert E. Ward (1968); *Tradition and Modernization in Japanese Culture*, ed. Donald H. Shively (1971); and *Dilemmas of Growth in Prewar Japan*, ed. James W. Morley (1971).

[32] For example, Hayami Akira, *Nihon keizaishi e no shikaku* (Tokyo: Tōyō keizai shimpōsha, 1968); and Shimbō Hiroshi, Hayami Akira, and Nishikawa Shunsaku, *Sūryō keizaishi nyūmon* (Tokyo: Nihon hyōronsha, 1975); Susan B. Hanley and Kozo Yamamura, *Economic and Demographic Change in Preindustrial Japan, 1600–1868* (Princeton, N.J.: Princeton University Press, 1977).

zation of democratization, a lack of emphasis on imperialism, a favorable view of the Meiji leaders, and the failure to relate modernization to imperialist developments) and made explicit the need to criticize the contemporary government's policies in any exposition of the Meiji Restoration.[33]

By the late 1960s the preoccupation of a new generation of American scholars with the Vietnam War produced an almost identical repudiation of the "modernization" school and its works. Now writings focused on the costs of modernization for the Japanese people and their neighbors and sought to relate such writings to American foreign policy.[34] Generational conflict was at work on both sides of the Pacific, however, for although a younger generation of American Japanologists was finding new merit in the Marxist writings of senior Japanese scholars, their contemporaries in Japan, weary of the student wars of the 1960s that had borne little fruit, were turning away from the formulaic denunciations of their mentors.

The newly sovereign Japan of the late 1950s and 1960s did not, in fact, seem to conform to the Marxist picture. Full civil and political rights had been extended; freedom to organize was at hand; civil rights had the full protection of law; and yet the masses did not seem to make use of them. The great campaign to prevent ratification of the United States–Japan Security pact that peaked with the demonstrations of 1960 left Japan no closer to a Marxist model. New movements of political participation pursued local and practical issues like pollution instead of larger ideological goals. The arguments and controversies began to seem dated and irrelevant. The Japan Communist Party, which expelled several thousand intellectuals from its ranks after the 1960 struggle, lost ascendancy and appeal. A history that spoke to Japan's new urban masses had to find new things to say.

It is not surprising that a fully "modernized" Japan, conscious of the wrenching discontinuities with its past, turned to reexamine the problem of national roots and distinctiveness. Prewar history that had focused on important leaders was ruled out, but so were sterile Marxist categories that had little room for people at all. Instead, new currents of "people's history" came to the fore. By 1968 the annual gathering of the once solidly Marxist Association for Research in History (Rekishigaku kenkyūkai) set its topic as "History of People's Thought," and in the

---

33 Tōyama, *Meiji ishin to gendai*, pp. 6–8.
34 Mikiso Hane, *Peasants, Rebels and Outcastes: The Underside of Modern Japan* (New York: Pantheon, 1982); and John W. Dower, *Origins of the Modern Japanese State: Selected Writings of E. H. Norman* (New York: Pantheon, 1975), pp. 3–101.

following years more and more effort was devoted to finding, publishing, and analyzing sources for the life, thought, and activities of ordinary Japanese. In this process the evaluation of categories through which the nineteenth-century past had been seen changed once more. When the scholar Ōtsuka Hisao translated and discussed Max Weber in the 1950s, it was his contention, then accepted by Marxists and liberals alike, that the "gemeinschaft" community (*kyōdōtai*) of Tokugawa times had been a bar to individualism and a hindrance to democratic development. In the 1960s, as rapid economic growth, urbanization, and industrialization brought impressive environmental pollution to Japan and as modernization became firmly associated with capitalism in ordinary speech, there was a preparedness to rethink and reevaluate the once-scorned "community" of the past. Individualism seemed a mixed blessing unless it retained the lateral cohesion and social solidarity of the premodern village that took care of its own. The hard-and-fast legal distinctions of twentieth-century Japan, the environmental degradation and anomie of modern society, made modernization less attractive as fact and as conceptual framework.

In the intellectual currents of the 1960s and 1970s these considerations moved in parallel with a rising interest in ethnology and folklore. This was associated with a revival of interest in Yanagita Kunio (1875–1962) and peaked with the centennial of his birth. Yanagita, a poet-scholar and sometime government official, had devoted his life to establishing folklore as a subject of academic study. He sought to elucidate the history of Japan by exploring and recording oral traditions in all parts of the country, thereby supplementing and strengthening the work of academic historians who relied on documents. "If there are no old records," he wrote, "we must search among the facts that have survived into the present."[35] Yanagita's valorization of the life and legends of ordinary people presented material for the observation of a Japan that was neither "good" nor "bad," a "success" or a "failure," but pregnant with possibilities for irrationality as well as orderly bureaucratization. His work contributed to that of the historians of "people's thought." These scholars were no less determined than were the Marxists to avoid the pitfalls for future error through the understanding of the roots of previous national aberrations. Within Marxist historiography as well, trends toward the same concerns and emphases replaced the rigid emphasis on the class struggle of the past.

For these historians the centuries of Tokugawa rule produced impor-

---

35 R. A. Morse, trans., "Introduction," *The Legends of Tōno by Kunio Yanagita* (Tokyo: Japan Foundation, 1975), p. xxv.

tant changes in the Japanese countryside that made the early modern village quite different from what it had been and equally different from the landlord-dominated village it was to become under twentieth-century capitalism. Obsequious deference to the military had all but disappeared during the prolonged absence of the samurai in their castle towns. The countryside had produced a natural elite of local notables whose education and responsibility prepared them for intellectual as well as social leadership. Government had increasingly relied on a traditional morality that depended on reciprocal respect among the classes, and village notables responded with a responsibility that was demonstrated by their willingness to defend and articulate local needs and expectations. In the "moral economy" of the countryside, diligence and propriety were expected, and oppression and greed from above brought resistance that was usually successful. Life was, in other words, less brutish and harsh than the Marxist proponents of immiseration had asserted, and the local elite less exploitive and grasping than it it had been portrayed. Meiji capitalism, on the other hand, and the prescription of clear-cut obligations under modern law, enforced by ubiquitous modern police, had changed these conditions for the worse as the local elite moved to the new cities and the *inaka shinshi* (local gentlemen) described by Meiji historians were replaced by, or degenerated into, exploitative employers.[36]

The gloomy evaluation of twentieth-century developments in Japanese society has, however, been tempered by a number of recent studies of landlord–tenant relations in modern Japan.[37] The "moral economy" of the people's historians who have described a more prosperous and caring countryside is probably not without its nostalgia for a better past, but the specific studies of rural discontent with Meiji policies and the evidence of vibrant possibilities for politics of an engaged and engaging rural elite that responded eagerly to the People's Rights movement in the late 1870s and 1880s have transformed the understanding of the Japanese countryside.[38] These debates and concerns have been reflected, though also somewhat muted, in Western writing about nineteenth-century Japan. One symposium volume

---

36 See Carol Gluck, "The People in History: Recent Trends in Japanese Historiography," *Journal of Japanese Studies* 38 (November 1978): 25–50.
37 Ann Waswo, *Japanese Landlords: The Decline of a Rural Elite* (Berkeley and Los Angeles: University of California Press, 1977); and more particularly, Richard J. Smethhurst, *Agricultural Development and Tenancy Disputes in Japan, 1870–1940* (Princeton, N.J.: Princeton University Press, 1986).
38 Irokawa Daikichi, *Meiji no bunka* (Tokyo: Iwanami shoten, 1970), translation edited by Marius B. Jansen as *The Culture of the Meiji Period* (Princeton, N.J.: Princeton University Press, 1985).

that combines the statistical work of economists and demographers with discussions of social organization and social scientists suggests some of the approaches called to bear in the effort to treat nineteenth-century Japan as a unit and the Meiji Restoration experience as transition rather than cataclysmic innovation.[39]

Nineteenth-century Japan speaks differently to each generation of students who pursue its themes, and Japanese continue to seek in it clues to their society's past and future. The movement for "people's history" has unearthed documentary and private sources that crowd our shelves. Knowledge that local leaders in remote mountain villages met regularly to debate the content of model constitutions in the 1880s, and evidence from private collections that shows how eager many people were to participate more fully in Japan's institutional growth makes it necessary to review long-standard generalizations about enlightened leaders who brought their backward countrymen into the modern world.[40] The tide of publications that illustrate the irreverent and even obstreperous communications with which ordinary people addressed and reproached their leaders gives the lie to sweeping generalizations about "inert commoners" who had no sense of larger issues.[41]

What was true in history has now become true of historians. The standard picture of the metropolitan scholar respectfully heard by obsequious provincials is changing today as centennial meetings to commemorate the inauguration of the People's Rights movement, and its milestones of the 1880s, attract participants who number in the thousands. The 1981 centennial of the founding of the Liberal Party drew seven thousand; the 1984 centennial of the Chichibu revolt attracted six thousand; and a 1987 centennial of the revival of People's Rights activities again drew as many. Founders of "people's history" have been astonished to find their country dotted with a network of local "people's history" societies as widespread as were the People's Rights societies of the 1880s. As was the case a century ago, local schoolteachers provide almost half the members and participants in these celebrations of Japan's modern history, and academic specialists make up the merest fraction. A field that E. H. Norman, almost half a

---

39 Jansen and Rozman, eds., *Japan in Transition*.
40 Irokawa, *The Culture of the Meiji Period*.
41 See William W. Kelly, *Deference and Defiance in Nineteenth-Century Japan* (Princeton, N.J.: Princeton University Press, 1985), for specific illustrations from Shōnai. To date, six volumes have appeared of a massive project reprinting memorials addressed to the government by ordinary people: Irokawa Daikichi and Gabe Masao, eds., *Meiji kempakusho shūsei* (Tokyo: Chikuma shobō, 1986–).

century ago, described as fertile, fallow, and awaiting cultivation has brought different harvests for workers in many seasons, but its riches are far from exhausted. It is our hope that the chapters that follow will encourage still others to share in that bounty.[42]

[42] E. H. Norman, *Japan's Emergence As a Modern State* (New York: Institute of Pacific Relations, 1940) p. 222.

CHAPTER 1

JAPAN IN THE EARLY NINETEENTH CENTURY

The first third of the nineteenth century in Japan was dominated by personalities and policies that appeared on the scene in the last decade of the eighteenth century. The reform measures of Matsudaira Sadanobu and the personal preferences of his shogun, Tokugawa Ienari, lent a considerable continuity to the Bunka (1804–18) and Bunsei (1818–30) eras.

In contrast with the devastation and famine that the crop failures of the 1780s had brought, the quarter-century that followed seemed something of an Indian summer of Tokugawa rule. The years were marked by good harvests. The long continuity of Ienari, whose half-century in office marked the longest tenure of any of the fifteen Tokugawa shoguns, was reflected in a lack of political surprises in bakufu or daimyo domains. Economic growth, both in agriculture and in the provision of materials for the great metropolis of Edo, a striking rise in the diffusion of schooling, and the impressive production of material for the growing reading public all contributed to the impression of well-being. Arbitrary status divisions laid down by the seventeenth-century founders had less relevance in a period of economic change and growth. At the top of the samurai ranks, hereditary income and privilege stood as a guarantee of continuity, but the great urban merchants lived as well as did the petty daimyo, and the lower ranks of the samurai military were considerably worse off than were the middling merchants and artisans. In the countryside a clear division between the landholding village leaders and the landless and tenants was making a mockery of the regime's "peasant" ideal.

These developments also contributed to strains that had been building through the eighteenth century. The blurring of class lines was not accompanied by any institutional resolution, with the result that the newly able were usually frustrated by the limits of opportunity open to them. The diffusion of literacy and the production of reading material came in a setting of censorship and suspicion that foreclosed all discussion of public and national policy and thus forced writers into the production of the ephemeral and the absurd. A culture of play, as Harootunian refers to it in a later chapter, was also one of avoidance. The regime in fact responded to innovation with increased rigidity and thereby fossilized a tradition that it professed to defend. Threatened by a diffusion of knowledge about the outside world, it responded with policies of censorship and tried to co-opt the scholars concerned. Puzzled by the advance of Western ships, it elevated "seclusion" into a cardinal policy of state. Consequently, the decades with which this chapter is concerned saw the growing contradiction between the growth of knowledge and of goods and the rigid restrictions caused by status and suspicion, and this often led to frustrations expressed in privatization and alienation in individual lives.

SHOGUN AND REGENT

The eleventh shogun, Tokugawa Ienari, was born to the Hitotsubashi (*sankyō*) cadet house in 1773, designated heir to Ieharu in 1781, and succeeded him as shogun in 1787. His fifty-year incumbency was the longest of the Tokugawa period, and even after he retired in favor of Ieyoshi (shogun from 1837 to 1853), he dominated politics from his retirement until his death in 1841. His reign began with the reforms of Matsudaira Sadanobu, inaugurated when the boy shogun was only thirteen, and went on to include a period of personal luxury and opulence that brought him the disapproval of later historians.

Ienari was something of a rarity in shogunal history, in that he combined with his long tenure a willful personality that made him dominate a half-century of rule. He began with disapproval of the officials and policies of the Tanuma era. Ienari replaced that administration with the reforms of Matsudaira Sadanobu, but the reform minister soon fell out with his strong-willed master. In part this was because Sadanobu, who blocked an effort by the Kyoto sovereign, Kōkaku *tennō*, to give his father the honors and title appropriate to a retired sovereign (the *songō*, or Title incident), was no more inclined to honor Ienari's desire to install his own father, Hitotsubashi Harusada, in the Chiyoda Castle with honors appropriate to a retired shogun. In the case at Kyoto, Sadanobu first offered his resignation, and after it was rejected, he raised the father's income without granting him the desired status. Thereafter he took a strong line to emphasize the bakufu's concern with propriety and status by securing the punishment of the nobles who had encouraged the court in its confrontation with Edo. But when Ienari sought honors for his father, the case was not as easy to handle. When Sadanobu submitted his resignation as chief minister in 1793, it was accepted. The young shogun then proceeded to have his way with his father's residential arrangements.

Ienari seems to have disapproved of Sadanobu's treatment of the Kyoto courtiers on other grounds as well. During his reign he accumulated some forty consorts and produced fifty-five children, maintaining what was probably the largest harem (ōoku) in Tokugawa history, a record that has led some historians to characterize his rule as the "Ōoku era." With so generous a supply of chessmen, Ienari was led to practice marriage politics on a scale previously unknown, placing sons and daughters in daimyo and *kuge* families. His principal consort was a daughter of the Satsuma *tozama* daimyo Shimazu Shigehide (1745–1833), who was first adopted into the great *kuge* house of Konoe, and he approved similar alliances between Tokugawa cadet houses and court families. Ienari further accepted for himself titles and office in the court hierarchy, becoming successively minister of the right (1816), of the left (1822), and minister of state (*dajō daijin*) in 1827. In consequence, the traditional restraints on ties between the shogunal family and the court aristocracy and with *tozama* daimyo that had been worked out by the Tokugawa system's founders in the seventeenth century were now discarded in favor of a more cosmopolitan and largely undifferentiated aristocracy. In the final decades of Tokugawa rule a number of major daimyo were closely related and at times half-brothers. This made for equanimity during the plentiful harvests and relatively smooth course of national events in the Bunka and Bunsei eras, but it probably also made it more difficult for the bakufu to rally its supporters in the crises of its closing years.

THE KANSEI REFORMS

The reforms carried out by Matsudaira Sadanobu are often compared with those of his grandfather, the shogun Yoshimune in the Kyōhō (1716–36) era. Like Yoshimune, Sadanobu tried to return the polity to the simpler samurai standards of earlier days. Also like him, he failed in his object. But although the full severity of the reforms was moderated after the departure of Sadanobu from national politics in 1793, their impact went well beyond his brief rule. Members of the Tanuma faction returned to high bakufu office in 1818, but the legislation that had been instituted in the Kansei reforms was never fully or formally recalled. Most of Sadanobu's policies with respect to education and administrative competence outlived his tenure as regent. The

Kansei reforms thus made important and permanent marks on nineteenth-century cultural and institutional life.

Matsudaira Sadanobu was determined to curb what he regarded as the corruption and misgovernment of the Tanuma years and based his reforms on Confucian assumptions of probity in public office.[1] He was also concerned with the primacy of the Edo over the Kyoto court, as the struggle about the *tennō*'s father showed, and he was equally concerned with the economic dependence of Edo on western Japan. Imports from other areas had increased Edo's dependence on merchants who arranged those imports, and control of merchant profits was a natural corollary of his political purposes. Sadanobu responded to these problems by imposing measures of austerity that called for limits on administrative spending, restrictions on merchant guilds, and cancellation of samurai obligations for loans contracted to merchants before 1784. After a series of efforts to lower the price of rice, he ordered the prices lowered in 1791. He restricted foreign trade by reducing the number of foreign ships permitted to call at Nagasaki and lengthened the interval between the Dutch factor's visits to Edo. At the same time he worked for more able administration by calling for uniformity in official teachings of Confucianism and made the bakufu's school a national institution.

As described in Chapter 9, the importance of Edo in the Tokugawa economy had been increasing throughout the eighteenth century as the metropolis progressed from being an importer of Kansei products to being a producer and arbiter of economic life in the Kantō plain. Sadanobu's measures reflected and built on these trends. In order to lessen Edo's dependence on imports of food, he ordered recent urban migrants to return to their villages and took steps to limit the number and weaken the monopoly rights of merchant guilds. Currency was strengthened by a recoinage that increased the proportion of precious metal and tried to lessen the price advantage of Osaka. Edo rice brokers for samurai (*fudasashi*) were restrained by the cancellation of loans to samurai and steps to control interest rates. House rents in Edo were controlled, and major merchant houses were selected as the regime's fiscal agents in an attempt to lower the cost of transporting rice and other essentials.

Measures of this sort were designed to reduce the size of the metropolis and the independence of its merchant houses, but they also illustrated the importance of those merchants in the life of the citi-

---

[1] The reforms are also treated by Isao Soranaka, "The Kansei Reforms – Success or Failure," *Monumenta Nipponica* 33 (Summer 1978): 154–64.

zenry and in fact provided new opportunities for merchant enterprises. Sadanobu's officials issued directives designed to encourage the development of local sources for *sake*, oil, cotton, and paper that had been imported from western Japan, but these orders strengthened the Edo merchants and made the city and its surrounding plain a far more viable economic area. The importance of Edo for the bakufu bureaucracy was also illustrated by a proliferation of offices and bureaus for control and information. Concerned by the evidence of social instability that had accumulated during the hardship years of the 1780s, Sadanobu built up the administrative structure in an effort to deal with poverty and the homeless. The Edo Town Office (Machi kaisho) grew in size as social services and official vigilance increased. New bureaus improved record keeping, surveillance, and security. After analyzing Edo's administrative expenses for the years before his taking up office, Sadanobu ordered a reduction by one-tenth. Of this he set aside one-tenth as a rebate to those who paid land taxes and 70 percent for aid and relief to the poor. Merchant houses were enlisted to augment the sum. Much of this went for rice that was stored in specially built granaries, and the remainder of the cash reserve was used for emergency loans at interest. Under its bureaucratic and merchant management, the fund so established had grown to nearly half a million *ryō* by the 1820s, with an additional quarter-million *ryō* out in loans and close to a half-million *koku* of rice in reserve. Thus the minister who deplored official corruption under his predecessor launched his administration on forms of state activity that were as likely to encourage new excesses as they were to ensure "moral government." Additional administrative offices were also required for new measures to guard and repair the city's many bridges, improve and clarify judicial responsibilities, regularize record keeping, control fires, and increase undercover surveillance. Circulating inspectors were ordered to observe and report virtuous conduct and instances of outstanding longevity as well as infractions of behavior, with particular attention to plans destructive to the polity. The result was a city much more carefully and predictably governed than it had been.[2]

Calls for official rectitude extended to the rural areas that the bakufu controlled. A purge of *daikan*, the officials responsible for rural administration, saw eight officials punished in two years, in some cases for wrongdoing done by their fathers or uncles. The officials who survived or who were appointed were urged to perform in the manner

---

2 Minami Kazuo, *Edo no shakai kōzō* (Tokyo: Hanawa shobō, 1969), pp. 22–35.

of model Confucian administrators. One such man, responsible for the rule of 182 villages that had been devastated by famine in the north Kantō plain, gained such fame for a program of birth statistics and special allowances for births which he instituted to control infanticide that he was posthumously enshrined as a deity (*daimyōjin*). *Daikan* were ordered to prepare injunctions to be read to village elders encouraging ability, diligence, and self-denial and to offer public praise and reward for outstanding instances of filiality and loyalty in order to popularize proper Confucian behavior. Such steps were not, of course, new; similar measures had been taken by outstanding daimyo in other areas. Nevertheless, such measures were diffused more widely, and spoken of more generally, after Sadanobu's efforts.[3]

The educational and ideological references of the Kansei years provided the most striking example of Sadanobu's determination to reverse the presumed decline of the late-eighteenth-century trends and to reaffirm and reify a Tokugawa "tradition." Since the days of the first shogun, members of the Hayashi family of Confucian scholars had served as rectors of education (*daigaku no kami*) and directed a family school that stressed the teachings of Chu Hsi Confucianism. This association with bakufu appointment created a presumption of bakufu support for one philosophical position, and representatives of other intellectual traditions had never held the post. The early shoguns, however, were relatively indifferent to philosophical distinctions and tended to favor a mixture of Buddhist and Shinto values. Ieyasu's enshrinement as the Great Deity of the East (Tōshōgū gongen) at Nikkō, despite his personal affiliation with Pure Land Buddhism and the institutional favor he accorded the Zen monk Tendai, stand as proof of this eclecticism. In personal preference Matsudaira Sadanobu too was not markedly enthusiastic about Sung Neo-Confucianism. What mattered, he wrote before his access to power, was how one lived and behaved; practical administrators should not spare time for philosophical ratiocination.[4]

But once in office, Sadanobu was concerned with order and soon decided that the luxuriant growth of competing philosophical schools in eighteenth-century Japan was a clear departure from the approved way. In the seventy-two years between 1716 and 1788, Chu Hsi teachers in domain schools barely outnumbered others (by a count of 273 to 224); of the nonconformists, the great majority were followers of the

---

3 Kumakura Isao, "Kasei bunka no zentei: Kansei kaikaku o megutte," in Hayashiya Tatsusaburō, ed., *Kasei bunka no kenkyū* (Tokyo: Iwanami shoten, 1976), pp. 62–3.
4 Kumakura, "Kasei bunka no zentei," p. 51.

rigorously philological teachings of Ogyū Sorai (118), and Itō Jinsai (49). This seemed to Sadanobu to portend diversity and struggle for the future. He was encouraged in this fervor by some of the more rigid and self-assured advocates of Chu Hsi Confucianists who were associated with the school of Yamazaki Ansai (1618–82), men who considered themselves "orthodox" and all others "heterodox." They argued that growing diversity in interpretation and emphasis would lead to confusion in morality.

In 1790 came the proscription of heterodoxy (*igaku no kin*). Sadanobu instructed the Hayashi family head to purge his school of teachers who were not followers of Chu Hsi. His directive asserted that the learning of Chu Hsi had enjoyed the confidence of "successive generations of the ruling house" since early Tokugawa days and that because "in recent times a variety of novel doctrines" had been preached, the prevalence of heterodoxy had ruined public morals. Hayashi was ordered to accept new appointees to his faculty, consult carefully with them, "sternly forbid heterodoxy to the students," and make every effort to reach agreement with other schools to pursue the orthodox learning and "advance men of ability."[5] Sadanobu thus inaugurated, in the name of a "tradition" that he had substantially invented, official bakufu commitment to Chu Hsi orthodoxy. This remained official bakufu policy for the rest of the Tokugawa years. The domain schools followed the Tokugawa example by a process of attrition and appointment. Thereafter, formal commitment to Sung Neo-Confucianism was the norm, even on the part of scholars whose personal preferences were for more eclectic inclusion of other interpretations that had flourished in the eighteenth century.

This shift entailed official interference with the Hayashi academy, which became more of a national institution than it ever had been. That development was by no means welcome to its administrators. The new institution, henceforth to be known as the Shōheikō, soon included faculty members from Tokushima and Osaka. When Hayashi died, the bakufu selected as the school's new head the third son of the daimyo of Iwamura, who was first adopted into the Hayashi family and who served from 1793 to 1839. Confucianism thus became more narrow and restricted in deference to orders from above at the same

---

5 See Robert L. Backus, "The Motivation of Confucian Orthodoxy in Tokugawa Japan" and "The Kensei Prohibition of Heterodoxy and Its Effects on Education," *Harvard Journal of Asiatic Studies* 39 (December 1979): 275–338, and 39 (June 1979): 55–106. For Yamazaki Ansai, see Herman Ooms, *Tokugawa Ideology: Early Constructs, 1570–1680* (Princeton, N.J.: Princeton University Press, 1985).

time that the school's clientele and faculty became more representative of Japan overall.

Sadanobu's purpose was the phrase with which he ended his directive, the advancement of "men of ability." Education had direct relevance to administrative service. Sadanobu instituted tests for military proficiency as well as examinations for literary competence. Under changing circumstances, officials returned to their books. There are stories of mature vassals who turned with determination to the discipline of study to prove themselves worthy of new or continued appointment. Examinations for officials were modeled to some extent on those of China, but Sadanobu's advisers managed to blunt his purpose and secure the elimination of questions on Chinese prose and poetry. Nevertheless, Confucian studies became increasingly important to advancement in bakufu office.

As with the bakufu, so with the domains. Samurai and official literacy was advanced nationwide by increased enthusiasm for founding schools throughout Japan. In this the reforms reflected trends that had begun before Sadanobu's rule: 59 domain schools were established between 1781 and 1803. But soon the pace accelerated. The next four decades saw the establishment of an additional 72 schools.[6] Domain schools represented an administrative response to the growing maturity and complexity of a society in which literacy among commoners was growing rapidly. The establishment of private academies and parish schools for commoners also accelerated dramatically in these years. Only 57 private academies (*shijuku*) were founded in the years before 1788, but between that date and 1829 an additional 207 were established, and from 1830 to the end of Tokugawa rule, 796 were begun. The trend with parish schools (*terakoya*) was the same. There were 241 before Kansei; 1,286 were established between 1789 and 1829, and 8,675 between 1830 and 1867.[7] Officials set higher standards for themselves, but the people over whom they ruled were becoming conscious of the importance of learning for themselves as well.

Because the morality and values of the entire structure of education were broadly congruent, these trends could accommodate many emphases without conflict. The development of national studies (*koku-*

---

[6] R. P. Dore, *Education in Tokugawa Japan* (Berkeley and Los Angeles: University of California Press, 1965), the classic study; and Herman Ooms, *Charismatic Bureaucrat: A Political Biography of Matsudaira Sedanobu, 1758–1829* (Chicago: University of Chicago Press, 1975).

[7] Richard Rubinger, *Private Academies of Tokugawa Japan* (Princeton, N.J.: Princeton University Press, 1982), p. 5.

gaku) could, it is true, produce sharp altercations among intellectuals over the relative merits of Chinese and national learning. But much Shinto learning derived from Yamazaki Ansai's blend of Chu Hsi and Shinto, and elaborate etymological explanations were available to demonstrate the ultimate identity of truth, although for national status, Japanese learning, by virtue of Japan's sacred and unchanging line of sovereigns, represented a nobler and more final version of that truth. So too with Dutch studies (*yōgaku* or *rangaku*), which emerged as an individual discipline in the waning decades of the eighteenth century. For some clearheaded specialists it seemed to require repudiation of much of the traditional wisdom of China because of its superior knowledge of the physical world, but to others its practical emphases in medicine or ballistics, the two areas of greatest relevance, seemed fully assimilable with the morality of the East.

Growing literacy rates and the burgeoning urban culture also presented Tokugawa officialdom with problems of control. This was particularly true of materials dealing with the outside world, but also with popular literature. The production of reading material for the literate sector of commoner society had had vigorous beginnings a century earlier in the Genroku era, as books and their production began to be commercialized. Publishers and lending libraries operated to speed the circulation of reading matter. Into the late eighteenth century, much of the popular literature was created by samurai intellectuals. Matsudaira Sadanobu himself, in fact, had had his own hand at such writing, with a short burlesque of a pompous daimyo.[8] Such stories, usually well illustrated, also usually included pleasure in esoteric references comprehensible only to initiates, as well as situational humor and word play. Sometimes they could, of course, go on to become thinly veiled satires directed against the existing social order. At that point they became of interest to an authoritarian regime.

Tokugawa publication was never free of censorship. From the first there had been three categories of concern. Works dealing with Christianity were the chief target in the seventeenth century, gradually becoming less feared as the danger lessened. A second category consisted of works harmful to the political order. These were few at the outset of the period, but they became increasingly frequent in the eighteenth century. A third category, which concerned public morals, provided a basis for censorship of works considered pornography. Before 1720 there had been fifty-eight works banned in the first cate-

---

[8] Haruko Iwasaki, "Portrait of a Daimyo: Comical Fiction by Matsudaira Sadanobu," *Monumenta Nipponica* 38 (Spring 1983): 1–48.

gory, thirteen in the second, and twenty-eight in the third.[9] The eighteenth century brought increased severity and detail in legislation. Yoshimune's provisions of 1720 ruled out discussions bearing on the *kōgi*, or polity, warned of agitating the public mind, forbade publishing genealogical listings that would reflect on the hereditary elite, and spoke vaguely of the danger of *mezurashii koto* (astonishing things) that might unhinge an easily misled and uninformed public. Thus it was to be expected that the Kansei reform years would reaffirm and expand these exclusions. Edicts appeared ordering all works to carry colophons making clear the issuing authority; infractions of guidelines would bring speedy judgment. New guidelines warned against useless novelty or unnecessary proliferation of publications and required approval from the magistrate's office; they ruled out anything of contemporary journalistic coverage or interest, warned against misleading readers, and forbade disturbing public morals with pornography.

These guidelines were sufficiently broad to provide the basis for the punishment of Hayashi Shihei, whose books discussed the Russian advance. They were ideally suited to bring judgment against the author Santō Kyōden, who had just published three popular works that were thinly concealed satires of the reform. The censors who had approved the works were dismissed, and the author and publisher were harshly punished. One-half the publisher's property was confiscated, and Kyōden was sentenced to fifty days in handcuffs. A number of other authors were similarly punished. Henceforth samurai who had written tended to shift to other topics, and commoners like Kyōden avoided the appearance of repeating their errors by developing alternative forms of fiction.

The Kansei reforms, like the Tempō reforms that Harold Bolitho takes up in Chapter 2 in this volume, have not had a good press from historians. Matsudaira Sadanobu was lavishly praised by the modern Japanese government in periods of official exhortation and moral posturing but was virtually ignored in the decades after World War II. Recent studies, however, have helped illustrate the complexity of Sadanobu's character and position. He emerges as a sensitive intellectual, as hard on himself as he was on his countrymen. For himself he set impossible standards of rectitude and sincerity, determined to overcome desire and self-gratification. Convinced of the importance of Confucian example for the realm, he privately harked back to the Shinto standards of earlier shogunal days and thought seriously of his

9 Ekkehard May, *Die Kommerzialisierung der japanishen Literatur in späten Edo-Zeit (1750–1868)* (Wiesbaden: Harrassowitz, 1983), p. 58.

own enshrinement as a *kami*. His edicts were by no means unprecedented, although the severity with which they were enforced did mark a new high. Each aspect of his governance – management of the Edo economy, encouragement of education, and censorship of morality – represented a consolidation of trends already in progress more than it did a dramatic shift.

But whatever the evidence of continuity, the reasons for selecting Kansei as the beginning of nineteenth-century trends are sound. Sadanobu's measures took the existing system as far as it could go in meeting its problems. His moves institutionalized and hardened tradition and increased government control, and left a regime less flexible and more consciously concerned with preserving a tradition that had now been defined. Literary controls and educational requirements for office discouraged samurai authors of popular literature but provided openings for some of them in the world of literate politics. The same controls increased support for studies of the West while they also channeled it into politically approved paths. In each area, periods of relaxation lay ahead, but in terms of precedent and policy, the Kansei measures made a lasting contribution to the future allocation of energy and resources in the final half-century of Tokugawa rule.

The Kansei era also marked, though it did not create, a greater richness and variety in social and educational life in Japan. The bakufu's espousal of education, quickly followed in the domains, led to a measurable increase in jobs for the educated. Increasingly, scholars were recruited for their ability, often from outside the domain. In their new roles as hired intellectuals, albeit with the perquisites of feudal status, such men were only nominally retainers of their new lords. Ability counted more than did status or place of origin. The domain of Hiroshima employed Rai Shunsui (1746–1816), a scholar who had been born into a merchant family. His son, San'yō (1780–1832), an eccentric but learned scholar and poet, violated most of the norms of Confucian conduct but wrote in Chinese *An Unofficial History of Japan* (Nihon gaishi) which became one of the most important sources of nineteenth-century imperial loyalism. San'yō presented a copy to the long-retired Matsudaira Sadanobu in 1827, and after the work was printed in 1842, it passed through numerous editions.[10] Status consciousness and significance weakened. Some samurai scholars could equally well be considered artists. Watanabe Kazan (1793–

---

10 Burton Watson, *Japanese Literature in Chinese*, 2 vols. (New York: Columbia University Press, 1976), vol. 2, pp. 122 ff.; and Noguchi Takehiko, *Rai San'yō: rekishi e no kikansha* (Tokyo: Tankōsha, 1974).

1841) of Tawara, and Kakizaki Hakyō of Matsumae (1763–1826) were better known for their paintings than for their politics. Hirose Tansō (1782–1856) of Hita, in Kyushu, of merchant stock, declined official appointment altogether but attracted the sons of many samurai to his private school. Horizontal ties began to compete with hierarchical obligations, and contractual relationships began to replace hereditary obligations. Daimyo engaged visiting scholars and preachers to speak throughout their realms, and educators could move from post to post. This trend became particularly marked as the century advanced and the daimyo and bakufu competed for the service of experts in economic and military policy.

Once unswerving hereditary obligations mattered less than did ability and willingness in the new intellectual climate, there was room for more individualism, friendship, and humanity in social relations. One can take as an example the case of Matsuzaki Kōdō (1771–1844), born a farmer's son in Higo, who after an early education in the Chinese classics determined to enter the Buddhist priesthood. At fifteen he changed his mind and traveled to Edo to take up Confucian studies. There a Buddhist temple took him in and helped him enter the bakufu's Shōheikō, where he distinguished himself in scholarly competition with the future Shōheikō teacher Satō Issai (1772–1859). Upon the completion of his studies Matsuzaki accepted employment with the lord of Kakegawa (a member of the bakufu's senior council) and used his first stipend to redeem the contract of a lady of the licensed quarter who had helped support him with her earnings during his student years. Matsuzaki's marriage to this woman brought him not shame but praise. His official stipend grew from rations for twenty to rations for fifty men, and Kakegawa refused to allow the domain of Higo (modern Kumamoto) to bid for his services. In scholarly life Matsuzaki held to the same unswerving standards of self-determined rectitude, and he was sharply critical of Satō Issai's cautious refusal to intercede with the bakufu for Watanabe Kazan in the affair that will be detailed later.[11]

The diffusion of education led also to a diffusion in knowledge of and writing in Chinese. The post-Kansei years produced the greatest outpouring of verse in Chinese (*kanshi*) that Japan had ever known. Poetry circles and clubs at the capital and in the provinces included leading commoners as well as samurai, and well into the Meiji period *kanshi* specialists corrected and appraised the products of provincial

---

11 Shin'ichirō Nakamura, "New Concepts of Life of the Post-Kansei Intellectuals: Scholars of Chinese Classics," *Modern Asian Studies* 18 (October 1984): 622.

poets anxious to improve their skills in versification. *Kanshi*, free from the limitations of the thirty-one-syllable *waka* or the seventeen-syllable *haiku* of the Japanese tradition, had resources of length and elegiac eloquence that permitted extended passages of description "for the treatment of philosophical, social, or political themes that could not, or by convention would not, be dealt with in native Japanese poetry. . . ." They became a "principal means of artistic expression for the scholars and patriots who led the movement to bring about the restoration."[12] Not a few poets, including Rai Mikisaburō (1825–59), son of San'yō, paid with their lives for their political views and activities. Kansei orthodoxy became a factor in the bakufu's rigid conservatism, but Kansei intellectualism and emulation of China also served to carry currents of revolutionary commitment and change.

Shortly after the signing of the treaties with Perry, the Shimoda area was hit by destructive earthquakes. The Buddhist priest Gesshō, friend of Chōshū loyalists, greeted the news of these disasters with these lines in Chinese: "For seven miles by the river hills the dogs and sheep forage; the hues of spring visit the wastes of quake-ridden earth. Only the cherry blossoms take on no rank barbarian stench, but breathe to the morning sun the fragrance of a nation's soul."[13]

TOWNS, TRAVEL, AND URBAN CULTURE

The role of cities in the late Tokugawa society is discussed in Chapter 8 of this volume by Gilbert Rozman. The Bunka–Bunsei decades witnessed significant shifts in urban concentrations. Osaka and Kyoto, the metropolises of the Kansai, ceased to grow and had begun to lose population. Edo, too, had reached some sort of plateau in the late eighteenth century, but with the growth of the Kantō economy and the growing dominance of Edo over that plain, it grew in economic importance. By 1800 "Edo ranked as one of the roughly 70 cities in the world (five were in Japan) with more than 100,000 residents, as one of about 20 cities (three in Japan) in excess of 300,000 population, and as probably the only city easily to surpass 1,000,000 inhabitants."[14] It had grown so large because of the political requirements that the bakufu had instituted for the *sankin kōtai* rotation of daimyo. Accompanied by vassals, servants, and hangers-on, this circulating elite had stimulated the enor-

12 Watson, *Japanese Literature in Chinese*, vol. 2, pp. 12, 14.
13 Watson, *Japanese Literature in Chinese*, vol. 2, p. 67.
14 Gilbert Rozman, "Edo's Importance in Changing Tokugawa Society," *Journal of Japanese Studies* 1 (Autumn 1974): 94.

mous growth of service and trade organizations to supply their estates and needs, and commoners in search of the city's higher wages headed for the urban metropolis. Employment centers on the city's outskirts served to funnel the constant tide of newcomers into urban society, and each daimyo residence tended to attract a regional provincial service population that clustered around its walls in rented quarters.

The splendor of the daimyo establishments struck many commentators as excessive, and the traditionalists deplored this. The author of *Seji kemmon roku,* who may have been an Edo *rōnin,* wrote under the name of Buyō Inshi an account of "events seen and heard" in 1816 that sums up his observations about samurai, farmers, priests, doctors, diviners, the blind, and the courts. This author provides numerous and specific examples of the state of affairs midway between the reforms of Matsudaira Sadanobu and those of Mizuno Tadakuni. He was harking back to the presumed simplicity and probity of earlier days, and he decried the luxury and commercialism of his times. Nothing upset him more than the leveling out of class lines and distinctions. In earlier days, he wrote, samurai had found it possible to reprove the Kyoto aristocrats for their wasteful and lazy life-style, but now, alas, they were no better themselves. Even highly placed samurai advisers seemed to slant the counsel they gave to daimyo to emphasize immediate interests and profit. Samurai seemed to overspend, flatter, and curry favor with their lords; they sold their valuables, frequented pawn shops, and struggled with interest rates as high as 20 percent for a three-month loan. Some samurai even stooped to rent out their space in the Edo barrack when they were not there on duty. Debtor–creditor relations were the only roles in which they were proficient, and moneylenders were the only enemies they knew. Adoptions were arranged for money instead of for ability. Even the bakufu's own housemen, Buyō Inshi charged, served only four or five days a month and spent the rest of their time trying to earn a few additional coppers. They had little knowledge of weapons. They did not even hesitate to make free with their lords' things when the opportunity presented itself. Their needs rose constantly, as they wasted their substance on luxuries better left to Kyoto nobles. Consequently, samurai were no longer able to stir respect or fear. The entire Edo military establishment had declined in effectiveness and power; indeed, the very splendor of the Edo mansions concealed the weakness of those who resided in them.

There are no longer limitations on the size of estates the daimyo maintain. In earlier days daimyo had to think about the number of men they could bring with them to Edo, and so their mansions did not have to be very large; at that time they apparently limited themselves to what seemed appropriate. They say that daimyo used to be careful about the number of men they brought with them, because if they came with too large a detachment there might be disorder in the castle town they left behind; also, the domain would be in trouble because of the expenses incurred. But now, although the establishments are five or ten times as large as they used to be, and although the buildings are splendid and beautiful, the samurai who stay in those mansions are effeminate and weak; they are worth about one fifth or one tenth of the ones that used to be there. So in real terms their numbers are smaller. The entire force daimyo bring with them for *sankin kōtai* duty is smaller, their Edo complement is smaller, there are fewer horses, fewer weapons, and less equipment for horses. Because of those reduced numbers, and the way they live, a hundred-thousand *koku* daimyo doesn't come up to a fifty-thousand *koku* lord of former days, ten thousand *koku* up to what used to go with five, or one thousand *koku* to what five hundred used to mean.[15]

Vigilance, courage, loyalty, and ancestral observances had gone by the board: Samurai had become like women, like merchants, or like workers; most of them knew neither shame nor duty, and only two or three out of ten still kept the faith.

The glamour and splendor of life in Edo, Osaka, and Kyoto, all of them under bakufu control as part of the *tenryō*, and the constant movement of goods along the highways and coastal waters to provision these great cities made them inviting targets for private and pleasure travel. Travel within Japan, whose volume had startled Kaempfer in the 1690s, grew until by the early nineteenth century, roads and station stops were more crowded than ever. Feudal authorities thought very poorly of this: A traveler, unless he were burdened with goods for the city, was absenting himself from productive work. By the early nineteenth century, most domains were legislating against anything that smelled of travel for pleasure, and the only acceptable excuse for travel was religious or medical. One could be a member of a fellowship bound for a ritual climb of Mount Fuji, could be headed for one or another temple and pilgrimage circuit, or even, on occasion, could join mass pilgrimages to the Grand Shrine at Ise. There is no need to doubt the sincerity of many of the immense number of pilgrims who chose these routes, but feudal authorities were probably well advised to note – as they usually did in their prohibitions, as Morioka did in 1813 – that "these days many people who petition for permission to visit the sacred places of Kinai really

---

15 Buyō Inshi, *Seji kemmon roku*, ed. Honjō Eijirō and Takigawa Seijirō (Tokyo: Seiabō, reprint, 1966), p. 96.

want to sight see."¹⁶ The great Ise pilgrimage year of 1830, when 4.5 million pilgrims are estimated to have visited the shrine between March and August, constituted an almost total breakdown of regulations in an outburst of religious fervor, that was, for many, a rite of passage into autonomy from familial and political responsibilities.

In normal times, *han* restriction could limit the travel time allowed on *tegata* passports (in Okayama: twenty days for men, ten days for boys; fifteen days for women, seven for girls). But in periods of mass enthusiasm, travelers slipped out of villages and past check stations to throw themselves on the generosity of the villagers whose homes they passed. "Regular" travelers also increased in number and with them the production of travel accounts and guidebooks describing accommodations, food, scenery, and the availability of female entertainment. With guide books came sets of prints of scenic places by popular artists. The classic graphic records of travel along the major highways, especially the Tōkaidō, were soon recognized as masterpieces among the Japanese and became immensely popular with Western collectors later in the century.¹⁷

The great cities, and especially Edo, constituted popular goals for travelers from other areas. A tradition of guidebooks had begun in the seventeenth century as inexpensive pamphlets, printed in the Japanese syllabary, made the wonders of the city known to common travelers. Kyoto, the first to develop, led in this; its four hundred temples and shrines, with three thousand more in the city's environs, were self-evident attractions. By the middle of the seventeenth century, guidebooks singled out eighty-eight, then over three hundred, places in the capital as particularly noteworthy. Similar guidebooks were written for Osaka, noting merchant specialties, local products, brothels, and courtesans; soon the skills of artists were added to illustrate the books. By the early nineteenth century, Edo too had become celebrated in popular fiction as well as in the guidebooks. As local and smaller centers grew in sophistication, the urban attractions of the great cities began to reappear, in muted form, elsewhere as well; that is, urban culture was gradually becoming national. Literacy, travel, and a lively economic interchange between areas had transformed and joined together what had still been separated culture zones at the beginning of the Tokugawa years.

16 Yokoyama Kazuo, " 'Han' kokka e no michi," in Hayashiya, ed., *Kasei bunka no kenkyū*, pp. 102–9, speaks of the rise of a "culture of travel" and gives numerous illustrations of attempted restrictions. See also Carmen Blacker, "The Religious Traveller in the Edo Period," *Modern Asian Studies* 18 (October 1984): 593–608.   17 Blacker, "The Religious Traveller."

Legend and lore stressed the individuality of the three great cities, the *santo*. Kyoto was famous for its water, mushrooms, temples, women, textiles, and bean curd; Osaka for its shipping, moats and bridges, *sake*, guilds, and stones and trees; and Edo for its fish, daimyo mansions, onions, and nuns. Kyoto was famous for its painstaking artisans and merchants, Osaka for the craft and parsimonious nature of its tradesmen, Edo for the samurai indifference to frugality that seemed to infect its merchants and drive them into bankruptcy. Each city had a different population mix: Kyoto its artistocrats, imperial court, temple priests, and private scholars and doctors; Osaka, its moats lined with the warehouses to which the daimyo shipped their surplus rice, its merchant princes to whom to that rice was consigned; and Edo its *bushi* population. Although Osaka and Kyoto were nominally off-limits to the ruling class, samurai interest was in fact ubiquitous. Eighty-six daimyo maintained stations in Kyoto, even though they themselves could not enter the city, for access to the silks of Nishijin weavers, and many domains stationed representatives in Osaka because of its importance to their treasuries.[18] But Edo was special. By the nineteenth century it had become the crossroads of Japan, celebrated in guidebooks and systematized in the handbooks that listed the crests, banners, income, and dates of residence of daimyo for the tradesmen who had to deal with samurai customers.

Edo had long grown in response to migration, but by the nineteenth century the tide of entrants had slowed, and the Edo born were becoming significant in number among the townsmen. (Thanks to the hostage system under which daimyo families and heirs had to stay in the city, most daimyo had long been Edo born.) The "Edokko," or child of Edo, was a commoner, both of whose parents had been born in the city, and popular wisdom had it that they constituted about 10 percent of the city's population. Recruits from the countryside continued to perform the myriad service functions necessary to a premodern, labor-intensive economy, those of porters, bearers, peddlers, watchmen, and the like. But the Edokko also became the standard focus of much popular fiction. Emphasis was now less on the taste (*tsū*) of the urban dandy who had starred in eighteenth-century romances than on the vitality (*iki*) of the irreverent and cocky commoner. Obsequiousness in the face of samurai was no longer as likely for commoners who had grown up witness to warrior poverty, punctilio, and pomposity. *Kirisute gomen*, the right to strike down a disrespectful commoner, had become a thing

---

18 Donald H. Shively, "Urban Culture," paper presented to the colloquium Edo Culture and Its Modern Legacy, London, 1981.

of the past in the city. The Edo *chōnin* (townsmen) considered themselves every bit as important to the realm as their samurai contemporaries were, and they also considered themselves superior to their counterparts in other cities because they were at the center of the nation's politics and economics. The cost of living in Edo might be one or even two times that in Kyoto or Osaka; the rents charged for the shop with the narrow quarters behind it in the city's labyrinth of merchant quarters might consume most of the wages of even a good carpenter, but the Edokko was secure in his place and his importance.[19]

Popular fiction, inexpensive woodblock prints, and daily rumors brought the scandals of the theater and entertainment world to the attention of the population. Literacy was at its highest in the cities, and schools were most common in Edo if only because literacy was so essential to daily life and enterprise there. R. P. Dore estimates that "somewhat more than 40 per cent of all Japanese boys and about 10 per cent of Japanese girls were getting some kind of formal education outside of their homes" by late Tokugawa times,[20] and the Edo figures would probably have been higher than those elsewhere. If the cost of living was high in Edo, the standard of living was also higher. Buyō Inshi, the author of *Seji kemmon roku,* wrote that in his day, parents were becoming too proud to put their daughters out to service, that serving girls dressed as well as did their employers, and that parents continued to support them in their pursuit of salable arts and skills in hopes of getting them decently or at least inexpensively placed. Life in the city included high standards in dress, which meant an infinite variety of patterns and weaves and a luxuriance of taste. Food became more varied, and the variety of noodle and marine delicacies began to approach the standard of modern times. Life in the capital was also remarkable for the frequence and regularity of its festivals and processions. When these paled, the growing profusion of small, semilegal *akusho* (evil places) where prostitution was available, or the daily experience of the bustle associated with the approach of one of the hundred or more daimyo always resident in the city, gave Edo life the individuality of which its residents boasted.

More important than the guidebooks was the outpouring of fiction with which publishers tried to win their readers' favor. There was an unappeasable hunger for reading matter among the inhabitants of Edo, who consumed everything that the publishers provided. The

---

19 See the sample budget breakdown as constructed by Kitajima Masamoto, *Bakuhansei no kumon,* vol. 18 of *Nihon no rekishi* (Tokyo: Chūō kōronsha, 1967), pp. 264–5. Rents might be paid daily by the least privileged.   20 Dore, *Education in Tokugawa Japan,* p. 254.

spread of literacy and the lowering of printing costs, along with advances in wood carving, put booklets written in the native syllabary (*kana*) within the reach of commoners. Shikitei Samba speaks casually of apprenticing a boy to a bookshop, and his stories' mothers boast as they gossip in the communal bath about their boys' precosity in gobbling up the books in the house.[21] Nevertheless, on the whole the margin of existence was too modest for most people to permit the growth of a book-owning public. Editions of the simplest *kanazōshi* (books written in *kana*) might go as high as seven thousand copies, but for works of substance and size, the answer lay in the spread of lending and renting libraries.

Bakufu regulations record the licensing of a guild for book renting in Kyoto in 1716. By the turn of the century such shops were everywhere in Edo and in the provinces, where the reading public was served by itinerant peddlars with boxes of books on their backs. Takizawa Bakin, perhaps the greatest and most successful of the authors of lengthy "reading books" (*yomihon*), wrote that his books were read even in distant Sado Island. Edo had some eight hundred book-lending shops (*kashihonya*) which were organized in twelve guilds in the Bunka era, and they rented books for periods of fifteen days. Assuming full utilization at some two dozen transfers a year, an edition of 750 might thus reach 19,200 readers.[22] Prefaces often make it clear that the author was aiming for the rental audience.

Publishers worked closely with authors to time editions advantageously, and serial episodes had to be ready on time lest the market interest waver. *Yomihon* sections had a fifteen-day lead time, but *ninjōbon* (romance books) needed less time and allowed only three days. Under such pressures a successful author was the center of a production team, with assistants and engravers at hand for the finishing touches and illustrations. In his diary Bakin reports that he and Santō Kyōden were probably the first authors to receive a regular form of payment, as opposed to the "thank you" gifts and banquets that had previously been the norm. Certainly they, Tamenaga Shunsui, and Jippensha Ikku (1765–1831) (whose books, Bakin wrote, were read

21 Dore, *Education in Tokugawa Japan*, p. 111; and Robert W. Leutner, *Shikitei Samba and the Comic Tradition in Late Edo Period Popular Fiction* (Cambridge, Mass.: Harvard University Press, 1985). Note also a mother's comment, "If you have two sons, you're in a perfect position to get the younger one adopted into some other family as an heir, aren't you?"
22 Ekkehard May, *Die Kommerzialisierung der japanischen Literatur*, p. 55, an excellent study from which these computations are taken; also Peter F. Kornicki, "The Publishers Go-Between: Kashihonya in the Meiji Period," *Modern Asian Studies* 14 (1980): 331–44; and the excellent study by Konta Yōzō, *Edo no hon'yasan: kinsei bunkashi no sokumen* (Tokyo: NHK Books no. 299, 1977).

even by daimyo) were immensely successful, prolific, and talented.[23] Authors also had to exercise caution. Kyōden's punishment in the Kansei era, one that was to befall Shunsui in the Tempō reforms, underscored the need to keep a wary eye on the censors. This also affected content. Because it was impossible to discuss contemporary affairs, news from other countries, and recent history, authors were restricted to ribald or fanciful themes. Shikitei Samba (1776–1822) exploited the street humor of daily life in Edo in works placed in a setting of bathhouse gossip. Humor was situational rather than subtle, as in the case of Ikku's wandering rogues who fall into privies, encourage others to step into scalding hot metal bathtubs, and lay siege to maids in roadside inns. All this was highly commercialized. Publishers did their best to retain the readers' attention for sequels, with writers' afterwords promising even more gripping adventures to follow. Small volumes, as in the eighty, and then eighty-four, facsimiles in which a Japanese translation of the *Water Margin* (Shui hu ch'uan) was issued, provided another way to minimize risks and hold a following. Subliminal advertising often accompanied the texts: Kyōden's for his tobacco shop, Shunsui's for books, and Samba's for medicines.

This satirical and situational humor, despite its lack of depth, can also be seen as a response to the strains and limitations in Edo society. It reversed the normal and accepted platitudes of duty and morality in the textbooks from which the commoners had learned to read. Kyōden, Samba, Ikku, and others described a world of play filled with raucous laughter, physical indulgence, and crudity. Samba's bathhouse patrons are a scruffy lot, remarkable for sores, flatulence, casual insult, and gross indecency. They live in a world in which people spend their lives in narrow quarters of the permissible and achievable. It is a society in which concern with the physical usually takes precedence over concern with the intellectual or spiritual.

Bakin (1767–1848), the most important of the names that have been introduced here, illustrated in his life most of the themes of commercialization, travel, and frustration that have been described. Of samurai stock, Bakin resigned his modest commission and income in order to be a professional writer, only to dedicate the products of his efforts to finance the restoration of his son and, after the son's death, his

---

23 Probably the longest lived and best known of the genre of "humor books" (*kokkeibon*) is Jippensha Ikku's *Tōkaidō dōchū hizakurige* (Travels on foot on the Tōkaidō), published between 1802 and 1822 and translated into English by Thomas Satchell as *Hizakurige or Shanks' Mare: Japan's Great Comic Novel of Travel and Ribaldry* (Kobe: 1929 and subsequent reprints). See Donald Keene, *World Within Walls: Japanese Literature of the Pre-modern Era, 1600–1867* (New York: Holt, Rinehart and Winston, 1976), pp. 412–14.

grandson to samurai status. Although he achieved a considerable amount of success as author of *kibyōshi* (literally, "yellow covers," illustrated tales notable for humor, irony, and satire) in close association with Santō Kyōden, even writing fiction for his mentor during his fifty days in handcuffs during the Kansei reform, Bakin despised frivolous literature and wanted desperately to concentrate his efforts on sterner stuff. His *yomihon* relied on Confucian values and Chinese precedents to glorify Japan's samurai tradition by creating a series of implausibly noble and selflessly loyal warriors whom he placed in pre-Tokugawa times. One of the major events of his life was a sight-seeing trip to Kyoto and Osaka that he described in detail in a travel account replete with comments on costs and the quality of food and women. He frequented the literary and cultural clubs in Edo, made the acquaintance of the Dutch scholar Sugita Gempaku, and requested his help in the investigation of "barbarian names." He was acquainted also with the painter Watanabe Kazan but knew better than to go to his defense when Kazan was swept up in the purge of Western scholars in 1839.

Bakin's greatest success was with his masterpiece *Nansō Satomi hakkenden*, on which he labored from 1814 to 1841. In it a warlord besieged in his castle promises the hand of his daughter to anyone who can produce his enemy's head and is nonplussed to have his faithful watchdog meet the conditions of his promise. When one of his retainers, anxious to release the daughter from this strange alliance, kills the daughter by mistake, eight heads, each for a Confucian virtue, rise to the sky and subsequently appear in the surname (*inu* = dog) of a samurai superhero. Together they restore the fortunes of the maiden's father. Bakin's evocation of a vanished past of samurai glories was immensely popular. When one section was issued in a small number of copies by a bookseller in the depths of the famine of 1837, a crowd of hundreds of frustrated customers milled about demanding that more copies be made available.

Bakin's needs for money to pay for his grandson's elevation to samurai status remained unmet, however, and in 1836 he agreed somewhat reluctantly to a testimonial dinner of the sort common in his day. He went around the city in a palanquin to distribute the invitations and reserved most of a large restaurant for the occasion. In response there was a gathering of poets, entertainers, publishers, artists, writers, printmakers, engravers, book and rental guild representatives, and government functionaries which required the provision of 1,184 meals. The guests brought gifts in return for the fans and food they received, and Bakin's finances were finally secure. Even so, his worries were not at an end. When Mizuno Tadakuni inaugurated the Tempō reforms in 1841 with a series of measures similar to those of Matsudaira Sadanobu a half-century earlier, Bakin's long and immensely popular novel seemed a likely target for punitive action despite its content. One Shōheikō Confucian pedant did in fact propose to ban *Eight Dogs*, but moderation prevailed with the conclusion that its only fault was a few objectionable illustrations. Free of that concern, Bakin devoted his remaining years to the completion of his giant work. Blind in both eyes, he was finally forced to dictate to his daughter-in-law, but he finally completed one of the world's longest novels. All in vain: His twenty-year-old grandson, a samurai at last, outlived him by only one year.[24]

THE COUNTRYSIDE: GROWTH, SURPLUS, AND THE PROBLEM OF CONTROL

In the early decades of the nineteenth century the Japanese countryside retained the monochrome character of earlier Tokugawa years. In most villages one or two substantial buildings signaled the presence of the local elite, whether *gōshi* (rural samurai) or *gōnō* (wealthy farmers). There were the men whose influence and affectations upset the Confucian political economists. Their wealth, literacy, and connections with authority made them the natural leaders in the establishment of village schools, the expression of village opinion, and the funding of village activities. Their white stucco storehouses stood out from the weathered gray of their residences and the handsome evergreens that dominated their small gardens. That same visibility made their residences the targets for occasional outbursts of village anger: At such times, storehouses, pine, and *sake* vats might be demolished after the crowd became unruly. Nevertheless, on the whole the village was drab. Sumptuary laws ruled out roofing tiles, and there was little ornamentation, few windows, *shōji*, or flowers.

In a sense the "Kasei era," as the Bunka–Bunsei years are often termed, was remarkable for plentiful harvests, relaxation of the severity of Matsudaira Sadanobu's restrictions, and the flowering of a material and artistic culture in the great urban centers. When compared with the turbulence of Europe in these decades or with the slow attenuation of Manchu power in China, Japan seems to have experienced a

---

24 Leon M. Zolbrud, *Takizawa Bakin* (New York: Twayne, 1967).

period of respite. Domain schools were being founded more rapidly than ever before; private academies mushroomed throughout the land; and over a thousand parish schools for commoners appeared. European visitors like Hendrik Doeff and Philip Franz von Siebold, at the two extremes of these decades, spoke with admiration of the order and prosperity they saw. Artists of the period, notably Katsushika Hokusai (1760–1849) and Andō Hiroshige (1797–1858) who became celebrities through the skill and number of their genre paintings and prints, left a record of a peaceful and smiling countryside that has attracted travelers ever since.

The social and economic history of the period nevertheless presents the historian with an abundance of problems that belie the apparently placid tenor of life. If the central fact of eighteenth-century Japan was the growth of merchant power and influence made possible by the growth of cities, nineteenth-century governments were no less troubled by their awareness of the growth of comparable commercialism throughout the countryside, especially near the great cities of Osaka and Edo. That spread was accompanied by a growing differentiation of wealth within the village, in the struggle of villagers for more responsive local government, in strains between village and metropolis as bakufu and daimyo tried to protect and control prices and distribution, and between domains and bakufu as the latter found itself improvising measures to respond to economic trends that had not respected the division of domain and fief.

The central fact of Tokugawa history was the bakufu's inability to improve the imperfect political controls with which it began the period throughout the two and one-half centuries of its rule. By accepting its role as the greatest of the feudal lords, the bakufu closed itself off from the possibility of devising a more rational centralized structure. At the same time its political controls, which centered on the rotation of the daimyo to the capital, led to ever-larger centralization in the market economy. With responsibility for the great cities but not for the areas that supported their needs, the bakufu had to deal with the effects of economic centralization without being able to respond with effective measures of allocation and control. In addition, the sixteenth-century measures that separated the samurai from the land made it impractical to control the countryside closely. Cadastral registers that were reasonably accurate at the beginning of Tokugawa rule continued to provide the basis for the daimyo's ritual and service obligations long after economic growth had rendered them obsolete. In a land at peace, in which ritual and status constituted the center of political attention, realignment would have caused repercussions comparable to those that follow reapportionment in contemporary democratic societies. Yet the daimyo themselves were seldom better off than the bakufu. Those that had lost territory to the Tokugawa victors had more warriors than their castle town could accommodate; Satsuma scattered them throughout the realm and retained feudal control and discipline into the nineteenth century. In contrast, the bakufu and its principal vassals had experienced a vast increase of territory without a compensating increase in manpower. Consequently the environs of the great cities, the most commercialized and the most productive, were also the least garrisoned, enjoyed the best leverage in negotiation over tax and monopoly, and became the least "feudal." There was thus a disjunction between political primacy and economic dependence, political rationalization and traditional decentralization. A rice-based revenue guaranteed that a regime with a grain-tax income would find itself disadvantaged in years when good harvests brought lower prices for rice. The Kasei period found this true.

The hardening of seclusion as the national doctrine had an additional impact on economic thought and policy. In late-eighteenth-century Japan a number of writers had envisaged the possibility of new economic measures that could promote expansion and increase productivity. Much of the fascination of European books for writers like Honda Toshiaki and other *keiseika*, as the political economists styled themselves, was the revelation of measures that might be taken to increase productivity and contribute to the public good. The decisions against such innovations symbolized by Matsudaira Sadanobu's reification of seclusion as mandated by tradition, however, suggested a ceiling on the sum total of productivity possible under the existing system. Consequently it seemed that growth in any sector could come only at the expense of other sectors. Rural well-being and especially, as samurai commentators saw it, opulence could mean only that villagers were taking more than their share and impoverishing the cities where the samurai lived. If so, planning required measures to take this back from them and to keep commercial ventures in authorized channels. This view had consequences for struggles within the village, between village and city, and at times between domain and bakufu. That such projections were mistaken is something that long escaped analysts: Both Meiji historians and twentieth-century economic determinists alike were inclined to accept the gloomy view of the potential of the late feudal order implicit in the acts of the bakufu planners. More recent analysts, however, working with demographic statistics, hold that as the nineteenth century began, an economy that had long been moribund slowly began to move again. Previously backward areas began to share in the economic growth that the urban plains had experienced earlier. A new trend of rising productivity was set in motion in the Kasei years that extended into the Meiji period.[25] Contemporaries, however, did not sense this and acted on the basis of their perceptions of a constant sum of foodstuffs and goods.

It has already been observed that below the high levels of society, class and status lines were blurred more than they had ever been. As education became more widely available, it was inevitable that ability would seek and sometimes find reward. The fixed income of the hereditary stipends and rations to which most samurai were held made *bushi* status less desirable for many able youths, but at the same time political and status perquisites made that status attractive to merchants seeking to endow their sons. The frequency of adoptions into, and resignations out of, samurai status was widely noted. Many contemporaries voiced a discouraging estimate of samurai martial competence; it would require the national crisis of the mid-century years to rekindle the warrior spirit. For many, ambition could be realized only by abandoning the restrictions of fixed status. Hiroshige, the descendant of a Tsugaru samurai who gave instruction in archery, found himself a member of the Edo fire brigade. As soon as he could, he passed on his fire brigade duties to a son so that he could concentrate on his art. Meanwhile, not a few commoners found it possible to purchase samurai status.

This flexibility of status arrangements might seem convenient to many, but traditionalists found it deplorable and alarming. Buyō Inshi, whose *Seji kemmon roku* has already been cited for its disapproval of daimyo and samurai life-styles, went on to dismiss agriculturalists. He described a countryside alarmingly divided between the wealthy and the exploited. The former, who seemed oblivious to their proper status,

> live luxuriously like urban aristocrats. Their homes are as different from those of the common people as day from night, or clouds from mud. They build them with the most handsome and wonderful gates, porches, beams, alcoves, ornamental shelves, and libraries. Some give money to the government and get the right to wear swords and take surnames . . . they wear fine

---

25 Nishikawa Shunsaku, *Edo jidai no poritikaru ekonomii* (Tokyo: Nihon hyōronsha, 1979), a masterful discussion with case studies from northern and western Japan.

clothes and imitate the style and airs of samurai on occasions like weddings, celebrations, and masses for the dead.[26]

The author's emphasis is on the deplorable indifference to status; a properly ordered society, the society that had once existed, should be based on status: "The lord nurtures the people with virtue; the people honor the lord by giving crops of grains and do not depart from the precepts of *jinsei* in the slightest."[27] But with this fracturing of society, in which "fifty out of one hundred" were seizing the opportunity to improve themselves at the cost of the remaining fifty, some were able to ingratiate themselves with officials, bribing them at tax assessment time to base their rate on their worst paddies, thereby forcing others to bear the heavier burden. Farmers had become litigious, appealing decisions and heading for the courts at the slightest provocation.[28] The poor, increasingly oppressed, had no recourse but to leave the villages for the cities; once out of agriculture they would never return. The wealth of the village elite was not only responsible for the indigence of the samurai, but in addition the poor were being driven to crime. The happiness of the few came at the cost of misery for the many. Not surprisingly, these conditions were farthest advanced near the great cities. Prosperous farmers in the vicinity of Edo had no hesitation to head for court, and they were no longer in the slightest fear of the magistrate's office.

It has to be granted that there is supporting evidence for this view of social disruption in the nineteenth century. The extent to which society had come unraveled was shown in the response of some village elders to their lord's request for additional loans some decades later. In 1856, a *hatamoto* with a holding rated at 700 *koku* received a response from three village leaders to his request for money that challenged him to prove that he needed and deserved the additional money. The statement pointed out he had made no effort to reduce his expenditures, that he was supporting a brother who was an "immoral idler," and that he was supporting more maids and housemen than he needed. The villagers threatened to resign their posts as elders if the bannerman did not put his house in order soon.[29]

---

26 Nishikawa, *Edo jidai no poritikaru ekonomii*, p. 100. Noted also by Thomas C. Smith, *The Agrarian Origins of Modern Japan* (Stanford, Calif.: Stanford University Press, 1959), p. 176, whose translation has been adapted here.   27 Buyō Inshi, *Seji kemmon roku*, p. 125.
28 Buyō Inshi, *Seji kemmon roku*, p. 108. See also on this point, Dan Fenno Henderson, *Village "Contracts" in Tokugawa Japan* (Seattle: University of Washington Press, 1975), for discussion and examples of justiciable arrangements in the late Tokugawa decades.
29 Example from Kozo Yamamura, *A Study of Samurai Income and Entrepreneurship* (Cambridge, Mass.: Harvard University Press, 1974), pp. 47–8, who translates the document.

In 1816 things may not have come to such a pass as yet, but there was little doubt in Buyō Inshi's mind that they were heading in that direction. He looked back wistfully to the reform spirit of Matsudaira Sadanobu, and he found little comfort in the society of his day. His jeremiad went on to complain of merchant wealth, the expense and demoralizing effects of popular amusement on stage and in books, and ended with a plaint that the feudal order, although clearly of divine institution, was being subverted by luxury and superstition. The Buddhist clergy was among his targets, and the image of Kyoto, with its unproductive luxury and pretensions to elegance, a particular bane. *Seji kemmon roku,* in other words, provides a picture of Japan by someone whose self-image was adversely affected by the social change to which he was witness.

We can be thankful for the evidence that many contemporaries felt differently and realized that economic differentiation was based on more than a diversion from approved channels of distribution. Books on economic management and growth were important products of the times and circulated in large numbers during the Bunka and Bunsei years. Ōkura Nagatsune (b. 1768) traveled widely in both the Kansai and Kantō areas, wrote on ways to increase yields of cotton and rice, and encouraged the cultivation of mulberrys to feed to silkworms. He served as a private commentator and as an adviser to several daimyo. He advocated sending experts into the villages and setting aside experimental plots of land in order to give the farmers a chance to see the results of new methods. Village leaders could then be persuaded to teach and persuade others. Ōkura and other writers stressed farm-family profits – exactly the kind of concern deplored in *Seji kemmon roku* – to urge on their readers. It was clear that such techniques would benefit the gifted and the energetic most immediately, but Ōkura wrote about lessening the labor of the masses and increasing the income of all. Agronomists like him did not, in other words, accept the view of a fixed total of agricultural productivity that animated the official moralists. With the spread of commoner literacy, such writings circulated widely as itinerant peddlars and lenders moved through the countryside with boxes of books on their backs. One book on sericulture had a first printing of three thousand copies.[30]

30 Thomas C. Smith, "Ōkura Nagatsune and the Technologists," in Albert M. Craig and Donald H. Shively, eds., *Personality in Japanese History*, (Berkeley and Los Angeles: University of California Press, 1970), pp. 127–54; and Iinuma Jirō, "Gōriteki nōgaku shisō no keisei: Ōkura Nagatsune no baai," in Hayashiya Tatsusaburō, ed., *Kasei bunka no kenkyū* (Tokyo: Iwanami shoten, 1976), pp. 397–416.

Material of this sort circulated most regularly near Japan's great cities, but the men who produced it traveled widely, and they had readers in many areas. Nevertheless there must have been a great deal of difference between the confidence of the rural elite in the Kansai and Kantō plains and the attitudes permitted by harsher conditions in other areas. In the Kyushu coastal province of Higo, for instance, commercialization was by no means absent, but village stratification was more a product of the superiority of the lowland paddies to the more recently developed upland and marginal lands. Village councils were dominated by those who held the older paddies. The domain began selling samurai commissions in the eighteenth century as a way of raising income, and wealthy farmers had been able to change their legal standing in return for paltry stipends that brought the status of swords and surnames. In the nineteenth century the figures for such transfers were not impressive; thirty commissions were sold during Bunka, and thirty during Bunsei. Yet commercialization was by no means absent. The domain administration developed a banking system by establishing a depository that issued certificates of deposit, offered loans, and stored goods and promises of future goods. In 1802 a desperate shortage of money in *han* coffers made it impossible to cover domain indebtedness and brought a collapse of consumer and creditor confidence that caused a run in which the "bank" building within the castle grounds was "besieged by hundreds of people from dawn till dusk who attempted to save what could be saved and even tried to force their way into the building."[31] *Han* administrators brought a halt to the run by the draconian device of publicly burning the instruments of deposit to indicate that they had no intention of honoring them. The next year the domain tried to recoup its prestige by shifting the system of tax assessment from the annual inspection (*kemmi*) system to an averaged (*jōmen*) tax, using as the basis the figures for the previous thirty years. This brought a new wave of protests, now led by rural leaders, who presumably feared that a fixed rate would allow less flexibility. They may also have been afraid of the survey that would be required to set the new tax rates. The *han* prevailed.

Clearly conditions were worse, and feudal authority was stronger, in Kumamoto than in the metropolitan areas. Visits of tax assessors from the castle town were of critical importance. They were greeted by village elders in formal dress with elaborate courtesy and food in the

---

31 Heinrich Martin Reinfried, *The Tale of Nisuke* (Wiesbaden: Harrassowitz, Studien zur Japanologie Band 13, 1978), p. 189.

hope of softening their requirements. After the harvest was in, guards were set up on all roads to make sure none of it left the village without authorization; and when the tax rice was delivered to the authorities, a procession of villagers leading packhorses prepared for the nervous process of tests for quality.

This tension was the subject of a samurai-administrator who noted the villagers' hardships in the account of an imaginary discussion he wrote in 1803. The participants in the discussion, entitled *Tale of Nisuke*, are a local official, a wealthy peasant, a village doctor and teacher, and two ordinary farmers who provide the foils for their wise contemporaries to instruct. The three men of standing agree strongly on one point: Buddhist priests represent idleness, waste, and superstition. The peasants they address, however, remain disinclined to risk whatever harm that supernatural intervention may add to their mortal ills. The author noted the village's resistance to the domain's policies of afforestation and tried to allay fears that runoff from the conifers would poison their paddies. He tried to assure them that the *jōmen* tax was fair and explained its practicality. But he had to admit the evils of other aspects of the system: rapacious officials who underweighed the harvest tax, and officials and merchants who took advantage of the villagers' distress to offer supplemental loans at ruinous rates.

Generalization is nevertheless difficult, for local variation in a Japan divided into hundreds of administrative principalities was inevitably very great. In the Shōnai *han* on the northwestern coast of Honshu there were enormous contrasts within the *han*. The original fields were lightly taxed and their elite favored, but more recently reclaimed land had a harder time of it. Merchant money became landlord money, and by the early nineteenth century, the Homma family holdings were of an order that made massive loans to the domain government a regular affair.[32] Northern Japan – Morioka and Tsugaru – was perhaps least commercialized of all. The domain of Morioka, despite a climate unsuited for the production of rice, used its resources of iron, lumber, and horses to balance its books. The role of the merchant houses located in central Japan was important. As early as 1716 there is a record of an Osaka merchant who paid 55,000 *ryō* for the right to cut cypress, and an 1806 record speaks of the harvesting of almost 700,000 trees in one district.[33] *Han* efforts to get additional tax income out of

---

32 William W. Kelly, *Deference and Defiance in Nineteenth-Century Japan* (Princeton, N.J.: Princeton University Press, 1985), a close study of Shōnai finance and politics in the nineteenth century.
33 Susan B. Hanley and Kozo Yamamura, *Economic and Demographic Change in Preindustrial Japan, 1600–1868* (Princeton, N.J.: Princeton University Press, 1977), p. 135.

its hard-pressed farmers were often unsuccessful and led to a series of peasant revolts. Collaboration with merchant capital provided a better route for administrative stability. Morioka taxed imports and sold samurai rank, and as early as 1783 the *han* provided the convenience of a price list for status, from 50 *ryō* for wearing a sword to 620 *ryō* for full warrior standing.³⁴ Such payments were, of course, beyond the means of most residents, and as the bakufu pressed the *han* for contributions to defenses in the north, the Morioka finances grew worse. Nevertheless there are indications of a steady rise in differentiation and a decline in old-style bondage. Economic historians find evidence that the proportion of *nago*, the poorest category of agricultural dependent, declined.³⁵ Even in Tōhoku Japan, contemporaries complained about luxury in the village in much the same way that Buyō Inshi wrote about the Kantō plain. In 1830 a Morioka man wrote about Sendai:

Everyone has forgotten the righteous way. Now everyone is working for profit. . . . In the villages we now have hairdressers and public baths. If you see houses you see flutes, samisen, and drums on display. Those living in rented houses, the landless, and even servants have *haori*, umbrellas, *tabi*, and clogs. When you see these people on their way to the temples, they seem better dressed than their superiors.³⁶

Buyō Inshi could not have put it better.

There were a number of responses to the acceleration of these trends in the early nineteenth century. One was internal to the village. Long subject to hereditary headmen or the purely formal alternation of headmen, villagers began to demand more of a say in the selection of their own notables. Usually the stimulus to such a demand was provided by insensitive or obsequious action on the part of headmen whose eyes were on the domain or bakufu authorities. In the more highly commercialized parts of the country, a series of demands and demonstrations found villagers on the whole having their way. Increasingly, the offices of village headmen tended to be filled with some regard for the wishes of the villagers whose lives and livelihood those worthies would affect.³⁷

Another result took the form of changes in village demonstrations and protests. In the Bunka years, village demonstrations averaged 16.6 per year for all of Japan. In Bunsei this declined somewhat to 13.3 annually, but the character of protests began to change subtly as they reflected complaints and strains within the village collectivity. More often than not the demonstration would end with the imposing

---

34 Ibid., p. 140.   35 Ibid., p. 156.   36 Quoted in ibid., p. 158.
37 Kitajima, *Bakuhansei no kumon*, p. 240.

houses of the wealthy in flames or demolished by the wrath of the crowd. This was noted by alarmed contemporaries. Matsudaira Sadanobu, living in retirement, had this to say in 1815:

> When it comes to peasant revolts, there is no need to be concerned just because a lot of people are involved. And that they are bitter about headmen (*shōya*) and lower officials (*yakunin*) and start riots to demonstrate about that doesn't amount to much either. But when they're close to starvation because of famine and decide to rise up rather than starve to death, and attack the homes of the wealthy and the rice dealers, or start setting fire to everything, it's time to look out. They are strongest when the fief holder's government is bad, for then they make him out to be the enemy. Moreover these risings are worst when there are additional complaints because of long-standing despotic government with heavy demands for taxation, transport, corvée, and forced loans.[38]

Village strains could also be affected by voluntary associations. The growth of young men's organizations (*wakamono gumi* or *nakama*) to some degree represented an assertion of rural autonomy in the face of an increasingly intrusive central government and economy. Such organizations had begun as socializing agencies within the village, but in the early years of the nineteenth century, they also became agents of communal compulsion, demanding additional holidays on which no villager dared near his fields, assessing dues for festivals, and ensuring conformity to communal desires for entertainment in the form of contributions for itinerant troupes of kabuki actors and dancers.

Wakamono gumi also assessed service duty for communal corvée. In many parts of Japan the condition for achieving full membership in the community was passage through such an organization. The organizations used ritual, formality, and fear to magnify the importance and secrecy of the process. Early-nineteenth-century village life was lived in the tension between prescriptive communal forms and a jealous concern for familial interest and accumulation; inevitably families of property put a higher priority on the second. Arrangements for communal obligations such as the rescue of ships in distress, the prevention of fire, the transport of tax rice, the cutting of wood, and riparian projects found the organizations utilized to ensure equity and efficiency. Frequently income from part of a village upland or grassy areas was allotted to the youth groups by the village assemblies. On occasion the groups might also have separate and specific fields to provide them with steady income for their projects. The allocation of

---

38 Quoted from Sadanobu's *Kantei hisetsu*, in Tsuda Hideo, *Tempō kaikaku*, vol. 22 of *Nihon no rekishi* (Tokyo: Shogakkan, 1975), pp. 80–1.

rest days gave the *wakamono gumi* particular power to influence the community. In some areas records indicate that upwards of seventy holidays, distributed throughout the year, were set aside as rest days, and any villager who went to work in violation of such pronouncements was likely to regret it.[39]

Some of these customs brought village youth groups into conflict with members of the village elite, and many brought communal interest into direct conflict with the governing authorities. Ultimately it was the central political authorities who tired of the friction and decided to ban the youth groups.[40]

Efforts for tighter regulation took place in a context of the need for law and order. Buyō Inshi had complained that class division and economic inequality were creating lawlessness in the countryside, and there does in fact seem to have been a rise in banditry and gambling, particularly in the Kantō area. In a number of cases, some celebrated in recent popular entertainment drawing its heroes from legendary Robin Hoods, chivalrous bandits attained almost mythical renown. The legendary Kunisada Chūji, a robber, bandit, and gang leader, won an instant response on the kabuki stage. The term "chivalrous figure" (*kyōkaku*) represented illegality as well as idealism. Late Tokugawa kabuki authors, especially Tsuruya Namboku, specialized in the depiction of such types. Conventional standards of morality went by the board, as did conventional standards of law. Namboku's drama showed strange misalliances of bandits and the highborn, and his oeuvre culminated in the spectacular *Tōkaidō Yotsuya kaidan* (Ghost story of Yotsuya on the Tōkaidō) in 1825.[41] A historian of manners cannot fail to note this fascination with the abnormal and the obsession with what was, in Confucian eyes, evil. Actor worship and the spread of prostitution quarters (*akusho*, "evil places") beyond the permitted areas to other parts of the great cities reflected this. So did the vogue for tattooing. In 1837 this reached into the very highest circles when a Kantō-area daimyo was ordered into retirement for having had himself tattooed.[42]

---

39 Michiko Tanaka, "Village Youth Organizations (*Wakamono Nakama*) in Late Tokugawa Politics and Society," Ph.D. diss., Princeton University, 1982.
40 Kitajima Masamoto, "Kaseiki no seiji to minshū," (Tokyo: Iwanami shoten, *Iwanami Kōza Nihon rekishi*, 1963), pp. 313ff.
41 Keene, *World Within Walls*, pp. 456–69; Noguchi Takehiko, "*Aku*" to Edo bungaku (Tokyo: Asahi shimbunsha, 1980), pp. 76ff. Abe Yoshio, in *Meakashi Kinjūrō no shōgai* (Tokyo: Chūō kōronsha, 1981) provides a fascinating close-up of the forty-six-year career of an eighteenth-century petty informer who operated on the borderline between the worlds of the police and gambling and thus illustrates the compromises that a premodern government had to make with illegality.
42 Kitajima, *Bakuhansei no kumon*, p. 248, for Kunisada, and p. 271 for the fad of tattooing.

In the 1820s the bakufu moved to tighten control by means of regulations that ranged from control of transport to sweeping police measures. It had become necessary to control the movement of commerce as well as the movement of people. With respect to commerce, it was important to retain the profit for the officially sanctioned guilds of the metropolis. These could be ordered to contribute to special government levies, and having made such contributions, they expected protection from their sponsors within the castle. The process can be followed in the Kansai plain before it took place in the Kantō.

Near Osaka the villages in the provinces of Settsu, Kawachi, and Izumi had been the target of bakufu orders forbidding the retailing of oilseeds as early as 1797. Seeds were to be sold only to Osaka wholesalers, and the farmers were also ordered to purchase the oil they needed from Osaka dealers. Forty-one villages requested a free market in these goods that same year, only to be turned down. Village petitions grew in number as urban cotton guilds pressed their case for monopoly rights. Outside merchants were forbidden entry into the provinces involved, and the farmers, presented with a narrowing market for their cash product, organized to protest. In 1822, sweeping bakufu regulations ordered the abolition of guilds that had handled consignments from thirteen provinces in western Japan to Hyōgo and Edo and substituted Osaka as the only legitimate entrepôt for vegetables and oil. The next year, 1,107 villages petitioned for a free market in these products, only to have their petition rejected. Next, 1,307 villages in Settsu, Kawachi, and Izumi petitioned again. The bakufu again refused, although the petitioning villages now constituted about three-quarters of the provinces involved. In all these cases the protests were clearly organized by village leaders, as they remained within bounds and used legal channels of request. Despite the formal bakufu rejection, however, relaxation came in piecemeal fashion, particularly with regard to cotton after yet another request from 1,007 villages. It should be noted that requests from so wide an area had to come from villages subject to widely different jurisdictions and that those submitting them recognized the increasing centralization of the economy and considered their "lords" of secondary importance in matters of daily economic livelihood.[43]

During these same years, the bakufu began to respond to the irrationality of Kantō landholding patterns with sweeping measures of control. From the first, holdings near Edo assumed a crazy-quilt pattern

43 Ibid., pp. 240ff.

that made police control difficult. The area constituted a large part of the shogunal *tenryō*, with many small *fudai* daimyo realms and numerous *hatamoto* and large *gokenin* villages included. Shrines and temple holdings also dotted the area. Much of the *tenryō* was administered by the Kantō *gundai*, a post long hereditary in the Ina family, which supervised other bakufu *daikan* (administrators). This important post, which was directly responsible to the Senior Council (*rōjū*), maintained control over highway taxation, made government loans to farmers and merchants, and monitored security through a series of observation elevations officially designated as Eagle Hunting Hills, yet its staff, including servants and foot soldiers, amounted to only 380 men. By the early years of the nineteenth century, commercialization was producing more and more travel for business and pleasure and with this came the development of hot springs, silk markets, and, inevitably, an increase of vagrants, robbers, and gamblers. Throughout Japan, disputes between people of different jurisdictions were supposed to come before bakufu courts in Edo, but the Kantō jurisdictions were so confused that many holdings consisted of parts of several villages and so made neighbors in many villages subject to different petty lords. As a result, almost any dispute was likely to end up in the shogunal courts. Added to this was the bakufu's penchant for moving and transferring holdings among its favorites. One village in the western outreach of the Edo plain, Gōdo, consisted of 111 households, with a population of 536 and a rating of 1,239 *koku* at the end of Tokugawa rule. It was sectioned into six holdings, each with a petty fief holder who tried to maintain his Edo standard of living through direct administration. He had to work through the local notables, and their attitude toward his "rule" was more one of tolerance than of awe.[44]

In 1798 the Ina family was relieved of its responsibilities, and the authorities tried for closer control. In 1805 steps were taken toward regional administration of law through the appointment of officials who were responsible for given areas, regardless of the stewardship of the villages involved. Eight circulating intendants were appointed from among veteran officials with ten or more years of experience. Each was given assistants, in some cases commoners, who were assigned the duty of patrolling large areas on a regular circuit. This system too proved inadequate, for the forces of "lawlessness" (usually designated as "bandits and gamblers") were better organized, and

[44] Tanaka, "Village Youth Organizations," pp. 202–7.

probably more numerous, than were the new guards. As a result, in 1827 a series of measures, which are usually termed the Bunsei reforms, addressed the issue. The following year the *wakamono nakama* were banned. Local autonomy was being redefined.

The declared purpose of the Bunsei measures was to provide guidelines for the reactivation of five-family joint-responsibility groups and to use them to eradicate banditry and vagrancy. Villages were also to be assisted in controlling expenditures. The ban on young men's organizations made it possible to restrain the proliferation of holidays and was designed to end the spending of village funds on entertainment like kabuki, sumo, dancers, and puppet plays. The regulations were also explicitly anticommercial. The Bunsei regulations established a vertically integrated judicial system in which a large village union, consisting of thirty to forty villages headed by a chief village at the center, would direct the activities of smaller groups of one to six villages. Their representatives were to meet every six months to coordinate financing for measures to maintain law and order. At the base of society, the regulations called for vigilance in maintaining the five-family units of mutual observation and control.

Regulations were issued that were to be read at village assemblies, and signed statements of compliance had to be forwarded by male villagers. It seems possible that the measures helped prevent large-scale insurrections throughout the area and that local notables found in this structure a means for limited participation in local government.[45]

The regulations provide fascinating evidence about the state of society. "In all villages there are households which have become wealthy because they have worked hard even on rest days," they state, and then go on to prohibit young men from harassing such villagers by spreading rumors about their daughters or by defiling their wells and houses. "Except for fishing, woodcutting and other traditional trades, no new businesses are to be established," says another regulation; the commentary goes on to discuss the virtues of productive simplicity. "Artisans of different trades are reported to be getting together to demand higher wages," says another, but this is forbidden; wages should be reduced and certainly not allowed to rise. "The number of beggars is rising greatly, causing difficulties for the population"; the solution proposed is to provide them no help and to arrest them if they try to force themselves upon villagers. "Rumor has it that in some places local officials gamble." If this is so, gambling will never be

---

[45] Tanaka, "Village Youth Organizations," pp. 208ff., and Kitajima, "Kaseiki no seiji to minshū," pp. 311ff.

controlled; they are to be denounced. All lotteries are illegal as well. Again, "It is said that professional litigants (*kujishi*) in villages disturb the tranquility of the countryside." Avoid litigation and preserve harmony, and denounce the would-be lawyers to the authorities. Additional regulations set standards of austerity for prisoners' thongs, prisoners' conveyances, and prisoners' food. The provisions end with the customary injunction to filiality and gratitude:

> The tenno has compassion for the people and is concerned to keep peace . . . the shogun has appointed new officials to serve good people. . . . No words are adequate to express our gratitude for the benevolence of the shogun. Village officials should understand this situation, keep out of trouble, work hard and encourage farming so that you can pay more taxes in rice. Then your village will prosper.[46]

It will be seen that the paternalistic, Confucian spirit of the Kyōhō, Kansei, and future Tempō reforms was alive and well. Read with a mirror, however, these injunctions have a good deal to say about social and economic change in the Kantō plain.

There were also other and more constructive solutions proposed for rural poverty. Agrarian reformers like Ninomiya Sontoku (1787–1856) and Ōhara Yūgaku (1797–1858), the former of peasant stock, became known for communal self-help programs based on embryo cooperatives. Sontoku, who was plunged into poverty early in his life when his father died, first scraped out a living for himself and his brothers, next revived the family fortunes, and then went on to advocate improved agronomy, more saving, and cooperative credit unions. He did this in a highly moral tone of preaching that drew on the congruence of social values with respect to hard work, frugality, and gratitude for the benefits bestowed by ancestors, lords, and nature. His *hōtoku* (return of virtue) cooperatives were so successful in reviving village economy and prosperity after the demoralization that accompanied the great famines of the 1830s that his help was requested by neighboring domains and finally by the bakufu itself.

Sontoku's evangelism for rural rationality and thrift made him a hero for future propagandists during the reactionary years of prewar Japan, but his teaching went far beyond the saccharine tones in which he was presented in school textbooks. He taught the importance of precise calculation of the water and fertilizer required for optimal yields. He argued that taxes should be reduced to encourage higher

---

46 Tanaka, "Village Youth Organizations," pp. 272–309, provides translations of the injunctions.

effort and productivity. So too with Ōhara Yūgaku, born near Nagoya, who traveled widely throughout the country to teach farming techniques and land reclamation. He too advocated thrift and diligence but added to these teachings a series of cooperative credit unions in which membership involved an investment contribution. These have been described as among the world's first industrial cooperatives, designed for the encouragement of small-scale enterprise as well as for agricultural improvements. The two reformers fared very differently: Sontoku became an ideal type for future state moralists, and Yūgaku, investigated for possible subversion, met personal ruin during his long prosecution and finally committed suicide. Nevertheless they shared to a high degree views of self-help and rationality. In Sontoku's famous phrase, "It is the Way of Nature to achieve great results by being careful about small things."[47]

During these years the rational approach to accumulation found an even more effective spokesman in Kaiho Seiryō (1755–1817), a political economist who argued the justice and morality of calculation and profit. Though born to rank and privilege, Seiryō chose the path of private teacher, adviser, and traveler, perhaps from the disillusion of seeing his father's fall from domain elder to *rōnin*. After a sound grounding in the Confucian teachings of Ogyū Sorai, Seiryō received and rejected opportunities for political office in favor of traveling throughout Japan to study geography, local resources, products, and customs. By the early Bunka years he was in the Kaga domain advising merchants and samurai about problems of production and the domain economy; he then returned to Kyoto where he opened his own school.

Kaiho Seiryō's writings used much of the language and many of the concepts of his predecessors in political economy, but he transformed their thrust to an advocacy of rationality. Everything, from material goods to personal service, he argued, was a commodity with an exchange value. Exchanges were to be based on a principle of precise calculation, equating name with content, that would permit objective measurement and help determine a just profit or interest.[48]

47 Kitajima, *Bakuhansei no kumon*, pp. 253–260; and for Sontoku, Thomas R. H. Havens, *Farm and Nation in Modern Japan* (Princeton, N.J.: Princeton University Press, 1974), pp. 25–7, and sources cited there. It should be noted that *kokugaku* nativism in these years made much of agrarian improvement and used books on agronomy to spread its teachings among farmers.
48 See Tetsuo Najita, "The Conceptual Portrayal of Tokugawa Intellectual History," in Tetsuo Najita and Irwin Scheiner, eds., *Japanese Thought in the Tokugawa Period: Methods and Metaphors* (Chicago: University of Chicago Press, 1978), pp. 23–24, for a discussion of Seiryō. See also Najita's more recent *Visions of Virtue in Tokugawa Japan: The Kaitokudō Merchant Academy of Osaka* (Chicago: University of Chicago Press, 1987).

This was a prelude to his advocacy of careful planning in order to generate wealth and profit. He argued that this was as important to domain administrators as it was to commoners whose profit lay in the exchange of goods or in the production of agricultural wealth. Seiryō noted that investment cooperatives were spreading from urban to rural areas, and he held up as models the calculation of merchant houses that based their profit on assiduous attention to small matters that, over time, combined to make a difference. The domain itself, in fact, should be thought of as a kind of enterprise, and its affairs should be administered with a view to maximizing income and minimizing waste.

All of this was consistent with universal principles. To Seiryō it made more sense than did the moral posturing, classical affectation, and wasteful irrationality that characterized samurai life and ideals. Indeed, the conventional derogation of merchant activity was clearly wrong; the towns and communication centers were neither parasites nor problems but probably were more in tune with the course of human affairs than were the samurai who, at all but the highest levels of power and affluence, found themselves strapped into patterns of expenditure that they could not afford.

Views of this sort, transformed by national emergency upon the coming of the West, could be related to domain and bakufu efforts to build wealth and strength (*fukoku, kyōhei*). At the time that Seiryō espoused them, they constituted important examples of the way that political economists could turn to deal with the actualities of late Tokugawa life.

THE IMAGE OF THE WESTERN WORLD

The Kansei and Kasei years also inaugurated a new awareness of possible danger from the Western world. That awareness began with knowledge of the Russian advance on East Asia from the north, and it intensified with information about the disorder that the Napoleonic wars had produced in the European state system. The major channel for such information was the Dutch trading station at Deshima (or Dejima) in Nagasaki, where the Dutch were required to submit regular reports (*fūsetsugaki*).

It has already been stated that the Tokugawa system was hardened and systematized by the Kansei reform. This was equally true of the system of national isolation. Indeed, the very consciousness of those regulations as a "system" came only in the nineteenth century, and the term for "closed country" (*sakoku*) was coined in 1801 by Shizuku Tadao when he translated the defense of the system incorporated in the closing chapter of Engelbert Kaempfer's *History of Japan*.[49] But by his day the limited number of apertures from which the West could be observed had had the effect of attracting viewers to those openings and probably of sharpening their focus. As that took place, the visits and materials of the Dutch, which had aroused little curiosity in the early Tokugawa years, began to make it possible to arrange structured access to books and information.

From 1641, when the Dutch trading station was moved from Hirado to Dejima, that fan-shaped fill served as Japan's window on the world and the world's peephole into Japan. Nagasaki also had a slightly larger, but similarly enclosed, area for Chinese traders, and in the seventeenth century Korean imports carried out by way of Tsushima provided access to important Confucian texts.[50] The China trade was less structured, however, and lacked the official status accorded to the Dutch East India Company. Dejima was about 650 feet in its longer and 550 feet in its shorter dimension, connected to the mainland by a carefully guarded stone bridge. All sides were surrounded by a stone wall to prevent exits. The island itself provided two rows of two-story buildings that provided warehousing and living space for the Dutch detachment. That detachment was headed by the chief factor (or *kapitan*, as the Japanese termed the *opperhoofd* from their prior trade with Portuguese) of whom there were 163 in 315 years. Normally there were also a few scribes, a barber-doctor, a butter maker – in all, from ten to fifteen men.

The number of Dutch ships, which normally arrived in the summer and left in the fall, varied over time but diminished steadily. The ships brought Chinese and Southeast Asian cargo of silks, spices, and exotica and in return loaded Japanese copper. Tokugawa political economists worried about the impact on Japanese coinage of the drain on copper, and periods of rigidity and reform at the beginning and end of the century included measures to reduce the volume and frequency of Dutch trade. Arai Hakuseki in 1715 and Matsudaira Sadanobu in 1790 sponsored major restrictions. The number of Dutch ships permitted to come fell from five, to three or four, to three, to two, and finally to

---

49 Ronald P. Toby, *State and Diplomacy in Early Modern Japan: Asia in the Development of the Tokugawa Bakufu* (Princeton, N.J.: Princeton University Press, 1984), p. 13.
50 The standard work on trade with Korea in Tokugawa time is by Tashiro Kazui, *Kinsei Ni-Chō tsūkō bōekishi no kenkyū* (Tokyo: Sōbunsha, 1981); and, more briefly, Kazui Tashiro, "Foreign Relations During the Edo Period: *Sakoku* Re-examined," *Journal of Japanese Studies* 8 (Summer 1982): 283–306.

one per year. Similarly, the count of smaller Chinese ships dwindled in number from seventy to thirty and finally to ten. Even so, between 1621 and 1847, a total of 715 Dutch ships reached Japan.

The Dutch were merchants in Nagasaki, but as representatives of a structured order they were required to schedule trips of homage and service to the shogun's court in Edo. As with the Japanese daimyo, these trips were at their own expense. They involved the preparation of gifts of appropriate quality and cost for some twenty categories of officials and hosts, beginning with the shogun and his senior councilors and extending to the masters of the inns prescribed for their use. The Dutch had to hire porters and provide for the needs of the inspectors and guards attached to their party as well as see to their own needs. The retinues moved slowly through the country, greeted, escorted, and seen off by representatives of each daimyo through whose land they moved. From 1633 to 1764 these visits took place annually; from then until 1790 in alternate years, and from 1790 to 1850, the last trip, they came every fourth year.[51]

Each year the Dutch were expected to file a report (*fūsetsugaki*) about developments in the outside world. For many years these were perfunctory in content and aroused little curiosity in Japan, but when Japan began to experience direct contact along its coasts from north and south, the reports began to be scrutinized more carefully. The Dutch also imported books. For many years these had been checked chiefly to make sure that they did not contain any taint of Christianity. The same was true of books brought in by Chinese traders at Nagasaki, where systematic arrangements were made for the inspection and approval of material from overseas. Bakufu officials had the first choice of books, as they did with goods, and by the nineteenth century they were able to order specific volumes through orders (*eischboek*) that they gave to the Dutch. This process produced a body of experts in foreign matters. Initially it was the Chinese books that mattered, as they included direct or indirect results of the Jesuit movement in China. Throughout the eighteenth century there was a brisk trade in Chinese texts. Books from China in the nineteenth century included translations by Protestant missionaries, and in the fourth decade of the century, there were Chinese accounts of the Opium War. These were accessible to all literate Japanese, and their role in awakening Japan to

---

51 The classic descriptions of such trips are the two provided by Engelbert Kaempfer in the 1690s in vol. 3 of his *History of Japan*, 3 vols., trans. J. G. Scheuchzer (Glasgow: James MacLehose and Sons, 1896). Practical aspects of this contact are described by Kanai Madoka, *Nichi-Ran kōshōshi no kenkyū* (Tokyo: Shibunkaku, 1986).

its danger has had too little emphasis in Western writing.[52] In the late eighteenth and early nineteenth century, however, it was Dutch books that mattered most to Japan's image of the West, and as the body of men able to read them grew, a distinct tradition of Dutch (*rangaku*) and later "Western" (*yōgaku*) studies came to matter in intellectual and political terms.

An understanding of nineteenth-century developments in Japan's image of the outside world requires discussion of the way that Dutch books, study and translation, and government policy were related. There were two groups of intellectuals who had direct access to the Dutch. At Nagasaki there were professional (and hereditary) interpreters. Four senior interpreters (*oppertolken*, as the Dutch termed them), with assistants, apprentices, and students, supervised a community of many more. In the 1690s Kaempfer spoke of a group numbering "no less than one hundred and fifty persons"; in the early nineteenth century there were fifty-two interpreters divided into three ranks of seniority, and by the late Tokugawa decades (when, of course, additional languages were required), Fukuchi Gen'ichirō described a group of one hundred and forty. These men enjoyed, and had it in their own interest to monopolize, whatever access the authorities permitted to the little group of resident Dutch. But access was not always helpful. The group of foreigners might include someone of intellectual quality and interest, but more often it did not. Only two of the chief factors left accounts that indicated a strong interest in things Japanese. Isaac Titsingh (in Japan from 1779 to 1784, in three visits that included two trips to Edo) and Hendrik Doeff (in Japan intermittently from 1799 to 1817, after 1803 as chief factor, unable to leave because of the interruption of contact with Holland) made major contributions. Titsingh's stay in Japan came during a period when the curbs were relaxed, with the result that he was able to meet many scholars and daimyo. After his departure he corresponded with Edo scholars and Nagasaki interpreters.[53] Johannes Edewin Nieman, who visited Edo as chief factor in 1838 and who met Watanabe Kazan, had studied geography in London, Paris, and Vienna. More important, however, was the role of the physicians attached to the Dutch settlement, who regularly accompanied the chief factor on his trips to Edo. Three of

---

52 Ōba Osamu, *Edo jidai ni okeru Tōsen mochiwatarisho no kenkyū* (Suita: Kansai University, 1967) provides the basic study of books imported from China. Ōba Osamu, *Edo jidai no Ni-Chū hiwa* (Tokyo: Tōhō shoten, 1980) includes accounts of imports relating to the Opium War.
53 Titsingh is discussed in C. R. Boxer, "Isaac Titsingh, 1745–1812," chap. 7 of *Jan Compagnie in Japan 1600–1850* (The Hague: Martinus Nijhoff, 1950).

the most remarkable were nationals of other countries. These were Engelbert Kaempfer, a German doctor whose stay in Japan from 1690 to 1692 included two visits to Edo and resulted in his celebrated *History of Japan*, Carl Peter Thunberg, a Swedish intellectual and later professor at the University of Uppsala, in Japan in 1775, and especially the German Philip Franz von Siebold, whose stay in Japan between 1823 and 1830 included a period in which he gave instruction in a medical school set up for him in Nagasaki.[54]

The Nagasaki interpreters enjoyed frequent access to these men, but their Edo counterparts were restricted to a few command occasions during the Dutch presence in Edo at the Edo inn where the missions were housed, the Nagasakiya. At Edo a larger group of scholars of Dutch learning was made up of doctors anxious to learn more about Western medicine and science.

The seventeenth century, which saw trade at its high point, found Japanese interest in the West at a low point. Over the course of a century, as Dutch-Japanese trade declined in volume and profit, the cultural cargoes became more appreciated. Books increasingly displaced Chinese silks as imports, and Japanese exports came to feature Arita ceramics, known as Imari for the port from which they were exported, which contributed to the development of Delft and other European ceramics.[55] The books that the Japanese imported had the greatest importance for future times. Thanks to these, "Dutch studies," (*rangaku*) became a vital intellectual tradition in the later eighteenth century and a matter for government concern at the century's end.[56]

Holland was, however accidentally, an appropriate bridge to the West for Japanese scholars. It was small enough to be unthreatening, squarely in the middle of European cultural exchange, and quick in its response to European learning, much of which was quickly translated into Dutch. Most of the major achievements of the Japanese translations effort were translations of Dutch translations of English and continental learning. The first great monument, the *Kaitai shinsho* of 1774, was a collaborative effort by three doctors: Sugita Gempaku (1733–1818), Maeno Ryōtaku (1723–1803), and Nakagawa Jun'an

---

54 Siebold is the subject of a magisterial biography by Kure Shūzō, *Shiiboruto sensei, sono shōgai oyobi kōgyō* (Tokyo: Hakuhōdō shoten, 1926) and a journal launched in 1982, *Shiiboruto kenkyū* (Tokyo: Hōsei University).
55 See T. Volker, *Porcelain and the Dutch East India Company 1602–1682*, and *The Japanese Porcelain Trade of the Dutch East India Company After 1683* (Leiden: Brill, 1954 and 1959.)
56 See Marius B. Jansen, "*Rangaku* and Westernization," *Modern Asian Studies* 18 (October 1984): 541–53.

(1739–1786). Their achievement was to translate the work of a Leiden professor, Gerard Dictin, who had translated the descriptive captions, but not the notes, of the 1722 work of the German physician, John Adam Kulmus, *Tabulae anatomicae in quibus corporis humani*. Sugita and his associates understood this project after viewing the dissection of an executed criminal and confirming their suspicion that the Western source was far more accurate than the Chinese texts in which they had been trained. Sugita later recalled, in memoirs written in 1815:

> On our way home we talked with excitement about the experiment. Since we had served our lords as doctors, we were quite ashamed of our ignorance of the true morphology of the human body, which was fundamental to the medical art. In justification of our membership in the medical profession, we made a vow to seek facts through experiment.

The three agreed to seek no assistance and began a tedious process in which "we translated by conjecture, word by word, and gradually these increased in number. . . . After two or three years of hard study everything became clear to us; the joy of it was as the chewing of sweet sugar cane."[57]

There had been earlier cases in which Japanese doctors had become aware of the discrepancy between anatomical facts and Chinese texts, which treated the body as the constituent part of a properly balanced cosmos, but this occasion remains highly important and historic. One notes the doctors' sense of shame that as specialist professionals, they had let down their daimyo. Their resolution to seek answers through experiment in the future and, by inference, to follow the facts where they might lead marked the real shift. This led to a readiness to relegate Chinese learning to its place as a great, but no longer the only, source of wisdom. When critics disparaged the conclusions of Sugita's work and forced him to respond, he did so in a dialogue in which he argued that China was only one country in the Eastern Seas and that true medical knowledge had to be based on universal grounds. The search for such knowledge led increasingly to Western books, until by the time of his memoirs, *Rangaku kotohajime*, Sugita could marvel that he had unwittingly launched an age of translation. As he put it,

57 Described in Donald Keene, *The Japanese Discovery of Europe* (Stanford, Calif.: Stanford University Press, 1969), pp. 22 ff.; and also discussed by Grant Goodman, "Dutch Studies in Japan Re-examined," in Josef Kreiner, ed., *Deutschland–Japan Historische Kontakte* (Bonn: Grundmann, 1984), pp. 69–88. The authoritative accounts in Japanese are by Satō Shōsuke, *Yōgakushi kenkyū josetsu* (Tokyo: Iwanami shoten, 1964), and *Yōgakushi no kenkyū* (Tokyo: Chūō kōronsha, 1980). The notes were later added in a revised translation by Ōtsuki Gentaku (1757–1827).

Today so-called *rangaku* is very widespread. Some people study it earnestly, and the uneducated talk about it thoughtlessly. . . . I never imagined that Dutch studies would become so important or make such progress. I think Chinese studies made only slow progress, but Dutch studies were more lucid and made rapid progress because they were written in plain and direct language.

And yet, he concluded, in a striking willingness to compare the current of thought and effort in which he had participated with the far more massive effort to domesticate the wisdom of China a millennium earlier, it might be that the training in Chinese studies "developed our mind beforehand."[58]

The Edo doctors were a far larger group than were the Nagasaki interpreters. Through the lords they served they had opportunity to request and borrow Dutch books, and through their presence and common concerns in the great metropolis they became an important and vital group. Edo was the center of samurai learning and society, and the information that reached curious minds there could easily reach others, stir response, and produce sponsorship for ever-more ambitious efforts. At the same time, suspicions of a Western advance, exaggerated or misunderstood, could produce more results in Edo than they could in Nagasaki.

The new awareness of danger from abroad began with news about the Russians. Russian probings to the north begun about a century before the Japanese became aware of them. The seventeenth and eighteenth centuries had brought a slow expansion of Russian activities into Siberia and the Amur region. Early Russian treaties with China (Nerchinsk, 1686, and Kiakhta, 1727) formalized commerce on a basis of relative equality. Russian caravans contacted authorized Chinese merchants at frontier stations and in Peking, somewhat in the way that accommodation with maritime foreigners was being worked out at Canton.[59] Forced to move north of the Amur basin by the Chinese presence in Manchuria, the Russians approached Japan from the north through Kamchatka and, after 1700, the Kurils. In 1702, Peter the Great ordered the subjection of Kamchatka and the collection of information about Japan in preparation for commerce. The advance through the Kurils was not

---

58 Discussed in Marius B. Jansen, *Japan and Its World: Two Centuries of Change* (Princeton, N.J.: Princeton University Press, 1980); and Haga Tōru, "Introduction," in *Nihon no meicho: Sugita Gempaku, Hiraga Gennai, Shiba Kōkan* (Tokyo: Chūō kōronsha, 1971), pp. 9–84.
59 Joseph Fletcher, "Sino-Russian Relations, 1800–1862," chap. 7 of John K. Fairbank, ed., *The Cambridge History of China* (Cambridge, England: Cambridge University Press, 1978), vol. 10: *Late Ch'ing*.

planned or coordinated, but it continued after Peter died in 1725. Two expeditions led by Bering and Spanberg, Danes in Russian service, explored the northern coasts and archipelago to make contact with Japan. Russian enthusiasm for seal pelts in the Kurils brought them ever farther south and into contact with the Ainu on the Kuril Islands. By 1770 Russians had completed their preliminary exploration and had been on almost every island in the Kuril chain.[60] During the same years Japanese merchants and explorers were pushing north from southern Hokkaido, trading with the Ainu in a pattern that gradually brought the Ainu into substantial subjection to the daimyo of Matsumae. The daimyo in turn delegated commercial dealings to merchants from Osaka, Edo, and Sendai. By the latter half of the eighteenth century the Japanese were becoming aware of the "Red Ainu" to the north, and the Russians, from their knowledge of Ainu trade patterns, sensed a major country to the south. Kudō Heisuke, a Sendai physician, wrote two accounts in the early 1780s advocating colonization and trade expansion to the north. That served as spur to plans for action by the councilor Tanuma Okitsugu. Matsudaira Sadanobu, however, put an end to such developments when he came into power, on the grounds that a diversion of resources to the north would serve to impoverish the southern domains.[61]

The Russian proximity was brought home to the Japanese in 1771 when a Hungarian nobleman, Moritz von Benyowsky, who had escaped from exile in Kamchatka, appeared in southern Japan with warnings that Russia was planning to attack Ezo (Hokkaido) from new fortifications in the Kurils. These warnings, quite without substance in fact, became further distorted in transmission and resulted in a good deal of alarm among those who learned of them. They contributed to the argument of a Sendai scholar, Hayashi Shihei (1738–93), who wrote two works, *Sankoku tsūran zuisetsu* and *Kaikoku heidan*, warning of Russian designs and advocating stronger maritime defenses to the north. Honda Toshiaki (1744–1821), a more widely oriented student of political economy, responded with plans for the sponsorship of merchant activities to the north and the development of Japan's natural potential there. Several of the memorials that he addressed to Matsudaira Sadanobu on the subject were without effect,

60 John J. Stephan, *The Kuril Islands: Russo-Japanese Frontiers in the Pacific* (Oxford, England: Clarendon Press, 1974), p. 50.
61 Satō, *Yōgakushi no kenkyū*, pp. 118 ff. for Tanuma's plans and their failure; John W. Hall, *Tanuma Okitsugu (1719–1788): Forerunner of Modern Japan* (Cambridge, Mass.: Harvard University Press, 1955), pp. 100ff.

but his writings, travels, and knowledge of the north, though never disseminated through publication, survived to influence later thinkers.[62] Hayashi Shihei fared less well, for he had the temerity to publish his books in an attempt to recoup his finances. His advocacy of maritime defense began to appear in 1787 in a few copies, and when the entire work was published in 1791, he was arrested under the provisions of the Kansei prohibition of publications on contemporary affairs. After a period of imprisonment he was sent to his domain of Sendai for confinement, and the plates for his books were ordered burned. He died the following year.[63]

But the Russian probings were not at an end. In 1792 and 1793 another expedition, this one led by Adam Laxman, was sent by Catherine the Great. Laxman tried to use the return of castaways as the occasion to investigate the possibility of opening commercial relations with Japan. He was courteously received in northern Hokkaido where he spent the winter and continued on to Matsumae in the summer of 1793 to confer with the representatives that the bakufu had sent there to head off any plans to visit Edo. The Japanese accepted the castaways, but not the credentials and letters. Matsudaira Sadanobu responded to Laxman's request with a statement that Japan had been bound "from antiquity" by orders to seize or destroy ships from countries with which it had no formal relations, that foreign ships, even when returning castaways, could call only at Nagasaki, that other foreigners were to be turned over to the Dutch for repatriation, and that intruding ships had to be destroyed and their crews imprisoned permanently. Curiously, however, Laxman was also given a permit to enter Nagasaki, from which he drew misleading conclusions. Sadanobu perhaps intended to communicate with him there, but Laxman took it as a sign of willingness to trade. What mattered, however, was that Sadanobu had now, as with his prescription of Confucian orthodoxy, identified a new policy – the armed expulsion of Westerners – as part of Tokugawa tradition.[64]

In 1798, with Sadanobu out of power again, the bakufu decided to send an expedition to investigate conditions in the north, and the following year it placed half of Hokkaido, including Kunashiri and

---

62 Honda is the principal subject of Donald Keene's *Japanese Discovery of Europe*.
63 Satō, *Yōgaku kenkyūshi josetsu*, pp. 106 ff., for the text of the indictment.
64 Documentation and translation of Sadanobu's reply from Bob Tadashi Wakabayashi, *Anti-Foreignism and Western Learning in Early-Modern Japan* (Cambridge, Mass.: Harvard University Press, 1986). The standard account of these events, based principally on Russian sources, is by George Alexander Lensen, *The Russian Push Toward Japan: Russo-Japanese Relations, 1697–1875* (Princeton, N.J.: Princeton University Press, 1959).

Etorofu, under its own rule; eight years later the rest of Hokkaido and Sakhalin were decreed bakufu *tenryō* as well, and Matsumae was reassigned elsewhere. This arrangement continued until 1821, when Matsumae was allowed to take over once again. During much of that period, programs of settlement and subsidization for the Ainu through the provision of clothing, food, metal, and road construction were carried out in the hope of solidifying Japanese control and erecting barriers to Russian infiltration south from Uruppu.

The permit to enter Nagasaki that Laxman had received led to additional Russian moves a decade later. In 1799 the Russian-American Company was established to administer northern territories and to increase trade, and its directors were made responsible for new efforts to approach Japan. In 1802 an ambitious expedition was launched to extend Russian maritime contact with the Pacific coast, and as part of these plans Captain Nikolai Rezanov appeared at Nagasaki in 1804 with a letter from Alexander I formally requesting the privilege of trade with Japan. Rezanov was kept waiting in Nagasaki harbor between October 1804 and April 1805 for a reply before his request, together with the presents he had brought, was refused.[65] Rezanov left in anger and encouraged two young lieutenants, Khostov and Davydov, to take stronger measures in a misguided attempt to force the issue. They thus carried out a series of raids on Sakhalin and the southern Kurils in 1806 and 1807 in the curious expectation that this would make the bakufu more amenable to talks about trade. The last raid was on Etorofu and routed the unprepared Japanese garrison, resulting in the suicide of its disgraced commander. The raids had not reflected formal Russian policy so much as they had the enthusiasm and immaturity of proconsular ambition. The Japanese response, however, did. The northern daimyo were ordered to mobilize, and in 1808 over one thousand troops were landed on Kunashiri and Etorofu. The bakufu now gave up its plans for economic development in the area in the expectation of early conflict.

Three years later a surveying expedition commanded by Captain Vasilii Golovnin appeared, anxious to avoid difficulty with the Japanese. It helped them little. Golovnin was captured during an effort to find supplies on shore, removed to Hakodate, and kept there for two years until he was exchanged for a Japanese merchant that his command had kidnapped. His *Narrative of a Captivity in Japan During the Years 1811–1812 and 1813* was an account of growing mutual toler-

---

65 A scroll in the possession of the Historiographical Institute of the University of Tokyo showing his procession to the magistrate's office to receive the bakufu's response is one of the best illustrations of the Nagasaki of his day.

ance and almost friendship with his guards. Local commanders on both sides realized the urgency of some agreement to demark Russian and Japanese interests. When Golovnin was released, letters from the Russian governor of Irkutsk and the commander at Okhotsk expressed regrets for the attacks of a few years earlier and urged the establishment of a boundary, but no action was taken. The focus of Japanese concern gradually shifted to the south. In 1821, local administration of the north was returned to the daimyo of Matsumae, and from then to 1853 there was little action or tension in the north.

Larger problems rose with reference to Europeans who came from the south. In the same year that the Japanese defenses were proving inadequate in the north, they were challenged in the south. In 1808 the English frigate *Phaeton* sailed into Nagasaki harbor, threatened to attack shipping there if food was not supplied, and succeeded in having its way despite orders from the Japanese commander that it be attacked and burned. This was a minor but disturbing flurry in the disturbances of the Napoleonic years.

During the 1790s a few private English vessels had attempted to trade along the Japan coast, but without success. The British East India Company had little interest in or expectation of trade with Japan. Great Britain seemed unlikely to interfere with Japanese seclusion. Hesitation to alter this state of affairs led the Dutch chief factor at Deshima to minimize in his *fūsetsugaki* the European disorders that followed the French Revolution. The news that French revolutionary armies had invaded Holland, that Napoleon's brother had been placed on the Dutch throne, and that the Dutch king had taken refuge in England would, the Dutch realized, have put Holland in a very poor light indeed. The Dutch at Batavia were able to charter American vessels to service their trade. During the ten years between 1797 and 1807, American vessels flying the Dutch flag visited Deshima nine times, and five European vessels were leased. Meanwhile the Dutch reported as little about events in Europe as they could. The *fūsetsugaki* of 1794 was the first to report that "great crowds of rioters have beset the French government, killed the king and crown prince, and thrown the realm into confusion. Neighboring countries including Holland have had to take up arms."[66] In 1797 further news was provided to the effect that the royalists had won out and the revolution put down but that Holland had gone to war with England and lost some of its colonies.

66 Surviving *fūsetsugaki* have been edited by Iwao Seiichi as *Oranda fūsetsugaki shūsei*, 2 vols. (Tokyo: Nichi-Ran gakkai, 1976 and 1979). For 1794, vol. 2, p. 94.

Not surprisingly, the deception did not escape the Japanese very long. The American ships looked different; their crews spoke a different language; and they carried different goods: The Japanese interpreters at Nagasaki were soon aware that something was wrong. In 1803 the Dutch admitted that the ship that entered port that year was a leased American vessel but provided no details. The matter was made worse by other American ships that soon appeared requesting trade. Java fell to the British in 1811, and from then to 1816 Deshima was the only spot where the Dutch flag still flew.

Worse still, the bakufu did not realize that America had become an independent country and still considered it an English colony. This was straightened out in the aftermath of the *Phaeton* incident of 1808 when a disturbed bakufu ordered the Nagasaki officials to prepare a special report on world affairs. In response to that order, the interpreters Ishibashi Sukezaemon and Motoki Shōzaemon questioned *opperhoofd* Hendrik Doeff on Deshima for days at a time. This finally brought the word of the colonies' success in extricating themselves from the rule of the English king and gave in outline form the structure of the United States, the prominence of a man named Thomas Jefferson, and especially of a great commander named George Washington whose fame was such that his countrymen, five or six years after his death, had constructed a new capital city named for him. Now for the first time it was possible to dismiss rumors that the ships calling at Deshima had really been English.[67]

After the Napoleonic interlude the East Indies were returned to Dutch sovereignty by an English government that had no interest in colonial involvement there. While Thomas Raffles served as governor of Batavia, he had tried to substitute his country for Holland in the trade with Japan, but he received little support from his political superiors or from the British East India Company itself. Suggestions that England seize the Bonins and make them a base for contacts with Japan and China were brushed aside.[68]

The impact of these events on Western studies, and of those studies on government policy, now became clear. On the one hand, the bakufu's control and restrictions on the study of the West had been shown by Matsudaira Sadanobu's punishment of Hayashi Shihei. Though unresponsive to Honda and the prosecutor of Hayashi, how-

---

67 Satō, *Yōgakushi no kenkyū*, pp. 145–9.
68 W. G. Beasley, *Great Britain and the Opening of Japan 1834–1858* (London: Luzac, 1951), p. 30.

ever, Matsudaira Sadanobu was not blind to the value of Western-style learning. He wrote in his autobiography:

I began about 1792 or 1793 to collect Dutch books. The barbarian nations are skilled in the sciences, and considerable profit may be derived from their works of astronomy and geography, as well as from their military weapons and their methods of internal and external medicine. However, their books may serve to encourage idle curiosity or may express harmful ideas. . . . Such books and other foreign things should therefore not be allowed to pass in large quantities into the hands of irresponsible people; nevertheless it is desirable to have them deposited in a government library.[69]

Sadanobu had also reduced the number of Dutch ships permitted to enter Nagasaki, lengthened the interval between Dutch trips to Edo from two to four years, and restricted access to the Dutch while they were in Edo. Edo scholars had earlier been free to bring their students to the question-and-answer sessions with the Dutch doctors, but after Kansei, such access was limited to daimyo doctors. It all made for difficult communication. In 1794 Ōtsuki Gentaku, unable to get the floor in Edo with a question he had prepared for the Dutch, reflected stoically that he would have to wait four years for another opportunity to get it answered.[70]

Some of the writings of *rangaku* scholars may be cited to illustrate the grounds for Sadanobu's decision that access to Dutch learning should be controlled. Kudō Heisuke's writings about developments to the north have already been mentioned; Sugita Gempaku, it will be remembered, as early as 1775 had written a dialogue in which he separated the country of China from the central cultural tradition of East Asia. He declared: "The earth comprises a single great globe, and the myriad countries are distributed upon it. Every place is the center. One can call any country the central country. China is only a small country on one border of the Eastern Sea." He then went on to say: "The books of China are concerned with techniques and not with principles; they are not lacking in principles, but the provenance of those principles is not clear." Dutch medicine, based on facts, was also based on principles, and those principles were equivalent to the true teachings of the sages, who sought to improve human life. Thus the practicality of Western medical science was fully compatible with explicit adherence to the Sages and the essence of the East Asian tradition.

69 Quoted in Keene, *Discovery of Europe*, pp. 75–6.
70 Tadashi Yoshida, "The Rangaku of Shizuki Tadao: The Introduction of Western Science in Tokugawa Japan," Ph.D. diss., Princeton University, 1974.

But then in 1807, in *Yasō dokugo*, Gempaku made it clear that in his opinion Japan, no less than China, had departed from the wisdom of that great tradition. In a dialogue (presumably not published, as it ends with injunctions to maintain secrecy) Gempaku now called for a restoration (*chūkō*) of the state before its illness should become terminal. Evidence of the problem was to be found in Russian encroachment on Japan's northern shores, followed by the appearance of Rezanov at Nagasaki in 1804. It was Japanese duplicity that had prompted the permit for Laxman to enter Nagasaki, and Rezanov's irritation on discovering that deception had led to the raids by Khostov and Davydov in the north. After all, the doctor's interlocutor in the dialogue explains, Russia is young and vigorous, an expanding nation that has accomplished wonders since its remarkable beginnings under Peter. In fact, its vigor is comparable to that Japan showed in the days of Hideyoshi and Ieyasu. Japan's leaders now face one of two choices: an affirmative response to the Russians' request, or preparation for the war that will follow rejection of that request. Unfortunately Japan's fighting qualities have disintegrated under generations of peace. "Bushido has waned by stages, so that even among *hatamoto* and *gokenin*, who ought to be the first to come forward, seven or eight out of ten are like women. Their spirit is mean, like that of merchants, and they seem to have lost their sense of honor as samurai." The bakufu's samurai are unable to make an arrow fly two feet and cannot ride horses even "when the horses are more like cats than steeds"; they are hopelessly encumbered by urban luxuries and the debts that accompany them; and they are not even very effective against unarmed peasant rabble. The Russians, in contrast, have recently been able even to stand up against the might of K'ang Hsi to gain the treaty of Nerchinsk.[71]

Arguments of this sort reappeared in future debates. The immediate danger was exaggerated (the Russians did not reappear for almost a half-century), but the alarm was not entirely misplaced because the West as a whole would shortly become steadily more intrusive. Sugita realized that Japan was virtually defenseless but had no solution to propose. Like Tokugawa Nariaki after the coming of Perry, Sugita proposed using whatever time remained to

foster the people, drill the troops, reform and sustain our customs, and put everything in order. . . . Our first priority is to save our world: if we are

---

71 Haga, ed., *Sugita Gempaku, Hiraga Gennai, Shiba Kōkan*, pp. 269–95, for text.

forced to permit trade for now, we must, even though it is a disgrace; at a later time we will be able to redeem our honor.

He then offered proposals for institutional reforms that would turn the clock back to an earlier day: Warriors should return to the land; there should be less commercialism; and the cities should be reduced in size. The bakufu should even out the distinctions between *tozama* and *fudai* daimyo in order to encourage a shared sense of crisis and duty, and it should make higher posts accessible to men of ability, even though their samurai rank might be low. Thus intellectual awareness of the West was accompanied by calls for retreat into an institutional past in order to hold that West at bay. A half-century later, similar reasoning would provide the first steps on a bridge to the reforms that produced modern Japan.

For scholars of Dutch learning, the aftermath of the Kansei punishment for unauthorized publications like Hayashi Shihei's was a closer identification with authority. Because Sadanobu and his successors collected books and saw value in them, government employment provided the best path to support and safety. Inevitably this had consequences for attitudes as well. The case of Ōtsuki Gentaku is instructive. In 1803 Ōtsuki and a friend were ordered to translate Lalande's astronomical tables. Shortly afterward Nagasaki officials tried to use him as a channel to power brokers in Edo. In 1809, in the hope of easing the financial hardships that the merchants were suffering because of the interruption of trade with the Dutch, the Nagasaki magistrate got the Nagasaki interpreters to have Ōtsuki propose that trade with the Ryūkyū Islands be authorized as a substitute. Ōtsuki's connection with authority soon became formal with the establishment in 1811 of a separate Translation Office in the Bureau of Astronomy. Now began the recruitment of other linguists to work on a large-scale project to translate selected portions of a 1743 Dutch translation of Noel Chomel's *Dictionnaire Oeconomique*. The work in question, a byproduct of the eighteenth-century encyclopedist tradition, promised information for every means "D'augmenter son bien et de conserver sa santé" and appeared frequently on the order lists that were given to the departing Dutch vessels thereafter. Although the project was never completed, three hundred articles were produced in 135 Japanese hand-sewn volumes. For the scholars so employed, Western learning (for from this time work also began on other European languages through the medium of Dutch) was no longer simply a matter of indulging personal interest and following knowledge where it might lead; increasingly, it also involved the subordination of personal preference to official needs. For some men, Ōtsuki among them, this resulted in a surge of pride that what had been considered idle interest could now be put in the service of the country. Ōtsuki went beyond this to modify his earlier dismissal of Chinese medicine, to criticize the superficial preference for everything Dutch that he thought characterized dilettantes like Shiba Kōkan,[72] and to argue that the new learning should be allowed to supplement the wisdom of the past where its superiority could be clearly demonstrated. He even lent his support for arrangements to control and monitor imported knowledge in order to prevent its use by the faddish and superficial who might otherwise gain a following by catering to the popular taste for novelty.[73]

Ōtsuki's response may not have been universal, but it is reasonable to suppose that his was a frequent reaction among specialists proud that their learning was at last deemed worthy of government sponsorship and enhanced position. Private meddlers like Hayashi Shihei had at their hand only incomplete and frequently out-of-date knowledge, and generalists like Shiba Kōkan might become so intrigued with the mix of artistry and technology that they garnered from Dutch books that they began to see the West as a distant utopia of benevolence, learning, and well-being. Responsible officials, men who shared their superiors' political priorities and took pride in their service to the late feudal state, should be made of tougher stuff.

The new vision of Western affairs conveyed by better books and punctuated by Western incursions presented a sharper challenge to Japan. Earlier bakufu edicts had provided for supplying distressed vessels with provisions to enable them to make a peaceful departure, but in 1825 these were nullified by instructions for instant attack. The bakufu now went Sadanobu's warning to Laxman one better:

Henceforth, whenever a foreign ship is sighted approaching any point on our coast, all persons on hand should fire on and drive it off. If the vessel heads for the open sea, you need not pursue it; allow it to escape. But if the foreigners force their way ashore, you may capture and incarcerate them, and if their mother ship approaches, you may destroy it as circumstances dictate. . . . [H]ave no compunctions about firing on [the Dutch] by mistake; when in doubt, drive the ship away without hesitation. Never be caught offguard.[74]

72 On whom, see Calvin L. French, *Shiba Kōkan: Artist, Innovator, and Pioneer in the Westernization of Japan* (New York: Weatherhill, 1974).
73 Satō, *Yōgaku kenkyūshi jōsetsu*, pp. 117ff.
74 Wakabayashi, *Anti-Foreignism*, p. 60. This is the *"ninen naku uchiharau"* (don't think twice! drive them out) edict.

This institutionalization of a zealot's stand came at the urging of the bakufu's director of the Translation Office. Takahashi Kageyasu (1785–1829) was the eldest son of Yoshitoki, a distinguished mathematician and official astronomer who had been commissioned to carry out the reform of the calendar in the Kansei period, had supervised Ōtsuki's translation of Lalande, and had sponsored a distinguished student, the geographer Inō Tadataka (Chūkei, 1745–1818), whose geographical surveys of the north served as the basis for Japanese maps throughout the entire nineteenth century. Kageyasu began with his father's skills in Chinese and Japanese mathematics and astronomy and succeeded to the family headship and the post of official astronomer in 1804. He supervised and supported the exploratory travels of his older contemporary Inō Tadataka. He mastered Dutch, translated part of Kaempfer's history, and also worked on Manchu, English, and Russian. From Deshima sources he obtained Kruzenstern's account of his explorations in the north, and he also obtained and translated an account of the Napoleonic wars. Thus it was from a background of the most solidly international orientation available in Tokugawa Japan that the head of the Translation Office proposed in 1824 that an edict be issued requiring the immediate expulsion of foreign ships from Japan. The *ninen naku uchiharau,* "don't think twice" edict stands as the final extreme of the seclusion system. Takahashi's argument was that unauthorized whaling ships were becoming more and more of a menace. They were taking advantage of Japanese benevolence, and the only solution was one of total separation and expulsion. Unauthorized landings and informal contact between Japanese commoners and foreigners would inevitably lead to forms of subversion in which the Westerners would take advantage of the credulity of ignorant commoners and prey on their curiosity to spread Christianity. It was wasteful to mobilize large numbers of men to deal with occasional incursions, Takahashi argued, and much better to follow what was actually international procedure: "When ships from a nation with whom diplomatic relations are not maintained try to enter, blank rounds are fired from the nearest cannon on shore. It is customary for those ships to leave the harbor after being informed in this way that entry is not permitted." The bakufu's order, when it banned entry by unauthorized foreign vessels, added a codicil affecting commoners: "If contacts with foreigners are covered up, the persons involved will be subject to the most severe punishment when the facts come to light."

Takahashi's story is full of ironies. His personal relations with Dutch residents at Deshima were entirely cordial. Hendrik Doeff, chief factor in the Napoleonic years, gave him, at his request, the Western name of Johannes Globius to honor his geographical achievements. Thus the bakufu's most far-reaching ban on foreign contacts did not come from the ignorance or indifference of an earlier day but had its origin in the recommendations of the finest scholar of the West of the day. It was justified not in terms of the "Sacred Ancestor's" precepts but in terms of Takahashi's understanding of the international procedures of the day.[75]

It is even more ironic that Takahashi himself next ran afoul of injunctions against purveying restricted information to foreigners and died while under investigation in the aftermath of the Siebold affair. Philip Franz von Siebold, mentioned as one of the most important of the doctors attached to the Dutch station at Deshima, arrived there in 1823. His distinction as a doctor and intellectual had recommended him to his Dutch employers, who gave him a special title as "surgeon major, authorized to conduct a survey of the natural history of this realm." His Japanese hosts quickly recognized his superior qualities. Nagasaki's rules were relaxed enough to make it possible for him to teach in an academy, the Narutakijuku, on the outskirts of the city. He also maintained a Japanese mistress by whom he fathered a daughter. In Nagasaki, Siebold lectured to a total of fifty-six students. Like many foreign teachers in Japan a half-century later, he had his students write essays in Dutch about their country, essays that provided material for his own publications about Japan. Thirty-nine such essays survive. Siebold himself drew up testimonial diplomas for his charges to certify their proficiency. Among his friends, and central to the breadth of his contacts, was Takahashi Kageyasu.

From Siebold, Takahashi obtained copies of Dutch translations of English explorers' accounts and of Krusenstern, and in exchange he presented Siebold with copies of Inō Tadataka's maps of Japan. While in Edo, Siebold also met daily with Mogami Tokunai, a member of the late-eighteenth-century expeditions to the north some decades earlier, who was able to tell him much about Ainu life, language, and northern geography. When Siebold was about to leave Japan, it became known, via Mogami, that he had exchanged information with Takahashi, and the investigation that followed led to the discovery of the maps of the north. Upon this, twenty-three of Siebold's students were taken into custody in 1828. Takahashi, the most highly placed and the most responsible for delivering proscribed materials into foreign hands,

---

75 Wakabayashi, *Anti-Foreignism*, pp. 102ff.

died under interrogation, and his corpse, preserved in brine, was sent to Edo for formal decapitation. Siebold himself was kept on Deshima for almost a year before being allowed to leave Japan. Alerted by his friends to what was coming, he had seized the short period of time available to copy the most important of the maps, so that they survived the confiscation and examination of his baggage.[76]

Takahashi's case serves to illustrate some of the ambivalence and constraints under which the foreign experts worked, an ambivalence that has its parallel in historical evaluations of their role. Although some writers have emphasized the trends toward modernity and liberation implicit in what the Western experts read and wrote, others have preferred to stress the government's co-option of their abilities and the increasing concentration on matters of defense. The growing crisis of the nineteenth century made for the practical application of intelligence that had begun as joyful and often idle curiosity on the part of the first *rangakusha*. Yet throughout the period, the scholars showed personal esteem and even, when possible, friendship for the foreigners they would contact, however they might combine that friendship with scorn and reprobation for "barbarians" in the mass. Sugita Gempaku considered the Russians to be barbarians, but able and dangerous, and Takahashi in his memorandum used the unpleasant figure of barbarians swarming like flies over Japan's rice bowl. Through it all, however, the intellectual curiosity of the best continued to be shown in translation efforts that were necessarily private, in fact covert, and hence unplanned and unsystematic. The most impressive product of all of this, Shizuki Tadao's rendition of a Dutch popularization of Newton, grew out of a letter from the translator, who was a Nagasaki interpreter, asking an Edo friend whether he knew of "any book you have there that describes stimulating and interesting theories of physics or astronomy, whether in Chinese or a Western language. I would particularly like to see a mathematics book on logarithms you said you

---

76 Keene, *Japanese Discovery of Europe*, provides sympathetic coverage of the affair, pp. 147ff. When the departure of the Perry flotilla for Japan neared two decades later, the United States Department of State requested its minister to The Hague to request copies of maps that Siebold was said to have brought with him, but neither the Department of Colonial Affairs nor the Dutch navy had knowledge of them. Siebold's book was at that time still in press. Manfred C. Vernon, "The Dutch and the Opening of Japan," *Pacific Historical Review* 27 (February 1959). Siebold later helped with the letter that William II of The Netherlands addressed to the shogun in 1844 and also sketched out the lines of a modern treaty for Holland. See J. A. van der Chijs, *Neerlands Streven tot Openstelling van Japan voor den wereldhandel* (Amsterdam: Muller, 1867). He visited Japan again in 1859 in service of the Dutch government, and his son Alexander was in British employ later in the decade. In this, Japanese suspicions of Western learning would undoubtedly have seen justification of their worst fears of a grand European plot.

were writing."⁷⁷ Nor was intellectual curiosity incompatible with official service, as the resources of officially sponsored projects provided the greatest opportunities. In later Tokugawa years the future president of Tokyo Imperial University, Katō Hiroyuki, reminisced that after he entered the Bansho shirabesho (Institute for the study of barbarian books) that was established after the coming of Perry: "I found other books, books not available to anyone else. When I looked into them I found them very interesting: for the first time I saw books about things like philosophy, sociology, morals, politics, and law . . . in view of that my ideas began to change." The utilization of such materials could be fully compatible in private conscience with the "good of the country" that officialdom might interpret more narrowly. Nishi Amane, sent to Leiden in 1862, wrote his adviser that in addition to his prescribed studies, he hoped to examine "those things advocated by Descartes, Locke, Hegel, and Kant, as "in my opinion, there are not a few points in the study of these subjects which will serve to advance our civilization. . . ."⁷⁸

But because the public advocacy of such catholicity of taste was impossible, this must also have brought frustration to many. The euphoria of Sugita Gempaku, who considered himself the founder of *rangaku*, did not extend to his grandson Seikei (1817–59), who was employed in the Chomel translation project. Ōtsuki Nyōden's history of Western studies notes that Seikei, having become acquainted with ideas of freedom (D. *vrijheid*) in his reading and being aware of the fate of scholars

> who had been seized for spreading foreign ideas, feared that he too was inviting trouble. He held himself in check and was very careful not to let the word *vrijheid* slip from his mouth. The only way he could find solace for the heaviness of his spirit was in drink, but when he was drunk he could not keep himself from shouting "Vrijheid!" "Vrijheid!"⁷⁹

A decade after the Siebold affair, the possibilities and limitations of *rangaku* under Tokugawa governance became dramatically manifest in what later became known as the "purge of barbarian scholars" (*bansha no goku*) of 1839. As with Sugita Gempaku's concern about the rejection of the Rezanov mission, this had its origins in misinformed scholars' ungrounded fears that the bakufu was risking disaster by rejecting

77 Yoshida, "The *Rangaku* of Shizuki Tadao."
78 Marius B. Jansen, "New Materials for the Intellectual History of Nineteenth Century Japan," *Harvard Journal of Asiatic Studies* 20 (December 1957): 592.
79 Satō, *Yōgakushi kenkyū*, p. 200, quoting Ōtsuki's *Yōgakushi nempyō*. This illustration was first brought to my attention by Haruko Iwasaki.

a Western approach that had already been turned back. Bureaucratic rivalry and police investigation led to serious charges and tragedy. In 1838 an American owned merchant ship, the *Morrison*, sailed for Japan from Macao with seven shipwrecked Japanese on board. In addition to a cargo of goods, presents, and documents, the ship carried three China coast missionaries, Peter Parker, Charles Gutzlaff, and S. Wells Williams (who later served as a documentary interpreter for Commodore Matthew C. Perry). It was hoped, as Williams later wrote, that the castaways

would form a good excuse for appearing in the harbors of that [Japanese] empire . . . [to create a] favorable impression of foreigners, and perhaps of inducing them to relax their anti-social policy. . . . It was hoped that the exclusive policy of that nation had become somewhat weakened since a foreign vessel had [not] visited any port other than Nagasaki, and that the influence of curiosity, and the nature of the errand, would at least secure a courteous reception.[80]

The bakufu was not impressed; the ship was driven off by shore batteries first at Edo and then at Kagoshima, and it returned to Canton with the missionaries and castaways still on board. About a year later the Dutch chief factor reported its identity to the bakufu on the basis of a Singapore newspaper story, mistakenly giving its nationality as British. Its possible return now became the subject for discussion in bakufu circles, and the story or some of it reached a circle of students of Western affairs.

The center of that circle was Watanabe Kazan (1793–1841), a leading retainer of the Tawara domain. Tawara, a small *fudai han* on the Mikawa coast, was hence charged with defense of its coast. Kazan was an accomplished intellectual and artist, born and bred in the national capital. After he was named a *han* senior councilor (*rōjū*) and placed in charge of its coast defense in 1832, he extended his earlier interest in Western painting to Western studies in general. He was not conversant with Dutch and so patronized and relied on men who were. His case marks a new step in Dutch studies, its extension beyond technicians of translation to statesmen of influence and position. Kazan's experts were Kozeki San'ei (1787–1839) and Takano Chōei (1804–50). Kozeki was a physician attached to the Translation Office which, briefly abolished after Takahashi's trial, had been reconstituted. Takano had been one of Siebold's best students; he had fled Nagasaki in

---

80 S. Wells Williams's account, "Narrative of the Voyage of the Ship Morrison, Captain D. Ingersoll, to Lewchew and Japan, in the Months of July and August, 1837" (Canton: *The Chinese Repository*, vol. 6, nos. 5, 8 [September, December 1837]; 1942 Tokyo reprint).

1828 to avoid implication with Takahashi, later set up a private medical practice in Edo, and began meeting with Kozeki and Kazan a few years later. A bakufu *daikan* named Egawa Hidetatsu, responsible for shogunal territory in Izu and Sagami and Kai, which included coastal areas, interested himself in Kazan's circle through a shared interest in coastal defense. The group itself was broad, experienced, cosmopolitan, and sophisticated.

Takano Chōei's response to the Morrison affair was a pamphlet, *Yume monogatari*, which circulated widely in handwritten copies. In it he deplored the bakufu's determination to repulse the ship, which he thought was still on its way, and protested:

Britain is no enemy of Japan . . . if the bakufu resorts to expelling them by force, Japan will be regarded as a brutal country incapable of distinguishing between right and wrong. The word will spread that we are an unjust country, and Japan will lose its good name as a country which respects propriety and courtesy. What disasters might befall us as a result are difficult to predict.[81]

Chōei's errors, which included the impression that the expedition would be commanded by the China scholar and missionary Robert Morrison, were less important than his intent to maintain seclusion by more courteous means: He thought the bakufu should accept the castaways, explain the seclusion system to the ship's commander, and send the mission back. For him *rangaku* was, as he put it, "useful and urgently needed practical scholarship." As he looked back, he felt his pamphlet entirely reasonable. To die for *rangaku* would be one thing, but "to die for *Yume monogatari* is something I cannot face without a feeling of regret."[82] Chōei was sentenced to life imprisonment but escaped in 1844 and lived in hiding, supporting himself by translation for another six years. Kozeki, more nervous and quick to despair, committed suicide rather than face the rigors of examination and imprisonment. Watanabe Kazan, with his friends within the bakufu and his larger circle of political and artistic acquaintances, was larger and more important game for the prosecution, which was responding to complaints by bakufu Confucianists.[83]

Kazan had written an essay on the state of international affairs for

---

81 *Yume monogatari* appears in translation in D. C. Greene, "Osano's Life of Takano Nagahide," *Transactions of the Asiatic Society of Japan* 41 (1913), p. 3.
82 From *Wasuregatami*, written in prison before Chōei's escape. Cited in Satō Shōsuke, Uete Michiari, and Yamaguchi Muneyuki, *Nihon shisō taikei* (Tokyo: Iwanami shoten, 1971), vol. 55, p. 182. Also D. S. Noble, "Western Studies and the Tokugawa World View: Watanabe Kazan, Takano Chōei, and the *Bansha no goku*," unpublished manuscript, January 1982.
83 Torii Yōzō, the scholars' chief accuser, was a member of the Shōheikō Hayashi family.

his friend Egawa, but at Egawa's request he had toned down the criticism in his first draft. After the arrests, a search of his quarters brought to light both the original version and a second tract, *Shinkiron* (A timely warning), which he had kept to himself. The West is ruthless, he wrote, powerful, and threatening; Japan is the only nation attempting to refuse to conduct relations with these countries. Appeals to tradition can lead only to "trivial squabbling, and in the end [will] give them a pretext for filling their avaricious designs. One may call them barbarians, but they will not resort to arms without an excuse." Britain, in particular, simply "bides its time, carefully plotting and sharpening its claws. Britain's persistence in what it wants from us is like that of flies . . . one may brush them away, but they always come flooding back again."

Kazan's discussion of the deeper roots of the crisis, however, was remarkable and forecast a fundamental reorientation of thought. Japan had come to its present predicament because of its uncritical adherence to "grand and lofty abstractions borrowed from China." As he laid out his essays on the world situation, Kazan showed himself ready to universalize civilization. The five great teachings – Judaism, Buddhism, Christianity, Islam, and Confucianism – all had their origins in Asia. But unfortunately the civilized lands of Asia had become soft and decadent, and "the world has entered an age in which it is dominated by the northern barbarians." In Asia, only Japan still retained its independence, China having been overrun by the Manchus, but the barbarians of today had become far more accomplished than had the nomads of the past. Those of the West, in particular, were different from the earlier predators, thanks to their accomplishments in the study of things, a sense of science, and a forward motion of events. "The root of this is their detailed knowledge of the world." Russia and the United States, in particular, represented a new dynamism. Russia had been raised under the dynamism of Peter into a source of raw power and strength. With regard to the United States, Kazan discussed the American Revolution and the establishment of the republic, to argue that it had become "the richest country in the world, apparently in the span of only fifty years." He went on to discuss the power of newspapers, public education, and the Americans' success in putting forward the "men of ability" sought by Confucian reformers in Japan. The Western structures that Kazan admired contained a congruence in which "the fundamental purpose of the natural sciences is to aid the other three major branches of knowledge represented by religion and ethics, government, and medicine, and to extend the basis upon which rest the various arts and techniques that are subordinate to them." Added to this was a social flexibility, (unattainable for Kazan, an artist who had been forced into the government because of his samurai status). In the West,

> an individual may select his own goals according to the bidding of his inborn nature, and devote himself to the study of ethics and government on the one hand, or arts and techniques on the other. Therefore no one's aspirations are looked down upon, and people are condemned only for failing to apply themselves to the tasks for which they are suited by nature.

As this shows, for Kazan the study of the West could lead ultimately to the path of complete transformation along Western lines.[84]

In the investigation that followed his arrest, Kazan protested that he was being tried and punished for some miscellaneous scraps of writing that he had meant to throw away; his supporter, Egawa, had decided against presenting Kazan's formal report to the government in any form. The intellectuals were as divided as were the officials: Matsuzaki Kōdō entered the lists with memoranda and letters arguing the injustice of Kazan's treatment, whereas Satō Issai, far from helping Kazan's cause, stood by his Shōheikō associates and looked the other way. Kazan was sentenced to permanent confinement in Tawara, a rustication he terminated with suicide two years later when it came to light that he had evaded the terms of his arrest by sending several paintings to Edo for sale.[85]

Within the bakufu the struggle continued. Kazan's accusers prevailed upon the authorities for more stringent restrictions on the translation and circulation of material from abroad. A series of edicts made it clear that such work should be limited to matters dealing with astronomy, military arts, and medicine. Nevertheless these measures were only temporarily suppressive and ultimately failed. The reactionaries never gained full control of the bakufu councils. Within a few months of Kazan's arrest, the first news of the Opium War in China entered Japan to put greater urgency behind the collection of information about the West; Chinese books that entered Nagasaki were fully accessible to educated Japanese, sometimes reissued in Japanese editions, and particularly important. But Western studies also profited from this new urgency. Dutch studies were further diffused through the great schools like that of Ogata Kōan (1810–63) in Osaka, which opened in 1838 and

---

84 Satō, in *Nihon shisō taikei*, vol. 55, p. 634, develops this point.
85 The trial can be followed in detail in Bonnie F. Abiko, "Watanabe Kazan: The Man and His Times," Ph.D. diss., Princeton University, 1982, pp. 180ff., who includes portions of the trial transcript.

became a mecca for students from all parts of the country. Partial records give the names of 637 students who passed through its gates, and the total in all probability exceeded 1,000. Dutch learning became a standard part of the training of physicians, and its relevance to national defense made it of increasing interest to samurai in many domains.[86] Ogata Kōan's students included many who later played central roles in Japan's nineteenth-century modernization.

PROBINGS TOWARD SYNTHESIS

Our discussion has considered the 1790s as a bench mark between the eighteenth-century awareness that urban and rural diversification was producing strains within the feudal order and the intensity of the concern that was focused on those problems in the light of the Western danger in the nineteenth century. Although the Bunka–Bunsei decades seem something of a plateau in the progression to political crisis and upheaval at mid-century, they also provided many indications of what might lie ahead. In the countryside the unwillingness of large numbers of villagers to accept political direction that involved economic cost showed that future solutions would require a slackening, and could not be based on a tightening, of feudal discipline. But in any case the agents for a tightening of discipline did not seem to be at hand. Buyō Inshi's unflattering description of the samurai of his day found echo in the opinions of Sugita Gempaku. Institutions had not changed, but society was changing and becoming more modernized, diversified, and fragmented.

What was still lacking was an overarching synthesis that could incorporate elements of many strands of thought to provide a vision around which a program of future action might be built. This too was in formation, and this too was firmly based on elements of eighteenth-century thought.

In Chapter 3 of this volume, Harry Harootunian describes the politicization of nationalist thought in late Tokugawa times. But for the purpose of our discussion it will suffice to place the synthesis of Aizawa Yasushi (Seishisai) (1781–1863), *Shinron*, in the context of Bunka and Bunsei.

Mito daimyo had led in the sponsorship of studies in Confucianism.

---

[86] Rubinger, *Private Academies*, chaps. 4, 5; and Ban Tadayasu, *Tekijuku o meguru hitobito: rangaku no nagare* (Osaka: Sōgensha, 1978), p. 89. For comments on the student body at the Tekijuku, Ogata's academy, and medical training, see Tazaki Tetsurō, "Yōgakuron saikōsei shiron," *Shisō* (November 1979): 48–72.

With the counsel of the Ming refugee Chu Shun-shui, who was permitted to take up residence at Mito some years after the fall of China to the Manchus and who taught the importance of unswerving loyalty to the sovereign, Mito sponsored the compilation of a massive history of Japan, constructed along the lines of Chinese dynastic histories, that carried the story up to Tokugawa times. As this project was nearing completion, a remarkable group of scholars was emerging into prominence. Fujita Yūkoku (1774–1826), his son Tōko (1806–55), and Aizawa Yasushi (Seishisai) [previous p.] transformed a regional scholarly tradition into one of national scope and influence.

Mito-style Confucianism with its emphasis on loyalism assimilated well with *kokugaku* (national learning). It will be remembered that a group of scholars culminating in Motoori Norinaga (1730–1801) combined literary and philological criticism with religious fervor to rekindle interest in the native tradition of Shinto. The politicization and further spread of this was preeminently the work of Hirata Atsutane (1776–1843), who reached out for what was available from other traditions and concluded triumphantly that Japanese learning was superior to all others because it incorporated elements of those others. At the same time, however, Hirata agreed fully that Japan's native traditions, best symbolized the unbroken continuity of the sovereign line, placed his country in a specially favored and divinely ordained position. In addition to politicizing *kokugaku*, Hirata also activated it. He developed a linkage with agricultural manuals that reached leading villagers in many parts of the country. The manuals that Hirata edited and sometimes published provided access to rural notables and helped identify *kokugaku* ideology with agronomy.[87]

Even apart from deliberate propaganda means of this sort, however, there is much evidence that a renewed interest in the national tradition and a heightened awareness of the imperial court had permeated rural leaders by the early nineteenth century. In the Shikoku domain of Tosa, for instance, resentment on the part of village heads (*shōya*) about the way they were regularly snubbed by petty samurai and urban representatives led to a demand, in 1832, for the dignity of surnames and swords. In the course of asserting their administrative importance, the heads used the ideology of imperial loyalism as the ultimate sense of authority. They complained about the "arrogant behavior of town officials" and charged that the treatment they were receiving constituted "a grave offense against the Imperial Way." In

---

87 See the opening pages of Jennifer Robertson, "Sexy Rice: Plant Gender, Farm Manuals, and Grass-Roots Nativism," *Monumenta Nipponica* 39 (Autumn 1984): 233–60.

the 1840s the Tosa village heads went on to form a league that circulated a secret document containing the startling assertion that the *shōya* who ran the villages were in fact more important than the urbanized samurai. "Should we not say that the *shōya*, who is the head of the commoners, is superior to the retainers who are the hands or feet of the nobles?"[88]

As one of the Tokugawa branch houses, Mito was in close touch with developments elsewhere in Japan, and its scholars linked such concerns with the foreign danger. Mito men were included in the bakufu's parties of exploration to the north, and they managed to get for their domain copies of the writings of Honda Toshiaki about the possibilities for Japan in the Kurils, Kamchatka, and Sakhalin.[89] In old age Aizawa remembered learning from his teacher, Fujita Yūkoku, about the disquieting probes made by the Russians. He recalled that as a boy of eleven he had derived pleasure from lashing with his whip a crude image of Adam Laxman. At the age of nineteen Aizawa had studied enough to write an account of the Kurils, in which he explained Russia's expansion to Asia by the fact that enemies blocked its path in Europe. He believed that the Russian occupation of Kamchatka had deprived Japan of part of what was once its territory, and he wrote about the transformation of Siberia under Russian control. Aizawa credited Russian dynamism to the ability of Peter the Great, who reformed his country and then extended its boundaries. Russia had done this not so much by conquest as through the enlightened tactics of suasion and bribery, in which innocent natives accepted gifts in return for allegiance to their new masters. Aizawa believed that the Russians made particularly adroit use of Christianity to capture the north and wrote that they now claimed all of Hokkaido as theirs. Such craft could be credited to Peter, who seemed dangerous precisely because of his great dedication and ability to inspire respect.

Within a few years Aizawa was able to interrogate some Westerners when a party of English whalers landed on the Mito coast at Ōtsuhama. Communication was imperfect. Aizawa knew no English and thought them Russian, for which he had prepared with a few phrases. But in several days' effort, he nevertheless gained enough impressions to confirm his suspicions of aggressive intent. This heightened his apprehension of the European advance. The Europeans, he con-

[88] Marius B. Jansen, "Tosa During the Last Century of Tokugawa Rule," in John W. Hall and M. B. Jansen, eds., *Studies in the Institutional History of Early Modern Japan* (Princeton, N.J.: Princeton University Press, 1968), p. 340.
[89] Wakabayashi, *Anti-Foreignism*, pp. 76–80.

cluded, "now endeavor to annex all nations in the world, The wicked doctrine of Jesus is an aid in this endeavor. Under the pretext of trade or whatever, they approach and become friendly with peoples in all areas, secretly probing to see which countries are strong and which are weak."[90]

The following year, in *Shinron* (New theses, 1825), Aizawa put together his synthesis. He rejected the idea that the simple bakufu fiat, in terms of the "don't think twice" edict, would keep the foreigners away. Foreigners were neither curious nor misinformed but bent on serious mischief. "Though interpreters may understand the barbarians' speech and be able to read their writings, they cannot understand the true 'barbarians' nature.' "[91] Men like Takahashi had underestimated the barbarian problem, for the Westerners had built a mighty force that relied on spiritual as well as material incentives. Japan's danger was less a military invasion than a corruption of its commoners through Christianity, cultural assimilation, and economic involvement. Western generals first secured beachheads, spread their goods, and then enlarged their armies with the numbers of their prisoners and dupes. It was possible that the West would use the Ainu against the Japanese and then the Japanese against the Chinese.

The only solution open to Japan was a counterstrategy of religious and cultural transformation combined with military strength. The use of Christianity as a state religion, and mass participation through education and conscription in the West could be offset only by the development of a similar dynamic in Japan. Japan had to emphasize its *kokutai*, or national essence.

Shinron thus opens with a defiant assertion: "The sun rises in our divine Land, and the primordial energy originates here. The heirs of the Great Sun have occupied the Imperial Throne from time immemorial." By such emphasis, its author felt, it was possible (though still somewhat dangerous, given the innocence of ignorant commoners) to recruit peasants to supplement samurai levies. Aizawa's remedies, the reform of bakufu institutions and policies to permit the daimyo to pursue military strength, would not suffice by mid-century, but in 1825 they constituted a mix of countermeasures based on the transformation of traditional institutions. His ideology – the emphasis of a state religion – made him seem prophetic after the imperial Japanese state had developed its national indoctrination at the century's end. Wakabayashi summed up the significance of Western learning for

90 Ibid., p. 90.   91 Ibid., p. 106.

Aizawa in these points: recognition, however dimly, of the nature of the emerging state, of the way in which it could make demands on its peoples, of the necessity for gaining the voluntary support of its people in the quest of national greatness, and of the fact that Japan was hopelessly placed to do so in its present situation. The unity of government and religion, ceremony, ritual, and belief that characterized the Christian West constituted a danger for Japan, and it would have to restore its original unity by returning to its true essence.[92]

Aizawa thus drew on several traditions: the Confucian, in which Japanese scholars had assimilated and domesticated the classics and asserted for their own country the place and status of Chūka, the central efflorescence, and even more the Shinto, whose invocation of the sun goddess and imperial divinity and continuity established the claim to national superiority and uniqueness, and Western learning, for a doomsday image of future national crisis.

In this manner the growing intrusions of the West, and the growing channels to information about the West, were to have as a result a growing affirmation of the importance of Japan and of the Japanese tradition.

92 Ibid., p. 122.

CHAPTER 2

THE TEMPŌ CRISIS

On the sixteenth day of the twelfth month of the year 1830, Japan entered a new era. By coincidence, that same afternoon, in a cottage not far from Shibuya, Matsuzaki Kōdō, a Confucian scholar, observed a flock of white cranes, "skimming over the hill" (as he wrote in his diary)[1] from the direction of Aoyama. He recorded their appearance the following morning, too, "wheeling northwards in the sunlight," his unmistakable delight suggesting just how reassuring it was that these stately and auspicious birds should show themselves at such a time. No era could have had so propitious an opening. Matsuzaki was equally happy with the new era name itself – "Tempō," or Heavenly Protection. It was well known that selecting era names was a delicate business, for the least carelessness – the use of Chinese characters already encumbered with unhappy associations, or those inviting ominous paranomasia – could well prejudice the prosperity of the entire nation. In this case, there seemed nothing to fear. The two characters for Tempō, as the elderly scholar construed them, paid tribute to two previous eras, the first being the Tenna era (1681–83) and the second, the Kyōhō era (1716–35). Matsuzaki did not need to remind himself that for scholars at least, both periods carried favorable overtones, suggestive of new hope, of depravity reformed, and of righteousness restored. This, too, augured well for the future.

Unhappily, in the course of the next fourteen years, these expectations were to miscarry. True, the Tempō era is remembered as one of Japan's great periods of reform. In the central government, the Tokugawa bakufu, it ranks with Kyōhō and Kansei as one of the "three great reforms," and equally significant, all around the nation, the provincial rulers, or daimyo, were also swept along on a wave of regenerative enthusiasm. Culturally, as well, the Tempō era saw one of Japan's great flowerings. This, after all, was the time of Hokusai's *Thirty-Six Views of Mount Fuji*, his *Eight Views of Ōmi*, and his famous

---

[1] Matsuzaki Kōdō, *Kōdō nichireki*, 6 vols. (Tokyo: Heibonsha, 1970–83).

waterfall series; when Hiroshige (whose *Fifty-three Stages of the Tōkaidō* began to appear in 1832), Kuniyoshi, Eisen, and Kunisada were at their peak. Some of Japan's most notable painters, too, men like Tanomura Chikuden, Tani Bunchō, and Watanabe Kazan, were active in the 1830s. The famous *Edo meishozue* appeared in the Tempō era, as did large sections of two of Tokugawa Japan's runaway literary successes – Takizawa Bakin's *Nansō Satomi hakkenden* and Ryūtei Tanehiko's *Nise Murasaki inaka Genji;* so did the complete version of a third, Tamenaga Shunsui's *Shunshoku umegoyomi*, which was published in 1832. Add to this the activities of thinkers as diverse as Hirata Atsutane, Ninomiya Sontoku, and Aizawa Seishisai, and we have a cultural profile as varied and distinguished as any part of the Tokugawa period can present.

Nevertheless, despite its auspicious opening, its reforms, and its cultural achievements, the Tempō era was to prove calamitous for both the common people of Japan and those who ruled over them. In terms of human misery and social dislocation, only the Temmei era (1781–88) caused more havoc, whereas for damage inflicted on Tokugawa Japan's system of government, the Tempō era had no peer. Indeed, Matsuzaki Kōdō quickly came to have his doubts. Just a few hours after his cranes had wheeled off toward Aoyama, he found himself speculating on two extraordinary phenomena: first, there had been earth tremors in Kyoto, a city in which they were virtually unknown, and second, the cherry trees had come into flower with uncanny disregard for the season. He was both puzzled and afraid at these portents: "Our ruler is virtuous, and our habits upright," he wrote, "so there should be no reason for any disasters. . . . All we can do is pray for the Heavenly Protection of yesterday's new era name." Two days later he was still uneasy, filling his diary with notes on previous earthquakes.

THE TEMPŌ FAMINE

In fact, his unease was premature, for real tragedy did not strike Japan until 1833, the fourth year of the Tempō era, and when it came, it proved to have nothing to do with earthquakes. The problem was the weather. It was unusually cold during the spring planting of 1833, exceptionally so during the summer growing season (to such a degree that in some areas farmers were obliged to bring out their padded winter clothing), and the autumn saw abnormally early snowfalls. Whereas the spring had been dry, itself an ominous sign, the summer was, unfortunately, wet, with high water covering the young rice plants for as much as four or five days at a time. The result was a general crop failure, in which rice, particularly sensitive to any but optimal conditions, was the chief victim but in which other staples like wheat, barley, and even bamboo shoots were also severely damaged as well.[2]

As was always the case, the worst effects were felt in the northeastern part of Japan, the Tōhoku. The cool climate there accommodated agriculture only grudgingly, and rice growing, needing an average temperature of twenty degrees centigrade during the crucial months of July and August, had always been particularly hazardous. In 1833, the Tōhoku yielded only 35 percent of its normal crop, and in some specific areas – Sendai, for example – it was much less than that. Farther to the south and west, in places like Hiroshima, the harvest was also poor.[3]

By itself, one bad season was an irritation rather than a tragedy. No doubt many would have reacted initially like the Sendai farmer at the beginning of 1834, writing laconically in his journal, "No New Year celebration; no *sake*."[4] Temporary suffering could always be alleviated by the distribution of food and seed. But tragically, 1833 was to be just the first in a run of bad harvests. The next two years were only marginally better, and the harvest of 1836 was infinitely worse. Even in Edo that year, as Matsuzaki Kōdō's diary shows, it rained almost incessantly throughout the summer. It was cold, into the bargain; on July 13 and 14 (5/30 and 6/1 by the lunar calendar), Matsuzaki was obliged to wear his winter cape, and on the night of August 25 (7/13 by the lunar calendar), one of his friends saw city roof tiles encrusted with frost. Once again the effects of this extraordinary weather were felt chiefly in the Tōhoku, where the harvest was estimated to be only 28 percent of normal, but this time they were spread over a far wider area. At Mito, 75 percent of the rice crop and 50 percent of the wheat and barley crop were lost, whereas at Tottori, over on the Japan Sea, only 40 percent of the harvest was salvaged. Indeed, there were complaints of crop damage as far afield as Hiroshima and even Kokura, in Kyushu.

There was a grim parallel to be drawn here, as contemporaries knew. Matsuzaki Kōdō certainly did: "The weather this year is almost exactly the same as it was in 1786," he noted in his diary, and so did

---

2 See, for example, Saitō Shōichi, *Ōyama-chō shi* (Tsuruoka: Ōyama-chō shi kankō iinkai, 1969), p. 101; *Miyagi-chō shi, shiryō-hen* (Sendai: Miyagi-ken Miyagi-chō, 1967), p. 700.
3 *Rekishi kōron* (Tokyo, 1976), vol. 9, pp. 33–4. 4 *Miyagi-chō, shiryō-hen*, p. 802.

Ninomiya Sontoku, observing what he called "the worst harvest in fifty years."[5] Just fifty years earlier, in 1786, a similar spell of weather had brought on the Temmei famine, with its legacy of deserted villages, unburied corpses, and tales of cannibalism. This time the season was almost as bad. Indeed, in some respects it was worse, for the bad weather was more widespread and affected some areas left largely untouched by the earlier catastrophe, like Tottori, for example, where officials estimated what happened in 1836 to be "worse than the fearful Temmei famine."[6]

As Susan Hanley and Kozo Yamamura have pointed out,[7] it is not easy to estimate how many died in the famines of the Tokugawa period. In 1836, we are told, over 100,000 starved to death in the Tōhoku, and in Echizen the following year the death rate was three times the normal figure. In Tottori, officials were claiming that of a total of 50,000 people in distress, 20,000 died. The difficulty is, of course, that these figures were all too often thrown together on the basis of hasty and confused impressions, as there was little real opportunity for counting heads. Officials, moreover, safe in the knowledge that no one would ever check, could afford to exaggerate the distress in areas under their care; in fact they could hardly afford not to, as aid would go only where the need seemed greatest.[8]

Nevertheless, there is ample evidence to suggest, if not prove or quantify, that the famine that reached its height in 1836-7 was a crisis of no ordinary proportions. The reports of people eating leaves and weeds, or even straw raincoats, carry a certain conviction; so do the instructions circulated in some areas to bury corpses found by the roadside as quickly as possible, without waiting for official permission. Nor is there any reason to disbelieve reports of mass movements out of the countryside, with people descending on towns and cities "like a mist," to be greeted by gruel kitchens if they were lucky or otherwise by doors hurriedly barred with bamboo staves by nervous householders. There is, too, the evidence of some reliable figures. In 1833, at the very beginning of the famine, the Tokugawa bakufu had received 1.25 million *koku* of tax rice from its widely dispersed holdings; in 1836, when the harvest was universally bad, that amount had dwindled to 1.03 million *koku*, an indication of something out of the

---

5 Kodama Kōta, ed., *Ninomiya Sontoku*, vol. 26 of *Nihon no meicho* (Tokyo: Chūō kōronsha, 1970), p. 452.   6 *Tottori-han shi* (Tottori: Tottori kenritsu toshokan, 1971), p. 610.
7 Susan B. Hanley and Kozo Yamamura, *Economic and Demographic Change in Preindustrial Japan, 1600-1868* (Princeton, N.J.: Princeton University Press, 1971), p. 147.
8 *Rekishi kōron op. cit*; *Tottori-han shi*, pp. 615, 621.

ordinary. The price of rice is also suggestive. In Osaka, during the summer of 1837, it was fetching three times its 1833 price; in Echigo the cost had risen fivefold. In Edo, a little later, it was more expensive than it had ever been.[9]

The effects of the Tempō famine were felt everywhere. They were felt first in the countryside, where those whose crops had failed were forced to compete for dwindling supplies with such little cash as they could muster. The cities were the next to suffer, as prices rocketed upwards. "What shall I do?" a despairing Matsuzaki Kōdō asked in his diary as rice suddenly grew more expensive, "What shall I do?" Nor were the samurai unscathed. All around Japan domain governments, anticipating lower revenues and higher costs, tightened their belts, reducing samurai salaries in the process. There was, too, a more general problem connected with the famine. "A sickness is spreading," wrote the Sendai farmer nervously in 1834, all thoughts of *sake* forgotten, and spread it did, right through the 1830s, in a variety of forms – pestilence, smallpox, measles, influenza – among those too weak to resist.[10]

CIVIL DISORDER

Not surprisingly, the people who suffered most from the hunger of the 1830s quickly made their unhappiness known. Popular unrest had always mushroomed during famines, and the 1830s proved to be no exception. What was now exceptional was the depth of the resentment displayed, for in the frequency, scale, and violence of its popular protests, the Tempō era came to surpass any previous period in Japanese history. The people were unusually fretful in the 1830s, and their behavior showed it. Indeed, even before the famine there were symptoms of abnormal ferment. As early as 1830, for example, there had been an extraordinary outbreak of *okagemairi*, the peculiar form of mass hysteria during which vast numbers of people, young farmers for the most part, spontaneously set off on a pilgrimage to the Grand Shrine at Ise. This in itself was not so unusual. *Okagemairi* had been erupting, at roughly sixty-year intervals, for a long time; the last one had taken place in 1771. By 1830, therefore, the sexagenary cycle having run its full course, Japan was due for another, so there was no

---

9 Imaizumi Takujirō, ed., *Essa sōsho* (Sanjō: Yashima shuppan, 1975), vol. 2, p. 311; Ōguchi Yūjirō, "Tempō-ki no seikaku," in *Iwanami kōza Nihon rekishi* (Tokyo: Iwanami shoten, 1976), vol. 12, p. 329.
10 Fujikawa Yū, *Nihon shuppei shi* (Tokyo: Heibonsha, 1969), pp. 62–3, 110–11.

surprise when it came. Nor was there surprise at concurrent reports of such miracles as shrine amulets floating down from the sky. Rumors of *prodigia* like this, spreading from village to village, were the customary call to pilgrimage. Rather, it was the scale of the 1830 outbreak that was so extraordinary. In 1771, two million had visited Ise; now within the space of four months, there were five million, jostling, singing, shouting, begging (or occasionally stealing), and all fighting their way into the shrine precincts.[11]

The authorities naturally were nervous. They were never comfortable when unruly bands of people strayed about the countryside, disrupting the placid agricultural round. But although they were not to know it, worse was to come. The 1830 *okagemairi* was soon to be dwarfed by developments that, if far less spectacular, were infinitely more threatening. From 1831 onwards, and particularly in 1836, Japan was struck by a wave of unprecedented popular protest. Opinions differ on just how much there was, but Aoki Kōji, whose research on the subject is by far the most detailed, has credited the Tempō era with a total of 465 rural disputes, 445 peasant uprisings, and 101 urban riots, the two latter categories reaching their peak, like the Tempō famine, in 1836.[12] There is general agreement that no matter how many incidents there were or how they are classified, Japan had never before seen such civil commotion.

Mere numbers alone, however, do not explain why the disorder of the Tempō era was so remarkable. To understand this, it is necessary to look at certain aspects of the incidents themselves, for they displayed features that were both new and alarming. The rural uprisings, for example, seemed to be of a new kind. Before, such protests had followed a fairly predictable pattern, with a delegation (normally composed of traditional village leaders), representing a fairly limited area (a few villages, at most), presenting local authorities with a list of demands – usually for tax relief, for freedom to sell their produce at the highest price, or for the replacement of officials seen to be dishonest or unsympathetic. After a ritual show of solidarity, these demands would be put politely, in the expectation of at least some concession. Elements of this tradition persisted into the Tempō era, but they were overshadowed by unmistakable signs of something quite new.[13]

First, the scale was different. Now, instead of a few villages, whole

---

11 Fujitani Toshio, *"Okagemairi" to "eejanaika"* (Tokyo: Iwanami shoten, shinsho ed., 1968), pp. 32, 78–9.
12 Aoki Kōji, *Hyakushō ikki sōgō nempyō* (Tokyo: San'ichi shobō, 1971), app. pp. 31–2.
13 Miyamoto Mataji, ed., *Han shakai no kenkyū* (Kyoto: Minerva shobō, 1972), p. 535.

regions were caught up; in 1831, in Chōshū, for example, a routine demonstration against the domain's cotton monopoly suddenly spilled over into fourteen similar incidents, in which more than 100,000 people terrorized the entire area.[14] In 1836, too, during the famine, the Gunnai region north of Mt. Fuji saw an incident involving an estimated 30,000 angry, hungry protestors – an event without parallel, according to one contemporary observer, "even in old military histories and chronicles." Just a month later, another 10,000 demonstrators plunged the province of Mikawa into uproar, while in 1838 almost the entire island of Sado – some 250 villages in all – rose in anger.[15]

Such numbers made it inevitable that the control wielded by traditional village leaders over the direction of protest would crumble. Uprisings on this scale simply would not respond to direction, as one of the initiators of the Mikawa rising found to his dismay when rioters included his house on the list of those to be burned down. Further, because almost all the participants were poor and often desperate, they were not nearly so amenable to the wishes of their richer fellows. At Gunnai, indeed, where the unrest was initiated by an elderly farmer (one of the poorest in his village) and a peripatetic mathematics teacher, the poor provided leaders as well as followers, and that was not all. One of the features of that incident was the enthusiastic participation of people from outside the area, "not just the poor," it was remarked, "but gamblers, vagabonds, and those posing as *rōnin*."[16] The new scale of rural protests may to some extent have reflected difficulties peculiar to the Tempō crisis, but their changing composition spoke eloquently of the social polarization through which many country districts had been split irrevocably into rich and poor. So, too, did the violence, for these incidents, no longer directed by gentleman farmers, were anything but gentlemanly. In fact, as often as not, the gentleman farmer class was the object of mob hatred. It was their houses, stores, granaries, breweries, and pawnshops that were ransacked and burned during the Tempō unrest. This was so in Chōshū, in Mikawa, and in Gunnai (where more than five hundred buildings were treated in this way); even on Sado Island 130 gentleman farmers felt the force of local discontent.[17]

Sooner or later, all these incidents subsided or were put down, leaving the authorities free to step in and make a few examples –

14 Aoki, *Hyakushō ikki sōgō nempyō*, pp. 225, 277–84.   15 Ibid., p. 242.
16 Aoki Michio, *Tempō sōdōki* (Tokyo: Sanseidō, 1979), pp. 194, 197.
17 Thomas C. Smith, *The Agrarian Origins of Modern Japan* (Stanford, Calif.: Stanford University Press, 1959), pp. 180–200.

torturing some, crucifying others, or imposing sentences of banishment or punitive tatooing. But all were concerned by the new kind of rural protest. "If we have another bad harvest," warned Tokugawa Nariaki, daimyo of Mito, in 1837, "I think there will be trouble."[18] They were to find urban unrest no less disconcerting. Tokugawa Japan had three of the world's largest cities – Edo, with over a million people, and Osaka and Kyoto, with something less than half a million each – as well as a further fifty or so substantial provincial centers, all with at least ten thousand inhabitants. Such concentrations of people, most of them highly vulnerable to food shortages and price fluctuations, had proved volatile before, during the Temmei famine. In the hunger of the 1830s they were to prove so again, with an unprecedented succession of riots, or *uchikowashi*, from the autumn of 1833 onwards. The Osaka authorities had to cope with eleven such incidents, whereas even in Edo, despite its intimidating preponderance of samurai, the common people rioted on three occasions. Elsewhere, too, there was unrest – in Kyoto, Sendai, Hiroshima, Nagasaki, and Kanazawa (where, in 1836, a mob of three hundred irate women broke into Zeniya Gohei's store demanding rice and money). Once again estimates vary, but Kitajima Masamoto claims no fewer than seventy-four urban riots for the Tempō era, a totally disproportionate 20 percent of all such incidents during the Tokugawa period.[19]

This was bad enough, but in 1837 Osaka saw planned – and very nearly executed – the most menacing urban disorder of all, on a scale unseen since the great conspiracy of 1651. The instigator was Ōshio Heihachirō, a former government official, then in his forty-fifth year. Some years earlier, allegedly disappointed at the corruption of his fellow officials in Osaka, he had surrendered his career as a police inspector to devote himself to reading, writing, teaching, and, apparently, collecting weapons. Then, early in 1837, at the height of the famine, he circulated copies of an angry document entitled *Gekibun* (A call to arms) to villagers around Osaka, summoning the common people to an attack on the city.[20] He carefully disclaimed any general challenge to the government, but the implications were obvious. "We must first punish the officials, who torment the people so cruelly," he wrote, "then we must execute the haughty and rich Osaka merchants.

---

18 Quoted in Kitajima Masamoto, *Mizuno Tadakuni* (Tokyo: Yoshikawa kōbunkan, 1969), p. 208.
19 Kitajima Masamoto, *Bakuhan-sei no kumon*, vol. 18 of *Nihon no rekishi* (Tokyo: Chūō kōronsha, 1967), p. 418.
20 I have used the version contained in *Koga-shi shi: shiryō kinseihen (hansei)* (Koga: 1979), pp. 695–7.

Then we must distribute the gold, silver, and copper stored in their cellars, and the bales of rice hidden in their storehouses." These sentiments, coming from one of Ōshio's former rank and current reputation, were disturbing. So, too, was the subsequent rising, in which Ōshio and three hundred supporters tried to take over the city. It was suppressed readily enough, within twelve hours, and succeeded in changing the condition of the poor only insofar as it burnt down 3,300 of their houses and destroyed an estimated forty to fifty thousand *koku* of rice.[21] Nevertheless it provoked a widespread sensation. Its reverberations were to be felt throughout Japan, in the "growing unease" noted by Fujita Tōko among the official class and in a general undercurrent of excitement among the common people, where it was fed by rumors and copies of Ōshio's *Gekibun,* surreptitiously distributed. It also found its emulators in smaller risings at Onomichi, Mihara, Nose, and, three months later, at Kashiwazaki, on the west coast of Honshū, where a group of insurgents, again led by a scholar from the samurai class, attacked government offices.[22]

THE FOREIGN THREAT

In the midst of this mounting unrest, Japan had to confront yet another difficulty, a threat from abroad. The policy of national isolation, imposed early in the seventeenth century, had remained intact for two hundred years, but by the beginning of the Tempō era there seemed reason to believe that it might not do so for much longer. The West was drawing nearer, as the ever-more frequent sightings of foreign vessels in Japanese waters attested. Already, to counter it, the Tokugawa bakufu had issued instructions in 1825 that all such ships were to be driven off at sight, but this was often more readily said than done. The Tempō era had hardly begun when Matsuzaki Kōdō wrote in his journal of reports of an armed clash in Ezo between local residents and foreign sailors.

The first really serious shock, however, came in the summer of 1837, while the authorities were still digesting the Ōshio rebellion. In August that year a privately owned American vessel, the *Morrison,* left Macao for Japan. On board were Charles King, an American businessman, whose idea the voyage was, and his fellow countryman, Samuel

---

21 Ōguchi, "Tempō-ki no seikaku," in *Iwanami kōza Nihon rekishi,* vol. 12, p. 336; *Koga-shi shi,* p. 698.
22 Okamoto Ryōichi, "Tempō kaikaku," in *Iwanami kōza Nihon rekishi* (Tokyo: Iwanami shoten, 1963), vol. 13, p. 218.

Wells Williams, a missionary; these representatives of God and Mammon were accompanied by seven Japanese castaways. Some days later, at a rendezvous in the Bonin Islands, the ship was joined by Dr. Charles Gutzlaff, a German missionary who had entered British employ at Canton as an interpreter. Ostensibly, the *Morrison*'s mission was to repatriate the castaways, but the trinity of God, Mammon, and Whitehall perhaps had other aspirations as well. Whatever they were, there was to be no opportunity to convey them – or the castaways either, for that matter – to the Japanese. On August 29, the *Morrison* anchored in Edo Bay, on the Tokugawa bakufu's very doorstep. The next morning, without any warning, it was driven off by gunfire from the shore batteries, a welcome that was repeated at Kagoshima a few days later.[23]

In itself, the *Morrison* incident, although unsettling to the Japanese, was of no great significance. Admittedly, they were taken aback to learn, the following year, that in repelling an unauthorized foreign vessel they had also, albeit unwittingly, condemned seven compatriots to permanent exile. This could never be construed as an act of Confucian benevolence, and the guilt was later to return, in grossly distorted form, to haunt them. Still, the memory of the *Morrison* was soon blotted out by more ominous developments. Later that same year it was rumored that Great Britain, already known as the reputed possessor of vast wealth, an extensive empire, and a limitless capacity for violence, was about to annex the Bonin Islands, some six hundred miles to the south. The report, as so often the case, proved exaggerated. British businessmen and officials had discussed the possibility in a desultory fashion for some years, but a survey in 1837 simply served to confirm what they all suspected: that annexation was pointless.[24] Nevertheless, to the Japanese, aware of the survey but not of its outcome, it was undeniably disquieting.

In 1840, when officials in Nagasaki received the first accounts of an armed conflict between China and Great Britain, the disquiet blossomed into panic. This time the rumors were not exaggerated, for the skirmishing between the British and Chinese at Canton the previous year had developed into a full-fledged war. The British proceeded to win it with a dispatch that, reported faithfully in Edo, left the Japanese in no doubt that their great and powerful neighbor faced a humiliating defeat. In the autumn of 1843, reports of the Treaty of Nanking confirmed their worst fears. Great Britain had come to the Far East to

---

23 W. G. Beasley, *Great Britain and the Opening of Japan, 1834–1858* (London: Luzac, 1951), pp. 21–6.   24 Ibid., pp. 16–20.

stay, and Japan, committed to a policy of national isolation and now saddled with a reputation for barbarism (for who but a barbarous country would fire on its own returning castaways and those befriending them?), could expect to come under foreign pressure as never before. Indeed, the Dutch in Nagasaki had been telling them as much for some time. Whether or not British policy toward Japan warranted such fears (and W. G. Beasley argues persuasively that it did not),[25] the very fact of an armed British presence a mere five hundred miles from their shores reminded the Japanese of something they had tended to forget – just how small and isolated they were.

CRITICS AND CRITICISM

The Tempō era had produced two major problems: on the one hand, an unsettled populace whose dissatisfactions (not least among them hunger) goaded them to unprecedented violence; on the other, a diplomatic situation more complex and threatening than at any time since the early seventeenth century. Alone, either of these would have been enough to dismay Japan's rulers. In combination, they brought on a crisis without parallel in Tokugawa history, shaking society to its very foundations.

Inevitably, that crisis was felt most keenly among the country's approximately half a million samurai. As bureaucrats, working either for the Tokugawa bakufu or for any one of the 264 daimyo governments, the peace and prosperity of the common people were in their hands.[26] The famine and the disorder had already raised questions about their stewardship. Equally, as Japan's standing army, it was their duty to spring to their nation's defense. As the diplomatic clouds gathered, however, their military capability, too, became an object of concern. It was a situation of some embarrassment. For more than two centuries they had laid claim to status, stipends, and privileges on the assumption that their innate wisdom and bravery entitled – indeed obliged – them to guide and protect the common people. Now, in the crisis of the Tempō era, they found themselves unable to do either. The samurai class was at a very low ebb indeed.

First, they had seen no blow struck in anger since the Shimabara Rebellion of 1637, so they were far from battle hardened. They were, into the bargain, undertrained and poorly equipped, simply because both training and equipment cost money, and nobody had any money

25 Ibid.
26 *Daibukan* (Tokyo: Meicho kankōkai, 1965), vol. 3, pp. 798–808, lists 264 daimyo in 1833.

to spare. Almost to a man, the samurai of the Tempō era were poorer than their ancestors had been.[27] They had their stipends, but inflation and rising expectations had combined to make a mockery of them. At best, the samurai's stipends had remained unchanged since the beginning of the Tokugawa period; all too often they had actually been reduced, whether on a temporary or semipermanent basis, by daimyo trying to cope with some particular emergency. For most samurai – perhaps all – only the moneylenders offered any respite, and even that was temporary, as debts (unless canceled unilaterally by government fiat) always had to be repaid. By the Tempō era, therefore, the samurai, although they had increased in bureaucratic skills, were a ragged remnant of what they had once been: poor, unwarlike, addicted to gambling, and so demoralized that it was not uncommon for them to report drunk for duty.

Those they served, whether the shogun or one of the 264 daimyo, faced similar problems and for similar reasons: the inroads of inflation combined with a more opulent life-style. More significantly, however, their incomes had shrunk. In part this was due to the damage inflicted regularly by fire, flood, and earthquake, and, of course, famines. But other factors, less obvious but even more detrimental, were also at work. The shogun and his daimyo were no longer milking the resources of their domains as effectively as they had once done, for taxation had failed to keep pace with either the speed or the direction of agricultural change. Throughout central Japan, in particular, the stable (and eminently taxable) population of subsistence farmers had long since begun to disappear, taking with it its absolute commitment to rice growing. In its place was a new kind of agricultural community, divided into wealthy landowners, at one extreme, and their tenants and laborers, at the other. Rather than producing for their own needs, farmers now grew commercial crops – cotton, tobacco, rapeseed, and indigo, among others – for sale. Some grew rich by it, and others did not; a fact that, as we have seen, helped transform the nature of civil disorder. But rich or poor, all were much more difficult to tax than their seventeenth-century forebears had been.[28]

Japan's daimyo rulers, in consequence, met the Tempō crisis in circumstances of chronic overspending and perennial indebtedness. Examples of this abound, each more bizarre than the last. The shogun's government in Edo went through the 1830s spending, each year, over half a million gold pieces more than it earned. In Tosa, over the

---

27 Kozo Yamamura, *A Study of Samurai Income and Entrepreneurship* (Cambridge, Mass.: Harvard University Press, 1974), pp. 26–69.   28 Smith, *Agrarian Origins*, p. 160.

same period, domain revenues never met more than 75 percent of its running costs, and few other domains would have been significantly better off. Almost inevitably, they all found their way to moneylenders. Chōshū, for example, amassed debts equal to twenty years' worth of domain income, and one-third of Kaga's revenue each year went to repay loans. These were not the conditions in which Japan's samurai would have chosen to meet the Tempō crisis, and they knew it all too well. "It is hard enough for us to keep going even under normal circumstances," acknowledged one daimyo morosely, "let alone in an emergency."[29] Unfortunately, an emergency was precisely what they now faced.

The general predicament was not new. Daimyo debts had been common in the eighteenth century, and so had bakufu penury; so, for that matter, had signs of decay among the samurai. Back in the seventeenth century, when most samurai had already left the countryside for the castle towns, there had been complaints of the corrosive impact of city life, with its unaccustomed pressures, expenses, and temptations. Their isolation certainly made the samurai less effective administrators; no less certainly their new life-style made them less effective warriors. During the Russian scare at the turn of the century, Sugita Gempaku noted the decline: "Today's samurai have lived in luxury for nearly two hundred years," he wrote, " . . . and have seen no fighting for five or six generations. Their military skills have disappeared, . . . and seven or eight out of ten are as weak as women."[30]

The situation was far worse by the Tempō era, for the Russian threat had receded too quickly to make any lasting impact on Japan's defenses, which therefore remained as inadequate as ever: some ancient cannon (many unused for decades) at a few points along the coast, and a scattering of tumbledown towers, still known by the anachronistic title *Karabune bansho,* or watchtowers for Chinese ships. Japan's ships, cannon, and small arms, too, all were substantially as they had been for the previous two hundred years. They could still pretend to be efficient bureaucrats and even put on plausible military displays on ceremonial occasions, but they could not transform themselves so readily into an effective fighting force. Before they could be confident of repelling foreign invaders or even of suppressing domestic rioters, the samurai class needed reorganization, a fresh sense of purpose, new weapons, and appropriate training. This all would cost

---

[29] Quoted in Miyamoto, *Han shakai no kenkyū,* p. 548.
[30] Numata Jirō, et al., eds., *Yōgaku (I),* vol. 64 of *Nihon shisō taikei* (Tokyo: Iwanami shoten, 1976), p. 296.

extra money, and money was precisely what the samurai, en masse and individually, did not have.

Nobody knew this better than the samurai themselves. They had greater access to information than anyone else did and, thanks to their education, a greater sense of historical perspective, so they could sense the dimensions of the problems facing them. As they knew all too well, the responsibility for doing something about it was theirs, so, in the Tempō era, they gave voice to their anxiety with an insistence, and to an extent, unique in Tokugawa history. Ironically enough, this criticism itself in its volume, scope, and variety added yet another element of uncertainty to an already unstable situation.

In one sense, the criticism was remarkably diverse. After all, it came from people of disparate status and experience. Daimyo of the eminence of Tokugawa Nariaki, ruler of the Mito domain, had much to say, but so too did humbler people: Hirose Tansō, a country schoolmaster, Takashima Shūhan, a provincial magistrate, and Ōshio Heihachirō, the retired Osaka policeman. Watanabe Kazan the artist, too, added his criticism, as did Takano Chōei the physiologist, Satō Nobuhiro the wandering scholar, and Sakuma Shōzan the gunner.[31] Naturally, too, all perceived the crisis in different ways. To Ōshio, the major problem was the Tempō famine and the extent to which it had been mishandled by callous bureaucrats. Watanabe Kazan, on the other hand, gave his undivided attention to Japan's diplomatic situation, compared luridly with that of "a hunk of meat left by the roadside" while Western predators prowled around it. Sakuma Shōzan, too, concerned with the same issue, was afraid that his country might have to fight a war without "the least hope of winning." For Tokugawa Nariaki – as for his adviser, Aizawa Seishisai, whose *Shinron* (New theses), written in 1825, circulated widely during the Tempō era – the crisis combined both foreign and domestic elements. "As you know," Nariaki warned in a memorial of 1838, "history shows us that internal disorder invites external difficulties, while external problems provoke internal unrest." Similarly, the criticisms took different forms. Ōshio's *Gekibun* was a public appeal, passed from village to village. The observations of Hirose Tansō and Satō Nobuhiro, on the other hand, circulated in manuscript, whereas Watanabe Kazan's

---

[31] Material in this section is drawn from the following: "Satō Nobuhiro," vol. 45, and "Watanabe Kazan" and "Sakuma Shōzan," vol. 55 of *Nihon shisō taikei* (Tokyo: Iwanami shoten, 1974 and 1977); *Koga-shi shi*, pp. 695–7; Arima Seiho, *Takashima Shūhan* (Tokyo: Yoshikawa kōbunkan, 1958); Konishi Shigenao, *Hirose Tansō* (Tokyo: Bunkyō shoin, 1943); Nakajima Ichisaburō, *Hirose Tansō no kenkyū* (Tokyo: Dai-ichi shuppan kyōkai, 1943).

were kept secret until uncovered in a police raid in 1839. Other criticism assumed the guise of formal memorials, offered to daimyo (as in the case of Sakuma Shōzan), specific officials (as with Takashima Shūhan), or the shogun himself (as with Tokugawa Nariaki). The tone, too, varied with the form. Ōshio's *Gekibun* was as strident and inflammatory as one would expect a call to arms to be. The scholarly analyses and memorials, on the other hand, were suitably clad in their respective camouflages of academic decorum and deferential concern.

Yet differences notwithstanding, there were some common threads running through the Tempō criticism, and one was dissatisfaction with the government. Ōshio Heihachirō, observing that "when the nation is governed by unworthy men, disasters come one upon the other," was more outspoken than others, but the view was nevertheless commonly held. Others also shared his conviction that government officials "accept bribes unashamedly"; both Watanabe Kazan, in his confidential *Shinkiron* (A timely warning), and Tokugawa Nariaki, in his 1838 memorial, said much the same thing. The latter, indeed, considered that "what we must first do is stamp out corruption, for unless this is done we shall succeed in nothing." Hirose Tansō, in his *Ugen* (Circumlocutions), written in 1840, extended his criticism to the daimyo and the entire samurai class, drawing attention to their besetting sins of arrogance and ignorance. Some, like Watanabe Kazan and Takano Chōei, condemned Japan's policy of national isolation as too provocative for the nation's own good. Takashima Shūhan and Sakuma Shōzan, on the other hand, endorsed it and drew attention instead to the lamentable state of national defense.

Governments do not usually accept criticism readily, and the Tokugawa bakufu was no exception. Adverse comment had been forcibly discouraged since the early seventeenth century, with considerable success, so the Tempō authorities were simply unprepared for what now poured in on them from all sides. They reacted in the conventional way. Watanabe Kazan and Takano Chōei, together with some of their associates, were arrested during a purge of amateurs of Western learning. Takano was subsequently jailed, as, on a different occasion, was Takashima Shūhan. Satō Nobuhiro was ordered to stay away from Edo. Watanabe was exiled from Edo to his domain, a fate he shared with Satō Nobuhiro and even Tokugawa Nariaki, rusticated to his domain in 1841. Ōshio Heihachirō, of course, had signed his own death warrant by launching a rebellion. He evaded capture for six months and, when he could do so no longer, took his own life.

Still, the criticism itself persisted. The fears and the complaints that the Tempō crisis had awakened remained, to be passed from hand to hand and mouth to mouth. So, too, did suggestions for reform which, despite their heterogeneity, were all equally dramatic, revealing a general conviction that only desperate remedies could cure a nation so desperately ill. Here Ōshio, demanding punitive carnage, was on his own; Japan was not quite ready for that. Yet other calls for change were in their own way just as radical. Several critics – Hirose Tansō, Sakuma Shōzan, and Tokugawa Nariaki among them – urged that samurai be sent away from the cities back to the countryside, to lead a national defense effort in which the common people, too, would participate. In effect, this proposal struck at the very foundations of the Tokugawa social order. The diplomatic order, too, was threatened by the demands of those like Watanabe and Takano, who urged that the country be thrown open to the world.

Other proposals were to attack the Tokugawa political order, calling into question the entire *bakuhan taisei*. Under this system, political authority was delegated by the emperor (whether he liked it or not) to the shogun, the head of the Tokugawa house. The shogun in turn, while commanding an establishment of his own to coordinate certain national functions like foreign affairs and defense, delegated much of the responsibility for local administration to 264 local rulers. These daimyo (or their bureaucracies) governed their own domains, collected their own taxes, and maintained their own armies. As vassals of the shogun, they were obliged to give him whatever assistance he might require, no matter what the cost to themselves, and so should they prove negligent or miscreant, their lands and rank were to be forfeited. At least, this was how it worked in theory. By the Tempō era, however, two hundred years of inactivity had seen the authority of the shogun and his government decline and the de facto independence of the daimyo grow. Few were ever called upon to do anything for the general good, and fewer still felt the sting of bakufu displeasure. For the most part the system worked well enough, as Japan's placid history for most of the Tokugawa period shows. On the other hand, it lacked the coordination needed to cope with a national emergency. The Tempō crisis, with its famine and its massive popular unrest, displayed once more the deficiencies of a system that fragmented local authority into 265 separate jurisdictions.

Much more significantly, however, the crisis drew attention to another and particularly serious inadequacy. Tokugawa Japan could not protect itself against invasion – not merely because the samurai class as a whole had grown indigent and flabby but, rather, because the system itself did not permit it. The Tokugawa bakufu had long ago decided that it could maintain itself in power and keep the country from civil war only by limiting the military capacity of the daimyo. In the early seventeenth century it had therefore imposed several restrictions on them. The *sankin kōtai* system of alternate attendance at Edo was one, aimed at limiting their opportunities for rebellion by keeping them in Edo one year in every two. There was also the hostage system, designed to secure their good behavior by threatening their wives and heirs. More relevant to the present context, however, they were forbidden to fortify their domains or to build vessels of warship dimensions.

All these restrictions served Tokugawa Japan well. Without them, it is quite certain that its history would not have been nearly so tranquil. Yet, in the Tempō crisis, people came to realize that in restraining each other from civil war, they had also left themselves defenseless. To many critics, therefore, it seemed obvious that the system would have to change; indeed, Aizawa Yasushi's *Shinron* (written in 1825, but – wisely – not published until 1857) had already suggested this, demanding that domains be allowed to fortify themselves, acquire better weapons, and build larger ships. Tokugawa Nariaki, Aizawa's patron, spent much of the next twenty years saying the same thing. To Sakuma Shōzan, too, it appeared time for the old restrictions to be relaxed. The prohibition against building large ships, he wrote, had been drawn up in the belief that it "would keep the nation peaceful in the future," but with circumstances so dramatically changed that "we need not hesitate to revise, for the common good, a law introduced for the common good." Behind all such suggestions lay the implicit assertion that Tokugawa Japan was far too centralized for safety. Aizawa had denounced Japan's defense system for "emphasizing the center and ignoring the periphery," and Sakuma Shōzan, too, suggested that the bakufu should "lighten the burdens it imposes on the nation's daimyo, so that their domain finances may be made easier and they may devote themselves to defense."

Yet there was an alternative to the decentralization they demanded, and this was to be found in the works of Satō Nobuhiro. His *Suitō hiroku*[32] and its subsequent elaborations and glosses suggested not that domains be set free to see to their own defense but the opposite. What Satō advocated was the creation of a state far more centralized than Japan had ever seen (or, indeed, was to see until the new Meiji order

32 A title that defies an elegant, or even an inelegant, translation. Perhaps "A secret treatise on bequeathing an enhanced patrimony to posterity" suggests its purport. The most readily accessible version is found in "Satō Nobuhiro," vol. 45 of *Nihon shisō taikei*, pp. 488–517.

thirty years later), a state in which every aspect of national life, including defense, would be made totally subject to unified central control.

Each of the critics, in his own way, was calling on Japan to reform itself before it was too late – to bring about more honest government, to return to old habits of frugality, to try new kinds of diplomacy or social organization, and to acquire new and better kinds of weapons. The call did not go unheard, as the reforms of the Tempō era were to show, but it had unforeseen results, nowhere more so than for the issue of state organization. This particular issue, underlying all the others, was to prove the most intractable and, ultimately, the most divisive.

DOMAIN REFORMS

Traditionally, in Tokugawa Japan, crisis was followed by reform, and there was no reason that the Tempō crisis, for all its unaccustomed features, should have been any different. Reform, expressed variously as *kaikaku*, *kaishin*, or *chūkō*, was the conventional response, reassuringly optimistic and comfortably vague. After all, who could possibly resist a program centered on (as such programs always were) economy, frugality, and the promotion of "men of talent"? It could not fail to appeal to domains in financial turmoil, as they all were to a greater or lesser degree, and unable to lay the blame anywhere but on human failings. In any case, economy and frugality were the most elastic of abstractions, able to be stretched in any number of directions, whereas the use of the term "men of talent" was nothing if not subjective; in practice most people tended to reserve it for themselves and their friends.

Indeed, the concept of reform was vague enough to accommodate a variety of responses – progressive or reactionary, utopian or pragmatic, self-seeking or altruistic – or even no response at all, provided that it was decently cloaked in the appropriate rhetoric. Just how flexible it was can be seen in the wide range of reactions to the events of the Tempō era, for though none remained untouched by them, Japan's 264 daimyo domains did not react alike. Nor was there any reason to expect them to do so. They were scattered over a country of considerable economic, climatic, and topographical diversity, so the crisis impinged on them in different ways and to different degrees. In central Japan, for example, the problems of rural unrest were quite unlike those in regions where commerce had developed more slowly. Then, too, the famine and its problems loomed larger in the northeast, which had seen so much more devastation than elsewhere; the southwestern domains, on the other hand, had much more reason to be concerned about foreign ships and the threat of invasion. Coastal domains, too, no matter what their location, tended to be more alert to defense issues than to those at a safer distance from the sea. One must also not forget that just as each domain had its individual problems, so too did it have its own range of options, and, to choose among them, its own administrators, with their individual preferences.

For all these reasons, the Tempō reforms, as they unfolded in the daimyo domains, could hardly have been more diverse.[33] To some domains, as to some critics, it appeared that the kernel of the problem lay in the failings of the samurai class. So at Tawara, for example, Watanabe Kazan's reforms emphasized education, in the hope that the samurai might learn once again their traditional morality, with its virtues of loyalty and filial piety. Elsewhere, similar demands were accompanied by warnings against the insidious temptations of city life. "Each one of you must be frugal in all things," the Okayama authorities told their samurai in 1833, "avoid wasteful expenditures, and set your behavior to rights."

In matters of economic policy, too, many domain reformers looked no farther than the traditional remedies. Programs of stringent economy were common enough, and as usual, one of the most convenient places to begin seemed to be the samurai stipends. These had always been the easiest of game, as there was so little risk of protest. Samurai morality, even though it condoned opposition to a daimyo under some circumstances, would never have done so over anything so contemptible as money. Domains like Echizen, therefore, could begin their reforms confidently enough by halving all stipends for a three-year period. Still, even this avenue to financial health was not without its risks. For one thing, it was a two-edged weapon, as those samurai with less money would be less effective in a crisis. At Tawara, too, it was found that salary cuts simply goaded the samurai into absconding; all they had to lose, after all, was their status, apparently not worth much, and their salary remnants, now worth even less. No less traditionally, daimyo saddled with crippling debts could choose the option of repudiating them. This was sanctioned, at least in theory, by the

[33] The term "Tempō reforms" is customarily used rather loosely, including not only those of the Tempō era (1830–44) but also those initiated slightly before or after. The information appearing here is drawn from a variety of sources, of which the most important are Miyamoto, *Han shakai no kenkyū*; Ōkubo Toshiaki, ed., *Meiji ishin to Kyūshū* (Tokyo: Heibonsha, 1968); Inui Hiromi and Inoue Katsuo, "Chōshū han to Mito han," in *Iwanami kōza Nihon rekishi* (Tokyo: Iwanami shoten, 1976), vol. 12.

wide gulf in status between the merchant who did the lending and the daimyo who did the borrowing; the former could have no possible recourse against the latter, should he be determined to default. Domains like Chōshū and Fukuoka, therefore, readily used this expedient, and Satsuma and Saga came exceedingly close, the former with an announcement that although its debts (amounting to five million gold pieces) would ultimately be repaid, the process might take some time – 250 years, in fact. In the case of Saga, the domain authorities magnanimously offered to settle with one of their Edo creditors, provided he was willing to accept just 20 percent of the principal. Yet this too, like slashing the samurai's stipends, had its dangers, for in practice the right to repudiate debts had to be exercised with discretion. Few daimyo could risk alienating the business community on whose expertise, goodwill, and cooperation the economic life of their domains had all too often come to depend.

In many parts of Japan the Tempō crisis seemed a signal to turn back the economic clock, with a reaffirmation of the agrarian roots of the *bakuhan taisei*. This, so reformers argued, could be done by restricting the private commercial developments that had polarized so many farming villages and, incidentally, cut deeply into domain tax revenues. Elements of such a policy are to found in areas as geographically, economically, and socially diverse as Mito, Satsuma, Chōshū, and Saga. In some domains, too – Saga and Kokura, for example – the emphasis was on land reclamation, the most traditional of all methods of augmenting income. There was, however, one other traditional step to financial health that the domains chose to ignore. They could have increased the land tax or else extended it so that it fell as heavily on undertaxed dry fields as on rice paddies. After all, in most parts of Japan, taxes had not been readjusted for more than a hundred years. But not even the Tempō crisis could tempt the domains to take such a dangerous step. It was discussed here and there but in the end was rejected. For one thing, the aftermath of the Tempō famine was obviously not the most opportune moment. For another, everybody knew that more taxation would be interpreted in the villages as either a break with tradition or a breach of faith and vigorously – even violently – resisted.

Together with these elements of conservatism in many of the domain reforms, there were several new initiatives that suggest how seriously the Tempō crisis was viewed. Of course, a wholehearted swing to innovation was rare. Much more usual was a blend, sometimes even a contradictory blend, of the novel with the traditional, but nevertheless the new elements were unmistakable. There were, first, signs of a new approach to the chronic problems of domain finances, which, thanks to the Tempō crisis, had been moved from the category of irritatingly inconvenient to that of downright dangerous. At its most basic, this was revealed in a change of attitude, in which commercial development – under the proper auspices and for the proper purposes, of course – came to be encouraged. The pivotal influence of castle towns on the domain economy, for example, was to be recognized in many parts of Japan. At Fukuoka, it was judged important enough to justify an extraordinary *volte-face*. Elsewhere, the authorities were urging (and often compelling) their samurai to be frugal, but in Fukuoka, in an effort to develop the town center, they were encouraged to patronize local theaters and wrestling matches and to buy lottery tickets. Similarly, at Kurume calls for frugality were perfunctory in the extreme and appeared as an afterthought at the very end of the domain reforms.

The attitude of some domains toward the business community, too, seemed to be changing. On occasion this took an unusually peremptory form, in which domain officials, rather than wheedle loans from individual mechants, were prepared to force money from them, either as "loans," or – in the case of Echizen, Kokura, and Funai, among others – as "gifts." Increasingly, though, and far more significantly, it took the form of cooperation, often symbolized by offers of samurai status to members of the business community in return for expert advice and assistance. Business expertise was at a premium in those domains already engaged in, or about to begin, enterprises of their own, like domain monopolies. Ever since the seventeenth century, a few daimyo had managed to monopolize certain key items produced within their domains, forbidding their sale to anyone but authorized buyers or at anything but the authorized price, kept artificially low. Not infrequently, indeed, producers were paid in the domain's own currency, printed as needed and largely worthless in any other part of Japan. The produce was then sold at Osaka or Edo, and the profits brought back into the domain reserves of hard currency that it would otherwise not have had. Sendai rice, Awa indigo, Tottori wax, and paper from Tsuwano and Karatsu all earned substantial sums and helped cushion their domains from the general financial malaise. At Awa, indeed, where the indigo monopoly brought a profit of one million gold pieces in 1830, it was the major element in domain finances.

Understandably, the older such monopolies, the more successful they were. Imposed later, on producers jealous of their profits and unaccustomed to interference, they often provoked resistance, most notably in the Chōshū riots of 1831. The Tempō reform program in some domains in fact saw these monopolies relaxed in an attempt to pacify the farmers: Chōshū, Usuki, and Funai all were obliged to do exactly that. Nevertheless, the prospect of controlling the domain's commercial produce was too strong for many daimyo to resist, and so the Tempō era produced a number of monopolies. Usually these were confined to products already well established – like cotton, wax, and seed oil – but not infrequently the daimyo were dazzled enough by the prospect to encourage experimentation with new products. At Mito, for example, it was hoped to add some new enterprises to the paper, tobacco, and *konnyaku* that the domain already produced, and steps were taken to begin making pottery and lacquer and growing tea. Satsuma, too, while intensifying its sugar monopoly (to such an extent, incidentally, that profit doubled during the Tempō era) also tried to introduce the production of silk, paper, indigo, saffron, sulfur, and medical herbs.

There was also fresh activity as domains looked long and hard at their defenses. Few had reason to be pleased with what they saw: soldiers armed with the weapons – swords, pikes, muskets, decrepit cannon – of their seventeenth-century ancestors and with ideas on strategy and tactics to match. Clearly, some drastic changes had to be made. Some domains contented themselves with reintroducing maneuvers or, as Utsunomiya did in 1842, with reviving target practice after an interval of twenty-six years (during which it had been considered too expensive).[34] Others, feeling more exposed, took stronger measures, streamlining their chain of command, regrouping to give greater prominence to musketeer units, or even moving samurai out of the towns into garrisons along the coast and forming peasant militia units, as the Tempō critics had urged. Mito, where Aizawa Yasushi had been calling for just such measures, was one of the first domains to do so in the 1830s. Some felt, with Takashima Shūhan and Sakuma Shōzan, that Japan needed new skills and new equipment to cope with the crisis, and this was particularly noticeable among the domains of the southwest. After its brush with the *Morrison* in Kagoshima Bay in 1837, Satsuma began to buy imported arms from Nagasaki dealers, to try making its own mortars, howitzers, and field guns, and to send men to be trained in Western gunnery at Takashima Shūhan's school. Fukuoka, Chōshū, and Kumamoto were doing the same, and so was Saga, where the main

---

34 Tokuda Kōjun, ed., *Shiryō Utsunomiya han shi* (Tokyo: Kashiwa shobō, 1971), p. 172.

thrust of domain reforms was toward self-defense. Saga began research into alternative artillery techniques in 1832 and, from 1835 onwards, produced a large number of high-quality homemade cannon.

The diversity of the domains' responses to the Tempō crisis, then, is clear enough. There were, however, two other elements in these local reforms so common as to be almost universal. One was the extent to which the reform programs, despite all the reassuring overtones of the concept itself, aroused bitter disagreement, particularly when they meant abandoning long-established practice and when they involved innovation. Inevitably, given the atmosphere of general crisis, each domain had its skeptics, sometimes passive, sometimes not, and all needing to be persuaded or bullied into silence. Invariably the operation demanded a high degree of daimyo support, so that in Chōshū and Fukui, for example, their Tempō reforms could not begin until the daimyo had been replaced by one either more committed or more malleable. It was this factor that delayed the "Tempō" reforms of domains like Hiroshima and Tottori until the Tempō era had come to an end.[35] Elsewhere, as in Saga, reform had to wait until the new daimyo had found his feet. In many cases, too, reinforcing the impression of energy and unconventionality, the actual planning of the reforms was entrusted to a new man, often of comparatively humble status, brought in as part of a larger administrative reorganization. For example, the key figure at Fukuoka was a physician, at Mito a scholar, at Tawara a painter, at Nakatsu and Satsuma tea ceremony attendants – even, at Tosa, a convert to Shingaku. To add to the ferment, technocrats like Ōhara Yūgaku and Ninomiya Sontoku could be brought in from outside. Understandably, factions would form, and feelings would run high. Reformers naturally saw themselves as the "men of talent" known to appear whenever a reform was begun; they customarily considered their opponents thoughtless at best or, at worst, stupid and corrupt. To their critics, on the other hand, the self-styled reformers, if radical, seemed power drunk and doctrinaire, or, if conservative, sycophantic and self-seeking. Politics was a superheated business during the Tempō crisis, as many, given time to ponder their mistakes in jail cells, came to understand. Not even the daimyo always escaped unscathed, and Tokugawa Nariaki of Mito was one who came perilously close to being repudiated by a domain unable to countenance either his personality or his politics.

The other common element in these local reforms was this. The

---

35 Yamanaka Hisao, "Bakumatsu hansei kaikaku no hikaku hanseishiteki kenkyū," *Chihōshi kenkyū* 14 (1954): 2–3.

Tempō crisis had shown the domains some unpalatable truths: their tenuous control over the common people, their bankruptcy, their vulnerability to outside attack. It had also made them aware that if they were ever to cope with this new and dangerous situation, it would have to be by their own efforts. Nobody else could help them, certainly not the bakufu, which had far greater problems of its own. The domains would have to husband their own resources, make their own money, and take care of their own defenses. No doubt it was a salutary lesson; rather, it might have been, had Japan some other form of government. As it was, it had the gravest consequences for the *bakuhan taisei*, that system of decentralized feudalism in which the Tokugawa bakufu and the daimyo domains joined to govern the country. The Tempō crisis forced domains onto their own resources as never before and obliged them to turn their attention inwards, to themselves and their own needs. The result was a surge of *sauve qui peut* domain nationalism. It surfaced during the famine, in the refusal of some domains to let food leave their borders, no matter how desperate were conditions elsewhere.[36] It surfaced as the domains began to use their monopolies to drive up prices and profits, competing with one another and with the bakufu, and, in the process, helping destroy the orderly commercial habits of two hundred years.[37] It surfaced, too, in an arms race, begun during the Tempō era, in which domains scrambled pell-mell for new weapons and new techniques, shattering the fragile balance of power that had kept Japan at peace since 1615. This attitude, potentially more damaging than the crisis that produced it, outlived both the Tempō era and the *bakuhan taisei* itself.

BAKUFU REFORMS

Neither the Tempō crisis nor the domains' reactions to it were to go unmarked in Edo. The shogun, who lived there, and his administration, which was based there, faced all the common provincial problems – famine, civil disorder, inadequate defenses, and an army undermanned, underpaid, and ill equipped. In this respect the shogun was a daimyo like any other.

But there was one crucial difference: The shogun administered, through his government, a far greater area than any other daimyo – almost six times as much as the largest provincial domain – and to that extent his responsibilities, in terms of taxes to collect, mouths to feed,

36 *Tottori han shi*, vol. 6, pp. 610, 613.
37 Osaka shisanjikai, ed., *Osaka-shi shi* (Osaka: Seibundō, 1965), vol. 5, pp. 640 ff.

area to police, and shores to protect, were that much more onerous. The resources of the shogun's domain were also much more difficult to coordinate – administratively, financially, and militarily – for where most daimyo domains were well-defined geographical units, Tokugawa land was scattered throughout forty-seven of Japan's sixty-eight provinces. Tax loss, therefore, and famine relief (whether in the form of reduced taxes in the villages or free gruel in the cities) bit heavily into bakufu finances, as depleted in 1836 as they had been for over a hundred years.[38] Civil unrest, too, had hit hardest at areas under bakufu control, in Gunnai in 1836; Osaka, Edo, and Kashiwazaki in 1837; and Sado in 1838.

The crisis in foreign affairs also was uniquely the shogun's concern. His very title, supreme commander of the pacification of barbarians (*sei-i tai shōgun*), made it impossible for that particular responsibility to go to anyone else. The port of Nagasaki, Tokugawa Japan's solitary link with the world outside, was part of his domain, and all decisions on national diplomacy were taken within the bakufu, his own personal administration. So, too, were those decisions concerning the deployment and coordination of all samurai, whether Tokugawa vassals or rear vassals. Therefore, as the foreign nations closed in during the 1830s and the prospect of invoking powers unused for two hundred years became imminent, so did the burden of this responsibility grow heavier.

The shogun's government, then, was caught up in the Tempō crisis to a far greater extent than was any single daimyo domain. Yet paradoxically, its reaction to that crisis seemed at first to lack a certain urgency. This is not to say that it remained passive in the face of mass starvation, civil disturbance, depleted resources, foreign penetration, and inadequate protection. No government could. The bakufu reacted, but precisely as it had always done, by reducing taxes in the famine areas, securing food supplies for its cities, distributing rations to its needy, quelling its riots, debasing its currency, and despatching fact-finding missions to its coastal fortifications. These were the tried and true responses to familiar emergencies, but in a situation that seemed to call for an entirely new approach, they were undeniably anachronistic. Elsewhere, as we have seen, in the daimyo domains, the crisis of the 1830s inspired a number of new initiatives, but whereas some domains defied tradition by entering the market place, and oth-

---

38 Furushima Toshio, "Bakufu zaisei shūnyū no kōkō to nōmin shūdatsu no kakki," in Furushima Toshio, ed., *Nihon keizaishi taikei* (Tokyo: Tokyo daigaku shuppankai, 1973), vol. 4, pp. 28–31.

ers by arming their peasants, the Tokugawa bakufu seemed to cling tenaciously to the status quo. Only in the middle of 1841, when three-quarters of the Tempō era had already passed, did the bakufu begin a reform program of its own.

On the face of it, the delay seems inexplicable. There is no reason to imagine, for example, that bakufu officials were ignorant of the problems confronting them. Individual ministers could hardly be unaware of popular unrest, and they were by no means insensitive to developments overseas. Nor, for that matter, could they turn a blind eye to the sorry state of bakufu finances, now so anemic that only regular transfusions from currency debasement could provide relief. In any case, the Tempō critics, from Ōshio Heihachirō to Tokugawa Nariaki, had been all too ready to alert the government to its shortcomings.

In fact, many bakufu officials had recognized them and had already given thought to their solution. But before anything could be done, they had to wait for an opportunity, and in 1841 that opportunity came. As so often, it came with a change in government. Where reform in domains like Chōshū and Fukui had waited for the accession of a new ruler, in the bakufu it followed the death of an old one – the extraordinary Tokugawa Ienari, the eleventh shogun, who had long dominated the Tokugawa political world. No other head of the Tokugawa house had reigned for anything like his total of fifty years. None of them had lived nearly as long, either, for Ienari was in his seventy-ninth year when he died. Nor, apparently, did any live quite so fully; that is, at least, if numbers of concubines (estimated at forty) and children (fifty-five) indicate a full life.[39] At a tender age, Tokugawa Ienari had come under the influence of Matsudaira Sadanobu, but he had resisted all his sanctimonious mentor's attempts to mold his character. Instead, for the next fifty years Ienari, with the help of members of his personal household, had done much as he wished. Even after his retirement in 1837, his political grip did not slacken, but at the beginning of 1841 Ienari fell seriously ill with severe abdominal cramps, and within three weeks, despite prayers offered at Nikkō and Zōjōji, he died, leaving behind him a number of grieving concubines and a government suddenly reinvested with authority and initiative. For a time, there was little outward sign of change. As at all shogunal deaths, music was forbidden within the palace; officials had their heads shaved; and an obligatory period of mourning was announced. But then, within three months, came the first portents of something

39 Kitajima, *Bakuhansei no kumon*, p. 295.

new. Three of Ienari's favorite officials, popularly known as the "three sycophants," were suddenly dismissed. Kawaji Toshiakira, writing in his journal[40] that "although I was not particularly friendly with these men, I am still astonished," reflected the general surprise and unease. Over the next few weeks scores of officials were dismissed or resigned under various pretexts, and all were replaced by fresh appointees. There was a sudden convulsion, too, at the very highest official level. Of five senior ministers holding office at the beginning of 1841, only two remained by the end of the year. Their three colleagues had resigned, pleading ill health. This was a fairly common, and occasionally legitimate excuse, and in this instance one of those in question proved his good faith by dying a week later. The other two, however, did not, for one, Ii Naoaki lived until 1850, and the other, Ōta Suketomo, was hale enough to find his way back to office some seventeen years later, apparently little the worse for wear.

Contemporaries, noting the haste of these changes ("since Ienari's death," observed one,[41] "it is as if everyone's eyebrows had been set alight"), had little difficulty in deciphering their meaning. This was a purge, and on such a scale as to foreshadow some correspondingly dramatic change in policy. It soon came. On 5/15/1841, just two days after Ii Naoaki's departure, the government made a curiously unemphatic announcement. It urged its officials to adhere to traditional principles and, in particular, "not to deviate from the policies of the Kyōhō and Kansei eras."[42] Only the reference to those two previous reform periods – the one under the eighth shogun, Tokugawa Yoshimune, early in the eighteenth century, the other more than fifty years later – under Matsudaira Sadanobu – intimated the onset of yet another paroxysm of reform. But there was no hint that this time the bakufu would be led into waters far deeper than earlier, more conventional, reforms had ever contemplated.

This, however, lay more than a year away. As the bakufu began its Tempō reforms in the summer of 1841, despite the magnitude and urgency of its problems, it seemed anxious first of all to address itself to the perennial and abiding concerns of all Confucian states. In this

40 Kawaji Toshiakira, *Shimane no susami* (Tokyo: Heibonsha, 1973), p. 327.
41 Quoted in Kitajima, *Mizuno Tadakuni*, p. 302.
42 The following account of the bakufu's Tempō reforms derives largely, although by no means exclusively, from the following: Kuroita Katsumi, ed., *Zoku Tokugawa jikki* (Tokyo: Yoshikawa kōbunkan, 1966), vol. 49; Naitō Chisō, *Tokugawa jūgodaishi* (Tokyo: Shin jimbutsu ōraisha, 1969), vol. 6; Hōseishi gakkai, eds., *Tokugawa kinreikō*, 11 vols. (Tokyo: Sōbunsha, 1958–61); Kitajima, *Mizuno Tadakuni*; Okamoto, "Tempō kaikaku"; Tsuda Hideo, "Tempō kaikaku no keizaishiteki igi," in Furushima Toshio, ed., *Nihon keizaishi taikei* (Tokyo: Tokyo daigaku shuppankai, 1965), vol. 4.

respect, much of the legislation that now issued from the Tokugawa bureaucracy might just as well have been written fifty or a hundred years earlier. Indeed some of it was, judging from the insistent references to, and, in many cases, direct repetition of, laws handed down in the Kyōhō and Kansei eras.

The bakufu appeared, for example, most concerned with the moral health of those over whom it ruled. Urban life held many temptations – drink, gambling, prostitution, pornography, and frivolity of all kinds – and these were nowhere more evident than in Edo, the nation's largest city and the center of the bakufu's domain. No reforming government could ignore them, and one of the strongest strands in the Tempō reform program, and also the earliest to develop, was its effort – in a manner that Tokugawa Yoshimune and Matsudaira Sadanobu would have recognized and applauded – to control them. "If we use this opportunity for reform and cleansing," wrote Mizuno Tadakuni, the chief minister, "and restore dignity to our way of life, . . . we will succeed in setting things to rights."[43]

Prostitution was a case in point. The Tokugawa bakufu had long since recognized this unruly industry as inevitable and, to minimize its impact on society, had segregated it, first in the Yoshiwara and then later in the Shin-Yoshiwara, on the northeastern fringe of the city, under the control of a group of officially recognized whoremasters. As with so much of Tokugawa Japan, however, by the Tempō era this tidy system had broken down. Edo's urban sprawl to the west and the south had gradually placed the official brothel quarter beyond the walking capacity of all but the most amorous. It was no more than natural, therefore, that people should seek consolation nearer home and that the forces of free enterprise, as irrepressible in this field as in any other, should mobilize to provide it. Consequently the Tempō government had to deal with irregular and unlicensed prostitution, scattered throughout the city in teahouses and restaurants where waitresses were known to behave "in a lewd fashion." These were ordered to close in 1842, and any premises used for such purposes declared liable to confiscation. It also tried to restrict other avenues by which women could make themselves available, denying them access to a number of professions, from itinerant hairdresser, music teacher, archery range attendant, and physician to cabaret artist (in which profession women were known to get up on stage "quite shamelessly, and sing most unseemly . . . Gidayū ballads" to customers not conspic-

---

43 *Tokugawa jūgodaishi*, vol. 6, pp. 2869–70.

uous for their musical interests).[44] Mixed bathing, too, was outlawed in an effort to bring cleanliness and godliness back together.

Equally, there were other perils for the city dweller, and the bakufu, as it had always done, warned against them. Gambling was prohibited yet again, particularly among the samurai, as were lotteries. So, too, was the practice of decorative tatooing, an important element in the gambling life-style. The publishing industry also invited bakufu intervention. Certain publications – the novelettes known as *ninjōbon*, for example, believed to have "a bad effect on morals," or erotica (even worse), or works on unorthodox religion, or ephemeral works on contemporary mores – were banned, and others were required to obtain prior approval and to carry the names of both author and publisher. Prints of a kind depicting either actors or prostitutes, too, were prohibited. Nor did the bakufu overlook the entertainment industry, particularly the large number of music halls, often unlicensed, in which diversions of an emphatically unimproving kind were offered. These were restricted in number, and their programs were to be confined to inspiring talks on religious and historical subjects. Nor did the legitimate theater (in itself a concept that Tokugawa Japan would not have recognized) escape attention. In 1842 appeared a nationwide instruction that itinerant actors, known for "ruining morals wherever they go," were to be reported to the authorities, while six months earlier the major Edo theaters had been forcibly removed from the downtown area. Their new home was to be at Asakusa, near the licensed quarter, where the two great hazards associated with them – fires and the contamination of decent folk – would be of less consequence.

Together with its attack on frivolity and immorality, the bakufu continued its constant war on other aspects of indecorum and in particular on an ever-present source of unease: the fact that people were living and spending in a manner inappropriate to their station. The traditional status system had long since been reduced to tatters, but it nevertheless remained one of the major principles informing legislative and administrative practice, and these reforms showed it. There was a torrent of sumptuary instructions: some of a general kind, some directed specifically at samurai extravagance, and others aimed at the farmers, among whom the least trace of self-indulgence seemed particularly seditious. Less than a week after declaring its commitment to reform, the bakufu warned its local officials to keep farmers from

---

44 Saitō Gesshin, *Bukō nempyō* (Tokyo: Heibonsha, 1968), vol. 2, p. 102.

spending too much on food, clothing, or festivities of any sort, communal and private. From time to time, as it condemned extravagance in general, the government also drew attention to more specific areas – lavish decorations at the Tanabata festival, for example, elaborate hats and kites, costly children's toys, certain brands of fireworks, sumptuous clothing, gourmet specialties, and expensive houses and garden furnishings (including lanterns, basins, and trees). Linked with this, too, was the bakufu's insistence that people not only spend according to their station but that they also behave in a suitable manner – so, for example, it was judged inappropriate that ordinary townspeople should study the martial arts or wear long swords (as these were the prerogative of the samurai) or that farmers should leave their productive (and taxable) calling to become factory workers, a position that, because it was regarded as neither worthy nor productive, was not taxed.

None of this was particularly novel. The bakufu had always hoped to achieve social stability and decorum by telling its subjects, in painstaking detail, just what they should and should not do. This was particularly marked during periods of self-conscious reform, but it was no less so in more normal times as well. The 1830s, for example, had seen a steady flow of just this kind of instruction. What does identify 1841 as the beginning of a bakufu reform period is, first, the mood of urgency, in which the steady flow of the previous decade welled into a flood and, second, a willingness, rather unusual in bakufu history, to make examples of those conducting themselves in an unseemly fashion. There were instances of mass arrest – thirty-six apprehended in connection with female cabaret performances in 1841, for example, and thirty extravagantly garbed girls from Asakusa jailed for three days the following year. In others, the bakufu deliberately fixed on celebrities, in the process making examples of Kuniyoshi and Tamenaga Shunsui, both of whom were put in manacles, the latter for his "obscene novelettes" and the former for caricaturing the shogun and his chief minister. Ryūtei Tanehiko, too, author of the best-selling *Inaka Genji*, received a reprimand, and the matinee idol Ichikawa Ebizō (later the seventh Danjūrō) was exiled for a life-style rather imperfectly attuned to economy and frugality.

This all was the familiar stuff of Tokugawa reforms, a series of minutely detailed exhortations aimed at teaching people how to behave and thereby restoring the moral fabric of the nation to that pristine condition that had obtained before two hundred years of peace and self-indulgence had taken their toll. The Kyōhō and Kansei reforms had been aimed at precisely the same sorts of target. In other areas, however, the bakufu's Tempō reforms were rather more innovative, rather less directed at recreating the conditions of some legendary golden age, and rather more concerned with reaching an accommodation, however painful, with changing circumstances.

Traces of this new attitude can be seen in the question of foreign affairs. Admittedly, as far as defense issues were concerned, 1841 marked no perceptible change in bakufu policy, for any subsequent foreign threat was handled precisely as before, that is, with a brief, nervous flurry of inquiries into defense capacity and contingency plans more or less based on them, but little practical result. On the general issue of foreign affairs, however, and in particular on the question of Tokugawa Japan's formidable xenophobia, the Tempō reforms do represent a slight, but significant, change of direction. During the 1830s the government had seemed quite adamant, ushering in the decade by executing a man for giving a map of Japan to a foreigner and, at the other end, arresting a number of amateurs of European studies, Watanabe Kazan and Takano Chōei among them. Yet in 1841, just a month before the Tempō reforms were announced, the bakufu seemed suddenly to mellow. Takashima Shūhan, whose memorial had urged the government to adopt Western military technology, was granted an audience and then, a few days later, was permitted to mount a demonstration at Tokumarugahara, with twenty mortars, a howitzer, three field guns, and eighty-five men.[45] The bakufu showed its approval by rewarding him with two hundred pieces of silver, buying two of his best guns, and arranging for him to pass on his skills to some bakufu officials, one of whom, Egawa Hidetatsu, was the following year assigned the task of training one hundred musketeers along European lines.

This in itself was a change of heart, but more was to follow. In 1842, after reports that Britain had lost patience with Japan's policy of seclusion, the bakufu issued the following directive:

In 1825 it was ordered that foreign vessels should be driven away without hesitation. However, as befits the current comprehensive reforms, in which we are recreating the policies of the Kyōhō and Kansei eras, the shogun has graciously intimated his wish that his mercy be made manifest. Therefore, in the event that foreigners, through storm-damage or shipwreck, come seeking food, fuel, or water, the shogun does not consider it a fitting response to other nations that they should be driven away indiscriminately without due knowledge of the circumstances.[46]

45 Arima, *Takashima Shūhan*, pp. 146–51.   46 *Tokugawa kinreikō*, vol. 6, document 4085.

Hereafter, foreign ships were to be supplied with whatever they needed (before being sent away, naturally), a development that must have afforded some satisfaction to those who, like Takano Chōei (now in jail at Demmachō), had been so critical over the *Morrison* incident. Such critics would have been equally pleased when, the following year, the bakufu changed its attitude to the repatriation of Japanese castaways, who could now be brought back in Dutch or Chinese vessels – an obvious response to the accusations of inhumanity circulating after the *Morrison* had been driven away. Obviously, too, the bakufu now felt that the Dutch and Chinese ghettos in Nagasaki had their uses, for in the same year questionnaires were issued to these two foreign communities asking for whatever information they could give on the size, strength, and disposition of British forces.

There were to be some significant changes of direction, too, in the bakufu's conduct of its economic affairs, although they took rather longer to appear. No government of the Tokugawa period could turn its back on tradition altogether, particularly not one assuming the dignified mantle of reform, and so to a large extent at first the Tempō government simply perpetuated the conventional policies. There were the usual fitful attempts, some of them obsessively minute, to reduce costs, including warnings to works officials and kitchen staff to watch their expenses, and requests to everyone to avoid unnecessary wear and tear on the Edo Castle tatami. There was also the customary inquiry into the reasons for the decline in bakufu income, followed up with a number of purposeful, if conventional, initiatives. It was decided, for example, that the *tenryō* – the shogun's own land – required more efficient administration. Such conclusions were a part of every reform and, in this case, given the gradual decline in tax revenues since the mid-eighteenth century, were hardly unreasonable. With the assistance of Ninomiya Sontoku, the agricultural consultant from Odawara, the bakufu elected first to reform its local administrators – to whose complacency, inefficiency, and plain dishonesty the decline in tax receipts was attributed – and during 1842 more than half of these officials in eastern Japan (including all of those in the Kantō) were transferred or dismissed. Later that year twelve of them were expressly ordered away from their comfortable Edo residences and back to their districts, with warnings that land tax revenues would have to be restored to their former level.

There was, too, the time-honored compulsion to bring more land under cultivation, to which end the bakufu had been canvasing local officials ever since the beginning of the reforms, looking for pockets of wasteland that might be cleared or drained. In fact, as they all knew, the choicest of opportunities lay close at hand: Along the lower reaches of the Tone River, forty miles northeast of Edo, ten thousand acres of potentially rich rice-growing land lay waiting to be reclaimed. The difficulty was that it also lay, most inconveniently, under three feet of water. This was the Imbanuma, the great swamp that, could it be drained, was believed capable of producing another 100,000 *koku* of rice each year – as much as the average daimyo domain. The prospect was an alluring one. Tokugawa Yoshimune, the eighth shogun, had been tempted to do something about it in 1724, and Tanuma Okitsugu, sixty years later, had also tried his hand. Both had failed, but in 1843, nothing daunted, the bakufu undertook its third and last attempt.

There were other initiatives equally conventional. For example, it had not escaped notice that falling revenues might be due as much to the decline in the number of taxpayers as to idle and corrupt officials. Large numbers of farmers had been selling their land and taking up employment as either agricultural laborers or workers in rural industries of one sort or another, thereby removing themselves from the tax register. Others were deserting their farms altogether and moving into provincial towns or, worse still, into Edo itself, where, as the government noted in 1842, "many vagrants and vagabonds are roaming the city, and not a few of them are engaged in questionable activities."[47] Rural depopulation, although common throughout much of Japan at this period, was especially severe in the area around Edo, and the bakufu, which viewed every homeless immigrant as a drain on city resources, a potential criminal, and an absconding taxpayer, was not anxious to encourage it. To halt and, if possible, reverse this drift away from productive agriculture was therefore a matter of some urgency. The bakufu tried the usual remedies, many of them from the Kansei era – prohibiting employment in rural manufacturing industry, discouraging mendicant religious sects, and ultimately driving, or tempting, people back to their native villages.

Naturally, the bakufu's economic responsibilities did not end there. It was equally committed to protecting those in charge from exploitation, whether stemming from their own folly (controllable, the government hoped, by sumptuary legislation) or the cupidity and duplicity of others. Here, too, on the whole, the Tempō administration trod a wellworn path. Confronted, for example, by an increasingly erratic market in which during the 1830s, the price of rice, despite violent fluctuations,

---

[47] *Tokugawa jūgodaishi*, vol. 6, p. 2926.

had risen threefold, and the prices of other commodities, in their turn, were behaving more and more unpredictably, the bakufu ultimately did what its predecessors had always done – it blamed the business community. The solution, it was believed, lay in more intensive policing of the commercial world, including lowering the prices of some commodities and freezing those of others – foodstuffs, of course, but also bathhouse fees, fuel, and even horses (not to be sold for more than thirty gold pieces, and only then if they were of top quality). Similarly, it was forbidden to speculate in rice futures or to corner the market, and limits were imposed on interest rates, pawnbroking charges, the gold–silver exchange rate, and the level of shop rents. To make sure that these were observed, special squads of inspectors were to patrol the streets and shops of Edo and Osaka.

None of this activity was particularly new, deriving to a large extent from standard bakufu policy both in its tone (which often simply echoed that of the Kansei era) and its general thrust, which was toward making the system work as its founders had intended. Yet there were some distinct changes of emphasis. Currency debasement, for example, anathema to earlier reformers, had now become far too important to be jettisoned altogether; indeed, during the 1830s it had provided the bakufu with a third of its revenue. So although no new mintings were proposed during the period of the Tempō reforms, there was never any suggestion of currency reform along Kyōhō or Kansei lines. There had been a similar modification too in the way that the bakufu had come to regard the business community. It was still seen as a nuisance, but no longer quite so unmitigated as before, as the bakufu, like some daimyo, had discovered it to be a source of revenue. Despite the unorthodoxy of such a practice, therefore, it was decided in 1843 that "to assist in Bakufu reforms," thirty-seven businessmen from Osaka, and several more from towns adjacent to it, would be obliged to "contribute" well over a million gold pieces to the treasury. Equally unorthodox, to help its samurai (acknowledged to be, as usual, "in difficulties, having borrowed money over many generations") the government refrained from a general repudiation of samurai debts. The Kansei reformers had taken this way out, with no lasting results, other than one that was neither anticipated nor welcomed: severe financial embarrassment for the *fudasashi*, the rice brokers. The entire samurai stipend system depended on the services of these men, and the government knew it, and so this time it largely left them alone and, instead, itself entered the moneylending business. From an office at Saruya-chō, samurai were to be able to borrow, at 7 percent interest (less than half the normal *fudasashi* rate) and could consider their debts discharged after twenty-five years of interest payments.

Undoubtedly, however, the most abrupt departures from traditional economic practice were in the field of price control. In the past, wherever possible, the bakufu had tried to regulate commercial activities through a system in which craft guilds, business associations, and the professions (including, as we have seen, the oldest) were guaranteed government protection in return for an annual fee. The fee itself was never particularly great, but that had never been too important: The value of the system was that it provided an avenue for government regulation. By the Tempō era, however, the emergence of independent, and more or less surreptitious, trade networks in the provinces had reduced the effectiveness of such semiofficial monopolies, whereas the current unease about prices made even a reforming government ready to question two hundred years of tradition.

In 1841, therefore, the bakufu was responsive to a complaint from Tokugawa Nariaki, by then the nation's chief complainer, attacking one of the most influential of these monopoly associations, the *tokumidonya*, a syndicate shipping such commodities as cloth, medicines, paper, and foodstuffs from Osaka, the commercial capital, to Edo, the consumer capital. As was his habit, Nariaki put his case in the most disinterested terms: "Would there not be some effect on rising prices," he suggested, "if they [the *tonya*] were totally abolished and all goods could be transported to Edo from anywhere in the land and sold freely?"[48] It was quite disingenuous, of course, for his hostility was not toward monopolies in general but only toward those that stood in the way of his own. Whether or not the bakufu was aware of this, it fell in with his suggestion, accusing the *tonya* of unspecified dishonesty and stripping them of their privileges. "There are to be no more associations calling themselves *tonya*, *nakama*, or *kumiai*," read the announcement, "and ordinary people may therefore trade freely in any of those goods shipped in the past, or indeed in any merchandise from anywhere in the land." The precise details were spelled out the following year in two notices, the second of which, observing in its preamble that "prices have increased of late, and the people are much distressed thereby" and predicting in its final sentence that goods would become cheaper, specifically linked the dissolution with the government's price policies.

The need to stabilize prices also lay behind another related, and no

---

48 *Mito-han shiryō* (Tokyo: Yoshikawa kōbunkan, 1970), app. vol. 1, p. 140.

less controversial, measure. During his twenty months as Osaka magistrate, a senior government official called Abe Masakura had investigated the whole subject of commodity prices and emerged with an answer. Prices were unstable, he said, because Osaka, once the distribution center for every kind of commercial product, was so no longer. Goods were going elsewhere, and Abe isolated two kinds of culprit. The first was the independent rural entrepreneur, thousands of whom were buying and selling, manufacturing and processing, with no reference to the traditional Osaka-based market system. The second was the daimyo, alert now as never before to the profits to be won from commerce, and doing much the same sort of thing. "The commercial produce hitherto sent to Osaka wholesalers by farmers and merchants," went Abe's report, "has of recent years been bought up by daimyo . . . [who have also] been buying up produce from other domains, claiming it to be from their own, and probably in not a few cases sending it off to wherever they please; . . . truly what they are trying to do is unbecoming to warriors."[49]

Back in Edo, the government had already precluded the first of these implicit recommendations. Whereas Abe wanted the government-sponsored monopoly system to be intensified, the bakufu, acting before his report was finished, abolished it. On the other hand, the second made an impression. At the end of 1842, a year after dismantling the merchant monopolies, the government turned on those operated by the daimyo. "Of late," its order read, echoing Abe's findings,

> daimyo of Kinai, Chūgoku, Saigoku, and Shikoku have been, by various methods, buying up the products not only of their own domains, but of other domains also; . . . sending them to their warehouses, and then selling them when the market price is high. . . . Consequently they are using their authority as daimyo to cause much mischief to commerce. . . . This is most irregular, particularly bearing in mind our frequent instructions to reduce prices.

Any daimyo continuing his monopolies was therefore to be reported and, presumably, made to regret it.[50]

It is perhaps not immediately apparent just how unusual this instruction was. No doubt any government as committed to price controls as this one might have been expected to turn its attention sooner or later to domain monopolies. For that matter, few Tokugawa governments derived any joy from the sight of samurai buying and selling, particularly not during periods of reform, when all aspects of commerce

---

49 Quoted in Harold Bolitho, *Treasures Among Men* (New Haven, Conn.: Yale University Press, 1974), p. 26.   50 *Tokugawa jūgodaishi*, vol. 6, p. 2924.

tended to come under censorious scrutiny. Nevertheless, in the context of the Tempō era, this particular prohibition was quite extraordinary. Monopolies were vitally important to the financial health, and therefore the security, of many domains; to others, they represented a hope – perhaps the only hope – for a stable future. The bakufu, itself administered by daimyo, can hardly have been ignorant of this. The prohibition of domain monopolies, therefore, carried implications far beyond any immediate issue of price controls. It implied, first, a certain disregard for regional needs and aspirations. More importantly, however, it implied a certain reappraisal of the relationship between the bakufu and the daimyo domains.

In 1642 there would have been nothing untoward about such interference in domain affairs, but in 1842, after two hundred years of peaceful coexistence, the daimyo could have been pardoned for believing that a strong central government was a thing of the past. Just a year earlier, in fact, the bakufu had been obliged to admit as much, publicly and humiliatingly: It had ordered three daimyo to exchange their domains and then suddenly retracted the order in the face of strong protests from daimyo all over Japan. "This was the first time such a thing had happened," noted the compiler of the *Tokugawa jūgodaishi*, "and from it one can see that bakufu authority was no longer what it had once been."

Nonetheless, expected or not, anachronistic or not, by forbidding access to commercial profit, the bakufu had reasserted its right to control the daimyo domains. During the next six months, from late 1842 to mid-1843, it was to do much more, challenging domain independence in one measure after another as it had not been challenged for generations. Not only monopolies but also domain currency, the very token of economic independence, was soon to be threatened. Before the year was out, money changers had been instructed not to handle any copper cash minted in the domains, and an investigation had been ordered into *hansatsu*, the local paper currency used so effectively in underpinning domain monopolies.

The onslaught assumed a slightly different form when in the spring of 1843, Ieyoshi, the twelfth Tokugawa shogun, left his castle for a period of eight days to worship at the tombs of his great predecessors: Tokugawa Ieyasu, who had founded the dynasty, and Tokugawa Iemitsu, who had consolidated it. This official progress to Nikkō, ninety miles away, may seem to have been no more than filial piety of the most praiseworthy sort. Its implications, however, were very different. First, it placed heavy demands on a number of daimyo. Three of them, at Iwatsuki, Koga, and Utsunomiya, were obliged to house the shogun and his retinue, both on the way to Nikkō and on the way back. The Utsunomiya domain records, which speak of "indescribable turmoil and confusion," suggest that this was no easy matter.[51] Other daimyo had to provide the shogun with an escort, amounting to some 150,000 men, and still others were given ceremonial duties, some guarding Edo Castle in the shogun's absence, or manning the Kantō's key strategic points – Usui Pass, Uraga, the Ōi River, and Hakone (where the daimyo of Sendai sent six thousand men). Because they cost money that none could afford, such movements provided a headache for those domains directly involved and a matter of concern for others that, if not called on this time, might well be so in the future. Beyond the immediate financial problem, however, loomed something less tangible but, in its way, far more ominous. The shogunal progress to Nikkō had once been an important, if intermittent, part of Tokugawa ceremonial life. Whether in its ostensible objective – an act of homage to the architects of Tokugawa supremacy – or in the manner in which large numbers of men from the daimyo domains were placed at the shogun's disposal, it was a symbolic celebration of Tokugawa rule and an affirmation of Tokugawa authority. That this costly and wasteful ritual should be revived now, after a lapse of nearly seventy years, by a government otherwise dedicated to economizing and frugality, was yet another tribute to the severity of the Tempō crisis and the extent to which it had goaded the bakufu into action.

By the middle of that year, the pattern was clear. Within the space of fourteen days, the bakufu reformers gave warning of their intention to restore not only conventional morality and economic stability but also the old early-seventeenth-century relationship between the Tokugawa shogun and his daimyo, characterized by unquestioned authority, on the one hand, and unquestioning obedience, on the other. One indication was the plan to drain the Imbanuma, for this project, designed to increase the shogun's own productive land, was to be carried out at the expense of five daimyo, who together were to share the cost of more than 200,000 gold pieces. It had been sixty years since daimyo had been forced to bear so heavy a burden for Tokugawa benefit.

Nor was that all. The Imbanuma project was announced in the middle of the most ambitious rearrangement of daimyo land for more than two hundred years. On the first day of the sixth month of 1843, a number of daimyo and *hatamoto* had received an unusual notice. The details differed, but the wording was roughly the same in each case:

51 Tokuda, *Shiryō Utsunomiya han shi*, p. 177.

A measure has now been announced by which, for administrative purposes, all land adjacent to Edo Castle is to become bakufu land. Therefore you are ordered to surrender land producing at least X *koku* from your fief in Y County, Z Province. In due course you will be given land in exchange. . . .[52]

In short, the bakufu was resuming land originally given to daimyo in fief. This first round of reappropriations affected land producing some 15,000 *koku*, but the next ten days were to see more, all in the vicinity of Edo. On the eleventh day, the scene shifted briefly to the west coast, with the appropriation of 600 *koku* of land from the Nagaoka domain – a relatively small area but a most important one, as it was the site of Niigata, the largest of the Japan Sea ports. Then, on the fifteenth day, came a further series of announcements, this time addressed to sixteen daimyo with land near Osaka Castle, requiring them to surrender a total of 100,000 *koku*.

In strategic terms, these measures, known collectively as *agechi rei*, were no more than reasonable. Obviously, if the nation were to face a foreign threat, then the land surrounding its two greatest fortresses should be under unified control, rather than, as was the case at Osaka, controlled by 165 different authorities. A similar case could have been made for joining Niigata to the other major ports – Osaka, Edo, Nagasaki, and Hakodate – under Tokugawa supervision. Nonetheless, as with the prohibition of domain monopolies, the *agechi rei* were significant in other respects. The bakufu did not hesitate to admit, for example, that it was reshuffling these fiefs to enhance its own financial situation at daimyo expense: "It is inappropriate," read the official statement, "that private domains should now have more high-yield land than the bakufu."[53] Therefore, the daimyo were to be required to give up their pockets of productive land around Edo and Osaka, taking in return some of the low-yielding land held by the bakufu in such large quantities. Once again, these measures were well within the bakufu's formal power; having originally bestowed the land on the daimyo, it could also take it away. Yet, nearly two centuries of freedom from interference had left the daimyo believing that despite formal subordination to the shogun and his government, their fiefs were inviolable, theirs to be held in perpetuity. Now they were reminded that this was not so and, ominously, informed that the bakufu contemplated extending the *agechi rei* into a large-scale rationalization of its landholdings. To any daimyo, condemned to discharging a whole range of administrative responsibilities on a dwindling income, it was a notably cheerless prospect.

52 Quoted in Kitajima, *Mizuno Tadakuni*, p. 425.   53 *Tokugawa jūgodaishi*, vol. 6, pp. 2955 ff.

Historians have often labeled the bakufu's Tempō reforms as conservative. In many respects they were. So much of the Tempō legislation was repetitious, self-consciously archaic, and irrelevant to the crisis that Japan faced. Nevertheless, certain aspects of the bakufu's reforms were extremely singular, and none more so than these efforts to reestablish its central authority over the daimyo and thereby to regain some kind of political and economic primacy. This, too, may have been conservative, as it was predicated on the revival of powers dormant since the mid-seventeenth century. Nevertheless it represents a dramatic departure from the pattern laid down by the earlier reforms, neither of which had compromised daimyo autonomy in any significant way. Here, at least, we can see the bakufu reacting appropriately to the demands of the Tempō crisis — appropriately, that is, from one point of view. With the nation fearful of civil unrest and foreign invasion, a central government — particularly one as weak as the Tokugawa bakufu — could legitimately call for more power. Unfortunately, the daimyo domains, subject to pressures equally intense, were less ready to listen than ever before. The Tempō crisis had spurred the domains into new and potentially divisive forms of behavior; it had now done no less for the Tokugawa bakufu. More than that, it had brought the domains and the bakufu face to face with each other's aspirations in a particularly peremptory fashion, and neither could be reassured by what they saw.

MIZUNO TADAKUNI

If the bakufu reforms were unusual, the man who had charge of them was more unusual still. Traditionally, in Tokugawa historiography, the reformer assumes his role at birth, displaying, with preternatural speed, every quality expected of a Man of Destiny. Tokugawa Yoshimune, initiator of the Kyōhō reforms, was tough, disciplined, and frugal; Matsudaira Sadanobu, father of the Kansei reforms, was talented, conscientious, and wise beyond his years. By contrast, Mizuno Tadakuni (1794–1851), architect of the Tempō reforms, was all too human. He was, for example, rather greedy. Conger eel, prepared in the Kyoto style, was his favorite dish, but his all-embracing absorption with food was well known, and Tokugawa Nariaki could contemplate winning his favor with boxes of salmon *sushi* and wild duck *tempura*. There were other weaknesses, too, for his appetites by no means halted at his stomach. In 1840, less than a year before launching his campaign to restore the nation to moral health, Mizuno Tadakuni was reputedly obsessed with sex. "I have been making surreptitious inquiries about [Mizuno's] tastes," reported one of Tokugawa Nariaki's agents, "but at the moment he cares for nothing but women," adding that the senior councilor was giving his servants money to make sure of a ready supply.[54]

A weakness for food and women, however unexpected in a Confucian reformer, was not unpardonable, but in this case there were other, graver, defects. Tokugawa Nariaki, though refusing to condemn Mizuno's passion for women, nevertheless considered him unfit for public office, citing the fact that "he does not care for soldierly things and prefers the ways of courtiers; his interests lie in court ceremonial and antiquarian information, rather than in weaponry. . . ." Mizuno's own avowed ambition, expressed at the beginning of his career, "to become senior councilor as quickly as possible and then relax," suggests that this judgment was not without foundation. Beyond this, however, and most serious of all, is the matter of Mizuno's demonstrable partiality to money. As a young daimyo, first at Karatsu and later at Hamamatsu, his financial situation had always been one of his chief concerns, and as he readily confessed, he undertook an official career confidently expecting to make something out of it. To some extent he was right. Office brought him a richly decorated mansion in Aoyama, surrounded by gardens full of rare plants and unusual rocks – "so splendid a residence," wrote a contemporary, "as to steal away the senses." It also brought something less welcome: a reputation for venality that most politicians, and reformers in particular, might have wished to avoid. "In the past people have asked [Mizuno] for favors," wrote one of Tokugawa Nariaki's informants in 1840, "and such is his nature that he has obliged them. He has, too, accepted bribes quite freely, although since this spring he has been wary and returned all gifts offered to him." Nevertheless, Tokugawa Nariaki considered him even more corrupt than the notorious Tanuma Okitsugu.

It is undeniably difficult to associate such a man with orthodox Confucian reforms. Hypocrisy was never too far below the surface of Tokugawa period morality, but exhortations to self-restraint must have rung more than usually hollow in the mouth of a known glutton, debaucher, dilettante, and taker of bribes. Yet it is still more difficult to associate Mizuno Tadakuni with the other, unorthodox aspect of the Tempō reforms. He was, after all, a daimyo and therefore subject to all the pressures of the Tempō crisis. More than that, his sympathies on this issue had never previously been in doubt. As the daimyo

---

54 Tsuji Tatsuya, "Tokugawa Nariaki to Mizuno Tadakuni," *Jimbutsu sōsho furoku*, no. 154 (Tokyo: Yoshikawa kōbunkan).

of first Karatsu and then Hamamatsu, he had consistently given priority to domain interests. In government, which he entered in 1815, he had endured, but not endorsed, the rule of Tokugawa Ienari. Then with Ienari dead, he proceeded to purge all those who had followed the eleventh shogun on his capricious and autocratic way. Clearly, to Mizuno, as to almost all of his predecessors in bakufu office, the best government was one in which the shogunal prerogative was curbed by senior officials who, daimyo themselves, saw the value of regional autonomy. Such was certainly the intent behind Mizuno's memorial to the twelfth shogun, in 1841, urging that he work through his daimyo ministers, and not, as his father had done, through personal cronies.[55]

This was not the kind of man suddenly to turn and savage his own class. But he did. His directives from late 1842 to mid-1843 – the abolition of guilds and domain monopolies, the shogunal progress to Nikkō, the *agechi rei*, the draining of the Imbanuma – all threatened, directly or otherwise, the regional independence that the daimyo had enjoyed since the mid-seventeenth century. Why did he change? The question is reasonable and straightforward enough, but unfortunately, it cannot be answered with any finality. Mizuno, like all but a few politicians of the Tokugawa period, has left us no substantial clues to the workings of his mind. The chronicle of events alone offers some assistance, but even that is tenuous. What there is, however, is suggestive. Mizuno had come to maturity in a society accustomed to isolation; nothing in his background or his earlier career could have prepared him for the hard diplomatic decisions, the rumors, and the atmosphere of impending catastrophe waiting for him in the Tempō era. Together with the critics – Tokugawa Nariaki, Watanabe Kazan, Takashima Shūhan, Sakuma Shōzan, and the rest – he would have shared fears of foreign invasion in 1838 and, like them, would have seen those fears, amorphous at first, take on British shape with news of the Opium War. "It is happening in a foreign country," wrote Mizuno, describing the affray in China in a letter to a subordinate, "but I believe it also contains a warning for us."[56] With responsibilities and access to information far more extensive than any of the Tempō critics, his concern would have been no less than theirs. Nor can Mizuno have been ignorant of the implications of the Chinese experience. If a great centralized state could be despatched so readily, then what chance had Japan – small, weak, and fragmented as it was? The

---

55 Bolitho, *Treasures Among Men*, p. 215.
56 Quoted in Inoue Kiyoshi, *Nihon gendaishi* (Tokyo: Tōkyō daigaku shuppankai, 1967), vol. 1, p. 89.

unpalatable truth about the *bakuhan taisei*, as politicians and critics were beginning to realize, was that it was inadequate to the needs of a country threatened by invasion. It was either too centralized (because the daimyo were forced to squander their resources paying court to the shogun in Edo) or not centralized enough (because the bakufu had no firm control over them).

There are indications that Mizuno, background and personal preferences notwithstanding, had come to incline to the latter view. One is to be seen in the bakufu's changing attitude toward Satō Nobuhiro. Satō was the critic who, more than any other, stood for stronger central government. It was not a position that won him many friends; on the contrary, in 1832 he had been ordered not to come within twenty miles of Edo. Ten years later, however, as the government began to digest the lessons of the Opium War, his works came to be read again by bakufu officials, Mizuno among them. At the beginning of 1843 Satō was pardoned and allowed back into the city where in 1845, at Mizuno's personal request, he compiled an abbreviated version of *Suitō hiroku*, the work in which he had provided the blueprints for a unified nation-state.

On its own, this is far from conclusive evidence of any change of heart. Yet taken in conjunction with Mizuno's policies, as they developed from late 1842 to the middle of the following year, it suggests that of the two possible lines along which the *bakuhan taisei* might have been modified – either in the direction of more regional autonomy or toward greater central control – Mizuno, for one, had made his choice. Events thirty years later vindicated his judgment, but this was far too late for Mizuno. All too soon he paid dearly for that choice at the hands of those infinitely less prescient.

THE AFTERMATH

It was one of the peculiarities of Tokugawa period reforms that they never reached a formal conclusion. How could they? They all began with a public commitment to precisely those virtues – honesty, frugality, the recognition of talent – most highly prized in conventional morality; no government could possibly confess itself no longer interested in such things. Nevertheless, all these paroxysms of reform subsided as quickly as they appeared. In the bakufu, the Kyōhō and Kansei reforms faded imperceptibly into the inertia of Gembun and Kyōwa. Domains like Tosa, proclaiming reforms in Genna, Kambun, Tenna, Kyōhō, Temmei, and Kansei, saw them all come to a halt. It was a fact universally recognized but never openly admitted. With so much to be done before the golden age could be restored and human nature transformed, it would not have been politic to confess that reforms could ever end.

The Tempō reforms proved no exception. In the domains they all ended, some whimpering their way into oblivion, others culminating in an explosion in which the reformers were dismissed (as with Watanabe Kazan at Tawara in 1837) and sometimes thrown into prison as well (as with Mabuchi Kahei at Tosa in 1843). Whatever the end, they were ignored until their resurrection as models for fresh reforms in the 1850s and 1860s.

In the Tokugawa bakufu, the climax was more spectacular. Toward the end of 1843, just two years after Mizuno had declared his reformist intentions, one year after he had fired his first shots against domain autonomy, and one month after the salvo of *agechi rei*, Mizuno was tumbled out of office and disgraced in a spasm of conservative revulsion. He was accused of "dishonesty," and his dismissal was said to have brought a crowd of irate citizens into the streets to pelt his house with stones. Exactly the same thing had happened to Tanuma Okitsugu, who had also tried to strengthen the bakufu at daimyo expense. Unlike Tanuma, however, Mizuno's career did not quite end there. Within nine months, in the middle of 1844, he was reinstated, the allegations of "dishonesty" and unpopularity forgotten in the confusion of yet another diplomatic crisis. The Dutch had just sent word of an important communication from their king, and Mizuno was recalled to deal with it. His rehabilitation was brief, however (just eight months), incomplete, and hampered by ill health (genuine, not assumed). Once again it terminated in humiliation, and Mizuno was obliged to resign for the second and last time. Before the year 1845 was out, he was forced into retirement, and 20,000 *koku* was stripped from his estates. Hori Chikashige, the only other senior councilor to have given him full support, was treated in much the same way, while two of Mizuno's subordinates were subsequently jailed, and a third was put to death. The bakufu's Tempō reforms, in this, the second year of the succeeding Kōka era (1844–8), were well and truly at an end. In fact, they had never really survived Mizuno's first dismissal, in the intercalary ninth month of 1843.

Did the Tempō reforms succeed or fail? This depends on one's perception of the reforms' aims and one's definition of success or failure. In their own terms, they failed. They made no lasting impact on human nature, certainly not to such an extent that the Japanese people thereafter turned again to righteousness and resumed the simple life they had once allegedly enjoyed. No reforms ever did. In Japan, as elsewhere, human nature was always ready to ignore or circumvent whatever arbitrary restrictions were imposed on certain inalienable rights (among them spending money, drinking, gambling, and pursuing sexual gratification, whether at the bathhouse, teahouse, or street corner). Incorrigible, the public continued to read frivolous and salacious books, and the publishers, after only a momentary check, continued to provide them. Printmakers, too, seemed largely to have ignored government prohibitions. In Edo, for example, there were more variety theaters than ever by 1845, and actors were no less in the public eye. Repression of this kind, whether originating in the bakufu or the domain governments, was always doomed to failure.

To the extent that the Tempō reforms aimed at restoring a measure of peace and prosperity to the Japanese people in the wake of the Tempō crisis, they enjoyed a measure of success. Most of this, however, was accidental, more a product of better seasons and increased food supplies than anything else. Government interference, wherever it took place, tended to be disastrous. In the case of the bakufu's dissolution of merchant associations, for example, insofar as these bodies ever complied with the government's order (and even this is questionable), the effect seems to have been not quite what officials had anticipated. In some areas it reduced the traditional commercial network to chaos, leaving "everybody engaged in trade much inconvenienced," as one village official complained in his diary.[57] It promoted confusion, shortages, and economic depression – even, ironically, higher prices, the very thing the bakufu had hoped to counter. On the other hand, it encouraged commercial and industrial activities of a kind even more difficult to control, whether in the hands of independent rural entrepreneurs or the daimyo domains. When this attempt failed, therefore, the bakufu promptly returned to more familiar measures, only to see those fail in their turn. It simply did not have the means to enforce its price restrictions and by early 1845 had apparently come to doubt not only the feasibility of such an enterprise but even its desirability, observing lamely that "naturally prices will rise and fall according to circumstances and according to the volume of goods available."[58] What is certain is that prices had remained high throughout Mizuno's tenure of office and were still the object of official complaint in 1845, on the eve of his final departure from the political world.

57 *Essa sōsho*, p. 312.   58 Quoted in Okamoto, "Tempō kaikaku," pp. 239–40.

Other social problems, too, remained untouched. It is debatable, for example, just what result was obtained by efforts to drive, or tempt, people out of the cities and back to their native villages. Some scholars deny any effect whatsoever; another detected a 5 percent fall in the population of Osaka between 1842 and 1843, but even this tells us little, as the measures were aimed not so much at reducing the number of city dwellers as replenishing Japan's farm population.[59] In either case, one wonders what lasting effect was likely to be achieved by measures that attacked the symptoms of rural decline while so transparently ignoring the causes. Similarly, the system of bakufu loans for samurai would seem to have fallen well short of its mark, although in this case it is not easy to judge how effective it might have been, for like so many of Mizuno's initiatives, it had been in operation barely a year before it was hastily reversed by his successors.

Insofar as the bakufu and the domains used their reforms to retrieve some sort of financial balance by reducing debts and expenses and increasing income, the judgment is a little less certain. Overall, it is difficult to escape the impression that they failed. Mito, for example, despite all its efforts at expanding and diversifying its economic base, really solved none of its problems. Echizen, too, continued to spend more than it made, prompting even the phlegmatic Yuri Kimimasa to complain that "you never see any money in Fukui," and this condition did not begin to improve until another set of reforms was instituted in the 1850s.[60]

It would appear, however, that in at least some domains, the reforms did work, and in this context, historians usually point to the great domains of the southwest, most notably Satsuma, Chōshū, Tosa, and Hizen. This is not unreasonable, in view of these domains' later economic strength and their considerable political influence; it is, however, open to question. Satsuma is perhaps the exception. The commercialization of farming and the emergence of rural entrepreneurs had never been a problem there; nor for that matter had peasant rebellions, which were virtually unknown. New crops and processing industries could therefore be introduced and closely supervised by the Satsuma government without provoking any local opposition, for their farmers apparently did not miss freedoms they had never enjoyed. Otherwise, however, there is room for doubt. Tosa had not one but

---

59 Compare, for example, the views of Tsuda, "Tempō kaikaku," p. 316; and Okamoto, "Tempō kaikaku," p. 222.
60 Quoted in Rekishigaku kenkyūkai, eds., *Meiji ishinshi kenkyū kōza* (Tokyo: Heibonsha, 1968), vol. 2, p. 216.

two sets of Tempō reforms, both of which ended in disgrace – the first with the resignation of the daimyo in 1843, the second with the imprisonment of Mabuchi Kahei, the domain's financial expert, a few months later. Chōshū, too, forced to abandon its plans of marketing domain products in 1843, saw Murata Seifū, its chief reformer, resign in 1844, his Thirty-seven-Year Plan in ruins. Like Echizen, Chōshū's financial rehabilitation had to await further reforms in the 1850s.

In the case of the bakufu, there can be no such doubts. Mizuno's attempts to restore bakufu finances were no more successful than was anything else he initiated. Ideas of developing and controlling the productivity of the bakufu's own domain dissolved in a storm of rural protest in which farmers, preferring to keep their agricultural surplus in their own hands, attacked government offices and destroyed their documents. Other initiatives, among them recoinage, levies on the business community, and the addition to the bakufu domain of land reclaimed from the Imbanuma, all were casualties of their author's fall from power. The final result, therefore, was a bakufu that had failed to restore itself to financial health. This was to have disastrous consequences in the future, particularly because domains like Satsuma had done so much better. For the present, its consequences were equally serious, simply because lack of money prevented the bakufu from reorganizing national defense. Had Mizuno remained in office longer, of course, the situation might well have improved. As it was, however, he spent just 2,739 gold pieces on defense, less than 3 percent of the cost of the shogun's progress to Nikkō.

There is one more measure of the success or otherwise of the Tempō reforms. The Tempō crisis, which had entangled daimyo and bakufu in civil unrest, financial malaise, and fears of impending diplomatic, and possibly military, confrontation, obliged them all to respond. Given their separate responsibilities, they could do so only from standpoints that were radically different and, ultimately, incompatible. The domains, looking to their finances and their defenses, saw the need to move outside bakufu control; the bakufu, equally preoccupied, began to reassert its right – indeed, its obligation – to control the domains as they had not been controlled for generations. Which side prevailed, then, in this most fundamental of struggles?

In one sense it was the daimyo domains. Where Mizuno's policies could be defied or circumvented, they did so – most obviously, of course, with domain monopolies, which continued everywhere, despite official prohibition. When resistance appeared no longer possible, then a concerted movement of daimyo – some inside the bakufu itself, others not – turned Mizuno out of office, crushing his policies in the process. The *agechi rei*, for example, were canceled six days before their author's dismissal; so potent a threat to domain autonomy could hardly have remained uncorrected. Work on the Imbanuma, too, was allowed to lapse ten days after Mizuno's dismissal and never resumed, although the project itself had been on the verge of completion. All that remained of the bakufu's attack on daimyo prerogatives, therefore, were the memories and the painful financial scars of the shogun's journey to Nikkō.

In Mizuno's place they ultimately installed a much more predictable successor. This was Abe Masahiro, whose qualities immediately commended themselves. He was sober, upright, conciliatory, and totally lacking in initiative. Abe made sure that once the controversial element of Mizuno's reforms had been dismantled, he would do nothing to offend anybody.[61] His government proceeded to ignore its financial problems, as it ignored matters of defense and foreign policy. Mizuno, however maladroitly, had tried to do something about them; Abe, on the other hand, conferred endlessly and did nothing. All three issues were swept out of sight, as they touched on the contentious question of the relative powers of the bakufu and the daimyo. Watanabe Shūjirō, Abe's biographer, observed that under his government, "all the daimyo were content."[62] We may be sure that they were. But on the other hand, with all the hard decisions about Japanese political organization pushed to one side, the rest of Japan paid dearly for that contentment in 1853, when it faced Commodore Perry with no central government worth the name.

There was another sense, however, in which the results of the Tempō reforms were not quite so well defined. True, the bakufu's reforms had been destroyed, and measures had been taken to see that daimyo interests would not be further threatened. But Mizuno had shown that the bakufu was not entirely without teeth, and several domains bore the marks for some time. Tokugawa Nariaki, for example, who never forgot an injury, had cause to remember this, for it was bakufu intervention that had aborted the Mito reform program. In

61 Scholarly appraisals of Abe have varied markedly and will no doubt continue to do so. W. G. Beasley, in his *Select Documents on Foreign Policy, 1853–1868* (London: Oxford University Press, 1955), p. 21, judges him "hardly the man best fitted to meet a serious crisis." By contrast, Conrad Totman, in *The Collapse of the Tokugawa Bakufu* (Honolulu: University of Hawaii Press, 1980), p. xx, impressed by his "repeated displays of political skill," considers him to have been an "astute" politician.
62 Watanabe Shūjirō, *Abe Masahiro jiseki* (Tokyo, 1910), vol. 1, p. 52.

Chōshū, too, they had learned a lesson: Murata Seifū had felt it politic to restrict the domain's commercial activities, to avoid open conflict with the bakufu. As a result, the Chōshū reforms had been ruined, and Murata himself was forced to resign. Mizuno, although he had lost, had alerted the daimyo domains to just how formidable an opponent the bakufu could still be. By raising this specter and not laying it completely, the Tempō reforms had left Japan with its fundamental dilemma still unresolved. How was the nation to be organized to meet a troubled future? This particular legacy of the Tempō crisis remained to bedevil Japan for the next thirty years. Other aspects of the crisis could be resolved, superficially at least, by the return of fine weather and good harvests, but not this one. The foreign problem, with all its attendant internal difficulties, had arrived. No amount of sunshine was likely to alter that.

THE IMPLICATIONS

The Tempō era had been one of critical importance for Japan. Even historians who agree on little else agree on this, detecting in these years of crisis the beginning of a chain of events that culminated thirty years later in the dismantling of Japan's ancien régime. Beyond this, of course, they disagree. To some historians, perhaps the majority, the Tempō era's most important contribution to Japan's future ferment was the informal alliance concluded across class barriers by the country gentry, on the one hand, and some sections of the samurai class – the so-called lower samurai – on the other, an alliance of the kind of men who, in 1868, put paid to an establishment that excluded them and installed themselves in its place.[63] Other scholars, to whom the Meiji Restoration was far more the result of political developments than social ones, contrast the failure of the bakufu's reforms with the success of those carried out in domains like Satsuma, finding the seeds of future instability in the poverty of the one and the wealth of the other.

My personal inclination is toward the latter view, yet not without some modification. Certainly the newfound affluence of the Satsuma government held serious implications for the *bakuhan taisei*. In the diplomatic crisis of the Tempō era, wealth was already equated with

---

63 This aspect of the Tempō reforms has been much analyzed by Japanese historians, many of whom interpret it as a development tending toward "absolutism." I refer interested readers to Ishii Takashi, *Gakusetsu hihan Meiji ishin ron* (Tokyo: Yoshikawa kōbunkan, 1968).

the acquisition of military power: new weapons, new ships, new training. All were necessary, but because all were expensive, few could afford them. If Satsuma could and the bakufu could not, then the balance of power that had kept Japan at peace for more than two hundred years was at risk. Yet there was a far more serious and far more general threat. Satsuma's success with its Tempō reforms was exceptional. Other domains, Mito and Chōshū among them, had tried and failed, their aspirations to wealth and power blocked by a central government that, too weak to offer them any protection, was at the same time too strong to allow them to prepare for their own. It is clear that such domains chafed at their economic impotence and at the military incapacity that inevitably accompanied it. The Tempō crisis had shown them all that the traditional balance of power was no longer workable, that one way or the other it would have to be changed; it had provided them with thesis and antithesis but, with the reforms so inconclusive, had suggested no synthesis. The dilemma was a real one. Obviously Japan needed to do something about its defenses, but nobody could decide what, because the subject was surrounded by too many uncomfortable issues. Who was to pay for the ships, the cannon and the small arms that Japan so desperately needed? Who would command them? How would they be used? Was there any guarantee that such weapons in bakufu hands would not be turned on the daimyo themselves, to complete by force the process that Mizuno had begun by edict? Conversely, if the daimyo acquired such weapons, might they not once again plunge the nation into turmoil? These were serious matters for a country in which regional autonomy had always been so prized, too serious for the Tempō era to produce a solution.

In fact, Mizuno's bakufu had already made it clear that given a choice between a Japan armed to the teeth and one helpless against foreign attack, it would prefer the latter to the former, with its implicit threat to internal stability. So much was apparent in a remarkable exchange of letters between Tokugawa Nariaki and Mizuno's government in 1843. "If you allow daimyo and shipowners to build stout ships," Nariaki argued, "it will not cost you a copper," adding later that to prohibit large ships simply because they might be misused was "like forcing everyone to wear wooden swords because a madman has unsheathed his in the palace." It was a reasonable point, but so, too, was the counterargument: "If we permit everyone to build warships," read the bakufu rejoinder, "who can tell what evils may ensue? The daimyo of the west country and elsewhere may begin to conspire and build unorthodox vessels; this will have a significant impact on our administration of the law."[64]

This reply was both honest and accurate, but it was not likely to satisfy any domain preparing to defend itself against foreign invaders. Nor were the bakufu's various interdictions – its attempt to keep Takashima Shūhan from teaching his gunnery techniques to samurai from the daimyo domains, for example, or its warning to the Astronomical Bureau (where Western works were translated) that translations of "calendars, medical books, works of astronomy, and all books on practical matters . . . are not to be circulated indiscriminately."[65] Many domains reacted, therefore, with mistrust, deception, and evasion – experimenting with three-masted ships, importing foreign arms and manuals in secret through Nagasaki gunrunners, and offering shelter to fugitives with particular skills (as Uwajima did for Takano Chōei after his escape from prison, and Satsuma for Torii Heishichi, a Nagasaki-trained gunner). It was an atmosphere in which the former *tairō*, Ii Naoaki, placing a translation of a Dutch work in his library in the autumn of 1843, could write on the box, in his own hand, instructions that it "be kept secret for a long period."[66] It was also one in which rumors flourished, particularly rumors involving those already viewed with official mistrust, "the daimyo of the west country." Satsuma, for example, was rumored in 1837 to have spirited Ōshio Heihachirō away from Osaka and into hiding aboard one of its ships; six years later it was rumored to have engineered Mizuno's dismissal. The roots of the *bakumatsu* arms race, which pitted the bakufu and the domains against each other so disastrously, can be found in this climate of mutual suspicion.

New political alignments, too, had their origins in the Tempō crisis. During these years Tokugawa Nariaki, the daimyo of Mito, became a national political figure, gathering around him the men who dominated the politics of the next twenty years. Date Munenari, soon to become daimyo of Uwajima, married Nariaki's daughter in 1839. The young Matsudaira Yoshinaga, recently made daimyo of Echizen, visited Nariaki at his Koishikawa mansion in 1843 with a list of questions on domain government and corresponded with him regularly thereafter; Shimazu Nariakira was a visitor from the late 1830s, as were the daimyo of Saga and Kurobane. Abe Masahiro, the bakufu's inoffensive senior councilor, although sharing many of Nariaki's friends – particularly Shimazu Nariakira and Matsudaira Yoshinaga (whose

---

[64] *Mito han shiryō*, pp. 173–82. [65] *Tokugawa jūgodaishi*, pp. 2855–6.
[66] *Hikone-shi shi* (Hikone: Hikone shiyakusho, 1962), vol. 2, p. 673.

adopted daughter became his second wife) – took a little longer to warm to Nariaki, but the two men had nevertheless become allies by 1846. The scholars in Nariaki's employ, Aizawa Seishisai and Fujita Tōko, were also far from idle. While their master forged his faction to defend daimyo prerogatives, they supported him by laying down the ideological barrage that, known to contemporaries as Mitogaku (Mito learning), was attracting students from domains as distant as Saga and Kurume.

As the political events of the 1850s and 1860s proved, this alignment of forces had particularly fateful consequences. So, too, did the issue of the arms race. The history of Japan would have been quite different without them. Yet the Tempō crisis produced something far more fateful than either. In 1837 Ōshio Heihachirō had begun his *Gekibun* by lamenting the disappearance of the emperor from Japanese political life: "From the time of the Ashikaga," he wrote, "the emperor has been kept in seclusion and has lost the power to dispense rewards and punishments; the people have therefore nowhere to turn with their complaints." Before another decade had passed, this situation was to change dramatically, as the imperial symbol was the obvious refuge – indeed the only possible refuge – for those wishing to justify political opposition. Increasingly, during the Tempō era, they sought shelter in it, and none more persistently than Tokugawa Nariaki. Privately, he lobbied with the court in Kyoto; publicly, he displayed his boundless respect by demanding that the bakufu repair the imperial mausolea. His scholars meanwhile worked feverishly to remind the nation that a government established by imperial consent could be disestablished by the same means.

In 1846, a year after Mizuno left office, the campaign had its effect. Sixteen years earlier, Matsuzaki Kōdō, observing the cranes, had felt his heart lift at the sight. The crane, after all, was the traditional symbol of happiness and longevity. It was also, by a convention equally venerable, a symbol of the emperor. In the flowery language of the court, the emperor's palace became "the Palace of the Crane," his command, the "Missive of the Crane," his voice "the Voice of the Crane." This time, in 1846, in an event unparalleled in Tokugawa history, the Voice of the Crane made itself heard in a formal expression of imperial concern that under Tokugawa leadership the nation was in grave danger. This time it presaged no thousand years of felicity; instead, the Voice of the Crane launched Japan on twenty years of turbulence, destroying in the process the last vestige of the Tempō world.

CHAPTER 3

LATE TOKUGAWA CULTURE AND THOUGHT

THE CULTURE OF PLAY

Japanese historiography has conventionally located the beginning of the end of the Tokugawa (*bakumatsu*) in the decade of the 1830s, when the regime and the several domains embarked on a series of reforms aimed at arresting economic failure and restoring public confidence. Historians who have concentrated on making sense of the signs of financial failure point to the implementation of the Tempō reforms as recognition of a gathering crisis. Some have established the revolt of Ōshio Heihachirō in Osaka in 1837 as the turning point in Tokugawa history. But regardless of the many opinions concerning the beginning of the end, most discussions of the end of the shogunate have used economic signs, political events, or a combination of both as criteria for periodization. Yet to establish the beginning of the end in the 1830s obliges us to accept a concomitant assumption that cultural events constitute a second order of activity; one that avoids organizing the world in terms of a base–superstructure dyad but still sees culture and ideas as determined by material forces. Culture is then made to appear as a dependent variable of economic and political processes, and the observer is diverted from recognizing that the production of culture may in fact possess a logic of its own, one that seeks to resolve problems belonging to an entirely different class of events and facts.

If we regard culture as something more than a pale reflection of changes detected earlier in the material realm, we will be persuaded to propose that the special culture of late Tokugawa culture did not begin in the 1830s, or even later, but probably in the late eighteenth century or the early 1800s.[1] Sometime in the 1830s there appeared a historic conjuncture between new forms of self-understanding, which consti-

---

[1] This is certainly the argument of Naramoto Tatsuya, *Nihon kinsei no shisō to bunka* (Tokyo: Iwanami shoten, 1978), pp. 65–214; Maruyama Masao, *Nihon seiji shisōshi kenkyū* (Tokyo: Tokyo daigaku shuppankai, 1953); and the more recent essay by Sugi Hitoshi, "Kaseiki no shakai to bunka," in Aoki Michio and Yamada Tadao, eds., *Kōza Nihon kinseishi*, vol. 6: *Tempōki no seiji to shakai* (Tokyo: Yūhikaku, 1981), pp. 17–70.

168

tute the content of culture, and the critical political and economic events that began to jar the viability of the *bakufu–han* system. The realization that the order was losing viability may well have been possible only after the formulation of new forms of self-understanding and the establishment of new modalities of relating things to one another.

An essay by Professor Hayashiya Tatsusaburō offers the possibility of using the *bakumatsu* as a metaphor or historical trope.[2] By constructing a model of *bakumatsu*, which draws on the common experiences of the late years of the Kamakura, Muromachi, and Tokugawa shogunates, Hayashiya has identified a number of conditions shared by the three and the cultural means whereby contemporaries sought to represent their own sense of an ending and recognized that they were living through a time of profound change. His metaphor thus tries to bring together political, social, economic, diplomatic, and cultural developments. In all three cases the dissolution of the political order was accompanied by a displacement of the authority of the military estates and wider participation in a broader arena of struggle. This explanation presupposes a theory of "crisis" that ultimately is expressed in the occurrence of a "rebellion." Hayashiya noted vast social changes in the wake of this political event that signify transformations in the structure of values and norms, swiftly followed by the development of equally important economic forces, such as shifts in patterns of landholding, the circulation of currency, and new forms of exchange and foreign and domestic trade. Finally, Hayashiya links to this the emergent cultural styles that characterize and shape the social, political, and economic transformations. These new styles were symbolized by terms like *basara* in the Kamakura period, *kabuki* in late Muromachi times, and *ki* and *i* in the Tokugawa. *Basara* referred to love of the gaudy and ornate and the self-indulgent and unauthorized behavior with which some warrior leaders set the example for their peers; *kabuki* meant "to lean" or "to tilt" and called forth the outlandish and playful, often associated with debauchery and perversity; and in late Tokugawa, *ki* invoked the strange, curious, and eccentric, whereas *i* signaled the different, uncommon, and foreign. Thus in each *bakumatsu* the prevailing attitudes were inscribed in style and conduct previously signified as different and nonnormative, even unthinkable and unimaginable.

It is important to recognize that these new styles were not reflec-

---

2 Hayashiya Tatsusaburō, ed., *Bakumatsu bunka no kenkyū* (Tokyo: Iwanami shoten, 1978).

tions of more basic material forces. Rather, the real function of this metaphor is to establish a different relationship between material conditions and symbolic or cultural representation. The historical trope allows us to glimpse a unified world, a universe in which discontinuous realities are somehow bonded and intertwined with one another, thereby suggesting a network of relationships among things that first seem remote. The trope manages to establish a momentary reconciliation between the material and spiritual worlds without assigning priority to one or the other and persuades us to acknowledge disparate elements as equivalents in relationships whereby each determines and is determined by the other. It is as if the interaction resembled a form of dialectical traffic that permits a transaction between the language of social change and cultural form.[3] Such an approach to late Tokugawa culture helps us read the content of the socioeconomic macrocosm, the massive substance of the "real," in terms of form and representations that appear as significations of it. *Bakumatsu* represents a rhetorical figure, a form in time, ordering a specific reality, but precisely at that moment when the most disparate facts order themselves around a model that will later offer "meaning."

In the late Tokugawa period we can note a confluence between the content of the real, transforming productive process and the production of new cultural forms that promised to make sense of what was occurring in social life. Yet the relationship between the effort to meet the consequences of newer productive forces and social relationships and the attempts to stabilize meaning between politics and culture had less to do with a simple reflection from one "base" to the "superstructure" than with the operation of mediations. The massive transformations in the social process were translated into the cultural sphere, and this placed great strains on the social image of Tokugawa Japan and its conception of cultural praxis.[4] The polity was called on to meet the contradictory demands of stabilizing conditions of private accumulation while responding to requests for social welfare. A search for

---

[3] Frederic Jameson suggested this conception of conjuncture in his *Marxism and Form* (Princeton, N.J.: Princeton University Press, 1971), pp. 3–59.
[4] The idea of a social imaginary was advanced by Corneilus Catoriadis, *L'Institution imaginaire de la société* (Paris: Seuil, 1975); and Claude Le Fort, *Les Formes de l'histoire: Essais d'anthropologie politique* (Paris: Gallimard, 1978). The concept of a social imaginary, as used by these writers, refers not to a specular image submitted to reflection but, rather, to the indeterminate ways in which society organizes the production of material goods and the reproduction of its members. The domain of the social imaginary therefore conforms not to the fact that humans must have resources to survive and reproduce but to the variety of ways in which they are able to do so, which builds on but surpasses the basic material conditions of life. It is the way that a society seeks, through forms of signification, to endow itself with an identity different from those of other societies and from chaos.

meaning and self-understanding in a changed environment was expressed in calls for benevolence and greater political participation at a time when urban expansion and cultural participation required new definitions. New forms of cultural production accompanying the expansion of cities collectively signified what we may call, from playful literature (*gesaku*), the "culture of play." By the end of the eighteenth century this had exceeded the limits of its own formal constraints to reveal in vague outline the possibility of constructing a social imagination vastly different from the one authorized by the Tokugawa. The culture of play then turned into a play of culture committed to finding stable and permanent forms that might best accommodate new demands and expectations by reconstituting the whole.

At the core of this cultural development was the search for new and different forms of knowledge and the search for ways to implement them. The explosion of new forms of knowledge in late Tokugawa Japan was increasingly difficult to assimilate to the categories of the existing political system. What occurred in the late eighteenth century was the recognition, first in the cities but soon exported to the countryside, that the opposition of ruler–ruled and external–internal had exhausted its productivity and was incapable of constructing a vision of the political that could accommodate the complexity and plurality of the social urban environment. The physical and demographic expansion of urban sites like Edo, Osaka, Kyoto, and Nagoya, not to mention lesser castle towns functioning as regional market centers, and the resulting differentiation of social and cultural life were presented as a spectacle of social surplus juxtaposed to the "rational" and organized structures of the Tokugawa "order" imagined by Confucian ideologues. According to Hayashiya this perception was proclaimed in the calls like Yoshida Shōin's for the "different" and the strange.[5] It was inscribed in countless practices associated with the new culture of play, and it called into question the suppositions of a political ideology rooted in the logic of similitude.[6] That logic neatly divided the political and hence the cultural spheres between the rulers, who possessed mental powers, and the ruled, who labored manually. The former were supposed to know, and the latter were enjoined to follow. The social identity of the ruled was fixed in a closed, hierarchic chain, resembling elements in a stable structure that reflected the order

---

[5] The term *social surplus* is my reading, not Professor Hayashiya's, of the sociopolitical scene.
[6] On the logic of similitude, see H. D. Harootunian, "Ideology As Conflict," in Tetsuo Najita and J. Victor Koschmann, eds., *Conflict in Modern Japanese History* (Princeton, N.J.: Princeton University Press, 1982), pp. 25–61.

found in nature. Yet the material expansion of Edo as the hub of a world not yet imagined made it possible to challenge these fixed identities through the proliferation of different subject positions. The multiplication of needs and the differentiation of services contributed to the city's expansion and to the concomitant blurring of fixed distinctions between ruler and ruled.[7]

At the heart of the culture of play was a system of signification that recognized that the fixed boundaries and social identities established to guide people had become increasingly uncertain as society grew larger and more complex. The new systems of meaning agreed that social space and differentiation of positions invalidated most earlier distinctions. With the observation that people who resided in the cities acquired multiple identities, the culture of play produced a threat to the social identity of society. When, for example, the Tokugawa authorities laid down the proscription of heterodoxy in the late eighteenth century, they were recognizing the threat to social identity that the new cultural forms were beginning to pose. But even Matsudaira Sadanobu, who promoted the prohibitions, acknowledged that "principle" and "reading books" fell short of grasping the "passions of the times" and equipping the ruled with proper instruments to prosecute their managerial duties.[8] What his edict disclosed was thus an acknowledgment of social surplus that seemed to elude the conventional forms of representing the social in the fixed dichotomy of ruler–ruled. His call for the promotion of men of talent and ability through the social formation still took for granted the received political divisions. Ironically, the edict contributed to the problem of surplus and difference rather than to its solution, by encouraging the development and sponsorship of new skills in science, medicine, and Japanese and Western studies that promised to supply the leadership with practical techniques to grasp the "passion of the times."

If late-eighteenth-century Japan appeared as a scene of social surplus and blurred identities, its cultural praxis expressing play sought not only to displace fixed boundaries representing the real but also to show how the real, the differentiated masses living in the cities required new modes of representation. Play (*asobi*) referred to a form of subjectivity that existed outside the "four classes" that operated within the space of the "great peace" *taihei*.[9] A sense of liberation, closely

---

7 See Hayashiya Tatsusaburō, *Kasei bunka no kenkyū* (Tokyo: Iwanami shoten, 1976), pp. 19–42.   8 Ibid., pp. 43–80, 343–95.
9 Hiraishi Naoaki, "Kaiho Seiryō no shisōzō," *Shisō* 677 (November 1980): 52.

resembling the nonrelated, insubordinated autonomy associated with the free cities of the late Middle Ages in Japan, demanded freedom from fixed positions as a condition for endless movement, best expressed in excursion narratives and tales of travel.[10] Yet the reference to movement evinced still another meaning associated with *asobi*, which was to authorize crossing established geographical and social boundaries. According to Kaiho Seiryō (1755–1817), the ideal of this playful subject was the "gaze that disconnects and separates" (*kirete hanaretaru moku*): Once the "spirit" was separated from the "body," it would be possible to carry on "independent play."[11] As a *rōnin* (masterless samurai), Kaiho had abandoned fixed positions of status in order to "play" within the "great peace"; as a traveler he journeyed to more than thirty provinces in his lifetime. The conception of play held by intellectuals like Kaiho was invariably related to the production of "playful literature," the deliberate decadence of "mad poetry," comic verse, and an inordinate taste for the different and exotic. This type of autonomous individual liberated from the collectivity in some sense resembled the person who buys and sells commodities as a condition of commercial capitalism, but the relationship was less causal than homologous. On numerous occasions Kaiho expressed best what many contemporaries believed and acted upon when he proclaimed that it was human nature for the self to love the body. He saw a world of universal principles dominated by substantiality, that is, things and bodies interacting with each other. In this arrangement, thing or object (*mono*) was increasingly identified with commodity (*shiromono*), and each person functioned as both buyer and seller. Rules that now constituted the social related more to calculation and self-interest than to moral imperatives of status, and they were mandated by the exchange of commodities.

Late Tokugawa cultural practice seemed to converge upon the body, making public what hitherto had remained private, whether in eating, drinking, speaking, bedding down with either a man or a woman, or relieving oneself, and often led to gargantuan indulgences coming from the joys of the flesh. Despite the variety of forms of verbal fiction that proliferated in the late eighteenth century to meet the rapid diversification of tastes, pleasures, and demands for greater "consumption," the content of playful culture invariably focused on the activities of the body. This concern for the autonomy of the body, expressed in Kaiho's "independent spirit" of movement, constituted the subject matter of

---

10 The argument is made by Amino Yoshihiko, *Muen, kugai, raku* (Tokyo: Heibonsha, 1978).
11 Hiraishi, "Kaiho Seiryō no shisōzō," pp. 52–3.

most of verbal fiction and woodblock illustrations. One of the distinguishing features of the culture of play was its tendency to juxtapose a part, whether limb, organ, face, or body itself, to a larger entity, not as a substitute for the whole, but, rather, as an adequate alternative to it. To dismiss the whole in this way was clearly to discount it. Centering on the body and its activities emphasized the physical and the manual; by the same token it called into question the superiority of mental over manual skills on which the older distinction between ruler–ruled, external–internal, and public–private had rested its authority. Finally, the emphasis on the body as the maker and consumer of things put daily life in the forefront and valued the things that composed it. Late-eighteenth-century Japan was a time when recalling Marx, "the frames of the old *orbis terrarum* had been broken" and "only now . . . was the earth opened up . . . ," when the search began to find ways to link real history, the daily life, to the space of the real earth.¹²

What the verbal fictions of the culture play first disclosed was a new form of time and its relationship to earthly space. This resulted in individualizing personal and everyday occasions, separating them from the time of collective life identified with the social whole, precisely at that moment when there appeared one scale for measuring the events of a personal life and another for historical events. When Hirata Atsutane sought to figure a narrative that would recount the tale of the folk collectivity, he was reacting to a culture that had already divided time into separate units and differentiated the plots of personal life – love, marriage, travel – from the occasions of history. In texts that provided the plot of "history" and the private plots of individuals, interaction between the two levels took place only at certain points – battles, the ascension or death of an emperor, transgressions – and then ended as they proceeded on their separate ways. Although political economists sought to reapprehend the relationship between the life of nature and that of humans in order to retain the category of nature, and nativists tried to naturalize culture in an effort to restore it to a place of primacy, the two were increasingly uncoupled under the new regime. Now the various events making up daily life – food, drink, copulation, birth, death – were denatured and separated from the conception of a whole and integrated life to become aspects of a personal life. Existence became compartmentalized and specialized.

Hence the life narrated in late Tokugawa fiction is presented as individual and separate sequences and personal fate. The social for-

---

12 This quotation is from M. M. Bakhtin, *The Dialectic Imagination*, trans. and ed. Michael Holquist and Caryl Emerson (Austin: University of Texas Press, 1981), p. 206.

mation was being differentiated into classes, groups, and specialized constituencies, each conforming to functional scales of value and each possessing its own logic of development. The activities of daily life that concentrated on bodily performance lost their link to common labor and a common social whole; instead, they became private and petty matters on which writers reported as though through a peephole.[13] Contemporaries increasingly saw that peephole as habit or custom and deportment and went to great lengths to classify its range and variety. And yet to discover and categorize it so also presumed a conception of the whole, of society itself, even though the *gesaku* writers consistently apprehended personal affairs as mere particularities that implied no conception of a larger whole or meaning.[14] The impulse to "pierce" the crust of custom necessitated paying close attention to detail. More often than not, tactility, rather than a discernible storyline, was figured as the plot of the narrative and usually told the tale that the author wished to pierce. The absence of any real story in many "narratives" in favor of continuous dialogue about the interaction of things attests less to a diminution of literary standards than to their being in contest. These literary productions of the culture of play managed to convey a sharp dissatisfaction with conventions of narrative closure. Writers seemed convinced that failure to attend to the way that things were arranged, people were dressed, and foods were presented risked losing any chance to penetrate the surface of affairs. Readers were required to recognize differing levels of meaning in order to plumb hidden intentions below the surface. By making the familiar objects that inhabited daily life seem "strange," they persuaded readers to believe that they had been living in a hole, and not the whole, a rut whose very surroundings had obscured a recognition of the way that things really were. The texts (*kokkeibon*, amusing books) of Shikitei Samba (1776–1822) and Jippensha Ikku (1765–1831) offered an endless stream of snapshots of the most mundane, familiar, and trivial activities that townsmen encountered in their daily life and on the road. But by rearranging them so that they appeared unfamiliar, by forcing readers to look at activities that they performed habitually and objects that they took for granted, writers could jar them into seeing custom in a new and different light. Laughter was recognition of the familiar made to appear strange and even alien. The

---

13 Nakamura Yukihiko and Nishiyama Matsunosuke, eds., *Bunka ryōran*, vol. 8 of *Nihon bungaku no rekishi* (Tokyo: Kadokawa, 1967), p. 60; see also Mizuno Tadashi, *Edo shōsetsu ronsō* (Tokyo: Chūō kōronsha, 1974), p. 17; and Nakamura Yukihiko, *Gesakuron* (Tokyo: Kadokawa, 1966), p. 137.   14 Nakamura, *Gesakuron*, p. 137.

world of Ikku's Tōkaidō travelers is peopled by characters who, when they are not about to seduce a maid or slip out of an inn without paying the bill, are preoccupied with farting, soiled loin cloths, and a round of trivial involvement. The conversations that Samba records in barbershop and bathhouse relate to the most mundane affairs in the daily life of readers who now see and hear themselves speaking. Both writers emphasize the details and particularity of life in conversation or movement, such as eating, bathing, drinking, burping, and farting, in which the readers recognized their quotidian existence. Even in the more solemn historical romances of Bakin or the books of emotion (*ninjōbon*) which were preoccupied with the trials of love, the effect was to confront the reader with the familiar in an entirely different context. Bakin's explorations into the grotesque and fantastic in the well-known *Nansō Satomi hakkenden,* for example, concern a dog who performs a meritorious act of loyalty and then demands the reward, which happens to be the daughter of his feudal lord. And Ryūtei Tanehiko's *Nise Murasaki inaka Genji monogatari* retells the Genji story in a different historical setting and projects contemporary custom and speech into the fifteenth century. At another level it still remained the world of the shogun Ienari, now identified with a familiar exemplar of corruption in the past.

Although the focus on the body as a maker and consumer of things emphasized the parts, it ultimately drew attention to the idea of a whole and a conceptualization of the social order, but in terms that were new and different from the officially sanctioned version. Bodily imagery in both verbal and illustrated texts signified a different kind of social reality with an inverted scale of priorities for the Edo townsmen. It was an order that had as its head the genitalia or anus and as its heart the stomach. Often, verbal fictions described the body, with its mouth and arms as a devouring, consuming totality; humans appeared as bodies that related to the world through their orifices rather than through public duties demanded by fixed social status and disciplined intention. Moreover, the body's needs were never satisfied and never completed; people continued to eat, drink, speak, make love, and evacuate ceaselessly without any prospect of an end. To portray the infinite details involved in partying, with its random arrangement of empty cups, vomit, and half-filled bottles the morning after, or to pay close attention to foods, eating, and the accompanying conversation – all recognizable as appropriate subjects (not objects) for representation – dramatized a world of activity and things that no longer referred to anything outside it. Tokugawa verbal fiction and woodblock illustrations enforced a new awareness of a world that people had habitually placed in the background by repositioning it in the foreground of represented experience. It also offered human alternatives to the world of public or official ideology. To the demands of the heavenly way (*tendō*), often satirized by writers, it provided space for play, laughter, and passion in anatomical representation, a veritable people's utopia, an arcadia of flesh, joy, and pain experienced by the body, a ceaseless delight that came from endless consumption and to the discharge of waste. In this regard, late Tokugawa fiction appropriated the common and customary to work on the dominant ideology in order to make it appear unfamiliar and to recast the somber requirements of official expectation within the world of play. By using immediate experience as its subject and making people aware of their daily lives and surroundings, writers were able to transform the quotidian experience into a system of knowledge that even the most common could possess and master. In this way, verbal fiction and the illustrator's art made the body into a text and reading an act of consuming knowledge.

Finally, the mass readership of late Tokugawa times was far more interested in identifying and recognizing contemporary custom than in retrieving ethical lessons from a history that, according to one authority, probably assaulted their sensibilities.[15] Early-nineteenth-century writers like Samba and Tamenaga Shunsui, for example, wrote with an eye for details and nuances of contemporary life among the different quarters of Edo. Their production of *gesaku* helped define the conception of a coherent social world signifying changing conditions propelled by the constant interaction of humans, making and consuming, even though it consistently opposed the part to the whole. The early-nineteenth-century kabuki playwright Tsuruya Namboku portrayed what he called a "world" (*sekai*) bounded by "living custom" (*kizewa*). But Tsuruya's world, often darkened by violence, bloodshed, and conflict, was still nothing more than a reminder that social life was the stage on which contemporaries acted out their encounter with custom. This increasing identification of the culture of play and the world of theater with society – life following art – was noted by contemporaries who could agree that "its plot resembles the puppet theater" and that "its world is like the kabuki."[16]

15 Sugiura Mimpei, *Ishin zenya no bungaku* (Tokyo: Iwanami shoten, 1967), pp. 3–22.
16 Quoted in Maeda Ichirō, ed., *Kōza Nihon bunkashi* (Tokyo: Misuzu shobō, 1971), vol. 6, p. 121.

THE PLAY OF CULTURE

There were contemporary moralists and thinkers like Buyō Inshi (?–?) and Shiba Kōkan (1747–1818) who alerted their contemporaries to the dangers inherent in conceptions of society grounded in play and enjoyment inspired by the world of theater. This new social criticism brought about a conceptualization of the whole, called *seken* or *seji*, that was able to accommodate the differentiation and fragmentation of life proclaimed by the culture of play. Whether such critics were openly opposed to contemporary social life (Buyō Inshi), saw in laughter a problem and not its solution (Hirata Atsutane), or envisaged a new set of arrangements conforming to the changes that had taken place since the middle of the eighteenth century (Shiba Kōkan), they believed that the culture of play had exhausted its productivity and imperiled the prospect of maintaining a stable public order. All seemed to agree on the necessity of restoring a conception of the social whole to counteract the baneful effects of the progressive particularization and privatization of life, but it was more difficult to reach a consensus on how the whole should be reconstituted. What concerned the critics most was the way that "custom" was generating new combinations of social relationships and eroding the older guarantees of solidarity. Buyō Inshi charged that the changes noted in his narrative of contemporary history (*Seji kemmonroku*, 1816) would inevitably undermine the political order by persuading people to turn away from their public duties for the private pleasures of the body.[17] Shiba Kōkan's *Shumparō hikki* (1818), a lasting testament to contemporary changes in its recording of an excursion to the south, condemned the widespread prevalence of private desire less as evidence of moral bankruptcy than of insufficient knowledge, which made unknowing people vulnerable to the temptations of self-indulgence.[18] Nobody would deny that changes in society had uncoupled the fixed relationship between culture as self-understanding and political purpose. Yet the resolution of the crisis, many believed, required a systematic effort to reconstitute society's self-understanding in such a way as to make it possible again to realign the various parts with a whole capable of instituting public order. Critics like Buyō Inshi looked to the seven-

17 Buyō Inshi, "Seji kemmonroku," in *Nihon shomin seikatsu shiryō shūsei* (Tokyo: Misuzu shobō, 1969), vol. 8, p. 656. See also Aoki Michio, *Tempō sōdōki* (Tokyo: Sanseidō, 1979), pp. 1–9, for a useful account of Buyō's jeremiad, as well as Sugiura, *Ishin zen'ya no bungaku*, pp. 23–46.
18 Shiba Kōkan, *Shumparō hikki*, in *Nihon zuihitsu hikki* (Tokyo: Yoshikawa kōbunkan, 1936), vol. 1, pp. 404ff., 435.

teenth century and to the even more remote past to find models for the present, whereas others, like Shiba, trained their sights elsewhere and began to envisage new possibilities for the eventual reunion of politics and culture.

The specific grievance that agitated many critics was that the relentless pursuit of private desire fed the process of fragmenting interests and blinded people to the necessity of collective purpose. Everywhere people seemed to be turning inward to satisfy private desires and human needs. Yet such behavior constituted a public act, for self-understanding came to mean self-indulgence. The crisis of self-identity underscored the need to find new forms of knowing and understanding that could offer meaning in the new social environment without compromising the chance for order and stability. Any reconsideration of knowledge would have to account for the vast transformations that had taken place in Japanese society since the middle of the eighteenth century, transformations that had been noisily announced by the culture of play: the discovery and valorization of daily life, the common world of things and objects, the particularity of experience, the dehistoricization of the present, the ceaseless obsession with the body, and the possibility of constituting subjects for knowledge. What ensued in the late Tokugawa period was a play of culture, which entailed finding the means to represent stable forms of identity and meaning in discourse and a coherent voice. Although social critics like Buyō Inshi and Shiba Kōkan grasped the importance of knowledge for a resolution of the crisis of identity, they differed widely over its content. Predictably, Buyō called for a return to proper moral knowledge as a sure antidote to the "bad knowledge" of townsmen, but this meant excluding commoners as knowers in order to recast them in the role of the ruled and make the present look like the past again. By contrast, from his study of Western painting, Shiba favored a concept of empirical investigation based on the plurality of perspectives in viewing an object in order to open the way for new principles of the organization of knowledge and society. Shiba's promotion of perspective offered the prospect of making knowledge accessible to any group or person.[19]

What this play of culture inspired was a broad search for new forms of knowledge adequate to explain to certain groups the spectacle of surplus and why the social image of the past no longer applied to the early nineteenth century. Once these new forms of knowledge were

19 Shiba, *Shunparō hikki*, p. 444; also Numata Jirō, Matsumura Akira, and Satō Shōsuke, eds., *Nihon shisō taikei*, vol. 64: (1) *Yōgaku* (Tokyo: Iwanami shoten, 1976), pp. 449, 484–5.

structured, they would be able to authorize the establishment of cultural constituencies and the representation of interests and claims that had hitherto not been granted entry into official discourse. Yet almost simultaneously these new configurations sought to find political forms consistent with the content of culture that they wished to designate. The play of culture differed significantly from the culture of play in just this capacity to envisage stable or permanent political forms consonant with the new cultural constituencies. This coupling of culture and politics was mandated, and even accelerated, by the apparently rapid deterioration of domestic order and the appearance everywhere of events that seemed to signify the inevitability of decline. Catastrophic events like violent and unseasonable rains throughout the Kantō area and elsewhere, earthquakes in Echigo and Dewa (1833), urban "trashings" (*uchikowashi*), and widespread peasant rebellions were taken as signs of uncontrollable and unmanageable disintegration. Prevailing political forms seemed inadequate to prevent disorder and to provide assistance, relief, tranquility, and the semblance of safety to needy peasants. It was within this framework that the foreign intrusion, which had already begun at the turn of the century, was added as one more sign confirming the generally held belief that the realm was doomed. Thus whereas groups sought to represent knowledge of themselves in the will to form discourses, the new discourses invariably sought correspondences between culture and politics. A good deal of this activity was poured into efforts to stem disorder and to provide relief, security, and assistance. Virtually all of the new discourses of the late Tokugawa period – Mitogaku (Mito learning), national learning, Western learning, and the new religions – tried to unite a conception of culture with politics. This impulse is surely reflected in the Mito identification of ceremony and polity, in nativist conceptions of *matsurigoto* (government as ceremony), the emphasis of the new religions on a community of believers free from hierarchy, and Western learning's formulations of science and morality. Moreover, when these new discourses spoke to vital issues of order and security, relief and assistance, equality and fairness, they were pressing not only a claim to represent interests constituted as knowledge but also the right to speak on questions directly affecting their constituencies. Gradually their "business," their interest, became society's business, just as their conception of culture and political organization became a substitute for the social formation as a whole. The claim of right to participate in and resolve problems of common concern, which meant survival, order, and defense, became the condition for creating a public realm in late Tokugawa society.

The new claims were often rooted in questions of productivity and security. When they were, groups were inadvertently led to challenge the authority of Tokugawa society, whether it was invested in the shogunal arrangement of power or in principles of a natural order of legitimacy. Such acts invariably resulted in defection from the center, the Tokugawa polity, at a time when authorities were finding it difficult to meet their own responsibilities and satisfy demands for "order" and "relief." Such withdrawals to the periphery were usually prompted by the conviction that if the Tokugawa structure could not live up to its obligations, then the groups would have to take care of themselves. Thus what appeared from the 1830s onwards was a progressive retreat from the center to the periphery, not as explicit acts of revolutionary sedition, but as an expression of diminishing confidence in the system's ability to fulfill its moral duties. The new cultural disciplines provided justification for groups to perform for themselves tasks that the Tokugawa polity was now unable to perform. This required the formation of voluntary associations, some of which ultimately flew in the face of a conception of a natural order that defined groups according to their natural and expected function. The occasion for this massive impulse to secede was provided by the way that contemporary history was grasped by those who acted to arm themselves with self-definition. The move to emphasize the production of wealth, the centrality of daily affairs, the importance of the communal unity for nativist thought and new religions, and the widespread concern of all groups with aid and relief, mutual assistance, equality in the distribution of resources, along with talent, ability, and utility did not so much "reflect" the conditions of *bakumatsu* as "interpret" such facts and events. Ultimately all these new cultural discourses sought to merge with power that knowledge based on principles of inclusion and exclusion of both objects and people. To appeal to new forms of knowledge that different groups could know meant talking about different conceptions of power. Each of these groups saw itself and its response to contemporary problems as a solution to the social, and imagined that the part that it represented was a substitute for the unenvisaged whole. The proper kind of knowledge, it was believed, would lead to a solution of the problems agitating society. All assumed that a decision on one part would disclose the shape of the whole. Hence Mito turned to the primacy of the autonomous domain sanctioned by the national polity (*kokutai*); *kokugaku* (national learning) concentrated on the self-sufficient village authenticated by its relation to the primal creation deities; *yōgaku* (Western learning) celebrated a crude form of the mercantilist state, propelled by virtue and science; and the new religions announced the establishment of new forms of sacred communalism in their effort to give permanence to a conception of epiphany and the liminal moment.

All of these new discourses were formulated in the early nineteenth century. All aimed to understand the world anew and lessen its problems by offering solutions. Yet they contributed as much to *bakumatsu* problems as they did to their resolution. They all were generated by a will to knowledge that masked more fundamental considerations of power. Every manifestation of how the new discourse sought to fix rules of formation and discipline disclosed an accompanying and almost obligatory concern for the foundations of knowledge and learning. Every discussion of the status of knowledge and learning inevitably raised questions concerning the identity of the knowers and what should be known.

GOOD DOCTRINE AND GOVERNANCE

The problem of defining cultural context and finding an adequate political form for it was engaged first by a generation of samurai intellectuals from the Mito domain (Fujita Yūkoku, his son Tōko, Aizawa Seishisai, Toyoda Tenkō, the daimyo Tokugawa Nariaki) and their spiritual associates, Ōhashi Totsuan, Yoshida Shōin, and Maki Izumi. As early as the late eighteenth century, Mito writers began to search systematically for ways to enunciate a program of practical discipline and education. Mito had long been the center of an ambitious historiographical project, the *Dai Nihon shi*, a lightning rod for serious-minded philosophic speculation in the Neo-Confucian mode. But there was a difference, if not a break, in intellectual continuity, between the meditations of the so-called early Mito scholars and the discourse of the latter Mito school.[20] Whereas the early Mito writers clung closely to a rather formal Neo-Confucianism, the later thinkers selected a syncretic position that mixed parts of Neo-Confucianism, nativist religious, and mythic elements to produce a comprehensive statement very different in structure and purpose from what had gone before. Politically, Mito was one of the three collateral houses of the

20 Bitō Masahide, "Mito no tokushitsu," in Imai Usaburō, Seya Yoshihiko, and Bito Masahide, eds., *Nihon shisō taikei*, vol. 53: *Mitogaku* (Tokyo: Iwanami shoten, 1973), p. 561. Hereafter cited as *Mitogaku*.

Tokugawa family and thus occupied a relatively privileged position near the center of power. But in economic terms, Mito, like so many domains in the late eighteenth and early nineteenth century, encountered problems that seemed to resist conventional solutions. Fujita Yūkoku (1774–1826), a middle-ranking retainer trained in the Mito historiographical bureau, called attention to the diminishing domainal financial resources and the consequences for people and government. His student Aizawa Seishisai (1781–1863) later specified the cause of the contemporary "crisis" when he proposed that it had stemmed from the decision to move the samurai off the land into towns and the consequent growth of the use of money and the dependence on the market. Mito writers were especially concerned with the economic impact of these changes on the ruling class, who had incurred deep indebtedness to meet daily expenses, as they adopted luxurious lifestyles inspired by the pursuit of private interests. What worried the critics was the way that these changes seemed to have affected agricultural productivity and contributed to the growing power of merchants and moneylenders who benefited from the samurai's need for cash.[21] Yet they were no less sensitive to the recurrence of famines and other natural disasters that undermined agricultural production. Both samurai and peasants suffered from the hardships caused by such events. Taxes were relatively high in Mito, Yūkoku noted in his *Kannō wakumon*, and the population had decreased steadily since the middle years of the century.

These developments were not unique or even exceptional for the times, but the Mito writers interpreted them as signs of impending disintegration. Yūkoku complained that a fondness for money and usury had already led to a number of disrupting abuses in the domain. The most serious by far in his inventory was the growing frequency of peasant rebellions. Here, he advised the leadership to take stock of its responsibilities to rule "virtuously." Instead of relying on laws and ordinances, always a sign of slackening control, it was necessary to promote a leadership skilled in the art of governance. In the context of the late eighteenth century, what this meant was a redefinition of virtue into practicality, and the training of administrators who would be able to understand the requirements of the times. Years later, Aizawa expressed grave misgivings regarding the invasion of gamblers

---

21 J. Victor Koschmann, "Discourse in Action: Representational Politics in the Late Tokugawa Period," Ph.D. diss., University of Chicago, 1980, p. 30. Published as *The Mito Ideology: Discourse, Reform, and Innovation in Late Tokugawa Japan, 1790–1864* (Berkeley and Los Angeles: University of California Press, 1987).

and idlers into Mito and saw their presence as a manifestation of moral decay. He concluded that such unwanted guests had been permitted to enter the domain because of administrative laxity and ignorance concerning the way that they could corrupt village morals and encourage peasants to abandon work for drink, gambling, and expensive foods. Underlying this was the belief that ordinary people naturally loved profit and were eager to pursue private interest whenever they were given the slightest opportunity. Aizawa also feared the influence of new religions like the Fuji cult (Fujikō), which had recently established itself in Mito and was beginning to recruit large numbers of followers among the peasantry.[22] But he reserved his harshest judgment for Christianity, a "cruel and unjust religion," which won over the minds of ignorant people and diverted them from the path of moral rectitude.

The Mito writers were convinced that the problems threatening domain integrity resulted from inadequate leadership. If the masses lost their way, it was because the managerial class had abdicated its responsibilities to provide moral examples.[23] Fujita Tōko (1806–55) lamented that the way of loyalty and filiality had disappeared. Order could be restored by clarifying these principles once more and redirecting the rulers to govern the realm properly. Yet, he noted, this would require an understanding of the part and the whole, between the leader and the people, the domain and the realm.

The sanction for the Mito effort to resolve the contemporary crisis lay in the reunification of learning and doctrine. Writers like Fujita Yūkoku argued the necessity of knowing how to rectify names (*seimeiron*) and straightening the arrangement of duties so that name would correspond to responsibility (*meibunron*). In the rectification of names he saw the general problem of social decay as a failure of representation in language. In this Yūkoku shared the assumptions of an eighteenth-century discourse that had already drawn attention to the problematic relation between words and the things they were supposed to denote. Because names and status no longer conformed to reality, it seemed imperative to realign name to truth.[24] A realignment along these lines made possible by language itself promised to retrieve the archetypical way of loyalty and filiality. According to Yūkoku,

In the realm, there are lords and retainers, and there are the upper and lower orders. If the designations of lords and retainers are not corrected, the divi-

[22] "Shinron," in *Mitogaku*, p. 105. *Shinron* has been translated by Bob Tadashi Wakabayashi in *Anti-Foreignism and Western Learning in Early-Modern Japan* (Cambridge, Mass.: Harvard University Press, 1986).   [23] Koschmann, "Discourse in Action," p. 34.
[24] "Seimeiron," in *Mitogaku*, p. 10.

sion between the aristocratic and nonaristocratic classes will blur, and distinctions between the upper and lower orders will vanish. The strong will come to despise the weak and the masses will be thrown into confusion and disorder.[25]

His son Tōkō went even further when, following the lead of contemporary nativists, he noted that even though in ancient times the Way had no name by which it was known, everybody naturally knew and understood its requirements. Although writing did not exist in that remote age, the meaning of the Way was conveyed through song and poetry (a point made earlier by Kamo Mabuchi in the *Kokuikō*), in manners, custom, deportment, education, and government. Yet when the effort was finally made to express the Way in written texts, its "true and original nature suffered."[26] Both writers believed that rescuing the Way in language in their times was the supreme duty of leadership and the first principle of education. The Mito conception of the Way differed from the more established Neo-Confucian view of the conviction that the Way could not be found in nature but only through human effort, a proposal they shared with the eighteenth-century philosopher Ogyū Sorai. Victor Koschmann has argued, in this connection, that " . . . representation . . . means precisely the objectification of the 'natural' state (the Way of heaven, unity between Heaven and Earth) through some form of 'unnatural' (linguistic, instrumental, demonstrative) action. The object to be represented through human mediation is Heaven itself, not a temporary arrangement."[27]

By calling attention to the operation of rectification and designation, the Mito writers were able to demonstrate the primacy of the domain as an adequate space for the realization of the necessary alignments. Much of their formulation was powered by a strategy that reduced the parts to an essential and original whole, to the primal origins of the realm as expressed in the term *kokutai* (national polity or body). *Kokutai* was identified as the whole for which the parts stood. For the Mito writers, the concept represented the indissoluble link between status and loyal behavior (*chūkō no michi*) and the corresponding network of designations and duties. It was their intention to show how the realignment of name and duty could again be implemented in the domain and how, in fact, the appeal to *kokutai* mandated the resuscitation of the domain along such lines. To argue in this fashion was to propose that a morally reconstituted domain serve as a substitute for the whole. This was surely the meaning of Yūkoku's enunciation, in

---

25 Takasu Yoshijirō, ed., *Mitogaku taikei* (Tokyo: Mitogaku taikei kankōkai, 1941), vol. 3, p. 382.   26 Koschmann, "Discourse in Action," p. 52.   27 Ibid., p. 61.

his *Seimeiron*, of the vertical ties of loyalty that stretched from the emperor down through the lower orders. But it is also evident that the lynchpin in this hierarchical chain was the domainal lord. "How can we strengthen the rectification of duties and designation," Yūkoku asked rhetorically, "How is the country of the bakufu to be governed today? . . . At the top we live under the heavenly descendants, and at the bottom we are tended by the various lords."[28]

With this strategy, the Mito writers were in a position to interpret the events they encountered in the early nineteenth century and make reality appear less problematic. They moved along a rather broad arc whose terminal points were marked by a profound distrust of the people and a moral sense of benevolence and compassion for them. Among the recurring anxieties expressed in their writings, none seemed more urgent and frightening than the prospect of imminent mass disorders in a countryside affected by foreign intrusion and, by implication, the incapacity of the Tokugawa bakufu to stem the swelling threat of mass civil disorder. The growing incidence of peasant rebellions since the late eighteenth century, they believed, related to the disabled status of the domain itself and reflected a widespread agreement that the general administrative machinery no longer functioned properly. Mito writers regularly complained that the shogunate had departed from its earlier role as the largest domain among equals to pursue policies deliberately designed to undermine the military and financial autonomy of its peers. By the end of the eighteenth century it was clear that these policies had made the domains more dependent on the bakufu. Resolving the domains' declining status required persuading the bakufu to accept a less exalted position in the arrangement of authority. But this move was prefigured by the Mito insistence on rectifying names, duties, and designations as a necessary condition for the moral realignment of the system. If the bakufu fulfilled the expectations associated with its name, it would cease acting in a self-interested manner.

Once the relationship between shogunate and domains was rectified, it would be possible to turn to the problem of the ruled. People can be governed, Aizawa announced, only when rulers rely on the Way of loyalty and filiality. This proposition was not based simply on a dim view of human nature – most members of the managerial class in Tokugawa Japan held that as an article of faith – but on a more complex conviction that because an agricultural population was neces-

---

28 Takasu, *Mitogaku taikei*, vol. 3, p. 388.

sary to the survival and welfare of order, it must be made to acknowledge its duty to produce as a moral trust. This was also what Fujita Yūkoku had meant when he proposed that "people are the basis of the realm. If they constitute a firm foundation, then the realm will also be stable."[29] Aizawa, who constantly referred to the people in uncomplimentary terms, believed that because they were predictably disorderly and forever prevented from acquiring the niceties of virtue, they were capable only of being led. But leading the people meant making sure they produced. "People properly should rely . . . on rules; they should not know them."[30]

Under the sanction of this conception of privilege, the Mito writers directed their rhetoric toward explaining the reasons that the people were "naturally" excluded from having knowledge and why they had to be ruled, which meant work. If the ordinary folk were left to their own devices and were not persuaded to perform their proper duties, Aizawa explained, they would act like children and pursue profit, pleasure, and personal luxury at every opportunity. The possession of knowledge entitled a few to rule and required the many to follow. Neither the exercise of coercion nor the accumulation of wealth was equivalent to knowledge as conditions for rulership. Those who "should not know" must always depend on the informed guidance of those who "know." This conception of knowing and knowers prompted the Mito writers to look harshly on all religions organized to enlist the people, because their doctrines invariably promoted forms of nonexclusionary knowledge accessible to all. Fujita Tōko declared rather excitedly in his commentary on the establishment of an academy in Mito (*Kōdōkanki jutsugi*) that heretical doctrines continue to "delude the people" and "bewilder the world." As a result, he discerned a causal relationship between the slackening of belief in the true Way and the dissolution of ties of dependence, currently reflected in the incidence of peasant uprisings. Yet he was convinced that these disturbances were only manifestations of new forms of knowledge that actually confused and confounded the people to embark on a course of disorderly conduct.

Hence, the Mito writers viewed disturbances as expressions of private interest encouraged by new opportunities for the pursuit of self-indulgence and new religious doctrines promising rewards to all. To offset such threats they recommended the establishment of a regime devoted to benevolence and compassion and advised the leadership to "love" and "revere" the people. Once love and reverence were actual-

---

29 Takasu, *Mitogaku taikei*, vol. 3, p. 179.   30 "Shinron," in *Mitogaku*, p. 147.

ized in concrete measures, they believed, the fears of the managerial class would diminish, and the incidence of "unhappiness" in the countryside would disappear. Despite Aizawa's scarcely concealed contempt for "mean people," he remarked that "loving the people" required hard commitments from the leadership. He believed with his teacher Yūkoku, who had earlier called for a program promoting people's welfare, in "assisting the weak and restraining the strong, fostering the old and loving the young, prohibiting laziness and idleness. . . ."[31] He sided with Tokugawa Nariaki who, upon becoming lord of Mito in 1829, announced the promise of a reform reflecting the leadership's duty to love and provide care for the people. "Virtue is the root," Nariaki declared, "commodities the branch"; a virtuous leadership cannot "avoid bestowing blessings on the people."

The issue that the Mito writers sought to resolve was how to increase productivity and exercise greater control. The "good teachings" of etiquette and civilization, which Aizawa believed only the leadership could know, were guarantees of permanent order and wealth. By equating the status ethic and its proper discrimination throughout the domain with "loving the people," the Mito thinkers could argue that if leadership "bestowed proper blessings upon the people," the realm would administer itself. Yet if the rulers abandoned "good doctrine," the people would, according to Tōko, "Avoid political laws as one avoids an enemy. Their yearning will be like that of a child for a mother's affection." When people are not under moral control, Tōko noted, recalling Ōshio's recent rebellion in Osaka in 1837, they will resemble a "product that first putrefies and then gives way to worms and maggots. People who are heretical are similar to those who are ill. Men who govern the sick will first promote their health; men who expel heresy will first cultivate the Great Way." Nariaki and later observers continued to assert that if the "peasantry bears a grudge or resents the upper class, it will not stand in awe of them." Control required providing assistance which, in this context, referred to restoring order in the Mito domain. "If we succeed in exhausting our intentions day and night to return the blessings, we will be able to sympathize with all our hearts. . . ." But control, through the blessing of conferring assistance and relief, required returning people to the land and increasing their productive labor. Earlier, Fujita Yūkoku had outlined a program for "enriching the domain" in *Kannō wakumon*, and in the late 1830s Nariaki and Tōko worked out a comprehensive

---

31 Takasu, *Mitogaku taikei*, vol. 3, p. 179.

land policy that included a land survey, a realignment of tax quotas, greater efforts for empathy to draw peasants and local officials more closely together, a study of new agricultural techniques, and, not least important, a recall of samurai from Edo back to Mito. This last plank, which announced the domain's intention to withdraw from the center for a reliance on its resources in the periphery, was more than enough to disturb large numbers of retainers who had become accustomed to city life.

The lord of Mito thought that the times were ripe for a "restoration of the domain" (*kokka o chūkōshi*) in the 1830s and a "renovation of custom for the unification of all." The purpose of the economic and educational reforms Nariaki announced in the late 1830s was to halt the fragmentation of social life that had spread throughout the domain. Fragmentation referred to "evil customs," and its elimination required economic and educational renovation. Aizawa had already indicated in *Shinron* (1825) that as loyalty and filiality become one, "the education of the people and the refinement of custom is accomplished without a word being spoken. Worship becomes government, and government has the effect of education. Thus, there is no essential difference between government and the indoctrination of the people."[32] This sense of unification, realized through identifying teaching and doctrine, became the special task of the academy in Mito, the Kōdōkan, whose task was to instruct samurai and commoners (through a network of village schools) in how to "refine custom" and reinstate proper morality. Tōko's commentary emphasized this sense of union in neat slogans designed to remove differences to reach the underlying similitude of all things: "the unification of Shinto and Confucianism," "the inseparability of loyalty and filiality," "*sonnō jōi*" (revering the emperor, expelling the barbarian, a term first coined in the proclamation establishing the school; it meant renovating the domestic system in order to be able to withstand external interference), "the union of military arts and civilian skills," and the "indivisibility of learning and practice." The purpose of the school was to reunify doctrine and government, which had become distinct in the course of the long peace. Duties and designation had to be reunited, and custom brought into line with morality.

Following Yūkoku and Aizawa, Nariaki used language that called attention to the basis, as against the unessential. The solution to the contemporary problem was to return to essentials. This meant reapplying the classic injunction of the "great learning": "The base of the

---

32 "Shinron," in *Mitogaku*, p. 56.

realm is the family; the foundation of the family is moral discipline," to the domain itself. In tightening moral relationships the domain was required to embark on far-reaching reforms in "custom" and "military preparedness." Aizawa observed in *Shinron* that a long peace had resulted in extravagant customs, indulgent lords, and the "bitterness of the poor," and Nariaki noted in his *Kokushiden* that

> with a tranquil realm we can never forget about rebellion . . . we have forgotten about the thick blessings that have been bestowed by peace today . . . and we have been concerned only with being well fed and well clad. The samurai have become effeminate and resemble a body that contracts with illness after exposure to cold, wind, or heat. They are idlers and wastrels among the four classes.[33]

In this way the Mito discourse came to see in the domainal space the only prospect for a genuine restoration. Toyoda Tenkō, in an essay composed along restorationist lines in 1833, wrote that even though the "ancients wrote that 'a restoration is always difficult to accomplish,' it must be even more difficult to do so today."[34] Yet he was convinced that the time and place were right. The ancients had linked the achievement of a restoration to the successful termination of a rebellion, but Tenkō saw the recent decline of the domain as equivalent to embarking on the difficult task. The logic for this conception of restoration had been powerfully articulated by Yūkoku in the late eighteenth century and was eloquently restated by Aizawa, who saw in the moment an opportunity that comes only once in a thousand years. Aizawa's proposals were propelled by his belief that the bakufu had willfully followed a policy of self-interest, in which the base had been strengthened at cost to the branches.[35] Aizawa charged that this represented a distortion of Ieyasu's original intention. Ieyasu had strengthened the center and weakened the periphery in order to head off rebellion and anarchy. He had done this by assembling the warriors in the cities, where their stipends were weakened, and by sheltering the people from a military presence.[36] "The military were lessened, and the masses were made into fools." But Aizawa believed that the time had now come to reverse this policy and to strengthen both the base as well as the ends by "nourishing" and "strengthening" the lords.[37] If the lords were permitted to play the role originally designated to them by the emperor, Yūkoku had asserted earlier, they could turn to the task of rectifying their own domains. Though he acknowledged the

---

33 "Kokushiden," in *Mitogaku*, p. 211.   34 "Chūkō shinsho," in *Mitogaku*, p. 197.
35 "Shinron," in *Mitogaku*, p. 73.   36 Ibid., pp. 73–4.   37 Ibid., p. 78.

overlordship of the Tokugawa shogun, Aizawa wrote in the *Tekii hen* that there was a reciprocal relationship between lord and subject. The vertical relationships outlined by Yūkoku thus gained new force in the context of domain reform in the formulations of Aizawa and Nariaki. The shogun should assist the court and govern the realm, just as local leaders should support the emperor and obey the bakufu's decrees in their provinces. But "the people who obey the commands of the daimyo are in effect obeying the decrees of the Bakufu."[38] Because the bakufu was limited by the court, it had not absolute authority over the Mito domain. What this meant for Mito ideologues was the elevation of the domain and the virtual reversal of the base–ends metaphor.

The intellectual sanction for this new edifice envisaged in the Mito discourse was the identification of the whole in a mystical body called *kokutai*. Elaboration of this seminal idea was provided chiefly by Aizawa in his *Shinron*. This construct was universal and absolute, but it could mobilize the rich tradition of Japanese mythohistory.

The heavenly ancestors introduced the way of the gods and they have established doctrine; by clarifying loyalty and filial piety they began human history. These duties were ultimately transferred to the first sovereign and they have since served the great foundation of the state. The emperor joined these divine ordinances to his own body.[39]

Just as the emperor looked up to the virtue of the heavenly descendants, Aizawa continued, so the people received in their bodies the heart of their ancestors and respected and served the emperor for an eternity. When the emperor receives the will of their ancestors, there can be no change in history. Similarly, the emperor himself, worshipping his ancestor the sun goddess, has realized the principle of filial piety and reveals this obligation to the people. Because the principle of loyalty and filiality had existed without needing to be articulated, daily practice – the practice of the body – signified the inseparability of worship, ceremony, and governance.

Such an ideal had always been represented in ritual. In the first book of the *Shinron*, Aizawa discussed how ancient rulers displayed filiality by carrying out worship at ancestral tombs and in performing the solemn ceremonies and rites.[40] The most important of these rituals was the *daijōsai*, the great food-offering ritual performed by each new emperor at the time of the first harvest after his succession. The rite

---

38 Koschmann, "Discourse in Action," p. 171; also Masao Maruyama, *Studies in the Intellectual History of Tokugawa Japan*, trans. Mikiso Hane (Princeton, N.J.: Princeton University Press, 1974), p. 305.   39 Koschmann, "Discourse in Action," p. 79.
40 "Shinron," in *Mitogaku*, pp. 81 ff.

consisted of offering new grain to the sun goddess (Amaterasu), but the significance of the ritual was its reiteration of archetypal themes such as the divine creation of the land and the benevolence of Amaterasu toward her people. Aizawa noted that in the actual ritual, subject and sovereign experience the presence of Amaterasu and ultimately "feel like descendants of the gods." For a moment, history is frozen; past flows into present; and the great principles of loyalty and filiality – dramatized by the exchange between sovereign, who presents the divine progenitor with riches she has made possible, and her subjects, who must return the "blessings" – are represented as timeless and universal norms. By invoking the example of this great ritual, Aizawa was able to show how mere history, a record of changing circumstances, differed from timeless truths reaching back to mythical origins. The *daijōsai* annuls history; the primal moment restores to each participant presence and self-identity. The ceremony should unify sovereign, subject, and descendants and thus dissolve the division between governance and worship. "If the whole country reveres the heavenly deities, then all will know how to respect the emperor." If civilization in Japan was to withstand the erosion of history, it was important for the people to know how to express respect as represented in ritual. The present was the appointed time, a unique opportunity, Aizawa said, "to inform the people of this principle and purify the public spirit." When this great enterprise had been accomplished, "past will be united to present," sovereign to people.

In this manner the essential national body, a mystical whole signifying origins and continual presence, validated the domain's claim to restore the great principles of loyalty and filiality. For the Mito writers, the ideal of *kokutai* functioned at several levels. It represented the whole to which the parts – the domains – could relate; it also provided the sanction for the domain, pledged to reinstate the timeless principles, to act as a substitute for the whole. *Kokutai* served to remind every generation of the essential beginnings from which all things had come and to which all things are reduced. This is surely what the Mito writers meant when they advised contemporaries "not to forget about the basis" and to "return the blessing to its origins." What could be more essential than the body of the realm, however shapeless, vague, and mystical, the *karada* (body) of the *kuni* (country)? "What is this body of the country?" Aizawa asked, and he answered, "If countries do not have a body, it cannot be made by men. If a country has no body, how can it be a nation?"[41] Aizawa envisaged

---

41 Ibid., p. 69.

this body as a form that distinguished the idea of a unified realm from chaos. It was his purpose to link the sense of the whole to a new political space represented by the autonomous domain. His actual proposals for reform were unexceptional and echoed Yūkoku's earlier suggestions and Nariaki's later measures. Yet they confirmed the belief in the inseparability of representation and action, learning and practice.

Changes in contemporary history altered the character of the Mito discourse. This is not to say that the Mito writers changed their minds about the veracity of their vision but only to suggest the possibility of varying emphases within the discourse. Whereas in the 1840s, Mito rhetoric was pressed into service to reconstitute the domain through a series of reforms, in the 1850s and 1860s, as the area of political space widened, the reformist impulse came to address national issues and to advocate direct action. Whereas the earlier goals aimed at rebuilding the domain without necessarily affecting the bakufu, the later course of action made the destruction of the shogunate a condition for realizing domainal autonomy. The generation of samurai intellectuals who had been attracted to the Mito discourse in the Tempō period, not to mention the retainers of the domain itself, turned gradually to representing the ideals in the form of direct action calling for a restoration of imperial authority and the destruction of the bakufu. Mito retainers themselves had taken matters into their hands in 1860 when they participated in the assassination of the shogunal counselor Ii Naosuke. Four years later the domain was torn apart by civil war. Yet the theoretical justification for extending representation to include direct action was provided by thinker-activists like Yoshida Shōin, Ōhashi Totsuan, and Maki Izumi. The general outline of this Mito theory of action was propelled by the recognition that in the new political arena of the 1850s, especially after the opening of the country (1854) and the subsequent signing of commercial treaties with Western nations, the bakufu no longer possessed either the authority or the will to speak for the nation as a whole. Such authority resided with the emperor, as the Mito writers had proposed earlier in their discussion of vertical relationships, and it was he who must now lead directly in the great accomplishment of renovation.

Yoshida Shōin (1830–59), a specialist in military instruction in the Chōshū domain, saw the signing of the commercial treaties as the opportunity to dramatize the failure of the bakufu. What he demanded of the shogunate was a domestic order that could withstand foreign contact. He recognized that the bakufu had succumbed to the treaties out of indecision and fear. But the new treaties affected the nation as a whole, not simply the shogunate or the domains. "If problems arise in the territory of the shogun," he wrote at the time, "they must be handled by the shogun; if in the domain of the lord, by the lord."[42] This was fully consistent with the Mito arrangement of authority and its corresponding definition of jurisdiction. The problems facing Japan in 1856–7 were not restricted to the shogun or indeed the lord but involved both because they now related to the security of the imperial land itself. It was the emperor, not the shogun, who had the right to make authoritative decisions concerning foreign demands, because the crisis imperiled all of Japan. "This affair (the signing of the treaties) arose from within the territory of the emperor." Hence, the shogunate had shown not only weakness but had actually committed treason by committing an act of lèse-majesté.

The bakufu had acted willfully and "privately" by agreeing to treaty negotiations. Yoshida proposed that its officials be punished and the institution dismantled for ignoring an imperial decree calling for the immediate expulsion of foreigners. The bakufu had committed a crime of unprecedented magnitude: "It has abjured heaven and earth, angered all the deities . . . it has nourished a national crisis today and bequeathed national shame to future generations. . . . If the imperial decree is honored, the realm will be following the Way. To destroy a traitor is an act of loyalty." To this end Yoshida, in his last years (he was a casualty of the Ansei purge of 1859) worked out a program that would best fulfill the requirements of direct action and loyal behavior. He called for a rising of "grass-roots" heroes, appealing principally to the samurai and independent villagers, willing to leave their homes and perform what he called meritorious deeds.

> If there is no rising of independent patriots, there will be no prosperity. How will these unaffiliated men reinstate the saintly emperor and wise lords? Men who follow my aims and are of my domain must follow this rising. Through the unauthorized power of the rising, small men will be excluded, evil men will be thrown out, and correct and able lords will be able to gain their place.[43]

Yoshida's call for an organization of grass-roots patriots willing to act directly was also the subject of Ōhashi Totsuan's (1816–62) meditation concerning the contemporary situation. Ōhashi, who came from the small domain of Utsunomiya, affiliated with Mito, and was contemplating the possibility for direct action at the same time that Yoshida

---

42 Quoted in H. D. Harootunian, *Toward Restoration* (Berkeley and Los Angeles: University of California Press, 1970), p. 219.   43 Ibid., p. 237.

was seeking to call his own followers to arms against the bakufu. Ōhashi was more consistently committed to classic Neo-Confucian arguments concerning the importance of differentiation between civilization and the barbarism represented by the West. Yet this philosophic conservatism merely elaborated Mito ideas on expulsionism (*jōiron*). Ōhashi's thinking on restoration first favored removing incompetents from high shogunal offices. This effort to rob the bakufu of its top leadership (favored by Yoshida as well) showed the later restorationists how to dramatize the issue of able leadership and also how to paralyze the bakufu. The failure of this tactic later encouraged others to consider raising a small army for an imperial campaign against the shogunate, something that was first suggested by the Satsuma retainer Arima Shinshichi (in 1862) and tried by Maki Izumi a year later. Ōhashi's most explicit statement on restoration appears in a work he completed in 1861 called *Seiken kaifuku hisaku* (A secret policy for a restoration of political authority). The work was written in response to the bakufu's attempt of 1860 to unite court and shogunate by securing Princess Kazu no Miya as the consort of the shogun. His plan sought to extend the culturalism of his earlier writings.

> Since the coming of the foreigner and the expansion of commerce, the Bakufu's position has not been good; it has carried temporizing to extremes, and the arrogance of the barbarians has been rampant . . . Bakufu officials are afraid of them. . . . Even though only one barbarian was permitted to enter in the beginning, now several have pushed their way in. . . . Although trade is not yet three years old, the rising prices of commodities, the exhaustion of domainal resources, and the impoverishment of the lower classes must be viewed as disasters.[44]

Ōhashi was also convinced that the bakufu had systematically undermined the "brave and loyal samurai" of "courageous domains." The only solution, he reasoned, was a call to arms under the "banner of an imperial decree."

Like Yoshida, Ōhashi believed that the decision to take Japan out of the hands of the barbarians belonged to the imperial court. Hence, he declared, all people, out of love of the emperor, lay waiting for the "august movement of the court. . . . As with the booming clap of a thunderous voice, once an imperial decree is promulgated all men must act, since all will be inspired. It will be like the collapse of a dam holding back a lake." Ōhashi believed that the bakufu had violated the strictures of *meibun* and had acted out of contempt of the court. He

---

44 Ibid., p. 270.

was convinced that nine of every ten men were alienated from the Tokugawa exercise of power. "The people of the realm," he urged, "must abandon the Tokugawa before it is too late, deepen their devotion to the imperial court, and move toward a revival of the emperor's power. The time must not be lost."

Ultimately Ōhashi's views on restoration melded into the organization of a small group of plotters – grass-roots heroes, recruited from Mito and Utsunomiya, willing to execute a plan to assassinate the shogunal counselor Andō Nobumasa. The plot was carried out in 1862 and is known as the Sakashitamon incident. Ōhashi saw the assassination as the occasion for both a rising of patriots and the promulgation of an imperial decree condemning the bakufu. Although he played no direct role in the attempted murder (Andō was wounded), he was willing to accept responsibility for his part in its planning.

The failure of Ōhashi's theory of restoration prompted a shift to the second method, that of raising an army of loyalists prepared to embark on an imperial campaign. This method was developed chiefly by the Kurume priest Maki Izumi (1813–64), an enthusiastic follower of the Mito discourse. The locus of activity also shifted from Edo to Kyoto, the site of the imperial court and the emperor. Whereas Ōhashi stressed the more formal Neo-Confucian elements in the Mito discourse, Maki, owing to his Shinto education, emphasized the native mythohistorical dimensions of the discourse. Maki was also critical of the meditative and quietistic tendencies of Neo-Confucianism, which he felt contained little sense of practicality. Neo-Confucianism, like Zen, was too abstract to use in understanding the contemporary situation. It was his intent to replace passivity, meditation, and self-cultivation with direct action.

Maki also plunged into national politics in the early 1860s after spending years in house imprisonment for activities in the Kurume domain. Almost immediately, he began to develop a theory of an imperial restoration to arrest the "unceremonial" behavior of the barbarians and to punish the "effeminacy" of the wavering bakufu. He was convinced that it was the court's duty to seize the initiative and to act. This was the moment, he wrote in 1861, to encourage the emperor to promulgate an expulsionist policy that would announce the restoration of imperial authority. In a letter to a Kyoto courtier, Maki outlined the way to accomplish a restoration: (1) Select talented men for positions of political responsibility; (2) reward men who act for the court with status; and (3) preserve the "great polity of the realm" by "returning to the prosperity of antiquity." Here, Maki brought together two themes – *kokutai* and the heavenly ordinance, both familiar conceptions within the Mito discourse, and pressed them into the task of formulating a new theory of emperor. To see the emperor armed with the moral authority of heaven and the divinity of the national ancestors and personalized by history (a tactic that the Mito writers failed to promote) became the condition for Maki's call for restoration. His theory sought to actualize the Mito conception of representation by calling up the historical characteristics of ancient emperors (although Mito merely summoned the principle, not the principal, of imperial authority) and rescuing the sovereign from his seat "beyond the clouds," as he put it, in order to liberate him from court concealment and return him to the world of politics. He believed that this conception of the emperor, now conforming to hard, concrete elements derived from actual history, corresponded to the requirements of contemporary political reality more closely than to the bland and abstract image envisaged by the Neo-Confucians.[45]

Maki saw the present as the moment in which to implement what he called, in his *Kei-i gusetsu*, a "great enterprise." He later translated the "great enterprise" into an "imperial campaign" against the bakufu. The idea of such an "imperial campaign," pledged to bring about a restoration, was authorized by historical examples. Emperors in the past had satisfied heaven's requirements to act. "Jimmu tenno had erected the great feudal system, established the teachings of Shinto, and unified the public spirit. . . . Temmu tenno expanded the skills in a hundred ways. He planned for the central administration, swept away abuses in the court, established a prefectural system . . ." Ancient imperial precedents showed contemporaries that current conditions necessitated a comparable response, what Maki called the "labor of the august Imperial Body." But completing this act in the present demanded commitment and heroism. In 1860 and 1861 Maki conceived of a plan to organize an imperial campaign aimed at overthrowing the bakufu. In an essay called the *Record of a Great Dream* he argued that the time had arrived for the emperor to exercise direct authority by issuing an edict branding the shogun a traitor and usurper. The edict would also call for an imperial campaign led personally by the emperor from a new base of operations established in the Hakone mountains. There, the emperor would take up residence and assemble shogunal officials for punishment. Next, he would summon the young shogun Iemochi and demand from him the return of former

[45] Matsumoto Sannosuke, *Tennōsei kokka to seiji shisō* (Tokyo: Miraisha, 1969), pp. 72–82.

imperial possessions. Finally, the emperor would enter Edo and seize the shogun's castle, which would become the new imperial capital, and issue a "proclamation announcing a great, new beginning." Because for Maki the whole purpose of the imperial campaign was to destroy the bakufu, he recommended a return to an antiquity before the shogun and military estates had appeared as a model for the present, even though he favored retaining the feudal order in form. As for the composition of the imperial campaign, the *Gikyō sansaku* (1861) advised that the first principle had to be the recruitment of loyal lords. Beyond appealing to feudal lords, Maki also looked to enlisting small guerrilla groups composed of samurai and upper-ranking peasants capable of carrying out lightninglike action. In the end, Maki, together with men from Chōshū, tried to bring about an imperial restoration in 1864 at the Imperial Palace in Kyoto. It was a desperate plan, and it failed. But Maki's concept for restoration was to become a rehearsal for a real and successful performance in 1868. In Maki, the Mito discourse, which had begun with Confucian statecraft for domain reform, had gone on to provide the validation of Shinto mythology for the organization of efforts for nationwide reforms and emperor-central revolution.

THE RESTORATION OF WORSHIP AND WORK

Just as the Mito discourse interpreted contemporary reality in order to establish the "real" and the "appropriate" as justification for the autonomous domain, so the nativists (*kokugakusha*) advanced a theory of the self-sufficient village as the substituted part for the unenvisaged whole. The nativists operated under similar constraints but sought, in contrast with Mito, to represent a different social constituency selected from the rural rich, such as the upper and middle peasantry and village leaders. They also proceeded from the assumption that the vast changes in the content of culture necessitated finding a political form adequate to the transformation. Like the Mito discourse, nativism originated at an earlier time in the late seventeenth century and initially concentrated on resuscitating the landmarks of the Japanese literary and aesthetic tradition. National studies represented an effort to structure what we might call native knowledge and matured under the guidance of scholars like Kamo Mabuchi (1697–1769) and Motoori Norinaga (1730–1801) in the eighteenth century. Toward the end of his life Motoori began to show sensitivity to contemporary conditions and recommended ways of averting social failure. Although he was the most gifted and original practitioner of *kokugaku*, a man whose range of interest was truly prodigious, it was one of his self-styled students, Hirata Atsutane (1776–1843) who virtually transformed the nativist discourse in the late eighteenth and early nineteenth century into a discipline of knowledge addressed to specific interests.

This transformation resulted in a radical shift from poetic studies (which were carried on by Motoori's adopted son and successor Motoori Ōhira) to practical religiosity and a preoccupation with daily affairs. Under Hirata's reformulation, nativism left the cities, where people like Motoori had lectured to wealthy townsmen and samurai, for the countryside, where the message was appropriated and even altered by the rural rich as a response and a solution to the apparent incompetency of the control system to provide security against disorder and assistance to the general peasantry. The immediate target of the peasants' discontent was invariably the village leadership and the rural rich. Thus nativism, as it became a discourse representing the leading elements in the countryside, constituted a break with its original purpose and character. This is not to say that Hirata and his followers abandoned their original tenets. Hirata had started his career as a conventional student of *kokugaku*, and his earliest writings in this idiom concentrated on poetry and aesthetics. Early in the nineteenth century he broke with the main line of *kokugaku* and began to emphasize a different position, but he was still very much dependent on earlier formulators like Kamo Mabuchi and Motoori Norinaga. Hirata tended to give weight and emphasis to ideas and elements in nativist thought that had, in earlier studies, remained recessive. The result was a new mapping of nativism and a plotting of its structure of thought to make it appear different. Hirata's mapping was virtually transformed into a new discipline, the study of the Japanese spirit (*yamatogokoro no gakumon*), whose subject would now be the "ancient Way" (*kodōron*) rather than language and poetry. Later followers like Ōkuni Takamasa (1792–1871) reshaped these new formulations into a systematic field of knowledge that Ōkuni called "basic studies" (*hongaku*) or into a unified doctrine that Yano Gendō (1823–87) referred to as "the study of basic doctrine" (*honkyōgaku*).

Adopted into a family of doctors, Hirata Atsutane appeared on the scene in the late eighteenth century and opened a school in Edo. He claimed to have studied with Motoori, but there is no record that he did. Almost immediately he became known as an outspoken critic of contemporary custom and urban mores. Intemperate to a fault, excitable but self-possessed, Hirata's special targets were scholars of all stripes, but especially Confucians (*bunjin*), whom he identified with writers of verbal fiction, and vulgar Shintoists. In his discussions on the practice of worship (*Tamadasuki*, 1828) he struck hard against contemporary preoccupations with poetic parody, wordplay, and *gesaku* fiction. Thus although he excoriated writers of verbal fiction for confusing people, his own concerns aimed at providing the ordinary folk with more useful instruction. Ordinary people served as both the subject of his lectures and the audience or object. He talked to them about themselves and their daily lives. Texts like the *Ibuki oroshi* and the *Tamadasuki* employed the language of daily speech, often the same idiom found in *gesaku*, and projected a vernacular voice studded with references to both the "ordinary person" (*bonjin*) and to things constituting their world. Yet it was precisely this juxtaposition between the "ordinary" and "extraordinary" (emphasized by Motoori in his discussions of aesthetic sensibility) that Hirata hoped to dramatize in his denunciations of contemporary scholars, poets, and writers. To underline this stance, he rejected the status of scholar for himself, as if by doing so he was cementing his ties to an audience of ordinary street people.

This humble person hates scholars. . . . The scholars of Edo do not devote themselves to bringing people together. Still, the ordinary people are not nauseating. Because it is good to assemble people together, I am fond of this kind of association. If you ask a commoner, he will speak, but ordinarily he does not like (to listen to) a scholarly tale.

Hirata boasted that there were many like himself among the ordinary folk, who simply did not consider themselves as scholars.[46] Specifically, "scholars are noisy fellows who explain the Way. Such people as Confucians, Buddhists, Taoists, Shintoists, and intuitionists broaden a bad list indefinitely. . . . " Scholars feared obeying the "sincerity of august national concern" and avoid "emphasizing the court" in their studies. In the end, Hirata added, they poisoned the people's intention and neglected the emperor. "Even though there is an abundance of men in society who study, what fools they all are!" The reason for this "habit" was that there were simply too many men "who despise the eye and respect the ear." It was far better to study the "words and sayings of men who are nearby, men of our country, rather than the sayings of foreigners or only the deeds expressed by ancient men." Hirata's criticism sought to show that arcane knowledge monopolized by scholars had no relevance to large numbers of people; the immediate was more

---

[46] Haga Noboru, "Edo no bunka," in Hayashiya, ed., *Kasei bunka*, pp. 183 ff.

useful than the mediate, and knowledge of what was "nearby" was prior to what was distant, remote, and foreign.

If Hirata left no doubt of his dislike for contemporary scholars who knew nothing about the present, he saw himself as a man devoted to studying the "true Way" and as one who possessed "extensive knowledge of the truth."[47] He believed that despite the army of erudite scholars inhabiting Edo, most were addicted to the good life, the arcane, and the strange. They all were essentially ignorant of the real goals by which ordinary people lived. His own lectures were first directed to reaching townsmen, but by the 1830s, the rural population. "Men of high rank have leisure time to read a great many books and thus the means to guide people; men of medium rank do not have the time to look at books and do not possess the means to guide people. . . ." Yet the ruled must be offered assistance and the opportunity to hear about the Way, as it was as relevant to those who might not be able to read well as to those who did have leisure time. "I would exchange one man who reads books for one who listens," he announced to his audience, "for those who hear the Way have realized a greater achievement than those who have reached it through reading."[48] Clearly Hirata was claiming the necessity of offering representation of a different kind of knowledge to the merely ordinary – those to whom Motoori had referred as ideal but rarely had specified or tried to reach. Hirata's tactic for creating a discourse designed for the ordinary person resulted in a shift to discussing the "ancient way" and showing that its content was no different from that of daily life. "Great Japan," he said, "is the original country of all countries; it is the ancestral country. From this standpoint the august lineage of our emperor has been transmitted successively and rests with the great sovereign of all nations. The regulations of all the countries are commanded and controlled by this sovereign." The bakufu and the managerial class were obliged to satisfy the "spirit of Japan," which came to mean fulfilling the "august obligation to the spirit of Tokugawa Ieyasu" by "serving" and "studying antiquity."

The immediate purpose of Hirata's thought was to allay popular fears concerning death and to provide consolation to the people. He believed that the popular mind had become confused by fashionable explanations that made people susceptible to the temptations of licentious and private behavior. It was for this reason, after the 1790s, that

47 Ibid., p. 184.
48 Muromatsu Iwao, ed., *Hirata Atsutane zenshū*, vol. 1: *Ibuki oroshi* (Tokyo: Hakubunkan, 1912), p. 2. Hereafter cited as *Hirata zenshū, 1912*.

he apparently turned his attention to the lives of the ordinary folk. Yet it would be incomplete to say that his only goal was to pacify the present. By centering on ordinary folk in discourse, Hirata provided a powerful warrant for independent action.[49]

Hirata's aim to offer consolation to ordinary folk involved a comprehensive strategy demonstrating the connection between all things and establishing a genealogy for that kinship. Connectedness showed family resemblances, and family resemblances revealed the relationship of all things, past and present, owing to the common and creative powers of the creation deities (*musubi no kami*). By promising unhappy contemporaries the prospect of consolation, Hirata and his followers resorted to a systematic classification capable of representing the relationship of all things. His own favored mode of relating was expressed in cosmological speculation (already pursued by a number of late-eighteenth-century thinkers) which presumed to explain why it was impossible for the spirits of people to migrate after death to the dreaded and foul world of permanent pollution (*yomi*). The purpose of this form of speculation was to provide comfort to the large numbers of ordinary folk who, Hirata believed, feared death and consequently expressed their anxieties and unhappiness in activities such as peasant rebellions, escape to the cities, and self-indulgence in the privatized pleasures of the culture of play. Hirata's explanation (articulated in *Tama no mihashira*, 1818) was rooted in a fundamental division between "visible things" (*arawanigoto*) and "matters concealed and mysterious" (*kamigoto*). Although this classification between the seen and the unseen had been initially authorized by the *Nihon shoki*, it now demanded apprehending phenomena as being related in the modality of the part–whole relationship, which permitted reducing one thing to function as a substitute for another. Nativists were able to make this move because they believed that both realms were ultimately produced by the creation deities. Yet they valued the world of "hidden things" more than the visible world of the living and made the latter dependent on the actions of the former. Because the invisible realm had been originally identified with the *kami*'s (deities') affairs, it was natural to see it as the source of the phenomenal world of living things. But by linking the visible to the invisible in this way and bonding conduct in the former to judgment in the latter, Hirata and his rural followers were able to offer representation and even meaning to the life

[49] Despite Hirata's apparent valorization of the ordinary folk, many contemporaries would have agreed with the writer Bakin's assessment that he (Hirata) was less concerned with commoners than he was with self-aggrandizement.

of groups who had remained outside or on the margins of official discourse. Judgment of performance based on an asessment of morally informed behavior usually meant work and productive labor. Each individual was obliged to perform according to the endowment (*sei*) bestowed on him at birth by the heavenly deities. Whatever one did in life was important and necessary.

Hirata's elaborate cosmology did more than simply enjoin the ruled, the ordinary folk whom he now called by the antique name *aohitokusa*, to fall into line and work hard.[50] The significant result of his reformulation of the relationship between divine intention and human purpose was to transform what hitherto had been regarded as an object into a knowing and performing subject. Accordingly, the ordinary folk now occupied a position of autonomy through the valorization of their quotidian life and the productivity of their daily labor. By arguing that the living inhabited the invisible world where the spirits and deities resided, Hirata was able to demonstrate the existence of a ceaseless transaction between creation and custom. Even though each realm was considered separate from the other, they were nonetheless similar in all decisive aspects, as the living were descendants of the spirits and deities. If creation was initially the work of the gods, it was maintained by humans who continuously created to fulfill their divine obligation of repaying the blessings of the gods. The two primal creation deities established the connection of the two realms at the beginning of heaven and earth.[51] For thinkers like Hirata, the conception of *musubi*, creativity and productivity, established the divisions, the classes of events and things, inner and outer affairs, human and sacred, visible and invisible, yet such categories attested to the integrated wholeness of life and its continuation from one generation to the next. The archetypal example of the creation deities making the cosmos continued to manifest its "necessity" down to the present in manifold ways: the procreation of the species, the production of goods, and the constant reproduction of the conditions of human community. *Musubi* also denoted linkages, the act of binding things together, and union, an observation made by Ōkuni Takamasa that served as the leading principle in the formulation of the theory of harmony (*wagō*).

---

50 This is the argument of Matsumoto Sannosuke, *Kokugaku seiji shisō no kenkyū* (Osaka: Yūhikaku, 1957). Following Maruyama's interpretation of nativism as an irrational prop capable of eliciting voluntary submission of the ruled to the emperor, Matsumoto shows how *kokugaku* was made to serve the ideology of the managerial class.

51 Tahara Tsuguo, et al., eds., *Nihon shisō taikei*, vol. 50: *Hirata Atsutane, Ban Nobutomo, Ōkuni Takamasa* (Tokyo: Iwanami shoten, 1973), p. 18. Hereafter cited as *Hirata Atsutane, Ban Nobutomo, Ōkuni Takamasa*.

Above all else, the most explicit sign for the continuing activity of the creation deities was agricultural work. Work constituted the guarantee that the creation would be reproduced in every generation and appeared as the bond holding the community together. Here, nativists offered it as an alternative to securing social solidarity, fully as effective as mere political obedience because it was associated with the sacred. In this way Hirata and his followers succeeded in shifting the emphasis from performing specific behavior-satisfying norms to the essence of life activity itself, work, now authenticated by the archetypal event of creation, as the measure of all real conduct in the visible realm. By altering an argument based on abstract principles governing power relationships to valorize concrete and practical mundane activities, the nativists had found a way to highlight the means of social reproduction and its realization as the content of discursive knowledge.

In rural Japan this nativist intervention had great consequences. The hidden world, once the domain of the gods, now became synonymous with the departed ancestors of the living. This identification between the hidden and the space occupied by the spirits of the living increasingly served to encourage folk religious practices emphasizing guardian deities, tutelary beliefs, and clan gods. Yet it also induced the community to concentrate on its own centrality in the great narrative of creation and the reproduction in custom. In texts like the *Tamadasuki* and the starchy enjoinment to daily worship, Hirata outlined in some detail the way that the most mundane forms of daily life interacted with worship and how the lives and activities of ordinary people represented a religious moment. Summoning daily life to such a discourse and linking it to worship and religious observances made archaism (*kodōron*) meaningful to wider audiences in rural Japan. To be sure, Hirata imagined these mundane activities as living examples of the archaic precedent and authoritative proof that no real disjunction separated the present from the preclass, folkic past. In his exposition the ancient Way, once identified with sincerity and ethics in poetry and theater, forfeited its privileged status to the ordinary folk living in the present. When peasant leaders who had passed through Hirata's school juxtaposed this concentration on the unity of work and worship, life and labor with their perception of rural unease, it appeared to offer a solution to unrelieved fragmentation, divisiveness, and the threat of decreasing productivity, as well as conferring a form of representation on their leadership. By rescuing the ordinary folk from the margins of official discourse, *kokugaku* could enforce a community of interests among the upper and lower peasantry and overcome the apparent ambiguity stalking the relationship between the village leaders and their followers.

That link was provided by the status of the ancestors and the centrality accorded to the village deities in binding the various parts of the village into a whole. Together, they constituted a world of relationships more real and fundamental than those found in the visible realm of public power. For the flow of ties, transactions, and traffic between the hidden world of the ancestors and tutelary deities and the visible realm of work and social relations disclosed a commonality of interest and purpose that transcended ascribed status and mundane ethical duties. The logic for this connection between work and worship in the rural setting was plainly prescribed by Hirata's systematization of ancestor respect within the larger framework of folkic religious practices. In these lectures, he was able to link people with their ancestors and the creation deities, explain the central importance of the clan deities (*ujigami*) and tutelary gods (*ubusuna no kami*), and show why the creation deities were so vital to the agricultural project. These explanations also became elements in the formation of a theory of village rehabilitation and self-strengthening. By identifying increased productivity and agricultural labor with religious devotion, by making work itself into a form of worship repaying the blessings of the gods, and by projecting a theory of consolation that promised immortality to the spirits and certain return to the invisible realms after death, Hirata and his followers were able to strike deeply responsive chords in the villages of the late Tokugawa period and present the prospect of resolving the problems of the countryside and reconstituting life anew along different lines.

The most obvious contact with village life was provided by the creation deities and the necessity to continue agricultural work. A variety of writers like Satō Nobuhiro (1769–1850) and Mutobe Yoshika (1798–1863) pursued this connection further by showing how wealth originated in agricultural production and how rural life corresponded to cosmic categories. Hirata had already, in the *Tamadasuki*, established the necessary linkages among the creation deities, the ancestors, and the households (*ie*) as indispensable to reproducing the social means of existence. He argued that the spirits of the dead inhabited the same place as the living and that they fixed the essential similarity between the invisible and visible realms. In an afterword to his inventory of daily prayers, Hirata noted that it was as important to make observances to one's ancestors as it was to other deities. Men who carried out household duties properly were also obliged to pray to the deities of the *ie* and to the shelf reserved for the ancestors. One should also worship the various clan deities and the deities of occupations.[52]

If the household represented the most basic and essential unit in Hirata's conception of the invisible world, then the village defined its outermost limits. Village, household, spirits (ancestors), and distant deities reaching back to the creation gods constituted a series of concentric rings, one within the other, linked by kinship. As Hirata's prayers to the ancestors called for protection and good fortune of the household, so his invocation to the tutelary gods and guardian deities served to secure protection and prosperity for the village community. "Grant all protection to this village (sato)," the prayer intoned, "Before the great tutelary deities we offer prudent respect. Protect the village day and night, and grant it prosperity."[53] Hirata related these village shrines to the hidden realm. "Regional spirits (kunitamashii) and the tutelary deities have been directed to share the administration of the realm among themselves and to assist Ōkuninushi no kami, whose basis of rule is concealed governance." Authority was manifest in the tutelary shrines of the various locales. While the deities conferred protection and prosperity, a thankful community should offer prayer, supplication, and hard work. Prayer and work meant the difference between continued wholeness (order) and fragmentation and decreased productivity (disorder). Indeed, in Hirata's thinking it was natural to move from formal religious observance to more enduring forms of gratitude, work. This identification of worship and work was refined by others, but it is clear that Hirata figured work as another way of talking about worship. His conception of work was rooted in a concern for repaying the blessings of the kami. This meant returning trust to the deities who had bestowed benefits. This trust, as he pointed out, meant both the land that produced food and the material from which clothing and shelter were made.

This sense of a powerful, hidden realm directing the fortunes of the living represented a structural similarity with the world of the household and rural community. It was a world symbolized by the authority of the tutelary shrines (which themselves represented a manifestation of the invisible world) and hence the place of the village, hidden, powerless in the realm of public authority, but nevertheless vibrant with "real" activity. Here the nativists, who, like the Mito writers, turned away from Edo, pitted a horizontal realm, close to nature and origins, against the vertical world of the Tokugawa daikan, daimyo,

[52] Hirata Atsutane zenshū kankōkai, eds., *Hirata Atsutane zenshū* (Tokyo: Meicho shuppan, 1977), vol. 6, pp. 4–19. Hereafter cited as *Hirata zenshū, 1977*. [53] Ibid., p. 217.

shogun, and even emperor. The hidden world of the village, deities, ancestors, and descendants was more "real" than was the visible world of power and consumption. Without the sanction of the hidden world, the idea of an autonomous village would not have been possible. At its most fundamental level, the world envisaged by the nativists was one of linkages and kin relationships. It was a realm where microcosm, the household and the village, served as a substitute for the macrocosm, the so-called national soil (*kunitsuchi*), where the emperor as a living deity met the tutelary deities and the ancestors administered by Ōkuninushi and where the vertical claim of public authority collided with the horizontal claims of village life.

In its rural appropriation, *kokugaku* sanctioned the elevation of the village as a substitute for the whole, as Mito had projected the domain. The argument for an autonomous and self-sufficient village, removed from the centers of power, relied on people's recognizing their duty to return the "blessings" to the creation deities from whom all things literally flowed. This meant replicating the archetypal act of creation through agricultural work and reproduction. Judgment and final authority lay in the hidden realm administered by Ōkuninushi no kami, not the "living deity" who was the emperor. Duty was described as a form of stewardship that, as stated earlier, referred to the actual event in which the creation gods gave something to the other deities, the imperial descendants, and the land itself as a trust. Trust required repaying the divine gift with work. Late Tokugawa *kokugakusha* like Miyauchi Yoshinaga (1789–1843), Miyao (or Miyahiro) Sadao (1797–1858), and Hirayama Chūeimon (?–?) (all priests or village leaders) saw the idea of entrustment as the means to emphasize the central importance of agricultural life. It was in this context that Miyao, a Shimōsa village leader, argued that the realm was founded on agriculture and that the village was the appropriate instrument for organizing people to work together in the countryside. Others saw the village and the household as one and the same. Miyauchi responded to what he believed were signs of fragmentation in rural life as an example of neglecting the imperial doctrine imparted by the two creation deities. Evidence appeared everywhere in "rebellion," "disorder," and "wastage," which Miyauchi attributed to improper leadership. Theoreticians like Ōkuni coupled this notion of proper village leadership with the idea of an administration pledged to taking care of the people (*buiku*). All agreed that *kokugaku* was a method for solving problems in the countryside. Even a high-ranking samurai nativist scholar like Ikuta Yorozu (1801–37) (who followed the route of rebellion) believed that peasant disturbances would cease if good doctrine and leadership were administered to the villages. Such a method was dramatized in the formulation of a conception of relief and assistance (used also by the new religious groups) that would program stewardship. In the end, stewardship or entrustment became the grounds for village self-sufficiency and the justification for secession from the center.[54]

According to the rural nativists, all of this would be possible if proper knowledge were available. Miyauchi, for example, saw knowledge as the proper definition of the boundaries of order, whereby all persons knew what they were required to do and what was sufficient for their livelihood. When people violated established boundaries, they invited disaster. "If one does not extend (through work) the boundaries imposed by the heavenly deities, one will surely neglect his productive duties and be impatient toward them. . . . In the end it destroys the household and is the source of disaster."[55] Miyauchi's *Tooyamabiko* (1834) is sensitive to the frequency of rebellions and disorder, and the text's apparent purpose was to understand their causes in order to arrest their occurrence. The question Miyauchi asked was how not to forget what one was supposed to do. Selfishness undoubtedly turned people away from the established divisions and tempted them to excess. Excess transcended boundaries and could lead only to unhappiness and ruin. Those who had "exceeded their own boundaries," neglecting "household duties," had gone beyond "endeavoring" and had ceased to work. Working for the household brought order; work out of that context meant disorder. Such duty represented "entrustment" from one's parents and beyond them from ancestors and deities. Following the lead of Hirata, Miyauchi enjoined people not only to work but also to worship the ancestral deities and pray at the tutelary shrines. Like other rural nativists, he tried to remind contemporaries that because people had become so habituated to the uses of money, they had forgotten the source of wealth. Treasure (*takara*) was the word that many nativists used to designate the peasants (*hyakushō*), and by that they meant people working in the fields. Such people reflected a blessing of the gods, whereas offenders of divine injunctions, men who committed polluting acts (*tsumibito*), resembled "annoying pests" who gathered together to destroy the house-

---

54 The idea of a self-sufficient village "movement" was developed by Haga Noboru in several essays and books but notably in "Bakumatsu henkakuki ni okeru no undō to ronri," in Haga Noboru and Matsumoto Sannosuke, eds., *Nihon shisō taikei*, vol. 51: *Kokugaku undō no shisō* (Tokyo: Iwanami shoten, 1971), pp. 675–84. Hereafter cited as *Kokugaku undō no shisō*.
55 Ibid., p. 333.

hold. Such concerns led Miyauchi to examine the function of tutelary shrines as a focus for life, work, and worship, with a constant reminder of the necessity to "repay the blessings" of continued good fortune.

So powerful was this impulse to restructure village solidarity around the tutelary shrine that it became the basis of a nationwide movement in the 1840s. Another Shinto priest, Mutobe Yoshika, devoted his major texts to elucidating the connection between such shrines and the two creation deities. In his cosmological *Ken-yūjun kōron*, he proposed that the creation deities responsible for the procreation of humans were indistinguishable from the gods associated with the tutelary shrines. "These . . . deities reside in their *gun, ken, mura*, native place (*furusato*), and it is decreed that their ordinances are to be regulated by the tutelary gods."[56] Elsewhere he argued that the division according to fixed boundaries and deities representing various regions in the country meant that each place had its own tutelary god. The purpose of these deities, he declared, was that they informed people regularly of the "secret governance" of procreation and its administration. "In these places people daily grasp in their lives both the spirit of activity and calm from . . . the shrines."[57] Although the invisible government was not seen by mortals, it was manifest symbolically in the precincts of the shrines. They represented a bonding between the invisible realm and the visible and a guarantee of the continuing presence of the former in the world of the living. "The shrines of tutelary deities are very important," Mutobe wrote in the *Ubusunashako*. "Because that is the case, we must first offer daily prayer to these deities; next we should make regular visits to these shrines."[58] When such devotion and respect was carried out faithfully, it would guarantee prosperity and abundance. Guided by this conviction, Mutobe was prompted in the 1840s to call for the establishment of a countrywide movement pledged to worship the tutelary deities.

Whereas writers like Miyauchi and Mutobe were shrine priests who emphasized the importance of worship, Miyao Sadao, who described himself as a "potato-digging village official," stressed the primary role of the village official. Yet his concerns for leadership and work reflected another way of talking about worship and respect and stressing the importance of making the village a self-sufficient economic and political unit. By advising peasants to understand and preserve the "commands of the *nanushi*, which are no different from the public ordinances (of the

---

56 Mutobe Yoshika, "Ken-yūjun kōron," *Shintō sōsho* 3 (October 1897): 2–3.
57 Ibid., p. 3.   58 *Kokugaku undō no shisō*, p. 229.

lord)," Miyao was envisaging the role of village leadership (in the manner of Mito writers writing about domainal leadership) as a substitute for the entrustment represented by the emperor, shogun, and daimyo, not as a challenge to officially constituted authority. His intention was merely to recognize that within the jurisdiction of the village, officials "must make the administration of the peasantry their chief duty." Most rural nativists acknowledged that the village, especially in bad years, would have to take responsibility for the extension of relief and assistance. This idea had been promoted earlier by agricultural writers of such differing persuasions as Ninomiya Sontoku and Ōhara Yūgaku. But assistance and relief, real necessities for village survival in the hardship years of the 1830s and 1840s, also underscored the primacy of collective purpose over private interest. It was seen as a method whereby the village, following the model of the household, would rely on its resources and its own efforts to reproduce the necessities of social life and thereby achieve a sense of the whole. This preoccupation with relief and mutual assistance, leading to the achievement of village autonomy and self-sufficiency, logically drew attention to the quality of local leadership. Promoting policies of strict economy meant urging the peasants to increase productivity for the sake of the village community as a whole under the informed guidance of agricultural sages, usually village officials, elders, and local notables (*meibōka*), instead of simply tightening their belts. Yet such leaders – Ninomiya, Ōhara, and rural nativists like Miyao believed – had to possess the right kind of knowledge of rural affairs in order to validate their authority.

For the rural nativists, knowledge meant "knowing about the *kami*." But to "know" about the *kami* meant also knowing about the ordinary folk. In other words, knowledge of the customary life of ordinary people was equivalent to knowledge of the deities, and vice versa. Village leaders were obliged to know both the divine intent of the gods and the conditions of daily existence that might satisfy the purpose of creation. Miyao described his own appointment as a divine trust that bound him – and all officials – to the duty of promoting self-sufficiency and economic self-reliance. This formulation concerning the identity of divine and human knowledge represented a transformation of an idea introduced earlier by Hirata. Whereas Ōkuni Takamasa catalyzed the formula into a discipline of learning in the 1850s, the rural nativists had already made its "content" a criterion for proper and authoritative leadership. Miyao in his *Kokueki honron* advised that the wealthy of the region properly instruct the people into the way of the *kami*. He shared with thinkers like Ninomiya and Ōhara the conviction that people had to be inculcated with the spirit of the work by showing them how their daily life related to a world larger than mere day-to-day subsistence and the paying of taxes. This meant teaching them about the necessity of producing children to increase the labor force and to ease the financial burden on the rural population.[59] By the same token, village leaders must attend to famines, natural disasters, and the general well-being of the community. "Uneconomical policies," he asserted, "result in shame for the village, and the shame of the village becomes the shame of the lord."[60] Improper leadership always revealed a lack of knowledge and lack of piety before the deities. What Miyao feared most was the ever-present threat of conflict and division within the village. Its officials should promote harmony and "guide ignorant peasants." Their trust to administer well was even greater in hard times because they had "replaced the *daikan*." "During times of bad harvests," Miyao stated, "one cannot rely on the assistance of the regional lords and officials. One helps oneself with one's own savings and effort. One must understand that one should not bother or depend on the leaders in bad times."[61] To say this was to recognize that local autonomy and authority prevailed in the countryside.

Suzuki Shigetane (1812–63), an independent student at the Hirata school and a casualty in the loyalist explosions of the 1860s, gave even sharper expression to this identification of trust and knowledge and the stewardship of local leadership. In *Engishiki norito kōgi* (1848) he presented the idea that officials do not differ from the emperor inasmuch as they are obliged to offer "mutual help and assistance in the great august policy . . . to preserve the household enterprises given by the gods and make substance for food, clothing, and shelter."[62] Suzuki was referring to the rural elite assigned to administer the communities under their jurisdiction. Although he accepted a division within society, he was convinced that each sector exercised a sacred trust to fulfill the divine obligations "to make things for other people in hard times." His student Katsura Takashige (1816–71), a village leader in Niigata, constructed an argument whereby Suzuki's conception of "making the *kunitsuchi* habitable for the people" was enlisted to promote the primacy of village administration. In fact, writers like Suzuki and Katsura simply spoke of the village as if it were the larger realm

---

59 Ibid., p. 293.
60 Miyao Sadao, "Minke yōjutsu," in *Kinsei jikata keizai shiryō* (Tokyo: Kyōbunkan, 1954), vol. 5, p. 317.   61 Ibid., p. 304.
62 Suzuki Shigetane, *Engishiki norito kōgi* (Tokyo: Kokusho kankōkai, 1978), pp. 13–14.

(*kunitsuchi*). In *Yotsugigusa tsumiwake* (1848), Katsura envisaged the village as the equivalent or adequate political form for the realm as a whole and local leaders as exemplars for peasants. This should require no reliance on coercive measures, laws, or ordinances, as trust bound ruler to ruled. Such trust was conveyed to the people through "preaching" and "exhortations" from elders and superiors. He explained how this was to be done:

> First, depend on the Great August intention (heart) which deepens and widens the *kami* learning of the people. . . . This learning is transmitted from court officials (priests) who have made their own intention identical with the Great August Heart, down to regional lords, county officials, village chiefs, and headmen, to the peasantry. The peasants also receive and transmit this intention to each household in the learning of the deities.[63]

The systemization of *kokugaku* into a discipline of knowledge was completed by Ōkuni Takamasa, who sought to show how "learning about the *kami*" amounted to "learning about the ordinary folk." The term, he believed, referred to the realm itself. In the age of the gods, he wrote in *Hongaku kyoyō*, there had been three instances of entrustment, and two in the age of men. The first of these was from the heavenly deities to Izanami and Izanagi; the second from Izanami and Izanagi to Amaterasu (the formation of the moon and sun); the third was Amaterasu's entrustment to the imperial ancestor Ninigi no mikoto.[64] For the human world, the two great grants were to Sukunobikana and Ōkuninushi to solidify the realm and to make it habitable. Here was the basis for a theory meant for local leaders searching for the authority to establish an arrangement of mutual assistance and relief in the interest of a productive and harmonious life, as well as the larger sanction for a restoration of antiquity. At the mythic level, this link was forged in the example of the grant to Ōkuninushi to render and restore the national soil to human cultivation and habitation, and at the historical level it appeared in demands for the local leadership and peasantry to live up to this trust.

Ōkuni structured these trusts and obligations within the framework of a discipline. He associated knowledge of the gods with knowledge of the ordinary folk, without whom the creation would be meaningless and "talk about ruling the realm useless." One must always view the times from the perspective of the ordinary people. No real distinction could be made between the customs of the gods and those of ordinary

---

63 Katsura Takashige, *Yotsugigusa tsumiwake* (Niigata, 1884), unnumbered pagination.
64 Hirata Atsutane, Ban Nobutomo, Ōkuni Takamasa, pp. 408–9.

people. In *Yamatogokoro* (1848) Ōkuni wrote that the human species was divided into two categories. The Chinese called these two categories "great" and "small" men, but in Japan it had been the learning of the gods and the customs of the ordinary people. "When one learns about the deities, then even the small person will become a lord and great man, and when the lord and great man learn about the *aoihitogusa*, they will become as ordinary people."[65] A knowledge of origins (*moto*) thereby taught that the official was the base, and one's body, the ends. Together, they formed a reciprocal relationship. Yet in recent times, he continued, the ordinary people had reversed the order of things and had begun to consider their "bodies as the base." To do so resulted in pursuing pleasure and neglecting household duties. Moreover, this habit had affected the lords as well. Ōkuni warned the lower classes against imitating upper-class habits and advised them to "learn well the customs of the deities." He worried most about conflict and disharmony, division and fragmentation. Even though men had different faces and appearances, they were fundamentally the same because they were human.[66] Owing to divine intention, all humans were linked to one another by "mutual concern." When people conformed to this intention, times were good, but when they went against it, disaster ensued.

"The deeds of the gods join base to ends." Actualizing divine intention in practice resulted in the organization of a human community. But the ends of human activity represented the making of products from the natural material of the land granted by the gods. If the "customs of the ordinary people" (work, mutual assistance, relief) were successfully reunited with the customs of the gods, as specified in the ancient texts, then the true meaning of a harmonious union would be recovered and made manifest in the present. Indeed, the customs of the gods were equivalent to the "desires of the deities." The human impulse to help others expressed the desire and deeds of the gods. If the identification of godly deeds and human nature comprised the core of Ōkuni's thinking about politics, the installation of a harmonious community, wherein all were united by mutual assistance, became the form he envisaged for it as a displacement for contemporary institutions and administration. Because this form of human community existed before the establishment of all historical political structures and ordinances but had been forgotten in time, the present generation was appointed to restore it from memory to resolve the contemporary "crisis."

65 Nomura Denshirō, ed., *Ōkuni Takamasa zenshū* (Tokyo: Yuko shakō, 1937-9), vol. 3, pp. 18, 43.   66 Ibid., vol. 5, pp. 32 ff.

The *kokugaku* conception of work and mutual assistance was brought to completion by another rural writer from the Shimōsa region, Suzuki Masayuki (1837–71). Suzuki's central text, written just before the Restoration, was the *Tsukisakaki*, which tried to demonstrate that work was fundamental to life and that activity and performance represented the fulfillment of the cosmic plan. He attributed the "generation of all living things" first to the primal creation gods and then to the ancestral spirits. The spirits, he believed, were actually *kami* who had formerly been humans. The meaning of creation was, therefore, related to the "generation of life." Since the beginning of time, all "have endeavored similarly for the enterprise of generating life." Such an enterprise prevented conflict and disharmony. Excesses everywhere, Suzuki noted, could be avoided if people pursued the completion of virtue by working to generate life. Yet the generating of life bespoke mutual assistance, much in the manner that it had been conceptualized by Ōkuni Takamasa. "To work by and for oneself," Suzuki wrote, "will, in general, fail to bring about an accomplishment" of the great enterprise.[67] Like many nativists, Suzuki appealed to the body as a model, not to specify never-ending pleasures, but to represent the unity symbolized by household and village. The eyes see, he declared, the ears hear, the mouth speaks, the hands hold, and the feet move; each part relies on "mutuality" in order for the whole – the body – to operate. Suzuki then projected this metaphor to describe people working together as the key to realizing the great enterprise. If any part fails to assist the other, the body will collapse into dysfunction, just as neglect of reciprocity in work will terminate the "generation of life" and plunge the realm into disorder.

Suzuki was convinced that destruction of the work ethic would drive the realm into riot and rebellion, forcing people to turn against one another and transforming Japan into the image of China. Ultimate responsibility for the interruption of life-generating activity, however, belonged to the lords, and not to village officials. Lords obstructed and often prevented people from performing work. Suzuki went further than most nativists to portray the disruption and discontinuity between ruler and ruled and showed how *kokugaku*, in creating a discourse centering on the producer – the ruled – would hold the leadership responsible for interfering in activities necessary to the continuation of life. The lord, like the parent, provided the conditions for life-giving activity; the land constituted the basis of this activity. But

---

67 Sagara Tōru, ed., "Tsukisakaki," vol. 24 of *Nihon no meicho* (Tokyo: Chūō kōronsha, 1972), p. 387.

although this arrangement reflected a positive good, it could also turn into evil. Work and productivity could be misused by the lord for private and selfish purposes. Private desire drove the realm into a "deep valley." Higher loyalties to the land and to the deities should be repaid with life-generating work. Suzuki's explanation of private desire rested on the conviction that confusion was caused by "evil doctrines." It was necessary to "jettison the evil and mistaken doctrines of foreign countries (China) and return to the original intention . . . to cast off contemporary abusive customs in order to study the ancient minds." In his last, post-Restoration text on local government, Suzuki pointed to the village as the crucible for carrying on life-generating activity and an autonomous administration as the surest defense of proper doctrine.

RELIGIONS OF RELIEF

Commenting on the contemporary religious situation, the author of *Seji kemmonroku* roared:

In today's society, the representatives of Shinto and Buddhism resemble national traitors. All the *kami* have ascended to heaven; the Buddhas have left for the Western Paradise; and all present and other worlds have fallen into disuse. Providence and retribution have been exhausted. All the Buddhist priests have fallen into hell and have ended (their mission) by becoming sinners.

Buyō Inshi's astringent condemnation of religious life in the Bunka–Bunsei area, like his sweeping renunciation of social life, may have been hyperbolic, but it signified a general playing out of older, more established religious forms at a time when people were beginning to search for new kinds of meaning and faith. Hirata Atsutane was already in the streets of Edo denouncing the vulgar Shintoists, the deceiving Buddhists, and the "stinking Confucianists." Provincial life was beginning to show renewed interest in more basic, nativist forms of religious practice. In the spring of 1830 large numbers of people from several areas of Japan streamed toward the Grand Shrine at Ise. This mass movement, numbering in the hundreds of thousands, was the most recent of periodic pilgrimages to the shrine of Amaterasu. The pilgrimage disintegrated into disorder and violence. It had no disciplined structure (although many groups were organized as *kō* for this explicit purpose), and it is not clear who its leaders were. But people were prompted to leave their households and villages – men, women, even children – to make the long and often perilous trek to Ise. The greater portion of pilgrims were from the lower classes, and even though they were proscribed from making the visitation, they nonetheless felt compelled to leave their work, families, children, parents, wives, and husbands to make the journey to Ise. Some writers proposed that the pilgrimages represented an enlargement of the late Tokugawa impulse for travel. If it is true that the pilgrim experienced momentary release, freedom, or even a sense of unconnectedness while traveling on the road, the pilgrimage was nonetheless religious or political in its intensity. Travel, propelled by religious zeal, offered temporary release from the harsh uncertainties of everyday life, the very same life that *kokugaku* scholars had made the centerpiece of their new discipline of learning. It also heightened awareness of the power that large groups could command. "We have stimulated an earthquake and unleashed the august virtue of the Grand Shrine; the heart moves Japan. We have unleashed the august good omen in the pilgrimage, and it is called an earthquake; the heart moves the country of Japan," so announced a contemporary riddle.[68] The pilgrimage of 1830 also dramatized questions of social surplus, fragmentation, poverty, and the prospect of even greater disorder. People went on such pilgrimages for many reasons. Some even had a good time, but many were driven by hopes of divine relief, assistance, and the desire for good fortune. The experience signified both a new religious zeal and a concomitant search for new forms of community. It also disclosed what had become disturbing and disquieting about the tenor of life for large numbers of ordinary people.

It was in this context of a massive search for divine assistance and relief, and the quest for new forms of communitarian and voluntary association, that a number of new religious groups appeared in the late Tokugawa decades. Along with the establishment of new, syncretic religious organizations, some older sects, like the *nembutsu* sects and Fujikō, also underwent renewal and revitalization. But it is important to note that the new religions, like Mitogaku and *kokugaku*, represented a departure from past and more established religious forms that, many believed, had been played out. Like other discourses in the late Tokugawa period, the new religious message reflected the operation of a strategy that sanctioned bringing together older ideas, elements, and practices into new combinations. Organizationally the new groups like Tenri, Konkō, Kurozumi, and Maruyama sought to real-

[68] Quotation from Fujitani Toshio, *Okagemairi to ee ja nai ka* (Tokyo: Iwanami shoten, 1968), pp. 168–9.

ize the promise of voluntary association (as against the involuntary association demanded by "nature") and horizontal relations by reconstituting themselves as autonomous communities. These new religions recruited their followers from the broad stratum of society but appealed largely to the lower classes. Their recruitment signified both the attempt of the people to represent themselves in a discourse, by centering themselves and their lives as its subject, and a criticism of Tokugawa social conditions. In this connection Professor Yasumaru Yoshio has written:

In order to criticize society as a whole from the standpoint of popular thought, which tended to make humility, submission, and authoritarianism as its substantive element, a great leap was necessary. The mediation that made this leap possible took on a . . . character that was, in many cases, religious. The new popular religions offered an ideal . . . that transcended the authority of the contemporary feudal system.[69]

Like *kokugaku*, many of the new religions were disposed to blend elements of myth with contemporary history as a means to create new forms of expression and interpretation. Moreover, they were often driven by the same impulse to ascertain the "real." Their solution, which led to even more radical secessions, disclosed an obsession with autonomy and the desire to remove their followers from the contagions of contemporary history and the corruption of the center. The most extreme example of this obsession was the *yonaoshi* (world renewal) movements and *ee ja nai ka* (ain't it grand?) outbursts of the last years of the Tokugawa period, whose constituencies were usually the same people against whom both Mito and *kokugaku* sought to find protection by granting relief and assistance. Recalling the intentionality informing both Mito discourse and nativism, the new religions consistently projected an unpolitical stance in the promotion of new programs and new relationships based on different conceptions of knowledge, even though their activities resulted in political consequences. Adherents to these sects often saw themselves as providing pockets of productivity and relief in a context of scarcity and unrelieved hardship, rather than as challenging the established world of politics and public authority. But when they sought to eliminate the divisiveness of politics by dissolving the collectivity into autonomous religious communities, they instead contributed to the very political fragmentation that they were seeking to displace. In the move to establish the principle of autonomy and wholeness, in which they apparently saw neither, the new religions withdrew

---

69 Yasumaru Yoshio, *Nihon kindaika to minshū shisō* (Tokyo: Aoki shoten, 1974), p. 90.

from the center and offered their own interpretation of contemporary history by rejecting it. At the periphery, they believed that they would find a place sufficiently removed from the corrosions of temporality to establish new political forms growing out of the content of culture. An apprehension of the world in this manner was equivalent to changing it in order to secure the necessary communal arrangements that conformed to the new forms of knowledge and conceptions of human nature. Nowhere was this commitment to act and change the world expressed in greater extremity than in those groups yearning for "world renewal" (*yonaoshi*).

If the new religions strove to recapture an original experience of wholeness, they also believed that the horizontal relationships that their belief authenticated came before the vertical ties demanded by the "discrimination of names" and the Tokugawa status system. This was their most distinctive and dangerous contribution to the general discussion in late Tokugawa society. All looked to the establishment of a genuine human order organized along horizontal relationships devoted to realizing equality. By the same token the new religions showed sensitivity to the way that distinctions caused social inequality. Consequently they announced their determination to find forms of organization calculated to diminish the reliance on hierarchy. The form favored by most recalled the traditional *kō*, groups of believers in which every member served as an equal partner, which characterized the groups participating in the *okagemairi* (i.e., Isekō) and merchant investment societies.[70] Under the sanction of an egalitarian organization, the new religions projected an image of relief, mutual assistance to all followers, and even reform of existing structures by calling for the equitable distribution of land and resources. At the heart of their programs was the valorization of daily life and its importance for maintaining the solidarity of community. Although their organizational principle emphasized human connectedness (the brethren) and the necessity of working and living together in mutual reciprocity as a solution to the fragmentation of more established social units that had taken place with the commercialization of the countryside, it also made equality the condition for sustaining community.[71] The new religions sought to console the spiritually and materially poor who occupied the lowest rungs of the social scale of Tokugawa Japan. In their understanding of the times, people who were "poor" were also

---

70 Murakami Shigeyoshi, *Kinsei minshū shūkyō no kenkyū* (Tokyo: Hōzōkan, 1977), pp. 21ff.
71 Yasumaru, *Nihon kindaika*, pp. 18ff.

"unhappy," and only association and mutual cooperation could alleviate that state.

What enabled the new religions to interpret contemporary reality in this way and to claim interest in the poor and unhappy was a special conception of knowledge and of learning. They all substituted faith and belief in the powers of deity for conventional sources of solace. Faith and belief appeared to be comparatively rational, as the new religions made an effort to discourage believers from relying on superstition and traditional magical practices.[72] In parting from the more structured sects of Buddhism in which Tokugawa regulations had required villagers to register, they also represented a direct search for new forms of knowledge and belief, often promising health and happiness, that met the needs of daily life. In this they could be related also to the focus on utility that characterized Mito and *kokugaku* thought. Thus Konkōkyō proposed that "learning (*gakumon*), without belief, never assists people," whereas the founder of Tenri, Nakayama Miki, advised her believers that only faith could enable people to know the exalted state and secure relief from contemporary suffering and hardships. Kurozumi Munetada, founder of the Kurozumi sect, constantly admonished his followers to stop "worrying about the Way" in order to "know and transmit the virtue of Amaterasu to people of the times."

It is important to note that many of the new religions originated in localities where newer commercial arrangements were in the process of disturbing older modes of production and social relationships and where economic distress seemed to be the most severe. In large part this observation describes the frequency and distribution of peasant rebellions as well and suggests why the new sects often ended up recruiting the same kind of people who were willing to join rural jacqueries. Owing to the regional nature of economic hardship, many of the new religions enlisted local nativistic practices and traditions to familiarize their messages when recruiting a followership. Yet, it is undeniably true that many struck deep roots in regional and village religious practices associated with Shinto and shamanism and that they derived their authority from a broadened base of shrine Shinto and religious conventions related to agricultural life.[73] But the appropriation of older, local practices frequently betrayed the limited appeal

---

72 Kano Masanao, *Shihonshugi keiseiki no chitsujo ishiki* (Tokyo: Chikuma shobō, 1969), p. 138.
73 Miyata Noboru, "Nōson no fukkō undō to minshū shūkyō no tenkai," *Iwanami kōza Nihon rekishi*, vol. 13 (*kinsei* 5) (Tokyo: Iwanami shoten, 1977), pp. 209–45.

of such groups and revealed the initimate relationship between regional hardship and the construction of consoling ideologies, even though many of these religions projected a universal message.

In general, these sects promoted doctrines calling for the regime of relief everywhere, according to the blessings of a single and all-powerful *kami* who represented a first principle (or principal), whether it was Amaterasu Ōmikami of Nyorai and Kurozumi, Tenri Ōmikami of Tenri, Tenchikane of Konkōkyō, Mt. Fuji of Fuji *kō*, or Moto no oyagami of Maruyama *kō*. Such deities supplied authority for claims promising to offer relief and assistance and contrasted dramatically with the rather discredited obligations of the feudal order to provide benevolence and aid in times of need. It is also true that nativists assigned a comparable role to the creation deities and to the tutelary shrines, even though they emphasized the human capacity for self-help. In many instances, these all-powerful gods were seen as creators of the cosmos and progenitors of the human species. And the reliance on a reliever who bore striking resemblance to the Buddhist Miroku (Maitreya) or simply one who possessed *kami* character explained to the poor and the beleaguered the necessity for help and assistance among humans and why it was absent in their time. The effectiveness of this explanation often depended on the powers of the founder of a sect to demonstrate the efficacy of his or her knowledge and charismatic powers. Unlike nativism, which often diminished the powers of the person for the spirit of the word (*kotodama*), the new religions relied principally on performance to validate the message. Part of this reliance on the performative act stemmed from a distrust for conventional forms of knowledge based on the primacy of words and abstractions, yet part of it was undoubtedly inspired by the emphasis on the body and on the importance of its movements, whether in play or in physical work, in late Tokugawa thought. What appears important is the emphasis on the performative powers of the body and its kinship with manual rather than mental activity. This projection, of course, reflected the primacy of daily life. It is, in any case, this factor that accounts for the difficulty in dissociating the religious career of the founders from the discourse that they helped construct and in separating actual demonstration and action from verbal utterance. Frequently, the performance model of the founder became a text for the followers to read, as a source for correct knowledge, just as the body served as a text in verbal fiction.

The founder's performance depended on a successful appropriation of elements from shamanistic practice related to *kami* possession and healing spiritual powers. Many of the new religions resorted to the convention of identifying the founder of the sect as a "living *kami*" (*ikigami*), a designation that the nativists reserved for the emperor. The act of describing the founder as a living god, mediating between the primal voice and the followers and supplying his or her body as a vessel to convey the deity's wishes to the faithful, added authenticity to the autonomous doctrine that each was trying to articulate. The process whereby in most cases this new persona was realized began with the founder's illness (later interpreted as time spent with the primal deity), followed by divine intervention and speedy recovery, which led to a change in personality, which in turn bore fruit in miraculous cures among the local inhabitants and was accompanied by periodic trances to reinforce the new charisma. The ritualization of the founder's life into a drama of living *kami* undoubtedly served the same purpose as the Mito celebration of the timeless presence represented by the Daijōsai and the nativist enshrinement of tutelary worship as a technique for securing continuous contact with the creation deities and the work of Ōkuninushi no kami.

To explain a world based on knowledge that only initiates could know (closely resembling *kokugaku*'s valorization of the activities of daily life) risked provoking conflict with the authority system, which had its own claims to a privileged knowledge entitling certain people to rule and its stated responsibility to provide benevolence. Even so, some of the new religions, like Tenri and Maruyama, developed doctrines announcing "world renewal" in the present and the beginning of a new heaven on earth. So powerful was the appeal of this ideal that by the end of the epoch, world-renewing rebellions and *ee ja nai ka* disturbances in cities like Kyoto and Osaka were proclaiming their cause in slogans of relief and assistance to the people. Despite the world renewal project, such revolutionary utopianism usually drew attention to this-worldly temporal orientations. All of the sects, including the revitalized *nembutsu* organizations like the *myōkōninden*, spoke of "extreme happiness in this world" and underscored the necessity to find contemporary answers to prayers requesting the *kami* to eliminate struggle and "correct illness and disease." Tenri insisted on making a "fresh start beyond death" and enjoined its followers to concentrate on their daily lives without fear or anxiety concerning their fate after death. Underlying this attitude was the conviction that humans, not nature, were the standard of action or behavior, just as the present, rather than some remote and transcendent sanctuary in the future or elsewhere, was the place for carrying out the duties of the daily life. Here again is a close resemblance to the claims of late Tokugawa verbal fiction and woodblock illustrations with its own elevation of human subjectivity as the maker of society and custom. In the case of the new religions, primacy of the human, regardless of status, was intimately related to the process of becoming a *kami*. Doctrines like Konkō and Tenri, for example, joined humans to the deities by employing such familistic metaphors as "children of the *kami*" or "family of the deities." Yet such reference to the divine merely reinforced the essential kinship that it was believed all humans shared, regardless of status, class, sex, or even race. To be human meant promoting programs of relief and assistance to all folk, whose destitute and often impoverished lives constituted the touchstone for recruitment into the new religions. Konkōkyō constantly dramatized the importance of "men who assist other men" as the major criterion of being human, whereas Nakayama Miki exhorted her followers to "never forget other men" – not just people of abundance, the rural rich, merchants, and managers, but the diligent and nameless people about whom official discourse had been silent, who now inhabited the "bottom of the valley" (*tanizoku*). Social division itself, it was held, set people against one another and created the circumstances of conflict and struggle between the rich and the needy. The purpose of programs pledged to relieving the poor was a radical presumption of the equality of all individuals and between the sexes and the promise to redistribute wealth and land. Behind this call was the sustaining power of human love for others and a dangerously optimistic belief in the essential goodness of human nature.

Among the late Tokugawa religions the most representative sects, which also captured the largest following, were Kurozumi, Tenri, and Konkōkyō. Kurozumi was the earliest and was founded by Kurozumi Munetada (1780–1850) in Okayama prefecture. He was born in a village in Bizen, the son of a Shinto priest of the Imamura Shrine, a guardian deity of Okayama Castle. His mother was the daughter of a priest. When Munetada was in his thirties, he contracted tuberculosis, after losing his parents who apparently also died of infectious disease, and was confined for a year and a half. His illness and confinement solidified his resolve to devote his efforts to securing assistance from the sun goddess for the ill, diseased, and downtrodden. It has been reported that he aspired to become a "living deity" and felt cheated because of the imminent threat of death, deciding that after death he would become a deity devoted to healing the ill. But Munetada survived and recovered after experiencing unity with Amaterasu while venerating the rising sun at the winter solstice. Upon recovering, he began a new ministry of cures, teaching his first followers the lesson he had learned about the sun and the benefaction and compassion of Amaterasu. Success led to disciples and the establishment of a formal organization.

Kurozumi's doctrine was based on conversion to the sun goddess. He advised people to know how to concentrate their devotion on the august virtue of Amaterasu; the light of the sun goddess had not changed for an eternity and wanted the "august intention of Amaterasu" and the people's intention to become united.[74] Like other founders, Kurozumi was convinced of the possibility of becoming identified with the deity. This devotion undoubtedly derived from his own religious background, but his focus on the singularity and superiority of the sun goddess also offered a way to overcome the claims associated with other deities prevalent among traditional agricultural believers. Hereafter relief and assistance were to be related to the saving powers of a single deity. In time such relief came to range from simple cures to the prolongation of life, abundance, having children, easy delivery, increased success in trades and business, bumper crops, and larger fishing catches, all things that would make life easier.[75] If Amaterasu were idealized as the sun and the source of life, then life itself would find meaning only within the confines of her powers. Hence Kurozumi advanced a conception of enclosure (found in other doctrines as well) bounded by belief and occupied by the faithful. In a letter he confessed that there "was no special way to relate this basic unity (between believer and sun goddess) outside this circle (○)."[76] This imagery of the circle was scattered throughout his writings and referred to an enchanted enclosure free from desire and misfortune. In the early 1840s he wrote:

> The Way is easy to serve, even though we can see that some do not serve it easily. To serve this Way is to live in it. This Way, as I have repeatedly stated, is Amaterasu Ōmikami. That is, it is the circular deity. As I have said before, things should be entrusted to this circle. It is easy to leave things to this Way, and it is very strange that people in China and Japan have not been aware of this. They are perplexed by the name of the Way. Men who have been separated from the true Way are all under heaven. Not to be separated from the true Way is the Way I have been talking about.[77]

If all things were done gratefully, the "august intention of Amaterasu Ōmikami" would be satisfied.[78]

To explain the grace provided by the circular enclosure made it

---

74 Kano, *Shihonshugi*, p. 138. See also Helen Hardacre, *Kurozumikyō and the New Religions of Japan* (Princeton, N.J.: Princeton University Press, 1986). 75 Kano, *Shihonshugi*, p. 139.
76 Ibid., p. 140; also, Murakami Shigeyoshi and Yasumaru Yoshio, eds., *Nihon shisō taikei*, vol. 67: *Minshū shūkyō to shisō* (Tokyo: Iwanami shoten, 1971), p. 130. Hereafter cited as *Minshū shūkyō to shisō*. 77 *Minshū shūkyō to shisō*, p. 115. 78 Kano, *Shihonshugi*, p. 114.

appropriate to develop an idea of order faithful to its requirements. The central principle lay in the deity's capacity to fulfill all requests. When individuals entrusted themselves to the the sun goddess's ordinances, they were immediately relieved of evil. To enter the enclosure meant leaving the world of suffering and misfortune; and as the epoch came to a close, followers increasingly read that to mean the Tokugawa social system. Kurozumi's message presupposed the power of the deity to deliver people's requests. By locating all blessings in the sun goddess, he was able to place his principal emphasis on the believers' faith in the deity and their willingness to make the effort to improve conditions. Kurozumi held that the unification of the believers' intention with that of Amaterasu meant that people themselves had to show by faith and goodness that they were deserving. Failure to secure grace or blessing revealed only one's unworthiness and lack of real faith. Next came the idea that all people were brothers and sisters. This, too, resulted from the conception of a united intention. "When assisting," he wrote in a poem, "there is life."[79] Life was accessible to all. Kurozumi believed that all people were ultimately children of the sun goddess. "There are none who do not give thanks sincerely; one truth is that all in the four seas are brothers."[80] With the universalistic thrust of this idea, its immediate purpose was to stem contemporary conflict and distrust. The idea promoted a powerful sense of equality and sharing. Things are important, Kurozumi wrote, but they do not constitute criteria by which to separate people between the esteemed and despised. Neither life nor death, high nor low can separate people from one another. In this connection Kurozumi sought to juxtapose the spirit of sun (light and happiness) to the principle of darkness. According to Kano Masanao, the dark, or *in* (*yin*), principle was the symbol for the peasants' circumstances; it was precisely the association manifest in the status order that made the peasant low man in the hierarchy. "The august belief in the sun goddess (projecting the symbol of light – *yō* (*yang*) – increasingly dispels the spirit of darkness." If too much attention were devoted to darkness, to the exclusion of the principle of light, it would ultimately lessen and destroy the spirit of light. Kurozumi believed that a balance between the two would fulfill the expectation of a perfect and complete society, perhaps the circle he had drawn to dramatize the sacred space designated for believers. His conception of the social order was revealed in his meditations on the

79 Ibid., p. 102. 80 Ibid., p. 116.

circle. For the circle, the sun, light, Amaterasu represented fullness, plenitude, presence, perfection – surely an attractive alternative when juxtaposed to the received arrangement of authority. Kurozumi saw the installation of this new age of the *kami* as a veritable utopia glowing in the midst of progressive social darkness. "The age of the gods and of the present are one; they offer compassion to all at the end of the world."

More than Kurozumikyō, Tenri was implicated in the trials of the oppressed and conveyed the sense that the present constituted a time of crisis. It was founded by a peasant woman near Nara, Nakayama Miki (1798–1887), who was oppressed by her family and her husband and knew hardship, pain, and personal suffering. Miki's biographers have attributed her zeal for helping people to her personal experience. But Nakayama Miki also had a keen grasp of political realities; she was a sensitive recorder of the Tempō famine and an understanding witness of the *okagemairi* pilgrims who passed through her village on their way to Ise. The pilgrimage and the famine signified suffering for her and showed the necessity of finding ways to provide relief and assistance. As with Kurozumi Munetada, Miki's life unfolded as a series of cases of caring for the needy and the poor. Self-sacrifice, ascetic zeal, and a sense of injustice propelled her on her ministry. According to Carmen Blacker, Miki's ministry was marked by a number of important "tribulations" in which she was able to demonstrate her powers to heal the afflicted.[81] In time she was credited with the powers of a local shaman (*yamabushi*). In one session, when Miki was beginning to chant the incantatory spells, her face began to contort, and she fell into a trance. While still possessed by a deity she replied to a question that she was Ten no shōgun, "the true and original god who has descended from Heaven to save mankind."[82] In the presence of her husband and others, the *kami* who had come to inhabit her body asked Miki to abandon her family to serve as the vehicle and messenger for the divine work of assistance. Should her husband refuse to comply, the deity threatened to cast the family under the pall of a curse. This trance lasted three days, and only after Miki's husband consented to the divine demand did Miki return to normal. She experienced subsequent signs of divine origin as part of her passage into a new state. The sudden fits of possession and her erratic behavior as a condition for her

---

[81] Carmen Blacker, "Millenarian Aspects of New Religions," in Donald Shively, ed., *Tradition and Modernization in Japanese Culture* (Princeton, N.J.: Princeton University Press, 1971), pp. 574–6. [82] Ibid., p. 575.

ministry led to ostracism and poverty, but her success in healing, especially with respect to painless childbirth, brought her followers and the beginnings of an organization.

Miki's transformation into a divine vehicle for relief began when, commanded to give up her possessions, she decided to distribute her family land. The act dramatized personal attachment to land and the belief that ownership itself was the source of all inequality. Because equal distribution under conditions of ownership is impossible to realize, true equality can be realized only through abject landlessness. Miki's behavior underscored her teaching that "one must fall into poverty." Poverty and relief from pain became the axis of her vision. This vision was further reinforced within the structure of a cosmological myth, derived from native myth, legend, and history. According to this, the world originated in a muddy ocean (the salty brine of *kokugaku*) inhabited by a variety of fish and serpents. Because the parent deities wished to create humans, they gave birth to myriads of people on the site of the Nakayama household in Japan. These grew to great size and died. After this, the deities had created birds and beasts and a variety of insects; these also died. All that was left were monkeys. From the monkeys, men and women were born; then heaven, earth, mountains, and plains were differentiated. Humans lived first in water for eons and eventually moved onto the land. It is interesting to compare this crudely evolutionary conception with Hirata's earlier assertion that all humans originated from the insect world. Although such notions were indispensable to the peasant experience, steeped as it was in a firsthand involvement in the cycle of growth, they also showed how earlier concerns for natural history had become part of a prevailing consciousness.[83] Moreover, such an evolutionary process demonstrated the common origins of equality among all people and validated Miki's articulation of a utopian vision in her hymn *Mikagurauta* (1869).

This long text, written in Nara dialect, focused on increased agricultural productivity. "The intention of everybody in the world requires fields and lands,"[84] "if there are good fields, everybody in a row will be cleansed of desire,"[85] and it would be possible to increase the abundance of Yamato through the unlimited powers of the deities.[86] Miki also sang her expectations of social reformation: "Drum beat, the New Year's dance begins/ How wonderful; if we erect a structure for teaching/ What prosperity! revering the body and securing health/ *yonaori*."[87] Related to the idea of "world renewal" was, of course, the

[83] See Kano, *Shihonshugi*, pp. 147–8, for an account of the Tenri mythology.
[84] *Minshū shukyō to shisō*, p. 184.   [85] Ibid., p. 185.   [86] Ibid., p. 181.   [87] Ibid.

ideal of mutual assistance which was the central theme of both the *Mikagurauta* and her instructions (*Ofudesaki*). The hymn opens with a celebration that all people will be one when they assist one another. Assistance will also confer the blessings of the spirit of light: ". . . If one speaks the faith in the wider world, one and then two will be cleansed by helping each other." Assisting people will bring freedom and an eternal abode in the heart of the *kami*. Disturbances can be dispelled by recognizing the fundamental equality of all humans. "When one compares humans from the standpoint of the body," Miki wrote, "they all are the same, whether high or low." Once more, it should be noted, we encounter the metaphor of the body and its centering as subject, known by acting; it is the body, not status, that confirms humanity; not the trappings of civilization, but the blessings of the gods.

To neglect the ordinances of the *kami* and to fail to work for universal relief and assistance was to incur divine wrath. In order to ward off anger and forestall misfortune, repentance was necessary. In this context Miki pointed to the quality of late Tokugawa leadership and its failure to deliver relief and help. She characterized the leadership as high mountains, remote and distant from the ordinary folk who dwelt in the valleys and in the real world. But the power of the *kami* was vastly stronger than the power of "those who are high and make the world's conditions as they are; will they know about the misfortunes of the deities?"[88] Indeed, she had no hesitation in calling attention to the "contrast in intention between the *kami* and those in high places." The false division between high and low constituted a sign of the way that things were and the conditions of life that had to be overcome. People would change, she was convinced, because humans were "the children of the gods" and possessed a good nature. Their problem was pride (*hokori*). Pride, for Miki, was the basic human evil and produced the "eight dusts" – desire, regret, sweetness, avarice, arrogance, hatred, rancor, and anger – qualities she associated with the powerful. The powerless were advised to trust themselves to the deity of world renewal, who held out for them the promise of a renovated moral life. How the gods were to bring about this idealized world was already prefigured in Miki's conception of assistance and relief. It was, as Yasumaru Yoshio explained it, the world vision of small cultivators and encompassed diligent and frugal peasants bound together in a community of cooperation.[89]

88 Yasumaru, *Nihon kindaika*, p. 83.   89 Ibid.

Konkōkyō was established by a peasant named Kawate Bunjirō (Konkō Daijin) (1814–83) in Bitchū, also part of present-day Okayama Prefecture. Adopted into a rural family, Kawate, unlike Kurozumi and Nakayama, was deeply versed in agricultural affairs. The area was marked by commercialization and a subsequent decline of smallholding farmers. The founder experienced a long life punctuated by hardship and poverty, and this undoubtedly prompted his deep concerns for the unrelieved hardship among cultivators of the vicinity. The boundaries of his own thought were marked by his desire to secure relief from contemporary circumstances and a zeal for bringing about order and prosperity. His religiosity was early revealed in a decision to make the trek to Ise with fellow villagers during the Ise *okagemairi* of 1830. Several years later (1846) Kawate made still another pilgrimage to the Grand Shrine. His personal ministry was interrupted by bouts of illness, and it ultimately brought on a trance that disclosed to him his true identity as the brother of Konjin, one of the calendar gods of the yin–yang tradition observed in rural areas. In folk belief this deity was capable of inflicting great harm or abundant prosperity, depending on how he was worshiped. Kawate received the ordinances of this god into his body which, as with Nakayama Miki, became the instrument for the "august intelligence" (*oshirase*). Kawate also received permission from the deity to be called the "family Kane no kami's lower leaves" and to take the divine appellation of "Bunji Daimyōjin."

Once Kawate, or as he now came to be called, Konkō Daijin, served as the vessel of Konjin's *oshirase*, the popular understanding of that *kami* was transformed. A figure that had been associated with curse and calamity became a *kami* of love who brought good fortune and abundance to those who followed his commandments. As the instructions of the *kami* proliferated and encouraged agricultural activity among believers, the cult spread.[90] In 1859 Konkō Daijin, on instructions from the *kami*, went into concealment. Empowered as a *daimyōjin*, Konkō Daijin now functioned as a living *kami*. Like Miki, he gave up all his possessions to demonstrate his faith in Tenchi Kane no kami. His new organization coincided with the critical events of the pre-Restoration decade. In an environment charged with political struggle and shogunal failure, a saying went, "How many distressed *ujiko* (members) there are in society! But if the *kami* help, the people will be able to live."[91] Nine years before the Restoration, when he returned from his concealment, Kawate established a formal religious organization.

90 Murakami, *Kinsei minshū shūkyō no kenkyū*, p. 177.   91 Ibid., p. 179.

More than other founders, Konkō Daijin stressed the importance of knowledge in the form of the *oshirase*. This is not to say that other groups were not interested in the question of knowledge. But Kawate was more systematic about the kind of knowledge that his followers should possess. While he served as the agency to transmit divine knowledge, the revelations he made in response to specific problems were not sudden. He received instructions in a conscious state, not in the circumstances of a trance, but he alone was able to recall the content of the divine instructions and interpret them to others.[92] Sharing with the founders of the other sects a profound distrust of conventional knowledge, Kawate's central text for the faithful condemned learning (*gakumon*) as something that "consumes the body" and as the product of mere "cleverness" and contrivance.[93] He freely granted that he did not have much formal learning and was not very literate:

Today's society is one of wisdom and knowledge. By permitting humans to become clever, we risk losing the virtue of the body. In this age the principal pollutant is desire. Let us be released from the use of the abacus. It is said that we are clever but have no skills. We show off our cleverness and rely on artifice. Let us separate ourselves from cleverness, contrivance, and wisdom. Let us depart from the assistance and customs of society. By leaving society, we will be able to entrust our body to the *kami*.[94]

Accordingly, acts of "listening" and "understanding" were supremely important. In the operation of listening and understanding, the body became the reservoir for intentionality and knowing similar to the way Konkō used his own body as agency for divinity. It was the action of the body, not the contrivances and ruses of mere knowledge extracted from books and conventional instruction, that promised to secure people relief from society's afflictions. The *Konkō Daijin rikai* reported that the founder disapproved of religious austerities and advised that "eating and drinking are important to the body."[95] The body required strength if it was to express its faith and belief by working and acting.

The knowledge valued by Konkō Daijin related to how people were to assist others. Like the other new religions, Konkōkyō stressed relief and assistance for others as the condition for faith. No other kind of knowledge was required. Here again, this idea pertained to contemporary society and custom which had failed to provide relief to the distressed. Konkō Daijin constantly called on people to leave society,

---

92 Seto Mikio, "Minshū no shūkyō ishiki to henkaku no enerugi," in Maruyama Teruo, ed., *Henkakuki no shūkyō* (Tokyo: Gendai jaanarizumu shuppankai, 1972), p. 67.
93 *Minshū shūkyō to shisō*, p. 364.   94 Ibid., p. 376.   95 Ibid., pp. 400, 404.

with all its contrivances and fragmenting propensities, and to entrust themselves to the *kami,* whose grace would manifest itself in people helping people. "Men, assisting men, are human."[96] Mutual help distinguished humans from other species and represented a special form of thanks to the *kami.* Just as the deities, at times of illness and disaster, offered assistance to humans, so humans should assist the needy in times of distress.

Such assistance was also based on the idea of human equality. Here Konkō proposed two interrelated notions: All people are members of the "family of the deity" (*kamisama no ujiko*), and they are capable of becoming deities themselves. Together they represented a new concept of community. "All under heaven," he advised, "are the *ujiko* of the deities of heaven and earth. There are no other kinds of men."[97] Because all were potentially *ujiko,* "one cannot look down on humans or befoul them." Closely associated with this sense of equality was the new status assigned to women. All the new religions elevated women to a status equivalent to men, and some, like Konkō, even tended to exalt them. "Women are the rice fields of the world," Konkō Daijin announced, and in the "teachings of the deities, if the rice fields are not fertilized and enriched, they will be of no value."[98] Life itself would not be possible. Hence Konkō proposed, employing familiar metaphors of samurai politics and power, that women were the *karō* (principal retainers) of the household; if there were no *karō,* there could be no castle. Thus women and peasants, precisely because they lacked access to the established disciplines of learning, became exemplars of what was truly human. Belief came from women; they were close to the deities. No doubt valuing women in this way stemmed from an idealized agricultural respect for productivity. Both Kurozumi and Tenri also showed real concern for women physiologically, especially with reference to problems and pain incurred at the time of childbirth.

Yet ultimately all people were capable of becoming godlike. "Deity and man," Kawate announced, "are the same." Whatever deity one worships, if he fails to correspond to the heart of man, he will not correspond to the heart of the *kami;* and if he fails to correspond to the heart of the deity, he will not conform to the heart of man."[99] Konkō Daijin wrote that as he had received the "august principle of *yin* (*okage*) to become a living deity, so you (*anatagata*) will receive the principle as well." A living *kami* was nothing more than someone

---

96 Ibid., p. 420.   97 Ibid., p. 401.   98 Ibid., p. 416.   99 Ibid.

doing the work of the deity in a human moment and was a status available to all. Hence he constantly played down his own exalted status as an intermediary and acknowledged personal "ignorance," as he was simply a man who "tills the soil and does not know anything." Irony notwithstanding, Konkō Daijin possessed the kind of knowledge necessary to make him and all followers living *kami*. The community of believers thus constituted a divine assembly, as "all receive their bodies from the *kami* of heaven and earth."[100]

In its elaboration of a new community of believers serving one another and withdrawn from official society, Konkō stressed, not least of all, the primacy of household work and agricultural cultivation. As he himself was a committed farmer, he paid close attention, as did the rural *kokugakusha*, to growing conditions and agricultural techniques. He was particularly interested in weather ("wind and rain" as he put it) but linked such conditions to the presence or absence of belief. He rejected the idea that a mere visit to the shrine would bring wind and rain at the right time. Proper conditions could be secured only if faith allowed the *kami* to enter one's body. Evidence of such faith was shown by attending to one's household duties. The believer's sense of joy, he noted, would make him feel obliged to tend to his household duties.[101]

DEFENSE AND WEALTH

In the late Tokugawa period, Dutch studies, as it was first called, combined with eighteenth-century discussions on political economy (*keisei saimin*) to create the possibility of a new discourse. Dutch studies expressed an interest in the new sciences of medicine, anatomy and physiology, natural science, astronomy, physics, and geography. Political economy aimed at uncovering the sources of wealth. As it was formulated in the early nineteenth century, the new discourse first emphasized maritime defense and related science and technology and then moved on to discuss national wealth. The impulses underlying such a discourse was the increasing presence of foreigners who were searching for adventure, trade, and empire, and the domestic economic failures, which the Tempō reforms were seeking to arrest. At the heart of this new discourse was a dissatisfaction, bordering on outright criticism, with the shogunal political arrangement and its evident incapacity to act decisively and effectively to find adequate sources of wealth for relieving the people (*saimin*).

100 Ibid.   101 Ibid., p. 366.

Writers at the turn of the century had already alerted contemporaries to the foreign menace and the need for adequate coastal defense and a firm national policy. Discussions on defense turned on the question of adequate military technology, but any consideration of science and technology invariably raised the issue of political decision making. An early proponent, Kudō Heisuke (1734–1800), saw the installation of new maritime fortifications as the fundamental condition for a new policy. "The first aim in governing the realm," he wrote, "is to deepen the power of our country. To deepen the strength of the country, we have first to allow the wealth of foreign countries to enter Japan." Trade was an absolute necessity, as it generated the wealth that many came to recognize as the key to a proper defense. Kudō went on to advocate the opening of new lands like Hokkaido and the systematic search for gold, silver, and copper. Another contemporary, Hayashi Shihei (1738–93), author of a famous geographic miscellany, *Sankoku tsūran zusetsu*, shared a similar view and was even more insistent about the merger of defense and the search for wealth.

It was Honda Toshiaki (1744–1821) who first grasped in global terms the problem of wealth and formulated a coherent statement yoking wealth to defense:

Because Japan is a maritime nation, crossing the ocean, transport, and trade are the primary vocations of the realm. In governing with the power of only one domain, the national strength weakens increasingly. This weakness affects the peasantry, and it is a natural condition for them to yearly decrease their productivity.[102]

He was convinced that policy must reach beyond a single domain to represent and employ the resources of the whole. Trade and markets were also necessary. Once Japan was thrown into the global market network, it would have to compete with other countries in a struggle for scarce resources. Appearing as a good mercantilist, Honda was persuaded that the search for trade and markets was prompted by the domestic scarcity of goods, products, and natural resources. Yet it was in Japan's national interest to promote foreign trade if the realm was to survive and overcome chronic domestic difficulties. Honda noted that Japan differed from other Western nations only in its scientific and technological inferiority, but he was convinced that the gap could be closed.[103]

---

102 Quoted in Maeda Ichirō, ed., *Kōza Nihon bunkashi* (Tokyo: Misuzu shobō, 1963), vol. 6, p. 58.
103 Tetsuo Najita, "Structure and Content in Tokugawa Thinking," unpublished manuscript, p. 54.

More than any other political economist, Honda recognized the relationship between trade as a source of national wealth and Japan's technological backwardness. To rectify both, he proposed in an unpublished essay, *Keisei hissaku* (1798), four urgent priorities: (1) the systematic manufacturing of explosives for military and civil purposes; (2) the development of mining, as metals were the backbone of the nation's wealth; (3) the establishment of a national merchant marine that would enhance the national treasury by selling products abroad and help avoid domestic famines; and (4) the abrogation of seclusion for a policy of colonial enterprises in nearby territories.[104] Collectively, these proposals were meant to show that Japan had pursued an unnatural course that had led to an economic dead end. Isolation was anachronistic, territorial decentralization destructive to the national interest, and agricultural primacy was a fiction in view of Japan's maritime position. Japan should promote a policy directed toward the opening of trade in order to meet, rather than to be subdued by, the European thrust in Asia.[105]

Any consideration of defense and wealth entailed employing a new knowledge capable of developing military technology and finding new sources of wealth. When thoughtful men turned to this question, they embraced a form of inquiry that validated the investigation of first principles, but they were also mindful to balance the inherent formalism of first principles with a conception of historicism that accounted for changing circumstances. As did other contemporary discourses, Western learning used a strategy that required reducing things to origins in order to demonstrate how the principle of the past authorized changes in the present. Whereas Mito, *kokugaku*, and the new religions resorted to primal deities and archetypal events to specify first principles, Western studies referred to paradigmatic heroes in the remote past whose accomplishments reflected the conviction that each age demanded policies adequate to its requirements. The discourse on defense and wealth, owing to its commitment to defend the realm as a whole rather than as a domain or a region, inched toward abandoning feudalism for a conception of a larger political unity. Ultimately, the cultural content of the discourse came to suggest the political form of the early modern state to satisfy the imperatives of national wealth and defense. If other discourses searched for ways to deliver relief and assistance to the needy, the discussions on defense and wealth saw a

---

104 Ibid., pp. 54–5; and Donald Keene, *The Japanese Discovery of Europe* (Stanford, Calif.: Stanford University Press, 1969), for a partial translation of *keisei hissaku*.
105 Najita, "Structure and Content," p. 60.

mercantilist state as the form most able to realize this goal. Honda early perceived in the state the agency to supply such services when he observed that the "several European nations are kingdoms that provide assistance to people; it is a heavenly duty of the kingdom to relieve hunger and cold with trade, overseas transport, and passage."[106] The state that such writers came to conceptualize was more mercantilist than despotic or absolutist and was based on social labor and productivity, manufacturing, and trade. In this regard, it was also more ethical than merely political, which many writers identified with the privatism of the Tokugawa bakufu. Although the practitioners of this discourse, as good mercantilists, shied away from thinking about an equitable redistribution of national resources, as did the Mito writers, they displaced the egalitarian impulse by turning to merit, talent, and ability as criteria for recruitment and advancement. The demonstration of talent (*jinzai*) depended on the mastery of expert knowledge useful to the necessities of the day. The discourse on wealth and defense envisaged human subjectivity as the maker of custom and history and agreed that the human species, even though people held different stations in life, originated from a single source. Although Western studies rejected the existence of qualitative distinctions among people, it did believe that status derived from the acquisition and demonstration of useful knowledge which constituted the only acceptable criterion of social and political preferment. But it also agreed with Mito that such knowledge was not available to all, even though it resisted making this conceit into a principle of preemptive closure. It is, furthermore, important to note that its followers frequently came from small and medium-sized domains, often *fudai* houses, and sometimes large merchant houses, men who were no doubt convinced that transforming the bakufu into a national organization devoted to promoting wealth and defense would save them as well.

The maturation of the discourse on wealth and defense occurred in 1830, with the establishment of the Shōshikai, two years after the famous Siebold incident. Two of the members of this group had previously been Siebold's students. By resorting to examination of the foreign scientist as a "spy" and condemnation for his chief contact, Takahashi Kageyasu, the authorities had raised the stakes for anybody desiring to pursue the new knowledge independently. One of the

106 Maeda, *Kōza Nihon bunkashi*, vol. 6, p. 59.

casualties of the incident and a former student of Siebold, Takano Chōei (1804–50) remarked in the wake of the persecution that because of the bakufu's policies, the "school of Western scholars was momentarily frightened, and Western studies began to decline."[107] As a result, organizing an independent study group in Edo years later constituted an act of calculated risk.

The Shōshikai's agenda was to explore new kinds of knowledge that promised to yield practical solutions to contemporary domestic and foreign problems; its heyday coincided with the Tempō famine, mounting peasant disturbances, violent urban uprisings, and Ōshio's Osaka rebellion. Writing years later in *Bansha sōyaku shoki*, Takano Chōei explained that the society aimed to supplement traditional samurai learning which, emphasizing elegance and ornamentation in expression rather than substance, prepared people for purely literary careers. He commented that this tradition "has not been useful for the relief of society" and recalled that when the group was founded, many believed it was necessary to "understand how to mend social abuses."

Since 1833, famines have occurred among the lower classes in the cities and the countryside. One can only conjecture at what is happening in the countryside. In response, there have been expressions of regret, and many have produced books concerning relief and ruin. Because many of these [books] investigated specific conditions relating to political economy, several domains implemented policies [to rectify the conditions] and tended to question the nature of political affairs itself. But because the problems have become exceedingly complex and so difficult to resolve, we decided to establish the Shōshikai.[108]

In addition, news concerning the intention and appearance of foreign ships, though frequently incorrect, seemed to appear more frequently during the 1830s and was used increasingly by shogunal critics to justify their demands for new policies.[109] One such rumor circulating throughout Edo prompted Takano and Watanabe to question the bakufu's expulsion policy. Takano's *Yume monogatari* (Tale of a dream) and Watanabe Kazan's report on foreign policy resulted in shogunal action leading to the dissolution of the society, imprisonment of its principal members, and Watanabe's eventual suicide. The inci-

---

107 Kitajima Masamoto, *Bakuhansei no kumon*, vol. 18 of *Nihon no rekishi* (Tokyo: Chūō kōronsha, 1966), p. 367.
108 Satō Shōsuke, Uete Michiari, and Yamaguchi Muneyuki, eds., *Nihon shisō taikei*, vol. 66: *Watanabe Kazan, Takano Chōei, Sakuma Shōzan, Yokoi Shōnan, Hashimoto Sanai* (Tokyo: Iwanami shoten, 1971), p. 190. Hereafter cited as *Watanabe Kazan, Takano Chōei, Sakuma Shōzan, Yokoi Shōnan, Hashimoto Sanai*.   109 Ibid., pp. 192, 193.

dent became known as *bansha no goku*, or the purge of barbarian scholars.[110]

It is important to note that the society, many of whose members had begun in Dutch studies with some proficiency in medicine, anatomy, and natural history, shifted its focus to investigating knowledge that might be put into the service of the country. Guiding this decision was the belief that appropriate policy could not be formulated unless it were informed by knowledge adequate to its objectives. This apparent coupling of knowledge and power was fully acknowledged by the society when it demonstrated how policies concerning famine relief drew attention to political conduct or when it made public the official insensitivity to questions relating to maritime navigation and defense. Yet it is important to add that the society's leading figures envisaged political criticism as an effect of a new conception of culture. Takano Chōei, for example, explained in his *Wasuregatami* (*Torii no nakune*) that it was possible to imagine changes in the content of culture and necessary to pursue a critical course if such changes were to be enacted. As evidence, he offered the example of his associate Watanabe Kazan who had been transformed from the status of a high-ranking samurai noted for his literary and artistic interests into a serious and committed student of Western learning. Despite his considerable achievements in traditional disciplines, art, composition, and his exquisite sensibilities, Watanabe had changed, Takano reported, after observing places marked by disaster and famine in recent years.

What provoked Watanabe to make this cultural "sea change" was his search for reasons explaining contemporary hardship and disorder. The rich, he observed, seemed to get richer, while the poor slipped farther down the scale of poverty. Everywhere the poor were resorting to rebellion. "Because tumult has spread throughout the society for one reason or another," Takano wrote, "he [Watanabe], impelled by a grieving heart, began excerpting selections from Dutch books on the *kokutai* of all countries and political affairs and circumstances revealing social conditions and the way people felt." Next, he had turned to examining the pros and cons of contemporary affairs, writing essays on the issues of the day and discussing these matters with other thoughtful men. "Even though he had studied the way of old, he had

---

[110] The novelist Ishikawa Jun wrote a moving account of this complex and concerned intellectual: *Watanabe Kazan* (Tokyo: Chikuma shobō, 1964). Marius B. Jansen, "Rangaku and Westernization," *Modern Asian Studies* 18 (1984), also described this early Westernizing impulse, based on a survey of the recent secondary literature.

become a person whose doubts could no longer be concealed."[111] In place of the traditional learning that served him so well before but that now fell short of providing an understanding of contemporary conditions, he sought to substitute science and technology. Watanabe himself confessed as much in a letter in 1840 to Maki Sadachika in which he asserted that no division existed between the Way and the reality of custom.[112]

Watanabe's views on Western culture confirmed the efficacy of this new content. Western learning represented a new orientation, he believed, and thus required new methods to achieve it. In *Gekizetsu wakumon*, he complained that the traditional discrimination between "civilized" and "barbarian" was bound to cause serious trouble for Japan in the future as it affected Western nations. Times changed, and the present could never be the same as the past. Men who apprehended the present from the standpoint of the past tried to anchor the *koto* (Japanese harp) to a support and were obliged to pull both harp and support when they moved. The learning of T'ang China was inapplicable to Japan's current needs and resembled a "dream within a dream." Watanabe relied on the explanatory powers of historicism to explain that great changes have occurred since antiquity. Among these changes, one of the most important had been the Western use of "things" (in physics). Although he plainly recognized a differentiation between practicality and doctrine (morality) in the *Shinkiron*, he also acknowledged that each could assist the other and form a complementary relationship. When juxtaposing the "Way of the West" to the "Way of Japan," it might be supposed that they were different, but because both were informed by reason (*dōri*), they were ultimately one and the same. Study showed that what distinguished Western societies from Japan was their discovery and development and science and technology, not their favorable climates (as Honda Toshiaki had thought), rich lands, or even vast populations. Western superiority disclosed the difference between diligence and indolence. For Watanabe, diligence meant wisdom, knowledge, and effort. Western schools prospered in subjects like political studies, medicine, physics, and religion, whereas Chinese learning was moribund. "Because the Western barbarians have concentrated chiefly on physics, they have acquired detailed knowledge of the world and the four directions." Fearing the West, the Japanese "hear the thunder and block their ears. The greater evil is to shut one's eyes because one detests

111 *Watanabe Kazan, Takano Chōei, Sakuma Shōzan, Yokoi Shōnan, Hashimoto Sanai*, pp. 179–80.   112 Ibid., p. 123.

listening. It is our duty to investigate not only the principles of creation but also the principles of all things and opinions."¹¹³ Technology, the application of scientific principles, as Watanabe understood them, was particularly important to this new endeavor, because it showed how to transform the physical landscape through methods of construction and excavation, to put up schools, hospitals, and poor houses; technology pointed to the way that culture might be changed.

Watanabe's faith in the practical use of science and technology inspired specific proposals. The foreign question had become particularly irksome, and Japan was the only country that did not have a relationship with the West. As a result, Japan has come to resemble a "piece of meat left along the roadside. How can the attention of wolves and tigers be avoided?" Without proper knowledge, Japan's security had acquired all of the "contentment of a frog in a pond."¹¹⁴ Politics originated on the basis of what was considered reliable, whereas misfortune ushered in the smug assumption that nothing was wrong. Today, Japan existed only because of the happy accident of geography that offered protection by distance and the seas. But it was no longer possible to depend on what others had relied on in the past and to be consoled by solutions that had worked before. China, once a vast and powerful land, was already heaving under the impact of seaborne Western intrusions. Hence, the first task for Japanese was to abrogate the seclusion policy and then to embark on a program of maritime trade and defense.

Watanabe saw that the globe had become a competitive arena for struggle among nations, but Japanese leadership had failed to see that Japan would involuntarily be drawn into this contest. T'ang learning had come to Japan in remote antiquity. Since that time empty studies had prospered continuously to divert men's minds from the real tasks at hand. The new learning demanded a commitment to preparing for the defense of Edo Bay. The bakufu's failure to recognize the necessity for such preparations revealed an even more basic incapacity to grasp the power offered by Western knowledge. Not even the bakufu's most reliable allies had yet been deployed to the region of the bay. Caustically, Watanabe described the situation as a sign of "domestic catastrophe" (*naikan*), rather than "external disaster" (*gaikan*): a failure of nerve rather than an outside threat.¹¹⁵

The threat of an invasion imperiling a defenseless Japan haunted Takano Chōei as well. Unlike Watanabe, Takano was a professional

---
113 Ibid., p. 78.   114 Ibid., pp. 69, 72.
115 Satō Shōsuke, *Yōgakushi no kenkyū* (Tokyo: Chūō kōronsha, 1964), p. 168.

student and translator of Western learning and a leading proponent of the utility of the new learning. This interest in medicine fostered in the discourse on Western studies continued even after many of its adherents shifted their focus to questions concerning defense and military technology, and it represented an impulse comparable to the effort of relieving the ill and diseased found among the new religions. As a principal participant in the Shōshikai, Takano had begun in the 1830s to direct his own interest toward resolving the perceived disjunction between the domestic policy of feudal fragmentation and the question of national defense. Upon learning of a proposed visit of an English ship in the late 1830s, he drafted an essay to express his alarm at the probable rejection of such a probe. Takano charged in *Yume monogatari* (Tale of a dream, 1838) that expelling the *Morrison* would be considered by the British as the act of a belligerent country that understood neither right nor wrong. The loss of virtue resulting from this action would result in untold disasters.[116] Years later, Yokoi Shōnan transformed this reading of national moral conduct in international affairs into a classic defense of trade and peaceful foreign relations against the noisy claims of xenophobic expulsionists.

While others joined the discussion on maritime defense in the early 1840s, the issue came to command serious attention by shogunal officials, who understood that a decision on defense meant a prior commitment to a different conception of knowledge. Even as Watanabe and Takano were trying to establish the outer boundaries of the discourse on defense, bakufu officials like Egawa Tarōzaemon and Torii Yōzō turned to formulating appropriate proposals for policy after making their inspections of Edo Bay. Egawa's views corresponded closely to those held by Watanabe, but Torii rejected any suggestion of entering into relations with countries like England. Torii (who has sometimes been portrayed as the archetype of malevolence) was not a simple witchhunter; his memorandum late in 1840 disclosed a keen awareness of weapons manufacture. But he also recognized that a new conception of the world was at the heart of the problem of defense. Unlike many contemporaries, he was not convinced of British technological superiority at this time and thought the English victory over China to be inconclusive. What distressed him about proposals calling for new measures of defense and the implementation of Western technology was that they were linked to a larger view of the world whose acceptance he rejected as vigorously as he denounced colonialism. Although the cannons used by

---

116 *Watanabe Kazan, Takano Chōei, Sakuma Shōzan, Yokoi Shōnan, Hashimoto Sanai*, pp. 168–9.

the West performed efficiently, he wrote, and might be especially useful for coastal defense, in Japanese warfare there had been little utilization of weapons useful chiefly for a precision strike applied in places where large numbers of men were concentrated in close quarters.[117] This difference dramatized the profound distinction between Japanese and Western customs. The West planned only for the pursuit of profit, in contrast with a society intent on rites and rituals; it waged war to compete, rather than to defend morality. Owing to the disparity between these two social orders, it was inappropriate for the Japanese to have any faith in Western science and technology. What Torii implied was that any acceptance of Western technique necessarily meant adopting the culture that had produced it. Writers like Watanabe and Takano had already demonstrated that their interest in the West was not restricted merely to cannons but included the whole matrix of education and customs on which its culture was based. The dangers of a policy aimed at incorporating Western culture, Torii warned, were great. "The first principle of defense entails encouraging the strengthening of traditional military and civilian skills. At the same time, it is important to eliminate frivolous military discipline and esteem competence."[118]

In response to Torii's critique of the new Western learning, Egawa argued that Torii had deliberately misrepresented the nature of British activity in China and had misunderstood the knowledge they employed. Although wise planning always involved the study and mastery of military skills, it also included an evaluation of methods that were strange and effective. In accord with the ancient advice to "know the other in order to know oneself," it was imperative for the Japanese to learn as much as possible about the English before formulating a policy. When the Chinese were confronted by the British, they had no knowledge of the adversary they faced. How could they have devised a wise plan? China's failure and its subsequent defeat by the British reflected a reliance on empty theories and useless knowledge. Egawa was confident that importing cannons and other hardware would not constitute a faddish whim. It was common knowledge that Confucianism and Buddhism had been imported from abroad, and it was well known that there were many foreign products esteemed for their convenience and value. If such goods had a useful purpose, they were not fads. To favor trifling and useless toys might be a waste, but it was not whimsy to adopt useful items.

In the ensuing debate, the real problem clearly lay in the relation-

[117] Sugiura Mimpei, *Nihon no shisō*, vol. 16: *Kirishitan, rangakushū* (Tokyo: Chikuma shobō, 1970), p. 353.   [118] Ibid., p. 354.

ship between employing foreign military technology for defense and adopting the whole system of knowledge that produced it. Torii rightly considered this enabling knowledge as a threat to the legitimacy of the Tokugawa order, and he derived little solace from Egawa's thinly disguised effort to justify importing discrete items rather than the whole cultural matrix. Provoked less by charges of official incompetence (which he could easily acknowledge) than by the threat to Tokugawa claims to legitimacy, Torii recognized that the importation of military technology would inevitably lead to incorporating the enabling culture and jeopardizing the foundations of the traditional world order. His fears were systematized in classic manner by Ōhashi Totsuan years later in a last-ditch defense of the Neo-Confucian conception of a natural order.

In the last decades of the Tokugawa era, the discourse on defense was transmuted into a coherent theory of cultural purpose capable of combining the claims of a traditional world view with the principles of scientific discovery. This task was accomplished by Sakuma Shōzan (1811–64) and Yokoi Shōnan. Although they were initially prompted by the project to find a fit between Neo-Confucianism, however they understood it by this time, and Western learning, they contributed to reinforcing the primacy of the new knowledge as the fundamental condition for understanding the world and acting in it. Their effort to secure entry into the new knowledge through the agency of received philosophical idiom attests to the importance they assigned to finding a way of using both. Yet their ultimate solution was to lay the foundations for the subsequent dismissal of nature in favor of a history that was crucial to later Meiji efforts to establish a system of useful and instrumental knowledge.

The key to this vast transformation lay in Sakuma Shōzan's decision to recognize in Western knowledge a source of power as great as morality. Both Watanabe and Takano had taken steps in this direction, but neither of them went as far as to propose systematically the equivalence between two different forms of knowledge. The nature of international events in the late 1840s and 1850s had changed considerably, and the frequent appearance of Western ships in Japanese waters undoubtedly persuaded Sakuma to conclude that the world had come to represent a stage on which nations acted out their claims. If Japan failed to compete in this struggle for power, it would be eliminated. Accepting Western learning under these circumstances, "controlling the barbarians with their own methods," resolved the problem of acquiring the necessary strength and power to compete effectively in the coming contest. But power really referred to knowledge and its enabling cultural matrix. It was necessary to grasp the very principles that produced the techniques that now promised to protect the realm against Western colonialism. Without it, Sakuma warned, Japan was doomed.

It is important to note that Sakuma's commitment to study Western weaponry failed to follow the usual course of appraising Neo-Confucian metaphysics first. During the 1830s he made two extended trips to Edo. On the first he studied with the prominent Confucian teacher Satō Issai (1772–1859), the mentor of many late Tokugawa figures. His second trip coincided with the controversy over the alleged *Morrison* visit, shogunal punishment of Watanabe and Takano, news of the first Anglo-Chinese war, and the continuing debate over the defense of Edo Bay, a debate fueled by Takashima Shūhan's memorial calling for a new program of cannon casting. During his residence in Edo, Sakuma also witnessed at firsthand Mizuno Tadakuni's shogunal reforms, which included the appointment of Shōzan's lord Sanada Yukitsura to the post of naval defense. Sanada selected Sakuma as his adviser and commanded him to begin studying military technology. In response, Sakuma enrolled in Egawa Tarōzaemon's school. This sequence of events suggests that Sakuma did not enter into Western studies through Neo-Confucianism, as if it constituted a logical extension of his philosophical position, but found himself involved in the immediate and practical problem of coastal defense and cannon casting, thanks to the initiative of his lord. The identification of power as a new element in global policies, and the urgency to define practical programs enabling Japan to compete, prompted him to think about the relationship between the claims of the new knowledge and Neo-Confucianism, his own intellectual endowment. Sakuma's appraisal of Neo-Confucianism proceeded from his encounter with the new knowledge.

Through his contact with Egawa, Sakuma learned of the imprisonment of members of the Shōshikai and secured knowledge of Watanabe Kazan's writings. His own thoughts concerning European kingship appear to be a replay of Watanabe's elaborate explanation of kings and their importance in the expansion of the state. Disappointed in Egawa, Sakuma soon left the school after deciding that it had nothing to offer comparable to the views articulated by Watanabe.

Following a lead forged first by Egawa, Sakuma argued that the promise of an investigative method (*kyūri*) had been smothered by excessive concern for textual studies and that the true meaning of "the investigation of things" had been lost. Since antiquity, the Japanese and Chinese had therefore been robbed of the fruits of investigation and had forfeited the means to build national power. He advised that it was essential to national survival to make the effort to know the enemy, even though such knowledge had been forestalled by cultural conceit and complacency. "The urgency for preparing to meet a foreign invasion does not begin just by knowing them (the foreigners). The method by which you know them lies not just in exhausting their skills but in combining their learning with ours."[119] If they had large ships, Japan should construct large ships; if they had large guns, so should Japan. Sakuma warned against using outmoded and ancient methods that could not ensure victory. To use new technologies from the West was the condition for containing the foreigner. The expansion of the West and the war in China had shown that mere ethical propriety was no longer an adequate defense against colonization. By recognizing the centrality of power over morality alone, Sakuma distanced his discussion from the Mito discourse and made the crucial distinction between the opportunity of power and moral opportunity.[120] His recognition of power drove him to abandon a view that foreigners were mere barbarians who knew nothing of the niceties of morality and civilization.

And yet Sakuma's concern with power compelled him to minimize the substantive difference between Japanese and Western societies. He condemned the Chinese for having lost to the British because of their unwillingness to see foreigners as something more than barbarians who were no different from birds and beasts. To slight the great powers as barbarous, he wrote to his lord in 1849, "is a principle of great injury and small benefit to the state." Ultimately, he saw no incompatibility between "customs of the West and Japan's conventions." "When . . . foreign studies are carried on prosperously, the beautiful customs of our country will gradually change," but "if there is distrust and doubt, then they (foreign studies) will be impeded."[121] Received learning, like any learning, had to demonstrate its universality before its validity could be established. Attachment to rites and propriety should not be restricted to China and Japan alone. Knowledge knew no boundaries; nothing was foreign if it proved useful in preserving the independence of the realm.

Thus Sakuma viewed the new knowledge as a form of power.

---

119 Shinano kyōikukai, eds., *Shōzan zenshū* (Nagano: Shinano Mainichi shimbunsha, 1922), vol. 1, p. 128.
120 Uete Michiari, *Nihon kindai shisō keisei* (Tokyo: Iwanami shoten, 1974), pp. 39–40.
121 *Shōzan zenshū*, vol. 2, p. 710.

Knowledge of military technology guaranteed power, and its mastery was mandated by the "welfare of the state." Although this view originally restricted the adoption of Western learning to military matters, (trade, he still believed in 1843, would result in the importation of useless products), Sakuma was to change his mind. The positive inducement of Western scientific technique would result in the expansion of contact with other nations. If "strength" was the criterion, then any policy, including opening the country, would be justified if it led to the realization and completion of national power. This opinion marked Sakuma's thought after the Perry mission (1854) and the subsequent signing of commercial treaties. In the wake of these events, he began to advocate maritime travel and foreign trade. He considered the opening of trade between Japan and the outside world as a corollary to his conception of power. Military prowess needed a sustaining source of wealth, and trade was the only policy by which a small Japan could accumulate national power to strengthen its military capacity. In one of his last petitions (February 1862) Shōzan eloquently made the case for greater contact with the West. "The skills and techniques of foreign countries," he wrote, "especially the inventions of Newton and Copernicus and the discoveries of Columbus, have progressed long distances and extended to things like physics, geography, shipbuilding, cannon casting, and the construction of fortifications." From their prosperous study of the steam engine, the Europeans had navigated steam-driven ships at sea and steam-driven trains on land. Such accomplishments depended on exploring for resources at home: iron for railways, and coals for foundries. "How can we enrich and strengthen the national power? We must deduce from the facts." In Japan, he continued, neither the bakufu nor the domains had made much of a start. "If, however, Japan exerts itself for the profit of trade, strengthens its national power, attends to preparing ships, casting cannons, and building warships, it will be able to resist any country. . . . Should we not unite with the great countries and formulate a plan . . . ?" Knowledge and superior technology, he believed, would lead to "mutual refinement" and "mutual growth."[122]

This argument rested on the conviction that countries such as Japan and China were inferior to the West in more than military ways. If Japan was to withstand the peril of the Western presence and preserve its independence, it would have to proceed from the basis of powerful knowledge and powerful learning. In the past the trouble had stemmed

122 *Watanabe Kazan, Takano Chōei, Sakuma Shōzan, Yokoi Shōnan, Hashimoto Sanai*, pp. 322–3.

from the failure to identify the essence of useful learning. This perception was linked to Sakuma's understanding of the "investigation of principles." He now tried to restructure Neo-Confucianism by rescuing an earlier tradition of philosophic monism and by superimposing the idea of *kyūri* on Western natural science. Rather than investigating to satisfy the needs of ethics, he emphasized grasping the "principle of things" in the natural, material world. What he proposed was a "correspondence" between Chu Hsi Confucianism, which he never rejected, and Western natural science.

The meaning of Chu Hsi's thought is to penetrate principle in conformity [with the needs of] the realm so as to increase knowledge. When the meaning of the Ch'eng-Chu school corresponds to such things as the investigation of Western conditions, the explanations of those two teachers will correspond to the world. If we follow the meaning of the Ch'eng-Chu school, even Western skills will become part of learning and knowledge and will not appear outside our framework.[123]

Sakuma saw no real conflict between Neo-Confucian claims to knowledge and Western skills. If conflict appeared, it would have meant postulating two distinct cultures, a "we" and a "they," which were foreclosed by his conception of power and global struggle. In a letter to a friend, he stated that "there are not two principles of the universe residing in different places. The learning skills developed in the West are conducive to the learning of the sages. . . ."[124] And to the shogunal official Kawaji Toshiakira, he wrote that because the Western science of investigating principles conformed to the intention of Ch'eng-Chu, their explanations should apply correspondingly elsewhere. In this reformulation of the traditional epistemology, Sakuma expanded the meaning of investigation to include measurement, proof, and evidence and concluded that they constituted the real bases of all learning, which was mathematics. All learning was cumulative, "refinement," as he put it. Because Sakuma saw no conflict or duality of principles but, rather, a correspondence, he was able to couple Eastern morality with Western science. His famous phrase in *Seiken roku*, bonding Eastern morality and Western science, was not an acknowledgment of a division but, rather, a recognition of particularistic manifestations of a universal science.

Sakuma's view of knowledge as power and his construction of a scientific culture implied a conception of politics. At one level his constant admonition "to explore the five continents" for knowledge put

---
123 *Shōzan zenshū*, vol. 2, pp. 549–51.
124 Miyamoto Chū, *Sakuma Shōzan* (Tokyo: Iwanami shoten, 1932), p. 53.

Japan in a wider world. Greater knowledge of that world prompted him to accept what it could offer to bolster Japan's strength. Although he never went as far as Yokoi Shōnan did to recommend complete political and social reorganization, he was willing to alter his view of political possibility to adhere to the requirements of a scientifically based culture. Even though he willingly acknowledged that Japan was weaker than the Western nations, he added that such weakness was physical and material and demanded systematic correction. However good the "American political system was," he wrote, "it could not be carried out in Japan" because history inhibited such a transfer.[125] The acceptance of Western knowledge did not mean abandoning the moral way. Just as science was universal, so, too, was the morality of the five relationships. Western nations did not yet possess these truths. By retaining the idea of a natural order with its specific sense of politics, Sakuma was prevented from envisaging a larger social entity. Ethics always ruled the inner realm, whereas the outer, the world of politics and history, was changeable and could be served only after making a proper investigation of contemporary conditions. Although the idea of a prior natural order militated against actually substituting society for nature, Sakuma's commitment to science resulted in consequences for the Tokugawa social imagination that he could not have foreseen.

Contemporary events required new attitudes. Japan was facing an emergency. "However important the rules of the past have been," Sakuma announced, "they have to be replaced because of the hardships they have brought." He was referring here to seclusion; it was natural to "reform the august laws that have been erected for the realm," as "it is a moral principle of Japan and China to follow ordinary law and procedures in ordinary times, and emergency measures in time of emergency."[126] His advice to abandon "old standards" (remarkably similar to Watanabe's earlier plaint) foresaw the possibility of a new political form. He imagined something higher than the "dignity of the Tokugawa house" and the court itself and pointed to what he called the "welfare of the realm" as a principle of legitimation. From this point he constructed an image of a nation-state, no doubt derived from his observations of Western countries, devoted to defending the wider realm and not just protecting the Tokugawa family. Sakuma, like many contemporaries, saw in Western knowledge the promise of immediate relief and assistance. The solution was a national community (*tenka kokka*) that could compete with comparable

---

125 Uete, *Nihon kindai shisō keisei*, p. 61.   126 *Shōzan zenshū*, vol. 1, pp. 98–9.

nations "throughout the five continents." Ultimately, he proposed the establishment of some sort of comity of nations, whereby each country would retain a uniqueness insofar as it would not disturb the continuation of harmonious relations. The "divine land" would become the Japanese state, and Japan would earn for itself a place among the nations of the world through the exercise of the "correct principles of civilization." This conviction led him to propose internal reforms. These fell short of total reorganization, but the core of his program was rooted in the recognition that proper and able leadership preceded all other considerations. Although he retained the imperial office, he identified its occupants with national kings like Peter the Great and Napoleon. Here, Sakuma came close to earlier views that had linked national strength to the power of kings who could lead their countries to power and wealth.

The intervention of Yokoi Shōnan (1809–68) in the discourse on wealth and defense resulted in refashioning this conception of king and country into a theory of political formation that favored the mercantilist state. If Yokoi shared a discursive world with Sakuma and Hashimoto Sanai, his predecessor in Fukui *han*, he differed significantly from these two thinker-activists in crucial areas of experience and study. Sakuma and Hashimoto had immersed themselves in the study of foreign languages and rudimentary science, but Yokoi had had only the slightest exposure to these disciplines. Yokoi was more deeply committed to a traditional Confucian metaphysic, and his examination of its claims derived from an internal struggle with its philosophical propositions rather than an awareness of a national crisis. Like Hashimoto, Yokoi served as an adviser to the lord of Fukui, Matsudaira Yoshinaga (Shungaku), who was himself a prominent figure operating at the center of national politics during the late 1850s and early 1860s.

Yokoi's philosophic differences with Sakuma are instructive and help explain the decision to denature the social as a condition for establishing a modern state in Japan. Whereas Sakuma envisaged the act of investigating principle as a form of natural science and even tried to reinterpret the scientific discipline as inquiry based on a rational and empirical method, Yokoi, closer to a received metaphysic, grasped the investigation of principle and the concomitant "examination of things" (*kakubutsu*) as the vital connection between "true intention" and a "correct heart."[127] As a result, Sakuma moved toward an "investigation of the

---

127 See Uete, *Nihon kindai shisō keisei*, p. 83.

natural world," whereas Yokoi rejected any tendency that sought to "make morality a small consideration and imprudent and to transform knowledge into extensive reading and memorization." This attitude toward knowledge would lead only to "vulgar Confucianism" and "mere uselessness." In actuality, the investigation of principle and the examination of things referred to grasping the "physics of daily use." Despite Sakuma's decision to couple *kyūri* with empirical investigative methods, he was never able to overcome the dilemma of studying a primary natural order with the techniques of a natural science. Undoubtedly Sakuma recognized that the two categories of nature differed substantively, even as he tried to bring them together in an impossible synthesis. But Yokoi, who declared his fidelity to the true tradition by summoning the exemplar of the three dynasties and the ancient sages, found a transcendent way valid for all times and places. At the heart of his discovery was a reconstituted conception of the social now free from the responsibility of mirroring nature, which he believed conformed to the experience of the archetypal sages of antiquity, Yao and Shun. Their great achievement, Yokoi proposed, was to construct a viable social and political order adequate to the needs of their time alone and thereby to bequeath to future generations the universality of this particular experience, not a timeless arrangement of authority. In this manner, the universalism of the ancient precedent liberated Yokoi from the Sung conceit of defending the idea of a static natural order as if it constituted a norm for all times to come. Even though Sakuma came close to making this move by positing his conception of universalistic principles, he failed to follow through on its consequences. By contrast, Yokoi explored the possibilities inherent in the universalizing of the ancient precedent and went on to conceptualize a new social image for Tokugawa Japan based on the production of wealth and the deployment of power.

Yokoi shared Sakuma's conviction concerning the relationships between knowledge and power. Early in his career, he drew attention to what he called the "vulgar learning of the useless" which he discerned in the contemporary practice to separate forms of knowing from political affairs. The essence of learning required disciplining the self for governance. If men failed to understand the site on which the ancients inaugurated their own project, they would inevitably become "slaves of antiquity." In Yokoi's thinking, the logic that identified knowledge with politics was provided by a commitment to understanding the practical details and necessities of daily life. That life itself exemplified the great lesson of antiquity and validated the very historicism authorizing men in each generation to change and to prepare for new requirements. Scholars of later generations, especially since Sung times, had missed grasping the importance of daily use because they had been consumed by efforts to understand books:

When thinking about how one should study Chu Hsi today, you must think about how Chu Hsi himself studied. Without doing so, you will become a complete slave of Chu Hsi when you take to reading books. When one thinks about composing a poem and how it should become, you have to consider the kind of things that Tu Fu studied, which means going back to the Han, Wei, and Six dynasties.

Underlying this approach was the deeper conviction that texts are constituted and subsequently implicated in the very time they have been produced. But their identity is not fixed for all times to come. Active thinking, not blind acceptance of established precedents and morally irrelevant pieties, must become the essential condition for all learning seeking the mastery of principle. Yet Yokoi recognized that the decision to abandon old precedents and cast off ancient abuses would not necessarily lead to an understanding of the "physics of the daily" unless it were accompanied by the proper intention, sincerity, and honesty, a kind of good faith motivating thoughtful men to investigate themselves first. Writing to a colleague, Yokoi asserted that despite living in a universe that is the proper place for "our thinking, our minds have not yet investigated the various things we encounter and penetrated their principle." When one practiced sincerity and relied on "daily experiences, then one will have movement or the exercise of minds."[128] Self-examination prompted by sincerity invariably demands an investigation of the outer world and, accordingly, distinguishes between the act of merely knowing and genuinely understanding.

By constantly exercising the mind, men would reach a "true understanding of the governing principles that are brought out from thought." The Sung theorists, Yokoi complained, remained mired in the pursuit of mere knowing and wrote learnedly about the act of investigation but never understood it as a technique for "improving the welfare of the people."[129] In their hands, the examination of things and the investigation of principle, *kakubutsu kyūri*, served as an instrument for speculation and never as a tool for grasping the external world in its constant flux and inducing men to make the appropriate responses. Under the sanction of this conception of knowledge and

---

128 Ibid. 129 Yamazaki Masashige, ed., *Yokoi Shōnan ikō* (Tokyo: Meiji shoin, 1942), p. 922.

understanding, there could be little room for the idea of a timeless and fixed natural order.

"The conditions of past and present are different," Yokoi announced in his discussions with Inoue Kowashi at Nuyama, when he was under house arrest, "and although today and yesterday correspond to principle, they are not the same." Here, following the historicist impulse of eighteenth-century political economism, he differentiated principle (*ri*) from conditions (*sei*).[130]

Principle consistently guided men during times of change and enabled them to grasp the reality of circumstances in order to devise appropriate courses of action. Compelling men to overcome the temptations of an inactive subjectivism, the idea of sincerity would motivate them to know their times and to "assist nature's work," which now meant political administration or what the classic of the Great Learning called "outward pacification." In this discussion, Yokoi revealed his own conception of political form. If a culture were ethical, as he surely believed, informed by sincere intent, "good faith," prompting men to meet changing conditions head-on, then its form should also be ethical. Practical action undertaken to confront the challenge of changing conditions must always aim to actualize benevolence, which in the context of late Tokugawa times had become widely synonymous with the "public interest." What Yokoi was to imagine as the nation-state was principally an ethical space in which rulers pursued the public interest by serving the people's welfare. In this way, he realigned the conduct of political affairs with the larger conception of an ethical imperative. Behind this reformulation of place and purpose were the classic formulae that the "realm belongs to the public" and the "people are the base of the realm." "If there are no people," Yokoi asked rhetorically, "how would it be possible to erect a realm? But if there is a realm, it must serve the people who make it up." In an 1860 text, *Kokuze sanron*, Yokoi specified this conviction by calling attention to the Tokugawa failure. The Tokugawa household had acted as despots, he explained, demanding financial support from the several regions even when resources were scarce, thereby embarking on a "private management" that served only the "convenience of one family." Political doctrine alone never managed to tranquilize the realm by making people into children. "Perry was correct when he called this a nonpolitics." Real politics always assisted the people.

---

130 *Watanabe Kazan, Takano Chōei, Sakuma Shōzan, Yokoi Shōnan, Hashimoto Sanai*, p. 506.

[For to] govern the realm means governing the people. The samurai are the instruments used to govern the realm. Even though it is fundamental to the way to teach filial piety, honesty, and loyalty to the samurai and the people, doctrine must also aim at bestowing wealth. . . . Wealth must be the most important task.[131]

Good leadership must always make sure that its conduct and policies conform to the public interest. Profit should exist only on behalf of the people. "The usefulness of benevolence . . . reaches men in the form of profit. . . . To abandon the self is to profit the people. The ideograph for profit is the name for unprincipled (action) when it is used privately. When one profits the people, its use is benevolent."[132] In these circumstances, the realm should encourage trade and maritime commercial relations in order to realize the requirements of the public interest.

According the *Kokuze sanron*, agriculture remained the source of livelihood, even if it were only one aspect of it. Without the innumerable products that people needed for their daily use, life would be impossible. These products were obtained through exchange. Trade and the circulation of currency affected the whole country. Because such a system had not been put into practice, contemporary Japan was a comparatively poor country. As a result, every effort should be made to prepare for the development of a variety of products in several areas. But before this could be accomplished, there had to be a system of markets for the distribution of goods. A market system and the flow of currency would prevent stagnation by regulating the exchange and distribution of products. It would keep in check the activities in the economic realm. In fact, Yokoi's writings show a gradual shift of emphasis to the market over the national defense among Western enthusiasts once the opening of the country had made international relations possible. Yokoi chose the *han* (especially Fukui) as the unit in which the new economic arrangements should be implemented, but he also believed that the form of *fukoku kyōhei* could be extended to other domains because the "proper administration of one realm can be expanded to the whole country." On the national level, Yokoi, like Sakuma, supported the project of large domains striving to bring about a reconciliation between the court and the bakufu in the establishment of a new conciliar arrangement. The importance of his mercantilist program was that it could be applied to the broader national

---

131 Ibid., p. 444. *Kokuze sanron* is translated by D. Y. Miyauchi in *Monumenta Nipponica* 23 (1968): 156–86.
132 *Watanabe Kazan, Takano Chōei, Sakuma Shōzan, Yokoi Shōnan, Hashimoto Sanai*, p. 504.

scene. At this time, Takasugi Shinsaku was already seeking to establish a comparable program in Chōshū, and Ōkubo Toshimichi was trying to transform Satsuma into a wealthy and powerful domain. Eventually, as Yokoi became committed to finding ways to account for the existence of plural interests, he drew his political model from the example of the United States.

Yokoi developed a coherent argument justifying claims for broader participation in issues relating to the welfare and security of society as a whole. The idea of "public discussion" (*kōgi yoron*) signified an effort to formalize this claim to speak about society's business. This arrangement meant that the bakufu should summon all talented men of the realm to Edo (because the "great urgency of the day is to confide in sincerity") "to bring together the able of the realm and its political affairs." This policy would "seek out the words of the people in the realm and transmit people's intention on benefit and injury, gains and losses."[133] Yokoi particularly envisaged the form of a unified structure that still allowed for the expression of domain interests, resembling most the American Federal Republic which he came to admire. He hoped to install a hedge against the divisiveness of the *bakuhan* system, which inevitably invited "private management," by resorting to the idea of public discussions that would equate ability with efficacy or utility, informed by expert and specialized knowledge, and mediated by an awareness of changing times and a concern for the people's will and feelings. He believed that he had found the appropriate means to express the Confucian imperative that made the private morality of the lord ("disciplining and cultivating oneself") equivalent to governing the realm in the public interest. Knowledge came to replace morality as the necessary criterion for leadership. This was revealed in his recommendation to Matsudaira Yoshinaga (Shungaku) of Echizen in 1862 which urged "the abandonment of the selfishness that the Tokugawa bakufu has shown since it acquired countrywide authority." It was the season to "reform the nonpolitics of the Tokugawa house" and to "govern the realm" in the interest of a larger public.

CULTURAL PRACTICE AND THE TRIUMPH OF POLITICAL CENTRALIZATION

Among late Tokugawa writers and activists, none came closer than Yokoi Shōnan to grasping in the "current situation" the play of differ-

---

133 Uete, *Nihon kindai shisō keisei*, p. 83.

ences represented by new discourses, the destruction of received political identities, and the need to find a way to accommodate the plural claims that were being made in the explosive environment of the 1860s. Yokoi's "reading" of contemporary circumstances proposed a resolution of the problems of security and assistance that involved installing a hegemonic arrangement capable of stabilizing the political order while retaining the differing articulations. In fact, the conjuncture of discursive claims ultimately became the terrain for a new hegemonic political practice.

Since the turn of the century, the steady increase of discourses augmenting distinctly articulated practices presented the spectacle of a ceaseless play of what might be called cultural overdetermination,[134] a process whereby multiple causes and contradictions reappeared regularly in condensed form to shape an image of rupture and fragmented meaning. The new practices all announced the importance of "difference" which, since the late eighteenth century, had been associated with blurred social identities that demanded accommodation. The culture of play reflected an experience of fragmentation and division as the starting point of literary, artistic, and intellectual production. The collapse of a view that divided political space between ruler and ruled, the gradual dismissal of a meaningful cosmic order within which people occupied precise and determined places, and the replacement of this view by a self-defining conception of the subject combined to launch Japanese society on a constant search to reconstitute its lost unity. Each discourse, including Mito, acknowledged in its way the end of a simple division between ruler and ruled, which had authorized a hierarchic order accountable only to itself and directed by a metaphysic based on the paradigm of nature. Under the sanction of Neo-Confucianism, the social body had been conceived as a fixed whole. As long as such a holistic mode of social imagination prevailed, politics would remain a mere repetition of the hierarchical social relations. What the several discursive "interpretations" disclosed was the recognition of the incessant need to find instruments for restructuring that society by identifying and articulating social relations. Each dis-

---

134 The term *overdetermination* has a venerable genealogy that, for our purposes, goes back to Sigmund Freud's *Interpretation of Dreams*, in which he applied the concept to describe the process when a dream's elements appear to have been represented in dream thoughts many times over. I am using *overdetermination* to refer to the presence of plural discursive representations during the late Tokugawa period, whereby the same elements appear time and again in different form. In brief, those elements (fear of disorder, concern for productivity, anxiety over questions of security, the idea of community free from fragmentation, new concepts of authority and legitimacy, and the like) that seem to have the most numerous and strongest supports acquire the right of entry into the content of discourses.

course revealed an overdetermination implied in annulling the contradiction among a growing number of differences, a plethora of meanings of the "social," and the difficulties encountered in any attempt to fix those differences as moments of a stable structure.

All of the discourses proceeded from the presumption that the issues they sought to understand and speak to constituted society's business, not other people's business. Henceforth, questions relating to order, security, productivity, relief and assistance, the centrality of daily life, and the practical knowledge needed to reproduce social conditions of existence required a concept of the social capable of being mobilized for the realization of its goals. The creation of public opinion in late Tokugawa discourse as a condition for considering issues vital to the collectivity made it possible to conceptualize a new political space. All of the discourses shifted the terms of legitimation from cosmic and natural principles to the agency of human performance and productivity. In this they contributed their greatest challenge to the established Tokugawa order, whose claims rested first on metaphysical principles and only second on the instruments of production. Driven by a common impulse to overcome the division between ruler and ruled, the several discourses all sought to place daily life in the forefront of attention by emphasizing the tangible and sensuous against the abstract. As a result, all of the discourses aimed at showing how knowledge derived from the daily life of a certain social constituency entitled its knowers to the power to make decisions affecting their lives. An effect of these new systems of knowledge was the disciplining of the body, whereby the proper mental attitude was made to correspond to certain mutual intentions, in order to offset the baneful influence of received arrangements that insisted on separating mental from manual and more recent customs in which the body played and performed, often to excess.

To make other people's business one's own required finding a different form of authority that would validate the act of centering on the activity of people who had hitherto been disenfranchised. Any discussion of politics or administration, as officially defined, among groups long considered ineligible because they lacked the proper knowledge risked danger; it also challenged the officials' claim to designate objects for political discourse. This move entailed displacing the center from politics to culture and rethinking the identity of social relations in areas of religion, science and technology, and economics in order to locate an arena capable of offering representation to such groups. By the same token the move to imagine a new arena of this sort permitted conceptualizing different political forms. Each one of the new discourses produced a vision of political form consistent with the social identity of the group that it wished to represent and that, it was believed, had emerged from the new content of culture. Mito emphasized the autonomous domain; the nativists projected the self-sufficient village; the new religions installed the sacred enclosure or community of believers; and the proponents of defense and wealth promoted the nation-state. Yet for the most part the institution of envisaging a stable system of "differences" had become overdetermined, was directed at solving the problem of the whole by substituting a part for it.

As a distinct process of articulation, the several discourses tried to move away from the center to a periphery, or envisaged a plurality of centers by creating a larger public space as a forum for discussing issues that affected society as a whole. This signaled both the dissolution of a politics in which the division of identities between ruler and ruled had been fixed for all time and a transition toward a new situation characterized by unstable political spaces, in which the very identity of the contesting forces was submitted to constant shifts and calls for redefinition. In the late Tokugawa period the discursive field was dominated by a plurality of practices that presupposed the incomplete and open character of the social. This signified challenging closure and finding a form of mediation between the general need to stabilize order and promote productivity and a local demand to guarantee the preservation of the various social identities produced by the will to discourse. Only the presence of a vast area of semiautonomous, heterogenous and unevenly developed discourses and the possibility of conflict made possible the terrain for a hegemonic practice competent to satisfy both order and difference. For many who belonged to the new discourses, the Restoration vaguely promised the possibility of accomplishing a hegemonic formation committed to stabilizing the social and preserving interests and fixed identities. Yet the existence of these various claims to interest and projections of social identity would soon become the problem, not the solution.

In a sense, the initial stage of the Meiji Restoration, or as it was called, *ōsei fukko*, appeared at the moment when many believed it was necessary to find a form that would contain and even represent the various interests that undermined Tokugawa control. It should be noted that each of the movements discussed, in its efforts to discredit the center and replace it with centers, supplied its own conception of political restoration: Mito had already announced the goals of *chūkō* (restoration); nativism lodged its appeal in an "adherence to foundations" (*moto ni tsuku*); the new religions epiphanized their image of a new order in calls for "world renewal"; and proponents of wealth and defense sought in some sort of conciliar arrangement (*dai kakkyo*) a way of rearranging the constellation of political forces that existed in the 1860s. Nor least important, all could easily support a restoration symbolized by the emperor and court that promised nothing more binding than a return to the age of Jimmu tenno, a "washing away of all old abuses" and a search for new knowledge throughout the world. Here, for a brief moment, was the necessary fit between the forces that combined to bring down the Tokugawa and a hegemonic political structure that promised to reinstate order and security and to distribute relief while preserving regional autonomy. Uncertain as to its future goals, *ōsei fukko* could project the image of a hegemony willing to take into account the interests of all groups by presupposing a certain equilibrium among the various forces. So powerful was the appeal of an *ōsei fukko* in 1867 that writers like Suzuki Masayuki were encouraged to declare (significantly in a *chōka*, an archaic long poem): "Even the despised people, will not be lacking/ The emperor (*oogimi*), hidden in the shade like a night flower, will flourish increasingly/ Everyone will rejoice in the prosperity of the august age."[135] This sentiment seemed to be shared widely throughout society, and people everywhere saw in the Restoration, albeit momentarily, a representation of their own hopes and aspirations.

Yet before long, other voices were beginning to condemn the Restoration as a deception and a deathblow to their most cherished ideals. In Yano Gendō's short, elegiac lament for the vanished glories of Kashiwara and the promise of returning to its golden age, all that was left by 1880 was a "dream that will never be."[136] Almost immediately after *ōsei fukko*, the prospect for a hegemonic formation of the Restoration polity disappeared in the construction of a modern bureaucratic state – the Go-Ishin – pledged to eliminating precisely the fragmentation, difference, and overdetermination that had defeated the Tokugawa system of control. The reorganization of an ensemble of bureaucratic administrative functions arranged by criteria of efficiency and rationality after 1870 aimed at removing the very antagonisms that had surfaced in the discursive articulations of late Tokugawa and that were necessary for the installation of a hegemonic order. The very conditions that produced new political subjects demanding order, relief,

---

135 Itō Shirō, *Suzuki Masayuki no kenkyū* (Tokyo: Aoki shoten, 1972), pp. 287–8.
136 This quotation from Yano's poem is from Hirose Tamotsu, ed., *Origuchi Shinobu shū* (Tokyo: Chikuma shobō, 1975), p. 386.

assistance, security, and the subsequent withdrawals from the center now constituted a problem that many believed had to be resolved. The contest down to the 1890s consisted of an opposition between proponents of discursive practices insisting on preserving a measure of autonomy, usually expressed in movements calling for local control, and a new leadership committed to the rational centralization of power and the elimination of all articulations requesting the reinstatement of a hegemonic arrangement in a genuinely constitutional policy.[137] This is not to say that the Meiji Restoration successfully terminated the several discourses. Mito had already taken itself out of the political field as a result of a destructive civil war in the early 1860s, even though the later Meiji government appropriated parts of its program. Through the support of courtiers like Iwakura Tomomi, nativism briefly sought to control the course of events in 1867 and 1868 by proposing the implementation of a new restorationist polity based on ancient models, but it was too late for the construction of an order more religious and mythic than political and more self-consciously archaic and agricultural than modern and industrial. As a discourse, it was dissembled into a state-controlled sect promoting the worship of Ōkuni no nushi, the god housed in the Izumo Shrine. Later it was transformed into a Japanese science of ethnology that once again was formulated to forestall the power of the new bureaucratic state. The new religions continued a checkered course of withdrawals, staging confrontations with the state, recruiting larger numbers of followers, and generating newer and more radical communities like Maruyamakyō and Ōmotokyō. Finally, the older discourse on defense and wealth continued its own efforts to curb the centralization of the Meiji state by trying to give substance to ideas of broader political participation and local autonomy, ending with a systematic attempt to "civilize" and "enlighten" Japanese society in the 1870s and 1880s as the condition for a permanent moral and rational order.

Yet the Meiji state, as it was completed in the 1890s, was also a solution to the *bakumatsu* problems that have been addressed. It was precisely the loss of control in late Tokugawa decades that catalyzed a contest over how the center, and hence the whole, was to be reconstituted. Fear of the continuing failure to arrest the disorder – first in the

---

137 The terms of this contest between *center* and *periphery* are documented in Michio Umegaki, "After the Restoration: The Beginnings of Japan's Modern State," forthcoming. New York University Press, while the proponents of the localist inflection have been romanticized in Irokawa Daikichi, *The Culture of the Meiji Period*, translation edited by Marius B. Jansen (Princeton, N.J.: Princeton University Press, 1985).

countryside and the cities – and of the inability to meet the foreign threat, plus the clear need to put an end to centrifugal forces set in motion by secessions and withdrawals served to impel a search for more effective ways to restructure society. In this restructuring, the struggle was seen increasingly as one between authority and community, between the effort of various groups to attend to society's business and the belief that that business was too important to leave to the public. The modern state managed to exclude surplus social meaning, by fixing the identity of the public interest in its quest for order and security while relegating communitarian claims to the margins of otherness. It should be recalled that all the late Tokugawa discourses projected an image of assistance and relief, even when, as in Mito, that image was an ambiguous mix of loving and caring for the people while treating them as dependent children. But the Meiji leaders recognized that politics must determine the content of culture, rather than the reverse, and felt that social identities must be made to comply with the necessity of the state because an opposite course would have encouraged a continuous generation of new subjectivities and divisive antagonisms. Once the state had arrogated to itself the modes of cultural production, it was possible to remove culture from play and employ it as an ideological instrument to depoliticize the masses. That act required reducing the polyphonic discourses of the late Tokugawa, with their many voices speaking about the same things, to the single voice of an authoritative discourse.

CHAPTER 4

THE FOREIGN THREAT AND THE OPENING OF THE PORTS

The second half of the eighteenth century witnessed a new phase of European expansion into the non-European world, stimulated by the mercantilist ambitions of European governments and made possible by a growing technological superiority. One consequence was a series of attempts to develop a profitable trade with the countries of East Asia, most of which, bound loosely together in a political and economic system centering on China, had shown little inclination previously to engage in commerce with other regions. Japan, committed to a policy of national isolation (*sakoku*) dating from the seventeenth century, gave no sign of responding to such overtures. With China, however, there grew up a trade in tea and silk that by 1800 was of considerable value. In the next fifty years or so, this trade became, first, the main focus of Western economic penetration in East Asia and, then, the *raison d'être* for a set of institutional relationships, known as the treaty port system, which was eventually extended to most of China's maritime neighbors. As one of those neighbors, Japan became part of it.

The nature of the treaty port system in the nineteenth century derived principally from the commercial policies of Great Britain. These, in turn, reflected a shift from the eighteenth-century doctrines of mercantilism to those of laissez faire, linked with the coming of the Industrial Revolution. In 1840, seeking above all an expanding market for the products of its factories, Britain seized the opportunity afforded by a dispute with China over the opium trade and the treatment of British merchants at Canton to demand the "opening" of China on terms of "equality," in accordance with the principles of free trade. What this meant in practice, as exemplified in the treaty settlement that ended the Opium War in 1842–3, was full access for British trade to specified Chinese ports; a low fixed tariff on goods entering and leaving those ports; and legal protection for British merchants in the form of extraterritoriality, that is, the right to be tried under British law, administered through British consular courts in Chinese territory. Support was given to these arrangements by the cession of Hong Kong to Britain as a colony and naval base. Other countries quickly negotiated similar agreements. The benefits accorded by these, insofar as they differed from the British model, were shared by all the powers through the device of a most-favored-nation clause, included in every treaty.

The agreements proved harder to implement than had at first been envisaged. In the 1840s and early 1850s the China trade failed to expand as quickly as had been hoped. The merchants attributed this to two factors: lack of direct access to markets in the interior of China, and the reluctance of Chinese officials in the open ports to give full effect to the advantages granted to foreigners in the treaties. They accordingly persuaded the British government to seek revision of the treaty terms in order to open additional ports, including some on the Yangtze River, and to provide for diplomatic representation in Peking, through which, it was believed, protests about the "obstructionist" behavior of Chinese provincial officials could be urged on the Manchu court. A chance to press these demands came in 1856, when a dispute occurred at Canton concerning a local vessel, the *Arrow*, registered at Hong Kong. Once again, as in 1839–40, local hostilities escalated into war. Once again, British victory – this time in alliance with France – led to a dictated peace. In the summer of 1858 the earl of Elgin concluded a treaty at Tientsin that incorporated the crucial features of the earlier settlement and added, despite strenuous Chinese objections, the opening of further ports on the Yangtze and in the north, as well as the right to establish a legation at Peking. This treaty, together with the supplementary commercial articles negotiated at Shanghai later in the year, became in the eyes of foreign residents in China the embodiment of their privileges and aspirations there. For the rest of the century the maintenance of "treaty rights" was the primary task that they expected their governments to undertake on their behalf.

Events in China were of critical importance for the "opening" of Japan. They created in the minds of Western diplomats, businessmen, and missionaries a number of assumptions: that the instruments fashioned to carry out policy in China (gunboat diplomacy) could economically and successfully be used against its neighbors; that the attempt to do this would encounter difficulties similar to those that had arisen in China; and that these could be overcome by the same institutional means (the treaty port system). What is more, China's defeat tended to condition Japanese officials to accept the inevitability of the extension of the treaty port system to Japan, making easier the foreigners' task of negotiating there. Even so, Japan's experience was not to be a carbon copy of China's. Its position, domestically and internationally, was different. Hence Japan entered the treaty port system in a significantly different way.

THE CHALLENGE TO NATIONAL ISOLATION

One difference was that Japan was not opened by the actions of Great Britain, even though in the first half of the nineteenth century there were several British initiatives, both public and private, directed to that end. Essentially, this was because the Japan trade was of much less interest to Britain than was that of Canton. Historically, Japan had traded with China in two ways, directly through southern Chinese ports and indirectly through those of Southeast Asia. Since about 1640 the direct link had been provided by Chinese junks sailing to Nagasaki. The indirect trade had been mostly in the hands of the Dutch East India Company, being carried in Dutch ships coming annually from Java. Neither the Dutch nor the Chinese had been able to develop a line of exports from Japan that had much prospect of finding a market in Europe or America. Both took the bulk of their return cargoes in Japanese copper, destined for Asian markets. Nor had they been able to create a substantial Japanese demand for anything but Chinese and Southeast Asian products. In fact, by 1800 the Dutch were generally thought to be continuing the connection more because of the profits it yielded to individual participants than for any larger advantages it might afford.

Knowledge of these circumstances discouraged the British East India Company from making any serious efforts to gain access to the trade, as was demonstrated during Stamford Raffles's attempt to establish relations with Japan in 1813–14. Raffles was appointed lieutenant governor of Java when Britain took over the island from the Dutch in the course of the Napoleonic wars. Talented and ambitious, he saw British occupation as an opportunity to convert the Dutch trade with Nagasaki into a British trade, anticipating, as he explained to the governor general in India in April 1812, that "if we are successful in once obtaining a footing, there will be no serious difficulty in extending the exportation to many commodities the produce of British India, for which there is no sufficient vend in Europe."[1] In 1813 Raffles sent

---

[1] T. S. Raffles, *Report on Japan to the Secret Committee of the English East India Company* [Kobe, 1929] (reprint, London: Curzon Press and New York: Barnes & Noble, 1971), p. 11. I have given a brief account of the incident in *Great Britain and the Opening of Japan 1834–1858* (London: Luzac, 1951), pp. 5–7.

a ship to Nagasaki. However, his plans were thwarted by the Dutch *opperhoofd* there, who persuaded Raffles's representatives that they would be wiser to present themselves to the Japanese as serving Holland, not Britain. This, he said, was because there was a risk of Japanese reprisals, arising from the high-handed actions of a British frigate, the *Phaeton*, which had entered Nagasaki in 1808 during a commerce-raiding operation directed against Dutch ships.

Raffles, undaunted, planned another voyage for the following year, noting meanwhile that at least the first one had shown a profit on the cargo of copper it had brought back. Officials in India doubted even this. The accountant general in Bengal, to whom the records of the venture were sent for comment, held that Raffles had overvalued the copper, as well as ignoring the commercial disadvantage of the fact that it would in any case compete with the British ore being marketed by the company in India. More generally, he argued, judging from the accounts of the company's attempts to trade with Japan in the seventeenth century, it seemed likely "that the Trade with Japan can never become an object of attention for the Manufactures and produce of Great Britain."[2] The governor general accepted the implications of this argument and forbade Raffles to make any further overtures. In May 1815 London concurred, noting that the trade's value and importance had been overrated but leaving the door open for another attempt if there ever seemed a reasonable prospect that it would be successful:

Such an intercourse has been so long held to be unattainable and at the same time so desireable, that tho' our own expectations of benefit from it, either to the Nation or the Company, have not been great, we are disposed to regard with approbation any fair attempt on the part of our Government in Java, which has that object for its ultimate end.[3]

The incident had no sequel, as Java was handed back to the Dutch soon after, but the lack of any real enthusiasm for commercial prospects in Japan was to persist among East India Company officials for a generation or more. When the company lost its monopoly of the China trade in 1833, it transmitted this attitude to its Foreign Office successors. Writing in January 1834 to Lord Napier, who was to be the British superintendent of trade at Canton, the foreign secretary, Lord Palmerston, having instructed him to take any safe steps that might enlarge British trade with China, added:

2 Raffles, *Report*, p. 193.   3 Ibid., p. 210.

Observing the same prudence and caution, . . . you will avail yourself of every opportunity that may present itself for ascertaining whether it may not be possible to establish commercial intercourse with Japan, . . . and you will report to this Department from time to time the results of your observation and enquiries.[4]

That this was not just an oblique way of prompting the superintendent to take an initiative was soon made clear. In 1835 the Hudson's Bay Company suggested that three Japanese sailors, wrecked on Vancouver Island and rescued from the Indians, might be made the pretext for an official mission seeking trade with Japan. Palmerston would have none of it. Napier's successor was told tersely "to send these men quietly home in any Chinese junk bound for Japan."[5] Nor did the fact that this proved impossible do anything to change Palmerston's view of the matter.

The Opium War produced a more favorable atmosphere for action, or so it seemed. On the China coast, at least, it brought widespread acceptance of the proposition that Japan, like China, must eventually abandon its restrictive policies. The first official manifestation of it came in 1844, when the king of Holland sent a letter to the Japanese government, appealing for a more liberal approach to questions of foreign trade. For Japan to stand in the way of the commercial ambitions that the Industrial Revolution and rising populations had created in Europe, the letter warned, might well bring upon it the same fate that China had already suffered:

The intercourse between the different nations of the earth is increasing with great rapidity. An irresistible power is drawing them together. Through the invention of steamships distances have become shorter. A nation preferring to remain in isolation at this time of increasing relationships could not avoid hostility with many others.[6]

This kind of half-threat, half-persuasion was to become a familiar ingredient in Western diplomacy in Japan in later years. At this stage it had little effect. The Tokugawa bakufu simply replied that seclusion could not be abandoned: "Since the ancestral law has once been fixed, posterity must obey."

Nevertheless, the dangers to which the Dutch referred were not illusory. In May 1845, Sir John Davis, British superintendent of trade and governor of Hong Kong, drafted secret plans for an expedition to

4 Quoted in Beasley, *Great Britain*, p. 15.   5 Ibid., p. 24.
6 D. C. Greene, "Correspondence Between William II of Holland and the Shogun of Japan A.D. 1844," *Transactions of the Asiatic Society of Japan* 34 (1907): 112.

Japan that would use the available naval force to mount "an imposing mission," capable of demanding for Britain the same kind of privileges in Japan as those obtained in China by the Opium War. Given that the Japanese knew about the war, he said, there was every reason to suppose that the bakufu would accede to his demands: "I can scarcely imagine the possibility of its doing otherwise than at once seeing the policy of consenting to a Treaty of Commerce, based in substance on the Treaty of Nanking. . . ."[7] The Foreign Office approved the proposal; but nothing came of it in the end, largely because a suitable naval force – deemed essential to the project, for fear that without it Britain might suffer a rebuff damaging to its prestige in China and India – proved not to be available at the time when Davis wanted it.

The exchange of correspondence between Davis and the Foreign Office in 1845–6 confirmed that British policy had not fundamentally changed since the days of Raffles. To the British government and its representatives, trade with Japan was desirable but not worth any great effort. Merchant opinion, preoccupied with the problems and prospects of trade with China, which had much greater potential, made equally little push to bring about a more positive attitude toward Japan. It is not surprising, therefore, that when the United States announced its intention of sending an expedition there in 1852, the British response was one of acquiescence, not rivalry. Lord Malmesbury – not a very forceful Foreign Secretary, to be sure – told his superintendent of trade that "Her Majesty's Government would be glad to see the trade with Japan open; but they think it better to leave it to the Government of the United States to make the experiment; and if that experiment is successful, Her Majesty's Government can take advantage of its success."[8]

This statement serves to emphasize, directly or by implication, two characteristics of free-trade imperialism as it had begun to operate in East Asia. One was the importance of access rather than exclusive privilege. Entry to a market having been gained by one of the powers, it could then be shared by others through treaties embodying a most-favored-nation clause of the Chinese type. In this sense, at least, commercial competition would not inevitably create international rivalry. The other characteristic arose from the overwhelming importance of China in the eyes of Westerners, which made China not only a model of what was to be sought in other countries but in some respects a lightning rod, drawing danger away from them. It was to have this role

---

[7] Beasley, *Great Britain*, p. 59.   [8] Ibid., p. 93.

in Japan's relations with Russia, even though these were not primarily commercial in aims or character.

Russian interest in Japan arose in the context of expansion into Siberia, the Amur region, and across the north Pacific into the American continent. Like other forms of European expansion, this received fresh impetus in the closing years of the eighteenth century, though its outcome was sometimes more complex than its advocates expected. Penetration of the Amur basin, for example, because it threatened China's Manchurian frontiers, seemed at one time likely to put in jeopardy Russia's existing trade with China by the land route across the steppes. Similarly, exploration and settlement in the islands south of Kamchatka brought contact, sometimes conflict, with hunters and fishermen operating from northern Japan in areas that were not yet clearly defined as being under either Japanese or Russian rule. This created a danger of Russo-Japanese political disputes, which in turn made it more difficult for Russia to open trade with Japan, though such a trade was highly desirable as a means of obtaining foodstuffs and other supplies for Russia's colonies on the Pacific seaboard of the Asian mainland.

In July 1799, Russian activities in the whole of this area were put under the control of the newly formed Russian-American Company, which, like the British and Dutch East India companies, was given powers to administer territory as well as carry on a monopoly trade. One problem it soon recognized was that of supplying its Far Eastern posts, because of the difficulty of the land route across Asia. Accordingly, a plan was formulated in 1802 for opening sea communications with the Pacific coast, with a view both to solving the problems of supply and to developing a maritime trade with China. Included in the plan was a proposal for trade with Japan, partly as a source of provisions for the Russian settlements and partly as a supplement to the China trade, as Japan was thought to be capable of providing Europe with tea, silk, porcelain, and lacquer.

An exploratory expedition set out from Kronstadt in 1803, commanded by Captain Adam Krusenstern and carrying Nikolai Rezanov, a major shareholder in the Russian-American Company, as envoy to Japan. It reached Nagasaki in October 1804. The request for trade, in a letter from Czar Alexander I, was duly announced to Edo while Rezanov remained at Nagasaki, where he was shown scant courtesy. Finally, in April 1805, a Japanese official came to inform him that neither his proposals nor his presents could be accepted. Angry, he left the port and made arrangements for two of his subordinates to carry out raids on Japanese settlements in Ezo, Sakhalin, and the Kurils, justifying this action to the Czar as being the only way "to force the Japanese to open trade."[9]

The raids, carried out during 1806–7, did not induce a change of policy in Japan. All they achieved, in fact, was an increase in Japan's military awareness of the northern frontier, manifested in 1811 in the seizure of Vasilii Golovnin, captain of a Russian survey vessel operating in the Kurils. Golovnin was not released until 1813, when Russian officials disavowed their earlier military action. Thereafter, for a generation or more, Russian interest in Japan was infrequent and was promoted by private individuals rather than sponsored by the government.

For Russia, as for Britain, the Opium War prompted a reappraisal of Far Eastern policy. In 1842, Czar Nicholas I established a committee to review Russia's position in the Amur region and Sakhalin in the light of British gains in China. From it there came proposals for a mission to extend Russia's trade with both China and Japan, to be led by Rear Admiral Evfimii Putiatin; but the plan was eventually dropped on the grounds that Russia's commercial interests in the area did not justify so substantial an undertaking. All that survived was a modest expedition to survey the Amur estuary. Nevertheless, this proved to be the beginning of something more extensive, having important implications for Japan. In 1850 the officer in charge of the survey announced – without any authority – that Russia claimed "the whole Amur region down to the Korean frontier as well as Sakhalien." His superior, Nicolai Muraviev, governor general of Siberia, went further. Writing to the Czar in March 1853, he argued that just as it had proved impossible for Russia earlier in the century to prevent the extension of the United States' authority over the greater part of the North American continent, so "it is highly natural also for Russia to rule over the whole Asian littoral of the Pacific Ocean."[10] The main obstacle, Muraviev noted, was that Britain might seek to check Russia's advance by preempting control of Sakhalin and the Amur estuary, from which it followed that Russia must consolidate its hold on Sakhalin, "whence her trade will inevitably develop with Japan and Korea. . . ." In April, Alexander gave his imprimatur to this policy by instructing the Russian-American Company to occupy the island. The decision opened the way for a penetration of the Amur territory under Muraviev's leadership; this was to become Russia's principal preoccupation in the Far East in the

[9] The most useful account of this expedition, and of other Russian activities in the area, is in George A. Lensen, *The Russian Push Toward Japan: Russo-Japanese Relations 1697–1875* (Princeton, N.J.: Princeton University Press, 1959), pp. 121ff. [10] Ibid., pp. 300–1.

next few years. It culminated in treaties in 1858 and 1860, by which the Amur became the frontier between Russia and China, and the Ussuri territory, including Vladivostok, passed into Russian hands.

Japan's role in all this was secondary but not insignificant. The Japan trade was still seen to have importance to the Russian settlements in the north. More urgent, there had to be some agreement delineating a Russo-Japanese frontier in the islands if constant friction was to be avoided. Accordingly, the news that the United States was planning an expedition to Japan – potentially another challenge to Russia's position in the Pacific – prompted a revival of the Russian plans that had been abandoned in 1843. Once again Putiatin was appointed to carry them out. Early in 1853 he left Europe with a small squadron, bearing orders to ensure that Russia was not excluded from any opening of Japanese ports that the Americans might achieve, and to seek an agreement covering territorial questions concerning Sakhalin and the Kurils. He reached Nagasaki in August, a few weeks after Perry arrived in Edo Bay.

To the Japanese, Russian moves in the north were a threat that matched, or even exceeded, the dangers arising from British commercial ambitions, as exemplified in China. Japanese debates about foreign policy in the 1850s reverted constantly to these two themes. Yet Japan, as events were to demonstrate, was in reality no more central to Russian policy than it was to British. For both powers it was geographically at the perimeter of an area of concern: China in one case; the region north and east of Manchuria in the other. It is for this reason that the opening of Japan was accomplished in the end by the United States, the only power to see Japan directly as a factor in its relations with China.

America's interest in Japan, like Russia's, had a Pacific ingredient as well as a commercial one. After about 1820, whaling vessels, of which a large proportion were American, began to appear off the Japanese coast. The national isolation laws, which prevented the ships from calling at Japanese ports for water and supplies, plus occasional Japanese ill treatment of shipwrecked sailors, caused resentment in the United States, bringing some pressure for a treaty to overcome these difficulties. More important, however, was the growing recognition, first voiced publicly at about the same time, that the acquisition of a Pacific seaboard by the United States would bring great economic opportunities, not least that of a possible trade between California and China. American trade with Canton, conducted from the East Coast via the Indian Ocean, was already of substantial size, second only to that of Britain. The prospect of giving it an extra dimension therefore seemed attractive.

Japan entered these calculations not only as a potential hazard to shipping but also as a useful staging point on the Pacific route to China. Thus when President Andrew Jackson sent Captain Edmund Roberts to China as his agent in 1832, he instructed him to open negotiations with Japan if he could do so without undue risk. Roberts obtained a treaty with Siam but died before attempting anything elsewhere, so nothing came of the initiative, except insofar as it may have encouraged a group of missionaries and merchants, who organized a private voyage in 1837 (the *Morrison* incident), seeking to use the return of some Japanese castaways as a means of gaining entry to Japanese ports. Like others before them, they were turned away unceremoniously.

The Opium War and the more extensive opening of China's ports seemed to some Americans, as it did to Britain's Sir John Davis, to make the opening of Japan both inevitable and easier to achieve. Accordingly, in May 1845, instructions were sent to the United States representative in China to test the prospects by making a visit to Japan or by sending the senior naval officer on the station, Commodore James Biddle, to do so in his place. He chose the latter course. Biddle duly went to Edo Bay in July 1846, only to find that the Japanese firmly rejected his overtures, reaffirming their policy of national isolation. Because he had orders to avoid any resort to force, Biddle was compelled to withdraw frustrated, despite an incident – he was jostled by a Japanese guard – that might have given him grounds to insist on some kind of concessions. China coast opinion saw the whole venture as having done more harm than good.

The next few years, however, witnessed a significant change in the situation arising from the fact that the United States established formal authority in Oregon and California. As Secretary of the Treasury Robert J. Walker commented in 1848, this was an economic as well as a political gain: "By our recent acquisitions on the Pacific, Asia has suddenly become our neighbor, with a placid, intervening ocean, inviting our steamships upon the track of a commerce greater than that of all Europe combined."[11] It was undoubtedly the China trade that Walker had most in mind, but Japan, too, had its place in the pattern. In 1849 Commander James Glynn of the USS *Preble* was sent to

---

11 Quoted in T. Wada, *American Foreign Policy Toward Japan During the Nineteenth Century* (Tokyo: Tōyō bunko, 1928), p. 59.

Nagasaki to secure the release and repatriation of a party of shipwrecked American sailors. Returning to New York at the beginning of 1851, Glynn joined in a campaign, backed by shipping interests, to persuade Washington to send an expedition to Japan, pointing out that not only did that country have supplies of coal, mined near Nagasaki, but was also "directly on the line from San Francisco to Shanghai." This made it of major importance to any trans-Pacific steamer route. Finding these arguments persuasive, Secretary of State Daniel Webster approved the proposal in June 1851. The mission was to be carried out by Commodore John H. Aulick, whose instructions emphasized the necessity of securing for Americans the right to buy coal for steamers on passage between California and China; proper protection for shipwrecked sailors; and permission for ships to dispose of cargo at one or more Japanese ports of call. He was also provided with a letter from President Millard Fillmore, addressed to the emperor of Japan, setting out these points and calling for "friendly commercial intercourse" between the two countries.[12]

In the event, the expedition was commanded not by Aulick but by Commodore Matthew C. Perry, whose squadron reached the entrance to Edo Bay on July 8, 1853. The long voyage across the Atlantic and Indian oceans had impressed on him anew the importance of coaling stations. It had also given him ample time in which to decide on an approach to his task. In the words of his official narrative: "He was resolved to adopt a course entirely contrary to that of all others who had hitherto visited Japan on a similar errand – to demand as a right, and not as a favor, those acts of courtesy which are due from one civilized nation to another. . . ."[13] Pursuing this policy, Perry insisted on handing over the president's letter at Kurihama with all appropriate formality and under the guns of his anchored ships; refused to go to Nagasaki to receive a reply, as the Japanese urged; and indicated in a letter of his own that although "as an evidence of his friendly intentions," he had brought only a small squadron on this occasion, he

---

12 The text, given in ibid., is similar, though not identical, to that of the letter eventually delivered by Perry.
13 F. L. Hawks, *Narrative of an Expedition of an American Squadron to the China Seas and Japan, Performed in the Years 1852, 1853, and 1854* (Washington, D.C.: Beverley Tucker, Senate Printer, 1856), vol. 1, p. 235. This official narrative can usefully be supplemented by Perry's own journal: Roger Pineau, ed., *The Japan Expedition 1852–1854: The Personal Journal of Commodore Matthew C. Perry* (Washington, D.C.: Smithsonian, 1968). The standard account of United States policy toward Japan in this period is by P. J. Treat, *The Early Diplomatic Relations Between the United States and Japan, 1853–1868* (Baltimore: Johns Hopkins University Press, 1917).

intended, "should it become necessary, to return to Yedo in the ensuing spring with a much larger force."[14]

This plan he carried out, having decided it would be wiser to withdraw to the China coast for a time, rather than to give the Japanese a chance to keep him waiting for their reply. Hence February 13, 1854, found him once again in Edo Bay, ready to negotiate. As on the previous occasion, he maintained a ceremonial aloofness, coupled with a firm refusal to give way on procedural points. The Japanese negotiators, for their part, had orders not to grant trade but to avoid precipitating hostilities. The result was an agreement, signed on March 31, 1854, that gave Perry the substance of what he sought: the opening of Shimoda and Hakodate as ports of call for American ships, at which coal and other supplies could be obtained; just treatment for shipwrecked sailors; the appointment of a United States consul at Shimoda; an ill-defined right to purchase goods at the open ports; and a most-favored-nation clause. It was not in the full sense a commercial treaty. Nevertheless, as Perry said in his report, it was a beginning:

Japan has been opened to the nations of the west. . . . It belongs to these nations to show Japan that her interests will be promoted by communication with them; and, as prejudice gradually vanishes, we may hope to see the future negotiation of commercial treaties, more and more liberal, for the benefit, not of ourselves only, but of all the maritime powers of Europe, for the advancement of Japan, and for the upward progress of our common humanity.[15]

These are free-trade sentiments, clearly enough. Written of China, they might have been held to reflect the aspirations on which policy rested. But applied to Japan, they were no more than a pious hope, seeking to give an attractive gloss to a treaty more concerned with facilities than trade. In much the same way, the British and Russian negotiations that followed Perry's were more political and strategic than commercial in motivation. Just as Perry had prepared the way for an American steamer route to China, plus ports of supply for whalers, so Putiatin settled problems associated with Russian expansion in the Pacific, and the British negotiator, Rear Admiral Sir James Stirling, established relations with Japan as a by-product of naval operations in the Crimean War.

Stirling's agreement came first. News of the outbreak of war with

---

14 The texts of the letters from the president and Perry are given in Hawks, *Narrative*, vol. 1, pp. 256–9; and also in W. G. Beasley, ed., *Select Documents on Japanese Foreign Policy 1853–1868* (London, England: Oxford University Press, 1955), pp. 99–102.
15 Hawks, *Narrative*, vol. 1, pp. 388–9.

Russia reached Hong Kong in May 1854. As senior naval officer on the China coast, it became Stirling's task to protect British ships from attack by Putiatin and, if possible, to hunt down his squadron. In pursuance of this task he visited Nagasaki later in the year, seeking a Japanese declaration of neutrality that would deny the Russians refuge in Japanese ports. But his interpreter, a Japanese castaway, completely failed to make this clear. As a result, Stirling, though without diplomatic credentials, was offered and accepted a convention on the Perry model, which was signed on October 14, 1854. His government duly ratified it, despite a good deal of criticism from the China merchants.

Putiatin, as we have seen, had already been sent to Japan in 1853 to protect Russian interests in the new situation created by the Perry expedition and to seek an agreement on boundaries in the north. He delivered letters announcing his mission at Nagasaki in August and then, like Perry, decided to withdraw to China to give Edo time to consider them. Returning in January 1854, Putiatin found the Japanese ready to settle frontier questions but adamant on the subject of trade. Unwilling to accept this, he again left Japan while the bakufu considered his objections. At this point his plans were upset by the outbreak of the Crimean War, involving him in a game of naval hide-and-seek with Stirling in the north Pacific, and so it was not until late in 1854 that he returned to Japan. In December, negotiations were resumed, this time at Shimoda and in the knowledge of what Perry had achieved. Notwithstanding the destruction of Putiatin's flagship as a result of an earthquake and tidal wave, the talks were soon brought to a successful conclusion, a convention being signed on February 7, 1855, that divided the Kurils between the two countries – though leaving unresolved the boundary questions concerning Sakhalin – and opened Nagasaki, in addition to Shimoda and Hakodate, as ports of call for Russian ships.

THE COMMERCIAL TREATIES OF 1857–1858

If the attractions of the Japanese market proved too small to prompt any determined effort on the powers' part to secure access to it, it is equally true that the development of a commercial economy in Tokugawa Japan did not produce within the country any significant political pressures to overthrow the policy of national isolation for the sake of trade. The events we have just described undoubtedly had important repercussions for Japan, but they were not related primarily to commerce. Among the samurai they brought a heightened awareness of maritime defense, one first taken up by Hayashi Shihei and Honda Toshiaki; in the next generation by the Mito scholars Aizawa Seishisai and Fujita Tōko; and after the Opium War by military experts like Sakuma Shōzan. In a number of domains it brought experiments in iron founding and other industrial skills, which led to the manufacture of cannon and the building of Western-style ships. But notwithstanding the importance of this for Japanese modernization in the longer term, it did not produce significant moves to change the fundamentals of Japanese foreign policy until after the first treaties had been signed.

All the writers that we have named recognized that defense had implications for domestic politics. Hayashi and Honda both urged far-reaching changes in Japanese society, designed to strengthen it against the foreign threat even at the cost of undermining the bakufu. Hayashi was arrested for publishing his views, whereas Honda survived only because he circulated his writings privately. The Mito scholars used much the same arguments to advocate a relaxation of bakufu controls over the great lords, which they saw as part of a "restoration" of the traditional social order, involving a reassessment of the role of the emperor. Sakuma envisaged the need for a new kind of patriotism and for the emergence of a nonhereditary leadership capable of putting it to use. In their various ways, all these proposals were symptomatic of a dissatisfaction with the Tokugawa regime and are relevant to any examination of the process by which it was brought down. However, they did not necessarily constitute an attack on *sakoku*, or the bakufu's policy of national isolation itself. Indeed, they did not all lead to the same conclusions about foreign policy. Hayashi, Honda, and Sakuma all thought it necessary for Japan to take initiatives of a broadly mercantilist kind, including the creation of a navy and a merchant marine, if it were to develop the means to defend itself. This implied at least the suspension of those sections of the national isolation laws that forbade Japanese to venture overseas. Mito, by contrast, was committed to a policy of *jōi*, or "expelling the barbarians," that is, keeping Japan's ports closed, pending a political regeneration that would make it safe to open them.

Given these differences among its critics, the bakufu was able to keep its policies and its authority intact during the first half of the nineteenth century, though not without some equivocation. Between 1799 and 1821 it took over from the feudal lord of Matsumae direct responsibility for the administration of Ezo, in order to improve the defenses of the area against Russia. In 1825, responding to clashes with whaling vessels in the previous year, it reissued the national isolation laws in a more severe form, announcing that foreign ships that approached the coast must be "driven away" (*uchiharai*). This policy was maintained until the Opium War, one of its victims being the American ship *Morrison* in 1837. Thereafter, a growing awareness of Japan's military weakness vis-à-vis the West, induced by knowledge of British victories in China, brought a note of caution. A decree of August 1842 renounced *uchiharai*, substituting an order that foreign vessels were, if necessary, to be supplied with food and fuel before being sent away and fired on only if they then refused to leave. Associated with this was an injunction to officials to give greater attention to coast defense, designed to disarm criticism within Japan. Tokugawa Nariaki, daimyo of Mito and principal spokesman for *jōi*, dismissed the decision as at best cosmetic and at worst calculated to induce a dangerous apathy. His influence contributed to Edo's uncompromising rejection of Dutch overtures to trade in 1844. Even so, the bakufu showed itself willing in the next few years to turn a blind eye to various clandestine dealings with foreigners in the Ryūkyū Islands, which were under the patronage of the daimyo of Satsuma.

The Japanese debate over national isolation, which had earlier been intermittent and mostly private, was made urgent and public by the Perry expedition. In the expectation of such an eventuality, Abe Masahiro, the senior member of the Tokugawa council (*rōjū*), had gone to some trouble in the previous year or two to reach an understanding with Tokugawa Nariaki, aimed at uniting men of influence in the Tokugawa house and bakufu behind the proposition that until coastal defenses could be made effective, the country's foreign policy had to be a cautious one. Following Perry's arrival in July 1853, he decided to try to extend this consensus to the feudal lords as a whole, by circulating translations of the letters that Perry had brought and asking for recommendations concerning them. What he hoped was that by the time Perry returned in 1854, there would be substantial support for a compromise agreement. What he achieved was to bring into the open the underlying divergencies of view within Japan's ruling class.

The replies to the bakufu circular revealed three main segments of opinion. A majority supported national isolation in principle – not always honestly – but coupled this with a desire to avoid any hostilities while Japan remained weak. This is what Abe had hoped. However, there were also two powerful and apparently irreconcilable minorities. One was led by key figures in the bakufu establishment, including Hotta Masayoshi, lord of Sakura, who succeeded Abe as head of the council in November 1855, and Ii Naosuke, lord of Hikone, who became regent (*tairō*) in 1858. Their main argument was derived essentially from Hayashi, Honda, and Sakuma: that Japan's defense could be ensured only by adopting new techniques, especially of warfare, a knowledge of which depended on establishing relations with the West. As Ii put it, "It is impossible in the crisis we now face to ensure the safety and tranquillity of our country merely by an insistence on the national isolation laws as we did in former times."[16] As a temporary expedient, the Americans would have to be given access to Japanese ports for fuel and supplies, he said. Trade was quite another matter. Better by far that Japan should build a merchant marine to trade overseas than that foreign merchants should come to Japan. In this way the foundations could be laid for building a navy, possession of which would enable the bakufu to deal with the foreigners on its own terms, even, if necessary, closing the ports again.

The alternative viewpoint was stated by Tokugawa Nariaki, supported by other members of the Tokugawa house and its collateral branches. To Nariaki, too, Western military technology was an element in Japan's defense. More important, though, was morale. This could be maintained only if the bakufu led in rejecting foreign demands, no matter how great the resulting risk of war: "If there be any sign of the Bakufu pursuing a policy of peace, morale will never rise, . . . and the gunbatteries and other preparations will accordingly be so much ornament, never put to effective use."[17] Like Ii Naosuke, Nariaki wanted the bakufu to do something positive. But unlike him, he identified positive action above all with sounding a call to arms, not with modernizing Japan's military establishment. Between the two of them, given that both had immense political influence, Abe was in a position of some embarrassment.

Early in 1854, facing an insistent Perry, he settled for a treaty that granted ports of refuge, but not trade. This overcame the immediate crisis but did not resolve the fundamental problem of foreign policy or reconcile the two groups that sought to shape it. There was nothing "positive" in it for either party, though Abe had enough political skill to ensure that the next phase of the debate between them did not come until Hotta had replaced him as senior minister at the end of 1855,

16 Beasley, *Select Documents*, p. 117. The basic Japanese work on the subject of feudal opinion and foreign relations is by Inobe Shigeo, published in the 1920s and early 1930s; see, for example, his *Bakumatsu shi no kenkyū* (Tokyo: Yūzankaku, 1927). Much of his research was later incorporated into the major political history of the period: Ishin shiryō hensan jimukyoku, eds., *Ishin shi*, 6 vols. (Tokyo: Ishin shiryō hensan jimukyoku, 1939–41); see vols. 1 and 2 for the treaties of 1853–8.   17 Beasley, *Select Documents*, p. 106.

when it was soon overshadowed by new dangers, occasioned by the outbreak of hostilities between China and the West in the *Arrow* war.

The first step toward reopening discussions was taken by the Dutch representative at Nagasaki, Donker Curtius. In January 1856, he secured a treaty granting some relaxation of the personal restrictions applied to Dutch residents hitherto and extending to them the privileges secured by other countries in their recent agreements with Japan. Trade, however, was to continue on its former footing, that is, under close official supervision at Nagasaki. Some months later he took up this point in a long letter to the bakufu, setting out his expectation that Britain would soon be demanding a full commercial treaty with Japan and arguing that it would be to the latter's advantage to enter into a trade agreement with Holland, thereby establishing a model that Britain might also be persuaded to accept. After all, he pointed out, Japan could not hope to fend off Europe's commercial pressures indefinitely.

Hotta found the argument persuasive enough to put it to bakufu officials for study early in September. The key role in the subsequent discussions was played by a group of "talented men," originally promoted by Abe and destined before long to become Japan's principal experts in foreign affairs. They quickly came to the conclusion that the opening of trade in some form was inevitable. To some of them, it even seemed desirable. The chief obstacle to any such policy, it was clear, was the likely opposition of Tokugawa Nariaki, but his objections were made a good deal less weighty by news of the war in China – specifically, the British attack on Canton – which reached Japan in February 1857. On March 19, Hotta commented: "Any attempt on our part to cling to tradition, making difficulties over the merest trifles and so eventually provoking the foreigners to anger, would be impolitic in the extreme. . . . Therefore while we are still in safety we must make a long-term plan. . . ."[18] Hotta's statement set in motion the drafting of a series of memoranda within the bakufu, designed to identify the kind of terms on which trade might appropriately be granted. Ostensibly the issue was that of Japan's national interests, both international and economic. But in reality, most officials equated it with the preservation of political society in its existing form, so that arguments about foreign policy also became arguments about domestic politics. The more cautious wanted Japan to proceed slowly in treaty negotiations, granting only such terms as the foreign-

18 Ibid., pp. 130–1.

ers insisted on. Their reasons, as one document explained it, was that because national isolation was an accepted part of a political structure that included government, to change one would be to weaken the other:

> [T]o make a parallel between the national system and the construction of a house, for example, to change the superficial structure of the house according to the tastes of the moment will do no great harm to the building, but to change the framework or replace the pillars and foundation-stones is to introduce weaknesses and cause complete collapse.[19]

National isolation, as they saw it, was one of the pillars or foundation stones. Their more forthright colleagues, taking their cue from Hotta, responded that so negative an approach would make disaster sure. If Japan were to do no more than this, "all will fall to ruin," they said. By contrast, for the bakufu openly to commit itself to pursuing trade "would be a means whereby it could bring the whole country under control and also lay the foundations of national wealth and military strength."[20]

Hotta, recognizing the grave political risks in affronting Nariaki, preferred to make no final choice between these rival viewpoints until there had been talks with Curtius. These took place at Nagasaki during the summer of 1857. They were intended to be preliminary discussions, but Curtius was able to persuade the officials who had been sent to him to turn them into proper negotiations, with the result that agreement was reached on a draft commercial treaty, which was duly sent to Edo for approval.

This was at the end of August. There followed a long silence, reflecting continued uncertainty in the capital. Meanwhile, news reached Nagasaki – inaccurately, as it turned out – that a British fleet was on the point of sailing from China to bring an envoy to Japan. To the Japanese negotiators, this information made it urgent that they make a decision on the Dutch agreement, in order that it could be signed before the British arrived and so serve formally as a model of what they could be offered. Yet Edo still made no reply to their request for instructions. Then on September 21, Putiatin arrived. Because he immediately added his voice to that of Curtius in demanding a treaty, the pressures on the Nagasaki officials were still further increased. Finally, on October 16, they took the momentous decision to sign agreements with both Holland and Russia without waiting any longer

19 Ibid., p. 138.   20 Ibid., p. 136.

for bakufu approval. It was, as one of them wrote to colleagues in Edo, "an act of the greatest temerity," justified only by the overriding need to "preserve Bakufu dignity" and avert "complete national collapse."[21]

The terms embodied in these treaties were the most that the more enlightened members of the bakufu, relatively well informed as they were about the world situation, could bring themselves to concede. Even so, they were essentially a modification of the conditions under which the Dutch had traded for two centuries or more, and not a complete break with the past such as would have been implied by treaties of the kind that the powers had imposed on China. There was no longer to be any limitation on the annual value of the trade at Nagasaki or on the number of ships that could call there. Transactions were not to be handled solely through the Nagasaki government office, as heretofore, though that office retained a monopoly of certain Japanese exports, such as copper, and all payments for goods bought and sold were still to be made through it. There remained a number of restrictions on the movement of foreign ships and merchants in and around the port. Above all, the general level of tariff duties was set at 35 percent.

It is not surprising that such terms were anathema to Townsend Harris, the American consul general who had been established at Shimoda in September 1856, for his orders were to negotiate a commercial agreement of the China type. On one occasion he went so far as to describe the provisions of the Dutch treaty as "disgraceful to all parties engaged in making them,"[22] though because he made the comment when arguing the advantages of free trade with Japanese officials, one should perhaps not take his strictures too literally. At all events, Harris set himself very different objectives from those that Curtius had pursued. After some months negotiating at Shimoda, during which it was agreed to amend the Perry convention with respect to such points as rates of exchange and conditions of foreign residence in Japan, he turned to larger issues. He had already announced his desire to visit Edo, so as to present a letter from the president and enter into discussion of "a most important matter affecting Japan." The fact that he had simultaneously made available a copy of the United States treaty with Siam suggested that trade was at the

---

21 Ibid., pp. 146–9.
22 M. E. Cosenza, ed., *The Complete Journal of Townsend Harris* (New York: Doubleday, 1930), p. 507. The journal of Harris's secretary is also available: Henry Heusken, *Japan Journal 1855–1861* (New Brunswick, N.J.: Rutgers University Press, 1964).

heart of the matter, and so during the summer of 1857, against the background of the talks going on at Nagasaki, the bakufu tried cautiously to discover whether a treaty of the kind being discussed with Curtius would satisfy Harris, too. Harris declined to show his hand without an audience with the shogun. Fearing that if frustrated he might, like the British, summon warships, Edo gave way. Late in September, only two days after Putiatin's arrival precipitated a crisis at Nagasaki, the Shimoda *bugyō* told Harris he was to be permitted to have an audience in the capital toward the end of the year.

Harris reached Edo on November 30, 1857, traveling in the state appropriate to a feudal lord. A week later he had his audience, handing over the president's letter to Hotta in the shogun's presence. This opened the way for the discussion of diplomatic business, which was inaugurated at Hotta's official residence on December 12, when the American delivered a two-hour lecture on the state of the world and its implications for Japan. His theme was much like that of the Dutch letter of 1844 and the arguments recently advanced by Curtius at Nagasaki. The steamship, he said, would soon make the whole world "like one family." No country had the right to stand aloof from others in this family. What is more, Japan did not have the power to do so. Britain was willing to fight to impose on Japan the same conditions for trade that it had obtained in China. Resisting, Japan might well imperil its own independence. It would be wise, therefore, not merely to abandon national isolation but to do so by making an agreement that would bring it into the family of nations without violence or dishonor. This was what America offered:

> If Japan should make a treaty with the ambassador of the United States, who has come unattended by military force, her honor will not be impaired. There will be a great difference between a treaty made with a single individual, unattended, and one made with a person who should bring fifty men-of-war to these shores.[23]

The fact that similar arguments had for some time been used by some of Hotta's own subordinates made what Harris said more credible; and in any case the bakufu had now committed itself in principle to opening commercial relations with the rest of the world. This left only the detailed arrangements for implementing the decision to be settled. A few days later Hotta made it clear that he was willing to enter into negotiations on the basis that Harris had proposed. In a

---

23 Beasley, *Select Documents*, pp. 163–4, quoting a translation of the Japanese summary of what Harris said. The summary in Harris's journal is much briefer: see Harris, *Complete Journal*, pp. 485–6.

notable analysis of the options open to Japan, he stated the view that simply to fob off the foreigners with a temporary agreement, accepting their demands in order to buy time for military preparations, was bound to fail, because "year by year we would lose ground." Equally, to precipitate war forthwith, as a means of uniting Japanese opinion, would inevitably leave Japan on the defensive, its strength steadily draining away. The only real chance of survival was to do what the rest of the world was doing, so as to build up Japan's own wealth and strength:

I am therefore convinced that our policy should be to stake everything on the present opportunity, to conclude friendly alliances, to send ships to foreign countries everywhere and conduct trade, to copy the foreigners where they are at their best and so repair our own shortcomings, to foster our national strength and complete our armaments, and so gradually subject the foreigners to our influence until in the end, . . . our hegemony is acknowledged throughout the globe.[24]

Harris asked for two major concessions: the right for Americans to trade freely at a number of Japanese ports, and diplomatic representation at the Japanese capital. On January 16, 1858, Hotta informed him that the proposals were acceptable as a starting point for discussion, though in view of the dangers of popular resentment within Japan, the open ports would have to be fewer than Harris had envisaged. Thus established, detailed negotiations were begun with the Japanese representatives, Inoue Kiyonao and Iwase Tadanari. Harris began by producing a draft of a possible treaty. It was in fact the substance of the eventual agreement, but it was not admitted as such until Harris had been through a frustrating round of explanations and repetitions, designed to persuade the Japanese to accept the norms of diplomatic behavior and political economy as understood in the West. There were lengthy debates about whether a foreign envoy need reside in Edo instead of Kanagawa. There were arguments about the number of ports to be opened and whether merchants should have the right to live in the cities of Edo and Osaka. There was a complete deadlock over the proposed opening of Kyoto, about which Harris finally gave way. It all engendered in the American a good deal of impatience and irritability. Writing up an account of the negotiations in his journal afterwards, he prefaced it:

I shall confine myself to the main leading facts of actual transactions, omitting the interminable discourses of the Japanese where the same proposition may

24 Beasley, *Select Documents*, p. 167.

be repeated a dozen times; nor shall I note their positive refusal of points they subsequently grant, and meant to grant all the while; nor many absurd proposals made by them, without the hope, and scarcely the wish, of having them accepted. . . .[25]

Notwithstanding these difficulties, by February 26, proposals for a treaty had been agreed. Its central point was that "Americans may freely buy from Japanese and sell to them any articles that either may have for sale, without the intervention of any Japanese officers in such purchase or sale, or in making or receiving payment for the same. . . ." (Article III).[26] To this end, the following ports were to be opened, in addition to Shimoda and Hakodate: Kanagawa (Yokohama) and Nagasaki from July 4, 1859, Niigata from January 1, 1860, and Hyōgo (Kobe) from January 1, 1863. Trade in Edo and Osaka was to be permitted from January 1, 1862, and January 1, 1863, respectively. An American diplomatic agent was to reside in Edo, and consuls in any or all of the open ports. Americans committing offenses in Japan were to be subject to American law, administered through consular courts. The trade regulations, annexed to the treaty, provided for a tariff of 5 percent on Japanese exports and a variable rate for imports, under which supplies for ships, as well as raw silk, would pay 5 percent, and most other goods would pay 20 percent. Opium was prohibited, except small quantities for medical use.

Any Western diplomat who had been involved in negotiations with China would have recognized most of this, apart from the ban on opium. Only the most-favored-nation clause was missing. Harris, therefore, had good reason to be satisfied with his work. Yet events were soon to show that in Japan, as in China, securing a treaty was easier than enforcing it; and even getting it signed posed major problems.

What Harris had done, using the argument of inevitable British insistence on freedom of trade, was to persuade the bakufu's key policymakers to accept a document that went well beyond their experience and their concept of what was proper. The Dutch treaty represented the limit of reasonable concession, as they saw it. The American one took the Japanese into unknown and dangerous territory. What is more, it changed the terms of the debate within Japan. Whereas in 1853–4, Abe Masahiro had set out to establish a consensus among the feudal lords, in the light of which he could take decisions

25 Harris, *Complete Journal*, p. 505. Harris is also the subject of Oliver Statler, *Shimoda Story* (New York: Random House, 1969).
26 Treaty text in Beasley, *Select Documents*, pp. 183–9; see also Harris, *Complete Journal*, pp. 578–89.

about negotiating with Perry, his successors found themselves on this occasion committed in advance to a detailed treaty, which they had somehow to get feudal opinion to endorse. The attempt to do so put at issue not only the nature of Japan's future relations with the West but also the extent of the shogun's authority in foreign relations.

Before leaving Shimoda, Harris had been warned by the senior Japanese interpreter Moriyama Takichirō (Einosuke) that Edo opinion remained deeply divided about the opening of the ports. Ominously, a number of daimyo had protested the decision to grant him an audience. There was nothing surprising, therefore, in the fact that when news of what was under discussion became more widely known during January and February 1858, it produced an outcry. The statement made by Harris to Hotta in December was circulated to officials and feudal lords for comment, much as Perry's letters had been. Of the replies, many proved to be routine recapitulations of traditional arguments, reflecting an awareness, though often unstated, that the bakufu had already taken its decisions and that this was its duty. A few lords were still adamant in supporting national isolation, arguing that to admit foreign trade and foreign religion to Japan would increase the risks of disrupting Japanese society and hence of political unrest. Rather more tried to identify expedients that offered a chance of minimizing Japan's concessions while avoiding war. There was nothing very new in this. Most men realized by this time that Japan had little liberty of choice in these matters. Even Tokugawa Nariaki admitted that a trade agreement of some kind could no longer be avoided, though he urged that instead of bringing foreigners to Japan, it should provide for a Japanese trade mission to be established overseas, headed by himself and composed of "unwanted" members of the community, like lordless samurai and younger sons.

Another powerful Tokugawa relative, Matsudaira Keiei (Yoshinaga, Shungaku) of Echizen, argued that overcoming the crisis required above all a review of bakufu policies within Japan:

[T]he service of capable men must be enlisted from the entire country; peacetime extravagance must be cut down and the military system revised; the evil practices by which the daimyo and lesser lords have been impoverished must be discontinued; . . . the daily livelihood of the whole people must be fostered; and schools for the various arts and crafts must be established.[27]

Specifically, he put these proposals in the context of choosing an acceptable candidate as heir to the ailing and childless shogun, Iesada,

27 Beasley, *Select Documents*, p. 180. Nariaki's memorandum is on pp. 168–9.

a recommendation that had the support of Tokugawa Nariaki, several of the most able bakufu officials, and some influential *tozama* lords, like Shimazu Nariakira of Satsuma. How else, they asked, could the bakufu retain the prestige that would enable it to impose a necessary but unpopular decision on a reluctant country?

There was in fact one way in which it might be able to do so, as Hotta realized: to seek the approval of the imperial court for what was proposed, postponing meanwhile the signing of the American treaty. This he decided to attempt. After all, powerless though the emperor was, an imperial decree would be an authoritative statement of national policy, giving a formal authority to the bakufu's stand and helping silence its critics. Nor was there any reason to suppose that the court would refuse it. As the negotiators told Harris, when asking him to be patient for a while, the bakufu could always expect to get its own way in Kyoto and "had determined not to receive any objections from the Mikado."[28]

Hotta's optimism proved ill founded. Sending first a representative and then going himself to Kyoto, he argued strongly in favor of the treaty, both as something that fell within the shogun's executive competence and as a step required to save Japan from a disastrous war. It was all in vain. On May 3, 1858, he was told officially that Edo must think again. Because the emperor feared that "to revolutionize the sound laws handed down from the time of Ieyasu would disturb the ideas of our people and make it impossible to preserve lasting tranquility,"[29] there must be further consultation with the lords, in order to establish agreed recommendations for the court to approve. In other words, having sought an imperial decree to unite the country, Hotta was told that he must unite the country before securing his decree. On June 1 he arrived back in Edo, his policy in ruins.

Behind Kyoto's rebuff lay not so much the court's antiforeign sentiment as its political caution. For an institution that over several centuries had had only a ritual function in politics suddenly to take sides in a matter that sharply divided the bakufu and the great lords was to invite catastrophe. Nor was it just the signing of the treaty that was at stake, controversial though that was. There was also the Tokugawa succession, an issue that was both sensitive and politically divisive. There were two candidates who might succeed Iesada. One, later to become shogun as Iemochi, was from the Kii branch of the house, closest by blood but very young. Traditionalists in Edo favored him.

28 Harris, *Complete Journal*, p. 539.   29 Beasley, *Select Documents*, p. 181.

The other, Hitotsubashi Keiki (Yoshinobu) was older, more able, and son to Nariaki, which made him the preferred candidate of those who wanted reform. Because they saw reform as a necessary concomitant of opening the ports – without it, they said, negotiations would be no more than an expedient for postponing foreign attack – their argument linked the two great questions of the time. It was this, Hotta was convinced, that had bedeviled his talks in Kyoto.

He was given no opportunity to test this belief by trying to achieve a compromise with Matsudaira Keiei and Nariaki over the succession. To conservatives in Edo, the situation he had brought about seemed to pose a threat to the bakufu itself, making it necessary now to use resolution rather than finesse. As a result, Hotta was swept aside. On June 4, Ii Naosuke became regent, setting himself the formidable task of saving the regime by selecting the orthodox candidate, Iemochi, as Iesada's heir while creating at least an appearance of unity among the daimyo on the subject of the treaty, so as to warrant a renewed application to the court.

While moves to achieve this were still secretly in progress, there came news of the signing of a British treaty with China at Tientsin, heralding, it was said, the imminent departure of a British fleet for Japan. Townsend Harris brought the information, hurrying back to Edo Bay from Shimoda in an American warship. The American treaty, he argued, must be signed at once, both to protect Japan and to fulfill Hotta's promises. Ii Naosuke would still have preferred to wait for imperial sanction, as he recognized the great political risks of acting without it, having gone so far, but other members of the council saw the foreign threat as more immediate and compelling. On July 29, the regent reluctantly gave way to their arguments. The treaty was signed the same day.

Harris was correct about Elgin's plans for coming to Japan, though not about the size of his fleet. On August 12 he arrived in Edo Bay with a single ship, bringing Harris's secretary from Shimoda as his interpreter. Putiatin and Curtius were already there. Within two weeks all had signed treaties modeled on that of the United States, but with the addition of a most-favored-nation clause: the Dutch on August 18, the Russians the next day, and the British on August 26. On October 9, Baron Gros for France followed suit, thereby completing the list of Japan's five original treaty powers.

By signing these treaties, Ii Naosuke offended the adherents of *jōi* and gave them a weapon to use against him, namely, his lack of imperial sanction for what he had done. By choosing the Kii candidate in the succession dispute, he offended those lords who advocated reform, some of whom would otherwise have supported him on the treaty question. Thus isolated, he determined to carry matters with a high hand. Bakufu officials who sympathized with the Hitotsubashi party, including Hotta, were removed from office. Feudal lords who might be expected to give countenance to the opposition or intrigue at court against the bakufu were forced into retirement or put under house arrest. Tokugawa Nariaki and Matsudaira Keiei were among them. Two senior ministers of the imperial court were replaced, whereas others, thought to be more open to persuasion, received handsome gifts. This done, a new emissary, Manabe Akikatsu, was sent to "explain" the treaties to the emperor. Despite the preparations, the process took some time.

Manabe reached Kyoto late in October 1858 and, after some preliminary sounding out of opinion, prepared a series of memoranda, designed to persuade the court nobility that the treaties, though undesirable, had been wholly necessary. His task was made more difficult by the emperor, Kōmei, who let it be known that he was personally opposed to the concessions that Edo had made. Manabe, informed of this, countered by claiming that the bakufu had done no more than carry out its public responsibilities and threatened that criticism, being politically motivated, would be firmly suppressed. Nor, he made it plain, could the treaty decision be reversed: "Whatever the orders of the court may be, to rescind the treaties at this time would be to invite both foreign and domestic dangers at once."[30] Coupled with this, however, was a hint of compromise. The court need not approve the treaties, only recognize that the bakufu had had no option but to sign them, thereby validating the shogun's authority. Prolonged talks along these lines at last brought settlement. On February 2, 1859, the emperor, in return for a bakufu undertaking to seek a means of returning to seclusion as soon as practicable, formally acknowledged that Edo had acted under *force majeure* and agreed in the interest of national unity to "exercise forebearance on this occasion."[31] On the face of it, Ii Naosuke had weathered the storm. The ports had been opened; a foreign war had been avoided; and a major political attack on the bakufu had been contained.

PROBLEMS OF IMPLEMENTATION

The opening of Japanese ports to trade – officially from July 1859, though a number of foreign merchants beat the starting gun – was

---

30 Ibid., p. 191.   31 Ibid., p. 194.

accompanied by changes in the role of the various Western powers in the country's foreign relations. Russia, having achieved its immediate territorial ambitions in the north and lacking any great commercial interests in Japan, dropped more and more into the background during the following decade. So did the United States, largely because of its preoccupation with domestic politics and the Civil War: Washington remained willing to support moves to put pressure on the Japanese government to maintain the West's commercial advantages but was no longer in a position to take the lead in doing so. This left the initiative in Japan, as in China, with Britain and France. Britain, in particular, dominant in Far Eastern trade and possessing the naval strength to defend its position, acquired in effect a power of veto over Western policy toward Japan. Without British cooperation, no action in Japan could succeed. France, as one would expect, found this situation irksome, not least because Japan quickly acquired economic importance as a supplier of silk.

In these respects, Japan's foreign relations lost some of their distinctive features, being absorbed into a wider international pattern centering on China. Indeed, they soon began to resemble China's foreign relations after the Opium War. In Japan, as in China, treaties reluctantly conceded proved difficult to enforce. In both, resistance brought conflict, involving the substantial use of force; and the outcome was a further period of negotiation, in which Western privileges were confirmed and extended.

One cause of controversy after 1858 was directly economic: Japanese criticism of the treaties arose in part from the stresses produced by bringing Japan's hitherto isolated economy into a relationship with that of the rest of the world. The currency disputes of 1859–60 illustrate the nature of this conflict of interest and the way in which the West insisted on a solution conforming to its own economic ideas.[32] During his treaty negotiations, Townsend Harris had maintained that trade would only develop if a proper exchange rate were established. This he identified as an exchange of appropriate Western and Japanese coins on the basis of weight for weight. Because the Mexican dollar, as used on the China coast, had a face value and an intrinsic value that were approximately equal, he foresaw no difficulties with this arrangement. Japanese officials, however, viewed things differently. Japanese silver coins, of which the most important was the *ichibu,* had a higher percentage silver content than did the Mexican dollar. Moreover, they passed in Japan at a face value that was not directly related to their

[32] The most useful account is by Peter Frost, *The Bakumatsu Currency Crisis* (Cambridge, Mass.: Harvard University Press, 1970).

intrinsic value, being notionally linked to monetary units whose value was defined in terms of gold. In Japan, the gold-to-silver ratio was about 1 to 5, compared with a world ratio of 1 to 15. Similarly, the silver *ichibu* was, by world standards, substantially overvalued in terms of copper. Thus, to relate the dollar and the silver *ichibu* on a weight-for-weight basis, as Harris required, was to enhance the value of the dollar with reference to Japanese gold and copper coins. By contrast, to have established an exchange rate based on Japanese gold values for the *ichibu*, as Japanese officials wished, would have raised the export price of Japanese goods to what foreigners would have regarded as an unacceptable level.

Unwilling to revise Japanese gold-to-silver ratios to bring them into line with those of the rest of the world, because of the considerable disruption this would cause to the domestic economy, the Tokugawa government sought instead to circumvent the treaties' provisions. In June 1859, in preparation for opening the ports, it issued a new silver coin, called the *nishu-gin*, having the weight of half a dollar and the face value of half an *ichibu*. Under the treaty's exchange stipulations, this would mean valuing the dollar at one *ichibu*. Because the silver *ichibu* coin in use at the time when Harris made his proposals had exchanged by weight at approximately three *ichibu* to the dollar, the effect of introducing the new coin was to treble the price of Japanese goods to the foreign buyer.

The trading implications of this did not at all perturb bakufu officials, as they were not in the least concerned with promoting Japanese exports, but it alarmed the foreign representatives in the treaty ports. Both Townsend Harris and Rutherford Alcock, the newly arrived British minister, protested vigorously. In August the bakufu withdrew the new currency. In September it agreed to supply silver *ichibu* to foreign traders at a rate of three *ichibu* to the dollar, subject to restrictions on the amount to be provided. This led to brisk competition among foreign merchants for supplies of coin, involving a host of fraudulent applications. It also brought a "gold rush" in the winter of 1859–60, as foreigners used their *ichibu* to buy Japanese gold coins at a gold-to-silver ratio of 1 to 5 and then exported them to the China coast for sale at the prevailing ratio there of 1 to 15. Profits were high enough to justify foreigners' paying premium prices for Japanese gold, thereby making ineffective all the bakufu's attempts to halt the trade by banning the sale of gold coins in the treaty ports.

The amount of gold lost to Japan by this means was probably less significant economically than were the measures adopted to check its export. Attempts to end the transactions by cutting off the supply of *ichibu* in November 1859 brought further protests from Harris and Alcock, as this involved the stoppage of the entire Japan trade, in contravention of the treaty. They warned that the consequence might well be war. This threat left the bakufu with little freedom of action. Beginning in February 1860, it began a complete revision of its currency arrangements, reminting old coins and issuing new ones, so as to bring Japanese coinage into line with world gold-to-silver-to-copper ratios and to ensure a rough correspondence between face value and bullion content. Once completed, this checked the export of gold coins. However, it did so at the cost of further debasing the currency and dislocating the structure of commodity prices, thereby contributing to the rapid inflation of the next few years. The treaties had other economic consequences, too. Foreign trade created a demand for Japanese tea and silk, which Japanese producers, despite increasing output, could not readily meet. This inevitably pushed up prices. In a different context, preoccupation with the needs of defense on the part of both the bakufu and the feudal lords led to heavy expenditures on Western-style weapons and military technology. After 1863, armed clashes with the West led to demands for indemnities, whose payment placed a further burden on feudal revenues and gave additional impetus to inflation. It is not surprising, therefore, that many Japanese, seeking reasons to justify their dislike of the "unequal treaties," should have seized on economic factors as one of them. It became almost a cliché of Japanese politics in the 1860s that rising prices could be blamed on the presence of foreigners. There was some substance in the argument, though it was not in itself a sufficient explanation.

Nevertheless, the main Japanese objections to the treaties had political rather than economic roots.[33] At one level they reflected the fears of a feudal ruling class that change would undermine the existing social order. At another they were manifestations of cultural conservatism, commonly taking the form of ritual repetition of inherited prejudice against Christianity ("ritual," because in the absence of any large body of missionaries to provide a focus of hostility, anti-Christian feeling in Japan acquired neither the emotional nor the popular appeal it had in contemporary China). There was, however, a more modern ingredient as well, in the form of incipient nationalism. Japanese, especially samurai, were becoming increasingly aware that what was at risk was not just a culture or a social and political order but a territory and a nation.

33 I have discussed this topic and related matters at some length in *The Meiji Restoration* (Stanford, Calif: Stanford University Press, 1972), esp. chaps. 5, 6, 7.

They differed widely in the means they proposed for defending them, but almost all recognized that a decision required political action. As a result, attempts to influence the foreign policy of the Tokugawa government became a major concern of politically minded Japanese as soon as the terms of the treaties became widely known.

A court noble, feudal lord, or bakufu official could hope to influence policy by more or less legal means, that is, through memorials or family connections. Lesser men, as Ii Naosuke had sharply demonstrated in 1858, could not. If they were to act at all, it had to be by either manipulating their superiors or creating a situation in which their superiors were forced to act for themselves. This meant violence, either terrorism or rebellion. Thus the opening of the ports coincided with an upsurge of violence in Japanese politics, as groups and individuals committed themselves to overturning the decisions on foreign policy already taken by the shogun's ministers.

One way in which they did so was to attack those ministers and the men who served them. The most famous such incident was the assassination of Ii Naosuke outside the gates of Edo Castle in March 1860, an event that gave great encouragement to all those activists who had taken as their slogan the phrase "honor the emperor, expel the barbarian" (*sonnō jōi*). As regent, after all, Ii had flouted the wishes of the emperor by signing treaties that admitted the barbarians. It seemed just that he should pay the ultimate penalty. So should foreigners. There were a number of individual attacks on foreigners and their employees in Yokohama. In January 1861, Townsend Harris's secretary, Henry Heusken, was murdered in the streets of Edo. Most such acts were motivated by simple resentment and frustration, but in July 1861, there came a more organized affair, involving a night attack on the British legation at Tōzenji by a band of samurai, in the course of which two members of the British staff were wounded and a number of Japanese, both guards and attackers, were killed. Action on this scale was clearly intended to do more than wreak vengeance on the foreigners. It was a political move, designed to embroil the bakufu in disputes with Britain.

The response of the foreign representatives to this situation was to insist on the bakufu's obligation to defend them and their countrymen, while taking such steps as they could to defend themselves.[34]

---

[34] For detailed accounts of the diplomatic events of these years, see Grace Fox, *Britain and Japan 1858–1883* (Oxford, England: Clarendon, 1969); Treat, *Early Diplomatic Relations;* and Meron Medzini, *French Policy in Japan During the Closing Years of the Tokugawa Regime* (Cambridge, Mass.: Harvard University Press, 1971). The most important Japanese work on foreign relations in this period is by Ishii Takashi, *Zōtei Meiji Ishin no kokusaiteki kankyō*, rev. ed. (Tokyo: Yoshikawa Kōbunkan, 1966).

After Heusken's murder, for example, the British and French ministers ostentatiously withdrew to Yokohama, refusing to return until their safety could be guaranteed (a gesture that was made less effective by Townsend Harris's refusal to join them). After the Tōzenji incident, Alcock landed marines to act as a legation guard, replaced later by an army detachment sent from Hong Kong. For the rest, they continued to insist that the treaties' provisions must be implemented fully. In particular, they condemned the bakufu's attempts to limit the economic effects of foreign trade by putting it – like much of domestic commerce – as far as possible in the hands of monopoly merchants under official patronage, a practice that in Alcock's view was reminiscent of Chinese restrictive practices earlier in the century at Canton.

The bakufu's response was to try to turn the turbulence to its own advantage. The rise in commodity prices and the emergence of political unrest reinforced official dissatisfaction with the original treaty settlement, providing additional motives for trying to modify it. They also furnished arguments that might be used to persuade the foreigners to relax their defense of it. In May 1861 the shogun's council put their case to the foreign envoys in Edo. "The price of things," they argued, "is daily increasing, in consequence of the large quantity of products which is exported to foreign countries." The result had been to strengthen the resentments already provoked by the abandonment of policies of national isolation, "deeply rooted in the national spirit," and thereby to produce a state of popular disquiet in which "it is very difficult, even for the power and authority of the government, so to manage that each one should clearly understand the future advantage, and so cause them to endure for a time the present grief."[35] The solution proposed was to postpone the opening of further ports and cities as laid down in the treaties (Edo, Osaka, Hyōgo, and Niigata), to give time for Japanese resentments to die down and for the bakufu to win wider acceptance of the treaty arrangements. To this end, a mission was sent to Europe to discuss the question with the governments of the treaty powers.

The subsequent negotiations were conducted principally between the British Foreign Secretary, Lord Russell, the British minister, Rutherford Alcock, and the senior member of the bakufu council, Kuze Hirochika. Both Alcock and Russell were willing to make concessions for the sake of continuing the trade, as the alternatives seemed to be withdrawal from Japan or to use naval force, as in China, to maintain treaty rights (which the value of the trade did not justify). They

---

35 A contemporary translation, published in *British Parliamentary Papers* in 1862, is given in Beasley, *Select Documents*, pp. 208–11.

required in return compensation for the attack on the legation at Tōzenji and such guarantees as it was possible to devise for the future conduct of trade relations with Japan. This much was agreed in Edo. Alcock then returned to London to take part in talks with the Japanese mission, led by Takeuchi Yasunori. These became little more than a formality. Russell's original instructions to Alcock on the subject had been that "so far from restricting or abandoning the trade of Japan, you are to maintain and, if possible, enlarge it."[36] Accordingly, the protocol signed in London on June 6, 1862, not only postponed the opening of further ports and cities until January 1, 1868; it also improved on the original treaties by reducing the import duties on wines, spirits, and glassware, as well as providing for the establishment of bonded warehouses. More widely, it embodied a promise by the bakufu to end all restrictions, "whether as regards quantity or price, on the sale by Japanese to foreigners of all kinds of merchandise," together with all restrictions "limiting the classes of persons who shall be allowed to trade with foreigners," including, specifically, feudal lords.[37] Failing fulfillment of these conditions by the bakufu, the powers would be entitled to require the immediate opening of the additional ports and cities under the terms of the 1858 treaties, revoking the postponement agreed in the protocol.

In the event, the London Protocol did not prove an instrument for solving the problems of the Japan trade, as Russell and Alcock had hoped. It was designed, in accordance with the principles of gunboat diplomacy, as worked out in China, to put pressure on a Japanese government, recognized as "legitimate," so as to persuade it to enforce the treaties within Japan. To this extent it reflected an ignorance of Japanese politics. It is true that within the bakufu, men in authority, especially those whose duties gave them direct knowledge of foreign affairs, had by this time come to accept that there were serious restrictions on Japan's freedom of action in dealing with the West. However, the further one moved from the centers of responsibility, whether inside the bakufu or outside it, the less this recognition obtained. Thus a number of powerful feudal lords, led by Shimazu Hisamitsu, father of the daimyo of Satsuma – although they were fundamentally in favor of developing relations with the West – tried consistently to exploit the shogun's difficulties by exacting a price for their concurrence in his policy. That price was a greater share of power within Japan, or at least a greater measure of independence from central

---

36 Russell to Alcock, November 23, 1861, in *Parliamentary Papers, 1862*, vol. 64 (2929), pp. 72–73.   37 The text is printed in Beasley, *Select Documents*, pp. 216–17.

control. By contrast, samurai activists, concerned above all about the "national dishonor" occasioned by the treaties, sought to transfer responsibility for the conduct of foreign affairs from the bakufu to the imperial court and its feudal associates, in the expectation that this would ensure a less compliant attitude toward Western privileges. Both movements, backed as they were by terrorism or the military resources of the domains, constituted a threat to bakufu authority. For this reason they produced divided counsels in Edo. Some officials continued to regard the West as potentially the greater danger. By implication, this meant that domestic opposition must be controlled or suppressed for the sake of avoiding a disastrous foreign war. Others, including powerful relatives of the Tokugawa, like Matsudaira Keiei, saw Edo's first priority as being to come to terms with domestic opposition in such a way as would establish national unity and provide a basis for agreement on foreign policy. This implied in the short term a temporizing approach to the question of the treaties. These disagreements were essentially those of the 1850s, now spread more widely through Japanese society and backed by force. Until they were resolved, Japan was unlikely to achieve a stable relationship with the outside world.

Even while the London Protocol was being negotiated, moves were afoot in Kyoto to force a public change in bakufu policy. The first to materialize was the dispatch of an imperial envoy to Edo, escorted by Shimazu Hisamitsu, in an attempt to bring about a basis for a court-bakufu agreement by securing the appointment of Matsudaira Keiei and Hitotsubashi Keiki to high office. This objective was achieved during July and August 1862, but hopes that it might provide a better atmosphere for the discussion of foreign policy were dashed by an incident that took place during Shimazu's journey back to Kyoto. On September 14 a party of foreigners from Yokohama, riding through the nearby village of Namamugi, fell foul of part of the Satsuma escort and were attacked. One, a British merchant called Richardson, was killed, and two were wounded. The affair brought an immediate uproar in Yokohama. When reported to London, it persuaded Russell that the making of concessions, as manifested in the London Protocol, had been taken by the Japanese to be a sign of weakness or indifference, as Satsuma refused to hand over the men responsible for the killing and the bakufu had shown itself unable or unwilling to seize them. Accordingly, Russell required exemplary satisfaction. His dispatch to the British chargé, St. John Neale, on December 24, 1862,[38]

---

38 *Parliamentary Papers, 1864*, vol. 66 (3242), pp. 1–2.

demanded a full formal apology and an indemnity of £100,000 from the bakufu. Moreover, arguing that Satsuma and other powerful lords "who could not easily be coerced by the Japanese government" must not be allowed to "escape, on that account, the penalty of their misdeeds," he specified that Satsuma must not only execute Richardson's murderers in the presence of British naval officers but must also pay a separate indemnity of £25,000. The senior officer of the British naval squadron in the China seas would be authorized to take appropriate measures "of reprisal or blockade, or both," against the bakufu and Satsuma if these terms were rejected.

Although Neale avoided threats of blockade, because he thought that foreign merchants at the treaty ports would be the chief sufferers from it, he made it clear to the bakufu on April 6, 1863, that on this occasion "Great Britain will not tolerate even a passive defiance of its power."[39] Because action would be taken directly against Satsuma in the event of "refusal, delay, or evasion," on the part of its feudal lord, he recommended that Edo send a senior official there to advise against "any obstinate or ill-advised conduct." This was the language of gunboat diplomacy, applied fully to Japan for the first time by Britain. It was backed by the assembly of a powerful naval squadron in Yokohama, eventually totaling seven ships mounting over a hundred guns.

Satsuma ignored all representations made to it. The bakufu's own response was bedeviled by what was happening in Kyoto. As a result of Shimazu's mission in the summer of 1862, followed by another under the patronage of Chōshū later in the year, it had been agreed that the shogun should go to the imperial capital in the spring of 1863, accompanied by his highest-ranking officials, to settle outstanding political issues, including that of foreign policy. Once he arrived there (April 21), he and his advisers became subject to heavy pressure, backed by renewed terrorism, to fix a date for the expulsion of foreigners from Japan. Deprived of any Satsuma support, partly because of the Namamugi dispute, and reluctant to use force on the scale that would have been necessary to restore control over the palace, they finally chose June 25 as the date for action, making the unstated assumption that because implementation of the decision would be the bakufu's business, "expulsion" could in practice be turned into a series of time-consuming negotiations with the treaty powers.

It was in the light of a knowledge of all this that the officials left

39 Ibid., pp. 40–4. Text printed in Beasley, *Select Documents*, pp. 236–40. Because of the time taken in communication by sea via the Indian Ocean, Russell's instructions did not reach Neale until the middle of March 1863.

behind in Edo had to deal with Neale. They were in no doubt at all that an indemnity would have to be paid. On the other hand, to pay it while the shogun was in Kyoto would seriously undermine what their superiors were attempting there. They managed to spin out the talks until the end of May, when one of Hitotsubashi Keiki's advisers, Ogasawara Nagamichi, arrived from Kyoto to take charge of the final stages. By this time Neale's patience was exhausted. Even so, Ogasawara held him off until June 24, when the first installment of the indemnity was at last handed over. The same day he notified all the foreign representatives that the bakufu wished to enter into negotiations for closing the treaty ports. Neale was predictably indignant. Edo must realize, he wrote,

that the indiscreet communication now made . . . is unparalleled in the history of all nations, civilized or uncivilized; that it is, in fact, a declaration of war by Japan itself against the whole of the Treaty Powers, the consequences of which, if not at once arrested, it will have speedily to expiate by the severest and most merited chastisement.[40]

While the bakufu was considering the implications of this response, Neale completed his preparations for an expedition against Satsuma. On August 6 he left Yokohama with the British squadron, reaching Kagoshima five days later and presenting an ultimatum that embodied Russell's demands. Receiving an unsatisfactory reply, he ordered the seizure of three Satsuma vessels lying in the anchorage, intending to hold them against the payment of the indemnity. But in moving to carry out these orders, the squadron came under fire from shore batteries, and a general engagement followed. A good part of the city of Kagoshima was damaged or destroyed. Ships of the British squadron also suffered damage, causing their withdrawal to Yokohama to make repairs. Thus both sides were able to claim a measure of success. Reflecting this, discussions between them at Yokohama in the autumn brought an agreement, signed on December 11, by which Satsuma was to pay an indemnity (borrowing money from the bakufu for the purpose) but, for the rest, promised only that the Namamugi attackers would be punished in the presence of British officers, if and when they were found. Because they had been present at Kagoshima during Neale's negotiations, this was disingenuous, to say the least.

The repercussions of "expulsion" on June 25 proved to be more complicated. On that date, Chōshū, taking the emperor's orders literally, opened fire on an American vessel passing through the Shi-

40 *Parliamentary Papers, 1864*, vol. 46 (3242), p. 75.

monoseki Straits. There were similar attacks on French and Dutch ships during the following weeks. This produced local punitive action from French and American warships, plus a vigorous protest to the bakufu from the representatives of the powers, but it quickly became apparent that the bakufu could do nothing and that Chōshū could be coerced only at the risk of widespread hostilities. None of the foreign envoys was willing to take this risk without the approval of his home government, so for the time being the straits remained closed to foreign shipping. Trade between Yokohama and Shanghai had to proceed by a route to the south of Kyushu.

At the end of September, Satsuma, its prestige within Japan much heightened by its reputedly successful resistance in the face of British attack, joined with the bakufu to expel the Chōshū men and their terrorist allies from the precincts of the imperial palace in Kyoto. The bakufu promptly exploited the situation by proposing a new basis for national agreement on foreign policy, which took the form of a plan to close Yokohama at the bakufu's initiative. This, it was thought, would be a gesture of reconciliation with the antiforeign movement, which might also be made acceptable to the powers as an alternative to closing Japan's ports entirely. It would have the further advantage of reaffirming the shogun's prerogatives in matters of foreign affairs, which had been seriously challenged by the actions of Satsuma and Chōshū during the summer.

Steps to implement this plan were taken during the early months of 1864. First, a mission was sent to France in February, in the hope of being able to win European acceptance of the closing of Yokohama, or at least to make negotiations on the matter last long enough to give the bakufu a worthwhile breathing space. Second, the shogun went to Kyoto again to undertake talks on outstanding issues, this time from a position of strength. Neither demarche produced quite the results that had been hoped. In Kyoto, Hitotsubashi Keiki, acting for the shogun, secured imperial approval to substitute his new proposal for the more "reckless" forms of expulsion advocated in the previous year but did so only at the cost of an open quarrel with Shimazu, who argued that the whole idea was unrealistic. The break with Satsuma that this initiated greatly reduced the chances of getting the policy accepted by feudal opinion at large. In Paris, Ikeda Chōhatsu, the bakufu envoy, met with a flat refusal to contemplate any such action as the closing of Yokohama. Questions of prestige apart, France was by this time becoming dependent on Japanese supplies of raw silk – almost entirely shipped through Yokohama –

because of silkworm disease in Europe. Ikeda therefore accepted the inevitable, signing a convention on June 24 that promised that the bakufu would open the Shimonoseki Straits again within three months, if necessary with French naval help. He then set off for Japan again, far sooner than Edo expected.

Meanwhile, on March 2, 1864, Rutherford Alcock had returned to Japan after several months' leave in England. Because the governments of Britain, France, Holland, and the United States all had agreed to leave decisions concerning Shimonoseki to their representatives in Edo, it was open to him to persuade his diplomatic colleagues of the course of action he thought best. Alcock himself quickly came to the conclusion that naval action against Chōshū would not only be legal, in view of the bakufu's denial that there was any official policy of expulsion, but also expedient, because it would help strengthen the "legitimate" Japanese government against its domestic enemies. On May 30, at his suggestion, the four ministers sent identical notes to the bakufu, rejecting the closing of Yokohama and calling for action to remove "the continuing obstruction to commerce" by Chōshū. This produced no more that a reiteration of earlier bakufu statements on the subject, but no further steps were taken immediately, pending the arrival of enough British reinforcements to ensure the defense of the foreign settlement at Yokohama in the event of general hostilities. The arrival of fifteen hundred marines in June, followed by a foot regiment from Hong Kong in July, gave assurance. Accordingly, on July 22 it was decided to act as soon as the naval commanders were ready. As a precaution against an attempt by any one of the powers to exploit the expedition to its own advantage, the document recording this decision included an undertaking by each of the ministers "neither to ask for, nor to accept, any concession of territory, nor any exclusive advantage whatever, either in the open ports or elsewhere in Japan," and to "abstain from all interference in the jurisdiction of the Japanese authorities over their people."[41] Behind this lay an awareness of what had happened when Britain took punitive action in China and France in Annam. In Japan, it was hoped, imperialism was to be more truly cooperative.

At this point two events intervened to postpone naval operations. The first was the return to Yokohama of two Chōshū samurai, Itō Hirobumi and Inoue Kaoru, who had been studying in London. They offered their services to Alcock as intermediaries to bring about a

---

41 *Parliamentary Papers, 1865*, vol. 57 (3428), pp. 62–6.

settlement between Chōshū and Britain, an offer that was at once accepted. Alcock sent them to Chōshū in a British warship, bearing a letter in which he set out his own views on the implications of the crisis.[42] Britain, it stated, was not concerned about the distribution of political power within Japan. If the Japanese believed that the treaties needed "the formal assent of the Mikado to make them legal and binding," or if the feudal lords wished to end the monopoly of foreign trade enjoyed by the bakufu, there was nothing in such proposals to cause difficulty to the foreign powers. Rather, what the latter wanted was recognition of "some sovereign authority" with whom treaties could be made in the expectation that they would be binding. By contrast, "a persistent attempt to expel foreigners from Japan, or even from Yokohama, . . . may bring armies to Kioto as similar conduct led the armies of Great Britain and France victoriously to Peking not five years ago."

Itō and Inoue lacked the influence in Chōshū to bring about a settlement on the lines envisaged in Alcock's letter. By August 12 it was evident that their intervention had failed. A week later, Ikeda Chōhatsu arrived in Yokohama, bringing the convention he had signed in Paris, by which the bakufu was bound to open the Shimonoseki Straits within three months. Again preparations for an expedition were suspended while the foreign envoys awaited Edo's reactions. These were prompt and clear: Ikeda was dismissed, his agreement repudiated. If they were to implement the convention, the shogun's council agreed, "civil war would immediately break out."[43] This decision removed the last reason for delay. A joint squadron of seventeen ships – nine British, three French, four Dutch, and one American – sailed for Shimonoseki under the command of Vice-Admiral Kuper, carrying out attacks on the Chōshū batteries in the straits during the first week of September. On September 14 Chōshū representatives concluded a truce on terms dictated by Kuper, stipulating the opening of the straits and the disarming of the batteries, plus a promise to pay an indemnity as ransom for Shimonoseki and reimbursement for military costs. This became the basis of a convention between the bakufu and the powers concerned, signed on October 22. It fixed the indemnity at three million Mexican dollars, to be paid in six equal installments. However, the foreign representatives, in a clause that reflected primarily the commercial interests of Great Britain, expressed themselves willing to consider the opening of Shimonoseki or another suitable

---

42 Ibid., pp. 72–3. The text is also found in Fox, *Britain and Japan*, pp. 133–4.
43 *Parliamentary Papers, 1865*, vol. 57 (3428), p. 84, bakufu note of August 25, 1864.

port as an alternative to payment of the indemnity, were the bakufu to propose it. The legal basis for holding the bakufu responsible in this way rested on documents captured in Chōshū. These showed that the orders for expulsion of the foreigners in 1863 had been issued by the imperial court with the shogun's knowledge and consent. In effect, this destroyed Edo's last tactical advantage, that is, its ability to keep negotiations with the West and negotiations with the court apart, holding them secret from the other party.

SETTLEMENT

Justifying his actions to a somewhat skeptical Russell late in 1864, Alcock produced a classic statement of the case for resorting to gunboat diplomacy in China and Japan.[44] Treaties negotiated under threat, he argued, could not be maintained "by a religious abstinence from the use of force":

> It is weakness, or the suspicion of it, which invariably provokes wrong and aggression in the East. . . . Hence it is that all diplomacy in these regions which does not rest on a solid substratum of force, or an element of strength, to be laid bare when all gentler processes fail, rests on false premises, and must of necessity fail in its object – more especially, perhaps, when that end is peace.

He was also able to claim success for what he had done: "A catastrophe has been averted, the danger of a war indefinitely deferred, if not altogether prevented, and our position at Yokohama secured from all immediate risk." To Russell, conscious of criticism in Parliament, the argument was not altogether convincing, though he accepted it. He was beginning to realize that the political situation in Japan was sufficiently unlike that in China to make the policies appropriate to the one inappropriate to the other. The essential issue, as Alcock's dispatches revealed, was that of the shogun's authority to conclude and enforce treaties. Accordingly, Russell's instructions to Alcock's successor, Sir Harry Parkes, when he was appointed in March 1865, required him to pursue the question of securing the emperor's confirmation of the treaties if that seemed desirable.

As it transpired, Parkes's task had been made a good deal easier by the bombardments at Kagoshima and Shimonoseki. Once they had taken place, there was no longer any significant group of officials in Edo willing to argue in favor of resisting foreign demands. In Satsuma and

---

44 Ibid., pp. 148–54, Alcock to Russell, November 19, 1864.

Chōshū, the hotheads, who had been willing to risk the consequences of attempting to expel the foreigners for the sake of political gains, had been discredited by the demonstrable disparity of strength between their domains and the West. Their successors took a more realistic view of what was feasible in foreign affairs. Moreover, an attempted coup d'etat in Kyoto in August 1864, spearheaded by Chōshū men and checked after heavy fighting by troops from Satsuma and Aizu, had led to the deaths or flight of most of the radical leaders associated with the court. As a result, the whole tone of the foreign policy discussions changed. The few members of the court – including Emperor Kōmei – who still clung to ideas of expulsion found themselves isolated and increasingly helpless. Thus although antiforeign sentiment remained a tactical weapon for use in the domestic struggle, the only real policy question to which it had relevance from this time on was not whether, but in what way, Japan should come to terms with the "unequal" treaties. This was demonstrated in 1865, when Parkes made his bid for their ratification by the emperor.

Parkes's experience before coming to Japan had been entirely in China. He was a good Chinese linguist; he had served as one of the commissioners administering Canton when it was occupied by British and French forces during the *Arrow* war; and he had been British consul in commercially the most important of the Chinese treaty ports, Shanghai. He was, therefore, both a well-informed and a convinced exponent of the kind of policies that had built up Britain's position of dominance on the China coast. These defined his objectives. For the means of attaining them he relied heavily on the advice of Alcock, under whom he had served when young and who had been his predecessor at Shanghai as well as in Edo. Alcock's views we have already touched upon. Parkes largely inherited them.

In April 1865, about two months before Parkes arrived, the bakufu had informed the foreign representatives that it did not wish to exercise the option of opening Shimonoseki instead of paying the indemnity of $3 million. Simultaneously, however, it asked that the payment of the second and subsequent installments of the indemnity be delayed, because it was having difficulty in raising so large a sum. The foreign envoys referred this request to their governments. Winchester, the British chargé, reporting it to Russell, took the opportunity to argue for a different approach entirely. As he saw it, the money for the indemnity could be raised only by imposts on the trade, which would be much to Britain's disadvantage. He therefore proposed that Britain offer to waive two-thirds of the indemnity, in return for the following concessions: (1) the opening of Hyōgo and Osaka earlier than had been specified in the London Protocol; (2) the emperor's ratification of the existing treaties; and (3) a reduction of import duties, establishing the basic rate at 5 percent. Russell's instructions approving this proposal reached Parkes in Japan in October 1865.

Because the indemnity convention had been a four-power agreement, it was necessary for Parkes to work in cooperation with the American, Dutch, and French representatives. The first two offered no objections, but the French minister, Leon Roches, was beginning to develop a line of his own with reference to policy in Japan, which did not entirely accord with that of Britain. Essentially, Parkes, following Alcock, sought to avoid committing Britain to any one group in Japanese politics, even the bakufu, preferring to await the outcome of the power struggle and then to secure acceptance of the treaties from the victorious party. Roches saw greater advantages for France in recognizing the bakufu as a legitimate government and supporting it accordingly. This implied avoidance, where possible, of any action or diplomatic pressure that might serve to weaken the shogun vis-à-vis his political rivals. Roches was wary of the British plan, on the grounds that it might further lower the bakufu's prestige.[45]

Parkes's determination, plus recognition that the proposals, if accepted, would greatly benefit all the treaty powers, not merely Britain, finally won over Roches. On October 30, 1865, the four ministers jointly replied to the original bakufu request for postponement of the indemnity payments, offering to accept it on the terms put forward by Britain. At the same time, noting that the shogun and his senior officials were again absent – this time in Osaka to organize a punitive expedition against Chōshū – they observed that this circumstance would render negotiations in Edo "if not impossible, at least illusory."[46] They therefore announced their intention of transferring the talks to Osaka. On November 4 they arrived at Hyōgo with a squadron of nine ships. The letter embodying their demands was presented to a senior bakufu official at Osaka three days later and gave a limit of seven days for a reply.

The discussions that followed during the next two weeks are of interest chiefly for the light they throw on developments in Japanese

---

45 The rivalry and political maneuvers of Parkes and Roches in Japan have long been a subject of controversy, but they are not directly relevant to the theme of this chapter. The most recent and detailed discussion can be found in Fox, *Britain and Japan*, chap. 7, and Medzini, *French Policy*, chaps. 8–14. Ishii, *Zōtei Meiji Ishin*, chaps. 5 and 6, also discusses this at length.
46 The French text of the memorandum is given in Beasley, *Select Documents*, pp. 293–6.

politics. The bakufu council, having demurred, briefly and ineffectively, over the opening of Hyōgo and Osaka, because of the difficulties this might cause to Kyoto, accepted the terms on November 13, only to find Hitotsubashi Keiki insisting that for the bakufu again to act without the court's approval in a matter of such sensitivity would be politically disastrous. The council reluctantly agreed. Keiki secured a promise from the foreign representatives of an extra ten days to accomplish the task, then set out to win imperial consent. Hostility from remaining antiforeign groups in the palace was something he expected and could confidently ignore, given the support of senior court officials, most of whom owed their appointment to the shogun's favor. More alarming was the stubborn opposition he encountered from Satsuma. It was not so much that Satsuma objected to the foreign proposals in themselves. Rather, it was that Ōkubo Toshimichi, Satsuma's key political figure in Kyoto, was determined that the bakufu must not be allowed to use the crisis to establish a position of dominance at court that would strengthen it against the great lords. Consequently, to Keiki's insistence on consulting the court he added a demand for consultation of the daimyo, notwithstanding the time it would take. He even offered to approach the foreigners directly, or through the court, to secure their consent to the delay.

One factor in resolving the resulting deadlock was Parkes's impatience. On November 21 he wrote a letter to the shogun threatening all kinds of evil consequences if the matter were not settled: "[D]isunion must bring upon your country the most grave disorders, as our Governments are firmly resolved to insist upon the faithful and complete observance by all parties, whether our enemies or our friends, of every condition of the Treaties. . . ."[47] More immediately significant, however, was a remarkable closing of the ranks within the bakufu itself. On November 18 the shogun, Iemochi, offered to resign in favor of Keiki. He accompanied this gesture with a memorandum that not only recommended acceptance of the demands presently being made by the foreign envoys but also urged an entirely new line of approach to the West, that of borrowing Western techniques to build up Japanese strength. Japan, he argued, must "follow the example of the foreigners in using the profits from trade to construct many ships and guns, adopting the strategy of using the barbarian to subdue the barbarian."[48] The idea was not new, for many Japanese had been advocating something of the kind in the years since Perry, but never before had

47 Ibid., pp. 299–300.   48 Ibid., pp. 297–9.

the bakufu given countenance to such a policy publicly in its dealings with the court. Backing it up, the senior bakufu officials in Kyoto, including Keiki, formally warned the court in a joint memorial that if Japan provoked hostilities over this issue, "we should have not the least hope of victory."[49]

Faced with this unanimity, the court gave way. The emperor gave his consent to the treaties, commenting that "unsatisfactory provisions" in them needed to be revised.[50] He refused to authorize any action regarding Hyōgo and Osaka, though the bakufu, in communicating with the foreign representatives, assumed this to mean that they could be opened in accordance with the London Protocol. There was to be further disagreement on this subject in 1867, when the court became aware of what had been said. No statement was made about tariffs, which had at no time been mentioned in the Japanese discussions. The fact reflects a characteristic of the treaty port system that was common to both China and Japan at this stage: Whereas the West saw the system in terms of commercial advantage, both Chinese and Japanese were preoccupied with the political disabilities it imposed on them. They made economic concessions almost without thought.

This is borne out by the bakufu's subsequent behavior. Because it had not met *all* the West's demands, it accepted the necessity of paying the whole of the Shimonoseki indemnity. Moreover, it agreed to negotiate a revision of tariffs. When talks about this began in January 1866, Parkes, who took the lead in the matter on behalf of the powers, promptly expanded them to include arrangements concerning currency, which was still causing difficulties; the establishment of navigation aids, such as lighthouses; and the removal of all those restrictions on trade to which reference had been made in the London Protocol. He refused to contemplate any further delay in the indemnity payments until a satisfactory agreement had been reached on these points. This was not to be until June 25, 1866, when a convention was at last signed by Britain, France, Holland, and the United States, to come into force at Yokohama on July 1 and a month later at Hakodate and Nagasaki.

The convention was in effect an addendum to the 1858 treaties, spelling out free-trade doctrine as it applied to Japanese conditions. Goods imported into and exported from Japan were to be subject to customs dues calculated at a general level of 5 percent, either in the form of specified amounts or *ad valorem*. Some items, such as books,

49 Ibid., p. 301, memorial of November 22, 1865.
50 Ibid., p. 304, court decision of November 22, 1865.

gold and silver, coal or grain, could be imported free of duty. Only opium was a prohibited import. Rice, wheat, barley, and saltpeter were prohibited exports, and unminted gold, silver, and copper could be sold only by the Japanese government. Export duties on tea and silk were to be subject to review on the basis of 5 percent *ad valorem* at any time after the first two years. The remaining duties were open to revision after July 1872. Other articles contained provisions concerning matters ancillary to trade that had been causing difficulty: bonded warehouses, provision of Japanese currency, navigational aids, and details concerning transactions at the open ports. More far-reaching were Articles VIII, IX, and X. The first of these permitted Japanese citizens to buy "every description of sailing or steam-vessel," save warships (which could be sold only to the Japanese government). Under Article IX the bakufu declared that "Japanese merchants and traders of all classes are at liberty to trade directly . . . with foreign merchants, not only at the open ports of Japan, but also in all foreign countries. . . ." Completing the pattern, Article X provided that all Japanese "may travel to any foreign country for purposes of study or trade," subject only to being provided with passports.[51]

Given that the emperor had confirmed the treaties and that Edo had been browbeaten into an almost routine compliance with foreign demands, the tariff convention of 1866 could be said to have completed the opening of Japan to foreign trade. Foreign diplomats began to find their advice more welcome and their problems easier to solve; and when Keiki became shogun, following the death of Iemochi in the autumn of 1866, he was careful to grant audiences to both Parkes and Roches. They reminded him that the time was approaching for opening Osaka and Hyōgo in accordance with the London Protocol. He made no demur. Indeed, he promptly raised the matter at court.[52] Once again, he was opposed by Satsuma there, this time on the grounds that a settlement of the dispute with Chōshū must take priority over the opening of Hyōgo. Once again, as in November 1865, he successfully forced a decision in the bakufu's favor. On June 26, 1867, the emperor granted permission for the shogun to fulfill his treaty obligations.

These events were an important stage in the process by which Keiki broke finally with the great lords, contributing to his resignation and fall from power later in the year. From the point of view of the country's

[51] The text of the convention and the new list of tariffs are given in *Parliamentary Papers, 1867*, vol. 74 (3758), pp. 1–6. There is a summary of the negotiations in Fox, *Britain and Japan*, pp. 182–5. [52] See Beasley, *Select Documents*, sec. 8, for a discussion of this incident.

foreign relations, however, they raised the question – substantially the point at issue between Parkes and Roches – whether a successor regime dominated by the bakufu's enemies would be able or willing to uphold the treaties that the West had signed. For a time it looked doubtful. During the crisis weeks of early 1868, when the bakufu was overthrown and Japan was plunged into civil war, there was an attack on foreigners in Hyōgo, followed by another in Sakai, which suggested that the expulsion movement was still very much alive. So it was, if one is to judge by the views of the loyalist rank and file. Yet the men who were now beginning to take charge of government in the emperor's name were by no means so naive or inexperienced as to believe that they could ignore pressures that the bakufu had found imperative. On the last day of February 1868, the six powerful feudal lords who had played the most conspicuous part in events in Kyoto submitted a joint memorial to the court calling for a fresh approach to foreign policy.[53] Japan, they said, must avoid "the bad example of the Chinese, who fancying themselves alone to be great and worthy of respect, and despising foreigners as little better than beasts, have come to suffer defeat at their hands." Expulsion had been shown clearly enough to be impracticable. It would therefore be more sensible to enter on "relations of amity" with the foreigners, summoning the foreign representatives to an imperial audience "in the manner prescribed by the rules current amongst all nations" and making the fact known publicly throughout Japan.

No significant group at court was likely to oppose the men who by this time provided the imperial government's only effective fighting force, though a few court nobles still had to be persuaded of their own helplessness. Hence the emperor's reply, dated March 10, recognized realities: "[T]he stipulations of the treaties . . . may be reformed if found to be hurtful, but the public laws observed by all nations forbid wanton disturbance of those arrangements as a whole. . . . The Imperial Government feels itself therefore compelled to entertain amicable relations under the treaties concluded by the Bakufu."[54] Realism had proved to be transferable. The effect was a little spoiled by an attempt to assassinate Parkes on his way to the imperial audience that followed this exchange, but the culprits were promptly punished and "amicable relations" remained undisturbed. If the new regime survived, it could be expected that the treaties would survive with it.

---

53 The text is translated in J. R. Black, *Young Japan: Yokohama and Yedo* [1881] (London: Trubner, reprint edition, 2 vols., 1968), vol. 2, pp. 178–81.
54 Text in ibid., vol. 2, pp. 181–3.

TRADE RELATIONS UNDER THE TREATY PORT SYSTEM

Because of a preoccupation with the study of modernization, much recent writing on Japan in the nineteenth century has tended to overlook the fact that for the first twenty-five years after the signing of the treaties, Japan's political and economic relationships with the outside world were very much like China's. Indeed, the two were closely linked. The treaties negotiated in 1858 had been "Chinese" not only in the sense of applying to Japan a number of policies and institutions that the powers found useful or appropriate on the China coast but also incorporating Japan into a treaty port system that essentially focused on China. For example, the consular courts established in Japan to try cases involving foreign residents were modeled on those already created in the Chinese treaty ports. Britain, the only country that tried to give the system an element of professional expertise, established a Supreme Court in 1865 to act as a court of appeal and exercise general supervision. It had jurisdiction in both countries but sat as a rule in Shanghai. The consuls who administered the local courts, few of whom in the early years had had legal training, had often begun their careers in China. So had the merchants with whom they had to deal. One consequence was that the foreign community in the Japanese ports tried to reproduce on a smaller scale what had been done in places like Shanghai, Tientsin, and Canton. Within a year or two of its opening, Yokohama had its club, its racecourse, and its chamber of commerce. In 1862 the local residents organized a municipal council to deal with matters like sewage, street lighting, and local police in the area set aside for foreigners, but for a variety of reasons the arrangement was never very successful. In 1867 most of these functions reverted to the Japanese local officials, acting through a foreign municipal director until 1877 and thereafter directly in their own official capacity. Kobe (Hyōgo), which with Osaka was opened on January 1, 1868, was the only other foreign community of significant size. Profiting from knowledge of the mistakes made at Yokohama, its settlement was better organized, surviving as a separate entity until the revision of treaties in 1899, but it never approached the scale and complexity, or the influence, of the foreign communities in China.[55]

[55] Useful information on these matters can be found in Black, *Young Japan;* and Fox, *Britain and Japan.* The only specialist study is by J. E. Hoare, "The Japanese Treaty Ports, 1868–1899: A Study of the Foreign Settlements," Ph.D. diss., University of London, 1971. Edo (Tokyo) was not opened to foreigners until January 1, 1869, because of the civil war; its foreign settlement was of negligible importance, as from an early date, foreigners were allowed to live outside it.

The total number of foreign residents in Japan grew from approximately one thousand in 1868, when the great majority were at Yokohama and most of the rest in Nagasaki, to just under ten thousand in 1894, when about half were in Yokohama and about one-fifth in Kobe. Of these, more than half were Chinese. This partly reflects the continuing development of traditional Sino-Japanese trade, but it was also due to the China connections of many Americans and Europeans. Merchants coming from the China coast to set up branch houses or new companies in Japan brought with them not only household servants, trained to cater to Western needs, but also compradors and other trading assistants. Yokohama soon acquired a Chinese quarter, as Nagasaki had had throughout the Tokugawa period. The nature and organization of Japan's foreign trade was certainly influenced by this Chinese presence. Chinese experts in the tea and silk business helped make Japan, already a producer, into a substantial exporter of these products (taking over part of China's market in the process). It is also possible that because the Chinese were established in these specialist capacities, the Japanese were inhibited from entering the kind of symbiotic relationship with Western merchants that is nowadays comprised under the label *comprador*. At all events, Japanese merchants in the tea and silk trades, originally serving only as a link between the domestic producer and the Western exporter in the treaty ports, quickly developed their own separate export channels to Western markets. The process was spearheaded by the Mitsui Bussan trading company, founded in 1876, though the diversion of Japan's foreign trade in general from Western to Japanese hands did not make much headway until after 1890. In 1887, it has been estimated, nearly 90 percent of it was still handled by foreign merchant houses.[56]

Turning to the scale and composition of the trade, one encounters the problem that no reliable statistics exist for the years before 1868.[57] Ishii's estimates suggest that Japanese exports rose from something over $4 million in 1860 to an annual average of about $14 million for

---

[56] The most detailed study of the organization of foreign trade in this period is by G. C. Allen and Audrey Donnithorne, *Western Enterprise in Far Eastern Economic Development: China and Japan* (London: Allen & Unwin, 1954). See also Fox, *Britain and Japan*, chap. 12. An example of how the Japanese bypassed Western merchants at the treaty ports can be found in Haru Matsukata Reischauer, *Samurai and Silk* (Cambridge, Mass.: Harvard University Press, 1986), in the chapters on Rioichiro Arai.

[57] There are detailed studies of the trade for 1859-68 in Japanese: Ishii Takashi, *Bakumatsu bōekishi no kenkyū* (Tokyo, 1944); and Yamaguchi Kazuo, *Bakumatsu bōekishi* (Tokyo, 1943). Statistics from 1868 onward are available in a number of works, of which the most detailed is Oriental Economist, *The Foreign Trade of Japan: A Statistical Survey* (Tokyo, 1935). A useful summary (with statistical tables) can be found in G. C. Allen, *A Short Economic History of Modern Japan 1867-1937*, 3rd rev. ed. (London: Allen & Unwin, 1972).

the five years between 1863 and 1867. Imports were less than $2 million in 1860 but averaged over $15 million annually in 1863–7, the rise taking place chiefly in and after 1865. By comparison, exports averaged $21.7 million a year between 1873 and 1877 and $34.5 million between 1883 and 1887, whereas imports stood at an average of $26.1 million for 1873 to 1877 and $27.2 million for 1883 to 1887.

The character of trade changed little over this twenty-five-year period. The earliest exports to develop on any scale were tea and silk. Most of the tea went to the American market, where it competed with China's. Raw silk and silkworm eggs found a ready demand in Europe in the 1860s because of silkworm disease in France and Italy.[58] These markets were supplied both directly and through British firms. Later, the American market for raw silk became increasingly important, so that it dominated Japan's export trade, other than that with China, by the end of the century. Exports to China were initially of Japanese natural products like seafoods, a pattern that did not change until the growth of the Japanese cotton textile industry in the 1880s.

Of imports, the most important during these early years were Western manufactured products. There was a steady Japanese market for cotton and woolen textiles. This was briefly supplemented in the late 1860s by a demand for ships and munitions, reflecting the political disturbances of those years. Then as the new government began a program of industrialization, Japan began to import significant quantities of machinery and other capital goods, much of which came from Britain. During most of this period, the value of imports regularly exceeded that of exports; Britain had the largest share of Japan's import trade, and the United States was Japan's best customer.

To summarize, until the 1880s Japan was as much a client state of the West as China was, which is what one would expect from the nature of the "unequal treaties" and the manner in which they had been made. Western citizens had legal privileges in Japan – often more than the treaties implied, because of the inefficiency of the consular courts – and lived in designated residential areas, where they assumed the right to organize their own police and public services. Their way of life was Western, even to having their own newspapers in the treaty ports. Their diplomatic representatives occupied legations guarded by their own troops and usually had gunboats at call. For ten years Britain maintained a large infantry force in Yokohama. Commercially, foreign-

---

58 On French trade, see Medzini, *French Policy*, chaps. 6, 10.

ers traded on favorable terms under a tariff structure that the Japanese government could not change at will. They sold Japan manufactured goods from the countries of Europe and America and bought in return natural products like silk and tea. Most of the trade was handled by foreign firms and carried in foreign ships.

It was a relationship that modern Japanese scholars call "semi-colonial." Yet beneath the exterior of subordination there were factors making for change, factors that distinguished Japan from China and made the subsequent histories of the two countries diverge sharply. The overthrow of the Tokugawa in 1868 brought to power in Japan a group of men who had the political will and the political backing to attempt radical reform. They greatly increased the authority of the central government, acting in the emperor's name. They turned to the West for models of military technology and organization. They encouraged commerce, set up pilot industries, and revised the tax structure. Thus while maintaining in due form the treaty system, they were taking steps toward the kind of national strength that would enable them to challenge its inequality. Some of those steps were premature and ineffective. In 1871 Japan's leaders tried without success to negotiate with China a treaty that would give them a modicum of Western-style privileges in the China trade. In 1871–2 their first overtures for revision of Japan's own unequal treaties were rebuffed in America and Europe. Nevertheless, they learned from their mistakes and had the patience to wait for better opportunities. In 1875 Japan concluded an agreement with Russia settling frontier problems in the Kurils and Sakhalin by an exchange of territory. In 1876 Japan imposed on Korea a treaty similar to what Perry had extracted from the bakufu in 1854. In the same year Mitsui Bussan was founded. In 1878–9 came the first negotiations in which Japan's treaty revision proposals could be said to have been taken seriously by the powers, even though nothing came of them. Few foreign observers, however well informed, seem to have recognized these straws in the wind for what they were. All the same, by 1880 Japan was well on the way to recovering from the setbacks it had experienced in the closing years of Tokugawa rule. Unlike China, the disabilities that Japan suffered under the treaty port system were relatively short-lived.

CHAPTER 5

THE MEIJI RESTORATION

The Meiji Restoration stands as one of the turning points of Japanese history. Although the actual events of 1868 constituted little more than a shift of power within the old ruling class, the larger process referred to as the Meiji Restoration brought an end to the ascendancy of the warrior class and replaced the decentralized structure of early modern feudalism with a central state under the aegis of the traditional sovereign, now transformed into a modern monarch. The Restoration leaders undertook a series of vigorous steps to build national strength under capitalist institutions and rapidly propelled their country on the road to regional and world power. Thus the Restoration constituted a major event for Japanese, East Asian, and world history. The process whereby this came about has inevitably become a central issue in Japanese historiography, for verdicts on its content and nature condition all appraisals of the modern state to which it led. The work of historians has been undergirded by a vast apparatus of sources preserved by a history-minded government concerned with its own origins, and the scholarship that has been produced illuminates the intellectual history of Japan's most recent century.

TROUBLES WITHIN, DISASTER FROM WITHOUT

Japan's political crisis of the 1860s was preceded by serious internal difficulties and foreign danger that brought to mind formulations of Chinese historians who habitually coupled internal decline with border incursions made possible by that decline: "troubles within, disaster from without" (*naiyū gaikan*). A great deal of historical inquiry has been directed to the questions of how severe the first would have been in the absence of the second. Once the ports had been opened, there was no mistaking the complementary vibration between internal and external problems, but in the absence of foreign aggravation, the possibility of an internal upheaval sufficient to bring about the collapse of the feudal order remains uncertain. What is clear, however, is that the almost total isolation of Japan before its "opening" by the West served to magnify the consequence of the foreign impact in the public imagination.

The regime's internal difficulties came into striking focus during the years of the Tempō period (1830–44), which receive detailed treatment in Chapter 2. During those years Japan was devastated by crop failures that caused ruinous famines in central and northern areas. These combined with governmental inefficiency and unresponsiveness to encourage or provoke popular resistance. The most spectacular revolt of this period was one led by a model Confucian samurai official in Osaka, Ōshio Heihachirō, whose emotional call to insurrection made him a hero for later historians who sometimes dated the loyalist revolts from his manifesto. Ōshio's uprising resulted in little more than the burning of large areas of Osaka, but the striking incompetence shown by bakufu officials in its suppression contrasted with his own courageous (though equally maladroit) performance to symbolize what was wrong with the regime. Ōshio's revolt, led by samurai and centered in the second most important city of the land, provided a national shock,[1] but it was only one of many risings in that period. Peasant insurrections and urban "smashings" had tended to grow in size with the interrelationships of Japan's increasingly close-knit economy, and popular risings often moved rapidly along lines of communication. An added phenomenon of the period was the increase of chiliastic and millenarian movements. The world renewal (*yonaoshi*) uprisings were frequently led by a self-sacrificing individual who willingly martyred himself for the eventual good of his fellows. Ōshio, too, came to take on such an appearance in popular thought.[2]

Nevertheless, the insurrections of the period proposed few alternatives to the social and economic system that gave them birth. Manifestoes and petitions usually focused on recent or threatened violations of what had come to seem as acceptable, though admittedly burdensome, government demands. Communication routes were natural conductors for such protest, as the villages along the right of way were ex-

---

[1] Tetsuo Najita, "Ōshio Heihachirō (1793–1837)," in Albert M. Craig and Donald Shively, eds., *Personality in Japanese History* (Berkeley and Los Angeles: University of California Press, 1970), pp. 155–79; and Ivan Morris, *The Nobility of Failure: Tragic Heroes in the History of Japan* (New York: Holt, Rinehart and Winston, 1975), pp. 180–216, provide the best coverage in English of the man and his revolt.

[2] Two essays that suggest the dimensions of the problems in such uprisings are Irwin Scheiner, "Benevolent Lords and Honorable Peasants: Rebellion and Peasant Consciousness in Tokugawa Japan," in Tetsuo Najita and Irwin Scheiner, eds., *Japanese Thought in the Tokugawa Period: Methods and Metaphors* (Chicago: University of Chicago Press, 1978), pp. 39–62; and Sasaki Junnosuke, "Bakumatsu no shakai jōsei to yonaoshi," in *Iwanami kōza Nihon rekishi*, vol. 13 (*kinsei* 5) (Tokyo: Iwanami shoten, 1977), pp. 247–308.

pected to provide the *sukegō* porter service that moved travelers and transport on human and animal backs. Needs for such services increased in late Tokugawa times.

Rural order was also reinforced by an interesting group of nonofficial rural reformers whose teachings of sobriety, thrift, mutual cooperation, and agricultural improvement were designed to give farmers a better livelihood. The agricultural technologist Ōkura Nagatsune (1768–1856), the rural reformers Ninomiya Sontoku (1787–1856), with his plans for mutual cooperatives, and Ōhara Yūgaku (1798–1858) all worked to restore the health of the rural areas. Significantly, all three focused on the reclamation of land left fallow, whether by bad government or famine or migration. Their teachings were usually moralistic and pietistic, stressing the maintenance and care of land as an essential part of filial piety and ancestral obligation. Such efforts, though surely helpful to the government, were also evidence of the government's inability to fulfill the paternal role it had long ago set for itself. Equally important, the appearance of genuine rural leaders of this sort testified to a rising level of scholarship and leadership among the commoner elite throughout the Japanese countryside.[3]

The bakufu's response to these troubled times took the form of the Tempō reforms launched by the *rōjū* Mizuno Tadakuni in 1841. As Harold Bolitho points out in Chapter 2, the reforms, which included edicts against migration from country to city, provided relief for bakufu retainers' debts, abolished merchant guilds, and attempted to rationalize and concentrate bakufu landholdings within a set radius of Edo and Osaka, struck at vested interests of townsmen and vassals, and ended in failure. Simultaneous reforms in some of the larger domains, notably Satsuma and Chōshū, were somewhat more successful, but none fully met its goals. The bakufu's failure was particularly important, for its inability to raise its revenues augured ill for the greater crises that lay ahead. Nevertheless the ambitious, though abortive, plans for more intensive bureaucratic control of society have provided the basis for some historians' interpretations of the Tempō years as inaugurating late-feudal nineteenth-century "absolutism." Although judgments of these issues differ sharply, undoubtedly the future Meiji leaders, "men of Tempō" who experienced that turmoil in their early years, built on those lessons to their loss or gain.

The bakufu that had to deal with these problems was in many ways

---

3 Thomas C. Smith, "Ōkura Nagatsune and the Technologists," in Craig and Shively, eds., *Personality in Japanese History*, pp. 127–54; and Miyata Noboru, "Nōson no fukkō undō to minshū shūkyō no tenkai," in *Iwanami kōza Nihon rekishi*, vol. 13 (*kinsei* 5), pp. 209–45.

a less flexible and less adequate instrument of government than it had been. Although the eighteenth-century administrators had felt able to experiment rather widely within the pattern of the past, the language of the nineteenth-century leaders increasingly stressed the "obligations of the past" (*sono sujisuji no gohōkō*) in a rigid adherence to tradition. Central authority, as Harold Bolitho's study of the *fudai* daimyo points out, had not grown;[4] if anything, the shift from strong to weak shoguns had resulted in bureaucratic immobility. Mizuno's effort during the Tempō reforms to reclaim some vassals' holdings roused a storm of complaint, and yet his abortive efforts anticipated the measures that would be found necessary by future reformers when the crisis deepened in the 1860s. The once pragmatic bakufu had become a rather fine-tuned instrument that found it difficult to proceed without the cooperation of a number of distinct interest groups. Institutionally it remained premodern. The senior counselors (*rōjū*) served on cycles of monthly rotation, and the adoption of regular responsibilities and the abolition of the rotation system came only on the eve of the Tokugawa fall in 1867. Internal disaffection and bureaucratic rigidity may not have reached the levels that characterized contemporary China, but both regimes operated in a setting in which custom and precedent placed limitations on central power. More important, both regimes were limited by an inadequate governmental share of the nation's product. The precedents set by the ancestors and the barriers set by established and deeply routinized patterns of administration made it difficult to initiate radical change. The bakufu, though charged with the responsibility for the national defense, had access to only the income of its own lands. A shogunal procession to Kyoto in the 1860s required most of its regular cash income for that year, and the cost of restoring traditional preparedness and purchasing modern arms was soon to become prohibitive.[5]

The crisis in foreign affairs that followed the Tempō years is treated by William Beasley in Chapter 4. As he points out, it was a crisis that had been developing for decades. A growing consciousness of the foreign danger had been one of the unsettling elements in the nineteenth-century climate of opinion among informed intellectuals. The defeat of China in the Opium War of 1838–42 brought this conscious-

---

[4] Harold Bolitho, *Treasures Among Men: The Fudai Daimyo in Tokugawa Japan* (New Haven, Conn.: Yale University Press, 1974).
[5] Conrad Totman, *The Collapse of the Tokugawa Bakufu, 1862–1868* (Honolulu: University of Hawaii Press, 1980), provides excellent brief discussions of bakufu finances in the 1860s, pp. 190ff.

ness home to a far larger public. The Japanese had ready knowledge of that disaster through the messages brought by Dutch and Chinese merchants to Nagasaki, and Chinese accounts of the problem, notably Wei Yüan's *Hai-kuo t'u-chih*, went through many editions in Japan, where they were immediately accessible to all who had received formal education. In a secluded island country whose great metropolises were collection points for the literate elite of all sectors, speculation inevitably led to uneasy fears that imperialist flotillas would next come to Japan.[6]

Such consciousness had also been advanced by changes in the world of thought, which are treated by Harry Harootunian in Chapter 3. The nativist thought of national scholarship (*kokugaku*) moved in increasingly extreme directions in the nineteenth century. In the teachings of Hirata Atsutane and his disciples, it combined an increasingly assimilative and syncretic utilization of non-Japanese thought with a religious fervor focusing on the sun goddess Amaterasu as a national deity. A new and compulsive ethnicity was in formulation. Still premodern and perhaps only protonationalistic, this thought lay at hand as a potent incitation to alarm and indignation when once the sacred soil and sparkling waters of Japan might be sullied by foreign boots and hulls.

Knowledge about the West, and consequently informed awareness of its capability, was also available through the rise of Western learning (*rangaku*). A practice of translating Western books, launched in 1771 with the discovery by several doctors that the human anatomy conformed more closely to Dutch than to Chinese anatomical charts, grew so rapidly that at the time of his death in 1817 Sugita Gempaku, one of the doctors involved, compared it with the translation movement from Chinese a millennium earlier. The bakufu did its best to channel such learning and also to appropriate that part of it that seemed useful, but restless minds and figures soon carried it beyond the bound of the permissible. In the *Morrison* incident of 1837 a group of "Dutch scholars" concluded that the rude rejection of an English emissary would subject Japan to great danger. The ship in question had in fact already been repulsed successfully, but political criticism of this sort provided the impetus for political repression of the scholars in the purge of 1839.

A third, and ultimately the most important, development in the thought world of the nineteenth century was a growing concern with the imperial institution, which was the product of the *kokugaku* tradi-

---

6 Ōba Osamu, *Edo jidai ni okeru Chūgoku bunka juyō no kenkyū* (Tokyo: Dōhōsha, 1984), pp. 388 ff., for bakufu orders of Wei Yüan's work.

tion. This cut across all groups, but it found its most forceful and powerful formulation in a blend of ethnic and Confucian teaching that associated loyalism with morality and justified – and even required – participation in the political process under its imperative. In the slogan "revere the emperor, drive out the barbarian!" (*sonnō-jōi*), loyalism wedded to antiforeignism became the most powerful emotion of mid-century Japan.

Historical scholarship has often limited its consideration of emperor-centered thought to treat it as a political tactic without considering its substance, in good measure as a result of and in reaction to the use made of the institution by the modern state.[7] In fact, however, it can be demonstrated that the development of loyalist thought had a long continuity in Tokugawa intellectual history and was not without its roots in Chinese thought as well. The dominant stream of Tokugawa Confucianism drew on the Neo-Confucian thought of Sung China, which developed at a time when the foreign danger in the form of northern barbarians was at the forefront of scholars' consciousness. The antiforeign thrust of Chu Hsi Neo-Confucianism became blunted in a China ruled by Manchus, but in Japan the nonfunctioning throne became idealized, and it ended as the focus of ethnic nationalism. In samurai minds the identification of "country" with "virtue" tended to make absolutes of duty and action. "Loyalty" (*chūgi*) became a "great duty" (*taigi*) and the supreme test of the moral individual. This primacy of political values became the more powerful because, as Maruyama Masao has pointed out, it carried with it the implication that it was the vassal's responsibility to "correct" or "admonish" as well as to "obey" his superior.[8] In the nineteenth century, Tokugawa Confucian scholarship stressed a hierarchical scheme of obligations in which sovereign came to stand above shogun. Chinese civilization gradually came to seem distinct from the country of its birth, particularly after the fall of the Ming to the Manchus in the seventeenth century. Indeed, many nineteenth-century writers referred to Japan as the central country.

There were also trends in Tokugawa policy that gave impetus to this trend of imperial loyalism. In the eighteenth century, the bakufu, increasingly responsive to Confucian morality, demonstrated its respect for the court by protecting and maintaining the imperial tombs

---

7 Nagahara Keiji, "Zenkindai no tennō," *Rekishigaku kenkyū* 467 (April 1979): 37–47; and Bitō Masahide, "Sonnō-jōi shisō," *Iwanami kōza Nihon rekishi*, vol. 13 (*kinsei* 5), pp. 41–86. See also Hershel Webb, *The Japanese Imperial Institution in the Tokugawa Period* (New York: Columbia University Press, 1968).
8 Maruyama Masao, "Chūsei to hangyaku," in *Kindai Nihon shisōshi kōza* (Tokyo: Chikuma shobō, 1960), vol. 6.

and by increasing the miserly stipends that the early shoguns had provided for the court and courtiers. Whereas Ieyasu and his immediate successors had taken care to sever the ties the court had had with the military class up to that time,[9] awards of imperial rank and title to the Tokugawa cadet houses now became expected. Gradually extended to other leading daimyo, such titles became a matter of prestige and pride and helped lead to daimyo–court connections against which the early shoguns had guarded. Gradually and almost imperceptibly, the bakufu's "virtue" came to be identified with its ability to protect and insulate the court and country from outside contact. *Sakoku*, begun as a measure to ward off domestic dissidence in the mid-seventeenth century, ended by becoming a criterion of shogunal loyalty and performance.

Intellectually this package of patterns and ideals found its most persuasive setting in the writings of a group of scholars in Tokugawa Nariaki's domain of Mito. Aizawa Seishisai's *Shinron* (1825) provided in particularly compelling form a warning of the power of the West, insistence on the sacred nature of Japan and its imperial polity, and reminders that that superiority was based on the benefits of the imperial family. Mito thought, and especially Aizawa's book, became widely read in the 1840s and 1850s, at a time when the Mito daimyo began to take a vigorous part in urging measures of moral and material rearmament and in extending his political contacts to the Kyoto court.

THE HARRIS TREATY AND ITS AFTERMATH

The opening of Japan to international contact, described by Professor Beasley in Chapter 4, produced problems that were made more difficult by these strains. Economic difficulties and military unpreparedness made it important for Japan to avoid military conflict until preparations had been advanced. This required information (gathered by the Bansho shirabesho, the new Institute for Western Learning established in 1855), money (collected through new taxes, forced loans, and government economies), and political consensus to provide a time of quiet during which plans could be prepared. The search for that consensus brought efforts to consult, and thereby to educate, the daimyo and the Kyoto court. That consultation had the effect of activating first them and then their vassals and subordinates. A broadening circle of concern among people who were often poorly informed about for-

[9] See Asao Naohiro with Marius B. Jansen, "Shogun and Tennō," in John W. Hall et al., eds., *Japan Before Tokugawa* (Princeton, N.J.: Princeton University Press, 1980), pp. 248–70.

eign affairs but who were anxious to use those issues for internal affairs came close to paralyzing government processes.

The bakufu's first response to the news of the Opium War was to relax its standing orders for the prompt repulse of foreign vessels and to order that supplies be provided for them when they requested them. This order, issued in 1842, brought a reminder from Emperor Kōmei four years later to be careful about coastal defense. However mild its wording, it was an early indication that the court would consider itself involved in matters of foreign policy and defense. A letter of warning from the king of Holland in 1844 and the Biddle mission of 1846 were successfully turned aside, but no one doubted that more such would follow. Bakufu orders to daimyo to be vigilant about coastal defenses were issued in 1849, but because of the general financial stringency of the times, no real advances had been made when the Perry mission arrived in 1853.

Abe Masahiro, an able conciliator who had been *rōjū* since 1845, sent the Perry letter to the court for information and to the Tokugawa vassals with requests for advice. Abe was aware of the need for change; he had promoted a number of low-ranking officers to key posts. He also had a keen awareness of Japan's military weakness and had established an office of coastal defense over which he himself presided and which he manned with his own followers. Abe tried to outmaneuver the leading exponent of exclusion, Tokugawa Nariaki of Mito, by appointing him to a key defense post. The opinions that the bakufu received from daimyo and lesser vassals revealed a wide range of views on the American request, but for the most part they agreed that conflict should be avoided. The bakufu made its decision without a great deal of reference to the views that came in; it was a full year before it sent the text of the Shimoda treaty that its negotiators had worked out with Perry to the daimyo and the court. At the same time its orders to the daimyo had sharp reminders of the importance of coastal defense, and police officials (*metsuke*) were given sharp warnings about the importance of quick and ruthless action to prevent contacts between foreigners and ordinary Japanese. Abe seemed to have resolved the first step, but even his political agility could not conceal the change that was to come. In 1854 the court issued an order to melt down temple bells for guns, the first time in the entire Edo period that Kyoto had taken it upon itself to issue a national directive. Matsudaira Shungaku (Yoshinaga, Keiei), the collateral house (*shimpan*) daimyo of Fukui, Abe's father-in-law, and a leading figure in national politics from then on, wrote to remind Abe that daimyo respect for the bakufu was contingent on the bakufu's respect for Kyoto. In the future, the bakufu's desire for daimyo support in difficult decisions would find it consulting them more frequently, and the court itself developed the tactic of suggesting that daimyo, or at least leading Tokugawa vassals like the *gosanke*, should be consulted again.[10]

The Commercial Treaty of 1858 negotiated by Townsend Harris marked the real opening of Japan to trade and residence. Harris drew his most effective arguments from the disasters that China met in the second round of warfare (the *Arrow* war) that ended with the Tientsin treaties in 1858. Oddly enough, the bakufu's fear of following the course of China into foreign subjection led it to accept treaties almost identical to those inflicted on China.[11]

The debates about the Harris treaty next became inextricably interwoven with the problem of shogunal succession. Tokugawa Iesada, who died in the summer of 1858, had no successor, and so adoption procedures had to be set in motion. The leading candidates were Hitotsubashi Yoshinobu (Keiki), an able young man who was in fact one of the many sons of Tokugawa Nariaki of Mito, and a still-immature descendant of the Tokugawa house of Kii (Wakayama), the future Tokugawa Iemochi. Iemochi's selection would be the more conventional, and in the maneuvering that took place, reference to an "able" heir was code language for choosing Hitotsubashi (later Tokugawa) Yoshinobu.

Hotta Masayoshi, who had succeeded Abe Masahiro as chief bakufu official, informed Townsend Harris that the regime would need the formality of court approval of the new treaty before signing it, and he arrived in Kyoto to secure that approval in the spring of 1858. To his astonishment, the court instructions he received a half-month later instructed the bakufu that because this was of utmost importance to the country, it should take up the matter once more with the three cadet houses (*gosanke*) and the daimyo. This marked the first time in the Tokugawa years that the court had presumed to disagree publicly with bakufu policy. What had happened was that a number of leading daimyo, among them Tokugawa Nariaki, had recognized in the com-

---

10 Abe's tactics and ability have received poor marks from most historians, but more appreciative verdicts are rendered by Conrad Totman, "Political Reconciliation in the Tokugawa Bakufu: Abe Masahiro and Tokugawa Nariaki, 1844–1852," in Craig and Shively, eds., *Personality in Japanese History*, pp. 180–208; and Bitō Masahide, "*Bushi* and the Meiji Restoration," *Acta Asiatica*, 49 (Tokyo, Tōhō Gakkai, 1985): 78–96.
11 The point is Ono Masao's in "Kaikoku," *Iwanami kōza Nihon rekishi*, vol. 13 (*kinsei* 5), pp. 1–39. Nakamura Tetsu, "Kaikokugo no bōeki to sekai shijō," however, points out that the Ansei treaties were superior to the Tientsin treaties because they did not legalize opium or permit missionaries and provided better tariff arrangements, pp. 108–9.

mercial treaty an issue on which they could use the court's xenophobic instincts to influence bakufu policy in the matter of shogunal succession. Henceforth they would propose that the court couple reluctant approval of the treaty with the condition of selecting an "able" and mature heir to the shogun.

When Hotta addressed his second request for approval to the court, he was close to having his way when eighty-eight Kyoto nobles joined to protest. As a result, instructions to consult the vassals were handed down a second time. With this the lines were drawn for a showdown. House succession went to the heart of Tokugawa policy and was an internal Tokugawa matter. As the *fudai* daimyo of Hikone, Ii Naosuke, put it in a letter, selection according to ability might be the "Chinese way," but it was not the way things were done in Japan. Last-minute bakufu lobbying blocked a court plan to call for an able shogun.[12]

The court's second rebuff came in a context of growing exasperation with Kyoto xenophobia and obstruction, and it brought hard-liners to the fore in Edo. Shortly after Hotta's return from Kyoto, Ii Naosuke of Hikone became regent (*tairō*) and took over the leadership role in the Edo councils. He now began a period of personal leadership that had no real precedent in the history of shogunal ministers. It seemed to him that the reassertion of bakufu control over dissidents was a matter of the highest priority and that other issues were secondary.

On June 25, Harris was promised that the treaty would be signed by September 4. Once again letters were sent off to the daimyo in apparent conformity with imperial instructions. But when Townsend Harris brought word of the Treaty of Tientsin and speculated that the British and French warships would probably proceed to Japan next, the treaty was hastily signed on July 29 before the results of the new survey were in hand and without court approval. Ten days later the bakufu announced that shogunal succession had gone to the young Iemochi of Kii. Thus Ii Naosuke had decided the two burning questions of the period within ten days, and quite on his own authority.

Ii now moved against the opposition. Bakufu moderates and foreign affairs specialists who had come to office under Abe and who had favored a cooperative and conciliatory policy toward the daimyo were dismissed, demoted, or moved to less important posts. The great

12 George Wilson, "The Bakumatsu Intellectual in Action: Hashimoto Sanai and the Political Crisis of 1858," in Craig and Shively, eds., *Personality in Japanese History*, pp. 234–63, quotes Ii's retainer Nagano: "To nominate a lord because of his intelligence is to have inferiors choose their superior and is entirely the Chinese style . . . the custom of our empire must be to respect the direct line of descent," p. 260. But Nagano was too dogmatic in this; the adoption system permitted great flexibility in succession to secure ability.

daimyo who had lobbied through their agents in Kyoto for the succession of Yoshinobu as heir were driven into retirement and, usually, house arrest. Matsudaira Shungaku of Fukui, Tokugawa Nariaki of Mito, Tokugawa Yoshikumi of Owari, and Yamauchi Yōdō of Tosa were only the most eminent of those punished.

Emperor Kōmei was furious at this flouting of his sentiment and even considered abdication to demonstrate his frustration. He ordered that the head of one of the three cadet houses (*gosanke*), or the *tairō* himself, come to Kyoto, only to receive the response that the house heads were being punished and that the *tairō* was too busy with national affairs to absent himself from Edo. A lesser *rōjū*, Manabe Akikatsu, was designated as emissary, and even that worthy delayed almost two months before setting out for Kyoto. The court struck back; its directive to the bakufu, in a totally unprecedented breach of channels and security, was transmitted to the Kyoto representative of Mito and sent on to Edo by him to the consternation of the bakufu, which forbade Mito to divulge its contents to other quarters. At Kyoto, low-ranking agents of the daimyo who had favored the Hitotsubashi cause urged on inexperienced courtiers in misguided efforts to have the court insist on a reversal of bakufu policy, the dismissal of Ii, and a reversal of the Harris treaty. Ii Naosuke had his own agent in Kyoto, one Nagano Shuzen, who reported all this activity to Edo and helped provoke the counterstrokes that followed.

By October, bakufu arrests of those agents began. Umeda Umpin, Mito agents, and others were arrested in Kyoto. Hashimoto Sanai, Matsudaira Shungaku's chief emissary, was arrested in Edo. The men arrested in Kyoto were transported to Edo in cages and under heavy guard, and once there they were severely interrogated by a judicial board of five that sat for only the most serious offenses. The sentences handed down were unexpectedly severe and made this one of the largest crackdowns in the history of the bakufu. Over one hundred men were sentenced. Eight were condemned to death, and six of them were beheaded like ordinary criminals.

While all this was in progress, *rōjū* Manabe was working to wring approval from a sullen and reluctant court for the treaty that had already been signed. His hand was strengthened as bakufu punishments approached the court itself, with a round of changes and retirements in courtier positions there. In the end the reluctant sovereign agreed that because the treaties had been signed, it was too late to stop them.

Ii Naosuke has had harsh treatment at the hands of historians, especially those who wrote before 1945. His personal rigidity and harshness were untypical of bakufu procedure and, indeed, of most of Japanese administrative history with its preferences for collegial decision making. Moreover, his victims included some of the ideal types revered by the future Meiji state. The Fukui counselor Hashimoto Sanai, trusted assistant of Matsudaira Shungaku, was clearly carrying out instructions from his lord. In character and attainments he had won universal respect and admiration. Despite this, his sentence read: He "should have remonstrated with his lord that this was a serious matter . . . and he acted without respect for Bakufu will."[13]

Even more serious and tragic in popular imagination was the fate of the Chōshū scholar-teacher Yoshida Shōin. Yoshida began as a low-ranking but brilliant student of military science. After traveling to Nagasaki and elsewhere he concluded that these places would not suffice to protect Japan. He came under the influence of the modernizer Sakuma Shōzan and tried to persuade Perry to take him back to America with him for a period of study in 1854. After Perry maintained his commitments to the shogunate and refused this request as illegal, Yoshida was discovered, arrested, and sent back to Chōshū. There he was given partial freedom to teach in a village academy that came to number among its students many of the future Meiji leaders. Furious at what he considered bakufu disrespect to Kyoto and the servility to foreigners shown in signing the Harris treaty, Yoshida schemed with Umeda Umpin to engineer the assassination of Manabe on his way to Kyoto. Arrested and extradited to Edo, Yoshida was executed after his fellow inmate Hashimoto Sanai. He became posthumously exalted as a martyr for emperor and country.

Postwar historians, however, have been kinder to Ii Naosuke. Freed from the compulsion of earlier historiography to side with those who fell in the "Ansei purge" and able to see courage and intelligence on both sides of the struggle that was to rend the political fabric of mid-century Japan, later writers have softened their denunciations. Yet in any case, Ii Naosuke did not long survive his triumph. On a snowy day in March 1860, as his entourage approached the Sakurada gate of the great Edo Chiyoda Castle, a group of swordsmen, seventeen from Mito and one from Satsuma, cut through his guards, whose swords were covered to protect them from the late winter snow, and took the *tairō*'s head. The assassins' manifesto attacked the regent personally rather than the government he had headed, but it made it very clear

---

13 Wilson, "Bakumatsu Intellectual: Hashimoto Sanai." The Japanese text charges Hashimoto with disrespect for the *kōgi*.

that Ii's crime had been that of indifference to the imperial will, and it urged all Tokugawa retainers to turn with shame to the sun goddess of Ise in penitence. The loyalist years had begun.

THE LOYALISTS

The purge that Ii Naosuke carried out had resulted in his murder; the persecuted loyalists had retaliated by assassinating the chief bakufu minister. These events ushered in a period of violence and terror that transformed the setting of late Tokugawa politics. The loyalists, known to their contemporaries and to history as *shishi* – men of high purpose – became an explosive element in local and national affairs and ended by serving as ideal ethical types for the ideology of the modern imperial state and also as models for young radicals in future periods of instability.

Shishi tended to be of modest rank, status, and income. Lack of status meant that they were little encumbered by official duty and office, which were reserved for higher samurai rank. They lived in a world that was less structured by ritual than was that of their superiors, and communication with men from other domains was also easier for them than it was for their superiors. Because the *shishi* were at the outer circumference of the ruling class, frustrations of limited opportunity and ritual humility often made them suspicious and critical of their cautious superiors. Poorly informed about the context of national diplomatic and political issues, they were inclined to the simplistic solutions of direct action. Calls for preparedness that accompanied the opening of Japan produced a lively expectation of war and led to a setting that was alive with rumor and that put new emphasis on the importance of the martial arts. Swordsmanship academies were crowded as never before with students, and together with tournaments they became settings for political bravado and self-assertion. The *shishi* were men of the sword.

The lower samurai's frustrations often meshed with the discontent of the rural samurai and village leaders. In the countryside, pseudo-samurai pretensions were symbolized by swords, surnames, and rudimentary scholarship. These could combine with the experience of administrative responsibility to encourage critical attitudes toward urban-based but underemployed samurai, sometimes with the conclusion that it was the leadership of the farm villages that really mattered. In Tosa, for example, a Shōya League of the 1840s produced complaints that summed up many of the frustrations and that harked back to a past order in which village leaders had carried out the court's commands without interference from castle town samurai. Tosa *shishi* included sons of rural leaders as well as lower samurai.[14]

Shishi learning varied widely, but it tended to include assertion of the primacy of sincerity demonstrated through action. The Satsuma hero Saigō Takamori was steeped in the views of Wang Yang-ming Confucianism which stressed the identity of knowledge and action. Others drew on popularized teachings of Chu Hsi and Mencius to emphasize the meaning of sincerity and a well-ordered polity and to draw quick conclusions from bakufu concessions to the imperialist powers and its apparent disregard of the wishes of the court. Although they were drilled in the virtue of loyalty and subordination (*meibun*) as the highest duty (*taigi*) of all, the *shishi* also accepted the retainer's obligation to correct his superiors when convinced of their errors. The bakufu itself accepted this in its death verdict against Hashimoto Sanai. He "should have remonstrated with his lord" instead of blindly carrying out his instructions in Kyoto. By the same logic, the *shishi* were ready to condemn bakufu officials for carrying out shogunal instructions in defiance of the sovereign's wishes. A popular history of Japan that was written from the standpoint of Confucian loyalism, Rai San'yō's *Nihon gaishi* (Unofficial history of Japan) circulated in increasing volume, first in its Chinese original and then in Japanese translation, to spread the praise of loyal servants of the court in former days. Rai Mikisaburō, a younger son of the historian, was executed in 1859, one of the victims of Ii Naosuke's purge.

The *shishi* began as loyal retainers, convinced of the identity of their lord's wishes and the desires of the court. Ii Naosuke's punishment of the daimyo who had advocated the Hitotsubashi cause and did their best to block the Harris treaty turned them against the bakufu minister in the name of loyalty to their lord. In the southwestern domain of Tosa, for instance, an oath signed in blood committed a group of young swordsmen to a loyalist party in the fall of 1861 with a statement that combined indignation at the humiliation of Japan by the barbarians and the punishment of "our former lord . . . who, instead of securing action, was accused and punished." "We swear by the gods," the statement concluded, "that if the Imperial Flag is once raised we will go through fire and water to ease the Emperor's mind,

---

14 Marius B. Jansen, "Tosa During the Last Century of Tokugawa Rule," in John W. Hall and Marius B. Jansen, eds., *Studies in the Institutional History of Early Modern Japan* (Princeton, N.J.: Princeton University Press, 1968), pp. 340–1.

carry out the will of our former lord, and purge this evil from our people."[15]

At the outset, ethnic nationalism, retainer loyalty, and imperial reverence could be combined in a devotion that was relatively free of moral dilemma. But once feudal loyalty seemed at variance with imperial reverence – when the daimyo chose the path of caution and pulled back from the loyalist cause – the *shishi* faced a difficult personal choice. Large numbers resisted renewed subordination to their superiors through flight from the domain jurisdiction, seeking protection and employment under the aegis of a domain perceived as more committed to the imperial cause (Chōshū long served as a protector of men from all over the country) or entering the employment of court nobles in Kyoto who had need for bodyguards, agents, and messengers as the political cauldron heated up. Participation in politics in this way was dangerous and often tragic for men who gave up the security of family, home, and safety, but it also proved stimulating and ennobling for many who contrasted the excitement of their new life with the tedium of the ritualized subordination that they had known at home. The Tosa activist Sakamoto Ryōma wrote his sister to contrast the importance of his activities with this old life at home, "where you have to waste your time like an idiot"; at another time he asserted that "the idea that in times like these it is a violation of your proper duty to put your relatives second, your domain second, to leave your mother, wife, and children – this is certainly a notion that comes from our stupid officials. . . . [But] you must know that one should hold the Imperial Court more dear than country, and more dear than parents."[16]

The loyalists did not have a structured view or program toward which they were working. They had slogans (of which the most important was *sonnō-jōi* – revere the emperor! drive out the barbarians!) but not programs. They were opposed to their authorities but not to authority; they were full of ethnic nationalism but only dimly aware of the possibilities of a true nation-state in which the two-sworded class would not stride forth as a special repository of virtue and privilege.

This point requires further comment. E. H. Norman's pioneering study of the Restoration[17] perceived a coalition of "lower samurai" and "merchants" at the center of the political movement, with implications

---

15 Marius B. Jansen, *Sakamoto Ryōma and the Meiji Restoration* (Princeton, N.J.: Princeton University Press, 1961), pp. 108–9.   16 Jansen, *Sakamoto*, pp. 174–5.
17 E. Herbert Norman, *Japan's Emergence As a Modern State: Political and Economic Problems of the Meiji Period* (New York: Institute of Pacific Relations, 1940 and later printings).

for future social change, but more recent writers have differed sharply over the utility of this as an analytical distinction. The "merchant" participation has proved even more difficult to examine, much less establish. W. G. Beasley's masterly summary of Restoration politics examined the evidence in a number of the most important domains to conclude:

> There is, therefore, a valid connection between low-rank – rank below that of hirazamurai, which qualified a man for domain offices of some responsibility – and rebellion, terrorism, or the threat of violence. The rōnin who were the placard-posters, the demonstrators, the conspirators, the assassins were characteristically men of lower standing than the "politicians."

The same argument extends, Beasley wrote, to others whose "claim to samurai status was tenuous or even nonexistent: the village headmen, rich farmers, and merchants who had perhaps bought the right to use a family name and wear a sword."[18] Tokugawa status divisions had no provision for the political participation of such individuals, and to participate at all was to set aside authority and to ally oneself with kindred spirits who had at least some claim to status. Thus the Tosa loyalists included a goodly number of rural samurai (gōshi) (including Sakamoto) and village heads or their sons whose normal horizons of political awareness would have been expected to be limited to the valley within which their acreage lay.

Albert Craig, who restricted his focus to Chōshū, found the "lower samurai" phrase imprecise and without analytical value. "Almost any large movement of samurai would by necessity be a lower samurai movement," he wrote, and the conventional definition of "upper" would fit only seventy or eighty (out of five thousand, or counting rear vassals, ten thousand) Chōshū samurai families. Moreover, in Chōshū there were high-ranking loyalists and low-ranking conservatives. "The samurai class," Craig concluded, given its disparity, "could not act as a class, a gentry class, with common class interests."[19] Thomas Huber, who also studied Chōshū but limited his attention to the students of Yoshida Shōin's academy, defined "lower" as an income of two hundred koku or less to conclude that the Chōshū movement, which included commoner village administrators, represented the interests –

---

18 W. G. Beasley, *The Meiji Restoration* (Stanford, Calif.: Stanford University Press, 1972), p. 171.
19 Albert B. Craig, *Chōshū in the Meiji Restoration* (Cambridge, Mass.: Harvard University Press, 1961), pp. 112–13; and "The Restoration Movement in Chōshū," in Hall and Jansen, eds., *Studies in the Institutional History of Early Modern Japan*, pp. 363–73.

or at least the discontents – of the "service intelligentsia," thus refining and improving Norman's argument and position.[20]

Even when one grants the frustration and occasional fury of low-ranking members of the Tokugawa military elite and grants the importance of their enthusiasm and violence in energizing a political situation theretofore torpid and somnolent, one is reminded that the story that unfolded after the loyalist years was one of action and decisions taken by domains. Loyalists *as such* were brought under control after 1864 and required the cooperation of men who held power. *Han* policy was set by men of rank with access to the narrow elite that monopolized the highest offices. That elite seldom moved until it was convinced that the perils of inaction outweighed the risks of participation. At the last, the danger of failing to join a common front was that of exclusion from a new political order and structure. Regional and family self-interest had to be calculated with the greatest precision by men who inherited status, authority, and wealth. The *shishi* helped create an atmosphere in which movement was possible. Many, perhaps most, of them, perished in that work. Those who inherited the fruits of their labors were for the most part middle- and upper-ranking samurai who moved their *han* into positions in the years that followed.

Han policy and the logic of events seemed to enroll most samurai in some domains, notably Chōshū, under the loyalist banner before the Tokugawa fall. But in 1867 Chōshū had the most to lose and the most to gain. In other areas the scales were balanced differently. But just as many – indeed, far more – similarly placed samurai in other domains responded differently in other contexts, remaining aloof or following other banners. The bakufu responded to disorder and terror in Kyoto and Edo by recruiting and organizing *shishi* or *rōnin* who, seeing the Chōshū–Satsuma force as regional and "selfish," proved potent instruments of counterviolence. Lower samurai of the Tokugawa domain of Aizu, who served to keep the peace in Kyoto through the final Tokugawa years, were subject to the same class interests and frustrations as were their Chōshū counterparts and probably included as many advocates of exclusion and imperial loyalism among their number. But they responded to different regional and historical affiliations, and their domain provided the single most effective counter to Satsuma and Chōshū military strength until the Aizu castle was put to the torch in

---

20 Thomas M. Huber, *The Revolutionary Origins of Modern Japan* (Stanford, Calif.: Stanford University Press, 1981).

the desperate siege of Wakamatsu in 1868 that ended the Aizu presence on the national scene.

COURT AND CAMP, DAIMYO STYLE

The domains of Satsuma, Chōshū, Tosa, and Hizen furnished the early Restoration leadership. With the notable exception of Mito, which destroyed its strength in a civil war, remarkably few other *han* achieved a clear-cut presence or identity in the Restoration movement. Among these, Saga was a latecomer and was co-opted only after 1867. It may have joined the charmed circle chiefly because its proximity to the port of Nagasaki, which it was required to defend, helped bring some able and experienced leaders to the fore. Consideration of the sources of Restoration leadership therefore leads immediately to inquiry into the special characteristics of a very small number of domains. If samurai constraints and frustration were roughly comparable in all parts of Japan, what additional factors distinguished those southwestern domains and the few others that counted in the late Tokugawa years?

Factors of size and location come to mind immediately. Satsuma was second, Chōshū ninth, Saga tenth, Mito eleventh, and Tosa nineteenth in assessed productivity among the feudal domains. Distance and tradition helped create pride and autonomy. Large-scale resources were necessary for mounting a significant military force through the purchase of Western ships and guns in the 1860s. Satsuma, Chōshū, and Tosa also had disproportionately large numbers of samurai. Satsuma and Chōshū had been on the losing side in the struggles that brought the Tokugawa to power in the early seventeenth century; they suffered a loss of territory and had compressed a large military force into a reduced area. Also, the three domains were integrated territorial units with defensible borders along land communication routes that permitted vigilance over contacts with contiguous areas. Satsuma, at the extremity of southern Japan, was particularly famous for its own exclusion system. Each was a *tozama* domain, although Tosa's status was special because the Tokugawa founder had installed a man of his own selection after expelling his predecessor. Consequently, the Tosa lord sought some way of combining gratitude with warning and worked out the suggestion for shogunal resignation. Elsewhere, compunctions of loyalty were weaker. The entire samurai class of Satsuma and Chōshū and the lower ranks in Tosa, many of them rear vassals who had served the previous daimyo, harbored a centuries-old resentment of Tokugawa rule.

Remoteness and secure borders made for a greater degree of autonomy and of self-consciousness. "Han nationalism," to use Albert Craig's term, guaranteed that strong competitive urges operated to drive men on and to exacerbate fears of being left behind or out of whatever new political order might eventuate. Remoteness also made for a smaller role and presence in Edo, for higher costs and greater inconvenience attached to the central bakufu control mechanism of *sankin-kōtai*, and for reliance upon the Osaka market over that of the shogunal capital. Distance and size made possible relatively autonomous responses to bakufu and imperialist demands, as when Satsuma refused to make amends for the murder by its retainers of an English trader who happened along its line of march on horseback (the Richardson, or Namamugi incident), and when Chōshū tried to expel the foreigners by shelling ships along its shores without bakufu authorization. These incidents brought both domains face to face with the superiority of Western military technology, demonstrated by the British fleet against Kagoshima in 1863 and a foreign flotilla against the Chōshū Shimonoseki batteries the following year.

Remoteness had other consequences. At a time when money economy, economic change, and social dissolution were making the domains along the main-traveled parts of the Osaka and Edo plains, most of them held by Tokugawa houses, less feudal, social and economic relationships in southwestern Japan were still backward and traditional. The higher ratio of samurai to commoners in southwestern Japan could also be used to inhibit commoner complaint or participation; this was particularly so in Satsuma. Traditional authority structures provided an effective base for efforts to bolster the domain economy, tap more of its surplus for the regime, and speed military reforms. The Tempō reforms failed in bakufu territory, but Tempō fiscal and economic reforms in Satsuma and Chōshū left those domains in much stronger position for the competition that lay ahead. In Saga, too, the mid-century decades witnessed a successful campaign to redistribute land equally once again on the lines of the old Heian *kinden* system, a "land reform" program that spoke volumes for the ability of the feudal administration to control its most important resource.[21]

At mid-century the great fiefs of the southwest also enjoyed strong and able leadership. Throughout Japan able daimyo were few and far

---

21 See, for Chōshū, A. M. Craig, *Chōshū in the Meiji Restoration;* for Tosa, M. B. Jansen, *Sakamoto Ryōma;* and for Satsuma and other *han*, Ikeda Yoshimasa, "Bakufu shohan no dōyō to kaikaku," in *Iwanami kōza Nihon rekishi*, vol. 13 (*kinsei* 5), 174–207.

between in the late Tokugawa years, and in Edo itself shogunal power was entirely in the hands of surrogate bureaucrats during the reigns of Iesada and Iemochi. In Satsuma and Tosa, however, a fortunate accession to power of able men, products of the adoption system, introduced strong direction at the center. Saga too had an able daimyo, though the Chōshū lord was a cypher. What counted was the presence of a generous number of unusually able and adroit subordinates in each fief, men who did not hesitate to speak their minds.

This combination of historical, geographical, and economic circumstances helps to account for the few domains that took leading roles. But it does not explain why so few other domains, some more or less comparably endowed, took vigorous part in national politics. In Mito, where the loyalist teachings of the Confucianists and the personal prestige of Tokugawa Nariaki made for a leading role in the 1850s, an internal power struggle that destroyed domain unity combined with a Tokugawa affiliation to remove the *han* once Tokugawa Yoshinobu became a bakufu leader. In Fukui, also a related Tokugawa house (*shimpan*), Matsudaira Shungaku's early leadership gave way to watchful waiting and hoping for the moment when political conciliation would again be possible. But most daimyo – and indeed most upper samurai – witnessing the dangers that could accompany wrong judgments, preferred to conserve their resources and keep their counsel until the situation was clarified. There was no "anti-imperial" party, but there was a good deal of suspicion, much of it well founded, that those who professed loyalty to Kyoto were chiefly interested in their own advantage. For Tokugawa adherents, on the other hand, the twists and turns of bakufu policy made it both difficult and dangerous to follow a consistent and active line.[22]

The assassination of Ii Naosuke was followed by a series of efforts to bring court and bakufu together in a new and more cooperative structure. It did not succeed. For Edo, as Beasley points out, it meant "a bolstering of bakufu authority by the use of the imperial prestige," while to the great lords involved "it implied a renewed possibility of intervening in politics in the Emperor's name so as to achieve, among other things, an increase in baronial privilege."[23] Yet these efforts were important, for they led to the Bunkyū reforms of 1862, reforms which so changed the political balance of power that a recent study begins its consideration of the Tokugawa fall at that point. Meanwhile for others the hopes they engendered returned at the last to inspire the

22 Totman, "Fudai Daimyo and the Collapse of the Tokugawa Bakufu," *Journal of Asian Studies* 34 (May 1975): 581–91.
23 Beasley, *Meiji Restoration*, p. 177.

Tosa proposal under which the last shogun agreed to surrender his powers in 1867.

The proposals are usually grouped under the slogan *kōbu-gattai*, for reconciliation of court (*kō*) and camp (*bu*). The first of these to be proposed was put forward by Chōshū, where the official Nagai Uta persuaded his daimyo to urge that a new agreement make it clear that the shogunate ruled "in accordance with the orders of the court," which would thus set policy while the bakufu carried it out. Having secured agreement with this in Kyoto, Nagai proceeded to Edo for negotiation. But there he was soon overtaken by a Satsuma proposal and mission that seemed to promise Kyoto a good deal more. This proposed pardon for all those who had been punished by Ii Naosuke in 1858 and dismissal of the principal bakufu leaders who had held office since then. More important, the court would designate certain daimyo to represent its interests in Edo; the two principal figures of the succession quarrel, Matsudaira Shungaku, daimyo of Echizen (whose vassal Hashimoto Sanai had been executed for advancing the candidacy of Tokugawa Yoshinobu), and Tokugawa Yoshinobu (Keiki) himself were to be appointed to newly created offices. Yoshinobu, who had been denied the shogunate, would serve as guardian (*kōken*) for young Iemochi, while Shungaku would be Supreme Councillor (*seiji sōsai*). This set of proposals was brought to Edo by the court noble Ōhara Shigetomi, and the escort was provided by a large Satsuma military force headed by the regent Shimazu Hisamitsu.

These plans had antecedents in thinking that began in the years following the arrival of Townsend Harris under the urgency of military reform. The great lords who had lobbied for the succession of Tokugawa Yoshinobu wanted cooperation to replace the costly control measures of the Tokugawa system. Yamauchi Yōdō, the Tosa daimyo, had proposed a seven-year moratorium on *sankin-kōtai* duty for daimyo at that time, and many large domains had developed steps for financial reform to make military spending possible. Saga had pushed the implementation of its land division program, and Tosa and Satsuma had developed programs for central merchandising of regional specialties to increase domain income – Satsuma with sugar from its southern islands and Tosa with its camphor and indigo. Modification of the ritualized alternate attendance at Edo would be the best possible economy measure.

Unfortunately the strains generated by Ii Naosuke's purge and the enforced absence through punishment of several of the daimyo who were most important to the Ansei reforms had changed this pattern of planned cooperation into one of competitive assertion and rivalry. The

Ōhara-Satsuma mission itself was soon followed by a third, this time accompanied by troops from Tosa.

While Yamauchi Yōdō was still in forced retirement, his chief minister had been assassinated by loyalists, who promptly moved to the center of the decision structure that surrounded the young successor daimyo. Takechi Zuizan, the leader and founder of the Tosa Loyalist Party, now proposed in his young lord's name that the court nobles Sanjō Sanetomi and Anegakōji Kintomo proceed to Edo with orders from the court that the bakufu prepare to expel the foreigners immediately. These plans went on to propose establishing the Osaka-Kyoto (Kinai) plain as the private realm of the court, granting the court clear political primacy, ending *sankin-kōtai* so that the daimyo could spend their money for defense, establishing seven or eight of the daimyo of southwestern Japan in Kyoto as support for the court, and establishing a private defense force of courageous *rōnin* from all parts of the country to defend the court. Costs of all this would be met by ordering wealthy merchants in the Osaka area to put up the money. This proposal was one of the most sweeping the loyalists put forward, and it serves to illustrate the way thinking became radicalized. But it did not get much farther, for much to Takechi's surprise his former daimyo, Yamauchi Yōdō, moved skillfully to oust the Tosa loyalists after he was released from house arrest. After lengthy interrogation Takechi was ordered to commit suicide in 1865 for insubordination.[24]

The Chōshū and Satsuma initiatives, however, produced results before the Sanjō-Tosa procession had reached Edo, and the changes that came are known as the reforms of the Bunkyū era. These changed the political setting so basically that a recent study of the Tokugawa fall begins with the assertion that "the Tokugawa bakufu's time of troubles began early in 1862 . . . [when] a series of political changes . . . reduced the bakufu to a secondary role in national politics."[25] In terms of politics, the most important changes were the implementation of the Ōhara mission proposals: Matsudaira Shungaku of Fukui was appointed *seiji sōsai* (Supreme Councillor) and Hitotsubashi (Tokugawa) Yoshinobu *kōken* (guardian), the latter appointment specifically announced as made at "imperial request." Japan's problems with the imperialist powers, the extent of court disaffection, the insecurity of top-level bakufu officials, several of whom had been assassin's targets, and the appearance of the strong Satsuma military force in Edo to accompany Ōhara had combined to suggest to

---

24 Jansen, *Sakamoto Ryōma*, pp. 131–7, and Ikeda, "Bakufu shohan," pp. 184–6.
25 Totman, *Collapse of the Tokugawa Bakufu*, p. 3.

bakufu officials the wisdom of retreating from Ii's insistence on traditional bureaucratic direction of bakufu and national affairs. Shungaku and Hitotsubashi were in any event from Tokugawa houses, and the appointments did not at first seem an undue participation by outsiders in bakufu and national affairs.

Unfortunately for those who thought in these terms, Shungaku saw his appointment as a first step in a sharing of power by the great lords who had been his allies in the succession dispute a few years earlier. He began by insisting on a general pardon for those who had been punished by Ii; having carried his point he went on to demand punishment for the bakufu officials who had helped direct the purge. There followed a stream of demotions. The house of Ii lost its mandate as protector of Kyoto, and Ii's retainer and adviser Nagano Shuzen was ordered to commit suicide. Soon additional pressures represented by the Sanjō-Tosa mission persuaded bakufu officials of the need to show good faith with the court by extending the punishments to almost all officials who had worked with the successor governments that followed the murder of Ii and to the men who had negotiated the treaties with the foreigners. In considering the remarkable equanimity with which most Tokugawa fudai saw the bakufu collapse a few years later, it is well to keep in mind the demoralizing effect that turnabouts of this sort must have had on vassals' loyalty and resolution.

The 1862 reforms went on to a series of steps that were cumulatively disastrous to bakufu primacy. The first of these was the moderation and virtual abolition of the system of *sankin kōtai*, undertaken in order to permit economies to facilitate domain military preparedness. The period of daimyo residence at Edo was reduced to one hundred days in three years. Many of the lords, freed from duty at Edo, now transferred their attention to Kyoto, which thereafter competed with Edo as center of a national politics. Within a year bakufu officials were trying to undo the effects of this; two years later the bakufu asked all daimyo to send their families to Edo as before. Some lesser lords complied, but the more important domains showed no interest in returning to the restrictions of earlier times. By 1865–6 the great lords hardly granted the bakufu the courtesy of a reply to its summons, and a bakufu survey of Edo mansions turned up the fact that some of the lesser lords had gone so far as to rent their residences to commoners.[26]

Another step that was undertaken to repair relations with Kyoto involved a visit to the imperial court by the young shogun Iemochi.

---

26 Ibid., p. 141.

No shogun had visited Kyoto since the third shogun Tokugawa Iemitsu had traveled south with a mighty retinue in 1634 to demonstrate his power. Iemochi's trip to Kyoto was a dramatic contrast to that of his ancestor. Iemitsu had gone to Kyoto to show his might; he had acted to sever daimyo connections with the court, and redirected daimyo residence and attendance from Kyoto to Edo.[27] Iemochi, however, went to Kyoto as part of an attempt to gain strength from reconciliation at a time when daimyo attention was shifting from Edo back to Kyoto. In one point the visits were comparable. Iemitsu had taken an imperial princess as consort, and the same course was now suggested for Iemochi. In an effort to further cement relations with the court an imperial princess (Kazu no Miya) was proposed as consort for the young shogun. The arrangements were made in apparent disregard of her own reluctance and that of the Emperor Kōmei, and the matter served to inflame loyalist indignation further as a demonstration of shogunal disrespect.

Iemochi's trip was planned to be a short one for reasons of economy and politics; bakufu optimists hoped that his presence would serve to reestablish the awareness of bakufu primacy in Kyoto. It worked out quite differently; before the young shogun could be extricated from the intrigues at the imperial capital four months had gone by. He was obliged to show ritual humility in processions to imperial shrines, and his ceremonial deference to the emperor left little doubt of his subordinate position. In 1634, in contrast, it was the emperor who had called at the shogun's Nijō castle. The shogun's position had always depended in the last analysis on force; it was therefore significant that bakufu ministers now thought it desirable to secure a specific court authorization of shogunal authority. Unfortunately, that commission included orders to drive out the barbarians. Further instructions reminded Iemochi to consult with daimyo on major questions and to respect "lord and vassals" relations. "Not since the Muromachi period," Totman observes, "had a shogun been given such a patently empty title of authority."[28]

The shogun's visit was an important step in the growing transfer of political centrality to Kyoto. Within months of his return to Edo proposals for a second visit were underway; he was to die at Osaka, still a youth, on his third visit in 1866. More and more daimyo now established headquarters in the ancient capital. Kyoto became a prime

---

27 Asao Naohiro, "Shogun seiji no kenryoku kōzō," in *Iwanami kōza Nihon rekishi*, vol. 10 (*kinsei* 2), pp. 13ff.
28 Totman, *Collapse*, p. 58.

object of political and military planning for the southwestern domains. It was preeminently the preserve, at least until 1864, of the radical loyalists and *shishi* who made its streets unsafe for suspected enemies. In one celebrated instance of symbolic rebellion, they lopped the heads off statues of the Ashikaga shoguns. In order to retain control of the capital the bakufu appointed Matsudaira Katamori, young lord of Aizu, protector (*shugo*) of the city in 1862, and as a result he became an important actor in the politics of the next decade. So important did Kyoto become to Edo policy that the fifteenth and last shogun, Tokugawa Yoshinobu, spent his entire period in office in the Kyoto area and never once felt free to take time for a return to Edo. All this added urgency to the bakufu's economic problems. The Kyoto visits of Iemochi were ruinous for bakufu finances, and the necessity of maintaining an ever larger force and presence three hundred miles from the Tokugawa heartland worsened an already difficult situation.

A fourth product of the Bunkyū reforms was cooperation with the great daimyo. This had indeed been at the very heart of the program of proposals grouped as *kōbu-gattai* from the first, and it constituted the platform on which the last shogun based his resignation in 1867. The great lords that mattered included, in addition to Matsudaira Shungaku and Tokugawa Yoshinobu, a number of leading lords: Yamauchi Yōdō of Tosa, Shimazu Hisamitsu of Satsuma, Date Munenari of Uwajima, Mōri Yoshichika of Chōshū, and Matsudaira Katamori of Aizu. They were intermittently drawn into conference to discuss court-bakufu relations and diplomatic problems. In theory this was supposed to prevent unilateral, "selfish" bakufu direction. But the meetings, which began in 1862 and continued sporadically thereafter, produced no real results. There was no agreed-upon program of procedure, and the lords themselves were at least as "selfish" as the bakufu, usually retiring to their domains when things did not go well. The Tokugawa members, meanwhile, inherited the suspicion of bureaucratic "regulars" in Edo. The first attempt ended particularly badly when Matsudaira Shungaku, Supreme Councillor who had brought the whole program into being, resigned and returned to Fukui, followed by a bakufu order that he place himself under house arrest. He was pardoned by the summer of 1863 and remained a major figure, but then and later his program of conciliar cooperation had no real basis in regional interest and bureaucratic politics. As far as bakufu leaders in Edo were concerned, Shungaku and the others were outsiders whose interest in and loyalty to the Tokugawa cause was quite different from their own. In addition, haughty daimyo had great difficulty in controlling irritation and overcoming disagreement. Confrontation was not a congenial mode of resolution for them. A system without provisions for retreat and conciliation found them bargaining by absence and boycotting meetings. Most important of all, however, was the fact that the Western pressure left no slack for the resolution of differences. The insistence of court xenophobes on undoing the treaties clashed directly with the deadlines that had been agreed upon with the Western powers.

The Bunkyū program foundered most importantly on the issue of foreign policy. Throughout most of the negotiation about restructuring power between Edo and Kyoto, Japan was facing diplomatic problems and military threats that required more effective central-government decision making at the very time that power was becoming more diffuse. Important figures at the Kyoto court never wavered in their distaste for the treaties that had been signed with the Western powers, and an inevitable effect of the increased attention to court wishes in the rhetoric of 1862 and 1863 was subscription to promises, however ambiguously worded, to get rid of the foreign plague.

The Ansei treaties opened to foreign trade Yokohama (Kanagawa), Nagasaki, and Hakodate; within four years (by January 1863) Osaka, Hyōgo (Kobe), Niigata, and Edo were to be opened. Hakodate proved of little importance, and foreigners soon lost interest in Niigata, but Osaka was a national center and located, together with Hyōgo, close to the imperial court at Kyoto. In the spring of 1862 the bakufu sent a mission to Europe to ask for delay in the opening of additional ports, and an attack on the life of Andō Nobumasa, just after the mission had sailed, underscored its assertions about domestic difficulties as grounds for the request. Trade had not yet assumed major proportions, and even Rutherford Alcock, British consul general and later minister, thought the request reasonable. A protocol delaying further openings until 1868 was worked out as a result.[29]

The agreement unfortunately unraveled quickly. Within Japan competitive jockeying for favor at court produced more extreme demands for exclusion of foreigners, while on the spot "exclusion" in the form of samurai and *rōnin* terrorist attacks on foreigners (and, in 1863, on the British legation itself) produced a negative response on the part of the imperialist powers. At Kyoto demands for exclusion were set in motion to embarrass the bakufu, which then confounded its critics by

---

29 Beasley, *Select Documents on Japanese Foreign Policy 1853–1868* (London: Oxford University Press, 1955), pp. 1–93, provides the most incisive account.

agreeing to exclusion even after many great lords had backed away from the prospect of unsuccessful war.

The Satsuma regent, Shimazu Hisamitsu, emerged as a force for moderation. On his way into Kyoto in 1862 his men crushed a *rōnin* conspiracy in which his retainers had taken a leading role, and upon his return from Edo (whither he had conducted the court noble Ōhara) he warned of the impossibility of exclusion. Unfortunately his samurai had also taken a major step in strengthening English policy by their murder of Richardson on the way back to Kyoto. Thereafter Hisamitsu was preoccupied with the impending threat of British reprisal (which took the form of shelling and burning of his castle town of Kagoshima), and he helped destroy the hopes for a successful council of great lords by leaving Kyoto for Satsuma.

In Chōshū during this same period the pendulum swung from conservatism to radicalism. The initial Chōshū initiative represented by the proposals of Nagai Uta had failed before the more sweeping counter initiative of Satsuma; Nagai was disgraced, retired, and ultimately ordered to commit suicide. By summer of 1862 Chōshū stood as the principal protector and instigator of radical *shishi* and *rōnin* activities at Kyoto. In the latter part of 1862 Chōshū strength was joined by that of Tosa after the loyalists had taken control of that domain.

Thus it happened that, as has been described, the Tosa-Sanjō mission to Edo carried with it the clearest call yet for immediate and unconditional exclusion of foreigners from Japan. The chief bakufu representatives in Kyoto, Matsudaira Katamori (guardian of Kyoto) and Tokugawa Yoshinobu (shogunal guardian), were inclined to the view that the bakufu would have to announce agreement with this demand to show sincerity, and meanwhile look for some way of delaying its implementation, but the regular bakufu officials at Edo were aghast at the dangers involved in even a verbal pledge of exclusion. Edo leaders were operating under the guns of foreign warships in Edo bay and in fear of an English bombardment of their city when they hurriedly agreed to pay over to Great Britain an indemnity for the murder (by Satsuma men, it will be remembered) of Richardson in the spring of 1863, just as Tokugawa Yoshinobu was returning from Kyoto where he had agreed to a court demand for a promise of expulsion. It seems probable that Yoshinobu and other officials hoped they could avoid a clear deadline for action, and that even when they accepted, reluctantly, the court-imposed date (June 25, 1863) they thought of it as a date on which negotiations would commence (and inevitably fail). In any event they passed it along to the daimyo but with instructions to avoid hostilities.

In Chōshū, however, the extremist-dominated administration seized the opportunity for full compliance and opened fire on an American merchant ship at anchor in the Shimonoseki straits and later on French and Dutch vessels as well. Thus the *kōbu-gattai* program ended in a shambles: the Satsuma lord in Kagoshima vainly trying to prepare for a British attack on his city; Matsudaira Shungaku, author of the program, in retreat in his domain in Fukui; the bakufu verbally committed to exclusion at the same time that it was paying damages to Great Britain for actions it had not committed; and a defiant Chōshū determined to carry out exclusion on its own.

THE TREATY PORTS AND FOREIGN INFLUENCE

The Western powers had created the bakufu's political problems, and they remained to complicate them by their presence in the ports that had been opened. From the time that Yokohama, Nagasaki, and Hakodate were opened to trade in 1859, the bakufu found itself faced with insoluble dilemmas in having to yield to foreign pressures at the same time that it was being pressured to end the foreign threat. The foreign presence, however, also contained elements of hope for the bakufu: Tariffs provided a new source of central income, and the purchase of foreign weapons and foreign assistance in training soldiers and sailors was more easily available to the bakufu than to other governments in Japan. But arrangements for capitalizing on these opportunities were slow in being planned and worked out, and long before they might have helped restore Tokugawa political and military primacy, the negative aspects of the foreign presence had dealt mortal blows to some of the institutional aspects of Tokugawa power.

In some ways, however, the Tokugawa political institutions proved surprisingly resilient in their capacity to accommodate the problems that the mid-nineteenth century brought, for the tradition of seclusion contained few of the expectations of international hierarchy and national centrality that bedeviled contemporary Chinese efforts to accommodate institutions to international society.[30]

From the first, Abe Masahiro entrusted negotiation with the Americans to men he had selected for their ability. By the summer of 1858 a new magistracy was set up to specialize in foreign affairs, the *gaikoku*

---

30 See, for China, Immanuel C. Y. Hsu, *China's Entrance into the Family of Nations: The Diplomatic Phase, 1858–1880* (Cambridge, Mass.: Harvard University Press, 1968); and Masataka Banno, *China and the West: 1858–1861, The Origins of the Tsungli Yamen* (Cambridge, Mass.: Harvard University Press, 1964).

bugyō, with the appointment of five men to serve in a collegial capacity. From then until 1867, when a more streamlined and responsible structure was worked out, a total of seventy-four officials served in it. This also demonstrates a difficulty: Institutional flexibility was there, but political instability and uncertainty made the post hazardous to occupy. Policy shifts required new teams, and the magistracy changed its occupants like a revolving door. The individual and career patterns of virtually all late-Tokugawa high officials show the political hazards. The board of *rōjū* showed a 100 percent turnover with the substitution of Ii for Hotta. Ambassadors sent to the United States in 1860 to ratify the Harris treaty disappeared into a (probably well deserved) obscurity upon their return to Japan. Lower-level interpreters and "technicians" like Fukuzawa Yukichi and Fukuchi Gen'ichirō, on the other hand, survived to travel again and become the commentators and pundits of the future.[31]

The bakufu sent a series of missions to the West in the 1860s. They became more frequent, more professional, and more serious. The first, in 1860, included seventy-seven men. The discovery that life was possible in the West without mountains of straw sandals and the full panoply of ritual that accompanied Tokugawa society made it possible to be more selective with future missions. In 1862, thirty-eight men went, the interpreters for a second time; this group stayed longer, worked harder, and learned more. Mission followed mission, and a sixth was abroad at the time of the shogun's fall in 1867. By then a number of leading domains, including Satsuma and Chōshū, had smuggled students abroad to study. It will be remembered that Yoshida Shōin, the Chōshū martyr, had himself wanted to sail with Perry to learn about the West. The shogunate too sent students to Leiden to study. Upon his return, one, Nishi Amane, was charged with drawing up a modern charter for the shogunal regime. Japan had an exhibit at the Paris Exposition of 1867, as did Satsuma, which sent its own exhibit and tried to work out independent status as ruler of the Ryūkyū Islands. The bakufu rescinded its ban on the construction of oceangoing ships as early as 1853: It permitted Japanese exhibitors to go to Paris and buried the last of the seclusion provisions in June 1866 with a tariff convention that removed all restrictions on Japanese trading at the open ports, on Japanese purchase of foreign ships and employment of foreigners, and on Japanese travel abroad. In legal

---

31 For figures of officials, *Dokushi sōran* (Tokyo: Jimbutsu ōraisha, 1966), pp. 648–51. Eiichi Kiyooka, trans., *The Autobiography of Fukuzawa Yukichi* (Tokyo: Hokuseidō Press, 1948), and many other studies. For Fukuchi, James L. Huffman, *Fukuchi Gen'ichirō* (Honolulu: University of Hawaii Press, 1979).

and institutional terms, in other words, the bakufu was able to move speedily to dismantle the barriers it had established between Japan and the outer world.

Politically it was another matter. The readiness of the bakufu officials to build bridges with Kyoto at the cost of the careers of the officials who had negotiated and approved the early stages of the opening meant that foreign affairs specialists' careers showed a dizzying, roller-coaster sequence. Obscurantism and xenophobia among the two-sworded men who cursed the foreign presence meant that it was dangerous to be known as an expert in the new specializations associated with the West. Fukuzawa Yukichi found himself in fear of his life when he returned from Europe and America with the material that he made into his best-selling book, *Seiyō jijō* (Conditions in the West). Prominent consultants like Sakuma Shōzan and Yokoi Shōnan who had the ear of decision makers were murdered on suspicion of being pro-Western and even, in Yokoi's case, pro-Christian. The most trusted retainer could find himself ordered into suicide when the wind changed for his lord.

Yet for those who had access to foreign travel or, in time, the products of such travel in books like Fukuzawa's, the power of Japan's overseas adversaries provided convincing proof of the need to open Japan in order to strengthen its institutions and arms. Nor was the evidence all baleful. Fukuzawa found much in the West to praise: George Washington was almost a culture hero in late Tokugawa Japan; so, too, was Peter the Great. The West offered attraction as well as repulsion. Repulsion was close to hand on the Shanghai coast. Japanese who traveled to Shanghai on missions to buy ships and arms for their domains saw in the conditions at Shanghai a glaring example of humiliation and insult they were determined to avoid for their own country. Others recognized power: Inoue Kaoru, a Chōshū loyalist and future Meiji leader, recognized in the "forest of masts" in the Shanghai harbor sure evidence that exclusion could never succeed, and Takasugi Shinsaku, his superior in that movement, was shocked by the incidence of Western arrogance and superiority he encountered in Shanghai.

Nevertheless few Japanese made that trip, and none were more consistent in xenophobic instincts than the court nobles and their loyalist allies. Iwakura Tomomi, who had worked for the success of a reconciliation with the bakufu and helped arrange the shogun's marriage with Kazu no Miya, found himself out of office and forced into hiding to protect himself from angry *shishi*.

The representatives of the Western powers were quick to credit the erratic course of Japanese politics to dishonesty and deception. Rutherford Alcock, who initially favored accommodating the bakufu's requests to delay the openings of additional ports, changed from an advocate of accommodation to one of retribution. Japan's inability to protect foreigners was seen as bakufu unwillingness to do so, and security was sought in the presence of foreign detachments – Britain's came to number fifteen hundred men, and French units added several hundred more. These inevitably brought new problems and resentments with them. In 1864 the arrival of Harry Parkes as British minister brought to Japan one of the most vigorous and choleric of the China-coast specialists in gunboat diplomacy. Parkes soon developed contempt for the bakufu's inability to control the daimyo and domestic violence, and before long he added doubts about the bakufu's *de jure* authority to the clear evidence of its deficiencies in de facto authority. Leon Roches, the French minister who preceded Parkes by a few months, on the other hand, never showed the slightest doubt about bakufu legitimacy and detected an opportunity for French leadership in providing military assistance, economic advice, and institutional suggestions to the Tokugawa leaders. Yet even Roches was quick to join his colleagues in joint demands for bakufu concessions, and he warned Tokugawa officials that it would be folly for them to try to stand against the foreigners' wishes. The foreign presence thus provoked antiforeign incidents, which in turn brought demands for additional concessions, with the result that the imperialist presence became a one-way ratchet opening Japan. It was a process that wounded the bakufu more than it did the daimyo, for it was the bakufu that claimed, but could not exercise, full authority. Meanwhile, the evidence of foreign influence and the fears of more to come stimulated and fed a sense of danger and crisis among the Japanese elite. This was only natural. In addition to the background information about the fate of China, there were stories closer at hand. There was a Russian "occupation" of Tsushima for several months in 1861, and the possibility of future danger in a contest between Great Britain and France for leadership, the one favoring the great lords and the other helping the bakufu.

The economic impact of the opening of the ports on the social unease and political turbulence of mid-century Japan requires particular attention. Japan entered the world trade system at its point of greatest growth and at a time when the English Industrial Revolution was the chief locomotive of the trade expansion. The nineteenth century saw an exponential growth in the rate of world trade: Beginning with the 1820s, the growth rates for the successive decades were roughly 33 percent, 50 percent, 50 percent, 80 percent (for the 1850s), and 44 percent for the 1860s, when the Civil War in the United States slowed trade. Exports constituted an ever-larger part of England's product, surpassing 60 percent in the 1850s. The unequal treaties with non-Western countries were important instruments of that advance. Persia (in 1836 and 1857), Turkey (in 1838 and 1861), Siam (in 1855), China (in 1842 and 1858), and Japan (in 1858), entered that system in quick succession. Commercial arrangements that had been worked out for other areas were easily and speedily applied to Japan. The Peninsula and Oriental Steamship Company (founded in 1840) steamers added Yokohama to their calls. At Yokohama and, secondarily, at Nagasaki, the trading houses, agencies, and banks that had been set up along the China coast extended their networks and assigned their men to the newly opened ports of Japan.

From the first the Japan trade exceeded the modest expectations that had been held of it. In 1860, imports stood at 1.66 million and exports at 4.7 million Mexican dollars, respectively; five years later, exports had quadrupled, and imports were up ninefold. At a time when world trade was complicated by the American Civil War and the China trade was disturbed by the Taiping Rebellion, the unexpected growth of Japan drew pleased surprise from British consular and trading representatives and doomed any hopes that bakufu optimists might have had of Western willingness to accept reduction or forgo the planned opening of additional ports.[32]

Japan's trade grew rapidly because of the integration and efficiency of the national market. Goods flowed naturally and easily to the new markets at the new ports. The same flow complicated and ultimately defeated bakufu efforts to control the course of trade and channel its profits into politically desirable hands. Indeed, foreign trade in open ports served to accelerate a shift from metropolitan commerce, channeled through authorized guilds, to regional centers of production. This shift was long in process, and it had long been a subject of contention and dispute.[33] Unfortunately for the bakufu, the metropolitan guilds were important to its control of the economy and to the profits of the merchant houses whose forced loans (*goyōkin*) it called on to meet the rising need for cash. An effort was made to channel trade through Edo in 1860, when "five products" (thread, cloth, wax, hair and lamp oil, and grains) were to be shipped through Edo. But as the

---

32 Nakamura Tetsu, "Kaikokugo no bōeki to sekai shijo," in *Iwanami kōza Nihon rekishi*, vol. 13 (*kinsei* 5), pp. 95–6, 111.
33 For a dispute of 1823 in which 1,007 villages resisted the jurisdiction of Osaka guilds, see William B. Hauser, *Economic Institutional Change in Tokugawa Japan: Osaka and the Kinai Cotton Trade* (New York: Cambridge University Press, 1974), pp. 97ff.

trade grew, its largest items were raw silk and tea. In 1863, at a time when the bakufu was ostensibly committed to closing Yokohama, the silk thread guild sought relief from taxes levied on its products that did not move through Edo, and for a time it virtually managed to close Yokohama by boycotting shipments. A year later the bakufu tried to reassert its authority by banning the planting of additional mulberry trees on lands under its control. Such efforts drew quick protests from the representatives of the foreign powers, so much so that some historians suggest that the naval demonstration against Chōshū in 1864 had as a secondary aim the intimidation of the bakufu's efforts to channel trade. The foreigners' demand coincided with that expedition and brought abandonment of the ruling that products move through Edo channels. The following year the powers succeeded in getting tax and tariff agreements against the imposition of internal transit taxes on goods bound for the ports. Foreign trade thus had the effect of weakening the bakufu's ability to control domestic commerce and opened Japan to the ports as well as opening the ports to the foreigners.[34]

The market for Japanese silk was made larger by the European silkworm blight that resulted in large exports of cards of silkworm eggs in 1865 and 1866. The consequence was a dramatic rise in the price of eggs and thread for the Nishijin weavers of Kyoto, whose raw material prices doubled almost overnight. The unemployment that resulted became an element in several urban riots. Urban handicraft laborers and fixed-income groups were the chief victims of price instability in products that had long seemed stable.

Foreign trade was, however, only one element in a wild inflation that sent the prices of all essentials spiraling upward in the early 1860s. The major element in this instability was the bakufu's need to recoin. A closed country had been able to maintain a 1:5 gold-to-silver ratio as long as neither could be exported. But the open ports brought in a flood of Mexican silver dollars from nearby Shanghai, where the international rate of 1 to 15 prevailed. The disruption that followed, in what one author called the "great gold rush," was countered by the bakufu in a basic recoinage program that was punctuated by charge and countercharge between foreigners and Japanese officials. Gold, silver, and copper coinage all were devalued. At the same time the hard-pressed bakufu grew more liberal with its permission to the daimyo to mint their own coin and to print paper currency. Currencies of this sort were not supposed to circulate beyond domain borders, but the integration of Japan's commercial economy guaranteed their

---

34 Ishii Takashi, *Bakumatsu bōeki shi no kenkyū* (Tokyo: Nihon hyōronsha, 1943).

spread. Satsuma, for instance, minted millions of copper coins and profited hugely from them. Counterfeit coinage added to the problem. At the time of the Restoration there were sixteen hundred issues of paper money in addition to the multiple varieties of coinage in circulation.[35] An economy that had always known a multiplicity of issues – the bakufu had first debased its coinage in the late seventeenth century and did so fairly periodically thereafter – in the short space of a decade now enormously increased the number, variety, and quality of its issues. Regular requirements of large payments to the foreign powers – for equipment, military needs, and indemnities – worsened the problem by skimming off a significant fraction of the gold and silver bullion available; such payments were assayed with the greatest care and exactness.

The consequence of all this was a galloping inflation that drove up the price of essentials, particularly rice, For the daimyo and upper samurai who measured their income in *koku*, this posed no discomfort, but the vast majority of the warrior class had long since had their incomes commuted to money. Emergency levies in the form of stipend reductions added to the injury. City dwellers were equally distressed. As early as 1862 the Edo city magistrate reported that inflation had raised commoners' living costs by 50 percent. Placards denouncing merchants and foreigners contributed to the tension and growing level of violence. During one month in 1863, "some twenty people were murdered in the city (Edo), and uncounted others were attacked and threatened. . . . One worrisome aspect of the situation was the extent to which the keepers of the peace were becoming the breakers of the peace."[36] In addition to undisciplined members of *rōnin* units, the bakufu had coopted to cope with policing problems, "members of the new Bakufu infantry units were suffering from demoralization, and some of them also became engaged in brawls and abuse of city folk." Open ports also brought disease. A major cholera epidemic coincided with the opening of the ports. Nationwide, births in 1861 were 12 percent fewer than the year before, and in some central provinces they were as much as 80 percent lower.[37] If one adds the earthquakes in Edo in 1854 and 1855 and the severe crop failures in 1866 and 1869, it becomes clear that the last years of Tokugawa rule were difficult for most Japanese.

35 This astounding count of currencies reflects the fact that none was ever fully withdrawn or retired, so that the money chargers had a constantly changing ratio to work out. See John McMaster, "The Japanese Gold Rush of 1859," *Journal of Asian Studies* 19 (May 1960): 273–87; and Peter Frost, *The Bakumatsu Currency Crisis*, Harvard East Asian Monographs, no. 36 (Cambridge, Mass.: Harvard University Press, 1970).   36 Totman, *Collapse*, p. 94.
37 Akira Hayami, "Population Movements," in M. B. Jansen and G. Rozman, eds., *Japan in Transition: From Tokugawa to Meiji* (Princeton, N.J.: Princeton University Press, 1986).

Finally, mention must be made of the monetary payments that the bakufu had to make to the foreign powers. The Richardson indemnity, paid for Satsuma violence, came to £100,000. The Shimonoseki indemnity was set at an astounding 3 million Mexican dollars. "During the early days of the seventh month of 1865," Conrad Totman noted, "officials at Edo secretly transported to Yokohama some 30,000 to 40,000 *ryō* per day for delivery to the foreigners as another $500,000 payment on the indemnity."[38] Even this was only part of the very large sums that were shipped to the ports to pay for costs involved in new shipyards, guns, batteries and missions abroad in the next few years. National politics, the visits of the shogun to Edo, support to needy daimyo, rebuilding the Kyoto palace (destroyed by fire in 1854) and Edo castle (destroyed by fire in 1863), and the movement of troops to the Kyoto area – all, or most such expenses, could be described as direct or indirect consequences of the opening of the ports. As the inflation worsened, all impoverished the city dwellers and also those on fixed incomes, and all weakened the political posture of the bakufu. Confidence can hardly have been raised by the series of impressive drives for special loans from merchants that were launched between 1862 and 1867; some specified numbers and amounts expected, and others established classes of contributions, for a total of 2.5 million *ryō* of gold, or three times the bakufu's regular annual income in specie.

BAKUFU RALLY

In 1863, loyalists at Kyoto and in the domains overplayed their hand. Satsuma recalcitrance against the English brought on the bombardment of Kagoshima, and Chōshū insistence on implementing exclusion without waiting for bakufu instructions resulted in the four-power naval demonstration at Shimonoseki and doomed the bakufu's efforts to stave off the opening of additional ports and to take up the closing of Yokohama. The Tosa loyalists' efforts to seize the initiative in the name of their former lord resulted in their punishment and elimination on grounds of insubordination after Yōdō was free to turn his attention again to the direction of domain affairs.

This series of miscalculations enabled the bakufu leaders in Kyoto to claim to be more effective implementers of the imperial orders for exclusion programs and to oust the loyalists from Kyoto. Their colleagues at Edo took heart from these developments and tried to

---

38 Totman, *Collapse*, p. 193.

reassert Tokugawa control more broadly. The latter part of 1863 and most of 1864 saw the bakufu leaders advocating reconciliation with the court, but this time to their own, and not to the great lords', advantage.

The loyalist military and political setbacks came in quick succession. In September 1863, Aizu troops staged a successful coup with the assistance of Satsuma to drive Chōshū units out of Kyoto and thereby make it impossible for Chōshū loyalist leaders to communicate with and claim the authorization of the court. In the Kyoto area two loyalist risings, one led by a Tosa figure and the other by a Fukuoka *shishi*, were crushed by bakufu units when they tried to rally rural leaders to the loyalist cause and set up a regional political base. Nearer to Edo, in the summer of 1864, a loyalist movement led by elements of the Mito samurai class that began as the product of confusion over bakufu purposes was exacerbated by obtuse leaders and erupted into full-scale civil war. When it was finally crushed five months later, the domain of Mito was for all practical purposes eliminated as an effective political force. Over one thousand men died in the fighting, and hundreds of the holdouts who had been taken prisoner were executed the next year. Also during the summer of 1864, Chōshū loyalist units tried to avenge their setback by staging a military invasion of Kyoto that was driven back, though at immense loss of property in the fighting and fires that swept through the ancient capital. Leading loyalist court nobles fled to Chōshū with the defeated loyalists, thus ridding the court of some of its most troublesome elements.[39] Though discomfited by the way that suppression efforts had revealed its military ineptness, the bakufu stood to gain from this new evidence of loyalist rashness and insubordination, and it now tried to demonstrate its own loyalty to the court's instructions. During the shogun's first visit to Kyoto, the bakufu had accepted the imperial order for exclusion, and Tokugawa Yoshinobu had been named supreme commander of Imperial Defense. Yoshinobu now assumed a steadily larger role in Kyoto, though not without incurring the suspicions of Edo bureaucrats that his apparent acceptance of expulsion was wrongheaded and impractical.

For a few months after the shogun's return to Edo in the summer of 1863, the bakufu basked in the discomfiture of its Chōshū critics. Unfortunately, however, Kyoto's approval still hinged on the imple-

---

39 The fullest account of the Mito rebellion in English can be found in Totman, *Collapse*, pp. 108–21. Chōshū loyalist reverses can be followed in Craig, *Chōshū in the Meiji Restoration*, pp. 208–46; Tosa in Jansen, *Sakamoto*, pp. 145–52; and loyalist reverses more generally in Beasley, *Meiji Restoration*, pp. 197–240.

mentation of promises of expulsion that were clearly impossible to keep. Within months the shogun was in receipt of an imperial order directing him to return to Kyoto to report on the progress he was making in closing Yokohama. Edo bureaucrats put off compliance as long as they could, citing the pressure of diplomatic efforts and national politics. Their arguments had a good deal of substance, for the early stages of the unrest that would result in the Mito rising were evident, and a disastrous fire had reduced much of the shogunal castle complex to ashes. But by early 1864 the shogun was back in Kyoto, now in much higher favor, privileged with a number of audiences with Emperor Kōmei and able, through his appointment of Matsudaira Katamori of Aizu as guardian of the capital and the exclusion of Chōshū, to exert exclusive authority over access to the court.

Unfortunately these "gains" were still premised on promises of expulsion. When the bakufu informed the daimyo that it had been decided to work toward the closing of Yokohama, it encouraged some to press for stronger measures at the same time that it convinced the foreign emissaries of its mendacity. And when bakufu bureaucrats tried to extend their reassertion of control over Kyoto with steps to move toward a return of daimyo residence at Edo, they received lame excuses that should have told them that their old political primacy could not be restored.

The high point of the new bakufu enthusiasm for *kōbu-gattai* – on its own terms – came in 1864 after the impetuous attack of the Chōshū loyalists had resulted in a devastated Kyoto and an indignant court purged of its most extremist nobles. Ironically, the bakufu's decision to punish Chōshū, which was demanded by the court in late summer, was made more attractive because of the prior demands of the foreign powers, who wanted retribution for the shelling of their vessels. At first the bakufu tried to tie that punishment to the closing of Yokohama, only to have the imperialist powers respond that they would then undertake it themselves at bakufu expense. They did so in late summer, before the bakufu expedition got under way, and submitted as their bill the demand for the indemnity of three million Mexican dollars, which they offered to waive in return for immediate opening of an additional port. Bakufu administrators, committed by their promises to the court to have fewer and not more ports, saw no alternative but to agree to pay the indemnity, although doing that also strained their understanding with the court.

The court now insisted that the bakufu go ahead with its own punishment of Chōshū, thereby adding further expenses to the heavily burdened regime. A ponderous allied force commanded by the Tokugawa daimyo of Owari, with Saigō Takamori of Satsuma as his chief of staff, got under way and seemed for a brief moment to represent the return of the kind of Tokugawa-led coalitions that had been formed in earlier centuries. Yet the conditions were very different; it was not in the interest of allied daimyo to deplete their own forces for bakufu purposes or to provide precedents for the future by crushing the Chōshū dissidents. Consequently, a compromise, one that disappointed both court hard-liners and Edo traditionalists, was worked out. The expedition was declared a success, and the armies were disbanded before Edo had given its full approval. Under the terms, Chōshū was to offer a formal apology, suppress the irregular militia companies that had attacked Kyoto, turn over the loyalist court nobles who had fled to Chōshū to Fukuoka for custody, and order the suicide of the three domain elders (*karō*) who had been responsible for the mistaken loyalist attacks. The nobles were duly transferred and the apology delivered, together with the heads of the three *karō*.

This settlement was acceptable to the bakufu leaders in Kyoto, but men in Edo anxious to reassert full Tokugawa primacy did not find it punishment enough. They wanted the terms strengthened to include the bringing of the Chōshū daimyo and his heir to Edo, as a symbol of submission and as a prelude to the return of other major daimyo to residence there. In short, the squelching of loyalist dissidence in the Kyoto and Edo areas and the encouraging evidence of ascendancy over Chōshū had brought personnel shifts that saw the hard-liners again take over bakufu policy positions. Some were seasoned specialists in foreign affairs, wanted an end to the charade of exclusion, and thought the time had come for closer coordination of policy planning and implementation. *Fudai* traditionalists in Edo were fully supportive of this and desirous that the influence of the "outsiders" who represented the Tokugawa cause in Kyoto be lessened. This medley of purposes produced a consensus that led to the preparation of a second Chōshū expedition, the death of young Iemochi in Osaka where he had gone to "lead" his armies, and the disasters of the second Chōshū campaign of 1866. By then daimyo awareness of Tokugawa purposes had also produced a very different political climate, one that made all such plans depend on a convincing military victory.

REGIONAL REFORM

With central power diminishing, the future of Japan was to be decided by a contest among regional powers, and the chief contestants were the great domains of southwest Japan and the bakufu itself. Preparation for the struggle was primarily military and secondarily administrative. What counted was the ability to marshal resources and to use them effectively within a social context of obsolescent status distinctions.

Military reforms had been anticipated in some of the frantic preparations for possible war that followed the coming of Commodore Perry. In the domain of Tosa in the 1850s, for instance, desperate efforts were mounted to procure and produce better weapons. Officials were sent to Satsuma to study efforts that had been made to build a reverbatory furnace for arms production. The most important Tosa innovation was probably the decision to form a people's corps (*mimpeitai*) made up of commoner formations commanded by rural samurai (*gōshi*). But these efforts were abandoned after a few years' experience; war with the West had not eventuated; and Yoshida Tōyō, the administrator who had sponsored these efforts, was assassinated by the loyalists. The loyalists who succeeded him in control of domain fortunes were men of the sword and not of the gun.

In Chōshū, however, loyalist extremism accommodated Western arms and methods. In that domain, military reforms began in the 1860s, and as extremism drove the *han* into solitary opposition to the bakufu and its allies, the sense of crisis served to speed up military reform. The innovation for which Chōshū was to become best known was the recruitment of militia companies (*shotai*) with complements drawn from both samurai and nonsamurai; of these the Kiheitai are the most famous. Some of these companies were set up by government action, and others collected around extremist samurai who lived away from the castle town. All the companies were made up of samurai and commoners. The commoners showed a wide range of origin (hunters, mountain priests, townsmen, and fishermen), but the largest category seems to have been sons of village headmen. Thus the leaders of these companies were the sort of men who exercised effective, as opposed to formal, authority in the countryside. The companies also included *rōnin* from other areas. In the fighting that followed in 1866 and 1868, these units fought with tenacity and even ferocity. They must have known that if they failed, neither the bakufu victors nor the highly placed Chōshū conservatives would have shown much compassion. More than any other domain, Chōshū was becoming a small-scale "nation in arms" of the sort that the Meiji modernizers wanted.

The capitulation of the Chōshū government to the first expedition mounted by the bakufu displeased loyalists of many sorts in Chōshū, but none more so than the military units that were to be disbanded by the terms of the settlement. One of these, led by Takasugi Shinsaku, revolted and seized a government office in Shimonoseki before the ink was even dry on the agreements, thereby producing an offer from the bakufu negotiators to provide a body of troops to help the domain regulars suppress them. The Chōshū administration, confident in its own ability to subdue the militia, declined, but its confidence proved misplaced. Within a short time, additional *shotai* victories had produced an advance on the castle town itself and a strong sentiment of criticism against the domain administration that had let the civil war come about. This situation was resolved by the emergence of a new domain administration in the early spring of 1865 that represented a coalition of extremist and moderate samurai. This group led the domain on its collision course with the bakufu and into the early Restoration government.

The Chōshū violence had elements of class or at least of status conflict, and yet it was not a contest between upper and lower in any simple sense. The new administration produced a commitment to the loyalist cause, yet it was also staunchly Chōshū centered in values and objectives. It was nominally antiforeign and exclusionist in its goals, and yet places of influence were beginning to be found for individuals who knew the West. Itō Hirobumi, one of the future leaders of the Meiji state, symbolized the course of a leadership generation in the shifts of his career: a student of Yoshida Shōin, then a student in England, an interpreter and translator in the concluding stages of the foreign bombardment of Shimonoseki, next a commander of a militia company, and finally a protégé and trusted lieutenant of Kido Takayoshi, probably the single most important figure in the new Chōshū administration. Itō was of modest rank and origin. Responsibility and opportunity sobered judgment, and information about the outer world gradually moderated the extremism of the young warriors. Yet what seemed to their elders reckless "extremism" had brought them to power within Chōshū, and their pursuit of the bakufu was not likely to be more conciliatory.

Satsuma, unlike Chōshū, experienced no internal violence or political upset. Its samurai numbers were large and needed no supplement of commoners; distinctions of rank and income within its samurai ranks were so large that rifle-bearing companies could be mounted with little of the status compunctions that hampered the bakufu levies. Most importantly, however, the Satsuma regent Shimazu Hisamitsu was able to maintain political control and enlisted the talents of Saigō Takamori and Ōkubo Toshimichi, men who had been tempered by danger and punishment in 1858. They helped suppress Satsuma extremists at the beginning of the *kōbu-gattai* movement in 1862, and by 1865–6 they recognized and acted on the need for the domain to know more about the West. Fourteen students were selected and sent to London under the guidance of domain officials. Once in Europe the students were set to studying a variety of technological and military specialties. Before long they were joined by a second group. Satsuma officials in Europe tried to secure for their domain status as an independent country for the Paris Exposition of 1867, citing as reason the domain's control of Okinawa. They negotiated a number of agreements for industrial and mining operations, and although little came of most of these, the purchase of five thousand rifles added important strength to the Satsuma military. Thus, whereas Chōshū, under great military pressure from without, underwent a political upset that placed power in the hands of "extremists" who had use for the advice of the Western-experienced Itō and Inoue Kaoru, Satsuma, without the goad that military crisis provided for administrative change in Chōshū, was, thanks to the English bombardment of Kagoshima, no less alert to the need for Western equipment. Expulsion, one may conclude, was now a dead letter (though it remained a useful slogan) after the shellings of Kagoshima and Chōshū. The overthrow of the bakufu, which was not a practical proposition before the reforms of 1862, had become a goal of many men by 1865.

The changes of the early 1860s had made the bakufu itself a regional power. No set of reforms was more impressive and more extensive than the changes that the Tokugawa leaders initiated in their Kinai and Kantō territories. The Osaka and Edo plains were under full foreign and Japanese observation and hence subject to all the interference that national and international politics could provide. These territories were also divided between those under direct bakufu administration and the lands of minor daimyo and *hatamoto* who administered their holdings independently. Cumulatively the largest holdings of any daimyo in the Tokugawa structure, the Tokugawa *tenryō* was also the most affected by urban and national commerce and communications, the most "modern" in economic developments, and the most lightly invested by resident samurai. In Tokugawa lands, samurai as a percentage of domain population were relatively few and highly urbanized. The bakufu thus faced particular problems in its military modernization.

The bakufu's Bunkyū reforms of 1862 included administrative and military changes as well as the relaxation of daimyo controls that have already been discussed. On the whole, the administrative changes were more successful than the political changes. New procedures were developed for the rapid promotion of able men. Unessential jobs were eliminated; so many, in fact, that the unemployment that resulted required special programs of aid and relief for the newly unfortunate.

Military reforms found the bakufu (and its rivals) struggling to acquire the most lethal weapons at a time when firearms were undergoing rapid change in the Western world. A second problem was to transform the corps of house retainers (*hatamoto* and *gokenin*) into rifle companies. This last was easier to do in theory than in practice, for the urbanized samurai, who were essentially an army of occupation that had spent many generations in peace and quiet, often resisted drill.[40]

Extensive plans were worked out for a modern army and navy within the confines of the troop strength that retainers were expected to be able to provide. Efforts were made to correlate income to the rank structure of the modern forces, and planners set the goal of drawing one-half of those forces from the bakufu's house retainers. Thus it was assumed from the outset that it would be necessary to augment samurai with commoner strength.

Naval training got its start when a small Dutch training contingent came to Nagasaki in the 1850s; in the early 1860s Katsu Kaishū was assigned the responsibility of organizing a naval training school at Hyōgo. Katsu's tendency to recruit his men from many areas alarmed bakufu conservatives, who saw the institution becoming a nest of loyalists, and so Katsu was replaced in 1864. The point is significant: Bakufu reformers tended to draw on men of many areas, but the great southwestern *han* could be exclusive and probably had more esprit de corps. Sustained efforts were devoted to the land arm of the new military structure. By 1864 some ten thousand weapons had been imported through Yokohama, and from then to the end of the bakufu, gunrunning to Yokohama and to Nagasaki (for the southwestern domains) proved one of the most lucrative aspects of trade at the ports. As the second expedition against Chōshū drew near in 1865, bakufu leaders were beginning to realize that their reliance on their retainers (and especially the landholding *hatamoto*) would have to change. First they tried to get them to provide conscripts as part of their feudal military service requirement, but before long it became clear that a better system of recruiting commoners was needed. As the forces took shape, the composition of the principal rifle-bearing units gradually

---

40 For Satsuma, Beasley, *Meiji Restoration*, p. 246; for bakufu military reforms, Totman, *Collapse*, pp. 25–7: (for Bunkyū), p. 182 (for 1864), and p. 199 (for 1865). Totman's discussion of technological changes involved in muzzle loaders, Minie rifles, breech-loading rifles, and multishot pistols, p. 25, is particularly useful.

became commoner based. By degrees, *hatamoto* military service requirements were becoming commuted to a money tax that was used to cover the costs of conscripting and training peasants. All of this affected only part of the Tokugawa vassal armies, but it was that part that indicated future trends.[41]

The Tokugawa military reforms required extensive foreign cooperation, but as the nominal government of the entire country, the bakufu had the best access to foreign assistance. Its first moves were by way of the traditional link with Holland, and in the fall of 1864 three navy officers were sent to the Netherlands to study shipyards and other Western military developments. Negotiations for a shipyard were begun with the Dutch and also for a warship; talks also began for the building of a warship (the future *Stonewall*) in the United States.

But the most important channel of foreign assistance was that with France. Minister Leon Roches, who arrived in Japan in April 1864, worked unceasingly to consolidate for his country the role of principal source for military – and, he hoped, political – reform in Japan. Those plans developed gradually; they represented Roches' enthusiasm and not that of his government. Foreign aid never assumed the dimensions that the bakufu's domestic rivals feared it would, because neither Tokugawa nor French leaders were prepared to take risks. Yet the plans were extensive and stand as reminders of the possible impact that imperialist competition could have had on a developing Japan.[42]

Roches began with specific goals: The French silk industry was in dire need of help from Japan because of a silkworm blight, and that made him the bakufu's most importunate customer. But he was free with additional suggestions. Before long he had secured the appointment of Kurimoto Joun as special liaison officer between himself and the *rōjū*, and by the end of 1864, bakufu officials had requested his help in planning for the construction of a naval yard and arsenal at Yokosuka. Gradually confidence in Roches' intentions developed. In 1865 a mission was sent to Europe to seek military assistance as well as machinery and equipment for Yokosuka. Arrangements for a mint and a military training mission took shape, and bakufu officials began to develop hopes of a special source of access to the technology and training they knew they needed.

41 Totman, *Collapse*, p. 182. For purposes of brevity, this discussion telescopes changes that came at different speeds in different periods and areas.
42 Mark David Ericson, "The Tokugawa *Bakufu* and Leon Roches," Ph.D. diss., University of Hawaii, 1978, p. 243, improves on the earlier work of Meron Medzini, *French Policy in Japan During the Closing Years of the Tokugawa Regime* (Cambridge, Mass.: Harvard University Press, 1971).

These experiments gathered momentum with proposals for an officially sponsored trading company that would generate funds for bakufu purchases abroad. The banker Fleury-Herard was invested as the bakufu representative in Paris and put in charge of purchasing equipment for a foundry and mint. French advice (though not, it should be noted, French money), began to pour into Tokugawa circles about ways to restructure Japan's economy and administration in order to speed modernization and build up power. Long before much could come of this, however, the Tokugawa forces were gathering in Osaka to carry out the second punitive expedition against Chōshū. When hostilities broke out in the summer of 1866, it was still a largely traditional congeries of bakufu vassal forces that tried to contest the issue with the more highly motivated Chōshū units.

The second war with Chōshū proved a disaster. Although elements of the bakufu's new units were employed, they were fielded together with old-style units from other *han*. The bakufu army was a coalition of vassals' armies, as had always been the case, enabling the Chōshū warriors to select their target and attack the Tokugawa forces where they were weakest. Bakufu efforts to attack Chōshū at each of its borders were poorly coordinated, and the forces were poorly led. While all this was in progress, the young shogun Iemochi died at Osaka.

When the full scale of the military disasters became clear, Tokugawa Yoshinobu, now the ranking figure on the bakufu side, reluctantly decided that the battle would have to be broken off and seized upon the shogun's death as a face-saving reason for a cease-fire. Yet the cease-fire left Chōshū troops occupying areas of bakufu and *fudai* land, and it dealt the shogunate a blow in prestige from which it never fully recovered.

The defeat of the bakufu armies by Chōshū gave the Tokugawa modernization movement new urgency. The last year of the Tokugawa shogunate saw sweeping changes that portended centralization, rationalization, and bureaucratization. Once Yoshinobu was fully invested as shogun, with full honors and titles, the reconstruction of the bakufu began in earnest. Foreign relations were regularized. Permanent missions were set up in capitals. Yoshinobu's younger brother Akitake was sent to France as the bakufu representative at the Paris Exposition of 1867, and plans called for him to spend years of study there to prepare him for future leadership. Appointive changes brought to office some of the most effective of the modernizing officials of the recent half-decade. The entire foreign diplomatic corps was invited to Osaka for an audience with the new shogun, who entertained them at a dinner prepared by a newly employed French chef. Western dress replaced Japanese at the shogunal court for that occasion.

Numerous requests for advice were addressed to Roches, and he answered during long sessions with senior officials and a private audience with the shogun Yoshinobu himself. The list of questions covered administrative changes, taxes, military development, mineral resource development, economic growth, queries about Switzerland and Prussia, and questions about the abolition of feudalism by European countries.[43] Administrative reforms followed; these set up a sort of cabinet system with specialized responsibilities replacing the monthly rotation of all-purpose generalists that had been the pattern. New personnel practices were designed to facilitate the selection of competent officials, with a regularized salary system for government departments. A great deal of time went into the preparation of diagrams laying out specific administrative responsibilities and procedures, and initial steps working toward the commutation of vassal lands and stipends developed. Shogunal power in the Edo area was strengthened by measures to call in small nearby fiefs in order to rationalize and centralize administrative procedures. Military reforms were pushed particularly rapidly. A French military mission arrived in January 1867. Western uniforms were adopted; obsolete forces were disbanded; and steps were taken toward the substitution of a monetized tax on house vassals as the basis for a peasant conscription system. Nishi Amane, newly returned from study in Holland, was ordered to draw up a more modern scheme of government and produced a parliamentary draft that envisioned a division of power among the court, an executive branch, and a bicameral legislature with an upper house of daimyo empowered to dissolve the lower house.

As a result, it can be asserted that the bakufu leaders were launching a modernization program – perhaps a "Tokugawa restoration" – that would in time have emulated at many points the programs adopted by their successors in the Meiji government. Seen in this light, it can be said that the civil war of 1868 was fought over the issue not of whether Tokugawa feudalism would survive but whether its demise would be presided over by Tokugawa or anti-Tokugawa leaders. It was no longer a matter of saving the bakufu system but of replacing it, now that it was collapsing. As Totman said of the period immediately before the summer war, "there was no longer in Japan an authority

---

[43] Ericson, "The Tokugawa *Bakufu* and Leon Roches," pp. 238ff.

symbol capable of moving the feudal lords. There was no national polity; the *bakuhan* system no longer existed."[44] Ironically, however, these needs were probably seen more clearly by the bakufu leaders than by the southwestern lords who opposed them.

RESTORATION

The changes launched in Edo are difficult to evaluate, for they did not mature in time to help the bakufu; it is always easier to sketch reforms than to carry them out. Nevertheless, the fear that they would result in a greatly strengthened shogunate was an important factor in impelling leaders in Satsuma and Chōshū to try to anticipate such success with efforts of their own to overthrow it. What they particularly feared was that the administration of Yoshinobu would use French military and administrative assistance to build a central government capable of destroying the daimyo, with the shogun serving as its chief executive officer.

In 1867, the death of Emperor Kōmei of smallpox brought changes at the court as well. Though consistently antiforeign, Kōmei had usually been well disposed toward the bakufu as represented by Tokugawa Yoshinobu, with whom he had established relations of considerable trust. With the succession of the boy Mutsuhito, the future Meiji emperor, court nobles had a new field for political maneuver. The most able and important of those courtiers was now Iwakura Tomomi, a shrewd judge of events and possibilities. By the fall of 1866 Iwakura was writing that the court had the choice of siding with the bakufu against Chōshū and, possibly, Satsuma, or maneuvering to make itself the center of a new united polity. Because bakufu prestige and power were in decline, he suggested that "the Emperor should issue orders to the Bakufu that from now on it must set aside its selfish ways, acting in accordance with public principle; that imperial rule must be restored; and that thereafter the Tokugawa house must work in concert with the great domains in the Emperor's service." To restore national prestige and handle the foreigners, the country would have to be united, and "for policy and administration to have a single source, the Court must be made the center of national government." In additional documents Iwakura sounded more and more like the Satsuma leaders with whom he communicated, as when he wrote: "In the heavens there are not two suns. On earth there are not two monarchs. Surely

---

44 Totman, *Collapse*, p. 291.

no country can survive unless government edicts stem from a single source. . . . Hence it is my desire that we should act vigorously to abolish the Bakufu" and relegate the Tokugawa house to the ranks of the great domains.[45] Some of this language was echoed in future proposals, as in a Satsuma–Tosa document worked out in the summer of 1867:

> There cannot be two rulers in a land, or two heads in a house, and it is most reasonable to return administration and justice to one ruler. . . . It is evident that we must reform our regulations, return political power to the court, form a council of feudal lords and conduct affairs in line with the desires of the people . . . only then can we face all nations without shame and establish our national polity.[46]

These notes of national danger, international prestige, and the need for an effective, single center of government recur in many pronouncements of late Tokugawa days. In fact Japan now had not only two governments but even two bakufus, given the presence of Yoshinobu in Osaka/Kyoto and the more Tokugawa-centered world of the bureaucrats at Edo.

Although such divisions of power seemed impossible to men like Iwakura and many others, they also made it troublesome for foreign representatives who wanted firm guarantees of their privileges and a clear understanding as to the channels of power. Roches accepted the bakufu as a legitimate national government and devoted his efforts to help it become a more effective one. His British counterpart Harry Parkes was not sure and suspected that Japan would not have a real government until basic changes in Edo–Kyoto relations took place. Though junior to Roches in time of residence, Parkes proved a ruthless competitor, on one occasion forcing his way into a private meeting between Roches and Yoshinobu to insist on equal treatment as Her Majesty's representative. When the bakufu requested postponement of the second installment of the enormous indemnity exacted for Shimonoseki because of the costs that had been incurred in the preparation of the second campaign against Chōshū, Parkes demanded an accounting of those costs. When the bakufu argued court opposition as grounds for delay on Hyōgo, Parkes demanded – and secured – explicit court approval of the treaties by staging a demarche at Osaka in November 1865. When he saw the bakufu's difficulties with its recalcitrant daimyo, Parkes concluded that England, in a spirit of neutrality, should cultivate those daimyo as possible future power

---

45 Beasley, *Meiji Restoration*, pp. 261, 266–7. 46 Jansen, *Sakamoto Ryōma*, p. 300.

holders, and he alarmed bakufu officials by visiting several castle towns in the southwestern domains, including Kagoshima. Parkes's interpreter Ernest Satow, probably the best informed foreigner in late Tokugawa Japan, maintained close friendships with the leaders of the southwestern *han* and wrote a pamphlet (which was immediately translated into Japanese) arguing that English policy should work toward the creation of a council of great lords, of whom the Tokugawa head would be one, under the emperor, in order to secure binding guarantees of foreign privileges and rights. This private opinion was widely taken to represent English policy and seemed to be in the process of implementation by the actions of Harry Parkes. Thus foreign as well as court and daimyo opinion was working to exacerbate unstable national politics.

As the great domains shook off their subordination to bakufu leadership, they began to negotiate private agreements among themselves. These were no longer the personal discussions of daimyo, as in the early years, but policy decisions reached by the bureaucratic leaders who staffed *han* administrations. The most important of these was an agreement between Satsuma and Chōshū that was worked out early in 1866 to lessen the possible dangers for Chōshū in the approaching second bakufu punitive campaign. The agreement was made possible by the efforts of Sakamoto Ryōma and Nakaoka Shintarō of Tosa who provided their good offices. In February 1866, Kido Takayoshi, for Chōshū, and Saigō Takamori, for Satsuma, agreed that Satsuma would provide its help in mediating for Chōshū at court; it would do its best to prevent the bakufu from crushing Chōshū; it would secure Kyoto if necessary; and it would join with Chōshū, once that domain had been pardoned, in working for "the glory of the Imperial country."

After the defeat of the bakufu armies at the hands of Chōshū, the Satsuma–Tosa agreement that has been mentioned added another agreement. The two domains agreed on a program for politics: The court should have full authority, and a council with two houses would be established in Kyoto, one chamber staffed with daimyo and the other made up of "retainers and even commoners." The shogunate as such would be abolished. New treaties would be drawn up with the foreign powers "on the basis of reason and justice"; institutions would be revised and brought up-to-date; and self-interest was everywhere to take second place to the consciousness of the larger national good.

This optimistic view of an unselfish future, clearly a legacy of the *kōbu-gattai* persuasion, represented a Tosa plan to secure a peaceful solution to Japan's political crises. Chōshū, flushed with its victories in the summer war, was still technically under the ban of both court and bakufu and determined to exploit its military advantage in further violence. Simultaneously, the treaty powers were demanding action on the opening of Hyōgo, which was scheduled for the summer of 1867. Once again the great lords assembled to discuss the crisis. Matsudaira Shungaku, Shimazu Hisamitsu, Yamauchi Yōdō, and Date Munenari proposed to Yoshinobu that the bakufu combine a solution to the two and proposed to the court a pardon of Chōshū together with court approval for the opening of Hyōgo. Yoshinobu, however, was inclined to hold out for the impossible condition of an apology from Chōshū, but because Hyōgo could not wait, he preceeded to wrest approval from the court for that opening on grounds of pressing national danger.

This stance confirmed Satsuma's discouragement with even a reformed bakufu and helped produce a new Satsuma–Chōshū agreement for a military coup against the shogunate in the summer of 1867. The Tosa leaders, holding a median position, still tried to head this off with a peaceful solution. Tosa's size made it fearful of losing out in a military showdown. Its relationship to the bakufu, which had treated the Yamauchi house favorably, was also one of obligation and loyalty. All this reinforced hopes of a negotiated settlement by which the shogun would agree to step down and become one of the great lords in a new conciliar structure under the aegis of the throne. Similar hopes had been at the heart of the *kōbu-gattai* movement since 1862. Matsudaira Shungaku reappeared on the scene once again. Sakamoto Ryōma, once a Tosa loyalist and then an associate of the bakufu official Katsu Kaishū, subsequently sheltered by Satsuma and central to the Satsuma–Chōshū agreement of 1866, now worked out an eight-point program that contained Tosa hopes for a negotiated settlement. The Satsuma leaders who willingly subscribed to this program in endorsing the Satsuma–Tosa compact in the summer of 1867 were quite willing to help propose the bakufu's voluntary dissolution and were prepared to use force if a peaceful settlement should fail.

These currents converged in November 1867. While Edo modernizers were pushing reforms to produce a more effective bakufu and Chōshū and Satsuma leaders were readying their troops for a military showdown, Tosa representatives in Kyoto presented Yoshinobu with Yamauchi Yōdō's proposal that he resign his office and titles. The proposal contained eight parts: The court would rule, but a two-house council, made up of daimyo and court nobles, would be established; new treaties would be worked out; an imperial army and navy would be established;[47] "errors of the past" in procedure and institutions would be abolished; "wrong customs" in the court would be reformed; and once again, self-interest would be put aside.

Yoshinobu accepted the proposal. He did so without consulting the Edo government leaders and after almost no consultation in Kyoto. Clearly he saw it as a way of escaping his predicament of responsibility without power and retaining the power base that his reforms were building at Edo. Once the court accepted his resignation as shogun, the Tokugawa polity of 267 years formally came to an end.

But there was still nothing to replace it. The council of daimyo did not materialize, for uncertainty was so widespread that only sixteen daimyo arrived in Kyoto in response to a court request for attendance. *Kōbu-gattai* proved no more viable in 1867 than it had been in 1862. Soon large contingents of samurai were being sent to Kyoto; parts of the Chōshū domain army, still unpardoned, were nearing the city. The Satsuma–Chōshū plans for a military coup were still intact, and tension grew steadily. On January 2 and 3, 1868, an assembly at the court was convened, dominated by Iwakura and Satsuma men. Yoshinobu and his closest supporters, suspicious of what was planned, declined to attend. The meeting resolved to transfer the palace guard from bakufu to non-Tokugawa hands, to abolish old offices, and to demand the surrender of Tokugawa domains to the "court." Yoshinobu, in doubt as to his next step, withdrew to Osaka.

For over three weeks, things were at a standstill. Court representatives ordered Yoshinobu to appear in formal contrition and surrender, only to have him propose that all daimyo dedicate a comparable fraction of their income and land to the court. Roches offered Yoshinobu such French aid as he could muster, an offer that was not accepted, but neither was the advice of bakufu leaders who wanted to fight. A powerful document from Yoshinobu to the court calling attention to Satsuma's duplicity and his own exemplary behavior was kept from the young emperor. The former shogun's indecision began to cost him the support of even Tokugawa houses. Finally, in late January 1868, Yoshinobu decided to return to Kyoto with a body of troops to remonstrate. His commanders did not expect to have to fight their way back; their formations and composition represented an unlikely mixture of modern and premodern companies. To their misfortune they were

---

47 The proposal read: "We must have a force which will have no equal in the world."

opposed and ambushed by modern Satsuma and Chōshū units that stopped them and drove them back. The civil war had begun; force would decide the issue.

Fighting at Fushimi-Toba went on for four days and produced a casualty count of five hundred dead and one thousand to fifteen hundred wounded. On both sides, units fought well, but the leadership and determination of forces committed to the Kyoto cause was superior to that on the bakufu side. The bakufu commanders seem to have let a fear of popular disorder keep them from using all their Western-trained and armed troops at the front, whereas their adversaries had their best units at the right places. The bakufu units, trying to advance along two narrow roads, one on either side of the Yodo River, had the harder task to carry out. In some units, morale was a problem, but others, notably those of Aizu, fought with dash and courage.

When the dimensions of this new disaster were apparent, Tokugawa Yoshinobu and his bakufu army headed north for Edo. Within two weeks the former shogun had decided against further resistance to his enemies, despite Roches' encouragement and advice that he try again. The bakufu army was dismantled as the daimyo took their units to their own domains, some to join and others to apologize and submit to the "imperial" armies that advanced from the south. In the spring of 1868 Edo itself was surrendered by the bakufu official Katsu Kaishū to an imperial army commanded by Saigō Takamori.

But the war was not over, for the fighting known as the Boshin conflict went on until May 1869, when the Tokugawa naval units that had sailed to Hokkaido and held out there under the command of Enomoto Takeaki surrendered. The war in the northeast had been carried on by a daimyo alliance headed by the Sendai domain. Its cause was really not that of the Tokugawa, which was clearly doomed, but, rather, that of its region against the distrusted southerners from Satsuma and Chōshū. This "Northeastern League," in fact, claimed that its members were more loyal to the emperor than were the "selfish and self-serving" southerners. The most fierce battle of the campaign came at Aizu castle in Wakamatsu, where the men of Matsudaira Katamori, former *shugo* of Kyoto and long a thorn in the side of Satsuma and Chōshū, fought desperately. The castle was put to the torch, and Aizu lost almost three thousand samurai in the war, more than the combined total of the opposition. After its defeat, the domain was broken up, and its ruling family was moved to a niggardly and inhospitable plot of ground unable to support the remnants of its former retainer force. Katamori himself was made a Shinto priest, guardian of the Tokugawa burial shrines. No other domain was treated as harshly, though a number of recalcitrant daimyo were forced into retirement and others into house arrest. Tokugawa Yoshinobu himself was ordered to retire as house head and withdrew to Numazu in Shizuoka where he did his best to maintain his retainers. By the 1890s he had been received by the emperor and restored to honor. His successor, Iesato, was first head of the House of Peers.

The regime that replaced the bakufu, as Chapter 10 makes clear, underwent many changes before becoming the Meiji government.[48] Its first institutional probings came in the January meetings that maneuvered Yoshinobu into opposition. The same meeting that declared bakufu offices abolished established a new three-tier structure of *sōsai*, *gijō* (councilors), and *san'yo* (junior councilors) and named Prince Arisugawa *sōsai* in order to make the greatest possible use of imperial legitimacy. Gradually, however, status and office filtered downward to the samurai leaders of the southwestern *han* whose lords dominated the original table of organization, and as that process matured, the Meiji government took form.

In a basic sense, the program of the new government was enunciated as early as the spring of 1868, at a time when the regime was still seeking to reassure the doubtful and to enlist the wavering. In April, one day after Katsu and Saigō negotiated the surrender of Edo, the young emperor was presented with what became known as the "Charter Oath," five articles that bridged the transition from the Tosa proposals of 1867 to the constitutional order of the modern Japanese state. These articles promised the creation of "deliberative councils" and the determination of policies on the basis of "general opinion," the cooperation of all classes in carrying out the administration of affairs of state, full opportunity for commoners as well as for officials, and the abolition of "evil customs of the past." They also proposed basing everything on the "just laws of nature." Finally, a search for knowledge "throughout the world" would follow in order to "strengthen the foundation of imperial rule." This was a document couched in terms sufficiently general to conform to the social structure of its day, but it also held out the possibility of changes so basic that it could still be cited as authorization for the democratic institutional changes that followed World War II.

---

48 See Albert Craig, "The Central Government," Marius B. Jansen, "The Ruling Class," and Michio Umegaki, "From Domain to Prefecture," chaps. 2, 3, and 4 in Jansen and Rozman, eds., *Japan in Transition*.

THE RESTORATION IN HISTORY AND HISTORIOGRAPHY

If the definition of the Meiji Restoration is limited to the events of 1867 and 1868, it constituted little more than a coup that shifted rule from one sector of the ruling class to another. But when it is considered as a larger process, one that began before mid-century and that culminated in the modern state at the century's end, it can be seen to have brought revolutionary changes in Japanese society. Studies of these events during the century that followed them have inevitably been intertwined with the climate of opinion within which they were carried on. The nature of the nineteenth-century historical process, and the motive forces involved, have provided basic problems of classification and analysis.

The orthodox view of Japanese history before 1945, and one that is by no means dead, was based on interpretations that emphasized the maturization of currents of imperial loyalism through the Tokugawa period. With the coming of Perry and the foreign danger, the textbooks explained, selfless patriots – the *shishi* – fought to reverse their *han* policies and to defeat the bakufu by wakening long-slumbering imperial and national consciousness. Saigō, Ōkubo, Iwakura, Kido, and all the heirs of Yoshida Shōin were portrayed as though foretold by anguished loyalists of earlier times. Laudatory biographies told their stories as they themselves would have wished to be remembered. Official historiographical institutes provided proportional representation for the southwestern *han* to make certain that the praise would be allocated equitably. These views were spread by a modern education system that was centered on patriotism and loyalty, reinforced by the popular press, and fortified by scholarly compilations. So brief a summary risks distortion. There was enough of substance in the commitment of Restoration figures, enough romance and color in what they did, and enough national pride in what they produced to retain for the loyalist leaders a secure place in any historiography. But the identification of their success with morality and patriotism also introduced a strong bias in much that was written in a highly nationalistic setting.

Yet the nationalist emphasis of prewar history had developed in a context of much more critical writing. By the 1880s, historians had begun to fit Japan's experience into international models of liberal and capitalist societies, and some were becoming troubled by the disparities they sensed between the "deliberative councils" that had been promised and the reality of the Imperial Diet they saw approaching. Japan seemed to be eclipsing the timetable of other countries in modernization, but the reforms granted "from above" were somehow different from the reforms won from below. By late Meiji times the conservative and pragmatic government leaders in power also seemed quite unlike the hotheaded, two-sworded idealists of romantic memory. To some, they were becoming Japan's new problem, and judgments of the bakufu softened as a result. By the early twentieth century a new generation of writers had begun to separate the leaders from what they had brought about, to minimize the conflicts, and to explain the Restoration and modernization programs by showing the material advances that had taken place in Japanese society under Tokugawa rule. Tokutomi Sohō argued that it was not the Meiji leaders but inexorable trends that had created the new Japan. He and others stressed the fragility of feudal society, and the growing independence of stouthearted rural leaders, as the critical factors in the overthrow of Tokugawa feudalism. In turn, such interpretations were usually related to political advocacy and the desire to find legitimacy for liberalism and to advance social reform in Japan.[49] By the 1890s, however, the flush of victory over China, soon to be followed by the conquest of Russia, the maturation of the ideology of the imperial state, and the completion of the network of national schools all combined to reinforce the official orthodoxy with its sanctification of the modern state. Tokugawa Yoshinobu himself, in his memoirs (1915) and in an authorized biography (1918), became a loyalist.

After World War I, Marxist analysis provided a new and powerful teleological expectation of what the Restoration should or could have produced. Economic instability culminating in the world depression, increased political and intellectual surveillance consequent to the formation of the Japan Communist Party in the form of the Peace Preservation Act of 1925, and the aggressive course of Japanese foreign policy all combined to encourage new evaluations of Japan's recent past. Marxist historians divided into the Labor-Farmer (*rōnō*) group, which was prepared to describe the Restoration as a basically bourgeois movement that had ended feudalism in Japan, and the gloomier Lectures (*kōza*) group which held that feudal relationships had lived on in the countryside through noneconomic and non-contractual

---

49 See Jiro Numata, "Shigeno Yasutsugu and the Modern Tokyo Tradition of Historical Writing," in W. G. Beasley and E. G. Pulleybank, eds., *Historians of China and Japan* (London: Oxford University Press, 1961), pp. 264–87, for the evolution of Meiji historiography within inherited, Chinese tradition; and Peter Duus, "Whig History, Japanese Style: The Min'yūsha Historians and the Meiji Restoration," *Journal of Asian Studies* 33 (May 1974): 415–36.

restraints on tenants as the basis of a new "absolutism" built around the "emperor system," a term that was utilized in the Japan Communist Party theses of 1932. Like their Meiji predecessors, these historians were directing and relating their views to problems of political advocacy.[50]

Japan's surrender in 1945 freed the air of "emperor system" orthodoxy (although it replaced it with equally compulsive derogation for a time) and produced immensely important work that retained some of the Marxist categories without repeating the simplistic formulas of much of the earlier writing. Nevertheless, the presentist orientation of historical evaluation continued, and many writers' concerns were to identify and eliminate feudal remnants and advance democracy.[51]

When the focus of research is brought closer to the decade in which the bakufu was toppled, problems still outnumber answers. The principal actors among the leaders have been clearly delineated, but the source of their backing remains a matter of dispute. Shibahara Takuji, after summarizing movements of popular discontent and disorder in Restoration times, did not hesitate to term agrarianists the "moving force" of the Restoration and saw popular antifeudal sentiments as the key historical ingredient in the events of the decade. On the other hand, Conrad Totman's analysis of the bakufu's fall, though recognizing commoners' antifeudal attitudes, concludes:

This anti-feudal mentality did not become an anti-Bakufu mentality, however, and the reason seems to be that the political contest of the 1860s was pitting some parts of the ruling or feudal elite against others. . . . In conse-

---

50 The immediate prewar years saw publication of authoritative summaries of the positions mentioned here: Tokutomi Iichirō, *Kinsei Nihon kokuminshi* for Duus's "Whig History"; the monument of government historiography, *Ishin shi*, 6 vols. (Tokyo: Meiji shoin, 1941); and the definitive statement of the *kōza* position that gave the school its name, *Nihon shihonshugi hattatsu shi kōza*, 7 vols. (Tokyo: Iwanami shoten, 1932–3). For a recent and cogent analysis of the Marxist struggle, see Yasukichi Yasuba, "Anatomy of the Debate on Japanese Capitalism," *Journal of Japanese Studies* 2 (Autumn 1975): 63–82. See also Germain A. Hoston, *Marxism and the Crisis of Development in Prewar Japan* (Princeton, N.J.: Princeton University Press, 1986), for its analysis of prewar Marxist writing.
51 See, for a brief comment on the contributions of Maruyama Masao, Ōtsuka Hisao, and Kawashima Takeyoshi in the postwar climate, Nagahara Keiji, *Rekishigaku josetsu* (Tokyo: Tokyo daigaku shuppankai, 1978), pp. 51ff. The most influential postwar summary of Restoration scholarship was Tōyama Shigeki, *Meiji ishin* (Tokyo: Iwanami shoten, 1951), which argued the "absolutist" thesis. Most recent and influential is a "people's history" that emphasizes the indigenous and internal development of Japanese history, focusing (as did Tokutomi to some extent) on rural elites at mid-century. Carol Gluck, "The People in History: Recent Trends in Japanese Historiography," *Journal of Asian Studies* 38 (November 1978): 25–50. An important statement of this school, Irokawa Daikichi's *Meiji no bunka* (Tokyo: Iwanami shoten, 1970), has appeared in translation as *The Culture of the Meiji Period*, ed. Marius B. Jansen (Princeton, N.J.: Princeton University Press, 1985).

quence one finds commoners in all camps and on all sides of major disputes. . . .[52]

One statistical examination of the incidence of popular revolts between 1865 and 1871 (a total of 545) found that they were least prevalent in future "Restoration-led" areas and most common in Tokugawa-ruled or related areas and related this to the relative prosperity and productivity of the Tokugawa areas and the relatively depressed and suppressed state of the antibakufu domains. Effective anti-Tokugawa *political* action cannot be related to such popular discontent, but Tokugawa efforts to maintain control and counter nonsamurai resistance were, presumably, hampered by the relatively less stable social base of the Tokugawa territories.[53]

No one can doubt the evidences of commoner restlessness and movement. Recent studies of a bizarre movement that swept the principal communications routes of central Japan during the final months of Tokugawa rule provide fascinating evidence of a widespread and rather joyous spirit of revelry and mischief that was so troublesome for Tokugawa forces of order that some were prepared to blame the outbreaks on loyalist suggestion and stimulation. Yet the mood of the crowds was overwhelmingly optimistic, more appropriate to festival than to fury, and more social than political. The wealthy, who were expected to provide food and entertainment because the gods had favored them with talismans of good fortune, paid the bills.[54] Nonetheless, it is clear that the bakufu leaders interpreted such movements as threatening their control of society. Spontaneous, large-scale febrile movements like this also related to the rising trend of popular pilgrimage to Ise in the nineteenth century. Occasionally they became associated, at least briefly, with sentimental homage to loyalist *shishi* killed in the Restoration violence.[55] There was much political satire in occasional wall writings and shrine placards, but these phenomena do not seem to have been sufficiently focused to grant them a very significant role. The search for an independent merchant interest and role has also been unprofitable. Some merchants did assist the *shishi*: Shiraishi Shōichirō, a Shimonoseki shipping guild merchant, was a man

---

52 Totman, *Collapse*, p. 458; Shibahara Takuji, "Hanbaku shoseiryoku no seikaku," in *Iwanami kōza Nihon rekishi*, vol. 14 (*kindai* 1) (Tokyo: Iwanami shoten, 1962), pp. 169–212.
53 Yoshio Sugimoto, "Structural Sources of Popular Revolts and the Tōbaku Movement at the Time of the Meiji Restoration," *Journal of Asian Studies* 34 (August 1975): 875–89.
54 Takagi Shunsuke, *Eejanaika* (Tokyo: Kyōikusha rekishi shinsho, 1979), pp. 209–34.
55 Onodera Toshiya, "Zannen san kō: Bakumatsu Kinai no ichi minshū undō o megutte," *Chiikishi kenkyū* 2 (June 1972): 46–67, discusses pilgrimages to the tombs of Yoshimura Toratarō and Yamamoto Bunnosuke around the time of the Restoration.

of culture and means whose diary includes the names of four hundred *shishi*, to whom he was generous with food, drink, and lodging. But even more merchants, whether or not by choice, assisted the bakufu, which based a good deal of its emergency financing on massive loans. It seems logical to conclude that in a setting of widespread disaffection with the state of political and social order, many commoners favored those who promised change. But it is also true that regional loyalty – and distrust – affected commoners as well as samurai.

Another series of debates centers on the foreign threat. The increasing intimacy of Leon Roches with the bakufu leaders in the closing years of their regime and the bluster with which Harry Parkes obstructed that contact have led many to emphasize the danger of imperialist competition for influence in Japan. There was at one point negotiation for a French loan that would be predicated on Hokkaido's resources, and Roches apparently offered Yoshinobu the services of the small French military mission after the Fushimi–Toba disaster in January 1868. But the danger of foreign intervention has probably been exaggerated. Satow's influential pamphlet on English policy was written, as his memoirs make clear, without the knowledge of his short-tempered chief, and Roches seems consistently to have extended his personal diplomacy, as he called it, beyond the authorization of his government, which had all the imperialist problems it could handle in Mexico and in Southeast Asia during those years. Even if the bakufu leaders had decided to commit themselves to French assistance, they would have found that there was very little to be had: Far from being able to negotiate loans, they had to pay for everything in advance and in cash. Yet it has also to be granted that none of this lessens the perceptions of foreign danger that the Japanese held in the 1860s. That impression itself was a fact impelling men to action, and the fear of entangling loans and foreign leverage lasted throughout the decades of nation building in the Meiji period.

The importance of the imperial institution and the role of the court present further problems for historical analysis. The policy of the Meiji government to keep that court area sacrosanct and to accept it as a basic element in national character and history produced an understandable reaction in post–World War II days when authors minimized its substance and stressed its use as a tactic and artifice of the Meiji planners. Yet clearly there was more than tactic involved. Although the Restoration leaders frequently lamented popular indifference to the existence of the court, they themselves clearly kept it uppermost as the quintessential center of national identity, and that emphasis was later diffused among the people through centralization, mobilization, and education. The emotion generated among the *shishi* by charges that the bakufu had somehow allowed the emperor to be disturbed – heightened at court, where nobles knew that the emperor was in fact indignant – was a powerful solvent of ordinary discipline and restraint. Yet the court itself, after the loyalist frenzy of the early 1860s, was much less a factor than it had been at the beginning of the process. As Totman put it: "It was *shishi* who gave effective voice and real content to this *sonnō-jōi* rhetoric, and so the prominence of the imperial role is primarily attributable to *shishi* success in making their views heard."[56]

The historian turns finally to the Restoration leaders, men of modest rank but immodest self-assurance, who gloried in the opportunity to establish for themselves, their friends, and their domain a visibility that had been denied them under the constraints of feudal discipline and status, and who saw their cause as pure and selfless because it held out the hope of winning for their emperor and country the place they felt they deserved among the nations. Those hopes were great and almost the reverse of the circumstances of their time. For a country humiliated by Western powers, they wanted a leading role in the world; for a sovereign restricted to secluded impotence, they demanded full authority over a country his ancestors had once ruled; for their domain, they wanted a full share in national politics instead of second-class vassalage and, for themselves, honored status as imperial servitors instead of vassals' rear vassals.[57]

Yet in the final analysis, most of this concerned the locus of leadership and not its goals. Most Tokugawa partisans wanted much the same thing. One is struck by the convergence of planning between bakufu and Restoration leaders in the last decade of Tokugawa history. Indeed, the bakufu leaders, charged with responsibility, approached the steps that their adversaries worked out later. Discussion of shogunal resignation and substitution of a council of great lords began in Edo quarters, found its way into Tosa councils by that route, and came to fruition in the Charter Oath's promise of "deliberative councils"; later it was integrated into Meiji political institutions. Military reforms found the bakufu, like its southwestern vassals, discover-

---

56 Totman, *Collapse*, p. 462.
57 Hopes and expectations of course changed dramatically with the intensification of political conflict and the revelation of bakufu incapacity during the 1860s. See Yoshio Sakata and John W. Hall, "The Motivation of Political Leadership in the Meiji Restoration," *Journal of Asian Studies* 16 (November 1956): 31–50; and Sakata Yoshio, *Meiji ishinshi* (Tokyo: Miraisha, 1960).

ing that samurai hauteur went poorly with the discipline and drill required for infantry companies and substituting, by steps, a personnel and then a money tax as basis for a conscription system that would displace the samurai altogether. The bakufu planners who worked this out were, like their adversaries from the southwestern *han*, of middle rank within their status hierarchy, *hatamoto* or petty daimyo who set about disestablishing their fellows. Needs of administrative retrenchment and rationalization produced programs for integrating the vassal domains nearest to the metropolitan centers, leading to rumors that a system of postfeudal, effective centralization was being prepared. The Meiji government, which used the Tokugawa lands as its own without parceling them out to daimyo after the civil war of 1868–9, kept them as the core for the centralization that was consummated by the return of feudal registers in 1869 and the establishment of prefectures in 1871. In brief, the pressures posed by opening and reconstruction revealed to friend and foe alike the impossibility of long continuing with the institutional structure of the *bakuhan* system and the need to replace it with the structure of a central state.

CHAPTER 6

OPPOSITION MOVEMENTS IN EARLY MEIJI, 1868–1885

Like all the great revolutions of the modern era, the Meiji Restoration generated intense opposition from groups and classes displaced and disadvantaged by revolutionary change. What sets the Meiji Restoration apart, however, is the apparent ease with which opposition to the revolutionary regime was defeated or co-opted. Peasant riots over the new conscription law, village protests against the land tax revision, revolts by disaffected samurai, early campaigns for representative government, and uprisings by dispossessed farmers all were contained or suppressed. The original leadership group stayed in charge and did not change its basic policies. Viewed positively, Japan enjoyed extraordinary continuity and stability in government; viewed negatively, conservative and bureaucratic politics prevailed.

Japanese and Western historians disagree sharply when explaining the failure of opposition movements to oust the ruling oligarchy or force changes in its agenda. Scholars in America and Great Britain influenced by modernization theory have generally viewed Japan as a model of peaceful transition from feudalism to modernity, a transformation in which core values of consensus and loyalty to emperor kept dissent within manageable bounds.[1] On the other hand, most Japanese and some Western historians credit the failure of the opposition movements to the authoritarian character of the Meiji state, emphasizing the incorporation of oppressive semifeudal structures into the Meiji polity and the oligarchy's control of the new state's efficient state security apparatus.[2]

Although there is some truth to both interpretations, neither of which is as simple as this summary might suggest, neither adequately explains the complex interaction between modernizing reforms and

[1] John W. Hall, "Changing Conceptions of the Modernization of Japan," in Marius B. Jansen, ed., *Changing Japanese Attitudes Toward Modernization* (Princeton, N.J.: Princeton University Press, 1965), pp. 7–41.
[2] E. Herbert Norman, *Japan's Emergence As a Modern State* (New York: Institute of Pacific Affairs, 1940); and Roger W. Bowen, *Rebellion and Democracy in Meiji Japan* (Berkeley and Los Angeles: University of California Press, 1980).

class interests, and neither takes into account the diverse nature of the social forces represented within the various opposition movements. The following analysis focuses on the social factors involved in political mobilization and the structures and conditions that restricted mass collective action.

EARLY RURAL PROTESTS

If the number of village protests and disturbances is a meaningful indicator of the degree of social unrest, rural Japan was anything but peaceful in the aftermath of the Meiji Restoration. According to Aoki Kōji's data, there were 343 incidents between 1868 and 1872.[3] Peasant protests, which had increased steadily at the end of Tokugawa, reached a historical peak of 110 in 1869. Beginning in 1870, however, the number of incidents declined rapidly, and in 1872 only 30 incidents were recorded.

What does this large number of rural disturbances signify? To put the data into perspective, nearly half of the incidents were local conflicts engendered by the malfeasance of village headmen, landlord–tenant relations, hoarding of rice, foreclosure of loans, and other issues that affected the popular welfare but did not directly involve the central government. Of the remainder, the most frequent cause was the land tax. It can be argued that in these protests, the peasants expressed their frustration that the overthrow of the Tokugawa bakufu had not brought relief from feudal levels of taxation. Shortly after the imperial coup d'état of January 1868, the new government, at the urging of Saigō Takamori, issued an edict promising tax reductions of up to 50 percent in territories belonging to the shogun. Subsequent edicts promised that the emperor would "alleviate the suffering of the people," and commoners were invited to petition the proper authorities in order to rectify the "evil practices" of the Tokugawa bakufu.[4] These early expressions of benevolent concern for the farmers' welfare were commendably Confucian and reflected a degree of genuine concern for the plight of poor peasants. The promise of tax reduction, however, was a deliberate strategy to foment rebellion in the shogun's home provinces and thereby weaken the bakufu's capacity to wage war. After the Tokugawa family and most vassal daimyo surrendered in the spring of 1868 without fighting a single battle, no more was said on the subject, for with victory assured, the new govern-

---

3 Aoki Kōji, *Meiji nōmin sōjō nenjiteki kenkyū* (Tokyo: Shinseisha, 1967), p. 36.
4 Ibid., pp. 15–16.

ment's most urgent need was to pay its bills. Meiji officials temporarily lowered taxes in districts where extraordinary conditions made relief unavoidable. In Aizu, for example, the war had disrupted farming and devastated crops, and farmers were granted reductions of 50 percent in that year's taxes.[5] Moreover, in areas that had experienced climate-related crop loss, officials accepted petitions for tax relief. Thus, the policy initially adopted by the Meiji government with respect to the land tax was to leave the feudal fiscal structure in place and permit traditional appeals for temporary aid.

If early Meiji tax officials were in fact behaving very much like their feudal predecessors, did protests over the land tax signify the farmers' discontent that things had not changed for the better? In some petitions, the villagers respectfully but forthrightly reproached the government for unfulfilled promises. A January 1869 petition from villages in the Chichibu district began by citing two years of destructive floods in requesting tax reductions and also commented on the government's failure to carry out a general tax reduction: "A benevolent order was issued at the time of the Restoration that the [tax] rate be made lower than last year's, but it was not carried out; in the end nothing more was heard of it."[6] However, the language, content, form, and sentiments of these petitions were identical to those of the peasant appeals of the Tokugawa era that asked for tax reductions when forces beyond their control drastically reduced harvests. Because of generally high rates of taxation under the *kokudaka* system, peasants farming small, subsistence-size holdings depended on daimyo benevolence to mitigate the effects of natural disasters, for without tax reductions and loans, many small farmers would be forced to mortgage their land or leave farming altogether. Realizing the daimyo's interest in retaining population and thereby protecting his tax base, the peasants frequently organized illegal "direct appeals" (*osso*) and staged large and raucous demonstrations (*gōso*) before the castle in the expectation that public embarrassment and fear of greater disorder would move the authorities to grant concessions.[7] Economic conditions in fact explain the large number of land tax–related protests in early Meiji. Beginning in 1867, Japan experienced three consecutive years of crop failure; by 1869, the peak year for disturbances, many rural districts were eco-

---

5 Shōji Kichinosuke, *Yonaoshi ikki no kenkyū* (Tokyo: Azekura shobō, 1970), pp. 319–22.
6 Aoki, *Meiji nōmin sōjō*, p. 17.
7 Especially in the early Tokugawa period when new land was being brought into cultivation, it was in the interest of the daimyo to provide sufficient aid and tax relief to keep peasants on the land. Stephen Vlastos, *Peasant Protests and Uprisings in Tokugawa Japan* (Berkeley and Los Angeles: University of California Press, 1986).

nomically exhausted, although famine was rare. We find the greatest concentration of protests in the districts of western Japan that had suffered the most severe crop losses, and in general the incidence of rural protests in early Meiji correlates with the timing and extent of crop failures.[8] Indistinguishable from the Tokugawa peasant movements in most respects, these protests did not indicate opposition to the Meiji Restoration.

Beginning in 1870, agriculture revived, and the number of protests and disturbances declined dramatically. However, during the first years of Meiji, farmers gained little from the change in government. Indeed, in some districts administered directly by the new regime, taxes had actually increased. When the government abolished feudal domains in 1871 and appointed governors to replace the daimyo, farmers sometimes protested. For example, in August 1871 villagers in Hiroshima tried to prevent the daimyo's entourage from leaving the domain. In September there were demonstrations in Takamatsu and Fukuyama, and in November over three thousand people gathered in Okayama to demand both the reinstatement of the former daimyo and lower taxes. However, in these and other demonstrations, the villagers linked their appeals for the return of their daimyo to the issue of taxation, much like the Tokugawa peasants who protested when the appointment of a new daimyo presaged higher taxes.[9] But their actions did not signify a preference for feudal administration as such.

The Conscription Act of January 10, 1873, gave rise to the most violent rural disturbances of this period. The law decreed compulsory military service of three years in the regular army and four in the reserves for commoners, thereby ending the long tradition of a hereditary (and privileged) warrior class. Many samurai were naturally displeased by the loss of an ancient birthright. But why did the farmers protest?

Most of the sixteen antidraft protests occurred in the spring and summer of 1873, soon after the law was made public.[10] Although the circumstances of each disturbance differed, the uprising in Misaka district illustrates their salient features. First, the villagers misunderstood the meaning of a passage in the edict and charge that "Western people call this a blood tax. This is because one protects his country verily with blood." The intended meaning of the wording of the edict, of course, was that the citizen soldier should be prepared to die in

---

8 Aoki, *Meiji nōmin sōjō*, pp. 39–40.
9 See Shōji Kichinosuke, *Tōhoku shohan hyakushō ikki no kenkyū: shiryō shūsei* (Tokyo: Ochanomizu shobō, 1969), pp. 186–8.   10 Aoki, *Meiji nōmin sōjō*, p. 38.

battle to defend his country. As one of the leaders of the Misaka riots testified, however, many believed that the army drained the blood of conscripts for sale to foreign countries. Even before publication of the conscription law, villagers in Misaka had become greatly agitated by recent edicts that either imposed additional financial burdens or offended local custom. They objected to the cost of compulsory education, the slaughtering of cows, the liberation of the outcaste communities, and new hair styles. When they first learned of the Conscription Act, the villagers discussed the possibility of voicing their concerns through traditional grievance procedures but concluded that petitions to officials in Tokyo would surely go unanswered. Suddenly rumors abounded that men dressed in white were coming to round up conscripts. Anxious farmers met and resolved to organize a demonstration. A few days later, amid new rumors of the imminent arrival of the "blood tax man," they convened a mass meeting at a local shrine at which the villagers also complained vociferously of the outrageously presumptuous behavior of former outcastes and demanded a return to old customs. According to a prearranged plan, someone reported having seen a man walking in the nearby mountains dressed in white and carrying a large glass bottle. Great commotion ensued, and those assembled were easily persuaded to march to the district magistrate's office. On the way, they attacked the homes and shops of wealthy farmers, moneylenders, and merchants; entering the town of Tsuyama, they surrounded the prefectural office. When officers appeared and attempted to quiet the crowd, farmers armed with hunting rifles and bamboo spears attacked, killing one official and injuring a second. As soon as the police fired back, the crowd scattered, but subsequently disturbances spread to every district in the prefecture, as crowds attacked schools, slaughterhouses, village headmen, outcaste communities, and government buildings.[11]

Ignorance and prejudice contributed to the Misaka "blood tax" riots and violent "antimodernization" protests triggered by laws that offended local customs and beliefs. If we look only at the immediate causes, we can dismiss such incidents as irrational reactions to modernization. Examined more closely, however, the demonstrations reveal a complexity of motivations and objectives. In Ikuno and Harima villages near the present-day city of Kobe, farmers first protested laws relating to outcastes but went on to demand tax reductions; next they drew up an eight-point list of grievances and vented their anger at the

---

11 Tanaka Akira, *Meiji ishin*, vol. 24 of *Nihon no rekishi* (Tokyo: Shogakkan, 1976), pp. 275–9.

government by destroying machinery at nearby state mines. Finally, they destroyed the property of wealthy commoners, especially moneylenders, merchants, and village officials. Thus one finds in these incidents a mingling of political and social grievances, for to some degree ordinary farmers harbored suspicions, which were not entirely groundless, that the new laws benefited the rich. Although the draft law contained a provision for hardship cases, poor farmers realized that the burden of conscription would fall most heavily on their shoulders. A wealthy farmer could buy exemption from military service for his sons by paying ¥270, a luxury that no ordinary farmer could possibly afford. But if a poor farm family lost a son's labor for three years, its very survival would be threatened.

These protests reveal understandable suspicions regarding laws that, it must be remembered, were promulgated by the central government without public discussion or consultation. To understand why poor farmers in Misaka called for a return to the old ways, we should recall that the Meiji Restoration did not bring popular participation in the political process. If anything, the centralization of authority made it more difficult for the villagers to influence the very policies that most affected them. With respect to the land tax, the most frequent cause of conflict, the Meiji state was infinitely better prepared to resist protest than was the bakufu or daimyo. Not infrequently, the peasants' protests in the Tokugawa period had succeeded in wringing concessions from lords, even though the leaders of illegal protests might be severely punished. However, the creation of an efficient national bureaucracy and modern police and army drastically undercut the efficacy of traditional forms of protest. In the case of the Misaka riots, the villagers considered petitioning the Tokyo government but decided that their appeals would be fruitless and so took matters into their own hands instead. Hence, the apparently irrational "blood tax" riots and related disturbances stemmed from the peasants' justified fears that political centralization had actually increased their powerlessness and vulnerability to the new government's arbitrary decisions.

THE MEIJI LAND TAX AND VILLAGE PROTESTS

After abolishing the feudal domains in 1871, the Meiji leadership grappled with the problem of how to reform the feudal land tax system to meet the demands of national development. The enormous financial costs of pensioning off the daimyo and samurai made their task all the more difficult. How the government persuaded daimyo to surrender peacefully their ancient rights and powers will be discussed in the next section. What concerns us here is the economic constraints on fiscal policy incurred by pensioning off the ruling class, for stipends and domain debts alone consumed most of the government's revenue in the early 1870s.[12]

There were few sources of additional revenue that the government was willing or able to tap. It rejected borrowing abroad because of the obvious perils to national security in case of subsequent default, and it was determined to tax commerce and industry as lightly as possible in order to speed capital formation. Meanwhile, the commercial treaties forced on Japan by the West had fixed tariffs at uniform low rates that limited the revenue from foreign trade.[13]

Although the leaders saw no alternative to maintaining the high taxes on agriculture, they could not afford to alienate the farmers' allegiance to the state. There was little reason to fear rural revolution. But even passive resistance in the form of withholding taxes would strain the treasury, and small, nonviolent protests always had the potential to escalate. Memories of *yonaoshi* (world rectification) and *uchikowashi* (urban smashing) uprisings that had erupted in the mid-1860s were still fresh. If the farmers violently protested the new tax, prefectural officials would be forced to mobilize ex-samurai bands to restore order. Unemployed retainers were only too willing to unsheathe their swords, but the central government judged the risks of unleashing them to be unacceptably high. Whatever the changes made in tax and property rights, the government needed the farmers' acquiescence.

The dilemma facing the Meiji government was how to ensure the farmers' cooperation with the new tax system without substantially reducing land tax revenues. Part of the solution involved eliminating feudal restrictions on landholding and legalizing capitalist relations of production, changes welcomed by most farmers and particularly beneficial to large landholders. In 1871 the government abolished the customary restrictions on land use. Early in 1872 it legalized the sale of private holdings and prohibited the daimyo and retainers from expropriating farmland in their former domains. Next, new land surveys were ordered, and certificates were issued. Finally, in July 1873 the government promulgated a law that fundamentally restructured the

---

12 Niwa Kunio, "Chiso kaisei to chitsuroku shobun," in *Iwanami kōza: Nihon rekishi*, vol. 15 (*kindai* 2) (Tokyo: Iwanami shoten, 1962), pp. 145–6.
13 The United States and the other major Western imperialist powers had forced the bakufu to sign commercial treaties that limited import and export duties to a flat rate of 5 percent.

land tax system while maintaining the old levels of taxation. It deserves closer scrutiny.

The Meiji land tax established uniform procedures for assessing taxes based on the market value of land as a fixed investment. The Tokugawa land tax had been based on estimates of productivity measured in output of rice, and both nominal and real rates of taxation varied considerably from fief to fief. However, the new tax was set at a uniform 3 percent of the monetary value of each parcel of land as determined by a complex formula that included estimates of land fertility, commodity prices, fixed production costs, and reasonable rate of return. The tax was paid in cash directly to the state by each owner; it was a fixed tax that initially made no provision for reduction in the event of natural calamities. In return, taxpayers were given title deeds that conferred full rights of ownership. No attempt was made to regulate landlord–tenant relations: Landlords were responsible for paying the yearly tax, after which they were free to charge whatever rents the market would bear.

Inasmuch as the 1873 revision of the land tax altered every feature of the old tax system, we should expect conflicts to have arisen. According to Arimoto Masao's data, there were ninety-nine rural protests between 1874 and 1881, the period during which the reform was carried out. Why did farmers protest, and how did they mobilize?

Initially, the most frequent complaint was not the tax rate itself but the way that the local tax commissions had determined land values and interim taxes. Often villages disputed the prices used to calculate the cash value of crops and to commute taxes previously collected in kind; for the lower the price, the lower the assessment. And because rice prices fluctuated from year to year and from one district to the next, some villages were likely to feel unfairly treated, especially if local soil, climate, and market conditions lowered the price of their crop.

One of the larger protests occurred in the Naka district of Wakayama Prefecture in 1876.[14] In February, Kodama Shōemon, the eldest son of the mayor of Nakayama village, petitioned the governor to complain that in commuting taxes formerly collected in kind, the tax commission had overcharged villages by assuming an unrealistically high rice price. Spurred by Shōemon's appeal, the mayors of twelve neighboring villages petitioned jointly and voiced the same complaint. When the governor responded by rejecting the petitions, Shōemon made yet another appeal in which he insisted that although the official

---

14 Arimoto Masao, *Chiso kaisei to nōmin tōsō* (Tokyo: Shinseisha, 1968), pp. 600–10; and Gotō Yasushi, "Chiso kaisei hantai ikki," *Ritsumeikan keizaigaku* 9 (April 1960): 109–52.

price accurately reflected conditions in other districts of Wakayama, the prices in his district were in fact considerably lower. Anticipating the objection that the procedures must be uniform, he lectured the governor on the proper function of laws: "Laws are made for the people, not people for laws."

At first, the villages disputed only the assessment of interim taxes, but they soon broadened their demands to include land values. As before, they insisted that the official rice price was too high and cited examples of more favorable treatment afforded by other tax commissions. In their petitions they also played on the fears of popular disturbances. Reminding the governor that the mayors stood "between the officials and the people," they warned of the hardship caused by the tax revisions, hardships so severe that "even the blind can stir up the people."[15]

Only after twenty-nine mayors and assistant officials had tendered their resignations did the governor attempt a compromise. He refused to accept the resignations and authorized a 5 percent reduction in the official price, about half of what the mayors had requested. However, instead of ending the protest, his actions stirred the hope of even greater concessions and swelled the ranks of the protesters. In April, 177 village officials jointly petitioned the governor to demand that prices be determined on a case-by-case basis according to the conditions in each district.

By contesting the use of uniform procedures, the protest threatened to cause interminable delay. As compromise had not produced a settlement, the governor now took a hard line. The mayors were summoned to a meeting and admonished; when they still objected, he fired them and arrested five ringleaders. Although the arrest of popular village officials provoked a large demonstration, within a few days the local authorities had restored order without resort to force. A company of infantry had been dispatched to Wakayama, but it was not necessary to deploy it in the countryside. Later large-scale arrests were made to set an example: Over 1,000 people were arrested, and 688 were convicted of encouraging public disturbances.

The protest of Wakayama was unusual in that most disputes that arose in conjunction with the tax law revision were resolved without fines or mass arrests. How, then, did the tax officials gain the consent of recalcitrant villagers, for the law required owners to agree to new assessments? The fate of the protests in Tottori suggests some of the answers.[16]

15 Arimoto, *Chiso kaisei*, p. 605.   16 Ibid., pp. 618–29.

In Tottori, more than twenty villages in the Yatsuhashi and Kume districts rejected the new tax assessments, and an equal number postponed making a decision. Hoping to quell the resistance before the revolt spread, the tax commission ordered representatives of the villages to the prefectural capital where they were subjected to intense pressure to give their consent. Most of the bullying was verbal, but one man reported being held ten hours a day in the back of the jail for eight consecutive days. Not surprisingly, some of the representatives gave in and agreed to the assessments; soon only seventeen holdouts remained. But then several villages that had previously consented reversed their decision and joined the protest. In December, thirty-six villages filed suit in the district court challenging the assessments, and the pendulum swung the other way. By February 1876, 112 villages were holding out. Again, the officials did their best and convinced eight powerful landlords to break ranks and sign individual consent orders. Because their holdings spanned many villages, the effect was to undermine resistance, especially by their tenants.[17] As a result, the number of holdouts had dropped in half by spring.

Opposition collapsed in July when the local tax commission invoked a recently adopted amendment to the land law that authorized binding on-site assessments as a last resort.[18] The commission appointed a committee of local notables to investigate conditions in the eight villages that had been at the forefront of the protest. To the surprise of no one, they reported that conditions in the villages did not warrant special consideration, a finding that gave ample warning of what to expect from on-site assessments. Soon after, most of the villages abandoned the protest. The reduction of assessments for seven of the remaining holdout villages ended all opposition. By December the tax commission reported to the main bureau in Tokyo that its work was done.

The largest number of protests occurred in the latter half of 1875 and 1876. Although revision of the land tax had begun in the spring of 1874, initially there were few protests, for in areas such as Hiroshima, Chikuma, and Yamaguchi local notables participated in the commissions, and the new assessments were generally lower than the old. However, in May 1875 a special agency was established in Tokyo to supervise the work of the local commissions and to speed implementa-

---

17 Almost half of all the land in the Yatsuhashi and Kume districts was tenant cultivated, and a few landlords controlled immense holdings. Their acceptance of the commission's assessments undermined resistance in all of the villages.

18 The law was amended in April 1876 to authorize assessments without consent when based on inspections carried out by the local commissions. Because the new assessments were generally lower than the old, in most cases it was necessary to invoke this provision.

tion. Thereafter, state interests tended to predominate.[19] Assessments were less generous to the farmers, for the commissions were given target quotas that, though not absolute, influenced their decisions. And to discourage villages from protesting, in May 1876 an amendment authorizing on-site inspections was adopted.

The tougher policy produced a sharp increase in protests. At the same time, however, samurai revolts erupted in southwestern Japan, and soon the government adopted a more conciliatory posture toward the farmers.[20] In January 1877, the land tax was lowered from 3 percent of market value to 2.5 percent, a reduction of 17 percent in the yearly tax. Later in the year, the law was further amended to permit reductions when crop loss due to natural disasters exceeded 50 percent. Finally, farmers in villages distant from marketing centers were allowed to pay part of their tax in produce.

The adoption of these measures was followed by a noticeable decline in protests, but it did not eliminate all resistance. The most stubbornly contested dispute over revised assessments occurred in the summer of 1878 in Ishikawa Prefecture.[21] Initially, 232 villages in seven districts refused to accept the newly published assessments, but as the prefectural commission applied pressure, resistance dwindled. In the 28 villages that continued to hold out, opposition was led by a group of very wealthy local notables who did not back down when the tax commission invoked the threat of on-site inspections, a tactic that had worked well against poor villages in Tottori. Rather, they borrowed the rhetoric of natural rights to justify their refusal to accept the new assessment, lecturing the authorities that "if liberty be our right, we will never accede to what is not just." To strengthen their hand, they sought outside support and made contact with the Risshisha, a liberal political society headed by Itagaki Taisuke that was campaigning for an elected national assembly and that sent Sugita Teiichi to help their movement. Experienced in legal matters, Sugita filed various suits on behalf of the villagers, and it is likely that the linking of the two movements caused the government considerable alarm.

Perhaps because the government feared the involvement of the Risshisha in land tax–related protests, the dispute was settled in Tokyo by Ōkuma Shigenobu, chief of the Finance Ministry, who ordered that the entire process be redone, starting with new surveys. When

---

19 Niwa Kunio, "Chiso kaisei," in Nihon rekishi gakkai, ed., *Nihonshi no mondai ten* (Tokyo: Yoshikawa kōbunkan, 1965), pp. 297–8.
20 Fukushima Masao, *Chiso kaisei* (Tokyo: Kyōbunkan, 1968), pp. 188–92.
21 Arimoto, *Chiso kaisei*, p. 631.

these were completed one year later, the result was not an unqualified victory for the landowners, for although the new assessments were substantially lower, the administrative costs charged to the villages amounted to more than twenty times the yearly savings in the land tax.[22]

What does this brief survey of resistance to land tax revision reveal? What can we conclude with respect to rural opposition to the Meiji land tax, an institution that fundamentally shaped the development of the Meiji state?

First, the revision of the land tax must be judged a political as well as an economic success. Given the magnitude of the changes and the interests involved, conflict was inevitable. It was naturally in the farmers' interest to seek lower assessments, although the government could not afford substantial reduction in revenue. In the light of these facts, the total number of protests was small: ninety-nine incidents between 1874 and 1881, of which thirty-seven were landlord–tenant conflicts and did not directly involve the state. Most of the disputes over assessments were eventually settled through negotiation and compromise without arrests or resort to armed force. In a handful of cases, the local officials were sufficiently alarmed to call in the national army and mobilize samurai bands. But compared to the "blood tax" uprisings, these were tame and orderly affairs.

The principal effect of the Meiji land tax was to equalize and rationalize tax assessments according to market value and thereby to eliminate the arbitrary factor in Tokugawa taxation. Under daimyo rule, the actual rates of tax extraction varied considerably depending on the rigor of fief administration; rice fields (*suiden*) were more heavily taxed than was unirrigated land (*hatake*), as was arable compared with residential and commercial land. By making the land tax fall more equally, Meiji tax assessments provided some relief to the majority of landholders.[23]

Not all classes of landholders benefited equally, however. The Meiji land tax caused special problems for the poor.[24] The tax had to be paid in cash, a provision that forced subsistence producers into greater

---

[22] The land tax is discussed in economic terms in Kozo Yamamura, "The Meiji Land Tax Reform and Its Effects," in Marius B. Jansen and Gilbert Rozman, eds., *Japan in Transition: From Tokugawa to Meiji* (Princeton, N.J.: Princeton University Press, 1986), pp. 382–99; and is described in James Nakamura, *Agricultural Production and the Economic Development of Japan 1873–1922* (Princeton, N.J.: Princeton University Press, 1966), pp. 177–96.
[23] Arimoto, *Chiso kaisei*, p. 637.
[24] Norman, *Japan's Emergence As a Modern State*, pp. 138–44.

dependence on the market and increased the risk of bankruptcy. Subsistence producers also lost the protection previously afforded by daimyo benevolence – the granting of tax reductions to mitigate the effects of crop failure. Farmers on the margins of the market economy had the greatest need of short-term aid, as they did not have the resources to withstand severe shortfalls. The Meiji land tax, however, initially allowed no exemptions at all and, when amended, permitted reductions only if the crop loss exceeded half of the harvest.

At the same time, the revised land tax system worked to the advantage of large farmers and especially landlords. The corporate features of the Tokugawa land tax were eliminated, as was payment in kind, and both of these changes gave capitalist farmers greater access to the market. Second, the feature of the Meiji land tax that caused the greatest hardship to poor farmers – the fact that taxes were held constant – proved highly profitable to those farmers who, through investment and technological innovation, boosted output and income, for taxes were not tied to profits. Of course, innovation and production for the market were not limited to the wealthy. Nevertheless, landlords and farmers with large holdings naturally reaped the greatest benefits of the decline of the land tax as a fixed cost of production. Third, as noted earlier, taxpayers were given full rights of ownership, even to the mortgaged land and paddy fields that tenants (or their ancestors) had brought into cultivation, and conditions of tenure would no longer confer customary right to permanent tenancy. Finally, landlords were legally free to sell land and renegotiate rents. Although the landlord who cared about social esteem was unlikely to put out all his holdings to the highest bidder, the courts and police – both vastly more efficient than were their feudal counterparts – would back him up if he did.

It is not surprising, therefore, that in the latter phase of land tax revision, and particularly after the general reduction ordered in 1877, the number of disputes between tenants and landlords increased. Between 1877 and 1881, twenty-nine of the forty-nine incidents recorded were landlord–tenant conflicts. The major issues of contention were rents and the customary rights of cultivators. The issue of rents was connected to the revised assessments because tenants expected reduced rents when taxes were lowered, but tended to resist rent increases if the tax had been increased. Customary rights were a more volatile issue. The best-known, and certainly the bloodiest, dispute over proprietary rights involved tenant farmers in Shindo village, Kanagawa Prefecture, who had mortgaged land "in perpetuity" – a

Tokugawa practice whereby the mortgagor retained use rights.[25] When the tax commission awarded title to the mortgage holder, a powerful landlord and village mayor, the tenants contested the ruling through the courts, persisting with appeal after appeal over a two-year period. Finally, after a direct but fruitless appeal to the Ministry of Finance, they attacked the landlord's house in frustration, killing him and seven of his relatives and servants. Despite the murders, it was the dispossessed cultivators who won the sympathy of local opinion. When they were brought to trial, fifteen hundred villagers signed a petition pleading for leniency.

Taken as a whole, village protests against land tax revision reveal the pivotal role of the local notable (gōnō) class of farmers in representing to the state the interests of the rural communities. With the exception of disputes between landlords and tenants, opposition to land tax revision was spearheaded by mayors and local notables. That they assumed this role is not surprising, for throughout the Tokugawa period, headmen had represented the village in all dealings with fief authorities. Under the Tokugawa tax system, taxes were assessed on the village rather than on individual householders, and it was the responsibility of the headman to see that they were paid. Legally responsible for all financial relations between the corporate village and the state, headmen were also perceived by the community to be, and themselves felt, morally responsible for safeguarding their communities' well-being. If landholders suffered crop failure or the lord increased taxes, it was the headman's duty to petition the authorities; if permissible appeals failed to achieve redress of grievance, the village head had a moral obligation to continue the petitioning process, even if this entailed breaking the law. Hence, we find the tradition of *gimin*, the extreme case of leaders who risked (or lost) their lives protesting onerous taxes and officials' malfeasance.[26]

To understand the political dynamic of village protest against land tax revision, we should remember that the headmen and notables had traditionally assumed responsibility in all matters involving the village's fiscal obligations and other financial dealing with the state.

---

25 Irokawa Daikichi, "Konmintō to Jiyūtō," *Rekishigaku kenkyū*, no. 247 (November 1960): pp. 5–6.
26 Irwin Scheiner, "Benevolent Lords and Honorable Peasants," in Tetsuo Najita and Irwin Scheiner, eds. *Japanese Thought in the Tokugawa Period* (Chicago: University of Chicago Press, 1979), pp. 39–62; and Anne Walthall, "Narratives of Peasant Uprisings in Japan," *Journal of Japanese Studies* 42 (May 1983): pp. 571–87. See also Yokoyama Toshio, *Hyakushō ikki to gimin denshō* (Tokyo: Kyōikusha rekishi shinsho, 1977).

Thus, mayors and notables acted out a familiar role when they participated in the implementation of land tax revision by overseeing the enormously elaborate and time-consuming work of surveying, grading, and registering the thousands of parcels of land in their communities. Although the Finance Ministry determined policy objectives, prefectural commissions necessarily relied on the cooperation of village heads and prominent citizens to supply the data used to calculate the new assessments. This gave heads and notables both power and responsibility to ensure a satisfactory outcome. Hence, most of the disputes between villages and local tax commissions involved issues that affected the interests of all farm households, regardless of the size of their holdings. The collective interests of villagers in lowering land evaluations and interim taxes permitted political mobilization within the tradition of Tokugawa village protests. As we saw in the conflicts in Wakayama, Tottori, and Ishikawa prefectures, when principled mayors and notables felt that the commissions had done them an injustice, these otherwise law-abiding citizens resisted stubbornly.

We can now analyze the political dynamic in village protests against land tax revision. First, responsibility for initiating protest rested with the village heads and local notables, and they acted only when the interests of all landholders were affected by the rulings of the tax commissions. The relatively small number of protests is therefore explained by the fact that the revised assessments, though higher than desired, were usually somewhat lower than the Tokugawa tax rates. Second, because high-status villagers assumed responsibility for representing the community's interests to the state and relied on petitions and legal process, the protests tended to be orderly and restrained. Generally, they did not mobilize the village poor – the most volatile and potentially most militant social class. With few exceptions, village protests against tax revision were settled through negotiation and compromise. Despite confrontation and the testing of wills, conflict occurred within the larger context of economic reforms that were welcomed by the majority of rural producers. One does not see villages protesting the principal provisions of the Meiji land tax, only specific rulings of the prefectural commissions. This limited the scope and intensity of the conflicts.

The real hardships caused by the Meiji land tax did not readily lead to collective action. The social classes affected most adversely – subsistence farmers forced into bankruptcy and cultivators dispossessed of customary rights – were relatively powerless. Because capitalist farmers profited from the system of unqualified ownership rights and fixed monetarized taxes, the village as a whole did not share a common interest in opposing these provisions of the Meiji tax. Moreover, the political obligations of the headmen and notables did not extend – or did so in only attenuated form – to hardship arising out of contractual and commercial relations; as landlords and moneylenders, they themselves might be party to such disputes. Thus the dispossessed were left to fend for themselves. Although *uchikowashi* and *yonaoshi* uprisings provided a model of collective action by the poor against both the rich villagers and the state, conditions favorable to the mass mobilization of small farmers did not materialize until the mid-1880s, well after the revision of the land tax had been completed.

SHIZOKU REVOLTS

In contrast with the generally peaceful and limited opposition movements of rural commoners during the first decade of Meiji, samurai opposition initially took the form of armed uprisings that sought to topple the government. The underlying cause of the rebellions was profound discontent and considerable economic distress within the former warrior class caused by early Meiji reforms that dismantled the feudal polity and all but abolished samurai elite status. To the extent that the rebellions expressed the frustration and resentment of former samurai, they represented the clearest and most forceful example of resistance to modernization in the early Meiji period. Viewed as the organized, political response of a dispossessed social class, the half-dozen *shizoku* rebellions between 1874 and 1877 can be explained as the predictably violent reaction of a traditional elite displaced by a modern revolution. There can be no doubt that materially and psychologically the samurai bore the major burden of rapid modernization; and because they were systematically disadvantaged by early Meiji reforms, they had an obvious interest in joining counterrevolutionary movements.

Nevertheless, important aspects of *shizoku* rebellion do not readily fit the mold of counterrevolution. The leaders of the rebellions were not defenders of the ancient regime, nor had they lost power and status as a result of the Meiji Restoration. Without exception, the rebellion leaders were young samurai from southwestern Japan who had early joined the anti-Tokugawa movement and continued to identify passionately with the imperial cause. Outstanding members of the revolutionary elite that seized power in 1868, they had been richly rewarded for their services. In fact, the leaders of the largest rebellions – Etō Shimpei, Maebara Issei and Saigō Takamori – all had served on the Council of State, the highest decision-making body, before breaking with the government. Before resigning in 1873 to protest the cancellation of the Korean invasion, Etō and Saigō supported, if somewhat grudgingly, sweeping reforms that all but ended feudalism and laid the foundations for subsequent modernization.

As we shall see, the *shizoku* rebellions were complex events that incorporated various political impulses. Insurrections led by disaffected leaders, they reflected personality conflicts and bureaucratic rivalry within the ruling elite; local protests against the increasing power and assertiveness of the government in Tokyo, they expressed sectional opposition to political centralization. Nevertheless, at least among the rank and file, the underlying impetus to armed resistance was the opposition to the loss of traditional warrior status and class privilege. Whatever the motivation of individual leaders, the social basis of antigovernment *shizoku* ferment in the mid-1870s was resistance to early Meiji reforms that, by dismantling the feudal polity and building a modern army and a centralized state bureaucracy, eliminated samurai class privilege.

The young samurai who came to power in 1868 had experienced the frustration of subordinate rank in feudal society, and they quickly ended the social distinctions based on hereditary status.[27] Having come to the realization that the traditional status system was an obstacle to national unity, they dismantled it one step at a time. Beginning in 1869, the government ordered the profusion of hereditary ranks within the samurai class reduced to two, *shizoku* (knight) and *sotsu* (foot soldier), and ended the archaic division of commoners into status groups – peasant, merchant, and artisan – based on occupation. Two years later, it freed outcaste communities from legal prescriptions that had enforced strict segregation. All commoners were required to adopt surnames and were informed that public acts of deference toward samurai, such as prostration, were no longer necessary or desirable. Samurai, on the other hand, were told that they need not wear swords in public, an oblique request that they abandon their swaggering ways of old. For the first time, warriors were authorized to take up farming, industry, and trade and were offered capital for starting new enterprises if they gave up their hereditary stipends. Samurai were also advised to cut off their topknots and adopt Western headdress, and

---

27 Some of the leaders of the *sonnō jōi* movement were discontented with the Tokugawa class system and ideologically committed to a meritocracy. See Thomas M. Huber, *The Revolutionary Origins of Modern Japan* (Stanford, Calif.: Stanford University Press, 1981).

soon Western-style clothing was encouraged – indeed required of certain government officials, as a final step toward eliminating the visible marks of traditional status.

The abolition of the feudal domains in 1871 accelerated the decline of the warrior class. Overnight, the samurai lost their traditional perquisites as retainers and sinecures as soldiers, functionaries, and administrators. The most dramatic and far-reaching of the early Meiji reforms, the transformation of the polity from feudalism to centralized nation-state did not so much spring from a social critique of feudalism as from a concern for national strength. The Meiji leaders realized that the Tokugawa political order, based on parcelized sovereignty, was fundamentally incompatible with the political and military mobilization required to preserve Japan's independence in the world of nineteenth-century imperialism. Kido Takayoshi, who among Restoration leaders was the most conscious of Japan's precarious international position and need to "hold its own in the world," early advocated greater centralization of state power and soon convinced Ōkubo Toshimichi of Satsuma and Itagaki Taisuke of Tosa. The central government was still too weak to compel the daimyo to give up power, but Kido, Ōkubo, and Itagaki persuaded the lords of their respective domains – who were moved as much by traditional rivalry as by patriotic duty – to surrender voluntarily their *han* registers, symbols of daimyo authority, to the emperor. As other daimyo followed their example, they were appointed "governors" and granted one-tenth of fief revenue as personal income, and the Tokyo government paid all the administrative costs. If anything, the daimyo were probably better off financially, and outwardly their power had not diminished drastically.[28]

Nevertheless, not all diamyo agreed to give up their hereditary rights and privileges, and the government waited two years before compelling compliance. In the meantime, Chōshū, Satsuma, and Tosa combined forces to create the embryo of a national army, the ten-thousand-strong Imperial Guard subject to the sole authority of the Tokyo government. With an army at their command, the Meiji leaders felt sufficiently secure to abolish the fiefs entirely. In August 1871, the emperor issued an edict that proclaimed the end of daimyo rule. Daimyo were offered various inducements: appointment as governors of their former domains, generous pensions, state assumption of fief debts, and, in time, titles of nobility in a new peerage. Later in 1871, the government eliminated the last vestiges of daimyo administration.

28 W. G. Beasley, *The Meiji Restoration* (Stanford, Calif.: Stanford University Press, 1972), pp. 335–49.

Daimyo were ordered to take up permanent residence in Tokyo; fief armies were disbanded; and many local officials were dismissed. Governors appointed by the Home Ministry, who were often outsiders and protégés of leading ministers, now administered the countryside.

Even a cursory account of the process by which the Tokugawa feudal polity was abolished suggests some of the reasons for the slow development of counterrevolution in the Meiji period. First, the daimyo class, which had little capacity for collective action, was divided vertically along traditional sectional lines as large southwestern fiefs, whose clansmen dominated the national government, were played off against one another, and then against the more numerous, but smaller, fiefs of eastern and northeastern Japan. Second, and more importantly, the preferential treatment of the elite ranks divided the warrior class horizontally, thereby vitiating the *kashindan* – hierarchically organized corps of retainers – as a vehicle of antigovernment mobilization. Daimyo and fief elders received lavish pensions, in addition to ranks and titles, and possessed a strong material incentive to accept the loss of traditional status without protest. On the other hand, the pensions of most samurai were less than subsistence livings, and even these were commuted to interest-bearing bonds in 1876. Thus, nonelite samurai had every reason to resist, but without the sanction of the domain leaders they could not use the existing (feudal) structures of collective action. Before the samurai could act in defense of their traditional rights as warriors, they would have to find a new basis for collective action.

If *shizoku* privilege was to be preserved, the new national army was the logical place. A minority within the leadership clung to the feudal ruling class conceit that as the inheritors of a thousand years of military service, the samurai were uniquely endowed with the requisite martial virtues – courage, loyalty, and honor. Maebara Issei wanted the army to be entirely *shizoku*. Kirino Toshiaki and Shinohara Kunimoto, Saigō's chief lieutenants and commanders of the Imperial Guard, violently opposed the induction of commoners and resisted all attempts to integrate conscripts into their force. Others saw the drafting of unemployed *shizoku* as a solution to a pressing social problem. Torio Koyata, a general from Chōshū, proposed that 20 percent of the revenue be set aside to create a standing army and national reserve large enough to enlist all *shizoku* between the ages of twenty and forty-five. Tani Kanjō of Tosa advocated first conscripting the sons of *shizoku* and, only later, after all able-bodied *shizoku* had been inducted, opening recruitment to commoners.[29] However, majority opin-

---

29 Masumi Junnosuke, *Nihon seitō shi ron* (Tokyo: Tokyo daigaku shuppankai, 1965), vol. 1, p. 113.

ion within the oligarchy supported universal conscription – in part because it was the system used in the West but mainly because of its intrinsic merits. Yamagata Aritomo, who succeeded Maebara Issei as head of the army, foresaw that samurai virtues were a mixed blessing in a modern army. *Shizoku* might well be fierce and brave fighters, but they were also likely to be fractious, undisciplined, and more loyal to their clansmen than to the central government. High regard for ascriptive status and particularistic loyalties were as much as part of *bushidō* as was unflinching courage. Yamagata correctly anticipated that the first task of the national army would be to suppress internal revolts and reasoned that among the *shizoku*, their strong emotional identification with fief and clansmen impaired unity.[30] Even as soldiers of the imperial army, the *shizoku* might act and think in terms of old loyalties.

Promulgated on January 10, 1873, the Conscription Act made all twenty-year-old males liable for seven years of military service – three in the regular army and four in the reserves – and required men between the ages of seventeen and forty-five to register for possible call-up. The immediate aim was to create a truly national army loyal to the central government and suited to the highly regimented military system recently adopted from the West, but the adoption of universal conscription widened the distance between conservatives who insisted that the *shizoku* remain the military and political elite and those who viewed ascriptive status as being incompatible with modern national development.

Saigō Takamori was the leading conservative in the Meiji government. In 1871 he submitted two memorials outlining a model of economic and political development very different from the "iron and coal" model favored by the majority of the oligarchs. The first memorial advocated not only the adoption of Shinto as the state religion but also the proscription of Buddhism and Christianity; a national tax on agriculture based on the feudal norm of half to the lord and half to the people; and a tax on manufacturing to pay in full all warrior stipends under 100 *koku*. The second memorial proposed specific measures to revitalize the rural economy: hiring foreign experts; appointing especially diligent farmers as headmen to instruct villagers in the virtues of filial piety, frugality, obedience, and sincerity; setting up agricultural research stations; selecting the best technologies of traditional farm practices and Western agronomy; invest-

---

30 Roger Hackett, *Yamagata Aritomo in the Rise of Modern Japan, 1838–1922* (Cambridge, Mass.: Harvard University Press, 1971), p. 61.

ing public funds in irrigation and flood control; and providing credit to individual farmers.[31]

Whatever the merits of specific proposals aimed at improving agriculture, Saigō's conception of political economy was thoroughly traditional. The 50 percent land tax he proposed would impoverish all but the richest farmers and inhibit investment and growth. Instead of promoting industrialization, the manufacturing sector would be heavily taxed to support the socially unproductive *shizoku*. In later proposals, Saigō came to support and even advocate reduction in the level of *shizoku* support, but there remained little common ground between his thought and the "iron and coal" school of modernization.

The issue that split the original leadership group ostensibly involved foreign relations rather than domestic policy. When Korea refused to open diplomatic and trade relations with Japan, Saigō proposed a venture in gunboat diplomacy that he secretly hoped would lead to war and the immediate mobilization of unemployed samurai.[32] He was supported by Itagaki Taisuke and Gotō Shōjirō of Tosa and Etō Shimpei and Soejima Taneomi of Hizen, who agreed that Japan should invade Korea and impose diplomatic and trade relations, as the West had done to Japan fifteen years earlier. However, Iwakura Tomomi, Ōkubo Toshimichi, and Kido Takayoshi, who had recently returned from an extended tour of the United States and Europe, argued forcefully against Saigō's plan. They did not object on grounds of principle: They agreed that it was Japan's destiny to rule the backward nations of Asia, if only to protect them from the predatory West. But they realized that despite the abolition of feudal political institutions, Japan remained weak and vulnerable compared with the countries that the Iwakura mission had visited between 1871 and 1873. The possibility of Chinese or Russian intervention if Japan invaded Korea raised the stakes considerably, for the costs of fighting a prolonged war would jeopardize the development of the very institutions on which Japan's future as a major power depended. Although initially outvoted, the "peace" party managed to reverse the vote in the Council of State in October after Iwakura was appointed chairman. With his group now in the majority, Iwakura reintroduced Saigō's plan, which, of course, was voted down; and despite vehement protests from the war party, he immediately presented the results to the emperor. Humiliated and outraged by tactics that violated the spirit, if

---

31 Gotō Yasushi, *Shizoku hanran no kenkyū* (Tokyo: Aoki shoten, 1967), p. 28.
32 Saigō volunteered to head an uninvited diplomatic mission to Korea, fully expecting to be attacked and very possibly killed, thereby precipitating war.

not also the letter, of collective rule, Saigō, Itagaki, Gotō, Etō, and Soejima resigned from the Council of State and left Tokyo. So did many of their followers in the bureaucracy and army.

Underlying the debate over policy toward Korea was the acute social crisis confronting the *shizoku* class. Even though the pensions paid to the *shizoku* provided less than a subsistence living, they drained the treasury of revenue needed to finance national development.[33] Clearly, the government could not live indefinitely with this arrangement; in 1873, before the debate over Korea, the Finance Ministry had introduced a plan for the voluntary conversion of pensions into lump-sum payments in interest-bearing bonds. Ideally, the *shizoku* would invest in farming, trade, or manufacture and thereby enhance economic development while freeing tax revenues for public investment. But relatively few *shizoku* accepted the offer, and of those who did, many soon lost all their money. As their economic situation deteriorated, they became increasingly alienated and restive. Saigō had earlier written to Ōkubo, who was in London with Iwakura, that he felt as though he was "sleeping on a powder keg," because of the dissatisfaction of the Satsuma men in the Imperial Guard. Perhaps he exaggerated; nevertheless, the prospect of immediate employment and the excitement and adventure of war seemed to offer a temporary solution. The army had only just begun to conscript commoners, and the *shizoku* constituted the only segment of the population with military training. In addition to providing immediate employment and salary, mobilization for war promised to resuscitate traditional martial values and to restore the *shizoku* to a position of honor and respect. War might also strengthen the hand of Saigō and Itagaki, the "old soldiers," against the professional bureaucrats.

Of the six councilors who resigned in the fall of 1873, all but Soejima ended up leading antigovernment movements. In January 1874, Itagaki and Gotō submitted a memorial to the emperor (Etō and Soejima also signed) asking the throne to establish an elected national assembly. Rebuffed, they returned to Tosa and began a national campaign for constitutional government. Saigō immediately sailed for Kagoshima. Renouncing all political involvement, he retired to the Satsuma countryside. Although three years later he would lead the greatest of all *shizoku* revolts, the 1877 Satsuma Rebellion, his first inclination was to withdraw entirely from politics.

After resigning from the Council of State, Etō Shimpei returned to

---

33 Masumi, *Nihon seitō*, p. 124.

Saga where he led the first major rebellion against the Meiji state. By birth a lower-ranking Hizen samurai, Etō had defied the orders of his daimyo while still a young man to leave Saga to join the ranks of activists leading the loyalist cause against the Tokugawa shogunate. He rose steadily within revolutionary circles, even though as a native of Hizen, he was something of an outsider. Appointed to the Council of State in 1873, Etō also held key posts in the ministries of Education and Justice. During his tenure as chief of the Ministry of Justice, he oversaw work on legal codes that laid the foundation of the Meiji legal system. He was personally responsible for several humanitarian reforms: outlawing the sale of women into prostitution and putting restrictions on contracts of indentured laborers.[34] However, he advocated an aggressive foreign policy in the belief that only forceful demonstration of Japan's military power would end extraterritoriality. Convinced that Japan's failure to chastise Korea would be interpreted as a sign of weakness, Etō sided with the war party.

The decisive factor in Etō's move from opposition to rebellion was his involvement with the Seikantō (Attack Korea Party), one of two *shizoku* groups in Hizen openly critical of the Tokyo government. The larger group, the Yūkokutō (Party of Patriots), was headed by Shima Yoshitake. Shima was also a veteran Restoration activist, revolutionary, and after the defeat of the bakufu he initially held several middle-ranking posts in the Meiji government. Unlike Etō, however, he lacked the skills and temperament to be a successful bureaucrat. He was also violently opposed to reforms that smacked of Westernization. The political program of the Yūkokutō was xenophobic and reactionary. In addition to restoring fiefs and warrior rule, the party advocated the proscription of Christianity to prevent contamination of the national gods, the revival of traditional martial arts as part of a program of moral self-strengthening, and a massive military buildup. The Seikantō, on the other hand, focused its criticism of the government entirely on foreign policy. It was made up mainly of young *shizoku* who hoped to escape poverty and tedium by enlisting for the war with Korea; they were sufficiently desperate to resolve to carry out an invasion on their own, even without government authorization. Meeting for the first time in December 1873, the society enrolled more than one thousand members. Soon after it sent a delegation to Tokyo to confer with Etō, who agreed to assume leadership.

It is by no means certain that Etō returned to Hizen with the intent

---

34 Sonoda Hiyoshi, *Etō Shimpei to Saga no ran* (Tokyo: Shin jimbutsu ōraisha, 1978), pp. 89–92.

of leading a rebellion. Rather, the government, alarmed by reports of an imminent uprising in Saga, forced his hand by sending an expeditionary force into the prefecture. Previously, the Yūkokutō disdained any association with the Seikantō, but its members too felt compelled to resist the entry of government troops. Ironically, Shima had gone back to Saga at the express request of Iwakura to forestall rash action by his compatriots when he learned en route that the government had already sent a force to occupy the prefectural capital. Meeting at Nagasaki on February 12, Shima and Etō agreed to organize armed resistance, even though they realized that they faced certain defeat. Etō had already received word of Saigō's refusal to join forces, and without Saigō, it was hopeless to expect the support of Itagaki and the Tosa faction. Although a rebellion limited to Saga could not possibly succeed, Etō decided the issue by exclaiming that because the government had already ordered troops into Saga, "we have reached that point where there is no room for discussion. Rather than die with hands at our sides, isn't it better to seize the initiative?"[35]

Two days later the Seikantō set up headquarters at a temple five miles north of Saga. There was little consultation with the Yūkokutō, which had commenced its own preparations. The rebellion started by chance at dawn on February 16 when a party of Yūkokutō warriors exchanged fire with sentries posted by the vanguard of the government force that had entered the city a few hours earlier. A successful attack on the army garrison followed, but this was the only rebel victory. Three days later the main body of the expeditionary force led by Ōkubo in person linked up with the garrison troops, which had managed an orderly retreat. The Imperial army counterattacked and quickly gained the upper hand. In addition to more than five thousand soldiers from the standing army, the government had enlisted an equal number of *shizoku* volunteers from neighboring prefectures who were more than willing to aid in the suppression of the rebellion. Regional and class loyalties helped the Saga rebels not at all. In fact, at least several hundred Saga *shizoku* led by Maeyama Ichirō turned against their clansmen and joined the government forces.[36]

The revolt lasted less than two weeks. Faced with certain defeat, the rebel soldiers surrendered or deserted after the first pitched battle. Etō and his lieutenants fled to Kagoshima where they made a final appeal to Saigō. They went on to Tosa where they were tracked down and returned to Saga, brought to trial, and summarily executed. Punish-

35 Ibid., p. 154.   36 Ibid., p. 157.

ment of the rank and file of the rebel force was relatively lenient. Of the several thousand who took up arms, about one hundred were given sentences ranging from three to ten years.

Two and a half years elapsed between the Saga rebellion and the next major *shizoku* insurrection, the Shimpūren uprising. That the Saga rebellion was not the last attempt by the *shizoku* to overthrow the Meiji government should not surprise us. During the intervening years the position of *shizoku* had become increasingly insecure financially and psychologically as the government pushed ahead with policies that eliminated the last vestiges of warrior privilege. Moreover, Western culture and customs were spreading beyond the treaty ports and largest cities to the provincial towns and even villages. The expansion of diplomatic relations with the West caused great displeasure to nativists for whom the pre-1868 revolutionary slogans, "revere the emperor" and "expel the barbarian" were not separable. At the same time the central bureaucracy, now dominated by Chōshū and Satsuma men, asserted itself in more conspicuous and decisive ways in local affairs. Thus, a variety of factors fed *shizoku* discontent in the mid-1870s.

The leaders of the Shimpūren were lower-ranking samurai in Kumamoto who had joined the movement to overthrow the bakufu but remained passionately committed to Shinto nativism. Their mentor, Hayashi Ōen, was a Shinto priest and scholar who had advocated resisting all demands from the West to enter into trade and diplomatic relations, whatever the short-term consequences. Like many loyalists in the *bakumatsu* period, he acknowledged Japan's military inferiority and foresaw initial defeat but held that defeat would prove salutary: Samurai of all ranks would unite in the traditions of old, and fierce resistance would make occupying Japan too difficult and costly for distant invaders to maintain for long. Having expelled the West, Japan could then freely decide the terms on which it would relate to the outside world.[37]

Hayashi died shortly after the Meiji Restoration, but his disciples founded a nativist political society in Kumamoto and remained true to his teachings. Many were Shinto priests who vehemently opposed Westernization and denounced diplomatic relations with the West as dangerous, offensive, and cowardly. They were especially aroused by the arrival in Kumamoto of a young American, Leroy L. Janes, the first teacher at the newly established foreign school. Janes was a dy-

[37] Araki Seishi, *Shimpūren jikki* (Tokyo: Daiichi shuppan kyōkai, 1971), p. 123.

namic and popular teacher and impressed many of his students with the virtues of Christianity. Not only staunch conservatives were shocked when in January 1876, thirty-five of Janes's pupils publicly swore an oath to "enlighten the darkness of the empire by preaching the gospel," if necessary at the sacrifice of their lives.[38]

In mid-1876 the government eliminated the last privileges and vestiges of warrior elite status. First, the commutation of *shizoku* pensions with bonds was made compulsory; in March the wearing of swords in public was prohibited, and in June schoolchildren were required to cut off their topknots and wear their hair short in the Western fashion.

For the Shimpūren the provisions outlawing swords provided the final impetus for rebellion. The sword was the very soul of the samurai, they declared, and carrying two swords was a sacred national custom without which life was not worth living. Recent government policies threatened to destroy Japan's unique polity, but if they rose up in the spirit of righteousness, brave and loyal warriors would rally from all sides. Even if the revolt failed and all perished, this was their destiny. After consulting an oracle and receiving an affirmative response, they began active preparations that initially included efforts to coordinate their rising with insurrections in neighboring prefectures. Shimpūren leaders met with Miyazaki Kurunosuke of Akitsuki and with leaders of bands of disaffected *shizoku* in Saga, Fukuoka, Tsuruzaki, and Shimabara. In Chōshū they made contact with Maebara Issei, a former leader of the Chōshū *shishi* movement who had left the government in the early 1870s. These efforts met with some success as both Miyazaki and Maebara promised support.

However, the Shimpūren leadership placed more faith in the wisdom of gods than in the benefits of acting in concert. After again consulting the oracles, they advanced the date of their uprising to October 24, which did not give their confederates in Akitsuki and Chōshū sufficient time to complete their preparations. They also refused to use rifles in the assault on the army garrison because firearms were of foreign origin. Nor did they enlist the support of the Gakkōtō, a rival conservative *shizoku* party in Kumamoto equally committed to overthrowing the Tokyo government. As a result, the uprising proved to be little more than a suicidal insurrection. Striking without warning, they succeeded in killing the commanding officers of the Kumamoto garrison and mortally wounding the prefectural governor. But vastly outnumbered and outgunned, they were quickly defeated, with

[38] F. G. Notehelfer, *American Samurai: Captain L. L. Janes and Japan* (Princeton, N.J.: Princeton University Press, 1985).

most members committing *seppuku* to avoid capture. The Akitsuki and Hagi uprisings were also quickly suppressed.

The last *shizoku* revolt, the 1877 Satsuma Rebellion, was by far the greatest. Unlike the minor insurrections that preceded it, the Satsuma Rebellion is rightly considered a civil war.[39] Commanded by Saigō Takamori, the Satsuma army fought unrelentingly for seven months. Although confined to the southern half of Kyushu, the scale and intensity of combat were far greater than in the Restoration wars. Defeat proved to be decisive, for the annihilation of the Satsuma army extinguished the threat of counterrevolution in the foreseeable future.

The leader of the "war party" in the debate over relations with Korea, Saigō had resigned from the Council of State and given up his commission as supreme commander of the armed forces immediately after his proposal for armed intervention was defeated. Enraged by the tactics employed by Iwakura and Ōkubo, Saigō realized that in the near future he would have little power to influence policy. If he remained in the government, his principal role would be the unrewarding and morally distasteful task of reconciling former comrades at arms in the army and bureaucracy to policies that further undercut the position of the *shizoku* class.[40] Saigō was disgusted by the pretentiousness, venality, and vanity of many of his colleagues. He had publicly insulted Inoue Kaoru, Kido Takayoshi's protégé, over his unsavory connections with the business world, and his relations with Yamagata, whom he respected, had recently become strained owing to the Yamashiroya incident.[41]

After resigning, Saigō insisted that he wanted nothing more to do with politics and refused to support either Etō's revolt or Itagaki's campaign for an elected national assembly. However, whatever his initial intentions may have been, the possibility of his living out his life as a gentleman farmer was greatly diminished by the actions of his followers. As soon as Saigō's break with the government became known, a large contingent of officers and soldiers from the Imperial Guard picked up their weapons and followed him back to Kagoshima. Soon they were joined by more than three hundred clansmen from the newly formed national police, who, like the guards, pointedly ignored appeals from the emperor not to desert. Together they formed the

---

39 Japanese historians use the term *seinan sensō* (southwestern war) rather than Satsuma Rebellion.   40 Masumi, *Nihon seitō*, p. 116.
41 Hackett, *Yamagata*, p. 71. Yamashiroya, a military supplier that Yamagata had trusted and favored, had embezzled funds.

nucleus of a potential rebel army; the only question was what Saigō would do.[42]

Saigō had not encouraged his followers to defect and may have been, as some argue, more dismayed than pleased by their actions. Nevertheless, six months after returning to Satsuma, he established a system of "private schools" (*shigakkō*) which closely resembled military academies. The success of the *shigakkō* was due in no small part to Saigō's patronage: He provided funds for the schools from the large salary he still collected from the government; his popularity among the Satsuma *shizoku* had only been enhanced by the circumstances surrounding his break with the government; and his status as a "founding father" of the Meiji Restoration contributed to the schools' prestige. Equally important was the support of the *shigakkō* system provided by local government officials. Governor Ōyama Tsunayoshi, a close friend of Saigō, used prefectural funds to pay the salaries of the schools' staff and to provide rations to students, and he even purchased guns and ammunition which were distributed throughout the *shigakkō* system. The directors of the schools served under Ōyama in the prefectural administration, and many graduates of the schools were appointed to positions in the lower ranks of the provincial bureaucracy. Before long the entire administrative apparatus of Satsuma was staffed by *shigakkō* people or by senior officials like Governor Ōyama who were in complete sympathy with the antigovernment movement.[43]

As the line separating public and private institutions became increasingly blurred, the authority of the central government in Kagoshima all but disappeared. Satsuma officials openly criticized, and even disobeyed, the policies and directives of the central government. Governor Ōyama ignored instructions from the Finance Ministry to pay the *shizoku* stipends in cash rather than rice, and he refused to impose a surtax on *shizoku* income. Opposed to universal primary education and the progressive features of the Meiji land tax, he refused to implement either law. But most egregious was the use of the *shigakkō* to recruit, equip, and train an army hostile to the central government. The first academies established in Kagoshima were known as the "infantry" and "artillery" schools; the teachers and most of the students were former officers and soldiers of the Imperial Guard. The curriculum included academic subjects such as the study of Chinese

---

42 Tamamuro Taijō, *Seinan sensō* (Tokyo: Shibundo, 1958), p. 11. See also Charles L. Yates, "Restoration and Rebellion in Satsuma: The Life of Saigō Takamori (1827–1877)," Ph.D. diss., Princeton University, 1987.   43 Tamamuro, pp. 29–39.

classics, but the daily regime stressed physical fitness, military tactics, drill, and troop maneuvers conducted on land donated by the prefecture. By 1876, branch schools had been set up in every district to enroll *gōshi*, rural samurai. For military-age males, attendance became practically compulsory.[44]

Nearly one-quarter of the population of Satsuma were *shizoku* who provided a very large pool of potential recruits to the antigovernment movement. The extraordinarily large proportion of the population in Satsuma that claimed samurai status was due to the fief's policy of including *gōshi*, "rustic warriors," within the warrior class.[45] In most fiefs the *gōshi* had lost their warrior status at the beginning of the Tokugawa period and were assimilated into the wealthy farmer (*gōnō*) class. However, the Satsuma *gōshi* were accorded elite status and continued to think and act as warriors. They served the fief as rural administrators – district magistrates, policemen, and, most commonly, village headmen. *Gōshi* headmen governed hamlets of up to twenty households and lorded over the peasants like the estate managers of the medieval period. Elsewhere in Japan during the Tokugawa period, villages enjoyed considerable autonomy, and peasants acquired de facto proprietary rights to the land they cultivated. However, in Satsuma, the *gōshi* headmen strictly supervised the village economy and treated the peasants like tenant farmers. They had the authority to assign land to individual cultivators and adjusted the tax rate from year to year to take from the peasants all but what was needed for subsistence.[46]

Meiji reforms struck at the very heart of *gōshi* privilege. Like castle town samurai, they were accustomed to thinking of themselves as an elite, superior in status, if not always in wealth, to commoners. And as the lowest-ranking status group within the warrior class, they perhaps felt even more keenly the loss of the symbols of elite status, such as the right to bear arms. More concretely, the 1873 land tax revision threatened their socioeconomic power in the village. By conferring ownership rights on peasant farmers and taxing individual proprietors, the Meiji land tax eliminated the feudal role of the Satsuma *gōshi* as petty overlords. Not surprisingly, they flocked to the *shigakkō* once branch schools were established outside the city and later joined the rebel army in large numbers.

44 Masumi, *Nihon seitō*, p. 156.
45 Elsewhere, samurai numbered 5 or, at most, 10 percent of the population.
46 Tamamuro, *Seinan*, pp. 18–20; and Robert K. Sakai, "Feudal Society and Modern Leadership in Satsuma-han," *Journal of Asian Studies* 16 (May 1957): 365–76.

The government did not attempt to counter the *shigakkō* movement until late 1876, in part because it remained ignorant of the actual state of affairs. Prefectural officials, who would normally inform Tokyo of antigovernment activity, were in complete sympathy with the movement; they remained silent and, if questioned, denied that there was any cause for alarm. Furthermore, Ōkubo and the other Satsuma men in the oligarchy did not want to believe that Saigō and their clansmen in Kagoshima were capable of sedition. As late as November 1876, Ōkubo argued that Saigō's refusal to support the Shimpūren, Akitsuki, and Hagi uprisings was sufficient proof of his loyalty and honor and held that as long as Saigō remained in command, Satsuma would never rebel. Events soon proved Ōkubo wrong, but he was not entirely mistaken in his estimation of Saigō's character, for Saigō authorized rebellion only after the actions of government agents forced his hand.

Late in 1876, the government sent police spies into Kagoshima to infiltrate the *shigakkō*. It appears that their mission was to gather intelligence, foment dissention, and in other ways undermine the movement. A few weeks after arriving in Satsuma, the spies were exposed and apprehended. Under torture, one agent confessed that he had been sent to assassinate Saigō. The only evidence was his confession, but the officers and many of the students of the *shigakkō* desperately wanted an excuse to go to war, and Saigō appears to have believed the facts as reported to him.

Because of the increasingly tense situation in Satsuma, the government next tried to remove munitions stored at the Kagoshima arsenal. Although a commercial steamship and civilian crew were employed to disguise the operation, *shigakkō* students soon discovered what was going on. Without Saigō's knowledge, they broke into the arsenal and began carting off guns and powder. The local police did not try to stop them; emboldened, the students went one step further and forcibly prevented the ship's crew from loading cargo. The captain immediately set sail and, upon reaching Kobe, telegraphed the news to Tokyo.

Although angered by the students' rash action, upon learning of the raid on the arsenal, Saigō met with his lieutenants and authorized preparations for war. His intention was to topple the ruling oligarchy headed by Ōkubo. Believing that opposition to the oligarchy was sufficiently great to realize this goal with a minimum of force, he tried with vague public announcements to maintain the appearance of legality. On February 9, Saigō, Shinohara, and Kirino formally notified Governor Ōyama that they would "shortly leave the prefecture," taking with them "a number of former troops." Ōyama obliged by announcing that Saigō was proceeding to Tokyo in order to investigate the plot against his life, that a large force of former government troops would accompany him, and that the emperor had been fully informed. Although clearly in rebellion, Saigō and his officers wore their old Imperial army uniforms, and Saigō issued orders as commander in chief. At first he even refused to enlist volunteers from neighboring prefectures in order to avoid charges of having entered into a confederacy.[47]

By using the *shigakkō* system, mobilization was carried out with great speed. By the end of the first week in February, even before Saigō had notified Ōyama of his intentions, armed men from the schools had begun to assemble in Kagoshima. Within a week, the vanguard and a four-thousand-strong First Division completed mobilization and departed the capital; soon after, the Second Infantry Division, rear guard, artillery, and finally Saigō's bodyguard started the march north. On February 20 the Satsuma army crossed into Higo Prefecture. Defeating an advance party of troops from the Kumamoto garrison, they marched into the city and laid siege to the former domain castle that now served as the army headquarters. Almost immediately, two local bands of *shizoku* – the Gakkōto and the Kyōdōtai – came over to Saigō's side. It was an auspicious beginning.

After a final attempt to dissuade Saigō, the government mobilized for war. Three thousand troops from the Tokyo garrison were immediately transported by ship to Kobe, and the Osaka and Hiroshima garrisons proceeded directly to Fukuoka in northern Kyushu. Prince Arisugawa assumed command of the hastily assembled army and immediately dispatched two divisions to block further advance by the rebel force. Thereafter, the Imperial army steadily gained the upper hand. Despite being outnumbered, the Kumamoto garrison did not capitulate, and contrary to Saigō's expectations, it repulsed repeated assaults. Meanwhile, the government not only mobilized the standing army and called up reserves, but it also enlisted thousands of *shizoku* volunteers as "police" auxiliaries. Fresh units arrived daily, and the well-equipped Imperial army counterattacked. After several days of fierce fighting, on March 20, the government forces captured the key pass at Taharazaka. Both sides suffered heavy losses. The Satsuma army executed an orderly retreat and set up a new line of defense. During the next two weeks, the Imperial army assaulted this line while additional units advanced on Kumamoto from the south. Threatened

47 August H. Mounsey, *The Satsuma Rebellion* (London: Murray, 1879), p. 119. Reprinted by University Publications of America, Washington, D.C., 1979.

with encirclement, Saigō abandoned the siege and retreated. Although not yet defeated, the rebellion had clearly failed. The government controlled all of northern and central Kyushu, which severely curtailed the recruitment of additional forces. Most ablebodied *shizoku* from Satsuma had already enlisted, and Saigō was forced to conscript peasants, who had little incentive to fight on behalf of the *shizoku*, and convicted criminals, who were not likely to be dedicated soldiers. Nevertheless, Saigō and what remained of his army continued fighting through the summer. By September, only Saigō and a few hundred troops were still in the field. On September 23, 1877, confronted by a vastly larger government force in the hills north of Kagoshima, Saigō refused a personal plea from Yamagata to surrender. The next day the army attacked; the rebel force was annihilated; and Saigō committed suicide on the battlefield rather than allow himself to be captured.[48]

Unlike previous *shizoku* uprisings, which were small and poorly organized, the Satsuma Rebellion severely tested the government's capacity to wage war. To defeat the large and well-trained rebel forces, the government had to mobilize the entire standing army and reserves and enlist an additional 7,000 *shizoku* as "police" auxiliaries. Of the 65,000 soldiers sent to the front, 6,000 were killed in action, and 10,000 were wounded. The financial cost of prosecuting the war was staggering. Direct expenditures totaled ¥42 million, a sum equal to 80 percent of the annual budget.

However costly the war had been to the government in men and coin, the oligarchy had reason to view the outcome with considerable satisfaction. The annihilation of the Satsuma army – eighteen thousand rebel troops were killed or wounded, and Saigō and his lieutenants died in battle or by suicide – eliminated the only *shizoku* force capable of threatening the central government. Moreover, the performance of the Imperial army vindicated the government's decision to adopt universal military conscription. Approximately two-thirds of the Kumamoto garrison were conscripts; although outnumbered and short of supplies, they withstood a fifty-day siege, thereby preventing Saigō's army from moving into northern Kyushu. To say that the victory proved commoner conscripts to be superior to samurai is nevertheless an oversimplification, for the majority of government soldiers were also *shizoku*. The Imperial Guards and "police" auxiliaries, which were exclusively *shizoku*, bore the brunt of the fiercest fighting. Nevertheless, the overall efficiency with which the govern-

---

48 The most detailed account of the military campaigns of the Satsuma Rebellion is contained in Mounsey, *The Satsuma Rebellion*, pp. 154–217.

ment prosecuted the war amply demonstrated the advantages of military modernization and particularly of centralized command and national recruitment.

The Satsuma Rebellion marked the final attempt by disaffected *shizoku* to overthrow the Meiji government. What does the failure of the greatest revolt reveal about the limits of *shizoku* rebellion?

After the first three weeks, Saigō's army was outnumbered and outgunned. The core of the Satsuma army consisted of six infantry regiments of 2,000 men each, in addition to artillery and the rearguard. After entering Kumamoto, they were immediately joined by two bands of local *shizoku*, the politically conservative Gakkōtō and the Kyōdōtai (an association of nominally progressive *shizoku* affiliated with the Popular Rights movement) and an additional 5,000 volunteers from nearby provinces.[49] Thus, at peak strength the rebel forces numbered no more than 22,000.

In contrast, the government initially fielded an army of 33,000 and sent an additional 30,000 before the end of the war. The rebel army was short of guns and munitions throughout most of the war. The looting of the Kagoshima arsenal secured an initial stock of guns and powder, but when the army marched out of Kagoshima in February, each soldier carried only one hundred bullets, enough for two to three days of combat. Attempts were made to purchase arms abroad, but even if the negotiations had succeeded, the Imperial navy's control of the sea would probably have prevented their delivery. The government occupied Kagoshima in April, cutting off the overland supply of munitions that were manufactured locally.

Tactical miscalculations, and especially the decision to lay siege to Kumamoto Castle, undoubtedly hastened defeat. Because of the strategic advantages enjoyed by the government forces, it was unrealistic to expect victory in a prolonged war. The best hope lay in a rapid advance to link up with sympathizers and create the impression of success before the government had time to mobilize. If Saigō had proceeded directly to Fukuoka and thereby carried the rebellion into northern Kyushu, additional groups might have declared for the rebellion. As the Shimpūren, Akitsuki, and Hagi uprisings of the previous autumn had demonstrated, *shizoku* disaffection was intense, and the decision of the "liberal" Kumamoto Kyōdōtai to join Saigō when it appeared that the rebellion might succeed suggests that the timing was indeed a critical factor. How long would Itagaki and the Risshisha

---

49 Tamamuro, *Seinan*, p. 139.

have held off if Saigō's army had crossed the Inland Sea? One does not have to be a cynic to recognize that opportunism was a powerful determinant of political alignments in the early Meiji period. But by failing to stay on the offensive, Saigō forfeited his one chance of victory – a general uprising against the Tokyo government.[50]

However, military defeat was inevitable given the very narrow political base of the rebellion. Although Satsuma had been made into a bastion of counterrevolution, the high level of mobilization achieved there between 1874 and 1877 depended on a combination of factors unique to the domain: size and composition of the warrior population, virtual autonomy from central authority, sanction and support of prefectural officials, and Saigō's prestige as a "founding father" of the Meiji Restoration. Because these conditions could not be duplicated, Satsuma stood alone. In fact, its strength was also its weakness, for the leadership's parochial political loyalties stood in the way of horizontal alliances. From Saigō's return to Kagoshima in the fall of 1873 until the attack on the Kumamoto garrison in February 1877, mobilization had been carried out entirely within the prefecture; no effort was made to encourage, aid, or link up with like-minded *shizoku* bands outside Satsuma. As we have seen, Saigō steadfastly held aloof, even in the autumn of 1876 when the disaffected *shizoku* in nearby Kumamoto, Akitsuki, and Hagi went on the offensive. When Saigō finally moved against the government and authorized sending emissaries in search of allies, the optimal moment for a general uprising had passed. Potential allies had already committed themselves to local uprisings, which produced little more than suicidal insurrections. Lacking advance notice of Saigō's rising, in some cases sympathizers were not able to act quickly enough.[51]

In short, Saigō failed to capitalize on his greatest asset. Arno Mayer observed that counterrevolutions are similar to revolutions in that both "feed on socio-economic dislocations, discontents and cleavages."[52] But despite widespread disaffection, frustration, and despair among the *shizoku* nationwide, the antigovernment movement in Satsuma remained stubbornly parochial. This doomed it to defeat. Because mobilization was restricted to Satsuma and did not tap *shizoku* discontent nationwide, Saigō's rising produced a formidable, but geographically limited, military threat. As Gotō Yasushi has observed, despite geographical proximity, similar grievances, and a common

50 Ibid., pp. 134–5.   51 Gotō, *Shizoku hanran*, pp. 174–84.
52 Arno J. Mayer, *Dynamics of Counterrevolution in Europe, 1870–1956* (New York: Harper & Row, 1971), p. 59.

enemy, the *shizoku* rebels were incapable of acting in concert; dispersed and isolated, each was defeated.[53]

The Satsuma leaders also failed to mobilize politically disaffected commoners. Class itself need not determine the scope of counterrevolutionary mobilization. Historically, recruitment to counterrevolution has depended on the degree to which "segments of different classes experienced or were apprehensive about declassment, defunctionalization, or alienation." It is not simply displaced elites and formerly dominant classes who make up the cadre of counterrevolution, but strata of all classes, "whose fears and anxieties [are] heightened by crisis conditions."[54] However, the Satsuma leaders showed no interest in propagandizing and agitating the rural poor, who, no less than the impoverished *shizoku*, constituted a "crisis stratum" whose grievances and fears might have been turned against the government. As we have seen, small landholders and tenants gained little benefit from Meiji land policies; indeed, in some areas they had violently opposed its social, educational, and religious policies. How great the potential was for inciting rural uprising and what effect extensive social disorder might have had on the outcome of the Satsuma Rebellion cannot be known. But when the Satsuma army first entered Higo and laid siege to Kumamoto, the poor farmers in the Aso district carried out widespread attacks against the homes and property of local landlords and moneylenders. Although not encouraged in any way by the rebel army, they apparently assumed that the Satsuma army represented the poor and disadvantaged and associated the Imperial army with the rich. Against a background of resentment of the new land tax and allegations of malfeasance by village headmen, rumors circulated that Saigō had abolished the land tax and canceled outstanding debts. But the Satsuma army showed no interest in the peasants, except as suppliers of food, labor, and draft animals. In fact, they treated the local population so roughly that before long opinion swung against them.[55]

Counterrevolution was defeated because none of the rebellions drew on more than a fraction of the potential recruits to the antigovernment cause. Because the leaders did not develop models of collective action suited to mass mobilization, they failed to tap the vast reservoir of discontent among the declassed samurai nationwide. Generally, the revolts replicated the patterns of mobilization that characterized the *tōbaku* (overthrow the bakufu) movement: voluntary associations of like-minded men, on the one hand, and the domain as the territorial

[53] Gotō, *Shizoku hanran*, p. 64. [54] Mayer, *Dynamics*, p. 41.
[55] Tamamuro, *Seinan*, p. 157.

and emotional unit of collective action, on the other. However, whereas limited mobilization of *shishi* (men of spirit) and militant action by Chōshū succeeded in toppling the Tokugawa bakufu in the crisis conditions of the mid-1860s, a decade later the fully centralized Meiji state managed to suppress any single group that rose up against it.

THE POPULAR RIGHTS MOVEMENT

Liberal opposition to the Meiji oligarchy can be traced back to the splintering of the original leadership group in October 1873. Unlike Saigō Takamori and Etō Shimpei, Itagaki Taisuke and Gotō Shōjirō, the leaders of the Tosa faction, rejected rebellion; instead, they organized a public campaign to establish an elected national assembly. Calling themselves the Aikokukōtō, "Public Party of Patriots," in January 1874, they enlisted a handful of prominent Restoration leaders – among them Etō Shimpei and Soejima Taneomi – and drafted a memorial urging the adoption of "a council chamber chosen by the people."[56] Although it was rejected by the government, the memorial raised for the first time a liberal challenge to the incumbent leadership and signaled the opening round in what became a decade-long campaign by a socially and politically diverse coalition known as the "People's Rights" (*jiyū minken*) movement. Espousing liberty, equality, and the right to elect government officials, the People's Rights movement brought together at various times former Restoration leaders and intellectuals, urbanites and villagers, *shizoku* and wealthy commoners, and, finally, radicals and impoverished farmers – all who shared an interest in opposing oligarchic rule.

As suggested by the circumstances leading up to the Aikokukōtō petition, Japan's first "liberals" were members of the original leadership who had lost out in the power struggle of 1873. Indeed, there is reason to question the depth of their commitment to liberalism as a political doctrine, for their interest in representative government coincided with their loss of power. Moreover, they were prone to jingoism and rarely passed up an opportunity to denounce the government's handling of Japan's international relations, insisting on early revision of the "unequal" treaties, an aggressive pursuit of national interests in Asia, and favorable resolution of territorial disputes with Russia. They also repeatedly protested high taxes, especially the land tax. What,

---

56 Text in Walter W. McLaren, "Japanese Government Documents, 1867–1889," *Transactions of the Asiatic Society of Japan* 42 (1914): pr. 1, p. 428. Hereafter cited as *JGD*.

then, was the connection between specific grievances and advocacy of an elected national assembly?

The most prominent feature in the Aikokukōtō memorial was its criticism of the oligarchic and cliquish character of the government. The petitioners charged that the incumbent leadership, much like the hateful Tokugawa bakufu, monopolized power, thereby excluding both the emperor and the people. "When we humbly reflect upon the quarter in which the governing power lies, we find it lies not with the Crown (Imperial House) on the one hand, nor with the people on the other, but with the officials alone."[57] Officials acting in the name of the emperor ruled in an "arbitrary" and "partial" manner, to the detriment of the imperial institution, which was losing prestige, and of citizens, who could not express legitimate grievances. The consequence, the memorial asserted, was internal conflict and discontent which imperiled the nation; the remedy lay in government by "public discussion." Representative government, it was urged, would fortify the nation, for national strength depended on "the people of the empire being of one mind."[58] If entrusted with political rights, the people of Japan would willingly assume the many duties of citizenship, manifest a new unity of purpose, and develop the spirit of enterprise that was known to exist among the populations of fully civilized countries.

One finds in the Aikokukōtō memorial many of the themes and contradictions that permeated liberal thought in the Meiji period. In support of representative government, the petitioners emphasized the likely benefits to national strength rather than the value of individual rights. Instead of directly challenging the principle of absolute monarchy, they denounced "despotic officials" who stood between the emperor and the people. By claiming the imperial and popular will to be harmonious, they argued that the expression of public opinion would eliminate dissension between ruler and ruled. To this extent they implicitly invoked Confucian concepts to justify liberal reforms. At the same time, however, they called on the authority of natural rights theory, boldly citing the "universally acknowledged" principle according to which payment of taxes conferred rights of representation on citizens.

Although rightly criticized by modern scholars as shortsighted and opportunistic, the tactic of evoking the emperor's authority to legitimate demands for representative institutions reflected the realities of the contemporary political landscape.[59] Although theoretically abso-

---

[57] Ibid., pp. 427–8.   [58] Ibid., p. 430.
[59] Gotō Yasushi, *Jiyū minken: Meiji no kakumei to hankakumei* (Tokyo: Chūō kōronsha), p. 43.

lute in every realm of public life, imperial authority had not yet been marshaled against progressive forces by conservative politicians and ideologues; the process of associating the throne with specific authoritarian structures had only just begun. On the other hand, the Meiji emperor symbolized the recent triumph over feudalism and Tokugawa-style despotism. Liberals, therefore, could make a strong claim to being the legitimate heirs of the 1868 revolution. After all, the first article of the Meiji Charter Oath – the most authoritative, if deliberately vague, statement of Restoration aims – promised deliberative assemblies and public debate of affairs of state. Nor were out-of-power politicians the only proponents of liberal reform. Generally, officials not aligned with the dominant Satsuma and Chōshū cliques favored broader political participation. In fact, the Sa-in, the lower chamber of the state council, formally adopted the Aikokukōtō argument, declaring that "the subject of the establishment of a council chamber chosen by the people is an excellent one" and urged the Council of State and Home Ministry to take appropriate steps.[60]

However, the oligarchs were not yet prepared to share power with elected officials. They ignored the Sa-in's favorable recommendation and replied that the great majority of the people were "ignorant and unlearned." Although some segments of the former warrior class were advancing intellectually, "the peasant and merchant classes are still what they have always been . . . satisfied in their stupidity and ignorance, and it has not yet been possible to arouse in them the spirit of activity."[61] To avoid disaster, public opinion would have to be guided and educated before representatives of such people could be entrusted with the power to make laws. Although they admitted that government in principle existed for the people, not the people for government, the most they were prepared to offer was an experiment with prefectural assemblies chosen by *shizoku* and well-to-do commoners that would be allowed to discuss, but not legislate, local matters.

Nevertheless, the oligarchs were sufficiently astute to recognize that the issue of representative government was a likely rallying point for the opposition, and they tried to forestall the growth of a broadly based movement by co-opting key leaders. They were most concerned about the activities of Itagaki Taisuke, who, after Saigō, ranked second among the military heroes of the Restoration. Itagaki and his clansmen had returned to Kōchi in February 1874 to build up a local party. There they founded the Risshisha, an association that functioned both as a

---

60 McLaren, *JGD*, pp. 432–3.   61 Ibid., p. 436.

self-help society for former samurai and as a vehicle for promoting liberal political thought. The Risshisha charter proclaimed that all Japanese were equally endowed with rights to life, liberty, property, livelihood, and the pursuit of happiness – rights that "no man can take away." To educate members to this new political philosophy, the association sponsored public lectures and talks that introduced the thought of Locke, Mill, Rousseau, and Bentham. Although the society was generally unsuccessful in managing economic enterprises, which included forestry, tea plantations, and credit unions, it attracted a large and enthusiastic following among the Tosa *shizoku*.[62] Consequently, the government became worried when the Risshisha tried to link up with other groups of disaffected samurai, as it did in 1875 by organizing the Aikokusha, a national "association of patriots." To deflate the challenge and restore a semblance of unity within the leadership's ranks, Ōkubo Toshimichi, the dominant figure in the oligarchy, agreed on the eve of the conference to issue an imperial edict promising "gradual progress" toward an elected national assembly. In return, Itagaki, Gotō, and Kido Takayoshi of Chōshū reentered the government.[63]

The agreement between Ōkubo and Itagaki is noteworthy, less for its immediate consequences than for what it revealed of the oligarchy's attitude toward the liberal opposition. The majority of the top leaders were not opposed to a constitution, or even in principle to limited representation. They were, however, determined to dictate the substance and pace of liberalizing reforms and to keep executive and bureaucratic power in their hands; as pragmatists they had no difficulty making token concessions to recent colleagues.

The announcement of the agreement between Ōkubo and Itagaki and the promise of progress toward an elected assembly upstaged the first meeting of the Aikokusha. However, inasmuch as Ōkubo and his colleagues had a very restricted notion of what constituted "progress," renewed conflict was inevitable. In October, Itagaki, by now convinced that he would have no real influence in the government, resigned once more and returned to Tosa. The stage was set for a resurgence of liberal agitation.

During the first phase of the People's Rights movement, that is, from 1874 to 1878, the Tosa leaders did not actively seek the support

---

62 Nobutake Ike, *The Beginnings of Political Democracy in Japan* (Baltimore: Johns Hopkins University Press, 1950), pp. 61–5.
63 Kido, the senior member of the Chōshū faction, had resigned in 1874 after failing to dissuade Ōkubo from sending a punitive expedition to Taiwan. Bringing Kido back into the government was essential to preventing a further narrowing of the oligarchy.

of commoners, for they too believed that former samurai, those with education and experience as administrators, were the people worthy of political representation. However, as wealthy farmers and local notables took up the liberal cause toward the end of the decade, the political and social character of the movement changed dramatically. The turning point came in the summer of 1879 when Sakurai Shizuka, a commoner farmer of moderate means from Chiba, published an appeal in which he denounced the oligarchy's failure to institute representative government and invited prefectural assembly delegates and concerned citizens throughout the country to join forces in a new campaign. Sakurai published his appeal in the *Chōya shimbun*, a Tokyo daily newspaper, and mailed thousands of handbills. The response was immediate and overwhelming. In Okayama, the prefectural assembly unanimously endorsed Sakurai's plan and authorized a mass petition campaign. From Iwate Prefecture in the northeast to Hiroshima in the west, assemblymen raised their voices in support and began circulating similar petitions.[64]

The stunning success of the petition movement was largely due to the broad support it received from the traditional village elite – headmen, landlords, and small-scale entrepreneurs who lent their prestige and influence to the campaign, thereby ensuring its success.[65] In March 1880, when the Aikokusha convened its semiannual meeting, ninety-six representatives from twenty-four prefectures attended, bringing petitions bearing a total of 101,161 signatures. Reconstituting themselves as the Kokkai kisei dōmei, "League for Establishment of a National Assembly," they authorized Kataoka Kenkichi and Kōno Hironaka to present the petitions to the government. Supremely self-confident, the delegates pledged to carry the campaign to a successful conclusion. Recognizing the importance of grass-roots support, they vowed to organize up to fifty new societies of over one hundred members each.[66]

With the national petition campaign of 1879, the initiative within the People's Rights movement passed to hundreds of local political societies, many located in villages and small towns. Among the earliest of the societies was the Sekiyōsha, established in 1875 in Ishikawa, a small and out-of-the-way mountain town in southern Fukushima. Kōno Hironaka, the founder of the Sekiyōsha, had been born into a once-prosperous *gōshi* family of Miharu fief and began his political career as a

64 Ei Hideo, *Jiyū minken*, vol. 25 of *Nihon no rekishi* (Tokyo: Shogakkan, 1976), pp. 80–5.
65 Irokawa Daikichi, *Jiyū minken* (Tokyo: Iwanami shoten, 1981), p. 26.
66 Gotō, *Jiyū minken*, pp. 100–1.

district officer in Ishikawa. If we can believe Kōno's autobiography, he read a translation of John Stuart Mill's classic *On Liberty* while en route to his new post. Perhaps directly influenced by Mill, or possibly following the lead of Itagaki Taisuke, Kōno organized within the year a political society dedicated to promoting popular rights and representative government. The charter of the Sekiyōsha boldly proclaimed: "We have come together because government is for the people . . . and inherent rights of life and personal freedom, which are higher than the mountains and deeper than the sea, will endure forever on this earth."[67] Unlike the Risshisha, which had restricted membership to Tosa *shizoku*, the Sekiyōsha welcomed all persons who supported the society's goals, irrespective of "class, wealth or station." In addition to discussing current political issues, its members studied political science, economics, history, and even the natural sciences, relying for the most part on translations of European and American texts. At weekly meetings, which were open to the public, they discussed such classics of Western political thought as *On Liberty, The Spirit of the Laws, The History of English Civilization*, and *Social Contract*.

Four years after founding the Sekiyōsha, Kōno took a new position in Miharu district. There he established a second political society, the Sanshisha, and an academy, the Seidōkan. Before long, the Seidōkan graduated young men imbued with ideas of liberty, equality, and democracy who set up popular rights organizations in nearby villages, including one mountain village with a mere forty households.

The burgeoning political activity in rural areas that began in the late 1870s is one of the remarkable developments of the Meiji period. According to recent data, 303 societies sprang up in the six provinces around Tokyo, at least 120 in the northeastern region of the country, and approximately 200 in western and southwestern Japan.[68] To be sure, the political and social character of the societies varied considerably. Not all actively supported the popular rights movement or even considered politics to be their main activity; some restricted membership to men of similar social and economic status; and others were founded with the express purpose of enhancing the leaders' prestige. Nevertheless, most of the societies were influenced to some degree by the Popular Rights movement and supported the constitutional movement.

We have seen that *shizoku* popular rights leaders Itagaki Taisuke and Gotō Shōjirō saw representative government as a vehicle for regaining

[67] Takahashi Tetsuo, *Fukushima jiyū minkenka retsuden* (Fukushima: Fukushima mimpōsha, 1967), p. 140. [68] Irokawa, *Jiyū minken*, p. 17.

influence in the national government. Although this was not their only motivation, their commitment to the concept of representative government was inextricably bound up with hopes of regaining their former positions as leaders of the Meiji government. This was not true, however, of the thousands of local notables who provided leadership and financial support for the constitutional phase of the Popular Rights movement. How, then, can we explain their commitment?

To some extent these men were reacting to political centralization, a process that reduced their local status and authority, especially after the government promulgated the so-called Three Laws on Local Government in 1878. The first of these invested the power to appoint prefectural governors in the Home Ministry and authorized prefectural governors to appoint district officials, thus giving the central government control over all but the village and town councils. The second law added a prefectural tax of up to 20 percent to the national land tax without granting taxpayers a say in how these revenues would be used. The third law provided what the more liberal-minded oligarchs hoped would be a first step toward institutionalizing limited popular participation in the governing process by establishing elected prefectural assemblies that had the right to discuss, but not initiate, legislation and to review the annual budget.

During the Tokugawa period the village headmen had performed many of the functions that now came to be carried out by the state bureaucracy. The erosion of their authority began in 1871 with the abolition of private fiefs, and by the latter half of the decade the extension of the powers of the state bureaucracy was becoming apparent. It is not surprising, then, that they were attracted to the doctrine of natural rights which accorded the propertied classes not only guarantees of private wealth but political participation as well. Moreover, natural rights justified both participation and the right to resist.[69]

However, neither the eclipse of traditional authority nor the desire to promote their economic interests accounts fully for the grass-roots support among local notables for the constitutional movement. We should not overlook the cultural dimension of the political ferment in the countryside that characterized this phase of the Popular Rights movement. As Irokawa Daikichi has argued, political activism at the village level expressed the desire of Japan's new citizens to transcend the narrow world of feudal culture.[70] Intellectually and socially, the Popular Rights movement opened up avenues of activity long denied

69 Bowen, *Rebellion*, pp. 303–13.   70 Irokawa, *Jiyū minken*, p. 49.

to commoners, a phenomenon that Irokawa's research on the community of Itsukaichi, a small market town located in the mountainous Nishitama district northwest of Tokyo, amply illustrates.

Early in 1880, the mayor of Itsukaichi and the heads of locally prominent families – the former mayor, the supervisor of the village school, the mayor of a nearby hamlet – founded the "Learning and Debating Society." According to the first article of the society's charter, its members pledged to "work together with indomitable spirit to develop liberty and improve society" and to relate to one another "as brothers of the same flesh and bone, with love and respect as if one big family."[71] Much like the Sekiyōsha and Sanshisha, politics began with self-education. Using translations of Western classics and secondary works, the members avidly absorbed the "new knowledge." In 1881, when the movement to draft a national constitution reached its climax, these mountain villagers, ostensibly the "ignorant and unlearned" whom the oligarchs declared "satisfied in their stupidity," eagerly debated the shape and substance of Japan's future constitution. A list of subjects discussed by the society included fifteen topics concerned with drafting a national constitution, nine with the legal system, and six with civil rights.[72] Several of the younger members of the society became accomplished political orators who campaigned actively on behalf of popular rights. One member, Chiba Takusaburō, produced a complete draft of a national constitution which, in terms of protection of citizens' rights, ranks high among the more than thirty extant draft constitutions.[73]

Intellectuals, most of whom were former samurai, played an instrumental role in publicizing natural rights theory and kindling enthusiasm for political reform. Nakamura Masanao and Fukuzawa Yukichi were pioneers of the Meiji "enlightenment" whose translations and essays first introduced Western culture and political institutions; younger, more radical thinkers like Ueki Emori, Nakae Chōmin, and Ōi Kentarō were ideologues as well as political activists.[74] But we should also note the contribution of many young intellectuals who dedicated themselves to the constitutional movement. Beginning in the late 1870s, scores of Tokyo journalists and amateur orators carried the

---

71 Irokawa Daikichi, *Kindai kokka no shuppatsu*, vol. 25 of *Nihon no rekishi* (Tokyo: Chūō kōronsha, 1966), p. 91.
72 Irokawa Daikichi, *Meiji no bunka* (Tokyo: Iwanami shoten, 1970), p. 105. Translation issued by Princeton University Press in 1985 as *The Culture of the Meiji Period*, ed. Marius B. Jansen. For a chart of organizations formed in villages near Tokyo, see p. 49.
73 Irokawa, *Meiji no bunka*, pp. 107–8.   74 Irokawa, *Kindai kokka*, pp. 86–90.

constitutional campaign directly to the people. Dressed dramatically in black capes and broad-brimmed hats, they popularized a new kind of politics – barnstorming.

Because of the comparatively high rates of literacy and urbanization at the start of the Meiji period, journalism provided a vocation for politically ambitious young men excluded from government service. Numa Morikazu and his colleagues in the Ōmeisha, an intellectual circle founded in 1873 to discuss Western legal institutions, exemplified this new type of urban intellectual. Numa, who had fought on the Tokugawa side during the Restoration wars, bought the *Tokyo–Yokohama Mainichi Shimbun* in 1879 and immediately used the paper as a forum for the constitutional movement, publishing twenty-seven editorials between November 1879 and January 1880 that advocated the early convening of a national assembly. At the same time, the Ōmei Society established a network of provincial branches that promoted discussion and debate of political issues. Some highly committed members toured villages and market towns; traveling by ricksha, horseback, and even on foot, they lectured at temples, schools, storehouses, and wayside shrines, wherever they could assemble a crowd. One young journalist delivered over twenty speeches during a two-month tour that took him as far north as Sado Island in the Japan Sea.[75]

With the support of hundreds of local political societies and countless dedicated individuals in villages and towns across the country, the constitutional movement generated a deluge of petitions. As we have seen, organizations affiliated with the Kokkai kisei dōmei had collected over 100,000 signatures by the spring of 1880, and although the government repeatedly refused to accept petitions, enthusiasm for the campaign showed no sign of abating. Even after the highly publicized failure of Kokkai kisei dōmei representatives Kataoka Kenkichi and Kōno Hironaka that April, leaders of provincial petition movements came streaming into Tokyo, if anything more determined to succeed. From Sagami came Amano Seiryū who arrived in Tokyo in June and vowed not to return home until the government received his countrymen's petition. Furuya Senzō of Yamanashi first sought an audience with Prince Iwakura and, when rebuffed, threatened to take his demands directly to the emperor during the next imperial tour, thus emulating the English nobles who had forced King John to sign the Magna Charta. And in an episode that symbolized both the remark-

---

75 Irokawa, *The Culture of the Meiji Period*, pp. 237–8.

able achievements of this phase of the Popular Rights movement and the limits of its power, Matsusawa Kyūraku persevered for fifty days in a futile effort to present petitions containing more than 25,000 signatures from his native Shinano.[76]

The constitutional campaign thus succeeded beyond all expectations in mobilizing popular support: sixty petitions and a quarter of a million signatures by the end of 1880, a mere year and six months after Sakurai Shizuka's seemingly naive appeal to his countrymen. Not surprisingly, this mass mobilization alarmed conservatives. In an often-quoted letter to Itō Hirobumi dated July 4, 1879, Yamagata Aritomo, chief of the army general staff, noted the growth of the Popular Rights movement and predicted, "Every day we wait the evil poison will spread more and more over the provinces, penetrate the minds of the young, and inevitably produce unfathomable evils."[77] In the same letter he voiced the fear that popular rights leaders hoped to overthrow the government when the time was right. Yamagata did not, of course, fear an armed rising. Until the mid-1880s the movement eschewed violence and at no point constituted a credible military threat, in marked contrast with the *shizoku* counterrevolution. Rather, what Yamagata and other conservatives feared was loss of control: The constitutional movement had given birth to new organizations, ideologies, and class alliances; it presented the ominous specter of the people acting not merely to protect parochial interest but also to demand a voice in determining the future of the nation. Consequently, conservative and pragmatic leaders favored concessions to preempt the goals of the mass movement while preserving the principal structures of oligarchic rule.

Until the mid-1870s the Meiji government had only local opposition movements with which to contend, but not a hostile public; no issue or party had transcended the various community, class, and status barriers to popular mobilization that were inherited from Tokugawa feudalism. But once opponents voiced demands for alternative institutions and the press joined the campaign, the oligarchs began to restrict free expression of opinion and citizens' rights to organize. The first target was the press. In 1875 and 1877 the government promulgated press and libel laws that were used to silence dissident journalists. As the Popular Rights movement gained momentum, the number of arrests increased, rising from approximately sixty in 1875 and 1876 to more than three hundred in 1880. Freedom of assembly was also

76 Irokawa, *Kindai kokka*, pp. 103–4.   77 Translation from Ike, *Beginnings*, p. 93.

restricted. The Ordinance on Public Meetings, published on April 5, 1880, while the first meeting of the newly formed Kokkai kisei dōmei was still in session, gave the police considerable authority to investigate and regulate the activities of political groups. All associations were required to submit membership lists and charters and to obtain permits before convening public meetings. Uniformed police attended all rallies and speeches and intervened if the speaker deviated from the approved topic or made statements "prejudicial to public tranquility." The law also denied soldiers, police, teachers, and even students the right to appear at political meetings.[78] Employed selectively but forcefully when the occasion demanded, the press and public meetings laws provided a legal framework for political repression. According to police records, 131 political meetings were disbanded in 1881 and 282 in 1882. Many more never took place because the police simply denied permits to assemble. In addition, editors and journalists critical of the government were fined or jailed, sometimes for seemingly modest proposals. For example, the editor of the *Azuma*, a Tokyo newspaper, was sent to jail for two years and fined ¥200 merely for voicing the opinion that the emperor, no less than other government officials, was a public servant.[79]

Nevertheless, the constitutional movement was ultimately defeated without resort to systematic repression. No such coercion was needed, for the oligarchs neatly defused the mass movement by conceding the very issue that had so aroused public enthusiasm. After extensive consultation among the leading ministers, consultations that revealed fundamental differences among them, Ōkuma Shigenobu, the only advocate of the early establishment of an English-style parliament and cabinet, was expelled from the government on October 12, 1881, at the very moment that the delegates to the semiannual meeting of the Kokkai kisei dōmei were debating proposals for convening a constituent assembly, and the government announced that the emperor would graciously grant a constitution and convene a national assembly before the end of the decade.[80]

Although much more than a tactical move to stem the tide of popular agitation, the imperial proclamation struck the Popular Rights movement at its most vulnerable point. From the beginning, liberal opponents of the oligarchy had steadfastly insisted on the harmonious

---

78 McLaren, *JGD*, pp. 495–9.   79 Ike, *Beginnings*, p. 90.
80 The controversy within the oligarchy over the constitution is described in detail in George Akita, *Foundations of Constitutional Government in Japan, 1868–1900* (Cambridge, Mass.: Harvard University Press, 1967), pp. 31–67.

relationship between the imperial and the popular will and staked their claim to legitimacy on the proposition that representative institutions would fulfill the aims of the imperial state by eliminating "despotic ministers" who stood between the emperor and the people, that is, barriers between ruler and ruled. Rhetorically committed to justifying liberal reform in the name of imperial sovereignty, advocates of popular rights were trapped when the oligarchs, speaking through the Meiji emperor, appropriated the issue of constitutional reform for the throne. Leaders of the Popular Rights movement could not continue agitation without disputing the imperial prerogative, even though it was apparent to all that in writing the imperial constitution, the oligarchs would be able to dictate the form and content of the new body politic. To reject this would have required a radical redefinition of liberal ideology and goals and a fundamental critique of the Meiji state. No leader, theorist, or faction subsequently demonstrated the capacity to reconstitute liberalism as a mass movement, and having failed to transform popular enthusiasm for representative government into institutions of independent political power, the liberals "won" a constitution while losing the war against oligarchic rule.

After October 1881, the Popular Rights movement splintered. There were at least four distinct developments: formation of national political parties, agitation for greater power in local and prefectural government, rise of an insurrectionist faction, and the emergence of a radical populist movement.[81] None enjoyed more than temporary success; each was suppressed or chose to disband well before the convening of the first elected national assembly.

The creation of a national political party to replace the Kokkai kisei dōmei came after the announcement of an imperial constitution in October 1881. Proposals for such an organization had been made the previous year, but disagreement between those who advocated building up local affiliates and those who wanted a strong metropolitan party had delayed implementation. The issue was first debated at the October 1881 plenary session of the Kokkai kisei dōmei, but no sooner had discussion begun than the delegates learned that the oligarchs had announced a specific date for promulgating an imperial constitution. In an atmosphere of urgency and confusion, the Tosa faction took control. Itagaki Taisuke was elected party president, and his allies and

---

81 Many historians consider the various conflicts between 1882 and 1885 as constituting a separate phase of the popular rights movement and label them collectively as "incidents of extremism" (*gekka jiken*). See Bowen, *Rebellion*, "Introduction."

Tosa followers filled the executive postions, virtually excluding the rural and commoner contingents.

Although the record of the Liberal Party (Jiyūtō) is mixed, on the whole it probably did more to hinder than to promote effective opposition to oligarchic rule. On the positive side, 149 local societies affiliated with it, thus creating for the first time a political party with elected leaders, a party platform, a permanent secretariat, and a national membership. In addition, it published a newspaper, set up a legal bureau, and provided at least some funding and advice to local movements. On the other hand, because the Tosa faction monopolized the top positions, factional rivalries intensified. Competing for public support with an eye to future elections, the Jiyūtō leaders put as much effort into attacking the Constitutional Progressive Party (Rikken Kaishintō), a rival liberal party headed by the Saga leader Ōkuma Shigenobu, as it did the government. Moreover, although he was undoubtedly a charismatic figure, Itagaki was at best an unsteady leader who often appeared to have been more interested in promoting his career than his party. He caused irreparable damage in 1882 when he allowed himself to be co-opted by the government for a second time after being persuaded by Gotō Shōjirō to embark on an extended tour of Western nations, one year after assuming the party presidency, apparently at government expense.[82] To make matters worse, he left Japan at a time when violent repression of the Fukushima Jiyūtō and a deepening agricultural recession created demands for direct action by the party rank and file. Leaderless, the Jiyūtō neither aided nor controlled radical groups acting in its name.

If the national Jiyūtō failed to define new goals, in some localities party leaders revived the mass movement by contesting the state bureaucracy's control of local government. The most effective local Jiyūtō leader was Kōno Hironaka, who, in the spring and summer of 1882, skillfully rallied liberal delegates to the Fukushima prefectural assembly. Kōno's campaign provoked a strong reaction, and eventual repression, at the hands of the governor, Mishima Michitsune, a loyal servant of the Home Ministry. What happened in Fukushima deserves our attention, for it illustrates both the strength of opposition movements supported by local elites and the limits to dissent that the state was prepared to tolerate.[83]

---

[82] Gotō, *Jiyū minken*, p. 95. In fact, the money was provided by Mitsui interests at government request.

[83] The conflict in Fukushima is given a different interpretation in Bowen, *Rebellion*, pp. 8–28.

When he was elected chairman of the Fukushima prefectural assembly in 1881, Kōno's first act was to introduce motions calling for universal male suffrage and the election of district magistrates and opposing recent increases in prefectural spending, especially for the governor's office and police. However, the issue that Kōno chose to dramatize was largely symbolic: the refusal of the governor to acknowledge the legitimacy of the popularly elected assembly's role as a forum for the expression of political opinion. Governor Mishima, a Satsuma samurai and former protégé of Ōkubo Toshimichi, ignored the assembly and failed to answer two assembly requests that he attend its discussion of the budget. Kōno called for a vote of no confidence with a speech that vividly expressed the tenor of the confrontation:

This assembly was established to represent public opinion, and therefore public policy should be carried out in accord with its opinions. Let there be no mistaking that today's world is not the world of the past and that today's people are different from the people of former days. . . . Yet, [Governor Mishima] has not attended one session of the assembly; not only has he failed to take the will of the people into consideration, but he has shown his contempt for this precious public assembly.[84]

After Kōno's oration, the assembly voted to suspend debate until the governor appeared in person in the assembly chamber. Mishima, who had allegedly warned against "robbers, arsonists, and the Jiyūtō" when he took office, refused to back down. The battle lines were drawn.

Because the assembly lacked the legal authority to reject the budget or withhold appropriations, the vote to suspend debate amounted to a strong vote of censure and marked the beginning of an aggressive campaign by the Fukushima Jiyūtō to create a groundswell of popular support, comparable to the earlier petition campaign, that the oligarchs would not be able to ignore. In this they succeeded, for local Jiyūtō speakers were soon attracting large and enthusiastic crowds. Governor Mishima responded by turning to the police, who frequently refused to issue permits for political meetings and who intervened as soon as criticism of the government was voiced. What happened at a Jiyūtō rally in Ishikawa district in August was typical. Speaking to the topic "Who Is to Blame?" a local activist developed the theme that repressive government bred revolution. Arguing that English misrule had brought on the American independence movement and that tyrannical emperors and aristocrats in Russia had given rise to anarchism,

84 Gotō Yashushi, *Jiyū minken undō* (Osaka: Sōgensha, 1958), p. 88.

he then turned his attention to Japan: "Do not the police seize on a single word or phrase to throw the speaker in jail and disband the meeting?" he asked. At this the policeman on the podium stepped forward and declared the meeting a threat to public order. The speakers were ordered to step down, and the audience was dispersed.[85]

Concurrent with, but independent of, the campaign led by Kōno Hironaka, the Aizu Jiyūtō in western Fukushima organized local opposition to a major road construction project that Governor Mishima had assigned top priority. Residents of Aizu wanted the roads built; in fact, they had already approved additional taxes and corvée labor as part of an agreement on funding that had been negotiated with Mishima's representatives. But when it was discovered that the central government was paying considerably less than had been promised and that the residents would have no say in planning the route, the local Jiyūtō mounted a petition drive and tax boycott. Because the Aizu Jiyūtō was made up of the local notables and many party members were village mayors, it was able to mount large and effective protests, at least in the countryside.[86]

Backed by the Home Ministry, Governor Mishima ordered his subordinates to break the boycott. Two hundred and thirty policemen were sent to Aizu; homes were raided; property was seized; and leaders were harassed and arrested. Strong-arm tactics intimidated some of the party members, but they also aroused popular passions. Although the local Jiyūtō leadership tried to avoid violent confrontation, on a fateful day late in November a large crowd of villagers, urged on by young Jiyūtō activists who had recently arrived in Aizu, marched on the district jail in Kitakata where two leaders of the boycott were incarcerated. In the course of the demonstration, someone in the crowd, very possibly an agent provocateur, threw stones at the station, breaking several panes of glass. Immediately the police, swords drawn, charged and attacked the unarmed crowd, killing one demonstrator and wounding several others. Mishima, who was in Tokyo when the incident occurred, seized upon the incident as a pretext for legal action against the Fukushima Jiyūtō. He immediately sent a secret communiqué to his secretary which began: "The rioting of the scoundrels in Kitakata provides an excellent opportunity to arrest them all, bar none."[87] Within less than a week, one thousand Jiyūtō party members and sympathizers in Fukushima had been arrested; many were tortured; and some died while in

85 Takahashi, *Fukushima retsuden*, p. 47.
86 Shimoyama Saburō, "Fukushima jiken shōron," *Rekishigaku kenkyū*, no. 186 (August 1955): 5.
87 Takahashi Tetsuo, *Fukushima jiken* (Tokyo: San'ichi shobō, 1970), p. 187.

police custody. Most of them had never set foot in Aizu during the period of the protest.

In incidents that are collectively known as the "Fukushima incident," Jiyūtō-led resistance to Governor Mishima is usually considered the first of the so-called *gekka jiken,* violent incidents that marked the final stage of the Popular Rights movement. Yet in most respects, Jiyūtō activity in Fukushima shared more with the second phase of the Popular Rights movement, the constitutional movement, than with subsequent insurrections. As in the campaign for constitutional government, the majority of its leaders were of the local notable class, respectable and solid citizens who naturally inclined toward peaceful politics within the law. But despite such limited goals and peaceful tactics, the authorities had responded with violence, finally bringing the full weight of the judicial system to bear on the opposition.[88]

Nevertheless, the Fukushima incident was indeed a turning point in the Popular Rights movement, for the authoritarian face of the oligarchy had been revealed for all to see, causing a decline in support for the Jiyūtō among more cautious party members to whom commitment to representative government was not worth the risks of continued agitation. In this sense, the "incident" was both an end and a beginning. Mishima broke the power of a deeply entrenched local opposition movement, as he had allegedly been instructed to do upon taking office; and to young radicals, who continued the struggle against oligarchic rule, violence now appeared to be politically and morally justified.

In the last years of the Popular Rights movement, opposition to the Meiji oligarchy turned violent. It is essential, however, to distinguish between popular uprisings driven by acute economic distress, as in the Chichibu revolt of 1884, and the several insurrectionist plots of which the Kabasan incident is perhaps the best example. Whereas local leaders in Chichibu who had only recently joined the Jiyūtō organized thousands of destitute farmers around economic issues, the sixteen Kabasan rebels acted without popular support in an ill-conceived attempt to bring about revolution by assassination. Whereas the principal goal of the Chichibu uprising was debt relief, revenge and despair with conventional politics motivated the young Jiyūtō radicals of Kabasan. Hence it is the contrasts between Chichibu and Kabasan

---

88 Fifty-seven party members of the Fukushima Jiyūtō were charged with treason. Although six party members, including Kōno, had signed a "blood oath" to overthrow the oligarchy, there was no other evidence that any of them were actually plotting an insurrection.

that are of the greatest significance, for each movement possessed elements of revolutionary mobilization while it lacked other, essential ingredients.

For the majority of the Kabasan conspirators, the initial motive was to assassinate Mishima Michitsune and thereby avenge the brutal suppression of the Fukushima Jiyūtō. Twelve members of the Kabasan group were natives of Fukushima and had either been arrested in 1882 or witnessed the crackdown. Still, revenge was not their only motive, and the assassination of government ministers was conceived to be more than an act of terrorism. The Kabasan rebels proceeded on the assumption that the simultaneous assassination of high-ranking officials would cause the government to fall and set the stage for a revolutionary seizure of state power. Nor were they alone in thinking that direct action was the only road open to opponents of the authoritarian state. After 1882, a sizable group in the Jiyūtō headed by Ōi Kentarō had begun to advocate insurrection, a strategy that proved to be profoundly wrong but that reflected the despair of many of the most committed party members.[89] The constitutional movement and the mass movement it had spawned were dead; the Jiyūtō party secretariat was controlled by the ineffectual and compromising Itagaki; and the naked use of state power against the Fukushima Jiyūtō had demonstrated the perils, as well as the futility, of legal agitation. Thus, the Kabasan group was exceptional in its choice of tactics – plans to use homemade bombs to kill officials attending a public ceremony – but not in its frustration with conventional politics.

The particulars of the adventures and misadventures of the Kabasan conspiracy need not detain us, for they have been recorded elsewhere and illustrate only the many pitfalls that await an amateur band of political assassins.[90] The more significant failure of the Kabasan group was the scant attention that it (and most of the radical Jiyūtō) paid to organizing support among the people. To some extent, its failure to recruit the local population to the cause of revolution reflected practical limitations – primarily the need to maintain secrecy – that the group's choice of tactics imposed. Moreover, most of the conspirators were *shizoku* or sons of wealthy farmers and not natives of the locale in which they established their headquarters. But most of all, the band proved to be naive in its expectations, believing that it could raise an

---

[89] Gotō Yasushi, "Meiji jūshichinen no gekka shojiken ni tsuite," in Horie Eichi and Tōyama Shigeki eds., *Jiyū minken ki no kenkyū: minken undō no gekka to kaitai* (Tokyo: Yūhikaku, 1959), vol. 1, p. 208. [90] Bowen, *Rebellion*, pp. 31–49.

army of sufficient size to march on Tokyo simply by appealing to the rural poor, recruiting gangs of miners, and freeing convicts, all without prior political work to explain the purpose of the revolt. Completely cut off from reality, they never posed a serious threat to state power.[91]

The conspirators' lack of interest in organizing the people is all the more surprising in light of the desperate economic situation of many small farmers and the signs of incipient unrest. Beginning in 1882, a severe depression that lasted more than four years racked the countryside. The collapse of the rural economy had been precipitated by antiinflationary policies adopted at the recommendation of Finance Minister Matsukata Masayoshi in the fall of 1881 to curb inflation and promote capital accumulation and industrialization. Over the next four years the government withdrew 36 percent of the paper currency in circulation and increased excise taxes more than fivefold. Prefectural and local taxes also rose as the costs of public works and services were transferred to prefectural and local government. At the same time, the government reduced expenditures, in part by selling off to private concerns most of the industrial enterprises it had established and run as state industries.

In purely economic terms, Matsukata's policies must be judged a success. Nearly bankrupt in 1881, the government increased the ratio of reserves to currency in circulation from 8 percent to 37 percent by 1886; the nation's balance of trade swung from a deficit to surplus; and interest rates declined, all of which encouraged long-term investment in a manufacturing sector with growing capital requirements. On the other hand, what benefited industry hurt agriculture, particularly the small and marginal producers who produced cash crops and had experienced the gains of the previous inflation of prices. The immediate effect of the deflation was to depress commodity prices, thus reducing farm income. Rice prices fell from a post-Restoration high of ¥14.40 per *koku* in 1881 to ¥4.61 per *koku* in January 1884; raw silk and cocoons, the principal cash crop in many districts of eastern Japan, declined by one-half between 1882 and 1884. At the same time that the farmers' incomes were falling, taxes rose. There were new taxes to pay on consumer goods, but in addition, the real burden of the land tax increased as commodity prices declined. Paid in cash, the land tax consumed a far greater portion of total household

---

91 Most of the insurrections of the period were discovered by the police well before the conspirators could act.

income, rising from an average of 16 percent of the national harvest in 1877 to 33 percent in 1884.[92]

All farmers suffered to some extent as a consequence of the Matsukata deflation. However, small-scale producers of cash crops, and especially farmers who customarily relied on short-term debt, were hit the hardest. Caught between the government and the local moneylender, saddled with drastically reduced income but high fixed costs, such farmers struggled to stave off bankruptcy. Even moderately well-to-do farmers caught in the same predicament often had to mortgage their land. As the full effects of the depression took hold, bankruptcies soared, rising nationally from 33,845 households in 1883 to 108,050 in 1885.[93]

It is not surprising then that rural unrest was on the rise. Beginning in 1883, hardpressed farmers in eastern Japan began to agitate for debt relief, typically banding together to demand debt rescheduling or suspension of interest payments. These locally organized movements, self-styled "debtor parties" (*shakkintō*) and "poor people's parties" (*kommintō*), appeared most frequently in sericulture districts among small producers for whom debt management was as much part of the productive cycle as was nurturing silkworm larvae and harvesting cocoons. According to one survey, there were sixty-two incidents of collective action by debtors in 1884, the trough of the agricultural depression, with the greatest concentration in Kanagawa and Shizuoka. These efforts were not entirely unsuccessful, for there were several cases in which creditors rescheduled loans and reduced interest rates.[94]

For the most part, the Jiyūtō, whose rural membership consisted largely of local notables and wealthy farmers, kept aloof from the debtor movement; some party members, moneylenders, and wholesalers in the silk trade were themselves the targets of agitation. But in Hachiōji, a market town west of Tokyo, Ishizaka Kōrei, a local leader of the Jiyūtō who had himself fallen into debt, organized a community

---

92 Irokawa Daikichi, *Kindai kokka*, pp. 345–6, who bases himself on the research of Niwa Kunio.
93 Ibid., p. 353. This is, however, an area of continuing controversy, its parameters outlined by Bowen's estimate of three million bankruptcies in the mid-1880s (*Rebellion*, p. 104) and a recent assertion that much of the increase in tenancy was for newly reclaimed land and that "real income per farm worker fell only 9.2 percent from 1879–1881 [inflationary years] to 1882–1884." Richard J. Smethurst. *Agricultural Development and Tenancy Disputes in Japan 1870–1940* (Princeton, N.J.: Princeton University Press, 1986), p. 60.
94 Irokawa Daikichi, "Kommintō to Jiyūtō," *Rekishigaku kenkyū*, no. 247 (November 1960): 1–30.

effort to mediate between debtors and local creditors with Jiyūtō connections. Although Ishizaka achieved only moderate success, it is likely that events in Hachiōji stimulated the much more vigorous movement that developed to the north in Chichibu, a movement that culminated in a full-scale uprising a few months later.

In Chichibu, a mountainous sericulture district northwest of Tokyo, debt-related protests developed into armed resistance by local farmers whose three-thousand-strong "Poor People's Army" sacked municipal offices and attacked moneylenders and credit companies.[95] The rebellion far exceeded the previous popular uprisings of the Meiji period, in terms of organization, militancy, and ideological articulation if not in numbers of participants. The Chichibu rebellion raises a number of questions. Why was its mobilization so successful? How radical were its goals and ideology? What was its relationship to the Jiyūtō, nationally and locally? And what, finally, does the Chichibu revolt tell us about opposition to oligarchic rule at the end of the People's Rights movement?

Debt relief, the issue around which the people of Chichibu organized, spoke to their most pressing need. In the 1880s, 70 percent of all households in Chichibu raised silkworms, and the local economy was devastated by the sharp drop in silk prices after 1881.[96] However, in contrast with the debtors' movements which originated among the poorest farmers and lacked politically sophisticated leadership, the Chichibu movement was led by middle and small farmers who had only recently fallen on hard times. The three men who initiated the campaign for debt relief in Chichibu – Ochiai Toraichi, Sakamoto Sōsaku and Takagishi Zenkichi – represented the middle stratum of village society: literate but without much formal education, economically self-sufficient but certainly not wealthy, respected by their peers but lacking the prestige and influence of local notables. Whatever their prior interest and involvement in the Popular Rights movement might have been, the first we learn of their political activity is a petition delivered to the district magistrate in 1883 urging measures to regulate usury. The next spring, discouraged by the government's failure to act on the debt issue and impressed by speeches denouncing the government's economic policies made by Ōi Kentarō during a recent tour, they joined the Jiyūtō. Nevertheless, when they organized a mass movement around the debt issue in August, they did not turn to the Chichibu Jiyūtō for help. Instead, they approached hard-

---

[95] Bowen, *Rebellion*, pp. 49–67.
[96] Inoue Kōji, *Chichibu jiken* (Tokyo: Chūō kōronsha, 1968), p. 12.

pressed small farmers like themselves and made the village the unit of recruitment and mobilization. By September, they had mobilized a core of more than one hundred committed supporters. The Chichibu Komminto (Poor People's Party) had been born.[97]

The Chichibu Komminto decided on armed resistance only after the police and courts refused to do anything about the debt crisis and local creditors rejected conciliation. Its leaders had tried to postpone the revolt as long as possible, first, in the hope that continued agitation would produce tangible results and, second, to allow sufficient time for preparations. The head of the Komminto, Tashiro Eisuke, and several of his lieutenants wanted at least one month to plan the uprising, arguing that success depended on simultaneous risings in neighboring provinces. However, they were forced to act prematurely because local farmers faced imminent foreclosures; by October Chichibu moneylenders had begun to call in their debts.[98] The final decision for revolt was made on October 25, and one week later the Komminto army assembled to hear Tashiro read out the orders of battle.

The brief success of the rebel army and its subsequent defeat were described and analyzed by Roger Bowen.[99] What concerns us here is not the collapse of the rebel army but the political character of the rebellion. Consider its military organization. The formal command structure contained a clearly articulated hierarchy of staff positions descending from Tashiro, the commander in chief, to batallion leaders, establishing clear lines of authority needed to formulate and implement strategy. In addition, the goals of the revolt were clearly outlined and were supported by the rank and file, many of whom insisted on the rightness of their actions even after their arrest. At least some units followed orders and fought spiritedly, even when outnumbered and outgunned. These and other facts suggest a level of political consciousness greater than that found in Tokugawa peasant revolts or the rural protests of the early Meiji period.

On the other hand, the sophisticated conception of military organization evident in the formal command structure broke down once the Komminto army took the field. On the third day of the revolt, when it was learned that the Imperial army was closing in, the batallion commanders disobeyed orders, creating such confusion that further attempts to coordinate operations ended. When Tashiro absconded the following day, the greater part of the army, which had grown to over five thousand men, melted away. As in traditional peasant revolts,

97 Ibid., pp. 41–43.   98 Ibid., p. 72.   99 Bowen, *Rebellion*, pp. 59–67.

participation was neither individual nor entirely voluntary; to a large extent it represented a collective decision made by each village. And if there is evidence that some of the rank and file understood their actions in explicitly political terms, there is also evidence that many used the traditional language of *yonaoshi* (world rectification) to "equalize wealth," "aid the poor," and create "the kingdom of peace and tranquility" to describe the purpose of the revolt. They also raised banners proclaiming Itagaki Taisuke, "lord of world rectification" and referred to the Jiyūtō as "poor people's gold." This is not to argue that the entire movement in Chichibu was predominantly traditional or millenarian, but there can be no doubt that outside the ranks of the leaders, pre-Meiji concepts of resistance to authority still informed political consciousness.[100] According to the transcript of Tashiro's interrogation, the purpose of the uprising was to force the government to protect farmers threatened with foreclosure, to control usury, and to reduce local taxes. Armed resistance was the means, but the strategy was to use force to compel the government to accept their demands. More immediate objectives included punitive attacks against unscrupulous moneylenders, raising funds for local relief by threatening the rich, and attacking courthouses to destroy debt vouchers, mortgage deeds, and tax records. For most of the local leaders, the goals were economic and limited in scope. This was not true, however, of Kikuchi Kambei and Ide Tamemichi, Jiyūtō activists from neighboring Nagano Prefecture who went to Chichibu late in October. They interjected a broader political vision with demands for reduction of the land tax and the immediate convening of a national assembly, on the one hand, and a rhetoric of revolution that had little to do with the popular movement, on the other. The distance between the radical faction, most of whom were from outside Chichibu, and the majority of the local Kommintō leadership was made clear at the first meeting between Tashiro and Kikuchi. Tashiro insisted that the principal objective was debt relief, and Kikuchi was so disappointed that he tried to persuade Ide to return home.[101]

Finally, the role of the Jiyūtō remained marginal. A number of the leaders of the Chichibu Kommintō had recently joined the Jiyūtō or, as in the case of Tashiro, were associated though not formally enrolled in the party. But the Jiyūtō group in the Komminto was not at all representative of the party membership, either locally or nationally. They had joined the Jiyūtō in 1884 out of concern for the plight of

---

[100] Moriyama Gunjirō, *Minshū hōki to matsuri* (Tokyo: Chikuma shobō, 1981), p. 113. See also Irokawa, *Culture of the Meiji Period*, pp. 159ff.   [101] Inoue, *Chichibu jiken*, p. 73.

impoverished farmers at the hands of local moneylenders. In the course of the campaign to negotiate relief measures, they had come to see the role of the state as the guardian of private property and contracts. In other words, they drew the crucial connection between state power and economic structure, and this gave a political dimension to their uprising. But the majority of the Jiyūtō members in Chichibu came from the well-to-do local notable class and took no interest in the campaign for debt relief. The same pattern prevailed in the Sakyu district of Nagano, which bordered Chichibu to the west. When Kikuchi led a force of several rebels there, hoping to attract new recruits, the well-established Jiyūtō gave them no help at all. Neither did Ōi Kentarō, head of the radical Jiyūtō faction in Tokyo. Informed of the rising in advance, Ōi sent a messenger with instructions to cancel the revolt. Nationally, Jiyūtō leaders condemned both Kabasan and Chichibu in an effort to disassociate themselves from the violence that they felt discredited the party. In fact, meeting in Osaka just before the Chichibu rebellion, the party executives voted to disband, partly out of recognition that they could not control radical groups acting in the party's name.[102]

With the voluntary dissolution of the Jiyūtō and the suppression of the Chichibu rebellion, the Popular Rights movement ended. Although Jiyūtō radicals plotted several more insurrections, each was discovered, and the conspirators were rounded up before they were put to the test.[103] What did the liberal movement accomplish?

Very little. The decade of agitation and ferment that began with the memorial of the Aikokukōtō in 1874 ended without achieving the institutional reforms needed to establish a democratic polity. It is true that the government, as it had promised, delivered a constitution in 1889 that provided the framework for limited representation at the national level. But the constitution written by the oligarchs so circumscribed the power of the elected lower house that it was another twenty years before the political parties gained a share of ministerial power, and it was 1918 before a parliamentarian became prime minister. Hence politics in the first half-century of modernization, the period in which the basic pattern of institutional and ideological articulation took shape, was bureaucratic and authoritarian. In most respects the

102 Irokawa, *Kindai kokka*, p. 241.
103 The final episode involved plans to send armed forces to Korea to aid the progressive faction in that country to seize power, thereby setting the stage for revolution in Japan. Marius B. Jansen, "Oi Kentarō: Radicalism and Chauvinism," *Far Eastern Quarterly* 11 (May 1952): 305–16.

society created by the Meiji oligarchy was "modern," being capitalistic, meritocratic, and scientific, but also politically and socially repressive and increasingly chauvinistic and militaristic. In the light of Japan's difficult task as an Asian nation industrializing in the predatory world of Western imperialism, it is impossible to predict how modernization might have differed under more liberal political leadership.[104] What we do know is that the liberals were excluded from power at the time when there was the greatest opportunity for progressive change.

Among the factors limiting the effectiveness of the People's Rights movement were factionalism, weak and compromising leadership, and a generally united oligarchy that did not hesitate to use the police and courts to harass and intimidate its opponents. But perhaps the fundamental weakness of Meiji liberalism was its acceptance of the imperial institution as the fountain of all legitimate political authority. Not only liberal polemics against the oligarchs but every constitution made public during the Popular Rights movement placed the imperial institution at the center of the new polity and stipulated joint rule by the emperor and the people.

The reliance of popular rights leaders on the Meiji emperor as a legitimizing institution signified an ideological commitment and not just a political stretegy aimed at swaying public opinion. Although it was opportunistic as well, in a more basic sense the linkage of the imperial with the popular will in the rhetoric of the Popular Rights movement points out the all-too-real confusion on the part of the first generation of Japanese liberals about the relationship between imperial and democratic institutions and demonstrates the limiting historical conditions that they faced. The emperor was the one political force that transcended all the particularistic social divisions of rank, class, domain, and family inherited from centuries of feudalism. Needing an emotionally compelling symbol of progressive political relationships, popular rights thinkers and activists wholeheartedly accepted the Meiji emperor. But though they were free to lay claim to the imperial will, they had no control over the institution to which they hitched their star. For the Meiji emperor, as well as being a potent symbol of the modern era, was also a political actor controlled by the oligarchs. As such, he could be used with devastating effect against any group that appealed uncritically to his authority.

---

104 The political parties that emerged in the Taishō period were scarcely less chauvinistic than most other groups in Japanese society and overall more jingoistic than the bureaucracy.

CONCLUSION

The leaders of the Meiji Restoration never surrendered power during their lifetimes, and despite attacks from both progressive and reactionary political forces, they stuck to their agenda of rapid, top-down transformation of political, social, and economic institutions. To understand why the leaders prevailed, we need to consider the social character of the opposition forces, their interests, and the choices the oligarchs made. Put simply, they made tactical concessions that reduced the friction between the emerging middle class and the state but crushed movements by socially marginal classes.

Confronted with protests against the land tax and the campaign for constitutional government, movements that mobilized propertied and educated segments of the population, the oligarchs offered concessions addressing the long-term class interests of these groups. By reducing the land tax in 1877, subsequently shifting the tax burden from property to consumption, and writing a constitution that gave substantial fiscal and legislative power to the elected lower house, the oligarchs deflected demands for more progressive reforms without either surrendering power or permanently alienating the future middle class. Despite relatively heavy property taxes and exclusion from the government, the wealthy farmers, landlords, entrepreneurs, and the commercial and educated classes benefited enormously from the progressive reforms of Meiji – especially reforms that brought citizen equality, meritocracy, protection of private property, and promotion of capitalist economic growth.

Early in this chapter we observed that historians in the West tend to credit traditional values such as consensus and loyalty to the emperor with minimizing "dysfunctional" conflict in Meiji, whereas most Japanese historians emphasize the repressive role of the state. But at least in the case of liberal opposition movements, it is interests rather than values that are salient. The propertied and educated had a sufficient material stake in the emerging social order to keep them from launching a truly radical attack on the government. Their class interests dictated compromise rather than unrestrained confrontation; they faced selective, and not massive, repression by the state.

However, the classes marginalized by the Meiji reforms, groups that were losing social power as a result of modernization, faced an entirely different situation. The traditional warrior and small-scale subsistence farmer did not fit into the new order, and the government sacrificed their social needs quite ruthlessly to speed national integration and capital accumulation. Victims of the particular development strategies pursued by the Meiji government, these groups suffered severe and irreversible decline in socioeconomic status. They had every reason to revolt, but why did their rebellion fail?

Historically, the ability of governments to repress rebellion has been profoundly influenced by interaction with world political and economic systems.[105] Japan in the mid-nineteenth century was no exception. In the decade preceding the Meiji Restoration, military and economic pressures of Western imperialism hastened the collapse of the Tokugawa bakufu. Commodore Matthew C. Perry's warships undermined the legitimacy of the shogun and created a sense of national crisis within the ruling class. Faced with a possible loss of national independence, the bakufu was forced to authorize a military mobilization that strained its own resources and strengthened the hostile daimyo. The commercial treaties imposed on the bakufu by the Western powers disrupted financial and commodity markets. Rampant inflation, food shortages, hoarding, and rice riots further weakened Tokugawa authority. In the end, only a few of the hereditary vassals of the Tokugawa house were willing to fight on its behalf. Overall, the victory of the *tōbaku* (overthrow the bakufu) movement was due less to its own strength than to the crippling effects of Western imperialism on the traditional bases of Tokugawa strength. In the absence of the acute foreign crisis, the *tōbaku* forces, which were numerically small, internally divided, and ideologically diverse, could not have seized power in 1868 without first achieving a much higher level of mobilization.

Conversely, in considering the defeat of opposition movements in early Meiji, we should not overlook the fact that the oligarchs were not subjected to new pressures from the imperialist powers. The commercial treaties imposed specific constraints on economic policy and reduced state revenues, and extraterritoriality continued to be a cause of national humiliation. But during the critical first decade of political and social reform, when tension between the government and the former samurai class was the greatest, the Western powers did not make new demands for diplomatic, trade, or territorial concessions. There is no doubt that the relaxation of external pressure enabled the government to push ahead with modernization. Fighting a major war in the 1870s would have strained the government's resources while strengthening the exponents of reaction both inside and outside the

---

105 Theda Skocpol, *States and Social Revolutions* (Cambridge, England: Cambridge University Press, 1979), pp. 23–4.

oligarchy; a prolonged conflict would have necessitated mobilizing the *shizoku*. Once the traditional warrior class had been rearmed, it is unlikely that the government could have eliminated its stipends and class privileges. And without these reforms, the basis of the alliance between the oligarchy and wealthy commoners and progressive *shizoku* – meritocracy, lower property taxes, and the 1889 constitution – would have vanished.

The second contextual factor that aided the government was the sequential, rather than simultaneous, rise of opposition forces. The oligarchs faced challenges from both reactionary and progressive movements, but they did not have to confront both at the same time. Although the *shizoku* revolts overlapped with protests against the land tax, the constitutional movement reached its apogee well after the danger of *shizoku* rebellion had passed. Moreover, the liberal phase of the Popular Rights movement coincided with a period of general prosperity. From the defeat of the Satsuma Rebellion to the Matsukata deflation, good weather, the strong export demand for silk, expansive monetary policies, and inflation that reduced the farmers' real taxes created unprecedented prosperity in the countryside – conditions more favorable to reformist politics than to radical movements. Finally, when the Matsukata deflation brought severe hardship to the villages in the 1880s, the constitutional movement was already in full retreat. And because the principal demand of the rural poor was debt relief, the Jiyūtō ignored them. Leaderless except in Chichibu, poor farmers did not mobilize effectively.

Without a conjuncture of external and internally destabilizing forces, revolts by *shizoku* and poor farmers could not possibly succeed so long as they remained localized movements. Mass mobilization along class lines was a precondition for success, yet in the end only a minority of *shizoku* and impoverished farmers took up arms against the state.

The very limited scale of antigovernment mobilization, despite the substantial decline in socioeconomic wellbeing nationwide, is the salient factor in the defeat of armed opposition to the Meiji oligarchy. Unlike the groups that rallied around the issues of property taxes and representative government, declassed *shizoku* and subsistence farmers had gained little and lost a great deal as a result of Meiji modernization. They had ample cause to take up arms, but comparatively few did.

There is very little evidence to support the claim that loyalty to the emperor, one of the traditional values assumed to have reduced political conflict in Meiji, had a decisive impact on the political behavior of ex-samurai who were faced with the dilemma between acquiescence in loss of status and social redundancy or revolt in defense of traditional privilege. As we have seen, the *shizoku* rebels of the 1870s had once been at the forefront of the Restoration movement, and there is no reason to believe that they were any less patriotic or that they regarded the imperial institution with less reverence than did the samurai who served the oligarchy. On the contrary, had they not already demonstrated a greater degree of personal commitment than had most of their peers?

If loyalty to the emperor was not the decisive factor inhibiting *shizoku* rebellion, then what was?

Shizoku in the 1870s lacked the organizational resources to mobilize around class interests because Meiji reforms had crippled traditional samurai structures of collective action. For nearly three centuries the feudal *kashindan* (daimyo retainer band) had defined the political world of the samurai. Living within pyramidal, rigid status hierarchies, samurai were subject to the absolute authority of daimyo and fief elders; stratified by hereditary rank within the domain, they were segregated from the samurai of other domains because of affiliation with a single military house. At least until the emergence of the activist *shishi* bands in response to the foreign crisis in the *bakumatsu* period, the *kashindan* stood as the only legitimate forum for political action. Consequently, when the government ordered the abolition of private fiefs in 1871 and disbanded the *kashindan,* it deprived the middle and low-ranking samurai – the strata least adequately compensated for the loss of traditional income and privilege – of familiar and authorized organizations for collective action. If they were to resist, they would first need to create new ideological and organizational structures. The vast majority were not able to do that.

Viewed from this perspective, it is not surprising that disaffected veterans of the *tōbaku* movement and not, for instance, Tokugawa loyalists led the *shizoku* revolts in the early Meiji period. Unlike their more conservative peers, they had already participated in voluntaristic political associations which to some degree transcended ascriptive status. Having once rebelled against established political authority, they could more easily authorize their own actions in terms of higher principles, even when this entailed breaking the emperor's laws. They did not, however, foresee the need to go beyond the organizations of the *tōbaku* movement, and they never developed class-based structures for political action. As we have seen, they continued to rely on local associations of like-minded "men of spirit," and these proved inadequate against the newly centralized state.

Meiji reforms also undercut the social basis of traditional village mobilization. As seen in village protests against the Meiji land tax, sustained opposition depended on the leadership of headmen and local notables. Although by no means entirely contingent on shared economic interests, the tradition of village officials leading protests against oppressive taxation was integrally bound up with the corporate features of the feudal tax system. But the Meiji land tax eliminated the village as a fiscal unit; landholding was fully privatized, and the payment of taxes was made an individual responsibility. Under these conditions, the impending bankruptcy of small farmers unable to pay the land tax became a class issue and ceased to be a matter of collective village concern. Moreover, the modernization of the legal system and security apparatus strengthened the position of the landlords and moneylenders. Unlike the bakufu and daimyo, the Meiji state provided policing at the village level, laws that protected private property, and courts to enforce them – all of which reduced local constraints on individual acquisition.

The sharp and permanent rise in tenancy during the agricultural depression of 1882–6 stands out as the most decisive change in rural relations in the early Meiji period. Deprived of the thin margin of protection that village solidarity had once provided, impoverished farmers suffered massive loss of land as a direct consequence of monetary and fiscal policies enacted by the oligarchy to spur capital accumulation and investment in industry. But only in Chichibu did they take up arms.

The conditions that made rebellion possible in Chichibu suggest the nature of the obstacles that existed elsewhere. In contrast with the situation in most areas, some, though not all, members of the local Jiyūtō took up the cause of indebtedness and foreclosures, thereby providing leadership. Second, the social structure favored collective action by the poor, inasmuch as a majority of farmers were threatened with bankruptcy. Nearly 70 percent of Chichibu farm household heads were small landowners who reared silkworms as a cash crop. In contrast with the cotton and rice export regions where subsistence farmers had already lost their land and become tenant farmers, most peasants in Chichibu were still struggling to keep their status as marginal cash-crop farmers. Third, as recently as 1866, under similar conditions of economic hardship and indebtedness among small-scale producers, the peasants of Chichibu had carried out massive attacks against moneylenders, local rice and silk dealers, and village officials in the name of "world rectification" (*yonaoshi*).[106]

In Chichibu, all the ingredients needed to pursue collective action were present: local leadership, a mass base, and familiar structures for peasant mobilization. However, whereas *yonaoshi*-type mobilization allowed the poor to carry out retribution against local propertied classes, it could not be sustained for a long period of time and had no chance of toppling the central government. The uprising dramatized the plight of impoverished farmers, but it did nothing to change the actual conditions of their lives.

It is part of the lore of Western historiography of the Meiji Restoration that in Japan, tradition aided rather than obstructed modernization. Although there is some truth to this interpretation, like many theories, it obscures even as it enlightens our understanding of historical process. What this analysis of the failure of the Meiji opposition movements suggests is that the Meiji reforms destroyed traditional structures of collective action that, if they had remained in place, would have permitted far broader mobilization against the programs of the Meiji government.

106 See Vlastos, *Peasant Protests*.

CHAPTER 7

JAPAN'S TURN TO THE WEST

Although Japan was never a "closed country" in the sense that *sakoku* literally implies, it did awaken from two hundred years of substantial "national isolation" in the last half of the nineteenth century to devote its full energy toward the realization of one goal – the establishment of a modern nation-state. This effort itself is better evidence of Japan's "turn to the West" than anything else, for the concept of a modern nation-state had yet to manifest itself in any non-Western country. In economic terms, a modern nation-state is a state that has experienced an industrial revolution; in social terms, it is a state with a centralized political system under which popular participation is structured through the parliamentary institutions of a constitutional order. By any measure, such characteristics of a state are thoroughly Western in nature and origin.

These distinguishing characteristics were not to be found in the Tokugawa *bakuhan* state. Nineteenth-century Japanese society was preindustrial, and its economy was based on forms of production that depended on animate rather than mechanical sources of power. A large bourgeoisie did exist to carry on commercial and financial enterprise, but it was excluded from participating in political decisions. The Tokugawa political structure was composed of a bureaucracy, representing feudally privileged classes that operated within a system that reconciled theoretically incompatible elements of feudalism and absolute shogunal "monarchy." Despite Japan's high level of cultural homogeneity – or perhaps because of it – the concept of a people as a "nation" that participated actively in the affairs of a "state" was unknown.

Confronted by an apparently superior "civilization" represented by the states of Europe, the Japanese confronted tasks of achieving modernity – making themselves into a "nation" and a "state" – following the opening of their country (*kaikoku*). To that end they had to create a central government, train bureaucrats to run the state, institute an army and a navy based on universal conscription, organize a legal system, foster capitalism, abolish feudal privilege, implement the "equality of the four status groups," consolidate a system of education, and reform their customs.

The individual who was perhaps most responsible for formulating these goals and was central to their execution in early Meiji years was Ōkubo Toshimichi (1830–78), a Satsuma leader who held real political power during the first decade of Meiji rule. Compared with his Chōshū colleague Kido Takayoshi (Kōin, 1833–77), Ōkubo was more conservative and less willing to sacrifice tradition in the quest for modernization. At the seashore near Osaka one day, Ōkubo gazed despondently at a clump of tree stumps – all that remained of a pine grove famous for its beauty – that had been leveled as a consequence of the policy of "foster industry and promote enterprise" (*shokusan kōgyō*), of which he himself was the leading proponent. Feeling the need to admonish the prefectural governor responsible for this insensitive act, Ōkubo composed the following poem:

> The pines at Takashi beach
> in spite of their renown,
> could not escape the ravage of
> historic tidal waves.[1]

Even for Ōkubo, however, the policy of "civilization and enlightenment" (*bummei kaika*) that Japan had adopted remained synonymous with Westernization. In an apparent belief that the Western powers were pure and simple embodiments of civilization, he wrote that "at present all the countries in the world are directing all their efforts toward propagating teachings of 'civilization and enlightenment,' and they lack for nothing. Hence we must imitate them in these respects."[2]

A revealing anecdote about the process by which the Meiji constitution was formulated points by extension to the larger question of preconditions within Japanese society that affected, assisted, and channeled the process of appropriating the Western example.

In 1883, Itō Hirobumi, the chief architect of the future constitution, led a delegation to Europe to study its various national constitutions. Because the Meiji government had already more or less decided to model its new constitution on that of Prussia, Itō and his delegates first visited the jurist Rudolf von Gneist (1816–95) in Berlin to seek his advice. Gneist's advice was cool and discouraging. He told them that several years earlier Bulgaria, one of several newly independent

---

[1] Nihon shiseki kyōkai, ed., *Ōkubo Toshimichi monjo*, vol. 9 (*Nihon shiseki kyōkai sōsho*, vol. 36) (Tokyo: Tokyo daigaku shuppankai, 1969), p. 347.
[2] Ōkubo Toshimichi, "Seifu no teisai ni kansuru kengensho," in *Ōkubo Toshimichi monjo*, vol. 3, p. 11.

and semiindependent countries that developed in the Balkans after the Russo-Turkish War, had asked for assistance in framing a constitution. Though all of Gneist's colleagues were hampered by a lack of knowledge about conditions in that country, one legal scholar had volunteered to go there to produce a constitution within six months' time, an offer that brought scornful amusement. True to his word, however, the man made good his boast. But upon his return to Berlin, he had provoked loud laughter among his colleagues with the quip, "After all, how long does it take to gloss over a bronze vessel with gold paint?"

Gneist went on to advise his Japanese guests as follows:

I am most grateful that you have chosen to come all the way to Germany on your mission. Unfortunately I know nothing of Japan, and have never studied it. Let me first ask you about Japan, about the relationship between ruler and ruled, its manners and customs, about the sentiments of its people, and about its history, etc. Clarify all these things for me first, and then I will think about them and provide you with an answer that might be of some assistance to you.[3]

In short, Gneist began by bluntly admonishing Itō that only those nations possessing a minimum degree of latent potential, that is, a certain level of cultural advancement, were capable of creating a truly meaningful constitution. To undertake such a task before acquiring the requisite capacity would merely result in an elaborately embellished piece of paper. Gneist then insinuated that in Japan's case the drafting of a constitution might very well be meaningless.

This brusque reply was thoroughly disheartening to Itō, the representative of a small, backward, East Asian country who stood face to face with a European civilization that was at the zenith of its power and glory and that was convinced of its own superiority as none other in recorded history had been. How could the words of a famous Berlin jurist fail to ring true in both East Asian and European ears?

Yet if as Gneist asserted, a constitution, the framework of a modern nation-state, "is more a legal document," if indeed it is "the manifestation of a people's spirit and the measure of a nation's capacities," then the fact that a modern nation-state did emerge in nineteenth-century Japan indicates that something in the "relationship between ruler and ruled," the "manners and customs," the "sentiments of its people," and its "history, etc." facilitated the creation of a new form of state based on the Meiji constitution. To put it differently, this process, and

---

3 Yoshida Masaharu, "Kempō happu made," in Oka Yoshitake, ed., *Kindai Nihon seiji-shi* (Tokyo: Sōbunsha, 1962), vol. 1, pp. 286–7.

indeed the rapidity, of Japan's Westernization indicates that the gap between Japan and the West at that time was entirely bridgeable.

Japan's "turn to the West" had to be carried out in two separate dimensions: (1) the importation and assimilation of modern ideas and institutions on a technical, formal level, such as Gneist's constitutional "legal document"; and (2) the adaptation of an indigenous, traditional culture and institutions to bring out their latent potential, in Gneist's terms, "the national spirit and capacities."

THE MEDIUM OF BOOKS: FIRST AWARENESS OF MODERN WESTERN CIVILIZATION

Dutch studies

Tokugawa society was culturally creative and produced much that we now consider "traditionally Japanese," but Japan was not by any means intellectually self-sufficient during its period of national isolation. Intellectual activity during the Edo period can be broadly classified into three categories: (1) Confucianism, which had a distinguished pedigree and possessed great prestige; (2) Japanese learning (*kokugaku*), which arose in mid-Tokugawa times as a reaction to the sinocentrism that then prevailed in scholarly circles; and (3) Dutch studies (*rangaku*), whose emergence was signaled by the translation into Japanese of a Dutch translation of a work on anatomy by the German doctor Kulmus, referred to as *Tafel Anatomia*, which was completed in 1774 by Sugita Gempaku and his colleagues. Dutch studies sprang up as an adjunct to medicine and gradually spread to other areas, such as language study, astronomy, geography, physics, chemistry, and military science. Although they appeared on the academic scene relatively late, Dutch studies had wide currency by late Tokugawa times, and the awareness of some Dutch studies specialists of the need to reconsider the system of national seclusion played an important role in bridging the intellectual gap between the West and Japan in the mid-nineteenth century.

It is significant that two of these three principal fields of Tokugawa learning derived from China and the West and were alien in origin. Japan remained in contact with China and Holland, the cultural homelands of Confucianism and Dutch studies, throughout the Edo period, although to be sure the degrees of contact differed greatly. Nevertheless, conventional generalizations about the period of "national isolation" (*sakoku*) prepare one poorly for understanding the amount and quality of information about the outside world that was accessible to Tokugawa thinkers. Chinese books, including Chinese translations of Western works, were imported every year from Ch'ing China. The Dutch East India Company maintained a Nagasaki outpost whose superintendent was required to submit reports on foreign affairs (*Oranda fūsetsugaki*) to the bakufu via the Nagasaki magistrate whenever Dutch ships made visits to that port. The same superintendent was obliged to travel to Edo at regular intervals for a formal shogunal audience, at first annually, then every other year, and finally every four years. On these trips he and his associates were able to convey information to doctors and astronomers there who were thirsting for knowledge about the West. There was thus direct, though limited, contact with representatives of European civilization. Just as Tokugawa Confucians reaped the benefits of Ch'ing philological and historical scholarship, Japanese students of Dutch studies profited from many of the modern scientific advances in contemporary Europe and America. Consequently, despite the restrictions imposed by national isolation, there was a considerable degree of openness and receptivity to East and West in the intellectual milieu of Tokugawa Japan.

Even so, one cannot fail to be struck by the extraordinary speed with which Dutch studies spread. That speed reflects both the intense curiosity of those Japanese who pledged themselves to this new exotic discipline and the enthusiasm with which they pursued it. Moreover, the seemingly unsystematic activities of the Dutch studies specialists belie a certain underlying regularity. All these elements – speed of diffusion, curiosity, enthusiasm, and selective approach – anticipate Japan's more ambitious, post-Restoration attempts to assimilate modern Western civilization.

In 1815, the eighty-two-year-old Sugita Gempaku (1733–1817) published *Rangaku kotohajime* (The beginnings of Dutch studies) in which he recalled the circumstances under which he, Maeno Ryōtaku, and their associates had begun the formidable task of translating a volume of anatomical tables, *Tafel Anatomia* (Ontleedkundige Tafelen), forty-three years earlier in 1771. It can be said that with that endeavor they initiated modern Japan's independent and eclectic assimilation of advanced Western civilization through the medium of books. Sugita decribed the speed with which Dutch studies subsequently spread and the strength of will displayed by its early proponents:

At present, Dutch studies are in great fashion throughout Japan. Those who have decided to pursue them do so avidly, although the ignorant among the populace praise and admire these studies in greatly exaggerated terms.

Reflecting upon the beginnings of Dutch studies, I realize that in those days, two or three friends and I decided to take them up almost on the spur of the moment. Yet close to fifty years have since elapsed, and how strange it is! When we began, I never in my wildest dreams thought that Dutch studies would achieve the popularity they enjoy today.

It was only natural for Chinese studies to develop and prosper gradually here in Japan. After all, in ancient times the government dispatched scholarly missions to China; later, learned clerics were also sent to the continent where they studied under Chinese masters. In either case, after their return to Japan, such persons were placed in positions to teach high and low, nobility and commoners, alike. But that was not the case with Dutch studies. . . .[4]

Sugita, probably like other Japanese intellectuals with a similar historical consciousness, saw his own efforts at assimilating Western culture as sharply at variance with Japan's established methods of assimilating Chinese culture, which had been followed for over a millennium. He posited three principal methods through which a foreign civilization could be assimilated: (1) experience, observation, and study abroad; (2) instruction by foreign or Japanese teachers; and (3) books. Between A.D. 607 and 894, the Japanese court had sponsored over a dozen scholarly missions to China for the direct observation of and instruction in Sui and T'ang culture. The contrast between these subsidized enterprises and Sugita's own humble efforts loomed large in his mind, for the sole medium of cultural assimilation accessible to him and his colleagues was books written in a language they could not read.

But despite these handicaps – the lack of official support and awesome linguistic difficulties – toward the end of his life Sugita remarked that Dutch studies had developed like "a drop of oil, which, when cast upon a wide pond, disperses to cover its entire surface," a process that "brings me nothing but jubilation." The advances made by Dutch studies had now reached a point at which, as Sugita noted, "every year new translations appear." With historical hindsight we can add that the tide of translations from the Dutch in early-nineteenth-century Japan may have been roughly comparable to the amount of translation from Japanese into Western languages a century or so later.

Sugita's jubilation was well founded, for unlike the days when Japan had imported Chinese civilization, study in the West was out of the question, and devotees of Dutch studies could not even get instruction from fellow Japanese, much less from foreign teachers, except for

---

[4] Odaka Toshio and Matsumura Akira, eds., *Nihon koten bungaku taikei*, vol. 95: *Taionki, Oritakushiba no ki, Rantō kotohajime* (Tokyo: Iwanami shoten, 1964), p. 473.

the bits and pieces of information they could cull from Japanese interpreters who accompanied the Dutch East India Company representatives during their stays in Edo. Deprived of even the most elementary language training, Sugita and his associates had to begin their translation of *Tafel Anatomia* by substituting Japanese equivalents of foreign names for parts of the body that appeared on anatomical diagrams.

For example, we spent a long spring day puzzling over such simple lines as "An 'eyebrow' is hair growing above the eye." We sometimes stared at each other blankly from morning to dusk, unable to decipher a single line from a one- to two-inch passage of text.

Nevertheless they gradually overcame these difficulties by application and enthusiasm:

Yet we believed that "Man proposes, Heaven disposes" and persevered. We would meet six or seven times a month and devoted ourselves body and soul to the project. No one ever begged off on the scheduled meeting days; we all assembled without being prevailed upon to do so, and we would read and discuss the text together. "Perseverance will prevail," we would reassure ourselves and pressed on.

After a year or so, our command of vocabulary gradually increased, and we naturally discovered a great deal about conditions in Holland. Later on, we became capable of reading as much as ten or more lines of text per day if the particular passage was not too difficult.[5]

Sugita's satisfaction in recollecting these experiences lay in the fact that the cultural legacy of Dutch studies to subsequent generations of Japanese owed its existence to the determination and zeal displayed by this small group of pioneers.

In the 1860s, Dutch studies and the Dutch language were abandoned in favor of English, which soon became the primary Western language for Japanese intellectuals. This transition from Dutch studies to Western learning was depicted by Fukuzawa Yukichi in his autobiography in which he described his experiences in the foreign sector of Yokohama after the ports had been opened in 1859. Fukuzawa tried to speak Dutch with foreigners only to find to his dismay that communication was impossible. Undaunted, he made up his mind to "devote himself to English." Fukuzawa was a pioneer in the study of English and became an enlightenment thinker who explained the development of Japanese history in Western terms. By emphasizing the importance of fundamental changes needed in Meiji Japan, he tended to slight Tokugawa achievements. Yet even Fukuzawa ex-

5 Ibid., pp. 515, 493, 495.

pressed his indebtedness to men like Sugita in the Dutch studies tradition. Having obtained a copy of Sugita's *Rangaku kotahajime*, Fukuzawa and Mitsukuri Shūhei sat opposite each other and read and reread it. When they reached the portion that compared the way that those pioneers had set out on the translation of *Tafel Anatomia* to sailors "drifting about in a boat without rudder or oar, helpless and baffled on a vast expanse of ocean," he wrote that they "sobbed wordlessly until they came to the end." Fukuzawa wrote: "Each time we read this book we realize how great their toil must have been; we are amazed at their courage; we feel their sincerity and singleness of purpose; and we try to hold back the tears."[6] Fukuzawa republished Sugita's book at his own expense in 1868, and in the foreword he related his feelings after having first read the work: "It was like encountering an old friend, someone I thought was dead, reborn and well." He wrote that the source of energy propelling Meiji Japan toward modernization could be traced to forerunners like Sugita and argued that "the beginnings of knowledge of Western civilization existed" a century before his time among scholars on this small island in East Asia, that "today's progress . . . is not a product of blind chance."[7]

The deciphering of *Tafel Anatomia* by Sugita and his associates illustrates Japan's positive response toward Western civilization. There are two explanations of this enthusiastic response. First, it reveals the Japanese intellectuals' unusually strong curiosity toward the outside world, and it shows that the value system to which they were committed did not emphasize intellectual self-sufficiency to the exclusion of new ideas: To a large extent, alien doctrines and learning could be absorbed and accommodated. Second, the personal motivation that sustained the pioneers demonstrates both their intellectual curiosity and their pragmatism. Maeno Ryōtaku "desired to make Dutch studies his life's work, to learn all there is to know about that language and thus to find out all there is to know about conditions in the West and to read numerous books,"[8] whereas Nakagawa Jun'an "had long been interested in what things were made of and wanted by this means to learn about Western products."[9] On the one hand we discover an orientation of almost purely intellectual curiosity and, on the other, one of practicability, both driving people toward Dutch studies. In Sugita's own case, the

---

[6] Quoted in "Rangaku kotohajime saihan no jo," in *Fukuzawa Yukichi zenshū* (Tokyo: Iwanami shoten, 1962), vol. 19, p. 770. [7] Ibid.
[8] *Nihon koten bungaku taikei*, vol. 95, p. 499. [9] Ibid., pp. 491–2.

motivation for translating *Tafel Anatomia* lay in his professional consciousness of being a physician. As he put it:

First and foremost, I wanted to make manifest the fact that actual dissections performed on human bodies confirmed the accuracy of Dutch anatomical diagrams and disproved Chinese and Japanese theories. Then I wanted to apply the Dutch theories in clinical treatment and to make these available to other physicians in order to encourage the development of new techniques.

Sugita's sense of mission had first been sparked by witnessing an autopsy performed at Kotsugahara in Edo in 1771. On the way home, he wrote, he discussed its results with Maeno and Nakagawa:

What a revelation that day's demonstration had been! We were truly embarrassed to discover our ignorance. Each of us, who was responsible for serving our lord as a physician, proved to be totally ignorant of the basic anatomical structure of man, which is fundamental to medical science. It was a disgrace that we had been carrying on our duties all along in this state of ignorance.

Some writers have tended to associate Dutch studies with a critical attitude toward feudal authority, but here we find one of its most devoted proponents troubled by the sense of "disgrace" stemming from his unworthiness to "serve his lord" properly. Such an ethos, emphasizing as Sugita did the responsibilities of a physician's hereditary status, easily transforms itself into an occupational ethic. The intensity of this spirit – related also to *bushidō* – and the ease with which it could be translated into an occupational ethic can be considered two key factors that made Japan's "turn to the West" possible at an early stage in its contact with the West, thereby distinguishing the Japanese experience from that of other non-Western countries.

The significance of Tokugawa lexicography

In the initial phase of contact between Western and non-Western peoples, most lexicography was a product of the burgeoning, expansive West. This is seen, for instance, in the *Vocabulario da Lingoa de Iapan* containing over thirty thousand entries compiled by the Jesuit Joao Rodriguez Tcuzzu in 1603. Later, however, non-Western peoples who perceived Europe to be "advanced" and strove to "catch up" with Western civilization seized this lexicographic initiative. The Japanese provide a good example. The growth of Dutch studies in Japan was ensured after 1796, when Inamura Sampaku published a Dutch-Japanese dictionary, the *Edo Halma*. This was an adaptation of François Halma's eighty-thousand-word Dutch-French dictionary in which Inamura substituted Japanese translations for the French equivalents. In the era of early encounters with English-speaking peoples that followed, Dutch-English conversations books, English-Dutch dictionaries, and then English-language dictionaries were used. Webster's dictionary first reached Japan via the Perry squadron; and later, in 1860, Fukuzawa Yukichi and Nakahama Manjirō each brought back a copy from San Francisco. The first English-Japanese dictionary, the six-thousand-word *Angeria gorin taisei*, was compiled at the bakufu's direction by the Nagasaki Dutch interpreter, Motoki Shōzaemon, in 1814; but Hori Tatsunosuke's *Ei-Wa taiyaku shūchin jisho*,[10] containing over thirty thousand entries and published in 1862, received far greater use. Hori used entries and sample phrases and sentences from the English-Dutch portion of H. Picard's *A New Pocket Dictionary of the English-Dutch and Dutch-English Languages*, eliminated the Dutch definitions, and supplied Japanese equivalents from the *Nagasaki Halma*, a Nagasaki version of the *Edo Halma* that had more colloquial expressions. Thus the study of English developed from that of Dutch, and knowledge accumulated rapidly. Among the dictionaries compiled by Americans in Japan is the *Wa-Ei gorin shūsei*, a work containing over twenty thousand words, published in 1867 by James Hepburn (1815–1911), Presbyterian medical missionary who came to Japan in 1859. But thereafter almost all the best dictionaries, whether English-Japanese, Japanese-English, German-Japanese, Japanese-German, French-Japanese, Japanese-French, or Russian-Japanese were compiled by Japanese.[11]

A nineteenth-century figure who perceived the significance of Tokugawa lexicography was Sakuma Shōzan (1811–64), a scholar of both Confucian and Western learning. Sakuma planned to publish a revised and enlarged edition of the *Edo Halma*, and to cover the expenses he borrowed twelve hundred *ryō* from his domain by pledging his own stipend of one hundred *koku* rice as collateral. Although this plan

---

10 Hori changed the "pocket" of Picard's pocket dictionary to a kimono sleeve; hence the character *shū*, as in *sode*.

11 Professor N. I. Konrad's *Japanese-Russian Dictionary*, a possible exception, remains unsurpassed by Japanese efforts, a fact that probably indicates Japanese priorities in foreign-language study. What has been said about Western-language dictionaries applies equally to Chinese. Morohashi Tetsuji's reference dictionary of classical Chinese, *Dai Kan-Wa jiten*, published in 1960 by a publishing house that had to set the work a second time after its plant was destroyed in 1945, is recognized as standard in all countries where Chinese characters serve as the written medium. Like the Western-language dictionaries, this work represents an attempt to assimilate a superior foreign culture by a less developed civilization, but it nevertheless surpasses all similar lexicographical achievements in China itself.

came to naught because the bakufu refused to grant permission, Sakuma's petition shows his perception of the importance and meaning of the enterprise he proposed:

> If only you would see this project as a way of laying the foundation for access to and mastery of proficiency in the arts and sciences, as a step toward adopting the strong points of countries on every continent in order to create a Japan forever able to maintain its autonomy in the world, then whatever criticism it might draw would be as inconsequential as the flapping of a mosquito's wings.[12]

The "science" referred to in Sakuma's famous slogan "Eastern morality, Western science" is often taken to mean only "technology," but in fact, his term has broader implications, including the arts and sciences that form the basis of that technology. This can be seen in comments he made to a correspondent:

> At present the learning of China and Japan is not sufficient; it must be supplemented and made complete by inclusion of the learning of the entire world. Columbus discovered a new world by "investigating principle"; Copernicus worked out the theory of heliocentricity; and Newton recognized the truth of gravitational laws. Since these three great discoveries were made, all arts and sciences have been based on them – each is true, not one is false.[13]

Sakuma believed that Confucianism was fully compatible with Western military technology and hence that Chinese and Western doctrines were ultimately identical. To him, dictionary compilation was an indispensable means to acquire this fundamentally identical knowledge. In the petition cited earlier, he also stated:

> Nothing is more important to the conduct of war, nor is there anything more pressing in present-day coastal defense, than Sun Tzu's adage "Know the enemy." Hence, I would like to see all persons in the realm thoroughly familiar with the enemy's conditions, something that can best be achieved by allowing them to read barbarian books as they read their own language. There is no better way to enable them to do this than publishing this dictionary.

The compilation and publication of this dictionary thus symbolized Sakuma's desire to understand foreign civilization in a fundamental and comprehensive manner. He was also eager to disseminate such understanding among his countrymen. The assimilation of Western culture through such a process of enlightenment was pursued on a national scale by the Meiji government a few years later, but to

---

12 "Haruma wo hangyō nite kaihan sen koto wo chinzu," in *Shōzan zenshū* (Tokyo: Shōbunkan, 1913), vol. 1, p. 128.
13 "Letter to Yanagawa Seigan," dated 3/6/Ansei 5 (1858), in ibid., vol. 2, pp. 845–6.

Sakuma, it still seemed as though the task hinged entirely on the bakufu's approval for publishing his laboriously brush-copied dictionary manuscript. Such was this Tokugawa intellectual's intensity on the eve of the Meiji Restoration.

The cultural and intellectual milieu of Dutch studies

Consideration of the setting within which Dutch studies was able to develop in Tokugawa times must include attention to general cultural traditions as well as an awareness of the specific trends of eighteenth-century intellectual life.

Tokugawa intellectuals began with an awareness of their ancestors' ability to adopt and adapt Chinese civilization; a millennium earlier, the Japanese had also thought of their land as existing on the outer fringes of a world cultural sphere. In a sense, nineteenth-century Japanese intellectuals needed only to transfer that center from China to the West. In this regard, the Japanese consciousness and problems differed strikingly from those of China, and consequently Japanese thinkers were probably better equipped psychologically for assimilating Western culture than were their Chinese counterparts. Just as they had earlier studied Chinese civilization under the slogan "Japanese spirit, Chinese skills," now they spoke of "Japanese spirit, Western skills."

The eighteenth-century pioneers in Dutch studies were fully aware of this parallel. Sugita Gempaku concluded his recollections of the growth of Dutch studies by asking: "Was it not because our minds had already been trained through Chinese learning that Dutch studies were able to develop this rapidly?"[14] Moreover, the "training" he had in mind had linguistic as well as attitudinal aspects. Unlike other East Asian peoples on the fringe of the Chinese cultural sphere, the Japanese early developed a method for adapting texts in classical Chinese to the syntactical rules of their own language, instead of reading classical Chinese as a foreign language. The result, known as *kambun* reading, was a complex and cumbersome procedure, but it involved rigorous intellectual training in translation that had as one consequence the nationalization of a foreign language.

Partly because of this and partly because of its relative isolation, Japan was never overwhelmed by Chinese – or Western – learning but retained a substantial cultural autonomy from which assimilation

---

14 "Rantō kotohajime," in *Nihon koten bungaku taikei*, vol. 95, p. 505.

could be managed. Just enough could be learned about the outside world to whet the curiosity of men seeking knowledge and instill in them admiration for the West without totally absorbing them into the "superior" culture. Given the physical isolation in which Tokugawa scholars of Dutch studies labored, there was never any possibility of their identifying themselves completely with the alien culture; their admiration for the West was fated to be pursued along purely intellectual lines. This geographical limitation contributed to the emphasis on retaining and strengthening the "Japanese spirit" while pursuing "Western skills." Hashimoto Sanai (1831–59) wrote that Japan should "adopt mechanical devices and techniques from the West but retain the benevolence, righteousness, loyalty, and filial piety of Japan."[15] Yokoi Shōnan (1809–69) agreed and urged his countrymen to "make manifest the Way of Yao, Shun, and Confucius and to obtain a thorough knowledge of mechanical techniques from the West."[16] Sakuma Shōzan also spoke of "Eastern morality and Western techniques." The future Meiji government accepted these goals under the slogan "Adopt what is best in the culture of Europe to compensate for shortcomings in that of Japan."

It is also useful to examine eighteenth-century intellectual trends that helped give rise to Dutch studies. For the most part, the era was characterized by empiricism, a development that arose also within Ch'eng-Chu Confucianism, the grand system of speculative philosophy that provided the principal current of orthodox learning during the Edo period. Those trends within Confucianism are treated elsewhere, and this discussion is limited to the development of empirical trends in relation to Tokugawa medicine, the womb from which Dutch studies emerged.

Japan first encountered Western civilization in the late sixteenth century, before the national isolation of Tokugawa times. In that warring era, survival of the fittest was the rule, and political leaders were keenly aware of the need to appropriate any new device that would increase their chances of achieving victory. They were utterly indifferent as to whether cultural accretions like firearms or surgery were of foreign or native origin. At that time the Japanese learned early Western-style surgery through direct observation of Iberian practice

---

15 "Letter to Murata Ujihisa," dated 10/21/Ansei 4, in Nihon shiseki kyōkai, ed., *Hashimoto Keigaku zenshū*, vol. 2 (*Nihon shiseki kyōkai sōsho*, vol. 47) (Tokyo: Tokyo daigaku shuppankai, 1977), pp. 471–2.
16 "Letter to Nephews Studying in the West," in Nihon shiseki kyōkai, ed., *Yokoi Shōnan kankei shiryō*, vol. 2 (*Zoku Nihon shiseki kyōkai sōsho*, vol. 40) (Tokyo: Tokyo daigaku shuppankai, 1977), p. 726.

rather than through written accounts, and a distinct school of "southern barbarian" surgery developed. It was a physician (Kurisaki Dōyū) trained in this school who treated the wounds sustained by the shogunal official Kira Yoshinaka in 1701 in the incident that led to the celebrated vendetta of the forty-seven *rōnin*. This school of surgery was dominant until it was superseded by techniques developed by students of Dutch studies, but it contributed almost nothing to the latter's emergence. The impetus behind Dutch studies lay elsewhere, in Tokugawa Confucianism.

Toward the end of the seventeenth century, a number of private scholars challenged the Ch'eng-Chu Confucian school that then dominated the Tokugawa scholarly world. One of the foremost was Itō Jinsai (1627–1705) of Kyoto, who propounded the so-called Ancient Learning (also known as the School of Ancient Meanings) which rejected medieval commentaries and sought the Way of the sages by going directly back to the *Analects*, the *Mencius*, and other Confucian classics. Thus Jinsai's school may be considered a form of antiquarian revivalism. Slightly later, Ogyū Sorai (1666–1728), also an advocate of ancient learning, had an even greater impact on the contemporary intellectual scene. The influence of these teachings was felt beyond the field of Confucian scholarship. For example, Japanese learning (*kokugaku*) held that the pristine "true Japanese heart" could be discovered only by rejecting the "spirit of China" that had come to muddy it in later ages and that this could best be done through studying the *Kojiki*, the *Manyōshū*, and other ancient Japanese classics.

Until the middle of the Edo period, Tokugawa medical thought was dominated by the Li-Chu school of Chinese medicine that had developed under Li Tung-yuan and Chu Tan-ch'i during the Chin and Yuan periods. It was a form of speculative philosophy that discussed human pathology in terms of *yin–yang*, the Five Elements, the Five Circulations, and the Six *ch'i*. But under the influence of mid-Tokugawa Ancient Learning, a movement arose among nongovernment scholar-physicians to reject such speculative ideas as latter-day inventions and to return to the "Way" that medicine had supposedly been practiced in ancient China, as depicted in works such as *Shang-han lun*.[17] This movement was related to the School of Ancient Learning in its emphasis on the empirical. Gotō Konzan (1683–1755), who was an admirer of Itō Jinsai, sent one of his own disciples, Kagawa

---

17 A medical text written by Chang Chung-ching of the later Han dynasty. The oldest extant edition was compiled by Wang Shu-ho of the Western Chin. Centuries later in the Sung, Lin I published a newly edited edition.

Shūan (1683–1755), to study at Jinsai's private academy. Under Kagawa there evolved a form of Confucian-medical thought that viewed Confucius' "Way of the sages" as being basically identical with a "Way of medicine." According to Kagawa, the sages and worthies of antiquity were staunch in their reverence for empirical fact, and latter-day speculative philosophers had obfuscated that emphasis. The School of Ancient Method, as it came to be known, repudiated such latter-day accretions in favor of a return to the direct study of ancient Chinese medical texts.

The critical basis for this antiquarian revivalism was a positivism that insisted that hypotheses be verified. In time this emphasis made its proponents skeptical of the validity of ancient as well as medieval medical texts. For example, one scholar, Nagatomi Dokushōan (1734–66), related the story of a T'ang palace painter, Han Kan, who, when ordered by the emperor to paint a horse, was offered pictures done by former palace artists for reference. He replied, "I have no desire to look at such pictures, for the horses kept in Your Majesty's stables will provide far better reference." The physician too, Nagatomi concluded, must work in this manner. The mere reading of texts was insufficient; the physician had to be free of preconceived notions, tend a real patient, conduct a close and direct examination, and use his own ingenuity to devise a cure. This process was known as *shinshi jikken* (personal examination and actual experience). Yoshimasu Tōdō (1702–73), who stressed this method of *shinshi jikken*, devoted himself to what is now called the "symptomatic treatment" of diseases. In his book *Medical Diagnoses* he wrote that "principles" (*li*), or a priori speculative theories, are subjective, vary with the people who hold them, and lack established standards by which they can be confirmed or disproved. Diseases, on the other hand, have specific symptoms. In short, a doctor should not employ subjective theories without careful and accurate diagnoses of the diseases. Yamawaki Tōyō (1705–62) was long skeptical of the traditional anatomical diagrams used by Tokugawa specialists of Chinese medicine. With encouragement from his teacher, Gotō Konzan, he dissected an otter. Next, after obtaining official permission, he performed an autopsy on an executed criminal in 1754 and recorded his observations in a work entitled *Account of an Autopsy*. This work shocked the Tokugawa medical world. Yamawaki became the object of much censure and attack, but he steadfastly maintained his views. In his *Account*, he wrote: "Theories [*li*] may be overturned, but how can real material things deceive? When theories are esteemed over reality, even a man of great wisdom cannot fail to err. When material things are investigated and theories are based on that, even a man of common intelligence can perform well."

Yamawaki and his colleagues brought to the autopsy a Dutch translation of a textbook on anatomy written by a professor at Padua University. They were astonished to discover how closely the book's diagrams matched the corpse's organs. Yamawaki had originally viewed Vesling's diagrams with some disbelief because of their great discrepancy with prevailing Chinese medical theories, but when he compared these Western diagrams with actual human anatomy and verified their accuracy, he realized how outlandish the Chinese versions were. As he put it: "He who treads the Way of fact reaches the same end though living ten thousand miles away. How can I suppress my admiration?" This reveals the idea that differences of nation or race are irrelevant to the quest for objective fact and the realization that the road to truth, which had been obscured in China since medieval times, paradoxically existed among those very Westerners normally considered barbarians.

There was thus a clear relationship between the textual rigor of the School of Ancient Learning and the practical and empirical emphases of Dutch studies. The connection can also be traced in personal as well as intellectual terms. Kosugi Genteki, a student of Yamawaki Tōyō who witnessed the autopsy, was a domain physician in Obama and thus a colleague of Sugita Gempaku. Another Yamawaki disciple, Kuriyama Kōan, himself performed two autopsies in Hagi, the castle town of Chōshū, and Sugita in 1771 managed to arrange and be present at an autopsy in Edo which he described as the starting point of his dedication to truth through experiment. The accuracy of the anatomical tables of the Kulmus volume he had with him that day so impressed him that he and his colleagues resolved to translate the entire work.

Sugita's memoirs no doubt risk exaggerating the role of this event in a tradition already being transformed, but it should at the least be considered symbolic if not pivotal. There is a sense, moveover, in which Sugita and his contemporaries followed Ancient Learning to go a step beyond the promising beginning made earlier by Yamawaki. Despite the rhetoric of practicality and observation found in Yamawaki and his contemporaries, they tended in practice to restrict themselves to the wisdom of antiquity and refrained from pushing their ideas to their logical conclusions.[18] Sugita, however, in his *Nocturnal*

---

18 For developments in medicine and thought on the eve of the rise of *rangaku*, see Fujikawa Hideo, "Kohōka to rangaku," in Fujikawa Hideo, *Seitō shiwa* (Tokyo: Tamagawa daigaku shuppanbu, 1974), pp. 9–20. For a general treatment of *rangaku* and Western learning, see Satō Shōsuke, *Yōgaku-shi kenkyū josetsu* (Tokyo: Iwanami shoten, 1964).

Dialogues with My Silhouette, described how his reading of Ogyū Sorai's treatise on military science, *Kenroku gaisho*, motivated him to try to formulate a systematic study of medicine based on empirical methods:

> Sorai writes that true warfare is very different from what so-called masters of the art of war teach us. Topography may be hilly or flat, and armies may be strong or weak. One cannot make identical cut-and-dried preparations that will be right for all times and all places; one cannot discourse on victory and defeat in unvarying, stereotyped fashion prior to the commencement of an engagement. . . . Victory or defeat are determined on a case-by-case basis by constant study of strategic principles and by the capacities of great generals.[19]

In this way, military strategy discussed by the leading proponent of Ancient Learning was transferred to the realm of medicine, combined with systematic observation (*shinshi jikken*), and applied to the appropriation and utilization of Dutch medical and scientific lore by the pioneers of Dutch studies in late-eighteenth-century Japan. A half-century later the crisis in foreign relations found the emphasis shifting back to military concerns; ultimately it flowered in the Meiji government's policies of selective Westernization. These developments were thus of momentous significance for Japanese thought and Japan's assimilation of Western culture.

FROM BOOKS TO EXPERIENCE: LATE TOKUGAWA AND EARLY MEIJI TRAVELERS

Japan's longing to see the outside world

One of the striking phenomena of mid-nineteenth-century Japan is the strong desire of educated Japanese to see the outside world. With an eighty-year history of Dutch studies behind them, many Japanese grew dissatisfied with relying solely on books to learn about the West. Presented with the evidence of Perry's "Black Ships" that Japan had fallen behind during its two-century absence from the stage of world history, many young men resolved to meet the challenge posed by technological superiority of Western civilization by investigating Western civilization at its source. Yamaji Aizan described the late Tokugawa zeitgeist as a "desire to speed to foreign shores and take up the great task of observing far-off lands."[20] Miyake Setsurei, in his *History*

---

19 Sugita Gempaku, "Keiei yawa," in Fujikawa Yū et al., eds., *Kyōrin sōsho* (Kyoto: Shibunkaku reprint edition, 1971), vol. 1, p. 106. This passage is also quoted in Satō, *Yōgaku-shi kenkyū josetsu*, p. 60.
20 Yamaji Aizan, "Niijima Jō ron," in Yamaji Aizan, *Kirisutokyō hyōron, Nihon jimminshi* (Tokyo: Iwanami shoten, 1966), p. 44.

of Our Times, wrote: "Only the ignorant and indolent among the samurai were surprised upon learning of [Yoshida] Shōin's plan to visit America, for not a few like-minded men were making similar preparations. Ultimately his plan was implemented in the form of sending a bakufu warship to San Francisco in 1860."[21] Thus the steam engines of Perry's Black Ships, considered symbolic of the West's superior technology, convinced Japanese of their country's inferiority; their "consciousness of crisis" dictated that "there is no more pressing need in our defense against the barbarians at present than 'knowing the enemy'." This realistic, empirical outlook made it a prime task to "investigate enemy conditions," a goal mirrored in the title of Fukuzawa Yukichi's best-seller, *Conditions in the West*.

That this determination was shared by different sorts of men can be shown by comparing the cases of Yoshida Shōin and Niijima Jō. At first glance they seem an unlikely pair. Yoshida (1830–59) is known to history as a fiery nationalist and exponent of total, unquestioning loyalty to the emperor. His fury at the bakufu's agreement to sign the humiliating unequal treaties led him into teaching and plotting so extreme that he was executed in the Ansei purge carried out by Ii Naosuke. His unwavering espousal of the imperial cause as the highest duty made him a rallying point and martyr for later nationalism and nationalists. As early as 1867 the Chōshū loyalist Takasugi Shinsaku, and as recently as 1970 the novelist Mishima Yukio, invoked his words in justifying ritual suicide in the national cause. Niijima (1843–90), on the other hand, is known to his countrymen as an ardent Christian and Westernizer, a runaway from feudal jurisdiction who found protection, kindness, and Christianity in America, was educated at Amherst College and Andover Seminary, and returned to Japan to found its first Christian university (Dōshisha) in Kyoto, the ancient capital and heartland of Japanese Buddhism. Nevertheless, Yoshida and Niijima shared a basic receptivity and curiosity regarding the West and a great desire to learn in the hope of preparing themselves and their country to accept the challenge posed by that West.

The case of Yoshida Shōin

Yoshida Shōin's encounter with the West came at the dawn of Japan's opening by the squadron of Commodore Perry's Black Ships. Perry arrived in 1853, left President Millard Fillmore's letter requesting

21 Miyake Setsurei, *Dōjidaishi* (Tokyo: Iwanami shoten, 1949), vol. 1, pp. 2–3.

formal diplomatic relations, and sailed away with a warning that he would return for a reply in the spring of 1854. In the interim Sakuma Shōzan counseled his young student Shōin that it would be worthwhile to try to leave Japan with the squadron when it returned in order to equip himself with direct knowledge of the West.

While Perry's ships were inspecting the harbor of Shimoda in April 1854, J. W. Spaulding, captain's clerk of the *Mississippi*, was ashore for a stroll one afternoon when two young men dressed as samurai approached him, ostensibly to examine his watch chain. Once within reach, one of them thrust a letter into the vest of the startled clerk. Flawlessly written in classical Chinese, which S. W. Williams, the American interpreter, could read, it stated: "We have . . . read in books, and learned a little by hearsay, what the customs and education in Europe and America are, and we have been for many years desirous of going over the 'five great continents'." The exaggerated metaphors of the *kambun* document reveal the intensity of Yoshida's desire to learn about the world outside Japan:

When a lame man sees others walking, he wishes to walk too; but how shall the pedestrian gratify his desires when he sees another one riding? We have all our lives been going hither to you, unable to get more than thirty degrees east and west, or twenty-five degrees north and south; but now when we see how you sail on the tempests and cleave the huge billows, going lightning speed thousands and myriads of miles, scurrying along the five great continents, can it not be likened to the lame finding a plan for walking, and the pedestrian seeking a mode by which he can ride?[22]

The abortive effort of the two young men to secure passage on the *Mississippi* in the dead of night, before an answer could be given to this document, is well known. Perry felt it poor policy to help them break the laws of their government against travel overseas so soon after securing the treaty he had come to negotiate, and he reluctantly denied their request after discussing it with them through the interpreter on board. What should be noted, however, is the recklessness of the attempt and the intensity and, no doubt, naïveté, of their behavior. This disregard for personal danger and single-mindedness of purpose earned the warmhearted understanding of S. Wells Williams, the interpreter, which can be inferred from Yoshida's *Account of a Spring Night*, Spaulding's *Japan Expedition*, and F. L. Hawks's *Narrative*.

22 Yamaguchi-ken kyōikukai, ed., *Yoshida Shōin zenshū* (Tokyo: Iwanami shoten, 1936), vol. 10, p. 876. Also in Francis L. Hawks, *Narrative of the Expedition of an American Squadron to the China Seas and Japan: Performed in the Years 1852, 1853, and 1854, under the Command of Commodore M. C. Perry, United States Navy, the Official Account* (Washington, D.C.: Beverley Tucker, Senate Printer, 1856), p. 420.

Spaulding's account described the consequences for the two:

A few days afterward, some of our officers in their strolls ashore ascertained that there were two Japanese confined in a cage at a little barrack back of the town, and on going there they were found to be the persons who had paid the midnight visit to our ships, and they also proved to be my unfortunate friends of the letter. They did not appear greatly down-cast by their situation, and one of them wrote in his native character on a piece of board, and passed [it] through the bars of his cage, to one of our surgeons present. . . .[23]

The officers of the American fleet discussed the possibility of intervening to save the men's lives, but the next time they went ashore, the two were nowhere to be seen. Rumor had it that they had been transferred to an Edo prison, and when an official they questioned gestured ominously with hand to throat, the Americans realized that the two had or would soon be executed. Spaulding, recalling that the writing on the letter that had been thrust into his vest appeared "neat and sharply defined," concluded that the writer was surely "a man of intelligence and taste," and Hawks's *Narrative* account of the initial encounter concurs that "the Japanese were observed to be men of position and rank, as each wore the two swords characteristic of distinction, and were dressed in the wide but short trousers of rich silk brocade. Their manners showed the usual courtly refinement of the better classes. . . ."[24] Clearly the Americans were impressed by the courageous sense of purpose shown by Shōin, convinced of his qualities, and sympathetic toward his fate. The affair no doubt served to convince them all the more strongly of the justness of their mission to open Japan.

The message written on a small piece of wood that Yoshida was able to hand to the American naval surgeon who happened to pass by his cage was described by Hawks as a "remarkable specimen of philosophical resignation under circumstances which would have tried the stoicism of Cato." It read in part:

When a hero fails in his purpose, his acts are then regarded as those of a villain and robber . . . while yet we have nothing wherewith to reproach ourselves, it must now be seen whether a hero will prove himself to be one indeed. Regarding the liberty of going through the sixty States [Japanese provinces] as not enough for our desires, we wished to make the circuit of the five great continents. This was our hearts' wish for a long time. Suddenly our plans are defeated. . . . Weeping, we seem as fools; laughing, as rogues. Alas! for us; silent we can only be.[25]

23 Hawks, *Narrative*, pp. 884–5.   24 Ibid.
25 *Yoshida Shōdin zenshū*, pp. 874–5; and Hawks, *Narrative*, pp. 422–3.

Yoshida lived another five years, during which he inspired a generation of Chōshū disciples in the academy that the domain authorities permitted him to direct during his confinement. As he explained to one such student, Shinagawa Yajirō:

> If one is loath to die at seventeen or eighteen, he will be equally reluctant at thirty, and will no doubt find a life of eight or ninety too short. Insects of the field and stream live but half a year, yet do not regard this as short. The pine and oak live hundreds of years, yet do not regard this as long. Compared to the eternity of Heaven and Earth, both are ephemeral insects. Man's life span is fifty years; to live seventy is a rarity. Unless one performs some deed that brings a sense of gratification before dying, his soul will never rest in peace.[26]

This was not to be; further plotting brought Yoshida's extradition to Edo and his execution in 1859. Yoshida described himself as one "who fails in every enterprise undertaken, who bungles every chance for power and fortune." All the schemes he concocted, not only his trip to America, seemed to go awry. Yet his determination to know the West and his fervent loyalism lived on in his students and caught the eye of a sympathetic writer as early as 1882. Robert Louis Stevenson learned of Yoshida Shōin through a student of his Chōshū school, Masaki Taizō, who was studying at Edinburgh, and the stories that Masaki told about his teacher became a chapter in Stevenson's *Familiar Studies of Men and Books*. Stevenson quoted Thoreau to the effect that "if you can 'make your failure tragical by courage, it will not differ from success' " and concluded that "this is as much the story of a heroic people as that of a heroic man." Stevenson's other heroes in this volume possessed characteristics similar to those with which Japanese admirers have associated Yoshida Shōin: bravery, self-reliance, tenacity of will, a high sense of honor, and fervent aspiration. They were qualities required by Japanese who resolved to travel to the West in late Tokugawa days, and they were suprisingly common.

The case of Niijima Jō

Yoshida Shōin and Niijima Jō were part of the same late Tokugawa phenomenon, an urge to experience the West directly. Yoshida's attempt was abortive partly because it was made too early, in 1854, and partly because he chose the official channels of Perry's fleet on its initial diplomatic mission. By contrast, Niijima's attempt came a decade later, in 1864, and through the private auspices of an American

---

26 "Letter to Shinagawa Yajirō," dated circa 4/Ansei 6, in *Shōin zenshū*, vol. 6, p. 318.

merchant ship. Moreover, during the ten intervening years there had been much exchange and travel. The Tokugawa warship *Kanrin maru* had sailed to the California coast to accompany the shogunal mission to Washington in 1860, the first of a series of ever-larger and ever-more observant official missions to the West as treaty relations intensified. In 1862 the shogunate had sent Nishi Amane, Enomoto Takeaki, and Tsuda Mamichi to Holland to study. In 1863, the domain of Chōshū violated shogunal law by sending Itō Hirobumi and Inoue Kaoru, students of Yoshida's, to study in England; and the southern domain of Satsuma was preparing a large mission of fourteen students to go to to England in 1865. Knowledge of such travel usually spread to at least the families of those involved. When the Chōshū samurai (and later foreign minister) Aoki Shūzō visited the castle town of Nakatsu in Kyūshū while Fukuzawa Yukichi was abroad as interpreter for one such official mission, Fukuzawa's mother was able to show him letters and photographs – the first Aoki had ever seen – from her distant son.

Nevertheless, individual travel was still quite different, and very dangerous. Niijima later described his eagerness to travel in English still far from perfect: "Some day I went to the seaside of Yedo, hoping to see the view of the sea. I saw largest man-of-war of Dutch lying there, and it seemed to me a castle or a battery, and I thought too she would be strong to fight with enemy."[27] The excitement felt by this late Tokugawa youth is apparent. Niijima was acutely aware of Japan's need to create a navy and of the important benefits to be had from seaborne trade.

Niijima was chosen by his domain of Annaka to study Dutch, and he learned to read books on natural science. ("I read through the book of nature at home, taking a dictionary of Japan and Holland.") He had studied at the bakufu's Naval Training Institute for a time but found this inadequate and unsatisfying and decided that he must go overseas himself. Niijima was motivated by precisely the same simple-minded directness that Yoshida had shown, and as in Yoshida's case, Americans – the captain of the *Berlin*, who smuggled him out of Hakodate against instructions, and the captain of the *Wild Rover*, to which Niijima transferred in Shanghai and who accepted responsibility for him during the year-long voyage to Boston – found themselves drawn to him by the intensity of his passion. In Boston, the Alpheus Hardys, owners of the *Wild Rover*, after reading Niijima's poorly composed

---

27 A. S. Hardy, *Life and Letters of Joseph Hardy Neesima* (Boston: Houghton Mifflin, 1892), p. 6.

English explanation for coming to America, generously paid his school fees and supported him through his undergraduate education at Amherst College and his theological training at Andover Seminary.

When Niijima discovered that the captain of the *Berlin*, who had taken him on board, had been dismissed for having helped him leave Hakodate, he made the following diary entry:

> Ah, I feel torn with guilt for having caused that good man such grief. But what is done is done, and cannot be undone. In the future, when my schooling is finished, I will do all I can to repay each and every one of his kindnesses to me. Maybe then I can make up for a small part of my wrongdoing against him.[28]

Westerners could no longer be considered "barbarians" by a man of such gratitude and conviction.

Individual Westerners, of course, could still provoke strong reactions. Niijima served as the captain's valet, "cleaning his cabin, waiting on him, washing his cups and saucers, and caring for his dog" — duties that he could stoop to perform only because there were no other Japanese to watch him. Having been trained in etiquette in Annaka, Niijima was well equipped to minister to the captain's needs, and we may imagine that he did so splendidly; but his samurai pride was often gravely injured. On one occasion he was reprimanded for not obeying directions given in English by a passenger whose services he had requested as a language teacher. An expert swordsman, Niijima raced back to his cabin, took his sword, and prepared to cut down the passenger when he remembered his mission and stopped. No doubt such endurance and self-restraint were required more than once during the voyage.

After transferring to the *Wild Rover* at Shanghai, Niijima asked its captain to take him to America and presented him with the longer of his two samurai swords as a token of his gratitude. He also had the captain sell the shorter sword for $8.00 so that he might purchase a translation of the New Testament in classical Chinese. This captain, whom Niijima admired greatly, was unable to pronounce Japanese and so called Niijima "Joe." In 1876, Niijima formally adopted "Jō" as his first name. He later wrote his name "Joseph Hardy Neesima" in English, using "Hardy" to express his gratitude to the Boston shipowner couple who had cared for him and for whom he "felt a greater sense of gratitude than for his own parents." Niijima, an eldest son, justified his violation

---

28 Diary entry, 9/13/Meiji 1, in *Niijima Jō sensei shokan shū zokuhen* (Kyoto: Dōshisha kōyūkai, 1960), p. 239.

of filial piety and his illegal departure from Japan in terms of serving his "Father who art in Heaven." He became a Christian, found a new father and mother in the Hardys, and pursued his studies in America with total peace of mind.

In time, official Japanese policy turned to support what had been the goals of Niijima's decisions for disobedience and flight. By the time of the Iwakura mission to the West in 1871–3, when Niijima was still studying in the United States, he was asked to serve as official interpreter for his country's highest officials, and upon his return to Japan in 1874 he was able to win the confidence and help of high officials like Kido Takayoshi (a member of the Iwakura mission) in gaining permission to found his Christian college in Kyoto. By then Japan's policy of "civilization and enlightenment" seemed virtually indistinguishable from Niijima's personal mission to convert his fellow Japanese to Christianity. At that time Niijima clearly had a linear view of progress, and he saw Westernization, civilization, and Christianity as a single goal to be sought. As he put it in an appeal for support for his college in 1884: "It is the spirit of liberty, the development of science, and the Christian morality that have given birth to European civilizations. . . . We cannot therefore believe that Japan can secure this civilization until education rests upon the same basis. With this foundation the State is built upon a rock. . . ."[29]

Two points emerge from these two dramatically different careers. The first is that Yoshida Shōin, no less than Niijima Jō, began with a warm, trusting, and optimistic view of a West whose strengths he proposed to appropriate for his backward but beloved country. The second is that Niijima Jō, no less than Yoshida Shōin, though committing himself to the West totally in terms of personal relations and spiritual beliefs, did so in the conviction that he was contributing to the "foundation of the state."[30]

Learning missions to the West

Yoshida Shōin and Niijima Jō were not the only Japanese longing to experience the West directly; high-ranking officials in the very bakufu

---

29 "Meiji Semmon Gakkō setsuritsu shishu," in *Niijima sensei shokanshū* (Kyoto: Dōshisha kōyūkai, 1942), pp. 1158–9.
30 I have discussed the attitudes toward America of Yoshida Shōin, Niijima Jō, and other mid-nineteenth-century travelers in Hirakawa Sukehiro, *Seiyō no shōgeki to Nihon* (Tokyo: Kōdansha, 1974), pp. 139–99.

that prohibited travel to foreign lands strongly desired to see the West with their own eyes and create a navy equal to those of Western nations. As early as February 6, 1858, Japanese representatives negotiating the Treaty of Amity and Commerce between the United States and Japan were reported by the American consul, Townsend Harris, to have

> proposed, if I [Harris] was willing, to send an ambassador in their steamer to Washington *via* California for that purpose! I told them nothing could possibly give me greater pleasure. That, as the United States was the first power that Japan ever made a treaty with, I should be much pleased that the first Japanese Ambassador should be sent to the United States.[31]

Japanese documents record this incident as follows: "Your nation has sent a total of three missions (including this one) to obtain this treaty. Now that it has been concluded, would it be possible for us to send a mission of our own to Washington for purposes of exchanging the documents?"[32]

Iwase Tadanari, who made this statement, probably did so in hopes of being sent himself, but two years of political upheaval, which included the Ansei purge, elapsed before the project was realized. Finally, in 1860, Shimmi Masaoki was selected as chief ambassador ("due to my father's achievements," as he put it); Muragaki Norimasa was deputy ambassador; and Oguri Tadamasa, superintendent and inspector (*metsuke*). Muragaki, a man of gentle disposition, left the detailed *Kōkai nikki* (Voyage diary) in which he described his feelings when he was summoned to Edo Castle and informed of his appointment:

> Although we did dispatch "official envoys" to T'ang China in ancient times, that neighboring land was only a strip of water away; but America lies a myriad miles beyond our Divine Land, and when it is daytime there, it is nighttime here.

> I humored [my daughters, boasting,] "a man could achieve no greater honor than to assume this heavy, unprecedented responsibility and thereby attain renown throughout the five continents." But on second thought I realized, "a foolish man like myself accepting this first of all missions to a foreign land? Should I fail to execute the shogunal decree, our Divine Land will suffer humiliations untold." Just then, the moon was shining so clear and bright that I felt moved to a toast in solemn thanks for shogunal confidence:

---

31 M. E. Cosenza, ed., *The Complete Journal of Townsend Harris* (Rutland, Vt.: Tuttle, 1959), p. 531.
32 Dated 12/23/Ansei 4, in *Dainihon komonjo: Bakumatsu gaikoku kankei monjo* (Tokyo: Tokyo teikoku daigaku, 1925), vol. 18.

> Henceforth foreigners as well
> will gaze
> upon the moon
> of our Japan.[33]

The tension in this poem contrasts with the following, which Muragaki composed upon his arrival in San Francisco:

> Foreign lands as well,
> lie beneath the same sky.
> Gaze upward and behold
> the mist-veiled spring moon.

Clearly, the sense of self-importance enabling Muragaki to carry out his duties had weakened. Finally, the following poem expressed his sentiments when he parted with the captain and crew of the *Powhatan* in Panama:

> Though a glance reveals
> that they are foreigners,
> the sincerity of heart they display
> differs not from our own.[34]

Thus Muragaki expressed his appreciation to the American crew. After traveling with them, he had discovered the universality of human nature.

After "the Tycoon's envoys" ratified the Treaty of Amity and Commerce between the two nations in Washington with Louis Cass, President James Buchanan's secretary of state, they made their way to New York. In his diary Muragaki described in detail their welcome there on 4/28/1860. Walt Whitman also described the festivities in his "A Broadway Pageant." The poem describes not only Broadway, which on that day "was entirely given up to foot-passengers and foot-standers" but also the joy of seeing the union of East and West and the oneness of the universe.

The welcome received by the members of the mission became known throughout Japan after their return home, and the mistaken image of Westerners as barbarians was modified, albeit gradually and among a limited number of intellectuals. In Yokoi Shōnan's remote Kumamoto country school, lectures on the *Analects* were revised. Shōnan's gloss on the first entry reads:

---

33 Muragaki Awaji no Kami Norimasa, *Kōkai nikki* (Tokyo: Jiji shinsho, 1959). This work was translated by Helen Uno as *Kokai Nikki: The Diary of the First Japanese Embassy to the United States of America* (Tokyo: Foreign Affairs Association of Japan, 1958). That translation has been modified here.   34 Uno, *Kokai Nikki*, pp. 38, 51.

[*Analects*]: "Is it not a joy to have friends come from afar?"

[Shōnan's gloss]: The phrase "have friends" means that when we appreciate learning and are eager to study, if we voluntarily approach, become intimate with, and speak to a man of virtuous repute whether he lives near or far away, that person will as a matter of course confide in us and become intimate with us in return. This is what is meant by the principle of "feeling and response" (*kannō*).

The term *friends* is not limited to scholar-friends. When we study to adopt the good points of any person, all men in the world are our friends.[35]

Then this scholar-statesman cited recent historical developments and advocated revising Japan's international relations on the basis of universal brotherhood:

Viewed from a wider perspective, this principle of "feeling and response" may be witnessed in the warm reception extended by the Americans to the recent bakufu embassy sent to their land. Their cordiality was deep indeed. By extending this meaning [of friends] to all people in the world, and not just to those in Japan, they are all our friends.

Because sentiments for *jōi* were intense in Kumamoto *han* in that era, a feigned champion of righteousness could have cut an imposing figure by dancing to this tune of the times. But in Shōnan's lecture notes, we see a different figure, that of a Japanese thinker responding in kind to the hand of friendship offered by Whitman and other Americans. Until after the Russo-Japanese War, when American attitudes toward Japan began to change, the Japanese people felt a friendliness toward Americans that differed from their feelings toward other Western powers.

Oguri Tadamasa, *metsuke* in the first bakufu embassy, refined his knowledge while in the United States. After returning to Japan he served as commissioner for foreign affairs and then naval commissioner (*gaikoku*, then *kaigun bugyō*), exercised his capabilities in finance, sought assistance from France, and built the Yokohama and Yokosuka foundry and shipyard. After the bakufu's defeat at Toba-Fushimi in 1868, Oguri opposed concessions by the shogun, was captured, and executed.

However, the most famous member of this embassy traveled on an auxiliary vessel, the *Kanrin maru*, which was the first Japanese ship to cross the Pacific. Fukuzawa Yukichi, then a young student of Dutch, requested and received permission to escort Kimura Yoshitake on this trip to San Francisco. The chapter of his *Autobiography* entitled "I Join the First Mission to America" contains many interesting epi-

---

35 Yokoi Tokio, ed., *Shōnan ikō* (Tokyo: Min'yūsha, 1889), pp. 447–8.

sodes, but perhaps the most surprising of these is that his reading of Dutch books and scientific training at the Ogata school in Osaka had given him enough of a background in natural science to facilitate his understanding of the explanations of the latest inventions made in America. By way of contrast, "things social, political, and economic proved most inexplicable." For example, when he asked "where the descendents of George Washington might be," an American replied, "I think there is a woman who is directly descended from Washington. I don't know where she is now." The answer was "so casual as to shock" this Japanese, who had more or less equated the social positions of Tokugawa Ieyasu and George Washington, both of whom had founded the political systems then existing in Japan and the United States.[36]

Katsu Kaishū (1823–99), the captain of the *Kanrin maru*, was originally a low-ranking Tokugawa official, but he rose to the highest positions of authority within the bakufu and ultimately became the person responsible for surrendering Edo Castle to the Restoration forces. Immediately after returning to Japan from this mission, Katsu earned the rancor of his colleagues by asserting that unlike the situation in Japan, all men in positions of leadership in America possessed leadership capacity. In the late Tokugawa era, knowledge of the West gradually proved effective in criticizing the existing order for its inability to deal satisfactorily with the crises confronting Japan.

After this first mission abroad, the bakufu sent large and small embassies abroad each year or every other year until its demise in 1868. The second embassy, led by Takeuchi Yasunori in 1862, toured the states of Europe to seek approval for postponing the opening of four additional treaty ports. The third mission, to France, was led by Ikeda Naganobu in a futile effort to secure the closing of Yokohama as a port. Shibata Takenaka led the fourth mission, which went to France and England in 1865 to negotiate conditions for constructing the Yokosuka foundry and shipyard. The fifth toured Europe and headed for Russia in 1866 when its chief ambassador, Koide Hidezane, conducted negotiations to establish the boundary between Japan and Russia on Sakhalin (Karafuto). The sixth mission, headed by the shogun Tokugawa Keiki's personal representative, Tokugawa Akitake, attended the Paris World's Fair in 1867. This last embassy was entrusted with the secret mission of persuad-

---

36 "Seiyō jijō," in *Fukuzawa Yukichi zenshū* (Tokyo: Iwanami shoten, 1959), vol. 7, p. 95. Also Eiichi Kiyooka, trans., *The Autobiography of Fukuzawa Yukichi* (Tokyo: Hokuseidō Press, 1948), p. 125.

ing France to increase its aid to the bakufu, and it was still in Europe when the bakufu collapsed in 1868.[37]

Although these "envoys of the Tycoon" had specific diplomatic assignments for dealing with the domestic situation or foreign relations at the time of their appointment, intentionally or not, they also made important contributions to Japan's study and assimilation of Western civilization. In addition, when we consider the students sent to Europe by the bakufu and (illegally) by the domains of Chōshū, Satsuma, or Hizen, we realize that the movement to study "in barbarian lands," launched by Yoshida Shōin in 1854, had expanded and developed to the bakufu or national level. If we include the crew of the *Kanrin maru* on the first bakufu mission abroad, over three hundred Japanese traveled to foreign shores before the Meiji period.

Each of these missions investigated the institutions and civilization of the nations to which it was dispatched, but the second led by Takeuchi Yasunori was the most thorough and systematic, having been instructed "to pay particular attention to politics, school administration, and military systems." The activities of Fukuzawa Yukichi, Matsuki Kōan (Terashima Munenori), Mitsukuri Shūhei, and other students of Western learning were noted in pamphlets bearing such titles as "An Investigation of England," "An Investigation of France," and "An Investigation of Russia." On the Takeuchi mission, Fukuzawa, who had already been to America two years earlier, did more than gaze at Europe with the bedazzled eyes of a tourist; he had discerned the inevitability of the sociopolitical transformation that would soon take place in Japan and began to see himself as an enthusiastic "engineer of civilization." Thus the beginning of Fukuzawa's enlightenment activities in Meiji times can be gleaned from his travel in Tokugawa service.

Fukuzawa's *Account of My Voyage to the West* and *Notes on My Voyage to the West* are full of memos scribbled in a hodgepodge of Japanese, Dutch, English, and French. A glance at these works shows Fukuzawa to be a virtual walking antenna, eager to absorb any and all information in these foreign lands. Whereas other Japanese became caught up in the small facets of Western civilization, Fukuzawa sought to integrate these facets and observe the overall organization that made this civilization function. For example, his colleagues might admire

---

37 Haga Tōru discusses these embassies in *Taikun no shisetsu* (Tokyo: Chūō kōronsha, 1968). The diplomacy in which they participated is the subject of Ishii Takashi, *Meiji ishin no kokusai kankyō*, rev. ed. (Tokyo: Yoshikawa kōbunkan, 1966).

the size of a locomotive, note how fast the train ran, or measure the width and height of its rails. But Fukuzawa went well past such concerns; his interests led him to investigate the composition of railroad companies, their banking activities, or the joint control enjoyed by England and France over Egypt's railways. In short, he tried to grasp not only the technology but also the social aspects of Western civilization. In his *Autobiography* he wrote:

> I did not care to study scientific or technical subjects while on this journey, because I could study them as well from books after I returned home. But I felt that I had to learn the more common matters of daily life directly from the people, because Europeans would not describe them in books as being too obvious. Yet to us those common matters were the most difficult to comprehend.

So while in Europe, "whenever I met a person whom I thought to be of some consequence, I would ask him questions and would put down all he said in a notebook. . . ."[38] After returning home, Fukuzawa organized the notes he had taken during these question-and-answer sessions, checked them against information found in books that he had bought abroad, and published them from 1866 to 1869 under the title *Conditions in the West* (Seiyō jijō).

Fukuzawa wrote the following account of one of these investigations in his *Autobiography:*

> A perplexing institution was representative government. When I asked a gentleman what the "election law" was and what kind of a bureau the Parliament really was, he simply replied with a smile, meaning I suppose that no intelligent person was expected to ask such a question. But these were the things most difficult of all for me to understand. In this connection, I learned that there were bands of men called political parties – the Liberals and the Conservatives – who were always fighting against each other in the government.
>
> For some time it was beyond my comprehension to understand what they were fighting for, and what was meant, anyway, by "fighting" in peacetime. "This man and that man are enemies in the house," they would tell me. But these "enemies" were to be seen at the same table, eating and drinking with each other. I felt as if I could not make much out of this. It took me a long time, with some tedious thinking, before I could gather a general notion of these separate mysterious facts. In some of the more complicated matters, I might achieve an understanding five or ten days after they were explained to me. But all in all, I learned much from this initial tour of Europe.[39]

Conditions in the West, the fruit of such labors, was the first systematic account of the structure of Western civilization written by a Japa-

---

38 *Fukuzawa Yukichi zenshū*, vol. 7, p. 107; *The Autobiography*, pp. 142–3.
39 *Fukuzawa Yukichi zenshū*, vol. 7, pp. 107–8; *The Autobiography*, p. 144.

nese, and it was phrased in language that anyone could understand. In one sense it was designed to heighten Japan's appreciation of the West, but in another, it provided a vision of the future Meiji state as envisioned through Fukuzawa's reformism. Thus, the bakufu missions abroad greatly contributed to the building of Meiji Japan by teaching numerous Japanese about the West and producing popular best-sellers such as Fukuzawa's *Conditions in the West* and Nakamura Masanao's translation of Samuel Smiles's *Self-Help*. The Meiji Restoration altered Japan's political leadership totally and strengthened a resolve to learn from the West that was already forming by 1868. The greatest of all the official missions followed the Restoration. On December 23, 1871, the new Meiji government dispatched Ambassador-Plenipotentiary Iwakura Tomomi to America and Europe as the head of a forty-eight-member delegation that took with it fifty-nine students of the ex-samurai class, five of whom were women.

At this point we should mention the subsequent course of antiforeign sentiment. On his way back to Japan in 1860, Katsu Kaishū playfully displayed on board the *Kanrin maru* the Western umbrella he had bought overseas. When he asked, "What would happen if I tried to use this in Japan?" other members of the delegation cautioned him not to invite assassination. In 1862, when Fukuzawa returned from his second trip, sentiment for *jōi* had become more intense. As a student of Western learning Fukuzawa lived in constant fear of being cut down by xenophobic extremists, and for ten years he refused to go out after dark, choosing instead to concentrate on translations and his own writing. But by 1871 this sentiment had spent its force. The appearance among the members of the Iwakura mission of seven-year-old Tsuda Umeko, carrying a doll, symbolized the return of peace. The idea of a girl studying overseas would have been unimaginable before the Restoration, but after her long sojourn in America, Tsuda returned to Japan and founded what later became Tsudajuku University for Women, an institution that along with Fukuzawa's Keiō University and Niijima's Dōshisha University, made important contributions to private higher education in modern Japan.

We can only marvel at the new Meiji government's stability, which allowed it to send the Iwakura mission to America and Europe for such a long period of time, even allowing for the fact that civil war had ended and peace had been restored. Only four years after its inception, the new government abolished the old domains and provinces of Tokugawa Japan and forced through the establishment of a modern prefectural system. Then only four months after that, leaders such as

Iwakura Tomomi, Kido Takayoshi, Ōkubo Toshimichi, and Itō Hirobumi went abroad and, extending the originally planned length of their overseas stay by almost a full year, returned to Japan on September 13, 1873, after a tour that had lasted 631 days. The Iwakura mission's ostensible objective was to revise the unequal treaties ratified and exchanged in Washington by the first Tokugawa mission to America in 1860, but its members' real intention was to discover conditions in the West and adapt these to Japan in order to create a new Meiji state. The Meiji leaders realized that to revise the unequal treaties, they would have to restructure Japan by putting it on a par with Western states and reforming domestic laws and institutions to bring them into line with those of the Western powers. Though the Iwakura mission was larger than those sent by the bakufu, its purpose and task were essentially the same: to study and learn from the West. One piece of evidence for this continuity of purpose can be found in the embassy's membership. Although its leaders were court nobles and prominent power holders from the domains that had emerged victorious in the Restoration wars, the secretarial staff supporting these leaders included many veteran diplomats, such as Tanabe Ta'ichi, who had served under the bakufu and were knowledgeable about or had actually traveled to the West.

The mission looked at chambers of commerce, schools for the deaf and dumb, museums, shipyards, biscuit factories, girls' schools, prisons, telegraph offices, army maneuvers – all at a whirlwind pace. Kume Kunitake, a student of Chinese learning, went as scribe and published *A True Account of the Observations of the Ambassadorial Mission to America and Europe*, which describes the embassy's brisk day-to-day routine:

No sooner had our train arrived and we had unloaded our baggage at the hotel than our tour began. During the daytime we rushed about from place to place, viewing machines that peeled and locomotives that roared. We stood amidst the acrid smell of steel with smoke billowing around us and became covered with soot and dirt. Returning to our hotel at dusk, we barely had time to brush off our dirty clothes before the hour of our banquet approached. At the banquet we had to maintain a dignified manner; if invited to the theater, we had to strain eyes and ears to follow what took place on stage, and all of this led to exhaustion. No sooner had we retired at night, than morning greeted us with an escort sent to guide us around a factory. In this way, strange sights and sounds filled our eyes and ears; our spirits sagged and our bodies were exhausted by all the invitations we received to this and that event. Though we might have wished to drink a cup of water or stretch out and nap with bent elbow for a pillow, we could not, for any personal slovenliness on our part would constitute a lack of propriety in negotiations between Japan and foreign nations.[40]

The daily schedule of Ōkubo Toshimichi, who concentrated his investigations on industry and economic systems, no doubt resembled this. He questioned factory foremen, sought advice from legal scholars, exchanged speeches with city mayors, and discussed issues with the foreign ministers of various governments. In London he experienced a blackout caused by striking electrical workers seeking higher wages and thus discovered the serious effects that labor disputes might have. He toured the East End after sunset to see the misery and wretchedness lurking beneath the surface of modern Western "civilization." Ōkubo concluded that "the prosperity of English cities occurred after the invention of the steam engine," and Kume noted that "the contemporary phenomenon of wealth and population in European states presented itself after 1800 and has become pronounced only in the last forty years." On the one hand, the members of the mission marveled at the cumulative nature of civilization in Europe, saying that "the light of civilization shines because knowledge has been accumulated through the ages," but at the same time, they braced themselves and stirred their often-flagging spirits by realizing that the gap between Japan and the West, which had just experienced the Industrial Revolution, could be bridged. Thus they resolved to overtake and surpass the West.

Like Fukuzawa's *Conditions in the West*, Kume's *True Account* was organized according to individual countries. Japanese thinkers ranked Western nations according to their relative "superiority" or "inferiority." The scholars of Dutch learning had already discovered that Dutch medical texts were mostly translations from German and thus learned of Germany's superiority in this field. In similar fashion, the Japanese, through their study of books, through traveling abroad, and through advice obtained from foreign teachers, chose to assimilate the best that each particular Western nation had to offer. Fukuzawa challenged his countrymen to turn away from scholars of Chinese learning, arguing that they were so oblivious to world developments as to be "little more

---

40 Kume Kunitake ed., *Bei-Ō kairan jikki* (Tokyo: Iwanami shoten, 1977), vol. 1, p. 12. For detailed information on the Iwakura mission, see Tanaka Akira, *Iwakura shisetsu dan* (Tokyo: Kōdansha, 1977); and Haga Tōru, *Meiji ishin to Nihonjin* (Tokyo: Kōdansha gakujutsu bunko ed., 1980), pp. 219–43. I have relied heavily on Haga for this presentation. For the Iwakura mission in English, see Marlene Mayo, "The Western Education of Kume Kunitake 1871–1876," *Monumenta Nipponica* 28 (1973). The daily experiences and observations of Kido Takayoshi can be followed in Sidney D. Brown and Akiro Hirota, trans., *The Diary of Kido Takayoshi*, vol. 2: *1871–1874* (Tokyo: University of Tokyo Press, 1985).

than rice-consuming dictionaries," and to adopt Western culture, which was based on practicality. By the same token he himself abandoned Dutch for English in 1859 after acknowledging the superior material civilization of the Anglo-Saxon nations. The Japanese modeled themselves after England for industrial and naval development; Prussia, which defeated France in 1871, provided a model for military organization; France offered the model of its centralized police system and educational and legal patterns; and America stimulated agricultural development in the northernmost island of Hokkaido. The Iwakura mission found in Prussia a model of a late-developing modernizer that seemed particularly appropriate to emulate. In regard to Prussia, which then was exporting agricultural products to obtain the capital necessary to develop its mining and industry, Kume wrote: "In establishing its national policies, Prussia has much that closely resembles conditions in Japan. We should find it more profitable to study Prussian politics and customs than those of England or France."[41] It was only natural for the Meiji Japanese to turn to America and Europe rather than to Asian countries in formulating plans to modernize their nation rapidly, and they were wise to select the strong points of each Western nation to further this process. Their selectiveness, based on considerations of efficacy, seems totally different from the traditional Confucian view of a world order centered on China.

Japan's knowledge of and experience with the West may seem to have progressed further during the Taishō and Shōwa eras than during the Meiji. But on closer examination we find that at least in regard to Japan's leaders, their knowledge of foreign countries did not improve qualitatively and quantitatively. The "elder statesmen of the Restoration," as they later were called, were on the one hand raised in accordance with traditional Tokugawa values, but at the same time they also knew a great deal about the West. The Restoration activists exercised a shrewd sensibility in their contact with foreigners. For the Meiji government leaders, the Iwakura mission provided firsthand contact with the Western world. For most of them it was their first trip, although Itō had gone to England as a young Chōshū student. What mattered was that the experience shared by Iwakura, Ōkubo, Kido, and Itō produced a consensus on Japan's future course. These men were convinced of the need for domestic reforms first of all, and upon returning home in 1873, they canceled the plans for invading Korea that had been prepared by the "caretaker" government in their

[41] Kume, *Bei-ō kairan jikki*, vol. 3, p. 298.

absence. This was the first case of a split in views on national policy engendered by the experience or lack of experience of the outside world and the knowledge or ignorance of foreign affairs.

TEACHERS OF "ARTS AND SCIENCES": FOREIGNERS IN MEIJI GOVERNMENT EMPLOY

Japan's use of foreign employees in late Tokugawa and early Meiji times presents an interesting and useful perspective on the larger "turn to the West," and it was also in some sense prophetic of the role of foreign advisers in the reconstruction of Japanese institutions after World War II. The relative success with which the Allied Occupation of Japan completed its work contrasts with the problem of American counselors in their efforts to channel reform in other developing countries. But when considered in regard to Japan's use of foreign advisers in the nineteenth century, it suggests that much of that "success" was actually Japan's. The Meiji government and society, like those of developing states in the twentieth century, were intensely nationalistic, but the country's skill in using and then replacing outside foreign employees is too often forgotten.

The rush with which Japan adopted foreign institutions and customs following the Meiji Restoration sometimes gave Westerners (and not a few conservative Japanese) the impression that Japan was scrapping its entire traditional civilization to appropriate all the material and spiritual attributes of modern Western states. Of course, much of this program was tactical. Britain's defeat of China, followed by the extension of unequal treaties to Japan in the wake of Matthew Perry and Townsend Harris, filled Japan's leaders with apprehension. Japanese felt themselves exposed to a military threat and concluded that if they were to enter the arena known as the family of nations, they too must equip themselves with the weaponry possessed by the Western powers. But they also realized that the basis of Western power was not limited to weaponry; to the extent that such power was based on a civil society that had undergone the economic and social transformations of the Industrial Revolution, Japan's quest for power also entailed the building of political and social institutions based on the Western model.

Although the overthrow of the Tokugawa bakufu was conducted under the slogan "revere the Emperor, expel the barbarians!" the Meiji regime that followed immediately implemented a policy of "open the country, establish friendly relations." After the "expulsion" of the "barbarians" was rejected in the light of the recognition of the international situation, the same nationalism that produced the slogan was transformed into a quest for "civilization and enlightenment." So too for "reverence" for the sovereign: The overthrow of the bakufu resulted not in a restoration of direct imperial rule as it had existed in antiquity, but in a new form of monarchy.

In pursuing its goals of following, achieving equality with, and even overtaking the West, the Meiji government created slogans for all aspects of its endeavors – "enrich the country, strengthen the army" (*fukoku kyōhei*), "civilization and enlightenment" (*bummei kaika*), and "revise the (unequal) treaties" (*jōyaku kaisei*). The government obtained the assistance of foreign teachers and technicians to achieve these goals. In their assimilation of Western culture, the Japanese, who had progressed from book learning to direct experience of the West, now adopted a state policy of inviting large numbers of foreign teachers.

Countries of origins and numbers

Immediately after the opening of the country, the foreigners under whom the Japanese studied were mainly Dutch, although the first systematic instructor in Western arts and sciences was a German, P. F. von Siebold (1796–1866), who arrived in Nagasaki as a physician with the Dutch trading post in 1823. While studying Japan's language, history, geography, animals, and plants, he practiced and taught medicine to Japanese students in a private academy set up for him, the Narutakijuku. In the Tokugawa years, Japanese curiosity began with Western medicine and astronomy, but by late Tokugawa times, their concerns had shifted to Western arms and military methods, reflecting the gravity of the international situation. In 1855 the bakufu set up a naval training institute in Nagasaki to which it invited a team of Dutch instructors to provide training in navigation. Thus Japan's first "foreign employees" were Pels Rijcken and a group of twenty-two instructors, who arrived in 1855, and Huyssen van Kattendycke and a team of thirty-seven, who came slightly later.

In 1858, parallel treaties were concluded with the United States, Holland, England, France, and Russia. Once Holland was no longer the sole avenue for studying Western civilization, Dutch prestige suffered precipitously, and as the Japanese discovered that England, France, Germany, and America were the leading Western powers, they discarded the Dutch language and began studying English,

French, and German. Thereafter, students were dispatched to England, America, France, and (in Meiji times) Germany to study.

Initially, few foreigners were employed, and most of them were from France and Britain. In its final conflicts with Satsuma and Chōshū, the bakufu sought closer relations with France, whereas Satsuma and Chōshū looked to England. In 1862, the bakufu, with help from France, built a shipyard in Yokosuka and began a foundry in Yokohama as well as establishing a French-language school there. Oguri Tadamasa, a leading official in these final bakufu reforms, remarked to a colleague: "The Tokugawa may have to transfer this old house [the bakufu] to someone else, but it will look a lot better with a new storehouse on the premises."[42] In fact, the Meiji government did take the decrepit bakufu structure off the hands of the Tokugawa a few years later and received the new Yokosuka arsenal "storehouse" as a bonus. Moreover, it is important to note that not only the plant itself but also the foreign employees operating it were taken over by the new regime. The Meiji government acquired new facilities as well as precious human talent in the form of Japanese who had been sent abroad in the late Tokugawa period, but foreign employees were by no means the least valuable assets it inherited.

In the Meiji period there was a rapid increase in the number of foreign employees serving in government and private capacities. The number of foreign government employees peaked in 1875 with approximately 520 persons employed, but by 1894 and after, the annual totals were fewer than 100. In contrast, the number of foreigners in private employ was small at first but reached a high of approximately 760 in 1897. By occupation in government, engineers and educators in the ministries of Industry and Education were most numerous, and in the private sector, the number of educators increased as time went on. Classified by nationality, among government employees, the British were most numerous as educators and engineers, followed by the Germans; in the private sector, American educators predominated. In regard to the relative influence of the different nationalities, it is interesting to note the changes in numbers of foreigners employed in the various government bureaus. In 1872, out of a total of 213 government-employed foreigners, 119 were from the United Kingdom, of whom 104 were engineers in the Ministry of Industry, and 49 were French, of whom 24 were shipbuilding technicians. By 1881, however, the statistics show 96 English, 32 Germans, 12 Americans, and 10 French. Areas in which particular

---

42 Fukuchi Gen'ichirō, *Bakumatsu seijika* (Tokyo: Min'yūsha, 1900), p. 266.

nationalities were particularly influential included the English in the ministries of Industry, Navy, and Communications; and the Americans in the development of Hokkaido.[43]

Budget figures are revealing: At some points, foreigners' salaries accounted for one-third of the Ministry of Industry's regular budget and one-third of the budget allocations for Tokyo Imperial University, the first modern university to be established in Japan. The foreigners' salaries clearly placed great strains on the budgets of all government ministries and bureaus, to say nothing of the costs of studying abroad. Yet perhaps it was precisely because of these great costs that the Japanese studied so assiduously under their expensive foreign teachers. These costs were heavy when the foreigners were conscientious and of good character, but when they assumed an attitude of superiority toward their Japanese employers, the costs must have seemed heavier still – all the more reason, no doubt, for the diligence with which the Japanese strove to master the new teachings.

What the Japanese desired

In November 1873 Itō Hirobumi, minister of industry, delivered a directive to mark the opening of the government's new Kōgakuryō, which later evolved into the Department of Engineering of Tokyo Imperial University. Itō pointed out that the new enterprises that Japan was developing should be considered the foundation of future greatness. To create a "great civilization" meant educating "high and low alike," and it had to be done quickly so that "Japan could take its rightful place among the nations of the world" in wealth and power. Because only few Japanese had mastered the skills required up to that point, the country had "no choice but to employ many foreigners to assist us at the outset." But it was not enough to rely on the skills of others; to do so might bring temporary gains but not the "wealth and strength that will endure through myriads of generations." Consequently, Itō concluded:

It is imperative that we seize this opportunity to train and educate ourselves fully. On this solemn occasion, I urge all ambitious youths to enroll in this school, to study assiduously, to perfect their talents, and to serve in their various posts with dedication. If this is done, then as a matter of course, we will be able to do without foreigners. We ourselves will fill the realm with

---

43 Umetani Noboru, *Oyatoi gaikokujin: Meiji Nihon no wakiyakutachi* (Tokyo: Nihon keizai shimbunsha, 1965), pp. 209–23. In English, see Hazel Jones, *Live Machines: Hired Foreigners in Meiji Japan* (Vancouver: University of British Columbia Press, 1980).

railroads and other technological wonders that will form the basis for further developments to continue for a myriad generations. The glory of our Imperial Land will shine forth to radiate upon foreign shores, while at home, high and low will share in the benefits of a great civilization. Therefore, let all ambitious youths throughout the land proceed vigorously with their studies.[44]

It is clear that the Meiji leaders intended foreign employees to play only a subsidiary and temporary role in Japan's development and wanted Japanese nationals to be trained to replace them as soon as possible. The Japanese realized that in order to "lay the foundations for national wealth and strength that will last a myriad generations," they would have to "train and educate" themselves and that they had no choice but to develop and increase their own capabilities. It was also Japan's good fortune that even in the West, scientific and technological development had a history of only a few decades. And so although it was totally dependent on foreign teachers and technicians at the beginning, Japan succeeded in transplanting Western industrial techniques and in producing enough talented men to become surprisingly self-sufficient in the relatively short span of fifteen to twenty years. Tokyo Imperial University's engineering department had a total of 411 graduates between 1879 and 1885. This number of trained technological leaders was not far below the number of foreigners employed by the Ministry of Industry since the beginning of the Meiji period.

Tokugawa Japanese had gained a fair understanding of Western science, a fact that can be discerned in the observations made by Fukuzawa Yukichi during his 1860 visit to America. He was not in the least surprised by the modern phenomena of the telegraph, metalworking, or sugar refining. As is generally true for backward nations, however, Japan began its own development by availing itself of advanced Western science and technology.

The entry of Western modes of life

The numerous foreigners employed by the Meiji government facilitated Japan's "turn to the West," not only by serving as teachers, but also in the broader sense of introducing new life-styles. For example, at one time during the first half of the 1870s, there were as many as twenty foreigners (most of them English) employed at the government mint, where it is reported that as early as 1870–1, Western clothing, the solar

---

44 Umetani Noboru, *Oyatoi gaikokujin* (Tokyo: Kajima kenkyūsho shuppan, 1968), p. 210.

calendar, and Sunday holidays were adopted. Western clothing became compulsory for government officials in November 1872, when a directive established Western clothing as the official ceremonial dress. In 1876, frock coats were decreed standard business attire.[45]

Calendar reform took place in November 1872, when the government decreed that the third day of the twelfth month of the lunar calendar would become January of the next year.[46] This was how the solar calendar was introduced to Japan.[47] The rationale behind calendar reform deserves a slight digression. The solar calendar was not unknown during the Tokugawa period, thanks to Dutch studies. As early as 1795, Ōtsuki Gentaku and his *rangaku* friends had celebrated the eleventh day of the eleventh lunar month as "Dutch New Year's Day." The actual use of the solar calendar after its adoption in 1872, however, was not particularly rapid or widespread. The traditional lunar-solar "Tempō calendar," intricately connected with the pulse of agricultural seasons, suited the Japanese life pattern well. For a time the new Meiji calendar was dubbed the "imperial court calendar," as opposed to the "Tokugawa calendar" to which the people were accustomed. Not until 1911 were the lunar listings of days removed from the calendars, and even today many Japanese feel a certain nostalgia for the old lunar calendar.

One reason that the new regime pushed through calendar reform so early probably stemmed from budgetary considerations. Because there was one intercalary month to be added to the lunar calendar every three years, changing to the solar calendar meant saving the intercalary month's expenditures. When the new government converted to the solar calendar in 1872 and "erased" two days, it withheld salaries for those days, not only for Japanese, but also for foreign employees whose salaries were drawn on a monthly rather than a yearly basis. The government mint, which took the lead in adopting Western dress and the solar calendar, also pioneered in Western accounting methods, reserve funds for work injuries, medical clinics, and other matters hitherto unknown in Japan. In addition, it quickly introduced gas lights and telegraph lines, which became symbols of "civilization and enlightenment" in Japan, even though none of these innovations was directly concerned with minting techniques.

Individual foreign teachers often had astonishing influence through

---

45 Tsuji Zennosuke, *Nihon bunkashi* (Tokyo: Shunjūsha, 1950), vol. 7, p. 18.
46 Satō Masatsugu, *Nihon rekigakushi* (Tokyo: Surugadai shuppan, 1968), p. 479.
47 The Julian method of intercalation was used at this time, but the Gregorian method was adopted in 1900.

the strength of their personal example and assumed almost oracular importance for young students who were only partly rooted in traditional values and eager to learn the inner strength of "civilization." The artillery Captain L. L. Janes in Kumamoto and the agronomist William Clark in Hokkaido proved to be more successful religious teachers than were the numerous missionaries who were sent to Japan after the government rescinded the prohibitions against Christianity in 1873, and major groupings of the small but influential Protestant church derived from the "Kumamoto Band" and "Hokkaido Group."[48]

In addition, many of the customs inherent in "civilization and enlightenment" or capitalist enterprise were introduced by foreign employees of the Meiji government. Christmas, for instance, which became a holiday in a non-Christian land, came with the foreign residents, as did many other aspects of contemporary life. Many aspects of Western life were taught by the foreigners through their daily life rather than through formal instruction. Along with the formal learning they dispensed, these foreigners thus provided the Japanese with opportunities to become acquainted with Western ways by observing foreign lifestyles and daily activities. The result, as is mirrored in the woodblock prints of mid-Meiji, with the strong, aniline dyes that replaced the subtler hues of Tokugawa times, was as uniquely Japanese as were the mixed forms of dress and architecture pictured there.

THE JAPANIZATION OF WESTERN THOUGHT AND INSTITUTIONS

When Western value systems came into contact with Japanese values, there were three possible outcomes: The two could conflict; the values might be adopted totally; or they might be altered in the process of being accepted. Christianity provides one example of Japan's alteration and transformation of Western values. Another example can be found in Japan's civil code, which was drafted under the guidance of the French jurist G. E. Boissonade. By examining this draft, we may discover Japan's reaction to "teachers of arts and science" who attempted to introduce Western morality as well.

Social order was well maintained in Tokugawa Japan, but not because the Japanese of that era were bound by written laws. The un-

---

48 John F. Howes, "Japanese Christians and American Missionaries," in Marius B. Jansen, ed., *Changing Japanese Attitudes Toward Modernization* (Princeton, N.J.: Princeton University Press, 1965), pp. 337–68. For Janes, see F. G. Notehelfer, *American Samurai: Captain L. L. Janes and Japan* (Princeton, N.J.: Princeton University Press, 1985).

equal treaties concluded by the bakufu in 1858 posed a new problem and need in this regard. They were inequitable and humiliating; Japan was forced to relinquish tariff autonomy and concede extraterritoriality to Westerners. To obtain equal status with the West, the early Meiji government would first have to prove that Japan was a "civilized" country, deserving equal status and treatment, and part of that process involved compiling legal codes similar to those possessed by the European states. Thus the adoption of a Western-style legal system was not simply a domestic matter; it was also essential to the resolution of an external problem that demanded an urgent solution.

When the French legal system first came to the attention of the Japanese in late Tokugawa, they greeted it with enthusiasm. The Tokugawa official Kurimoto Joun, who traveled to France in 1867, noted in his memoirs:

"Deciding a lawsuit with half a word" is something that requires the wisdom of Tzu-lu and is beyond the capability of men of only average abilities and intelligence. How much more impossible for a man without human feelings. The complete elimination of argumentation in court would have been impossible even for the sage Confucius. That, at any rate, was what I thought until I learned of this Napoleonic code. . . . I was overwhelmed with admiration and envy.[49]

The reason for Kurimoto's praise was that two Japanese merchants who had accompanied his party had been arraigned and brought to court, where he saw the French judge "base his decision and pronounce sentence in accordance with Article X, Provision Y of the Napoleonic code."

In 1869, the Meiji government ordered Mitsukuri Rinshō to translate all five French law codes. At that time Etō Shimpei suggested that they "merely translate the French civil code verbatim, call it the 'Japanese Civil Code,' and promulgate it immediately."[50] His aim was to revise the unequal treaties: The laws need not be perfect, and it would be sufficient if they were part of a new judicial system. This would convince the West that Japan was indeed a "civilized" nation.

A group under Etō's direction began compiling a civil code based on Mitsukuri's translation. In 1872, the French lawyer Georges Bousquet was hired to assist them, and the next year Gustave Emile

---

[49] This opening phrase is a quotation from *The Analects* of Confucius. Kurimoto Joun, "Gyōsō tsuroku," in Nihon shiseki kyōkai, ed., *Hōan ikō* (*Zoku Nihon shiseki sōsho*, vol. 4) (Tokyo: Tokyo daigaku shuppankai, 1975), p. 24.
[50] Etō Shimpei, "Furansu mimpō wo motte Nihonmimpō to nasan to su," in Hozumi Nobushige, ed., *Hōsō yawa* (Tokyo: Iwanami shoten, 1980), pp. 210–13.

Boissonade de Fontarabie (1825–1910) followed;[51] the latter worked in Japan until 1895. In addition to their work of compilation, these men served as instructors in Western legal concepts at the Ministry of Justice. Before this, Inoue Kowashi (1854–95), who deserves much credit for his work to implement Western institutions, had been sent to France by the Ministry of Justice, where he had studied under Boissonade, who was then a professor of law at the Sorbonne. In Japan, Boissonade cooperated with Inoue on many projects. In public law, he strove to establish concepts like the principle of legality and the principle of evidence and to abolish torture. He also drew up criminal and penal codes, which were Japan's first modern law codes. In private law, he worked on the civil code, drawing up sections on property, securities, and evidence. In addition he was influential in determining what was to go into the sections on personal and family relations and property acquisitions. Boissonade's drafts passed final review in the Privy Council and were scheduled to go into effect in 1890. A noteworthy aspect of his draft was the ideal of equality between individuals in the inheritance of property. But these provisions drew sharp criticism from those who held that they would threaten the primacy of the house (ie), and as a result, implementation of the code was held up just before it was to become law. Boissonade's provisions were rejected and replaced by requirements that the household head inherit all property. In sum, the Meiji government placed more emphasis on maintaining the "house" (ie) as a structural unit than on respecting the individual's right to inheritance.[52] This "civil code issue" raged for several years.

The controversy over the new code had many facets, but in general terms it can be viewed as a conflict between the universalistic, theoretical legal thought espoused by French jurists of natural law and a more particularistic and empirical set of ideas advanced by proponents of historicist legal thought who drew their arguments from English and especially German traditions. The latter group argued that the concept of "house" (ie) and the sentiments it engendered were an intrinsic part of particularistic and traditional Japanese society and values. Hozumi Yatsuka, a spokesman for the latter group, became famous for his

---

51 See Ōkubo Yasuo, *Nihon kindaihō no chichi: Bowasonado* (Tokyo: Iwanami shoten, 1977) for a discussion of this consultant.
52 On the compilation of the civil code and the "civil code issue," in addition to Ōkubo, *Nihon kindaihō no chichi;* see Ishii Ryōsuke, ed., *Meiji bunkashi: Hōsei-hen* (Tokyo: Genyōsha, 1954), p. 515. This work is vol. 2 of the Centennial Cultural Committee Series, *Meiji bunkashi* and was translated by William Chambliss as *Japanese Legislation in the Meiji Era* (Tokyo: Pan-Pacific Press, 1958).

catchphrase "Loyalty and filial piety will perish with the enactment of the civil code." He wrote:

With the spread of Christianity in Europe, a self-righteous "Father who art in Heaven" has come to monopolize the love and respect of all men. Perhaps for that reason, Westerners neglect the worship of ancestors and the Way of filial piety. With the spread of doctrines like equality and humanity, they slight the importance of ethnic customs and blood ties. Perhaps that is why no "house" system exists among them anymore; instead they create a society of equal individuals and try to uphold it by means of laws centered on the individual.

Japan has never forgotten the teaching of ancestor reverence because of the coming of foreign religions. However, the spirit in which this civil code is drafted will bring repudiation of the national religion and destruction of our "house" system. The words *house* and *household head* do appear briefly, but the draft obscures the true principles of law, and thus, is worse than if it were a dead letter.

Alas, these men are trying to enact a civil code centered on extreme individualism, ignoring three thousand years of indigenous beliefs![53]

Hozumi explained why the proposed civil code would lead to "the loss of Japan's individuality": (1) The section on property, by idealizing unlimited freedom of contract for individuals, might raise society's productive capacities, but at cost of widening the gap between rich and poor, thereby producing conflicts between owners and workers, "contradictions inherent in capitalism"; and (2) the section on personal and domestic relations, based as it was on an imitation of Western individualism, had been drafted with the idea that husbands and wives, and elder and younger brothers were separate individuals. Consequently there was danger that the code would break up Japanese society, which had always been upheld by teachings of reverence for ancestors, who continued to be central to the house.[54] Instead, Hozumi advocated the enactment of a civil code that would emphasize "a spirit suited to the nation" and "the familial relations of the 'house system'."

As a result of this civil code issue, the Diet (parliament) voted to postpone until 1896 the enactment of the civil code scheduled to go into effect the following year. It was still in limbo when Boissonade, who had poured heart and soul into the code during a residence of over twenty years in Japan, returned to France in 1895. Inoue Kowashi

---

53 Hozumi Yatsuka, "Mimpō idete, chūkō horobu," in *Hōgaku shimpō*, vol. 5 (August 1891).
54 On Hozumi's theory of state, see Richard Minear, *Japanese Tradition and Western Law: Emperor, State, and Law in the Thought of Hozumi Yatsuka* (Cambridge, Mass.: Harvard University Press, 1970).

composed a commemorative poem in classical Chinese for Boissonade from his sickbed and died soon after. New forces came into play.

The code was in effect recompiled by a new commission headed by Itō Hirobumi and Saionji Kimmochi, and their new code was finally enacted in 1898. Their two guiding principles, which together defined the Meiji civil code, are of great interest to us: (1) Indigenous Japanese institutions and practices should be taken fully into account; and (2) the strong points of legislative theories from all Western nations should be adopted, and not just those of France and Italy, as had been the case previously.

The section on property was left virtually unchanged. It incorporated principles of legal equality between the sexes and the former social-status groups as well as the principles of individual choice, personal ownership of property, and liability arising from negligence, all based on the spirit of individualism. It also contained a system of real and obligatory rights based on the idea of equal rights and duties. However, the section on social relationships was greatly revised to establish the power of the household head by means of special provisions for family heads, parents, and fathers. As a result, individuals were constrained by being placed within a status hierarchy of family relationships. According to Western historical concepts, Japan's civil code was thus based on a dual structure, whose two layers were logically inconsistent: the return of the individual to a gemeinschaft-type of "house" unit in personal relationships versus the recognition of that person's status as an individual in capitalistic society. A modern society is presumably made up of individuals, but the Japanese people were continually forced to adjust themselves to a system burdened with a "house system" in which each individual was rooted.

That the enactment of Japan's civil code went through these vicissitudes and that the end product came about by such contradictory compromises are hardly surprising. Quite the contrary: The civil code epitomizes the basic pattern taken by Japan's "turn to the West." Etō Shimpei, who, as mentioned earlier, once suggested that Japan enact a word-for-word translation of the French civil code, is said to have given the following instructions to Inoue Kowashi when the Ministry of Justice sent him to France:

The most vital task for all of you who are being sent to Europe is to inspect various European countries and institutions and then adopt their strong points while discarding their weaknesses. You are not being sent to study about the conditions in each country and to import Western ways wholesale into Japan. Hence, you should no longer think in terms of learning from Westerners, but instead, observe them in a spirit of critical inquiry. As Japan proceeds along the path of civilization, it is vital to adopt Western institutions and ways to improve our governmental processes. Nevertheless we must not become so infatuated with the West that we fail to discern its defects. If that is the case, the institutions and ways we adopt with so much toil and trouble will not be fit for our use.[55]

In his memoirs Inoue stressed that the Meiji constitution and all other areas of reform in which he had had a hand in implementing show the spiritual characteristics of Japan. In contrast, Saionji Kimmochi (1849–1940), who spent ten years of his youth in France and who placed his faith in the universality of civilization, criticized such particularism as follows: "Usually, what is termed 'particular to' a certain nation or race is a shortcoming or idiosyncracy.... Most traits that present-day educators in Japan babble about as being distinctively Japanese would distress men of learning...."[56]

Hozumi Yatsuka, who overemphasized the importance of the "house system" and the "teaching of ancestor reverence," was derided by the intellectuals of his day. It must be noted here that when the sections on family relations and inheritance in Japan's civil code were drastically revised during the American Occupation in 1947, the concept of "house" was thoroughly repudiated. Many Japanese, however, still opposed such "morality" imposed from abroad and feared that Western-style individualism would weaken family ties and create new problems in caring for the elderly, a problem that was of great concern by the 1980s. Thus opposition to aspects of Western "morality" represented more than a conservative, emotional reaction, for it was reinforced by a desire to make Japan achieve "modernity" while avoiding the alienation and atomization of human relationships inherent in capitalistic society.

THE SPIRIT OF CAPITALISM: FIRST TRANSLATIONS FROM WESTERN LITERATURE

Robinson Crusoe

The great number of translations from Western literature made during the Meiji period and after provides another striking indication of

---

[55] Matono Hansuke, *Etō Nampaku* (Tokyo: Hara shobō reprint, 1968), vol. 2, p. 107.
[56] Miyazawa Toshiyoshi, "Meiji kempō no seiritsu to sono kokusai seijiteki haikei," in Miyazawa Toshiyoshi, *Nihon kenseishi no kenkyū* (Tokyo: Iwanami shoten, 1968), pp. 134–5.

Japan's "turn to the West." During the early decades, however, translators were concerned more with causes than with literature. From the last days of Tokugawa rule through the first decades of Meiji, numerous translations were really practical tracts of agitation, often known as "political novels," that reflected the conditions of the time. More often than not, they were translated to suit the convenience of those who supported a cause or political position. Regardless of their literary value or lack thereof, however, these translations are interesting for what they reveal about the way that Japanese in that era reacted to the foreign intercourse that followed the breakdown of national isolation.

Japanese intellectuals began reading accounts of castaways toward the end of the Edo period. Japanese castaways who returned to Japan were often interrogated by bakufu officials, who transcribed their accounts of conditions overseas. Against that background, two translations of *Robinson Crusoe* appeared before the Meiji Restoration. The first was a partial translation from a Dutch version, entitled *The Account of a Castaway* by Kuroda Kōgen, a student of Dutch studies, which was completed before Perry's arrival. The following preface to the Dutch edition was also included in Kuroda's translation:

Robinson Crusoe of England was a man with a desire to traverse the four quarters. He set out to sea and lost his ship in a tropical storm. He managed to stay alive but was cast adrift in a lifeboat, captured by pirates, and finally sold to a fisherman. Later, he escaped from that fishing boat and, while fleeing from pursuers, was unexpectedly rescued by a Portuguese merchant vessel. He grew sweet potatoes and became very wealthy, but his misfortunes at sea did not deter him from returning to it in a great vessel he constructed. He ran into many storms, was shipwrecked, and then marooned on a desert island. He used all his wits to survive on this island for twenty-eight years before an English ship chanced to come and take him home.

Any reader of these accounts cannot help but be overwhelmed with admiration. When it was published in England, readers devoured it and rushed to buy it in droves; at one point its publication reached forty thousand copies. Its Dutch translation is being read more avidly than was the English original. Moreover, this book supplements gaps in our knowledge of geography. Although there are numerous other accounts of sea voyages, these merely describe stormy seas or the contours of lands discovered; none reports anything like the miraculous nature of Crusoe's achievements. Readers who learn of his countless hardships and his resourcefulness in overcoming these cannot but develop their own mental faculties.

I personally feel that although life is full of vicissitudes, no one has experienced as many as Crusoe. Each account of his experiences on that deserted island has great relevance to our own understanding of affairs in society. You should never forget the sufferings Crusoe experienced and become conceited and self-indulgent.

Moreover, Crusoe was adept solely in navigation, not in any other technical skills. Yet the mind of man is indeed a marvelous thing! Once he landed on the deserted island, he sewed his own clothes, gathered his own food, built his own house, constructed his own ship, made his own pottery, grew his own vegetables – succeeded in meeting all his personal needs by himself. . . .[57]

This translator was apparently unaware that *Robinson Crusoe* was a fictional product of Daniel Defoe's pen and instead believed that it was a true account. Furthermore, *Robinson Crusoe* was not considered a children's story by the Japanese of that era but, rather, a true account of a castaway, meant to be read by adults.

Translations of this type suggest Japan's initial orientation toward the sea, as well as their yearning for information about foreign affairs. In the case of Niijima Jō, for example, his desire to find out about conditions abroad was accelerated by reading a translation of *Robinson Crusoe* lent to him by his teacher of Dutch studies. He then smuggled himself out of Japan. After spending well over a year at sea, he found himself in America in 1865, engaged in manual labor with no idea of what the future held in store for him: "Exhausted after each day's labor, I would fall asleep as soon as my head hit the pillow. When I awoke each morning, my entire body ached so badly that I could hardly move."[58] This continued for weeks. Then he bought a copy of *Robinson Crusoe* in the original English. This book, along with a Dutch book about Christ and a Bible translated into classical Chinese, were what induced him to become a Christian. Niijima too believed that Crusoe was a real person and seems to have compared his own experiences with those of that solitary castaway. When he was stranded in Boston, he was insulted by burly sailors and found out about the grim living conditions caused by post–Civil War inflation. In that black hour, he is said to have gained the strength to carry on by repeating Crusoe's prayer.

This is a most interesting account of the circumstances surrounding the conversion of one Japanese to Protestantism. Today we are used to reading editions of *Robinson Crusoe* rewritten for children and forget the emphasis on Divine Providence in Defoe's original. The author's intention, scholars tell us, was to edify readers and impress them with the importance of moral behavior. *Robinson Crusoe* was a parable of the role of Providence in human affairs, and accordingly, Niijima's

---

[57] Kokusho kankōkai, ed., *Bummei genryū sōsho* (Tokyo: Kokusho kankōkai, 1913), vol. 1, p. 136.   [58] "Hakodate yori no ryakki," in *Niijim sensei shokanshū*, p. 1137.

interpretation was probably truer to the original than is that of most modern readers.

Protestantism enlarged upon this idea of diligence and work based on the individualism of a God-fearing person, and for that reason it is often associated with the flowering of capitalism. What Defoe depicted in *Robinson Crusoe* was an individual in relation to an absolute God, and that relationship made for an autonomous individual. Niijima perceived in Crusoe such a religious man, but he also saw the prototype of those who would later develop capitalism.

After returning to Japan, Niijima established the Dōshisha English School in Kyoto in 1875. His goal was to foster "talented men of conscience," a phrase that suggests Max Weber's "spirit of this-worldly asceticism." One might even suggest that with the abolition of feudal society, Niijima and his associates set out to reconstruct and transform the ethics of the samurai, who had been taught to "do everything humanly possibly and trust in Heaven's fate" in Meiji society through the medium of Protestantism.

Except for a period in the 1880s when the number of converts to Protestantism seemed to be growing rapidly – a phenomenon not unrelated to the exigencies of treaty reform – the young Meiji church probably did not enroll more than about thirty thousand converts. They were a strategic and able group of educated and usually ex-samurai youths. Prejudice in Kumamoto brought L. L. Janes's "Kumamoto Band" to Niijima's Dōshisha, and the association of Protestantism with Western dynamism by adventurous and able youth made the influence of Protestantism much larger than the modest number of its adherents would suggest. Yet its significance can also be exaggerated, for adherents to the new faith as often came from a commitment to this-worldly values as they did to other-worldly, transcendent beliefs.

Self-Help

During the "civilization and enlightenment" of early Meiji, the first Western ideas to enter Japan were generally those associated with English and American thinkers like Mill, Bentham, Spencer, de Tocqueville, Guizot, and Buckle – utilitarianism, civil liberties, natural rights, and rational positivism. Slightly later, French republicanism associated with Rousseau arrived and spread. Together, these ideas destroyed the hierarchical status system of Tokugawa times and ushered in an ethos of "achieving success and rising in the world" (*risshin shusse*). This ethos was powerfully stated in the phrases of Fukuzawa Yukichi's *Gakumon no susume* (An encouragement of learning) in 1872: "People are not born exalted or base, rich or poor. It is simply that those who work hard at their studies and learn much become exalted and rich, while those who are ignorant become base and poor."[59] This later became the Meiji government's ideology.

Japan's traditional work ethic was instilled anew in early Meiji youths in the form of this demand for a modern education. As a result, an enthusiasm for "personal cultivation" spread. Under slogans such as "hard work and application" or "thrift, diligence, and effort," Meiji youths prepared to carry out their future duties and to acquire knowledge from the West in various capacities – as pupils in the newly created school system, as apprentices in traditional crafts, as live-in disciples in the homes of famous scholars, and as students studying in universities abroad.

In 1883 a new translation of *Robinson Crusoe* by Inoue Tsutomu appeared as *An Extraordinary Adventure: An Account of Robinson Crusoe, the Castaway*. In his preface, Inoue treated Crusoe as a fictional character, not as an actual person, but he also asserted that the novel was no mere adventure story and that it served to teach young Englishmen to overcome hardship. Inoue interpreted *Robinson Crusoe* in the following terms: "This book should not be thought of as trivial, for if men read it carefully they will see that it shows how an island can be developed by stubborn determination."[60]

But it is the reception given to *Self-Help* that best shows the dominant hold maintained by the work ethic in Meiji Japan as it was applied to rendering service to society. After Fukuzawa Yukichi, Nakamura Masanao was the most influential exponent of "enlightenment" in the early Meiji era. Half of Nakamura's influence stemmed from his translation of John Stuart Mill's *On Liberty;* the other half, from Samuel Smiles's *Self-Help*. Nakamura was born in 1832 to a low-ranking samurai family but was admitted to the bakufu's Shōheikō academy on the basis of his scholarly promise. His education was fundamentally Confucian, but he was also drawn to Western studies and to Christianity, which he embraced in 1874. Just before the Restoration he was sent to England as the supervisor of a group of young

---

59 "Gakumon no susume (shohen)," in *Fukuzawa Yukichi zenshū*, vol. 3, p. 30. This work has been translated into English by David Dilworth and Umeyo Hirano as *An Encouragement to Learning* (Tokyo: Sophia University Press, 1969).
60 Inoue Tsutomu's translation was published in Tokyo by Hakubunsha in 1883. See also George B. Sansom, *The Western World and Japan* (New York: Knopf, 1950), p. 419.

bakufu students. When he returned to Japan after a sojourn of a year and a half, he brought back copies of *Self-Help* (which was a gift from a friend) and *On Liberty*. At that time, the bakufu was collapsing, and Nakamura joined a group of loyal retainer-intellectuals who retreated to Shizuoka with the Tokugawa house.

Nakamura now became an educator and translator. He completed a translation of Smiles's *Self-Help* in 1871 and published it as *A Collection of Stories about Success in the West* and another of J. S. Mill's in 1872 as *The Principle of Liberty*. Both books were immediately successful, as the Japanese of that era were thirsting for knowledge of the West. *On Liberty* became a fountainhead of liberalism during the Meiji enlightenment, and *Self-Help* was read by all Meiji youths. The latter work was a best-seller in England and America as well, selling 250,000 copies by the end of the nineteenth century. But in Meiji Japan, where it appeared as an account of real Western men whose experiences were anchored in real social conditions, it is said to have sold 1 million copies. It certainly was a best-seller, being reprinted into the 1920s.

In recent years *Self-Help* has been dismissed as part of the "success-story genre," but Nakamura's goals were moral as well as materialistic, and he stressed (by length and language) moral responsibility and the national interest. His translation was couched in classical language congenial to samurai readers, but he achieved a sonorous style that still strikes a respondent chord in many people, especially his opening rendition of Smiles's language:

The proverb, "Heaven helps those who help themselves" is a truism, empirically verifiable. In this adage lies the success or failure of everything in human affairs. "He who helps himself" means the ability to be autonomous and independent, to refrain from relying on others. The spirit of self-help is the basis from which man derives intelligence. In broader terms, when the majority of a nation's people "help themselves," that state is filled with vigor and is strong in spirit.[61]

When Nakamura, a model Confucian scholar who had studied in England, pointed to the path that Japan should follow, Meiji youths obeyed him implicitly. His puritan individualism and utilitarian morality could be transplanted in Japanese soil without much opposition because they could be grafted onto traditional Japanese ideas almost naturally.[62] This is indicated by the following episodes.

In a book that Kōda Rohan (1867–1947) wrote to instill the success

[61] For Nakamura's original text from which this was translated, see Ishikawa Ken, ed., *Nihon kyōkasho taikei: Kindai hen 1* (Tokyo: Kōdansha, 1961), p. 25.
[62] Marius B. Jansen, ed., *Changing Japanese Attitudes Toward Modernization* (Princeton, N.J.: Princeton University Press, 1965), p. 67.

ethic in young people, the first book that its hero is said to have read is Ninomiya Sontoku's *Account of Recompensing Virtue* (Hōtoku-ki). But when Smiles's book became popular, Rohan changed the title of his hero's inspiration to make it Nakamura's translation of *Self-Help*. Yet the hero's exclamations, "The fruits of your labors will derive from Heaven's boundless abundance" or "This book made me what I am," fit either source of inspiration equally well.

Kunikida Doppo, in *An Uncommon Common Man*, sympathetically portrays Katsura Shōsaku, a youth fully imbued with the spirit of *Self-Help*. Katsura idealizes Watt, Edison, and Stevenson, saves his money, and goes to Tokyo to work his way through school. Though poor, he exhibits none of the heedlessness toward life's necessities that is usually depicted as a virtue (or a vice) in the traditional swashbuckling hero-gallant of East Asia. Instead, Katsura supports his brother while going on to become an electrical engineer who is earnestly "absorbed in the work he is performing." He walks around and around some equipment, checking to discover the cause of its malfunction and then repairs it. Such an uncommon common man who has set his mind to do something fits Smiles's description of "a man devoted to his trade," one who is "able to endure long periods of tribulation and possesses true mettle." The reason that Japan could follow the example of Western peoples (whom Nakamura hailed in exclamations like "Ah, how happy Western peoples are today!") so quickly and could enjoy the benefits of electrical lighting in rural villages so early is that the majority of Japanese shared Doppo's sympathy with Katsura: There was a large reservoir of uncommon common men toiling diligently in the Meiji era.

As might be expected in a nineteenth-century English work, Smiles lists many "creators of new inventions" among his heroes in *Self-Help*. He devotes several pages to an anecdote about Richard Arkwright's invention of the cotton reel. One admiring reader of this anecdote was Toyoda Sakichi, who himself succeeded in inventing an automatic loom in 1897. His descendents went on to make automobiles. The lessons preached by Smiles were quickly transplanted into Japanese soil and became the foundation for "overcoming adversity" and for "earnest application" in Meiji youths.

The philosophy implied in these slogans – that possibilities were unlimited for the individual with ability and that everything depended on personal application – fit the realities of early Meiji society. This philosophy was also expressed in common parlance. However, one should also keep in mind the less glamorous reasons when explaining why this transplantation took place so smoothly. One reason is that at least superficially, the lessons contained in *Selp-Help* are arbitrarily and conclusively stated. In both the original and the translation, the doctrines are asserted with categorical authority. This arbitrary though edifying style, which is rather at odds with the work's purpose, was probably congenial to men born and raised in a feudal, authoritarian, moral value system. As George B. Sansom wrote, "It was unfortunate that, when at last the Japanese had time to consider the nobler efforts of the Western mind, it was the dreary ratiocinations of Herbert Spencer or the homiletic of men like Benjamin Franklin and Samuel Smiles which seemed best to stay their intellectual pangs."[63] A Japanese raised within the Tokugawa Confucian tradition could accept the injunctions of Smiles and Franklin precisely because he was accustomed to their style of homily.

In 1878 the Meiji empress translated Benjamin Franklin's "Twelve Virtues" into traditional Japanese poems. Regarding industry, Franklin had written in his *Autobiography:* "Industry: Lose no time; be always employed in something useful; cut off all unnecessary actions." The young empress, who had learned Franklin's "Virtues" from her Confucian imperial tutor Motoda Eifu as part of her education, transcribed this in traditional poetic form and "bestowed it upon the Tokyo Women's Normal School" whose students had previously accompanied her procession at the school's opening ceremonies. The poem, adopted to music composed by Oku Yoshihisa, soon gained popularity and was sung in every part of the country:

> If unpolished, even the diamond
>   loses its jeweled radiance.
> Without education, people too,
>   will ne'er emit true virtue.
> If one begrudges the sunlight
>   working throughout the day,
> As ceaselessly as the hands of a clock,
>   all things can be accomplished.[64]

The tendency to modernize from above is discernible in all late modernizing countries, but in the Meiji era, when the need to "foster industry and promote enterprise" was felt especially keenly, the royal poetess saw in Franklin's "Virtues" a new morality for civil society

---

63 George B. Sansom, *Japan, a Short Cultural History* (London: Cresset, 1932), p. 504. See also Earl H. Kinmonth, *The Self-Made Man in Meiji Japanese Thought: From Samurai to Salary Man* (Berkeley and Los Angeles: University of California Press, 1981).
64 See Inoue Takeshi, ed., *Nihon shōkashū* (Tokyo: Iwanami shoten, 1958), pp. 48–9.

and took the initiative of Japanizing and introducing it to the people through the medium of traditional poetry.

Of course, the virtues of diligence and application were not new to the Japanese people in the Meiji period. The school song composed by the empress was, to be sure, Franklin's injunction in one sense, but in other respects, it was fully Japanese. In Tokugawa times there was a saying that "hardships polish one into a jewel." The thirteenth-century Zen monk Dōgen wrote: "The jewel becomes a jewel through polishing. Man becomes benevolent through training. No jewel shines in its natural state. No novice is characterized by keenness of insight from the very beginning. They must be polished and trained."[65] If we go back even farther, we will find virtually the same injunction in the *Book of Rites:* "Unless the jewel is polished, it does not become a jewel; unless men study, they do not learn the Way."[66] Precisely because this idea of character building had a long tradition in Buddhism and Confucianism in East Asia, the Japanese were able to educate themselves so diligently and in such a sustained fashion during the Meiji "civilization and enlightenment" period. Indeed, Ninomiya Sontoku's asceticism of self-restraint and moral cultivation was an ethos that dominated the rural villages until the end of World War II, and his *Account of Recompensing Virtue* (Hōtoku-ki) is far from neglected even today.

Every age has its fashions. Today, for example, "becoming a success and rising in the world" sounds old-fashioned and pretentious, but when rephrased as "self-realization," the same aspiration becomes modern and chic. Similarly, in early Meiji times, when everything traditionally Japanese or Asian seemed anachronistic, young hearts were not inspired by quotations from Dōgen or the *Book of Rites*.

Masaoka Shiki, a great Meiji reformer of Japanese poetry, read Franklin's *Autobiography* when ill with tuberculosis and was deeply impressed by it. Shimazaki Tōson, later a naturalist writer of great renown, used Franklin's *Autobiography* at a country school when he was a young teacher. These details illustrate what the Japanese were concerned about during the period of their nation's rise to statehood in the early Meiji era.

Finally, we must consider that just as the activities of citizens in Western societies, many of them Protestants, later supported national-

---

65 *Nihon koten bungaku taikei*, vol. 81: *Shōbōgenzō, Shōbōgenzō zuimonki* (Tokyo: Iwanami shoten, 1965), p. 397.
66 This is from the chapter "Music" in *The Book of Rites*. See *Kokuyaku kambun taisei*, vol. 24: *Raiki* (Tokyo: Kokumin bunko kankōkai, 1921), p. 351.

ism, the "diligence and application" of Meiji youths also became linked with nationalism in Japan. Self-cultivation did not stop at the personal level for Meiji youths but became associated with preserving Japan's independence in the face of Western encroachment. Morality and application came together in service to the larger community. As Fukuzawa Yukichi put it, again in *An Encouragement of Learning*, "When we compare Oriental Confucianism with Western civilization, we discover that what is possessed by the latter and is lacking in the former is (1) mathematics in the realm of the tangible and (2) the spirit of independence in the realm of the intangible."[67] Fukuzawa advocated cultivating the individual's spirit of independence. Based on Mill's view that "the independence of a nation grows out of the independent spirit of its people," Fukuzawa proposed that every Japanese "establish his own independence, and then Japan would be independent." This proposition is identical to one put forth by Smiles quoted earlier: "When the majority of a nation's people 'help themselves,' that state is filled with vigor and is strong in spirit." So it is interesting to note that the Confucian spirit repudiated by Fukuzawa functioned quite smoothly in this process, as Confucianism held that "personal cultivation and regulation of family affairs" was requisite to "ordering the realm and bringing peace to all under Heaven." Each citizen's "personal cultivation" in the form of "self-help" led directly to "ordering the realm" in the sense of "national wealth and power" (or its synonym, "national independence"). Thus, it was fortunate for Japan that "overcoming hardship through diligence" and "becoming a success and rising in the world" in private life were in complete harmony with Japan's fortunes as a state. In this sense, self-help was by no means at odds with traditional Japanese values; quite the contrary, it was reinforced by them.[68]

This simple unity between "hard work" and "rising in the world" dissolved in time, but only after Japan's "turn to the West" had advanced to a further stage in which Japanese accepted Western literature as literature and began writing modern novels themselves. The youthful characters in Futabatei Shimei's (1864–1909) *Floating Clouds* lived in the world of Meiji self-help, but the author no longer believed that "the success or failure of everything in human affairs" could be

---

67 "Kyōiku no hōshin wa sūri to dokuritsu," in *Fukuzawa Yukichi zenshū*, vol. 3, p. 198. See also Kiyooka, tr., *The Autobiography*.
68 On the influence that Franklin and Smiles had on Meiji Japan, see Hirakawa Sukehiro, "Furankurin to Meiji Kōgō," in Hirakawa Sukehiro, *Higashi no tachibana, nishi no orenji* (Tokyo: Bungei shunjūsha, 1981), pp. 53–88.

related to the saying that "heaven helps those who help themselves." Instead of general exhortations, Futabatei focused on the life of an average youth agonizing over conflicting values in a real society in which new ranks had begun to form.

THE RETURN TO JAPAN: A CONSCIOUSNESS OF SELF IN MEIJI YOUTH

The reaction against slavish Westernization

During the first two decades of the Meiji era, it seemed as if the entire nation was determined to Westernize itself completely, but in the late 1880s a reaction set in. Nevertheless, this "return to being Japanese" was not a reversion to the blind xenophobia of late Tokugawa times.

In 1887, Foreign Minister Inoue Kaoru was pursuing a policy of Westernization symbolized by balls and garden parties in the Rokumeikan that were designed as an aid to procuring treaty revisions from the Western powers.[69] Inoue spoke of the "recovery of judicial authority" for Japan, but in reality he was willing to accept the Westerners' treaty demands that foreign judges continue to preside in all cases involving foreign nationals. When an opposition faction headed by Inoue Kowashi learned of this, they leaked certain secret documents, thereby inciting fierce antigovernment agitation. Among those documents was a criticism by Boissonade of the government's frivolous Westernization policy. Boissonade pointed out that at that time in all areas – the armed services, administration, finance, education – in which foreigners served as employees or advisers, they were not permitted to obtain government posts or to wield actual government authority. Any system under which judicial authority was delegated to foreigners, he stressed, would be injurious to Japan's national interests and would open the door to foreign intervention in domestic affairs.[70]

It is noteworthy that foreign employees like Boissonade were critical of Japan's craze for Westernization. Nevertheless, the "return to being Japanese" was not triggered solely by the advice of such well-intentioned foreigners. What is more important is that some Japanese began to criticize Westerners in terms of the universal principles of

---

[69] See Donald H. Shively, "The Japanization of Middle Meiji," in Donald H. Shively, ed., *Tradition and Modernization in Japanese Culture* (Princeton, N.J.: Princeton University Press, 1971), pp. 77–119.
[70] See "Bowasonaado gaikō iken," in *Meiji bunka zenshū*, vol. 6: *Gaikō-hen* (Tokyo: Nihon hyōronsha, 1928), pp. 451–2.

"civilization" they had learned from the West. One example was the *Normanton* incident.

In 1886, the *Normanton*, an English ship, sank off the Wakayama coast. Its English captain and foreign crew scrambled to safety in lifeboats, leaving all the Japanese passengers to drown. Despite widespread public indignation, a consular court in Kōbe exonerated the captain and crew of charges of criminal negligence. The reaction was predictable: "The news spread like lightning throughout the four quarters, and all people, whether in or out of government, were overwhelmed with grief and righteous indignation. Newspapers were filled with editorials and articles treating the incident in a tragic or righteously indignant light."[71] This sense of outrage played its part in bringing to a close the craze for Westernization symbolized by Inoue Kaoru's balls at the Rokumeikan.

What provoked Japanese ire about the shipwreck and the court's verdict, in addition to the realization of racial prejudice, was the fact that the English captain and court had not lived up to the West's self-avowed standards. The Japanese originally were inspired by Smiles's *Self-Help* because of its many anecdotes of "benevolence even at the cost of death." For example, one story proclaims that when a British ship sank off the coast of Africa, the English army officers turned over the lifeboats to women and children. Nakamura's translation reads: "This group of heroes sank to the depths of that raging sea without a word of regret on their lips or a teardrop of lament on their cheeks." The hearts of Meiji readers were struck by "these gallant, yet quiet models of English manhood." The rule that "a captain goes down with his ship" was followed again and again until the end of World War II, not only in the Imperial navy, but also in Japan's merchant marine. Japanese youths had devoted themselves to creating a modern Japan based on Western models precisely because the injunctions and exemplars contained in *Self-Help* seemed to conform to their own ethical ideals. When these overly idealized images were betrayed and exposed as false by the actual deeds of living Englishmen, the Japanese reaction was to explode with anger and indignation.

To be sure, this incident itself should not be interpreted as ending Japan's "turn to the West." The "return to being Japanese" manifested by intellectuals was not a wholesale rejection of the West in

---

71 For journalism on the Normanton Incident, see *Shimbun shūsei Meiji hennenshi*, vol. 6 (Tokyo: Rinsensha, 1936), pp. 350, 356–7, 361, 365. See also Richard T. Chang, *The Justice of the Western Consular Courts in Nineteenth Century Japan* (Westport, Conn.: Greenwood Press, 1984).

favor of a total return to traditional foundations so much as a genuine appropriation of the best in Japanese tradition.

A composite sketch of Meiji nativism: Lafcadio Hearn's "A Conservative"

In *The Western World and Japan*, George B. Sansom wrote as follows about the Japanese (in this case, Baba Tatsui) who reembraced their native land during the Meiji period:

An interesting chapter of modern Japanese history could be written by tracing the careers of clever young men educated in liberal surroundings in England or America who returned to Japan flushed with domocratic enthusiasms and in course of time lapsed into a bitter nationalism accompanied by a strong dislike of the West, which had nourished their youthful ardours. Not long ago an able and experienced member of this class observed to me that most of his contemporaries, products of Western education, had turned against the Western democracies feeling that their liberalism was a sham.[72]

The phenomenon of the Westernized intellectual returning to native traditions is by no means restricted to Japan but is also found in thinkers and leaders in Russia and in other Asian countries. The trend toward a "return to Japan" was already evident in the 1890s, when Lafcadio Hearn wrote "A Conservative," a short story that he included in *Kokoro*. The piece is worth noting for the subsequent appeal it had to young Japanese. Its plot dealt with the intellectual development of a young man in changing historical conditions.

Hearn's protagonist was a high-ranking samurai born and raised in the castle town of a 300,000-*koku* domain. Trained in the martial arts and schooled in Confucian and other traditional values, he was disciplined to honor the spirits of his forebears and to scorn death. This warrior witnessed the coming of Perry's Black Ships; soon "barbarians" were employed as teachers within his castle town. After the Meiji Restoration, the protagonist left home to learn English in Yokohama under a foreign misssionary. At first he believed that love of country required him to learn about enemy conditions in a detached, cool manner, in keeping with the dictum "Know the enemy." But before long he was deeply impressed by the overwhelming superiority of Western civilization and decided that because the basis of its power lay in Christianity, he was duty bound as a Japanese patriot to accept this higher religion and encourage all his countrymen to convert. So in-

---

[72] Sansom, *The Western World and Japan*, p. 418.

tense was his conviction that he became a Christian against his parents' opposition. To discard the faith of his ancestors was cause for more than a moment's distress: He was disowned by his family, scorned by his friends, deprived of all the benefits accompanying his noble status, and reduced to destitution. Still, the samurai discipline of his youth enabled him to persevere with fortitude despite all the hardships to which he fell victim. As a true patriot and seeker of the truth, he ascertained where his convictions lay and pursued these without fear or regrets.

However, Hearn's protagonist was soon disturbed to discover that the knowledge derived from modern science, which had enabled his missionary-teachers to demonstrate the absurdity of Japan's ancient beliefs, could also be used to demonstrate absurdities in the Christian faith. The Western missionaries were often surprised and shocked to discover that the more intelligent their Japanese students were, the sooner they tended to leave the church. So it was with this youth, who became an agnostic in religious matters and a liberal in political affairs.

Forced to leave Japan, he went to Korea and then to China, where he earned his living as a teacher for a time before making his way to Europe. There he lived for many years, observing and obtaining a knowledge of Western civilization matched by few Japanese. He lived in many European cities and engaged in various types of work. The West appeared to him a land of giants, far greater than he had ever imagined. On both the material and the intellectual fronts, Western civilization seemed far superior to his own. Yet its power of intellect was too often employed to destroy the weak. With this realization, Hearn's hero gained two articles of faith: (1) Japan was being forced by necessity, not by choice, to learn Western science and to adopt much from the material culture of its enemies; and (2) nevertheless there was no compelling reason to discard completely the concepts of duty and honor and ideas of right and wrong that had been inherited from the past. The prodigality inherent in Western life taught him to value the strength found in his country's honorable poverty. He would do his utmost to preserve and protect the best in Japan's traditions.

What was of value and beauty in Japanese civilization – things that could be comprehended and appreciated only after coming into contact with foreign culture – now seemed clear to him. Thus, he had become a man longing to be allowed to go back home, and on the day that he set out for his return to Yokohama, he did so not as a blind xenophobe of *bakumatsu* times but as "a conservative" who was "returning to Japan."[73]

Hearn's character portrait can perhaps be considered a composite of the samurai-intellectuals who came to grips with Western civilization in the early Meiji era. It was so with many of the early Dōshisha student Christians, not a few of whom came as "band" members from Kumamoto where Hearn was teaching. Even Uchimura Kanzō, the leading member of the early Hokkaido Christian group, wrote of a moment in the United States when his homeland began to appear "supremely beautiful" to him. Another example can be found in the physician-writer Mori Ōgai, who, like Hearn's conservative, received a samurai education in a castle town. As a child Ōgai was often warned by his parents in no uncertain terms: "You are the son of a samurai, so you must have enough courage to cut open your belly." Others, like Nakamura Masanao or Uchimura Kanzō, studied under missionaries and accepted Christianity out of a sense of patriotic duty. Many converts, however, subsequently repudiated Christianity. In fact, although this is a little-studied area in modern Japanese thought, the great majority of Japanese thinkers seem to have "returned" to Japan in some sense. "China activists" like Miyazaki Tōten and journalists such as Tokutomi Sohō were both Christians at one time.[74] Baba Tatsui was a liberal who took refuge abroad, and Shiga Shigetaka and the periodical *Nihon oyobi Nihonjin* (Japan and the Japanese), bring to mind the intellectual who returned to Japan bent on discovering its true "national essence."

Hearn's piece, in that it foreshadows a floodtide of weltschmerz stemming from an observation of the darker aspects of Western civilization, has something in common with Natsume Sōseki's later critique of modern Western civilization, and Hearn's short story contains many aspects of thought and action that matches those of later Japanese intellectuals. Stated conversely, later Japanese intellectuals, for all the surface brilliance and diversity of their variegated philosophical spectrum, have much in common with Hearn's hero on a deeper level

---

73 "A Conservative," in *Kokoro*, vol. 7 of *The Writings of Lafcadio Hearn* (New York: Houghton Mifflin, 1922), pp. 393–422. For a detailed analysis of "A Conservative," see Hirakawa/Sukehiro, "Nihon kaiki no kiseki – uzumoreta shisōka, Amenomori Nobushige," *Shinchō* (April 1986):6–106.
74 Miyazaki's autobiography was translated by Etō Shinkichi and Marius B. Jansen as *My Thirty-three Years' Dream: The Autobiography of Miyazaki Tōten* (Princeton, N.J.: Princeton University Press, 1982). Tokutomi is treated by John D. Pierson, *Tokutomi Sohō, 1863–1957: A Journalist for Modern Japan* (Princeton, N.J.: Princeton University Press, 1980).

of feeling. In these respects, "A Conservative" is a composite sketch and a precursor of many modern Japanese intellectuals.

The Japanization of education

Upon his arrival in Japan in the early Meiji period, Basil Hall Chamberlain, who later became the dean of foreign Japanologists, lectured on "the life of Nelson" and similar topics in his post as instructor in the then fledgling Imperial Japanese Navy. About the young Japanese naval officers, successors of the Tokugawa samurai, whom he taught, he wrote that they were "fairly fluent in English, and dressed in a serviceable suit of dittos, might almost be a European, save for a certain obliqueness of the eyes and scantiness of beard."[75] He noted that the Meiji naval officers were quite fluent in English. This held true beyond the students in Japan's naval academy, for the generation born around 1860 produced an elite better able to communicate in foreign languages than could its successors. Men like Okakura Tenshin (b. 1862), Uchimura Kanzō (b. 1861), and Nitobe Inazō (b. 1862) all wrote books in English; and Mori Ōgai (b. 1862) probably did more than anyone else to introduce Western literature to Japan.

Natsume Sōseki (1867–1916), who was born a few years later, graduated from Tokyo Imperial University in 1893, took over Lafcadio Hearn's chair as the first Japanese lecturer in English literature in 1903, and then in late Meiji left academic life to concentrate on his writing. His remarks about the capabilities of Japanese students in English over time provide a revealing insight into the "Japanization" of Meiji higher education. The students' command of English was declining, he noted, because of the proper and predictable progress achieved by Japanese education:

> In my generation, all instruction at regular schools was done in English. In all courses – geography, history, mathematics, botany and biology – we used foreign-language textbooks. Most students who came a little before us even wrote their answers in English; and by my generation, there were some Japanese instructors who taught in English.[76]

In that era, he went on, English was only one aspect of an excessive subordination to foreign culture: "Men would show off by dangling gold watches, wearing Western dress, growing beards, and interject-

---

[75] Basil Hall Chamberlin, *Things Japanese* (Rutland, Vt.: Tuttle, 1971), p. 1.
[76] "Gogaku yōseihō," in *Sōseki zenshū* (Tokyo: Iwanami shoten, shinsho ed., 1957), vol. 34, pp. 233–4.

ing English phrases when speaking ordinary Japanese." Not only was English fashionable, but modern knowledge was as yet inaccessible in Japanese:

Because we had so much English training outside regular English classes, our ability to read, write, and speak developed naturally. But we all are Japanese in mind, and considering our independence as a nation, such an educational system is, in a sense, a disgrace. It invokes in us the feeling that we are no different from India, that we are subjects of England. We all agree on the importance of Japan's nationality; it is not something to be exchanged for a mere knowledge of English. Hence, as the foundations for our state's survival are solidified, the aforementioned educational system ought naturally to fall into disuse; and in fact, this is precisely what is taking place.

Not enough had been translated yet, and the use of many foreign textbooks was still unavoidable. But scholarship was universal, and once there were adequate materials and competent Japanese teachers, Japanese students were increasingly taught in their own language.

From the standpoint of widely diffusing scholarship in society, it would be best to teach in Japanese, the language in which our students have been brought up and which they use naturally. . . . The declining use of English is natural and to be expected.

But government policy also came into play and might even have proved more important than these cultural aspects. As Sōseki saw it:

The biggest cause for declining English abilities in Japan was man-made, in the form of a policy adopted, I believe, when the late Inoue Kowashi was minister of education [1892–6]. The decision was to teach all subjects except English in Japanese as much as possible. While emphasizing the importance of the Japanese language in teaching, Inoue sought to revive Japanese literary and classical Chinese studies as well. . . . This man-made decision to suppress the use of foreign languages [in education] is an overwhelmingly important factor behind the present decline in language abilities.

In early Meiji years, the "modernization" of institutions and ways was construed as "Westernization." However, in that the desire to modernize was generated by an external crisis that caused independence for the Japanese people and nation to be established as a categorical imperative, it was inevitable that Japanese students studying abroad would, upon their return home, appropriate the positions temporarily held by foreign employees in and out of government.

Inoue Kowashi, too, advocated modernization with less Westernization. Like many other Meiji leaders, his objective was not "the importation of things Western" but, rather, "Western-style production" in Japan. After the "political crisis of 1881," he submitted a political program to the government in which he outlined the educational policies that he thought the state should adopt. Two clauses in his program read:

The Promotion of Chinese Studies:

Since the Restoration, English and French studies have had high priority, and this has caused the sprouts of revolutionary thought to appear in our country for the first time. However, for teaching the Way of loyalty to ruler, love of country, and allegiance – values in danger of disappearing at present – nothing equals Chinese studies. We must revive these values and thereby maintain a balance.[77]

Encouraging the Study of German:

Under our present educational system, the only students who study the German language are found in medicine. Students studying law and related subjects all learn English and French. It is only natural that those who study English admire English ways, and that those who study French envy French government. But of all nations in present-day Europe, only Prussia is similar to us with regard to the circumstances of its unification. . . . If we want to make men throughout the land more conservative minded, we should encourage the study of German and thereby allow it, several years hence, to overcome the dominance now enjoyed by English and French.[78]

It was Inoue who, with Motoda Eifu, drafted the Imperial Rescript on Education which was promulgated in 1890. In the preceding passage we can see that as early as 1881 Inoue wanted to return to East Asian traditions and to uphold national unity by means of a philosophy stressing virtues such as loyalty to ruler, love of nation, and allegiance to superiors.

However, we must not forget that among the generation that studied directly under foreign teachers in Japan, there was a clarity of understanding regarding international affairs that proved lacking in later days. Naval officers are a case in point. Officers in the Russo-Japanese War for the most part fought on warships made in Britain. Unlike the officers in World War II, who fought on ships and flew in planes manufactured in Japan, they went to Britain or other foreign countries, observed how ships were built there, and delivered the finished products to Japan themselves. At times they might witness British laborers staging strikes, for example, and this broad range of experience made navy men international minded. After that generation retired in the 1920s, the naval officers, like the ships they com-

---

[77] "Kangaku wo susumu," in Inoue Kowashi denki-hensan iinkai, ed., *Inoue Kowashi-den, shiryō* (Tokyo: Kokugakuin daigaku toshokan, 1966), vol. 1, p. 250.
[78] "Doitsugaku wo okosu," in *Inoue Kowashi-den, shiryō*, pp. 250-1.

manded, were "made in Japan." This was true also for the leaders in all other areas of government. In the 1930s the entire nation was seized by a very narrow nationalism. That nationalism was partly due to conditions external to Japan, but it was able to gain ground in part because of the parochialism of Japanese education in that era.

From the Charter Oath to the Imperial Rescript on Education

The Charter Oath issued in 1868 and the Imperial Rescript on Education promulgated in 1890 may be considered official proclamations that mark the beginning and end of an era. In regard to the West, the Charter Oath states:

Evil customs of the past shall be abandoned and everything shall be based upon the just laws of Nature.

Knowledge shall be sought throughout the world so as to strengthen the foundations of Imperial rule.

These two articles were declared by the victorious loyalists (*sonnō-ha*) to be the cultural and political policies to be undertaken by a unified new Japan. It is interesting to note that once the antiforeign loyalists had toppled the bakufu and seized power themselves, they immediately proclaimed a policy of peace and opened the country to foreign trade and diplomatic intercourse. This fact exposed the slogan "revere the emperor, expel the barbarians" for what it had really been – a catchphrase devoid of meaningful content that was used to unite and mobilize the energies of dissident samurai activists.

Yet the new Meiji government's declaration that "knowledge shall be sought throughout the world" should not be interpreted as a simple by-product of its policy to establish peace and open the country. Yoshida Shōin, who defied bakufu law, had also "sought knowledge throughout the world," and his purpose too was "to strengthen the foundations of Imperial rule." The commitment to abandon "evil customs of the past" was clearly indicative of the realization that Japan in 1868 was as yet unequipped to be a modern nation-state and showed a singular desire to learn from the West.

As opposed to the Charter Oath, which sought models to adopt in foreign nations perceived to possess cultural superiority, the Imperial Rescript on Education issued twenty-two years later in 1890 sought these models in a transcendent Japanese historical character. The rescript reads:

Be filial to your parents, affectionate to your brothers and sisters; as husbands and wives be harmonious, as friends true; bear yourselves in modesty and moderation; extend your benevolence to all; pursue learning and cultivate arts, and thereby develop intellectual faculties and perfect moral powers; furthermore, advance public good and promote common interests; always respect the Constitution and observe the laws; should emergency arise, offer yourselves courageously to the State; and thus guard and maintain the prosperity of Our Imperial Throne coeval with heaven and earth. . . .[79]

These virtues appealed deeply to feelings traditionally held by the people. Moreover, the rescript asserts that "ever united," the Japanese people "have from generation to generation illustrated the beauty" of those virtues, thus pushing national unity and the source of national morality far back to the historical origins of the Japanese people. Conversely, such historicism posits the continued existence of national unity and morality throughout all periods of Japanese history, thereby giving birth to the concept of a historically transcendent "national essence" (*kokutai*).

Not that the rescript was anti-Western in thrust. The exhortations to "pursue learning and cultivate arts, and thereby develop intellectual faculties and perfect moral powers; furthermore, advance public good and promote common interests; . . ." are almost identical to those put forth by Smiles in *Self-Help*. Thus, although it is often characterized as a simple piece of Confucian reaction, elements meeting the demands of a new age are to be found in this document. The rescript did not assert that Japanese traditions were universal principles; rather, it proclaimed that values then regarded as universal in nature really conformed to traditional Japanese ways.

Yet it is also evident that foreign nations disappeared from view in the rescript. One distinguishing characteristic of post-*bakumatsu* history is that unlike the period of national isolation, an inescapable influence was exerted on Japan by foreign, mainly Western, nations. In the Charter Oath, we find a declaration that for Japan, a latecomer to international society, to preserve national independence, the Japanese people must learn from foreign countries and progress along the road to civilization and enlightenment. By contrast, the only reference to Japan's relations with foreign countries mentioned in the Imperial

---

[79] Translated in R. Tsunoda and W. T. de Bary, eds., *Sources of Japanese Tradition* (New York: Columbia University Press, 1958), pp. 646–7. For the genesis of the rescript, see also D. H. Shively, "Motoda Eifu: Confucian Lecturer to the Meiji Emperor," in D. S. Nivison and A. F. Wright, eds., *Confucianism in Action* (Stanford, Calif.: Stanford University Press, 1959), pp. 302–23.

Rescript on Education is "should emergency arise, offer yourselves courageously to the State; and thus guard and maintain the prosperity of Our Imperial Throne coeval with heaven and earth . . . ," which posits a hypothetical state of war.

The Imperial Rescript on Education, which totally ignored the existence of foreign countries and extolled the virtues of Japan's "national essence," was by no means indicative of recovered national self-confidence. The omission of foreign nations actually suggests a Japan filled with doubt and anxiety, a Japan unable to reject foreign influences completely and therefore driven to rely all the more on indigenous values. Such doubt and anxiety are revealed in the fact that as opposed to the Charter Oath, the rescript depicts foreign nations in a negative, almost menacing, light. The rescript's aim is to create internal solidarity among the people by maintaining a common national morality and a consciousness of that morality as stemming from shared origins in Japan's past. This aim is manifested from the beginning: "Our Imperial Ancestors [stemming from the sun goddess, Amaterasu] have founded Our Empire on a basis broad and everlasting, and have deeply and firmly implanted virtue; Our subjects ever united in loyalty and filial piety, . . ." to the end: "It is Our wish to lay it to heart in all reverence, in common with you, Our subjects, that we may all attain to the same virtue."

Thus, the Imperial Rescript on Education clearly decreed the end of a fervent "turn to the West," whose start was symbolized by the Charter Oath. Whereas the Charter Oath posited "the just laws of Nature," a value assumed to be hitherto lacking in Japan, as a goal to be attained, the Rescript asserted that a "national essence," whose values were already mainfested in Japan's feudal past, should be the foundation for future action.

The Charter Oath can be compared to a small child just beginning to understand what is going on around him who seeks to absorb things from his environment; in short, it shows the desire to identify with the world. Conversely, toward the end of the 1880s, after deciding that its "turn to the West" had been too sudden and extreme, Japan sought an identity of its own, and part of this straining to confirm an identity can be seen in the Imperial Rescript on Education of 1890.

Japan, a non-Western nation, adopted from the West a tremendous amount of what was fundamental and essential to modernization during these twenty-two years. Without those ideas and institutions, the establishment of a national identity would have been impossible, and the existence of an independent Japan within a society of nations dominated and ordered by the West could not have been maintained. But at the same time, because of this wholesale borrowing from the West, the basic establishment of a "self," which had to be attained and upheld by the Japanese themselves, became a process filled with anxiety and uncertainty. In short, the assimilation of Western culture was dictated by reasons of state, yet such efforts were fraught with an uneasiness that Japan's cultural self-identity might be violated. Because this psychological problem – a sense of pride easily injured – lay constantly at the bottom of Japan's modernization process, the Japanese displayed what might be called a strange fanaticism in every subsequent foreign crisis involving the West. The fact that the slogan "uphold the national essence" had such a powerful hold over Japanese hearts is undoubtedly also closely related to this psychological problem.

CHAPTER 8

SOCIAL CHANGE

Japan's nineteenth-century history is the crossroads for three overlapping, but normally distinct, perspectives on social change. Each perspective constitutes a search, respectively, (1) for the origins of rapid modernization, (2) for the unraveling of the premodern social order, and (3) for the consequences of sweeping reforms. No one of these searches is yet near completion, but together they already offer convincing evidence of far-reaching changes in social structure. When bolstered by information from abundant materials such as local histories, which are rich in detail but eschew broad generalizations, the scholarship associated with these three perspectives provides an unusually strong historical foundation for attempts to summarize the main lines of social change in a nineteenth-century, still little modernized country.

Exploration of the origins of rapid modernization derives from questions about contemporary Japan. In search of the fundamental and distinctive qualities of Japan's "economic miracle," a number of social scientists have turned back to the organizational characteristics, the work attitudes, and the general social structure that immediately preceded the modern era. Historically based catchphrases such as Chie Nakane's "vertical society" (*tate shakai*)[1] and Hayami Akira's "industrious revolution" (*kimben kakumei*)[2] are suggestive of the results of this retrospective inquiry, conveying the impression of a people prepared even before modern reforms were initiated for directed, concerted, and diligent action. In like manner, others eager to discover the roots of Japan's unusual modern development continue to find evidence for extraordinary qualities already widely dispersed among the Japanese people in the nineteenth century.[3]

[1] Chie Nakane, *Japanese Society* (Berkeley and Los Angeles: University of California Press, 1970).
[2] Hayami Akira, "Keizai shakai no seiritsu to sono tokushitsu," in Shakai keizaishi gakkai, ed., *Atarashii Edo jidai shi zō o motomete* (Tōyō keizai shimpōsha, 1977), p. 13.
[3] Evidence for Japan's distinctive premodern social conditions can be found in Cyril E. Black, Marius B. Jansen, Herbert S. Levine, Marion J. Levy, Jr., Henry Rosovsky, Gilbert Rozman,

The second perspective evident in recent scholarship is a growing interest in nineteenth-century social change as an outcome of earlier currents and "contradictions." The more that historians of the Tokugawa period recognize the dynamic qualities of Japan's so-called centralized feudalism (*shūkenteki hōkensei*), the more they will look ahead to the gradual unraveling of that carefully structured system during the eighteenth and especially the nineteenth centuries. Often applying concepts originally drawn from the Marxist historical lexicon but nevertheless broadly relevant, they amass evidence in support of a far-reaching transformation variously denoted by such labels as the "crisis of feudalism" or the "origins of capitalism."[4] When well grounded in empirical research, this perspective helps see beyond the relatively stable facade of the *bakuhan* system into its internally evolving social structure. The results of these studies are informative about many types of social change never before seen in Japan and only rarely and recently evident elsewhere in the world of the nineteenth century.

In the general histories, a third historical perspective overshadows either of these approaches to social change in nineteenth-century Japan. It is less controversial, as it specifically focuses on the sweeping and well-documented policy changes of the Meiji Restoration and the years that immediately followed, rather than on the long-range and often gradual changes occurring largely independently of, or beneath the surface of, official decision making. The challenge remains of reinterpreting the policy changes of the 1860s and 1870s within the context of the other, long-term perspectives, that is, of showing how the transition from the Tokugawa to the Meiji period built on the preexisting foundation for modernization and on the internally generated transformation of the Tokugawa social order.[5]

Henry D. Smith II, and S. Frederick Starr, *The Modernization of Japan and Russia: A Comparative Study* (New York: Free Press, 1975). The authors single out as important to modernization such qualities as experience of a large, circulating service-oriented elite, the presence of social controls capable of balancing family loyalties, high levels of resource accumulation and of urbanization, and the spread of secularized education.

4 For criticisms of excesses in applying Marxist categories without adequate attention to historical detail, see Hayami Akira, *Nihon keizaishi e no shikaku* (Tōyō keizai shimpōsha, 1968), chap. 1; and Susan B. Hanley and Kozo Yamamura, *Economic and Demographic Change in Preindustrial Japan, 1600–1868* (Princeton, N.J.: Princeton University Press, 1977), pp. 12–28. Despite the validity of these criticisms, one should recognize the importance of information obtained from testing Marxist propositions regarding landownership, labor relations, village solidarity, and social classes.

5 Beginnings toward this are made in Marius B. Jansen and Gilbert Rozman, eds., *Japan in Transition: From Tokugawa to Meiji* (Princeton, N.J.: Princeton University Press, 1986).

ASSUMPTIONS REEXAMINED

Explanations for the abrupt policy shifts associated with the Meiji Restoration invoke many of the prevalent interpretations of the sources of social change. Japan faced an international threat that forced a sharp turnabout in its foreign relations. Divisions within the leadership on how best to counter the foreign menace and to adjust to the altered international situation produced social unrest and widening conflict. From this environment emerged a new leadership prepared to make massive policy changes in areas touching numerous facets of the society. Although there is disagreement about the significance of the Meiji Restoration in terms of class motivation and about why Japan's social reforms came so quickly and penetrated so deeply, the scenario for change is reasonably clearly understood, and the causal arguments center on such standard factors as foreign demands and leadership changes. Political history appears to be more salient than social history, at least for explaining how change originated.

The other two perspectives in nineteenth-century Japan pose more of a challenge to once-prevailing assumptions about the origins of social transformation and draw historians more immediately into sociological problems. Contrary to views about modern social change popularly accepted for other countries, which were not among the first to modernize, the roots of modern development in Japan appear to lie more in the thrust of past social change and organization and less in long-standing diffusion from the first countries to modernize, in the specific foreign relations occurring in the late nineteenth century, in the will of new leaders, or even in parallels to particular currents of social change popularly associated with the histories of west European states. Attention centers on the organization and development of Japan's premodern social structure.

Sources of change often credited with transformative powers in other premodern societies were notably minimal in Japan. So-called free cities or merchant self-governing organs associated with the dynamism of medieval Europe may have had clear counterparts among the ports and commercial centers of sixteenth-century Japan, but by the following century, such cities were fully incorporated into the directly administered territory of the shogun or into the various domains (*han*). Merchants on the rise in Tokugawa Japan did not follow the prescribed path by assuming control over the full range of urban government or by mounting any direct challenge to national representation and power.

Popular assumptions about the role of international relations or of a "world economy" do not prove any more applicable than do the assumptions about free cities. As is well known, the self-imposed *sakoku* policies isolated Japan from the burgeoning foreign trade, the international division of labor, and the national competition seen by many as primary causes of domestic social changes elsewhere. Although the Japanese became aware of the expansion of the imperialist sea powers long before the country was forcibly opened to the world in 1853, one can also rule out the notion that earlier military threats or ambitions provoked any major reorganization of Tokugawa society as they had, for instance, in Russian society.

There is also no basis in the historical record for claiming that a push for absolutist leadership by the shogun (and certainly not by the isolated emperor) could account for the record of Tokugawa social change. For close to two and one-half centuries, Japan was notably bereft of disruptive political struggle and absolutist ambitions as well as military destabilization and realignments. If political leadership propelled major changes, its stimulus in Japan occurred for different reasons and at different levels in the national hierarchy than are customarily assumed elsewhere. It is also easy to reject the notion that popular rebellions, either peasant uprisings or more broadly based revolutions, produced important social change. Although it has become popular to add up the scattered incidents of village protest or violence (*ikki*) and of urban unrest or violence (*uchikowashi*), the total impact of these actions did not amount to much until the very end of the Tokugawa period.

Another set of explanations attributes massive behavioral and organizational changes to the development of new religious beliefs comparable to a "Protestant ethic" and to a rejection of previous other-worldly assumptions that had narrowed the horizons of the possible as far as this-worldly pursuits were concerned.[6] One cannot doubt that popular consciousness was changing on many issues, but without a struggle among religious movements or a pattern of religious conversions or awakenings one is hard-pressed to find a stimulus for new entrepreneurial activity or other social change that in any meaningful way resembles what is presumed to have occurred in Europe's Reformation.

---

6 On equivalents of the Protestant ethic, see Robert N. Bellah, *Tokugawa Religion: The Values of Pre-Industrial Japan* (Glencoe, Ill.: Free Press, 1957); but modified, however, in Robert N. Bellah, "Baigan and Sorai: Continuities and Discontinuities in Eighteenth Century Japanese Thought," in Tetsuo Najita and Irwin Scheiner, eds., *Japanese Thought in the Tokugawa Period* (Chicago: University of Chicago Press, 1978).

If the evidence does not support assumptions based on "free cities," a "world economy," military pressures, absolutism, popular rebellions, and an equivalent of the "Protestant ethic," what did produce the social changes for the period before 1868 and that continued to form the background for Meiji policy initiatives and for early modernization late in the century? Scholarship on Japan has not arrived at any simple or straightforward answer to this question. Consistent with recent currents in historical social science writings, the approach here is to examine relatively detailed and exact evidence from, for example, demographic and urban history.[7] This chapter will first introduce the findings drawn from quantitative social science evidence and then develop, in a necessarily hypothetical way, some linkages among them that may help explain the general pattern of social change. Because many of the European-based assumptions are obviously inapplicable, the reader will look in vain for a number of the themes stressed in treatments of premodern social change elsewhere.

To reject the assumptions of historical causality associated with European history is not to deny common themes in social science history. Many of the directions of Japanese social change are anticipated in studies of premodern societies elsewhere. The gradual transition from samurai-dominated cities to merchant-dominated ones indicates the rise of the bourgeoisie, albeit not according to a scenario that calls for "free cities." The shift from commerce based on the lord's economy to that based on the peasant economy (*nōmin keizai*) parallels the transformation of the peasantry away from self-sufficiency elsewhere. Increased specialization for national and regional markets alters the functions of cities and intensifies rural-urban interdependence as was occurring in western Europe. The individual household adapted to such changes by diversifying its income and its options for long-term advancement, in the process apparently coming to view children as resources whose numbers should be controlled, whose abilities should be cultivated through education, and whose labor from the teenage years should be used away from home where the wages were higher. These changes are in many ways reminiscent of changes observed in parts of Europe, which is noted in the brief comparisons in the concluding section.

[7] There may be no parallel to the mass of detailed, local studies of premodern social conditions now available for villages, cities, and local areas in Tokugawa Japan. Most studies are descriptive with little use of modern social science approaches; however, since the mid-1960s, research on historical demography and on wages and prices has led in the introduction of quantitative methods to local studies. A report on these trends is presented in Umemura Mataji, et al., *Nihon keizai no hatten: Kinsei kara kindai e* (Nihon keizai shimbunsha, 1976), vol. 1.

Assumptions regarding periodization are also evident in the labels used for Japanese society. There is near unanimity in Japan that the concept of "feudal" (*hōken*) society applies to the Kamakura, Muromachi, Sengoku, and Tokugawa periods and that within this feudal rubric the Tokugawa period forms the bulk of the "early modern" (*kinsei*) era which follows the "medieval" (*chūsei*) era. Furthermore, Western authors who define "feudal" more narrowly than do Marxists also apply the label to most or all of these same periods, although with some qualifications, such as John Hall's reference to "the declining feudal content of many political and social practices."[8]

The "feudal" label implies a considerable degree of continuity in Japanese society before 1868 and a sharp discontinuity with the following period. There is ample reason for accepting these implications even if one is aware of notable examples of social change during the first two-thirds of the century as well as of salient continuities that lingered until the end of the century and beyond. The basic social class hierarchy remained intact until the 1860s. The privileged samurai were entrenched at the top of the social ladder without granting access or equality to the *chōnin* (townspeople). Change in the peasant economy did not result in substantial diminution in the high tax obligations that went largely for samurai stipends and expenses. The castle cities (*jōkamachi*) continued to be the primary political and economic centers even when the flow of population was shifting to the smaller cities with less political importance. In almost all walks of life, the formal social structure and the legal system retained their early Tokugawa character, and it is little wonder that the currents of change were long minimized or overlooked in an emphasis on continuity.

In the absence of agreed-upon labels for further subdividing feudal or early modern, historians have applied the concepts of the rise and fall of a society. Accordingly, for the first two-thirds of the nineteenth century, Japanese "feudal" society is viewed as declining, and then it is seen as being replaced by a new type of "capitalist" (modernizing) society on the rise. Stated somewhat simplistically, (1) the Bunka and Bunsei (often abbreviated as Kasei) reign periods from the 1800s through 1820s are depicted as a time when the old social system, if not vibrant, was still capable of functioning, although the Kansei reforms of the late 1780s and early 1790s had not succeeded in setting back the clock to the social structure of a century earlier; (2) the Tempō crisis of

---

8 John W. Hall, "Feudalism in Japan – A Reassessment," in John W. Hall and Marius B. Jansen, eds., *Studies in the Institutional History of Early Modern Japan* (Princeton, N.J.: Princeton University Press, 1968), p. 48.

the 1830s and the abortive reforms in the 1840s are taken as evidence of the incapacity of the existing system and its "do nothing policies" to cope with continued social changes; (3) the *bakumatsu* period appears as a time when external and internal forces combined to destroy the old order; (4) the early Meiji period is characterized by massive reform and social engineering; and (5) the final decade of the century, the mid-Meiji period, witnessed the beginning of modern economic growth. Although this chapter is not organized chronologically, it is necessary to return from time to time to these five periods, each of which is associated with a particular phase of social change in the nineteenth century.

The labels "feudal," in both its broad and its narrow meaning, and "early modern" convey some information about social structure and have been reinterpreted to accommodate the growing awareness of social change in Japan. Nevertheless, they are originally based on assumptions drawn from European history and are not carefully worked out for comparative purposes. The use of these labels turns the focus primarily to the decline of a particular social order rather than to the foundation being built for a new order or the long-term processes of social change not easily encapsulated under the chosen label.

SOCIAL STRATIFICATION

The three broad categories of any premodern population are the ruling class, the bourgeoisie, and the peasantry. Explanations of social change center on the competition for income, power, and prestige among the three social classes and on the relationships of groups within each of these broad categories, for example, the relationship within the peasantry between landlords and tenants. The division of Tokugawa society into samurai, *nōmin* (peasants), and *chōnin* (townspeople) is no exception. Although the idealized hierarchy of that time (borrowed from the Chinese social outlook) divided the *chōnin* into artisans (*shokunin*) and merchants (*shōnin*), most historical studies concentrate on the general category of *chōnin* and find other subdivisions, such as that between the upper and lower strata in wealth, which are more useful in interpreting social change than is the distinction between artisan and merchant.

From the late sixteenth century until 1868, Japanese acknowledged a fixed, formal status order referred to as *mibunsei*. It was premised on two principles that called for a complete and permanent separation of social classes: that between the samurai and peasants (*heinō*) and that between the merchants and peasants (*shōnō*). The lines separating the former groups were drawn sharply when the samurai were removed from the land and from part-time agricultural employment. Agriculturalists, in turn, were denied all access to the symbols and training that characterized the samurai way of life. The lines were also drawn sharply between the agriculturalists and the merchants, and indeed townsmen in general. Each of the three social classes was to be residentially segregated and occupationally distinct, have a separate life-style, and recruit exclusively from its own ranks.[9] Allowance for social mobility by adoption was a concession that reaffirmed the general principle. The status order on which the Tokugawa social order rested was designed to freeze the character and relative position of each social class and to shield it from contamination, especially that which might emanate from the commercial activities.

Separate and unequal did not necessarily mean subordinate in all walks of life. Hall has suggested the phrase "rule by status" for the exercise of authority in the Tokugawa era. In place of paternalistic relationships based on locally exercised private authority, authority was exercised impersonally over a population separated into self-regulating units under the direct control of the daimyo:

As society became divided according to status levels and units of administration, it segmented into a series of boxes or containers which confined the individual but also served to limit the arbitrary exercise of authority upon him. To the extent that the administrative system became impersonalized, the individual gained a certain impartiality of treatment from the exercise of government. Rule by status assured an equality of treatment under law appropriate to the status of each individual.[10]

During the Tokugawa period, controls became less personal and arbitrary. The rigid class barriers set clear limits on what was permissible without precluding opportunities for mobility and competition under relatively impartial regulations. Large numbers of *chōnin* and *nōmin* seized the opportunities within the Tokugawa social order to advance their positions. In the process, they created a force for social change that gradually cast in doubt the very premises on which "rule by status" was based.

Japanese authorities recognized that the *chōnin* represented the greatest threat to their objective of maintaining the status quo in class

---

9 Honjō Eijirō, *Honjō Eijirō chosaku shū 3: Nihon shakai keizaishi tsūron* (Osaka: Seibundo shuppan kabushiki kaisha, 1972), pp. 232–305.
10 John W. Hall, "Rule by Status in Tokugawa Japan," *Journal of Japanese Studies* 1 (Autumn 1974): 45.

relations. Through commercial transactions and the accumulation of wealth, the *chōnin* might in one way or another undermine the privileges and martial discipline of the samurai. On the other hand, they might entice the farming population away from purely agricultural pursuits or make them dissatisfied with their frugal way of life. Quarantining the *chōnin*, to the extent it could be achieved through policies affecting each of the three classes, meant controlling such things as the use of money, the production and distribution of various kinds of goods, migration, intermarriage, and the flow of ideas.[11] Nevertheless, as developments in the late Tokugawa period demonstrate, the impact of the *chōnin* could not be contained. And so it is to this group that one should look first in the search for the sources of social change.

Chōnin

The narrow Tokugawa definition for this category is restricted to property-holding residents of officially designated urban areas (*machi*), but the reality is a more diverse and scattered collection of people engaged in activities characteristic of townspeople. E. S. Crawcour formulated what is widely documented in Japanese sources of commerce: Successive types and groups of merchants rose to the fore during the Tokugawa period.[12] Initially, the *goyō-shōnin* (special procurement merchants or quartermasters) operated as close associates of the emerging daimyo. They served the needs of wartime and domain consolidation, enjoyed exemptions from services and taxes as well as grants of monopoly over various forms of domain commerce, and supervised the *chōnin* community that was forming in the shadow of the daimyo's castle. Then, in the face of rapidly expanding interregional trade and urgent needs to convert local rice into cash for meeting expenses in Edo, the daimyo became deeply dependent on the central merchant financiers who were concentrated primarily in Osaka and Kyoto. By the early eighteenth century, as trade prospered and became more diversified between the castle cities across Japan and the three central cities, specialized wholesalers and shippers known as *ton'ya* gained control through their integrated commercial practices and broad marketing networks. Finally, from the late eighteenth cen-

---

[11] Controls on *chōnin* are discussed by Takeo Yazaki, *Social Change and the City in Japan* (Tokyo: Japan Publications, 1968), pp. 156–61, 199–223.

[12] E. S. Crawcour, "Changes in Japanese Commerce in the Tokugawa Period," in Hall and Jansen, eds., *Studies in the Institutional History of Early Modern Japan*, pp. 189–202.

tury a new challenge appeared from the *zaikata shōnin*, or rural and small-city merchants. In his study of the Osaka area, William Hauser has referred to the Kasei period from 1804 to 1830 as a time of "breakdown in urban-centered marketing networks."[13] In Edo too, the beginning of the breakdown of the *ton'ya* system is identified with this period.[14] The commercialization of agriculture, the low rate (or absence) of taxation on expanded commercial production, and the increased availability of capital in local areas all contributed to the rise of local merchants.

The succession of merchant groups, especially the serious competition offered in the early nineteenth century by local merchants without official authorization, testifies to the dynamism of commercial relations. No sooner had one group won recognition and a share in the privileges awarded by the local daimyo or the shogunate, than another group intensified its struggle to broaden the circle of authorization and privilege still further. Continuous competition and the growing prosperity of large numbers of *chōnin* marked the Tokugawa period. Social stratification among the merchant population became even more complex as each of the competing groups lingered on with its own sphere of operations.

Studies of the *chōnin*'s impact convey an impression of governments on the defensive, reacting chiefly in the face of harsh economic realities. Struggling to improve their debt-ridden finances, to extricate the samurai from a growing perception of impoverishment relative to the *chōnin*, to stabilize prices and supplies, the bakufu and *han* authorities repeatedly shifted their terms of cooperation with the merchant groups. It was hoped that somehow readjustments in the relationships between lord and merchant and among various merchant groups could solve the pressing problems. In the long run, however, national reform programs, including the Tempō reforms of 1841 to 1843, as well as occasional desperate acts of debt cancellation and arbitrary levies, failed to reassert national authority or to reverse the trends of decontrol and prosperity.

Most samurai commentators tended to see merchant gains as government, or even as samurai, losses, but this is certainly a distortion. The motif of class conflict, perceived by both contemporaries and histori-

---

13 William B. Hauser, *Economic Institutional Change in Tokugawa Japan: Osaka and the Kinai Cotton Trade* (Cambridge, England: Cambridge University Press, 1974), p. 51.
14 Hayashi Reiko, "Edo dana no seikatsu," in Nishiyama Matsunosuke, ed., *Edo chōnin no kenkyū* (Tokyo: Yoshikawa kōbunkan, 1973), vol. 2, p. 106.

ans,[15] must be balanced against that of mercantilist cooperation. In this latter view, tolerance and recognition of successive groups of merchants were seen as a means of raising domain prosperity. Seizing opportunities for improving their finances and pressed by the economic imperatives of bakufu government policies and of competition among the *han*, governments struggled to expand commerce and became even more reliant on the merchants.

Excluded from political affairs, the merchants spearheaded social change through their struggles for business success. They redirected their energies from one set of customers to another, from one set of products to another, and from sources of capital in one type of community to those in other types of communities. More than any other group, the merchants were in the vanguard of social change in Tokugawa Japan, all the more so under the relaxed controls in the first half of the nineteenth century.

The transformation of the *shokunin* (artisans) occurred more slowly than that of the *shōnin*. Both groups had been concentrated (through incentives as well as forcible migration) in the castle cities of the daimyo. Market forces increasingly operated rather than production for orders by powerful houses. The prized military craftsmen originally resided in close proximity to their lord, often within the castle grounds. Then, as the plan of the castle city called for greater residential segregation and specialization of land use, the artisans were moved to separate wards, or *machi*. More often than the merchant wards, those settled by artisans were named for the prevailing occupation and were organized as a community of households engaged in the same activity. Gradually, however, the forces of urbanization and impersonal markets overtook even the artisans. The lords could not justify or afford the small scale of production and duplication of services. Many artisans lost their earlier privileges. Some relocated in the central cities to which the daimyo were turning for mass-produced goods. Single-profession communities broke up as households moved to locations dictated by market forces. Nonetheless, the *shokunin* were slower to disperse than were the *shōnin*, and professions tied to *han* power were slower to disperse than were those oriented to domain consump-

---

15 The simplified version of class conflict is presented in Charles David Sheldon, *The Rise of the Merchant Class in Tokugawa Japan: 1600–1868* (Locust Valley, N.Y.: Association for Asian Studies, 1958). For a critique of the widely expressed notion that economic distribution in Tokugawa Japan was a zero-sum game, see Hanley and Yamamura, *Economic and Demographic Change*, pp. 12–27.

tion.[16] The castle city merchants easily outdistanced the artisans in establishing their independence both financially and symbolically and in their rate of population growth.[17] As military expenditures declined, the merchants' dominance became even more apparent.

In the nineteenth century, artisans in both the large central cities and the dispersed castle cities had to struggle with competition from the local (*zaikata*) producers. In some areas, such as the north Kantō region, the development of local textile production was so concentrated and occurred on such a large scale that it has been cited as evidence of the rise of manufacturing.[18] On a smaller scale, many forms of industrial production, especially the processing of agricultural goods such as saké and soy sauce, spread to the countryside. Across much of Japan, local crafts emerged as part of what Thomas Smith has described as the spread of side employments during the second half of the Tokugawa period.[19]

Kozo Yamamura has offered two reasons for investments becoming concentrated in rural Japan and thus posing a challenge to the urban *chōnin:*

> For the economy as a whole, this [roughly between 1760 and 1830] was a period of rapid increase in commercial and premodern manufacturing activities. [The alternative of investment in large urban centers] was closed to the village entrepreneurs for two major reasons. One was that city guilds, though their power was weakening, were still able to rebuff the incursions of outsiders. The other was the absence of institutional arrangements to enable the transfer of capital from the villages to the cities.[20]

Although the merchants and artisans could not readily shift their residences and shops (usually the two were joined in one building) from the city to the countryside or to the local marketing towns, the hired laborers (*hōkōnin*) were more mobile. This third category of *chōnin* (the term *hōkōnin* includes, among others, servants and day laborers) was at the same time the heir to the hereditary servants who

---

16 Nishikawa Koji, *Nihon toshishi kenkyū* (Tokyo: Nihon hōsō shuppan kyōkai, 1972), pp. 225–6, 255–6.
17 Nakamura Kichiji, ed., *Nihon keizaishi* (Tokyo: Yamakawa shuppansha, 1967), p. 156.
18 Japanese sources place considerable emphasis on the rise of rural manufacturing. See, for example, Kawaura Yasuji, *Bakuhan taisei kaitaiki no keizai kōzō* (Tokyo: Ochanomizu shobō, 1965).
19 Thomas C. Smith, "Farm Family By-Employments in Preindustrial Japan," *Journal of Economic History* 29 (December 1969): 687–715.
20 Kozo Yamamura, "Pre-Industrial Landholding Patterns in Japan and England," in Albert M. Craig, ed., *Japan: A Comparative View* (Princeton, N.J.: Princeton University Press, 1979), pp. 295–6.

performed household and military service duties for the samurai and the precursors of the modern proletariat employed by capitalists as wage labor in manufacturing and transportation.

Originally the *hōkōnin* of the samurai moved around with their masters and were treated as long-term dependents. The legal freedom of these people became increasingly secure in the early seventeenth century as the bakufu repeatedly issued prohibitions on slavery, on selling servants, and even on long-term service. At the same time, a severe labor shortage in the burgeoning cities improved the labor market for the poor. Soon annual, seasonal, and increasingly more short-term, even daily, wages prevailed.

Samurai on fixed incomes were finding that they often could not even afford labor in the face of rising wages offered by the chōnin.[21] As Kozo Yamamura makes clear, rising wage levels continued through the second half of the Tokugawa period.[22] Even the city merchants and artisans could not offer high enough wages to attract as much labor as they could before. These circumstances altered both the length of the service obligations and the extent of status dependency. Even when the employer was a samurai and the employee a poor servant, the relationship between employer and employee became largely a function of the labor market.

In the last century of Tokugawa rule, the urban lower strata, along with the merchants and artisans – all categories of *chōnin* – were largely free of the personal bonds to lords and bosses that had once regulated their existence. If the Genroku era (1688–1704) marked the florescence of a well-to-do *chōnin* society, then, according to Nishiyama Matsunosuke, the Tanuma era three-quarters of a century later witnessed the establishment of a lower-class society in the city of Edo.[23] The lower-class presence was increasingly felt in various facets of city life. The poor inhabited the backstreets. They numbered among the renters who, as is clearly shown in a detailed study conducted in 1828,[24] comprised as much as 60 to 80 percent of the *chōnin* population within numerous districts of Edo.

From time to time, the large numbers of hired labor, some temporarily unemployed, also posed a threat to urban order, as during the riots

---

21 Nakabe Yoshiko, *Kinsei toshi shakai keizaishi kenkyū* (Tokyo: Kōyō shobō, 1974), pp. 96–110.
22 Yamamura, "Pre-Industrial Landholding Patterns," pp. 293, 295–6, 300.
23 Nishiyama Matsunosuke, "Edo chōnin no sōron," in Nishiyama, ed., *Edo chōnin no kenkyū*, vol. 1 (1972), pp. 28–33.
24 Matsumoto Shirō, "Bakumatsu, ishinki ni okeru toshi no kōzō," *Mitsui bunko ronsō* 4 (1970): 105–64.

that gripped Edo in 1787. Whereas, on the one hand, the bakufu frequently reorganized privileged merchant associations in the hopes of solving commercial problems, it also repeatedly addressed the problems of the urban lower strata in an effort to preserve order. It responded to homelessness and unemployment through policies to return migrants to their native villages, through welfare measures, and through tighter controls within the city, including a system of guarantors to be held responsible for recent migrants.[25] The bakufu and *han* governments kept reacting to social change among the *chōnin*, but their policies did not reverse the relatively autonomous growth of a diversified urban population, including the alarming development of a distinct lower-class society.

It would be wrong to conclude that bonds of community and personal loyalty among *chōnin* became negligible during the Tokugawa period. Many themes of historical research refute such a view: The emphasis on self-government, albeit limited, and community cooperation within each urban ward; the identification of close main and branch store (*honke-bekke*) connections and of apprentice (*deshi*) relations, with prospects of gradual promotion through seniority and perhaps adoption; the emergence of powerful merchant houses that branched out from their home areas; and the presence of labor bosses (*oyakata*) who acted as intermediaries in the labor market. These features, as well as the provisions for holding workers at times of labor shortage, and the presence of paternalistic forms of management are among the conditions that might be said to anticipate twentieth-century employment practices.

Any discussion of the dynamism of *chōnin* life would be incomplete without mentioning the widely accepted concept of *chōnin bunka* (merchant culture). This concept, associated with the Genroku period but really a cumulative development continuing into the nineteenth century and reaching another peak in the Kasei period, refers to the emergence of a mass urban culture. It included, first, leisure-oriented interests in the arts and in the thriving nightlife that catered to urban males.[26] Second, it incorporated, and indeed was based on, the substantial advances in education, literacy, and knowledge that were made by large numbers in the urban population. Perhaps even more impressive than the qualitative advances in literacy were the advances

---

25 Tokoro Rikio, "Edo no dekaseginin," in Nishiyama ed., *Edo chōnin no kenkyū*, vol. 3 (1974), pp. 263–308; and Minami Kazuo, *Edo no shakai kōzō* (Tokyo: Hanawa shobō, 1969), chap. 2.
26 Nishiyama, "Edo chōnin no sōron," pp. 9–13.

in its distribution, for it eventually reached many of the urban poor and the rural population.[27] Third, the term also conveys overtones of a distinctive approach to life that was conveyed in the codes of the great merchant houses and elsewhere. Bearing many similarities to the samurai codes of conduct, this approach stressed duty to the household to make one's business prosper, loyalty to superiors as expressed in devoted service, and frugality and sacrifice in order to make one's way up through seniority.[28] Hard work, respect for learning, a mass reading audience, and diversionary entertaining were among the signs of a new urban consciousness. Over time, the differences between samurai and *chōnin* culture diminished, especially as the mass culture of the *chōnin* became part of the samurai world view and as the *chōnin* assimilated many of the samurai ideals depicted in literature and theater.

Changes in the *chōnin* population appear no less dramatic when viewed quantitatively. Over the first half of the Tokugawa period, the number of *chōnin* may have tripled or quadrupled, resulting in an urban population of merchants, artisans, and hired laborers together with their household members well in excess of three million.[29] Over the second half of the period, some decreases in the population of Osaka, Kyoto, and many of the castle cities were probably more than made up for by widespread increases in small cities, marketing centers, and even villages. A period of dramatic growth was followed by a period of deconcentration, and the consequences of the latter must have been great for the impact of commercial activities on the lives of the Japanese people.

In Edo, where approximately 600,000 *chōnin* resided,[30] the second phase was not marked by decreasing population. In other respects, however, there was a demographic transformation that was echoed in many other urban centers. The sex ratio dropped from roughly 140 males for every 100 females to little more than parity, and household size continued to fall.[31] Although in the 1840s, as many as one-third of the city population still came from outside, the figure fell over the next

27 Ronald Dore, *Education in Tokugawa Japan* (Berkeley and Los Angeles: University of California Press, 1965).
28 Johannes Hirschmeier and Tsunehiko Yui, *The Development of Japanese Business 1600–1973* (Cambridge, Mass.: Harvard University Press, 1975), pp. 43–66.
29 Urban population figures are given in Gilbert Rozman, *Urban Networks in Ch'ing China and Tokugawa Japan* (Princeton, N.J.: Princeton University Press, 1973), p. 102. The breakdown into social groups on pp. 81 and 88 must be supplemented by an estimate for hired laborers.
30 Gilbert Rozman, "Edo's Importance in the Changing Tokugawa Society," *Journal of Japanese Studies* (Autumn 1974): 101–2.
31 Nomura Kanetarō, *Edo* (Tokyo: Shibundo, 1966), p. 107.

two decades to under one-quarter.³² By the *bakumatsu* period, a more stable, family-centered *chōnin* population largely residing in small household units predominated. Demographically as well as occupationally, changes in the composition of the *chōnin* population proceeded at a rapid pace.

Awareness of the various changes in the *chōnin* class leads us to question two long-popular assumptions, that (1) the *chōnin* did not challenge samurai power because of their weak economic position and great dependency on state power, and (2) Meiji entrepreneurs were largely samurai because the *chōnin* were accustomed to following samurai and were unwilling to innovate. Kozo Yamamura cast doubt on the adequacy of the evidence cited in support of the dominance of samurai among Meiji entrepreneurs.³³ What remains to be done is to establish more clearly the links between *chōnin* dynamism during the Tokugawa period and their newly appreciated entrepreneurial vigor after 1868. The evidence suggests that the *chōnin*'s entrepreneurial impact was a continuous and generally growing force in Tokugawa as well as Meiji Japan.

For merchants and artisans, the reforms that ushered in the Meiji era were double-edged: They liberated the *chōnin* from burdensome restrictions and at the same time threatened them by opening the gates to competition. In just a few years the new Meiji government established freedom of occupation for all, freedom of travel and residence, freedom of commercial transactions, and other rights that, at least in principle, had been absent before. Large numbers of *chōnin* lost out with the elimination of the security of *han* monopolies, restricted domain markets, guild restrictions, and a concentrated demand from samurai customers. They faced new competition from samurai who turned to commerce, favored with bonds in lieu of their earlier stipends and from local, often part-time, merchants already on the ascendancy in the late Tokugawa era. Conditions were in flux: New export markets opened; imports replaced certain handicrafts; taxes in kind gave way to cash payments; and government enterprises were founded and then sold off.

Under these circumstances, the transformation undergone by *chōnin*

---

32 Takeuchi Makoto, "Kansei–Kaseiki Edo ni okeru shokaisō no dōkō," in Nishiyama, ed., *Edo no chōnin kenkyū*, vol. 1 (1972), pp. 387–90.
33 Kozo Yamamura, *A Study of Samurai Income and Entrepreneurship: Quantitative Analyses of Economic and Social Aspects of the Samurai in Tokugawa and Meiji Japan* (Cambridge, Mass.: Harvard University Press, 1974), pp. 137–62.

in Tokugawa times may have greatly aided the capacity of a number of them to adapt. Johannes Hirschmeier and Yui Tsunehiko have referred to "the astonishing pace of adaptation of the House of Mitsui to the conditions of the Meiji economy," noting their familiarity with "advertising techniques and customer service approaches which remind one very much of modern retailing."[34] Accustomed to a competitive environment and flexible in their commitments, the Mitsui reflect the evolving commercial conditions of the late Tokugawa period. Many *chōnin* proved adept at organizing to meet new circumstances, whether through the merchant houses with their elaborate rules and stringent demands of loyalty, the newly proliferating formal organizations modeled on Western examples, or the numerically predominant small-scale family enterprises. Modern organizational skills and their functional equivalents were widely dispersed across Japan. The acceptability of adoption and other employment mechanisms to ameliorate problems of nepotism in a family-oriented environment can be traced back to Tokugawa practices for expanding business operations and operating branch stores.

By the mid-Meiji period, Japan had a high proportion of women (well over half the total) among blue-collar workers. Unskilled, unmarried, short-term workers in light industry, these females were the heirs to the late-Tokugawa-era women who increasingly left home to take employment and, in the process, sharply reduced the sex ratio in the cities. Hazama Hiroshi, following Ōkochi Kazuo, refers to these women as "*dekasegi*-type" (sojourning for work away from home) workers, as they were only temporarily in their jobs and maintained a close relationship with their farm families.[35] The work conditions were grim; dormitory living was closely supervised; and contracts were made with the household head, who accepted money as an advance against wages. But the rural households benefited, and the growth of a self-conscious urban proletariat was slowed, although by the late 1880s the poor districts were becoming crowded with hired laborers, peddlers, porters, and others who formed the nucleus of a proletariat.

Early Meiji reforms that gave businessmen and workers legal rights comparable to those found in more modernized countries occurred with little pressure from below. They were granted by leaders who assigned high priority to economic growth. Intense competition re-

---

[34] Hirschmeier and Yui, *The Development of Japanese Business*, p. 66.
[35] Hazama Hiroshi, "Formation of an Industrial Work Force," in Hugh Patrick, ed., *Japanese Industrialization and Its Social Consequences* (Berkeley and Los Angeles: University of California Press, 1976), p. 29.

sulted. Three groups – the developing modern business community, the emerging industrial labor force, and the large number of merchants engaged in the still vital traditional sector – each became an amalgam of diverse social backgrounds. The ease with which entrepreneurial talent of all sorts was used must be attributed to the heritage of social change in the Tokugawa era. In short, the surge of reforms of early Meiji recognized and brought to fruition currents already widely visible in the Kasei era at the start of the century's counterreforms in the Tempō era. By the mid-Meiji period the new momentum given to these currents of social change contributed to the beginning of rapid modernization.

Nōmin

Change also permeated village life, transforming social conditions long before the Meiji Restoration and the land settlement that followed. Despite the goals of stability that the bakufu had for the rural areas, conditions were continuously transformed.

The goals of the Tokugawa leaders for rural life were embodied in four concepts: the separation of samurai and peasants, the *kokudaka* system, the emergence of *hombyakushō*, and the suppression of *nōmin keizai* (commercial activity by the peasants). The *heinō* (samurai-peasant) split was one of the founding principles of Tokugawa society. It signified the separation of the military from the peasantry, both physically and in terms of rights over the use of land and labor. Peasants were barred from entering the samurai class, and, in principle, from moving to the cities, from switching to nonagricultural pursuits, and from selling or using their land as they might see fit. Samurai were increasingly cut off from their land base as multilayered or proprietary landownership was eliminated. The restrictions on samurai interference in village pursuits proved more effective and enduring than were the restrictions on peasant economic diversification. The simplification and impersonality of controls actually opened the way to rapid social change for the *nōmin*, as it had for the *chōnin*.

On the basis of a national land survey and the establishment of a new landholding system in the 1580s, households, villages, tax administered territories, domains, and even samurai stipends all were expressed and set in *kokudaka* (estimated rice yield) levels. The system was founded on careful measurement and may have laid the foundation for a statistically oriented society. As a result of the *kokudaka* system, there was a high level of consciousness of relative standing (among *nōmin* as well as among the daimyo and the samurai) and, in turn, of household efforts for improving one's status. The system demanded clear delineation of land rights under the principle of "one land, one ruler." Although the initial taxes were burdensome and probably drained all of the surplus away from the peasant, the system did offer predictability. With improvements in agronomy and in yield and in the absence of new surveys and taxes, there was also an incentive to raise production. Together with the separation of the social classes, the *kokudaka* system swept away many of the structural impediments to the peasants' self-betterment and initiative. What the leadership had not anticipated was that the fruits of *nōmin* industriousness would increasingly escape the assessment process and the reach of the military elite. Throughout the 1860s this system continued to offer a secure and generally equitable foundation for household and community planning, while rural management and landholding patterns continued to change.

Taxes were assessed on the village and were allocated by village leaders drawn from owner-cultivators (*hombyakushō*). Through the listing of many marginal agricultural laborers as taxpayers, the *hombyakushō* system gave the village a substantial measure of autonomy from the city-based samurai rulers. This system produced a subdivision of land, a more contractual and impersonal relationship between the original large landholders and their former dependent laborers, and incentives to increase total output. Despite lingering corvée and collective obligations, the peasants were largely free to use their time as they saw fit, and even to engage in side employments to the extent that opportunities were available. Thomas Smith traced "the general weakening of the role of cooperation and obligation farming,"[36] contrasting the dependent farming of the seventeenth-century village with the new market-type relationships that evolved. These included tenancy based on autonomous economic units. Smith referred to changes "of great importance for Japanese history, perhaps justifying comparison with the agricultural revolution in Europe . . . as a whole they fell mainly in the Tokugawa period, and their central feature was a shift from cooperative to individual farming."[37] Small-scale management of agricultural resources advanced markedly as new methods and new farmers' handbooks became widely distributed.

Whereas management became fixed at the household level, the scale of landownership increased to some extent. Kozo Yamamura has con-

---

36 Thomas C. Smith, *The Agrarian Origins of Modern Japan* (Stanford, Calif.: Stanford University Press, 1959), p. 140.   37 Ibid., p. 9.

curred with Japanese scholars that landholding during the last 150 years of the Tokugawa period became more concentrated and the village more differentiated. In explanation, he offered the increased demand for labor, the increase in the value of labor vis-à-vis that of land, and, after 1830, the impact of "rampant inflation and an increased competitiveness in commercial and manufacturing activities due to the decline of the guilds and the rise of the village entrepreneurs."[38] Yamamura concludes that in both Japan and England "landholding patterns and contractual arrangements were changed to make agriculture increasingly efficient."[39] During the final third of the nineteenth century, when there was a big increase in the percentage of arable land controlled by landlords as their status rose under the new social system,[40] the *hombyakushō* system, which had provided a framework for expanded equality and homogeneity in the Japanese village, was disappearing.

John Hall has observed that the ideal economic world envisaged by Tokugawa administrators "postulated a fundamentally agrarian economy with minimum development of trade – a society in which the samurai governed, the peasants produced, and the merchants took care of distribution."[41] Delivering their rice directly to local officials, the peasants were minimally affected by commercial transactions. Officials initially suppressed *nōmin keizai* based on the direct commercial activity of the peasants, for fear that it bore the seeds of undesired social change. Their fears were justified as rural commerce grew markedly, and *han* finances and the relative position of the samurai fell into decline. Japanese scholars often depict the peasant economy as surging past the lord's economy by the early eighteenth century and continuing to forge ahead.[42] Referring to the late Tokugawa period, Hall concludes, "At the village level it was as much as anything the spread of landlordism and commercial activity which led to the breakup of the traditional village economy and to many of the social dislocations which troubled the authorities."[43] William Hauser has cited as one of the factors behind a sharp decline in imports from the countryside to Osaka after 1830 "the increased participation of both the cultivators and rural processors and the rural merchants in the marketing process."[44] Increased commercial agricultural production undermined

38 Yamamura, "Pre-Industrial Landholding Patterns," p. 300.   39 Ibid., p. 323.
40 Ann Waswo, *Japanese Landlords: The Decline of a Rural Elite* (Berkeley and Los Angeles: University of California Press, 1977), pp. 16–21.
41 John W. Hall, *Japan: From Prehistory to Modern Times* (New York: Dell, 1970), p. 204.
42 See, for example, Nakamura, *Nihon keizaishi*, pp. 98–104.
43 Hall, *Japan*, p. 203.   44 Hauser, *Economic Institutional Change*, p. 51.

not only the mechanisms for controlling trade but also an entire system premised on a fixed division of labor among various social strata and various types of settlements.

The Tokugawa period thus witnessed the fall of one type of landlordism and the rise of another. The former type existed in a relatively nonmonetized economy in which powerful peasants formed the core of small bands of households who owed diffuse labor services and, in turn, received unspecified amounts of assistance in times of need. In mountainous villages and in regions remote from Japan's economic arteries, relations of this type continued into the nineteenth century, often involving households linked by kinship bonds such as *honke-bunke* (main and branch households set up through unequal inheritances) or the survival of *dōzoku* (common lineage) bonds. In most areas diffuse and proprietary (so-called vertical) labor relations gave way earlier to more equal, "horizontal links" among households based on the subdivision of land, the transfer of risks to owner-cultivators, and the decline in mutual obligations for services and benefits.

The new type of landlords operated in an increasingly commercialized economy. Known as *gōnō* (wealthy peasants), they often diversified their investments. Especially in the late eighteenth century and during the first half of the nineteenth century, these landholders cum entrepreneurs gained ascendancy in the rural areas.[45] They acquired titles legally through investments in reclamation or by getting around laws against the alienation of land, for example, through mortgages. The *gōnō*, including substantial landholders of the past and households whose principal wealth derived from commercial enterprises, formed a new village leadership.

The impact of the new landlords, without the hereditary privileges often observed in other societies, transformed village society in the final century of the Tokugawa period. First, their rural investments expanded the demand for labor, driving up the wages necessary to attract workers, and altering household decisions about labor allocation, landownership, and migration. Second, their reliance on tenant farming or on wage labor made contracts the foundation for rural social relations, reducing the significance of the personal bonds that had earlier predominated in rural communities. Third, their flexibility in choosing among diverse and largely productive uses for their capital contributed to local economic growth in all sectors. Heavy invest-

---

45 Yamamura, "Pre-Industrial Landholding Patterns," p. 296.

ments in irrigation systems and fertilizers helped make commercial agriculture more profitable, and transfers of funds into marketing centers contributed to the development of local commerce and industry. Fourth, their role as investors and managers fostered entrepreneurial skills in the rural sector. Fifth, the *gōnō* joined with the earlier village elite to form a group capable of emulating urban life. John Hall described this process of cultural diffusion as follows:

> Together they [the new and old wealth peasants] formed a village upper class, often well educated and in close contact with samurai officialdom, able to partake of the cultural products of the castle town or the great cities. Rural society eventually acquired something of a higher cultural life of its own and was able to produce substantial leadership in local administration and economic development.[46]

Despite their improved situation, Japanese landlords operated under various constraints until what Ronald Dore refers to as "stage 1 land reform" followed the Meiji Restoration.[47] The new government's policies dispossessed the daimyo and others who had enjoyed inherent ownership rights (however removed they might have been from the exercise of these rights apart from the collection of income that more closely resembled taxes than rents). In the late nineteenth century the landlord elite reached its peak. The full establishment of private property rights permitted this group to increase its holdings rapidly, and the end of rigid class barriers removed occupational and investment barriers and sumptuary laws.

Ann Waswo has singled out the landlord elite as innovators and promoters of progress. Her analysis supports the conclusion that the actions of this rural elite were important to bringing about sustained advances to Japanese agriculture during the Meiji period and that the investments, managerial skills, and upwardly mobile sons of this elite contributed mightily to growth in other sectors. It was not until the late and post-Meiji years that increasing numbers of absentee landlords diverted funds away from local investments. Waswo took exception to the postwar Japanese scholarship that characterizes landlords as parasites and obstacles to progress:

> Most landlords lived comfortably, and a few, elegantly. But a large proportion of their wealth was used productively, not dissipated in conspicuous display. They were actively concerned with improving agriculture and village

---

46 Hall, *Japan*, p. 204.
47 Ronald Dore, "Land Reform and Japan's Economic Development," *Developing Economies* 3 (December 1965): 487–9.

life. Again in contrast to the stereotype, there is little evidence that they found trade and industry repugnant.[48]

There are many reasons to associate the transformation of landlords with the aforementioned social changes in the *chōnin* class. Large numbers of the local (*zaikata*) merchants on the rise in the late Tokugawa period were none other than *gōnō*. The new landlords responded to opportunities for commercial agriculture, transferred capital back and forth between landholdings and commercial enterprises, emulated urban practices, and competed for labor after the demand for it had grown rapidly in the urban sector. In short, the continuing investigation is turning up changes in commercial activities as explanations for each stage in the process that transformed a countryside dominated by patrimonial landlords to one characterized by deconcentrated, relatively egalitarian landholders, and finally to one with new concentrations held by entrepreneurial landlords, who, after 1868, were free to work toward larger holdings still.

For every change in the landlord stratum, there was a corresponding change in the stratum of tenants and agricultural laborers. The polarization of landholdings (often referred to as the "disintegration" of the peasant class) through the nineteenth century greatly increased the number of landless and marginal agriculturalists. It has often been assumed that the emergence in the last century of Tokugawa rule of a rural "semiproletariat" attests primarily to the expropriation of the poor by the rich, to the greedy manipulation of the terms of trade or of credit, and to the catastrophic impact of the Temmei and Tempō famines that drove impoverished peasants to turn over their land.[49] Yet the statistics on prices, wages, rents, taxes, and standards of living give credence to a different explanation for the disposal of many small plots of land. The positive factors encouraging small owner-cultivators to reallocate their household labor and to reduce their landholdings may well have surpassed the negative factors pushing them off their own land.

Clearly the situation of the rural lower strata changed markedly over the Tokugawa period. After they were legally released from personalized dependency relations with samurai and landlords alike, they gradually gained independence in other ways as well. They established separate households and residences. As labor services were discontin-

---

[48] Waswo, *Japanese Landlords*, p. 5. See also Richard J. Smethurst, *Agricultural Development and Tenancy Disputes in Japan, 1870–1940* (Princeton, N.J.: Princeton University Press, 1986).
[49] Sasaki Junnosuke, *Bakumatsu shakai ron* (Tokyo: Hanawa shobō, 1973), p. 15.

ued, agricultural laborers and owner-cultivators could use their time more efficiently. Direct participation in local markets also improved their position and added to the incentives for increasing and diversifying production in order to earn a larger income. Increased opportunities to move to the cities and to earn higher wages there also could not fail to influence the aspirations of potential migrants in the countryside and to put pressure on others who needed work to meet the standards of the competition. Indeed, by the nineteenth century, it appears that the term *hōkōnin* was as likely to refer to rural servants or hired labor as it was to their urban counterparts.[50] The convergence of wage labor in the urban and rural sectors and the gradual shift in destination from the cities to the countryside form the background for the changes in observed landholdings.

Susan B. Hanley and Kozo Yamamura have been virtually alone in bringing together the widely available evidence on the Japanese labor market in order to explain the situation of the rural lower strata. They have shown that in the final century of the Tokugawa period, the labor available for agriculture declined to such an extent that, unlike the seventeenth century when the population had grown rapidly, a shortage of labor developed. Because of large-scale migration to the cities and the expanding participation in side employments by peasants still in the village, there was inadequate labor left for agriculture. To summarize, what made possible a labor shortage was (1) the ease of movement to the cities and the high demand for labor there after the seventeenth century; (2) the existence of "labor markets, both in the agricultural and in the non-agricultural sectors, [that] were competitive by the beginning of the eighteenth century, if not before";[51] (3) increases in the number of "peasants engaged in commerce and manufacturing on a part- or full-time basis . . . [at the same time that] rural manufacturing and commercial establishments, growing larger and more efficient, could offer wages attractive enough to keep the labor for their needs";[52] and (4) slowdown in population growth.

The results of the labor shortage reverberated through rural and urban areas in similar ways. Many who enjoyed high status found that they could no longer afford hired labor – virtually the only form of extra household help still available. Others who were in a better position to readjust their use of scarce resources retained a declining num-

---

50 Hayami Akira and Uchida Nobuko, "Kinsei nōmin no kōdō tsuiseki chōsa," in Umemura et al., eds., *Nihon keizai no hatten*, pp. 67–98.
51 Hanley and Yamamura, *Economic and Demographic Change*, p. 86.   52 Ibid., p. 98.

ber of workers with the likelihood that improved skills would be well rewarded. The laborers themselves were in a position to improve their career prospects and standards of living. In the villages, Hanley and Yamamura noted that the shortage of labor stimulated directly or indirectly (1) an improvement in agricultural methods and other more efficient uses of resources; (2) an increase in wage levels and in benefits such as the number of holidays for hired laborers; (3) an improvement in the terms of contract for tenant-cultivators; (4) in some less commercialized regions, a further decrease in the number of *nago* (landless peasants) who still cultivated small plots of land and provided labor services in exchange for their plot; (5) an increase in peasant demand for diverse consumer products; (6) a reduction in the average duration of employment, as laborers found it advantageous to jump from job to job; and (7) a continued reallocation of landholdings, particularly as small and marginal peasants left the land in order to improve their living standards. Hanley and Yamamura summarized their findings on many of these points as follows:

The movement of labor to nonagricultural activities resulted in a shortage of labor in agriculture, which had the consequences of raising the wages of agricultural laborers and servants and of improving the terms of contract for tenant farmers. Under these circumstances, some arable land remained unworked, and the efforts of the ruling class to stabilize wages in defiance of the dictates of the labor market usually proved unsuccessful. The increasing returns to labor, imputed for tenants or paid to wage earners, necessitated the more efficient use of labor. In the manufacturing industries this often took the form of an increased scale of production. In agriculture, the result was for many to change the size of their unit to make it as close as possible to what would be optimum, given the prevailing level of wages, relative advantages in the types of crops that could be grown, climate and topographical conditions, and the market conditions (relative prices of crops and volume of demand) at the time.

For holdings to approach optimum size, some owner-cultivators had to increase their holdings, while some of the largest landholders began to lease part of their land to tenant cultivators, even though it meant they had to offer tenants terms of contract promising them a return for their labor equivalent to what they could earn by migrating to towns, by engaging in rural commerce on a part- or full-time basis, or by becoming agricultural wage laborers.[53]

Thus what had been described as the pauperization of excess or overtaxed rural laborers now becomes characterized as an intense, competitive bidding for scarce labor. Incentives increased and re-

---
[53] Ibid., p. 323. See also the elaboration on some of these themes in Yamamura, "Pre-Industrial Landholding Patterns," pp. 292–302.

sources were allocated more efficiently. Under these circumstances, it is understandable that the peasants became more industrious, that agricultural productivity rose, and that side employments became more competitive with urban production. Just as both the rural landlords and the least well-to-do laborers benefited from the significant institutional changes launched from above in the late sixteenth and seventeenth centuries, both groups also benefited from the perhaps equally significant changes emerging from below over the eighteenth and much of the nineteenth century.

Hayami Akira has introduced two expressions to refer to these changes in the lives of the rural masses: "economic society" (*keizai shakai*) and "industrious revolution."[54] The increase in the peasants' dependence on the market, the independence of the small peasant household as a participant in the market, and the formation of a national network for marketing goods all are aspects of an "economic society." Hayami included as part of this concept the substantial movement of people for economic purposes and the development of mass education, mass entertainment, the mass media, and other forms of mass culture. The convergence of rural and urban labor markets, involving high rates of migration with flexible choice of destinations, facilitated the diffusion of many characteristics of urban popular culture to the rural masses. Hayami's "economic society" is also a mobile and informed society; he regards it as a necessary but not sufficient condition for capitalism.[55]

Noting that agricultural productivity increased several times over during the Tokugawa period, Hayami cites as a factor increased labor input per agricultural laborer. The small-family producing unit whose members increasingly enjoyed longer life expectancies and improved conditions of life responded to incentives to increase their labor input in order to raise their living standards. Hayami declares that this period witnessed the birth of an industriousness still present among Japanese peasants today.[56] Gains in productivity through highly labor-intensive methods, with little population growth and with little, although increasing, inputs of capital, demanded that households maximize the effectiveness of their labor inputs.

However much the balance between landlord and tenant may have shifted after 1868 in the landlord's behalf (especially by denying tenants rights long sanctioned by local custom),[57] the long-term impact of the tenants' improved position was not easily obliterated. A degree of

---

54 Hayami, "Keizai shakai no seiritsu to sono tokushitsu," p. 318.   55 Ibid., p. 9.
56 Ibid., p. 13.   57 Waswo, *Japanese Landlords*, pp. 17–23.

tenant independence is deeply rooted in the social changes of the Tokugawa period.

One of the five articles in the Charter Oath issued by the new Meiji government in April 1868 asserted: "The common people, no less than the civil and military officials, shall each be allowed to pursue their own calling so that there may be no discontent." To that end, a series of decrees over the next five years raised the status of the majority of the people and established a broad category of commoners (*heimin*). Above all, two decrees of 1873, the land settlement and the conscription law, granted new opportunities while at the same time imposing new responsibilities. The former clarified landownership and regularized tax payments in cash, both resulting in a heightened orientation to the market and to land and labor as commodities. Freedom to move, to plant, and to sell formalized the free market in agriculture. Unlike land settlements aimed at eliminating the land-based aristocracy or at granting land to the previously landless, the Meiji settlement brought little redistribution. Several of its chief effects were to centralize regulations in a country long divided, to give uniform legal backing to practices that had defied earlier official restrictions, and to confirm the primacy of impersonal market forces. Free rein was given to the household to pursue its prosperity. Small-scale holdings continued to prevail, although by the end of the century the amount of land rented to tenants had increased sharply, and a group of powerful landowners had emerged.

The Meiji land settlement enhanced the authority of landlords in both tenancy relations and village life. It gave landowners clear title to the land, leaving tenants more vulnerable. In some cases the tenants protested the loss of common land or of customarily recognized permanent tenancy rights or high rent burdens, but they continued to accept the landlords as village leaders and referred to the relationship in kinship terms.[58] Over the final decades of the nineteenth century, they followed the example of the landlords in introducing new farming techniques, in sending their children to the newly established modern schools, and in joining new rural associations. Levels of agricultural productivity, rural literacy, and local organizational growth were extraordinary for a country just beginning modern economic development. The conclusion is inescapable that changes in Tokugawa village conditions left a rural population well endowed for modern development.

---

58 Ibid., pp. 23–4.

The conscription law was a principal step in abolishing the legal distinction between samurai and commoner. At age twenty-one, males were made liable for military service. Although there were exemptions and the possibility of commutation through payment, a considerable number of rural men were called up for service. Along with the educational reforms designed to achieve compulsory schooling, conscription played a crucial role in widening the horizons of the village residents, imparting new skills and organizational experience, and inculcating the attitudes of a modern military force imbued with a samurai heritage and guided by a European model. By the mid-Meiji period, military prowess and success had confirmed the significance of the military career, while also demonstrating that the qualities (literacy, discipline, readiness to learn, and so on) of Japan's rural recruits would not be easily matched elsewhere.

Of course, both old and new inequalities limited homogeneity of Japanese society. The right to intermarry with samurai granted in 1871 broke down artificial barriers without basis in wealth but did not result in much mingling of high and low. If most *nōmin* were unlikely to have the means to emerge from their day-to-day agrarian existence, the pariahs of the old society – *eta* and *hinin* – faced a still more insurmountable barrier. They were legally freed in 1871 from severe restrictions of occupation and residence, at the same time losing monopolies of occupation and nontaxed status. But despite legal equality, the adjustment was not easy, and more than a century later the stigma remained on their descendants (then called *burakumin*). Just as rigid, legal inequality did not prevent an easing of income differentials in the late Tokugawa period, reforms that provided for equality before the law did not prevent widening income inequalities during the Meiji era.

Any discussion of social relations in rural Japan would be incomplete without mentioning community relations. The Japanese village of this period had many elements of cohesiveness and solidarity, that is, *kyōdotai*, gemeinschaft, or community spirit. This concept appears predominantly in the following contexts: (1) the communal use of resources, especially in the context of a rice-producing economy with shared water rights, that is, conditions of production that demanded a good deal of cooperation; (2) the unity that resulted from the government's levying a lump-sum tax on the village and the collective concern that the number of households not increase too greatly or that the land be redistributed so unequally that meeting fiscal obligations would prove difficult; (3) the group responsibility for discipline and order embodied in village self-regulation and codes that called for ostracism or exclusion (*mura hachibu*) and other powerful controls in support of "governance by consensus";[59] (4) the existence of village assemblies and other leadership bodies that promoted collective endeavors and represented a generally unified village to the outside; and (5) the religious and ceremonial unity (*miyaza*) centered on the village Shinto shrine. Citing some of these factors, Harumi Befu described the Tokugawa village as a corporation:

> The village was a corporate body, a legal entity which owned, bought and sold property; loaned and borrowed money; and sued, was sued by, and entered into agreements with other villages. The fact that the village had such corporate qualities is important. It indicates the degree of commitment by village members toward the village as a unit and the degree of solidarity they expressed. It is this solidarity which enabled villagers to enforce their self-made laws and invoke sanctions against any members who transgressed them.[60]

Japanese rural communities varied in their degree of *kyōdotai*. By late Tokugawa times it seems to have been decreasing; in some cases it was an artifact of domination by an entrenched and hereditary elite, perhaps able to manipulate conditions to its own benefit. Many villages apparently had only nominal functions for the government-directed *gonin gumi* (five-household organizations, though they actually varied in numbers) intended for mutual surveillance and responsibility. Evidence of conflict is not hard to find. Nineteenth-century redistributions of labor and land increased the potential for conflict, especially after the controls became lax in mid-century. Nevertheless, there was a high degree of cohesion, continuity, and community on the village level, based on the strong roots maintained by the households (*ie*) identified as continuing for generation after generation, at the same time that there was great flux in the actual employment of each household's resources.

In the late Tokugawa period, the *nōmin* may have been experiencing even greater effects from social change than the *chōnin* were, for the locus of expanded migration and commercial vitality had shifted to local centers and villages. In comparison with the conditions that had prevailed a few centuries earlier, ordinary peasants were now more economically independent, market oriented, and industrious, and they were guided by diverse incentives and were educated and in-

---

[59] Dan Fenno Henderson, *Village "Contracts" in Tokugawa Japan* (Seattle: University of Washington Press, 1975).
[60] Harumi Befu, "Village Autonomy and Articulation with the State," in Hall and Jansen, eds., *Studies in the Institutional History of Early Modern Japan*, p. 308.

formed. Many of these social changes paralleled and came in the wake of similar changes among the *chōnin*.

Into the Meiji era – and beginning earlier in the growing port cities – the *chōnin* again took the lead in social change, which was dubbed "civilization and enlightenment" (*bummei kaika*). The urban sector led the way in introducing the symbols of Westernization – new haircuts in place of the shaved head and topknot, Western-style dress, and much more – and organizations and technology as well. In comparison with other latecomers to modernization, however, the Japanese rural sector does not appear to have lagged very far behind the urban sector, for example, in the spread of literacy. The earlier responsiveness of the late Tokugawa *nōmin* to urban-initiated change suggests that similar mechanisms operated in two periods.

Samurai

Whereas the other two social classes experienced much social change, the samurai did not after the *bakuhan* system became firmly entrenched in the mid-seventeenth century. From 1550 to 1650 the warrior's style of life had been transformed and bureaucratized. Assembled in cities, deprived of former associations with particular villages and plots of land, denied interference in local taxation and administration, and given some form of employment as members of governmental bureaucracies, the samurai had largely become civil administrators. The accumulated weight of their administrative experience and expanded educational training no doubt continued to raise the level of their performance in various capacities, but on the whole they probably had less incentive for superior achievement. After this formative period, there was little social mobility, either intergenerational or intragenerational. Eligibility for bureaucratic posts was generally limited to samurai of a specific rank. Duties continued very much as before, involving military, administrative, and ceremonial obligations. Especially in the higher ranks, almost no change was possible in hereditary status, although there was continual movement in and out of the lower ranks, to which honor and reward were less important. Regulations minutely governed performance on the job and much conduct off the job as well. The possibilities of new appointments for younger sons were vanishing. Stipends, both in actual amounts and in real purchasing power, remained scarcely altered. Although there is reason to argue that the early Tokugawa regrouping of the elite into an organized force for administration, based on ideals of dedicated service and high standards of performance, gave Japan a distinct advantage in the eventual formation of a modern bureaucracy, bureaucratic practices did not emphasize performance or responsiveness to changing social conditions. The *kashindan* (house retainer band) under each lord was too tradition bound and ascriptive – and too caught up in an intricate web of checks and balances defined in lord–vassal terms – to respond to gradual social changes. The rigidly structured existence of the samurai – their lack of flexibility in securing an income and in spending stipends – allowed scant opportunity to respond to new economic forces.

Nevertheless, the samurai perceived their position as changing. The origins of this perception can largely be traced to two conditions: the routinization and seeming irrelevance of many of their activities, and the awareness of improvements in the circumstances of the other social classes. Kozo Yamamura has discussed both of these conditions, describing job assignments or the absence thereof that must have left many without adequate motivation or a sense of accomplishment. The picture that emerges is very different from the picture of peasant industriousness painted by Hayami Akira referred to earlier:

> The continued peace of the Tokugawa period gradually changed the shogun's retainers from the samurai of the battlefields into bureaucrats, underemployed soldiers, and unemployed idlers. . . . Life was no longer unpredictable and dangerous, but full of monotonous routine for the former warriors who now spent hours working on the Tokugawa equivalent of interoffice memoranda, inspecting fire damage, and supervising the repair of river banks. . . . The working days of many bureaucrats decreased during the eighteenth century. Most worked two days with the third off in order to give employment to their fellow bannermen. A large number of supervisory bannermen and even some in other positions took turns on the job on a monthly basis. . . .[61]

The roughly two million samurai, including five thousand to six thousand bannermen (*hatamoto*), along with their household members, that Yamamura studied, were too numerous to be employed productively or to be rewarded to their satisfaction. Especially the *tozama* daimyo found that they "had more [vassals] than they needed or could afford."[62] Hard-pressed for funds, the daimyo repeatedly borrowed from their retainers, reducing their stipends at the very time that other social strata were making economic gains. Perhaps just as

---

61 Yamamura, *A Study of Samurai Income and Entrepreneurship*, p. 70. The work is based on Yamamura's study of the bakufu bannermen (*hatamoto*).
62 Harold Bolitho, *Treasures Among Men: The Fudai Daimyo in Tokugawa Japan* (New Haven, Conn.: Yale University Press, 1974), p. 71.

demoralizing was the absence of meaningful employment or opportunity to excel in their jobs.

Daimyo could not, in general, fire samurai and, at the same time under conditions of peace, had little or no work for perhaps as many as half of them. They ensured loyalty in part through a system of lifetime employment – a forerunner of the modern reluctance in Japan to lay off workers.

Problems of morale as well as of finances led to efforts to revitalize the bureaucracies. Herman Ooms has proposed the expression of "moral rearmament" to depict a prominent part of the two eighteenth-century reform programs intended to revitalize the bureaucracy – Yoshimune's response to routinization and Sadanobu's to corruption.[63] Discipline, frugality, mutual loyalties and obligations, a return to martial vigor, a sense of social commitment, and other aspects of the samurai ethic were called upon on these occasions and in the Tempō reforms of the 1840s to alleviate the growing sense of crisis and to renew the performance of the society's elite. But the tide was never reversed. It proved difficult to reconcile (1) the Confucian view that the samurai were the meritorious, or at least the rightful, leaders of society with the increasing irrelevance of many of their duties; (2) "the old tradition of the bushi as a militant man of action and the new concept of the ruler as a gentleman"; and (3) "the status of enfeoffed vassal" and "that of salaried official."[64] *Bushidō*, the way of the warrior, seemed increasingly irrelevant, as it expressed a formalism that offered little practical guidance for the changing times.

Merchants and landlords each comprised about the same order of magnitude as the samurai in the Tokugawa population, perhaps 5 to 6 percent. However, the ranks of these strata were adjusted by social mobility and prolonged competition. The samurai were immobilized from similar feats of adaptability and from "survival of the fittest" by their fixed residences, by official restrictions on (and disdain for) commercial involvement, and by the absence of occupational choice. But the impact of the forces generated by the *chōnin* penetrated this group too; samurai sought improvements in their situation while remaining loyal to their lords.

The major changes affecting the samurai in the eighteenth century and the first two-thirds of the nineteenth century were financial. First, they became increasingly reliant on loans, some of which were canceled from time to time, after which credit would dry up. Second,

63 Herman Ooms, *Charismatic Bureaucrat: A Political Biography of Matsudaira Sadanobu, 1758–1829* (Chicago: University of Chicago Press, 1975).   64 Hall, *Japan*, pp. 197–8.

their stipends were cut in difficult times by hard-pressed daimyo. Third, the severe inflation of the final decades of Tokugawa rule drove up commodity prices faster than the rice price on which the samurai's income depended. Fourth and most important, over the centuries their aspirations grew while their income remained relatively constant. Yamamura has suggested that in the eighteenth century "the bannerman's increasing poverty was caused by increasing wants."[65] Beset with heavy fixed expenses to maintain their positions, the samurai were also exposed every day to urban consumption practices that intensified their own demands. By late Tokugawa times the perception of impoverishment was probably reinforced by an actual decline in real income.

Yamamura concluded that large numbers of samurai became scarcely distinguishable from the *chōnin*, and in some cases the *nōmin*, in their life-styles and even in their real employment. So-called side employments became "common for all but a limited number of high-ranking and well-off samurai."[66] Many samurai were poor, performed odd jobs, and became a virtually indistinguishable part of a broad urban culture. Yamamura referred to "economic necessity . . . as a powerful equalizer of Tokugawa society" and wrote of class distinctions that became virtually nonexistent.[67]

Many important questions about the samurai remain under consideration, even though they have long been high on the agenda of Japanese studies. How did a growing sense of relative deprivation influence the samurai's attitudes toward their leaders and the *bakuhan* system? Why did such a large and firmly entrenched elite tolerate a shift in the distribution of income in favor of others? What accounts for the relative lack of resistance to the social policies that dethroned the samurai after the Meiji Restoration? What leadership roles did the samurai assume in the last decades of the century? Answers to these questions appear in other chapters. Only the last two questions require some comment here.

The "declassing" of an entrenched elite occurred remarkably smoothly.[68] In 1869 the daimyo accepted appointment as governors, ceding their hold on local power. In 1871, the complex classification of former samurai was simplified into two ranks, *shizoku* and *sotsu*, of which the latter was soon abandoned. Shortly thereafter, they were

---

[65] Yamamura, *A Study of Samurai Income and Entrepreneurship*, p. 48.
[66] Ibid., p. 131.   [67] Ibid., pp. 132, 133.
[68] See Marius B. Jansen, "The Ruling Class," in Jansen and Rozman, eds., *Japan in Transition*, pp. 68–90.

given the right to engage in all professions without loss of rank; the samurai's stipends were adjusted in steps and then, in 1876, were replaced by government bonds. There were instances of opposition – even armed resistance – but the transition from hereditary, privileged vassals to masterless individuals fending for themselves proceeded with astonishing speed. Why did the samurai so readily accede to the loss of their special status with corresponding changes in occupation, residence, and life-style? One part of the answer is the way that it was carried out, carefully in stages and with compensation. Another part of the answer is the nature of the samurai as a concentrated, disciplined, service-oriented elite with an increasing educational level. Although some samurai no doubt clung to their privileges as the only hope for security in the emerging Meiji society, others had confidence in their knowledge and experience and may have welcomed the opportunity to be freed of the virtually frozen status hierarchy of the *kashindan*. A third part of the answer must be the atmosphere of national peril and opportunity for service that inspired those who expected the Meiji leaders to honor their pledge to select talent on the basis of ability.

That the lower samurai assumed many high leadership positions after they were freed from the rigid status distinctions of their class testifies to the positive, if belated, effects of social mobility for bringing talent to the fore. The succession of new types of leaders was now well along in all three classes. Each succession produced a shift from ascriptive rewards to achievement, from privilege conferred by the leaders to a position earned largely by initiative and talent. Each succession involved a transition from urban to rural and from the big city to the small town; in the case of the samurai, many took up employment in local areas as teachers, police, and local administrators, applying skills learned in many generations of service to their lords. It is also likely that each succession of new social groups brought an increase in entrepreneurial skills and in the abilities necessary for exploiting commercial opportunities. Slow to engage directly in commercial enterprises, the samurai nonetheless had other skills that helped many make a rapid adjustment. For all classes, the succession process did not result in a complete displacement of the earlier top group, but a widening of the top circle and a transitional period when some might make the adjustment to the new methods of operation.

In each case, too, the initial sharp separation of classes helped determine the course of succession. For example, the urban *chōnin*, who were in many ways cut off from rural society, could not readily take command of the emerging rural commercial forces. Landlords, permanently separated from the samurai elite, could not rely on outside support to protect their claims on labor and land. The samurai faced the most barriers to shifting their resources out, but they also enjoyed the most protection in keeping their status intact. After 1868 the pent-up forces for rechanneling stifled energies operated as one of the major sources of social change. Thomas Smith identified this samurai response as the explosion of individual energies after the abolition of status distinctions.[69] The samurai legacy became a potent model for the entire society at the very time that rigid status barriers were becoming merely a memory. The government consciously employed samurai ideals in the new legislation and organizations of the Meiji era.

Above all, the samurai heritage (a mixture of military vassalage and Confucian hierarchical social relations embodied in a code known as *bushidō*) is reflected in the emphasis on loyalty and service to superiors. The cult of the emperor established a source of authority capable of keeping these values alive. As centralization continued and a reaction to unthinking Westernization set in, the educational system of the late 1880s incorporated a strong emphasis on ethics. Like the samurai before them, all Japanese were asked to submerge their individualism for the sake of larger causes. Modern nationalism and militarism found the samurai heritage fertile soil in which to grow. Meiji family law – its clear recognition of the authority of the household head, its favoritism for the eldest son, and its marked subordination of females to males – was also more fully rooted in the samurai tradition than in the practices of other social groups. The ability to keep alive and to diffuse samurai ideals was clearly one aspect of the anomalous combinations of traits observed in Japan since the earliest phases of its modernization: high degrees of social mobility combined with intense consciousness of social status; emphasis on achievement accompanied by a downgrading of individualism; and an entrepreneurial spirit combined with group orientation. In form, the samurai way prevailed, but in practice, the *chōnin*-led transformation continued its relentless course.

URBAN TRANSFORMATION

The level of urbanization in Japan remained fairly constant from the early eighteenth century until the 1880s, but there were many signs of

69 Thomas C. Smith, "Japan's Aristocratic Revolution," *Yale Review* 50 (March 1961): 3.

significant changes. Three perspectives on the cities reveal substantial changes in the cities and in urban-rural relations: (1) the network perspective that centers on the distribution of settlements by size and function; (2) the ecological perspective that focuses on the internal city plan and how the various physical features and population groups are distributed; and (3) the organizational perspective that considers how particular urban environments, governments, or work arrangements affect the lives of the inhabitants. In the case of Japan, the first of these perspectives often leads to singling out at least three levels of cities: the three central cities at the top of the settlement hierarchy, the more than two hundred *jōkamachi* or castle cities at an intermediate level, and various varieties of *zaigōmachi* or local centers at the lowest level.

The concentrated effort to freeze society in a newly created pattern is no less evident in Tokugawa urban policies than in stratification policies. A wave of new construction according to a highly structured plan – both for land use in the city itself and for the place of each city within its region – occurred in the early seventeenth century. The gradual breakdown of the original urban plans through the Tokugawa era parallels the transformation of social classes already discussed.

Tokugawa Japanese leaders envisioned a society in which each settlement had a distinct function. Villages were to be exclusively agricultural centers, relinquishing military and administrative activities along with the samurai who performed them and transferring embryonic commercial and craft enterprises to other types of settlements. The main concentration of nonagricultural functions would be in the *jōkamachi*, the centers of the domains into which four-fifths of the country were divided. Literally, "city below the castle," the *jōkamachi* expressed the authority of the daimyo: his monopoly of military and administrative functions within the domain; his mobilization of the area's resources through taxation and marketing; and his planned relocation of temples, shrines, merchants, artisans, and samurai in successively closer proximity to his castle headquarters.[70] Unlike the Sengoku pattern of multiple-branch castles grouped under a single lord, only a single castle city was permitted in each domain. To the extent possible, all urban functions were concentrated in this one administrative complex.

On a nationwide scale, it was of course impossible to preserve the simplicity of this stark dichotomy between village and *jōkamachi*. The

---

70 Nakabe Yoshiko, *Jōkamachi* (Kyoto: Yanagihara shoten, 1978).

Tokugawa plan took this into account by recognizing several additional urban types, all originating in earlier periods of Japanese history. There were the central cities, especially in the Kinai region, on which local elites had long been dependent for specialized production and services. There were the *shukubamachi*, or post towns, required as transportation centers along the roadways that linked the *jōkamachi* to the central cities. Also indispensable in some areas were the *shijōmachi*, or market towns, in the *tenryō* (lands directly under bakufu rule) and in the large domains where the *jōkamachi* could not absorb the marketing activities in all localities. Relatively cheap transport by sea also demanded a network of ports, not all of which could be sufficiently centrally located and meet historical expectations for local integration in order to serve simultaneously as *jōkamachi*. In addition, there remained *monzenmachi*, literally, towns in front of the gate (to a Buddhist temple or a Shinto shrine), and *jinaimachi*, or towns on the grounds of a religious establishment. Some of these centers managed to survive the transition from an era when powerful religious organizations had provided the necessary security and concentration of resources for urban development, usually by virtue of their capacity to perform other functions, as *shijōmachi* or *shukubamachi*. Apart from the central cities, each of these other types could be expected to serve only a peripheral and residual role in supplementing the primary urban functions centered in the *jōkamachi*. As far as possible, their functions were to be absorbed by the *jōkamachi;* indeed, *jōkamachi* count prominently among the places listed as filling each of the other categories.

Implicit in this precise division of labor among settlements was a corresponding division of labor among the regions. The regions of the central cities – the Kinai and Kantō regions – monopolized the nationally specialized activities. In fact, to a considerable extent, the three cities divided certain of these activities among themselves. On the one hand, Kyoto, the historical leader in crafts, and Osaka, the developing commercial leader, drew on the Kinai region's superior commercialized agriculture and numerous smaller urban places to dominate Japan's interregional specialized production.[71] On the other hand, Edo's role as an administrative and consumption city assumed far less commercialization in the Kantō region; rather, the city largely depended on a supply network stretching from scattered domains and, above all, from Osaka. The other regions, from Tōhoku in the northeast to

---

71 The literature on interregional marketing is rich in detailed local information. On Osaka's marketing significance, see Ōishi Shinzaburō, *Nihon kinsei shakai no shijōkōzō* (Tokyo: Iwanami shoten, 1975), chap. 3.

Kyūshū in the southwest, were to be largely self-sufficient in meeting their own needs, despite some variations in their secondary products after rice. The trickle of specialty items and luxuries from the central cities to the *jōkamachi* would only slightly offset the heavy flow of grain and other primary production to the center.

By the early nineteenth century, it was clear that this carefully ordered urban and regional differentiation was in flux. The main source of dynamism came not from administrative, military, or religious functions, but from commercial, craft, and transportation functions. Changes in the distribution of the urban population, beginning with the central cities, provide clear evidence of these developments. At each level, Japan's cities were changing remarkably.

Central cities

Two compelling central forces shaped Japan's national urban system during the seventeenth century and continued to operate throughout the Tokugawa period: the concentrated commercialization of the Kinai region, often referred to as the growth of a "national market," and the political centralization in Edo, in large part a consequence of the *sankin kōtai* system of alternate residence. Operating in concert, the two forces made possible unprecedented urbanization and, at the same time, stifled the development of regional urban centers elsewhere.

The Kinai region had enjoyed an extraordinary preeminence. Osaka, Kyoto, and other major cities such as Sakai, all under direct bakufu administration, gave this area an urban population in the early Tokugawa decades that I estimate, based on the city statistics that I have gathered, as close to one-half of the urban total for Japan. In addition, the Kinai was divided into administrative units (small fragmented *han* and large amounts of *tenryō* under the bakufu) that did not raise any serious barriers to specialized production and regional integration. Bakufu policies acknowledged the fundamental fact of the commercial superiority of this region and capitalized on it by building up Osaka as the "kitchen" of Japan and by encouraging the development of relatively inexpensive sea transport centered on that city.

A high level of urbanization in the Kinai region may have been indispensable to the transformation of Japan's system of cities, but the leadership in that transformation came primarily and increasingly from Edo.[72] Its unparalleled population growth – from an inconspicu-

---

72 Rozman, "Edo's Importance."

ous branch castle before 1590 to the largest city in the world, with roughly 1.1 million inhabitants after 1720 – led Japan's nationwide urbanization. Moreover, the promotion of residence in Edo stimulated the continued mobilization of increasing quantities of materials and people into cities throughout Japan. Edo's significance stems, above all, from the demands of the *sankin kōtai* system for the massive conversion of domain resources in order to meet the expenses of residence in the city. The daimyo maintained approximately one thousand residential complexes in prescribed locations in the city. There were ten complexes of Tottori *han* alone, and Hikone *han* had four with over 3,000 occupants.[73] Some one-half to two-thirds of the roughly 250,000 to 300,000 persons in these complexes consisted of those left permanently in Edo in connection with this system; the remainder were persons who accompanied the daimyo on their regular treks to and from the *jōkamachi*.[74] Far more than the numbers involved, the resources they commanded and felt pressure to expend attest to the significance of this regular migration. If one adds the irregular requisitions or assessments for projects such as castle construction or rebuilding after one of the many costly fires that swept across the city, then the demands placed on the daimyo directly or indirectly in support of Edo's development reach truly staggering proportions – perhaps one-third of all their expenses. Because of the importance of the Osaka market for converting domain rice into cash, rising expenses in Edo added also to Kinai prosperity. The huge Edo market relied on the Kinai cities for many of its supplies.

Other samurai resided in Edo as direct vassals of the bakufu. All together these *hatamoto*, *gokenin*, and their household members and servants totaled over 200,000 and made substantial claims on the production of bakufu-controlled land (*tenryō*) for their stipends.[75] Their presence added to Edo's luster as a consumption center.

Among the central cities, it was primarily Edo that gained from the narrowing of price differentials that had long favored the Kinai market, from the improving transportation network to outlying areas of the country, and on long-distance routes that made direct shipments feasible, and from the increased scale of exchange as a mass market expanded. The early magnate merchants in the Kinai region had profited from their indispensability under undeveloped conditions; the later, more differentiated commercial organizations were more broadly

---

73 Nishikawa, *Nihon toshishi kenkyū*, p. 278.
74 Fujioka Kenjirō, ed., *Nihon rekishi chiri sōsetsu: kinsei hen* (Tokyo: Yoshikawa kōbunkan, 1977), pp. 248–9, 260–1.   75 Ibid.

distributed, a reflection of Edo's increasing claims as a second national marketing center. At its peak, the population of the three central cities approached two million, of which over one-half lived in Edo. The proportion increasingly shifted to Edo's advantage, and by the mid-nineteenth century, Edo's *chōnin* population alone outnumbered the declining totals of Osaka and Kyoto combined. Explanations for the discrepancy in development among these central cities are diverse: the challenge to the large Kinai cities from newly prosperous commercial centers and *zaigōmachi* in southwest Japan; the continuation of the trend for commerce to bypass Osaka and proceed directly to Edo; the expanded production in the Kantō region to meet Edo's needs locally, often at the expense of earlier Kinai sources; and the greater stability of Edo's market due to the continued required residence of samurai, including those present by virtue of the *sankin kōtai* system. Over the last century of Tokugawa rule, Edo's impact across Japan became more direct and pronounced.

Above all, the impact of Japan's central cities rests on the large volume of resources accumulated therein, the large number of individuals (including the elite from all across Japan) who migrated there, and the great extent to which new patterns of consumption and styles of living filtered out to other cities and eventually to the countryside. The concentration of individuals with both the means and the motivation to mobilize resources from across Japan created an irrepressible force for change and a powerful demonstration effect that can be observed especially in the *jōkamachi* with which the central cities were directly connected. Few other premodern societies could boast as much as 6 percent of the total population in great cities; only much larger China exceeded Japan's record of three cities in excess of 300,000 population, and it is likely that Japan alone until the early nineteenth century supported a city as populous as 1.1 million. It required a few decades of reorganization: Edo's population fell with the Ansei earthquake; there was an exodus following the end of the *sankin kōtai* system in 1862; and after the abolition of samurai status, most cities recovered their earlier population levels and then began to expand rapidly at the end of the century. Until then, with little expansion in the percentage of its population in large cities, Japan already possessed an adequate urban base for launching modern economic growth. The percentage of Japan's population in cities of 100,000 or more was no higher (6 percent) in 1897 than it had been in the eighteenth century, and the number of cities at this level had only risen from five to six.

At the end of the nineteenth century, six cities dominated: Tokyo, Osaka, Kyoto, Nagoya, Kobe, and Yokohama. Tokyo's continued predominance (1.3 million residents in 1897) reflected its position as the center of a centralized, national government as well as its importance in modern finance and education. Osaka grew rapidly at the end of the century (750,000 in 1897), having reestablished itself as the center of large-scale manufacturing. Kobe and Yokohama, neither of which had been significant before the 1850s, were the leaders in urban growth (each nearing 200,000) because of their role in foreign trade. Nagoya, which along with Kanazawa had long ranked as one of the two largest castle cities, proved the most successful of any city of its type in converting to new functions (whereas Kanazawa declined below the 100,000 level, Nagoya doubled to 250,000 residents). Of the six largest cities, Kyoto grew the most slowly, but it still managed to accommodate itself fairly quickly (330,000 people in 1897) to the new industrial and commercial demands of the modern era. One city that was slow to pull out of the early Meiji decline was Nagasaki, which had lost its foreign trade monopoly to other ports; only the expansion of continental trade at the end of the century gave it new importance.

The long period of intense, domestic competition before the 1858 treaty that opened Japan to foreign trade helped prepare the population in the largest cities for organizational change under conditions of uncertainty. With the elimination in the late 1860s of trade monopolies and restrictions binding groups to particular occupations, the competition intensified. It centered in part on influencing government decisions about the location of offices and the establishment of modern enterprises. Much depended on the vigor of local leadership and its quest for prosperity under a centralized administration that granted the business community a heightened measure of autonomy. A major step toward urban self-government was the 1888 administrative reform, which recognized as cities (*shi*) settlements of 25,000 or more people. New organizations (e.g., police, banking, and manufacturing) proliferated in cities throughout the country, demonstrating how quickly modern structures were adopted by urban residents.

Jōkamachi

Close to two hundred cities with a total population of approximately 2 million comprise a second level in the planned hierarchy of Tokugawa cities. The individual populations of these castle cities varied from under 1,000 to over 100,000. As a rule of thumb, John Hall has suggested that the *jōkamachi* population equaled one-tenth the number of *koku* (estimated rice yield) of the *han*.[76] (The number of *koku* often approximates the number of people.) Japan's largest *han*, with hundreds of thousands of *koku*, boasted cities with tens of thousands of residents, whereas the numerous small *han* with 10,000 to 30,000 *koku* produced small *jōkamachi* generally below 3,000 in population. Fujimoto Toshiharu analyzed in some detail this relationship between city population and *kokudaka*, determining that in the northeast and along the Japan Sea, the *jōkamachi* were generally larger than expected, whereas in the southwest and along the Pacific and Inland Sea coasts the opposite pattern prevailed.[77] He explained that the latter regions had a denser concentration of population in other cities apart from the *jōkamachi*, that these regions tended to have larger *han* with greater commercialization. The *han* located in the Kinai and Kantō regions also generally produced relatively small cities because their domain land was not compact and was interspersed with *tenryō* directly under the bakufu and with the small holdings of distant daimyo granted to help them meet expenses in Edo and Osaka.

In comparison with other premodern settings, the castle cities supported surprisingly large proportions of their domain populations for many reasons: (1) the forced concentration of samurai and some *chōnin;* (2) the widespread prohibition on commerce in other areas within and often throughout the domain; (3) the lure of incentives in the form of tax exemptions, monopolies, and the like, for *chōnin;* and (4) the construction of a transportation system centered on the castle city and discriminating against other possible urban points within the domain.[78] Within the domain, the castle city not only concentrated existing nonagricultural activities, but it also promoted their further development and generated new ones. Rising demand in the central cities and growing pressures on the daimyo to increase revenues available for use in Edo spurred castle city growth over roughly one century and also continued the transformation of functions. The *jōkamachi* played an indispensable intermediate role in the national market, and in turn, much of its vitality depended on these intermediate links between the rest of the *han* and the central cities. Over this period of expansion, the *jōkamachi* shifted its central focus from the military, to the administrative, and then to the economic. The cities became functionally more complex, and the daimyo's control over them declined.

76 John W. Hall, "The Castle Town and Japan's Modern Urbanization," in Hall and Jansen, eds., *Studies in the Institutional History of Early Modern Japan*, pp. 182–3.
77 Fujimoto Toshiharu, *Kinsei toshi no chiiki kōzō: sono rekishi chirigakuteki kenkyū* (Tokyo: Kokin shoin, 1976), pp. 39–42.   78 Fujioka, ed., *Nihon rekishi chiri sōsetsu: kinsei hen*, p. 185.

The continued erosion of the domains' economic autarchy made the castle cities vulnerable to adjustments in the ties between local and national markets. The reorganization of national merchant groups in favor of more regularized, economically efficient ties was one such adjustment. A second was the entrance of the mass of rural producers directly into the marketing process. At both ends of the flow process, conditions became more competitive. The rapid-growth phase of the castle cities turned into a period of stagnant population and eventually, for many cities, decline. Thomas Smith and Nakabe Yoshiko separately assembled data that show the castle cities declining an average of 15 to 20 percent in *chōnin* population over more than a century.[79] Exceptions were largely in backward regions or inland. In contrast, the declining cities were disproportionately situated in the Kinki and Inland Sea areas of the southwest; many were ports, and mostly they defied provincial trends of population increase.

The gradual loss of population in the *jōkamachi* (some of the loss may be due to unrecorded suburbanization) in the late Tokugawa era can be largely attributed to their declining importance in four respects: transportation, commerce, industry, and consumption. In transportation, these cities along with many *shukubamachi* were increasingly bypassed by traffic seeking the cheapest possible routes. Official regulations on the old routes drove up prices and made them noncompetitive. At the same time, the castle city ports were not necessarily the most convenient for long-distance trade and for new *han* monopolies of specialized products. The more competitive flow of goods broke down the *jōkamachi* transport monopolies. In commerce, the castle cities gradually lost some of their marketing functions within the domain. Merchant monopolies in the castle city kept prices high, and restrictions on periodic markets within the *han* could not be maintained in the face of expanding rural economies. Nakajima Giichi determined that the small castle cities (especially those in *han* under 20,000 *koku*) often lacked a critical mass to support periodic markets of their own or could not attract enough commerce to compete with the prosperous *zaigōmachi* just outside the *han* borders.[80] Regions varied in the prevalence of markets. Tōhoku and much of the Chūbu region had many markets that met each fifth day (or perhaps only each tenth day), whereas the Kinai region and certain parts of the south-

---

[79] Thomas C. Smith, "Pre-Modern Economic Growth: Japan and the West," *Past and Present* 43 (1973): 127–60; and Nakabe, *Jōkamachi*, pp. 306–9.
[80] Nakajima Giichi, *Shijō shūraku* (Tokyo: Kokin shoin, 1964); and Nakajima Giichi, "Ichiman goku daimyō no jōka," *Shin Chiri* 10 (September 1962): 1–15.

west had primarily daily commerce in more substantial urban centers.[81] Whether the competition came from periodic or daily markets, the *jōkamachi* with their outmoded legacy of commercial exemptions and monopolies often fared badly.

In industry, the outlying settlements also proved more inventive and more strategically located close to raw materials, water power, cheap labor, and local markets. Led by the Kinai and Kantō regions, industrial activities spread widely through the countryside.

Finally, with respect to consumption, the deteriorating financial position of the *han* and the resultant reductions in the samurai's stipends lowered expenditures in the *jōkamachi*. To the extent that the *sankin kōtai* system and life in Edo became more expensive, the fixed revenues of the daimyo forced cutbacks at home. In this and in other respects, the center of the daimyo's life shifted to Edo.

On the whole, the *jōkamachi* relied too much on *han* power to be competitive and proved inconveniently large for meeting new, local, developmental opportunities.[82] Faced with pressing financial problems, the daimyo let their chief cities slide into decline. Indeed, both the policies aimed at preserving embattled sources of revenue and those generating new revenue outside the castle city contributed to the local urban transformation.

The interior transformation of the castle cities proceeded in step with the changes in their external role. The early-seventeenth-century castle city reflected the preeminence of military and administrative functions and the clear separation and regulation of diverse activities. By the mid-nineteenth century, as Yamori Kazuhiko has carefully analyzed, urban land use had changed in a number of ways.[83] In the area of military functions alone, several changes can be noted. The castle continued to lose military significance, although it remained the center of samurai administration. The temples, shrines, and post stations on the city outskirts were increasingly identified with recreation rather than with defense or control over movement. Some of the winding roads inside the city designed to help thwart an invasionary force were straightened and widened in order to thwart a more imminent danger, that is, fire. And the lower samurai – many called *ashigaru* – located close to the periphery turned to home-industry side employments that lessened their military interest and effectiveness. The military factor remained more pervasive in cities of the *tozama* daimyo, for

---

81 Fujioka, ed., *Nihon rekishi chiri sōsetsu: kinsei hen*, pp. 232, 276–8, 295.
82 Nakabe, *Jōkamachi*, pp. 310–23.
83 Yamori Kazuhiko, *Toshi puran no kenkyū* (Tokyo: Ōmeido, 1970).

example, in the Chūbu region, but they too experienced a general demilitarization.[84] Taking into account a wide range of urban activities, Nishikawa Kōji concludes that from the Genroku to the late Tokugawa periods, the *jōkamachi* changed substantially, for instance, through the dispersal of professions and the reorientation toward *chōnin* consumption.[85]

The proportion of urban population who were samurai first decreased and then later (when the *chōnin* population declined) increased, and the land area occupied by this group remained very large. Nakabe Yoshiko calculates the average number of samurai in a castle city as 70 to 80 percent of the number of *chōnin;* yet she noted that in backward regions, the samurai might be more numerous even to the extent of outnumbering *chōnin* by three to one.[86] Fujioka Kenjirō clarifies the size of the samurai group (*kashindan*), pointing out that its totals were greatest relative to the size of the *han* in the far northeast and southwest in which military localism was powerful.[87] Yamori Kazuhiko presents data on the percentage of urban land given over to samurai estates, showing in some cities as much as three-quarters of the city and, in large *han* in general, over 50 percent.[88] The population density in the *chōnin* wards was far higher than in the samurai districts; the turnover rate was higher; and the neighborhoods were more fluid. Yet the differences were smaller away from the castle where the lower samurai lived. Urban sprawl along the roads leading out of the city tended to disperse the *chōnin* population. The growth of cities at their outskirts can be attributed to their growing orientation to rural needs. In backward regions, urban periodic markets met more frequently in order to serve rural needs. Elsewhere, daily commerce and crafts inside the city also showed a greater dependence on the rural market, and specialty products from other sections in the *han* contributed to a reorientation toward the outskirts. Nishikawa Kōji finds evidence of this shift in the decline of certain professions and the rise of others within Hikone City.[89] The overall trend in the *chōnin* areas was from concentration to dispersal, from serving the centrally located samurai to meeting the internal urban demand of the more dispersed *chōnin*, to competing for the growing market of the scattered rural population. The initial commercial center near the castle, known as

---

[84] Fujioka, ed., *Nihon rekishi chiri sōsetsu: kinsei hen*, p. 250.
[85] Nishikawa, *Nihon toshishi kenkyū*, p. 326.   [86] Nakabe, *Jōkamachi*, pp. 304–5.
[87] Fujioka, ed., *Nihon rekishi chiri sōsetsu: kinsei hen*, p. 199.
[88] Yamori, *Toshi puran no kenkyū*, pp. 292–306.
[89] Nishikawa, *Nihon toshishi kenkyū*, pp. 257–9.

honmachi, declined as multiple and secondary commercial centers formed.

After 1868, military, administrative, and educational activities contributed to urban growth in new ways. Former castle cities continued to hold the bulk of Japan's urban population outside the national centers. Fujimoto Toshiharu examined the fate of these cities before 1920.[90] He found that cities in rather large *han* of 100,000 to 300,000 *koku* remained relatively stagnant even when they were chosen as the administrative centers of the new *ken* (prefectures). Concentrated in the Tōhoku, Hokuriku, and Sanyin regions, that is, along the Japan Sea, they were centers of agricultural surplus in areas of rice monoculture. With the removal of closed domain units of administration, they lost central place functions. In these backward areas for modern industry, the city's handicraft base could not endure after *han* protectionist policies were ended with the Meiji Restoration. For these cities the administrative factor was crucial to survival.

In contrast, former castle cities that began to grow rapidly in the late nineteenth century were in areas of greater commerce, more local cities, higher population density, and diversified agriculture. Other cities that had not been *jōkamachi* and grew rapidly became new military and textile centers, many in the nearby hinterlands of central cities such as Tokyo. The fate of castle cities after 1868 can be predicted not on the basis of their growth rates in the second half of the Tokugawa period but on the basis of their success in becoming diverse, multifunctional cities competitive under commercial conditions and capable of forging new links with smaller, and with central, cities. This explains the paradox that the declining *jōkamachi* of the late Tokugawa period emerged in the best position for growth in the Meiji period.

Meiji leaders forged a centralized, nationwide urban system largely on the basis of more than two hundred castle cities that had functioned as independent centers of local domains. They accomplished this through administrative reforms after the old domain system was abolished in 1871. Controls on appointments, finances, and legislation secured the central government's power. The swift transformation from *jōkamachi* to prefectural or district (*gun*) center had its roots in the evolution of a well-integrated and center-oriented urban system during the Tokugawa period. Despite the continuation in many respects of autonomous domain markets and administra-

---

90 Fujimoto, *Kinsei toshi no chiiki kōzō*, pp. 345–81.

tion, the underlying integrative forces had advanced far before Meiji centralization.

The last third of the nineteenth century was a period of adjustment for cities formerly protected by domain insularity and national isolation. For growth reorientation was essential, especially to specialized industries that could meet demands in large cities and abroad. It helped to be located along newly built railroad lines and to have the capital and human resources of an energetic *chōnin* community. Some places with excellent port facilities developed as naval centers. The opening up of Hokkaido also contributed to urban growth. Other cities, however, failed to readjust. Once-lavish samurai residential districts were left desolate, and farmers cultivated lots where shops had once stood.

Zaigōmachi

The initial suppression of the *zaigōmachi* was seen as a means of boosting the castle cities, that is, to simplify the settlement hierarchy much as the status hierarchy had been reduced to a small number of clearly defined classes. Many periodic markets and small craft centers (if they did not receive authorization as *shukubamachi* or in some other narrowly defined official capacity) were relegated to rural legal status, if, indeed, their nonagricultural functions survived at all. If they did survive, local rules allowed these centers to meet the peasants' supply needs with trade in agricultural tools, items of daily consumption, sake, and other goods that primarily supplemented the functions of the *jōkamachi*. The expansion of commerce through the seventeenth and into the eighteenth century made more of these settlements indispensable for *jōkamachi* prosperity. Conditions and timing varied from area to area, but the general pattern was for the central marketing activities of the castle city within the large *han* to gain by funneling resources through these local places.

Over the last century of the Tokugawa era, many of these small centers posed a threat to *jōkamachi* interests as they did to central city monopolies also. For instance, in 1787 the *shōnin* in Matsuyama petitioned to stop local trade and to move local merchants to the castle city, and in 1823 a coordinated effort by 1,007 villages caused the bakufu to reconsider its protection of the cotton monopoly granted to Osaka merchants.[91] Neither the Kansei reforms nor the Tempō re-

---

[91] Matsumoto Shirō, "Kinsei kōki no toshi to minshu," in *Iwanami kōza Nihon rekishi*, vol. 12 (*kinsei* 4) (Tokyo: Iwanami shoten, 1976), pp. 99–100; and Hauser, *Economic Institutional Change*, p. 181.

forms a half-century later succeeded in protecting the *jōkamachi* interests. Small and scattered local centers were also important to new *han* commercial objectives and could not be simply abolished without dire financial consequences. Increasingly through direct ties to the national market and outside merchants, favorable locations for accumulating *han* specialty products (*tokusanbutsu*) and access to rural capital and labor, these centers met the competition of the castle cities. Especially in the commercialized Inland Sea area, they even managed to win a measure of independence. Through the reorganization of trade routes, small centers found markets outside their own *han* and at odds with *han* monopolies and restrictions.

One of the major developments over the final century of Tokugawa rule was the adjustment in rural-urban relations led by the growing *zaigōmachi*. Drawing on the rural poor for labor and on their sales for capital, the *zaigōmachi* created a bridge between urban and rural. The indicators of change are many: the population growth in these nonadministrative centers; the change in the destinations of migrants from urban jobs to *zaigōmachi* labor that often allowed a return to the land at times of peak demand;[92] the increasing scale of production in these scattered towns; and the intense competition among the *zaigōmachi* that caused some periodic markets unable to develop new specializations to lose their rural exchange functions as well. The long-run importance of local growth centers of a semiurban character is recognized by specialists on economic development and undoubtedly should be counted along with Japan's high premodern level of urbanization as an asset important to the modern transformation undertaken in the Meiji period.

The population of both the semiurban *zaigōmachi* and other cities that were not *jōkamachi* was rising, with the addition of both full-time and part-time merchants, artisans, and hired laborers. If one adds (1) the population of Nagasaki, Sakai, and other major cities (neither *jōkamachi* nor among the three central cities); (2) the residents of the increasing number of intermediate ports in such areas as the Inland Sea; and (3) an estimate of the nonagricultural inhabitants of substantial local commercial and craft centers, then a total in excess of one million persons is indicated. This represents a major and growing component of the national urban total, which was in excess of five million.[93]

The elimination of castle city restrictions had both positive and negative consequences for competing centers. Both castle city and

---

92 Hayami and Uchida, "Kinsei nōmin no kōdō tsuiteki chōsa," p. 84.
93 Rozman, *Urban Networks in Ch'ing China and Tokugawa Japan*, p. 102.

zaigōmachi residents were freed from regulations affecting residence and business activities. The outcome varied greatly from area to area. Some towns maintained their late Tokugawa dynamism and overtook nearby castle cities as local centers, whereas others lost their competitive edge as the castle cities managed to rebound from the earlier population decline and an exodus of samurai in early Meiji.

Between 1872 and 1900, Japan's gainfully employed population rose from 21.4 million to 24.4 million as the number in agriculture fell slowly from 17.3 million to 16.4 million.[94] Thus the percentage outside agriculture grew from one-fifth to one-third. Most of the increase occurred after 1885 as the urban population growth accelerated. Under the impetus of initial, modern economic growth, the social composition of Japan's cities changed considerably. Unlike the previous major transformation two decades earlier as samurai resettled, the cities became crowded when commerce and industry flourished.

The dynamism of Japan's city system bears a number of resemblances to that of its social-class hierarchy. On the surface, much remained the same over the second half of the Tokugawa period. The *jōkamachi* were no more directly assailed than were the samurai who occupied their central areas. Despite some decline, both emerged in a strong position to take advantage of the new opportunities – administrative, military, educational, and industrial – after 1868. Change before the 1860s came gradually through reorganization; merchants in the national centers pushed through commercial developments that left the *jōkamachi* and the samurai more vulnerable; and merchants and landlords in the *zaigōmachi* seized new opportunities that whittled away at the prerogatives and security of castle city life.

In both the city system and the class system, one finds an initially highly rigid, planned arrangement persisting in important respects, whereas in other less obvious, but perhaps no less important, respects, it yielded to a highly competitive, fluid arrangement. Increasingly the forces of competition spread until even the countryside was engulfed.

In the case of the urban system, there are comparative data that document Japan's extraordinary achievement. As of 1800, and for the previous century or so, Japan's approximately 17 percent urbanization (in cities of three thousand or more plus one-half the total in smaller but still substantial commercial and/or administrative centers) approaches the highest levels in Europe and exceeds by a factor of two or three the levels reached after long histories of city building in Russia

---

94 Robert E. Cole and Tominaga Ken'ichi, "Japan's Changing Occupational Structure and Its Significance," in Patrick, ed., *Japanese Industrialization and Its Social Consequences*, p. 58.

and China.[95] The foundation of the late Tokugawa urban transformation was a high level of urbanization. In 1800 Edo retained its century-long position as probably the largest city in the world, and the closely bunched Kinai cities combined to produce a comparable urban market. A second foundation for urban change was the force generated by these two great urban complexes – at the end primarily by Edo. Thomas Smith described the second half of the Tokugawa period as rural-centered development.[96] Although the urban base remained substantially intact, the most visible changes spread through the countryside. A third foundation for change can be seen in Japan's powerful mechanisms for transmitting urban social currents into the countryside. All of these foundations continued to operate in the new circumstances after 1868.

Just as the dropping of social-class restrictions in early Meiji opened wide the gates of competition, the removal of settlement restrictions resulted first in a flurry of movement and, over several decades, an intense competition for urban growth and prosperity. The competition for markets, transport improvements, administrative functions, and many other plums occurred in a period of slow economic growth and urbanization. Separate households and community organizations faced severe readjustments in the face of the relocations of samurai, the elimination of domains, and the entry of international competition. Under these circumstances, it is noteworthy how little disruption there was in social control and economic activity. Massive urban reorganization proved a prelude to rapid urbanization, which was already under way in the mid-Meiji period.

HOUSEHOLD DECISIONS

In many largely agricultural premodern settings in which survival, even in ordinary times, required hard work, there was frequently little scope for flexible decision making. Marriage was arranged at an early age; the stream of births counteracted the stream of deaths, especially among infants; residence and occupation did not change from generation to generation or within a lifetime; and little thought was given to education or leisure. Although urban environments displayed some peculiarities in these matters, their impact on the countryside remained slight. On the contrary, those rural dwellers who managed to make their way into the cities brought with them the conventions of

---

95 Rozman, *Urban Networks in Russia*, p. 245.
96 Smith, "Pre-Modern Economic Growth," pp. 127–60.

country living, creating a sizable urban mass with scarcely more scope for flexibility than its rural counterpart had. One study after another over the past two decades has demonstrated that Tokugawa Japan moved away from this sort of fixed social order. Increasingly in the eighteenth and nineteenth centuries the household unit faced alternatives and made choices unanticipated in the early Tokugawa decades. The cumulative effect of these changes is registered in a number of social indicators established for selected villages and, in some cases, estimated for the country as a whole.

The reasons for these many changes are not necessarily obvious or easily demonstrated. Historians have long assumed that conditions such as a regionally stationary or declining population resulted from economic hardship and famine and that the peasants were pushed off the land into hired labor or migration. But recent empirical studies should lay to rest such assumptions. Other interpretations center on Japan's distinctive family system, on its community structure, and on the forces of commercialization and urbanization just discussed. At this early stage of research using quantitative data, it is still difficult to establish causal relationships with confidence. Nevertheless, in presenting the findings from various studies, the section that follows mentions some suggested explanations and relates them to the preceding sections on social stratification and urban transformation. Before proceeding, however, it is important to examine the basic structure of Japan's family system in order to establish the context in which household decisions were made.

The ie

The term for household, *ie*, refers to a corporate body expected to endure from one generation to the next. Its continuity rested on external and internal conditions. Viewed from the community, the *ie* was regarded as a legal unit under a head who had full authority over the family members and as a producing unit required to meet tax and other customary obligations. Official policies and local customs favored the continuity and viability of this unit in order to protect social order and community solidarity and to ensure sufficient land or income to satisfy all financial obligations. The household itself owed a responsibility not only to the community but also to its ancestors, who were regularly venerated through tablets and rituals. Its members were expected to work hard and to act together in order to ensure continuity and to strive for improved status. Its streamlined organization enhanced the chances for maintenance or improvement in status. Only one child, normally the eldest son of the head, inherited all property and authority. Adoption was readily accepted as a means to provide continuity or to bring a meritorious successor into an important post. Continuation of the blood line clearly was a lower priority than was perpetuation of the *ie*. Responsibilities to lineages and to other relatives outside the immediate household were slight. Robert Smith has noted that his study of members of small families

> identified an extremely limited range of kin by specific terms and "cousin usages" [that] appear to have been [as] ambiguous in eighteenth-century Japan as they are in contemporary Britain and the United States. The Japanese were early possessed of what some writers have claimed is a kin terminology closely associated with modern urbanized industrial societies with highly developed commerce, attenuation of kin ties, high rates of mobility, and increasingly universalistic relationships.[97]

A number of important features of family systems pertain to the formation of new households and the continuity of old ones. Among these are inheritance, adoption, and the dependence of the household on kinship or community organizations. That all of these features operated to stabilize the precise composition and number of households appears highly likely from the data available on individual village and social groups. It comes as no surprise, of course, that samurai households both persisted and remained quite constant in number after the early seventeenth-century formative period.[98] The size of the retainer band (*kashindan*) was basically fixed; younger sons had virtually no chance of being appointed bannermen. In a lord–vassal relationship preserved largely through primogeniture and by adoption if there was no male issue, stability in numbers is to be expected. What is more surprising is the pattern observed in village studies. In Susan Hanley's lists of the number of households in four villages, we find such narrow fluctuations, as between 109 and 112, over sixteen recorded years for Fujito between 1794 and 1826, between 69 and 73 over fourteen consecutive years for Nishikata, and between 68 and 70 over nineteen recorded dates from 1822 to the end of the Tokugawa period in Numa.[99] Hayami Akira's larger list of villages shows more

---

97 Robert J. Smith, "Small Families, Small Households, and Residential Instability: Town and City in 'Pre-Modern' Japan," in Peter Laslett, ed., *Household and Family in Past Time* (Cambridge, England: Cambridge University Press, 1972), p. 442.
98 Yamamura, *A Study of Samurai Income and Entrepreneurship*, p. 10.
99 Susan B. Hanley and Kozo Yamamura, "Population Trends and Economic Growth in Pre-Industrial Japan," in D. V. Glass and Roger Revelle, eds., *Population and Social Change* (London: Arnold, 1972).

variability in numbers of households, especially before the mid-eighteenth century when the population growth remained considerable.[100] But Hanley's general point appears valid in comparative terms: Japanese communities registered a relatively stable number of households. Regulations against subdividing land among sons accompanied by restrictions on the number of marriages to one in each generation preserved a fairly stable number of households. As some fell into extinction (*zekke*), some branch families (*bunke*) were permitted. Paradoxically, the denial of social change in this dimension encouraged it in others.[101]

The average household size declined markedly during the Tokugawa period. Hayami Akira and Uchida Nobuko explain the timing of that change:

The most common explanation given today is that small families or households consisting of one married couple and several children became common throughout the nation between the sixteenth and eighteenth centuries, and took the place of the larger households of earlier periods, many or most of which had more than one married couple apiece. A persistent and uninterrupted decline in average household size continued throughout the Tokugawa era, so that by the middle of the eighteenth century, the usual family size reached that common today, four or five members.[102]

Their data for 22,274 households show a persistent decline from an overall MHS (mean household size): 7.04 for 1671 to 1700, 6.34 for 1701 to 1750, 4.90 for 1751 to 1800, 4.42 for 1801 to 1850, and 4.25 for 1851 to 1870. Over these two centuries, communities in Suwa county became increasingly similar in their average household size. Furthermore, for three of the four districts studied (the fourth being a remote mountainous area), the values of MHS had already leveled off in the late eighteenth century.

Hanley cites additional evidence for the stability of average household size after the late eighteenth century. She proposes that the size of each household tended to remain constant, despite any changes in the village economy, because of constant social pressure to maintain one's relative status. However, villages also took current economic conditions into account in timing events that would increase family

---

100 Hayami Akira, *Kinsei nōson no rekishi jinkōgakuteki kenkyū* (Tokyo: Tōyō keizai shimpōsha, 1973), pp. 68–72.
101 Agreement on the need to control the number of households contributed to such changes as new controls on the size and composition of the household. The fullest statement of this argument is found in the writings of Susan B. Hanley, including *Economic and Demographic Change*, pp. 226–66.
102 Hayami Akira and Uchida Nobuko, "Size of Household in a Japanese County Throughout the Tokugawa Era," in Laslett, ed., *Household and Family in Past Time*, p. 473.

size, in particular, marriage.¹⁰³ Hanley explains that a family consciously regulated tended to return to its usual number of members whenever the number rose or fell from that level.

The question of how family size was regulated can be considered in the context of major life decisions. Before that, it is important to consider why household size declined and then why it remained remarkably constant. What social conditions contributed to this far-reaching transformation of Japanese households? Hayami Akira addressed the question of decline in MHS, noting in his explanation: (1) the decline of dependent laborers living with their proprietors in large households, a process that occurred primarily during the seventeenth-century transition in village relations; (2) the suitability of the resultant relatively small households for efficient agriculture production; and (3) proximity to the castle town: The closer the community was to the castle town and to convenient transportation on the plain, the earlier its household size would be stabilized at the new level, indicating the impact of the urban market on rural behavior.¹⁰⁴ Hanley takes up the question of household stability, attributing it to (1) the overriding concern with the perpetuation and status of the *ie*, which, given its practice of single-son inheritance and easy acceptance of adoption, would not be served by draining the family's resources on additional children who were not essential to the family's success; (2) the intense pressure to conform to community expectations, which were premised on the attitude that families should control their numbers in order to maintain their status and standard of living; (3) the general tendency for the family's economic base – and its need for farm labor – to remain constant or to change gradually in rough parallel with that of others in the village, requiring that it maintain the same number of members in order to preserve its status in the village.¹⁰⁵ At the root of these explanations are impressions of an extraordinary family system that is both demanding in its concern for status and flexible in its acceptance of adoption and family limitation as means to these ends. Also required is an unusual degree of community solidarity capable of formulating villagewide objectives and eliciting conformity from households in reaching them. Finally, one can discern economic conditions such as a fluid labor market and predictable market opportunities that gave house-

---

103 Susan B. Hanley, "Changing Life-Styles and Demographic Patterns in Tokugawa Japan," in *The Cambridge History of Japan*, vol. 4: *Early Modern Japan*, ed. John W. Hall (Cambridge, England: Cambridge University Press, forthcoming).
104 Hayami, *Kinsei nōson no rekishi*, pp. 100–2.   105 Hanley, "Changing Life-Styles."

holds the confidence and the incentives to plan their size for the future generation.

The stability of the community and the *ie* should not be confused with a static hierarchy of property and wealth. On the contrary, plots often changed hands. Thomas Smith has found that 50 percent of the holdings in the village that he studied increased or decreased by more than 20 percent from one tax register to the next, an average interval of twelve years. He further noted "the extraordinary difficulty that large holders had in keeping their place in the village [and that] small holders had even more difficulty."[106] Competing peasant families experienced frequent changes in household circumstances.

Marriage

One of the main reasons for the decline in household size is the change in marriage patterns that occurred during the eighteenth and nineteenth centuries. At the beginning of the Tokugawa period there is reason to believe that a sizable number of agricultural laborers dependent on and perhaps residing with patrimonial landlords did not marry. However, it was not long before the widespread establishment of independent households increased the marriage rate. But the rate did not stay high for long, for there was another pattern that gained ascendancy. Various village studies have demonstrated a gradual and long-term decrease in the percentage of married women that accompanied the decline in household size. Analyzing one set of village data, Hayami Akira and Uchida Nobuko found that the variable most highly correlated with household size was the number of married couples per household.[107] The small-household pattern, usually characterized by only one married couple, spread from one area to the next until by the early nineteenth century it had blanketed the areas studied.

Susan Hanley and Thomas Smith separately found evidence in other village data that marriage was largely restricted to the head of the household or his successor, limiting the number of childbearing couples to one per household.[108] Those who did not become family heads often did not marry, and heirs often married when they were in their late twenties in order to maximize the period of the family's peak

---

106 Thomas C. Smith, *Nakahara: Family Farming and Population in a Japanese Village, 1717–1830* (Stanford, Calif.: Stanford University Press, 1977), pp. 117–21.
107 Hayami and Uchida, "Size of Household," pp. 493–7.
108 Hanley and Yamamura, *Economic and Demographic Change*, pp. 246–52; and Smith, *Nakahara*, p. 133.

farming efficiency. The heir would still be young enough so that it was likely he could raise his children; yet postponed marriage prolonged the phase of high family-working capacity and delayed the release of noninheriting sons and daughters.

Computations of the ages at first marriage for females also reveal a tendency to late marriages, although not nearly so late as in parts of western Europe in the same historical epoch. Controlling family size and composition by controlling the age of marriage signifies a powerful means for promoting the welfare of the *ie*. Of course, short-term economic conditions were a factor in the calculations too; improved conditions led to a contraction in marriage ages, and in times of famine, marriage was delayed. Income differences also had an impact on women. Women from poorer families, many of whom worked away from home for a considerable amount of time, married later. Controlling for migration, income differences do not appear to have affected the age of marriage.[109]

The consequences of marriage patterns for the birthrates were direct and considerable. Birthrates dropped along with nuptiality in the eighteenth century as increasing numbers of individuals failed to marry and as women married late and shortened their span of childbearing. The new marriage patterns helped in these ways to reduce the ratio of dependents to producers and thus to improve the standard of living.

Childbirth

Along with controls on who married and at what age, birth control and/or infanticide within marriage made it possible to maintain a relatively constant household size. Analysis of household registration data, albeit for a small number of villages, strongly indicates that Japanese households deliberately limited the number of children they had and controlled the timing and sexual distribution of those that survived. Why did they do so? Famines caused some population limitation, but they were by no means responsible for the persistently slow or even negative rates of population growth. Even in times of relative prosperity and among households with sizable landholdings, the viewpoint appears to have prevailed that additional children represented a burden to be avoided if possible. Wealth must not be dispersed; status must be maintained. Hanley and Yamamura went so far as to hypothe-

---

[109] Smith, *Nakahara*, p. 95.

size that in the eighteenth century, villagers "began to choose to 'trade off' additional children for goods and services or for the accumulation of wealth needed to improve or maintain their standard of living and their status within village society."[110] For Thomas Smith, who emphasizes the role of infanticide in family limitation, the objectives in the villages he studied were "an equilibrium of some sort between family size and farm size; and advantageous distribution of the sexes in children; possibly the spacing of children in a way convenient to the mother; and the avoidance of a particular sex in the next child."[111] The results from various studies may not yet fully support these hypotheses or the exact means by which family limitation was carried out, but they do point to a pervasive planning mentality in this dimension of life, as in others.

The evidence for the presence of family limitation within marriage derives from the analysis of the timing and sexual distribution of births. In comparison with those societies in which there was no birth control, eighteenth- and nineteenth-century Japan exhibited a short span of childbearing for women, a low average age of the women at the last birth, and long average interbirth intervals. Hanley and Yamamura reported that "the average woman bore children for only about a dozen years."[112] In her mid-thirties a woman bore her last child. Thomas Smith found variation in the sex ratio by birth. After the second birth, "families tended to eliminate infants of the sex already predominant, and to eliminate girls somewhat more often than boys."[113] Infanticide as a form of family limitation gave parents the choice of sex at the same time that it enabled them to control the size of the family.

The demographic rates in the late Tokugawa villages were remarkable for a premodern society. After falling from seventeenth-century levels, the crude birth and crude death rates were in the twenty to thirty range rather than in the forty to fifty range often observed in the recent history of less developed countries before death rates plummeted. Life expectancy at New Year's after birth (Japanese age two) reached into the forties. On the basis of these findings, Hanley and Yamamura conclude that "all evidence points to a remarkable similarity with pre- and early industrial population trends in Europe and no similarity at all between Tokugawa Japan and the other nations of Asia today."[114]

110 Hanley and Yamamura, *Economic and Demographic Change*, p. 318.
111 Smith, *Nakahara*, p. 83.
112 Hanley and Yamamura, *Economic and Demographic Change*, p. 318.
113 Smith, *Nakahara*, p. 66.
114 Hanley and Yamamura, *Economic and Demographic Change*, p. 318.

Although infanticide (often in the form of drowning babies shortly after birth) apparently continued to be practiced, changes in sex ratios reveal a shifting pattern in its application.[115] The changes do not seem to be a result of official disapproval of this much-condemned practice, but of a shift in the relative desirability of boys and girls. High sex ratios in the early eighteenth century indicate a strong preference for boys, but by the mid-nineteenth century the sex ratio was close to normal, and to the extent that infanticide was still practiced, it seems less a response to dire conditions than one means to achieve the desired family size and composition. The heightened value of female labor, as seen in the large number of female migrants and in their increasing age at marriage, may help explain the more equal treatment given to girl babies.

Thomas Smith has studied the relationship between the sex ratio and the presence of trade, industry, and cities. Examining one set of data for Chōshū in 1843, he found that "the higher the per capita income and the more commercial the economy, the lower the sex ratio."[116] Using nationwide urban data for 1875 and regional sex ratios of 1846, he discovered almost the same correlation (-0.38) between the level of urbanization and the sex ratio. He concluded that "the development of nonagricultural employments seems to be associated with a declining sex ratio."[117] Again the evidence points to the strong impact of the urban sector and of commercialization spreading from the cities on late Tokugawa village household decisions.

Migration

In order to explain changes in landholding patterns, in the distribution of cities, in the age of marriage, and in other aspects of social structure as well, it is necessary to consider migration. The ideal of the essentially closed community bound by custom, collective responsibility, and corporate relations endured. Yet the high rates of migration not only made the realization of this ideal impossible in the urban periphery; residential instability also characterized the inner *chōnin* wards, many originally established for collective service in a given occupation. Increasingly during the second half of the Tokugawa period, high rates of migration became evident also in the villages, much of it directed to other villages and to local towns other than the castle cities. A mobile rural population did not give up its strong roots in the *ie* and

---

115 Hayami Akira, "Tokugawa kōki jinkō hendō no chiikiteki tokusei," *Mita gakkai zasshi* 64 (August 1971): 77.   116 Smith, *Nakahara*, p. 154.   117 Ibid., p. 156.

thus in its home villages. Rather, the timing and purposes of the departures were carefully regulated to meet household objectives. Relocations of labor proved generally responsive to changing employment opportunities.

The *sankin kōtai* system brought a distinctive form of migration that remained highly stable until the early 1860s. It involved the daimyo and the samurai who accompanied them and promoted a major redistribution of wealth to Edo and the other central cities with corresponding pressures for mobilizing resources in the castle cities. This fully formalized movement of the elite between alternate residences had ramifications for other forms of migration and for marketing, but itself did not represent an arena of social change.

A second massive flow of population to the cities also developed during the early Tokugawa period. This flow,

which in all essential respects should also include hōkōnin entering bushi service, differed from the first in bringing to the city persons mostly rural in origin, younger on the average, more predominantly male (although the migration of samurai also involved an unspecified surplus of males over females), and with rare exception poorer. Unlike samurai migrants, these would-be chōnin arrived in Edo without guaranteed incomes, jobs or places of residence, although not necessarily without contacts from their native areas which could ease the transition.[118]

Over time, females became roughly as numerous as males in this rural-urban flow, although the numbers involved diminished. Because local wages had increased and employment opportunities were more plentiful, those who chose to go to the city were likely to be less impoverished. This type of migration continued to replenish the ranks of those who rented lodgings in Japan's large urban sector.

Robert Smith offered evidence for a high degree of turnover in urban residences. Using household registers for thirty-six years between 1757 and 1858, he found "a social environment of constantly shifting composition. Although the continuity of the house-owners is more marked than that of the renters, even they move as households with great frequency."[119] The presence of large numbers of mobile, small households and of single persons temporarily engaged in hired labor in the city anticipates modern conditions. A continuous flow of rural-urban and then urban-rural migration on a considerable scale had various impacts, some more difficult to measure than others. Much speculation could be presented on its effect on rural attitudes

---

[118] Rozman, "Edo's Importance," p. 101. [119] Smith, "Small Families," p. 440.

and behavior, for example, on consumption and leisure tastes, but there is little hard evidence to demonstrate how urban practices were diffused. However, in one respect, the urban impact has been measured through correlational analysis. Dividing Japan into fourteen regions, Hayami Akira has examined the relationship between urbanization and population growth. He discerned a significant inverse relationship: Rural and overall population growth occurred largely in areas with relatively low urbanization.[120]

The repressive functions of the urban population resulted from several conditions: (1) In some cases as many as 50 percent of the migrants stayed in the city and did not return to the village; (2) the death rates in the city exceeded the birthrates, and the birthrates were below those in the village; and (3) the average age of marriage for returning migrants was higher than the average for other villagers. In short, the city swallowed migrants and depressed population growth in the surrounding region.

The natural rate of population growth was negative in the cities; that is, the cities needed migration from the countryside in order to maintain their total populations. But in the villages, the natural growth rate was normally positive. Hayami depicted one village in which the crude birthrate exceeded the crude death rate by 8.4 percent, but migration kept the population quite constant.[121] Then in the 1840s, migration (as *hōkōnin*) declined to both cities and local destinations. Following this decline, village populations grew by roughly 1 percent per year. The repressive effect of migration was eliminated.

Migration out from the villages also stabilized the village class structure. There was a continuous flow of downward mobility. Many lower-strata households died out, especially through migration. At the same time, the noninheriting sons of upper-strata households descended the social ladder through the establishment of branch households (*bunke*) and adoption. A fairly constant number of households does not mean that there was no replacement process. Substantial levels of migration were vital to this circulation of households that opened outlets for social mobility.

Across Japan, areas varied in their rates of migration. The highly urbanized hinterlands of Edo and Osaka-Kyoto and the south Kantō and the Kinki regions experienced substantial population losses, apparently through the effects of migration to the cities. Meanwhile, in southwest Japan, with a lower rate of urbanization, the population

---

120 Hayami Akira, "Kinsei kōki chiiki betsu jinkō hendō to toshi jinkō hiritsu no kanren," *Kenkyū kiyō* (Tokugawa rinseishi kenkyūjo, 1974), pp. 230–44.   121 Ibid., p. 232.

grew relatively rapidly during the second half of the Tokugawa period. Hayami also distinguished a different type of migration, more short term and mainly responsive to conditions pushing people out of the villages rather than to conditions pulling people into the cities.[122] At times of famine, this type of migration prevailed in the severely hit areas of northeast Japan. In contrast, migrants normally were not acting out of desperation but were responding to labor opportunities, wage differentials, household needs, and property differences at home in order to maximize the long-term success of the *ie*.

Hayami also related the population change to the declining sex ratio by region.[123] In areas of population decline, sex ratios had tended to be high in the early eighteenth century. The fact that they fell rapidly testifies to the even greater decrease in the male than in the female population. Especially in remote areas of Japan, the late Tokugawa period was marked by a rapid decline in the number of males as the small, independent household became nearly universal.

Hanley and Yamamura have argued that occupational and geographical mobility were factors in the rising living standards of Japanese peasants. From the eighteenth century onwards, income rose, as it became common for young men and young women to work away from home, often for several years before marriage. They summarized the studies on this topic as follows:

Migration allowed the efficient allocation of labor, higher wages, the permanent or temporary adjusting of village population, and the regulation of numbers in individual households through marriage, adoption, and migration in or out for employment. It also undoubtedly had an effect on fertility, both by delaying marriage for some and preventing it for others (second sons) and by lowering marital fertility in families in which the husband worked away from home for years at a time.[124]

Clearly a remarkable impression is left if one takes into account the extraordinary urban-urban migration of the *sankin kōtai* system, the high levels of rural-urban migration necessary to produce and to sustain the unprecedented Tokugawa urbanization, and the massive rural-rural and small-town migration that emerged in the second half of the Tokugawa period. These conditions of large-scale migration figured importantly in the transformation of social stratification and of the urban system as well as the decision making of households.

---

122 Ibid., p. 236.
123 Hayami Akira, "Kinsei Seinō nōmin no idō ni tsuite," *Kenkyū kiyō* (Tokugawa rinseishi kenkyūjo, 1977), pp. 295–6.
124 Hanley and Yamamura, *Economic and Demographic Change*, p. 255.

Although a modern census was not taken until 1920, the old system of obligatory registration at Buddhist temples (for all but a few categories of the population) and nationwide enumerations at six-year intervals from 1721 was replaced by a registration law in 1871. There are apparent deficiencies in the enumerations of the Meiji period, but they provide a general indication of population trends.

In the *bakumatsu* period and following the Meiji Restoration, the population growth accelerated. Whereas over the first half of the nineteenth century, growth was slight, over the second half, the total rose from roughly 30 million to 31 million to 44 million. The first phase of increased growth resulted in an annual rate of increase of about 0.5 percent in the early 1870s. The second phase produced a rate of about 1.0 percent in 1900. Birthrates appear to have risen somewhat at the end of the century, whereas death rates may have remained stable or fallen slightly. Whatever may be the explanation for increased growth, vital rates and the rate of natural increase remained relatively low in Japan – conditions generally considered favorable to economic growth.

Education and knowledge

With increasing standards of living and choice with regard to both work and consumption, Japanese gave more attention to bettering the prospects of their households. Fewer children and longer life expectancies permitted greater investments of time and resources in the education of each child. These opportunities were quickly seized. Ronald Dore has traced a chronology of change and wrote that by 1868 Japan was transformed into a literate society.[125] By 1700 there was widespread literacy in the big cities; many commercial publishers catered to a mass market; and routinized administration produced a flood of documents that required even village headmen as well as virtually all samurai to be literate. By 1800, the education of commoners had emerged as a goal of some domains for purposes of moral upbringing and the restoration of old virtues and also for the dispersal of new administrative and production techniques and skills. Authorities did not fear the spread of education, and popular attitudes did not resist it. Popular acceptance of schooling hinged on its relevance to mobility aspirations. Secular and practical, popular education responded to the widespread desire for self-improvement and to opportunities to apply improved skills. There was a steady growth in the number educated

125 Dore, *Education in Tokugawa Japan*.

and a gradual evolution to the content and purposes of education. Not only the actual knowledge imparted, but also rationalism, selflessness, sense of nation, training in being trained, and other attitudes involved in the educational process spread among the population. Dore estimated that by the 1860s as many as 40 to 45 percent of boys and 15 percent of girls were receiving some formal schooling outside their home.[126] In 1803 there had been but 550 *terakoya* (temple schools). At the time of the Restoration there were more than 11,000 that met the educational needs of a large part of the population.[127]

With the spread of education, extrafamilial sources of respect, prestige, and instruction gained in most villages. Nineteenth-century government directives thus could be understood, and impersonal means for the evaluation of achievement could be readily accepted. A good basis existed for the rapid achievement of universal schooling in the final decades of the century.

The Meiji Restoration brought a more fluid society. The legacy of the earlier spread of education was vital to the new society in many ways: (1) the acceptance of the possibility of self-improvement and at the same time of national improvement; (2) the readiness of those who "in childhood had submitted to some process of disciplined and conscious learning . . . to respond to further training, be it in a conscript army, in a factory, or at lectures arranged by his village agricultural association"; thus ensuring "that the generation which had passed childhood in 1870 did not have to be written off as lost";[128] (3) the foundation for a competitive society in which talent could be encouraged and applied; and (4) the acceptance of education for all not as a factor threatening the power of the samurai but as a means for a more just social order and a more skilled population. Neither did the ex-samurai fear mass education nor did the ordinary household reject it as irrelevant to personal needs. Largely through the spread of education, both before and after the ordinance of 1872, a diverse population once frozen into separate social classes became increasingly homogeneous.

The Meiji Charter Oath proclaimed as one of its five articles "the seeking of knowledge throughout the world in order to strengthen the foundations of the Throne." In 1872 a national plan of education called for a nationwide, three-tier network of public schools for all. Modifica-

---

126 Ronald Dore, "The Legacy of Tokugawa Education," in Jansen, ed., *Changing Japanese Attitudes Toward Modernization*, p. 100.
127 Richard Rubinger, *Private Academies of Tokugawa Japan* (Princeton, N.J.: Princeton University Press, 1982), and "Education: From One Room to One System," in Jansen and Rozman, eds., *Japan in Transition*, pp. 195–230.
128 Dore, *The Legacy of Tokugawa Education*, pp. 101, 104.

tions occurred through the next decades as leaders recognized that their initial plans had been overly ambitious, and by the 1880s, the system became more centralized. Standardized textbooks, ethics courses, and uniforms prevailed. With the Imperial Rescript on Education of 1890, the moralistic tone of education was set for the next half-century.

Whatever the items chosen for inclusion, the picture would likely be the same: Japanese household behavior changed markedly over the eighteenth and nineteenth centuries, reflecting increasing independence, long-term calculation, and scope for decision making. Social indicators such as mean household size, birthrates, death rates, life expectancy, sex ratios, migration, and literacy increasingly came to resemble those in modern societies. The explanations for these changes center, on the one hand, on urbanization, commercialization, improved standards of living, and a labor shortage near the major cities. But on the other hand, they also center on the nature and durability of the household organization and on the solidarity and social pressure aroused by village organization. Regarding conditions a century later, observers were still noting the curious combination of some types of change accelerated by urbanization or other conditions associated with the modern sector and other types accelerated by the distinctive organizational characteristics of Japanese society.

CONCLUSIONS AND COMPARISONS

The social changes described for the final century or so of the Tokugawa period can be instructively compared with the social changes during the first half of the Tokugawa period. Both periods witnessed considerable dynamism, but one can distinguish systematic differences in the main forces, the main locations, and the main groups that produced the changes. For social stratification, both continuities and contrasts are apparent between the two periods. Whereas in the earlier period, urban-based, specialized merchants prospered from increasingly regular and large-scale interregional trade, in the latter period local and perhaps part-time merchants tapped new or underutilized rural resources, including labor diverted from agriculture into side employments. Already in the earlier period, hired labor was becoming predominantly contractual; in the latter period rising wage levels (until the rising inflation of late Tokugawa) and local employment opportunities contributed to widespread participation in hired labor as a phase in the life cycle. The earlier primacy of the part-feudal, part-bureaucratic samurai ethic was yielding to the flowering of a mass urban culture emanating largely from the *chōnin* yet spreading to the other classes as well. A period of dramatic growth in the number of *chōnin* gave way to a period of deconcentration of their ranks and diffusion of their tastes and practices. The *chōnin*, especially the merchants, continued to be in the vanguard of social change. Although tightly limited in certain respects, the rise of the bourgeoisie characterized Japanese social development as it did the development of various other countries.

For the peasants the shift from cooperative to individual farming and the division of large landholdings once under the control of patrimonial landlords were followed by a period of increased concentration of holdings under a new type of commercially oriented landlord. In both periods the evidence indicates that peasant industriousness grew under the dual impetus of broadened incentives and concentrated social (community and household) pressures. On a larger scale than in the earlier period, landholders cum entrepreneurs accumulated resources, invested in diverse productive activities, and emulated urban consumption practices. Although village conditions in some areas spurred some outmigration, the intense competitive bidding for scarce labor created opportunities for ordinary peasants, thereby encouraging their economic independence, market orientation, and skill development. There was less and less justification for applying to Japan the stereotypes of parasitic landlords and impoverished peasants. Through mechanisms such as marketing, migration and formal education, the rural population broadened its horizons to an extent that perhaps few premodern societies could match.

For the samurai, the first period brought a routinization of tasks and rewards, a reorientation from military to administrative duties, and an urbanization of living conditions. The later Tokugawa period did not produce such abrupt changes in actual circumstances, but the impact on perceptions was by no means negligible. The samurai more and more doubted their relevance and questioned their material position relative to others. With respect to types of employment as well as life-styles, the samurai (with the exception of the upper ranks) and the *chōnin* were converging, as were the *nōmin* and the *chōnin*. In all three classes – but not so openly among the samurai until the 1870s – one finds a shift toward achievement criteria and an impersonal labor market and also a continued consciousness of status differences and group obligations. In comparison with other premodern elites, the samurai, by virtue of their skills and perceptions, were better prepared for coping with the loss of their elite status.

Japan's urban transformation during the last century or so of Tokugawa rule clearly did not produce the tumultuous changes that had preceded it; nonetheless, the changes that did occur had important implications. There was no longer an explosive growth in the population of the three central cities; instead, there was a redistribution away from Osaka and Kyoto, and Edo gained a more direct hold at the head of the national urban system. Moreover, the once-burgeoning castle cities began gradually to lose population. These declining cities, predominantly located in the Kinki and Inland Sea areas, could not meet the competition of the nonadministrative places, that is, the nearby ports, and of the small centers of crafts and commerce. That the largest and most numerous of the smallest cities prospered suggests the forging of a more direct link within the urban hierarchy, a redistribution conducive to commercialized agriculture and local specialization and to centralized transport and services. Although temporarily in decline, many castle cities became restructured in a manner conducive to eventual growth in the Meiji era. The dispersal of professions and the reorientation toward *chōnin* consumption continued from the earlier period, whereas commerce became more dependent on the rural market, and cities became more diverse and multifunctional in forming new links with the outside. A sharp contrast with the earlier period is particularly visible in the accelerated population growth and prosperity of the small towns. Their role in the dissemination of urban patterns to the countryside and in the accumulation of scattered rural resources became increasingly prominent in the nineteenth century.

Household decisions also were altered sharply in the nineteenth century, in ways often unanticipated in the seventeenth century. Efforts to control the number of households in a village and to maintain or perhaps to elevate the status of one's household under new economic conditions were factors in the popularity of new decisions reflected in the use of household resources. Household size declined sharply and then stabilized. Marriage rates declined as women married later or, in a small but growing number of cases, not at all. Family limitation was realized, in part through sex-selective infanticide aimed at males as well as females. Large numbers migrated, increasingly to other villages for wage labor. In particular, the high rates of migration to cities depressed village population growth. Improved standards of living, life expectancies, and opportunities in the choice of work and residence encouraged families to concentrate more resources on the training of each child. In turn, levels of literacy rose sharply from those of the eighteenth century. Responding to unusual conditions of urbanization, commercialization, and labor demand as well as to social pressures on behalf of the long-term needs of household and village organizations, ordinary families changed their behavior markedly during the second half of the Tokugawa period. On these matters, there is little evidence of similar rural household changes during the prior period or of a comparable intensity of change in other premodern societies.

Given this premodern history, it is no wonder that Meiji Japan was dynamic in many of the same respects. The new impetus came from legal changes, eliminating occupational and residential restrictions and freeing all groups to pursue their interests. The samurai heritage was transformed with the assistance of foreign advisers and Japanese missions abroad into a rapidly growing, modern bureaucracy. The *chōnin* legacy was invigorated through entrepreneurial talent from all backgrounds and was now virtually unfettered in its pursuit of profit. The *nōmin* tradition advanced in a more market-oriented economy following the land settlement. By the end of the century, day-to-day administration was under the competent grasp of a new elite chosen for its educational performance. Financial and industrial growth was spurred by the emerging zaibatsu, who led in the reorganization of business activities. Land was increasingly concentrated in the hands of landlords, who marketed a large part of agricultural production. The new groups were heirs to the old, both biologically and in terms of the skills and attitudes that had been transmitted.

Meiji cities and household decisions also were infused by reforms that speeded trends already under way. Urban hierarchies and functions changed, particularly with the exodus of the samurai from their exclusive residential zones in the castle cities, as resources continued to flow efficiently into local and national centers. Population growth increased, but the factors that limited fertility continued to operate. Initially high levels of urbanization, along with close urban-rural linkages and low levels of population growth based on early forms of family limitation, were of great importance in avoiding during the Meiji period the problems of cities without adequate jobs and adequate impact on the countryside and of excess population growth. Perhaps more clearly than in any other area, the continuities between Tokugawa and Meiji education show how far the premodern society had brought Japan along the path to modernization that it was following in the late nineteenth century.

In at least four ways, the transition to modernization was facilitated by the premodern foundation: (1) Intense group solidarities offered a measure of control and coordination important to both preventing deviant behavior and pressuring conformity in the pursuit of new goals; (2) large numbers of households engaged in nonagricultural activities (including an elite exposed through required urban living and alternate residence for many in Edo, merchants in local areas able to challenge their big-city rivals, and landlords successful in entrepreneurial undertakings) were prepared for new opportunities in the labor market; (3) high levels of urbanization, the presence of very large urban centers at the forefront of changes, and the proliferation of small, local growth centers formed a chain of communications and interaction capable of mobilizing resources and creating opportunities throughout the society; and (4) demographic and educational rates indicated a pattern of household decision making that promised to ease the task of controlling consumption and training a new generation for new tasks.

Over the past three decades, nineteenth-century Japan's comparative standing as a premodern society has been subjected to a series of reappraisals. In the process, the old perceptions of a backward population with outmoded social-class relations, oppressive urban and rural organizations, and desperate household behavior have been largely discredited. Comparisons of class relations, including landholding patterns, urban literacy, and demographic rates, all show Japan as an unusual premodern society in the midst of internally generated, rapid change.

In virtually every instance in which a quantitative indicator has been introduced, Japan's rate has turned out to be extraordinary for a premodern society. Repeatedly, the country chosen as most similar to Japan has been England, which elsewhere in the comparative literature normally appears as an exceptional case at the forefront of social development.

Several types of organizations were instrumental in producing social change. First administrative bodies, both regional and national, are singled out for their deep commitment to social planning, especially in the late sixteenth and seventeenth centuries but continuing throughout the Tokugawa period and greatly reactivated with the Meiji Restoration. Strong government direction emerges as a key element. Second, community organizations assumed a crucial role in leadership and coordination, for example, in controlling the number of households. The village community and other organizations possessed a high degree of solidarity and a rare capacity to mobilize

CONCLUSIONS AND COMPARISONS 567

social pressure. Third, household organizations engaged in the long-term planning of their resource needs and allocations. The distinctive qualities of the Japanese household came increasingly to the fore in the more competitive setting of the nineteenth century before and after 1868. All of these levels are distinguished by the considerable role of conscious planning, the high degree of group solidarity, and the substantial capacity for social control. In an environment of widespread opportunity and intense competition, these organizations combined tradition and leadership.

The basic trend during the Tokugawa period was for more and more initiative to be seized from below. Rigid administrative controls, monopoly merchant practices, patrimonial landlords, collective community obligations, concentrated castle city privileges, and other control devices gave way to more decentralized or dispersed practices. The panoply of restrictive regulations was never fully abolished, but many were successfully challenged or allowed to persist in name only. By the mid-nineteenth century, the household had gained a wide measure of autonomy. Unlike the previous period, during the second half of the Tokugawa era major social changes originated largely from below within the limitations imposed by the existing social system. Earlier scholarship emphasized those limitations, but recent scholarship offers a persuasive corrective with its stress on the social changes that were achieved. The speed and thoroughness of the early Meiji reforms as well as the rapid transition that followed should be seen against the backdrop of earlier dynamism.

The preceding emphasis on continuities through the nineteenth century should not detract from the recognition of the sweeping changes that came one after another in a span of one to two decades in the *bakumatsu*–Meiji transition. These changes constituted first a challenge to the Tokugawa social and political order, then a repudiation of it, and finally a legal foundation for modern development. Without them it is inconceivable that late Tokugawa dynamism, however extraordinary its scope, would have given way to modernization.

The transition brought changes with diverse significance for Japan's long-term transformation. Certain unprecedented events, such as the refusal of local merchants to ship their export goods through Edo and its guild channels, reveal how the actual social hierarchy was little more than a pale reflection of the officially supported social order. Resistance of this sort, rooted in earlier social change, gave impetus to the pressures for reform that won out in the late 1860s. Late Tokugawa changes also helped speed up the reform process. Fissures and new outlooks among the samurai were even more important than those among the merchants to galvanizing the forces of reform. Restoration politics exacerbated already-strained samurai loyalties, bringing many to opt for new rather than old loyalty. At the same time, the legacy of the old order left its deep imprint on the nature of the response, and dangers of foreign origin led to a reemphasis on the samurai tradition, especially its military and service orientations. New steps taken during the 1860s also foreshadowed what was to come, as when the bakufu and its enemies turned to mixed samurai–peasant armed units to secure an effective fighting force reorganized in new-style formations and equipped with foreign weapons. In this way, expedient measures in a period of turmoil were a stepping-stone to reform programs.

CHAPTER 9

ECONOMIC CHANGE IN THE NINETEENTH CENTURY

At the beginning of the nineteenth century, Japan was a preindustrial agricultural economy with technology and living standards not greatly different from those of other preindustrial areas of Asia. If a Frenchman of 1600 had been able to see the Japan of 1800, he would have been impressed by obvious differences in dress, manners, and architecture, but most features of economic life would have been readily understandable to him. Had the same Frenchman visited Japan a century later, he would have been bewildered. By the end of the century, the nation's output of goods and services had increased fourfold, and the proportion contributed by industry had at least doubled, whereas the contribution of agriculture had declined to less than half the total output. Much of the infrastructure necessary for the development of an industrial economy, such as transport, communications, ports, and financial institutions, had been created, and a modest but crucial nucleus of modern factory industry was becoming a viable growth sector. This was a century of economic change, and the change was at an increasing rate.

Explanations for this change represent both a variety of ideologies and a variety of views of the facts. Most Japanese historians have viewed it as a transition from a feudal to a capitalist society within the framework of the Marxian theory of stages of economic development. Even granted that a relative latecomer such as Japan might be able to take advantage of some shortcuts, it was not easy to see how such a change, which took centuries in Europe, could occur within a few decades in Japan. Japanese historians have been divided on how to explain this problem. The Rōnō (laborer and farmer) school, so called from its journal of the same name, made an adjustment at the beginning of the process and, while maintaining the idea that premodern Japan was basically feudal, stressed the emergence of capitalist elements in the century before the Meiji Restoration of 1868, which is usually taken to mark the beginning of Japan's modern period. According to this school, therefore, the gap between the Japan of 1868 and the Japan of the early twentieth century was not as great as that between feudal and capitalist Europe. The Kōza (lectures) school, which took its name from its major publication, *Nihon shihonshugi hattatsu shi kōza* (Lectures on the development of Japanese capitalism),[1] made the adjustment at the latter end and stressed the premodern aspects of the Japanese economy throughout the Meiji period and beyond, as exemplified by the survival of noneconomic factors in the relations between landlords and tenants and between employers and employees, the immaturity of Japanese capitalism, and the absolutist nature of the Meiji state. Neither school seriously questioned the assumption that the process of economic change in Japan was essentially similar to the earlier European experience.

Before the Pacific War, Western observers emphasized the importance of state power in alliance with powerful business groups in exploiting Japanese workers and poor farmers in the interests of building a strong nation as rapidly as possible. Their view may well have been colored by fears of what they saw as "unfair" competition in international trade supported by low wages in Japan. After the war, Western scholars devoted much attention to explaining Japan's economic development in terms of what were identified as preconditions for economic change. In essence, this was an attempt to see whether explanations of economic change in Europe based on such factors as the Protestant ethic and the agricultural revolution could be applied to the Japanese case by identifying analogues to these factors in the Japanese experience. The results were unsatisfactory for two reasons. First, the implied assumption that economic development could not take place in the absence of factors that were thought to be important to European development proved to be invalid. Moreover, when equivalents were found in Japan, such as a merchant ethic analogous to the Protestant ethic, similar conditions were found to exist in other countries, such as China, where modern economic growth did not occur. Second, these studies on the whole took insufficient account of the fact that economic changes in Japan occurred a century or more after the industrialization of western Europe and North America. Not only had the world changed in the meantime, but Japan was able to draw on the experience of the advanced industrial countries.

Since then, explanations of Japan's economic development have mostly been in terms of the quantitative relationships among economic variables such as capital formation, the labor force, technology, the

---

[1] 7 vols. (Tokyo: Iwanami shoten, 1932–3).

structure of production and consumption, prices and other aggregates, and the ways in which they affect the rate of growth of national income. In comparison with prewar studies, these quantitative analyses are less explicitly concerned with the role of government and the exercise of power as a means of influencing economic activity. Attention so far has centered more on the behavior of the economic aggregates themselves than on the less quantifiable forces that modified the operation of free-market mechanisms.

There are particular difficulties in applying these quantitative methods to the study of the Japanese economy in the nineteenth century, for most of which quantitative data on a national scale are lacking. What follows in this chapter must therefore be largely descriptive. Because conditions varied widely from one part of Japan to another, descriptions of economic life in one village or region, of which there are many, cannot be taken as representative of the whole country. This chapter will nevertheless attempt to describe the economic system as a whole and the changes in the way that system operated.

THE ECONOMY AT THE BEGINNING OF THE NINETEENTH CENTURY

Japan in 1800 was in most respects typical of a preindustrial Asian country. The population was about 30 million to 33 million, less than a quarter of the present population, and was growing slowly. Some 80 to 85 percent of this population lived in rural villages. Of the remainder, nearly 2 million lived in the three very large cities – Edo (modern Tokyo), Osaka, and Kyoto – and upwards of a million and a half lived in the castle towns, the administrative centers of the domains, that varied in size from a few thousand to nearly 100,000 inhabitants. At least half a million lived in ports and communication centers. For administrative purposes, the bulk of the population was divided into four main classes – samurai, farmers, artisans, and merchants.

With very few exceptions, such as Buddhist or Shinto priests, doctors, and professional teachers, who were outside the four main classes, those who lived in rural villages were officially classed as farmers. They produced all of the country's food including marine products, and industrial crops such as cotton, oilseeds, flax, tobacco, indigo, vegetable wax, and the raw materials for papermaking and sericulture, and they provided nearly all of the tax revenue. But they also produced a large and increasing part of the industrial output and conducted the local trade, commerce, transport, and construction. In some regions, such as around Osaka Bay and along the Inland Sea, villagers officially classed as farmers spent on average as much as half their time in nonagricultural pursuits. In more remote regions where opportunities for industrial employment were fewer, as many as one-third to one-half of the villagers spent the slack agricultural season or periods of a year or more working away from their villages, and at least half of this work was nonagricultural. The importance of industrial and commercial activity was therefore much greater than the classification as farmers of 80 to 85 percent of the population would suggest.

In Edo and the castle towns, about half of the population consisted of samurai and their dependents. As well as forming a standing military force whose function was mainly internal security, the samurai staffed the administrative and clerical levels of the government services. Samurai and their dependents made up some 6 to 7 percent of the country's population, but at any given time at least half of them had only nominal duties. The civilian population of these administrative centers consisted of artisans, wholesale and retail traders, and construction workers whose function was originally to supply the needs of the samurai establishment, but by the early nineteenth century much of the demand for their services came from the civilian population itself and from the growing role that these centers played as entrepôts for the commerce of the surrounding districts. Osaka, with a much smaller samurai establishment, was Japan's commercial center par excellence. Tax rice and essential agricultural and manufactured products were channeled into it and, sometimes after further processing, were redistributed to Edo and other parts of the country. Osaka's highly developed commercial institutions were a key point in the government's system of economic controls. Kyoto, the seat of the imperial court, was the traditional center of the industrial arts and also an important financial market. With the diffusion of such crafts as silk weaving and ceramics to other parts of Japan during the eighteenth century, Kyoto craftsmen specialized in products of high quality and artistic excellence for the court and senior samurai. Unlike the townsmen of Edo, few of whom had been in the city for more than a generation, many of the civilian inhabitants of Kyoto had been established there for two or three centuries before 1800 and were proud of their traditions.

Because of Japan's mountainous geography and long coastline, most interregional traffic went by sea along a chain of ports that ran right around the main islands. Ports like Hakata, Niigata, Sakata, Tsuruga, Obama, Shimonoseki, Shimizu, and Chōshi had populations of ten to twenty thousand and provided services that were adequate for the needs of the Japanese shipping of the time. Nagasaki, the only official international port, was a city of fifty or sixty thousand, not including the Dutch and Chinese settlements. Sakai, the major port for interregional trade, especially with Hokkaido, was about the same size.

The urban population tended to be a shifting one, and information on urban population is much less reliable than that on the rural population. In all, at least 10 percent of the population lived and worked in cities of ten thousand or more, and perhaps another five percent lived in towns of five thousand to ten thousand inhabitants.[2]

Urbanization on this scale, while low by modern standards, implies a good deal of commercial activity. Although the theories of the political economy of Tokugawa Japan were predicated on subsistence farming with all the surplus being drawn off in taxes, urban consumption centers had to be supplied with food, clothing, fuel, and other necessities, and thus the system itself required commercial development and production for the market as well as the delivery of taxes in kind. Tokugawa economic policy was aimed at securing these supplies without putting cash into the hands of rural producers who might use it to express their own competing demands for the products of the market. For administrations whose incomes were in taxes in kind but whose expenditures were in the cash market, any growth of civilian demand represented unwelcome competition, and this situation became both a basic problem of economic policy and the source of economic change.

Economic policy and its administration

Under the *bakuhan* system, responsibility for economic policy and its administration was shared by the Tokugawa government (bakufu) and some 270 domain (*han*) administrations. The bakufu held nearly a quarter of the country's land, by ratable value, as its own domain. In addition, it held all the cities of major economic importance containing nearly half the urban population. It also controlled all gold and silver production and had a monopoly of issuing coinage. The bakufu could also give guidance or even issue orders to the daimyo, the titular heads of the domains, who would comply more or less enthusiastically according to their own interests and their relationship with the bakufu; but because they were ultimately responsible to the bakufu for the good government of their domains, they tended to follow its lead. In

---

2 Sekiyama Naotarō, *Nihon no jinkō* (Tokyo: Shibundō, 1966), pp. 114–15. I have added a figure for samurai and others not included in this source.

general, the economic aim of both the bakufu and the domains was to take in tax as much of the production of their people as they could while maintaining and, if possible, increasing the productive capacity of their territories. In the early years of the *bakuhan* system, these aims of the bakufu and the domains did not seriously conflict with one another, but by 1800 production for the market had developed to a point where competition for the profit on the marketing of these products led to chronic conflict between the policies of the domains and the bakufu and between merchant groups allied with one or the other or seeking independence from both.

The principal aim of the bakufu's economic policy, as of its policy in general, was the maintenance of stability and the preservation of the agricultural economy which was its main source of income. Both the bakufu and the domains believed that the function of the agricultural population was to produce tax revenue, and this belief rather than any interest in the welfare of the villagers underlay their efforts to maintain the viability of the rural village and to increase the production of rice and other crops. Thus in the bakufu territories a village could be punished for failing to get the maximum amount of production from its land, planting commercial crops on land assessed as taxable rice land, or neglecting farming in favor of other occupations. Despite these efforts, the yield from taxes on agriculture had already reached its peak before 1800, and attempts to raise it increasingly encountered strong resistance.

Fiscal policies of both the bakufu and the domains aimed to spend no more than was received as revenue, but this aim was seldom achieved. With their regular income fixed within narrow limits, governments tried to find other sources of income and to limit expenditures as far as possible. In these respects, the situation of the bakufu differed from that of the domains, and the possibilities available to the domains themselves also differed from one another.

The bakufu had separate budgets for rice and cash. Records of these budgets are fragmentary and inconsistent, but all point to a deterioration in the financial position of the bakufu. The regular rice tax income of the bakufu was actually falling at the opening of the nineteenth century. Even in the famine decade of 1782–91 its rice tax receipts averaged 613,000 *koku*, net of collection costs and local administrative expenses, leaving an average annual surplus of just 38,000 *koku*. In the following two decades, receipts rose slightly, but so did expenditures. In the decade of 1812–21, however, rice tax receipts fell sharply to 566,000 *koku* per year, and the bakufu was forced to draw on its stocks. These figures do not appear to include the revenues of the *hatamoto*, or bannermen. Regular cash revenue, including various license fees, also fell over the same period, whereas cash expenditures increased.[3] From time to time the bakufu requested loan subscriptions from the virtually untaxed merchant communities of Edo, Osaka, and some other cities in its domains. Five requests between 1800 and 1813 yielded a total of over half a million *ryō*, about half the amount requested. The cash deficit was financed largely by resort, not to the printing press, as the bakufu did not issue paper currency, but to debasement of the coinage which was subject to rather more practical restraints. Nevertheless, the results were similar, and because about a quarter of the total cash expenditures were financed in this way, inflationary results could be expected.[4] That prices did not rise much until the 1830s and 1840s was due partly to the increasing demand for cash to finance a rising level of cash transactions, as people came to buy more and more things rather than produce them themselves or barter their produce for them, but it also depended largely on price control.

Efforts to reduce expenditures took two forms. First, the bakufu, like the domains, tried to reduce the amount of goods and services bought by itself and its retainers. Official exhortations to frugality were included in its "Regulations for Samurai" and repeated with particular zeal in times of financial crisis, but they seem to have been singularly ineffective.[5] The economic circumstances of the samurai depended on relative movements in the price of rice in which their incomes were denominated and in the prices of the goods and services on which they spent their incomes. As Yamamura has suggested, the real incomes of the bakufu's retainers seem to show no long-term falling trend in the last century of Tokugawa rule, but in the nineteenth century they fell sharply as rice prices fell, whereas the general price level remained relatively stable.[6] Using five-year averages to even out year-to-year fluctuations, the real value of the incomes of bannermen fell by 15 percent between 1791–5 and 1796–1800 and by a further 13 percent between 1796–1800 and 1801–5, and it was a long time before the levels of the last decade of the eighteenth century were

[3] *Nihon zaisei keizai shiryō* (Tokyo: Zaisei keisai gakkai, 1922–5), vol. 10, pp. 436–57.
[4] Satō Jizaemon, *Kahei hiroku* in *Nihon keizai sōsho* (Tokyo: Nihon keizai sōsho kankōkai, 1914), vol. 32, pp. 327–8.
[5] Ishii Ryōsuke, ed., *Tokugawa kinrei kō* (Tokyo: Sōbunsha, 1959), 1st ser., vol. 1, pp. 61–75; and Takayanagi Shinzō and Ishii Ryōsuke, eds., *Ofuregaki Temmei shūsei* (Tokyo: Iwanami shoten, 1958), pp. 481–92.
[6] Kozo Yamamura, *A Study of Samurai Income and Entrepreneurship* (Cambridge, Mass.: Harvard University Press, 1974), p. 41.

regained. It was thus in the bakufu's interests to maintain and stabilize the price of rice, while making every effort to prevent rises in the cost of other commodities. These efforts consisted of regulating competing demands for goods from the rural population and attempting to control prices in the cities.

Regulation and control were indeed the cornerstones of economic as of other administration at all levels in Tokugawa Japan and particularly of the economic administration of the bakufu. Economic policies were directed at people rather than at economic variables such as the money supply, incomes, and employment. It was well known, for example, that

> rising prices are due to an overabundance of money. After all, the annual production of goods is fixed while there is no natural limit to the annual amount of increase in the money supply. The greater the increase the worse the effects. It is just like trying to relieve a famine by cutting the meat into smaller portions.[7]

Faced with a deficit, however, the bakufu preferred to regard deficit financing as inevitable and to put the blame for rising prices on the people for spending the money that it thus put into their hands.

The people, particularly the peasant farmers, were regarded as existing and working for the support of the government. All that they produced was, in principle, at its disposal, but because the government accepted responsibility for the peasants' livelihood, it allowed them to keep just so much as they needed to keep body and soul together. In principle, too, every aspect of the village's economic life was controlled, and farmers were required to devote all their efforts to producing food and other useful crops. Any other activity that interfered with this was forbidden. Even if work of any kind was available outside the village, it could not be accepted without permission, and the authorities had to be satisfied that the move would not reduce production from the land. Even an overnight absence from the village required an official exeat. Failure to work from dawn to dusk was described as "laziness" and was a punishable offense. A farmer who failed to cultivate his land so as to produce the maximum crops possible with the existing technology and weather conditions – even though his income might be higher if he devoted his time to other pursuits – not only incurred social penalties but was guilty of dereliction of duty and could be punished for the crime of neglecting his proper duties.

Granted that these regulations were not always strictly enforced, it

---

7 Satō, *Kahei hiroku*, p. 320.

is clear that the bakufu did not rely on the operation of market forces and indeed regarded them as working against its interests. Restriction of consumption by fiat, wage fixing, compulsory procurement of all essential products at regulated prices, and processing and marketing through organizations that acted in many ways like government agents were the time-honored ways of restricting rural demand, ensuring a steady supply of essential goods to the administrative centers, and keeping prices down. If despite all this, prices in Edo rose, the bakufu simply ordered wholesalers and retailers to reduce them. If the market price of rice fell following a bumper harvest, the bakufu ordered the rice dealers to increase their stocks, sometimes lending them funds to do so. Under such a closely regulated system, the free market operated, as it were, on the fringes and was countenanced only when it was of a petty nature or when it could be made to work to the benefit of the authorities. The situation was in this respect not unlike that in a country such as the People's Republic of China. In terms of producing economic growth, the controlled economy was a failure, but then economic growth was not a principal aim of the policy. As we shall see, even in terms of the economic policy of the time, it failed to achieve the stability that the bakufu desired.

As well as its monopoly of the coinage, control of national commerce and agriculture, and consumption in its own domains, the bakufu controlled foreign trade and most mining and forestry. Foreign trade was officially limited to a small traffic with the Dutch and Chinese through Nagasaki, Japan's only authorized international port, but a considerable trade with the Ryūkyūs operated by Satsuma was tolerated and seems to have included as well as Okinawa sugar, some goods of Chinese, Southeast Asian, or even European origin.

Despite such an array of powers, the financial position of the bakufu and its ability to control the economy declined as the century progressed. The causes of this decline included, as we shall see, the growing fiscal demands of foreign relations and defense, the diminishing power to enforce collection of revenue, a slow but steady fall in the proportion of national product produced by agriculture, a number of poor harvests, and, not the least, the frustration of its system of commercial and financial controls by actions of the domains attempting to shore up their own finances.

Because the domains were denied the right to issue coinage, their deficits represented an increase in their indebtedness, and with rising costs, especially of traveling to and from Edo and maintaining an establishment there, almost all the domains were accumulating a mounting burden of debt despite a range of measures to increase revenue. These included raising the rate of agricultural tax, imposing new taxes, promoting land reclamation, "borrowing" or withholding part of the retainers' stipends, levying contributions from leading merchants of the domain, issuing paper money, encouraging production and processing of industrial crops, and sharing in the profit from their production and sale through monopoly marketing boards operated by the domain itself or through its agents. The scope for increasing revenue by most of these measures was limited. Despite the encouragement of reclamation projects, the output of rice and other staple crops that provided the traditional tax base grew only slowly; and the higher the tax rate was, the more profitable it was for farmers to direct their energies to other kinds of production. Hence the steady flow of edicts forbidding neglect of staple agriculture for other occupations and hence, too, their general lack of effect. Growing and processing industrial crops was far more profitable than was growing rice to be taken in tax. If the taxes were too heavy, the farmers absconded and left the land to go to waste, thus reducing the domain's income and offsetting schemes to increase acreage by expensive land reclamation projects. Even the Satsuma domain, which maintained tighter control than most over its farming population and where alternative occupational opportunities were relatively limited, had by 1820 accumulated debts to the tune of five million *ryō*, equal to about ten years' regular revenue.

In a society that had come to expect that traditional practices would be maintained, imposition of new kinds of tax provoked discontent and sometimes actual rebellion. Levies on merchants and borrowing from retainers tended to alienate the very groups on which the domain authorities relied for support. Denied the right to issue coinage, the domains turned to issuing paper notes. The bakufu had placed strict controls on such issues in 1759, but with the growth of local industry and commerce in the early years of the nineteenth century, there was a demand for means of local payments, and so many domains issued notes backed by cash, rice, or goods. Those notes (*hansatsu*) were legal tender for certain purposes within the domain, and some enjoyed limited acceptance beyond its borders. By the 1860s such issues reached very large proportions, circulated at a heavy discount against cash, and contributed heavily to the inflationary pressures of the last decades of the Tokugawa period. Their direct inflationary effects were, however, largely confined to the domain that issued them, and their effect on national price levels was less than that of the massive increase in bank advances associated with domain borrowing during these decades. At the start of the century, however, the harmful effects of *hansatsu* were not intolerable, even though such issues already involved some conflict with the monetary policies of the bakufu.

Whereas all these measures were to a greater or lesser extent negative, in that they did not promote economic development but rather the opposite, attempts by domains to obtain a share of the profits from production other than staple agriculture had far-reaching consequences. The Tokugawa theory of political economy was rationalized in terms of Confucian maxims that the state could not prosper unless the people were prosperous, understood in the context of subsistence agriculture in which the state's primary function was to maintain law and order rather than to promote economic growth. Promotion of production for the general market, as opposed to encouragement of production for the lord's use, clearly ran counter to the theory. For a domain government to promote such production and trade for its own financial gain was not only ideologically unorthodox but in fact brought the domain into conflict with the bakufu. The reason was that in setting up marketing boards that acquired, either directly or through commercial agents, the more profitable products of the domain at fixed prices and sold them not only locally but on the national market, they competed with the marketing system sponsored and controlled by the bakufu. Nevertheless, some domains had adopted these measures quite early – the Sendai domain's rice and salt monopolies and the Yamaguchi domain's paper monopoly, for example, had been in operation since the seventeenth century.

By the early nineteenth century, many domains had abandoned the orthodoxy of the early Edo period and were actively encouraging new crops and industries, usually in collaboration with merchants from their castle town or from the more advanced Kinki region. From the late eighteenth century, the Tōhoku domains of Aizu, Shinjō, and Yonezawa actively encouraged industrial arts such as weaving and lacquer making, as did the Mito domain in northern Kantō. In the Chūbu region from Kanazawa to Nagoya – with almost a quarter of Japan's arable land, population, and rice production – sericulture, silk and cotton weaving, paper, lacquer ware, and wood and bamboo products were important local industries by 1800. Silk-crepe weaving technology was introduced to Gifu as early as 1730 by a few refugees from a fire in Nishijin. By 1819 Gifu crepe broke the monopoly of the Kyoto industry by marketing its products through the official channels of the powerful Owari domain, to the advantage of the producers, local merchants, and the domain itself. The introduction of striped-cotton weaving in Mino was thanks to another Kyoto fire in the 1780s. Here finance and marketing were through merchants from Ōmi. Tokushima's indigo monopoly, Matsue's ginseng, Uwajima's and Yamaguchi's paper monopolies, and several domains' salt monopolies all brought considerable profits to the domains' treasuries. The operations of these monopoly marketing boards were linked with the issue of local paper currency, as local purchases were paid for in *hansatsu* and sales in the national market were for cash or credits convertible to cash.

Promotion and sale of industrial crops and industrial products by the domains was central to the economic changes taking place in the first decades of the nineteenth century. Those changes were at least as much the results of and reactions to government controls as of spontaneous activity by the population at large. The spread of industrial production in their domains, as commercial agents in the bakufu's cities sought cheaper sources of supply in the countryside, prompted the domain administrations to try to appropriate the profits from it in competition with the city merchants and to promote and control further growth to increase their own resources. Heavy taxes on mainstream agriculture and relatively light taxes on other occupations induced a move from rice culture to industrial crops and processing industries like textiles. This shift was supported from the demand side by a relatively elastic demand for industrial products and a relatively inelastic demand for rice.

Apart from small-scale local peddling, which was countenanced as a form of unemployment relief, commercial activity was controlled at all levels, but control also provoked resistance at all levels. City merchants struggled to maintain the privileges granted to them by the bakufu and to prevent the domains' selling directly to urban consumption centers. Merchants in the castle towns, usually with the backing of their domain authorities, struggled to maintain their privileges against rural merchants. The producers struggled for freedom to sell their products wherever they could obtain the best price, but seldom with much success, as escape from control at one level was generally replaced by control at another. In the process, however, production grew and incomes rose correspondingly, but the increase in income was distributed unevenly. Much went to the city population and helped produce the flowering of city culture that characterized the first years of the century, but a good part went also to the rural traders and manufacturers who came to be characterized as "rich peasants" (*gōnō*).

The village economy

The rural village, the basic unit of administration and taxation, which had once been almost completely self-sufficient, was changing rapidly around 1800, though the pace of change varied from region to region. Variation among regions and even among neighboring villages was so great that it is not possible to speak of a typical or representative village. A village might consist of six or seven households or two hundred or more. In some villages, landholdings were distributed fairly equally; in others the majority held no land at all, and the tax burdens varied from one domain to another and even among neighboring villages. By 1800, regional specialization had produced different patterns of village economic activity from region to region.[8]

Parts of northern Kantō, Tōhoku, and Kyushu and isolated villages throughout the country had changed little in the century before 1800. An average "backward" village consisted of about forty to fifty households, most of which held some land, though the distribution of landholdings could be uneven. In general, however, the scale of farming was limited to what could be cultivated by household labor, generally around half a hectare. Few of the larger landholders were still able to call on the customary labor services of dependent households, and most leased what they could not cultivate to those who held little or no land of their own. Rice was grown to pay taxes in kind, and in an average season, little was left after the tax rice was delivered. For the rest, wheat, barley, soybeans, and coarse grains were grown for household consumption, with the surpluses traded in small local markets or between households. In such areas the opportunities for commercial farming were limited, and industrial employment was also scarce. There was little incentive to use commercial fertilizers or to introduce new technology, and so agricultural productivity rose very slowly – if anything, backward areas were becoming relatively more backward.

Taxation tended to be heavy relative to output, as the domains tried to maintain establishments and styles of living comparable to those of their peers from more prosperous areas. In a poor season some farmers, unable either to pay their taxes or to support themselves, simply walked off their farms and sought employment elsewhere. Because those who remained in the village were held responsible for cultivating and paying the taxes on land so abandoned, this could result in progressive agricul-

---

8 Horie Eiichi, ed., *Bakumatsu ishin no nōgyō kōzō* (Tokyo: Iwanami shoten, 1963).

tural decline and create serious problems for the domains as well as the farmers. Laws prohibiting farmers from leaving the land were reinforced by prohibitions against neglecting agriculture for more profitable occupations that might have enabled them to hold on. But rather than punish those who had left their land, the bakufu gave subsidies in the form of tools and rations to induce them to return to agriculture; some domains even paid child endowment to try to build up the farm population. Encouragement of agriculture, which was the source of government revenue, and suppression of industry and rural commerce was rationalized by the theory that agriculture was the backbone of the economy, whereas other occupations were unproductive.

In the rice-growing areas of Mutsu and Dewa, improved techniques and some use of commercial fertilizers produced a surplus of rice for sale after taxes were paid. Those who held more land than they could cultivate with the labor of their own households employed labor either by the year or by the day. To operate a commercial farm successfully, however, required some capital, and those with very small holdings either became farm laborers or migrated in search of employment. By 1800 the gap between rich and poor was already widening and was taking a different form, as control over people progressively gave way to control over other resources and the richer were combining commercial farming with trade. To the disgust of one official observer, rich farmers in the Sendai domain never soiled their hands with farm work but lived in luxury, amusing themselves with music, theater, poetry, and archery.[9] Such a life-style must have been for a small if conspicuous minority. In the Kumamoto domain (southern Kyushu) in 1810, a farmer and his wife with just over half a hectare of paddy field and one-third of a hectare of dry field paid half of their crop of rice, barley, and millet in taxes and spent over half of the remainder on wages and food for hired labor. They owned a horse and bought processed foods, tools, equipment, seed, and fertilizer. As a solid owner-cultivator, the farmer's only luxuries were a trip to the temple during the slack season and a new straw hat. At that he would have broken even, had it not been for the horse's falling ill and needing a visit from the veterinarian.[10] Success or failure for a commercial rice grower depended on the quality of his land, his labor costs, and his tax assessment. A substantial farmer with one hectare of good rice land and some dry field in

---

9 Tamamushi Jūzō, *Jinsei hen*, in Honjō Eijirō, ed., *Kinsei shakai keizai sōsho* (Tokyo: Kaizōsha, 1926), vol. 7.
10 Kodama Kōta, *Kinsei nōmin seikatsu shi* (Tokyo: Yoshikawa kōbunkan, 1958), pp. 276–84.

Mito was able to save six or seven *ryō* a year. Another with the same amount of less productive land could save less than two *ryō*.[11] For those who could accumulate some capital, the region's export of rice, other grains, and dried fish, and its imports of manufactured goods, provided profitable trading opportunities.

In northern Honshū and Kyushu, the inadequacy of subsistence agriculture and rice monoculture as a revenue base was apparent by the middle of the eighteenth century and was highlighted by the crop failures of the 1780s. Many domains encouraged and often financed cultivation and processing of industrial crops such as paper, mulberry, wax, lacquer, and silkworms. The domain monopolized the products and took the lion's share of the proceeds. Although farmers were in effect working for a government enterprise, such innovations also enhanced the viability of the village economy.

In central Honshū, village life was more commercialized; industrial crops were widespread; and village industry was an important source of rural income. A sharp line cannot be drawn between this region and the rice-growing regions of the north. Although the Shōnai domain exported little but rice, other parts of Dewa grew, processed, and exported *benihana* (a red dye), and the Yonezawa domain began to encourage industrial crops, especially sericulture, in the 1790s in an attempt to make up for falling revenues from agriculture. Echigo, just south of Dewa, exported substantial quantities of silk crepe as well as rice. Further south again, the huge Kaga domain produced and exported silk, linen, and cotton cloth, marine products, umbrellas, livestock, lacquer ware, salt, and paper, but rice still accounted for 40 percent of all exports from the domain. The industrial exports themselves were the result of domain development policies dating back to the mid-eighteenth century, and their production and marketing were largely a domain enterprise.

It was in the southern provinces of central Japan from Owari to Harima, and particularly in the provinces of Izumi, Kawachi, and Settsu around Osaka Bay, that village life was most involved with the market. Here farmers worked for profit rather than for the domain administration; indeed with few powerful domains in the area, controls on production were few and ineffective. Many villages specialized in growing cotton and oilseeds to the extent that they imported rice from other areas. These crops required heavy applications of commercial fertilizers, such as oil cake, fish meal, and night soil, and farmers

11 Ibid., p. 284.

carefully balanced their expenditures on fertilizers against the extra income that it could expect to return. An average village in this area consisted of about fifty landholding households and perhaps as many who held little or no land of their own. There was a strong demand for labor, and those with no land of their own found employment in cotton spinning and weaving or as agricultural laborers. Labor was scarce, not, as in the north, because depressed farmers were leaving the area, but because industries were growing rapidly. As a result, wages were relatively high, and those with more land than they could cultivate themselves found it more profitable to rent their surplus land to tenant farmers than to hire labor. Conditions were similar in western Owari where cotton spinning was a major activity.

In all these areas, the villagers spent more time in spinning, weaving, and trading than in farm work. A villager with land sufficient only for a house and garden would have been impoverished in the less commercialized areas of the north, but here he might make a living as a weaver or even be a prosperous trader. Taxes were relatively light, but controls on marketing depressed the prices paid to producers.

The Kantō region, the hinterland of Edo, was developing rapidly in the 1800s as a direct supplier to the Edo market; silk weaving was established in Kiryū, Ashikaga, Hachiōji, and Chichibu; cotton weaving was also widespread; Noda soy sauce was replacing shipments from Osaka; and Edo was supplied with fresh vegetables from its surrounding villages. About a quarter of the rural population was employed in handicrafts and commerce. According to one contemporary source,[12] about half the population indulged in manufacturing, commerce, or sheer idleness, leaving the remaining half to do all the hard agricultural work. Many of these nonagricultural workers had migrated to Kantō from areas farther north where they had been unable to support themselves on their small farms.

All over Japan, village trade was prohibited or discouraged on the grounds that it diverted farmers from their proper work of producing income for the domain and led to luxury and laziness. Some domains permitted peddling so long as it was done on the villagers' own time or when the villager had no other means of support. Where commercial crops were grown with the domain's encouragement or permission, one or more villagers – often village officials – were authorized to collect the produce at the village level and forward it to licensed merchants or domain agents. Retail shops, however, were in principle

12 Buyō Inshi, *Seji kemmonroku* (1816), in *Kinsei shakai keizai sōsho*, vol. 1, pp. 55–6.

restricted to officially nominated towns (*machikata*). This was not easy to enforce, and in many parts of Japan there were villages with shops selling farm equipment, consumer goods of all kinds, and even, according to official reports, luxury goods inappropriate to farmers. The development of rural commerce was affecting the trade of established merchants in the cities and towns, who frequently appealed to the authorities to protect them by forbidding village trade.

The urban economy

Japanese cities were centers of adminstration, consumption, and commerce. Although each domain's castle town or capital combined all three functions, the bakufu's administrative headquarters was in Edo, and its main commercial center, and that of the whole country, was in Osaka. Osaka was the entrepôt to which the products of central and western Japan were sent and from which they were reexported to the great consumption center of Edo and to other parts of the country. This trade was handled by a sophisticated structure of wholesalers (*ton'ya, toiya*) organized in licensed associations (*kabunakama*) which were granted monopoly privileges in return for acting as the bakufu's agents for the control of the national commerce. Shipments from Osaka to Edo were the monopoly of twenty-four groups of authorized wholesalers who were required to consign their goods to ten similarly authorized groups in Edo. This system was under official supervision at every point and operated to keep city consumer prices stable and at the same time to restrict rises in rural incomes. In the century before 1825, this system was effective, and the value of goods channeled through the system rose fourfold or fivefold (much more for some commodities), and prices remained relatively stable. The quantity of cash in circulation at least doubled over this period, with a corresponding profit on the coinage going to the bakufu. That such an increase in the money supply did not produce inflation was due largely to the increased need for money as the volume of transactions increased, but it also reflected the effectiveness of the controls.

Osaka was also the main financial center. At the apex of the financial system of Osaka and of most of the country was a small group of bankers known collectively as the Ten Exchange Houses (Jūnin ryōgae) who performed some of the functions of a central bank, acting as a lender of last resort to correspondent banks, lending to domain governments, controlling the level of bank credits, and controlling the market between gold-denominated cash and silver-denominated bank money. This last was of particular concern to the bakufu. Because wholesale transactions were in silver credit and retail sales in cash, a change in the ratio affected retail price levels. The gold–silver market also reflected the ratio of bank credit to the cash supply. Bank loans financed trade and industry through advances to wholesalers who in turn advanced funds to producers repayable on delivery of the goods. The banks also provided facilities for remittances between Osaka and Edo (and some other centers) by bills of exchange which set off payments by Edo merchants for purchases from Osaka against transfers of official funds from Osaka to Edo. The Osaka banking system also made substantial loans to domains both to cover current deficits and to finance industrial and agricultural development projects.

Industry had once been concentrated in cities, but as the demand for industrial products increased during the eighteenth century, industries such as textiles, pottery, and lacquer ware spread to many parts of Japan. By the 1800s, urban manufacturing was declining, although Kyoto was still the center of high-quality silk weaving and the decorative arts, and Osaka was a major processing center. The construction trades flourished in all the major cities, and the demand for their services was maintained by frequent fires. Artisans in the construction industry were officially under the control of master craftsmen appointed by the bakufu or the domain, a system dating from the time when their function was to build castles and other public buildings; *sake* brewers, wax refiners, oil pressers, and some master weavers were subject to the rules and regulations of their trade associations. The larger cities, especially Edo, contained large numbers of unauthorized immigrants from rural areas who led a hand-to-mouth existence as casual workers, day laborers, and peddlers. Precarious though their livelihood was, they resisted attempts to send them back to their villages, much as the inhabitants of shantytowns on the outskirts of some Third World cities do today.

In each domain, the castle town acted as the commercial as well as the administrative center and performed at the domain level the functions analogous to those that Osaka and Edo performed at the national level. Licensed or "privileged" merchants acted as agents for the collection, distribution, import, and export of goods from the domain, financed and often managed domain enterprises, and backed and managed domain note issues (*hansatsu*).

This description of the Japanese economy at the beginning of the nineteenth century indicates tight economic as well as political control. Staple agriculture was supervised by the local authority in the interests of maintaining revenue. The growing, processing, and marketing of industrial crops were controlled by domain administrations, usually in association with commercial agents inside or outside the domain with whom they shared the profits, leaving small returns to the producers. The national commerce was controlled by the bakufu through licensed associations of merchants in the key cities to maintain adequate supplies of essential goods to Edo and other large cities at stable prices while restricting the growth of incomes and purchasing power in the countryside.

It was clearly in the interests of producers, local merchants, and the domains themselves to evade these controls, as they could usually sell at a higher price in the free market. How effective were the controls? Enforcement became more and more difficult through the first half of the nineteenth century wherever free-market demand was increasing. Faced with a relative decline in their agricultural tax base, moreover, more and more domains adapted to the growth of industry and commerce relative to agriculture by encouraging and exploiting industry and trade as sources of revenue, and those that did not do so soon found increasing difficulty in enforcing controls designed to maintain an economic system that was becoming an anachronism over a growing area of the country. The reforms of the Tempō era represented the last in a series of attempts by the Tokugawa bakufu to salvage its system of economic controls and adapt it to changing economic conditions. Efforts to control economic activity in the interests of the state did not, however, end with the Meiji Restoration, and their changing forms have been a central factor in Japan's economic development ever since.

THE TEMPŌ REFORMS

The transformation of the Japanese village from a community cultivating its land for the benefit of its overlord to a collection of households, each working for its own economic betterment, was well advanced in some regions by the early nineteenth century, and the process accelerated through the century, drawing in more and more areas as it went.

By the 1820s many of the new industrial crops and processing industries introduced by the domains or the city merchants were well established, and output rose quickly, with most of the product marketed through official channels in Osaka or Edo under the control of the bakufu. At about this time, however, the domains, local merchants, and producers themselves could see opportunities to get better prices for their products by selling outside these channels through their own agents in Osaka or Edo or directly to other parts of the country. Almost all the domains were heavily in debt – Satsuma owed thirty-three times its annual revenue in the 1830s, and Chōshū owed twenty-three times its annual income by 1840. A condition of many of these loans was that the domain consigned its produce to its creditors in Osaka, but to do so meant that after the interest and repayments were deducted, little remained. The domains therefore tried to avoid Osaka and to market through other ports or directly to Edo. As a result, shipments to Osaka fell by as much as 30 percent between the 1820s and 1840. In the process, the domains' credit ratings in Osaka fell, and they were forced to seek the cooperation of merchants nearer home and increasingly to rely for revenue on a share of the profits from rapidly growing local industry and trade. Domain restrictions on rural industry and commerce were therefore progressively eased in return for license fees, inspection charges, and other levies or a share in the profits.

Rural traders increased their business at the expense of merchants in the castle towns who had been granted privileges in return for the commercial and financial services they had provided in the eighteenth century or earlier when the rural trade network had not yet developed. These castle town merchants had been the commercial agents and financial backers of the domain monopolies in the late-eighteenth and early-nineteenth centuries, but by the 1830s, even though the total volume of commerce was increasing rapidly, their business was declining as village trade expanded. In Echigo, Shinano, Kii, Tottori, and elsewhere, castle town merchants complained that they were being ruined by competition from traders in villages where trade was supposed to be forbidden. The response of many domains was to reorganize their marketing boards to include village traders as their grass-roots agents.[13]

By the 1830s a national market had developed for cotton, silk, indigo, wax, paper, sugar, tea, *sake*, pottery, matting, hardware, and lacquer ware apart from and in competition with the bakufu's procurement system, and with new market opportunities opening up, industry and trade became increasingly profitable as compared with agriculture. A survey of the Chōshū domains at the southwestern end of Honshū in 1842 showed that the average gross nonagricultural income

---

13 See Andō Seiichi, *Kinsei zaikata shōgyō no kenkyū* (Tokyo: Yoshikawa kōbunkan, 1958).

was about as much as the net agricultural income.[14] The main reason for this was that agricultural income was taxed at the rate of 39 percent of net output, whereas nonagricultural income was taxed at less than 10 percent. Agricultural income after tax and production costs were deducted did not even cover reasonable living costs, but nonagricultural pursuits yielded a good profit. On the Inland Sea side of the domain, the proportion of nonagricultural net income was even higher. In northern Honshū about half of farm income came from sericulture, and in Kawachi almost three-quarters came from the cotton industry which by the 1830s produced two million lengths of cloth a year. In the cotton-processing areas of western Owari and Izumi, only 20 percent of output was from agriculture by 1840. Wherever industry developed, it provided cash income which in turn provided the basis for local commerce. In regions such as parts of Tōhoku which enjoyed no comparative advantage in industry, cash income could be obtained only by seeking employment elsewhere, and despite official restrictions, many laborers migrated to the cities or to areas where industry was expanding. In one village in Fukushima, half of the registered landholding families had disappeared by 1841, and 20 percent of the village land was left uncultivated. This was no isolated example – many villages in Tōhoku and outer Kantō were in a similar situation. Often such migration was through personal connections, but in some areas there seem to have been regular labor recruitment agencies.

It should not be imagined that these migrant workers went out in the expectation of making their fortunes. Although it was the existence of employment opportunities elsewhere that made migration possible, it was poverty and hardship that drove people to leave their economically depressed villages, and their willingness to work for little more than subsistence wages tended to keep the general wage level low. Complaints of shortages of wage labor and rising labor costs came mainly from farmers on the outskirts of the major cities who were trying to maintain their relative economic position in areas where nonagricultural activity was expanding rapidly. Overall, however, migration of labor from areas where nonagricultural activity was less

---

14 *Bōchō fūdo chūshin an.* See Akimoto Hiroya, "Bakumatsu-ki Bōchō ryōkoku no seisan to shōhi," in Umemura Mataji, et al., eds., *Suryō keizaishi ronshū,* vol. 1: *Nihon keizai no hatten* (Tokyo: Nihon keizai shimbunsha, 1976), pp. 137–58. For a discussion of this document, see Shunsaku Nishikawa, "Grain Consumption: The Case of Chōshū," in Marius B. Jansen and Gilbert Rozman, eds., *Japan in Transition: From Tokugawa to Meiji* (Princeton, N.J.: Princeton University Press, 1986), pp. 421–46.

productive to areas where it was more productive tended to raise average productivity and incomes over the country as a whole.

Cooperation among producers, local traders, and domain authorities could be very productive. In the early nineteenth century, the linen-thread producers of the Kaga domain operated on advances from Ōmi merchants to whom they were forced to sell their thread at low prices. Approaches to the domain to establish a system of finance and marketing that would bring better returns failed, and rather than sell the yarn for such a poor return, the producers, with the assistance of the domain, experimented with weaving their thread into linen crepe. By the 1820s the industry was well established, with finance and marketing facilities arranged by the domain authorities, who opened a marketing office in Edo in 1828. So successful was the venture that in the 1830s the villagers went into cotton weaving as a supplement to linen, for which demand was seasonal. The domain was asked to handle the new product but refused on the ground that the quality was still too uneven. A local merchant involved in the linen trade then offered to finance and market it himself if the domain would lend him the capital. The domain agreed, and by 1861 one district alone was producing a million lengths of cotton a year, and the domain had assumed direct responsibility for quality control and marketing.[15] Even though in such cases, the domain's main object was to secure a source of revenue, the prices to producers and middlemen rose. Producers were no longer prepared to work for the domain for little or no return, and attempts to force them to do so usually provoked vigorous protests. In Kinki and Shikoku where commercial production developed early, such protests were common in the 1790s, and by the 1830s they occurred whenever the producers could get significantly better returns outside the domain monopoly system.

In principle, producers and local merchants were not free to trade unless specifically permitted to do so, and when permission was granted there were usually conditions attached. Local merchants in Okayama gained freedom to export directly from the domain in the 1830s but were required to surrender the hard currency they obtained thereby in return for *hansatsu* which could be used for purchases within the domain but could be converted to cash only at a discount. Although the apparent profits of the local merchants rose, the system operated to help meet the domain's expenses in Edo and Osaka rather

---

15 Andō, *Kinsei zaikata shōgyō no kenkyū*, pp. 165–70.

than to strengthen the value of its paper currency within the domain, and thus in effect it taxed local trade.

Trading without permission was, however, widespread and difficult to suppress. The authorities were tolerant of peddling by villagers with no other means of support, but larger-scale trading, especially outside the domain or to the detriment of agriculture, was another matter. Nevertheless, there was unauthorized trade (*nukeni*) wherever commercial opportunities presented themselves and restrictions were easier to evade than to police. Having been forced by financial straits to license some village trading in return for license fees in 1825, the Tottori domain found that by 1846 there was so much of it that there was a shortage of cultivators. An attempt to correct the situation by putting the delinquent peasants to forced labor in land reclamation turned out to be a ludicrous anachronism. As the prices to producers rose, it became more and more profitable to leave agriculture for industry and trade, and as rural incomes thereby increased, so did the rural demand for manufactures of all kinds, thus adding fuel to the whole process. By the 1840s most villages in the more advanced regions of Kinki, Chūgoku, and Shikoku were served by shops selling a full range of consumption goods, and villagers bought in cash most of their requirements other than staple grains.

The gains of the domains and the rural producers meant a relative decline in the position of the shogunate. The traditional agricultural tax base was declining as a proportion of total output for domains and shogunate alike, but as possibilities for the domains to profit from the growth of industry and trade increased, the mechanisms by which the shogunate had been able to control national commerce to its advantage became less and less effective. This is indicated by a sharp decline in shipments to Osaka accompanied by rising prices, whose causes were diagnosed in a report prepared in 1841–2 under the direction of Osaka City Magistrate Abe Tōtōmi-no-kami.[16] Based on a survey of twenty-one commodities, the report found that although improper commercial practices were tending to raise prices, more importantly, the development of markets in the countryside was often diverting goods from Osaka and its control system. Attempts to strengthen and extend control to the hinterland of Osaka had failed when they encountered the massive resistance of the 1820s. In eight cases the report found that the operations of the domain monopolies were the major factor. Domains marketed their products elsewhere and forbade private ship-

16 This comprehensive report on problems of price control is printed in full in Osaka-shi sanjikai, ed., *Osaka-shishi* (Osaka: Osaka shiyakusho, 1926), vol. 5, pp. 639–86.

ments to Osaka. If they found it convenient to market in Osaka, they used their monopoly power and the threat of going elsewhere to obtain higher prices. The report recommended abolition of domain monopolies and renewed efforts to enforce regulations requiring producers to ship their products to Osaka, an across-the-board price cut of 20 percent (except for rice), and reorganization of the Osaka licensed trade associations. It appears that the report was never submitted to Edo but was overtaken by the progress of the Tempō reforms.

The reforms

Mizuno Echizen-no-kami Tadakuni, the prime mover of the Tempō reforms, had become governor of Osaka Castle (Osaka jōdai) in 1825, soon after the more-or-less successful protests by thousands of Kinki villagers outraged at being forced to supply the Osaka market at procurement prices to compensate, as they thought, for the increasing evasion of the system elsewhere. Though Mizuno's two-year term in Osaka was relatively quiet, his first years as senior councilor were marked by harvest failures, rising prices, financial crisis, and widespread revolts against the system of government as a whole and especially its economic administration.

Following disastrous harvests, the price of rice in 1836 rose to about double the average of the previous decade and rose by a further 50 percent the next year. But although the rice price subsided over the following three or four years, the prices of other commodities remained high, and in 1840–1 the ratio between the prices paid by the bakufu and its retainers for their purchases as against the price of rice, in which they received a good part of their income, was the highest since the 1770s. At the root of this inflation was the breakdown of trade and price controls in the face of the development of "free" markets, but the situation was aggravated by continuing budget deficits and large issues of currency. If we neglect silver bars (*chōgin, mameitagin*) which had gone out of general use by this time, the amount of currency in circulation had increased by about 75 percent in the twenty years before 1838 and was still rising. From 1839 to 1841 new issues of currency, mainly silver quarter-*ryō* pieces (*ichibugin*), totaled close to two million *ryō*, and the gold coinage had been debased to the extent that it was worth only half as much as the better-quality coins of the Keichō, Kyōhō, and Bunsei eras. At the same time, with more and more people earning cash incomes by handicrafts and buying more of their requirements for cash, there was a shortage of the copper currency used for these transactions, and so between 1835 and 1841 the bakufu issued new copper coins to the value of about 580,000 ryō. The bakufu seems to have rather overestimated the demand for these coins, because by 1842 their value had fallen further than was thought desirable.

With an increase of about 80 percent in the money supply between 1816 and 1841, substantial inflation could be expected. Although prices rose steeply in famine years, the underlying rise in prices in Edo over the same period was of the order of 50 to 60 percent, or a rather modest 2 percent a year. It seems clear that as well as a growing transaction demand for cash, there was also a considerable rise in the output of goods over the period. That inflation in Edo was relatively modest suggests that most of the increase in currency flowed to the developing rural areas where it was most needed and also that the fall in the flow of goods to Edo through Osaka was largely compensated for by shipments direct from the producing districts in the Kantō hinterland and elsewhere. Nevertheless, deficit financing turned what had until about 1820 been a falling price trend into a rising one.

Although the national output was growing, the bakufu's regular tax income was falling. It had, in fact, been on a declining trend since the mid-eighteenth century. Tax receipts in the famine year of 1836 were the lowest for 125 years, but even when harvests improved, attempts to increase tax revenue met with determined resistance.

The bakufu's first reaction, like that of the domain governments faced with similar problems, was to reduce its own expenditures, suppress competing demands for goods, and try to get more resources back into basic agriculture which was its main source of tax income. The large Kaga domain had embarked on this traditional course as early as 1837 and had anticipated most of the measures taken by the bakufu in the early stages of the Tempō reforms. Faced with financial crisis, the Kaga domain "borrowed" from its samurai by withholding part of their salaries, declared a moratorium on its loans to samurai, introduced price control, imposed export taxes, sent farmers back to their villages, and exhorted villagers to frugality while trying to prevent them from leaving agriculture for other occupations. In an order of 1844 the domain noted that higher wages in weaving were producing a shortage of farm laborers. Village officials should not lightly give permission to engage in industrial employment, and farmers must not pay more than officially determined wage rates – which were graduated from 7,500 *mon* of copper cash (about 1.15 ryō) per year for a first-class male farmhand down to 2,000 *mon* for a third-class female servant – and additional seasonal payments must not exceed the customary level.[17] Even though board and lodging were provided, they were at extremely low standards. Farm laboring was a hard life for little reward, and it is hardly surprising that few workers were disposed to accept it if other work were available at even slightly higher wages.

Mizuno himself was trying to implement similar measures in his own domain of Hamamatsu, with very limited success. Nevertheless, such attempts at turning the clock back seem to have been de rigueur for any major reform.

The bakufu announced its reforms in 1841 on the shogun's birthday. A survey of the extent of nonagricultural activity in its villages confirmed that there had been a substantial drift from agriculture, and an order was promptly issued forbidding villagers to engage in nonagricultural work or to seek such work outside the village. The ban was repeated the next year – and the year after and again in 1845 – but all attempts to keep the people down on the farm seem to have been ineffective.

Both the bakufu and the domains attributed the problems of agriculture to a decline in peasant morality leading to neglect of their proper, but unprofitable, work in the fields for more rewarding occupations. Peasants are not what they were, complained a bakufu order. Instead of wearing coarse clothing and tying their hair with straws, they were wearing cotton garments and using hair oil and fancy hair ties. And in wet weather, instead of straw capes they were using raincoats and umbrellas! Peasants would do almost anything to get out of farming, even to the extent of having themselves disinherited and struck off the village register so that they would be free to leave for more profitable employment elsewhere.[18] Such action could hardly have been taken lightly and indicates the desperation of some of the village population.

Government expenditure, the lifeblood of the Edo merchant community, was slashed; bans were placed on luxuries and amusements; and officials were appointed to police the bans throughout the city. Within a month Echigoya (modern Mitsukoshi Department Store) reported a drop in sales of 5,830 *ryō* from the previous month, Daimaru was down by 2,800 *ryō*, and Shirokiya (modern Tōkyū Department Store) by 3,670 *ryō*. Although all three survived, and indeed survive to this day, this indicated a major business recession.

17 Oda Kichinojō, ed., *Kaga han nōseishi kō* (Tokyo: Tōkō shoin, 1929), pp. 578–9.
18 *Tokugawa kinrei kō*, 1st ser., vol. 5, p. 192.

Even so, prices did not fall far enough for the bakufu, and after a survey of the marketing system based on reports from the wholesale trade associations (*ton'ya nakama*), it became clear that these organizations were no longer effective channels for bringing goods into Edo. Other channels had been developing for some time, bringing in goods from the rapidly growing production of Edo's own hinterland in the Kantō region. The bakufu itself favored this growth in the region in which it could best exercise direct control. By 1821, shipments of soy sauce from Osaka had been replaced by the products of Noda and other parts of the Kantō which were cheaper and whose stronger flavor appealed to Edo tastes. The wholesalers' associations whose business was bound up with the Osaka trade invoked their monopoly privileges in an effort to obstruct the marketing of Kantō products in Edo. But by the 1840s Kantō producers had captured 40 percent of the Edo market for cottonseed oil, and silk textiles from Ashikaga, Kiryū, and elsewhere in Kantō were selling in substantial quantities through Edo merchants who set up business in opposition to the chartered associations. Cotton cloth, tea, and other products of the Kantō region were entering the Edo market in increasing quantities.[19]

With supplies via the Osaka route dwindling, to give preference to Osaka goods in the Edo market meant restricting these growing supplies from Kantō and elsewhere. Moreover, the Kantō region was close to Edo, safe from blockade by sea, and because it was largely in the control of the bakufu either directly or through its retainers and branches, it was a potential base for a bakufu system of monopoly procurement along the lines of those so successfully operated by a number of domains. With such considerations in mind, the bakufu moved early in 1842 to withdraw its support from the Osaka route and to abolish the monopoly privileges of the chartered trade associations (*kabunakama*), beginning with those most closely involved in that trade. Anticipating, though not fully, the confusion likely to follow such a radical departure, the bakufu set up an office under one of the Edo city magistrates, but staffed by civilians, to observe and report on the operation of the new system and to control abuses.

In the spring of 1842 the order to dissolve such trade associations was extended to the domains. By no means all domains complied, and those that did appear to have done so for their own reasons. The Owari (Nagoya) domain, for example, held by one of the senior branches of the Tokugawa family, complied on paper but maintained existing

[19] See Hayashi Reiko, "Bakumatsu ishin-ki ni okeru Kantō no shōhin ryūtsū," *Chihōshi kenkyū* 20 (April 1971): 28–41.

controls on a number of trades. The monopoly privileges of its licensed cotton cloth dealers who handled one of the domain's major exports were abolished but were replaced by a marketing board nominally run by the domain itself but with former licensed dealers (*ton'ya*) involved in its operation. Some domains, like Aizu and Satsuma, ignored the order, and the Suwa domain actually licensed a new association of traders to control the marketing of its textiles.[20]

The monopoly marketing boards by which the domains profited from the growth of industry and trade had irked the bakufu for some time, as they were the main mechanism by which the domains were increasing their financial strength relative to that of the bakufu, which was unable to benefit in the same way. At the end of 1842, therefore, it denied domain claims that their monopoly marketing boards were official business and insisted that their products be marketed freely. The response was scarcely encouraging. With agricultural tax income falling and expenses mounting, profits from the marketing boards were essential to keep the domains reasonably solvent. The Matsushiro domain in Shinano, forced for internal reasons to abandon its control of the silk cloth market at this time, found itself heavily in debt within eight years.[21] Suspecting, with some reason, that the bakufu was considering establishing its own monopoly trading system or even moving toward some form of nationwide control of commerce, domains like Chōshū and Satsuma strengthened their own systems rather than relinquishing them.

By early 1843 the thrust of the reform was clearly toward shifting the balance of economic power in favor of the bakufu. At the beginning of the year the bakufu carried out a survey of issues of *hansatsu* (domain notes) but stopped short of banning them. Four months later it tried to restrict the domains' activities by forbidding auctions of goods in ports outside its own territory.

Meanwhile, the bakufu was attempting to reduce both its own expenses and the domains' profits by ordering a general 20 percent price cut in Edo and Osaka, accompanied by cuts in wages and rents. In doing so, it anticipated that the reductions would be passed back to the suppliers, especially the domain marketing boards, which would in turn be forced to lower the prices paid to local suppliers and eventu-

---

20 See Tsuda Hideo, *Hōken shakai kaitai katei kenkyū josetsu* (Tokyo: Hanawa shobō, 1970), pp. 222–3.
21 Yoshinaga Akira, "Han sembai seido no kiban to kōzō: Matsushirohan sembutsu kaisho shihō o megutte," in Furushima Toshio, ed., *Nihon keizaishi taikei* (Tokyo: Tōkyō daigaku shuppankai, 1965), vol. 4, pp. 225–62.

ally to cut the rates paid to the producers themselves. This would have the added advantage of reducing the relative attractiveness, however small, of industry and trade over agriculture. Had there been no outlets for goods other than the major bakufu cities, this would not have been an unreasonable expectation. In fact, however, a substantial demand had developed in many other parts of the country, and as long as sales could be made there, the domains and rural businessmen were not prepared to cut their margins. Payments to spinners, weavers, and other producers, however, had never been high, and their real incomes had been reduced by inflation. To have reduced them further would certainly have provoked resistance and forced more destitute villagers to move to the cities in search of a livelihood. Thus the supply price of goods did not fall as expected, and Osaka's wholesale prices fluctuated around a level 36 percent above the average of the 1830s.

The price controls were strictly policed under the direction of the Edo city magistrate and financial comptroller Torii Yōzō, Mizuno's right-hand man and a remarkably capable and hardworking official who for those very reasons was generally detested. The result was a substantial diversion of goods from Edo to other markets almost certainly accompanied by some fall in production. Bakufu officials attributed shortages in Edo to the machinations of unscrupulous merchants, but given the extent to which Japan had by then become a commercialized society, they were a natural consequence of its price control policy.

Like other governments, the bakufu seems to have been better at producing recessions than encouraging development. Within six months of the price control order, deteriorating conditions in the countryside were forcing more people out of the villages and exacerbating the problem of destitute itinerants in Edo. At the end of 1842, numbers of these were rounded up and either sent back to their villages or put to work in labor camps. This was followed by a general order to all those in Edo without authorization to return to their villages and their proper agricultural occupations. At this time Ninomiya Sontoku and Ōhara Yūgaku were active in reconstructing Kantō villages on a model in some respects analogous to the modern agricultural cooperative, based on the concept that if farmers were no longer willing to work for their lord, they might still be persuaded that they should work for the good of the village community. This idea, considered novel at the time, achieved only modest success, but it became the prototype for an important element in the organization of modern Japanese society.

By holding down interest rates in its territory, the bakufu had hoped to lighten the burden of debt carried by its retainers. Its effect was, however, to dry up the sources of finance on which they had become dependent, making their financial situation more difficult than ever. In the spring of 1843, therefore, the bakufu took steps to improve their situation and to keep both its retainers and their creditors afloat.

The bakufu itself had made substantial loans to its fief-holding retainers through its Bakuro-chō finance office. Seeing little chance of repayment, the bakufu wrote off half the amount outstanding, or some 200,000 to 250,000 *ryō*, and declared the remainder repayable in easy installments free of interest. Retainers who received their salaries in rice were in the habit of borrowing from their financial agents (*fudasashi*). Some were in debt for large amounts accumulated over generations. To help them, the bakufu worked out an arrangement by which it would lend to its retainers on very favorable terms through the Saruya-chō finance office on condition that the funds be used to repay their debts to the *fudasashi*. The *fudasashi* for their part would follow the example of the bakufu and relieve the financial burdens of their smaller debtors by remitting or lowering interest and arranging for the repayment of capital in small installments. The bakufu pointed out that compared with previous repudiations, this was generous treatment. Before this arrangement was implemented, however, Mizuno was dismissed, and his successor seems to have insisted that all amounts owing to the *fudasashi* be repaid over twenty years free of interest, although the details are unclear. Coming only five years after the *fudasashi* had been ordered to contribute 100,000 *ryō* toward rebuilding part of Edo Castle, it was a serious blow, and a number temporarily closed their doors.[22]

The Mizuno administration seems to have believed that it could finance these rescue operations and put its own finances on a sounder basis by a number of means. As a short-term measure, a forced loan (*goyōkin*) was imposed on the merchant communities of Osaka, Sakai, Hyōgo, and Nishinomiya. Such loans had been raised from time to time, usually to finance rice price support operations. The leading merchants, mainly bankers, were required to lend to the government roughly in proportion to their standing in the business community, for periods of up to twenty years at low rates of interest, very much as Japan's banking system is required to take up government bonds today. The operation of 1843, however, was on a much larger scale than were any of its predecessors. The original target was to raise

---

22 Koda Shigetomo, *Nihon keizaishi kenkyū* (Tokyo: Ōokayama shoten, 1928) pp. 76–83.

about 2.25 million *ryō* at 2.5 percent repayable over twenty years. Given the lower risk factor, this rate of interest compared favorably with the return on loans to domains. The amount actually taken up was about 1.15 million *ryō*, but even at that it was about twice as much as had ever been raised before. Beyond the financing of the Bakuro-chō scheme, which was said to require not more than 250,000 *ryō*, no clear reason was given for raising so large a sum, but Mizuno seems to have had in mind some other operation that would require a large amount of capital.[23]

Mizuno was aware of the work of the scholar Satō Shin'en and is said to have commissioned one of his best-known works, *Fukkohō gaigen*.[24] In this and other writings Satō recommended a state monopoly trading system on a national scale, decisively transferring the control of production and the profits of marketing from the domains to the bakufu.

Implementation of some such scheme within the bakufu's own territory was certainly a possibility, and the Kantō region had developed to the point that it could provide a good base. Even before the Osaka loan was finalized, the bakufu announced that it proposed to consolidate its territories by resuming under its direct control all land within a radius of about twenty-five miles of Edo and within about twelve and a half miles of Osaka. Those whose territory was resumed would be compensated with comparable lands elsewhere. One reason for this proposal was the needs of national defense, but another was the need of the bakufu for a strong economic base from which it could compete with the domains and perhaps eventually extend its economic control throughout the country.

Opposition to the plan was widespread among the domains and, combined with opposition from the *hatamoto* who would have been most affected, was sufficient to bring about Mizuno's dismissal. Plans for direct economic control at the national level were abandoned, and reclamation work in Kantō, which if successful would have added considerably to the bakufu's revenue, was stopped. Mizuno's successor, Doi Ōi-no-kami Toshitsura, professed himself unsure of the purpose of the large Osaka loan and suggested that in the circumstances, the money might be returned! Even when Mizuno returned to the government for a few months the following year, plans for, as it were, nationalizing the domains' trading monopolies were not revived.

Nevertheless, the Tempō reforms brought about changes that were

---

23 Ibid., pp. 437–8.
24 Satō Nobuhiro (Shin'en), *Fukkohō gaigen*, in Takimoto Seiichi, ed., *Nihon keizai taiten* (Tokyo: Shishi shuppansha and Keimeisha, 1928), vol. 19.

irreversible. They made it clear that the process by which economic power was shifting away from the bakufu could not continue without sweeping changes. A realistic program of national defense required the mobilization of resources on a national scale, but the domains were clearly not prepared to surrender their economic powers to the bakufu. At the same time, in dismantling the outworn system of control through the Osaka trade route, the bakufu cleared the way for further changes. These changes were beyond the bakufu's power, but its plans were taken over and largely implemented by the Restoration government some twenty-five years later.

THE OPENING OF FOREIGN TRADE

In the course of the Tempō reforms, the bakufu abandoned attempts to control the economy through the Osaka–Edo marketing system. In its place it had hoped to institute a new system that would give it control of production and commerce throughout the country, but it lacked the political and financial means to carry out its plans in the face of opposition from the domains. The plans were not, however, completely abandoned. Reestablishment of the wholesale traders' associations in 1851 did not represent a return to the pre-Tempō situation, but a move toward more widely based controls. The new associations were not intended to keep out outsiders but to bring them in. Thus they were granted no monopoly privileges, and membership was open to all bona fide traders. Instead of restricting rural traders, the bakufu encouraged them to join the new associations, and in 1852 membership was made compulsory. The jurisdiction of these associations did not extend to the domains' territories, but the new system was comprehensive enough to include all traders through whom the domains sold their goods in the major cities, thus bringing them, nominally at least, under the bakufu's surveillance.

It was into this somewhat uneasy situation that Commodore Matthew Perry arrived in 1853 with instructions to open Japan to foreign trade. The prospect of foreign trade and its actual opening in 1859 dominated the economic as well as the political life of Japan until the Meiji Restoration and beyond. If Japan had been moving toward economic change in the 1840s, the opening of foreign trade ensured that change would be rapid and far-reaching. It produced severe inflation, changed production and relative prices, and focused the struggle between the bakufu and the domains on the issue of control of foreign trade.

The effect of the deflationary measures of the Tempō era was relatively short-lived. By 1850, prices were again rising under the influence of the bakufu's and the domains' deficits and a continuing rise in rural demand. It was the opening of foreign trade, however, that turned comparatively mild price rises into serious and accelerating inflation, and the question of the exchange rate was a major factor.

In the negotiations leading up to the opening of trade, Townsend Harris, representing the United States, insisted that foreign currency – in practice Mexican silver dollars – should exchange for Japanese currency on a weight-for-weight basis. This was the system used in trade with China and other parts of the East where currency, mainly silver, was valued by weight. Silver by weight (*chōgin, mameitagin*) did exist in Japan, and at the official rate of 60 *momme* to the gold *ryō* exchanged for gold at very close to the international ratio of 15.5 to 1, but by the 1850s it formed less than 3 percent of the Japanese currency and was no longer in general use.

The Japanese currency of the 1850s consisted of gold one-*ryō* pieces and smaller-denomination gold coins and silver pieces representing fractions of a gold *ryō*. Most of these latter were silver quarter-*ryō* pieces (*ichibugin*), of which about 200 million had been minted since 1837. As the Japanese negotiators pointed out to Harris, the weight and fineness of these subsidiary coins was immaterial, as they circulated as tokens for one-quarter of a gold *ryō*, irrespective of their intrinsic value, which was much less. If a foreigner were to be allowed to exchange Mexican silver dollars for Japanese token silver coinage by weight, a dollar would exchange for three *ichibu* coins, which in Japan respresented three-quarters of a gold *ryō*. Thus for 1.33 dollars the foreigner would be able to obtain a Japanese gold coin worth over three times that amount, or about 4.59 dollars. Harris's insistence on what he should have realized was a grossly unfair exchange not only complicated the negotiations but also forced the Japanese government to reform its currency in such a way as to make massive inflation inevitable.

The first reaction of the Japanese was to remove the anomaly by reminting the subsidiary silver coinage. Just before the trade was due to start, the bakufu began minting large one-eighth *ryō* silver pieces, two of which weighed rather more than a Mexican silver dollar. At this rate a gold *ryō* would be equivalent to 4.48 Mexican dollars, very close to its value on the international market. Had the bakufu proceeded with its announced intention to remint all its subsidiary silver coinage in this way, it would have reduced the face value of currency in circulation by some 14 million *ryō*, or about 26 percent, with deflationary results. As soon as the new coins appeared at the treaty ports, however, the foreign representatives protested that they were not genuine Japanese coinage in general circulation but a device to prevent foreign traders from making profits in the spirit of the treaties. Forced to withdraw the new coins, the bakufu did all it could to avoid exchange at the anomalous rate specified in the treaties but, under continuing pressure, was unable to prevent the export of up to 500,000 *ryō* of gold over the following six months. In January 1860, however, the bakufu announced that the situation would be corrected by reminting the gold coinage and that in the meantime, silver *ichibu* would exchange in Japan for gold *ryō* at the rate of 13.5 to 1. In April the new gold coins, slightly more than one-third the size of the old ones, were issued at the rate of three new coins for one old one. As a result, the total amount of currency in circulation increased almost 2.5-fold. The British government later apologized for the whole sorry episode, but the damage had been done.

Whether the exchange anomaly introduced by the treaties was removed by reforming (regrading) the silver subsidiary coinage or by reforming (degrading) the gold coinage, the effect on the relationship between the two was the same. The effect on other price relationships, however, was vastly different. The former would have cut the dollar's purchasing power in Japan to one-third and reduced price levels in Japan, or at least would have prevented them from rising. The latter left the exchange value of the dollar intact but led to massive inflation and consequent changes in the distribution of wealth and income in Japan. Within a year the general price level had risen by over 30 percent and by 1866 it was over four times the pretrade level.[25]

Once the exchange situation was resolved, trade grew rapidly. In 1860, the first full year of trade, exports (in terms of Mexican dollars) were 4.7 million and imports 1.7 million. Exports rose to 10.6 million in 1864 and 12.1 million in 1867; and imports, including ships, rose to 8.1 million and 21.7 million, respectively. From the opening of trade until the Restoration, foreign trade resulted in an overall export surplus of just over 4 million. Raw silk was by far the biggest export, accounting for 50 to 80 percent of annual export value. The major imports were woolen and cotton textiles, with arms and vessels becoming important

---

25 Shimbo Hiroshi, *Kinsei no bukka to keizai hatten: zenkōgyōka shakai e no suryōteki sekkin* (Tokyo: Tōyō keizai shimpōsha, 1978), p. 282.

(20 percent) as the Restoration approached. The prices of export products rose much faster than those of items not affected by trade. The price of raw silk rose threefold in the first year of trade and doubled again over the following five years. Export demand eventually stimulated a large increase in output, but its initial effect on the Japanese silk-weaving industry was disastrous. In the silk-weaving center of Kiryū, the opening of trade produced an immediate rise in the price of first-grade raw silk, from 94 *ryō* per picul to 267 *ryō* per picul, and in Suwa the price per picul rose from 80 *ryō* to 200 *ryō*. With 30 to 50 percent of production being exported, the shortage of raw material for the Kyoto silk-weaving industry was so severe that the city magistrate anticipated riots and ordered a number of the richer merchants to set up soup kitchens for unemployed weavers.[26]

Currency reform and inflation had the effect of redistributing wealth and income. Reform of the gold currency brought a windfall gain of 200 percent to those who held gold currency, mainly substantial merchants, bankers, and landowners. Inflation benefited traders, especially those engaged in the export trade, but brought hardship to those, such as laborers and lower-ranking samurai, whose incomes were relatively fixed. By 1865 the real wages of carpenters in Osaka were half of what they had been in the 1840s,[27] and high prices and falling real incomes produced a wave of protests and riots in both rural and urban areas. Fuel was added to inflation by a large increase in bank credit. Loans by the banking system to the domain administrations between 1850 and 1867 amounted to about 21 million *ryō*, so large an amount that the value of bank credit instruments in terms of gold cash fell by half over the same period despite the threefold increase in the volume of gold currency.

The effects of the opening of trade on production were far-reaching. Production of raw silk doubled between 1858 and 1863, and new silk-reeling technology spread rapidly. New devices such as the Wakao and *zakuri* reelers, some of them water powered, doubled output per worker and produced raw silk of better and more even quality. Comparable advances were made in the production and processing of tea. These and other industrial crops increasingly replaced rice and other staple food crops, despite official restrictions on converting rice land to other uses. The opening of foreign trade and the

---

26 Ishii Takashi, *Bakumatsu bōekishi no kenkyū* (Tokyo: Nihon hyōronsha, 1944), 312, 52–4, 176–85, 318.
27 Shimbo, *Kinsei no bukka to keizai hatten*, p. 276. Although these particular wage data may not be representative, the general lag in wages was considerable.

expectations it generated provided an impetus for change throughout the country, notably in areas outside the economically advanced Kinki and Kantō regions, and greatly accelerated the changes in patterns of production and trade that had been proceeding since the beginning of the century.

The opening of foreign trade precipitated a crisis in relations between the bakufu and the domains. The bakufu's plans to impose national economic controls following the Tempō reforms were frustrated by political and financial weakness and domain opposition. If, however, the bakufu could control foreign trade, it could greatly increase its revenue and acquire the resources to organize a nationwide system of trading under its control and thus shift the balance of power decisively in its favor. Because all the ports opened to foreign trade were in bakufu territory, this was by no means a far-fetched scenario.

The bakufu made its first move early in 1860 as foreign trade was beginning to get under way, by declaring that as an interim measure to avoid domestic shortages – such as were affecting the silk-weaving industry – grains, vegetable oil, vegetable wax, textiles, and raw silk were to be sold to bakufu-controlled bodies in Edo which would determine quotas for export. There is clear evidence that the bakufu was planning a much more comprehensive control system that would have supplanted the domain trading corporations and in effect given it a monopoly of domestic as well as overseas trade.[28] An indication of the potential gains involved can be found in an offer by the Kyoto raw silk dealers' association to pay 500,000 *ryō* a year for the right to control that trade. Had the bakufu succeeded in its plan, its revenue would have increased by up to 50 percent. Even the interim measure, however, ran into immediate and stiff opposition from all sections of the raw silk export trade as well as from the domains, and when Harris warned that any form of control or restriction of exports would constitute a violation of the treaty, the bakufu was forced to withdraw once again and allow direct export sales subject to notification and an export permit. Permits seem to have been given freely until 1863, when the bakufu made another attempt to exercise control through export quotas. The result was a drastic fall in deliveries of raw silk and something approaching chaos in Yokohama, where Japanese silk traders whose quotas were restricted paid domain representatives as much as 18 *ryō* per packhorse load to include their consignments with domain silk against which it seems to have been more difficult to enforce the

---

28 Ishii, *Bakumatsu bōekishi*, pp. 448–67.

quota system. Some resorted to hiring masterless samurai to terrorize the export authorities into issuing licenses. No export permits were processed for about four months, and by February 1864 trade was almost at a halt. Again the bakufu was deluged with complaints from traders, the foreign community, and particularly from domains against whose direct trade the move was ultimately directed. Faced with a warning from the foreign consuls that there was nothing in the treaties to prevent the domains opening their own ports if they wished, the bakufu resumed processing export permits but continued to explore means of enforcing a monopoly of the export trade until October, when the combined foreign flotilla, fresh from the bombardment of Shimonoseki, entered Edo Bay with a show of strength that forced the bakufu to retreat once more.

The bakufu nevertheless continued to explore the idea of a national marketing monopoly right up to its fall, and the question of control of trade was a key factor in forming the attitudes of both the bakufu and individual domains toward foreign relations and the movements leading up to the Restoration.

THE MEIJI RESTORATION: CONTINUITY AND CHANGE

In the context of centuries of Japanese history, the changes following the Restoration appear to have been almost instantaneous and the restrictive apparatus of the old order to have been removed, as it were, at a stroke. But in fact these changes took at least ten turbulent years. The Restoration signaled far-reaching changes but had little immediate impact on the economy other than to exacerbate the existing uncertainty and disruption. Nor did it solve any of the economic problems that had beset the bakufu in its last years. Although the new government appreciated the need for change, the situation was not promising, and for a decade it moved, tentatively at first, from approaching the problems of the economy within the framework inherited from the old system toward entirely new solutions.

One of its first problems was to resolve the struggle for economic control between the central government and the domains. The problem was made more acute by the need to finance the considerable cost of the Restoration itself. Taking up the bakufu's abortive plans to establish a national system of economic control, the Meiji government within six months established an office (Shōhōshi) for the purpose, operating branches (Shōhō kaisho) in Tokyo, Osaka, and Hyōgo. These were organized very much along the lines of the old domain monopolies, with both commercial and financial operations entrusted to merchants of the major trading associations under government supervision. Just as the domains had financed their trading corporations by issuing paper currency, the Meiji government issued its own nonconvertible notes (Dajōkansatsu) through these offices. The system failed and for reasons similar to those that had frustrated earlier attempts by the bakufu. Opposition from the foreign powers prevented control of foreign trade; the new paper currency was not well accepted; and the domains' trading organizations continued to compete with that of the central government.

After only ten months of operation, the Shōhōshi were abolished and replaced by the Tsūhōshi which operated through the trading companies (tsūshō gaisha) and finance companies (kawase gaisha) established in eight major cities. Formed by substantial merchants and bankers such as the Mitsui and Ono groups under government control, their objectives and functions were similar to those of their predecessors. Although they helped to restore some degree of order to Japanese commercial life, by 1872 changing circumstances had rendered them inappropriate. In preparing for reform of the currency from ryō to yen in 1871, the finance companies were ordered to maintain a cash backing of 100 percent for their notes, a requirement that broke some of the participants, and when a new system of national banks was introduced in 1872, they either dissolved or were reorganized as national banks. Abolition of the domains as semiautonomous units in 1871 altered the position of the trading companies by opening the way to entirely new financial and economic policies that would supersede the idea of trade monopolies.[29] After this rather unpromising start, the first decade saw major institutional changes. In retrospect these changes were essential for modern economic growth, but at the time they represented responses to financial necessities rather than a commitment to economic or social progress.

The major preoccupation of the Meiji government was to create a sound fiscal base sufficient for its needs. Neither the bakufu nor a majority of the domains had achieved this, and the new government inherited not only their current fiscal deficits but also a mountain of accumulated debts and further debts that it had itself incurred during the Restoration campaigns. As we have seen, the Meiji government failed in its attempts to augment its income through monopoly corporations, as some domains had done. The most pressing problem was to

---

29 See Shimbo Hiroshi, *Kōbe keizaigaku sōsho*, vol. 7: *Nihon kindai shin'yō seido seiritsushi ron* (Tokyo: Yūhikaku, 1968).

acquire a stable source of tax revenue, and both the predominance of agriculture in the economy and reluctance to arouse further opposition by imposing revolutionary new taxes ensured that this would take the form of a tax on agriculture. Experience both before and after the Restoration clearly indicated that however redistributed or stabilized, agricultural taxes could not be raised much above their existing level without provoking dangerous levels of resistance.

At that rate the new government could expect at least as big a deficit as those of its predecessor unless it could drastically reduce some item of expenditure. Because some 30 percent of revenue went to pay the samurai's stipends, this was an obvious area for consideration. Other savings had been made. Roughly 20 percent of domain revenue had traditionally been taken by the costs of maintaining establishments in Edo under the system of "alternate attendance" (*sankin kōtai*), and this was no longer necessary. Thus if the yield of agricultural tax could be assured, irrespective of fluctuations in harvests and rice prices, and hereditary samurai stipends reduced or abolished, there seemed some hope of meeting the costs of government, even allowing for new commitments.

Attempts to reduce the fiscal burden of samurai stipends began at the end of 1869 when their total was reduced from 13 million *koku* (1 *koku* equals approximately 180 liters) to 9 million *koku*, and in 1871 the total was further reduced to 4.9 million *koku*. With the reform of the land tax, any hope that samurai may have had of retaining rights to income from land was extinguished, and the Conscription Law of 1873 removed their military *raison d'être*. Those who had refused earlier inducements to surrender their entitlements were required to do so in return for a lump-sum payment, mainly in the form of government bonds redeemable by lot over thirty years beginning in the sixth year after issue. This was well below the samurai's expectations, and the Satsuma Rebellion of 1877 was a forceful expression of their dissatisfaction. Over the next few years, inflation further reduced the real value of their compensation, and by the end of 1880 the market value of 7 percent commutation bonds was only 60.7 percent of their face value. In this way the Meiji government greatly reduced its recurrent expenditure for an outlay of ¥173 million in bonds and ¥730,000 in cash. Redemption of such a large bond issue was itself no easy matter, but without commutation of the samurai's stipends, the government's financial situation would have been hopeless. Those samurai who received comparatively large sums were encouraged to invest in the new national banks by a change in the regulations allowing the use of commutation bonds as capital. Some invested in railway or other joint stock companies, but most were reduced to earning their own living or sinking into poverty.

Reform of the agricultural tax system began in 1873 and took nearly six years to complete. The new tax was payable in cash on the assessed value of land, and the taxpayer was given title to his land. To assess the value of the land, the average crop was valued at the prices used to convert tax payments in kind into payment in cash, with some regard to local market conditions. From the gross value of the crop thus calculated were deducted allowances for seed, fertilizer, and national and local taxes to arrive at the value of the net product, which was capitalized at rates varying from 4 to 6 percent to give the assessed land value. The national land tax was set at 3 percent of this figure, and the local tax at one-third of the national tax.

There has been some discussion as to whether the farmers' tax burden became heavier or lighter as a result of the change. The government's intention was that the total tax yield be as nearly as possible unchanged. Before the reform, however, many domains imposed a number of more-or-less minor taxes in addition to the *seiso*, or tax proper. Villages were also responsible for local works, such as the building and maintenance of roads and bridges, as well as for their own administrative expenses. Because the extent of these is unknown and in any case varied from village to village, a direct comparison is impossible, but it seems likely that the new tax as a proportion of output was no higher, and in most cases lighter, than the old. Because the incidence of the new tax was on the whole more equitable, however, there may well have been cases of previously lightly taxed individuals' having to pay more. Nevertheless there was a good deal of opposition to the new tax, and in 1877 the rate of national tax was reduced to 2.5 percent and the local tax to one-fifth of that rate. This lowered the tax burden considerably, but over the following four years on-farm prices of agricultural products almost doubled while the land tax remained the same. Although there is no indication that the volume of agricultural production fell – it probably rose – the burden of the land tax as a proportion of farm output was by then well under half what it had been before the Restoration.

Although the object of the land tax reform was to secure a stable source of revenue, its effects went far beyond that. Land became a capital asset that could be freely and legally sold, and with taxes fixed in money terms, landowners – and not overlords – received the benefits from agricultural improvements, specialization, falling transport costs, and price rises. These incentives could be expected to have resulted in some increase in the first half of the Meiji period, but it is difficult to measure. Because these benefits went to the landowners, rather than to the cultivating tenants, the more land that a farmer owned in these circumstances, the more he would benefit, and the result was a noticeable concentration of landholdings and an increase in tenancy over this period.

Despite these drastic measures, the government was still heavily in deficit, and between the end of 1877 and the end of 1880 the government note issue rose from ¥105.8 million to ¥124.9 million, largely to cover the cost of suppressing the Satsuma Rebellion. Relaxation of the national bank regulations intended to facilitate the issue of commutation bonds allowed an increase in bank notes over the same period from ¥13.4 million to ¥34.4 million. The paper currency in circulation thus rose by a third in three years, and by the beginning of 1881 it was circulating at a discount of 70 percent against coin.

In the midst of its fiscal problems, the government somehow found the means to start building the infrastructure of communications essential to further development. The government regarded this as a matter of urgency, partly for internal security reasons and partly to forestall foreign investors who had shown a keen interest in direct investment in this area. Beginning with the Tokyo–Yokohama railway financed by a foreign loan, 64 miles of government railways had been built by 1877, and 2,827 miles of telegraph line had been installed by the same year. A semigovernment shipping company was formed in 1870 but failed after about a year of operation. This was followed by a mail steamer service using ships inherited from the bakufu and the domains, but this also failed. In 1875 the government handed over thirty ships free of charge to Iwasaki Yatarō's Mitsubishi Company, along with an operating subsidy of over ¥200,000 a year. This measure too was prompted by internal security considerations and anxiety to eliminate foreign shipping companies, the American Pacific Mail Line and the British P & O Steamship Company which had captured the coastal trade between the treaty ports. Within a year the foreign shipping companies were convinced that their role was over, and further subsidies to Mitsubishi for services during the Satsuma Rebellion put it on the road to becoming one of Japan's largest enterprises and a key participant in the construction of modern industry and commerce.

In land transport, the government-controlled system of packhorses based on post stations was abolished in 1871, and the business was opened to private enterprise. The old system of official couriers was retained with little more than a change of name for the first few years, but a modern-style postal service between Tokyo and Osaka was inaugurated in 1871. In 1872 there were still only 21 post offices, but the number rose to 3,224 by 1874, and in 1877 Japan joined the Universal Postal Union.

In addition to providing these essential physical services, the government created the institutional framework for reorganizing the banking system which culminated in the establishment of a central bank, the Bank of Japan, in 1882. The old financial system, which had served Japan's needs well for many years, had been left in disarray by the events of the Restoration. The government also provided the legal basis for insurance and joint stock companies and encouraged their formation and took the initiative in founding chambers of commerce and trade associations. Until 1885, government activity in the field of infrastructure was at least as great a contribution to economic development as was direct government investment in and promotion of modern industry.

ECONOMIC DEVELOPMENT, 1868–1885

National economic statistics before the 1890s are not available, and although estimates of national income aggregates and levels of production have been prepared back to 1878, the margins for error are great,[30] and the estimating procedures involve assumptions about economic relationships for which little evidence exists. An attempt at quantitative economic analysis of this period would therefore give a spurious impression of accuracy.

The best-documented and most conspicuous area of industrial development is the establishment of new industries based on imported technology. In terms of their proportion of Japan's industrial output at the time, their contribution was negligible, but as vehicles for introducing new technology and modes of production, their long-run significance was immense.

The Meiji government inherited a number of Western-style ironworks, munitions plants, and shipyards from the bakufu and some domains that had developed them for defense purposes.[31] The Saga domain had built Japan's first successful reverberatory iron furnace in

---

[30] See Nakamura Takafusa, *Nihon keizai: Sono seichō to kōzō*, 2nd ed. (Tokyo: Tokyo daigaku shuppankai, 1980), pp. 12–13.
[31] See Thomas C. Smith, *Political Change and Industrial Development in Japan: Government Enterprise, 1868–1880* (Stanford, Calif.: Stanford University Press, 1955).

1850 and cast iron guns in considerable numbers from 1853. Satsuma, Mito, and the bakufu itself followed suit. The bakufu's shipyard at Nagasaki built a steamer as early as 1857, and a comprehensive foundry, workshops, and shipyard were under construction at Yokosuka at the time of the Restoration. Satsuma, Saga, and Mito had built steamships, and several other domains had built Western-style sailing vessels. Just before the Restoration, Satsuma had installed a modern integrated cotton-spinning and weaving plant, and Saga had modernized its Takashima coal mine with British technical assistance.

Thus the new government found itself in possession of all Japan's munitions plants and shipyards. In addition it acquired about half of the country's forests and all the major mines, including the Sado gold mines, the Ikuno silver mines, the Miike and Takashima coal mines, the Ani and Innai copper mines, and the Kamaishi, Nakakosaka, and Kosaka iron mines.

Between 1868 and 1881 the government continued to develop these facilities and to establish new ones. Its motives were primarily twofold. First, it gave priority to developing defense industries to meet what it saw as a pressing foreign threat. It keenly appreciated the important role of military power in the negotiations connected with the opening and the conduct of foreign trade and was determined that future negotiations should be on the basis of equality. It was for such reasons that priority was given to munitions plants, although in retrospect their contribution to the development of general engineering proved to be significant. Second, the foreign trade surpluses of the pre-Restoration period soon gave way to mounting deficits. From 1868 to 1880 these deficits totaled ¥77 million, and the prospects for balanced trade were not bright. Foreign yarns and textiles, which in the 1870s made up half of the value of all imports, were much cheaper and of better quality than the Japanese products, and with the demand for them rising, there was an urgent need for import-replacement industries in Japan. Without adequate supporting infrastructure and services, technological background, and the means of mobilizing investment funds on the comparatively large scale required, private Japanese investors could not be relied on to undertake such a task. Direct foreign involvement could not be expected in import-replacement industries, and although it might well have been forthcoming in the production of bulky construction materials such as glass, bricks, and cement, Japanese were convinced that the superiority of foreign enterprise would overwhelm local business and be difficult to control.

It was for these reasons that the government, starting from the Sakai cotton textile mill inherited from the Satsuma domain, bought two more two-thousand-spindle cotton spinning plants in 1878 and installed them in Aichi and Hiroshima. The following year it bought ten more such plants for sale on very easy terms to private investors, mainly people already prominent in the traditional cotton textile industry, and financed the purchase of three more. The indifferent profit performance of these plants was attributed to their small scale, and so later spinning mills were larger. The Senju woolen mill was founded in 1879 for the same import-replacement purposes.

Third, the government hoped that its new nonmilitary industries would have a demonstration effect in familiarizing Japanese with factory production, training administrative and technical staff, and accumulating experience that could be made generally available. Whether or not these industries were expected to make profits is not clear, but in fact most ran at a heavy loss. The government was also active in the promotion and technical improvement of export industries and agriculture. The Tomioka silk filature was established in 1872 to improve technology in Japan's leading export industry, and a number of experimental stations and farms investigated the most modern overseas technology.

It has been estimated that over ¥36.4 million was invested in government enterprises between 1868 and 1881,[32] and in the difficult fiscal circumstances of the time this was a substantial commitment. As we shall see, the nonmilitary enterprises were sold off in the 1880s, and their transfer to private hands was an important factor in the formation of "Meiji capitalism."

The contribution of the new industries to production in the early Meiji period was, however, minimal, and agriculture and traditional industry continued along pre-Restoration lines. Estimation of agricultural production for this period is a serious problem, with important implications for our understanding of the growth process of the following decades. Ohkawa estimated the average annual value of agricultural production between 1878 and 1882 at ¥432 million in current prices.[33] Nakamura, basing his arguments on a reexamination of crop yields and reported acreage, raised this estimate by as much as 80 percent.[34] Ohkawa later revised his estimate to give a value about

---

[32] Ibid., p. 69.
[33] Kazushi Ohkawa, *The Growth Rate of the Japanese Economy Since 1878* (Tokyo: Kinokuniya, 1957).
[34] James I. Nakamura, *Agricultural Production and the Economic Development of Japan 1873–1922* (Princeton, N.J.: Princeton University Press, 1966).

50 percent higher in real terms than his earlier estimate.[35] The upward revisions were certainly in the right direction, but the question can hardly be said to have been settled.

In 1874 the government ordered a survey of physical production on lines similar to those carried out by the bakufu and the domains before the Restoration.[36] It revealed that agricultural products formed 60 percent of physical output, industrial products 30 percent, and the products of extractive industries (forestry, fishing, and mining) 9 percent. There is a good deal of double counting involved, as the value of silk textiles, for example, includes the value of the raw silk used in their production, which in turn includes the value of the cocoons from which it was reeled.

Of the total value of crops produced, rice accounted for 63 percent, other food crops 23 percent, and industrial crops 12 percent. Most crops were cultivated to some extent in most parts of the country, but production was regionally specialized to the extent that for most crops, about one-ninth of the sixty-three prefectures produced between them one-third to a half of national output. Industrial output consisted mainly of *sake* and processed foods (42 percent) and yarn and textiles (28 percent). The value of *sake* produced was astonishingly large, more than the value of all silk and cotton textiles and three times the value of raw silk output. Commercial production in the economically advanced regions of Kinki, Shikoku, and Kantō was about three times as much per prefecture as in the relatively backward regions of Tōhoku, Kyushu, and the Japan Sea coast.

A survey of the occupational distribution of households in the same year listed 77 percent as "agricultural," with only 3.7 percent (mostly carpenters) as "industrial," 6.7 percent as "commercial," and 9 percent as "miscellaneous, servants, and employees." Clearly a large proportion of handicraft production and trade was the work of households listed as "agricultural."

A survey of nongovernment "factories" in 1884 showed that of 1,981 establishments, 1,237 were in rural villages. Over a third of all "factories" had no more than five workers, and only 176 of them employed more than fifty. Only 72 were steam powered; 47 percent were water powered; and the rest were operated entirely by hand. By industry, textiles accounted for 61 percent, ceramics for 12 percent,

---

35 Ōkawa Kazushi, ed., *Chōki keizai tōkei*, vol. 1: *Kokumin shotoku* (Tokyo: Tōyō keizai shimpōsha, 1974).
36 This and the following paragraph are based on Yamaguchi Kazuo, *Meiji zenki keizai no bunseki* (Tokyo: Tokyo daigaku shuppankai, 1956), pp. 1–73.

food processing for 9 percent, and metalworking industries for 8 percent.[37]

The outlines that emerge from these surveys are similar to our impressions of Japanese economic life in the 1850s and 1860s. Advances in production of raw silk and tea in response to export demand, some diffusion of indigenous technology, greater specialization, and recovery from the disruption surrounding the Restoration probably raised the real value of farm output above the levels of the early 1860s. Consumption of cotton textiles rose faster than imports, indicating both growth in the domestic industry and some rise in standards of living. Insufficient though the evidence is, however, there are no signs of drastic change or of a sudden spurt in Japanese economic activity.

THE TRANSITION AND ITS NATURE

By 1880 it was clear that inflation was not only a serious fiscal problem but was also hampering economic development. The adverse balance of payments had led to a loss of ¥60 million to ¥70 million of specie, and because silver was depreciating abroad faster than in Japan, most of this was in the form of gold. Japan's reserves of specie had fallen so low that they provided only 4.5 percent backing for the note issue.

When Matsukata Masayoshi became minister of finance in 1881, he took on the task, begun by Ōkuma, of reducing the volume of paper currency in circulation and restoring its parity with specie. Matsukata later recalled the situation as follows:

At that time [1880] we fell into a condition which filled all classes of the country with anxiety. The real income of the government was reduced by nearly one-half. Among the people, those who lived on interest from government bonds, pensions, and other fixed incomes were suddenly reduced to dire straits. Bonds dropped sharply while commodity prices, especially the price of rice, rose to new heights. The land tax was in reality sharply reduced, while the value of land appreciated greatly. The farmers, who were the only class to profit from these circumstances, took on luxurious habits, causing a great increase in the consumption of luxury goods.... Consequently imports from foreign countries were increased and the nation's specie supply further depleted. Merchants, dazzled by the extreme fluctuations in prices, all aimed at making huge speculative profits and gave no heed to productive undertakings. As a result, interest rates were so high that no one could plan an industrial undertaking that required any considerable capital.[38]

---

37 Ibid., Table 17 facing p. 104.   38 Quoted from Smith, *Political Change*, pp. 96–7.

By drastic retrenchment, new taxes, and skillful financial management helped by what seems to have been a fortuitous cyclical downturn in business conditions,[39] Matsukata's measures reduced the note issue from ¥159.4 million in 1881 to ¥118.5 million by 1885, slightly below the 1877 level. Specie backing rose to 35.7 percent, and the value of paper currency returned very nearly to par. The process produced a severe recession that reversed many of the effects of the inflationary boom, transferring resources back to the government, the banking system, and stronger and more competitive businesses, especially those with government connections who ultimately benefited from the sale of government enterprises forced by financial stringency. The growth of the traditional economy was checked as deflation helped turn resources toward the sectors where they would ultimately be most productively employed. Whether intentionally or not, the Matsukata deflation established the strategy of giving priority to the modern sector which eventually proved successful in its own terms, although inevitably at some cost to the average Japanese both at the time and for many decades later.

But financial management, however skillful, cannot by itself increase the availability of real resources for development. Growth in production no doubt provided some, but what evidence we have suggests that this growth was not nearly as fast as was once thought. The economic transition of the Meiji period thus required some reallocation of existing resources, and the changes that occurred between the Restoration and the end of the Matsukata deflation in fact resulted in the redistribution of both income and wealth.

The commutation of samurai stipends effected a substantial redistribution of income. Before the Restoration, samurai incomes in terms of rice had totaled about nine million *koku*. After allowing for the cost of providing the services that they had performed and of providing for their basic consumption needs, commutation converted income to capital to the value of some three million *koku* a year, enough to cover over half of the total investment in the early Meiji period. Reform of the land tax and the subsequent sequence of inflation and deflation tended to concentrate income in the hands of those rural landowners and businessmen who were likely to invest it.

The monetary changes of the Restoration, particularly the abolition of the silver credit unit, resulted in a large transfer of assets away from

---

[39] Teranishi Shigeo, "Matsukata defure no makuro keizaigakuteki bunseki," *Gendai keizai* 47 (Spring 1982): 78–92.

those who held their assets in that form, mainly conservative bankers and wholesalers closely associated with the old economic order. In the post-Restoration settlement of the bakufu's and the domains' debts, their creditors were forced to write off an estimated ¥47 million, thus transferring assets from the traditional banking system to the government. In the process of redeeming domain paper currency (*hansatsu*), compensation was only about a third of their face value, inflicting heavy losses on the rural population who held them. Most of these changes tended to transfer income and wealth from consumers to potential investors.[40]

One of the most interesting questions that arises from a study of the Japanese economy in the nineteenth century is that of the relationship between the pre-Restoration economy and the transition to modern economic growth. A number of studies have tried to find features and trends in the pre-Restoration economy that might be considered "preconditions" of modern development. In fact these are not very evident. Levels of income per head were on the high side for a preindustrial economy, but they were far below the initial levels in any other country that achieved modern economic growth in the nineteenth century. Moreover, Nakamura's thesis that the Japanese growth rate at this time was not particularly high implies that Japan's success depended significantly and perhaps critically on the ability of the Meiji government and its supporters to restrict consumption in the interests of industrial and military investment. Indeed, consumption over the whole period up to 1945 appears so low and so weakly correlated with national income as to be difficult to reconcile with the usual experience in a free economy.

There has been almost a surfeit of discussion and controversy among Japanese scholars about the nature of Japanese capitalism and the workings of the Japanese economic system, but it has not been widely reflected in Western scholarship, and possibly for good reason. To what extent, however, are we justified in analyzing Japan's early economic growth as though it had taken place in the context of a free-market economy? As we have seen, until the 1870s at least, it was very far from that. Byron Marshall argued that the ethical foundations of classical free-enterprise utilitarianism – faith in the "invisible hand" and the philosophy of laissez faire – were unacceptable in prewar Ja-

---

40 E. S. Crawcour, "Nihon keizai ikō no arikata: Kinsei kara kindai e," in Shimbo Hiroshi and Yasuba Yasukichi, eds., *Kindai ikōki no Nihon keizai* (*Sūryō keizaishi ronshū*, Vol. 2; Tokyo: Nihon keizai shimbunsha, 1979), pp. 15–28.

pan and that business activity was rationalized in terms of service to the community and the state.[41]

Although traditional economic activity, and the small-business sector that succeeded it, became increasingly free and competitive, Japanese governments have, in the areas that they considered most important, generally put more faith in manipulation than in free competition and the market mechanism. This chapter has suggested that the heritage of manipulation may have contributed as much to Japan's economic development as did the heritage of individual enterprise. As a comparative late developer, Japan was able to take advantage not only of advanced industrial technology but also of advanced techniques of manipulation. Whether the latter should be counted among the "advantages of backwardness" is an interesting question and one that should exercise the minds of all who study the modern development of Japan.

41 Byron K. Marshall, *Capitalism and Nationalism in Pre-war Japan: The Ideology of the Business Elite, 1868–1941* (Stanford, Calif.: Stanford University Press, 1967).

CHAPTER 10

MEIJI POLITICAL INSTITUTIONS

The overthrow of the Tokugawa in 1867–68 carried implications of important changes in the political institutions of Japan, as well as in the location of power. Yet when Tokugawa Yoshinobu (Keiki) resigned as shogun in November 1867, this did not seem by any means inevitable. He might well have been succeeded, so contemporaries believed, by some kind of baronial council, in which he would still hold a preponderant place, thereby putting the authority of the shogun into the hands of a group of great lords, of whom he would be one. The palace coup d'état of January 3, 1868, engineered by Satsuma and Chōshū, ended that prospect, at least in the sense of ensuring that the Tokugawa would be excluded from any successor regime to which those domains belonged. There followed some months of civil war, which confirmed and extended Japan's political polarization, ensuring that all the lords and most of their retainers had to commit themselves to one side or the other. After this there was no going back. Because the Tokugawa had been defeated and there had emerged no single victorious feudal lord who could aspire to the office of shogun – Satsuma came closest – the country's new rulers had then to work out an alternative framework through which authority could be exercised. Japanese tradition and recent history ensured that it must focus on the emperor, but devising institutions appropriate to it was to take a whole generation, that is, until the promulgation of the constitution in 1889 and the associated regulations concerning central and local government.

There are two contexts within which these events can be examined. One is that of modernization and the pursuit of national strength. The men who came to power in 1868, like the politics that brought them to it, had been deeply influenced by an awareness of Japan's weakness in the face of the Western threat. One important motive for the reforms they undertook was the desire to evolve ways of meeting that threat and averting the danger of a total Japanese submission to imperialism. Politically, this translated into a search for strong government and national unity. Both strength and unity involved the West, though not necessarily in the same way. Whereas unity depended in some degree on Japaneseness, that is, on the maintenance of certain traditional attitudes and the institutions embodying them, the strength of government required elements of Western technology, like modern weapons and communications. To some it seemed that it might be the more readily ensured by adopting Western institutional models as well. Military organization was a case in point. Laws and bureaucratic structure were others. Moreover, Western models had a measure of propaganda and diplomatic value, insofar as their adoption might persuade foreigners of Japan's right to the label "civilized," and hence to their respect. There was here a question of direct political significance, because the tension – or the choice – between tradition and modernity aroused powerful emotions. Historians of Meiji political institutions must confront it when they consider, as they must, the nature and extent of foreign influences on Japanese life.

It is also necessary to take a view on the subject of political typology. If one regards the Meiji Restoration as initiating a process by which state institutions were adjusted to underlying shifts in the distribution of wealth and social standing, it is possible to characterize what followed it in two different ways. The first is to identify the Western experience as the norm: to stipulate that it was one in which the development of capitalism was accompanied by an extension of political rights to a larger proportion of the population, usually through an elected parliament; then to measure Japan's subsequent achievements in terms of how fully and how quickly they approximated those of Western democratic societies. Many Meiji politicians tended to take this line, sometimes in criticism, sometimes in praise of what was done. So have some later historians, both Japanese and Western. Starting from quite different assumptions, as Japanese Marxists do, one can treat Meiji institutions as having been both objectionable and differently motivated. The argument, briefly stated, is that the emergence of capitalism in Japan – there is some disagreement about dating the phenomenon – brought an inevitable movement toward a bourgeois revolution, such as had been manifested in Europe under similar circumstances, but that the Meiji Restoration provided a means by which the movement was halted, although powerful elements of feudalism still survived. This left Japan at a stage labeled Meiji "absolutism" (*zettaishugi*), defined as one in which political groups associated with the emperor and the military were able to achieve a balance between the feudal landowners and the bourgeoisie, playing off one against the other and thereby securing absolute power for themselves. This formulation is central to the Marxist critique of modern Japanese society, as well as to its explanation of the nature of Japanese imperialism and the origins of World War II.

The two contexts, which can for convenience be described as those of modernization and democracy, are sometimes connected through the question of Japan's relationship with the West. One can illustrate this with reference to German influence on Meiji political institutions, especially on the constitution of 1889. This influence can be explained in two distinct ways. One can attribute it to a basic similarity in the social structure and political development of the two countries, which brought the Meiji leadership to recognize that German problems and German solutions – rather than British or American problems and solutions – were relevant to Japan. Alternatively, one can argue that the similarity is in the situation rather than in the societies: Japan, like Germany, as a "late developer" in the catching-up phase, found authoritarian government a more effective framework for modernization than democracy was. Put in this way, the problem clearly extends beyond the bounds of a discussion of political institutions, narrowly defined. Nor can an answer to it be wholly restricted to the Meiji period.

INITIAL DECISIONS

Japan's political tradition was not exclusively feudal. In the seventh and eighth centuries there had come into existence a form of government, modeled on that of China, that asserted a claim to rule the whole of Japan through a hierarchy of appointed officials. It is true that imperial power was always less than imperial pretensions; but when the emperor was eventually reduced to a merely ceremonial role, first by the reassertion of aristocratic privilege under the Fujiwara and then by the rise of de facto feudal rule under successive houses of shogun, he remained the nominal head of the governmental structure, largely because it was more convenient to use him than to find another source of legitimacy. Accordingly, Japan's political institutions remained notionally monarchical and autocratic, like those of medieval Europe; the shogun closely controlled the court but acted in the emperor's name. This tradition was reinforced during the Tokugawa period by two developments. The first was the spread of a knowledge of Confucian philosophy within the feudal class, tending to increase the bureaucratic element in Japanese feudalism and to create a wider awareness of the differences between the Chinese and Japanese imperial systems.

The second was a resurgence of Shinto ideas, carrying with it a new emphasis on the emperor's divine descent.

Thus those who sought to replace feudal government (the bakufu) did not have to look outside Japan to find an instrument ready for their purpose. In all the disputes that followed the opening of the ports, men turned to the emperor for validation of their actions, thereby giving the court a new contemporary importance.[1] It became clear that any regime succeeding the Tokugawa would have to act in the emperor's name, as the shogun had always done. Moreover, as criticism of the Tokugawa shaded into criticism of the system – on the grounds that it promoted disunity and deprived Japan of effective leadership against the West – the various alternatives that were propounded all appealed in some way to the emperor's authority. Some, put forward by samurai activists of the early 1860s, envisaged an increase in the actual wealth and influence of the court within a continuing feudalism, so as to afford opportunities for the advancement of those whose low feudal status – and illegal actions – denied it to them as things stood. Yet others cherished ambitions of a return to the prefeudal ideal, when the emperor's government had been the government of Japan.

What gave a degree of realism to the last of these was evidence of a possible stalemate in the struggle among competing feudal alliances. In the closing months of 1867 it seemed by no means certain that the various opponents of the Tokugawa could be held together long enough to overthrow the bakufu. In fact, Iwakura Tomomi and Ōkubo Toshimichi, the one a court noble, the other a Satsuma samurai, who organized the final stages of the Restoration movement, found it necessary to bring into existence for that purpose a coalition of feudal lords, whose political objectives were in many respects diverse. It was Iwakura who drew up a draft of a new political structure for Japan, the first that can be attributed to those who were to have a central part in the formation of the early Meiji government.[2] It set out the ultimate desideratum as being "to make the sixty-odd provinces of the country into a single imperial stronghold and so ensure the people's unity." Iwakura recognized, however, that this would require an independent military force at the disposal of the central authority, which the court could not provide or command. He therefore compro-

---

[1] I have discussed these topics at some length in chaps. 12 and 13 of *The Meiji Restoration* (Stanford, Calif.: Stanford University Press, 1972).
[2] The Japanese text, dated 1867, third month, is printed in *Iwakura Tomomi kankei monjo*, 8 vols. (Tokyo: Nihon shiseki kyōkai, 1927–35), vol. 1, pp. 288–300.

mised by putting the proposals in a feudal framework. The daimyo were to retain their lands but be subordinated to the court through a supervisory level of regional officials, "men of talent appointed from among the imperial princes, court nobles, and feudal lords."

Because of its authorship, this document can be taken as an authoritative statement of intent on the part of key political figures, though it was never put to or agreed by the members of the antibakufu coalition. Yet it was not the only influence that has to be taken into account in examining the background to early Meiji institutions. For several years the Japanese had been acquiring a knowledge of Western political ideas, both from Western residents in Japan and from Japanese students sent to Europe and America. Most of the advice based on them was channeled to the bakufu, which used it principally to devise a number of expedients that might serve to reconcile feudal opinion to a continuation in some form of the shogun's power. At the end of 1867, for example, Nishi Amane, who had spent two and a half years studying at Leiden, produced at Edo's request an outline of a constitution for Japan, under which the emperor's largely ceremonial functions would be specified and defined and the bakufu would retain executive authority. Legislation was to be entrusted to a bicameral assembly of daimyo and samurai, whose recommendations would be subject to imperial approval, obtained through the shogun.[3]

For different reasons, the same kind of devices appealed to some of the bakufu's opponents. It was already evident by the autumn of 1867 that Satsuma and Chōshū would seek to dominate the coalition of antibakufu lords and push it into more extreme measures than many would wish. The probability was that success, if achieved by their efforts, would leave them in a position to control the new government. Their less powerful allies consequently sought means of forestalling this eventuality, occasionally using a Western-style constitutionalist argument for the purpose. Thus Tosa, urging Keiki to resign in September 1867, put forward plans for a political structure, under which the right to govern Japan would revert to the imperial court, acting through a bicameral council of lords, samurai, and commoners.[4] The advantage of this from Tosa's point of view was that it would eliminate

---

[3] Thomas Havens, *Nishi Amane and Modern Japanese Thought* (Princeton, N.J.: Princeton University Press, 1970), pp. 62–3. The most detailed study of the influence of Western political thought before 1871 can be found in Asai Kiyoshi, *Meiji ishin to gunken shisō* (Tokyo: Ganshōdō, 1939).

[4] Marius B. Jansen, *Sakamoto Ryōma and the Meiji Restoration* (Princeton, N.J.: Princeton University Press, 1961), pp. 300–1, 316–17, gives a translation of the text of the proposal, together with the terms of the earlier agreement with Satsuma on which it was based.

the bakufu, while preventing its replacement by an equally unwelcome hegemony on the part of Satsuma and Chōshū. In other words, constitutionalism, which the bakufu saw as a cloak for continued Tokugawa rule, Tosa saw as a restraint on dangerous rivals.

Despite Tosa's efforts, events in the winter of 1867-8 gave the advantage increasingly to Satsuma and Chōshū. They did not do so decisively enough, however, to make those domains independent of the other great lords who had cooperated in the final coup d'état, with the result that in its early decisions, the Meiji government manifested a readiness to conciliate the widest possible spectrum of political views. This is apparent in the wording of the emperor's Charter Oath, issued on April 6, 1868. The document went through several drafts. The first, prepared by Yuri Kimimasa of Echizen in February, following court discussions about the government's need for financial and political support, gave some emphasis to the part to be played by commoners as well as samurai. Fukuoka Kōtei of Tosa then revised it along the lines of the earlier Tosa proposals for an assembly, giving greater attention to provisions that would secure a closing of the ranks within the ruling groups in Kyoto. Finally, several weeks later, the wording was modified – becoming even less precise – by Satsuma and Chōshū members of the government's inner circle. As issued, the text read as follows:

(i) An assembly widely convoked shall be established and all matters of state shall be decided by public discussion.

(ii) All classes high and low shall unite in vigorously promoting the economy and welfare of the nation.

(iii) All civil and military officials and the common people as well shall be allowed to fulfil their aspirations, so that there may be no discontent among them.

(iv) Base customs of former times shall be abandoned and all actions shall conform to the principles of international justice.

(v) Knowledge shall be sought throughout the world and thus shall be strengthened the foundation of the imperial polity.[5]

Two points need to be made concerning this. One is that it is an appeal for unity, not a statement of immediate policy, despite the guarded references to a new kind of relationship with the West. Implicit in it is a rejection of the bakufu's overbearing habits and a promise to avoid them for the future, though without a specific indica-

---

5 This is the English version given in Ryōsuke Ishii, *Japanese Legislation in the Meiji Era* (Tokyo: Tōyō bunko, 1969), p. 145. The fullest discussion of the drafting of the document can be found in Inada Masatsugu, *Meiji kempō seiritsu-shi*, 2 vols. (Tokyo: Yūhikaku, 1960-2), vol. 2, pp. 1-22.

tion of how this would be done. The second point is that it is an "imperial" document, not merely because it refers to "the imperial polity," but still more so because it takes the form of an undertaking by the emperor personally, not through some *kampaku* or shogun acting in his name. This signaled a change in Japanese constitutional practice, by which the emperor was to be much more closely associated with the actions of the state than for several centuries past. By public appearances, like reviewing troops or naval forces; by granting audiences to foreign envoys; by giving his name to a growing list of decrees and rescripts outlining various aspects of policy; by making awards to deserving members of the population, especially officials – in all these ways, the emperor indicated that what was done was done by the emperor's will, making opposition to it a form of lèse-majesté. For the Meiji leadership, especially as power fell more and more into the hands of relatively low-born samurai, some such prop was a pragmatic necessity, as Japanese society was one in which feudal loyalties remained strong and status still depended above all on birth. Nevertheless, whether or not intentionally, the practice carried important institutional implications, which the 1889 constitution eventually spelled out.[6]

The break with constitutional custom is also seen in the arrangements concerning official apppointments early in 1868. During the Tokugawa period the bakufu had exercised its control over the court through a range of offices, headed by that of *kampaku*, which had originated with the Fujiwara. These offices, like the Fujiwara families whose members inherited them, were therefore deemed to be part of the probakufu establishment. This made it desirable for the Restoration government to avoid using them. Fortunately it had a means of doing so that did not involve a prolonged search for new concepts and terminology. The slogan "restoration of imperial rule" (*ōsei fukko*), under which power had been seized, was soon taken to justify not only the working out of a new role for the emperor but also a reversion to a system of court administration dating from pre-Fujiwara days, that is, to the Chinese-style structure that had been introduced in the seventh and eighth centuries.

The first step was the negative one of dismantling the old order. On

---

6 On the emperor, see John W. Hall, "A Monarch for Modern Japan," in Robert Ward, ed., *Political Development in Modern Japan* (Princeton, N.J.: Princeton University Press, 1968), pp. 11–64; and Herschel Webb, "The Development of an Orthodox Attitude Toward the Imperial Institution in the Nineteenth Century," in Marius B. Jansen, ed., *Changing Japanese Attitudes Toward Modernization* (Princeton, N.J.: Princeton University Press, 1965), pp. 167–91.

January 3, 1868, once the approaches to the palace had been secured, a hastily convened imperial council – excluding bakufu sympathizers – abolished all existing senior offices and substituted for them a three-tier hierarchy of officials and advisors. At the top was a chief executive (*sōsai*), who was an imperial prince. Below him came a group of senior councilors (*gijō*), comprising a few high-ranking court nobles, together with the principal feudal lords of the anti-Tokugawa coalition. Below this again were the junior councilors (*san'yo*): lower-ranking court nobles, plus samurai from those domains whose lords were appointed as *gijō*. The functions to be performed by these men were not at first made clear, as the primary purpose of the appointments was to hold together the victorious coalition in the face of bakufu resistance. This is evident from the huge number of appointments made during the first five months. By June 11, when there was a major reorganization following the surrender of Edo to the imperial forces, 30 men had held office as *gijō*: 5 imperial princes; 12 court nobles; and 13 daimyo (or their close relatives). The *san'yo* were even more numerous, totaling 102: 43 court nobles, 6 court officials not of noble rank, and 53 samurai, the great majority being from the middle and upper levels of the samurai class.[7]

It was not until the middle of February 1868, when the departments of state were established, that these officials were given something to administer. The departments had eighth-century names and modern-sounding functions – home, foreign, and military affairs, finance and justice – except for the department of Shinto religion, whose special standing served to underline the importance of the emperor's prerogatives, deriving from divine descent. A general supervisory department (Sōsaikyoku) was added later in the month. All department heads and their chief subordinates were senior or junior councilors. This in theory gave members of the council an executive role; but in practice, of course, despite the growing list of domains that had "submitted" to the emperor, virtually all Japan was still ruled by feudal lords, and so the principal task of imperial officials was to persuade the daimyo to cooperate in fighting a civil war. The formal submission of Tokugawa Keiki in May changed all this by putting the Tokugawa lands, or a

---

[7] I have analyzed these and other appointments in "Councillors of Samurai Origin in the Early Meiji Government, 1868–69," *Bulletin of the School of Oriental and African Studies* 20 (1957): 89–103. There are lists of officials in Robert A. Wilson, *Genesis of the Meiji Government in Japan 1868–1871* (Berkeley and Los Angeles: University of California Press, 1957). The question of the origins of Meiji officialdom is also discussed at length in Bernard S. Silberman, *Ministers of Modernization: Elite Mobility in the Meiji Restoration 1868–1873* (Tucson: University of Arizona Press, 1964).

large part of them, at the court's disposal. In June, therefore, came a revision of the government structure. The number of departments was reduced to five – religion, military affairs, foreign affairs, justice, finance – and they were put under the control of the Executive Council (Gyōseikan), headed by two court nobles, Sanjō Sanetomi and Iwakura Tomomi, who had long had close political ties with Chōshū and Satsuma, respectively. Senior administrative posts continued to be held by senior and junior councilors, but the numbers of these were substantially reduced. In the fourteen months until the next reorganization there were only twenty-one *gijō* and twenty-two *san'yo* (nineteen of whom were representatives of key domains, mostly men with administrative experience).

To compensate others for the loss of status implied by this streamlining of the system, a legislature (Giseikan) was created, consisting of an upper chamber of *gijō* and *san'yo* and a lower chamber of nominees from the domains and from former Tokugawa territories now administered by the court. This body, renamed the Kōgisho early in 1869, became a sounding board of feudal opinion, through which the Meiji leadership hoped to keep in touch with the ideas of the men to whom it still looked for political and military support. Significantly, however, such men came to Kyoto only in an advisory capacity. Insofar as Japan had a central government at all, it consisted of the group of court nobles, feudal lords, and samurai who held office as *gijō* and *san'yo*. It is convenient at this point to identify its most influential members.

No other court nobles were as important as Sanjō and Iwakura, who continued to act as senior ministers for several more years. Among the daimyo, Matsudaira Keiei (Yoshinaga, Shungaku) of Echizen, Date Munenari of Uwajima, and Nabeshima Naomasa of Hizen, all "men of ability," remained in major posts until 1871. The rest, nearly all figureheads in their own domains, soon gave way to men of lower rank, mostly samurai. Of these, the key figures were the men who had held together the antibakufu movement in the immediate pre-Restoration years: Ōkubo Toshimichi and Saigō Takamori of Satsuma, Kido Takayoshi (Kōin) of Chōshū, and Gotō Shōjirō of Tosa. They were joined by others from the same domains, some having special skills, like a knowledge of the West, and some being younger men, just emerging into prominence. The best known were Terashima Munenori, Matsukata Masayoshi, and Ōyama Iwao from Satsuma; Inoue Kaoru, Itō Hirobumi, and Yamagata Aritomo from Chōshū; and Fukuoka Kōtei and Itagaki Taisuke from Tosa. The Hizen domain had been "neutral" in the earlier struggles, but its connection with Nagasaki had given it a place of some importance in the introduction of Western military technology. Recognition of this brought several Hizen samurai, as well as their lord, into the early Meiji government, notably Ōkuma Shigenobu and Soejima Taneomi. There were perhaps twelve or fifteen other samurai, largely from the same domains, who also held posts of some responsibility.

The ministerial changes of the next few years continued the trend, established in 1868-9, of dispensing with the men whose original apppointment had been designed, either as a gesture toward groups that had a "public image" role to play, like the court nobles, or as a recognition that the regime needed the support that the daimyo could marshal, even though the daimyo themselves were not always welcome as recruits to office. This marks a shift in emphasis from maintaining an anti-Tokugawa alliance – significantly, the next reorganization came in April of 1869, after the last military resistance of bakufu adherents in Hokkaido ended, just as the reorganization of June 1868 had followed the surrender of Edo – to forming a government, even, as some historians have seen it, creating an oligarchy. The process raised problems. The most critical was that of the status of the new leaders and the standing of the regime to which they belonged. Their diverse social and geographical origins, which in traditional terms were bound to make it difficult for the imperial councilors to work together publicly, was to some extent overcome by previous political experience as members of an "illegal" form of opposition movement. Conspirators had no option but to deal with one another, however uneasy the relationships this implied. What caused more difficulty was that they had now to establish a relationship with other senior members of the body politic, including, for the samurai among them, their own feudal lords.

There was a traditional solution to this kind of problem. An autocrat, whether emperor or daimyo, could always raise the rank and income of the men in his personal entourage to a level commensurate with their importance to him. Some of the samurai had already enjoyed this kind of promotion. However, there were disadvantages to using the device any more extensively. Quite apart from the fact that in existing circumstances it might imply a transfer of loyalty from lord to emperor – which "loyalist" samurai were making in any case for a variety of reasons but which others would find objectionable – such elevation of the lowly would certainly offend the susceptibilities of many conservatives whose cooperation was still necessary in the task of manipulating the political structure as it stood. The Satsuma samurai showed themselves especially conscious of this. As a result, the process of putting together a government in the emperor's name forced its members to confront another question, involving their personal stake in it. Because there was no dominant personality who could make himself shogun or *kampaku* and demand obedience, what was to be the basis of the government's authority? Was its authority to be nominal, one that depended on persuasion and influence? Or was it to be real, giving the emperor's ministers, no matter what their origin, the power to command? In practice, this meant raising an issue that was central to any decision about the nature of Japan's political institutions, namely, that of feudal separatism, or the independence of the domains (*han*).

THE ABOLITION OF THE DOMAINS

A variety of arguments in favor of abolishing the domains (*haihan*) was being pressed on the Meiji government in 1868–9. Diplomats like Sir Harry Parkes, the British minister, had two reasons for recommending it. One was that they associated the whole domain structure with the existence – and immunity from punishment – of samurai who had shown themselves eager to attack foreigners. The other was that feudalism belonged to Europe's past, something long since superseded by a commercial and industrial society. So if Japan were to be modern, manifesting a stability that was as important to foreign trade as it was to national strength, then it needed, in Parkes's view, to rid itself of an outmoded form of government.

This second argument appealed strongly to some of Japan's new leaders, especially those who had visited Europe or America. Itō Hirobumi, for example, was one who urged an appeal to the lords to surrender their lands to the emperor. It could be made attractive to them, he wrote early in 1869, by an offer to make them members of a reconstituted aristocracy, give them substantial stipends, and open their way to office; whereas their followers could be conciliated by being incorporated into the national army and bureaucracy or enabled to return to the land. This was similar to the plan that was eventually followed.[8]

Such reasoning was reinforced by traditionalist sentiment and by a widespread dissatisfaction with things as they were. Many samurai,

---

8 This section is chiefly based on Beasley, *Meiji Restoration*, chap. 13; Wilson, *Genesis*, chap. 5; and Asai, *Meiji ishin*, pp. 105–300. See also Masakazu Iwata, *Ōkubo Toshimichi: The Bismarck of Japan* (Berkeley and Los Angeles: University of California Press, 1964), chap. 5.

who had been highly critical of the way in which feudal superiors, both shogun and daimyo, had reacted to the foreign threat, felt rather imprecisely that better things could be expected from an emperor who embodied all that was best in Japanese tradition. They were ready to see him made a real, not a nominal ruler, even at the cost of a major upheaval in the social order. From a different viewpoint, merchants and rich peasants, at least in some rural areas, had become resentful of their own low status in feudal society and felt little desire to perpetuate it. They had, indeed, often given material support to loyalist samurai in the turbulent years after the opening of the ports. Leaving aside the difficult question of how much weight one should attach to these factors, it is nevertheless clear that there existed at least some political basis for action to limit or destroy the independence of the domains, quite apart from the predilections of the emperor's own more "enlightened" councilors.

Two things held the government back, however. One was the knowledge that many lords and upper samurai, including some on whose support the court continued to depend, would be resentful of such a move, perhaps to the point of open opposition. The other was an uncertainty about how to "manage" a situation to which familiar techniques would cease to apply. After all, the samurai members of the council had risen to power partly by learning to manipulate their feudal lords, rarely moving to the center of the stage themselves. It is not surprising that they felt some qualms about abolishing the system by which they had been able to climb.

The test of the practicability of a measure in these circumstances was the extent to which Ōkubo and Iwakura could be brought to support it, for they were the politicians par excellence of the ruling group. Following discussions within Chōshū, Kido took up Itō's ideas for getting the lords to surrender their lands and broached the matter to Ōkubo at the beginning of November 1868.[9] Ōkubo was sympathetic, and they agreed that as a first step, opinion in the other key domains should be quietly sounded out. Their inquiries soon revealed that the plan, if put forward officially, was likely to meet a mixed reception. As an interim measure, a decree of December 11, 1868, imposed a decree of supervision and uniformity on the domains, requiring all daimyo to effect a clear separation between "public" and "house" business and to ensure that the selection of officials was deter-

9 Kido can be followed from his diary in Sidney Devere Brown and Akiko Hirota, trans., *The Diary of Kido Takayoshi*, vol. 1: *1868–1871*, vol. 2: *1871–1874*, and vol. 3: *1874–1877* (Tokyo: Tokyo University Press, 1983, 1985, and 1986).

mined by talent, not just by birth. The change substantially increased the government's ability to influence administrative policy in Japan as a whole, partly by ensuring that its views would get a ready hearing locally and partly by requiring each domain to appoint an official to represent it in the capital. To go beyond this and challenge the lord's title to his land seemed to some, as one of Matsudaira Keiei's followers put it, of no practical advantage and likely "to bring the country into confusion and disorder."

Coming from such a source, comments like this were bound to induce caution. Early in 1869, therefore, the central government representatives of Satsuma, Chōshū, Tosa, and Hizen decided to put forward in the name of their lords a memorial that would enable them to test more widely the extent and intensity of the opposition to these proposals. This was submitted to the court on March 5. Briefly referring to the fact that the creation of the office of shogun in the distant past had led to the sequestration by the great military houses of what were properly "the emperor's lands," the document agreed that the overthrow of the Tokugawa provided an opportunity to put this right and give Japan "one central body of government." It then went on to offer to surrender the land registers of the four domains to the emperor,

> asking that the court dispose of them at will, bestowing that which should be bestowed, taking away that which should be taken away; and we ask that the court issue such orders as it may deem necessary, disposing of the lands of the great domains and deciding changes in them, as well as regulating all things, from institutions, statutes, and military organization down to regulations concerning uniforms and equipment, so that state affairs, both great and small, may be in the hands of a single authority.[10]

The wording of this memorial left open several options. The court – dominated by the men who had drafted the document – could take it at face value and impose similar action on all the domains in the name of national unity. Alternatively, if opposition seemed to make such a step politically unwise, the offer could simply be treated as an expression of loyal sentiment, requiring no action on the part of the government, beyond a confirmation of existing territories, in the manner befitting a new feudal overlord.

Reactions were in fact confused. Openly, most domains followed the lead given by Satsuma, Chōshū, Tosa, and Hizen, forwarding similar memorials. But privately, many lords and upper samurai ex-

10 Text in *Iwakura Kō jikki*, 3 vols. (Tokyo: Iwakura Kō kyūseki hozonkai, 1927), vol. 2, pp. 670–2. There is a translation (differing slightly from mine) in W. W. McLaren, ed., *Japanese Government Documents*, in *Transactions of the Asiatic Society of Japan* 42 (1914): pt. 1.

pressed misgivings. The Kōgisho, where domain representatives discussed the question in June and July, was sharply divided. A significant minority opted for the kind of arrangement that Itō had proposed, but a majority preferred to retain feudalism in one form or another, subject to confirming the emperor's preeminence. In effect, this meant that the government had to make a decision and implement it, taking such account of feudal opinion as seemed wise. Ōkubo concluded that the matter was one for "gradual action." Kido, though with reservations, concurred. Iwakura accordingly drafted a compromise plan, accepted by senior officials early in July, which was designed to ensure that the daimyo would surrender their hereditary rights in name but retain enough authority in practice to satisfy, or at least conciliate, the more conservative. As announced on July 25, 1869, this meant apppointing them imperial governors (*chiji*) – not on an hereditary basis, thanks to Kido – of the lands they had formerly held in fief, allowing them to retain a generous one-tenth of their revenues as household expenses but requiring them to use the rest in ways specified by the central government. One corollary was to be a new peerage (*kazoku*), combining court nobles and feudal lords. Another was a review of samurai stipends and a simplification of samurai ranks, implying that although the samurai would remain a privileged class, their status and perquisites would now be subject to central direction. These decisions were supplemented in October of the following year, by regulations requiring the new governors to spend at least three months in every three years attending meetings in the capital, and laying down various restrictions on the powers of local officials in such matters as finance, legal jurisdiction, and the raising of armed forces.

Despite the considerable increase in central authority that these changes represented, there remained a number of anomalies. The lands taken over from the Tokugawa, which were extensive, had been made into prefectures (*ken*), in which all officials were appointed from the capital. Here government policy was carried out without question. Elsewhere, the extent of conformity depended a great deal on circumstances. Even within the "loyal" territories of Satsuma, Chōshū, Tosa, and Hizen, there was a good deal of variation. Both Tosa and Hizen were in the hands of reforming samurai, who pressed on with measures of the "modernizing" kind that found their chief spokesmen in Kido and Ōkuma, but in both Satsuma and Chōshū there were powerful conservative groups who would not always do the bidding of their colleagues in the capital. The same differences of emphasis existed in other parts of the country, and so it became clear before long that the surrender of domain registers (*hanseki-hōkan*) in the summer of 1869 had by no means solved the problem of national unity.

One reason was that some of the things that the government was trying to do were socially divisive. The handling of the samurai's stipends is an outstanding example. Finance was at this time a major difficulty, partly because the need to fight a civil war with inadequate resources had put the regime in debt from the start, giving fresh impetus to the inflationary trends inherited from the Tokugawa. Given that stipends had always been a heavy, regular burden on domain finances, they were an obvious target for economies. However, the effect of another government policy, that of "promoting men of talent," was to make the incidence of these economies very uneven, because the method chosen was to cut most hereditary stipends, sometimes savagely, while maintaining or increasing those that were paid for holding office. As a result, able bureaucrats did well, and other samurai did badly, often being forced to seek supplementary income from farming or commerce. This helped confirm the loyalty of officials to the government, especially as it was accompanied by relaxation or abolition of the status requirements for appointment; but to the great majority, who did not benefit from this, it raised serious doubts about the government's virtues. There were a number of outbreaks of samurai unrest in 1870–1, including an important one in Chōshū, attributable directly or indirectly to this cause.

Senior administrators in some domains, especially small ones, or those with particularly intransigent economic problems, found these difficulties of finance and disaffection beyond their power to solve. Increasingly, they began to see advantages in making their territories into prefectures, thereby relieving themselves of worrying responsibilities. Several petitioned Tokyo to this effect and were incorporated voluntarily into the prefectural system. Members of the government for their part found in these developments additional reasons for taking up again the question of abolishing the domains. As they saw it, it was not merely that some domains were becoming trouble spots. More generally, there was a rising level of popular disturbances, a continuation of the peasant revolts of the late Tokugawa period, damped down briefly during the immediate aftermath of Restoration but recurring once it became clear that the change of regime had done nothing to reduce grievances in the countryside. These had to be suppressed if Japan were to be made strong. If the domains, which in the past had always had the task of maintaining order, were no longer able to carry it out, then it seemed that other means must be found. A national army, loyal to the emperor and not to a variety of feudal lords, was one obvious desideratum. Yet creating it would entail a further attack on samurai privilege, and financing it would require funds that at present were allocated to the domains. There was here another argument for a greater measure of centralization, which government ministers appear to have had in mind early in 1871.

They were also aware that a divided council could never hope to impose on the country a policy so calculated to provoke resentment as abolition of the domains was likely to be. Hence, pushing through the 1869 decisions to their logical conclusion, which had always seemed to Ōkubo and Iwakura a matter of timing not one of principle, came to depend on ensuring the unity of the ruling group. In the summer of 1870 they took steps to limit the influence of Ōkuma, Itō, and their reforming friends (who were established in the ministries of Finance and Civil Affairs) with a view to making possible a rapprochement with those, especially in Satsuma and Chōshū, who had objected to the policies followed with respect to samurai status and stipends. Then in the autumn Ōkubo made overtures to Saigō Takamori to persuade him to rejoin the government. Kido undertook similar discussions with men in Chōshū. Finally, in February 1871 Iwakura proceeded as imperial messenger to both domains, providing a cover for Ōkubo and Kido to complete their arrangements. As a result, Shimazu Hisamitsu and Mōri Yoshichika, representing the two daimyo houses, agreed to come to Tokyo and give the government countenance.

At some point during these discussions the decision was taken to go ahead with abolishing the domains; and at the end of March, when all the men concerned were back in the capital, it was agreed to bring in reliable troops from Satsuma, Chōshū, and Tosa, in case the action was resisted. Saigō was to command them. In August – there was a delay because Mōri had died and Shimazu had second thoughts – the government was reorganized in preparation for the final announcement: Saigō, Kido, Ōkuma, and Itagaki were made councilors (*sangi*), demonstrating the solidarity of the four leading domains; and Ōkubo became minister of finance, providing an additional guarantee that the reform party would be restrained. This done, the abolition of the domains was announced in an imperial edict dated August 29, 1871. Such daimyo as were in the city were summoned to the palace and brusquely informed that the prefectural system was to be extended to the whole of Japan. There was no pretense of consultation or debate. The edict, which was read to them, simply stated:

> We deem it necessary that the government of the country be centred in a single authority, so as to effect a reformation in substance as well as in fact.... All this is for the purpose of doing away with superfluity, for issuing in simplicity, for removing the evils of empty forms and in order to avoid the grievance caused by the existence of many centres of government.[11]

It would be difficult to exaggerate the significance of this step. Quite apart from the authoritarian manner in which it was carried out, the act itself had implications of fundamental importance for the future of Japanese political institutions. For most of Japan and the great majority of its people, the domains had for centuries provided the formal structure within which life was lived. Without them, the Meiji leaders had to devise a machinery for administering the large areas hitherto ruled by feudal lords, and recruit officials for running it; to organize a military and police force to do what the samurai had done as part of their feudal duty; to introduce courts and codes of law to replace those established by feudal custom; and to create a tax system that would provide a central revenue, making good the loss from feudal dues. In sum, this required that the Japanese government now be organized on entirely fresh principles. The availability of Western models for the most part determined what they should be. Indeed, there was little real choice, as China's institutions, to which Japan had always turned in the past, had been as much discredited by recent history as Japan's had been. China's military organization had shown itself incapable of putting down large-scale rebellions or of defending the country against quite small British, French, and Russian forces. China's tax arrangements, under which only a small proportion of the total revenue found its way to the central government, had failed to provide the resources required for military reform or effective government. They had also occasioned disputes with the powers, leading to the development of a customs administration almost entirely under foreign control. Similarly, the working of Chinese courts of law had long been a source of friction with the foreigners. Given the influence that Western diplomats could exercise in Japan, it was idle to suppose that the Chinese institutional alternative was any longer a realistic one.

Even before the fall of the Tokugawa there had been a good deal of experiment with military reform in Japan, involving both the bakufu and the domains. Edo had invited a French military mission to Japan,

---

11 Translated in Ishii, *Japanese Legislation*, p. 717; also in McLaren, *Documents*, pp. 32–3. See also Michio Umegaki, "From Domain to Prefecture," in Marius B. Jansen and Gilbert Rozman, eds., *Japan in Transition: From Tokugawa to Meiji* (Princeton, N.J.: Princeton University Press, 1986), pp. 91–110.

officers from which had remained with bakufu troops during the civil war. Britain had produced a similar naval mission, arriving in October 1867. Satsuma, Wakayama, and other domains had applied various forms of Western organization to their samurai forces. Chōshū had devised irregular units in which commoners played an important part. Thus there was no lack of precedents for the new administration when it turned to the task of creating armed services of its own. Its principal military expert in the early period was Ōmura Masujirō of Chōshū, who as vice-minister in the Department of Military Affairs, put forward proposals in July 1869 for a conscript army, whose members were to be recruited from the domains but would be required as one of their conditions of service to sever their domain connections. The samurai's hostility to this plan was one of the reasons for Ōmura's assassination at the end of the year. However, his work was later continued by his young protégé, Yamagata Aritomo, who was in Europe at the time, studying the military organizations of Britain, France, and Germany.

Yamagata returned to Japan in September 1870 and was appointed to a senior post in the military department. Almost at once he secured a decision in favor of standardizing Japanese military practice on French lines; orders to this effect were sent to the domains in October. In April 1871, regulations were issued for a form of conscription broadly in accordance with Ōmura's ideas, but in practice nothing was done to implement them before the abolition of the domains, which changed the context in which reform would take place. Thereafter Yamagata became vice-minister in the department. Later in the year, jointly with his two Satsuma subordinates, one of whom was Saigō's younger brother, Tsugumichi, Yamagata put forward fresh plans for organizing a regular army which eventually became the basis of Japanese policy. These recommended that conscripts be "trained and drilled in Western tactics," and "organized into units regardless of whether they be samurai or commoners." After their period of service they would return to their own localities, forming a reserve that could be used to maintain civil order. Stability at home and defense against foreign attack, as Yamagata saw it, "were aspects of a single problem."[12]

These proposals met with serious opposition from men who resented the adoption of any kind of military structure that did not give the samurai an entrenched position. Because this was a sensitive issue,

---

12 Roger F. Hackett, *Yamagata Aritomo in the Rise of Modern Japan: 1838–1922* (Cambridge, Mass.: Harvard University Press, 1971), pp. 61–2. For the conscription policy in general, see ibid., chap. 2; and Ishii, *Japanese Legislation*, pp. 186–97.

progress toward a decision remained slow. In fact, it was not until the end of 1872 that the government was ready to proceed with the regulations drafted during the year by Yamagata and his colleagues (who included a Leiden-trained, former bakufu official, Nishi Amane). On December 28 an imperial rescript announced "a nationwide conscription law" designed to "lay the basic foundation of national security." A government statement accompanying this rescript condemned the samurai class in blunt language for "living a life of idleness for generations"; claimed that what was now to be instituted would clear the way for "the unity of soldier and peasant"; and argued that hereafter no distinction would be made between samurai and commoner "in the service they render to their country."[13]

The conscription law itself was promulgated on January 10, 1873. Conscripts were to be called up at age twenty for three years' service with the colors, followed by four years with the reserve. Eventually there were to be six army districts, their combined strength totaling some 31,000 men, though in practice a start was made only in Tokyo during 1873, and it was some years before the whole force came into existence. There were a good many loopholes by which men could escape service altogether: by reasons of health or family status, as national or local government officials, as students in specified schools, or by paying for substitutes to replace them. Such loopholes seem to have been used widely. In addition, there continued to be objections to the system from both samurai and peasants, which were sometimes violently expressed. Nevertheless, Japan acquired by this step an instrument that soon showed itself capable of imposing order at home. During the next ten years or so, peasant rebellion was gradually suppressed. Even the Satsuma samurai were successfully put down when they rebelled in 1877.

Proposals for land tax reform were at least as contentious as were those for conscription.[14] The subject had first been raised with reference to the land taken over by the imperial government from the Tokugawa in 1868 – about one-quarter of Japan – which was sufficiently scattered and diverse to pose unaccustomed problems to samurai officials drawn from close-knit domains. Two arguments emerged

---

13 Translations are in Ishii, *Japanese Legislation*, pp. 723–4. For a comment on the social implications, see E. H. Norman, *Soldier and Peasant in Japan: The Origins of Conscription* (New York: Institute of Pacific Relations, 1943).
14 For a summary of the land tax discussions, see Beasley, *Meiji Restoration*, pp. 390–400. Of the many studies in Japanese, two are particularly useful: Fukushima Masao, *Chiso kaisei no kenkyū* (Tokyo: Yūhikaku, 1962); and Seki Junya, *Meiji ishin to chiso kaisei* (Kyoto: Minerva, 1967).

among these officials as justifying some kind of reform. One emphasized the question of law and order, pointing out that the considerable variations in the land tax among the localities had produced much popular unrest which the government so far lacked means to control. This line of reasoning led the prefectural governors, backed by the department of civil administration in the capital, to urge both a standardization and a reduction of the taxes. By contrast, finance officials, especially in Tokyo, gave more attention to the rapid growth of state expenditure and the erosion of the value of the revenue by inflation. This, they said, meant that an upward revision of tax rates was vital to the financial needs and hence to the very existence of the imperial regime. One of them, Kanda Kōhei (Takahira), a former bakufu expert employed in the Finance Ministry, went so far as to propose in 1869 and 1870 that the tax in kind should be replaced by a tax in cash, based on a valuation of landholdings. This, he claimed, would be easier to administer than would be feudal dues, would be payable in kind, and would provide a more stable revenue from year to year without in any way harming the farmers' interests.

These differences of viewpoint prevented any substantial progress toward an agreement on policy before the summer of 1871. The abolition of the domains then made urgent some kind of action. Many more areas, each with its own local customs and dues, had then to be incorporated into a theoretically unified administration, greatly increasing the possibilities of discontent. Moreover, the Finance Ministry inherited heavy commitments to set against its additional revenue, as one condition of abolition had been that the government would permit the daimyo to retain a tenth of their former revenues as private income, as well as taking over responsibility for the payment of domain debts and samurai stipends. In these circumstances, it is not surprising that the initiative in Tokyo passed to the finance officials. In the autumn of 1871 Matsukata Masayoshi, deputy head of the tax section, submitted a memorial that argued for a new kind of land tax as part of a general agrarian reform, designed to stimulate production by abolishing restrictions of every kind. This was taken up by his superiors, Ōkubo as finance minister and Inoue Kaoru as vice-minister, who put to the council proposals for a land tax payable in cash, representing a percentage of a stipulated valuation of the land. Arriving at such a valuation, they noted, would require creating a market in land by raising the feudal ban on its sale or purchase.

These points having been agreed in principle, it was left to the Finance Ministry to prepare the various regulations for putting them into effect. This necessitated many drafts and much discussion, lasting nearly two years. In March 1872 the ban on sale of land was abolished, and regulations were announced covering the issue of landownership certificates. In August, the option of paying dues in cash, already standard in the former imperial prefectures, was extended to the whole of Japan. As a final stage, officials then turned to the problem of land valuation and tax rates. The first draft of regulations on this subject, apparently dating from the autumn of 1872, set out a complex system of calculating values, involving owners, village assemblies, and local officials, whose intention was to set the tax rate at 30 percent of the crop's net annual value. This was thought to have been the national average under the Tokugawa, though basing it on an up-to-date valuation would undoubtedly have increased the current yield to the advantage of the government. At all events, it brought protests from many influential groups. Rich landlords, whose wealth frequently reflected in part their success in paying lower real tax rates than did their fellow villagers, sought assurance that increases in the tax burden would, for an interim period, be limited to 40 percent in any individual case. By contrast, samurai groups sought to ensure that their own notional land rights – stipends had nominally become payable in the remote past as a substitute for fiefs – would be recognized by requiring cultivators to buy out surviving feudal rights in their land, the funds so raised being used to finance samurai stipends and other public expenditures.

The political importance of landlords and samurai ensured that opposition of this kind could not be ignored. In the spring of 1873, the whole range of issues, including that of stipends, was put to a conference of local officials in Tokyo, whose meetings were presided over successively by Inoue Kaoru and Ōkuma Shigenobu. On stipends it was impossible to reach agreement, at least at this level, because the conflicting arguments about possible samurai unrest and government financial imperatives were not really negotiable. On tax rates there were some acrimonious exchanges between Finance Ministry representatives and the rest, but in the end their differences were resolved. One decision was to add a further charge for local taxes, thereby raising the total annual levy from 3 percent to 4 percent of the land's capital value, the extra 1 percent being for local use. The other major cause of dispute, which was the method of valuation, involved assumptions about dividing the product of the land among cultivator, landlord, and tax collector. Here the interests of the landlord and the tax collector were more vigorously defended, with the result that the formula as finally agreed on envisaged that 34 percent of the yield would be needed to pay for tax, whereas in the case of tenanted land, 34 percent would go to the landlord and only 32 percent to the tenant. Given that the landlords were in a better position than the tenants were to protect themselves in the subsequent discussions about implementing the rules in the villages and prefectures – estimating values and making surveys was not completed until 1876 for arable land, 1891 for forest and waste – one consequence of the tax changes was to make landlordism more profitable.

Another was to give the government a stable and predictable revenue, which, because it was payable in cash, transferred the commercial risk of putting crops on the market to the private citizen. The imperial decree announcing the regulations, dated July 28, 1873, declared their purpose as being to ensure that the "tax be levied impartially in order that the burden may be shared equally among the people."[15] This fairly reflected the concerns of many prefectural officials, anxious to prevent further disorder. On balance, however, the rather different aims of the Finance Ministry seem to have been more successfully pursued.

Much the same can be said about the commutation of samurai pensions.[16] The crucial fact about them, as seen by Finance Ministry officials, was that in 1871 the department had to take over responsibility for annual stipends that cost something like a third of the yield from land tax, which was itself overwhelmingly the greatest part of government revenue. Because the domains had several times reviewed the payments in recent years, cutting back hard on all the larger ones, there was little more that could be done by way of pruning the list. Consequently, if spending was not to be crippled by this charge, the government had either to find new sources of revenue or to accept the political risks inherent in shedding much of the burden in some fairly drastic way. To tax commerce, which was one alternative, would imperil many of the plans for modernization. By contrast, to end entitlement to stipends would be a further step toward dismantling the privileges of those samurai who had little to contribute to the military and administrative machine. Thus logic argued for the conversion of stipends into capital sums; politics for caution in carrying out the decision.

15 Translation in Ishii, *Japanese Legislation*, p. 722.
16 See Beasley, *Meiji Restoration*, pp. 382–90. The most detailed Japanese study of the stipend question is by Fukaya Hakuji, *Kashizoku chitsuroku shobun no kenkyū* (Tokyo: Takayama shoin, 1941).

The first attempt to solve the problem was a proposal from the Finance Ministry early in 1872 that Japan should raise a foreign loan, part of which could be used to capitalize the stipends at four times their annual value, this amount to be paid to stipend holders in marketable bonds over a six-year period. Several members of the council, including Kido and Iwakura, thought this much too severe, hence politically dangerous. The idea was therefore dropped. It was not put forward again until November 1873, when Ōkubo and Ōkuma, despite objections from Kido and Itō, pushed through another Finance Ministry scheme, this time to tax stipends on a sliding scale – in effect, reducing them – while offering to holders of the smaller ones the option of commuting them at a four-year valuation for life stipends and a six-year valuation for hereditary ones. This decision was announced in December. It did little to overcome the financial difficulties, however, and it was soon clear that something else would have to be done to reduce expenditures under this head. In November 1874, the option of commutation was extended to all samurai, not just the poorer ones. Finally, in March 1876, Ōkuma proposed that commutation be made compulsory. This was agreed, and in August, the terms for commutation were announced. The very smallest hereditary stipends were to be surrendered for government bonds at fourteen times their annual value, bearing interest at 7 percent; for the very largest the figures were to be five times the annual value and 5 percent; others would be at points between these two extremes. Life stipends were to be converted at half these rates.[17]

For the government, commutation reduced the charge on the budget by approximately 30 percent; ultimately, because of inflation, much more. For the more affluent samurai and their feudal lords, it provided useful capital sums in treasury bonds, which could be used to finance investment in land or some forms of modern enterprise. For the poorest, it completed the process of impoverishment that had been going on for generations, forcing them back to the land or into other kinds of productive employment. In all these ways it made a useful contribution to economic modernization, achieved at some human cost. Inevitably, it also brought unrest and discontent, which played a significant part in the origins of the Satsuma Rebellion of 1877. More important in the long term, it signaled the end of the first stage in a transformation of the regime's political base. The daimyo and some upper samurai now joined the court nobles in a comfortable and digni-

---

17 Translations of the relevant decrees (December 27, 1873, and August 5, 1876) are in McLaren, *Documents*, pp. 557–66.

fied way of life, marked by social prestige and political obscurity. Among their retainers, a minority found successful careers in the bureaucracy and armed forces, becoming the core of Japan's governmental elite. The rest sank back into relative anonymity, often respected but no longer privileged, either becoming, like the landlords and merchants, part of an emerging bourgeoisie, or descending into the ranks of peasants and laborers. It was this new class configuration that Meiji political institutions were to reflect in the next twenty years.

CENTRAL AND LOCAL GOVERNMENT

The surrender of domain registers had been followed on August 15, 1869, by a major restructuring of the central government, of which the chief characteristic was a further strengthening of the executive, now renamed the Dajōkan.[18] Power was to be restricted to a very small number of persons. The senior post was that of minister of the right (udaijin), held by the court noble Sanjō Sanetomi. Immediately below him came three great councilors, one of whom was Iwakura Tomomi, another the former daimyo of Hizen, Nabeshima Naomasa. Below this again came the councilors (sangi), whose numbers varied between two and seven during the next two years, all being samurai from Satsuma, Chōshū, Tosa, and Hizen. Collectively, these men were responsible for advising the emperor on matters of state. Executing their decisions was entrusted to six ministries: Finance (Ōkurashō), Civil Affairs (Mimbushō), Foreign Affairs (Gaimushō), War (Hyōbushō), Justice (Kyōbushō), and Imperial Household (Kunaishō). These were headed by high-ranking court nobles or feudal lords, but in practice they were usually controlled by samurai vice-ministers. This meant that authority rested with a close-knit group of men who had a good deal of political experience. The figureheads of 1868–9 had largely been discarded.

Because this arrangement gave effective direction to the central government's activities, there seemed no need to make sweeping revisions after the abolition of the domains in 1871. Such changes as were made still further increased the degree of centralization within the executive, which was now divided into three chambers. The Central Chamber (Sei-in) – often equated with the Dajōkan as a whole, be-

---

18 For details of central government in this period, see Ishii, *Japanese Legislation*, pp. 115–35; Wilson, *Genesis*, pp. 66–8; Albert M. Craig, "The Central Government," in Jansen and Rozman, eds., *Japan in Transition*, pp. 36–67; and Suzuki Yasuzō, *Dajōkansei to naikakusei* (Tokyo: Shōwa hankōkei, 1944).

cause it was so important – consisted of the chancellor (*dajōdaijin*), ministers of the left and right (*sadaijin*, *udaijin*), and several councilors (*sangi*). This was the body that met in the emperor's presence and made recommendations to him. It was advised by a Right Chamber (U-in), consisting of ministers and vice-ministers of the executive departments, and a Left Chamber (Sa-in), nominally an appointed legislature but in fact never achieving a position of any great importance.

The central group of officials remained much the same as before, though the number of its members shrank still more, and the samurai among them emerged more openly as men in authority. Sanjō was appointed chancellor in August 1871, remaining in that post until it was abolished in 1883. The office of minister of the left remained vacant. Four samurai were appointed councilors at the beginning – Saigō of Satsuma, Kido of Chōshū, Itagaki of Tosa, and Ōkuma of Hizen – and there were only nineteen more in the fourteen years for which the office existed. All but one – Katsu Kaishū, a former bakufu official – came from the same four domains that were nominated in 1871. Ōkubo Toshimichi was made minister of finance, not councilor, the first samurai to attain that kind of recognition, though before long such promotions became quite common. Moreover, a few samurai, like Yamagata Aritomo in the War Ministry, found themselves vice-ministers of departments in which there was no minister, a fact that made their influence more substantial.

There were a few significant adjustments in the names and functions of ministries, mostly related in some way to the extension of the central government's power over the country or to plans for modernization. The Ministry of Justice was renamed Shihōshō in August 1871 and given responsibility for organizing a system of national and local courts. It inherited a criminal code based on Chinese and traditional Japanese precedents, which had been approved in February 1871; but a revision of this, completed in 1872 and issued in July 1873, was already beginning to show French influence.[19] It was superseded in 1882 by a new criminal code based entirely on French models. In 1875 the Supreme Court (Daishin-in) was created to strengthen the judiciary and serve as a court of appeal. The Ministry of Education (Mombushō), established in September 1871, took over the supervision of various institutions for the training of officials and specialists, previously administered by the bakufu, but gave most of its attention to devising a system of national primary education, which was an-

---

19 See Paul Heng-chao Ch'en, *The Formation of the Early Meiji Legal Order: The Japanese Code of 1871 and Its Chinese Foundation* (New York: Oxford University Press, 1981).

nounced in September 1872. In January 1873 it absorbed the functions concerned with propagating Shinto, which had formerly been performed by the Jingikan. That body, which had been reduced to the status of a ministry (Jingishō) in 1871, was abolished.

The two principal innovations made at this time stemmed directly from the decisions to introduce conscription and abolish the domains. Introducing Western-style methods of organization and training for the armed forces had important implications for the relevant bureaucratic structures, which themselves came to rely heavily on Western experience. In April 1872 this was reflected in the division of the Hyōbushō into the Army Ministry (Rikugunshō) and the Navy Ministry (Kaigunshō). In 1878, following evidence of command and planning weaknesses during the campaign to suppress the Satsuma Rebellion, an army general staff was established on German lines, independent of the War Ministry and reporting directly to the emperor as commander in chief. This was to have important long-term consequences for Japanese politics.

Equally important were the decisions made about governing the lands and people relinquished to the emperor by the domains in the summer of 1871, amounting to approximately three-quarters of Japan. The Department of Civil Affairs, which had earlier borne the chief responsibility for matters concerning the imperial territories, was discontinued in 1871, some of its functions being transferred to the Finance Ministry, others to a new Ministry of Public Works (Kōbushō), dating from December 1870. This proved to be an unsatisfactory arrangement, as there was then no single office to coordinate central policy toward the various local and regional units into which the country was divided. Accordingly, in November 1873, when Ōkubo and Iwakura emerged as the dominant figures in the government, the Home Ministry (Naimushō) was established, and Ōkubo was made its head. Its powers and duties, as defined in February 1874, were extremely wide. It was to select local and prefectural officials; carry out surveys in connection with land tax assessment; administer the census; organize road building and coastal shipping; supervise the mails and local sanitary services; and so on. In short, it was to resume and expand on behalf of the central government a whole range of functions that had for centuries been performed by feudal lords. Moreover, it clearly proposed to do so by subjecting officialdom itself to tight controls, as it proceeded to issue regulations in November 1875 by which similar duties – plus provision of a police force, responsibility for schools, and care of shrines and temples – were imposed on the prefectural governors (*chiji*) and their subordinates, whose appointment, promotion, and dismissal were made subject to Home Ministry decisions, based on regular inspections and reports.[20]

The local administrative entities to which these rules applied were also changed.[21] When the domains were abolished, their territories were made into prefectures (*ken*), of which there were 302, varying enormously in size, in addition to the three urban areas (*fu*) of Tokyo, Kyoto, and Osaka. In January 1872 a process of consolidation reduced the number of *ken* to 72 (later to 43). For the purpose of preparing house registers as a preliminary to enforcing conscription, these units were subdivided into districts called *ku*, each under an appointed official, who in 1872 became the local representative of government, replacing the traditional headman. The final stage in this development came in a law of July 1878, when the *ku*, divided into wards (*chō*), were retained only as sections of the urban *fu*, and the prefectures were subdivided into districts (*gun*) and villages (*mura* or *son*). Headmen of *ku* and *gun* were appointed by the government and had official status; those of *chō* and *son*, being less important politically, were to be elected by residents. Thus the supervision exercised over prefectural administration by Tokyo was extended into the larger local communities.

Staffing this expanding system, as it could no longer be done by calling on samurai to serve as part of their feudal duty, required the creation of a bureaucracy.[22] Many of those whom the Meiji leaders appointed to subordinate positions were predictably men on whose loyalty they could rely because of past political associations, or "experts" possessing useful skills, such as a knowledge of Western methods and technology. Bernard Silberman, analyzing sixty-two officials who held major posts in government ministries between 1875 and 1900, has shown that about half met both these tests, and nearly three-quarters met one or the other. Indeed, at this level the overwhelming majority were samurai from Satsuma, Chōshū, Tosa, and Hizen, whose domain affiliation was presumably some kind of evidence of

---

20 For the translated text of the orders establishing the Home Ministry, see McLaren, *Documents*, pp. 37–40; for the 1875 regulations, ibid., pp. 259–64.
21 For local government in the early Meiji period, see Ishii, *Japanese Legislation*, pp. 198–231; and Kurt Steiner, *Local Government in Japan* (Stanford, Calif.: Stanford University Press, 1965), pp. 19–29.
22 See, in particular, Silberman, *Ministers*, passim; Bernard S. Silberman, "Bureaucratic Development and the Structure of Decision-Making in Japan, 1868–1925," *Journal of Asian Studies* 29 (1970): 347–362; and Sidney D. Brown, "Okubo Toshimichi and the First Home Ministry Bureaucracy 1873–1878," in Bernard S. Silberman and H. D. Harootunian, eds., *Modern Japanese Leadership* (Tucson: University of Arizona Press, 1966), pp. 195–232. In Japanese, the most useful work for the Meiji period is still by Tanaka Sōgorō, *Kindai Nihon kanryō shi* (Tokyo: Tōyō keizai shimpō, 1941).

reliability. Appointments to office of lower standing show less consistency. Sidney Brown, studying the Home Ministry, found that of the fifty-one officials serving Ōkubo between 1873 and 1878, only two came from Satsuma and three from Chōshū, which was far fewer than in comparable positions in the ministries of Finance and War. By contrast, thirty-four out of seventy-three prefectural governors in this period came from the four leading domains. One can compare this with Silberman's figures. Taking a random sample of prefectural governors between 1875 and 1900, Silberman identified 86 percent as being samurai in origin; fewer than one in four as having had some Western education; and only one in seven as having worked his way up through the bureaucracy from the bottom ranks. The implication seems to be that the two types of qualification did not necessarily apply to the same kind of jobs. When expertise was required, feudal background could be overlooked – some experts had even served the bakufu – but in posts that were politically sensitive, loyalty, measured by a man's feudal "connections," was of preeminent importance. Certainly in choosing senior prefectural officials – except in Satsuma, which was a special case because of its record of samurai turbulence – care was taken to avoid men who had previously belonged to a local domain.

This brings us to a point where we can summarize the nature of the changes taking place in Japanese government during the first decade of Meiji rule. The main features are obvious enough: a concentration of power at the center in the hands of an oligarchy of court nobles and ex-samurai, and an authoritarian control, exercised by the bureaucrats of the capital over governmental organization in the provinces and extending the boundaries of administration far beyond the traditional ones of collecting taxes and maintaining order. Politically, this was a logical response to the "general crisis," occasioned by the threat of foreign attack and an apparent disintegration of domestic society. Institutionally, it operated through a choice of models that were on the surface "Chinese," in that they derived from the earliest, China-dominated era of Japan's political culture. Nearly all the names of offices and departments were taken from eighth-century originals, as was much of the formal terminology of imperial pronouncements. Yet the reality they were required to serve had, by the middle of the 1870s, less and less to do with Japan's ancient past. "Wealth and strength," though a classical slogan, was everywhere being interpreted in ways that owed more to Europe's example than to China's, looked more to industry and Western military science than to agriculture and a feudal soldiery. Some consequences of this were already being manifested in government organization, as we have seen. The next decade was to see this trend accelerate, so that over the whole range of political institutions, Japan moved decisively to Western models.

Rapid progress was made in the development of a professional and politically reliable army. In 1881 the military police (*kempeitai*) was organized, primarily to ensure the loyalty of servicemen to the regime. An imperial "Rescript to Soldiers and Sailors," issued in January 1882, admonished them: "Neither be led astray by current opinions, nor meddle in politics, but with single heart fulfil your essential duty of loyalty."[23] In 1884 an army staff college began training officers under the supervision of a German adviser, its work being supplemented in the next few years by specialist military schools for medicine, engineering, and artillery. The navy established an officers' training college in 1888 and a separate gunnery school in 1893. It acquired its own general staff in 1891, though it was not until 1893 that this became independent of the Navy Ministry. There were parallel developments in the organization of the civilian police, originally set up in 1872 under the Ministry of Justice and the prefectural governors. Yamagata Aritomo as home minister between 1883 and 1890 brought them under firm Home Ministry control, provided them with a training school on the German model, and gave them substantially greater powers over press censorship and political offenses.

The aim of much of this was to make a "strong" government more efficient by making it more Western, the decisions being taken against a background of rising criticism at home about the arbitrary behavior of the Meiji leadership and a series of clashes with China over Korea, which in 1884–5 brought the two countries close to war. The same concern with political stability and strength was evident in the creation of a Western-style peerage. An imperial decree of July 1884 announced that the emperor wished to honor two groups: those who were "high-born descendants of illustrious ancestors" and those who had distinguished themselves "in the restoration of my rule."[24] For this purpose, he established new ranks and titles, those of prince (or duke), marquis, count, viscount, and baron. The names of five hun-

---

23 Translated in R. Tsunoda et al., eds., *Sources of Japanese Tradition* (New York: Columbia University Press, 1958), pp. 705–7. See also James B. Crowley, "From Closed Door to Empire: The Formation of the Meiji Military Establishment," in Silberman and Harootunian, eds., *Modern Japanese Leadership*, pp. 261–87.   24 Translated in McLaren, *Documents*, pp. 88–90.

dred men were put forward for initial appointment to them. Most of these were members of the old court and feudal nobility, who were to be accorded appropriate levels of prestige to ensure their continuing cooperation, notwithstanding their loss of many traditional privileges. They were to provide the basis for a reliably conservative House of Peers in the new constitution then under discussion. However, thirty of the names were those of government ministers, generals, and admirals, mostly ex-samurai, who were at last to be given a status commensurate with their political importance. Significantly, the head of the Tokugawa house became a prince, and Ōkuma, Itagaki, and Gotō, now in opposition, were omitted altogether. Evidently, the principle of selection was present usefulness, not past performance.

There was as great a need to reconcile inherited status with contemporary power within the government itself as there was in the wider circle of the privileged. The Dajōkan system had not solved all the problems of welding men of disparate origin into a governing elite. Although the feudal lords had vanished from the political scene, there remained a tension between samurai "upstarts" and surviving court nobles, particularly as several of the latter had potentially powerful positions in the emperor's entourage. The death of Iwakura in 1883 removed the man best able to mediate these differences. At the same time it weakened the influence of the nobility, creating an opportunity of institutional adjustment that Itō, aspiring to overall leadership in the government, was eager to take. There were also internal differences about coordinating government policy, which assumed an added importance in the atmosphere of foreign crisis during 1884–5. Coordination between the dominant Central Chamber of the Dajōkan and the advisory body of senior executive officials, the Right Chamber, had been achieved by a variety of devices: by interlocking appointments, ensuring that some councilors (*sangi*) were also departmental ministers; by the use of an informal Inner Council (Naikaku) to provide a forum in which key officials could discuss major issues; and by exploiting the personal links among former members of the antibakufu movement. Some of these devices provoked opposition from men who found themselves becoming "outsiders," like Ōkuma and Itagaki. Others were being weakened by time. Nearly all the first generation of Restoration leaders from Satsuma and Chōshū were dead by 1883: Ōmura in 1869, Kido and Saigō in 1877, Ōkubo in 1878. Without them the system worked clumsily, betraying its origins as a form of government designed to hold together the heirs to the victorious coalition of 1868. In the conditions of the 1880s there was much to be said for putting it on a better-defined and more coherent footing.

In 1884, therefore, Itō took the initiative in proposing the replacement of the Dajōkan by a Western-style cabinet (though using the term Naikaku).[25] Discussions were delayed for some months by the crisis with China, which made it necessary for Itō to go to Tientsin, but on his return early in 1885 he overrode objections from Sanjō, who feared that the cabinet proposal might upset the delicate balance between the Satsuma and Chōshū factions, and entrusted the task of drafting suitable regulations to Inoue Kowashi, his principal assistant in constitutional matters. In some respects Inoue exceeded his brief, for he not only envisaged raising the status of samurai in government by making them eligible for the ministerial title of *daijin*, hitherto reserved for court nobles – a step parallel to that which had made them members of the peerage the year before – but also proposed to strengthen the government's public authority by providing for the emperor's personal participation in cabinet meetings (making the cabinet in this respect a continuation of the Sei-in). Itō, following discussions with Sanjō, ordered a revision of this clause. Accordingly, when the new structure was announced in December 1885, prefaced by an imperial decree that identified the government's intentions as being to abolish "circuitous methods," economize expenditures, and "promote efficiency in the public service," the chief coordinating role was entrusted to the minister president, or prime minister (*sōri daijin*). All laws and ordinances issued by the government were to be signed jointly by him and the appropriate departmental minister. The prime minister was also to receive reports on the work of the various ministries and to be responsible for major matters of general policy. Thus, although the ministers continued to be in theory responsible directly to the emperor in departmental matters, they were in fact clearly subordinated to the prime minister in a manner similar to that laid down in the Prussian regulations of 1810, on which the Japanese ones were chiefly based.[26] That this was a personal triumph for Itō, who became the first prime minister, is beyond doubt. Sanjō, hitherto the nominal head of the government as chancellor, withdrew to the lesser post of imperial household minister. The fact that this was not to carry

25 For relevant texts and discussion, see McLaren, *Documents*, pp. 90–7; Ishii, *Japanese Legislation*, pp. 370–4, 389–93; and Inada, *Meiji kempō*, vol. 1, pp. 732–58.
26 The prime minister lost some of his powers of supervision and countersignature when the regulations were revised in 1889, but in the long term, this did not do as much to weaken his position as did other institutional developments.

membership in the cabinet underlined the reality of the decision to remove the emperor from an active involvement in politics.

Reinforcing the cabinet arrangements of 1885 were detailed regulations concerning the organization of the bureaucracy.[27] In 1880 the government had issued rules for the conduct of official business, which set out at length the duties and authority of the minister and his subordinates in each department. A few days after the announcement about the cabinet in December 1885, a revised version calling for restriction of the number of officials, clear definition of functions, and careful enforcement of discipline was sent as an instruction from Itō to other ministers. It struck a very moral tone, emphasizing the need for attention to the officials' character, as well as avoidance of nepotism, undue present giving, or anything that might mar "the dignity and credit of the government." These instructions were incorporated into an imperial ordinance in February 1886, to which were added numerous rules regarding the handling of correspondence, the circulation of drafts, the keeping of archives and entry books, methods of making payments, and so on. Finally, another ordinance (July 1887) codified the requirements regarding personal behavior: a ban on bribery and accepting lavish entertainments, an injunction against "habits of dissipation or improvidence," and an official secrets clause prohibiting the passing of information on government matters to private persons or even courts of law.

Under these various regulations, Japanese civil servants were classified into three distinct grades: at the top, *chokunin*, appointed personally by the emperor, a group that included vice-ministers and prefectural governors; next, *sōnin*, middle-grade officials appointed on the recommendation of ministers; and finally, *hannin*, men holding minor posts, appointed by a minister under delegated authority. Given that the choice of men at all levels had so far been mostly personal – and of a kind that gave credence to the criticism that power was too much monopolized by Satsuma and Chōshū – there were clearly some arguments in favor of devising rules for appointment and promotion that would both disarm such opposition and make for smoother working of the kind of bureaucracy that was taking shape after 1885. Earlier proposals to use Chinese-style examinations for this purpose had come

---

27 For texts of the regulations issued between 1880 and 1887, see McLaren, *Documents*, pp. 55–75, 99–127. On the development of an examination system, see Robert Spaulding, *Imperial Japan's Higher Civil Service Examinations* (Princeton, N.J.: Princeton University Press, 1967), chaps. 2, 5–7.

to nothing because of the leadership's preoccupation with the need for unity and strong central direction.

In 1884, however, Itō raised the matter again. At his instigation a draft was prepared, envisaging examinations in law, economics, and political science, by which candidates would be admitted to posts at appropriate levels. The first step toward implementing it was taken with reference to judicial posts, because foreign criticism of the Japanese legal system was holding up progress on treaty revision; but in December 1885, Ito included a statement of intent about recruitment by examination in the instructions that he circulated to the ministers. During 1886 a scheme was worked out at his request by Kaneko Kentarō, which made examinations the main means of recruitment to *sōnin* and *hannin* ranks and coupled the qualifications for entry to them with attainments in the state educational system. Despite continued opposition from those who thought the requirements were too strict, Itō put the scheme into effect in July 1887. There remained some exceptions. Those already holding office were exempt from the new tests. So were the *chokunin* posts, which were still to be filled at government discretion. Graduates of the new imperial university in Tokyo were to be admitted to *sōnin* rank without examination after a period of training (a privilege they lost in 1893). All other recruits to government posts would have to pass the relevant examinations.

This completed the move away from inherited status as the prime qualification for government office. Although it was still true that samurai descent and the family connections that went with it remained a considerable advantage in seeking an official career, ensuring both access to education and valuable patronage, Japan hereafter relied in recruiting its governmental elite on the selection of "men of talent" through education and examinations. It was a Confucian concept, as many of the discussions leading up to its adoption had emphasized. However, it was not in any other respect Chinese. The examinations in question were designed to test skills that were entirely Western in origin and methodology. In the long term they were to be an instrument of social mobility. Immediately, they aroused much opposition, both from conservatives, who saw in the change a turning away from Japanese values, and from men whose own inherited status had been their only guarantee of livelihood. At the same time, the groups who were eventually to benefit – the landlords and merchants, for whose sons education was to be the route to political influence – remained in the 1880s more conscious of the authoritarian character of the Meiji government than of its career opportunities. There was, therefore, still something to be done by way of reconciling both kinds of critics to the new structure of power. A written constitution, combining a traditional rationale of imperial sovereignty with what seemed to be a compatible form of Western political thought, was the chosen means for achieving it.

THE MEIJI CONSTITUTION

Japan's earliest moves toward limiting the power of the central authority derived, like Europe's, from ideas of feudal separatism. During the closing years of Tokugawa rule, several proposals had been put forward for a kind of baronial council, involving some of the great lords and even representatives of their retainers. From this came two developments. One was a bakufu attempt to fend off complete disaster by making the shogun the president of such a council. This merged in the months after the Restoration into plans by Tosa and Echizen, in particular, to check the ambitions of Satsuma and Chōshū within the Meiji government. The other was the use of a similar device by the Meiji leadership as a means of conciliating those whose role in the political structure was assumed to be passive: the large numbers of court nobles, feudal lords, and samurai who had to be persuaded to accept the decisions taken by a minority on their behalf. In both contexts it was possible to appeal to Western models and precedents. In time it was recognized that there was good reason for doing so, namely, the desire to give Japan an international image of "enlightenment," which would reinforce its efforts to revise the unequal treaties of 1858. These motives – the wish by lesser members of the political elite to restrain the ministers' arbitrary authority, the value to government of marshaling the support of "public opinion," the need to impress the treaty powers – all were to continue, though with varying degrees of importance, to influence Japanese discussions of representative institutions throughout the events leading to the announcement of a written constitution in 1889.[28]

The first step in that direction was the creation of the Kōgisho in 1869. This was a legislature, comprising nominees from the domains,

[28] On the late Tokugawa and early Meiji background to the constitutional movement, see Nobutake Ike, *The Beginnings of Political Democracy in Japan* (Baltimore: Johns Hopkins University Press, 1950), pp. 24–43; and Osatake Takeki, *Ishin zengo ni okeru rikken shisō*, rev. ed., 2 vols. (Tokyo: Hōkōdō, 1929).

which was formed to discuss matters put to it by the executive. It had a turbulent history and was quickly abolished, though its existence served to stimulate the emergence of similar assemblies in a number of domains. When the Dajōkan was reorganized in 1871, the legislative function was entrusted to the Left Chamber (Sa-in). It seemed even less likely to weaken the essentially authoritarian character of the regime than its predecessor was.

What changed this situation was the development of a split within the oligarchy. During 1872 and 1873, when leading members of the government took part in an exploratory mission to America and Europe under Iwakura, the Satsuma and Chōshū leaders, Ōkubo and Kido, began to diverge in their views concerning the course that Japan should take to secure international equality. Ōkubo, impressed by Britain's industry and Bismarck's authority, sought to make these his models. Kido began instead to dwell on the importance of consent as an ingredient in national unity and of a written constitution as providing a necessary framework for it. At his request Aoki Shūzō, then a student in Germany, drew up a draft of a constitution for Japan, which Kido submitted to his colleagues in November 1873, following their return from Europe. It provided for the emperor to have extensive powers, which the Dajōkan would wield in his name: to superintend the administration, appointing and dismissing officials; to conduct foreign policy; to command the armed forces; and to issue emergency ordinances having the force of law. A bicameral assembly would share the legislative authority with him. It would consist of an upper house (Genrō-in), appointed from among officials of *chokunin* rank, and a lower house (Gi-in), ultimately to be elective but in the short term to be chosen from the nobility and prefectural governors. The emperor would have the right to veto legislation and dissolve the assembly, but an amendment of the constitution would require the consent of both houses, and the budget would have to be passed by the Gi-in. Ministers would be responsible to the emperor, not to the legislature.[29]

Ōkubo's response to this document was cool. He agreed that Japan needed a constitution to "establish harmony between the ruler and the people"; accepted that this implied the kind of monarchy under which

---

29 Kido's memorial of November 1873, supporting these proposals, is in McLaren, *Documents*, pp. 567–77. The draft constitution is translated in George M. Beckmann, *The Making of the Meiji Constitution: The Oligarchs and the Constitutional Development of Japan, 1868–1891* (Lawrence: University of Kansas Press, 1957), pp. 100–10.

"state affairs are conducted according to the constitution," avoiding "monarchial absolutism . . . which had no fixed laws"; but he insisted that what was done must be "consistent with our conditions, customs, and tendencies." This he interpreted as requiring the retention of "the supreme power of the emperor."[30] In fact, Ōkubo was well enough satisfied with the Dajōkan as it stood, that is, a strong executive, a legislature (Sa-in), consisting of members of the nobility and others "specially selected," and a clear separation of powers, which denied to the legislature any executive role. Because by this time he had emerged as the strong man of the Meiji government, taking over the newly formed Home Ministry, it seemed likely that his views would prevail.

There was, however, a more serious disagreement that soon had to be taken into account. During the late summer and autumn of 1873 there had been a bitter dispute among members of the government, focusing at first on Japan's policy toward Korea, but broadening into an assessment of national aims as a whole. As a result of it, several of the established leaders, including Saigō of Satsuma, Gotō and Itagaki of Tosa, and Soejima of Hizen, had resigned. In January 1874 the last three, together with six other influential samurai, took up the arguments that Kido had put forward a few weeks earlier, but giving them a different thrust. Kido had called for a constitution, binding ruler and people together, as an element in Japanese defenses against foreign attack, urging – much as Ōkubo did from his more authoritarian standpoint – the need to end feudal separatism for the sake of unity. "If a country is divided among a multitude of petty rulers, each one having full authority in his own district," he had written, " . . . the national strength is dissipated." Itagaki and his friends dwelt more on social cohesion, writing of "no taxation without representation," of terminating arbitrary rule, and of an assembly "chosen by the people" having substantial powers.[31] Their memorial was thus a deliberate challenge to the men in office. They followed it up by organizing a public campaign to introduce representative government in Japan, seeking support especially among disaffected samurai. Given the widespread unrest that already existed, because of such measures as conscription and the handling of samurai stipends, they had to be taken seriously.

It was not only samurai discontents that were at issue. It is significant

---

30 Ōkubo's memorial in reply to Kido, translated in Beckmann, *Making*, pp. 111–19.
31 Memorial of January 17, 1874, in McLaren, *Documents*, pp. 426–32. For the quotation from Kido, p. 570.

that both Kido and Itagaki came from areas in which nonsamurai – the well-to-do of the countryside and towns, men often on the fringes of the samurai class – had played an active part in the events leading to the bakufu's overthrow. In another memorial, early in 1874, Itagaki commented that if an assembly were established, the franchise should initially be limited to "the samurai and the richer farmers and merchants, for it is they who produced the leaders of the revolution of 1868."[32] In this he was reflecting the political aspirations of men who had achieved a measure of wealth and local influence in the economic conditions of the late Tokugawa period but had so far been denied any share in running the affairs of the country. They were the kind of men whom it was important to conciliate. In many parts of Japan the mass of the villagers, oppressed by tax collectors, exploited by landlords, and bewildered by the commercialization of agriculture, were in a state of turbulence and occasional rebellion. Without the cooperation of rural elites, it was doubtful whether the army and police force could yet maintain order; and if they failed to do so, Japan might again face the combination of foreign and domestic dangers that had brought down the Tokugawa.

Because of these circumstances, the Popular Rights movement (Jiyū minken undō) of the 1870s, marshaled by Itagaki and Gotō through political party organizations like the Aikoku kōtō and the Risshisha,[33] contributed to a shift in government policy away from a preoccupation with feudal opinion and toward the assimilation of new groups into the Japanese ruling class. It was not a sudden change. Nor was it something inexorably forced on the leadership by its political opponents. Rather, it reflected several converging influences: a steady improvement in the government's facilities for suppressing samurai and peasant unrest; a growing awareness of the need for a wider base of support within the population, if Japan were to be strong in any Western definition of the term; and a recognition that leaders were available who could organize an alternative regime, should those in power fail. Working out an institutional pattern appropriate to this situation took time. It also required that the remaining members of the governmental oligarchy come to an accommodation with one another, a process that took place largely behind closed doors.

One step that could be taken with relatively little controversy was to

---

32 Memorial of February 20, 1874, in ibid., pp. 440–8.
33 On the subject of the *minken* movement and its significance, see Ike, *Beginnings*, pp. 60–86; and George Akita, *Foundations of Constitutional Government in Modern Japan: 1868–1900* (Cambridge, Mass.: Harvard University Press, 1967), pp. 6–30.

provide for wider participation in local government. Under an agreement between Ōkubo and Kido early in 1875, an assembly of prefectural governors (Chihōkan kaigi) was established as a partial substitute for a national legislature. One of the proposals put to it in June of that year concerned the possibility of extending and regularizing the local assemblies already established in some regions by the former domains, so as to ensure that there would be one in each urban area (*fu*) and prefecture (*ken*). Action was delayed by the outbreak of the Satsuma Rebellion and other manifestations of samurai unrest in 1876–77, but the plan was brought forward again in 1878, approved by the Chihōkan kaigi, and implemented in July. The regulations then issued stated that the electorate was to be limited to males over twenty-five, paying at least ¥5 in annual land tax; that assemblymen were to serve four years, with half retiring every two years; and that decisions were to be taken by simple majority vote. The main business to be conducted by the assemblies was raising and spending that part of the land tax designated for local use. They were entitled to discuss other matters put to them by the governor; but to make sure that they did so in a suitably responsible manner, any action they recommended was subject to veto by the governor and approval by the home minister.[34]

In April 1880 these arrangements were supplemented by the creation of similar advisory assemblies for towns (*chō*) and villages (*son*), with the difference being that the heads of *chō* and *son*, who had no formal official authority, were to be elected, whereas those of larger areas were still to be appointed by government. The whole system was then codified under the influence of German advisers in the 1880s, when Yamagata was home minister. The chief change then made was the introduction of districts (*gun*) and cities (*shi*) as intermediate units within the prefectures, each having an elected assembly and an appointed head. Another consequence of the revised regulations – issued in 1888 for cities, towns, and villages; in 1890 for prefectures, urban areas, and districts – was that the members of the prefectural assemblies were thereafter elected indirectly by those of cities and districts. Paralleling these developments but causing much more difficulty was a series of decisions taken within the oligarchy about the nature of a national parliament.[35] The first stage was in February 1875, when Ōkubo, Kido, and Itagaki,

[34] Regulations of July 22, 1878 in McLaren, *Documents*, pp. 272–6. On local government assemblies and their powers in general, see Hackett, *Yamagata*, pp. 107–15; and Steiner, *Local Government*, pp. 25–54.
[35] The discussions within the oligarchy leading to these decisions are treated in some detail in Akita, *Foundations*, pp. 31–57; and Beckmann, *Making*, pp. 26–61. In Japanese, see Inada, *Meiji kempō*, vol. 1, chaps. 6–11.

with the help of Itō as an intermediary, agreed to reorganize the Dajōkan so as to replace the Left and Right Chambers by a bicameral legislature, comprising a senate (Genrō-in) and the assembly of prefectural governors (Chihōkan kaigi) already mentioned. This was announced in April in an imperial rescript promising that constitutional government would be established "in gradual stages." The change did not in any way reduce the authority of the executive, acting through the Center Chamber (Sei-in), but it did set up a machinery for constitution making. In September 1876 the Genrō-in was instructed to prepare constitutional proposals, a task entrusted to a small committee and completed in June 1878. The scheme it produced had some similarities to what Kido had put forward nearly five years earlier, as well as to the constitution that was eventually introduced in 1889. Nevertheless, in a number of respects it betrayed the influence of the kind of thinking that both Iwakura and Itō were inclined to describe as un-Japanese. Thus, although it referred to the imperial line as "unbroken for ages" and the emperor as "sacred and inviolable," possessing "the power of administration," it also described the legislative power as "divided between the Emperor and Parliament." Ministers were to be appointed and dismissed by the emperor but were to take an oath of loyalty to the constitution and could be impeached by the upper house (Genrō-in). The lower house, which was to be elected under rules similar to those being introduced for the prefectural assemblies, was to have the sole right of approving the budget.[36]

Much of this was unacceptable to senior members of the Center Chamber. Itō and Iwakura promptly told the Genrō-in to revise its draft to make it more in keeping with the "national polity," that is, to strengthen the imperial prerogative, but the version that was finally produced in December 1880 still did not satisfy them. For example, it did not provide for the emperor to have the right to issue ordinances having the force of law, or free the government from budgetary dependence on parliament, both of which were measures they deemed necessary. Consequently, the proposals were not accepted, and the drafting committee was abolished early in 1881. Meanwhile, ministers had been canvased for their views. All but one agreed that some kind of constitution was needed, that it must protect the imperial sovereignty, and that it must be approached gradually, after careful preparation. Yamagata envisaged a legislature consisting of appointed members for an interim period or indirectly elected by the prefectural assemblies,

---

36 The draft is translated in Beckmann, *Making*, pp. 120–5.

but in any case one that would not be able to challenge the executive. Itō proposed as a first step an enlargement of the Genrō-in, in order to give more members of the nobility and the prefectural assemblies some experience of state affairs, as these were the men to whom Japan must look for sober political judgment. In general, he claimed, Japan's leadership must seek to disarm its critics, but not at the cost of ceding real power. We must "relax our hold over government but not yield it."[37]

The one voice that broke the unison was that of Ōkuma Shigenobu of Hizen, who had been councilor since 1871 and minister of finance from 1873 to 1880. He had long been the government's outstanding modernizer. Now that Ōkubo was dead and Iwakura was getting old, the contest for overall leadership seemed to lie between Itō and Ōkuma, which gave the latter's views a particular importance. He did not submit them until March 1881. They then proved to be a great deal more radical than any of his colleagues had expected, not least in recommending that a parliament be established almost immediately, so that elections could be held in 1882 and the first session convoked in 1883. Not only was this very much faster action than any of the other ministers wanted, but it also was action of the wrong kind: Ōkuma envisaged a constitution on the British model, in which power would depend on rivalry among political parties and the highest office would go to the man who commanded a parliamentary majority. "Constitutional government is party government," he wrote, "and the struggles between parties are the struggles of principles."[38] Implicit in this was a challenge to the Satsuma and Chōshū domination of the Meiji government. Itō at once took it up, threatening to resign if anything like Ōkuma's proposals were accepted. This enabled him to isolate Ōkuma and force him out of the council later in the year.

In the interval, Itō consulted privately with Iwakura about the constitutional question, working out a set of ideas that on July 5 were put to the Dajōkan in Iwakura's name as a statement of "general principles." The memorial accompanying them rejected the proposition that Japan move "suddenly" to a British system, which made "the administration of the government responsible to the majority in parliament," and expressed a preference for that of Prussia, in which parliament had only legislative power and "the organization of the chief officers of the administration" remained "the prerogative of the ruler." In Iwakura's words, the situation of Japan made it more appropriate to

---

37 The memorials by Yamagata and Itō are translated in Beckmann, *Making*, pp. 126–35.
38 The memorial is translated in ibid., pp. 136–42.

"advance gradually on the model of Prussia, thereby leaving room for future improvements."[39] Specifically, he identified three points as crucial to the choice: that the emperor retain the right to appoint and dismiss ministers and senior officials; that the cabinet not be subject to "the intervention of parliament," the ministers being directly responsible to the emperor in departmental matters; and that the government be freed from financial control by the parliament by providing for the budget of the previous year to be continued in force whenever the parliament rejected the current budget proposals. On October 11, 1881, the Dajōkan accepted Iwakura's statement as the basis for its future action. The next day an imperial decree promised that a constitution, designed to ensure "that our imperial heirs may be provided with a rule for their guidance," would be gradually worked out and brought into effect in 1890.[40]

Two themes ran through all these documents, except that of Ōkuma. One was that parliamentary government in Japan would be weak or even subversive government, destroying the firm central direction on which the whole future of the country depended. The other was that Prussia, not Britain, was the relevant model for Japan, because Prussia's problems and experiences were much more apposite to a country that had not yet attained the economic and social foundations needed for parliamentary rule. These considerations were to continue to dominate the discussions that led to the actual drafting of a constitution during the next eight years. They were manifested, first, in the muzzling of opposition through the enforcement of strict controls over press and public meetings, culminating in the Peace Preservation Law of 1887, through which the police were given the power to remove from the capital any person "who plots or incites disturbance, or who is judged to be scheming something detrimental to public tranquility"[41]; and, second, in the arrangement by which the drafts were prepared under the direction of Itō, working in seclusion with the help of German and German-influenced advisers.

Insofar as the debates over a constitution were part of a struggle for power, it was one in which the position of the men in office grew steadily stronger. Following the imperial announcement of October 1881, those who wished to push the government in the direction of a constitution that would give parliament genuine authority organized

39 Iwakura's memorial is translated in ibid., pp. 143–8.
40 Text translated in Ishii, *Japanese Legislation*, pp. 720–1.
41 Text of December 25, 1887, translated in McLaren, *Documents*, pp. 502–4. For the press laws of 1875 and 1887, pp. 539–50.

themselves into political parties and conducted vigorous campaigns.[42] Ōkuma's Reform Party (Kaishintō), founded in March 1882 with the backing of some urban intellectuals and wealthy merchants, pressed hard for a parliament of the British type, but its broad acceptance of the main elements in Meiji modernizing held it back from taking any action that might be genuinely disruptive. The government had little to fear from gradualism of this kind, especially as the movement was without any solid commercial or industrial base. Itagaki's Liberal Party (Jiyūtō) had no similar inhibitions. Initially controlled by dissident ex-samurai, many of whom had been influenced by French political thought, it attracted widespread support in the early 1880s from landlords and farmers in the countryside. Under the pressures of a deflationary monetary policy, which reduced farm prices and caused considerable distress, some of these turned to demonstrations of force, more in the tradition of peasant rebellion than party politics. This had two effects. It provided the government with ample excuse for the use of army and police, on the grounds that the party was acting illegally, and it frightened the more moderate leaders into breaking with the radicals. The Jiyūtō was dissolved in 1884, and the scattered outbreaks of violence with which it was associated were suppressed by the following year.[43] Thereafter there was little really effective opposition of which the oligarchy needed to take account in its task of writing a constitution.

One purpose of having a constitution was to consolidate this gain, that is, to ensure that men of substance would see enough advantages in the regime to make them want to cooperate with it, leaving the police to deal with the rest. In this sense one cannot divorce the formal written constitution from the decisions that were being taken during the 1880s regarding recruitment to the bureaucracy and the nature of local assemblies, though neither of these was to be the subject of specific provisions in the document of 1889. The latter also had another function, however: to persuade the world of Japan's enlightenment. To this, too, other decisions were relevant. Changes in the peerage and cabinet system, for example, were made not only for reasons of elite unity but also because they would present Japanese institutions to the West in a familiar and favorable form. Yet in pursu-

---

42 The fullest account in English is by Ike, *Beginnings*, pp. 101–68.
43 For discussions of rural disatisfaction as it related to the *minken* movement, see Roger Bowen, *Rebellion and Democracy in Meiji Japan* (Berkeley and Los Angeles: University of California Press, 1980); and Irokawa Daikichi, *The Culture of the Meiji Period*, ed. and trans. Marius B. Jansen (Princeton, N.J.: Princeton University Press, 1985).

ing the path of Westernization, Japan's leadership faced a critical difficulty. The rationale on which its own power rested was that of imperial absolutism, deriving from the emperor's divine descent. Belief in divine descent was part of a complex of traditionalist sentiments that were spread widely through Japanese society. Westernizing was frequently offensive to those who held them. It was necessary, therefore, to find a constitutional formula that would reconcile Western norms with the Japanese imperial tradition, if the maximum advantage was to be gained.

Early in 1882 it was agreed that this task be entrusted to Itō, who would visit Europe to study Western models. He left Yokohama in March, proceeding directly to Berlin – a logical destination, in view of Iwakura's references to the Prussian constitution in the previous July and the German origin of Kido's original proposals of 1873. There he consulted constitutional experts like Rudolph Gneist and his pupil Albert Mosse. He then went to Austria to hear lectures from Lorenz von Stein. Thanks to those men, he wrote to Iwakura in August, "I have come to understand the essential features of the structure and operation of states. In the most crucial matter of fixing the foundations of our imperial system and of retaining the prerogatives belonging to it, I have already found sufficient substantiation. . . . "[44]

By the time he returned to Japan in the summer of 1883, following brief visits to Paris and London, Itō was in a position to put flesh on the bones of Iwakura's "general principles." For various reasons the actual drafting did not begin until 1885. It was then protected from political pressures – within the establishment, as well as outside it – by being conducted, first, in Itō's residence in Tokyo and then in his summer villa on an island in Tokyo Bay. Five men, apart from Itō, were principally concerned with it. Two were German: Albert Mosse, invited specially from Germany for this work, and Hermann Roesler, who had been an adviser to the Foreign Ministry in Tokyo since 1878. The others were Japanese: Inoue Kowashi, the most influential of them, who had been associated with both Ōkubo and Iwakura in constitutional discussions; Itō Miyoji, a former interpreter in English and secretary to the Dajōkan, and Kaneko Kentarō, a graduate of Harvard and a secretary in the office of the Genrō-in.

The political ideas that most influenced their discussions were those

---

44 Quoted in Akita, *Foundations*, p. 61. For accounts of Itō's work in drafting the constitution and of the subsequent discussions, pp. 58–75; Beckmann, *Making*, pp. 69–95; and Ishii, *Japanese Legislation*, pp. 366–408. Vol. 2 of Inada, *Meiji kempō*, is almost wholly devoted to this subject.

of "social freedom" and "social monarchy," current above all in Germany.[45] The former implied freedom within the law, involving the regulation of social groups through legal institutions, in order that all might enjoy the benefits of security and stability. In the modern state, the argument ran, the main threat to this freedom arose from the struggle between capital and labor, which, if not regulated, could cause anarchy. It was the function of a constitution to impose a framework of law such as would moderate this struggle and harmonize competing interests. The role could not be performed by an elected parliament, because those who were elected to it would be representatives of the groups that were in conflict. Instead, it belonged to a monarch, standing above the struggle and embodying in himself the general interest. To perform it effectively, he must not be placed under the control of parliament. Nor must his ministers, who must be free to act under his direction in a manner contrary to the wishes of those who might at any given time possess a majority there. Yet this was not to be mere personal absolutism, subject to no limitations. It must operate within a framework of law, which it existed to uphold, a restraint symbolized by the requirement that the ruler's executive actions required the countersignature of a minister, just as his legislative actions required the consent of parliament.

In a memorandum of June 4, 1887, drawn up in response to questions from Inoue Kowashi, Roesler set out this argument as it applied to Japan.[46] Japan was already entering the age of commerce and industry, he maintained. It followed that the bourgeoisie would emerge eventually as the most powerful class and that its demands for a political voice would have to be met. Satisfying it, however, would put in jeopardy the interests of the rural population, both landlords and propertyless. They would become the groups whom it would be the state's task to protect, and as the traditional defender of the weak it would be above all the emperor who must protect them.

The kind of constitutional conclusions to which this argument led – ministerial responsibility to the emperor, a strong House of Peers, the denial of full budgetary rights to the Lower House, property qualifications for the electorate, and a bureaucracy independent of parliamentary control – were clearly the sort of thing the Meiji leadership de-

---

45 See especially Joseph Pittau, *Political Thought in Early Meiji Japan: 1868–1889* (Cambridge, Mass.: Harvard University Press, 1967), pp. 131–95; and Johannes Siemes, *Hermann Roesler and the Making of the Meiji State* (Tokyo: Sophia University Press, 1966), pp. 3–35.
46 Summarized in Siemes, *Hermann Roesler*, p. 32. The full Japanese text is given in Inada, *Meiji kempō*, vol. 2, pp. 142–8.

sired. Indeed, Roesler had played a part in drafting Iwakura's "general principles," from which the discussions had begun. Nevertheless, there was a key issue on which Roesler was out of step with his Japanese colleagues. One reason that the draft constitution produced by the Genrō-in had been rejected in 1879 was, as Iwakura wrote to Sanjō at the time, "because there are parts which do not conform with the national polity."[47] By this he meant that the treatment of the imperial institution was not in accordance with Japanese custom and tradition. Precisely the same objection was made by Itō Hirobumi and Inoue Kowashi to Roesler's drafts in the 1880s, even though they were in other respects in line with their aims and interests. Roesler's justification of the imperial prerogative, after all, was theoretical and European in its derivation, owing nothing to Japanese circumstance beyond the general statement that the monarchy's historical survival demonstrated its appropriateness to Japanese conditions. There was no trace in it of the mystique of Japan's "national polity" (*kokutai*). Most Japanese understood *kokutai* to connote the existence of a uniquely Japanese emperor, ruling by right of divine descent and having a relationship with his people of a kind not paralleled in other societies. Unless the essence of this belief found expression in the constitution, many of them would regard it as no more "Japanese" than the cabinet system, or French criminal law, or an army recruited by conscription and dressed in foreign-style uniforms.

Consequently, although the European concept of "freedom within the law" found its way into the final drafts of the constitution, that of "social monarchy" did not. In an article published twenty years later, Itō gave an account of the origins of the constitution that helps explain his thinking on this subject.[48] Japan, he argued, faced in the Meiji period the necessity of securing the "recognized status of membership upon an equal footing in the family of the most powerful and civilized nations of the world." Because of the country's small size, success in this depended on cohesion and efficiency. Yet the heritage of feudalism meant not only that there were "centrifugal forces" to be overcome, but also that the people were "merely a numerical mass of governed units." For Japan to become strong, therefore, "it was a matter of prime necessity that these units . . . should combine and cooperate as a solid and compact organization for the attainment of the common weal," to which end the government had "to train the mass of

---

47 Quoted in Akita, *Foundations*, p. 11.
48 "Some Reminiscences on the Grant of the New Constitution," in S. Ōkuma, ed., *Fifty Years of New Japan*, 2 vols. (London: Smith, Elders, 1909), vol. 1, pp. 122–32.

the people to modern ideas of public and political life." It did this, first, through prefectural and district assemblies, then by the introduction of a national assembly. Indeed, Itō wrote,

the problem to be solved and the object to be attained by the constitution in our country was not only the harmonising and conciliating of conflicting tendencies of different interests within the State, as is the case in the majority of constitutional monarchies, but also the imparting of a new vitality to the public life and citizens – a new and increased creative energy to the public functions of the State itself.

In other words, "social monarchy" was not enough.

The special significance of the imperial institution in this connection was something that Itō emphasized in a statement to the Privy Council in June 1888, when that body was discussing the final draft of the constitution.[49] In Europe, he said, history and religion had together provided a basis for constitutionalism, about which there was "a fundamental consensus." Without some equivalent foundation in Japan, "politics will fall into the hands of the uncontrollable masses." Religion could not provide it: Shinto was too weak, and Buddhism was in decline. Only the imperial house could become "the cornerstone of our country." Hence "the first principle of our constitution is the respect for the sovereign rights of the emperor." The section of the final document that embodied this principle was the work of Itō himself and Inoue Kowashi, not of their German colleagues; of the politicians, that is to say, not the jurists.

The draft constitution, together with related documents – the Imperial Household Law, the Law of the Houses of the Diet, the Election Law, and so on – was ready by April 1888. At the end of that month the government created the Privy Council (Sūmitsu-in), initially to scrutinize the drafts and subsequently to act as the highest authority on matters concerning constitutional interpretation and revision. Itō resigned as prime minister in order to become president of the council, though he continued to attend meetings of the cabinet by special imperial command. The discussions that followed took almost nine months and led to a few amendments of some importance – for example, giving the legislature (the Diet) the right to initiate laws, as well as to discuss and vote on them – but did not change the fundamental character of the proposals. They were announced publicly from the throne on February 11, 1889, that is, Kigensetsu, the supposed anniversary of the accession of the first emperor, Jimmu.

49 Quoted in Pittau, *Political Thought*, pp. 177–8.

The first chapter of the constitution concerned the emperor.⁵⁰ It described him as "sacred and inviolable" and as "the head of the Empire, combining in himself the rights of sovereignty." He was to exercise legislative authority "with the consent of the Imperial Diet," which he could convoke, prorogue, and dissolve. He had the power to sanction laws; to issue ordinances having the force of law, subject to subsequent approval by the Diet; to exercise supreme command of the army and navy; and to declare war, make peace, and conclude treaties. In sum, as Itō put it:

All the different legislative as well as executive powers of State, by means of which he reigns over the country and governs the people, are united in this most exalted personage, who thus holds in his hands, as it were, all the ramifying threads of the political life of the country.⁵¹

What is more, none of this depended on any kind of social contract or the performance of a particular function. The emperor ruled because he was descended from "a line of Emperors unbroken for ages eternal."

The second chapter of the constitution dealt with the rights and duties of subjects. Their rights included those of appointment to civil or military office, regardless of inherited status; of trial according to the law; of property; of religious belief; and of liberty of speech, publication, and political association "within the limits of the law." Their duties involved military service and the payment of taxes. All rights were subject to the special ordinance powers of the emperor "in times of war or cases of national emergency." Itō took pains to emphasize this: "[I]t must be remembered that the ultimate aim of the State is to maintain its existence . . . [so] in times of danger the State will have to sacrifice, without hesitation, part of the law and of the rights of the subjects, in order to attain its ultimate end."⁵²

Chapter III established a bicameral Diet (Gikai), consisting of a House of Peers and an elected House of Representatives, whose composition was set out in detail in separate laws. Neither house was given superiority over the other. All legislation required the consent of the Diet, both houses having the right to initiate proposals and make repre-

---

50 The text of the constitution is available in English in a number of works, for example, Beckmann, *Making*, pp. 151–6; and Ishii, *Japanese Legislation*, pp. 725–33. The official commentary, published under the name of Itō Hirobumi, is *Commentaries on the Constitution of the Empire of Japan* (Tokyo: Igirisu hōritsu gakkō, 1889); it follows closely Roesler's commentary, except for the chapter on the emperor. There is a shorter commentary, also in Itō's name, "The Constitution of the Empire of Japan," in A. Stead, ed., *Japan by the Japanese* (London: Heinemann, 1904), pp. 32–63; this is arranged under the same headings as the English text of the constitution itself.
51 Itō, "The Constitution," p. 34.   52 Ibid., pp. 43–4.

sentations to the government. Sessions were to be for three months in every year; votes to be by simple majority; and deliberations to be public except when specifically ruled to be secret. Ministers were to have the right to attend and speak in either house. They were required (Chapter IV) to "give their advice to the Emperor, and be responsible for it," as well as to countersign relevant laws, ordinances, and rescripts. Itō's summary was that the Diet "takes part in legislation, but has no share in the sovereign power," whereas ministers served "as media, through which the imperial commands are conveyed. . . . "[53] In no sense were the ministers responsible to the Diet. Nor did they have a collective responsibility as members of the cabinet.

Chapter VI spelled out the limitations on the Diet's budgetary powers. The annual budget needed its consent, but there were a number of significant exclusions. The expenditures of the imperial household required Diet approval only when they were to be increased. Fixed expenditures arising from "powers appertaining to the Emperor" under the constitution or from "the legal obligations of the government" – which covered most costs of regular administration, including pay for the armed forces – "shall be neither rejected nor reduced by the Imperial Diet, without the concurrence of the Government." Finally, when there was no Diet vote on the annual budget or the budget proposals had not been passed, "the Government shall carry out the budget of the preceding year." These provisions were to be the main focus of conflict between the cabinet and the lower house in the following decades.

POLITICAL SOCIETY AFTER 1890

The constitutional provisions concerning the imperial institution were to be a major source of weakness in Japanese political life. As we have seen, they were formulated in terms of a mystical absolutism, based not on the emperor's responsibilities in government, but on his legitimating role, which derived in turn from his place in an "eternal" lineage. Appropriately, this kind of emperor became steadily more aloof: his public appearances few and ceremonial and his rescripts hortatory and lofty in tone.[54] From remoteness he sanctioned policy, making the decisions of his ministers those of the state. It is true that as an individual he was able to influence the decisions informally, as

---

53 Ibid., pp. 34, 50.
54 See Marius B. Jansen, "Monarchy and Modernization in Japan," *Journal of Asian Studies* 36 (1977): 611–22; also David A. Titus, *Palace and Politics in Prewar Japan* (New York: Columbia University Press, 1974), pp. 1–57.

could members of his household acting in his name, but there was no constitutional procedure by which he could do so formally. Roesler's proposal that the emperor should regularly preside at meetings of the cabinet had been rejected by Itō. As a result, the emperor became an autocrat whose powers, absolute in theory, were strictly limited in practice. The judicial power had to be exercised by the courts according to law; use of the legislative power required the consent of the Diet; executive action was the subject of advice by ministers, who had to countersign all decrees and similar documents. Thus it became the accepted interpretation of the constitution that ministers enjoyed a dictatorial authority, "since the cabinet's conduct was regarded in a legal sense as the exercise of an imperial prerogative legitimately based on the advice of imperial ministers."[55]

There was nothing very new about this in Japanese history. Under the Fujiwara, the Minamoto, the Ashikaga, and the Tokugawa, for centuries the emperor's role had been much the same. In all these cases, however, there had existed, apart from the emperor, a continuing center of power, whether aristocratic or feudal, from which Japan was actually governed. In the Meiji period this condition no longer obtained. Following the restoration of imperial rule (ōsei fukko), Japan had on the surface reverted to an earlier, bureaucratic type of political organization. Itō and his colleagues had then shaped this into a pluralistic constitution, in which office depended on merit, not birth, and the emperor's prerogatives were separately institutionalized in such bodies as the cabinet, the Privy Council, the Diet, and the general staff. By doing so they severed old links without always substituting effective new ones. No one institution could challenge the legitimacy of another, provided that it acted within its "proper" sphere; the emperor himself was removed from everyday politics; the officials of his household lacked the political weight to take over the coordinating role that was his in name; and there was no longer a feudal system that could operate independently of central direction.

The bonds that held this structure together were provided, as was logical, by the men who devised it, the "oligarchs," though not without considerable difficulty. Their first attempt at constructing a policy-making organ, the Dajōkan, had been abandoned as too clumsy and not "modern" enough. The cabinet replaced it, but the cabinet's cohesion was imperiled by the desire to avoid a doctrine of collective responsibility, because it might carry connotations of British parlia-

---

55 Ishii, *Japanese Legislation*, p. 387. See also Sakata Yoshio, *Tennō shinsei* (Kyoto: Shibunkaku, 1984).

mentary rule. Itō had tried to fill the gap by arranging for the prime minister to have overriding powers; that is, in the words of his commentary of 1904, "to indicate, according to his pleasure, the general course of policy of the State," and to exercise control over "every branch of the administration."[56] Sanjō and Yamagata apparently believed that this was a dangerous degree of individual authority. They accordingly introduced regulations in December 1889 by which the prime minister lost many of his supervisory functions. As a substitute they provided for the cabinet as a whole to discuss matters of general importance, but in a period when significant differences over both home and foreign affairs were emerging among the members of the central group, this proved ineffective.

The solution that was eventually worked out was extraconstitutional, like so much else that matters in Japanese politics. It comprised the gradual evolution of a process of regular consultation on key questions, including the choice of a prime minister, among those who were recognized as having a preponderant influence in the regime.[57] These men, the *genrō*, or elder statesmen – Itō, Yamagata, Matsukata Masayoshi, Inoue Kaoru, Kuroda Kiyotaka, and one or two others – personified the power of Satsuma and Chōshū. Because of their standing, they could make themselves coordinators of policy in their capacity as personal advisers to the emperor. Because they acted outside the written constitution, they could do so flexibly and confidentially. Until death removed them, they were able to supply the piece that had been missing from the machinery of government. Thereafter the problem recurred, for they had no comparable successors. In the twentieth century the lack of an acceptable means of mediating among the different segments of government, which often prevented agreement on national priorities, played an important part in the events leading to World War II.

By comparison, the development of the bureaucratic machine itself – at the levels where policy was implemented rather than – was comparatively smooth.[58] There was some revision of the examination arrangements in 1893, chiefly to reduce the privileges of direct appointment enjoyed by graduates of Tokyo Imperial University and to separate out the candidates for the diplomatic service. But for the

---

56 Itō, "The Constitution," p. 51. On the powers of the prime minister, see also Ishii, *Japanese Legislation*, pp. 384–94.
57 See Roger F. Hackett, "Political Modernization and the Meiji Genrō," in Robert W. Ward, ed., *Political Development in Modern Japan* (Princeton, N.J.: Princeton University Press, 1968), pp. 65–97.
58 See Hackett, *Yamagata*, pp. 198–203; Spaulding, *Higher Civil Service*, pp. 88–120; and Silberman, "Bureaucratic Development."

most part, the transition from a civil service recruited among samurai, usually through personal connections, to one recruited through the national education system, went ahead with remarkably little friction. The one important source of disagreement was the method of appointment to the highest (*chokunin*) ranks, which included vice-ministers and prefectural governors. Because these were filled by nomination of the government – technically, appointed by the emperor in person – they fell outside the examination system. And as the strength of political parties grew, Yamagata, in particular, began to fear that senior posts in local and central government might become part of a system of "spoils." He took several steps to prevent this while prime minister between 1889 and 1900. First, he changed the regulations concerning *chokunin* appointments, so as to give an advantage to those who had already served as *sōnin*, that is, had entered by examination, and to those who had had other kinds of administrative experience, which made it unlikely that they would be mere political nominees. Second, he extended the powers of the Privy Council, including in them the review of legislation concerning education and the bureaucracy, thereby making it difficult for any future party government to change the rules. Finally, he gave formal recognition to an existing practice whereby the posts of army and navy minister were limited to generals and admirals on active duty. All this helped protect the bureaucracy, both civil and military, from political meddling. What it did not do, as the twentieth century was to demonstrate, was to prevent the bureaucracy from meddling in politics.

Because the privileges of both oligarchs and bureaucrats had been firmly entrenched, there was from the outset a predictable clash between those who already wielded power and those, the political parties, who sought to acquire it through votes in the House of Representatives. The oligarchy's view of the cabinet's relationship with the Diet was that it must be "transcendental." Itō stated it as follows in a speech to the presidents of the prefectural assemblies in February 1889: "The emperor stands above the people and apart from every party. Consequently, the government cannot favor one party above the other. It must be fair and impartial. And the prime minister . . . who assists the emperor, must not allow the government to be manipulated by the parties."[59]

[59] Quoted in Akita, *Foundations*, p. 70. For an account of parliamentary politics between 1890 and 1900, see especially Akita, *Foundations*, chaps. 6–10; W. W. McLaren, *A Political History of Japan During the Meiji Era: 1867–1912* (London: Allen & Unwin, 1916), pp. 208–26, 242–73; and Robert Scalapino, *Democracy and the Party Movement in Prewar Japan* (Berkeley and Los Angeles: University of California Press, 1953), chap. 5.

Yamagata made a similar observation in an address to the prefectural governors in the following year: "Because administrative rights are the sovereign prerogatives of the emperor, those who are given the responsibility of their exercise shall stand outside the various political parties."[60] Nevertheless, there was, as we have seen with reference to bureaucratic institutions, a certain lack of articulation in the constitution, and this was manifested also in those sections that specified the respective powers of the government and the lower house. The result was to leave openings that the parties were able to exploit. In particular, the Diet's ability to block any *increases* in the budget proved to be a much more potent weapon than Itō had expected, given that the first parliamentary decade was to be that of Japan's first modern war and the beginnings of its overseas expansion.

In July 1890 the first elections gave a majority in the lower house (160 votes out of a total of 300) jointly to the three parties led by Gotō Shōjirō, Itagaki Taisuke, and Ōkuma Shigenobu, all former members of the Dajōkan, who were now openly at odds with the men still in office. Through several turbulent sessions – and intervening elections – they concentrated their attacks on the budget, forcing ministers to adopt a variety of illegal or suspect devices in order to get their proposals through. Matsukata, for example, tried to manipulate the 1892 elections by an extensive use of bribery and the special powers of the police. The outcome was twenty-five people killed, but only ninety-three representatives supporting the government returned to the Diet. In the next session, Itō had recourse to a personal message from the emperor as a means of getting a favorable budget vote. Despite a political truce during 1894–5, because of the Sino-Japanese War, such deadlocks recurred, and it began to seem that if the parties could not rule Japan, they could make it almost impossible for anyone else to do so constitutionally.

Neither Itō nor Yamagata wanted the constitution to break down, as this would seriously damage the country's international reputation. Itō, however, was willing to go much further than Yamagata in trying to make it work, even to the point of admitting the parties to a share of office. In 1893 he had begun a limited cooperation with Itagaki's Liberal Party, only to find in the end that the opposition of other *genrō*, notably Yamagata, prevented him from paying Itagaki's price, which was a post in the cabinet. In 1896 he was willing to pay that price, and in 1898 he gave his support to the formation of a joint

---

60 Quoted in Scalapino, *Democracy*, p. 153, n. 8.

Ōkuma–Itagaki government, but this collapsed in a matter of weeks because of its own internal divisions. As a last resort, therefore, Itō turned to forming a party of his own, one whose members would back "government" policies in return for some access to cabinet appointments for themselves, that is, a party that would be satisfied with influence, not power. Taking over the surviving membership and organization of the Liberal Party, he founded the Rikken Seiyūkai (Association of Friends of Constitutional Government) in September 1900. This marked a parting of the ways between Itō and Yamagata, the former relying thereafter on manipulating the Diet and the *genrō*, the latter on exploiting his base of support within the army and the Home Ministry bureaucracy. It also opened the way for a gradual infiltration of "outsiders" into the corridors of power, men like Hara Takashi (Kei), who countered Yamagata's moves by establishing ties between the parties and senior bureaucrats. Itō, optimistically, saw the resulting changes as evidence of a recognition by both sides that "the spirit of tolerance and conciliation, together with the tacit and mutual consent to place the welfare of the nation high above party politics or party passions, were necessary for the vitality and harmonious working of any constitutional government."[61] Later commentators have been less generous. Be that as it may, events in the 1890s had certainly demonstrated that the exclusion of elected representatives from positions of authority need not be as complete or as permanent as a first reading of the constitution would suggest.

There had also during the same period been a broadening of the electorate, which was equally indicative of things to come.[62] In 1890 the vote was confined to males over twenty-five, who had lived for a year in the electoral district and paid annually at least ¥15 in national taxes. This meant that the total electorate was less than half a million, approximately 1.5 percent of the population. Electoral districts were small and were based on the census figures, not the distribution of qualified voters, and so the number of votes required to secure election varied, according to area, from under one hundred to over four thousand. Because the voters qualified chiefly by paying land tax – other tax rates were low – there was a substantial overrepresentation of rural interests, chiefly those of the landlords, and an underrepresen-

61 Itō, "Some Reminiscences," p. 131.
62 There is a good summary of the electoral system between 1890 and 1900 in George E. Uyehara, *The Political Development of Japan: 1867–1909* (London: Constable, 1910), pp. 168–79. For a detailed study of the system in action, see R. H. P. Mason, *Japan's First General Election, 1890* (Cambridge, England: Cambridge University Press, 1969), esp. pp. 27–58.

tation of urban ones. This did not entirely accord with the oligarchy's assessment of the desirable course of national development, especially after Japan's victory over China. Hence Itō and Yamagata both tried to secure electoral reform, starting in 1895. Early bills for this purpose failed to get past the landlord vote in the lower house, but Yamagata finally succeeded in getting one approved in 1900. It created larger, multimember electoral districts, using the single, transferable vote; reduced the tax qualification for voting to ¥10 and made it less dependent on land tax, thereby increasing the electorate to about 1.7 million; and established separate electoral districts for all municipalities with a population of more than thirty thousand. Thus it ensured that the twentieth-century Diet would be more representative of Japan's growing commercial and industrial class.

In conclusion, let us return to the question, raised at the beginning of this chapter, of how Meiji political institutions can be characterized as a whole. One negative statement can be made at once. The liberal democracy, which Western Europe and America developed during the nineteenth century – and sought eagerly to export – found its principal advocates in Japan among those who criticized the regime, not those who created it. Nor was this phenomenon in isolation. Japan before 1900 was not yet fully industrial or even capitalist, whether viewed in a political, economic, or social context. Its government did not pursue liberal economic policies, any more than it pursued liberal democratic ones, and the bourgeoisie remained less powerful than the ex-samurai or landlords. It is easy to be misled by the enthusiasm with which Japanese translated Samuel Smiles or Herbert Spencer into believing that the liberal tendency in Japan was stronger than it really was.

Contemporary opponents of the Meiji government, mostly liberals themselves, saw it as feudal and autocratic: an alliance of factions (*hambatsu*) institutionalizing the power of men from a small number of domains (Satsuma, Chōshū, Tosa, and Hizen) who had come together to overthrow the bakufu in 1867–8. As a description of the origins of the leadership and of the bonds that held it together for the first twenty years, this emphasis on the feudal has much to commend it. Moreover, it was a feudal society that had to be transformed. Samurai origins and connections, especially for families belonging formerly to those four powerful domains, have continued to be politically important in the twentieth century. In social and economic institutions, too, feudal attitudes and values have often proved remarkably enduring. Nevertheless, as a means of identifying a stage of political development, the *hambatsu* label is inadequate. It does not sufficiently differentiate between the importance of being a samurai and the importance of belonging to a particular domain. More serious, it does not give enough weight to the nature of the common policies that the members of the Meiji government pursued. These had modernizing and centralizing dimensions that make an explanation in terms of the geographical and status origins of the leadership too narrow and possibly misleading.

There are two later interpretations that have wide currency. One is that of "social monarchy," which emphasizes the German theme in Meiji political institutions and identifies points of similarity between the two countries in social structure (Junkers and samurai) and stages of growth (late developers). This view, which is essentially concerned with theories of modernization, has a good deal of substance. It serves to underline the element of choice exercised in Japan's approach to the West. The German constitution was selected for study by Iwakura and Itō because of its apparent relevance; it was not just "copied" because it was there. It also identifies correctly the kind of Western ideas that were most influential within the Meiji government, where there was a clear recognition that the example of "advanced" countries, like Britain, was one that Japan was not yet ready to follow, notwithstanding the appeal of Britain as an example of what modernization might achieve. Finally, it introduced an element of lasting importance into Japanese political thought, notably the kind of university training given to aspiring civil servants. One could even argue that the concept of "social monarchy," as a justification of conservative reform on bureaucratic initiative, was more influential in Japan in the twentieth century than in the nineteenth.

Yet this label, which implies a Western frame of reference for an analysis of Japanese political development, may be a source of misunderstanding. This is not least because it purports to apply specifically to the monarchy. As we have seen, it was precisely in this context that Itō and Inoue Kowashi moved away from the recommendations of their German advisers. In their eyes, even within a Western-style constitution the emperor had to remain a traditionally Japanese symbol and legitimating authority. There were sound reasons for this, related to Japanese nationalism and the advance of national unity, but the result of accepting them was the creation of institutional anomalies that were a continuing source of difficulty in Japanese politics. They were resolved only in 1946 by abandoning the whole Japanese rationale on which the monarch's constitutional role had rested.

The alternative "absolutism" theory is as much sociological as historical. In a narrow sense, in which it may be said to identify the Meiji leaders as samurai who were able, by using the imperial institution, to detach themselves from their feudal origins and seize power without becoming dependent on the support of any single social class, it is an extension of the *hambatsu* approach. In addition, by asserting that absolutism of this kind was possible in the later decades of the nineteenth century only because there was an approximate balance of forces among a declining feudalism, a rebellious peasantry, and a rising bourgeoisie, it provides a satisfying formulation of the relationship between political events and socioeconomic change (though like most such statements it cannot be proved). There are two possible explanations of the origins of Meiji absolutism. One is E. H. Norman's argument that it was "only through an absolutist state that the tremendous task of modernization could be accomplished,"[63] which tends to emphasize the Tokugawa heritage and the foreign threat. The other is the argument that peasant unrest in Japan was an independent factor working in the same direction, that is, stimulating the ruling class's fear of populist revolution and thereby making absolutism an acceptable alternative.[64] Similarly, there are different ways of extending the theory into the twentieth century: to claim that Meiji absolutism succeeded in checking an incipient bourgeois revolution, thereby "distorting" Japanese historical development, or to see it as a stage in the transition to a distinct type of bourgeois society, characterized by a symbiosis between absolutist bureaucrats and entrepreneurs. Such interpretations are far too wide in their implications to be examined in a chapter of this scope. The point of this paragraph is simply to remind the reader that they exist and that they are controversial. They also make it unlikely that any scholarly consensus about the nature of Meiji political institutions will last very long.

[63] E. H. Norman, *Japan's Emergence As a Modern State* (New York: Institute of Pacific Relations, 1940), p. 102.
[64] See, for example, the discussion of this subject by Tanaka Akira, "Ishin seiken-ron," in *Kōza Nihonshi*, vol. 5: *Meiji ishin* (Tokyo: Rekishigaku kenkyūkai, 1970), pp. 147–75.

CHAPTER 11

MEIJI CONSERVATISM

The Meiji period bequeathed to modern Japan a powerful conservative tradition that dominated government and society in the twentieth century. Meiji conservatism took shape at the end of the nineteenth century in reaction to the sweeping reforms and Western influence that had held sway in the first two decades of Meiji. Those reforms, which brought to fruition the demands for change that had grown during the late Tokugawa, drew their inspiration from Western ideas and institutions that were the products of the Enlightenment and of the liberal philosophies that accompanied the emergence of commercial capitalism and a bourgeois class dissatisfied with traditional forms of government in Europe. The Meiji ruling group, after initially adopting many of the ideas and institutions of the Enlightenment, subsequently promoted a powerful conservative program in order to sustain its power and the social order on which it rested.

Conservatism, in the sense used here, is not simply a tendency to maintain the status quo. Rather, it is a distinctly modern phenomenon that first developed in the West in the late eighteenth and early nineteenth centuries in reaction to the dominant themes of the Enlightenment and to the implications of the French Revolution. Although conservatism had distinctive features in different European countries, owing to their divergent histories and social structures, certain common features became apparent wherever it arose in the West. It is worthwhile to examine our topic in the context of European conservatism, in part because the Japanese conservatives drew inspiration from their European counterparts and in part because comparisons will prove meaningful in understanding the nature of Meiji conservatism.

The origins of conservatism have generally been associated with Edmund Burke and the reaction to the consequences of the French Revolution. However, students of this style of thought, like Karl Mannheim and Klaus Epstein, trace its origins more precisely to a reaction to the ideas of the Enlightenment. They show that conservative doctrines were already formed before 1789. To be sure, the polarities among categories of liberal, radical, and conservative were more sharply defined after the French Revolution, but it was the implications of the European Enlightenment that first called forth a coherent philosophy of conservatism.

The dominant themes of the Enlightenment in Europe included an optimistic faith in the ability of humans to mold their environment according to their own designs. This faith was rooted in the achievements of natural science and the belief that it was possible through the application of reason to construct a social order in accord with nature. In the same way that rational science had made progress possible in the mastery of the physical world, human affairs, too, could be improved because they were believed to be governed by natural laws whose workings, once discerned, could be used to bring ever-greater improvement in society. Accordingly, traditional values and beliefs associated with organized religious practice were dismissed in favor of a new view of humanity and its place in the world. By disseminating the new scientific knowledge and liberating humanity from the obscurantism and religious parochialism of the past, a new era would dawn. Government must become enlightened by recognizing the "rights of man" and by sweeping away the old class restrictions and establishing a new social equality through a wide array of reforms. It was necessary to eliminate all artificial restrictions, especially state regulations, that inhibited the natural workings of the economy. Because all human beings were subject to universal laws, all peoples and races were seen as progressing toward a uniform civilization. The Enlightenment, accordingly, embodied a negative view of the particularistic culture and traditions of all societies.

Those who opposed this new world view, who became known as conservatives, rejected the notion that society could successfully be remade simply through the application of the rational will. They stressed the idea of the historic growth of societies and the "collective wisdom" that existing customs and traditions embodied. Institutions would be more useful if they were the product of gradual growth than if they were constructed anew by individuals. Conservatives did not oppose change but said that it should be evolutionary. Society was like an organism; it had grown as a whole, as a system with its parts interrelated and fitting one another. Such a holistic conception of society required that a change of institutions be made by gradual adaptation. Because nations were the products of organic growth, institutions could not be transferred arbitrarily from one nation to another. Conservatism and nationalism found a natural affinity in their glorification of the particular traditions and institutions of a people. The universalist themes of the Enlightenment, its affirmation of the potential similarity of all human beings and of the progress of all peoples and races toward a uniform civilization, were countered with the particular claims of distinctive national patterns of historical development.

THE CHALLENGE OF THE JAPANESE ENLIGHTENMENT

Modern Japanese conservatism had its origin in response to dominant themes of influence exercised by Western culture during the period of "civilization and enlightenment" (*bummei kaika*) that held sway in the first two decades of the Meiji period. The full sweep of European Enlightenment and nineteenth-century liberal thought was introduced into Japan in a very short space of time. Positivism, materialism, utilitarianism – there was little opportunity to sort out and pursue the logical development of ideas. They were introduced in no particular order. For example, Nakamura Masanao published a translation of John Stuart Mill's *On Liberty* in 1871, but it was eleven years before Jean-Jacques Rousseau's *Social Contract* was translated by Nakae Chōmin.

The *bummei kaika* brought a wholesale delivery of the entire Western liberal tradition. The Enlightenment writers associated with the society known as the Meirokusha – Fukuzawa, Nishi, Tsuda, Mori, Kanda, Katō, and others – were among the most self-conscious initial advocates of the cultural revolution that swept over Japanese society in early Meiji. Subsequently, the ideologues of the People's Rights movement, like Ueki Emori and Nakae, further elaborated the political implications of the Western liberal tradition; and in the 1880s a new generation of writers, of whom Tokutomi Sohō was the most representative, sought to press the *bummei kaika* ideals to their ultimate conclusion by demanding the Westernization of every aspect of Japanese society. Western liberal civilization challenged Japan's traditional beliefs, its traditional social organization, and its traditional system of government with such ceaseless persistence as to throw nearly every area of life into a state of turmoil. The details of the *bummei kaika* are described in this volume. Here we shall try only to summarize the main themes that subsequently evoked the conservative response.

First, *bummei kaika* thought was dominated by a negative view of Japan's traditional institutions and the learning that underlay them. Fukuzawa Yukichi summed up this sweeping rejection of his heritage:

If we compare the knowledge of the Japanese and Westerners, in letters, in techniques, in commerce, or in industry, from the smallest to the largest matter . . . there is not one thing in which we excel. . . . Outside of the most stupid person in the world, no one would say that our learning or business is on a par with those of the Western countries. Who would compare our carts with their locomotives, or our swords with their pistols? We speak of the yin and yang and the five elements; they have discovered sixty elements. . . . We think we dwell on an immovable plain; they know that the earth is round and moves. We think that our country is the most sacred, divine land; they travel about the world, opening lands and establishing countries. . . . In Japan's present condition there is nothing in which we may take pride vis-à-vis the West. All that Japan has to be proud of . . . is its scenery.[1]

Despite this thorough rejection of Japanese civilization, the *bummei kaika* writers held almost limitless hope for the future. As with the Enlightenment in Europe, there was an optimistic belief that human effort could master the sociopolitical environment, just as science had made it possible to master the physical environment. A second dominant theme of the Japanese enlightenment stressed the cultural example of the West. Because universal laws of nature governed human behavior, if Japan developed in accord with these laws, it could progress in the same way that the Western nations had. Progress, in other words, was unilinear; it was determined by universal forces of historical development rather than by the particular trends of national history. Civilization in the West had progressed further along this universal path of development, and therefore, it could be looked to as an example. The liberal economist Taguchi Ukichi explained that the object of *bummei kaika* was not simply to "Westernize" Japanese society but, rather, to follow the path of universal progress that the West represented:

We study physics, psychology, economics, and the other sciences, not because the West discovered them, but because they are the universal truth. We seek to establish constitutional government in our country, not because it is a Western form of government, but because it conforms with man's own nature. We pursue the use of railways, steamships, and all other conveniences, not because they are used in the West, but because they are useful to all people.[2]

Taguchi was bold and consistent in his pursuit of the *bummei kaika* themes. Civilized development meant not only that people would use

---

[1] Albert M. Craig, "Fukuzawa Yukichi: The Philosophical Foundations of Meiji Nationalism," in Robert E. Ward, ed., *Political Development in Modern Japan* (Princeton, N.J.: Princeton University Press, 1968), pp. 120–1.
[2] Kenneth B. Pyle, *The New Generation in Meiji Japan: Problems of Cultural Identity, 1885–1895* (Stanford, Calif.: Stanford University Press, 1969), p. 90.

similar machines; they would also think and behave in similar ways, eat the same kinds of food, wear the same kinds of clothing, live in houses of similar architecture, and enjoy the same kinds of art. In short, it was the implication of his *Nihon kaika shōshi* (A short history of civilization in Japan) that civilized people would become more and more aware of their common humanity and that no nation would have a peculiar message.

A third dominant theme of the *bummei kaika* was a wholehearted commitment to science, technology, and utilitarian knowledge. The classical curriculum in the schools must be replaced by practical learning that was useful for day-to-day life. Fukuzawa's well-known condemnation of Tokugawa scholars as "rice-consuming dictionaries" concluded that "managing your household is learning, business is learning, seeing the trend of the times is learning."[3] The principles governing the physical universe could no longer be seen as identical with Confucian ethical principles. "First there are things and only afterward ethical principles"; Fukuzawa wrote in his *Bummeiron no gairyaku* (Outline of civilization), "it is not that principles come first and that things emerge afterward."[4]

As a fourth dominant theme, the *bummei kaika* writers promulgated a new view of humanity with revolutionary implications for society and the state. Fukuzawa's ringing words that opened *Gakumon no susume* (The progress of learning), "Heaven did not create men above men, nor set men below men," succinctly summarized a rejection of inflexible hereditary status. Signifying a new, open, and mobile society, he went on to explain that a young man's position in society should be determined by his grasp of practical knowledge. In *Bummeiron no gairyaku* he wrote that the fundamental flaw of Japanese culture was its most basic institution – the Japanese family system. The *bummei kaika* writers blamed the family for destroying the spirit of individual initiative and independence on which, they believed, modern scientific civilization depended. They said that the family system inculcated values of absolute power on the one hand and unquestioning deference on the other and, therefore, that it provided the foundation for authoritarian government. What was necessary was the fostering of a new set of values on which democratic, constitutional, and

---

3 Carmen Blacker, *The Japanese Enlightenment: A Study of the Writings of Fukuzawa Yukichi* (Cambridge, England: Cambridge University Press, 1964), p. 52.
4 Craig, "Fukuzawa," in Ward, ed., *Political Development*, p. 122. For the entire work, *An Outline of a Theory of Civilization*, trans. David A. Dilworth and G. Cameron Hurst (Tokyo: Sophia University Press, 1973).

enlightened government could be founded. The *bummei kaika* was by no means democratic in the twentieth-century sense of advocating universal suffrage or economic equality, but it did oppose old forms of social stratification and government by a closed elite. It favored an open and mobile society in which economic rewards would be commensurate with individual talent and effort. It stood for a new social ethic that would free the individual from group control – an ethic that would cultivate self-support, self-expression, and self-responsibility. The *bummei kaika* advocates frequently expressed hope of replacing the extended hierarchical family groups with independent nuclear households consisting of only parents and children and marked by the elevation of women to a new status. These writers generally argued for a parliamentary government that would function through rational deliberation and enlightened legislation, with responsible ministries and an impartial law-abiding administration. They espoused Manchester free-trade ideals and put their faith in an emerging internationalism. Fukuzawa, in a section entitled "Countries Are Equal" of *Gakumon no susume*, saw little future for a narrow nationalism: "A country is a gathering of people. Japan is a gathering of Japanese and England is a gathering of Englishmen. Japanese and English alike are members of a common humanity; they must respect each others' rights."[5] Taguchi Ukichi was typically even more bold and provocative in arguing an emerging internationalism. In an article in the first issue of the journal *Kokumin no tomo* in 1887, he described nationalism as a foolish and outmoded conception that had caused needless disputes. Nationality ought to be ignored, so that an Englishman living in Tokyo was "a Tokyoite" just as much as was a Kagoshima man living in Tokyo. *Kokumin no tomo*, the journal of Tokutomi Sohō that evoked enthusiastic response from educated youth, represented the carryforward of *bummei kaika* themes and ideals to a new generation of Japanese. *Heiminshugi*, as Tokutomi called his ideas, proclaimed the emergence of "a new Japan," making a clean break with its past and becoming a wholly Western, liberal, democratic, industrial society. There was no room here for a Japanese cultural identity.

EARLY MEIJI CONSERVATIVES: THE MORAL IMPERATIVE

It was in confronting individual elements and themes of the *bummei kaika* that a conservative philosophy began to take shape. From the

---

5 Ibid., p. 118.

very outset of the Meiji period, of course, there was reactionary opposition to the reforms that were introduced. This opposition drew its greatest strength from the activities of those who were politically alienated from the new regime. Saigō, for example, left the government, returned to Satsuma, and led an uprising, already described in this volume, that sought to turn back the clock on many of the Meiji reforms. There were other reactionary efforts such as the Shimpūren in Kumamoto, which were prepared to use violence against the agents of Western-inspired reform.

In contrast with such reaction and a wish to return to the past, the beginnings of a coherent conservative philosophy depended on a reasoned response to the premises of the *bummei kaika*. Above all, it was the challenge that the Enlightenment offered to fundamental Japanese social institutions and values that evoked the beginnings of Meiji conservatism. Except for the imperial institution, the *bummei kaika* advocates could not have attacked any part of traditional society to which the Japanese felt a deeper emotional attachment than they did to the values that underlay family life.

Even the advocates of reforming these values found it difficult to practice their proposals within their own families. Fukuzawa, for example, had advocated a modern education and individual rights for women but brought up his own daughters in the strictest orthodoxy. Mori Arinori had published a reformist "Essay on Wives" in the periodical *Meiroku zasshi* but found trouble in being consistent. For his first marriage, he insisted that it be in the form of a contract – Fukuzawa was a witness! – to demonstrate the equality of the partnership. Subsequently, however, he dissolved the marriage, explaining that his wife had become "peculiar and flighty" as a result of the new relationship and that "to attempt a marriage like that with an uneducated Japanese woman was my mistake."[6]

The early Meiji education system was the prime target of conservative wrath because it replaced traditional Confucian moral teachings with a utilitarian spirit stressing a view of learning as an investment in worldly success. The preamble of the Education Ordinance of 1872 stated that the purpose of education was to enable a student to "make his way in the world, employ his wealth wisely, make his business prosper, and thus attain the goal of life." Some of the values that were

---

6 Michio Nagai, "Mori Arinori," *Japan Quarterly* 11 (1964): pp. 98–105. For Mori's "Essay," see *Meiroku Zasshi: Journal of the Japanese Enlightenment*, trans. William R. Braisted (Cambridge, Mass.: Harvard University Press, 1976). For Fukuzawa's raising of his daughters, see Blacker, *Japanese Enlightenment*, pp. 157–8, note.

introduced in the new school system may have had a basis in Japanese experience and in the background of the Meiji Restoration. Those values that emphasized ambition, hard work, the value of education, and the utility of science clearly had the force of history behind them. Other values, however, which were drawn from the Western liberal tradition and emphasized the natural rights of humans, the freedom of the individual, the rights of women, and so on, had little basis in Japanese experience and relatively little social support.

In fact, traditional ideals of loyalty and obligation, solidarity, and duty to superiors, which had deep roots in the family ethics and the feudal experience of Japanese, retained vast social support in Meiji and well into the twentieth century. This was partly owing to the "limited" nature of the Meiji Restoration which had not brought to power a wholly new class espousing a revolutionary set of values. Above all, there was no revolutionary change in the basic nature of the farming classes. Extraordinary continuities in the mode of Japanese farming all the way up to World War II helped perpetuate old values in the countryside. Accordingly, it was no surprise that the clean sweep of traditional values wrought by the *bummei kaika* in the educational system should soon come under attack. Conservatives had a vast social basis for the reassertion of old values.

The beginnings of a coherent, conservative defense of traditional Japanese values can best be found in the thought of several Confucian-oriented writers who supported some of the Meiji reforms but who regarded the disappearance of a clear, accepted moral code as a failing of the new period. They concentrated their criticism particularly on the new educational system, advocating instead a return to prescribed, Confucian-based values. Their ideas had something in common with the views of intellectuals in the late Tokugawa years who advocated a combination of *Tōyō dōtoku* (Eastern ethics) with *Seiyō geijutsu* (Western techniques).

The two most prominent advocates of this position were Motoda Eifu and Nishimura Shigeki, both of whom were Confucian in their fundamental views. Motoda, who served as tutor and personal adviser to the Meiji emperor for twenty years beginning in 1871, was the more conservative of the two because he still held in significant ways to the universal applicability of Confucian values.[7] Though accepting the

---

[7] Three essays by Donald H. Shively are useful in understanding the early stages of this Confucian-oriented protest: "Motoda Eifu: Confucian Lecturer to the Meiji emperor," in David S. Nivison and Arthur F. Wright, eds., *Confucianism in Action* (Stanford, Calif.: Stanford University Press, 1959), pp. 302–33; "Nishimura Shigeki: A Confucian View of Modernization" in Marius B. Jansen, ed., *Changing Japanese attitudes Toward Modernization*

irreversibility of the Western technological adoptions, he maintained that Confucian ethics must remain the core of education. Virtue and knowledge could not be separated:

> The advocates of enlightenment completely mistake the basic meaning of virtue when they contend that whereas the province of wisdom is broad and boundless, the sphere of virtue is narrow and limited. Originally, virtue was a name which embraced myriad excellences, while wisdom was one part of virtue with no province outside it.[8]

Motoda began a crusade to restore traditional Confucian ethical training shortly after the Ministry of Education decided in 1872 to replace Confucian ethics in the courses in moral training (*shūshin*) with translations of American and French moral texts. As lecturer to the emperor he was able to press his views within the government, often through documents drafted for the Meiji emperor to promulgate.

In 1879 he wrote a document describing the emperor's dismay at what he observed in schools on an imperial tour of inspection to the Tōhoku region. The damage that Western-style ethics texts was inflicting could be overcome if instruction were "founded upon the Imperial ancestral precepts, benevolence, duty, loyalty, and filial piety, and Confucius were made the cornerstone of our teaching of ethics."[9] Issued as an imperial rescript, the Kyōgaku taishi (The great principles of education) put the emperor's prestige behind the preservation of Japan's "customary ways" as part of every Japanese child's schooling. The rescript of 1879 regretted that "in recent days, people have been going to extremes. They take unto themselves a foreign civilization whose only values are fact-gathering and technique, thus violating the rules of good manners and bringing harm to our customary ways."[10] To reverse the decline in the moral climate required restoration of the "ancestral teachings" and, particularly, the "study of Confucius" to priority among the objectives of instruction.[11]

The rescript of 1879 spelled the beginning of the end of the *bummei kaika* era in education. A new minister of education decreed a greater

---

(Princeton, N.J.: Princeton University Press, 1965), pp. 193–241; and "The Japanization of the Middle Meiji," in Donald H. Shively, ed., *Tradition and Modernization in Japanese Culture* (Princeton, N.J.: Princeton University Press, 1971), pp. 77–119. An essay more sharply focused on our interests here is by Matsumoto Sannosuke, "Meiji zenpanki hoshushugi shisō no ichi danmen," Sakata Yoshio, ed., *Meiji zenpanki no nashonarizumu* (Tokyo: Miraisha, 1958), pp. 129–64.
8 Shively, "Motoda," in Nivison and Wright, eds., *Confucianism in Action*, p. 315.
9 Ibid., p. 327.
10 Herbert Passin, *Society and Education in Japan* (New York: Columbia University Press, 1965), p. 227.
11 Ivan Parker Hall, *Mori Arinori* (Cambridge, Mass.: Harvard University Press, 1973), p. 347.

centralization of education and stipulated that moral instruction in loyalty and filial piety be the chief end of education.[12] What was more, at the urging of Itō Hirobumi, the government issued the Public Assembly Ordinance in 1880 which denied to both pupils and teachers the right "to attend or to join as members in assemblies organized for the purpose of political lectures and debates."[13] Itō's primary intent was to undercut the influence of the People's Rights movement in the schools, but the ordinance also had the effect of adding to the conservative tide in education.

Nonetheless, although the liberal ideals that had guided education in the 1870s were mortally wounded by the initiatives of Motoda and other conservatives with the personal backing of the Meiji emperor, there were sharp disagreements among the conservatives. Itō, Inoue Kowashi, Mori Arinori, and others in the bureaucracy opposed the reintroduction of Confucian moral doctrine and the establishment of a "national doctrine" (*kokkyō*) through the educational system.[14] They favored a secular, statist approach in contrast with what they regarded as Motoda's reactionary and crude attempts at Confucian ideological orthodoxy. Itō already envisioned a modern though limited constitutional monarchy, whereas Motoda sought imperial rule and the unity of court and government.

Despite these disagreements, the conservative trend gained momentum. Influential officials, particularly those around the emperor, began to compile new moral textbooks. Among them was Nishimura Shigeki, who had been a founding member of the Meirokusha and was one of the early advocates of Western institutions but whose *bummei kaika* enthusiasm faded after his appointment as a lecturer to the emperor in 1876. Outside the court, Nishimura's views often had greater influence than Motoda's did, as he was not so uncritical of Confucian values as Motoda was. Nishimura found fault with Confucianism as a comprehensive and universal doctrine and for its lack of progressive spirit, but he believed that it formed the basis for a code of moral values that could serve modern Japan. While pointing out the shortcomings of Confucianism, he proposed to adopt selectively from both Confucianism and Western philosophy in order to build a new morality for modern Japan. In practice, the result was a watered-down Confucianism:

12 Passin, *Society and Education*, p. 84.
13 Hall, *Mori Arinori*, p. 346.
14 See Helen Hardacre, "Creating State Shintō: The Great Promulgation Campaign and the New Religions," *Journal of Japanese Studies* 12 (Winter 1986): 29–63.

> The Confucian way which has formed the morality of the Japanese people since the times of our ancestors, cannot be discarded even if we were to try to discard it. Especially the Four Books – the *Analects, Mencius, Great Learning,* and the *Mean* – in my opinion, can be said to be so far the best teachings in the world. Therefore, it is most proper to establish the foundation of moral education in Confucian books today. . . . When the Confucian Way is used, its spirit alone should be taken, and I hope the name Confucianism will not be used. The name Confucianism has for some time been disliked by the people, so that there are many who would not believe in the substance because of the name.[15]

In 1886, Nishimura published a treatise, *Nihon dōtoku ron* (Discourse on Japanese morality), in which he summarized his views. The faults with Confucianism, he wrote, were its lack of progressive spirit, its idealization of the past, and its rigid hierarchical views of the social order. Western philosophy alone, however, was inadequate because it did not give sufficient attention to personal conduct and was too contentious to provide a basis for a strong moral system. Japan would selectively have to build its own system, retrieving the basic Confucian spirit and updating it with appropriate maxims from Western philosophy.

Nishimura and Motoda also pressed during the 1880s for a "sacred rescript" to establish the basis of a moral orthodoxy for education. But Itō, who became prime minister in 1885, and Mori, whom he appointed education minister, opposed the idea of creating a rigid national orthodoxy. It was not until after Mori's assassination in 1889 that Nishimura and Motoda succeeded. In 1890, Premier Yamagata Aritomo and Minister of Education Yoshikawa Akimasa gave their support to the idea of an imperial edict because they thought it would contribute to the stability of the new constitutional era. The final document, issued shortly before the opening of the Diet (parliament) on October 30, 1890, was the product of drafts by many in the government, including Motoda. Until 1945, it remained the fundamental statement of ethical principles to govern the behavior of teachers and students and, in fact, the entire nation.

The Imperial Rescript on Education read as follows:

> Our Imperial Ancestors have founded the Empire on a basis broad and everlasting. . . . Our Subjects ever united in loyalty and filial piety have from generation to generation illustrated the beauty thereof. This is the glory of the fundamental character of Our Empire, and herein lies the source of Our Education. Ye, Our Subjects, be filial to your parents, affectionate to your brothers and sisters; as husbands and wives be harmonious; as friends true. . . . Pursue learning and cultivate arts, and thereby develop intellectual

---

15 Shively, "Nishimura," in Jansen, ed., *Changing Japanese Attitudes*, p. 238.

faculties and perfect moral powers; furthermore, advance public good and promote common interests; always respect the Constitution and observe the laws; should emergency arise, offer yourselves courageously to the State; and thus guard and maintain the prosperity of Our Imperial Throne coeval with heaven and earth.

Conservatives faced a dilemma to which Nishimura alluded when he wrote that the name Confucianism should not be used in the document because "there are many who would not believe in the substance because of the name." In the new age, Confucian values lacked the automatic sanctions to command belief that they had once had when the entire Confucian world view was accepted. The dilemma is nowhere better illustrated than in the work of Inoue Tetsujirō, a conservative professor of philosophy at Tokyo Imperial University who was asked by the Ministry of Education to prepare a commentary on the education rescript. In his *Chokugo engi*, Inoue set out to justify traditional values to a new generation raised on scientific and utilitarian thought. His purpose, he said, was to explain a rational basis for loyalty and filial piety. He wrote that traditional values must be justified inductively if they were to command belief. Accordingly, he gave the values of the rescript a utilitarian explanation. Filial piety, for example, was justified by self-interest, for "inevitably everyone grows old and weak.... Therefore, if you want your children to feel filial tenderness for you in the future, you must set the example.... If you do not, you cannot expect anyone to take care of you."[16]

It was typical of this formative period of conservative thought that such clumsy attempts at rescuing traditional values should be made. Inoue's blatant utilitarianism was indicative of the conservatives' desperate attempt to justify the traditional values, to which they were still attracted, in terms of the new rationalist thought that was intellectually satisfying to them.

Other young conservatives found distasteful such a defense of traditional moral values. The brightest and most influential of a new conservative group that came to the forefront in the late 1880s was the young editor of the newspaper *Nihon*, Kuga Katsunan. Well read in European conservative thought, he understood the kind of premises on

---

[16] Pyle, *The New Generation*, pp. 127–8. See also Minamoto Ryōen, "Kyōiku Chokugo no kokkashugiteki kaishaku," in Sakata Yoshio, ed., *Meiji zenpanki no nashonarizumu* (Tokyo: Miraisha, 1958), pp. 165–212. The standard reference on the framing of the rescript is Kaigo Tokiomi, *Kyōiku Chokugo seiritsushi no kenkyū* (Tokyo: Tokyo daigaku shuppankai, 1965). For the development of nonofficial interpretations of that document, Carol Gluck, *Japan's Modern Myths: Ideology in the Late Meiji Period* (Princeton, N.J.: Princeton University Press, 1985).

which a viable conservative philosophy must be built. The fundamental claim of the *bummei kaika* that Japan must follow the historical development of the West must be combated. The *bummei kaika* writers contended that this process was a fixed, universal pattern of development to which all progressing nations must conform. Accordingly, they held that the values of *bummei kaika* were of universal validity. On both theoretical and practical grounds, Kuga attacked these premises. His editorials, which had a wide and influential audience, argued that the liberals failed to understand the meaning of history and of the nation-state that established the framework within which Japanese reform must take place if it were to be effective and enduring. He was fond of asserting that the *bummei kaika* theorists "failed to grasp the historic, that is to say, organic, relationship between the nation and the individual."[17] A Japanese acted not as a member of a bloodless humanity governed by universal values; he acted rather as a member of his own vibrant people, inspired by Japan's own national spirit.

Kuga did not embrace traditional values, as Motoda and Nishimura had, from confidence in their universal validity. Nor did he try to legitimize them, as Inoue Tetsujirō attempted, in terms of the new rationalist thought. Instead, he gave them a nationalist justification. Referring to the rescript's provisions, he stated: "Filial piety, brotherly affection, marital harmony, and the loyalty of all to the Imperial Throne are Japan's distinctive national ethics. They are the historic customs of the Japanese people, the basic elements that support her society." He concluded pointedly that these values "cannot be deduced by academic reason (*gakuri*), but (only) by the emotions (*kanjō*)" of Japanese.[18]

Further, on practical grounds Kuga added that the preservation of traditional morals and customs was psychologically necessary to the nation because they provided the binding, integrative basis on which Japan's cultural identity and nationalism could be built. Kuga feared the social disruption that the values of the *bummei kaika* would cause, which in the heyday of Western imperialism could lead to national destruction:

> If a nation wishes to stand among the great powers and preserve its national independence, it must strive always to foster nationalism (*kokuminshugi*). . . . If the culture of one country is so influenced by another that it completely loses its own unique character, that country will surely lose its independent footing.[19]

17 Pyle, *The New Generation*, p. 97. 18 Ibid., p. 127. 19 Ibid., p. 75.

This argument became the most powerful in the conservative arsenal: that nations could not be subdued by force alone, that cultural acquiescence could prove to be self-defeating.

Promulgation of the Imperial Rescript on Education was accompanied by much pomp and circumstance. Copies of the imperial portrait and the rescript were sent to all the schools as sacred symbols to be used for regular ceremonies. When Uchimura Kanzō, a Christian recently returned from a period of extended study in the United States and now teaching at the First Higher School, abstained from ceremonial obeisance to the portrait on the occasion of a reading of the rescript at the school, it set off a controversy as to whether Christianity was compatible with Japanese nationalism. Inoue Tetsujirō wrote an essay denouncing Uchimura's behavior that became the center of the controversy. His essay, entitled "The Clash Between Religion and Education," held that Christian beliefs in individualism, universal brotherhood, and denial of the emperor's divinity could not be reconciled with the spirit of the rescript.

Kuga, much more astute than Inoue, saw the controversy in a somewhat different light. If Christianity could be stripped of its foreign customs and ties and assimilated to Japanese circumstances, as Buddhism had been, then Christianity need not be regarded as inevitably in conflict with Japanese moral education. In a period of intense competition among nations, as a matter of national survival, moral education was necessary to foster the "common sentiments" of the Japanese people to enable them to work together to deal effectively with their domestic and international problems. Uchimura, in fact, later attempted to foster a Japanese-style Christianity shorn of its foreign customs and ties. It was not his goal to turn Japanese into "universal Christians" who, he said, "turn out to be no more than denationalized Japanese."[20] He founded the "nonchurch" movement (*mukyōkai*) which deliberately divorced itself from outside influences. But Christianity in Japan after the rescript and the rise of conservative ideological movements in the 1890s was on the defensive. Traditional values of Japanese society became inextricably intertwined with partriotism and loyalty to the Japanese nation. In the heyday of imperialism, to adhere to beliefs introduced by missionaries coming from the Western

---

20 Marius B. Jansen, *Japan and China: From War to Peace, 1894–1972* (Chicago: Rand McNally, 1975), p. 99. For a study of Uchimura, see John F. Howes, "Uchimura Kanzō: Japanese Prophet" in Dankwart A. Rustow, ed., *Philosophers and Kings: Studies in Leadership* (New York: Braziller, 1970), pp. 180–207.

imperial nations was to leave oneself open to suspicion of disloyalty and subservience.

CONSERVATIVES AND THE PROBLEM OF FOREIGN RELATIONS

The struggle over the nature of moral instruction in education was the first issue around which conservative opinion began to crystallize. Another issue that early attracted the conservatives' attention was the problem of Japan's relations with the treaty powers. Until 1894, revision of the unequal treaties was one of the prime political issues whose influence was felt in both domestic and foreign affairs. More than any other issue at the time, it forced the conservatives to define their views of the Japanese nation.

The *bummei kaika* had posited a rather benign view of the treaty powers. Its advocates were disposed to overlook, at least for the time being, the violations of Japanese sovereignty imposed by the system of extraterritoriality that the powers maintained. Such infringements were attributed to Japan's backward nature; but as it adopted civilized values and institutions, these infringements, they believed, would disappear. Nations as they progressed would become more alike, and with the advancement of civilization, conflicts among them would recede. The nation-state, in fact, would become less important.

Tokutomi Sohō, whose views as a young writer in the 1880s can be seen as the culmination of *bummei kaika* themes, saw the militant phase of civilization being replaced by an industrial phase. Under the influence of Herbert Spencer, Tokutomi foresaw the decline of warfare and emergent internationalism. The rise of industrial civilization was accompanied, he wrote, by free-trade policies and economic interdependence that would overcome divisions among nations. Economic, rather than military, strength would determine the survival of societies. Accordingly, the most important measures that Japan could undertake were the adoption of the modern technology, civilized institutions, and liberal values that were common to the advanced industrial societies. Reaction to such a sanguine world view became a major issue, evoking a conservative response to the *bummei kaika*.

The treaties to which the bakufu had submitted represented an infringement of Japanese sovereignty. They permitted foreign residents and trade in certain leased territories and ports, and under the system of extraterritoriality, foreign residents were subject to the jurisdiction of their consular courts. Japanese tariffs were under international control. For a quarter of a century after the Restoration, it was a primary goal of Japanese foreign policy to revise the treaties and join the international system on an equal footing with the Western powers. To achieve this goal, the Meiji leaders pursued a pragmatic course of adopting the legal institutions that were deemed necessary for acceptance into the company of civilized nations who controlled the international system of late-nineteenth-century imperialism. Foreign Minister Inoue Kaoru put it succinctly in 1887 when he told his colleagues, "It is my opinion that what we must do is to transform our empire and our people, make the empire like the countries of Europe and our people like the peoples of Europe. To put it differently, we have to establish a new, European-style empire on the edge of Asia."[21]

The Meiji leaders went to great lengths to accommodate to the rules and mores of the international system. They pressed for adoption of Westernized legal codes in order to impress on the powers the civilized progress of Japan and so to hasten treaty revision. Many of the other Meiji reforms, including constitution making, had treaty revision as one of their motives. The lengths to which the oligarchs were willing to go to accommodate their Western visitors were dramatized by the opening in Tokyo in 1883 of the Rokumeikan, a gaudy Victorian hall where foreign residents were entertained with Western music, cards, billiards, masked balls, and other social functions. A dancing master was hired from abroad to instruct the oligarchs and their wives in the "civilized" social graces.

Conservatives were outraged and made the Rokumeikan a symbol of cultural subservience to the Westerners, but it was Inoue Kaoru's efforts at treaty revision that elicited a clearer focus of conservative views of the importance of cultural autonomy. Inoue convened representatives of the treaty powers in Tokyo in 1886 and proposed a number of concessions in return for the abolition of consular jurisdiction. He offered to establish "mixed residence," which would allow foreigners to travel and engage in commerce in the interior, and promised determination of all Japan's legal codes "according to Western principles."

The intense conservative opposition to these proposals was led by Tani Kanjō, minister of commerce and agriculture. Tani was a former army general who, along with other military figures, had opposed some of the liberal trends of the 1870s and had organized a party to

---

21 Marius B. Jansen, "Modernization and Foreign Policy in Meiji Japan," in Ward, ed., *Political Development in Modern Japan*, p. 175.

urge a conservative version of the constitution. The oligarchs had given him a cabinet position that took him on a tour of Europe where he was impressed by the spirit of nationality that was preserved from country to country. He returned from the trip at the time that Inoue was pressing his proposals. Tani expressed sharp opposition to them on the grounds that the promise to transform Japan's legal codes after the pattern of Western ones was humiliating and destructive of the Japanese spirit of nationality. Tani issued a dramatic resignation from the cabinet and led a vociferous opposition, both in the bureaucracy and outside the government, forcing Inoue to resign and ending his effort to revise the treaties.

Nonetheless, the government followed it with another effort at revision. This time the attempt was by the new foreign minister, Ōkuma Shigenobu, appointed in 1888. In his negotiations with the powers, Ōkuma extracted more concessions than Inoue had, but he did not gain an unconditional end to extraterritoriality. Moreover, the commitment to adopt Western legal principles remained a part of the agreement. When the details were revealed, controversy once again erupted; Ōkuma was driven from office; and negotiations were suspended.

The treaty revision controversy galvanized conservative opposition to *bummei kaika* views. It brought into focus the relationship between cultural borrowing from the West and the establishment of national self-esteem and pride. This issue was the prime concern of a new generation of intellectual conservatives. A group of young journalists and publicists emerged who expressed a more moderate conservatism than Motoda or Nishimura had. Educated after the Restoration in the new schools, they had been imbued with Western values from the early days of their education. They were not backward looking; they favored change and reform; but they believed it must be consistent with the Japanese character. Such concerns, they believed, were essential to national survival in an age of keen competition among nation-states and, particularly, in the heyday of Western imperialism. We have already considered Kuga Katsunan, the most articulate of them, the one most impressive for the clarity of his reasoning. He and others of this group formulated arguments against the *bummei kaika* notion of a universal civilization toward which all nations were progressing and against the belief that cultural distinctions from the West would ebb as Japan advanced. He held that the concept of "civilization" was relative, that social progress was not governed by universal laws. Not only was progress compatible with a diversity of cultures, but in fact, "world civilization progresses through the competition of different cultures." He sought to distinguish his own views from the more traditionalist reaction by arguing for careful, selective borrowing:

We recognize the excellence of Western civilization. We value the Western theories of rights, liberty, and equality; and we respect Western philosophy and morals. We have affection for some Western customs. Above all, we esteem Western science, economics, and industry. These, however, are not to be adopted simply because they are Western; they ought to be adopted only if they can contribute to Japan's welfare. Thus we seek not to revive a narrow xenophobia, but rather to promote the national spirit in an atmosphere of brotherhood.[22]

When he argued for selective borrowing from the West, his liberal critics charged that this would make a "patchwork" of society, because there was a certain spirit and set of values that underlay and motivated institutions in Western society. Kuga argued, however, against a monolithic conception of Western societies, pointing to cultural differences among the European countries and their fierce preservation of their own separate nationalities. The artist and writer, Okakura Tenshin, who was joining at this time with an American, Ernest Fenollosa, in a movement to preserve the distinctive Japanese traditions of aesthetics, made a similar point:

Where is the essence of the West in the countries of Europe and America? All these countries have different systems; what is right in one country is wrong in the rest; religion, customs, morals – there is no common agreement on any of these. Europe is discussed in a general way, and this sounds splendid; the question remains, where in reality does what is called "Europe" exist?[23]

Kuga adopted the historicist and holist arguments characteristic of conservative theorists in any country, to counter the *bummei kaika* themes of universalism and individualism. There was rarely apparent in his thought nostalgia for the past. Certainly there was no longing for an archaic utopia, for example, antedating Western or even Chinese influence on Japan. Rather, Kuga argued for the idea of the historic growth of society over time. This was, in short, moderate conservatism that sought piecemeal change – selective borrowing, for example – to improve society. Japan's development must be organic and

---

22 Pyle, *The New Generation*, pp. 94–7. A treatment of Tani Kanjō and other conservatives of his group is found in Barbara Joan Teters, "The Conservative Opposition in Japanese Politics, 1877–1894," Ph.D. diss., University of Washington, 1955. See also Barbara Joan Teters, "The Genro-In and the National Essence Movement," *Pacific Historical Review* 31 (1962): 359–78; and Barbara Joan Teters, "A Liberal Nationalist and the Meiji Constitution," in Robert K. Sakai, ed., *Studies on Asia* (Lincoln: University of Nebraska Press, 1965), vol. 6, pp. 105–23.

23 Pyle, *The New Generation*, p. 74 note. For Fenollosa, see Lawrence W. Chisholm, *Fenollosa: The Far East and American Culture* (New Haven, Conn.: Yale University Press, 1963).

holistic; it must grow gradually so that all the parts interrelated and worked together.

A group of young intellectuals and writers, with whom Kuga was closely associated, known as the Seikyōsha and led by Miyake Setsurei, founded a journal *Nihonjin* (The Japanese) in 1888 whose express purpose was the "preservation of the national essence" (*kokusui hozon*). The phrase became popular among writers of the day, and there was much debate over the nature of the national essence that should be preserved. The difficulty they had in this regard was indicative of a conservative dilemma. These young writers had a Western education and were perturbed by reactionaries who used their arguments to make a sweeping defense of traditional civilization. They sought a middle way between such traditionalism and the Westernism of the *bummei kaika*. In a word, they sought to be both modern and Japanese.

The fundamental issue in the deliberations of these young conservative writers is one not fully resolved today, namely: What is the nature of social progress? They, of course, fully accepted the notion of progress, but was it compatible with diverse social structures? Or did the functional necessities of industrial society inevitably overcome the diversity of social and cultural forms? Today, in the late twentieth century, there is plenty of evidence to show that industrial societies retain aspects of their traditional social structure, but for the Japanese in the late nineteenth century, as the first non-Western people to pass through the Industrial Revolution, the issue was particularly perplexing. Young liberals, like Tokutomi Sohō, who had a broad following in the 1880s and 1890s believed that industrial development required passage through universal, evolutionary stages. As it advanced, Japan would inevitably come to resemble the more advanced Western nations; Japan's progress, in fact, could be measured by its success in acquiring similarities to Western societies.

Such views made Japanese self-esteem vulnerable. For example, when the first session of the Diet failed to operate smoothly, many liberals were depressed because the experience reawakened doubts about Japan's ability to establish successful parliamentary institutions that were regarded as the essence of the *bummei kaika*.

Miyake Setsurei's most successful contribution to formulating a conservative argument was an essay, *Shin-zen-bi Nihonjin* (The Japanese: truth, goodness, and beauty), written in 1891 amidst disappointment over the outcome of the first Diet. This essay set forth a concept of world civilization progressing through competition among nations having diverse talents that resulted from different experiences and environments. The culture of Western nations might be the highest stage that civilization had so far attained, but progress would require other cultural forms and values if civilization were to move on to a higher state. In other words, cultural nationalism was not only a matter of self-defense, as Kuga argued, it was also a contribution to the progress of man. In his preface, Miyake wrote: "To exert oneself on behalf of one's country is to work on behalf of the world. Promoting the special nature of a people contributes to the evolution of mankind. Defense of the homeland and love of mankind are not at all contradictory."[24] It was a billiant argument designed to appeal to the young by persuading them that preserving Japanese cultural values was not a reactionary stand against progress but was, rather, a contribution to the development of civilization in the world.

Miyake described the ways in which his concept of world civilization, with its corollary of national mission, could be pursued by the Japanese and thus contribute to the realization of the ideals of truth, goodness, and beauty, which he defined as the ultimate goal of world civilization. Japanese, because they were familiar with both Asia and Europe, could make a unique contribution to truth by correcting the Western-centric view of scholarship. Spencerian sociology, for example, did not deal adequately with Asia, and the Japanese could offer new scholarly theories based on broader knowledge than Western scholarship possessed. Similarly, Japanese had a mission to contribute to goodness by building their military strength, protecting Asian nations from Western imperialism, and thus promoting justice. Finally, the Japanese had a mission to conserve their unique conception of beauty, with its emphasis on the delicate and exquisite, rather than simply adopting the grand styles characteristic of Western art and architecture.

These young conservatives had many able spokesmen, and we cannot doubt their wide influence in appealing to the nationalist predilections of the first generation to go through the Western-oriented Meiji schools. They were instrumental in forestalling the treaty revision effort of Inoue and Ōkuma. They also lent support to the opponents of the new legal codes that had been drafted and that would have introduced many significant Western legal concepts. For a generation, Japanese bureaucrats and scholars had been working with foreign advisers to develop new codes to cover the law of the family and

---

24 Pyle, *The New Generation*, p. 151.

private transactions as well as the law of civil procedure. Tokugawa customary law, in unrecorded form and highly diverse from place to place, was incapable of dealing with the social relations and commerce of the Meiji state. Adherents of French or German or other Western legal traditions argued for the adoption of their favored patterns of legal codes. The complex controversies were important, to say the least, because of the effects that the codes were bound to have on the future social order. The growing influence of conservatism in the 1890s induced much greater caution. The Code of Civil Procedure went into effect in 1891, but the civil code was postponed and debated further until 1898, and the commercial code was delayed until 1899.

Similar controversies between the universalism of the *bummei kaika* and the growing influence of cultural nationalism and conservatism took place in many fields of human endeavor. Literature and the arts were directly affected. Okakura and Fenollosa led a movement against the prevailing adulation of Western styles in the arts. The *bummei kaika* had brought to adherents of Westernism control of the government apparatus of art training and patronage, but the traditional arts and crafts languished in neglect and disrepute. Okakura, a contributor to *Nihonjin,* and Fenollosa tried to chart a middle position between the liberal, utilitarian, and pro-Western circles, on the one hand, and the traditionalists and xenophobes on the other. They tried "to create a new basis for Japanese art in an amalgam of East and West, old and new, subjective and objective."[25] Similarly, literati struggled over new forms of prose. Tsubouchi Shōyō's *Essence of the Novel* in 1885 pointed the way toward a new realistic literature that Futabatei Shimei's novel *Ukigumo,* published two years later, in prose close to the colloquial, sought to attain.[26]

The 1890s was, in short, a kind of watershed in the public discussion of cultural issues raised by the Meiji reforms. Japanese conservatism in its formative phase became deeply imbued with cultural nationalism. The younger generation had clearly succeeded in articulating a more thoughtful and balanced conservatism than Motoda, Nishimura, and others had in the early 1880s. The perceptive journalist, Yamaji Aizan, distinguished between the two styles of thought:

Whereas the conservatism that appeared in 1881 and 1882 was nothing more than a rebirth of Chinese learning, the conservatism of the late 1880s repre-

---

25 John M. Rosenfield, "Western-style Painting in the Early Meiji Period and Its Critics," in Shively, ed., *Tradition and Modernization in Japanese Culture,* p. 204.
26 Translated by Marleigh G. Ryan as *Japan's First Modern Novel: Ukigumo of Futabatei Shimei* (New York: Columbia University Press, 1967).

sented the development of national consciousness. Of course, in the latter case, many backwoods priests and Confucianists were delighted to plunge into the movement but . . . the leaders of the group had an understanding of Western culture. They absorbed the spirit of European nationalist movements, and regarded the attempt to make Japan over into a Western state as a most dangerous tendency. They observed that Western powers, through their language, literature, and customs, strove to preserve their nationality. Ultimately, they reversed the intellectual trend, and national spirit (which those who did not sympathize called conservative spirit) finally prevailed.[27]

The successive public controversies over the unequal treaties with the powers diminished the appeal of the *bummei kaika's* benign view of international relations and helped make the conservatives' case for preserving cultural autonomy a basis for maintaining the strength of the Japanese state. Tokutomi saw his Westernism declining in influence before the growing strength of "the new conservative group." In an eloquent appeal he admonished his countrymen:

If you hate damage to national pride and therefore entrance into the civilized world . . . then feeling for Japan will grow and feeling for the world will wane, then the ideal of the state will flourish and the ideal of the people will wither, then the spirit of conservatism will appear and the spirit of progress will die, and our country will have lost its vital energy. . . . Stop treaty revision, but don't halt the progress of nineteenth century Japan![28]

More than any other event, the outbreak of the Sino-Japanese War in 1894 and its extraordinary release of patriotic emotion gave sway to the conservative cause and overrode the universalism and liberal ideas of the *bummei kaika*. Not until 1945 was public opinion again so receptive to the appeals of reform as it had been in the early Meiji.

For a generation an effective foreign policy had implied a successful reform movement. But by 1890 the mood was changing. The new order was largely in place, and the international environment was changing. East Asia became the locus of fierce competition among the powers. Yamagata and the heads of the military services concluded that the security of the Japanese islands could be imperiled by the way in which the vacuum of power on the continent was filled. The Western powers became primarily adversaries rather than models of reform.

Treaty revision was achieved, and national pride, so long submerged by the tasks of the *bummei kaika*, welled up with the great military

27 Pyle, *The New Generation*, p. 108.
28 Ibid., p. 106. For a comprehensive treatment of Tokutomi, see John D. Pierson, *Tokutomi Sohō, 1863–1957: A Journalist for Modern Japan* (Princeton, N.J.: Princeton University Press, 1980).

victories of 1894–5. Abandoning his liberal views in a *volte-face* that attracted immense symbolic interest, Tokutomi Sohō exulted:

> Now we are no longer ashamed to stand before the world as Japanese.... Before, we did not know ourselves, and the world did not yet know us. But now that we have tested our strength, we know ourselves and we are known by the world. Moreover, we *know* we are known by the world![29]

Fukuzawa, the leading symbol of an era now past, could scarcely contain his joy:

> One can scarcely enumerate all of our civilized undertakings since the Restoration – the abolition of feudalism, the lowering of class barriers, revision of our laws, promotion of education, railroads, electricity, postal service, printing, and on and on. Yet among all these enterprises, the one thing none of us Western scholars ever expected, thirty or forty years ago, was the establishment of Japan's imperial prestige in a great war.... When I think of our marvelous fortune, I feel as though in a dream and can only weep tears of joy.[30]

THE EMERGENCE OF BUREAUCRATIC CONSERVATISM

The Meiji leaders looked at the problems of cultural nationalism and the lack of moral standards in a somewhat different light than did the journalists and intellectual leaders. The oligarchs were less concerned with the issues of cultural pride than with the practical problems of stabilizing the new order and, at the same time, mobilizing mass support for the national goals of economic and military power.

European conservative thought became increasingly relevant to the Meiji leaders in the early 1880s. They had already implemented many of the revolutionary ideas that they had held when they came to power, including the abolition of the rigid Tokugawa social order, the establishment of a national conscript army, the introduction of universal education and a new curriculum, and the promotion of an ambitious industrial policy. Other reforms still awaited completion, including the constitution, the local government system, parliamentary institutions, and the codification of law. But in the implementation of these programs in the 1880s, an increasingly conservative tone was evident. After the crisis of 1881, Meiji leaders, purged of liberal elements and determined to reestablish order and unity in political

---

29 Pyle, *The New Generation*, p. 175.
30 Kenneth B. Pyle, trans., "The Ashio Copper Mine Pollution Case," *Journal of Japanese Studies* 1 (Spring 1975): 347. From *Fukuzawa Yukichi zenshū*, 21 vols. (Tokyo: Iwanami shoten, 1958–64), vol. 15, pp. 333–7.

life, were less inclined to hold up their revolutionary example to the younger generation. Itō Hirobumi, for example, described the early 1880s as "an age of transition":

The opinions prevailing in the country were extremely heterogenous and often diametrically opposed to one another. We had survivors from former generations who were still full of theocratic ideas and who believed that any attempt to restrict an imperial prerogative amounted to something like high treason. On the other hand, there was a large and powerful body of the younger generation educated at a time when the Manchester theory was in vogue, and who, in consequence, were ultraradical in their ideas of freedom. . . . A work entitled *History of Civilization*, by Buckle, which denounced every form of government as an unnecessary evil, became the great favorite of students of all the higher schools, including the Imperial University. . . . At that time we had not arrived at the stage of distinguishing clearly between political opposition on the one hand and treason to the established order on the other.[31]

In order to realize the immense task of building an industrial society in the course of their generation, the Meiji leaders had to find some means to spur the populace to prodigies of self-sacrifice and effort and, at the same time, to maintain social stability. This, of course, is a fundamental problem of nation building, for modern development entails the awakening of increasing numbers of people to the national political community, and it engenders new divisions of the population. The challenge that Meiji leaders faced, therefore, was to balance economic development with political integration. What is particularly impressive about the statecraft of the Japanese leaders is the clarity with which they understood the historical process through which they were leading the nation. This owed much to their sensitivity to the experience of the more advanced industrial societies of the West. As Itō wrote in 1880 of the People's Rights movement and the demands for democratic government to which the *bummei kaika* had given rise.

The present political disturbance is symptomatic of a general trend sweeping the whole world and is not limited to a single nation or province. About a hundred years ago, the revolutions in Europe started in France and spread gradually to other European nations. The momentum of those revolutions gained strength and has come to constitute a tremendous force. Sooner or later practically all nations . . . will feel the impact of this force and change their form of government. The change from old to new was accompanied by violent disturbances. The disturbances have lasted to this very day. An enlightened ruler and his wise ministers would control and divert the force towards a solidifying of the government. To achieve this, all despotic conduct

[31] George M. Sansom, *The Western World and Japan* (New York: Knopf, 1950), pp. 347–8.

must be abandoned, and there can be no avoiding a sharing of the government's power with the people.

Itō was confident that Japan could avoid the revolutionary violence that had accompanied the historical process elsewhere: "Even as we control the trends, there will be no violence, and even when ideas are given free reign, they will not lead the people astray. Progress will be orderly and we will set the pace of progress, and the passage of time will bring about the normalization of trends."[32] Itō believed that the trend toward popular participation in government was irreversible but that it could be controlled.

The oligarchs needed to find ways to avoid the severe antagonism in society that would undermine the effort to achieve their national goals. They found their answer to this need in the conservative reform tradition of German political-economic theories. Influenced by this tradition, the oligarchs foresaw the necessity of accommodating new groups into the political order so as to maintain the social consensus necessary to control the development of society. The concept of social monarchy was influential – up to a point – in the development of the oligarchs' attitudes toward the institutional framework. The thinking of Lorenz von Stein and Rudolf von Gneist was particularly influential in forming the oligarchs' conservative reformism. Stein saw the development of industrial capitalism as creating acquisitive instincts that if unchecked, would lead to the dominance of the bourgeoisie at the expense of the other social classes. The result was likely to be social upheaval. Therefore, it was the necessary role of the socially conscious monarch and his bureaucracy to stand neutral above class interests and to act in the interest of the whole. In order to build a strong nation-state, the government would intervene in the economy to prevent class conflict and to maintain a harmonious social balance, integrating the lower classes into the national community "by means of social legislation and an active administrative policy that works for the physical and spiritual welfare of the lower classes."[33]

It was not only the Germans who gave conservative advice. There was plenty of it from other Western countries, much of it originating from evolutionist thought. Ivan Hall called it "overcompensating conservatism on the part of Westerners, a tendency to lean over backward away from their own liberalism in order not to push Japan too rapidly down

---

32 George M. Beckmann, *The Making of the Meiji Constitution: The Oligarchs and the Constitutional Development of Japan, 1868–1891* (Lawrence: University of Kansas Press, 1957), app. 5.
33 Johannes Siemes, *Hermann Roesler and the Making of the Meiji State* (Tokyo: Sophia University Press, 1966), p. 32.

the road of progress."³⁴ Herbert Spencer, for example, advised Mori that constitutionalism not be introduced too rapidly, that institutional growth follow an evolutionary or organic pattern: "I explained how botany teaches that vegetation transplanted from a foreign land will not produce the same flowers and fruits as in its native soil; that constitutions follow a principle identical with this botanical law. . . ."³⁵

The Meiji leaders were committed to finding ways to accommodate and, thus, to control the increasing politicization of the lower orders. Yamagata, more conservative than many of his colleagues, wrote in his 1879 "Opinion on Constitutional Government" that although political parties and other forms of opposition to the government were wrong and immoral, the governed should be given an opportunity to participate in order to overcome divisions within society, popular estrangement from the government, and economic discontent: "If we gradually establish a popular assembly and firmly establish a constitution, the things I have enumerated above – popular enmity toward the government, failure to follow government orders, and suspicion of the government, these three evils – will be cured in the future."³⁶ It became an *idée fixe* of bureaucratic conservatism that the people should be brought into the governing process, not as a natural innate right, but, rather, to achieve national unity. Thus, conservatives in Japan favored – in fact, conservatives generally took the initiative in bringing about – popular participation in local government, a national assembly, and, later, universal suffrage.

After Ōkuma, whose constitutional views were an extension of *bummei kaika* thought, was expelled in 1881, Itō went to Europe to prepare for the development of a conservative constitutional order and, in particular, to study Prussian experience firsthand. "By studying under two famous German teachers, Gneist and Stein," he wrote to a fellow oligarch,

I have been able to get a general understanding of the structure of the state. Later I shall discuss with you how we can achieve the great objective of establishing Imperial authority. Indeed, the tendency in our country today is to erroneously believe in the works of British, French, and American liberals and radicals as if they were Golden Rules and, thereby, lead virtually to the overthrow of the state. In having found principles and means of combatting this trend, I believe I have rendered an important service to my country, and I feel inwardly that I can die a happy man.³⁷

---

34 Hall, *Mori Arinori*, p. 321. 35 Ibid., p. 138.
36 Beckmann, *The Making of the Meiji Constitution*, p. 130.
37 Nobutaka Ike, *The Beginnings of Political Democracy in Japan* (Baltimore: Johns Hopkins University Press, 1950), pp. 175–6.

Itō found in German constitutional thought the elements needed to legitimate the new order in terms other than natural rights philosophy. Popular participation in government would be permitted under conditions that channeled it in nationalist directions. As was pointed out in Chapter 10 of this volume, Herman Roesler was retained as an adviser, but his ideas were filtered through the oligarchs' own determination to make the emperor into an unchallengeable and invulnerable centerpiece of the government, giving the Japanese people the sense of identity that conservative intellectuals had seen as so necessary to the new era. As Itō wrote:

> What is the cornerstone of our country? This is the problem we have to solve. If there is no cornerstone, politics will fall into the hands of the uncontrollable masses; and then the government will become powerless. . . . In Japan [unlike Europe] religion does not play such an important role and cannot become the foundation of constitutional government. Though Buddhism once flourished and was the bond of union between all classes, high and low, today its influence has declined. Though Shintoism is based on the traditions of our ancestors, as a religion it is not powerful enough to become the center of the country. Thus, in our country the one institution which can become the cornerstone of our constitution is the Imperial House.[38]

The imperial myth became the ideological glue that held together the new political structure. As we have seen, it was enunciated again in the Imperial Rescript on Education, laying the foundation for the more fullblown ideology of the family state. The new order was, therefore, at its core given a Japanese cast that departed sharply from the vision that the *bummei kaika* had held out for a new Japanese nation. Though embodying some limited aspects of liberal political principles, it was fundamentally based on a conception of a unique Japanese polity – the Japanese *kokutai* – which was rooted in the history and traditional cultural values of the people. Conservatives interpreted this *kokutai* in different ways. Itō held to a rational, secular view of the *kokutai* which treated it as the product of a long evolutionary process and certainly capable of change and development in the future.

But there was another interpretation that had more in common with the views of conservatives like Motoda. In this interpretation the *kokutai* was a moral, religious, almost mystical entity. The rescript on education described the imperial house as "coeval with Heaven and Earth," almost a personification of the Confucian cosmological order. Conservative legal scholars like Hozumi Yatsuka, dean of the law

---

38 Joseph Pittau, *Political Thought in Early Meiji Japan* (Cambridge, Mass.: Harvard University Press, 1967), pp. 177–8.

faculty at Tokyo Imperial University and one of the most influential interpreters of the constitution at the turn of the century, elaborated this religious conception of the *kokutai* by stressing the themes of the family state and of ancestor worship. His was a blend of Confucian, Shinto, and German statist thought. Japanese society, according to Hozumi, was founded not on a social contract but, rather, on racial unity that was preserved through ancestor worship. All Japanese were ultimately descended from a common imperial ancestor:

> The ancestor of my ancestors is the Sun Goddess. The Sun Goddess is the founder of our race, and the throne is the sacred house of our race. If father and mother are to be revered, how much more so the ancestors of the house; and if the ancestors of the house are to be revered, how much more so the founder of the country.[39]

Hozumi was the chief opponent of the French-influenced draft of a civil code that was debated from 1892 to 1898. The draft, based on natural rights theory, would have greatly curtailed the power of the family head. But Hozumi and other opponents argued that the Japanese *kokutai* was based on the authority of the househead, in both the family and the state. "Our family state," he wrote, "is a racial group. Our race consists of blood relatives from the same womb. The family is a small state; the state is a large family"[40] The section on family law in the revised civil code issued in 1898 represented a victory for Hozumi's views. The notion of the family state was, likewise, increasingly evident in the school texts for moral education. Hozumi, himself, headed the Ministry of Education Commission that recommended revision of the textbooks in 1908.

The conservative interpretations of the new order were soon disseminated through the educational system. As we have seen, the tide had already turned in a conservative direction by the early 1880s, when the liberal morals texts were removed, and a reassertion of traditional values began. When Mori Arinori was appointed minister of education in 1885, the momentum picked up.

Mori, an apostle of the *bummei kaika* in the 1870s, helped push

---

39 Richard H. Minear, *Japanese Tradition and Western Law: Emperor, State, and Law in the Thought of Hozumi Yatsuka* (Cambridge, Mass.: Harvard University Press, 1970), p. 73. For a splendid treatment in Japanese, see Matsumoto Sannosuke, *Tennōsei kokka to seiji shisō* (Tokyo: Miraisha, 1969).
40 Minear, *Japanese Tradition*, p. 74. For treatment of the civil code controversy, see Tōyama Shigeki, "Mimpōten ronsō no seijishi kōsatsu," in Meiji shiryō kenkyū renrakukai, ed., *Minkenron kara nashonarizumu e* (Meijishi kenkyū sōsho, IV) (Tokyo: Ochanomizu shobō, 1957). In English, see Dan Fenno Henderson, "Law and Political Modernization in Japan," in Ward, ed., *Political Development*, pp. 387–456.

education in a conservative direction during the succeeding decade. He and Itō had conferred at great length regarding the role of education while they were in Europe in 1882. Both agreed that "the foundations of education should be established with a view to the future stability of the nation." Education should not be confused with the "aimless promotion of intellectual prowess" or with "the struggle to get ahead." Rather, its purpose was "to elevate the spirit of the entire nation."[41] Under Mori's leadership the educational system was recast to place it at the service of the state rather than the individual. It was to create an elite of talent so as to promote "the economic growth and viability of the Japanese state."[42] Mori told local officials in 1887:

Reading, writing, and arithmetic are not our major concern in the education and instruction of the young. Education is entirely a matter of bringing up men of character. And who are these men of character? – they are the good subjects required by our Empire. And who are these good subjects? – they are those persons who live up fully to their responsibilities as Imperial Subjects.[43]

Mori's was a secular vision of the state that contrasted with the views of Motoda and later theorists like Hozumi whose views approached a mystical conception of the Japanese state. Mori was, in fact, assassinated in 1889 for his purported slights in ritual during a visit to the Ise Shrine. At the time, Kuga reminded the readers of *Nihon* that the ceremonies conducted at Ise were not religious services to worship Shinto deities, but rather they were national political ceremonies to reverence the imperial household, because Ise had been built to honor the emperor's ancestors. The distinction was an important one for Kuga and for most conservatives: the imperial household was the most important symbol of Japan's historical continuity and its unique cultural traditions.

The growing popular reverence for the imperial institution was apparent after 1890. We have already seen the reaction to Uchimura Kanzō's reluctance to bow before the imperial portrait in 1891. The same year, a Tokyo Imperial University professor, Kume Kunitake, published an article describing Shinto as the "survival of a primitive form of worship." Writing in objective, historical fashion, he traced the origins of court ceremonies, of the imperial regalia, and of the Ise Shrine to forms of primitive worship in the Orient that had existed in prehistoric Japan. Shintoists attacked the article as sacrilegious and forced Kume out of his university position. Moderate conservatives

---

41 Hall, *Mori Arinori*, pp. 362–3.   42 Ibid., p. 458.   43 Ibid., p. 398.

like Kuga made no attempt to defend a literal belief in Shinto myths, but they abhorred detached objective criticism of the imperial court, which they regarded as an historic symbol of national unity, essential to national cohesion. Kuga wrote:

It is our moral obligation to refrain from making a public issue of anything that relates to the Imperial household, lest . . . what began as an academic dispute result in jeopardy to the security of the nation. People like Mr. Kume are aware of their status as scholars, but they tend to forget their obligation as subjects.[44]

The *bummei kaika* had never had a deep social basis for many of its ideas. There was a ready audience for conservative views, and the public mood of Japan changed dramatically. The pressures to conform, as Marius Jansen has pointed out, came not so much from the government as from "forces within Japanese society. Colleagues, neighbors, publicists, relatives – these were the people who hounded the Kumes, the reformers, and the liberals."[45]

The new ethics texts adopted the conservative ideology to explain the basis of the new political order. In the early 1890s, over eighty texts were privately produced. They stressed the sacred authority of the emperor, the family state, and ancestor worship. To maintain control of the new developing orthodoxy, the Education Ministry began, in 1903, to compile an official set of ethics textbooks. There is some indication that the bureaucracy felt that the conservative trend was going too far, for the 1903 edition is regarded by many as representing a somewhat liberalizing trend. Nevertheless, they contained the basic teachings of the family–state ideology on which the subsequent edition of 1910 was built.[46] The new imperial ideology drew on the traditional language of loyalty and obligation and on a mythical past to imbue the new order with the aura of sanctity and legitimacy that would inhibit political opposition and dissent. As one scholar has put it, "The emperor became a substitute for the charismatic leader so prominent in the modernization of most non-Western societies of a later period, a substitute that was more permanent, more deeply rooted in the culture, and more invulnerable to attack."[47]

---

44 Pyle, *The New Generation*, pp. 124–5.
45 Jansen, *Changing Japanese Attitudes Toward Modernization*, pp. 80–1.
46 Wilbur M. Fridell, "Government Ethics Textbooks in Late Meiji Japan," *Journal of Asian Studies* 29 (1970): 823–34. The standard authority is Karasawa Tomitarō, *Kyōkasho no rekishi* (Tokyo: Sōbunsha, 1960).
47 Robert A. Scalapino, "Ideology and Modernization: The Japanese Case," in David E. Apter, ed., *Ideology and Discontent* (New York: Free Press, 1964), p. 103.

THE CONSERVATIVE APPROACH TO INDUSTRIAL SOCIETY

The Meiji leaders in their drive to promote industry had always advocated one of the main enlightenment themes, namely, the advancement of science, technology, and utilitarian knowledge. In that sense they might not be considered conservatives. As Benjamin Schwartz observed in his essay on conservatism in modern China, modernization of industrialization would seem to be "the very antithesis of conservatism" because it involves "the systematic universal application of technological rationalism both to nature and society," which was one of the main premises of enlightenment thinking that the conservatives were said to oppose. Modernization, Schwartz continued,

> thus seems to be the very paradigm of the deliberate effort to shape the social order according to conscious ideas in people's heads. Yet the fact is that as modernization has proceeded, it too has come to be viewed more and more as a sociohistoric process independent of human wills. It has thus also come to be viewed as a kind of organic societal growth which has already achieved a mature state of development. While there no doubt have been forms of aristocratic conservatism in Europe which resisted industrialization, the fact is that conservatism of the Bismarckian variety wholeheartedly based itself on bureaucratic and industrial nationalization and clearly perceived the link between industrialization and national power.[48]

The Bismarckian variety of conservatism formulated under the impact of Germany's maturing industrialism, fear of social revolution, and the ideals of German unification was uniquely relevant to Japanese circumstances and, in fact, exercised great influence on the Meiji bureaucratic leaders. German thought helped them anticipate the social and economic effects of industrialization and plan ways in which political initiatives could be taken to maintain conservative control of industrial society.

The German historical school of economics was particularly influential. It had risen in the nineteenth century to challenge the laissez-faire liberalism of Adam Smith. The historical school rejected the notion that the same body of theory was valid for all times and places. It rejected the materialism and universalism of both the Manchester school and the socialists. Instead, it saw economic issues as inseparable from the society, culture, and history in which they arose. Economic

---

[48] Benjamin I. Schwartz, "Notes on Conservatism in General and on China in Particular," in Charlotte Furth, ed., *The Limits of Change: Essays on Conservative Alternatives in Republican China* (Cambridge, Mass.: Harvard University Press, 1976), p. 14.

issues, moreover, could not be left free to work themselves out as the Manchester liberals had contended. Economics should be studied from an ethical point of view, with the purpose of advancing the good of the whole society. German historical economics, therefore, favored the intervention of the state to maintain social welfare. Otherwise, pursuit of individual self-interest would lead to class cleavages and to social revolution. The socially conscious monarch and his bureaucracy were the only neutral force in the conflict of social classes. In order to build national greatness and to prevent the alienation of the lower classes, it was necessary to protect them from exploitation and to integrate them into the political community. Under the influence of these economists, Bismarck's government proposed factory inspection laws, social insurance plans, state encouragement of consumers' and producers' cooperatives, state ownership of railroads, and minimum wage laws.

Conservatism in the modern world since the French Revolution came to have a direct relationship to social revolution. As one observer puts it, "The historic mission of political conservatism in the West has been not to defeat but to forestall revolutions, not to crush but anticipate them."[49] In Japan, bureaucratic conservatism had as a principal motivation the forestalling of social revolution.

German historical economics came to have very great influence in shaping bureaucratic conservatism in Japan. Its introduction was primarily the work of Kanai Noburu (1865–1933) who was the first major academic economist in Japan, the one most responsible for introducing the new industrial economics, and the teacher of many of Japan's subsequent academic and bureaucratic leaders.[50] The writings of his school greatly expanded the understanding of incipient social problems inherent in the process of industrialization that Roesler had touched on in his advice to the oligarchs.

In 1890, after four years of study in Europe, principally in Germany where he had immersed himself in studying the historical school and in observing Bismarck's conservative policies, Kanai was appointed professor at Tokyo Imperial University. Kanai's early writings criticized the *bummei kaika* writers, attacking their universalism and arguing that economic theory must be based on the particular history and cultural heritage of a nation. They had followed Manchester views. Fukuzawa, for example, wrote in *Seiyō jijō* that economics, like chem-

---

49 Clinton Rossiter, "Conservatism," in *International Encyclopedia of the Social Sciences* (New York: Macmillan and Free Press, 1968), vol. 3, p. 292.
50 Kanai is described in Sumiya Etsuji, *Nihon keizaigaku-shi* (Kyoto: Mineruva shobō, 1958).

istry and physics, was governed by fixed laws. Similarly, Taguchi Ukichi, one of the most bold and consistent of the enlightenment writers, wrote in his *Keizairon no rompō* (1884): "Economic truth does not change according to the times or the national conditions. The law that is useful in one country is useful in every country. . . . One plus two is always three."[51] Kanai rejected the free-trade notions and the faith in individual pursuit of self-interest that the *bummei kaika* had introduced. He held that liberalism had failed in Europe because it permitted conditions in the new industrial societies to deteriorate until revolution became a serious possibility. Kanai was instrumental in introducing discussion of the social problems (*shakai mondai*) created by industrialization and the positive role required of the state to prevent such problems. He wrote in 1891:

> If workers are treated like animals, then after several decades unions and socialism will appear. If now we concentrate on protection we can prevent unions and the spread of socialism. This is the policy of prevention. An illustration of the failure to act is not far to seek; it is in every country of the West.[52]

Kanai's theme of preventive action became an important element in Meiji conservative thought. The timing of Japan's industrialization gave it an opportunity to learn from the experience of the more advanced Western societies, to act early to forestall social problems. A second theme in Kanai's writing was his emphasis on thought guidance (*shisō zendō*) as an important preventive for social unrest. He held that social problems originated as much in the awakened consciousness of the lower classes as they did in objective living conditions. Accordingly, it was necessary for the state to lead the lower classes toward a positive and harmonious social attitude. Another important theme of Kanai's that was also essential to the conservative view was his emphasis on social solidarity as necessary to success in foreign affairs. He wrote:

> Ultimately the highest object of social policy in modern times is to bring back together again the various social classes which are daily becoming more and more separated; and it must establish a socially cooperative life based on intimate relations of mutual help and interdependence. . . . That is to say, social policy, which is the greatest need in domestic politics, is not just a

---

51 Kawai Eijirō, *Meiji shisōshi no ichi danmen: Kanai Noboru o chūshin to shite*, reprinted in *Kawai Eijirō zenshū* (Tokyo: Shakai shisōsha, 1969), vol. 8, p. 195. This account of economic thought in Meiji, centering on Kanai and written by his son-in-law, himself a well-known political economist, is a valuable source.
52 Kenneth B. Pyle, "Advantages of Followership: German Economics and Japanese Bureaucrats, 1890–1925," *Journal of Japanese Studies* 1 (1974): p. 143.

noble human ethic, it is an effective method to achieve success in foreign policy.[53]

Social policies of the government would introduce reforms, not as a matter of justice or right, but because they would strengthen national cohesion. Max Weber, in his 1895 Freiburg inaugural lecture, explained the motivation of German economists: "It is not the purpose of our work in social policy to make the world happy, but to unite socially a nation split apart by modern economic development, for the hard struggles of the future." And he added, "Not peace and human happiness we have to pass on to our descendants, but the maintenance and up-breeding of our national kind." Japan was not yet "a nation split apart by modern economic development."[54] Japanese conservatives were determined to prevent that.

In 1896, Kanai's disciples established the Shakai seisaku gakkai (Organization for the study of social policy), a group modeled on the Verein für Sozialpolitik, which had been formed by the German historical economists in 1872 to advocate state intervention in the economy in order to ease class conflicts through social welfare legislation. The Gakkai became the principal professional organization for Japanese economists, including nearly everyone teaching economics in universities as well as those in the bureaucracy and in business who were considered economists.

Increasingly, after the Sino-Japanese War, the Meiji conservatives found themselves as much concerned about the socialists and other radicals as they were about the liberals. The declaration of principles issued by the Shakai seisaku gakkai defined a middle course between the liberals and the socialists. It professed to discern already in Japan the beginning of a clash between labor and capital:

We oppose laissez-faire because it creates extreme profit consciousness and unbridled competition, and aggravates the differences between rich and poor. We also oppose socialism because it would destroy the present economic organization, obliterate capitalists, and therefore impede national programs. We support the principles of the present private enterprise system. Within this framework we seek to prevent friction between classes through the power of government and through individual exertions and thereby preserve social harmony.[55]

Kuwata Kumazō, who was a prime mover in the founding of the Shakai seisaku gakkai, wrote in an 1896 essay, entitled "The State and

---

53 Ibid., p. 144.
54 Ralf Dahrendorf, *Society and Democracy in Germany* (New York: Doubleday Anchor, 1967), p. 41.   55 Pyle, "Advantages of Followership," pp. 145–6.

the Social Problem," that although the nineteenth century had been one of political revolutions, the new century promised to be one of economic revolutions. Whereas the Western countries were accomplishing the economic revolution in the same way as they had accomplished the political revolution – at the cost of great strife and bloodshed – Japan could avoid this, as it had already proved: "The fact that the Japanese people established a constitutional system without shedding a drop of blood is a matter of great distinction in modern history. In the coming economic revolution, too, why should it be impossible to solve this great problem peacefully?" He argued that German social policy was appropriate to the Japanese experience because of Confucian injunctions to a ruler to take a benevolent interest in the well-being of his people and to instruct them in moral principles. Kuwata, who lectured on industrial policy at the Imperial University of Tokyo and served on many governmental commissions, recommended specific measures that the government should enact:

1. Factory legislation to regulate working hours, conditions, and female and child labor.
2. Regulations to protect the interests of tenants.
3. Poor relief laws.
4. Compulsory workers' insurance.
5. Credit cooperatives to protect and aid small farmers.
6. Progressive tax policies to ease the burden of low-income groups.

After the Sino-Japanese War, with the political order established and underwritten by a powerful ideology and with the goal of treaty revision accomplished, the Meiji leaders had to turn their attention to the problems of the industrial revolution. It was a new era. The term *shakai mondai* (social problem) became a frequent theme of public discussion. The naive optimism about the future that had characterized the *bummei kaika* was fading and was replaced by a more balanced assessment of what was entailed by modern economic development. The term *bummei byō* (civilization sickness) became a common phrase to indicate the problems that afflicted Western industrial societies – class hostilities, labor strife, destruction of the peasant village, decadence, materialism, radical ideologies, the decline of cooperation, and its supporting values. Would Japan be inevitably afflicted by the same problems as it passed through its industrial revolution? Many Japanese feared so. There were already harbingers. Socialist writings appeared in the 1890s, and the first socialist groups, small as they were, were accorded much attention. The first socialist party did not have a long history – it was closed down by the Home Ministry several hours after it had announced its formation in 1900.

The Ashio Copper Mine problem was seen as an early symptom of *bummei byō*. The mine, situated at the headwaters of the Watarase River, near Nikkō, represented one of Japan's important industries. Through the application of modern technology, the mining complex had undergone impressive expansion, but in the process, through deforestation, the river's watershed was destroyed. Floods brought appallingly polluted waters downstream, inundating villages and contaminating fields in the northern Kantō plain. In 1896, thirteen thousand households were flooded, and a national protest movement began. Ashio became a symbol of the sacrifice of agriculture to industry and of community values to economic growth.[56]

Ashio was only one of the more dramatic indications to the Japanese of what was likely to come as the industrial revolution proceeded. By the turn of the century, there was a rising awareness of the need to take preventive measures and a sense that Japan had a special advantage as a "follower country" to profit from the Western experience. The young economist (later to be a socialist), Kawakami Hajime wrote in 1905:

We have the history of England's failure and there is no need to repeat that history. Are there not opportunities for countries that lag behind in their culture? . . . The history of the failures of the advanced countries (*zenshin-koku*) is the best textbook for the follower countries (*kōshin-koku*). I hope that our statesmen and intellectuals learn something from this textbook.[57]

As the comments of one official, Kaneko Kentarō, indicated, the Japanese bureaucrats were sensitive to the lessons of history. We should learn from the "sad and pitiful" history of British industrialization, because, Kaneko added, "it is the advantage of the backward country that it can reflect on the history of the advanced countries and avoid their mistakes."[58] This style of thought soon infused the thinking of officialdom, even at the highest levels. Ōkuma Shigenobu wrote in 1910 that Japan was in an advantageous position to secure the cooperation of labor and capital: "By studying the mistaken system that has brought Europe such bitter experience in the past several decades, businessmen, politicians, and officials in Japan can diminish these abuses." Relying on the force of laws and family customs, they

---

56 See "Symposium: The Ashio Copper Mine Pollution Incident," *Journal of Japanese Studies* 1 (1975). 57 Pyle, "Advantages of Followership," pp. 129–30.
58 Ronald P. Dore, "The Modernizer As a Special Case: Japanese Factory Legislation, 1882–1911," *Comparative Studies in Society and History* 11 (1969): 439.

could "prevent a fearful clash" and plan the conciliation of capitalists and laborers. Similarly, Prime Minister Katsura wrote in 1908:

We are now in an age of economic transition. The development of machine industry and the intensification of competition widens the gap between rich and poor and creates anatagonisms that endanger social order. Judging by Western history, this is an inevitable pattern. Socialism is today no more than a wisp of smoke, but if it is ignored, it will some day have the force of a wild fire, and there will be nothing to stop it. Therefore, it goes without saying that we must rely on education to nurture the people's values; and we must devise a social policy that will assist their industry, provide them work, help the aged and infirm and, thereby, prevent catastrophe.[59]

Thus, by the turn of the century, a conservative approach to industrial society had taken root in the bureaucracy. It was heavily influenced by Bismarckian social policy and German economic thought. It was influenced, as well, by the conservative belief that Japanese society was indeed different and should be unique, that by preserving its own values of social harmony it could avert the social consequences of industrialism evident in many Western societies. Finally, and perhaps most important, it was motivated by the urgency of the time. Success in foreign affairs depended on a united nation and rapid economic growth.

THE SOCIAL PROGRAM OF THE CONSERVATIVES

The most clearly defined initial objective of the bureaucratic conservatives in addressing industrial society was the passage of a factory law to regulate the working conditions of industrial labor. Actually, far in advance of an organized labor movement demanding it of the government, the bureaucracy took the initiative in drafting it and in organizing support for its passage. In fact, the bureaucracy's efforts were so early, Dore points out, that when the Ministry of Agriculture and Commerce began to study foreign factory laws in 1882, there were fewer than fifty factories using steam power in all of Japan![60]

In the 1890s, the Ministry of Agriculture and Commerce circulated to various chambers of commerce the draft of a law that would establish minimum health and safety standards and limit the working hours of women and children employed in factories.[61] After the Sino-Japanese War, the government pressed factory legislation with greater

---

59 Horio Teruhisa, "Taisei sai-tōgō no kokoromi to teikoku ideorogii no keisei," *Nihon seiji gakkai nempō* (1968): 164. See also Pyle, "Followership," pp. 130, 159.
60 Dore, "The Modernizer As a Special Case," p. 437.   61 Ibid., pp. 437–8.

urgency. Beginning in 1896, the government convened a series of national conferences to discuss the state of the economy. Bureaucrats brushed aside the contention of businessmen that working conditions in Japan were good, with the argument that it was necessary "to create the laws necessary to maintain in the future the balance between capital and labor, and harmonious relations between employers and employees, thereby protecting in advance against any disorders."[62] At the same time, steps were taken to prevent the growth of union powers. The Peace Police Law of 1900 virtually denied the unions the primary function of organizing.

A factory law was eventually passed in 1911, and in the meantime, there were other steps taken in the cities to prepare for industrial society. On the whole, however, before World War I, the bureaucracy depended primarily on its police power to maintain control in the urban sector and, for a number of reasons, showed far more concern for the countryside. First, that was where 80 percent of the population still lived at the turn of the century. If the new order were to have a powerful counterrevolutionary bulwark, it would most effectively be in the towns and villages. Second, industrialization in Japan frequently had a rural setting and was dependent on village labor and farm side employments. The commercial spirit had already begun to invade the countryside and to affect the solidarity of the village community. Third, ever since the *bummei kaika* had made its effect felt on the cities, the towns and villages had come to symbolize the essence of what was historically Japanese. Finally, there was traditional sanction for such a view. Tokugawa political thought had regarded agriculture as the basis of society. Ogyū Sorai put it this way: "To take care of the roots and to keep the branches under control, this is the principle taught by the sages of old. The root is agriculture; the branches, industry and commerce."[63]

The Shakai seisaku gakkai devoted much attention to studies of the way in which industrialization in Western countries had led to the disintegration of the peasant village. Already, this society's members saw dangers in the countryside. Rising government expenditures for industrial capital formation and military enterprises were creating a growing tax burden for the citizenry. Central government expendi-

---

[62] Byron K. Marshall, *Capitalism and Nationalism in Prewar Japan* (Stanford, Calif.: Stanford University Press, 1967), p. 54. Discussion of bureaucratic efforts to develop factory and labor legislation can be found in Sheldon Garon, *The State and Labor in Modern Japan* (Berkeley and Los Angeles: University of California Press, 1987).
[63] Ronald P. Dore, *Land Reform in Japan* (London: Oxford University Press, 1959), p. 57.

tures tripled in the decade before the Russo-Japanese War, and responsibilities for public works and education were increasingly delegated to local government. Local taxes rose sharply, and the town and village assemblies, which were dominated by wealthy families, enacted a variety of regressive taxes. This growing tax burden, the increasing concentration of land ownership, and the attractiveness of the city to ambitious peasant youth portended social problems in the countryside that the government could ill afford. As Tani Kanjō wrote in 1898, a secure yeomanry was critical to Japan because it would serve as a barrier to radical ideologies, provide a reliable source of able-bodied soldiers, and ensure self-sufficiency of food in time of war. To prevent destruction of the cohesiveness and harmony of the village, the Gakkai proposed a tenancy law to regulate landlord–tenant relations, and the establishment of credit facilities and industrial cooperatives.

The bureaucracy thus came to the conclusion that if the cohesion of the countryside could be preserved, then the tensions that industrialism was certain to create could somehow be managed. The oligarchs, particularly Yamagata, had always regarded local administration as critical to the future stability of their rule. For that reason, Yamagata had taken an intense, firsthand interest in the establishment of the new system of local government, which culminated in the Town and Village Code of 1888.

To infuse this system with the new national ideology and to establish a stable conservative social base for the difficult transition to an industrial economy, the government embarked on an ambitious and comprehensive program of conservative reforms in the countryside. The Rural Improvement movement (Chihō kairyō undō), which the Home Ministry launched at the turn of the century, was the archetype of the bureaucratic approach to modern Japanese social problems. It demonstrates the pragmatic effort of Japanese conservatives to make limited reforms within a nationalist framework as a means of cushioning society from the traumatic effects of the industrial revolution. The objectives of the movement were to promote both economic development and social harmony. It thus sought to strengthen the financial resources of the new administrative towns and villages and to build national loyalties among all classes at the local level.

One of the most impressive manifestations of social policy thought in the bureaucracy's approach to rural society was its promotion of agricultural cooperatives. Through the efforts of a leading bureaucrat, Hirata Tōsuke, who was a close associate of Yamagata and who had studied social policy in Germany, the Diet passed in 1899 the Industrial Cooperatives Law which encouraged the establishment of credit, consumer marketing, and producers' cooperatives. Just as the factory law had not depended on the demands of discontented laborers for its promotion and passage, so the Industrial Cooperatives Law was not the result of demands from farmers or farm pressure groups. Rather, the bureaucracy took the initiative in drafting it in order to prevent the kind of agrarian impoverishment and disruption that had occurred in the West. Hirata's justification of the measure is noteworthy for us here. He regarded cooperatives as a form of "social education" that would establish a strong collectivism at the local level. They would become "communities working in behalf of the nation" (*kokka no tame no kyōdōtai*). Hirata reasoned that if "we come to have the great class divisions that exist in every Western country, it will be cause for immense concern and regret. Therefore before this calamity occurs we should let the lower class people share in the blessings of civilization along with the great capitalists." Cooperatives would "protect the security of society" and promote economic development by helping the small producer who was "the center of the industry."[64] Following the enactment of the Industrial Cooperatives Law, the government mounted a vigorous propaganda campaign throughout the countryside. It relied on the teachings of the Tokugawa peasant-scholar, Ninomiya Sontoku, which stressed mutual aid and cooperation in the village, conciliation and cooperation between landlord and tenant, careful long-term planning and budgeting, the dignity of manual labor, thrift, and the payment of taxes as a moral obligation. Ninomiya's followers had, in fact, formed societies known as *hōtokusha* which had functioned as crude credit associations. By 1921, over 13,700 cooperatives had been organized in conformance with the new law, and nearly one-half the farm families were members of a cooperative.

The Rural Improvement movement took a number of steps to strengthen the new administrative towns and villages that, following the Town and Village Act of 1888, had been formed by joining many of the old hamlets. By the time of the Russo-Japanese War, over 76,000 natural villages or hamlets (*buraku*) that had existed in the Tokugawa period had, through mergers, been reduced to some 12,000 administrative towns and villages. The intention was to transfer re-

---

64 Kenneth B. Pyle, "The Technology of Japanese Nationalism: The Local Improvement Movement, 1900–1918," *Journal of Asian Studies* 33 (1973): 51–65. The best description of the Local Improvement movement in Japanese is by Miyachi Masato, *Nichi-Ro sengo seijishi no kenkyū* (Tokyo: Tokyo daigaku shuppankai, 1973). Another major work is by Kano Masanao, *Shihonshugi keisei-ki no chitsujo ishiki* (Tokyo: Chikuma shobō, 1969).

sources, including all communal lands and property, from the hamlets to the new administrative units.

As part of the same effort, the Home Ministry announced in 1906 its determination to enforce a sweeping merger of Shinto shrines at the local level so that hamlet shrines would be replaced by a single central shrine in each administrative village. Worship at the hamlet shrines had centered on the daily concerns of local inhabitants – such matters as clement weather, good harvests, and healthy offspring. Under the new program, worship was to focus chiefly on the imperial family and national festivals.[65] Priests were placed under the disciplinary regulations of regular civil government officials.

Inspiration for this program, as Hashikawa Bunsō and others noted, came from the visits that bureaucrats made to the West where they were impressed with the cohesive power of religion and the dominance of churches in local society. The instrumental use of religious rites to support the state, of course, can be traced back in Japanese history to the ideas of Ogyū Sorai and beyond. In this way, what Itō had envisioned as the cornerstone of the nation – the imperial ideology or what was later called state Shinto – was established at the local level. This was not something that welled up spontaneously from the people and their folklore and traditions. To the contrary, there was much resistance at the local level to the attempt to merge shrines and override the simple local devotions of the past.

The bureaucracy, however, persisted in other methods to create national loyalties and inculcate the national ideology at the grass-roots level – most effectively through organizations that Professor Ishida Takeshi has called half-bureaucratic/half-popular organizations – because they were organizations that had their origins at the local level and that were used by the bureaucracy as effective vehicles of the new nationalism and were encouraged to develop much more elaborate structures. The most important of these organizations were the youth groups (*seinenkai*) and the military associations (*zaigō gunjinkai*).[66]

The modern youth group movement was begun in the 1890s by a Hiroshima Prefecture schoolteacher, Yamamoto Takinosuke, who

65 Wilbur M. Fridell, *Japanese Shrine Mergers, 1906–1912* (Tokyo: Sophia University Press, 1973). See also Hashikawa Bunsō's excellent essay on the bureaucracy's efforts to extend its power to the local level: *Kindai Nihon seiji shisō no shosō* (Tokyo: Miraisha, 1968), pp. 35–73.
66 Ishida Takeshi, *Meiji seiji shisōshi kenkyū* (Tokyo: Miraisha, 1954) and Ishida Takeshi, *Kindai Nihon seiji kōzō no kenkyū* (Tokyo: Miraisha, 1956) are the standard sources. Also essential is Fujita Shōzō, *Tennōsei kokka no shihai genri* (Tokyo: Miraisha, 1966). In English, see Richard J. Smethurst, *A Social Basis for Prewar Japanese Militarism* (Berkeley and Los Angeles: University of California Press, 1974).

published in 1896 a tract entitled *Inaka seinen* (Rural youth). In this and subsequent writings, he exhorted and praised rural youth as the backbone of the nation: They exemplified virtues of hard work, thrift, filial piety, and national spirit. They were uninfected by the "civilization sickness" (*bummei byō*) that afflicted city youth. The Home Ministry, seeing the value that such grass-roots organizations could have in mobilizing support at the local level, set out to organize village youth groups in a national hierarchy under its guidance. By the end of the Meiji period, youth groups were said to number 29,320, with a membership of 3 million.

The local military associations (*zaigō gunjinkai*) had similar grass-roots origins. Established after the Satsuma Rebellion as fraternal organizations for former members of the military, they took leadership of youth activities, community service projects, and patriotic ceremonies. The government organized them into a national hierarchy, and by the end of the Meiji period, virtually every community in the nation had a branch. The youth groups and military associations became mass organizations (along with the credit associations) at the grass-roots levels and were increasingly effective in the twentieth century as instruments for mobilizing nationalist support of the great effort required to achieve military and industrial success.

The keynote of the Rural Improvement movement was sounded by the issuance of the Imperial Rescript of 1908, known as the Boshin shōsho. As Professor Sumiya Mikio observed, this rescript symbolized the government's intention to press a campaign of national mobilization, exhorting all Japanese to unite in hard work, thrift, and cooperation so that the nation could achieve its destiny as one of the world's great military and industrial powers.[67] In part it read:

In order to keep pace with the constant progress of the world, and to participate in the blessings of its civilization, the development of the national resources is manifestly a requisite of prime importance.... We desire all classes of Our people to act in unison, to be faithful to their callings, frugal in the management of their households, submissive to the dictates of conscience and calls of duty, frank and sincere in their manners, to abide by simplicity and avoid ostentation, and to inure themselves to arduous toil without yielding to any degree of indulgence. The teachings of Our revered Ancestors and the record of our glorious history are clear beyond all misapprehension. By scrupulous observance of the precepts thus established, the growing prosperity of our Empire is assured.

---

67 Sumiya Mikio, *Nihon no shakai shisō* (Tokyo: Tokyo daigaku shuppankai, 1968), pp. 65–6.

The ease and speed with which mass mobilization was achieved under bureaucratic initiative is sometimes exaggerated and is still the subject of controversy. What was clearly accomplished by the late Meiji period was mobilization for nationalist purposes of the "local notables" – village headmen, school principals, prominent landlords, and Shinto priests. It was this stratum of grass-roots leadership that Yamagata had referred to as the "strong middle men" (*chūken jimbutsu*) who could mediate between the new national administrative system and local society. Charged with responsibility for achieving the national destiny, they attained enhanced respectability by exercising patriarchal leadership of the youth groups, the industrial cooperatives, and the military associations.[68]

THE LEGACY OF MEIJI CONSERVATISM

By the turn of the century, the public mood of Japan had been transformed, and a powerful conservative orthodoxy held sway. The millennial vision of the *bummei kaika* had faded, and liberals and reformers were in disarray. Their optimism had given way to ambivalence. Many of them now had a more balanced perspective on the impact of the science and industry in which the *bummei kaika* advocates had put their faith. The new technology was creative but also destructive. It offered new hope and opportunities, but at a high cost in human disruption and hardship. The reformer, Tanaka Shōzō, expressing moral revulsion toward the commercialization of values and the decline in cooperation, said in the Diet in 1910 that modern civilization was destroying "moral structures that have taken five hundred or a thousand years to build." Reflecting on the Ashio pollution case, he wrote in his diary that "progress of material, artificial civilization casts society into darkness. Electricity is discovered and the world is darkened."[69] Some of the liberals like Tokutomi Sohō, the leader of the reform cause, had abandoned the faith and thrown in their lot with the conservatives. The journalist and reformer Kinoshita Naoe wrote of his disillusion with the Spencerian vision of the future that Tokutomi had offered in the 1880s: "Weren't we fools! We were afire with hope when we first heard Spencer's prophecy that society was evolving from

---

68 A recent assessment of the success of bureaucratic efforts at the local level is by Ariizumi Sadao, "Meiji kokka to minshū tōgō," in *Iwanami kōza Nihon rekishi*, vol. 17 (*kindai* 4) (Tokyo: Iwanami shoten, 1976), pp. 221–62.
69 Alan Stone, "The Japanese Muckrakers," *Journal of Japanese Studies* 1 (1975): 402.

the militant to the industrial stage, that wars would cease, that loyalty and patriotism would disappear, and that there would be a golden age of peace and freedom!" Instead, material civilization had brought "depravity, ruin, and normlessness."[70]

Liberal despair over the course of industrial civilization was compounded by the oppressive orthodoxy that pervaded public discourse. Most young Japanese had little of their predecessors' optimism about reforming society. They felt powerless to change the social and political order. "The atmosphere that surrounds us youth," the poet Ishikawa Takuboku wrote, "is suffocating. The influence of authority pervades the entire country. The existing social organization reaches into every nook and cranny." It was this kind of despair that radicalized socialists like Kōtoku Shūsui and impelled them to extremes.[71]

Even moderate conservatives were dismayed at the extent to which the conservative reaction had gone. Those like Miyake Setsurei and Kuga Katsunan had attacked some of the main themes of the Japanese enlightenment, including its dismissal of Japanese history, its naive internationalism, and its adulation of Western society and politics. But by the turn of the century, they were appalled at the distortion of their ideas. The term they had originated, "preservation of the national essence" (*kokusui hozon*), had become a pretext for opposing needed reforms. Moderate conservatives had argued for cultural autonomy, for a modern industrial society that was in keeping with historical traditions, but they lamented the narrow views that now stigmatized change as inconsistent with the national character.

This dramatic reversal of the liberal cause came about because many of the main themes of the *bummei kaika* had lacked a strong social constituency to defend them. When they were challenged, particularly from within the government and the imperial court, as in the case of the liberal education reforms, they were easily displaced. The extreme adulation of the Western cultural model could not sustain itself once the vogue had passed and, particularly, once the motivation of treaty revision had disappeared. Free trade and internationalism never had many self-interested supporters and, in the age of imperialism that dawned in the 1890s, could scarcely be sustained. Many of the new social values introduced during the *bummei kaika* ran counter to the mores of the Japanese but, above all, were incompatible with the institutions of the countryside where the great majority of the popu-

70 Ibid., p. 404.
71 Pyle, *The New Generation*, p. 200. On Kōtoku, see F. G. Notehelfer, *Kōtoku Shūsui: Portrait of a Japanese Radical* (Cambridge, England: Cambridge University Press, 1971).

lace had its roots. Finally, by the turn of the century, there was an emerging awareness that industrial society in the Western countries was subject to disruptions and strife that made it much less worthy of emulation. For these reasons, the public mood changed rapidly in the 1890s.

The oligarchs led this change in mood, placing the full weight of their power behind the new conservative tide. Historiographical controversy regarding Meiji conservatism has tended to center on assessment of its motivations and its legacy. E. H. Norman's classic work, *Japan's Emergence As a Modern State* (1940), locates the motivation of the Meiji leadership in the desperate exigencies of the time:

> Time was short, resources scanty, and it is a cause for amazement that Japan's leaders accomplished so much rather than a cause for blame because they had to leave so much undone in the way of democratic and liberal reform. . . . Speed was a determining element in the *form* which modern Japanese government and society assumed. The *speed* with which Japan had simultaneously to establish a modern state, to build an up-to-date defense force in order to ward off the dangers of invasion . . . , to create an industry on which to base this armed force, to fashion an educational system suitable to an industrial, modernized nation, dictated that these important changes be accomplished by a group of autocratic bureaucrats rather than by the mass of the people working through democratic organs of representation. These military bureaucrats were so far in advance of the rest of their countrymen that they had to drag a complaining, half-awakened nation of merchants and peasants after them.[72]

In a later work, written in 1943 during the height of the Pacific War, Norman was more negative and harsh in his assessment. Repression and counterrevolution were the driving motives of the oligarchs. In *Soldier and Peasant in Japan* he wrote that

> any possibility of a steadily rising standard of living, a broadening out of popular liberties (all of which would have directed Japanese energies into channels other than . . . expansion, aggression, and wars) was resolutely blocked by the calculating Japanese Metternichs. . . . As soon as the people of Japan could stand upright and breathe the intoxicating air of freedom following the overthrow of the Bakufu, they were burdened with fresh exactions and taxes; their relative advance in terms of social and political freedom was soon drastically checked.[73]

This judgment has been widely shared by postwar Japanese historians who have elaborated themes of a nascent democratic-populist movement that supported the People's Rights movement and subsequently resisted bureaucratic institutions of control in the 1890s and

---

72 John W. Dower, ed., *Origins of the Modern Japanese State: Selected Writings of E. H. Norman* (New York: Pantheon, 1975), p. 154.   73 Ibid., p. 23.

later. Recent historiography in the West, which has tended to emphasize the success of Japanese modernization, has accorded a more favorable assessment. Most striking in this regard is Professor George Akita's judgment that the Meiji leaders were enlightened heroes determined to share their power with their countrymen by "force-feeding 'liberalization' to a citizenry reluctant to accept the rights and duties of participation in government affairs. When the results were not what had been expected and were threatening the socio-political structure, the Meiji leaders continued to take further steps calculated to relax their own hold."[74]

It is important for us to remember that there were different shades of conservatism within the bureaucracy. Some bureaucrats were moved by a primary reliance on the imperial myth to circumscribe narrowly the limits on institutional innovation; others were more pragmatic and tolerant of change. There was, in fact, a strong strain of conservative reformism in the bureaucracy that was motivated by nationalist concerns. These reform-minded bureaucrats came to the conclusion, principally from their sensitivity to the experience of the Western industrial societies, that to prevent social disruption and maintain a strong nation-state, it was necessary for a government to adopt an early social policy and intervene in the economy to accommodate the lower classes into the political order. Their strategy for building this national solidarity was twofold. On the one hand, they pressed for social reforms like factory legislation and agricultural cooperatives. On the other hand, they relied on schools, youth groups, military associations, and the shrines to propagate the collectivist ethic.

This dual strategy characterized the government's approach to the problems of industrialism in the post–World War I years. Reform-minded bureaucrats worked for institutional changes that would conciliate tenant–landlord and labor–management problems. Similarly, they pressed for extension of the suffrage. Along with their social policy, they promoted the national ideology as a means of mass mobilization. The Local Improvement movement, which served as a model of this dual strategy, was followed by a succession of bureaucratically sponsored movements in the 1920s and 1930s, each one designed to maintain social cohesion and to prod the populace to the greater efforts required by the forced march to industry and empire.

This conservative strategy of early establishing institutions and an ideology to cope with social problems helped Japan avoid some of the

---

[74] George Akita, *Foundations of Constitutional Government in Modern Japan, 1868–1890* (Cambridge, Mass.: Harvard University Press, 1967), p. 174.

horrors to which the industrial revolution gave rise in England – but it had its price. Ralf Dahrendorf, reflecting on the German experience, wrote that an "early social policy serves to prevent rather than to promote the reality of the citizen role" and that "social policy always went too far in holding citizens in tutelage."[75] In Japan, too, the bureaucratic strategy weakened support for parliamentary politics and for open confrontation of competing ideas and interests. A premium was placed on national unity. Reforms did not keep pace with the growing social problems. As problems of the economy worsened, threatening Japan's precarious international position, the rhetoric of national strength and exclusiveness was continuously strengthened. Meiji conservatism had set a pattern for handling the problems of industrial society that tended under these circumstances to lead to more and more extreme measures.

75 Dahrendorf, *Society and Democracy in Germany*, pp. 70–1.

CHAPTER 12

JAPAN'S DRIVE TO GREAT-POWER STATUS

THE FOREIGN POLICY OF A MODERN STATE

Nothing is more striking, in tracing Meiji Japan's foreign affairs, than the fact that the Meiji period coincided with the emergence of several "modern states." The half-century before the outbreak of World War I in 1914 witnessed political, economic, social, and intellectual developments in the West that coalesced into the development of national entities, outlines of which have remained to this day. England, France, Germany, Italy, and other European countries, as well as the United States, evolved as centralized and integrated mass societies that, for want of a better term, have been called modern states. Although no two modern states were exactly alike, they were generally characterized by centralization of state authority, on the one hand, and mass incorporation into the economy and polity, on the other. These developments had, of course, been preceded by the democratic and the industrial revolutions of the late eighteenth and the early nineteenth century, but it was in most instances only after the 1860s that these earlier, and ongoing, revolutions conspired with other trends to create conditions for unified state systems.

The twin phenomenon of centralization and mass incorporation may be illustrated by the United States, the country that held the greatest fascination for the Japanese during the two decades after Perry. The America of Perry's days was not yet a full-fledged modern state. It was a country with serious cleavages between regions and economic interests. Although shared mythologies of the American Revolution generated a sense of common heritage, what a later generation would call a "civil religion," and although a sense of nationhood was buttressed by economic opportunity (a theme that Alexis de Tocqueville stressed in the 1830s), there also grew an apparently insoluble dispute about the nature of the American state. Those following Andrew Jackson, who believed in the integrity of national unity as expressed by the government in Washington, were increasingly on the defensive in the face of "nullifiers" like John C. Calhoun, who argued that the very essence of the nation lay in a compact among units to form a larger entity so that any of them retained the freedom to secede from the entity when the latter seemed to infringe on its rights. When the first Japanese embassy, led by Shimmi Masaoki, visited the United States in 1860, they were being unwitting witnesses to a drama that preceded the dissolution of the union.

The situation was vastly different when the second embassy, this time dispatched by the fledgling Meiji state and headed by Iwakura Tomomi, reached the United States in 1871. The four-year-long Civil War had settled the question about the inviolability of national unity. The country was to be governed as one political unit under a federal government with powers to emancipate and enfranchise slaves, regulate internal commerce, and use troops for maintaining domestic order. "Rebel states" in the South would never again attempt to create their separate sovereignty; instead they would try to promote their welfare within the larger national framework. The national government was now more centralized than before the Civil War, with civil reforms recruiting bureaucrats whose loyalty was to the new order. The armed forces, too, were increasingly bureaucratized. Although in the immediate postbellum years both the army and the navy dwindled in size, the nucleus of modern armed power remained, and its leaders were committed to the rationalization of organization, ordnance, and command.

The centralization of political authority reflected and confirmed economic integration. The United States grew as a huge national market, its agricultural sector producing all that its citizens needed, and much more. Railroads crisscrossed every region, and the newly developed technology of refrigeration and canning enabled farm and dairy products to travel thousands of miles to reach the consumer. Inevitably, problems arose in arbitrary railway tariff charges, unsanitary conditions of meats, or falling prices of wheat due to overproduction, and in every instance the federal government was viewed as an arbiter and regulator of conflicting interests. The government's most crucial contribution to the national economy, however, lay in its tariff policy. Protectionism provided a setting in which industrialization could grow apace. Capital for industrialization came from largely European, particularly British, sources, rather than from domestic savings, but the late nineteenth century also created a class of fabulously rich American capitalists who, by controlling the railways and expanding factories, were so influential in linking segments of the national economy that the government felt obliged, in 1890, to enact the first antitrust measures. But they did little to stem the trend toward the creation of a national economic order.

Mass incorporation into the national economy and polity was an integral part of this phenomenon. In the United States, it is true, the people had enjoyed greater freedom and opportunity than in most other countries since the late eighteenth century. Still, the situation after the Civil War was unique in that on the one hand, the federal government as well as the political parties were committed to the idea of national economic development through industrial, transportation, and financial development, whereas on the other hand, rapid economic change created significant social dislocations severely affecting the lower strata of society who often had recourse to organized political action. Both phenomena tended to deepen the government's involvement in the people's economic and social affairs – what Morton Keller has termed "the affairs of state" – while at the same time developing a pervasive sense of the people's common identity as workers, consumers, and often victims of forces beyond their control. In all this process a mass society was being created, a society that was at once more heterogeneous racially and socially, and more integrated politically, than earlier. Whether this was a desirable phenomenon for the health and growth of America was a question hotly debated by its leaders. Some urged a return to a less complicated era characterized by homogeneous local communities, and others sought to forge a new unity on the basis of cooperation among different interest groups under the benevolent leadership of the state. Still others advocated a class struggle as the only way to improve the living conditions of the masses. These alternatives pointed to a central question of the modern state: how to preserve order amid change. Given the rapid technological development and economic change, the state authority had to devise means for preventing unmanageable upheavals, but a politically conscious populace would not be satisfied with a stale stability that gave them no feeling of participation in public affairs and opportunities.

Thus both the state authority and the masses were gaining power. Whether one would grow at the expense of the other was never satisfactorily resolved, but on the whole it may be said that various mechanisms were devised to prevent either development and to maintain a balance between state and society. One such mechanism was party politics, and another was organized interest groups. These institutions mediated between governmental leadership and bureaucracy, on the one hand, and mass interests and aspirations, on the other. Also important were the intellectuals, professionals, social workers, and educators who served as intermediaries among the different groups, and between them and the government. They were the experts capable of understanding – so it was thought – the forces of modern transformation. They would work to make the process of modernization more beneficial and less painful to the society at large; they would provide technical expertise for public administrators to cope with complex issues of the industrial age; and they would put brakes on both governmental power and popular power lest they should get out of hand and undermine social unity. Usually called reformers or liberals, these were the individuals who were the country's leaders without being part of the state, and who spoke for the masses without being totally identified with them. Thus functionally they were against state dictatorships, mass revolutions, and class struggles. Rather, they were reformists trying to accommodate forces of change within manageable frameworks. Their task was not an easy one, for they had to chart a middle course between revolution and reaction and between authoritarianism and anarchy.

Such, in rough outline, were the forces that were shaping American society after the Civil War. Although the existence and abolition of slavery made the country unique, in most other instances the experience was similar to those elsewhere in the West. The European countries, too, had their domestic strife and civil wars before they emerged as centralized states with civilian and armed bureaucracies, national markets, and mass politics and culture. When the Japanese awoke to the importance of turning to the West, then, they were presented with precisely those features that made them modern states. Of course, they may not have been aware that this was a rather recent development, a stage in Western history. But they were naturally more interested in the present than in the past, and they could not have chosen a more suitable moment for transforming their own country. They had models everywhere they looked, and it required no unusual imagination for them to pattern their national development after these models. They did not pick just one model, but several, and so they borrowed certain institutions from Britain, some from Germany and France, and still others from the United States. Such selectivity is not surprising in view of the fact that Western nations, too, were avidly copying one another with a view to transforming themselves into powerful modern entities.

The emergence of modern states inevitably had serious repercussions on international affairs. First, a modern state by definition had greater military resources at its command. Its armed forces were better organized and more effectively mobilized than earlier because of the state's centralized system of bureaucracy and taxation. The armed forces represented the state, both internally to maintain law and order (against "public enemies" such as dissidents, subversives, and sometimes even strikers) and to demonstrate national power abroad. Military organization, ordnance, and intelligence were improved, and vast strides were made in building faster ships, better fortifications, and more efficient systems of communication. Because these developments were taking place simultaneously in most countries, it was not surprising that they should have intensified, rather than contributed to diminishing, a sense of insecurity in each country, which would now be confronted with potential adversaries with larger ships and better-equipped soldiers. Under the circumstances, the idea of national defense expanded. Basic to the new definition was a global perspective. All regions of the world were perceived to be interlinked because of technological improvements and increased armament, and for a nation to maintain secure defenses it was considered imperative to adopt a global strategy. As Alfred Thayer Mahan noted in the 1890s, "Defense means not merely defense of our territory, but defense of our just national interests, whatever they be and wherever they are." Echoing such a view, an American army officer wrote in 1892, "Now we have interests abroad which are endangered by threats of aggression far from our own borders."[1] The broadened concept of defense was a characteristic feature of the late nineteenth century and reflected the emergence of centralized states. It compelled strategic reformulation and produced certain ideas that remained influential through World War I. They included the quantitative enlargement and qualitative improvement of armed forces, the acquisition of bases and coaling stations, and the development of a geopolitical outlook that might call for a combination of "land powers" against "sea powers," as Mahan advocated, or for the establishment of an economically viable regional bloc such as "Mitteleuropa," an idea developed by some German economists and military thinkers.[2]

Equally important were military alliances. As ultimately exemplified by Britain's decision to terminate its "splendid isolation," the capitals of Europe became aware at this time that no one country

---

[1] Graham Cosmas, *An Army for Empire: The United States Army in the Spanish-American War* (Columbus: University of Missouri Press, 1971), pp. 35–7.
[2] David E. Kaiser, *Economic Diplomacy and the Origins of the Second World War* (Princeton, N.J.: Princeton University Press, 1980), p. 5.

would be able to maintain its security in a world of expanding armament and improving technology. It would be necessary to form alliances and ententes to pool several countries' resources and labor power against contingencies. At the outset, when an alliance was concluded between Germany and Austria-Hungary in 1879, few could have foreseen that this presaged a rigid structure of alliances that led ultimately to war. At that time, this and other similar undertakings appeared to be temporary expediencies designed to provide their signatories with a sense of security; they would be replaced by other alliances as conditions changed. However, within less than thirty years after 1879, there had emerged two groups of powers into which the major European countries had become divided: the Triple Alliance of Germany, Austria-Hungary, and Italy, on the one hand, and the Triple Entente of Britain, France, and Russia, on the other. They vied with one another for more efficient armed forces, and within each group its member states exchanged strategic and mobilization plans. Peace was maintained precariously in the form of a balance of power between the two camps. But it could give way to conflict, and when it did, it was likely to involve all these countries and even more.

Strategic implications, however, were not the only by-product of the emergence of modern states. Also crucial was the fact that each state was committed to rapid economic development, particularly overseas trade and domestic industrialization. Sometimes called *neomercantilism*, this commitment was different from seventeenth-century mercantilism in that it stressed the growth of national economic units as producers and as markets in the global economic system. The state encouraged the expansion of worldwide trade and investment activities, while at the same time facilitating the growth of domestic industry. Western nations were economically linked to one another by a gold standard that made national currencies convertible into gold and other currencies. But the states remained economic units, and governments fostered the creation of national marketplaces by establishing transportation networks, encouraging cooperation between capital and labor, and protecting domestic industry and agriculture against foreign competition. All these activities could be carried out more efficiently than formerly now that each government had built up a system of administration by career bureaucrats. Their task was to ensure the stability of the gold standard and the success of industrialization. These were linked to foreign affairs in that they sustained the new modern states, providing them with revenue for further armament expenditures. Increased armaments, in turn, were seen as a means of protecting the country's trade routes and overseas possessions that were linked to the domestic economy.

This last phenomenon, that is, the incorporation of overseas possessions and spheres of influence into the domestic economic and strategic system, was then and has since been termed *imperialism*. Although the term has been so broadened as to include almost any type of domination by one country over another – even by a noncapitalist or underdeveloped state over another – it also connoted something specific, a development that coincided with the emergence of centralized industrial states.[3] Although not all such states undertook imperialist policies, the nations that did were invariably "powers" that were going through the process of political centralization and economic modernization. This was because they had enough economic, military, and administrative resources to dominate the less powerful and less developed areas of the world. Their bankers, industrialists, and merchants sought to maximize their profits through finding and enlarging overseas markets and through obtaining cheap raw materials and foodstuffs in the tropical regions for consumption at home by the laboring population. Although these activities had been going on since the inception of the Industrial Revolution in the eighteenth century, at the end of the nineteenth century their endeavors were more readily supported, and often encouraged, by the state. Its bureaucratic and military apparatus could be used to seek overseas markets as well as bases; they provided the labor power necessary to protect rights and prerogatives obtained; and both economic and military activities enhanced the state's prestige and power. Somehow it was believed that all successful modern powers must expand overseas. Much of this expansion, of course, deviated little from more traditional forms of expansion such as emigration to the American continent or trade with other advanced countries. However, there was also great concern with incorporating less developed parts of the globe into modern state systems. These "peripheral" areas would constitute the fringes of the modern states geographically and politically; they would never be fully integrated into the polity. But they would serve as dependable markets, as *raisons d'être* for large armed establishments and bureaucracies and as symbols of status and power in international affairs.

This last was very important, particularly with regard to the masses in the metropolises whose tax contributions as well as votes were necessary for an imperialist program. Their support could be obtained by

---

[3] Various interpretations of imperialism are aptly summed up by Wolfgang Mommsen, *Theories of Imperialism*, Engl. ed. (New York: Random House, 1980).

painting a picture of an expanding empire as an invigorating and noble enterprise in the service not only of the state but also of civilization and humanity. Because the empire now contained tropical regions and populations, it could be presented as a duty – even a "burden" in Rudyard Kipling's famous construction – incumbent upon more advanced and civilized peoples to provide the former with order and purpose. If metropolitan voters and taxpayers were not in a missionary mood, then they could be told that the new possessions gave them added opportunities to better themselves. If they did not fare well at home, they could always go to these areas where they would be treated as superior beings and would be guaranteed protection by their government. Their nationalism, which was daily being cultivated through news of international rivalries as well as promoted by domestic policies of centralization, could be counted on to support acts that resulted in additions of more territory under the country's control. Some political parties took advantage of this expansionist sentiment by identifying themselves with imperialism in order to obtain a mass following. In a sense they mediated between government and people. By channeling mass emotions away from domestic issues, which, as George Bernard Shaw noted, could lead to revolution, and deflecting them to the support of imperialism, the parties ensured domestic order at the expense of international stability.[4] But this phenomenon – sometimes referred to as *social imperialism* – could go much beyond obtaining mass satisfaction with the polity. An emotionally aroused public opinion could be transformed into irresponsible jingoisms not easily controllable even by the government. If that should happen, foreign policy issues would seriously undermine domestic order. The modern state, in this way, was built on a precarious balance between obtaining mass support for military strengthening and overseas expansion and avoiding mass extremism that could unleash far more emotional and irrational forces than could be accommodated in the political apparatus.

THE MEIJI POLITY AND SOCIETY

This brief sketch helps put Meiji Japanese foreign affairs in context and perspective. It is important to recall that Japan, too, was transforming itself as a modern state. Its foreign relations were an aspect as well as a product of that process. Other chapters in this volume treat the domestic developments at greater length, so it should be sufficient

---

4 On social imperialism, see Bernard Semmel, *Imperialism and Social Reform: English Social Imperial Thought, 1895–1914* (London: Allen & Unwin, 1960).

here to note that between 1868 and 1912 – the forty-five years of the Meiji emperor's rule – Japan came to acquire almost all of the ingredients of a modern state that other countries were also in the process of obtaining. First, internal administrative unity replaced the cumbersome Tokugawa system. The new Tokyo government quickly established a bureaucratic apparatus so that within a few years after 1868 it boasted of a multitude of ministries of Finance, Home Affairs, Foreign Affairs, and others for which "enlightened" elites were recruited. These elites were mostly former samurai who had been active in bakufu and *han* affairs in the years before the Restoration, and many of them had spent several years studying in the West. They were technical experts whose loyalty was to the new regime under the nominal head of the emperor. The latter symbolized the fact that the country was now administratively and politically centralized, a system in which professional bureaucrats would play a pivotal role. Their work was sustained and protected by the newly created armed forces that, too, represented central authority against latent localism. The suppression of the Satsuma Rebellion of 1877 marked a successful alliance of Japan's new bureaucrats and armed forces, some recruited from peasant families, against the remnants of the old order.

Administrative centralization was accompanied by the development of a national economy. Even before 1868, of course, the country had been unified as a national market through commerce, uniform currencies, and domestic travel. But the Meiji government was intent on providing national leadership for economic development so that the country as a whole would "increase production and create industry," as one of the slogans put it. This was essentially an administrative task, involving tax reforms so as to obtain revenue from the agricultural sector and to turn it over for industrialization. The government took steps to identify and protect merchants and industrialists, to establish model factories and quality inspection stations, and to instill in the people the idea that "enriching the country" was just as important a goal as was "strengthening its defense."

Mass incorporation into the new polity, in the meanwhile, grew quickly. This took various forms, ranging from a comprehensive system of population registers to universal military conscription. The idea was to create an administratively effective system so that the government would be able to reach out to the entire population as citizens of the state. Their services were needed not only as potential soldiers and loyal subjects but ultimately as the backbone of the modern Japanese nation. An educated, enlightened citizenry was considered an essential part of the entity. Hence there was an early emphasis on education, both at the schools and in various political and professional activities. The people had to be politically conscious and economically developed if they were to support the new arrangements as citizens, producers, and taxpayers. This process of mass incorporation, of course, was destined to give rise to social movements that were not all supportive of the state. Although the awakening of political consciousness was a vital part of the formation of the modern state, it could develop into a force of protest against specific governmental decisions, general thrusts of national policy, or even the Meiji state itself. These forces, broadly termed the "Freedom and People's Rights" movement, made their appearance during the 1870s, evidence that Japan was already acquiring yet another characteristic of a modern state. For mass movements were a necessary component of a society that was undergoing political and economic centralization. Although such movements could, and often did, present obstacles in the way of centralization, functionally there could be no centralized modern society without politically conscious citizens.

The two could be related in a number of ways. The twentieth century has produced such extreme examples as the totalitarian mass societies in Nazi Germany and Stalinist Russia, or the "mass-line" politics in Maoist China. They all linked the masses with the state through centralized indoctrination, party dictatorship, and mass meetings. Few institutions stood between the state and the people. In the late nineteenth century, however, almost all modernizing states retained family, church, business, community, and other institutions that mediated between them. They functioned as checks on state power, on the one hand, and as agents of modernization, on the other, in the sense that through them the people would be socialized, educated, and developed into citizenry. Most important, there were political parties that spoke for both the state and the people. They provided personnel for the government and also represented the diverse interests and viewpoints of the people.

Meiji Japan fitted into this pattern. Already by the 1870s numerous political parties, study groups, and community organizations had come into being, superimposed on traditional family and religious institutions. Their growth was ensured by the government's policy of encouraging education, social mobility, economic development, and political consciousness. Both those who benefited from such developments and those who felt left out found it easy to organize. Early political parties were an amalgam of divergent interests and viewpoints, some urging the state to do more for modernization and others opposing the process as too swift and confusing. Even the latter, however, lent their hands to the modernization process in that they contributed to political organizing efforts and to arousing mass interest in national affairs. After all, they had no recourse for seeking amends other than through organizing themselves and demonstrating their causes in accordance with the various grievance procedures that were being set up. In the end, the bulk of the "premodern" dissidents found themselves joining existing political parties or being co-opted into working for the state.

It does not mean, of course, that Japan as a modern state did not have special characteristics of its own. All nations are unique. But uniqueness generally lies in historical diversity. Although Japanese history made the country different, the same was true of other countries. Moreover, some peculiar features of Meiji Japan should probably be considered within the framework of its development as a modern state, that is, as minor variations on a common theme. Among such variations two stood out in the Meiji era: the emperor system and the military's "right of supreme command." Although most modern states at that time were monarchies, the Japanese case was unique in that the imperial institution was consciously used to create a centralized bureaucratic system. By identifying the new arrangements as rule by the sacred emperor, an aura of sanctity was accorded to them. Japan's armed forces and bureaucrats would be "the emperor's soldiers and officials," making them perhaps less vulnerable to partisan attacks than might have been the case in other societies with shorter periods of dynastic history. By combining a newly created bureaucracy, civilian and military, with the prestige of a fifteen-hundred-year-old institution, the Meiji leaders succeeded in giving modernization almost instant legitimacy. Second, they early perceived the need to separate military administration from strategic affairs, and in 1878 they established a general staff independent of the Ministry of War. The former would control strategic planning, tactical decisions, and military intelligence. These, comprising matters pertinent to "the right of supreme command," would enable the general staff to report directly to the emperor, thus sustaining its separate status from civilian bureaucracies. The system was learned from Prussia, but it grew into an extremely important aspect of the Japanese state, because the "independence" of the supreme command was combined with the imperial institution. Already by 1879, army leaders such as Saigō Tsugumichi and Ōyama Iwao were arguing that as the civilian and constitutional government was expected to expand, it would be desirable to maintain the separate existence of the military.[5]

It is these characteristics that have led some historians to define the Meiji state as "emperor absolutism." Presumably such a definition makes sense in stressing the pivotal roles played by the emperor and the military. Evidently the two were under much less restraint than in other modern states, perhaps with the exception of czarist Russia. These features, however, do not alter the fact that Japan was emerging as a modern state in the late nineteenth century. The imperial institution and the military right of supreme command represented the centralizing forces, the first prerequisite for such a state. Whether these institutions made Japan an "absolutist" state cannot be discussed in the abstract. To the extent that their appearance coincided with that of the civilian bureaucracy and popular movements, it may be said that all were aspects of modern transformation. To the degree that these latter weakened relative to the power of the emperor and the military, Japan became less "democratic" and more totalitarian. The key question was whether there developed a mutually reinforcing relationship between state and society so that both the central government and the people benefited from the new arrangements.

Japanese foreign relations become significant in such a context. How Japan's emergence as a modern state determined its foreign relations; how the latter in turn affected the nature of the modern Japanese state and how Japanese society's unique features resulted in peculiar foreign policy decisions are among the most interesting questions that arise. Unfortunately, there are few systematic treatments of the subject, although the Foreign Ministry has been scrupulous about publishing its documentary compilations.[6] Most writings are little more than conventional narratives of diplomatic relations, as illustrated by the multivolume *Nihon gaikō shi* (History of Japanese diplomacy) by Kajima Morinosuke.[7] These volumes, some of which have been translated into English, are simplistic compendia of official documents, with little analysis. Where interpretation is attempted, it is almost invariably in the framework of justifying Japan's actions. Less parochial but similarly oriented to chronological treatment are the few other general histories of Meiji foreign relations that have been pub-

---

[5] Yamanaka Einosuke, *Nihon kindai kokka no keisei to kanryōsei* (Tokyo: Kōbundō, 1974), pp. 64–8, 70.
[6] Gaimushō, *Nihon gaikō bunsho*. Over 151 volumes, reaching the year 1926 in 1986.
[7] Morinosuke Kajima, *The Diplomacy of Japan, 1894–1922*, 3 vols. (Tokyo: Kajima Institute of International Peace, 1976–80); in Japanese, Kajima heiwa kenkyūjo, *Nihon gaikō shi*, 34 vols. (Tokyo: Kajima kenkyūjo shuppankai, 1970–73 and *Nihon gaikō shi, bekkan*, 4 vols. (1971–4).

lished, such as Hanabusa Nagamichi's *Meiji gaikō shi* (History of Meiji diplomacy) and Shinobu Seizaburō's *Nihon gaikō shi* (History of Japanese diplomacy).[8] This last contains systematic essays by Marxist-oriented historians and provides the best survey to date of Meiji foreign affairs. There are also numerous monographs that describe in laborious detail various diplomatic incidents and negotiations of the Meiji era, most of which, however, are conventional diplomatic history in that they document intergovernmental relations, with little attention paid to the interplay between them and domestic developments. Many of them focus on a few individuals so that the foreign affairs as presented are little more than a sum total of what they said and did.

One looks in vain for studies that transcend a parochial, nationalistic treatment, or antiquarian diplomatic history. At this stage of scholarship, the most plausible approach would seem to be a comparative one in which Japanese foreign affairs are comprehended in comparison with those of other modern states. Such a study would be useful not only to students of Japanese history but also to modern international history. Unfortunately, these latter have all but ignored Japan or manifested only the most superficial knowledge of its history and politics. Note, for instance, that virtually all historians who, for the past thirty years, have been engaged in fierce and productive debate on the nature of modern imperialism have had little to say about Japanese imperialism. Wolfgang Mommsen's *Theories of Imperialism* (English edition, 1980), though a splendid synthesis of the key interpretations that have been offered by students of modern imperialism, does not once mention Japan. There is thus a regrettable gap between these two groups of specialists. It is in part to fill this gap that the following sections have been written.[9]

CONSOLIDATION OF DOMESTIC AND FOREIGN AFFAIRS, 1868–1880

The awareness that domestic and external affairs were intimately linked was, of course, always present during the Tokugawa era. After all, the Edo regime built its administrative and legal system on the basis of curtailing and controlling all foreign contact. The assumption, from the time of Tokugawa Ieyasu, had been that such contact would

---

8 Hanabusa Nagamichi, *Meiji gaikō shi* (Tokyo: Shibundō, 1960), and Shinobu Seizaburō, ed., *Nihon gaikō shi: 1853–1972*, 2 vols. (Tokyo: Mainichi shimbunsha, 1974).
9 This gap will be more difficult to justify since the appearance of Ramon H. Myers and Mark R. Peattie, eds., *The Japanese Colonial Empire, 1895–1945* (Princeton, N.J.: Princeton University Press, 1984).

be detrimental to domestic order. This was ultimately because international affairs were seen as disorderly, confusing, and constantly shifting, in which countries vied with one another for power and material gains. Obviously, international disorder could not be allowed to intrude on domestic order. Toward the end of the eighteenth century, the shogunate allowed a few individuals to have access to the Westerners in Nagasaki, but the intention was to use this contact to strengthen the regime. The policy eventually backfired, as various domains, too, came to appreciate the value of Western arms, artifacts, and ideas as a means for their own strengthening and for bringing about a change in the country's political system.

Given this background, it is not surprising that from the beginning the Meiji regime should have sought to establish control over foreign affairs as an essential prerequisite for consolidating its power at home. In March 1868, the imperial government in Kyoto (eleven months before it moved to Tokyo as the new capital) issued a proclamation calling on the people to cooperate with its foreign policy. "Domestic conditions are unstable," it said, but "external dealings are extremely important." In such a situation, the new regime's stability appeared to depend on the willingness of various factions to deal with foreigners only through the government, and on the readiness of the foreigners to cooperate in this process. Such were, the proclamation said, the "trends of the times" (*jisei*).[10] This was a delicate process, but on the whole the new leaders succeeded in preventing foreign affairs from exacerbating domestic tensions and in using external issues to stabilize internal order. In this sense, the story of Japan during the 1860s and 1870s is comparable to that of Prussia in the same period, in which external and internal affairs likewise developed in a symbiotic fashion. The situation was different in the neighboring country of China, in which a brief period of "restoration" after the turmoil of the Taiping Rebellion – a restoration that was supported by the Western powers – was followed by a sustained period of antiforeign attacks, decentralization of political authority, and mass disaffection, a situation that proved to be fertile ground for further foreign encroachment.

Japan's relative success in the years after 1868 was due fundamentally to the recognition of the intimate link between domestic and foreign affairs that the new leaders shared. They thus took foreign relations with the utmost seriousness lest they render ineffective their

10 Shinobu Seizaburō, ed., *Nihon gaikō shi* (Tokyo: Mainichi shimbunsha, 1974), vol. 1, p. 74; Inau Dentarō, *Nihon gaikō shisō shi ronkō* (Tokyo: Komine shoten, 1965), vol. 1, pp. 42–3.

effort to establish a new domestic order. A few examples will illustrate how this was done.

First, antiforeign attacks were banned and, when they did take place, were severely dealt with. The new regime knew all too well how indiscriminate assaults on foreigners could undermine its claim as the government of the country; similar attacks had fatally wounded the Tokugawa shogunate's standing in the international sphere. Foreign complications would serve only to keep the country in turmoil, which in turn would invite further diplomatic incidents. To deal with these dangers, the government had to improve its system of law enforcement and legal procedure. It also engaged in an extensive propaganda campaign to inform the populace that antiforeign attacks were against "the laws of the world." The country was now going to develop in accordance with these laws, and therefore its people should not act on the basis of "old, stained habits." By accepting the laws of the universe, Japan would be able to "assert its prestige throughout the world."[11] The people were exhorted to join this task. It was a brilliant strategy, combining the prohibition of antiforeignism with the vision of a glorious future, both calculated to consolidate the government's authority and prestige. Apparently, within a few years after 1868 virtually all segments of the population and all factions among the former samurai accepted the new orientation, so that antiforeign incidents visibly abated.

The issue of antiforeign assaults was closely connected to that of legal reforms in the country, looking eventually to the abolition of extraterritoriality. To the extent that the Meiji government successfully stamped out antiforeign outbursts, the country would be safe for foreign residents. Foreigners would no longer have to be confined to restricted areas to protect them from violence. They would be free to travel and live in the interior. All this would assume that the Japanese people would treat overseas visitors with deference. At the same time, such a situation would make obsolete the special system of legal protection that had been granted to foreigners in the form of consular jurisdiction. There would no longer be much justification for its existence, and foreigners would have to be asked to obey Japanese laws like anybody else. If extraterritoriality were abolished, it would be a sign that foreigners were perfectly safe in Japan and that the country had a system of laws that they could accept. In both cases, the government would be credited with having transformed Japan into a modern legal state. Its prestige, both internally and externally, would be enhanced.

[11] Shinobu, *Nihon gaikō shi*, vol. 1, p. 74; Inau, *Nihon gaikō shisō shi*, vol. 1, pp. 64–5.

Already in April 1869 Iwakura Tomomi noted the need for treaty revision, as the presence of foreign troops in the country and the foreigners' extraterritorial rights were a violation of Japanese independence.[12] Few would have disputed the view, and in 1871, when Iwakura led a large mission to the United States and Europe, the emissaries were entrusted with the task of initiating preliminary discussions of treaty revision. They were not to undertake formal negotiation, for the Meiji leaders felt that the country's internal reforms had not yet progressed to the point that it could boast a completely modernized system of laws. As the government's instruction to the ambassadors pointed out, "nations must possess equal rights" in their treaty relationships, but Japan had been deprived of such rights because of "the defects of its traditional custom and Oriental political institutions." These deficiencies, however, were now being overcome, and a new legal system was being established. It would take a few more years to complete the task by drastically revising civil, criminal, tax, trade, and other laws. The mission was in part intended for an extensive observation of Western legal institutions and political systems so that the "political institutions of the most enlightened and powerful nations" could be introduced to the Japanese people.[13] In Kume Kunitake's *Bei-Ō kairan jikki* (*True Account of Observations of America and Europe*), one sees a massive documentation of the embassy's observations, ranging from scenery and architecture to the politics, economy, and history of the Western countries.[14] It is not surprising that one of the things that struck the visitors most was the way in which governments and people appeared to be struggling for common goals such as national strengthening and well-being. They carried away the strong impression that a modern nation must have not only a strong central government but also an enlightened and motivated populace. Because this was the very theme of the emerging states in the West, the trip could not have taken place at a more opportune moment. Particularly pertinent was the German example, as the Japanese visit coincided with the establishment of the newly unified nation and Prince Otto Bismarck frankly explained to the Japanese the need for realism and hard work if they hoped to succeed in their own task of nation building.

After the embassy's return, legal reforms proceeded apace, and in 1880 the government promulgated new criminal laws. But treaty revi-

---

12 Shinobu, *Nihon gaikō shi*, vol. 1, p. 78.   13 Ibid., p. 85.
14 Marlene Mayo, "The Western Education of Kume Kunitake 1871–76," *Monumenta Nipponica* 28 (1973): 3–67.

sion could not be easily achieved. On the one hand, foreigners sought to hold onto their privileges and reminded the Japanese that their modern reforms were still not complete; they would need to revise further their civil, tax, and commercial laws. Domestic travail, as evidenced by Saigō Takamori's resignation from the government in 1873 and his open rebellion four years later, was not calculated to give confidence to foreigners regarding Japan's political stability. Although negotiation for revision was not interrupted by the rebellion of 1877, the foreign governments were unwilling to concede that their nationals could subject themselves to Japanese jurisdiction. Tokyo's leaders sought to mollify them by offering to appoint foreign judges in Japanese courts in cases involving foreign residents, but even such concessions produced no immediate response by the powers.[15]

Equally important, the government's seeming lack of success and willingness to consider concessions such as the appointment of foreign judges aroused the resentment of the politically active segments of the population that strengthened in proportion to the delay in the treaty revision negotiations. To the extent that one may speak of "public opinion" or "mass politics" in Japan during the 1870s, the treaty question played a major part in their development. A vocal minority from the beginning was opposed to "mixed residence," that is, the opening of the interior for foreign residence, business, and property ownership. Although opinion was divided on this and other specific issues, newspapers and nascent political organizations – Aikoku kōtō (Public Party of Patriots) was organized in 1874 – were adept in taking advantage of the treaty question to demand more "freedom and people's rights." They insisted that the best way to put an end to the foreigners' extraterritorial privileges was to mobilize and organize popular opinion by convening a national assembly. The establishment of such an assembly, which was an institution in almost all Western states, would not only demonstrate that Japan was now as modern a country as theirs but would also be effective in presenting a massive national sentiment in favor of treaty revision. Foreigners would thus be persuaded to relinquish their special privileges and accord to Japan the status of an equal, sovereign nation.

Thus ironically, mass integration into the polity was being achieved because of the government's alleged failure to have the powers recognize the country as an independent, modern state. The only solution to the dilemma, according to government leaders, was to push for

---

15 The best concise summary of treaty revision negotiations remains Inoue Kiyoshi, *Jōyaku kaisei* (Tokyo: Iwanami shoten, 1955).

further legal and political reforms, so that foreigners would have no excuse for treating the country as semicivilized, while at the same time making certain that during the 1870s movements for popular rights and for treaty revision were aspects of the same drive for the nationalization of the Japanese polity.[16]

In the meantime, the government became interested in regaining tariff autonomy. All existing treaties stipulated that duties imposed on foreign imports were to be determined by agreement between Japan and other governments. This "treaty tariff" system was viewed by the Japanese government and public as an infringement on sovereignty, just as consular jurisdiction was. It deprived the country of much needed revenue as it undertook economic modernization. Public finance was in a chronically critical situation, in which taxes had to be raised. The people, too, were quick to establish a connection between their heavy tax burden and the absence of tariff autonomy. As Foreign Minister Terashima Munenori pointed out in 1876, such a sentiment could revive antiforeign hysteria. In order to "satisfy public sentiment, maintain law and order, and expand foreign trade," it was imperative to "regain our national rights" by seeking the restoration of tariff autonomy.[17] Between 1876 and 1879 Terashima concentrated on this issue, rather than extraterritoriality, as the first priority in treaty revision negotiation. He achieved modest successes when the United States, Russia, Italy, and several others indicated their willingness to restore tariff autonomy to Japan, but Britain, France, and Germany stood adamant, and the efforts bore no immediate result. Although the Western countries' trade with Japan was minuscule at this time, amounting in most instances to less than 1 percent of their total volume of trade, they all viewed export trade as an important ingredient of national economic growth. Treaty tariffs provided an effective means for maintaining their "informal empires" overseas. Some powers, notably the United States, took the position that trade would expand even after Japan regained tariff autonomy; in fact, the friendly relationship that would result from it could be calculated to tie the two countries closer together economically. Moreover, the United States under the Republican administrations was practicing a highly protectionist trade policy, causing Japanese officials like Itō Hirobumi to call for a protectionist policy of their own as beneficial to the country.[18]

16 Shinobu, *Nihon gaikō shi*, vol. 1, p. 112; Sakeda Masatoshi, *Kindai Nihon ni okeru taigaikō undō no kenkyū* (Tokyo: Tokyo daigaku shuppankai, 1978), p. 7.
17 Shinobu, *Nihon gaikō shi*, vol. 1, p. 108.
18 Shimomura Fujio, *Meiji shonen jōyaku kaisei shi no kenkyū* (Tokyo: Yoshikawa kōbunkan, 1962), p. 80.

Although protectionism was practiced by few other countries at that time, all believed that industrialization and extensive trade went hand in hand. Ultimately, then, the question of tariff autonomy hinged on the readiness of the Western nations to permit an economically modernizing Japan to enter their system of international relations. As of the 1870s, few of them were.

Treaty revision graphically illustrated the close links between domestic political developments and foreign affairs. No less important in this context were the territorial questions. Modern history has shown that few issues arouse as intense a popular passion as territorial issues do, and few are regarded as a more telling index of a state's ability to govern or of a government's claim to legitimacy. A modern state is defined as a territorial entity in which center and periphery are united in a conception of national unity and defense. It is no accident that during the second half of the nineteenth century the geographical boundaries of such countries as the United States, Italy, Germany, and the Low Countries became more clearly defined and that where there were ambiguities, as was the case in Alsace and Lorraine and most notably in the Balkans, in which Russia, Austria-Hungary, and Turkey had conflicting claims, there was always a strong likelihood of armed hostilities. Nationalistic sentiment could easily be mobilized through government propaganda and the press whenever it was felt that a country's justifiable territorial claim was being violated; on the other hand, the government would be held accountable for ensuring territorial integrity and security so that its authority would be seriously undermined when it gave the impression of succumbing to external pressures on a territorial question.

Meiji Japan was no exception. The new leaders assumed as a matter of course that one of their first tasks would be to establish clearly definable national boundaries. This could have been a relatively easy undertaking, compared with the complex situation in Europe where historical, ethnic, and religious diversities never quite corresponded to distinct geographical boundaries. Japan was characterized by no such complexity, and during the Tokugawa period its domain had been confined to the four major islands. Beyond them, however, were regions of ambiguous definition that had not been incorporated into another power's domain. For this reason, the Japanese were eager to establish clear demarcations for these areas. Such incorporation would not only define the limits of the new Japanese state to come under the jurisdiction of the central government; it would also enable the latter to plan for national defense and development. The populace, in the meantime, would have a new conception of the nation so that they would be under the protection of the new government anywhere within the new boundaries.

Reflecting such perceptions, the Meiji government early showed an interest in establishing a clear boundary to the north of Hokkaido. There lay the large island of Sakhalin and the chain of smaller islands, the Kurils, that arched the northwestern Pacific from Hokkaido to Kamchatka. In the mid-nineteenth century both these territories were sparsely populated by Russians and Japanese. The latter were a minority, mostly fishermen, but they would have to be protected if indeed they were living in Japanese territory. The perpetuation of mixed residence, in which the two nationals lived together in ambiguous status, appeared undesirable. Japan could have drawn a line close to Hokkaido so that Japanese living in Sakhalin and the Kurils would be considered beyond the protection of the government, or else they would be told to return to Japan proper. (This has been the situation since 1945.) But this was an option that the Tokyo government found hard to accept. It would imply a retreat and damage the new regime's domestic and external prestige. It would bring Russia that much closer to Japan proper. Russian ships had temporarily seized the island of Tsushima (lying between Kyushu and Korea) in 1861, causing a near panic among Japanese in that part of the country. Similar incidents could recur if Russia gained Sakhalin and the Kurils. On the other hand, there was little compelling reason that those territories should belong to Japan. Territorial enlargement would complicate the question of administration and defense; it could give rise to further problems with Russia, as it would bring Japan closer to Russia's territory in Siberia and the Maritime Provinces; and it was not at all clear whether the government and the people of Japan were prepared to divert their resources to the economic development of Sakhalin and the Kurils when they had just begun a project for settling and developing Hokkaido.

In the end, Tokyo's response showed the government's receptivity to domestic pressures. In 1874 it decided to evacuate Japanese residents from Sakhalin, intimating a decision to concede the whole island to the Russians. At the same time, Japan insisted on its claim to the whole of the Kuril island chain. This was for reasons of prestige; it would placate domestic opposition unhappy about the Sakhalin retreat and also demonstrate to the other powers that Japan would make concessions only on a quid pro quo basis. All this would add to the sense of national unity and clarify the limits of state administration. It was symbolic of the concern with national unity that the government should have turned to Enomoto Takeaki, one of the staunchest supporters of the late shogunate against the new regime, who had established an ill-fated republic in Hokkaido before being captured and imprisoned and who had been released from prison only in 1872, to go to St. Petersburg to negotiate a settlement of the territorial question. In 1875 Enomoto successfully concluded a treaty along the lines of his instructions, resulting in an "exchange" of Sakhalin for the Kurils. Henceforth Russia was to control the entire island of Sakhalin but was to cede all of the Kurils to Japan. The treaty was popular, as it was the first significant settlement with a Western power in which Japan had been treated like an equal and had not been forced to make humiliating concessions.[19]

Somewhat more clear-cut was the disposition of the Ryūkyū kingdom, consisting of the island of Okinawa and its vicinity. Standing almost equidistant from Kyushu, Korea, and Taiwan, the islands had been governed as part of Satsuma *han,* but their rulers had also sent tributary missions to the Chinese court under the Ch'ing dynasty. Ethnically and culturally, the people of Ryūkyū were distinct from, though related to, both the Chinese and the Japanese, although their language was closer to Japanese. The question that the Meiji government faced was whether the island population should now be incorporated into the Japanese state, extending to them the jurisdiction and protection of the central authority. From the beginning there was little hestitation to answer the question in the affirmative, the national government placing the kingdom of Ryūkyū under the jurisdiction of Kagoshima Prefecture (formerly Satsuma *han*) in 1871. It was resolved that because the Tokugawa regime had, indirectly through Satsuma, ruled over the kingdom, the Tokyo government should do likewise but also go a step further and turn it into an administrative district of the country. This entailed extending the national government's protection to the Ryūkyū population, a matter that suddenly surfaced as a grave national issue when in 1871 some fifty-odd island fishermen who had been shipwrecked and drifted to Taiwan were massacred by aborigines.

The incident was a test of the Meiji regime's ability to affirm its leadership of a modern state. If those fishermen, Ryūkyū subjects, were to be considered Japanese citizens, it would be incumbent upon the government to seek satisfaction for their tragedy from the Chinese government, which had control over Taiwan, a province of China. If

19 On the Sakhalin–Kurils "exchange" treaty, see John J. Stephan, *The Kuril Islands: The Russo-Japanese Frontier in the Pacific* (New York: Oxford University Press, 1975).

they were not viewed as Japanese citizens, Japan's claim to the Ryūkyūs would, of course, be destroyed. This was something the leaders could not concede, especially in view of an aroused domestic opinion. Both within and without the government, voices called for strong action to avenge the damages done to Japanese citizens and to "punish" the "uncivilized" people of Taiwan who had dared to assault Japanese subjects. The vocabulary was similar to what Westerners had used in retaliating against Japanese attacks on their nationals. (Commodore Perry, in fact, had dealt severely with Okinawan authorities when one of his sailors was killed by local residents.) Inaction in the face of such an assault would be taken as a sign of weakness, as evidence that Japan was not yet as strong a state as America and the European countries.

Presumably, satisfaction could have been obtained from the Ch'ing government, but the latter was unwilling to discuss the issue on the grounds that the massacre had been caused by "uncivilized people," beyond the reach of Chinese "politics and religion."[20] Such an argument, of course, revealed the Chinese authorities' lack of understanding of the responsibilities of a modern state – which is not surprising in that they were similarly irresolute and insensitive when a far more serious incident arose closer to home, the massacre of French missionaries in Tientsin, in the same year, 1871. (Several years afterwards, Chinese officials resorted to Japanese and Western language in their efforts to hold the United States government responsible for the killing of Chinese immigrants in western states.) For two years after 1872, when the incident became known, Japanese and Chinese officials engaged in inconclusive talks over the incident, but in the end the former decided to act unilaterally by sending a punitive expedition to Taiwan. This was fundamentally in response to domestic pressures. These years saw a series of critical clashes and confrontations among the country's political leaders, the most dramatic of which was the 1873 dispute on the Korean question, resulting in the resignation from the government of several influential men. In such a situation, those who remained in power – Ōkubo Toshimichi, Ōkuma Shigenobu, and others – felt they needed an issue that would dissipate some of the dissidents' unhappiness, coalesce national opinion, and reaffirm the regime's prestige. An expedition to Taiwan was chosen as a viable solution. It was officially approved at a cabinet meeting of February 6, 1874, and an expeditionary force of 3,000 was organized under Saigō

20 Shinobu, *Nihon gaikō shi*, vol. 1, p. 90.

Tsugumichi. They landed in Taiwan on May 22, and after incurring some 573 casualties, all but 12 of which were due to tropical diseases, they established control over the areas inhabited by the aborigines.

The fact that the Taiwan expedition came more than two years after the massacre took place indicates that it was less a reactive move than a deliberate response to domestic needs. This explains why the Japanese government informed foreign governments of the impending expedition at the very last moment and did not even bother to tell China about it until after the expedition had taken place.[21] From the Japanese point of view, the important thing was to carry out the expedition to placate domestic opposition and, by having the Chinese recognize its legitimacy, to assert control over the people of Ryūkyū as Japanese citizens. After some protracted postexpedition negotiations in Peking, in which Ōkubo himself took part, the Ch'ing court acquiesced in recognizing the "justice" of the expedition, in return for Japan's evacuation of Taiwan. Because the seizure of that island was never an original Japanese aim, this was accomplished without arousing domestic resentment. It was enough that the Japanese had acted like the other powers in protecting its nationals by a show of force.

The Chinese-Japanese agreement on the settlement of the Ryūkyū massacre was a blow to China's prestige, especially in view of the 1871 treaty between the two countries that had established normal diplomatic relations between them and granted mutual extraterritoriality. The treaty also included a provision for mutual assistance and mediation in case one of the signatories entered a dispute with a third power. But the Taiwan expedition threatened to undermine the framework of friendly relations that such provisions implied. The Japanese were aware that their policy of incorporating the Ryūkyūs into their national boundaries – which was to be effected in 1879 – would create tensions with China. But they reasoned that as a modern state, Japan could no longer acquiesce in an anomalous situation in which the island people were not fully integrated into the nation. Moreover, if these people were to be considered Japanese subjects and protected by Japanese arms, it would become necessary to assume responsibility for the defense of the islands. Japan might have to build a naval base there to station a fleet and also to cope with a potential internal turmoil – the Okinawan king did not conceal his displeasure at the abolition of his own kingdom – through military means. All these measures would be tantamount to extending Japanese control into a region close to

21 Ibid., p. 94.

Taiwan and the Chinese mainland. It is not surprising, under the circumstances, that Chinese officials should have become increasingly alarmed over the situation and that during the second half of the 1870s a sense of acute crisis should have developed between the two countries. That in turn would confront the Japanese with the need for strengthening their military and for defining their strategic priorities. Though little was done in those areas at this time, it should be noted that Japan was following the pattern of other states in that the delimitation of territorial boundaries went hand in hand with a redefinition of security needs, resulting in calls for increased armament and long-range war plans. The transformation of China in Japanese perception in the 1870s, from a friendly neighbor of equal status to a potential adversary, is a good illustration of the way in which a modern state stressed power considerations in its external affairs.

Power in a modern state, however, meant more than armament and war plans. It also developed in combination with economic and social forces at home. For the state to have an effective foreign policy, it was vital to mobilize domestic resources to the full. We have seen this in connection with treaty revision. Equally significant for the 1870s was the developing crisis with Korea. Nowhere were the links between domestic and foreign affairs more graphically demonstrated, and nowhere were the promise as well as the frustrations of modernization more tellingly revealed, than in the tangle of events and decisions that dotted Japanese-Korean relations after the Meiji Restoration. Meiji leaders early recognized the clear links between the Korean question and the establishment of domestic order. As Kido Takayoshi wrote in 1869, a vigorous assertion of policy toward Korea "would instantly change Japan's outmoded customs, set its objectives abroad, promote its industry and technology, and eliminate jealousy and recrimination among its people."[22] Behind such bombast lay historical factors that had defined a tortuous pattern of relationship between the two countries. The Japanese liked to talk of "restoring" an ancient relationship between the two countries now that they had effected their own internal "restoration." The Tokugawa regime had dealt with the Korean kingdom through the lord of Tsushima, and the Koreans had viewed such connections as distinctly inferior to their tributary relationship with China. Perpetuation of the existing arrangements would imply

---

[22] Key-Hiuk Kim, *The Last Phase of the East Asian World Order: Korea, Japan, and the Chinese Empire, 1860–1882* (Berkeley and Los Angeles: University of California Press, 1980), p. 125. Kido reversed his position after taking part in the Iwakura mission to the West and also opposed the Taiwan expedition.

that Japanese-Korean relations were still comprehended within the traditional world order defined by China. If Japan were to "restore" domestic arrangements to eradicate feudalism and if part of that undertaking involved the establishment of a new framework of foreign affairs, then it followed that Japanese-Korean relations, too, must be placed on a new footing. The matter was complicated, however, because it was never clear how that footing was to be defined and because division on this question threatened the very domestic stability in Japan that was the basic objective of the Meiji leaders.

Kido's assertion just cited revealed a widely shared view that a strong stand toward Korea would be a good way to unify domestic opinion and consolidate the base of the new leadership in Japan. But ironically, the Korean issue almost destroyed the nascent Meiji government. There is not enough space here to chronicle the fascinating story of internal strife in Japan during the 1870s which brought about the defeat of *sei-Kan ron* (the movement for a Korean expedition). As one Japanese historian has pointed out, even Saigō Takamori, usually identified with that movement, was initially opposed to the use of force.[23] He wanted to use diplomacy, such as the dispatch of a high-level embassy to Seoul headed by himself, to solve the impasse in Korea, in which the Yi dynasty refused to accede to Japanese demands for a new diplomatic relationship. But his political opponents, such as Kido, Iwakura, and Ōkubo, feared that a successful consummation of the project could enhance Saigō's prestige, thus undermining their own power. Because they were dedicated to consolidating the Meiji state, they had to oppose Saigō's plans. Frustrated, he in turn came to call for a more militant policy in Korea so as to embarrass the Kido–Iwakura faction. The conflict ultimately led to the Satsuma uprising of 1877. In all these developments, Korea was but a context in which domestic rivalries were played out.

It was obvious that the government had to achieve some diplomatic success quickly. Its passivity would be contrasted not only with the growing tide of *sei-Kan ron* but also with Saigō's advocacy of a diplomatic solution. What the Kido–Iwakura leadership carried out was close to what Saigō had advocated: the dispatch of a high-level mission to Korea to seek to establish diplomatic relations between the two countries. The government also hoped to silence advocates of forceful measures by dispatching three gunboats to Korean waters in 1875.

23 Shinobu, *Nihon gaikō shi*, vol. 1, p. 92.

When one of them was fired on at Kanghwa Bay, it retaliated by bombarding some coastal batteries. Thus provided with a pretext for sending an emissary, Tokyo dispatched an embassy headed by Kuroda Kiyotaka in January 1876. Fully conscious of the parallel between his own and the Perry expedition, Kuroda was accompanied by three warships and succeeded in concluding a treaty with the Korean kingdom roughly similar to the treaties that Japan had been forced to negotiate during the 1850s. The Korean treaty stipulated that the kingdom was "an independent nation," thereby putting an end to its tributary relationship with the Chinese empire. The opening of three ports for Japanese trade was provided for, as was Japanese consular jurisdiction in Korea. Compared with the Japanese-Chinese treaty of 1871, this was clearly one that established an unequal relationship between Japan and another country.

It would be wrong to conclude, however, that the 1876 treaty with Korea was the product of a premeditated plan for expansion and that it was the first step for Japan's continental imperialism. It was more a case of the Japanese leaders' eagerness for a diplomatic success in order to consolidate their power at home. In this they achieved their goal. The treaty was hailed as a sign that Japan was now in a position to enjoy some of the same rights in another country that Westerners had gained in Japan. It was the first nation to have opened up Korea to foreign intercourse. The resulting prestige enhanced the power of the Meiji leadership, although this very success led dissidents under Saigō to stage the unsuccessful Satsuma Rebellion of 1877.

The story of Japanese foreign affairs between 1868 and 1880, then, should primarily be seen as subsidiary to domestic developments. The consolidation of centralized power at home and the incorporation of larger segments of the population into the new polity had first to be achieved, and external issues had to be put in that context. This is hardly different from other countries, in particular Germany and the United States, which, too, were just then emerging as modern states. Of course, compared with theirs, the Japanese economy was far less industrialized, and its trade was still largely controlled by foreign merchants enjoying treaty privileges. It was hardly surprising that a key goal of the Japanese state should have been to seek revision of the treaties. At the same time, the Meiji leaders shared the views of their Western counterparts that national power must be defined broadly, in terms of the people's productivity, education, and discipline, as well as an efficient system of administration. They understood that a modern state must have clearly defined geographical boundaries as well as a sense of nationhood on the part of the people living within them. Although threatened with periodic internal turmoil, the Japanese state was on a firmer footing at the end than at the beginning of the 1870s, in many ways the crucial decade in modern international history. The result was that after 1880, when the tides of change in the world moved faster, Japan was in a position to understand, identify with, and use them for its further strengthening.

DOMESTIC POLITICS AND OVERSEAS EXPANSION, 1880–1895

After the 1880s European international relations entered a phase of colonial expansion and imperialist rivalries. Although neither colonialism nor power politics was a new phenomenon and although during the preceding decade Britain and Russia had signaled the opening of the Near Eastern question by clashing in Afghanistan and Turkey, it was in the 1880s that the tempo quickened, with France, Britain, Germany, and other states avidly extending their power to areas hitherto either loosely tied to European powers or lying beyond their control. In 1881 France established a protectorate over Tunis; in 1882 Britain occupied Egypt; in 1883 Germany began its colonial activities in Southwest Africa; during 1884–5 France and Britain extended their respective sways to Indochina and Burma; and in 1889 Germany, Britain, and the United States divided up the Samoan kingdom into three segments for their tripartite condominium. By the mid-1890s most of the Middle East, Africa, Asia, and the Pacific had fallen under the domination of one or another of the Western powers. China, Japan, and Korea were among the few noncolonized states in 1880, but by 1895 China and Korea had lost part of their sovereignty, thanks largely to Japanese expansionism.

Such a brief listing makes the conclusion inescapable that Japan joined the ranks of imperialist states and began behaving like them overseas. No amount of apologetic writing alters the fact that between 1880 and 1895 Japan did establish colonial enclaves and spheres of dominance over Korea, Taiwan, and parts of China. It is surprising, however, how little effort writers have made to fit Japanese expansionism into the general history of late-nineteenth-century imperialism and to fit the Japanese case into theories of imperialism. Most European writings on imperialism concentrate on Britain, France, and Germany. American historians, on their part, have written volumes about the emergence of the United States as an imperialist in the late

1890s but have on the whole tended to treat the phenomenon in isolation, separate from European and Japanese imperialism. Russian scholars, quite predictably, do write a great deal about czarist imperialism. They have also published far more about Japanese imperialism than have historians of other European countries; perhaps this reflects the fact that the rivalry between Russia and Japan was a key feature of the age of imperialism in East Asia. However, virtually all Soviet writings on the subject are presented in Marxist-Leninist formulations, and they are as susceptible to criticism as are similar accounts of British, French, or German imperialism. If anything, Leninist concepts are much more difficult to apply to less developed economies such as Russia and Japan at the turn of the century than to Britain and other countries. Despite this, Japanese writings on imperialism have also tended to be largely couched in Marxist-Leninist terms. The result is that when Japanese imperialism is fitted into the general history of modern imperialism, it is usually little more than a mechanistic exercise in applying rigid theories to the country. This has taken the form of locating the emergence of capitalism, the bourgeoisie, monopoly interests, and the like, as they are credited with having brought about late-nineteenth-century and early-twentieth-century imperialism. As with Marxist interpretations of European imperialism, however, it has been difficult to establish a correspondence between economic developments and specific instances of overseas expansion.

Neo-Marxists such as Andre G. Frank and Harry Magdoff have presented less rigid and more usable generalizations, although few of them have worked specifically on Japan.[24] It is their contention that regardless of the different rates of capital accumulation or levels of industrialization, the Western nations had, by the late nineteenth century, linked themselves to other parts of the world, turning the latter into their "satellites." These "satellites" provided raw materials, markets, and infrastructures, thereby making themselves dependent on the metropolitan economies. The result, according to this argument, was the perpetual underdevelopment of non-Western countries, which was in a symbiotic relationship with the development of the West. These writers term this total structure of dependency *imperialism*. Japan, obviously, is one exception to this pattern of Western domination, a fact that Frank has explained rather tautologically, saying that it escaped the dependency status by not becoming a satellite of the

---

24 A. G. Frank, *Latin America: Underdevelopment or Revolution* (New York: Monthly Review Press, 1970); Harry Magdoff, *The Age of Imperialism: The Economics of U.S. Foreign Policy* (New York: Monthly Review Press, 1969).

West. At least such a framework is useful, as it takes into account that despite its relative underdevelopment, Japan in the 1880s was not incorporated into a global economic system as a satellite of an advanced capitalist nation. On the contrary, as this chapter has emphasized, the country was on its way to becoming a centralized mass society, that is, a modern state. The country's basic political and bureaucratic framework had been established; the leadership had just survived a serious challenge to its authority; and the ground was being laid for the promulgation of a constitution and the convening of a national assembly, the Imperial Diet. More important than such institutional provisions was the fact that the populace had been educated and politicized. Often they had grown more politicized than the leaders had bargained for; the movement for "freedom and people's rights" throughout the 1870s had indicated that segments of the population were well educated, versed in political theory, and intent on resisting the growth of state authority. But those who held power recognized the importance of a politically alert opinion, and they had tried to channel it in the direction of national cohesiveness. The result, at the beginning of the 1880s, was that the politically essential preconditions for turning Japan into a modern state had been sufficiently fulfilled.

These basic achievements meant that in the 1880s, when the European powers stepped up their tempo of imperialist domination, the Japanese state, with a centralized bureaucracy and aroused public opinion, was in a far better position to understand and respond to these developments than were the other countries of Asia, the Middle East, or Africa. Japan's own imperialism must be understood in that context. In other words, its foreign dealings were now backed up by a stronger, more centralized government and were affected by domestic opinion and interest groups with greater self-assertiveness than before. Power, summing up armed forces, public opinion, and economic resources, could be better mobilized, just as it was being mobilized by other advanced countries. To the extent that the disparity between stronger and weaker power areas throughout the globe provided the setting for imperialist pressures, as David Landes has noted, it followed that Japan would represent the former and hence develop as an imperialist.[25]

In some such fashion, the Japanese began their story of overseas expansion, which culminated in the establishment of control over vast

25 David Landes, "Some Thoughts on the Nature of Economic Imperialism," *Journal of Economic History* 21 (1961): 496–512.

areas of Asia within thirty years. It should be pointed out, however, that expansion was always considered in the context of the growth of the modern Japanese nation and that as such it took many forms, not just formal colonial domination. The latter was not an end in itself, a premeditated goal for its own sake, but an aspect of Japan's development in a world environment defined by the major powers.

Basic to such a conception was a view of international affairs that the Japanese had begun to develop through their contact with Western countries and peoples during the 1870s and that was confirmed by the latters' overseas expansionism in the new decade. That view was expressed in such phrases as "war without warfare," "economic warfare," or "the struggle for survival," all expressions common in Japanese utterances at this time. That the international arena was controlled by the powerful, industrializing nations of the West was already clearly recognized. Added to this was the idea that those powers were constantly struggling with one another for greater national strength, not necessarily through war but through other means as well. There were, in fact, few, if any, armed hostilities among Western powers at that time. But this did not mean that they were not preparing for such conflict or that they were not constantly trying to augment their power. Even more important, not simply armies and navies but the total resources of a given country seemed to be committed to these goals. The people in these countries, the Japanese found, were energetic, vigorous, and aggressive, sharing with their leaders a sense of devotion to power, prestige, and wealth. They were, in short, engaged in a "war without warfare" or, as it came to be called in the 1890s, a "peacetime war." That the Japanese should do likewise was taken for granted by virtually all who spoke or wrote on the matter, although, as elsewhere, they differed among themselves as to the means for achieving the same ends. They were unanimous in believing that vigorous foreign policies and enterprises were a sign of internal health and power. Conversely, overseas activities by Japanese would rebound to the benefit of the home country. This was the theme of "expansion" broadly defined, a theme that came to be repeated with almost monotonous regularity in the 1880s and the subsequent decades. This was also imperialism, but it would be best to reserve that term for expansion into less powerful and less developed areas, such as Korea and China. There the Japanese came into contact with other imperialists and engaged in imperialist rivalries. But it should not be forgotten that there were other kinds of activities, such as emigration to Hawaii and trade with the West, that were equally important.

Japanese-Korean relations during the 1880s reflected a sense of power and urgency not visible earlier. As befitting a leadership that had survived a serious domestic challenge to its authority, the Meiji government in the late 1870s and early 1880s launched a program for extending its political and economic control over the peninsular kingdom. Export trade to Korea expanded phenomenally, not only bringing Japanese goods (matches, copper, and so on) there, but also shipping Western commodities from Japan to Korea (only 11.5 percent of total Japanese exports to Korea in 1882 consisted of goods made in Japan). Korea's rice and soybeans were imported into Japan in growing volume, Japan almost always purchasing 90 percent of all Korean exports. In 1881 a military advisory group was dispatched from Japan to start working on a modernized army for Korea.[26] These moves were obviously connected with the perceived needs of the Japanese state. Economic control over Korea was considered both desirable and feasible. Both the revenue from the export trade and the grains imported from the peninsula were considered important to Japan's industrialization, and the supervision of Korean military affairs ensured that nothing would happen to disrupt these emerging economic ties. It is unlikely that much thought was given at this time to imperialist rivalries in Asia in general, although the Japanese were quite aware of Russian expansionism in the north and its French and British counterpart in the south. Rather, it appears that it was considered desirable to use the opportunities provided by the nearby kingdom for the enhancement of Japanese power, economic and political.

This objective was supported by the populace. If anything, politically active segments of the population – the antigovernment press, dissident leaders who gathered around Ōkuma Shigenobu and created a minor crisis in 1881, and various political organizations – became even more interested in Korean affairs than the government was. Political movements evolved around the domestic issues of constitutional government and the convening of a national Diet, but the dissidents and popular rights activists often called on the nation to turn their attention overseas and promote reforms in China and Korea. Many of them felt frustrated in their challenge to the domestic leadership and believed that the best strategy was to arouse popular opinion about the government's alleged passivity toward Korea. Some were convinced that reforms in Japan would follow those in Korea. Others went further and advocated an alliance of Japanese and Korean reform-

26 Hattori Shisō, *Kindai Nihon gaikō shi* (Tokyo: Kawade shobō, 1954), p. 105.

ers so as to enlighten and civilize their countries. Tarui Tōkichi expressed such opinions in his famous *Dai–Tō gappō ron* (Unification of great Asia), written in 1885, calling on the two countries to unite to become a strong Asian power. (Fukuzawa Yukichi's even more famous *Datsu–A ron* – On leaving Asia – was also published that year and sought to refute Tarui's argument by asserting that it would be impossible to unite with a more backward country like Korea.)

In this way, both government and populace came to incorporate Korean issues into their own respective visions of national power and domestic arrangements. Expansionism was domestic politics by extension. It soon became apparent, however, that events in Korea itself were equally crucial to determining the course of Japanese expansionism. In a way similar to the circumstances in the "peripheral areas" that created and strengthened European imperialism in Africa and the Middle East, events in Korea played a key role in affecting the specific course that Japan was to take. In 1882, followers of the Taewongun, the de facto ruler of Korea between 1864 and 1873 who had been forced into retirement by the supporters of Queen Min for his extreme antiforeign policies, staged a coup against the Min and their alleged Japanese allies. The insurgents killed the Japanese officers in charge of training the new army and attacked the legation in Seoul. Minister Hanabusa Yoshitomo and his aides barely escaped and returned to Nagasaki on board a British ship. The Taewongun was restored to power, only to be forcibly taken to China by Chinese troops that were dispatched to Seoul to prevent further disorder.[27]

The Japanese might have decided to disengage themselves from the Korean peninsula then and there. Such a decision would have spared them from becoming involved in complex Korean politics and, even more important, with China. It might also have compelled them to turn their attention elsewhere, such as Sakhalin or Taiwan. However, the leaders in Tokyo considered inaction an admission of failure and were unanimous that something had to be done. Nongovernmental opinion also called for a quick response; it would surely seize upon government inaction as a failure of leadership. Tokyo's approach to the crisis was twofold. On the one hand, it would eschew hasty military action against the Korean government, as it would exacerbate the tensions already mounting between Japan and China. Instead, Japan would try to conclude an agreement with the Korean court to prevent a recurrence of similar outbursts. At the same time, the Japanese

27 Kim, *Last Phase*, pp. 316–25.

would make plans for a possible military engagement with Korea and, possibly, with China. The first approach led to the conclusion of an agreement in August 1882, stipulating that the Korean government would send a mission of apology to Japan, indemnify for the loss and damages to Japanese lives, and agree to the stationing of Japanese troops to guard the legation in Seoul. The second stipulation brought about a plan for strengthening armaments in preparation for a possible war with China over the Korean question. Particularly urgent appeared to be naval construction, in which Japan was believed to lag far behind China's naval building program. It would be necessary, Iwakura noted, to construct larger and faster ships. Because the Meiji regime eschewed large-scale foreign borrowing, funds for this had to come from domestic resources, that is, increased taxes. Popular opposition to them could be mitigated by a rhetoric of national defense and an image of China as a potential adversary. The press and political organizations generally cooperated by accepting such rhetoric. As many historians have pointed out, from around this time, patriotism and national assertiveness came to characterize popular movements in Japan. Opinion leaders such as Fukuzawa Yukichi, as well as most political parties, supported the government's stand in Korea and the military-strengthening programs as a way to enhance national prestige and obtain recognition by the powers that Japan was one of them.[28]

The growth of such patriotic sentiment deserves examination, for it came to provide a domestic context for Japanese foreign policy. Patriotism in the sense of particularistic ethnocentrism had, of course, existed throughout Japanese history, fostered by geographical isolation, relative racial homogeneity, and cultural self-consciousness. It had manifested itself in an extreme form when bands of samurai attacked and cut down the foreigners who came to Japan in the 1850s. Thirty years later, however, this indigenous sentiment had been reinforced by deepening contact with other countries, East and West, and had also become more organized. It found its expression in the press, political movements, and educational institutions. As such, it was little different from the patriotism and "jingoism" in the West, which were also aspects of its modern transformation. It may be, however, that in Japan traditional ethnocentrism had developed into modern patriotism without a substantial metamorphosis, whereas in the West, nationalism had intervened in the process. Nationalism as it grew after the late eighteenth century was not simply an exclusive, particularistic

28 Shinobu, *Nihon gaikō shi*, vol. 1, pp. 124–6.

sentiment. In its inception, it had been part of the democratic revolution, in which national identity was sought less in a country's ethnic and historical uniqueness than in the belief that it embodied certain universal values such as freedom and human rights. That sentiment never completely disappeared from the emotive vocabulary of the modern states in the late nineteenth century, and in fact the tension between it and more romantic, particularistic emotions, extolling the greatness of a country for its culture and soil, provided a theme in the self-perceptions of modern peoples. In Japan, too, there were currents of thought that stressed the universality of goals of modernization. Industrialization, constitutionalism, popular enlightenment, and similar objectives were viewed as universally valid, and it was thought that Japan would be considered a more self-respecting nation in proportion as it approximated these goals. But except for a small number of writers and activists, these objectives did not easily provide a vision for a more ideal international order. In the West, nationalism could often be transformed into internationalism because a nation could envision a world order that embodied some of the universalistic principles that it exemplified itself. Serious and sustained efforts in this direction were made by the Japanese only after World War I. In the late nineteenth century, universalistic objectives were usually viewed as a means for particularistic ends, for the strengthening and enrichment of the country. Or else they would provide the vocabulary for an activist policy in Korea or China in the name of Asia's "awakening," a geographical particularism.[29] It is not surprising, then, that movements for popular rights or constitutionalism could easily turn into patriotic moves or that the leaders of those movements would more often than not find themselves impelled to take a lead in chauvinistic adventures overseas.

Such considerations help one understand the growing support during the 1880s for the use of force against Korea or China. It was not, as is so often alleged by historians, that the Japanese felt superior to their Asian neighbors and resorted to military action; rather, they couched their belligerence in some universalistic vocabulary. They decided to prepare for possible armed hostilities with Korea and China for reasons that had to do more with the consolidation of the modern Japanese state than with any ideology. But they found it convenient to justify their action by stressing the need for Japan to emulate the West and "leave Asia," in Fukuzawa's famous words of 1885. Here patriotic assertiveness was combined with the language of universalism (that is,

---

29 Sakeda, *Kindai Nihon*, pp. 63–5.

Westernization). It was obvious that the former was a more potent force than the latter was. It was because of this that patriotism could be a double-edged instrument, for it would be boundless and might arouse national expectations that could not be fulfilled. Subsequent history showed that quite often the government had to restrain popular patriotism in carrying out its foreign policy. Here too, one sees an instance in which mass incorporation into the polity was a fundamental feature of the foreign relations of a modern state.

All these factors contributed to the development of Japanese relations with Korea and China after 1882. The struggle for power in Korea between the followers of the Taewongun and Queen Min was now joined by that between the "independence faction" and the "conservatives," the former seeking Japan's support and the latter China's. An attempted coup by the "independence" group, openly assisted by Japanese minister Takezoe Shin'ichirō and his hundred-man legation guard, was executed at the end of 1884, resulting in the brief establishment of a pro-Japanese government under the reigning king, dedicated to the "independence" of Korea from Chinese suzerainty. However, this proved short-lived, as "conservative" Korean officials requested the help of Chinese forces that had been stationed in Korea. Two thousand troops marched to the palace and surrounded it. The coup collapsed, and an angry Korean mob retaliated by killing ten Japanese officers and thirty other Japanese residents in Seoul. Some leaders of the "independence" faction, including Kim Ok-kyun, fled to Japan. The result was a further exacerbation of Chinese-Japanese relations.[30]

The situation tested the Japanese government's ability to maintain domestic control, for national opinion was aroused by news of the humiliation, and pressures mounted for punitive action against China. The use of force was called for in the popular press in order to occupy Seoul, protect Japanese lives, and, if necessary, diminish and eliminate Chinese influence in Korea. Those steps would enhance Japanese power and honor, it was asserted, and unite further the leaders and the people of the country. The Tokyo government was well aware of the need to respond to those pressures, but it considered the further use of force premature. Reinforcement of Japanese troops and ships would surely provoke countermeasures by the Chinese, and a situation would be created in which the two countries would find it difficult to avoid an open clash. Because Japan had just begun a program for an arma-

30 See Hilary Conroy, *The Japanese Seizure of Korea: 1868–1910* (Philadelphia: University of Pennsylvania Press, 1960) for an excellent treatment of the 1884 incident.

ment buildup, its military leaders were virtually unanimous in counseling caution, at least for the time being. A premature war with no assurance of victory would not only devastate the national economy but would also cause the government's leadership to be questioned and lead to domestic turmoil. Civilian officials, too, were inclined to take a less belligerent stand in view of the fact that Foreign Minister Inoue Kaoru was in the middle of serious negotiations for treaty revision. A foreign war would certainly complicate those negotiations. At the same time, it was considered dangerous to national prestige and domestic stability to acquiesce in China's military presence in Korea, a symbol of humiliation for Japan. The most plausible solution, then, had to be an agreement with the Chinese for a mutual reduction and evacuation of forces in Korea. With this as the key objective, Itō Hirobumi went to Tientsin to confer with Li Hung-chang, the Chinese negotiator. The 1885 Li–Itō convention was, in terms of the objective, a success. The two governments agreed to withdraw their troops from Korea; furthermore, they pledged to give each other prior notice should it become necessary once again to send armed forces to the peninsular kingdom.[31]

The agreement, however, could not silence Japanese domestic opinion, which had been aroused by the rhetoric of national power and patriotism. Disappointed by what they took to be the government's passivity, advocates of stronger action in Korea or toward China continued their agitation, often in clandestine meetings and secret plots for creating disturbances in the neighboring countries. They often employed the rhetoric of Asianism to present their arguments. The idea was that it was incumbent upon the Japanese to take the lead for the salvation of all Asia, in particular Korea and China. They should be willing to go to these countries, engage in efforts to eliminate corrupt and weak regimes, reform their institutions, and urge their people to join together to stop avaricious European nations.[32] The emergence of Asianism in the mid-1880s marked the beginning of an interesting phenomenon in Japan's modern relations with the neighboring countries: the activities of individual Japanese, without official backing, in Korea, China, and other countries whose behavior could often be an embarrassment but at times useful to the government in Tokyo. They

[31] See Bonnie B. Oh, "Sino-Japanese Rivalry in Korea, 1876–1885," in Akira Iriye, ed., *The Chinese and the Japanese: Essays in Political and Cultural Interactions* (Princeton, N.J.: Princeton University Press, 1980).
[32] On Asianism, one must still go back to the pioneering study by Marius B. Jansen, *The Japanese and Sun Yat-sen* (Cambridge, Mass.: Harvard University Press, 1954).

were, in essence, little different from Western missionaries, explorers, and filibusters who roamed all over the world; they had no explicit official sanction for their acts but could turn to their home governments for protection when necessary. But the Japanese case was notable because of its close connections with the internal politics of all countries, including Japan. Frequently, those Japanese – many of them were called *shishi* (heroes) – started out in opposition to the government and sought to influence domestic politics in their own country by bold acts in Korea or China. These acts were usually of a conspiratorial nature; they would contact antigovernmental factions and individuals in Korea or China and plot to undermine, if not overthrow, the existing regimes. If successful, their endeavors would be rewarded by changes in Japan's domestic politics. In this sense, they were a potential threat to internal political authority. On occasion, however, their activities might be useful for extending Japanese power on the continent, just as missionaries provided an opportunity for Western nations to obtain and extend their rights abroad. Japanese activists, in contrast with Western missionaries, were, at the same time, driven by the ideology of Asianism, and this made their support awkward for Tokyo's officials, particularly during the 1880s when they were trying to Westernize legal and commercial institutions so as to obtain their goal of treaty revision. In this sense, Asianism functioned as the antithesis of the official dedication to Westernization. Those who felt revulsion toward the fad of Western clothes, manners, dancing, and the like found in the Asianist ideology an alternative that could give them a vocabulary with which to assault the government.

For all these reasons, continental issues became bound up with domestic developments in the years after 1885. Political movements at home tended to challenge public authority and threatened to nullify the efforts of the government and military to obtain treaty revision and maintain calm on the Korean peninsula while strengthening the armed forces. It would be wrong to say, however, that this rift menaced the foundation of the modern Japanese state. On the contrary, it could be argued that all these popular movements were indications of an aroused national sentiment and that regardless of their Asianist opposition to the government's Westernizing programs, they revealed a heightened sense of patriotism that, combined with stronger arms, could eventually be put to use in foreign wars. In that sense, there was no fundamental contradiction between public and private activities; they might differ on means, and they might represent their acts in contrasting rhetorical frameworks, but they both were solidifying the basis of the Japanese state as it staged its first imperialist ventures.

Moreover, it is worth noting that the use of force in Korea and armament expansion were not the sum total of the efforts that went into the consolidation of the Japanese state. Treaty revision negotiations went on throughout these years, as did the domestic reforms that led to the promulgation of the constitution in 1889 and the convening of the Diet in 1890. Efforts were being steadily made to regain control over Japanese trade from foreign merchants, to improve the quality of products for export, and to reduce imports by encouraging domestic industrialization in textiles and other light manufactures. These efforts were considered just as important to national wealth and strength as military activities. In fact, some writers and officials believed that it was in the nonmilitary spheres that the struggle for power among nations was being waged and must be won. This harked back to an earlier emphasis on "enriching the nation," but the situation was more urgent in the 1880s because the Western powers were visibly growing in economic strength and expanding rapidly all over the globe. It would not be enough, under the circumstances, for Japan to seek to maintain a balance of power on the Korean peninsula. Such an aim paled in significance beside the far larger goal of mobilizing the resources of the whole country for economic growth and expansion. This, too, was an important part of the story in the period before the Sino-Japanese War.

It was from the 1880s onwards that foreign trade established itself as a serious objective of the Meiji state. The fiscal retrenchment policy of Finance Minister Matsukata Masayoshi, in office between 1881 and 1892, had the effect of reducing government expenditures, encouraging private industry, discouraging foreign imports, and making Japanese commodities more competitive in overseas markets. Between 1880 and 1885, total Japanese exports increased from ¥28.4 million to ¥36.7 million. Still an insignificant volume (world trade during the decade of the 1880s amounted to over £3 billion), it nevertheless marked a significant trend. Exports from Japan to Korea, for instance, increased by over 90 percent between the mid-1880s and the early 1890s, of which commodities made in Japan increased by 160 percent from ¥511,000 to ¥1.313 million.[33] These consisted of cotton yarn, piece goods, and other manufactured items, products of industrialization. Regardless of political and military issues, there was little ques-

33 Hattori, *Kindai Nihon*, p. 107.

tion that here was a fundamental development in Japanese capitalism that was finding a ready market nearby.

Equally important was the beginning of Japanese emigration overseas. It was more an idea than an achievement, but already during the 1880s, writers were stressing the need for resettling the country's surplus population so that they would contribute to the nation's wealth and strength. In one of the earliest treatises on the subject, Mutō Sanji, a businessman, wrote in 1887 that Japan's lower, laboring classes should be resettled in large numbers overseas, particularly in Hawaii and the west coast of the United States. It would not only give them better opportunities to earn a livelihood but would also contribute to enriching the nation through their remittances home.[34] At the time, it is true, there were fewer than five thousand Japanese in Hawaii, and only a little over one thousand in California and other western states.[35] But these figures were roughly equal to the number of Japanese in Korea and China. Whereas those in the neighboring countries were engaged in commercial, educational, and, frequently, political and military activities, quite often under the supervision of the Japanese authorities, Japanese who crossed the Pacific were predominantly agricultural and manual workers. To men like Mutō, these were far more productive pursuits and far more beneficial in the long run for the country, for the rich climate and soil of Hawaii and America, as well as the high cost of white labor, ensured that Japanese would have no trouble obtaining employment and contributing to the economic growth of the host territories. Even more important, they would become better known to Americans and other Westerners through their overseas immigration, settlement, and hard work. That in turn should redound to enhance the country's prestige.

It is interesting to note that the theme of augmenting national power by engaging in "peaceful warfare" throughout the world never disappeared in the 1890s, despite the continuing tensions with China that ultimately led to war in 1894. If anything, treaty revision, trade expansion, and emigration were pursued with even greater vigor than earlier. As during the 1880s, this reflected the Japanese leaders' perception of both domestic needs and the further growth of the West's economic and military power. On the domestic front, the convening of the first session of the Diet under the new constitution, taking place in

---

[34] Akira Iriye, *Pacific Estrangement: Japanese and American Expansion, 1897–1911* (Cambridge, Mass.: Harvard University Press, 1972), p. 23.
[35] *Nichi-Bei bunka kōshō shi: Ijū hen* (Tokyo: Yōyōsha, 1955), pp. 50, 382.

November 1890, established a basic framework for political action. The first election gave the voters – albeit with a restricted franchise, enabling only 1.1 percent of the population to vote – an opportunity to experiment with a Western system of political choice. Political parties now geared their activities toward gaining influence in parliamentary politics; they sometimes supported, and at other times collaborated with, men in power in order to gain their influence. The unenfranchised, of course, would seek to organize themselves and agitate for their rights, but here too, the framework was largely defined by the new parliamentary system. Henceforth it would be the political parties that would mediate between government and people, as was the case in most Western nations.

If domestic developments were gradually falling into place, continued Western power and influence defined Japanese perceptions of external affairs. What particularly attracted their attention was the fact that the Western powers that had steadily extended their spheres of action, incorporating ever-wider regions of the world into their domains, now appeared to be bent on massive undertakings in Asia and the Pacific. Having established control over Burma, Indochina, and the Maritime Provinces, they seemed to be pushing for the interior of China as well as Korea, as exemplified by the launching of the construction of the Trans-Siberian Railway in 1891 and the various powers' attempts to gain influential positions in Korean politics by providing the kingdom with financial and military advisers. In the West, moreover, voices began to be heard, stressing that the future of world politics would be decided in Asia and the Pacific. Alfred Thayer Mahan, Henry Norman, Charles Pearson, and others started writing alarmist tracts, urging their readers to pay close attention to this region for its geopolitical and economic significance. Having penetrated Africa and the Middle East, it now seemed incumbent upon the Western powers to extend their influence to Asia and the Pacific. The region was of strategic significance because of its landmass and the wide ocean; it contained a majority of humankind; and it was rich in natural resources. Rivalries among the powers were likely to be increasingly played out and determined in this area.[36] Such activities and views were well known to the Japanese, heightening a sense of urgency that they too must act more energetically, both in the passive sense of avoiding victimization by the more aggressive West and also in the sense of extending their own power in order to join the ranks of the

---

36 Iriye, *Pacific Estrangement*, pp. 19–20.

great powers. As Inagaki Manjirō, who had studied with Robert Seeley at Cambridge University, asserted in *Tōhōsaku* (Eastern policy, 1891), a work comparable to the English historian's expansionist writings, Japan must understand its geopolitical requirements and strive to strengthen itself economically and militarily. The two went hand in hand, but the most urgent need was for further economic growth through commerce and industrialization. This would be a momentous task but a crucial one, for the center of world politics was shifting to Asia and the Pacific. The powers that emerged victorious in the competition in that part of the world were destined to be the leaders in the coming century.[37] Few would have disagreed, and similar ideas made their appearance throughout the first half of the 1890s. That this was no idle talk can be seen in specific instances of economic strengthening. For example, 1893 marked the year when domestically manufactured cotton yarn surpassed imports for the first time since the 1860s. Although imported cotton products still surpassed exports, the gap was steadily narrowing, thanks to phenomenal increases in the export of cotton yarn to Korea and China.[38] Equally significant, overseas expansion through emigration, colonization, and even outright seizures of some tropical islands came to be vigorously advocated in the early 1890s. It was around then that the term *hatten* (expansion) took on the connotation of establishing Japanese communities and enclaves throughout the globe as a source as well as a symbol of national power. As writer after writer noted, only a vigorous, expansionist people, willing to take risks and fight against obstacles in strange countries, deserved to be powerful. Like Westerners, the Japanese must go abroad, work hard, and bring as many areas of the world as possible under Japanese influence. Because the country was far from prepared militarily to push for such expansion and because Western nations, too, appeared to be enlarging their domains through peaceful means such as commerce and emigration, Japan should do likewise. It should particularly look to regions that were relatively sparsely populated but richly endowed with natural resources. Many writers thus pointed to the importance of the South Seas. Expansion in the south, they asserted, recalling the memories of Japanese activities in the Philippines, Siam, and elsewhere in the sixteenth century, would prove to be the answer not only to Japan's population problem but also to its quest for great-power status. There were others, however, who continued to believe that Hawaii and the American continent would prove to be

37 Ibid., pp. 35–6.
38 Sumiya Mikio, *Dai Nihon teikoku no shiren* (Tokyo: Chūō kōronsha, 1965), pp. 66–7.

even more advantageous. Already in 1892 there were 4,500 Japanese in America; in 1893, there were 22,000 Japanese in Hawaii. They were viewed as a spearhead of much larger waves of emigration across the Pacific. In order to assist in such activities and to find other suitable areas for "colonization through peaceful methods," a colonization society was organized in 1893 by some of the leading publicists and politicians of the time.[39] Summing up this rising expansionist sentiment, Tokutomi Iichirō (Sohō) declared on the eve of the Sino-Japanese War, "Certainly our future history will be a history of the establishment by the Japanese of new Japans everywhere in the world."[40]

The crisis in Korea that culminated in the Chinese war in 1894 should be put in the context of this expansionist sentiment. Extending Japanese power and influence on the continent of Asia was part of a larger vision, such as Tokutomi's. Only by developing itself through expansion, it was believed, would the Japanese nation be able to emerge as a power in the world arena and to cope with the expanding powers of the West. At the same time, expansionism would provide a new national objective for the Japanese people. Instead of being preoccupied with internal squabbles and domestic concerns, they would be driven by a vision of boundless opportunities overseas. "Overseas settlement," as the manifesto of the colonization society put it, "is a vital aspect of the national policy, adopted at the Meiji Restoration, of elevating our spirit, broadening our vista, introducing new knowledge, and reforming people's minds." Having just had their first national election for the convening of the Diet, it was as if the Japanese people were now being exhorted to concern themselves with grandiose schemes for overseas expansion, not just with internal political matters. In this fashion, overseas expansionism could serve as a device for turning national opinion outward. Whether consciously or unconsciously, the country's literary and educational leaders, too, delighted in stressing patriotic themes and exhorting readers and students to consider Japan's unique history and traditional beauty as well as its modernizing achievements. The focusing on these themes, however, did not mean the fostering of a neoisolationist mentality. Rather, they were cited as evidence of the strengths and virtues of the Japanese nation on the threshold of overseas expansion. They would give confidence to the people as they sought to pursue activities abroad. It is true that some thinkers took strong exception to patriotism as a basis for expansion. They were more interested in individual liberty, human

---

39 Iriye, *Pacific Estrangement*, pp. 40–1.   40 Ibid., p. 44.

rights, and other Western values. In some instances the conflict between the two was unbridgeable. In most cases, however, it would appear that the Japanese managed to embrace patriotic themes while holding onto a more universalistic rhetoric. After all, that was what they thought they observed in Western countries. Whether complacent or uneasy about the juxtaposition of such visions, the Japanese found themselves defining their personal and national objectives in an environment of deepening contact with the outside world.[41]

Given this background, the war with China from 1894 to 1895 was viewed with equanimity and often enthusiasm by most Japanese. It seemed to fit into their policies, economic programs, and expansionist mentality. The occasion for war was provided by a rebellion (led by the Tonghaks, a banned organization) in Korea, impelling the court in Seoul to seek Chinese assistance in putting it down. Over two thousand Chinese soldiers landed at the western port of Asan. The situation threatened to test the Chinese-Japanese agreement of 1885, according to which the two countries were to coordinate their action in case they decided to reintroduce forces into Korea. As it turned out, the Korean authorities were able to suppress the rebels even while the Chinese forces were confined to Asan. But the Japanese government decided to seize this opportunity to reduce Chinese power and extend Japanese influence in the peninsula. Such a decision implied war, and the Japanese leaders were well aware of it. In fact, such men as Foreign Minister Mutsu Munemitsu and other cabinet members welcomed the opportunity, for military action could be presented to the populace and the Diet as a necessary step for obtaining more rights in Korea and otherwise expanding Japanese influence on the continent of Asia. They correctly judged that they would obtain national support. The Diet, which had caused trouble to the cabinet on budgetary issues, quickly fell into line, and the press was similarly compliant. Japan's armed forces, too, were judged to be ready. Since the 1880s they had been steadily augmented. Moreover, it had been considered most likely that they would first be used in Korea. This was because of the view, which Yamagata Aritomo had expressed openly at the first session of the Diet in 1890, that national independence hinged on the defense of the country's "lines of interest." Every country, he asserted, must protect its boundaries by defending these lines. Such views were similar to strategic conceptions being developed in the West and expressed the eagerness of the Japanese to identify with the

---

41 Irokawa Daikichi, *Kindai kokka no shuppatsu* (Tokyo: Chūō kōronsha, 1966), pp. 464–78.

advanced Western countries by accepting their formulations of national defense. And it was clear in Yamagata's speech, as well as in more secret military plans being worked out in the early 1890s, that these "lines of interest" primarily meant the Korean peninsula. If Japan were to consider Korea of immediate relevance to the national defense, it followed that its military spending and war plans would have to be geared to at least maintaining the status quo in the peninsula through a balance of power between Japan and China. But such an objective might lead to armed clashes with China, and thus preparations had been made for a hypothetical war with that country.

Here again, Japanese behavior fitted into the general pattern of the modern Western states which, too, were engaged in making elaborate war plans and armament programs as means for augmenting national power. What is particularly notable about the Japanese case is that it was the first non-Western state that was now joining the ranks of the militarily strong, imperialistic powers. It is significant that on July 16, 1894, Japan finally achieved its goal of concluding a new treaty with Britain, providing for the abolition of extraterritoriality in five years in return for the opening up of the country for "mixed residence." Unlike earlier treaty drafts, the Japanese-British treaty contained no provision for an interim appointment of foreign judges in cases involving foreigners. The successful consummation of this agreement, after close to thirty years' efforts, symbolized the growing status of Japan as a modern state and the willingness of the West to recognize it as such. The Japanese people, whose views were now channeled through the political parties and expressed in often-acrimonious debate in the Diet, were not united in welcoming the prospect of foreigners residing in the interior of the country, but they nevertheless took the signing of the new treaty as evidence that Japan was emerging as a major power, now in a better position than before to assert itself in the world arena, in particular in the developing crisis with China.

War was declared against China only sixteen days after the signing of the British treaty. Actually, the first shot was fired on July 25, when the Japanese fleet off the west coast of Korea attacked Chinese warships; four days later, Japanese troops that had been dispatched to Korea engaged Chinese forces in Asan. By then Japan's objective in Korea was no longer the maintenance of a balance between Japan and China, but the ejection of Chinese influence from the peninsula. This goal could be achieved by destroying Chinese land forces in Korea and ships in the Yellow Sea, which was accomplished with relative ease by September. After October, the Japanese expanded their spheres of action, invading the Liaotung peninsula, later Weihaiwei in Shantung Province, and engaging in a sea battle with China's Peiyang fleet. By March 1895, Japanese forces had occupied Lushun (Port Arthur), Talien (Dairen), and Weihaiwei and had destroyed most of the Chinese fleet. The Chinese government saw no alternative but to seek to end the war. On March 18 it approached the United States minister in Peking to obtain America's good offices as a mediator.

The war was enormously popular. The political parties vied with one another in expressing their support and voting funds for military supplies and manpower. They, as well as the press, considered the conflict eminently justifiable in view of Korea's need for reform and China's alleged refusal to promote it. Japan, as the most modernized nation in Asia, had the obligation, it was asserted, to come to the aid of its weaker neighbor and to punish the Chinese who had not awakened to the importance of cooperating with the Japanese to spread civilization in Asia. All such rhetoric reflected Japan's self-perception that the nation was now behaving as a modern power, one prerequisite for it being a willingness to extend national horizons to assume responsibility for the peace and stability of nearby areas. Perhaps one of the most notable statements about the war was made by Tokutomi Sohō when he asserted, two days before the opening of hostilities, "I do not advocate war just for the sake of it. I am not advocating plundering of other lands. But I insist on war with China in order to transform Japan, hitherto a contracting nation, into an expansive nation."[42] By waging war, Japan would establish a beachhead in Asia and be recognized as an expanding nation, a symbol of its great-power status. Self-consciousness about overseas expansion emerged as the most significant product of the Chinese war. The few thousands that had already gone abroad, to Asia, Hawaii, and North America, would now be joined by hundreds of thousands, just as the expanding countries of the West had been sending overseas waves of merchants, settlers, and adventurers. The Japanese would dedicate themselves to the task of expansion, for only by doing so would they be counted among the world's great nations. In short, they would join them as an imperialist nation.

IMPERIALISM AND MILITARISM, 1895–1912

Imperialism, as we noted, characterized part of the external behavior of modern states in the late nineteenth and early twentieth centuries.

---

[42] Iriye, *Pacific Estrangement*, p. 44.

It expressed the energies, orientations, and interests of a modern state at that particular period, but not necessarily of modern capitalism at a certain stage of development. Obviously, Japanese capitalism and industrialization were just getting under way when war with China came, and it would be impossible to treat them as sources for Japanese imperialism in the way that one might treat the subject for more mature capitalist countries. Industrial and finance capitalism, rather, should be viewed as one ingredient in a modern state, but not always the most predominant factor. It was the state that undertook the overseas expansion. And the key to this phenomenon was the coalescence of domestic forces toward both the creation of centralized authority and the generation of mass society. Imperialism affirmed and further strengthened these trends. Japan was no exception. It undertook military action in Korea and sought to entrench its power on the continent of Asia because it was politically and militarily equipped to do so and because national opinion firmly supported such action. The war and its aftermath, in turn, strengthened the centralizing tendencies of the polity, contributed to industrialization, and militarized society. As in other modern nations, however, these developments in turn created new divisions and tensions among segments of the population. Although external expansion never ceased to be a driving objective of both state and society, this did not prevent a rift between the two about the mode of expansion and about the ways in which the benefits of expansion might be distributed. Like Europeans and Americans, the Japanese began to recognize the burden as well as the glory of empire; although all partook of the latter, the burden was unevenly shared, giving rise, at least in the minds of some, to questions about the inequities of the modern Japanese empire. The years after the Sino-Japanese War, then, may be seen as a period in which imperialism came to occupy a central position in the politics, economy, and culture of the Japanese state and in which tensions as well as convergence characterized national opinion.

Victories on land and sea caused Japanese politicians, publicists, and citizens to dream of empire, just as a war three years later would drive the American people in the same way. Empire connoted prestige and power and also fitted into the vision of implanting Japanese interests and influence extensively abroad. But specific questions had to be raised about the immediate goals of expansion. Expulsion of Chinese power from Korea – the so-called independence of Korea – no longer satisfied the expansionist urge. Both government and people assumed, after all the victories, that the nation deserved more. The army thought a foothold in the Liaotung peninsula indispensable for defending the now enlarged concept of national defense; the navy looked southward to Taiwan; the political parties insisted that Japan should aim at obtaining these and more, including some provinces in China proper; and the country's press generally took the view that the war was but an opening chapter in Japan's new status as an empire.[43] The final terms of peace that the Japanese delegation, headed by Itō, presented to Li Hung-chang at Shimonoseki in April 1895 reflected such optimism and ambitions. China was to recognize that Korea was an independent state, cede the Liaotung peninsula and Taiwan to Japan, pay Japan an indemnity of 200 million taels (about ¥300 million) in seven years, open up four treaty ports, grant Japan most-favored-nation status as well as the right to navigate the Yangtze River, and give the Japanese the right to engage in manufacturing in China.

These terms, which the Chinese had no choice but to accept, albeit reluctantly and after prolonged negotiations, represented the view, as Itō told Li, that a "victor is of course entitled to claim any place he likes" for territorial cession and that if the Chinese refused them, Japan would continue the war and claim even more.[44] Fundamentally, Japan's peace terms expressed the country's perceived requirements as a major power. The securing of the "lines of interest," overseas territorial acquisitions, equal status with the Western powers in China, economic rights on the continent, and an indemnity payment to enable Japan to continue with its industrialization program – these were considered to be indispensable to the nation if it were to make good its pretensions as a power. Domestically, too, these cessions would appeal to the people's expansive sentiment, unite opinion and stifle opposition, and justify additional military expenditures. The war and the resulting peace, publicists never tired of asserting, established Japan's reputation as a great power, and the Japanese would gain the respect that they had coveted so long from Europeans and Americans.

Subsequent developments showed that the Japanese did gain such a reputation and respect but that these did not end their problems. If anything, they created complications in Japan's external affairs, which in turn deepened cleavages at home. As was the case in the West, imperialism, considered a prerequisite for modern states, threatened to undermine domestic order by generating expectations that could not always be fulfilled, by increasing governmental expenditures that had to be financed through taxation, by strengthening the bureaucracy

---

43 Ibid., p. 46; Sumiya, *Dai Nihon*, p. 36.
44 Morinosuke Kajima, *The Diplomacy of Japan, 1894–1922* (Tokyo: Kajima Institute of International Peace, 1976), vol. 1, pp. 235–41.

and the armed forces in defense of empire, and, most fundamentally, by creating new issues of national and personal identity. In Europe these problems and tensions provided an environment in which the modern imperialist states dealt with their external and internal affairs and which ultimately produced a calamitous war among them. At the same time, serious efforts were made to prevent war through such means as armament reduction, arbitration treaties, pacifism, various types of internationalist organizations, and the fostering of economic interdependence. This last was considered particularly crucial if international affairs were to reduce tension in the world and within each society. Although economic interdependence would not develop as the guiding concept of capitalist international relations until after the World War, it began to be presented as an alternative to imperialism at the turn of the century. According to its theorists, such as John A. Hobson, Andrew Carnegie, Norman Angell, and others, imperialism was not a necessary condition or an inevitable phase of modern capitalism; it was, rather, a perversion. Modern states, they insisted, could maintain amicable relations externally and stable order domestically by engaging in peaceful pursuits of business activities. Other analysts disagreed, asserting that modern capitalism inevitably led to imperialism and that imperialism produced war abroad and class tensions at home, both leading to revolutionary upheavals until noncapitalist, nonimperialistic societies emerged to ensure world peace.

These and other kinds of debate on the nature of modern capitalism and imperialism were taken seriously by the Japanese, now that they, too, had joined the ranks of imperialists. They would participate in the drama of imperialist politics and contribute to the debate. Like Westerners, they had to consider how domestic stability could be preserved while they undertook overseas expansion and whether such expansion would lead to increased international tensions and war or to greater harmony and interdependence among nations.

There was no easy answer. Immediately after signing the Shimonoseki treaty, Japan's confidence and optimism were jolted when Russia, France, and Germany presented their "friendly counsel" that Japan retrocede the just-obtained Liaotung peninsula to China. The tripartite intervention expressed the powers' alarm at the quick tempo of Japanese expansionism and their determination to preserve as much of China as possible for their own exploitation. There was little unusual about such maneuvers, but the intervention made an indelible impression on Japanese minds that imperialist politics was ruthless and kept nations in a perpetual state of potential conflict. This was a confirmation of earlier views about the ambitiousness of the West, but it showed the Japanese that their achievement of great-power status had not changed the situation. All that happened was that Japan was now in a position to play the same game. Thus instead of giving up their dream of Asian empire, they took this incident as a merely temporary setback, determined that once opportunity presented itself, they would regain the foothold. In this sense their imperialism led to further imperialism and, because war would be inevitable in the process, armament and militarization. Likewise, there was also trouble in the other territorial acquisition, Taiwan. Although no power disputed its transfer to Japan, the Chinese and native Taiwanese on the island put up a fierce struggle against its incorporation into the Japanese empire without their consent. Hoping that the tripartite intervention in Manchuria could be extended to Taiwan, they resisted the Japanese army of occupation, numbering 60,000 troops. In the end the uprising was suppressed, but only after causing 4,600 deaths among the Japanese through fighting and tropical diseases.[45] Still, few Japanese thought they should give up the island as unworthy of the effort. Huge expenditures to suppress the uprising could be justified only by maintaining it under colonial rule. Further expenses would be forthcoming to establish a system of administration for law and order, education, and the health of the island's population.

Nor did Korea's alleged independence end all the problems on the peninsula. "Independence" amounted, in Japan's conception, to replacing Chinese with Japanese influence, and steps were taken to "reform" the Korean government and military administration by introducing to the country the kinds of measures that Meiji Japan itself had undertaken in the late 1860s. These measures provoked Korean resistance, and many, including the Taewongun and Queen Min, sought to undermine Japan's influence by turning to foreign powers, particularly Russia, the very country that the Japanese blamed for initiating the tripartite intervention in Manchuria. In October 1895, Japanese authorities in Seoul staged a coup to eliminate supporters of Queen Min and pro-Russian forces. The attempt ended up in the murder of the queen but not much else, and it produced fierce anti-Japanese agitation throughout Korea. Russian influence increased further. Thus, even Korean "independence," the initial aim of Japanese policy that had led to the war with China, could no longer be taken for granted.

---

[45] On the Taiwanese resistance movement, see Hsü Shih-k'ai, *Nihon tōchika no Taiwan* (Tokyo: Tōkyō daigaku shuppankai, 1972); and Hung Chao-t'ang, *Taiwan minshukoku no kenkyū* (Tokyo: Tōkyō daigaku shuppankai, 1970).

Yet despite all these frustrations, the Japanese were determined to push ahead with their imperialism, rather than abandoning it as too frustrating and hopelessly complicated. The Diet obligingly passed one military expansion bill after another, budgetary allocations for armed forces increasing from ¥24 million before the war to ¥73 million in 1896 and ¥110 million in 1897. The political parties supported these increases as a matter of course, for they all accepted imperialism as a necessary and desirable attribute of the Japanese state. If Westerners seemed interested in pushing the Japanese out of Manchuria and if the Chinese, Taiwanese, and Koreans appeared hostile to their schemes, they would respond by affirming, rather than retreating from, their imperialism. Again, this was the standard response of the imperialist powers at that time. The costs were enormous, but it was generally believed that in domestic political terms, the cost of retreat and retrenchment would be even more devastating. Moreover, if the advanced capitalist countries of the West were holding onto their imperial and colonial domains despite their obvious expense, it seemed even more imperative for Japan to do likewise, for otherwise the Western powers would further extend their control and grow even more powerful. It would then be too late, and far too expensive, to undertake Japan's own expansion. Such appeared to be the case when, starting in 1897, the European nations obtained bases, leaseholds, and concessions in China, so that within a year the whole of China had been divided into their spheres of influence. Although it was far from clear what specifically Japan would gain by acting likewise and although Japanese capital for building railways and developing mines in China was meager, Tokyo did not hesitate to join the scramble for concessions, successfully inducing the Chinese to consider Fukien Province, opposite Taiwan, Japan's sphere of influence where the Japanese would have prior rights.

There was general approval of such acts in part because they took place simultaneously with industrialization which, in turn, was considered one of the keys to modern states. Industrial production, primarily of cotton and silk textiles but also including iron and steel, grew rapidly after the Sino-Japanese War, more than doubling in volume between 1895 and 1900. Some of this would have taken place even if the war and the resulting colonization had not taken place. But part of the industrial revolution was undoubtably linked to these external affairs. For instance, cotton textile exports, surpassing imports for the first time in 1897, were tremendously aided by the opening of more treaty ports in China as a consequence of the war and by an optimism prevailing among industrialists at the time in investing capital in machinery. The iron and steel industry, for its part, was a clear response to the needs of the armed forces. The Yawata Iron Works, created by an act of the Diet in 1895, was a typical example. It began producing iron by 1901, the first successful development in heavy industry in Japan. Likewise, the shipbuilding industry was given impetus by naval construction, the government subsidizing shipyards to construct merchant ships to be used in the expanding opportunities of Korea and China.[46]

Imperialism, then, coincided with rapid industrialization, confirming the prevailing view that all these, as well as great-power status, were part of a single historical development. The Japanese state, it appeared, was now a bona fide member of the community of modern, industrial, great powers. The *Asahi* newspaper echoed this view when it asserted that imperialism was an expression of basic national energy made manifest through the organization of the state. Just as other countries had their dissenters from such a perception, however, in Japan too there existed currents of thought that questioned this equation's alleged inevitability. One strain, comparable to some of the antiimperialist views in the West, was the theme of peaceful expansion, as opposed to militarism and imperialism. Perhaps the most influential writer in this vein at the turn of the century was Kōtoku Shūsui, who published *Nijū seiki no kaibutsu teikokushugi* (Imperialism, the monster of the twentieth century) in 1901. In it he castigated patriotism, militarism, and imperialism as a waste of national resources that brought nothing but suffering to the people. He was not, he wrote, opposed to peaceful economic expansion through trade, production, and the spread of civilization. Another influential writer, Ukita Kazutami, did not condemn imperialism so harshly, arguing that the nation had no choice but to practice it if it were to maintain its independence and participate actively in world politics and civilization. At the same time, however, Ukita echoed Kōtoku's stress on peaceful expansion, asserting that "peaceful, economic, and commercial" expansion in Asia, the Pacific Ocean, and the Western Hemisphere was as crucial to the national well-being as was more frankly militaristic control over Korea and Taiwan.[47] Both writers, and numerous others who shared their views, assumed it would be possible to engage in less militaristic, more peaceful overseas expansion. They did not consider imperialism inevitable, but at the same time they took it

46 Sumiya, *Dai Nihon*, pp. 61–75.   47 Iriye, *Pacific Estrangement*, pp. 78–80.

for granted that the country would continue to industrialize, expand its trade, and raise the people's level of education and well-being by means of peaceful activities overseas. They were echoing the strain of thinking in the West that eventually created an outlook known as liberal internationalism.

Although this strain identified itself with comparable developments in the West, another strand of dissent took a more particularistic, Asianist stand. Asianism, as noted earlier, had tended to be sporadically mouthed by those who were impatient with the government's foreign policy. After 1895 the situation changed, with the Japanese having established themselves above other Asian peoples. This imperialism, however, did not altogether stifle Asianist activities. If anything, it encouraged the growth of Pan-Asianist ideology and organized movements for a number of reasons. First, there was a psychological need to justify Japan's seizure of Taiwan or establishment of spheres of influence in China, not merely as something the nation had to do to emulate Western imperialists or to defend its "lines of interest," but also as a way to awaken and reform Asians by providing them with law and order and introducing them to the benefits of modern civilization. Japan had an obligation to do so as the only modernized country of Asia. Even though Japan had now joined the ranks of the great powers, some felt that it remained, and should remain, an Asian power, as Asia was where Japan lay geographically and historically. Japan, therefore, had a special mission to perform in this region. This type of thinking produced a cultural and philosophical Pan-Asianism best exemplified by Okakura Tenshin who asserted in 1902 that "Asia is one." All countries and peoples east of the Suez seemed to be united in certain fundamental principles, as opposed to those in the West. This view could be used to rationalize the idea that the aim of Japanese imperialism was to reunite all of Asia against Western imperialism. Although no such sweeping view would be advocated until the 1930s, the concept of Asian uniqueness was sufficiently influential for it to give rise to a number of movements and organizations. Among the most powerful was the Tōa Dōbun Shoin (East Asian common cultural association), founded by Konoe Atsumaro in 1898 and dedicated to the cooperation of the Chinese and Japanese. The two peoples, Konoe asserted, were destined to work together for the regeneration of Asia. There were, in addition, many smaller organizations and societies with similar objectives. They were carryovers from the earlier activities by the *shishi*, but they now found their spheres of action much enlarged and better protected because of the expansion of Japanese control over the continent. Some of them, like Miyazaki Torazō, were interested in assisting Chinese revolutionaries, whereas others helped the constitutionalists like Liang Ch'i-ch'ao. There were many underground networks of personal ties between Chinese and Japanese, all imbued with the idea that the two peoples shared a common destiny. In all such movements, it was an article of faith that Japan must not be satisfied with great-power status but must do something to give meaning to its national existence.[48]

Japanese foreign affairs after the turn of the century, then, may be examined in terms of these various developments. Imperialism defined the basic framework, and it had a history of its own, but interlocked with it were other themes such as peaceful expansion and Pan-Asianism which, too, affected official policy and popular perceptions. All these, moreover, must be seen against the background of domestic political and economic developments. The Meiji state was, by 1900, over thirty years old, and few thought it possible to challenge its legitimacy. The only direct threat came in 1910, when Kōtoku, now an anarchist after having spent a few years in the United States, plotted to assassinate the emperor.[49] But the state was too powerful to be destroyed by isolated violence. More important was the way in which state authority would be restrained by the maturing of the political parties and the growing self-assertiveness of the Diet. Moreover, as Japanese capitalism continued to make strides, giving rise to financial combines (zaibatsu) at one level and to the socialist movement at another, it remained to be seen whether the modern Japanese state would be able to accommodate these economic and social developments and what new definition of domestic order and stability might emerge. Japanese imperialism both affected and was affected by the outcome of such questioning.

The diplomacy of imperialism, that is, the interrelationship among the powers, fully incorporated Japan, and Japanese action in Asia played a crucial role in its evolution after the turn of the century. Nothing better illustrates this than the signing of the Anglo-Japanese alliance in 1902. A product of careful deliberations and cumbersome negotiations which historians have minutely described,[50] the alliance finally recognized Japan's status as a major power. In 1900–1, Japan

[48] Marius B. Jansen, *Japan and China: From War to Peace, 1894–1972* (Chicago: Rand McNally, 1975), pp. 137–8, 162–4; and Miyazaki Tōten, *My Thirty-Three Years' Dream*, trans. Etō Shinkichi and Marius B. Jansen (Princeton, N.J.: Princeton University Press, 1982).
[49] See F. G. Notehelfer, *Kōtoku Shūsui: Portrait of a Japanese Radical* (Cambridge, England: Cambridge University Press, 1971).
[50] Ian Nish, *The Anglo-Japanese Alliance: The Diplomacy of Two Island Empires 1894–1907* (London: Athlone, 1966).

participated in the international expedition to China to fight against the Boxers and in the subsequent conference with the Ch'ing authorities to restore order. Whether one interprets the Boxer uprising as a manifestation of Chinese nationalism or of more traditional antiforeignism, there is little doubt that Japan played a role as a protector of Western interests in China, dispatching as many as ten thousand soldiers, about the same number as the troops sent by all the Western powers combined. The Japanese were rewarded by being invited to the peace conference, the first time that Japan attended an international conference as a full-fledged member. After 1901 Japan became one of the "Boxer protocol powers," with the right to station troops in the Peking–Tientsin region. Its newly won status made the country a factor in power politics among nations, with Britain willing to allot Japan a role as its principal partner in Asia, and Russia sought to counter the trend by entrenching itself in Manchuria. But the impact of the Anglo-Japanese alliance was not confined to Asia. Although the subsequent chain reaction was but dimly foreseen in 1902, it is possible to link it to the great war of 1914. For the alliance had the effect of forcing France closer to Britain, as the French, allied with Russia after 1894, feared an involvement with the British on account of the Japanese-Russian rivalry in Asia. The British-French entente of 1904, mutually recognizing their spheres of influence in Egypt and Morocco, was a harbinger of further strengthened ties between the two powers that eventually came to include strategic coordination against Germany. Russia, in the meantime, moved steadily closer to Britain, forming its own entente with the latter in 1907 over colonial questions. Because the world war of 1914 pitted the entente powers (Britain, France, and Russia) against Germany and its allies (Austria and Italy), its origins, as far as the power-political aspect was concerned, went back to the formation of the Anglo-Japanese alliance which, in turn, was a response to the rise of Japan as an imperialist power.

There is little doubt that the Japanese welcomed the British alliance as an added confirmation of their status in the world. But the alliance was by no means the only alternative open to them. Some of their leaders, such as Itō, favored a Russian alliance to settle the dispute over Korea. Because it had been Russian influence that had been ascendant in Korea after 1895, and Russia that had seized the Liaotung peninsula in 1898, they argued that only through some understanding with that power would Japan be able to attain its objective, which was defined in a cabinet decision of 1903 as the "securing of national defense through the protection of Korean independence."

What Japan sought was the powers' recognition of its special interests in Korea and, as a longer-range goal, elsewhere in China. The Russians' recognition of Japan's special interests would have been just as acceptable as a British alliance, but in the end Tokyo's officials judged that more would be gained through the latter option. What is striking was the assumption by the Japanese that this sort of imperialist collusion and understanding was the best means for protecting their rights. They were confident that the major powers would seriously consider a Japanese alliance. They were not disappointed, and after 1902 imperialist Japan established itself as a key factor in world politics.

In that situation, it might have been possible to arrive at some understanding with Russia so that the latter would recognize Japan's special position in Korea, in return for Japanese acquiescence to Russian interests in Manchuria. An "exchange" of Manchuria for Korea would have been in accordance with the imperialist practices of the day. Despite protracted negotiations between the two countries, however, Tokyo and St. Petersburg were unable to come to terms, thus convincing the Japanese that their position in Korea would be vulnerable so long as Russian influence remained predominant in southern Manchuria. Even so, it might have been possible to continue talks in the hope that domestic conditions in Russia, China, or Korea or the international situation might change in such a way as to induce the Russians to loosen their grip on Manchuria. Certainly, there was no optimism that a war with Russia could be won or that Japan was economically prepared to finance it.

The decision for war, made by the cabinet in early February 1904, can be understood only in the domestic context. The Russian presence in Manchuria was reported in sensational fashion by the press and helped create the impression that the czarist regime would persist in its intransigence unless Japan showed its determination to use force. Political parties, publicists, and intellectuals organized prowar movements and put pressure on the government. Their argument was that the struggle between the two powers in Korea would not end until one of them retreated; because it was unthinkable for Japan to do so, it must be prepared to use force to reduce Russian power. As seven Tokyo Imperial University professors asserted in a memorial that they presented to Prime Minister Katsura Tarō in June 1903, "a fundamental settlement" of the Manchurian problem was needed if Japan were to secure its position in Korea. They were supported by middle-echelon officials in the Foreign Ministry and the service ministries, who were convinced that Japan should strike before it was too late.

Their argument could easily have been countered on practical and theoretical grounds, but it is suggestive that the only organized movement against the war was carried out by some socialists, several of Christian persuasion: men like Kōtoku Shūsui, Sakai Toshihiko, and Uchimura Kanzō. Socialism in a country that was just beginning to industrialize could not boast the authority and history that its counterpart in Europe did, but it nevertheless suggested an alternative to the definition of the modern state as an imperialist that was taken for granted by the supporters of an assertive policy toward Russia. Japanese socialists called for arms reduction and racial equality and condemned chauvinism and war as serving only the interests of the aristocracy and the military but not the welfare of the people. Although recognizing that the majority of the people appeared to be clamoring for war, the socialists, who published their views in their organ, *Heimin shimbun* (People's daily), opposed it as unjust and wasteful of resources. In a famous editorial written shortly after the declaration of war, they appealed to the Russian people to join forces with the Japanese to condemn the two governments' imperialistic ambitions that had led to war. "Patriotism and militarism are our common foes," the editorial asserted, expressing a clearly alternative view of modern states and interstate relations.

The enormous clamor for war revealed that such ideas were not widespread in Japan at that time. Patriotism, militarism, and imperialism were accepted as necessary conditions for the existence of the nation. If successfully waged, war would further enhance Japan's prestige and standing among the community of great powers. And even if unsuccessful, as many leaders feared, the war would have shown that the Japanese would fight for their "self-defense" and "rights" rather than meekly submit to Russian pressure and reduce themselves to the status of a second-rate nation. It was such a sentiment rather than specific gains that drove Japan's leaders and people to war with mighty Russia.[51] This, of course, does not make the Russo-Japanese War any less imperialistic. It was quintessentially an imperialistic war, fought between two powers over issues outside their national boundaries, at the expense of the Koreans and Chinese who had no say in the matter. But it was not a product of economic interests in any immediate sense. Japan was so poor financially that it had to borrow over ¥100 million in London and New York, an amount that accounted for more than

---

[51] The best recent treatment of war jingoism prior to the Russo-Japanese War is in Sakeda, *Kindai Nihon*, chap. 4. The most authoritative account of the coming of war is by Ian Nish, *The Origins of the Russo-Japanese War* (London: Longman Group, 1985).

one-third of the total cost of the war, whereas Russia relied on the financial markets of Paris. Japanese trade with Korea was extensive, to be sure, but that alone was not the cause of the difficulties with Russia. Japan's economic interests in Manchuria were not negligible, but they hardly comprised a substantial portion of the country's total trade. There was as yet no significant investment overseas. The war was not produced by economic pressures but by the sentiment inside and outside the government that it was the only alternative if the country were to remain a viable entity as a modern power.[52]

At first it appeared as if this judgment were a correct one. Not only did the country's armed forces achieve impressive military victories, but it also succeeded in raising loans abroad. Its prestige rose as never before, and the people once again showed unity and cooperation in executing the war. Patriotism, militarism, and imperialism were reaffirmed, and they in turn contributed to strengthening the Japanese state. At the peace conference in Portsmouth, New Hampshire, the Japanese gained the southern half of Sakhalin as well as most of the rights that the Russians had enjoyed in southern Manchuria, including the ports of Dalny (Dairen) and Port Arthur and the branch of the Chinese-Eastern Railway between Changchun and Dairen. Moreover, before the end of the war Japan took the unilateral step in Korea to turn it into a protectorate. Not one outside power protested this or the peace settlement. Having consolidated its hold on Korea, extended its sway over south Manchuria, acquired the southern half of Sakhalin, and destroyed the Russian fleet, Japan had, by late 1905, emerged undisputably as a major power, even the key power in Asia. That was the moment of glory the Japanese had dreamed of since the humiliating days half a century earlier.

The glory, however, did not end the quest for great-power status abroad and social order at home that would be commensurate with each other. If anything, a new search began almost instantaneously after the end of the war, a search that in many ways would continue for several more decades. It was symbolic of the uncertain situation that the signing of the Portsmouth treaty should have been the occasion not for jubilation and thanksgiving but for mob attacks on police stations and official residences in Tokyo. The public, whose expectations had been raised by military successes and whose patriotic fervor had added fuel to insular arrogance, expressed their anger at what they viewed as meager fruits of victory. They thought they deserved more than was

---

[52] For a discussion of the economic aspect of the war, see Shimomura Fujio, "Nichi-Ro sensō no seikaku," *Kokusai seiji* 3 (1957): 137–52.

obtained at the peace conference and blamed this on the government and the United States, who had mediated between the two combatants. It was as if domestic order was unraveling at the very moment when it should have been solidified.[53] The state of confusion at the moment of glory was well described by the novelist Tokutomi Roka, who had initially joined his countrymen in calling for a punitive war against Russia but later, before the end of the conflict, turned to pacifism. In a memorable essay written soon afterwards, Roka asserted that Japan's "joining the great powers" had done little to ensure its security or economic interests. These were still dependent on the armed forces, alliances with other powers, and colonial products. Moreover, Japanese victory had aroused the fears of other nations which would try to cope with the new development by augmenting their own military forces. There was also a danger of racial antagonism. Because Japan was the only nonwhite power, its victory might embolden colored races throughout the world and, by the same token, antagonize the white peoples. This would surely lead to a racial conflict. All these problems indicated, he wrote, that the victory over Russia was a hollow one; it was a victory filled with "melancholy." The only solution, according to him, was to end Japan's reliance on military force and to transform the country into one devoted to peace and justice.[54]

Few accepted Roka's pacifism and idealism, but many shared his diagnosis. It is one of the ironies of modern Japanese diplomatic history that at the very moment when the country had gained recognition as a formidable power, its sense of isolation, insecurity, and lack of direction were also enhanced. As Itō wrote in 1907, Japan had never been so isolated in the world.[55] Although in 1905 the British alliance had been renewed and in 1907 a new entente was signed with Russia for maintaining the postwar status quo in Asia, the country was faced with many other problems. The United States, the country that in the late 1890s had expanded into Asia and the Pacific simultaneously with Japan, now posed a challenge because of its naval expansion, its opposition to exclusive rights and interests in Manchuria, and, above all, its hostility toward Japanese immigrants. The immigration crisis arose as a result of the influx of Japanese into California after the turn of the century and particularly after the Russo-Japanese War. In Japanese perception the immigrants were to have been the spearhead of an expanding nation, a bridge between the two countries. But the Ameri-

---

53 See Shumpei Okamoto, *The Japanese Oligarchy and the Russo-Japanese War* (New York: Columbia University Press, 1970).
54 Akira Iriye, *Nihon no gaikō* (Tokyo: Chūō kōronsha, 1966), pp. 4–5.   55 Ibid., pp. 9–10.

cans rejected such expansionism and began talking of war on racial grounds. Britain, Japan's ally, sided with the United States on this issue. In the meantime, the Koreans, Chinese, and other Asians grew increasingly resentful of Japanese imperialism. Although some of them openly expressed their pleasure at Japan's defeating a Western power, they soon came to view Japanese imperialism as no less evil than the West's. If anything, the sense of injustice was all the greater as they viewed the Japanese as Asians who dared to copy Westerners in subjugating fellow Asians. A nationwide boycott of Japanese goods in China in 1908 and the assassination of Itō Hirobumi by a Korean nationalist in 1909 clearly revealed the kind of trouble that the Japanese now faced in Asia. If they were not accepted in America and were opposed in Asia, where and how could they expand?

That Japan should continue to be an expanding nation was taken for granted by virtually all publicists. Even Tokutomi Roka supported it, but in his case expansion was to be primarily a moral movement, in which Japan took the lead in spreading "justice in the four seas." His brother, Sohō, wrote that Japan's mission lay in promoting the harmony of the white and yellow races as a way to leading mankind to a world of humanism. Less abstract were those like Ozaki Yukio and Kayahara Kazan who exhorted their readers to "venture out to all parts of the world" as emigrants and settlers.[56] Then there were others who thought the time was opportune for undertaking a massive expansion of trade. "Just as England tremendously expanded its foreign trade after the victory over Napoleon," wrote Kaneko Kentarō, who had raised loans in the United States during the war, "so can Japan be expected to take advantage of the new situation to increase trade and promote national strength."[57] Finally, the official policy of "postwar management" referred to extending Japanese influence in Korea and Manchuria politically and economically. As much as ¥200 million was provided as initial capital for the operation of the South Manchuria Railway and its feeder lines. With the railway as the artery in southern Manchuria, private business entered the scene and invested in coal mines, soybean exports, and the importation of textiles. In Korea, in the meantime, Japanese advisers instituted monetary and police reforms; efforts were made to settle Japanese farmers by having crown lands distributed to them; and large numbers of poor merchants and

---

[56] Iriye, *Pacific Estrangement*, p. 100; and Akiya Iriye, "Kayahara Kazan and Japanese Cosmopolitanism," in A. M. Craig and D. H. Shively, eds., *Personality in Japanese History* (Berkeley and Los Angeles: University of California Press, 1970), pp. 373–98.
[57] Iriye, *Pacific Estrangement*, p. 128.

laborers from Japan sought quick riches by attaching themselves to the colonial establishment.

The more the Japanese expanded, and the more they talked of further expansion, the greater appeared to be the obstacles in the way. Diplomatic complications, naval rivalries, and racial disputes mounted. These were inevitable by-products of expansionism, but few were willing to question the premise that expansion was vital to the country's development as a modern state. Although the government tried in vain to cope with the mounting crises overseas, it also directed its attention to the domestic base of imperialism. It strengthened martial laws to cope with internal disorder, modernized its armed forces, and extended compulsory education from four to six years, with an emphasis on ethics.[58] But the people were now more politically and socially aroused than before the war, and they were less willing to accept what was given them. Constitutionalism and industrialization, which had earlier provided a focus for national energies, were no longer sufficient as objectives. It was not modernization but the future of a modern society that concerned the public. Patriotism, which had defined its mission as the making of a great power, proved incapable of providing new aims, wrote Ishikawa Takuboku, the poet.[59] Prime Minister Katsura shared the sense of crisis and sought to cope with the situation by having the emperor issue a new rescript in 1908, calling on the people to cooperate with one another, avoid waste, and work hard. This was a stale program, hardly enough to provide a vision of ideal domestic order.

Publicists fared little better. They all accepted the need for solidifying a domestic basis for overseas expansion and exhorted the people to continue to develop commerce and industry. But these were ineffectual ideas in the face of social unrest. Some leaders tried to define the nation's domestic goals by talking of the importance of "creating a new Japanese people," as the Social Education Association, organized in 1906, proclaimed. The new people were to be "a great cosmopolitan people" oriented toward peace and humanism. By molding themselves into such a people, they would contribute to both internal and international peace. The association typified these postwar concerns by stressing education and social harmony as means for avoiding a serious crisis in Japan's domestic and foreign affairs. These were to be made symbiotic so that domestic order would approximate, as well as contribute to, international order. As Takada Sanae, a famous economist and a founder of the association, remarked, the Japanese must cultivate "a

---

58 The best recent treatment of postwar state control is by Ōe Shinobu, *Nichi-Ro sensō no gunjishiteki kenkyū* (Tokyo: Iwanami shoten, 1976).   59 Sumiya, *Dai Nihon*, p. 344.

talent for engaging in worldwide activities through harmonizing international and national tendencies."[60] This was a plausible argument, anticipating the internationalism of the 1920s. But it had little specific to offer for coping with domestic problems. Education, designed to make the Japanese more cosmopolitan and tolerant, was about the only specific program that Takada and others like him could propose. Even then, there was no assurance that a more educated populace might not begin to question the basic premises of the Japanese state or that the intellectuals might not turn inward, aloof from the mundane concerns of society. In the meantime, cosmopolitanism was not yet effective enough to enable the nation to understand, let alone cope with, the issues of racial prejudice in the West or of antiimperialist movements in Asia – the twin challenge that was to baffle the Japanese for many more decades.

The Meiji era ended in uncertainty, in both its external relations and its internal affairs. The last years of the Meiji emperor (1910–12) saw the formal annexation of Korea as a colony, another renewal of the British alliance, and the signing of commercial treaties with the United States and Britain, providing for Japan's tariff autonomy for the first time. These were achievements in line with the country's great-power status. The period also coincided with revolutionary movements within China, culminating in the overthrow of the Manchu dynasty in 1912, and nationalistic upheavals in the Balkans that threatened the stability of empires in Europe and the Middle East. Unbeknownst to all but a handful of the most prescient, the great powers were fast sliding into a state of confrontation from which there could be no escape but war. All that the Western states, and Japan, had accomplished in the preceding half-century would go up in smoke in a fierce struggle for no other cause than power, prestige, and patriotism. The Great War was a failure of the modern states to define a viable world order, and it also demonstrated how fiercely and blindly the central authorities and the people in these states would concentrate their resources in order to destroy one another.

Japan was spared much of this destruction. Instead, it even took advantage of the European conflict to extend its hold on the Asian continent. By so doing, it ran headlong into antiimperialism in China and Korea, a clear manifestation of mass nationalism that became the basis for their own eventual emergence as modern states. In the meantime, the Japanese people began to question the national objectives

60 Iriye, *Pacific Estrangement*, p. 127.

and domestic arrangements that had been defined for them as part of the nation's growth as a modern state. They stressed other themes and looked for an alternative order at home. In so doing, they created a cleavage in their midst, between those oriented toward change and those entrenched in the existing order. The struggle did not end until after another major war.

Japan's drive to great-power status during the Meiji era, then, was one device by which the nation's leaders sought to establish a connection between domestic and external relations. Political and economic change at home, and the assertion of power and influence abroad, reinforced each other so that within forty-odd years after the Meiji Restoration, the nation was a modern state and an imperialist power. Like other countries, the Japanese accepted the two as interdependent, as two sides of the same coin. Only a small number questioned the equation, and the majority of Japan's leaders and public opinion assumed that all viable modern states were also imperialist. It would be left to a future generation to recognize that this was not necessarily so and that the nation need not be militaristic or imperialistic in order to undertake domestic modernization.

WORKS CITED

Abe Yoshio. *Meakashi Kinjūrō no shōgai*. Tokyo: Chūō kōronsha, 1981. 阿部善雄, 目明し金十郎の生涯, 中央公論社

Abiko, Bonnie F. "Watanabe Kazan: The Man and His Times." Ph.D. diss., Princeton University, 1982.

Akimoto Hiroya. "Bakumatsu-ki Bōchō ryōkoku no seisan to shōhi." In Umemura Mataji et al., eds. *Sūryō keizaishi ronshū: 1 Nihon keizai no hatten*. Tokyo: Nihon keizai shimbunsha, 1976. 穐本洋哉, 幕末期防長両国の生産と消費, 梅村又次等編, 数量経済史論集: 1 日本経済の発展, 日本経済新聞社

Akita, George. *Foundations of Constitutional Government in Modern Japan: 1868-1900*. Cambridge, Mass.: Harvard University Press, 1967.

Allen, G. C. *A Short Economic History of Modern Japan 1867-1937*. 3rd rev. ed. London: Allen & Unwin, 1972.

Allen, G. C., and Audrey Donnithorne. *Western Enterprise in Far Eastern Economic Development: China and Japan*. London: Allen & Unwin, 1954.

Amino Yoshihiko. *Muen, kugai, raku*. Tokyo: Heibonsha, 1978. 網野善彦, 無縁・公界・楽, 平凡社

Andō Seiichi. *Kinsei zaikata shōgyō no kenkyū*. Tokyo: Yoshikawa kōbunkan, 1958. 安藤精一, 近世在方商業の研究, 吉川弘文館

Aoki Kōji. *Hyakushō ikki sōgō nempyō*. Tokyo: San'ichi shobō, 1971. 青木虹二, 百姓一揆総合年表, 三一書房

Aoki Kōji. *Meiji nōmin sōjō no nenjiteki kenkyū*. Tokyo: Shinseisha, 1967. 青木虹二, 明治農民騒擾の年次的研究, 新生社

Aoki Michio. *Tempō sōdōki*. Tokyo: Sanseidō, 1979. 青木美智男, 天保騒動記, 三省堂

Araki Seishi. *Shimpūren jikki*. Tokyo: Daiichi shuppan kyōkai, 1971. 荒木精之, 神風連実記, 第一出版協会

Ariizumi Sadao. "Meiji kokka to minshū tōgō." *Iwanami kōza Nihon rekishi*. Vol. 17 (*kindai* 4), 1976. 有泉貞夫, 明治国家と民衆統合, 岩波講座日本歴史

Arima Seiho. *Takashima Shūhan*. Tokyo: Yoshikawa kōbunkan, 1958. 有馬成甫, 高島秋帆, 吉川弘文館

Arimoto Masao. *Chiso kaisei to nōmin tōsō*. Tokyo: Shinseisha, 1968. 有元正雄, 地租改正と農民闘争, 新生社

Asai Kiyoshi. *Meiji ishin to gunken shisō*. Tokyo: Ganshōdō, 1939. 浅井清, 明治維新と郡縣思想, 巌松堂

Asao Naohiro. "Shōgun seiji no kenryoku kōzō." In *Iwanami kōza Nihon rekishi*. Vol. 10 (*kinsei* 2), 1975. 朝尾直弘, 将軍政治の権力構造
Asao, Naohiro, with Marius B. Jansen. "Shogun and Tennō." In John W. Hall et al., eds. *Japan Before Tokugawa*. Princeton, N.J.: Princeton University Press, 1980.
Backus, Robert L. "The Kansei Prohibition of Heterodoxy and Its Effects on Education." *Harvard Journal of Asiatic Studies* 39 (June 1979): 55-106.
Backus, Robert L. "The Motivation of Confucian Orthodoxy in Tokugawa Japan." *Harvard Journal of Asiatic Studies* 39 (December 1979): 275-338.
Ban Tadayasu. *Tekijuku o meguru hitobito: rangaku no nagare*. Osaka: Sōgensha, 1978. 伴忠康, 適塾をめぐる人々, 蘭学の流れ, 創元社
Banno, Masataka. *China and the West: 1858-1861, the Origins of the Tsungli Yamen*. Cambridge, Mass.: Harvard University Press, 1964.
Beasley, W. G. "Councillors of Samurai Origin in the Early Meiji Government, 1868-69." *Bulletin of the School of Oriental and African Studies* 20 (1957): 89-103.
Beasley, W. G. *Great Britain and the Opening of Japan 1834-1858*. London: Luzac, 1951.
Beasley, W. G. *The Meiji Restoration*. Stanford, Calif.: Stanford University Press, 1972.
Beasley, W. G. *Select Documents on Japanese Foreign Policy 1853-1868*. London: Oxford University Press, 1955.
Beasley, W. G., and E. G. Pulleyblank, eds. *Historians of China and Japan*. London: Oxford University Press, 1961.
Beckmann, George M. *The Making of the Meiji Constitution: The Oligarchs and the Constitutional Development of Japan, 1868-1891*. Lawrence: University of Kansas Press, 1957.
Befu, Harumi. "Village Autonomy and Articulation with the State." In Hall and Jansen, eds. *Studies in the Institutional History of Early Modern Japan*.
Bellah, Robert N. "Baigan and Sorai: Continuities and Discontinuities in Eighteenth Century Japanese Thought." In Najita and Scheiner, eds. *Japanese Thought in the Tokugawa Period*.
Bellah, Robert N. *Tokugawa Religion: The Values of Pre-Industrial Japan*. Glencoe, Ill.: Free Press, 1957.
Bitō Masahide. "Mito no tokushitsu." In Imai Usaburō, Seya Yoshihiko, and Bitō Masahide, eds. *Mitogaku*. Vol. 53 of *Nihon shisō taikei*. Tokyo: Iwanami shoten, 1973. 尾藤正英, 水戸の特質, 今井宇三郎, 瀬谷義彦, 尾藤正英編, 水戸学, 日本思想大系, 岩波書店
Bitō Masahide. "Sonnō-jōi shisō." *Iwanami kōza Nihon rekishi*. Vol. 13 (*kinsei* 5), 1977. 尾藤正英, 尊王攘夷思想
Bitō Masahide and Shimazaki Takao, eds. *Andō Shōeki/Satō Nobuhiro*. In *Nihon shisō taikei*. Vol. 45. Tokyo: Iwanami shoten, 1974. 尾藤正英, 島崎隆夫, 安藤昌益／佐藤信淵, 日本思想大系, 岩波書店
Black, Cyril E. et al. *The Modernization of Japan and Russia: A Comparative*

Study. New York: Free Press, 1975.
Black, J. R. *Young Japan: Yokohama and Yedo* [1881]. London: Trubner, reprint edition, 2 vols., 1968.
Blacker, Carmen. *The Japanese Enlightenment: A Study of the Writings of Fukuzawa Yukichi.* Cambridge, England: Cambridge University Press, 1964.
Blacker, Carmen. "Millenarian Aspects of the New Religions." In Shively, ed. *Tradition and Modernization in Japanese Culture.*
Blacker, Carmen. "The Religious Traveller in the Edo Period." *Modern Asian Studies* 18 (October 1984): 593–608.
Bolitho, Harold. *Treasures Among Men: The Fudai Daimyo in Tokugawa Japan.* New Haven, Conn.: Yale University Press, 1974.
Bowen, Roger W. *Rebellion and Democracy in Meiji Japan.* Berkeley and Los Angeles: University of California Press, 1980.
Boxer, C. R. *Jan Compagnie in Japan 1600–1850.* The Hague: Martinus Nijhoff, 1950.
Brown, Sidney D. "Ōkubo Toshimichi and the First Home Ministry Bureaucrary, 1873–1878." In Silberman and Harootunian, eds. *Modern Japanese Leadership.*
Brown, Sidney D., and Akiko Hirota, trans. *The Diary of Kido Takayoshi.* 3 vols. Tokyo: University of Tokyo Press, 1983–6.
Buyō Inshi. "Seji kemmonroku." In *Nihon shomin seikatsu shiryō shūsei.* Vol. 8. Tokyo: Misuzu shobō, 1969. 武陽隠士、世事見聞録、日本庶民生活史料集成、みすず書房
Chamberlin, Basil Hall. *Things Japanese.* Rutland, Vt.: Tuttle, 1971.
Chisholm, Lawrence W. *Fenollosa: The Far East and American Culture.* New Haven, Conn.: Yale University Press, 1963.
Cole, Robert E., and Ken'ichi Tominaga. "Japan's Changing Occupational Structure and Its Significance." In Patrick, ed. *Japanese Industrialization and Its Social Consequences.*
Conroy, Hilary. *The Japanese Seizure of Korea: 1868–1910.* Philadelphia: University of Pennsylvania Press, 1960.
Cosenza, M. E., ed. *The Complete Journal of Townsend Harris.* Rutland, Vt.: Tuttle, 1959.
Craig, Albert M. "The Central Government." In Jansen and Rozman, eds. *Japan in Transition.*
Craig, Albert M. *Chōshū in the Meiji Restoration.* Cambridge, Mass.: Harvard University Press, 1961.
Craig, Albert M. "Fukuzawa Yukichi: The Philosophical Foundations of Meiji Nationalism." In Ward, ed. *Political Development in Modern Japan.*
Craig, Albert M., ed. *Japan: A Comparative View.* Princeton, N.J.: Princeton University Press, 1979.
Craig, Albert M. "The Restoration Movement in Chōshū." In Hall and Jansen, eds. *Studies in the Institutional History of Early Modern Japan.*
Craig, Albert M., and Donald Shively, eds. *Personality in Japanese History.*

Berkeley and Los Angeles: University of California Press, 1970.
Crawcour, E. S. "Changes in Japanese Commerce in the Tokugawa Period." In Hall and Jansen, eds. *Studies in the Institutional History of Early Modern Japan.*
Crawcour, E. S. "Nihon keizai ikō no arikata: kinsei kara kindai e." In Shimbo Hiroshi and Yasuba Yasukichi, eds. *Sūryō keizai ronshū.* Vol. 2, *Kindai ikōki no Nihon keizai.* Tokyo: Nihon keizai shimbunsha, 1979. 日本経済移行の有方：近世から近代へ，新保博，安場保吉編，数量経済論集，近代移行期の日本経済，日本経済新聞社
Crowley, James B. "From Closed Door to Empire: The Formation of the Meiji Military Establishment." In Silberman and Harootunian, eds. *Modern Japanese Leadership.*
Dahrendorf, Rolf. *Society and Democracy in Germany.* New York: Doubleday Anchor, 1967.
Dai Nihon komonjo. Bakumatsu gaikoku kankei monjo. Vol. 18. Tokyo: Tokyo teikoku daigaku, 1925. 大日本古文書，幕末外國関係文書，東京帝國大学
Dilworth, David, and Umeyo Hirano. *An Encouragement to Learning.* Tokyo: Sophia University Press, 1969.
Dore, Ronald P., ed. *Aspects of Social Change in Modern Japan.* Princeton, N.J.: Princeton University Press, 1967.
Dore, Ronald P. *Education in Tokugawa Japan.* Berkeley and Los Angeles: University of California Press, 1965.
Dore, Ronald P. "Land Reform and Japan's Economic Development." *The Developing Economies* 3 (December 1965): 487–96.
Dore, Ronald P. *Land Reform in Japan.* London: Oxford University Press, 1959.
Dore, Ronald P. "The Legacy of Tokugawa Education." In Jansen, ed. *Changing Japanese Attitudes Toward Modernization.*
Dore, Ronald P. "The Modernizer As a Special Case: Japanese Factory Legislation, 1882–1911." *Comparative Studies in Society and History* 11 (1969).
Dower, John W., ed. *Origins of the Modern Japanese State: Selected Writings of E. H. Norman.* New York: Pantheon, 1975.
Duus, Peter. "Whig History, Japanese Style: The Min'yūsha Historians and the Meiji Restoration." *Journal of Asian Studies* 33 (May 1974): 415–36.
Ericson, Mark David. "The Tokugawa *Bakufu* and Leon Roches." Ph.D. diss., University of Hawaii, 1978.
Etō Shimpei. "Furansu mimpō wo motte Nihonmimpō to nasan to su." In Hozumi Nobushige, ed. *Hōsō yawa.* Tokyo: Iwanami shoten, 1980. 江藤新平「フランス民法をもって日本民法と為さんとす」，穂積陳重編，法窓夜話，岩波書店
Etō, Shinkichi, and Marius B. Jansen, trans. *My Thirty-Three Years' Dream: The Autobiography of Miyazaki Tōten.* Princeton, N.J.: Princeton University Press, 1982.
Fletcher, Joseph. "Sino-Russian Relations, 1800–1862." In John K. Fairbank,

ed. *The Cambridge History of China*. Vol. 10, Cambridge, England: Cambridge University Press, 1978.
Fox, Grace. *Britain and Japan 1858-1883*. Oxford, England: Clarendon, 1969.
French, Calvin L. *Shiba Kōkan: Artist, Innovator, and Pioneer in the Westernization of Japan*. New York: Weatherhill, 1974.
Fridell, Wilbur M. "Government Ethics Textbooks in Late Meiji Japan." *Journal of Asian Studies* 29 (1970): 823-34.
Fridell, Wilbur M. *Japanese Shrine Mergers, 1906-1912*. Tokyo: Sophia University Press, 1973.
Frost, Peter. *The Bakumatsu Currency Crisis*. Harvard East Asian Monographs, no. 36. Cambridge, Mass.: Harvard University Press, 1970.
Fujikawa Hideo. *Seitō shiwa*. Tokyo: Tamagawa daigaku shuppanbu, 1974. 富士川英郎, 西東詩話, 玉川大学出版部
Fujikawa Yū. *Nihon shippei shi*. Tokyo: Heibonsha, 1969. 富士川游, 日本疾病史, 平凡社
Fujimoto Toshiharu. *Kinsei toshi no chiiki kōzō: sono rekishi chirigakuteki kenkyū*. Tokyo: Kokon shoin, 1976. 藤本利治, 近世都市の地域構造：その歴史地理学的研究, 古今書院
Fujioka Kenjirō, ed. *Nihon rekishi chiri sōsetsu: kinsei hen*. Vol. 4. Tokyo: Yoshikawa kōbunkan, 1977. 藤岡謙二郎編, 日本歴史地理総説, 吉川弘文館
Fujita Shōzō. *Tennōsei kokka no shihai genri*. Tokyo: Miraisha, 1966. 藤田省三, 天皇制国家の支配原理, 未来社
Fujitani Toshio. *"Okagemairi" to "eejanaika."* Tokyo: Iwanami shoten shinsho edition, 1968. 藤谷俊雄, 「おかげまいり」と「ええじゃないか」, 岩波書店
Fukaya Hakuji. *Kashizoku chitsuroku shobun no kenkyū*. Tokyo: Takayama shoin, 1941. 深谷博治, 華士族秩禄処分の研究, 高山書院
Fukko ki. 16 vols. Tokyo: Naigai shoseki, 1929-31. 復古記, 内外書籍
Fukuchi Gen'ichirō. *Bakumatsu seijika*. Tokyo: Min'yūsha, 1900. 福地源一郎, 幕末政治家, 民友社
Fukushima Masao. *Chiso kaisei no kenkyū*. Tokyo: Yūhikaku, 1962. 福島正夫, 地租改正の研究, 有斐閣
Fukushima Masao. *Chiso kaisei*. Tokyo: Yoshikawa kōbunkan, 1968. 福島正夫, 地租改正, 吉川弘文館
Fukuzawa Yukichi. *An Outline of a Theory of Civilization*. Translated by David A. Dilworth and G. Cameron Hurst. Tokyo: Sophia University Press, 1973.
Furushima Toshio. "Bakufu zaisei shūnyū no dōkō to nōmin shūdatsu no kakki." In Furushima, ed. *Nihon keizaishi taikei*, vol. 6, 1973. 古島敏雄, "幕府財政収入の動向と農民収奪の画期", 日本経済史大系
Furushima Toshio, ed. *Nihon keizaishi taikei*. 6 vols. Tokyo: Tokyo daigaku shuppankai, 1973. 古島敏雄編, 日本経済史大系, 東京大学出版会
Gaimushō, ed. *Nihon gaikō bunsho*. Over 151 vols., reaching the year 1926 in 1986. 外務省編, 日本外交文書
Gluck, Carol. *Japan's Modern Myths: Ideology in the Late Meiji Period*. Princeton, N.J.: Princeton University Press, 1985.

Gluck, Carol. "The People in History: Recent Trends in Japanese Historiography." *Journal of Asian Studies* 38 (November 1978): 25-50.
Goodman, Grant. "Dutch Studies in Japan Re-examined." In Josef Kreiner, ed. *Deutschland-Japan: Historische Kontakte*. Bonn: Grundmann, 1984.
Gotō Yasushi. "Chiso kaisei hantai ikki." *Ritsumeikan keizai gaku* 9 (April 1960): 109-52. 後藤靖, 地租改正反対一揆, 立命館経済学
Gotō Yasushi. *Jiyū minken: Meiji no kakumei to hankakumei*. Tokyo: Chūō kōronsha, 1972. 後藤靖, 自由民権：明治の革命と反革命, 中央公論社
Gotō Yasushi. "Meiji jūshichinen no gekka shojiken ni tsuite." In Horie Eichi and Tōyama Shigeki, eds. *Jiyū minken ki no kenkyū: minken undō no gekka to kaitai*. Vol. 2. Tokyo: Yūhikaku, 1959. 後藤靖, 明治十七年の激化諸事件に付いて, 堀江英一, 遠山茂樹編, 自由民権期の研究：民権運動の激化と解体, 有斐閣
Gotō Yasushi. *Shizoku hanran no kenkyū*. Tokyo: Aoki shoten, 1967. 後藤靖, 士族反乱の研究, 青木書店
Grappard, Alan. "Japan's Neglected Cultural Revolution: The Separation of Shinto and Buddhist Deities in Meiji (*Shinbutsu bunri*) and a Case Study: Tonomine." *History of Religions* 23 (February 1984): 240-65.
Greene, D. C. "Correspondence Between William II of Holland and the Shogun of Japan A.D. 1844." *Transactions of the Asiatic Society of Japan* 34 (1907): 99-132.
Greene, D. C., trans. "Osano's Life of Takano Nagahide." *Transactions of the Asiatic Society of Japan* 41 (1913): pt. 3.
Hackett, Roger F. "Political Modernization and the Meiji Genrō." In Ward, ed. *Political Development in Modern Japan*.
Hackett, Roger F. *Yamagata Aritomo in the Rise of Modern Japan: 1838-1922*. Cambridge, Mass.: Harvard University Press, 1971.
Haga Noboru, "Bakumatsu henkakuki ni okeru kokugakusha no undō to ronri." In Haga Noboru and Matsumoto Sannosuke, eds. *Nihon shisō taikei*. Vol. 51, *Kokugaku undō no shisō*. Tokyo: Iwanami shoten, 1971. 芳賀登, "幕末変革期における国学者の運動と論理, 芳賀登・松本三之介編, 国学運動の思想, 日本思想大系, 岩波書店
Haga Noboru. "Edo no bunka." In Hayashiya, ed. *Kasei bunka no kenkyū*. 芳賀登, 江戸の文化, 林屋編, 化政文化の研究
Haga Tōru. *Meiji ishin to Nihonjin*. Tokyo: Kōdansha gakujutsu bunko edition, 1980. 芳賀徹, 明治維新と日本人, 講談社
Haga Tōru, ed. *Nihon no meicho: Sugita Gempaku, Hiraga Gennai, Shiba Kōkan*. Tokyo: Chūō kōronsha, 1971. 芳賀徹編, 日本の名著：杉田玄白, 平賀源内, 司馬江英, 中央公論社
Haga Tōru. *Taikun no shisetsu*. Tokyo: Chūō kōronsha, 1968. 芳賀徹, 大君の使節, 中央公論社
Haga Tōru et al., eds. *Seiyō no shōgeki to Nihon*. Tokyo: Tokyo daigaku shuppankai, 1973. 芳賀徹等編, 西洋の衝撃と日本, 東京大学出版会
Hall, Ivan Parker. *Mori Arinori*. Cambridge, Mass.: Harvard University Press,

1973.
Hall, John W. "The Castle Town and Japan's Modern Urbanization." In Hall and Jansen, eds. *Studies in the Institutional History of Early Modern Japan.*
Hall, John W. "Changing Conceptions of the Modernization of Japan." In Jansen, ed. *Changing Japanese Attitudes Toward Modernization.*
Hall, John W. "Feudalism in Japan — A Reassessment." In Hall and Jansen, eds. *Studies in the Institutional History of Early Modern Japan.*
Hall, John W. *Japan: From Prehistory to Modern Times.* New York: Dell, 1970.
Hall, John W. "A Monarch for Modern Japan." In Ward, ed. *Political Development in Modern Japan.*
Hall, John W. "Rule by Status in Tokugawa Japan." *Journal of Japanese Studies* 1 (Autumn 1974): 39-49.
Hall, John W. *Tanuma Okitsugu (1719-1788): Forerunner of Modern Japan.* Cambridge, Mass.: Harvard University Press, 1955.
Hall, John W., and Marius B. Jansen, eds. *Studies in the Institutional History of Early Modern Japan.* Princeton, N.J.: Princeton University Press, 1968.
Hanabusa Nagamichi. *Meiji gaikō shi.* Tokyo: Shibundō, 1960. 英修道, 明治外交史, 至文堂
Hane, Mikiso. *Peasants, Rebels, and Outcastes: The Underside of Modern Japan.* New York: Pantheon, 1982.
Hanley, Susan B., and Kozo Yamamura. *Economic and Demographic Change in Preindustrial Japan, 1600-1868.* Princeton, N.J.: Princeton University Press, 1977.
Hanley, Susan B., and Kozo Yamamura. "Population Trends and Economic Growth in Pre-Industrial Japan." In D. V. Glass and Roger Revelle, eds. *Population and Social Change.* London: Arnold, 1972.
Hardacre, Helen. "Creating State Shintō: The Great Promulgation Campaign and the New Religions." *Journal of Japanese Studies* 12 (Winter 1986): 29-63.
Hardacre, Helen. *Kurozumikyō and the New Religions of Japan.* Princeton, N.J.: Princeton University Press, 1986.
Hardy, A. S. *Life and Letters of Joseph Hardy Neesima.* Boston: Houghton Mifflin, 1892.
Harootunian, H. D. "Ideology As Conflict." In Tetsuo Najita and J. Victor Koschmann, eds. *Conflict in Modern Japanese History.* Princeton, N.J.: Princeton University Press, 1982.
Harootunian, H. D. *Toward Restoration.* Berkeley and Los Angeles: University of California Press, 1970.
Hashikawa Bunsō. *Kindai Nihon seiji shisō no shosō.* Tokyo: Miraisha, 1968. 橋川文三, 近代日本政治思想の諸相, 未来社
Hashimoto Hiroshi, ed. *Daibukan.* 3 vols. Tokyo: Meicho kankōkai, 1965. 橋本博編, 大武鑑, 名著刊行会
Hattori Shisō. *Kindai Nihon gaikō shi.* Tokyo: Kawade shobō, 1954. 服部之総, 近代日本外交史, 河出書房

Hauser, William B. *Economic Institutional Change in Tokugawa Japan: Osaka and the Kinai Cotton Trade.* Cambridge, England: Cambridge University Press, 1974.

Havens, Thomas R. H. *Nishi Amane and Modern Japanese Thought.* Princeton, N.J.: Princeton University Press, 1970.

Havens, Thomas R. H. *Farm and Nation in Modern Japan.* Princeton, N.J.: Princeton University Press, 1974.

Hawks, Francis L. *Narrative of the Expedition of an American Squadron to the China Seas and Japan: Performed in the Years 1852, 1853, and 1854, Under the Command of Commodore M. C. Perry, United States Navy, the Official Account.* Washington, D.C.: Beverley Tucker, Senate Printer, 1856.

Hayami Akira. "Keizai shakai no seiritsu to sono tokushitsu." In Shakai keizaishi gakkai, ed. *Atarashii Edo jidai shi zō o motomete.* Tokyo: Tōyō keizai shimpōsha, 1977. 速水融, 経済社会の成立とその特質, 社会経済史学会編, 新しい江戸時代史像を求めて, 東洋経済新報社

Hayami Akira. "Kinsei kōki chiiki betsu jinkō hendō to toshi jinkō hiritsu no kanren." *Kenkyū kiyō* (Tokugawa rinseishi kenkyūjo), 1974, pp. 230-44. 速水融, 近世後期地域別人口変動と都市人口比率の関連, 研究紀要, 徳川林政史研究所

Hayami Akira. *Kinsei nōson no rekishi jinkōgakuteki kenkyū.* Tōyō keizai shimpōsha, 1973. 速水融, 近世農村の歴史人口学的研究, 東洋経済新報社

Hayami Akira. "Kinsei Seinō nōmin no idō ni tsuite." *Kenkyū kiyō* (Tokugawa rinseishi kenkyūjo), 1977, pp. 280-307. 速水融, 近世西濃農民の移動について, 研究紀要, 徳川林政史研究所

Hayami Akira. *Nihon keizaishi e no shikaku.* Tokyo: Tōyō keizai shimpōsha, 1968. 速水融, 日本経済史への視角, 東洋経済新報社

Hayami, Akira. "Population Movements." In Jansen and Rozman, eds. *Japan in Transition.*

Hayami Akira. "Tokugawa kōki jinkō hendō no chiikiteki tokusei." *Mita gakkai zashi* 64 (August 1971): 67-80. 速水融, 徳川後期人口変動の地域的特性, 三田学会雑誌

Hayami, Akira and Nobuko Uchida. "Size of Household in a Japanese county Throughout the Tokugawa Era." In Laslett, ed. *Household and Family in Past Time.*

Hayami Akira, and Uchida Nobuko. "Kinsei nōmin no kōdō tsuiseki chōsa." In Umemura Mataji et al. eds. *Nihon keizai no hatten: kinsei kara kindai e.* Tokyo: Nihon keizai shimbunsha, 1976. 速水融, 内田宣子, 近世農民の行動追跡調査, 梅村又次等編, 日本経済の発展:近世から近代へ, 日本経済新聞社

Hayashi Reiko. "Bakumatsu ishin-ki ni okeru Kantō no shōhin ryūtsū." *Chihōshi kenkyū* 20 (April 1971): 28-41. 林玲子, 幕末維新期における関東の商品流通, 地方史研究

Hayashi Reiko. "Edo dana no seikatsu." In Nishiyama, ed. *Edo chōnin no kenkyū.* Vol. 2. 林玲子, "江戸店の生活", 西山松之助編, 江戸町人の研究

Hayashiya Tatsusaburō, ed. *Bakumatsu bunka no kenkyū.* Tokyo: Iwanami shoten, 1978. 林屋辰三郎編, 幕末文化の研究, 岩波書店

Hayashiya Tatsusaburō. "Bakumatsuki no bunka shihyō." In Hayashiya, ed. *Bakumatsu bunka no kenkyū*. 林屋辰三郎, 幕末期の文化史評, 林屋辰三郎編, 幕末文化の研究

Hayashiya Tatsusaburō, ed. *Kasei bunka no kenkyū*. Tokyo: Iwanami shoten, 1976. 林屋辰三郎編, 化政文化の研究, 岩波書店

Hazama, Hiroshi. "Formation of an Industrial Work Force." In Patrick, ed. *Japanese Industrialization and Its Social Consequences*.

Hearn, Lafcadio. *Out of the East and Kokoro*. Vol. 7 of *The Writings of Lafcadio Hearn*. New York: Houghton Mifflin, 1922.

Henderson, Dan Fenno. "Law and Political Modernization in Japan." In Ward. ed. *Political Development in Modern Japan*.

Henderson, Dan Fenno. *Village "Contracts" in Tokugawa Japan*. Seattle: University of Washington Press, 1975.

Heusken, Henry. *Japan Journal 1855–1861*. New Brunswick, N.J.: Rutgers University Press, 1964.

Hiraishi Naoaki. "Kaiho Seiryō no shisōzō." *Shisō* 677 (November 1980): 46–68. 平石直昭, 海保青陵の思想像, 思想

Hirakawa Sukehiro. "Furankurin to Meiji Kōgō." In Hirakawa Sukehiro. *Higashi no tachibana, nishi no orenji*. Tokyo: Bungei shunjūsha, 1981. 平川祐弘, フランクリンと明治皇后, 東の橘・西のオレンジ, 文芸春秋社

Hirakawa Sukehiro. "Nihon kaiki no kiseki - uzumoreta shisōka, Amenomori Nobushige." *Shinchō* (April 1986): 6–106. 平川祐弘, 日本回帰の軌跡：埋もれた思想家；雨森信成, 新潮

Hirata Atsutane zenshū kankōkai, eds. *Shinshū Hirata Atsutane zenshū*. 15 vols. Tokyo: Meicho shuppan, 1976–80. 平田篤胤全集刊行会編, 新修平田篤胤全集, 名著出版

Hirosue Tamotsu, ed. *Origuchi Shinobu shū*. Tokyo: Chikuma shobō, 1975. 広末保編, 折口信夫集, 筑摩書房

Hirschmeier, Johannes, and Tsunehiko Yui. *The Development of Japanese Business 1600–1973*. Cambridge, Mass.: Harvard University Press, 1975.

Hoare, J. E. "The Japanese Treaty Ports, 1868–1899: A Study of the Foreign Settlements." Ph.D. diss., University of London, 1971.

Honjō Eijirō. *Honjō Eijirō chosaku shū 3: Nihon shakai keizaishi*. Osaka: Seibundō shuppan kabushiki kaisha, 1972. 本庄榮治郎, 本庄榮治郎著作集；日本社会経済史, 清文堂

Honjō Eijirō. *Kinsei hōken shakai no kenkyū*. Tokyo: Kaizōsha, 1928. 本庄榮治郎, 近世封建社会の研究, 改造社

Honjō Eijirō. *Nihon keizai shi gaisetsu*. Tokyo: Nihon hyōronsha, 1933. 本庄榮治郎, 日本経済史概説, 日本評論社

Horie Eiichi, ed. *Bakumatsu ishin no nōgyō kōzō*. Tokyo: Iwanami shoten, 1963. 堀江英一編, 幕末維新の農業構造, 岩波書店

Horio Teruhisa. "Taisei sai-tōgō no kokoromi to teikoku ideorogii no keisei." *Nihon seiji gakkai nempō* (1968): 139–90. 堀尾輝久, 体制再統合の試みと「帝

国」イデオロギーの形成，日本政治学会年報

Hōseishi gakkai, eds. *Tokugawa kinreikō*. 11 vols. Tokyo: Sōbunsha, 1958-61. 法制史学会編，徳川禁令考，創文社

Howes, John F. "Japanese Christians and American Missionaries." In Jansen, ed. *Changing Japanese Attitudes Toward Modernization*.

Howes, John F. "Uchimura Kanzō: Japanese Prophet." In Dankwart A. Rustow, ed. *Philosophers and Kings: Studies in Leadership*. New York: Braziller, 1970.

Hozumi Yatsuka. "Mimpō idete, chūkō horobu." *Hōgaku shimpō* 5 (August 1891). 穂積八束，民法出でて，忠孝滅ぶ，法学新報

Hsü Shih-k'ai. *Nihon tōchika no Taiwan*. Tokyo: Tokyo daigaku shuppankai, 1972. 許世楷，日本統治下の台湾，東京大学出版会

Hsu, Immanuel C. Y. *China's Entrance into the Family of Nations: The Diplomatic Phase, 1858-1880*. Cambridge, Mass.: Harvard University Press, 1968.

Huber, Thomas M. *The Revolutionary Origins of Modern Japan*. Stanford, Calif.: Stanford University Press, 1981.

Huffman, James L. *Fukuchi Gen'ichirō*. Honolulu: University of Hawaii Press, 1979.

Hung Chao-t'ang. *Taiwan minshukoku no kenkyū*. Tokyo: Tokyo daigaku shuppankai, 1970. 黄昭堂，台湾民主国の研究，東京大学出版会

Iinuma Jirō. "Gōriteki nōgaku shisō no keisei: Ōkura Nagatsune no baai." In Hayashiya, ed. *Kasei bunka no kenkyū*. 飯沼二郎，合理的農学思想の形成：大蔵永常の場合

Ike, Nobutaka. *The Beginnings of Political Democracy in Japan*. Baltimore: Johns Hopkins University Press, 1950.

Ikeda Yoshimasa. "Bakufu shohan no dōyō to kaikaku." In *Iwanami kōza Nihon rekishi*. Vol. 13 (*kinsei* 5), 1977. 池田苟正，幕府諸藩の動揺と改革

Imaizumi Takujiro, comp. *Essa sōsho*. 19 vols. Sanjō: Yashima shuppan, 1932-. 今泉鐸次郎編，越佐叢書，三条：野島出版

Inada Masatsugu. *Meiji kempō seiritsu-shi*. 2 vols. Tokyo: Yūhikaku, 1960-62. 稲葉正次，明治憲法成立史，有斐閣

Inobe Shigeo. *Bakumatsu shi no kenkyū*. Tokyo: Yūzankaku, 1927. 井野辺茂雄，幕末史の研究，雄山閣

Inoue Kiyoshi. *Jōyaku kaisei*. Tokyo: Iwanami shoten, 1955. 井上清，条約改正，岩波書店

Inoue Kiyoshi. *Nihon gendaishi*. Tokyo: Tokyo daigaku shuppankai, 1967. 井上清，日本現代史，東京大学出版会

Inoue Kōji. *Chichibu jiken*. Tokyo: Chūō kōronsha, 1968. 井上幸治，秩父事件，中央公論社

Inoue Kowashi denki-hensan iinkai, ed. *Inoue Kowashi-den, shiryō*. 6 vols. Tokyo: Kokugakuin daigaku toshokan, 1966-77. 井上毅伝記編纂委員会編，井上毅伝史料，国学院大学図書館

Inoue Takeshi, ed. *Nihon shōkashū*. Tokyo: Iwanami shoten, 1958. 井上武士編，

日本唱歌集, 岩波書店
Inui Hiromi and Inoue Katsuo. "Chōshū han to Mito han." In *Iwanami kōza Nihon rekishi*. Vol. 12 (*kinsei* 4), 1976. 乾宏巳, 井上勝生, 長州藩と水戸藩
Iriye, Akira, ed. *The Chinese and the Japanese: Essays in Political and Cultural Interactions*. Princeton, N.J.: Princeton University Press, 1980.
Iriye Akira. *Nihon no gaikō*. Tokyo: Chūō kōronsha, 1966. 入江昭, 日本の外交, 中央公論社
Iriye, Akira. *Pacific Estrangement: Japanese and American Expansion, 1897-1911*. Cambridge, Mass.: Harvard University Press, 1972.
Irokawa, Daikichi. *The Culture of the Meiji Period*. Princeton, N.J.: Princeton University Press, 1985.
Irokawa Daikichi. *Jiyū minken*. Tokyo: Iwanami shoten, 1981. 色川大吉, 自由民権, 岩波書店
Irokawa Daikichi. *Kindai kokka no shuppatsu*. Vol. 25 of *Nihon no rekishi*. Tokyo: Chūō kōronsha, 1966. 色川大吉, 近代国家の出発, 中央公論社
Irokawa Daikichi. "Konmintō to Jiyūtō." *Rekishigaku kenkyū* 247 (November 1960): 1-30. 色川大吉, 困民党と自由党, 歴史学研究
Irokawa Daikichi. *Meiji no bunka*. Tokyo: Iwanami shoten, 1970. 色川大吉, 明治の文化, 岩波書店
Irokawa Daikichi. *Meiji seishinshi*. Tokyo: Chikuma shobō, 164. 色川大吉, 明治精神史, 筑摩書房
Irokawa Daikichi and Gabe Masao, eds. *Meiji kempakusho shūsei*. Tokyo: Chikuma shobō, 1986-. 色川大吉, 我部政男編, 明治建白書集成, 筑摩書房
Ishida Takeshi. *Kindai Nihon seiji kōzō no kenkyū*. Tokyo: Miraisha, 1956. 石田雄, 近代日本政治構造の研究, 未来社
Ishida Takeshi. *Meiji seiji shisōshi kenkyū*. Tokyo: Miraisha, 1954. 石田雄, 明治政治思想史研究, 未来社
Ishii Ryōsuke. *Japanese Legislation in the Meiji Era*. Translated by William J. Chambliss. Tokyo: Pan-Pacific Press, 1958.
Ishii Takashi. *Bakumatsu bōekishi no kenkyū*. Tokyo: Nihon hyōronsha, 1944. 石井孝, 幕末貿易史の研究, 日本評論社
Ishii Takashi. *Gakusetsu hihan: Meiji ishin ron*. Tokyo: Yoshikawa kōbunkan, 1968. 石井孝, 学説批判:明治維新論, 吉川弘文館
Ishii Takashi. *Zōtei Meiji ishin no kokusaiteki kankyō*. Rev. ed. Tokyo: Yoshikawa kōbunkan, 1966. 石井孝, 増訂明治維新の国際的環境, 吉川弘文館
Ishikawa Jun. *Watanabe Kazan*. Tokyo: Chikuma shobō, 1964. 石川淳, 渡辺崋山, 筑摩書房
Ishikawa Ken, ed. *Nihon kyōkasho taikei: kindai hen*. Tokyo: Kōdansha, 1961. 石川謙編, 日本教科書大系, 近代編, 講談社
Ishin shiryō hensan jimukyoku, ed. *Ishin shi*. 6 vols. Tokyo: Meiji shoin, 1939-43. 維新史料編纂事務局編, 維新史, 明治書院
Itō, Hirobumi. *Commentaries on the Constitution of the Empire of Japan*. Tokyo: Igirisu hōritsu gakkō, 1889.

Itō, Hirobumi. "The Constitution of the Empire of Japan." In A. Stead, ed. *Japan by the Japanese*. London: Heinemann, 1904.
Itō, Hirobumi. "Some Reminiscences on the Grant of the New Constitution." In S. Ōkuma, ed. *Fifty Years of New Japan*. Vol. 1. London: Smith, Elders, 1909.
Itō Shirō. *Suzuki Masayuki no kenkyū*. Tokyo: Aoki shoten, 1972. 伊藤至郎、鈴木雅之の研究, 青木書店
Iwakura Kō jikki. 3 vols. Tokyo: Iwakura Kō kyūseki hozonkai, 1927. 岩倉公実記, 岩倉公舊蹟保存会
Iwakura Tomomi kankei monjo. 8 vols. Tokyo: Nihon shiseki kyōkai, 1927–35. 岩倉具視関係文書, 日本史籍協会
Iwao Seiichi, ed. *Oranda fūsetsugaki shūsei*. 2 vols. Tokyo: Nichi-Ran gakkai, 1976, 1979. 岩生成一編、和蘭風説書集成, 日蘭学会
Iwasaki, Haruko. "Portrait of a Daimyo: Comical Fiction by Matsudaira Sadanobu." *Monumenta Nipponica* 38 (Spring 1983): 1–48.
Iwata, Masakazu. *Ōkubo Toshimichi: The Bismarck of Japan*. Berkeley and Los Angeles: California University Press, 1964.
Jansen, Marius B., ed. *Changing Japanese Attitudes Toward Modernization*. Princeton, N.J.: Princeton University Press, 1965.
Jansen, Marius B. *Japan and China: From War to Peace, 1894–1972*. Chicago: Rand McNally, 1975.
Jansen, Marius B. *Japan and Its World: Two Centuries of Change*. Princeton, N.J.: Princeton University Press, 1980.
Jansen, Marius B. *The Japanese and Sun Yat-sen*. Cambridge, Mass.: Harvard University Press, 1954.
Jansen, Marius B. "Modernization and Foreign Policy in Meiji Japan." In Ward, ed. *Political Development in Modern Japan*.
Jansen, Marius B. "Monarchy and Modernization in Japan." *Journal of Asian Studies* 36 (August 1977): 611–22.
Jansen, Marius B. "New Materials for the Intellectual History of Nineteenth Century Japan." *Harvard Journal of Asiatic Studies* 20 (December 1957): 567–97.
Jansen, Marius B. "Oi Kentarō: Radicalism and Chauvinism." *Far Eastern Quarterly* 11 (May 1952): 305–16.
Jansen, Marius B. "Rangaku and Westernization." *Modern Asian Studies* 18 (October 1984): 541–53.
Jansen, Marius B. *Sakamoto Ryōma and the Meiji Restoration*. Princeton, N.J.: Princeton University Press, 1961.
Jansen, Marius B. "Tosa During the Last Century of Tokugawa Rule." In Hall and Jansen, eds. *Studies in the Institutional History of Early Modern Japan*.
Jansen, Marius B., and Gilbert Rozman, eds. *Japan in Transition: From Tokugawa to Meiji*. Princeton, N.J.: Princeton University Press, 1986.
Jippensha Ikku. *Tōkaidō dōchū hizakurige*. (Travels on foot on the Tōkaidō). Translated by Thomas Satchell as *Hizakurige or Shanks' Mare: Japan's Great*

Comic Novel of Travel and Ribaldry. (Kobe, 1929, and subsequent reprints). 十返舎一九，東海道中膝栗毛

Jones, Hazel. *Live Machines: Hired Foreigners in Meiji Japan*. Vancouver: University of British Columbia Press, 1980.

Kaempfer, Engelbert. *History of Japan*. 3 vols. Translated by J. G. Scheuchzer. Glasgow: James MacLehose and Sons, 1896.

Kaigo Tokiomi. *Kyōiku chokugo seiritsushi no kenkyū*. Tokyo: Tokyo daigaku shuppankai, 1965. 海後宗臣，教育勅語成立史の研究，東京大学出版会

Kaikoku hyakunen kinen bunka jigyōkai, ed. *Nichi-Bei bunka kōshō shi: ijū hen*. Tokyo: Yōyōsha, 1955. 開国百年記念文化事業会編，日米文化交渉史：移住編，洋々社

Kajima, Morinosuke. *The Diplomacy of Japan, 1894–1922*. 3 vols. Tokyo: Kajima Institute of International Peace, 1976–80.

Kajima Morinosuke. *Nihon gaikō shi*. 34 vols. Kajima heiwa kenkyūjo. Tokyo: Kajima kenkyūjo shuppankai, 1970–3. 鹿島守之助，日本外交史，鹿島平和研究所

Kano Masanao. *Shihonshugi keiseiki no chitsujō ishiki*. Tokyo: Chikuma shobō, 1969. 鹿野政直，資本主義形成期の秩序意識，筑摩書房

Kano Masanao. "Yonaoshi no shisō to bummei kaika." In Kano Masanao and Takagi Shunsuke, eds. *Ishin henkaku ni okeru zaisonteki shochōryū*. Tokyo: San'ichi shobō, 1972. 鹿野政直，"世なおしの思想と文明開化"，鹿野政直，高木俊輔編，維新変革における在村的諸潮流，三一書房

Karasawa Tomitarō. *Kyōkasho no rekishi*. Tokyo: Sōbunsha, 1960. 唐澤富太郎，教科書の歴史，創文社

Kawai Eijirō. *Meiji shisōshi no ichi dammen: Kanai Noboru o chūshin toshite*. Vol. 8. Reprinted in *Kawai Eijirō zenshū*. Tokyo: Shakai shisōsha, 1969. 河合榮治郎，明治思想の一断面：金井延を中心として，河合榮治郎全集，社会思想社

Kawaji Toshiakira. *Shimane no susami*. Tokyo: Heibonsha, 1973. 川路聖謨，島根のすさみ，平凡社

Kawaura Yasuji. *Bakuhan taisei kaitaiki no keizai kōzō*. Tokyo: Ochanomizu shobō, 1965. 川浦康治，幕藩体制解体期の経済構造，御茶の水書房

Keene, Donald. *The Japanese Discovery of Europe, 1720–1820*. Stanford, Calif.: Stanford University Press, 1969.

Keene, Donald. *World Within Walls: Japanese Literature of the Pre-Modern Era, 1600–1867*. New York: Holt, Rinehart and Winston, 1976.

Keiō Gijuku, ed. *Fukuzawa Yukichi zenshū*. 21 vols. Tokyo: Iwanami shoten, 1962. 慶應義塾，福澤諭吉全集，岩波書店

Kelly, William W. *Deference and Defiance in Nineteenth Century Japan*. Princeton, N.J.: Princeton University Press, 1985.

Kim, Key-Hiuk. *The Last Phase of the East Asian World Order: Korea, Japan, and the Chinese Empire, 1860–1882*. Berkeley and Los Angeles: University of California Press, 1980.

Kitajima Masamoto. *Bakuhansei no kumon*. Vol. 18 of *Nihon no rekishi*. Tokyo:

Chūō kōronsha, 1967. 北島正元，幕藩制の苦悶，日本の歴史，中央公論社
Kitajima Masamoto. "Kaseiki no seiji to minshū." In *Iwanami kōza Nihon rekishi*. Vol. 12 (*kinsei* 4), 1963. 北島正元，化政期の政治と民衆
Kitajima Masamoto. *Mizuno Tadakuni*. Tokyo: Yoshikawa kōbunkan, 1969. 北島正元，水野忠邦，吉川弘文館
Kiyooka, Eiichi, trans. *The Autobiography of Fukuzawa Yukichi*. Tokyo: Hokuseidō Press, 1948.
Kobata Atsushi et al. *Dokushi sōran*. Tokyo: Jimbutsu ōraisha, 1966. 小葉田淳等，讀史總覧，人物往来社
Kodama Kōta. *Kinsei nōmin seikatsu shi*. Tokyo: Yoshikawa kōbunkan, 1958. 児玉幸多，近世農民生活史，吉川弘文館
Kodama Kōta, ed. *Ninomiya Sontoku*. Vol. 26 of *Nihon no meicho*. Tokyo: Chūō kōronsha, 1970. 児玉幸多編，二宮尊徳，日本の名著，中央公論社
Koga-shi shi hensan iinkai, ed. *Koga-shi shi: shiryō kinseihen* (*hansei*). Koga, 1979. 古河市史編纂委員会，古河市史，史料近世編(藩政)，古河
Kokumin bunko kankōkai, ed. *Raiki*. In *Kokuyaku kambun taisei*, Vol. 24. Tokyo: Kokumin bunko kankōkai, 1921. 国民文庫刊行会，禮記，國譯漢文大成
Kokusho kankōkai, ed. *Bummei genryū sōsho*. 3 vols. Tokyo: Kokusho kankōkai, 1913–14. 国書刊行会，文明原流叢書
Konishi Shigenao. *Hirose Tansō*. Tokyo: Bunkyō shoin, 1943. 小西重直，広瀬淡窓，文教書院
Konta Yōzō. *Edo no hon'yasan: kinsei bunkashi no sokumen*: 近世文化史の側面 Tokyo: NHK Books no. 299, 1977. 今田洋三，江戸の本屋さん，NHKブックス
Kornicki, Peter F. "The Publishers Go-Between: Kashihonya in the Meiji Period." *Modern Asian Studies* 14 (1980): 331–44.
Koschmann, J. Victor. *The Mito Ideology: Discourse, Reform, and Insurrection in late Tokugawa Japan, 1790–1864*. Berkeley and Los Angeles: University of California Press, 1987.
Kumakura Isao. "Kasei bunka no zentei: Kansei kaikaku o megutte." In Hayashiya, ed. *Kasei bunka no kenkyū*. 熊倉功夫 "化政文化の前提：寛政改革をめぐって"
Kume Kunitake, ed. *Bei-Ō kairan jikki*. 5 vols. Tokyo: Iwanami shoten, 1977. 久米邦武編，米欧回覧実記，岩波書店
Kure Shūzō. *Shiiboruto sensei, sono shōgai oyobi kōgyō*. Tokyo: Hakuhōdō shoten, 1926. 呉秀三，シーボルト先生，その生涯及功業，吐鳳堂
Kurimoto Joun. *Hōan ikō*. In Nihon shiseki kyōkai, ed. *Zoku Nihon shiseki sōsho*. Vol. 4. Tokyo: Tokyo daigaku shuppankai, 1975. 栗本鋤雲，匏菴遺稿，日本史籍協会，続日本史籍叢書，東京大学出版会
Kuroita Katsumi, ed. *Zoku Tokugawa jikki*. In *Kokushi taikei*. Vol. 49. Tokyo: Yoshikawa kōbunkan, 1966. 黒板勝美編，続徳川実記，国史大系，吉川弘文館
Laslett, Peter, ed. *Household and Family in Past Time*. Cambridge, England: Cambridge University Press, 1972.

Lensen, George A. *The Russian Push Toward Japan: Russo-Japanese Relations 1697-1875*. Princeton, N.J.: Princeton University Press, 1959.
Leutner, Robert W. *Shikitei Samba and the Comic Tradition in Late Edo Period Popular Fiction*. Cambridge, Mass.: Harvard University Press, 1985.
Lockwood, William W., ed. *The State and Economic Enterprise in Japan*. Princeton, N.J.: Princeton University Press, 1965.
Maeda Ichirō, ed. *Kōza Nihon bunkashi*. Vol. 6. Tokyo: San'ichi shobō, 1963. 前田一良編, 講座日本文化史, 三一書房
Marshall, Byron K. *Capitalism and Nationalism in Prewar Japan: The Ideology of the Business Elite, 1868-1941*. Stanford, Calif.: Stanford University Press, 1967.
Maruyama Masao. "Chūsei to hangyaku." In *Kindai Nihon shisōshi kōza*. 8 vols. Tokyo: Chikuma shobō, 1960. 丸山真男, 忠誠と反逆, 近代日本思想史講座, 筑摩書房
Maruyama Masao. *Nihon seiji shisōshi kenkyū*. Tokyo: Tokyo daigaku shuppankai, 1953. 丸山真男, 日本政治思想史研究, 東京大学出版会
Maruyama, Masao. *Studies in the Intellectual History of Tokugawa Japan*. Translated by Mikiso Hane. Princeton, N.J.: Princeton University Press, 1974.
Mason, R. H. P. *Japan's First General Election, 1890*. Cambridge, England: Cambridge University Press, 1969.
Masumi Junnosuke. *Nihon seitō shi ron*. 7 vols. Tokyo: Tokyo daigaku shuppankai, 1965-80. 升味準之輔, 日本政党史論, 東京大学出版会
Matono Hansuke. *Etō nampaku*. 2 vols. Tokyo: Hara shobō reprint, 1968. 的野半介, 江藤南白, 原書房
Matsumoto Sannosuke. *Kokugaku seiji shisō no kenkyū*. Tokyo: Yūhikaku, 1957. 松本三之介, 国学政治思想の研究, 有斐閣
Matsumoto Sannosuke. "Meiji zempanki hoshushugi shisō no ichi dammen." In Sakata Yoshio, ed. *Meiji zempanki no nashonarizumu*. Tokyo: Miraisha, 1958. 松本三之介, "明治前半期保守主義思想の一断面" 坂田吉雄編, 明治前半期のナショナリズム, 未来社
Matsumoto Sannosuke. *Tennōsei kokka to seiji shisō*. Tokyo: Miraisha, 1969. 松本三之介, 天皇制国家と政治思想, 未来社
Matsumoto Shirō. "Bakumatsu, ishinki ni okeru toshi no kōzō." *Mitsui bunko ronsō* 4 (1969): 105-64. 松本四郎, 幕末, 維新期における都市の構造, 三井文庫論叢
Matsumoto Shirō. "Kinsei kōki no toshi to minshu." In *Iwanami kōza Nihon rekishi*. Vol. 12 (*kinsei* 4), 1975. 松本四郎, 近世後期の都市と民衆
Matsuzaki Kōdō. *Kōdō nichireki*. In Tōyō bunko series. 6 vols. Tokyo: Heibonsha, 1970-83. 松崎慊堂, 慊堂日暦, 東洋文庫, 平凡社
May, Ekkehard. *Die Kommerzialisierung der japanischen Literatur in der späten Edo-Zeit (1750-1868)*. Wiesbaden: Harrassowitz, 1983.
Mayo, Marlene. "The Western Education of Kume Kunitake 1871-1876." *Monumenta Nipponica* 28 (1973): 3-68.

McLaren, Walter W., ed. "Japanese Government Documents, 1867-1889." *Transactions of the Asiatic Society of Japan* 42 (1914): pt. 1.

McLaren, Walter W. *A Political History of Japan During the Meiji Era: 1867-1912*. London: Allen & Unwin, 1916.

McMaster, John. "The Japanese Gold Rush of 1859." *Journal of Asian Studies* 19 (May 1960): 273-88.

Medzini, Meron. *French Policy in Japan During the Closing Years of the Tokugawa Regime*. Cambridge, Mass.: Harvard University Press, 1971.

Meiji bunka zenshū. 24 vols. Tokyo: Nihon hyōronsha, 1927-30. 明治文化全集，日本評論社

Meiji hennenshi hensankai, ed. *Shimbun shūsei: Meiji hennenshi*. 15 vols. Tokyo: Tōkyō zaisei keizai gakkai, 1934-6. 明治編年史編纂会，新聞集成；明治編年史，東京財政経済学会

Meiroku zasshi (Journal of the Japanese Enlightenment). Translated by William R. Braisted. Cambridge, Mass.: Harvard University Press, 1976.

Minami Kazuo. *Edo no shakai kōzō*. Tokyo: Hanawa shobō, 1969. 南和男，江戸の社会構造，塙書房

Minamoto Ryōen. "Kyōiku chokugo no kokkashugiteki kaishaku." In Sakata Yoshio, ed. *Meiji zempanki no nashonarizumu*. Tokyo: Miraisha, 1958. 源了圓，"教育勅語の国家主義的解釈，" 坂田吉雄編，明治前半期のナショナリズム，未来社

Minear, Richard H. *Japanese Tradition and Western Law: Emperor, State, and Law in the Thought of Hozumi Yatsuka*. Cambridge, Mass.: Harvard University Press, 1970.

Mito-han shiryō. 5 vols. Tokyo: Yoshikawa kōbunkan, 1970. 水戸藩史料，吉川弘文館

Miyachi Masato. *Nichi-Ro sengo seijishi no kenkyū*. Tokyo: Tokyo daigaku shuppankai, 1973. 宮地正人，日露戦後政治史の研究，東京大学出版会

Miyagi-chō shi, shiryōhen. Sendai: Miyagi-ken Miyagi-chō, 1967. 宮城町史，史料編，仙台，宮城県宮城町

Miyake Setsurei. *Dōjidaishi*. 6 vols. Tokyo: Iwanami shoten, 1949-54. 三宅雪嶺，同時代史，岩波書店

Miyamoto Chū. *Sakuma Shōzan*. Tokyo: Iwanami shoten, 1932. 宮本仲，佐久間象山，岩波書店

Miyamoto Mataji, ed. *Han shakai no kenkyū*. Kyoto: Mineruva shobō, 1972. 宮本又次編，藩社会の研究，ミネルヴァ書房

Miyao Sadao. "Minka yōjutsu." In *Kinsei jikata keizai shiryō*. Vol. 5. Tokyo: Yoshikawa kōbunkan, 1954. 宮負定雄，民家要術，近世地方経済史料，吉川弘文館

Miyata Noboru. "Nōson no fukkō undō to minshū shūkyō no tenkai." In *Iwanami kōza Nihon rekishi*. Vol. 13 (*kinsei* 5), 1977. 宮田登，農村の復興運動と民衆宗教の展開

Miyazawa Toshiyoshi. "Meiji kempō no seiritsu to sono kokusai seijiteki haikei." In Miyazawa Toshiyoshi, ed. *Nihon kenseishi no kenkyū*. Tokyo:

Iwanami shoten, 1968. 宮澤俊義, 明治憲法の成立とその国際政治的背景, 宮澤俊義編, 日本憲政史の研究, 岩波書店
Mizuno Tadashi. *Edo shōsetsu ronsō*. Tokyo: Chūō kōronsha, 1974. 水野稔, 江戸小説論叢, 中央公論社
Morinaka Akimitsu, ed. *Niijima Jō sensei shokanshū zokuhen*. Kyoto: Dōshisha kōyūkai, 1960. 森中章光編, 新島襄先生書簡集続編, 同志社校友会
Morinaka Akimitsu, ed. *Niijima sensei shokanshū*. Kyoto: Dōshisha kōyūkai, 1942. 森中章光編, 新島先生書簡集, 同志社校友会
Moriyama Gunjirō. *Minshū hōki to matsuri*. Tokyo: Chikuma shobō, 1981. 森山軍治郎, 民衆蜂起と祭り, 筑摩書房
Morley, James W., ed. *Dilemmas of Growth in Prewar Japan*. Princeton, N.J.: Princeton University Press, 1971.
Morris, Ivan. *The Nobility of Failure: Tragic Heroes in the History of Japan*. New York: Holt, Rinehart and Winston, 1975.
Morse, R. A., trans. *The Legends of Tōno by Kunio Yanagita*. Tokyo: Japan Foundation, 1975.
Mounsey, August H. *The Satsuma Rebellion*. London: Murray, 1879. Reprinted by University Publications of America, Washington, D.C., 1979.
Muragaki (Awaji no kami) Norimasa. *Kōkai nikki*. Tokyo: Jiji tsūshinsha, 1959. 村垣(淡路守)範正, 航海日記, 時事通信社
Murakami Shigeyoshi. *Kinsei minshū shūkyō no kenkyū*. Tokyo: Hōzōkan, 1977. 村上重良, 近世民衆宗教の研究, 法蔵館
Murakami Shigeyoshi and Yasumaru Yoshio, eds. *Nihon shisō taikei*. Vol. 67, *Minshū shūkyō to shisō*. Tokyo: Iwanami shoten, 1971. 村上重良, 安丸良夫編, 民衆宗教と思想, 日本思想大系, 岩波書店
Muromatsu Iwao, ed. *Hirata Atsutane zenshū*. 15 vols. Tokyo: Ichidō, Hirata gakkai, 1911-18. 室松岩雄編, 平田篤胤全集, 一致堂, 平田学会
Mutobe Yoshika. "Ken-yūjun kōron." In Nakajima Hiromitsu, ed. *Shintō sōsho*. Vol. 3. October 1897. 亡人部是香, 顯幽順考論, 中島博光編, 神道叢書
Nagahara Keiji. *Rekishigaku josetsu*. Tokyo: Tokyo daigaku shuppankai, 1978. 永原慶二, 歴史学叙説, 東京大学出版会
Nagahara Keiji. "Zenkindai no tennō." *Rekishigaku kenkyū* 467 (April 1979): 37-45. 永原慶二, "前近代の天皇"歴史学研究
Nagai Hideo. *Jiyū minken*. Vol. 25 of *Nihon no rekishi*. Tokyo: Shogakkan, 1976. 永井秀夫, 自由民権, 日本の歴史, 小学館
Nagai, Michio. "Mori Arinori." *Japan Quarterly* 11 (1964): 98-105.
Naitō Chisō. *Tokugawa jūgodaishi*. 6 vols. Tokyo: Shin jimbutsu ōraisha, 1969. 内藤耻叟, 徳川十五代史, 新人物往来社
Najita, Tetsuo. "The Conceptual Portrayal of Tokugawa Intellectual History." In Najita and Scheiner, eds. *Japanese Thought in the Tokugawa Period*.
Najita, Tetsuo. "Ōshio Heihachirō (1793-1837)." In Craig and Shively, eds. *Personality in Japanese History*.
Najita, Tetsuo, and Irwin Scheiner, eds. *Japanese Thought in the Tokugawa*

Period: Methods and Metaphors. Chicago: University of Chicago Press, 1979.
Nakabe Yoshiko. *Jōkamachi.* Kyoto: Yanagihara shoten, 1978. 中部よし子, 城下町, 柳原書店
Nakabe Yoshiko. *Kinsei toshi shakai keizaishi kenkyū.* Tokyo: Kōyō shobō, 1974. 中部よし子, 近世都市社会経済史研究, 晃洋書房
Nakajima Giichi. "Ichiman goku daimyō no jōka." *Shin chiri* 10 (September 1962): 1-15. 中島義一, 一万石大名の城下, 新地理
Nakajima Giichi. *Shijō shūraku.* Tokyo: Kokon shoin, 1964. 中島義一, 市場集落, 古今書院
Nakajima Ichisaburō. *Hirose Tansō no kenkyū.* Tokyo: Dai-ichi shuppan kyōkai, 1943. 中島市三郎, 広瀬淡窓の研究, 第一出版協会
Nakamura Kichiji, ed. *Nihon keizaishi.* Tokyo: Yamakawa, 1968. 中村吉治編, 日本経済史, 山川出版
Nakamura Naokatsu, ed. *Hikone-shi shi.* 3 vols. Hikone: Hikone shiyakusho, 1960-9. 中村直勝編, 彦根市史, 彦根市役所
Nakamura, Shin'ichirō. "New Concepts of Life of the Post-Kansei Intellectuals: Scholars of Chinese Classics." *Modern Asian Studies* 18 (October 1984): pt. 4, 619-30.
Nakamura Tetsu. "Kaikokugo no bōeki to sekai shijō." In *Iwanami kōza Nihon rekishi.* Vol. 13 (*kinsei* 5), 1977. 中村哲, 開国後の貿易と世界市場
Nakamura Yukihiko. *Gesakuron.* Tokyo: Kadokawa, 1966. 中村幸彦, 戯作論, 角川書店
Nakamura Yukihiko and Nishiyama Matsunosuke, eds. *Bunka ryōran.* Vol. 8 of *Nihon bungaku no rekishi.* Tokyo: Kadokawa, 1967. 中村幸彦, 西山松之助編, 文化繚乱, 日本文学の歴史, 角川書店
Nakamura, James. *Agricultural Production and the Economic Development of Japan 1873-1922.* Princeton, N.J.: Princeton University Press, 1966.
Nakamura Takafusa. *Nihon keizai: sono seichō to kōzō.* 2nd ed. Tokyo: Tokyo daigaku shuppankai, 1980. 中村隆英, 日本経済:その成長と構造, 東京大学出版会
Nakane, Chie. *Japanese Society.* Berkeley and Los Angeles: University of California Press, 1970.
Naramoto Tatsuya. *Nihon kinsei no shisō to bunka.* Tokyo: Iwanami shoten, 1978. 奈良本辰也, 日本近世の思想と文化, 岩波書店
Nihon shihonshugi hattatsu shi kōza. 7 vols. Tokyo: Iwanami shoten, 1932-3. 日本資本主義発達史講座, 岩波書店
Nihon shiseki kyōkai, ed. *Hashimoto Keigaku zenshū.* 3 vols. (*Nihon shiseki kyōkai sōsho*). Tokyo: Tokyo daigaku shuppankai, 1977. 日本史籍協会編, 橋本景岳全集, 日本史籍協会叢書, 東京大学出版会
Nihon shiseki kyōkai, ed. *Ōkubo Toshimichi monjo.* 10 vols. (*Nihon shiseki kyōkai sōsho*). Tokyo: Tokyo daigaku shuppankai, 1969. 日本史籍協会編, 大久保利通文書, 日本史籍協会叢書, 東京大学出版会
Nihon shiseki kyōkai, ed. *Yokoi Shōnan kankei shiryō.* 2 vols. In *Zoku Nihon*

shiseki kyōkai sōsho. Tokyo: Tokyo daigaku shuppankai, 1977. 日本史籍協会編，横井小楠関係史料，続日本史籍協会叢書，東京大学出版会
Nish, Ian. *The Anglo-Japanese Alliance: The Diplomacy of Two Island Empires 1894-1907*. London: Athlone, 1966.
Nish, Ian. *The Origins of the Russo-Japanese War*. London: Longman Group, 1985.
Nishikawa Kōji. *Nihon toshishi kenkyū*. Tokyo: Nihon hōsō shuppan kyōkai, 1972. 西川幸治，日本都市史研究，日本放送出版協会
Nishikawa Shunsaku. *Edo jidai no poritikaru ekonomii*. Tokyo: Nihon hyōronsha, 1979. 西川俊作，江戸時代のポリティカル・エコノミー，日本評論社
Nishikawa, Shunsaku. "Grain Consumption: The Case of Chōshū." In Jansen and Rozman, eds. *Japan in Transition*.
Nishikawa Shunsaku. *Nihon keizai no seichōshi*. Tokyo: Tōyō keizai shimpōsha, 1985. 西川俊作，日本経済の成長史，東洋経済新報社
Nishio Minoru et al., eds. *Shōbōgenzō, Shōbōgenzō zuimonki*. In *Nihon koten bungaku taikei*. Vol. 81. Tokyo: Iwanami shoten, 1965. 西尾實編，正法眼蔵：正法眼蔵随聞記，日本古典文学大系，岩波書店
Nishiyama Matsunosuke, ed. *Edo chōnin no kenkyū*. 5 vols. Tokyo: Yoshikawa kōbunkan, 1973. 西山松之助編，江戸町人の研究，吉川弘文館
Nishiyama Matsunosuke. "Edo chōnin no sōron." In Nishiyama, ed. *Edo chonin no kenkyū* Vol. 1 (1972). 西山松之助，江戸町人の総論
Nivison, D. S., and A. F. Wright, eds. *Confucianism in Action*. Stanford, Calif.: Stanford University Press, 1959.
Niwa Kunio. "Chiso kaisei." In Nihon rekishi gakkai, ed. *Nihonshi no mondai ten*. Tokyo: Yoshikawa kōbunkan, 1965. 丹羽邦男，地租改正，日本歴史学会編，日本史の問題点
Niwa Kunio. "Chiso kaisei to chitsuroku shobun." In *Iwanami kōza Nihon rekishi*. Vol. 15 (*kindai* 2), 1963. 丹羽邦男，地租改正と秩禄処分
Noguchi Takehiko. *"Aku" to Edo bungaku*. Tokyo: Asahi shimbunsha, 1980. 野口武彦，「悪」と江戸文学，朝日新聞社
Noguchi Takehiko. *Rai San'yō: rekishi e no kikansha*. Tokyo: Tankōsha, 1974. 野口武彦，頼山陽，歴史への帰還者，淡交社
Nomura Denshirō, ed. *Ōkuni Takamasa zenshū*. 7 vols. Tokyo: Yūkōsha, 1937-9. 野村傳四郎編，大國隆正全集，有光社
Nomura Kanetarō. *Edo*. Tokyo: Shibundo, 1966. 野村兼太郎，江戸，至文堂
Norman, E. H. *Japan's Emergence As a Modern State: Political and Economic Problems of the Meiji Period*. New York: Institute of Pacific Relations, 1940 and later printings.
Norman, E. H. *Soldier and Peasant in Japan: The Origins of Conscription*. New York: Institute of Pacific Relations, 1943.
Notehelfer, F. G. *American Samurai: Captain L. L. Janes and Japan*. Princeton, N.J.: Princeton University Press, 1985.
Notehelfer, F. G. *Kōtoku Shūsui: Portrait of a Japanese Radical*. Cambridge, England: Cambridge University Press, 1971.

Numata, Jiro. "Shigeno Yasutsugu and the Modern Tokyo Tradition of Historical Writing." In Beasley and Pulleybank, eds. *Historians of China and Japan.*

Numata Jirō et al. *Yōgaku (I)*. In *Nihon shisō taikei.* Vol. 64. Tokyo: Iwanami shoten, 1976. 沼田次郎等編, 洋学(上), 日本思想大系, 岩波書店

Ōba Osamu. *Edo jidai ni okeru Chūgoku bunka juyō no kenkyū.* Tokyo: Dōhōsha, 1984. 大庭修, 江戸時代における中国文化受容の研究, 同朋社

Ōba Osamu. *Edo jidai ni okeru Tōsen mochiwatarisho no kenkyū.* Suita: Kansai University, 1967. 大庭修, 江戸時代における唐船持渡書の研究, 吹田:関西大学

Ōba Osamu. *Edo jidai no Nitchū hiwa.* Tokyo: Tōhō shoten, 1980. 大庭修, 江戸時代の日中秘話, 東方書店

Oda Yoshinojō, ed. *Kaga han nōseishi kō.* Tokyo: Tōkō shoin, 1929. 小田吉之丈編, 加賀藩農政史考, 刀江書院

Odaka Toshirō and Matsumura Akira, eds. *Taionki, Ōritakushiba no ki, Rantō kotohajime.* Vol. 95 of *Nihon koten bungaku taikei.* Tokyo: Iwanami shoten, 1964. 小高敏郎, 松村明編, 戴恩記, 折たく柴の記, 蘭東事始, 日本古典文学大系, 岩波書店

Ōe Shinobu. *Nichi-Ro sensō no gunjishiteki kenkyū.* Tokyo: Iwanami shoten, 1976. 大江志乃夫, 日露戦争の軍事史的研究, 岩波書店

Ōguchi Yūjirō. "Tempō-ki no seikaku." In *Iwanami kōza Nihon rekishi.* Vol. 12 (*kinsei* 4), 1976. 大口勇次郎, 天保期の性格

Oh, Bonnie B. "Sino-Japanese Rivalry in Korea, 1876–1885." In Iriye, ed. *The Chinese and the Japanese: Essays in Political and Cultural Interactions.*

Ohkawa, Kazushi. *The Growth Rate of the Japanese Economy Since 1878.* Tokyo: Kinokuniya, 1957.

Ōishi Shinzaburō. *Nihon kinsei shakai no shijō kōzō.* Tokyo: Iwanami shoten, 1975. 大石慎三郎, 日本近世社会の市場構造, 岩波書店

Oka Yoshitake. *Kindai Nihon seiji shi.* Vol. 1. Tokyo: Sōbunsha, 1962. 岡義武, 近代日本政治史, 創文社

Okamoto Ryōichi. "Tempō kaikaku." In *Iwanami kōza Nihon rekishi.* Vol. 13 (*kinsei* 5), 1963. 岡本良一, 天保改革

Okamoto, Shumpei. *The Japanese Oligarchy and the Russo-Japanese War.* New York: Columbia University Press, 1970.

Ōkawa Kazushi, ed. *Kokumin shotoku.* Vol. 1 of *Chōki keizai tōkei.* Tokyo: Tōyō keizai shimpōsha, 1974. 大川一司, 国民所得(長期経済統計), 東洋経済新報社

Okubo Akihiro. "Bakumatsu ni okeru seijiteki hanran to shijuku." In Kano Masanao and Takagi Shunsuke, eds. *Ishin henkaku ni okeru zaisonteki shochōryū.* Tokyo: San'ichi shobō, 1972. 小久保明浩, 幕末における政治的反乱と私塾, 鹿野政直, 高木俊輔編, 維新変革における在村的諸潮流, 三一書房

Ōkubo Toshiaki, ed. *Meiji ishin to Kyūshū.* Tokyo: Heibonsha, 1968. 大久保利謙編, 明治維新と九州, 平凡社

Ōkurashō, ed. *Nihon zaisei keizai shiryō*. Vol. 10. Tokyo: Zaisei keizai gakkai, 1922-5. 大蔵省編, 日本財政経済史料, 財政経済学会

Ono Masao. "Kaikoku." In *Iwanami kōza Nihon rekishi*. Vol. 13 (*kinsei* 5), 1977. 小野正雄, 開国

Onodera Toshiya. " 'Zannen san' kō: Bakumatsu Kinai no ichi minshū undō o megutte." *Chiiki shi kenkyū* 2 (June 1972): 47-67. 小野寺逸也, "残念さん"考: 幕末畿内の一民衆運動を巡って, 地域史研究

Ooms, Herman. *Charismatic Bureaucrat: A Political Biography of Matsudaira Sadanobu, 1758-1829*. Chicago: University of Chicago Press, 1975.

Ooms, Herman. *Tokugawa Ideology: Early Constructs, 1570-1680*. Princeton, N.J.: Princeton University Press, 1985.

Oriental Economist. *The Foreign Trade of Japan: A Statistical Survey*. Tokyo, 1935.

Osaka-shi sanjikai, ed. *Osaka-shi shi*. 7 vols. Osaka: Osaka shiyakusho, 1911-15. 大阪市参事会編, 大阪市史, 大阪市役所

Osatake Takeki. *Ishin zengo ni okeru rikken shisō*. Rev. ed. 2 vols. Tokyo: Hōkōdō, 1929. 尾佐竹猛, 維新前後に於ける立憲思想, 邦光堂

Osatake Takeki. *Meiji ishin*. 4 vols. Tokyo: Hakuyosha, 1946. 尾佐竹猛, 明治維新, 白揚社

Passin, Herbert. *Society and Education in Japan*. New York: Columbia University Press, 1965.

Pierson, John D. *Tokutomi Sohō 1863-1957: A Journalist for Modern Japan*. Princeton, N.J.: Princeton University Press, 1980.

Pineau, Roger, ed. *The Japan Expedition 1852-1854: The Personal Journal of Commodore Matthew C. Perry*. Washington, D.C.: Smithsonian, 1968.

Pittau, Joseph. *Political Thought in Early Meiji Japan: 1868-1889*. Cambridge, Mass.: Harvard University Press, 1967.

Pyle, Kenneth B. "Advantages of Followership: German Economics and Japanese Bureaucrats, 1890-1925." *Journal of Japanese Studies* 1 (1974): 127-64.

Pyle, Kenneth B. "The Ashio Copper Mine Pollution Case." *Journal of Japanese Studies* 1 (Spring 1975): 347-50.

Pyle, Kenneth B. *The New Generation in Meiji Japan: Problems of Cultural Identity, 1885-1895*. Stanford, Calif.: Stanford University Press, 1969.

Pyle, Kenneth B. "The Technology of Japanese Nationalism: The Local Improvement Movement, 1900-1918." *Journal of Japanese Studies* 33 (1973): 51-65.

Raffles, T. S. *Report on Japan to the Secret Committee of the English East India Company* [Kobe, 1929]. Reprint. London: Curzon Press and New York: Barnes & Noble, 1971.

Reinfried, Heinrich Martin. *The Tale of Nisuke*. Wiesbaden: Harrassowitz, Studien zur Japanologie Band 13, 1978.

Reischauer, Haru Matsukata. *Samurai and Silk*. Cambridge, Mass.: Harvard University Press, 1986.

Rekishigaku kenkyūkai, eds. *Meiji ishinshi kenkyū kōza*. 7 vols. Tokyo: Heibonsha, 1968. 歴史学研究会編，明治維新史研究講座，平凡社

Robertson, Jennifer. "Sexy Rice: Plant Gender, Farm Manuals, and Grass-Roots Nativism." *Monumenta Nipponica* 39 (Autumn 1984): 233-60.

Rosenfield, John M. "Western-Style Painting in the Early Meiji Period and Its Critics." In Shively, ed. *Tradition and Modernization in Japanese Culture*.

Rozman, Gilbert. "Edo's Importance in Changing Tokugawa Society." *Journal of Japanese Studies* 1 (Autumn 1974): 91-112.

Rozman, Gilbert. *Urban Networks in Ch'ing China and Tokugawa Japan*. Princeton, N.J.: Princeton University Press, 1973.

Rubinger, Richard. "Education: From One Room to One System." In Jansen and Rozman, eds. *Japan in Transition*.

Rubinger, Richard. *Private Academies of Tokugawa Japan*. Princeton, N.J.: Princeton University Press, 1982.

Ryan, Marleigh G. *Japan's First Modern Novel*: Ukigumo *of Futabatei Shimei*. New York: Columbia University Press, 1967.

Sagara Tōru, ed. *Hirata Atsutane*. Vol. 24 of *Nihon no meicho*. Tokyo: Chūō kōronsha, 1972. 相良亨編，平田篤胤，日本の名著，中央公論社

Saitō Gesshin. *Bukō nempyō*. 2 vols. Tokyo: Heibonsha, 1968. 斉藤月岑，武江年表，平凡社

Saitō Shōichi. *Ōyama-chō shi*. Tsuruoka: Ōyama-chō shi kankō iinkai, 1969. 斎藤正一，大山町史，鶴岡：大山町史刊行会

Sakai, Robert. "Feudal Society and Modern Leadership in Satsuma han." *Journal of Asian Studies* 16 (May 1957): 365-76.

Sakata Yoshio. *Meiji ishin shi*. Tokyo: Miraisha, 1960. 坂田吉雄，明治維新史，未来社

Sakata Yoshio, *Tennō shinsei*. Kyoto: Shibunkaku, 1984. 坂田吉雄，天皇親政，思文閣

Sakata, Yoshio, and John W. Hall. "The Motivation of Political Leadership in the Meiji Restoration." *Journal of Asian Studies* 16 (November 1956): 31-50.

Sakeda Masatoshi. *Kindai Nihon ni okeru taigai kō undō no kenkyū*. Tokyo: Tokyo daigaku shuppankai, 1978. 酒田正敏，近代日本における対外硬運動の研究，東京大学出版会

Sansom, G. B. *Japan: A Short Cultural History*. London: Cresset, 1932.

Sansom, G. B. *The Western World and Japan*. New York: Knopf, 1950.

Sasaki Junnosuke. "Bakumatsu no shakai jōsei to yonaoshi." In *Iwanami kōza Nihon rekishi*. Vol. 13 (*kinsei* 5), 1977. 佐々木潤之介，幕末の社会情勢と世直し

Sasaki Junnosuke. *Bakumatsu shakai ron*. Tokyo: Hanawa shobō, 1973. 佐々木潤之介，幕末社会論，塙書房

Satō Jizaemon. *Kahei hiroku*. In *Nihon keizai sōsho*. Vol. 32. Tokyo: Nihon keizai sōsho kankōkai, 1914. 佐藤治左衛門，貨幣秘録，日本経済叢書，日本

経済叢書刊行会
Satō Masatsugu. *Nihon rekigakushi*. Tokyo: Surugadai shuppansha, 1968. 佐藤政次，日本暦学史，駿河台出版社
Satō Nobuhiro. *Fukkohō gaigen*. In Takimoto Seiichi, ed. *Nihon keizai taiten*. Vol. 19. Tokyo: Shishi shuppansha and Keimeisha, 1928. 佐藤信淵，復古法概言，瀧本誠一編，日本経済大典，史誌出版社
Satō Shōsuke. *Yōgakushi kenkyū josetsu*. Tokyo: Iwanami shoten, 1964. 佐藤昌介，洋学史研究序説，岩波書店
Satō Shōsuke. *Yōgakushi no kenkyū*. Tokyo: Chūō kōronsha, 1980. 佐藤昌介，洋学史の研究，中央公論社
Satō Shōsuke et al. *Watanabe Kazan/Takano Chōei/Sakuma Shōzan/Yokoi Shōnan/Hashimoto Sanai*. In *Nihon shisō taikei*. Vol. 55. Tokyo: Iwanami shoten, 1977. 佐藤昌介等，渡辺崋山，高野長英，佐久間象山，横井小楠，橋本左内，日本思想大系，岩波書店
Scalapino, Robert A. *Democracy and the Party Movement in Prewar Japan*. Berkeley and Los Angeles: University of California Press, 1953.
Scalapino, Robert A. "Ideology and Modernization: The Japanese Case." In David E. Apter, ed. *Ideology and Discontent*. New York: Free Press, 1964.
Scheiner, Irwin. "Benevolent Lords and Honorable Peasants." In Najita and Scheiner, eds. *Japanese Thought in the Tokugawa Period*.
Schwartz, Benjamin I. "Notes on Conservatism in General and on China in Particular." In Charlotte Furth, ed. *The Limits of Change: Essays on Conservative Alternatives in Republican China*. Cambridge, Mass.: Harvard University Press, 1976.
Seki Junya. *Meiji ishin to chiso kaisei*. Kyoto: Mineruva shobō, 1967. 関順也，明治維新と地租改正，ミネルヴァ書房
Sekiyama Naotarō. *Nihon no jinkō*. Tokyo: Shibundō, 1966. 関山直太郎，日本の人口，至文堂
Seto Mikio. "Minshū no shūkyō ishiki to henkaku no enerugii." In Maruyama Teruo, ed. *Henkakuki no shūkyō*. Tokyo: Gendai jaanarizumu shuppankai, 1972. 瀬戸美喜雄，民衆の宗教意識と変革のエネルギー，丸山照雄編，変革期の宗教，現代ジャーナリズム出版会
Sheldon, Charles David. *The Rise of the Merchant Class in Tokugawa Japan: 1600-1868*. Locust Valley, N.Y.: Association for Asian Studies, 1958.
Shiba Kōkan. *Shumparō hikki*. In *Nihon zuihitsu hikki*. Vol. 1. Tokyo: Yoshikawa kōbunkan, 1936. 司馬江漢，春波樓筆記，日本随筆筆記，吉川弘文館
Shibahara Takuji. "Hanbaku shoseiryoku no seikaku." In *Iwanami kōza Nihon rekishi*. Vol. 14 (*kindai* 1), 1963. 芝原拓自，反幕諸勢力の性格
Shimbo Hiroshi. *Kinsei no bukka to keizai hatten: zenkōgyōka shakai e no sūryōteki sekkin*. Tokyo: Tōyō keizai shimpōsha, 1978. 新保博，近世の物価と経済発展：前工業化社会への数量的接近，東洋経済新報社
Shimbo Hiroshi. *Nihon kindai shin'yō seido seiritsushi ron*. Vol. 7 of *Kōbe keizaigaku sōsho*. Tokyo: Yūhikaku, 1968. 新保博，日本近代信用制度成立史

論，神戸経済学双書，有斐閣
Shimbo Hiroshi, Hayami Akira, and Nishikawa Shunsaku. *Sūryō keizaishi nyūmon*. Tokyo: Nihon hyōronsha, 1975. 新保博，速水融，西川俊作，数量経済史入門，日本評論社
Shimomura Fujio. *Meiji shonen jōyaku kaisei shi no kenkyū*. Tokyo: Yoshikawa kōbunkan, 1962. 下村富士男，明治初年条約改正史の研究，吉川弘文館
Shimomura Fujio. "Nichi-Ro sensō no seikaku." *Kokusai seiji* 3 (1957): 137-52. 下村富士男，日露戦争の性格，国際政治
Shimoyama Saburō. "Fukushima jiken shōron." *Rekishigaku kenkyū* 186 (August 1955): 1-13. 下山三郎，福島事件小論，歴史学研究
Shinano Kyōikukai, ed. *Shōzan zenshū*. 5 vols. Nagano: Shinano Mainichi shimbunsha, 1934-5. 信濃教育会編，象山全集，長野：信濃毎日新聞社
Shinobu Seizaburō, ed. *Nihon gaikō shi: 1853-1972*. 2 vols. Tokyo: Mainichi shimbunsha, 1974. 信夫清三郎編，日本外交史，1853-1972，毎日新聞社
Shively, Donald H. "The Japanization of the Middle Meiji." In Shively, ed. *Tradition and Modernization in Japanese Culture*.
Shively, Donald H. "Motoda Eifu: Confucian Lecturer to the Meiji Emperor." In Nivison and Wright, eds. *Confucianism in Action*.
Shively, Donald H. "Nishimura Shigeki: A Confucian View of Modernization." In Jansen, ed. *Changing Japanese Attitudes Toward Modernization*.
Shively, Donald H., ed. *Tradition and Modernization in Japanese Culture*. Princeton, N.J.: Princeton University Press, 1971.
Shively, Donald H. "Urban Culture." Paper presented at colloquium, Edo Culture and Its Modern Legacy. London, 1981.
Shōji Kichinosuke. *Tōhoku shohan hyakushō ikki no kenkyū: shiryō shūsei*. Tokyo: Ochanomizu shobō, 1969. 庄司吉之助，東北諸藩百姓一揆の研究：史料集成，御茶の水書房
Shōji Kichinosuke. *Yonaoshi ikki no kenkyū*. Tokyo: Azekura shobō, 1970. 庄司吉之助，世直し一揆の研究，校倉書房
Siemes, Johannes. *Hermann Roesler and the Making of the Meiji State*. Tokyo: Sophia University Press, 1966.
Silberman, Bernard S. "Bureaucratic Development and the Structure of Decision-Making in Japan, 1868-1925." *Journal of Asian Studies* 29 (1970): 347-62.
Silberman, Bernard S. *Ministers of Modernization: Elite Mobility in the Meiji Restoration 1868-1873*. Tucson: University of Arizona Press, 1964.
Silberman, Bernard, and H. D. Harootunian, eds. *Modern Japanese Leadership*. Tucson: University of Arizona Press, 1966.
Smethhurst, Richard J. *Agricultural Development and Tenancy Disputes in Japan, 1870-1940*. Princeton, N.J.: Princeton University Press, 1986.
Smethurst, Richard J. *A Social Basis for Prewar Japanese Militarism*. Berkeley and Los Angeles: University of California Press, 1974.
Smith, Robert J. "Small Families, Small Households, and Residential Instability: Town and City in 'Pre-Modern' Japan." In Laslett, ed. *Household and*

Family in Past Time.
Smith, Thomas C. *The Agrarian Origins of Modern Japan.* Stanford, Calif.: Stanford University Press, 1959.
Smith, Thomas C. "Farm Family By-Employments in Preindustrial Japan." *Journal of Economic History* 29 (December 1969): 687–715.
Smith, Thomas C. "Japan's Aristocratic Revolution." *Yale Review* 50 (March 1961): 370–83.
Smith, Thomas C. *Nakahara: Family Farming and Population in a Japanese Village, 1717–1830.* Stanford, Calif.: Stanford University Press, 1977.
Smith, Thomas C. "Ōkura Nagatsune and the Technologists." In Craig and Shively, eds. *Personality in Japanese History.*
Smith, Thomas C. *Political Change and Industrial Development in Japan: Government Enterprise, 1868–1880.* Stanford, Calif.: Stanford University Press, 1955.
Smith, Thomas C. "Pre-Modern Economic Growth: Japan and the West." *Past and Present* 43 (1973): 127–60.
Sonoda Hiyoshi. *Etō Shimpei to Saga no ran.* Tokyo: Shin jinbutsu ōraisha, 1978. 園田日吉、江藤新平と佐賀の乱、新人物往来社
Soranaka, Isao. "The Kansei Reforms – Success or Failure." *Monumenta Nipponica* 33 (Summer 1978): 151–64.
Sōseki zenshū. 34 vols. Tokyo: Iwanami shoten shinsho edition, 1956–7. 漱石全集、岩波書店
Spaulding, Robert. *Imperial Japan's Higher Civil Service Examinations.* Princeton, N.J.: Princeton University Press, 1967.
Statler, Oliver. *Shimoda Story.* New York: Random House, 1969.
Steiner, Kurt. *Local Government in Japan.* Stanford, Calif.: Stanford University Press, 1965.
Stephan, John J. *The Kuril Islands: The Russo-Japanese Frontier in the Pacific.* New York: Oxford University Press, 1975.
Stone, Alan. "The Japanese Muckrakers." *Journal of Japanese Studies* 1 (1975): 385–407.
Sugi Hitoshi. "Kaseiki no shakai to bunka." In Aoki Michio and Yamada Tadao, eds. *Tempōki no seiji to shakai.* Vol. 6 of *Kōza Nihon kinseishi.* Tokyo: Yūhikaku, 1981. 杉仁、"化政期の社会と文化,"青木美智男、山田忠雄編、天保期の政治と社会（講座日本近世史 6）、有斐閣
Sugimoto, Yoshio. "Structural Sources of Popular Revolts and the Tōbaku Movement at the Time of the Meiji Restoration." *Journal of Asian Studies.* 34 (August 1975): 875–89.
Sugita Gempaku. "Keiei yawa." In Fujikawa Yu et al., eds. *Kyōrin sōsho.* Vol. 1. Kyoto: Shibunkaku reprint edition, 1971. 杉田玄白、形影夜話、富士川游編、杏林叢書、至文閣
Sugiura Mimpei. *Ishin zenya no bungaku.* Tokyo: Iwanami shoten, 1967. 杉浦明平、維新前夜の文学、岩波書店
Sugiura Mimpei. *Kirishitan, rangaku shū.* Vol. 16 of *Nihon no shisō.* Tokyo:

Chikuma shobō, 1970. 杉浦明平, キリシタン／蘭学集, 日本の思想, 筑摩書房

Sumiya Etsuji. *Nihon keizaigaku shi.* Kyoto: Mineruva shobō, 1958. 住谷悦治, 日本経済史, ミネルヴァ書房

Sumiya Mikio. *Dai Nihon teikoku no shiren.* Vol. 22 of *Nihon no rekishi,* Tokyo: Chūō kōronsha, 1965. 隅谷三喜男, 大日本帝国の試煉, 日本の歴史, 中央公論社

Sumiya Mikio. *Nihon no shakai shisō.* Tokyo: Tokyo daigaku shuppankai, 1968. 隅谷三喜男, 日本の社会思想, 東京大学出版会

Suzuki Shigetane. *Engishiki norito kōgi.* Tokyo: Kokusho kankōkai, 1978. 鈴木重胤, 延喜式祝詞講義, 国書刊行会

Suzuki Shigetane. *Yotsugigusa tsumiwake.* 3 vols. Edited by Katsura Takashige, Niitsū, Niigata: Katsura Takateru, 1884. 鈴木重胤, 世継草摘分, 桂誉重編, 新津, 新潟：桂誉輝

Tahara Tsuguo et al., eds. *Hirata Atsutane, Ban Nobutomo, Ōkuni Takamasa.* Vol. 50 of *Nihon shisō taikei.* Tokyo: Iwanami shoten, 1973. 田原嗣郎, 平田篤胤, 伴信友, 大國隆正, 日本思想大系, 岩波書店

Takagi Shunsuke. *Eejanaika.* Tokyo: Kyōikusha rekishi shinsho, 1979. 高木俊輔, ええじゃないか, 教育社歴史新書

Takahashi Tetsuo. *Fukushima jiken.* Tokyo: San'ichi Shobō, 1970. 高橋哲夫, 福島事件, 三一書房

Takahashi Tetsuo. *Fukushima jiyū minkenka retsuden.* Fukushima: Fukushima mimpōsha, 1967. 高橋哲夫, 福島自由民権家列伝, 福島：福島民報社

Takasu Yoshijirō, ed. *Mitogaku taikei.* 10 vols. Tokyo: Mitogaku taikei kankōkai, 1941. 高須芳次郎編, 水戸学大系, 水戸学大系刊行会

Takayanagi Shinzō and Ishii Ryōsuke, eds. *Ofuregaki Temmei shūsei.* Tokyo: Iwanami shoten, 1958. 高柳真三, 石井良助編, 御觸書天明集成, 岩波書店

Takeuchi Makoto. "Kansei-Kaseiki Edo ni okeru shokaisō no dōkō." In Nishiyama, ed. *Edo chōnin no kenkyū.* Vol. 1. 竹内誠, 寛政化政期江戸における諸階層の動向

Tamamuro Taijō. *Seinan sensō.* Tokyo: Shibundo, 1958. 圭室諦成, 西南戦争, 至文堂

Tamamushi Jūzō. *Jinsei hen.* In Honjō Eijirō, ed. *Kinsei shakai keizai sōsho.* Vol. 5. Tokyo: Kaizōsha, 1926. 玉虫十蔵, 仁政篇, 本庄榮治郎, 近世社会経済叢書, 改造社

Tanaka Akira. "Ishin seiken ron." In *Kōza Nihonshi.* Vol. 5, *Meiji ishin.* Tokyo: Rekishigaku kenkyūkai, 1970. 田中彰, 維新政権論, 講座日本史, 明治維新, 歴史学研究会

Tanaka Akira. *Iwakura shisetsu dan.* Tokyo: Kōdansha, 1977. 田中彰, 岩倉使節団, 講談社

Tanaka Akira. *Meiji ishin.* Vol. 24 of *Nihon no rekishi.* Tokyo: Shogakkan, 1976. 田中彰, 明治維新, 日本の歴史, 小学館

Tanaka, Michiko. "Village Youth Organizations (*Wakamono Nakama*) in Late Tokugawa Politics and Society." Ph.D. diss., Princeton University, 1982.

Tanaka Sōgorō. *Kindai Nihon kanryō shi.* Tokyo: Tōyō keizai shimpōsha, 1941. 田中惣五郎, 近代日本官僚史, 東洋経済新報

Tashiro, Kazui. "Foreign Relations During the Edo Period: *Sakoku* Re-examined." *Journal of Japanese Studies* 8 (Summer 1982): 283–306.

Tashiro Kazui. *Kinsei Ni-Chō tsūkō bōekishi no kenkyū.* Tokyo: Sōbunsha, 1981. 田代和生, 近世日朝通交貿易史の研究, 創文社

Tazaki Tetsurō. "Yōgakuron saikōsei shiron." *Shisō* (November 1979): 48–72. 田崎哲郎, 洋学論再構成試論, 思想

Teranishi Shigeo. "Matsukata defure no makuro keizaigakuteki bunseki." *Kikan gendai keizai* 47 (Spring 1982): 78–92. 寺西重郎, 松方デフレのマクロ経済学的分析, 季刊現代経済

Teters, Barbara Joan. "The Conservative Opposition in Japanese Politics, 1877–1894." Ph.D. diss., University of Washington, 1955.

Teters, Barbara Joan. "The Genro-In and the National Essence Movement." *Pacific Historical Review* 31 (1962): 359–78.

Teters, Barbara Joan. "A Liberal Nationalist and the Meiji Constitution." In Robert K. Sakai, ed. *Studies on Asia.* Vol. 6. Lincoln: University of Nebraska Press, 1965.

Titus, David A. *Palace and Politics in Prewar Japan.* New York: Columbia University Press, 1974.

Toby, Ronald P. *State and Diplomacy in Early Modern Japan: Asia in the Development of the Tokugawa Bakufu.* Princeton, N.J.: Princeton University Press, 1984.

Tokoro Rikio. "Edo no dekaseginin." In Nishiyama, ed. *Edo chōnin no kenkyū.* Vol. 3, 1974. 所理喜夫, 江戸の出稼人

Tokuda Kōjun, ed. *Shiryō Utsunomiya han shi.* Tokyo: Kashiwa shobō, 1971. 徳田浩淳, 史料宇都宮藩史, 柏書房

Tokutomi Iichirō. *Kinsei Nihon kokuminshi.* 100 vols. Tokyo: Jiji tsūshinsha, 1960–5. 徳富猪一郎, 近世日本国民史, 時事通信社

Totman, Conrad. *The Collapse of the Tokugawa Bakufu, 1862–1868.* Honolulu: University of Hawaii Press, 1980.

Totman, Conrad. "Fudai Daimyo and the Collapse of the Tokugawa Bakufu." *Journal of Asian Studies* 34 (May 1975): 581–91.

Totman, Conrad. "Political Reconciliation in the Tokugawa Bakufu: Abe Masahiro and Tokugawa Nariaki, 1844–1852." In Craig and Shively, eds. *Personality in Japanese History.*

Tottori-han shi. 7 vols. Tottori: Tottori kenritsu toshokan, 1971. 鳥取藩史, 鳥取:鳥取県立図書館

Tōyama Shigeki. *Meiji ishin.* Tokyo: Iwanami shoten, 1951. 遠山茂樹, 明治維新, 岩波書店

Tōyama Shigeki. *Meiji ishin to gendai.* Tokyo: Iwanami shoten, 1968. 遠山茂樹, 明治維新と現代, 岩波書店

Tōyama Shigeki. "Mimpōten ronsō no seijishiteki kōsatsu." In *Minkenron kara nashonarizumu e.* Tokyo: Ochanomizu shobō, 1957. 遠山茂樹, 民法典論争の

政治史的考察，明治史料研究連絡会，民権論からナショナリズムへ，御茶の水書房
Treat, P. J. *The Early Diplomatic Relations Between the United States and Japan, 1853-1868*. Baltimore: Johns Hopkins University Press, 1917.
Tsuda Hideo. *Hōken shakai kaitai katei kenkyū josetsu*. Tokyo: Hanawa shobō, 1970. 津田秀夫，封建社会解体過程研究序説，塙書房
Tsuda Hideo. *Tempō kaikaku*. Vol. 22 of *Nihon no rekishi*. Tokyo: Shogakkan, 1975. 津田秀夫，天保改革，小学館
Tsuda Hideo. "Tempō kaikaku no keizaishiteki igi." In Furushima, ed. *Nihon keizaishi taikei*. Vol. 4, 1965. 津田秀夫，天保改革の経済史的意義，古島敏雄編，日本経済史大系，東京大学出版会
Tsuji Tatsuya. "Tokugawa Nariaki to Mizuno Tadakuni." *Jimbutsu sōsho furoku*, no. 154. Tokyo: Yoshikawa kōbunkan. 辻達也，徳川斉昭と水野忠邦，人物叢書付録，吉川弘文館
Tsuji Zennosuke. *Nihon bunkashi*. Vol. 7. Tokyo: Shunjūsha, 1950. 辻善之助，日本文化史，春秋社
Tsunoda, R., and W. T. de Bary, eds. *Sources of Japanese Tradition*. New York: Columbia University Press, 1958.
Uete Michiari. *Nihon kindai shisō no keisei*. Tokyo: Iwanami shoten, 1974. 植手通有，日本近代思想の形成，岩波書店
Umegaki, Michio. *After the Restoration: The Beginnings of Japan's Modern State*. New York: New York University Press, 1988.
Umegaki, Michio. "From Domain to Prefecture." In Jansen and Rozman, eds. *Japan in Transition*.
Umemura Mataji et al., eds. *Nihon keizai no hatten: kinsei kara kindai e*. Vol. 1. Tokyo: Nihon keizai shimbunsha, 1976. 梅村又次等編，日本経済の発展：近世から近代へ，日本経済新聞社
Umetani Noboru. *Oyatoi gaikokujin: Meiji Nihon no wakiyakutachi*. Tokyo: Nihon Keizai shimbunsha, 1965. 梅渓昇，お雇い外国人：明治日本の脇役たち，日本経済新聞社
Uno, Helen. *Kokai Nikki: The Diary of the First Japanese Embassy to the United States of America*. Tokyo: Foreign Affairs Association of Japan, 1958.
Uyehara, George E. *The Political Development of Japan: 1867-1909*. London: Constable, 1910.
van der Chijs, J. A. *Neerlands Streven tot Openstelling van Japan voor den wereldhandel*. Amsterdam: Muller, 1867.
Varley, H. Paul. *Imperial Restoration in Medieval Japan*. New York: Columbia University Press, 1971.
Vernon, Manfred C. "The Dutch and the Opening of Japan." *Pacific Historical Review* 27 (February 1959): 39-48.
Vlastos, Stephen. *Peasant Protests and Uprisings in Tokugawa Japan*. Berkeley and Los Angeles: University of California Press, 1986.
Volker, T. *The Japanese Porcelain Trade of the Dutch East India Company After 1683*. Leiden: Brill, 1959.

Volker, T. *Porcelain and the Dutch East India Company 1602-1682.* Leiden: Brill, 1954.
Wada, T. *American Foreign Policy Toward Japan During the Nineteenth Century.* Tokyo, Tōyō bunko, 1928.
Wakabayashi, Bob Tadashi. *Anti-Foreign Thought and Western Learning in Early Modern Japan.* Cambridge, Mass.: Harvard University Press, 1985.
Walthall, Anne. "Narratives of Peasant Uprisings in Japan." *Journal of Japanese Studies* 42 (May 1983): 571-87.
Ward, Robert E., ed. *Political Development in Modern Japan.* Princeton, N.J.: Princeton University Press, 1968.
Waswo, Ann. *Japanese Landlords: The Decline of a Rural Elite.* Berkeley and Los Angeles: University of California Press, 1977.
Watanabe Shūjirō. *Abe Masahiro jiseki.* 2 vols. Tokyo, 1910. 渡辺修二郎, 阿部正弘事蹟
Watson, Burton. *Japanese Literature in Chinese.* 2 vols. New York: Columbia University Press, 1976.
Webb, Herschel. "The Development of an Orthodox Attitude Toward the Imperial Institution in the Nineteenth Century." In Jansen, ed. *Changing Japanese Attitudes Toward Modernization.*
Webb, Hershel. *The Japanese Imperial Institution in the Tokugawa Period.* New York: Columbia University Press, 1968.
Williams, S. Wells. "Narrative of the Voyage of the Ship Morrison, Captain D. Ingersoll, to Lewchew and Japan, in the Months of July and August, 1837." Canton: *The Chinese Repository*, vol. 6, nos. 5, 8 (September, December 1837); 1942 Tokyo reprint, pp. 209-29, 353-80.
Wilson, George. "The Bakumatsu Intellectual in Action: Hashimoto Sanai and the Political Crisis of 1858." In Craig and Shively, eds. *Personality in Japanese History.*
Wilson, Robert A. *Genesis of the Meiji Government in Japan 1868-1871.* Berkeley and Los Angeles: University of California Press, 1957.
Yamaguchi Kazuo. *Bakumatsu bōeki shi.* Tokyo: Chūō kōronsha, 1943. 山口和雄, 幕末貿易史, 中央公論社
Yamaguchi Kazuo. *Meiji zenki keizai no bunseki.* Tokyo: Tokyo daigaku shuppankai, 1956. 山口和雄, 明治前期経済の分析, 東京大学出版会
Yamaguchi-ken kyōikukai, ed. *Yoshida Shōin zenshū.* 11 vols. Tokyo: Iwanami shoten, 1934-6. 山口県教育会, 吉田松陰全集, 岩波書店
Yamaji Aizan. "Niijima Jō ron." In Yamaji Aizan, *Kirisutokyō hyōron, Nihon jimminshi.* Tokyo: Iwanami shoten, 1966. 山路愛山, "新島襄論"山路愛山, 基督教評論, 日本人民史, 岩波書店
Yamamoto Shirō. "Taishō seihen to goken undō." *Rekishi kōron* 9 (1976): 30-41. 山本四郎, 大正政変と護憲運動, 歴史公論
Yamamura, Kozo. "The Meiji Land Tax Reform and Its Effects." In Jansen and Rozman, eds. *Japan in Transition.*
Yamamura, Kozo. "Pre-Industrial Landholding Patterns in Japan and

England." In Craig, ed. *Japan: A Comparative View.*
Yamamura, Kozo. *A Study of Samurai Income and Entrepreneurship: Quantitative Analyses of Economic and Social Aspects of the Samurai in Tokugawa and Meiji Japan.* Cambridge, Mass.: Harvard University Press, 1974.
Yamanaka Einosuke. *Nihon kindai kokka no keisei to kanryōsei.* Tokyo: Kōbundō, 1974. 山中永之佑, 日本近代国家の形成と官僚制, 弘文堂
Yamanaka Hisao. "Bakumatsu hansei kaikaku no hikaku hanseishiteki kenkyū." *Chihōshi kenkyū.* 14 (1954): 47–56. 山中壽夫, 幕末藩政改革の比較藩政史的研究, 地方史研究
Yamazaki Masashige, ed. *Yokoi Shōnan ikō.* Tokyo: Meiji Shoin, 1942. 山崎正董編, 横井小楠遺稿, 明治書院
Yamori Kazuhiko. *Toshi puran no kenkyū.* Tokyo: Ōmeido, 1970. 矢守一彦, 都市プランの研究, 大明堂
Yasuba, Yasukichi. "Anatomy of the Debate on Japanese Capitalism." *Journal of Japanese Studies* 2 (Autumn 1975): 63–82.
Yasumaru Yoshio. *Nihon kindaika to minshū shisō.* Tokyo: Aoki shoten, 1974. 安丸良夫, 日本近代化と民衆思想, 青木書店
Yazaki, Takeo. *Social Change and the City in Japan.* Tokyo: Japan Publications, 1968.
Yokoi Shōnan. *Kokuze sanron.* Translated by D. Y. Miyauchi, *Monumenta Nipponica* 23 (1968): 156–86.
Yokoi Tokio, ed. *Shōnan ikō.* Tokyo: Min'yūsha, 1889. 横井時雄編, 小楠遺稿, 民友社
Yokoyama Kazuo. "'Han' kokka e no michi." In Hayashiya, ed. *Kasei bunka no kenkyū.* 横山俊夫,「藩」国家への道
Yokoyama Toshio. *Hyakushō ikki to gimin denshō.* Tokyo: Kyōikusha rekishi shinsho, 1977. 横山十四男, 百姓一揆と義民伝承, 教育社歴史新書
Yoshida, Tadashi. "The Rangaku of Shizuki Tadao: The Introduction of Western Science in Tokugawa Japan." Ph.D. diss., Princeton University, 1974.
Yoshinaga Akira. "Han sembai seido no kiban to kōzō: Matsushiro-han sambutsu kaisho shihō o megutte." In Furushima, ed. *Nihon keizaishi taikei.* Vol. 4, 1965. 吉永昭, 藩専売制度の基盤と構造：松代藩産物会所仕法をめぐって, 古島敏雄編, 日本経済史大系, 東京大学出版会
Zolbrud, Leon M. *Takizawa Bakin.* New York: Twayne, 1967.

GLOSSARY-INDEX

Abe Masahiro 阿部正弘, *rōjū*, (senior councilor), 6, 17–18, 19n, 273–5, 280–1, 315–16, 326
absolutism (*zettaishugi*), as description of Meiji state, 619, 673, 732
agechi rei 上知令 (bakufu confiscation of Kantō lands), 153–4, 157, 159, 163
Aikokukōtō 愛国公党 (Public Party of Patriots), 402–3, 424, 654, 737
  see also people's rights movement
Aikokusha/Kokkai kisei dōmei 愛国社/国会期成同盟 (League for the Establishment of a National Assembly), 406, 410, 412–13
Aizawa Yasushi (Seishisai) 会沢安(正志斎), 12, 111–15, 117, 129, 132, 137, 167, 182–4, 186–92, 272, 314
Aizu domain 会津藩, 324–5, 343, 358
Alcock, Sir Rutherford (British diplomat), 286, 289–90, 295–9, 333, 338
alternate attendance, system of, *see sankin kōtai*
American Pacific Mail Line, 609
ampo 日米安全保障条約(安保) (U.S.-Japan Security treaty), 45
Andō Hiroshige 安藤広重, 72, 74, 117
Andō Nobumasa 安藤信正 (bakufu official), 196, 333
Anegakōji Kintomo 姉小路公知, 329
Angell, Norman, 768
Ansei purge (*Ansei no taigoku*) 安政の大獄, 18–19, 194, 318–19, 328, 330
  see also Ii Naosuke
Aoki Shūzō 青木周蔵
  and Fukuzawa Yukichi, 453
  as student in Germany, 652
Arai Hakuseki 新井白石, 88
Arima Shinshichi, 有馬新七, 195
Arisugawa Taruhito 有栖川熾仁, prince, 359, 397
Ashikaga bakufu 足利幕府, 8–9

Ashikaga Yoshimitsu 足利義満, 9
Ashio Copper Mine pollution incident 足尾銅山, 709, 716
Asianism (pan-Asianism), as justification for actions in China and Korea, 756–7, 672–3
asobi 遊び (play, culture of), 168–77
  contemporary critiques of, 178–82
Awa (Tokushima) domain 阿波(徳島)藩, 130

Baba Tatsui 馬場辰猪, and Japan's "return to Japan", 489, 491
bakufu 幕府 (shogunal government)
  economic role, 573–8, 591, 597–8
  see also agechi rei; Bunkyū reforms of 1862; foreign relations/trade; Kansei reforms; Meiji Restoration; Tempō reforms
bakuhan system (*bakuhan taisei*) 幕藩体制, *bakufu-han* political order
  contrasted with modern nation-state, 432
  nature of, 131, 573
bakumatsu 幕末, as historical metaphor, 168–70
Bakuro-chō 馬喰町 (bakufu finance office), 598–9
Bank of Japan 日本銀行, 31–2
bansha no goku 蕃者の獄 (purge of scholars of foreign learning), 106, 235–6
Bansho shirabesho 蕃書調所 (Institute for the Study of Barbarian Books), 106, 314
basara 婆娑羅・時勢粧 (ostentation), 9, 169
benihana 紅花 (safflower), 583
Bentham, Jeremy, 480
Benyowsky, Moritz von, 94
Biddle, Commodore James, 17, 268, 315
Boissonade, Gustave Emile, and Japanese civil code, 472–5, 487

813

Bonin Islands (Ogasawara Shotō), 98, 125
Book of Rites (Li Chi), 485
Boshin Civil War of 1868-9 戊辰戦争, 18, 21-2, 357-9
Boshin shōsho (Imperial Rescript of 1908) 戊辰詔書, 715
Bousquet, Georges, and use of French legal code in Japan, 473
Boxer Rebellion 義和団, 774
Buchanan, President James, and Treaty of Amity and Commerce, 457
Buckle, Henry Thomas, English historian, 480, 697
Buddhism 仏教, and Japanese national character, 663, 687, 700
bugyō 奉行 (magistrate), 278
bummei byō 文明病 (civilization sickness), 708-9, 715
bummei kaika 文明開化 ("civilization and enlightenment"), 676-83, 686, 688, 690-2, 694-5, 697, 699-701, 703, 705-6, 708, 711, 716-17
Bunkyū reforms of 1862 文久改革, 22, 327, 329-33, 384-9
see also kōbu-gattai
Bunsei reforms of 1827-8 文政改革, 14, 84-5
burakumin 部落民, (oppressed class) 526
bureaucracy, 644-5, 649, 659, 661, 672, 729
Bureau of Astronomy (Translation Office), 14, 101, 103, 166
Burke, Edmund, and European conservatism, 674
bushi 武士 (warrior), 74
Buyō Inshi 武陽隠士, author of Seji kemmon roku, 63-4, 74-6, 81, 178-9, 215

cabinet, creation of, 648-9
calendar reform, 471
Cass, Louis, and Treaty of Amity and Commerce, 457
Central Chamber, 641, 647-8, 656
centralized feudalism, 500
Chamberlain, Basil Hall (British scholar), 492
Charter Oath, 6, 18, 24, 26, 28-9, 35, 359, 365, 404, 561-62
Chichibu komminto 秩父困民党, 422-4
Chichibu rebellion 秩父事件, 32, 417, 421-4, 430-1
chihō kairyō undō 地方改良運動 (rural improvement movement), 713-13, 715
chihōkan kaigi 地方官会議 (assembly of provincial governors), 655-6
chiji 知事 (governors), appointment of, 631, 644-6, 668
childbirth and birth control/infanticide, 554-6
China
  colonization of, 759, 767
  dispute with, over Ryūkyūs: 742-4
  as model, 443, 634, 642, 645, 649
  and Western imperialism, 770
  see also foreign relations/trade
chiso kaisei (land tax reform), 28, 272-82, 430, 607-8, 615, 636-9
chokunin 勅任 (Imperial appointee)
  differentiated from sōnin 奏任 and hannin 判任, 649-50;
  as rank, 652, 668
chōnin 町人 (townspeople)
  differentiated into artisans (shokunin 職人) and merchants (shōnin 商人), 505, 509, 545
  merchant culture (chōnin bunka 町人文化), 512-13, 563
  in Tokugawa society, 504-16, 527-8, 530-3, 538, 540-1, 543, 545, 556, 564
Chōshū domain 長州藩 bakufu expedition against, 345
  in bakumatsu politics, 21-5, 28, 128, 293-8, 323-9, 334-6, 343-7, 351, 353, 355-8
  economy, 19, 20, 23
  Tempō reforms, 135, 137-8, 161-2, 164-5
  victory of loyalists in, 346-7
Christianity, 28, 114, 287, 472, 481, 489-91, 677
  and Niijima Jo, 449, 479-80
Chronicle of the return to antiquity, 35-6
Chu Hsi 朱熹, Confucian philosopher 55-6, 245
civil code, 34, 474-6
"civilization and enlightenment," see bummei kaika
civilization sickness, 708-9, 715
Clark, William S., and Hokkaido school, 472
clothing, Western, official use of, 471
Code of Civil Procedure, 694
  see also civil code

Confucianism, 442, 444–5, 486, 579, 620, 650, 678, 680–5, 695, 701, 708
Conscription Act, 386, 607, 636, 643
Constitutional Progressive Party, 414
currency crisis (*bakumatsu*), 285–7, 331–2, 601–2
Curtius, Donker, 275–8, 283

daijin 大臣 (minister), 648
daijōsai 大嘗祭 (imperial ceremony), 191–2
daikan 代官 (intendant), 54–5
daimyōjin 大明神 (deity), 55
Dai Nihon shi 大日本史 (History of Great Japan), 182
Daishin-in 大審院 (Supreme Court), 642
dajō daijin 太政大臣 (minister of state), 52, 642
Dajōkan 太政官 (Council of State), 28, 32, 641, 647, 652–3, 656–8, 660, 666, 669
dajōkansatsu 太政官札 (Meiji government currency), 606
Date Munenari 伊達宗城 (daimyo of Uwajima), 166, 332, 356, 626
Defoe, Daniel, and reception of *Robinson Crusoe* in Japan, 479–80
dekasegi 出稼ぎ (sojourning for work away from home), 515
Department of Civil Affairs, early role of, 643
Department of Rites, 643
Deshima (Dejima) 出島, Dutch trading system in Nagasaki, 3, 22, 87–8, 97–8, 103, 104, 105
Diet, Imperial, bicameral legislature established by Meiji constitution, 32, 664–6, 668–9, 671, 684, 692, 712, 716, 749, 751, 758–60, 762
Discourse on Japanese morality, 684
Doeff, Hendrik, 72, 90, 98, 103–4
Doeff ("Halma") Dictionary, 14, 440–1
Dōgen 道元, (thirteenth century Zen monk), ideas compared to those of Benjamin Franklin, 485
Doi Toshitsura 土井利位, successor of Mizuno Tadakuni as *rōjū*, 599
domain schools (*hankō*) 藩校, 57
Dutch East India Company, 3, 436, 438
Dutch studies, *see yōgaku/rangaku*

Echigoya 越後屋, forerunner of Mitsukoshi department store, 594

economy
  Bunka-Bunsei period, 13–14, 571–3
  commercialization, 14, 580
  effects of foreign trade on, 286–7, 600–5
  Meiji policies, 605–14
  policy and administration of, 573–9
  rural, 71–84, 127–8, 148, 183, 581–5
  Tempō reforms and, 82, 148–55, 587–600
  urban, 587–7
Edo 江戸, Kansei reforms and, 53–4, 62–7, 143, 536–8
Edokko 江戸っ子, 66–7
Edo Town Office 江戸町会所, 54
education
  Kansei reforms and, 55–8
  in Meiji, 560–2
  Ordinance of 1872, 680
ee ja nai ka ええじゃないか (ain't it grand? movement of 1867), 217, 221, 365
Egawa Hidetatsu (Tarōzaemon) 江川英龍 (太郎左衛門) (bakufu intendant), 108–10, 146, 239–42
election law, 663
Elgin, James Bruce, 8th Earl of, 283
emigration, 759, 761–2
Enlightenment, the Japanese, 674–7, 680
Enomoto Takeaki 榎本武揚, 358, 453, 741
eta and *hinin* 穢多・非人 suppressed classes, *See burakumin*
Etō Shimpei 江藤新平, early Meiji leader, 28, 383, 388–91, 402
  see also Saga rebellion
Etorofu, 96
expansionism (*hattenshugi*) 発展主義, 761–2, 765, 780
extraterritoriality, 735–6, 764
  See also unequal treaties and treaty revision

factory laws, 708, 710–11, 713
Fenollosa, Ernest
  and neotraditional movement, 691, 694
feudalism, 504–5, 619–22, 628, 631, 662, 671, 681, 745
Fillmore, President Millard, and Perry mission, 449–50
foreign employees of Meiji government, distribution by ministry, 468–9
foreign relations/trade, 9–10, 12, 124–6, 146–7, 259–307, 314–20, 324–42
  with China, 3, 88–9, 261, 754–7, 761

foreign relations/trade (*cont.*)
  domestic debate over, *bakumatsu*, 271–84, 287–303, 314–20
  domestic opposition to, 288–9, 291, 298, 303, 320–4
  effects of, on domestic economy, 286–7, 339–42
  with France, 283–5, 294–5, 299, 338, 350–1
  with Great Britain, 97, 125–6, 261–4, 270, 283–5, 289–93, 298–303, 306, 338, 764, 774, 778, 781
  with Holland, 3, 87–91, 97–8, 261, 275–7, 283, 294
  and imperial court, 282, 284, 298–303
  with Korea, 3, 5, 31–2, 88, 387–8, 744–7, 751–8, 761, 777
  opening of ports, 20, 270, 280, 304–7, 333
  with Russia, 93–7, 265–7, 271, 276–7, 284–5, 338, 459, 776–8
  with Ryūkyūs, 3, 5
  treaties, 31, 270–1, 301–2, *see also* unequal treaties and treaty revision
  with United States, 45, 267–70, 277–85, 294, 306, 316, 339, 458, 765, 778, 781
  volume of late Tokugawa, 305–6, 339–40
France
  colonialism, 747
  as model, 465, 472–4, 635, 642, 701
  see also foreign relations/trade
Franklin, Benjamin, influence in Japan, 484–5
French Revolution and definition of liberal thought, 674–5
fudai 譜代 (hereditary vassals) 18
fudasashi 札差 (rice brokers), 53, 598
Fujikō 富士講 (Fuji cult), 184, 216, 220
Fujita Tōko 藤田東湖, Mito thinker, 12, 112, 124, 167, 182, 184–5, 187–9, 272
Fujita Yūkoku 藤田幽谷, Mito thinker, 112–13, 182–91, 193
Fukkoki 復古記 (Chronicle of the return to antiquity), 35–6
fukoku kyōhei 富国強兵 (rich country, strong army), 87, 467
Fukuchi Gen'ichirō 福地源一郎, 327
Fukui (Echizen) domain 福井（越前）藩, 20, 134, 136, 161–2
Fukuoka domain 福岡藩, 135–8

Fukuoka Kōtei (Takachika) 福岡孝弟, and Charter Oath, 623, 626
Fukushima incident 福島事件, 32, 405–8
  see also Kōno Hironaka; Mishima Michitsune
Fukuzawa Yukichi 福沢諭吉, 38–9, 336–7, 409, 449, 453, 458–62, 464, 470, 481, 486, 676, 678–80, 696, 705–6, 752–4
Funai domain 船井藩, 136–7
fūsetsugaki 風説書 (reports of Dutch factors), 87, 89, 97
Futabatei Shimei 二葉亭四迷, author of *Ukigumo* (*Floating Clouds*), 486–7, 694

gaikoku bugyō 外国奉行 (foreign affairs magistrate), 335
gekka jiken 激化事件 (violent incidents), 417
"gemeinschaft," 46, 526–7
genrō 元老 (elder statesman), 667, 669–70
Genrō-in 元老院 (senate), 219, 652, 656–7, 660, 662
Germany (Prussia)
  colonialism, 747
  as model, 433–4, 464–5, 620, 643, 646, 648, 655, 657–8, 660–3, 672, 698–701, 704–5, 708, 710, 731
  see also foreign relations/trade
gesaku 戯作 (literature of play), 171, 177
Gi-in 議院 (lower house), 654
gijō 議定 (councilor), 359, 625–6
gimin 義民 (martyr), 380
giseikan 議政官 (legislature), 626
Glynn, Commander James, 268–9
Gneist, Rudolph, and Meiji constitution, 433–5, 660, 698–9
gokajō no seimon 五ヶ条の誓文, *see* Charter Oath
gokenin 御家人 (bakufu retainer), 83
Golovnin, Vasilii, 96–7, 266
gonin gumi 五人組 (five-household organization), 527
gōnō 豪農 (wealthy farmer), 71, 519–20
gosanke 御三家 (collateral houses of the Tokugawa), 18
gōshi 郷士 (rural samurai), 71
gōso 強訴 (demonstration), 369
Gotō domain 五島藩, 20
Gotō Konzan 後藤艮山, and Chinese medical thought, 445–6
Gotō Shojirō 後藤象二郎, Meiji political

GLOSSARY-INDEX

leader, 387–8, 402, 405, 407, 414, 626, 647, 653–4, 669
goyōkin 御用金 (forced loans), 330, 598
goyō shōnin 御用商人 (quartermasters), 507
Great Britain
  colonialism, 747
  as model, 465, 657–9, 672
  see also foreign relations/trade
Great Principles of Education, 682
Gros, Baron, 283
Guizot, François, 480
gun 郡 (county), 209, 644
Gutzlaff, Charles, 107, 125
Gyōseikan 行政官 (Executive Council), 626

Hagi rebellion 萩事件, 22
  see also Maebara Issei
haihan chiken 廃藩置県 (abolition of domains), 25, 384–5, 628, 633–5, 637, 643
Halma, François, 440–1
hambatsu 藩閥 (domain clique), 671–3
han 藩 (domain)
  alliances between, 355
  and bakufu economic policies, 573–80
  and education, 57
  roles in Restoration, 324–35
  trade between, 20
  travel, 65
Hanabusa Yoshitada 花房義質 (minister to Korea), 752
han nationalism, 326
hansatsu 藩札 (domain currency), 152, 578–80, 586, 590–1, 596, 616
hanseki hōkan 藩籍奉還 (return of domain registers), 24–5, 628–30, 632, 641
Hara Takashi (Kei, Satoshi) 原敬 Seiyūkai politician, 670
Hardy, Alpheus, and Niijima Jō, 453–4
Harris, Townsend, U.S. consul, 17–18, 277–83, 285–6, 289, 316–17, 456, 566, 601, 604
Hashimoto Sanai 橋本左内, Fukui domain samurai, 247, 318–19, 321, 328, 444
hatake 畑・畠 (dry field), 378
hatamoto 旗本 (bannerman), 75, 537, 575
Hawaii, Japanese emigration to, 750, 759, 761–2
Hawks, Francis L., and Perry mission, 450–1
Hayashi Shihei 林子平, *keiseika* (political economist), 59, 94–5, 98–9, 101–2, 232, 272, 274
Hayashiya Tatsusaburō 林屋辰三郎 8–10, 169, 171
Hearn, Lafcadio, on Japan's "return to Japan," 489–92
heimin 平民 (commoners), 525
Heimin shimbun 平民新聞 (People's daily), socialist newspaper, 776
heiminshugi 平民主義 (democracy, "common people"), and Tokutomi Sohō, 679
Hepburn, James, author of *Wa-Ei gorin shūsei*, 441
Heusken, Henry, 288–9
Hijikata Hisamoto 土方久元, 36
Hirata Atsutane 平田篤胤, 112, 117, 174, 178, 199–206, 208, 210, 215, 226, 312
Hirata Tōsuke 平田東助, 712–13
Hirohito 裕仁, Shōwa emperor, 35
Hirose Tansō 広瀬淡窓, 61, 129–31
Hiroshima domain 広島藩, 20, 138
Historiographical Institute 史料編纂所, 36–7
Hitotsubashi (Tokugawa) Harusada 一橋治済, 51
Hizen domain 肥前藩, 161
Hokkaidō (Ezo) 北海道/蝦夷, 1, 5, 12–15, 29, 32, 94–7, 272
hōkōnin 奉公人 (hired laborers), 510–11, 522, 558
Holland, 263, 315, 352, 467
  see also foreign relations/trade; *yōgaku/Rangaku*; Deshima
Honda Toshiaki 本多利明, *keiseika* (political economist), 94–5, 98, 232–4, 237, 272, 274
Hori Chikashige 堀親寰, 159
Hori Tatsunosuke 堀達之助, author of *Ei-Wa taiyaku shūchin jisho* (English-Japanese dictionary), 441
hōtoku 奉徳 (return of virtue), 85
Hotta Masayoshi 堀田正睦, 18, 273–6, 278–9, 281–4, 316–17, 336
House of Peers 貴族院, 32, 647, 661, 664
House of Representatives 衆議院 664, 668
Hozumi Yatsuka 穂積八束, on Japanese civil code, 474–5, 477, 700–2
hyakushō 百姓 (peasant) (*see also nōmin*), 208, 517–19, 576
Hyōgo (Kōbe) 兵庫(神戸), 304–5

Ichikawa Ebizō (seventh Danjūrō) 市川海老蔵(団十郎VII), 145

ie 家 (house), 205, 474–7, 549–54, 556
igaku no kin 異学の禁 (proscription of heterodoxy), 56
Ii Naoaki 井伊直亮, 142, 166
Ii Naosuke 井伊直弼, *tairō* (great councilor), 18–19, 22, 193, 274, 283–4, 288, 317–21, 327, 330, 336, 449
Ikeda Chōhatsu (Nagaoki, Naganobu) 池田長発, 294–6, 454
ikki 一揆 (violent protest), 502
Ikuta Yorozu 生田万, 207–8
Imbanuma reclamation 印旛沼干拓, 148, 153, 157, 163
imperial court 朝廷, 19–20, 195, 318–20, 342–5, 365
Imperial Household Law, 663
imperial institution, 618–21, 624, 628–9, 631, 652–3, 656, 658, 660–9, 672, 680, 689–99, 697, 700–3, 719, 731
imperialism
 Japanese, 748–50, 765–7, 769–71, 773–4
 Western, 760, 768, 770
 see also foreign relations/trade
Imperial Rescript of 1908 (*Boshin shōsho*), 715
Imperial Rescript on Eduction 教育勅語, 6, 494–7, 562, 684–5, 687, 700
Imperial Rescript to Soldiers and Sailors 軍人勅諭, 646
Inagaki Manjirō 稲垣満次郎, author of *Tōhōsaku* (Eastern policy), 761
Inamura Sampaku 稲村三伯
 author of *Edo Halma*, 440
 see also Halma, François
Industrial Cooperatives Law of 1899, 712–13
"industrious revolution" (*kinben kakumei*), concept of Hayami Akira, 499, 524
Inō Tadataka 伊能忠敬, explorer and cartographer, 103
Inoue Kaoru, 井上馨, Meiji oligarch, 36, 295–6, 337, 348, 393, 453, 487–8, 626, 637, 667, 689–90, 693, 756
Inoue Kiyonao 井上清直, 279
Inoue Kowashi 井上毅, Meiji leader, 250, 474–7, 487, 493–4, 648, 660–3, 672, 683
Inoue Tetsujirō 井上哲次郎, 686–7
Institute for the Study of Barbarian Books, 106, 314
Ise, Grand Shrine 伊勢神宮, 64–5, 120, 215–16, 702
 see also okagemairi
Isekō 伊勢講, 218
Ishibashi Sukezaemon 石橋助左衛門, 98
Ishikawa Takuboku 石川啄木, poet, 717, 780
ishin 維新 (restoration), 11
Ishin shi 維新史 (history of the Restoration), 36
Itagaki Taisuke 板垣退助, Jiyūtō leader, 28–30, 36, 379, 384, 387–8, 390, 393, 400, 402, 404–5, 407, 413–14, 418, 423, 626, 633, 642, 647, 653–5, 659, 669–70
 see also Jiyūtō; "People's Rights" movement
Itō Hirobumi 伊藤博文, Meiji statesman, 7, 30, 32–4, 295–6, 347–8, 434–5, 453, 463, 465, 469, 470, 476, 626, 628–9, 631, 633, 640, 647–50, 656–8, 660, 662–72, 683–4, 697–700, 702, 714, 738, 756, 767, 774, 778–9
Itō Jinsai 伊藤仁斎, 56, 445–6
Itō Miyoji 伊東巳代治, 660
Iwakura mission of 1871–3 岩倉遣外使節, 26, 28, 37, 455, 462–3, 465
Iwakura Tomoni 岩倉具視, early Meiji leader, 257, 337, 353–4, 357, 387–8, 390, 393, 410, 463, 465, 621, 626, 629, 631, 633, 640–1, 643, 647, 652, 656–8, 660, 662, 672, 722, 736, 745, 753
Iwasaki Yatarō 岩崎弥太郎, founder of Mitsubishi, 609
Iwase Tadanari 岩瀬忠震, 279, 456

Janes, Leroy L., 40, 391–2, 472, 480
Japan Communist Party 日本共産党, 42, 45, 362
Jimmu, Emperor 神武天皇, legendary first emperor of Japan, 663
Jingikan and Jingishō 神祇官・神祇省 (Department of Rites), 643
jinsei 仁政 (benevolent government), 75
jinzai 人材 ("men of talent"), 235, 650
Jippensha Ikku 十返舎一九, 68–9, 175–6
Jiyū minken undō 自由民権運動, *see* "People's Rights" movement
Jiyūtō 自由党 (Liberal Party), 29–30, 32, 34, 413–18, 420–1, 423–4, 428, 659, 669
 see also Itagaki Taisuke; "People's Rights" movement
jōiron 攘夷論 (expulsionism), 195

jōkamachi 城下町 (castle towns), 504, 534–47
jōmen 定免 (fixed tax rate), 77–8
jōyaku kaisei 条約改正 (revision of unequal treaties), 467
   see also foreign relations/trade
Jūnin ryōgae 十人両替, see Ten Exchange Houses

Kabasan incident 加波山事件, 417–19
kabuki かぶき, 9, 169
kabunakama 株仲間 (licensed commercial associations), 150–2, 585, 595
Kaempfer, Engelbert, 64, 88, 90–1
Kaga domain 加賀藩 128
Kagawa Shūan 香川修庵, 446
Kagoshima 鹿児島, 23, 297, 326, 334, 342
Kaiho Seiryō 海保青陵, 86–7, 173–4
kaikaku 改革 (reform), 133
   see also Kansei reforms; Tempō reforms
kaikoku 開国 (opening of country), 432
kaishin 改新 (reform), 133
Kaishintō 改新党 (Reform Party), 659
Kakegawa domain 掛川藩, 61
Kakizaki Hakyō 蠣崎波響, 61
Kamakura bakufu 鎌倉幕府 8–9
kami 神 (deity), 60
Kamo Mabuchi 賀茂真淵, 185, 198–9
kampaku 関白 (regent for mature emperor), 624, 628
Kanai Noburu 金井延, 705–8, 711
kana zōshi 仮名草紙, 68
Kanda Kōhei (Takahira) 神田孝平, and land tax reform, 637, 676
Kaneko Kentarō 金子堅太郎, 36, 650, 660, 709, 779
Kansei reforms 寛政改革, 5, 7–8, 12, 50–62, 70, 148–9, 172, 645
   see also Matsudaira Sadanobu
Karafuto, 266, 271, 307, 459, 740–1, 777
   see also Sakhalin
kashindan 家臣団, (retainer corps), 385
Kataoka Kenkichi 片岡健吉, 406, 410
Katō Hiroyuki 加藤弘之, 106, 676
Katsu Kaishū (Awa, Rintarō) 勝海舟 (安房, 麟太郎), late Tokugawa official, 349, 356, 358, 459, 462, 642
Katsura Takashige 桂誉重, 211–12
Katsura Tarō 桂太郎, Meiji leader, 710, 775, 780
Katsushika Hokusai 葛飾北斎, 72, 116–17
Kattendycke, Huyssen van, foreign employee of late Tokugawa government, 467
Kawaji Toshiakira 川路聖謨, 142, 245
Kawakami Hajime 河上肇, early Marxist thinker, 709
kawase gaisha 為替会社 (exchange houses), 606
Kawate Bunjirō (Konkō Daijin) 川手文治郎 (金光大神), 228–31
Kayahara Kazan 茅原華山, on expansionism, 779
kazoku 華族 (peerage), 25, 631, 646–7, 659
Kazu no Miya 和宮, imperial princess, 195, 331, 337
keiseika 経世家 (political economist), 73
keisei saimin 経世済民 (political economy), 231
kaizai shakai 経済社会 (economic society), concept of Hayami Akira, 524
kemmi 検見 (annual tax assessment), 77
kempeitai 憲兵隊 (military police), 646
ken 県 (prefecture), 209
kibyōshi 黄表紙 (illustrated tales), 70
Kido Takayoshi (Kōin) 木戸孝允, early Meiji leader, 22, 25–8, 347, 355, 384, 387–8, 393, 405, 433, 455, 463, 465, 626, 629, 631, 633, 642, 647, 652, 654–6, 660, 744–5
kigensetsu 紀元節 (anniversary of supposed accession of first emperor), 663
kiheitai 奇兵隊, 346
Kim Ok-kyun 金玉均 and Korean "independence" movement, 755
Kimura Yoshitake (Kaishū) 木村喜毅 (芥舟), and first Japanese mission to the U.S., 458
kimben kakumei 勤勉革命, see "industrious revolution"
King, Charles, American merchant, 124–5
Kinoshita Naoe 木下尚江, 716–17
Kira Yoshinaka 吉良義央 and "southern barbarian" surgery, 445
Kirino Toshiaki 桐野利秋, 385, 396
kōbu gattai 公武合体 (unity of court and bakufu), 22, 325–35, 344–5, 355–7
Kōda Rohan 幸田露伴, and *Self-Help*, 482–3
kodōron 古道論 (ancient way), 199, 204
kōgi 公儀 (polity), 59
kōgisho 公議所 (early Meiji chamber), 626, 631, 651
Koide Hidezane 小出秀実, leader of 1866–7

bakufu mission to Europe, 459
Kojiki 古事記 (Record of Ancient Matters), 445
Kōkaku, Emperor 光格天皇, 51
kokkeibon 滑稽本 (amusing books), 175
kokkyō 国教 (national doctrine), 683
koku 石 (measure of capacity), 54
kokudaka 石高, 360, 516, 574
kokugaku 国学 (national learning, nativism), 57–8, 86n, 198–217, 219, 221, 226, 233, 257, 312, 435, 445
Kokumin no tomo 国民之友 (*The Nation's Friend*), and Tokutomi Sohō, 679
kokuminshugi 国民主義 (nationalism) and Kuga Katsunan, 686–7
Kokura domain 小倉藩, 20, 135–6
kokusui hozon 国粋保存 (preservation of the national essence), 692, 717
kokutai 国体 (national polity), 38, 185, 191–3, 496, 662, 700–1
Kōmei, Emperor 孝明天皇, 23, 282, 284, 298, 301, 303, 315, 317, 331, 344, 353
Konkō Daijin 金光大神, *see* Kawate Bunjirō
Konkōkyō 金光教, 216–17, 219, 222, 228–31
Konoe Atsumaro 近衛篤麿, founder of Tōa Dōbun Shoin, 772
Kōno Hironaka 河野広中, 32, 406–7, 410, 414–16, 417n
Konrad, N. I., and Japanese-Russian dictionary, 441n
Korea
  colonization of, 759, 763–4, 766, 769, 771, 774–5, 779–81
  plans to punish (sei-Kan ron), 387–9
  Western attempts to influence, 760
  see also foreign relations/trade
Kosugi Genteki 小杉玄適, 447
Kōtoku Shūsui 幸徳秋水, anarchist thinker, 36n, 717, 771, 773, 776
Kōzaha 講座派 (lectures factions), 41–3, 361–2
Kozaki Hiromichi 小崎弘道, 37
Kozeki (Ozeki) San'ei 小関三英, 107–8
Krusenstern, Adam, 265
Kudō Heisuke 工藤平助, 94, 99, 232
Kuga Katsunan 陸羯南, opposition to indiscriminate westernization, 685–7, 690–1, 693, 702–3, 717
kuge 公家 (court nobility), 52
  see also kazoku
"Kumamoto band" 熊本バンド, 40

Kumamoto domain 熊本藩, 77, 137
Kume Kunitake 久米邦武, 26, 463–4, 702, 736
Kunikida Doppo 国木田独歩, 483
Kunisada Chūji 国定忠次, 81
Kuper, Vice-Admiral, 296
Kuril islands (Chishima) 千島列島, 1, 5, 28, 94–6, 271, 307
Kurimoto Joun 栗本鋤雲, 350, 473
Kurisaki Dō-u 栗崎道有, 445
Kuriyama Kōan 栗山幸庵, 447
Kuroda Kiyotaka 黒田清隆, Meiji leader, 667, 746
Kuroda Kozan 黒田湖山, and translation of *Robinson Crusoe*, 478–9
Kurozumikyō 黒住教, 216–17, 219–20, 222–5, 229
Kurozumi Munetada 黒住宗忠, 219, 222–5
  see also Kurozumikyō
Kurume domain 久留米藩, 136
Kusaka Genzui 草坂玄瑞, 10
Kuwata Kumazō, 桑田熊蔵 and Shakai seisaku gakkai, 707–8
Kuze Hirochika 久世広周, 289
kyōdōtai 共同体 ("gemeinschaft"), 46, 526–7
Kyōgaku taishi 教学大旨 (great principles of education), 682
Kyōhō reforms 享保改革, 5, 52, 148–9
  see also Tokugawa Yoshimune
kyōkaku 俠客 (chivalrous adventurer), 10, 81
Kyoto 京都, 62, 64–7, 330–2

land tax reform 地租改正, 28, 372–82, 430, 607–8, 615, 636–9
Law of the Houses of the Diet, 663
Laxman, Adam, 95–6, 100
League for the Establishment of a National Assembly, 406, 410, 412–13
Left Chamber (Sa-in), 642, 652–3, 656
Liang Ch'i-ch'ao 梁啓超. Chinese reformer, 773
Liaotung peninsula 遼東半島
  cession to Japan, 767–8
  cession to Russia, 774
Liberal Party, *see* Jiyūtō
Li Chi 礼記 (*Book of Rites*), 485
Li Hung-chang 李鴻章, 756
literacy, 67–8, 512–13
literary culture, 68–71

local administration, 31–2, 54–5, 82–4
local assemblies, 659, 663, 712
local improvement movement, 719
London Protocol, 290–1, 299, 301–2
loyalist samurai, see *shishi*

Mabuchi Kahei 馬淵嘉平, 159, 162
machikata 町方 (towns officially permitted to have retail shops), 584–5
Maebara Issei 前原一誠, 22, 383, 385–6, 392
  see also Hagi rebellion
Maeno Ryōtaku 前野良沢, 91–2, 436, 439–40
Mahan, Alfred Thayer, on defense, 725, 760
Maki Izumi 真木和泉, 182, 193, 195, 196–8
Manabe Akikatsu 間部詮勝, 284, 318–19
Manchester school, 704–5
Manchuria 満州, Japanese development of, 779
Mannheim, Karl, 674
Manyōshū 万葉集 (eighth century poetry anthology), 445
marriage in Tokugawa period, 553–4, 558, 564
Maruyamakyō 丸山教, 216–17, 220–1, 257
Marxist interpretation, 500, 504, 569, 619–20, 733, 748
  see also Kōzaha and *rōnōha*
Masaoka Shiki 正岡子規, 485
Matsudaira Katamori 松平容保, daimyo of Aizu, 332, 334, 344, 358–9
Matsudaira Sadanobu 松平定信, 5–8, 12, 50–60, 80, 88, 94–6, 98–9, 101, 141, 155, 172, 530
  see also Kansei reforms
Matsudaira Yoshinaga (Keiei, Shungaku) 松平慶永（春嶽）(daimyo of Fukui), 166–7, 252, 281–4, 291, 315–17, 319, 327–32, 335, 356, 626, 630
Matsukata deflation 松方デフレ 30–1, 36, 419–20
Matsukata Masayoshi 松方正義, Meiji leader, 29, 614–15, 626, 637, 667, 669, 758
Matsumae domain 松前藩, 94–6, 272
Matsuzaki Kōdō 松崎慊堂, 61, 110, 116–21, 167
Meiji 明治, origin of term, 11, 23
Meiji Constitution 明治憲法, 6, 29–30, 32, 412–13, 424, 433, 618, 620, 622, 624, 651–65, 672, 689, 758
Meiji emperor (Mutsuhito) 明治天皇（睦仁）, 23, 353, 424, 682–3, 781
Meiji empress, 484–5
Meiji Restoration 明治維新, 1, 11, 19, 21–5, 34–49
  events, 353–9
  intellectual background, 312–14
  interpretations, 360–6
  opening and its impact, 314–18
  role of activists, 320–5
Meirokusha 明六社, 676, 683
Meiroku zasshi 明六雑誌, 680
"men of high purpose," see *shishi*
"men of talent," 235, 650
merchants, organization of houses and businesses, 512
metsuke 目付 (police official), 315
mibunsei 身分制 (status order), 505–6
migration, internal, 556–9
military reform, 349–50, 634–6, 643
Mill, John Stuart, influence of *On Liberty*, 480–2, 486, 676
millenarianism, 21–2, 27
  see also ee ja nai ka, *okagemairi*
mimpeitai 民兵体 (people's corps), 346
Min, Queen of Korea, 752, 755, 769
Ministry of Education (Mombushō) 文部省, 642–3, 682, 685, 701, 703
Ministry of Finance (Ōkurashō) 大蔵省, 29, 643, 645
Ministry of Foreign Affairs (Gaimushō) 外務省, 660, 775
Ministry of Home Affairs (Naimushō) 内務省, 643–5, 653, 670, 709, 712, 714–15
Ministry of Justice 司法省 (Shihōshō), 642, 646
Ministry of Public Works (Kōbushō) 工部省, 643
Ministry of the Army (Rikugunshō) 陸軍省, 643
Ministry of the Navy 海軍省 (Kaigunshō) 643, 646
minshūshi 民衆史 (people's history), 45–8
Mishima Michitsune 三島通庸, 414–18
  see also Fukushima incident; Kabasan incident
Mishima Yukio 三島由紀夫, as admirer of Yoshida Shōin, 449
Mito domain 水戸藩, 111–15, 135, 137–8, 161, 165, 325, 327–9, 334,

Mito domain (cont.)
   343
   see also Tokugawa Nariaki
Mitogaku 水戸学 (Mito learning), 167,
   180-94, 216-17, 219, 234-5, 255-8,
   314
Mitsui Bussan 三井物産, 305, 307
Mitsukuri Rinshō 箕作麟祥 and French
   legal code, 473
Mitsukuri Shūhei 箕作秋坪 and Dutch
   studies, 439, 460
Miyake Setsurei 三宅雪嶺, 448-9, 692-3,
   717
Miyao (Miyahiro) Sadao 宮負定雄, 207-11
Miyauchi Yoshinaga 宮内嘉長, 207-9
Miyazaki Tōten (Torazō) 宮崎滔天(寅蔵)
   and Chinese revolutionaries, 773
Mizuno Tadakuni 水野忠邦, 8, 16, 71,
   143, 155-67, 242, 310-11, 592, 594,
   597
   see also Tempō reforms
modernization theory, 43-5
Mogami Tokunai 最上徳内, 104
monopolies, domain, 579-80
Mori Arinori 森有礼, Meiji leader, 676,
   680, 683-4, 699, 701-2
Mori Ōgai 森鴎外, writer, 491-2
Morioka (Nambu) domain 盛岡藩(南部藩),
   64-5, 78-9
Moriyama Takichirō (Einosuke) 森山多吉
   郎, 281
Mōri Yoshichika 毛利慶親, daimyo of
   Chōshū, 332, 633
Morohashi Tetsuji 諸橋轍次, editor of *Dai
   Kan-Wa jiten* (Chinese-Japanese
   dictionary), 441
Morrison incident, 16-17, 107, 124-5,
   147, 268, 273, 312
Mosse, Albert, and drafting of Meiji
   constitution, 660
Motoda Nagazane (Eifu) 元田永孚, 484,
   494, 681-4, 690, 694, 700, 702
Motoki Shōzaemon 本木庄左衛門, 98, 441
Motoori Norinaga 本居宣長, 112, 198-201
Motoori Ōhira 本居大平, 199
Muragaki Norimasa 村垣範正, deputy
   ambassador on first Japanese mission
   to the U.S., 456-7
mura hachibu 村八分 (ostracism), 527
Murata Seifū 村田清風, 162, 164
mura 村 (village), 209
   and land holding, 507-24, 527, 581-5
Mutobe Yoshika 亡人部是香, 205, 209

Mutō Sanji 武藤山治, 759
Mutsu Munemitsu 陸奥宗光, Meiji leader,
   763
myōkōninden 妙好人伝 (popular faith
   Buddhist sect), 221

Nabeshima Naomasa 鍋島直正, Saga
   daimyo, 626, 641
Nagai Uta 長井雅楽, 328, 334
Nagano Shuzen 長野主膳, 318, 330
Nagasaki 長崎, 3, 22, 305
Nagatomi Dokushōan 永富独嘯庵, 446
nago 名子 (low status farm laborer), 79
naikaku 内閣 (inner council), 647
   Cabinet, 648
naiyū gaikan 内憂外患 (troubles within,
   disaster from without), 308
Nakae Chōmin 中江兆民, 39, 400, 676
Nakagawa Jun'an 中川淳庵, 91-2, 439-40
Nakahama Manjirō 中浜万次郎, 441
Nakamura Masanao 中村正直, 409, 462,
   481-3, 488, 491, 676
Nakaoka Shintarō 中岡慎太郎, 355
Nakatsu domain 中津藩, 138
Nakayama Miki 中山みき, 219, 222,
   225-8
Namamugi incident 生麦事件, see
   Richardson incident
Nansō Satomi hakkenden 南総里見八犬伝
   (Takizawa Bakin), 70-1, 117, 176
nanushi 名主 (village headman) (see also
   shōya), 209
Natsume Sōseki 夏目漱石, 491-3
Neale, Sir John, British diplomat, 291-3
nembutsu sects 念仏, 216, 221
neomercantilism, 726
new religions, 215-31, 234, 257-8
New Theses, see Aizawa Yasushi
Nieman, Johannes Edewin, Dutch factor,
   90
Nihon 日本, newspaper, 685, 692
Nihonjin 日本人, journal, 692, 694
Niijima Jo 新島襄, Christian leader, 449,
   452-5, 462, 479-80
Nikkō 日光, procession to, by Tokugawa
   Ieyoshi, 152-3, 162-3
ninen naku uchiharau decree 無二念打払令,
   14, 102-3, 273
ninjōbon 人情本, 68, 144
Ninomiya Sontoku 二宮尊徳, 85-6, 117,
   119, 138, 147, 210, 310
Nishi Amane 西周, founding member of
   Meirokusha, 106, 336, 352, 453, 622,

636, 676
Nishimura Shigeki 西村茂樹, *Nihon dōtoku ron* (Discourse on Japanese morality), 684
Nitobe Inazō 新渡戸稲造, 492
nōmin 農民 (farmers), peasant economy, 503, 505, 516–21, 523, 531, 580
"nonchurch" movement 無教会運動, and Uchimura Kanzō, 687
Norman, E. Herbert, 48–9, 673, 718
Norman, Henry, 760
Normanton incident, influence on Japan's view of the West, 488
nukeni 抜け荷 (unauthorized trade), 591
Numa Morikazu 沼間守一, 410
Nyoraikyō 如来教, 220

Ogasawara Nagamichi 小笠原長行, 293
Ogasawara Shotō 小笠原諸島 (Bonin Islands), 98, 125
Ogata Kōan 緒方洪庵, 110–11
Oguri Tadamasa 小栗忠順, 456, 458, 468
Ogyū Sorai 荻生徂来, 56, 86, 185, 445, 448, 711, 714
Ōhara Shigetomi 大原重徳, 328–9, 334
Ōhara Yūgaku 大原幽学, 85–6, 138, 210, 310
Ōhashi Totsuan 大橋訥庵, 182, 193–6, 241
Ōi Kentarō 大井憲太郎, 409, 418, 421, 424
okagemairi 御蔭参 (pilgrimage to Ise shrine), 120, 218, 228
  see also Ise
Okakura Tenshin 岡倉天心, 492, 691, 694, 772
Okayama domain 岡山藩, 20, 65, 134
Ōkubo Toshimichi 大久保利通, early Meiji leader, 26–8, 252, 300, 347, 384, 387–8, 390, 393, 396, 405, 415, 433, 463–5, 621, 626, 629, 631, 633, 635, 637, 640, 642–3, 645, 647, 652–3, 655, 657, 660, 742–3, 745
Ōkuma Shigenobu 大隈重信, Meiji political leader, 29–30, 377, 412, 414, 614, 627, 631, 633, 638, 640, 642, 647, 657, 659, 669–70, 690, 693, 699, 709, 742, 751
Ōkuni Takamasa 大国隆正, 199, 203, 207, 210, 212–14
Ōkura Nagatsune 大蔵永常, 76, 310
Ōmotokyō 大本教, 257
Ōmura Masujirō 大村益次郎, 635, 647
ōoku 大奥 (women's quarter), 52

Osaka 大坂・大阪, 62, 64–7, 123–4, 572, 585–6, 588, 591–2, 596
Osatake Takeki 尾佐竹猛, 40, 41
ōsei fukko 王政復古 (return to imperial rule), 255–6, 624, 666
Ōshio Heihachirō's rebellion 大塩平八郎の乱, 8, 16, 123–4, 129–31, 166–7, 309
osso 越訴 (direct appeal), 369
Ōtsuki Gentaku 大槻玄沢, 92n, 99, 101–2, 471
Ōyama Iwao 大山巌, 36, 626, 731–2
Ōyama Tsunayoshi 大山綱良, 394, 396–7
Ozaki Yukio 尾崎行雄, 779

Parker, Peter, 107
Parkes, Sir Harry, British minister, 297–303, 338, 354–5, 364, 628
Peace Police Law of 1900, 711
Peace Preservation Law of 1887, 658
Pearson, Charles, 760
peasant protest, 79–80, 121–4, 309–10, 363, 368–82
Peninsula and Oriental (P & O) Steamship Company, 339, 609
People's Daily, 776
people's history (*minshūshi*), 45–8
"People's Rights" movement (*jiyū minken undō*), 7, 18, 27, 29–31, 39, 47, 402–31, 676, 683, 697, 718, 730, 749
Perry, Commodore Matthew C., 6, 16–17, 244, 267, 269–70, 273–4, 281, 315, 319, 441, 449–50, 452, 448–9, 466, 489, 600, 721, 742, 746
Phaeton incident of 1808, 12, 97–8, 262
Picard, H., author of *A New Pocket Dictionary of the English-Dutch and Dutch-English Languages*. 441
police, 646, 458–9, 669, 711
popular culture, 67–71, 174–77
population, 550–6, 541, 571–3
Privy Council 枢密院, 32, 474, 663, 666, 668
prostitution, 143–4
"Protestant ethic" in Japan, 570
Public Assembly Ordinance, 683
Public Party of Patriots, see Aikokukōtō
publishing, 58–9, 67–8, 144
purge of scholars of foreign learning, 106, 235–6
Putiatin, Evfimii, 266–7, 270, 276, 278, 283

Raffles, Thomas Stamford, 261–2

Rai Mikisaburō 頼三樹三郎, 62, 321
Rai San'yō 頼山陽, 60, 321
Rai Shunsui 頼春水, 60
rangaku 蘭学 (Dutch learning), see *yōgaku/rangaku*
Reform Party (Kaishintō), 659
Rekishigaku Kenkyūkai 歴史学研究会 (Association for Research in History) 45
restoration, 193–8, 255–8
Razanov, Nikolai, 12, 14, 96, 100, 265–6
Richardson (Namamugi) incident 生麦事件, 22, 291–3, 326, 334, 342
Right Chamber (U-in), 642, 647, 656
Rijcken, Pels, foreign employee of late Tokugawa government, 467
Rikken Kaishintō 立憲改新党 (Constitutional Progressive Party), 414
Rikken Seiyūkai 立憲政友会 (Association of Friends of Constitutional Government), 34, 661, 670
Risshisha 立志社 early Meiji political organization, 404–5, 407, 654
Roches, Leon, French minister, 299, 302–3, 338, 349, 352, 354, 357–8, 364
Roessler, Herman, 71, 660–2, 664n, 666, 700, 705
rōjū 老中 (senior councilor), 18
Rokumeikan 鹿鳴館, 487–8, 689
rōnin 浪人 (masterless samurai), 63
Rōnōha 労農派 ("Labor-Farmer" faction), 41–3, 361–2
rural improvement movement (*chihō kairyō undō*), 712–13, 715
Russia
  influence of, in Korea, 769
  as threat, 751, 754–5
  see also foreign relations/trade
Russo-Japanese War, 776–7
ryō 両 (unit of gold currency), 54, 575
Ryūkyū/Okinawa 琉球・沖縄, 1, 3, 5, 28, 273, 577, 741–3
  see also foreign relations/trade; Satsuma domain
Ryūtei Tanehiko 柳亭種彦, 117, 145, 176

sadaijin 左大臣 (minister of the left), 642
Saga (Hizen) domain 佐賀藩, 23, 135, 137–8, 325–8, 334–5
Saga rebellion 佐賀の乱, 389–91
  see also Etō Shimpei

Saigō Takamori 西郷隆盛, Restoration leader, 21, 27–8, 37, 321, 345, 347, 355, 358, 368, 383, 386–8, 390, 393–402, 626, 633, 642, 647, 653, 680, 737, 745–6
  see also Satsuma Rebellion
Saigō Tsugumichi 西郷従道, 635, 731–2, 742–3
Sa-in 左院 (Left Chamber), 642, 652–3, 656
Saionji Kimmochi 西園寺公望, 476–7
Sakai 堺, center of domestic sea trade, 573
Sakai Toshihiko 堺利彦, and opposition to Russo-Japanese War, 776
Sakamoto Ryōma 坂本竜馬, Tosa activist, 322–3, 355–6
Sakashitamon incident 坂下門外の変, 196
  see also Ōhashi Totsuan
Sakhalin (Karafuto) 樺太, 266, 271, 307, 459, 740–1, 777
sakoku 鎖国 (closed country), 88, 432, 435, 502
Sakuma Shōzan 佐久間象山, 129–32, 137, 157, 241–8, 251, 272, 274, 319, 337, 441–4, 450
samurai class 侍・武士, 528–33, 537, 542, 547, 563, 575, 599
  bushidō ideology, 530, 533
  commutation of stipends, 27, 631–3, 638–40, 653
  economic problems, 74, 126–7, 149–50
  in Meiji period, 531
  sale of status, 79
Sanada Yukitsura 真田幸貫, 242
sangi 参議 (councilor), 633, 641–2, 647
Sanjō Sanetomi 三条実美, 35, 329, 626, 641–2, 648, 662, 667
sankin kōtai 参勤交代・参覲交代 (alternate attendance), 1, 2, 19–20, 22, 62–4, 132, 328, 536–8, 542, 557, 559, 607
sankyō 三卿 (Tokugawa cadet houses), 51
Sansom, Sir George B., 484, 489
Santō Kyōden 山東京伝, 59, 68–70
san'yo 参与 (junior councilor), 359, 625–6
Saruya-chō 猿屋町 (bakufu finance office), 598
Satō Issai 佐藤一斎, 61, 110, 242
Satō Nobuhiro (Shin'en) 佐藤信淵, 129–30, 132–3, 158, 205, 599
Satow, Sir Ernest, 355, 364
Satsuma domain 薩摩藩
  bakumatsu politics, 21, 23–5, 28, 73, 291–4, 298, 300, 302, 324–9, 334,

336, 347-8, 353-8
and court participation in politics, 19
relations with Ryūkyū, 3, 568
in Restoration, 347-8
Tempō reforms. 15-16, 135, 137-8, 161, 164-5
trade with other domains, 20
Satsuma Rebellion (seinan sensō), 27-8, 393-402, 607, 609, 636, 640, 643, 655, 680, 715, 729, 737, 746
Schwartz, Benjamin, 704
Seeley, Robert, 761
Sei-in 正院 (Central Chamber), 641, 647-8, 656
seiji sōsai 政事総裁 (supreme councilor), 329
sei-Kan ron 征韓論 (proposal to punish Korea), 27, 465, 653, 745
see also Korea foreign relations/trade
Seikyōsha 政教社 692
seinan sensō 西南戦争, see Satsuma Rebellion
seinenkai 青年会 (youth groups), 714-15
Seiyukai, see Rikken Seiyukai
Seji kemmon roku 世事見聞録, see Buyō Inshi
Sendai domain 仙台藩, 358
Shaw, George Bernard, 728
Shiba Kōkan 司馬江漢, 102, 178-9
Shibata Takenaka 柴田剛中, bakufu emissary, 459
Shiga Shigetaka 志賀重昂, 33, 491
shijōmachi 市場町 (market towns), 535
Shikitei Samba 式亭三馬, 68-9, 175-7
Shima Yoshitake 島義勇, 389-90
see also Saga rebellion
Shimazaki Tōson 島崎藤村, 485
Shimazu Hisamitsu 島津久光, Satsuma regent, 290-1, 328, 332, 334-5, 347, 356, 633
Shimazu Nariakira 島津斉彬, Satsuma daimyo, 166, 282
Shimazu Shigehide 島津重豪, Satsuma daimyo, 52
Shimmi Masaoki 新見正興, leader of 1860, Japanese embassy to U.S., 456, 722
Shimonoseki, shelling of, 下関, 22-3, 293-9, 301, 324-5, 342, 344, 354
Shimonoseki, treaty of, 下関条約, 34, 768
shimpan 親藩 (Tokugawa collateral houses), 315
Shimpūren uprising 神風連の乱, 391-3,
680
Shinagawa Yajirō 品川弥二郎, student of Yoshida Shōin, 452
shingaku 心学 ("heart study" merchant class ethical movement), 138
Shinohara Kunimoto 篠原国幹, 385, 396
Shinron 新論 (*New Theses*), see Aizawa Yasushi
shinshi jikken 真摯実験 (examination and experience in medical study), 446, 448
Shinto 神道, 527, 621, 625, 643, 663, 700-3, 714, 716
Shionoya Tōin 塩谷宕陰, 17
Shiraishi Shōichirō 白石正一郎, 363-4
shishi 志士 (activists, "men of high purpose"), 320-4, 627, 629; in Korea and China, 757, 772-3
shizoku 士族, early Meiji status category, 22, 25, 382-402, 427-9
see also samurai class
Shōheikō 昌平黌 bakufu academy, 57-7, 61
Shōhōshi, Shōhō kaisho 商法司・商法会所 (Meiji commercial bureaus), 606
shokusan kōgyō 殖産興業 (foster industry and promote enterprise), 433
Shōnai domain 庄内藩, 78
Shōshikai 尚歯会, 234-5, 239, 242
shōya 庄屋 (village headman), 80
see also nanushi
shūkenteki hōkensei 集権的封建制 (centralized feudalism), 500
shukubamachi 宿場町 (post towns), 535, 541, 545, 609
shūshin 修身 (moral training), 682
Siebold, Philip Franz von, 13-14, 72, 91, 104-5, 234, 467
silk-reeling technology, 603
Sino-Japanese War 日清戦争, 7, 669, 671, 695, 707-8, 762-5
Smiles, Samuel, author of *Self-Help*, 462, 481-4, 486, 488, 496, 671
Social Education Association, 780
social monarchy, 661-3, 672, 698
Soejima Taneomi 副島種臣, 28, 387-8, 402, 627, 653
songō 尊号事件 (title) incident, 51-2
sonnō jōi 尊皇攘夷 (revere the emperor, expel the barbarian), 189
sōri daijin 総理大臣 (prime minister), 648
sōsai, sōsaikyoku 総裁(局) (supervisory department), 359, 625

sotsu 卒, lower samurai status category, 25
South Seas, Japanese expansion in, 761
Spaulding, J. W., and Perry mission, 450-1
Spencer, Herbert, 39, 480, 484, 671, 688, 693, 699, 716
Stein, Lorenz von, and drafting of Meiji constitution, 660, 698-9
Stirling, Sir James, 230-1
Sugita Gempaku 杉田玄白, 70, 91-3, 99-101, 105-6, 128, 312, 437-40, 447-8
Sugita Seikei 杉田成卿, 16, 106
suiden 水田 (paddy), 369
sukegō 助郷 (corvée), 310
Suzuki Masayuki 鈴木雅之, 214-15, 256
Suzuki Shigetane 鈴木重胤, 211-12

Taewongun 大院君, Korean regent, 752, 755, 769
Tafel Anatomia, 437-40
Taguchi Ukichi 田口卯吉, 39-40, 676-9, 706
Taiping Rebellion 太平天国, 734
tairō 大老 (great councilor), 166
Taiwan 台湾, 7, 27, 741-3
  colonization of, 767, 769, 771-2
Takahashi Kageyasu 高橋景保, 13, 103-5, 114, 234
Takano Chōei 高野長英, 107-8, 129-31, 146-7, 166, 235, 238-42
Takashima Shūhan 高島秋帆, 129-30, 137, 146, 157, 166, 242
Takasugi Shinsaku 高杉晋作, 252, 337, 346-7
Takata Sanae 高田早苗, and Social Education Association, 780-1
Takechi Zuizan 武市瑞山, 10, 329
Takekoshi Yosaburō 竹越与三郎, 39-40
Takeuchi Yasunori 竹内保徳, 290, 459-60
Takeuchi Yoshimi 竹内好, 42
Takezoe Shin'ichirō 竹添進一郎, and Korean problem, 755
Takizawa Bakin 滝沢馬琴, 68-71, 117, 176, 202n
Tamenaga Shunsui 為長春水, 68-9, 117, 145, 177
Tanabe Taichi 田辺太一, and Iwakura mission, 463
Tanaka Mitsuaki 田中光顕, 36
Tanaka Shōzō 田中正造, and *bummei byō*, 716
Tani Bunchō 谷文晁, 117

Tani Kanjō 谷干城, 387, 689-90, 712
Tanomura Chikuden 田能村竹田, 117
Tanuma Okitsugu 田沼意次, 5-6, 52-3, 94, 148, 159
Tarui Tōkichi 樽井藤吉, *Dai-Tō gappei ron* (Unification of great Asia), 752
Tashiro Eisuke 田代英助, 422-3
tate shakai 縦社会, see vertical society
Tawara domain 田原藩, 134, 138
taxation, 368-9
Tcuzze, João Rodriguez, author of *Vocabulario de Lingoa de Iapan*, 440
Temmei famine 天明の飢饉, 119, 521
Tempō famine 天保の飢饉, 117-20, 521
Tempō reforms 天保改革, 8, 11, 15-16, 20, 71
  appraisal of, 164-7; 310-11
  in bakufu, 139-55
  in domains, 133-9
  Mizuno Tadakuni's role, 155-8
  results, 158-64, 508, 545-56, 587, 592-601, 604
  see also Mizuno Tadakuni
Ten Exchange Houses (*Jūnin ryōgae*), function as Tokugawa bills clearing house, 585-6
tennō 天皇 (emperor), 51
tennōsei 天皇制 (emperor system), 42
Tenrikyō 天理教, 216-17, 219-22, 225-7, 229
tenryō 天領 (Tokugawa house lands), 1, 64, 535-6, 540
terakoya 寺子屋 (parish school), 57, 561
Terashima Munenori (Matsuki Kōan) 寺島宗則(松木弘庵), 460, 626, 738
Thunberg, Carl, 91
Titsingh, Isaac, 90
Toba domain 鳥羽藩, 20
tōbaku 倒幕 (overthrow the bakufu), 401
Tocqueville, Alexis de, 480, 721
Tokugawa Akitake 徳川昭武, 342
Tokugawa Yoshinobu (Hitotsubashi Keiki) 徳川(一橋)慶喜, 20-1, 23, 37-8, 283, 291, 294, 300-3, 316, 318, 327-30, 332, 334, 343, 351-4, 356-9, 361, 364, 459, 618, 625
Tokugawa Ieharu 徳川家治, tenth shogun, 51
Tokugawa Iemochi 徳川家茂, fourteenth shogun, 19, 282-3, 300, 302, 316, 328, 330-2, 351
Tokugawa Ienari 徳川家斉, eleventh shogun, 13, 15, 50-2, 141-2, 157,

176
Tokugawa Iesada 徳川家定, 13th shogun, 281-3, 316
Tokugawa Iesato 徳川家達, 359
Tokugawa Ieyasu 徳川家康, first shogun, 459
Tokugawa Ieyoshi 徳川家慶, twelfth shogun, 51, 152-3
Tokugawa Nariaki 徳川斉昭, Mito daimyo, 12-13, 15-16, 18, 123, 129-32, 138, 150, 156, 163, 166-7, 182, 188-91, 193, 273-5, 281-4, 314-17, 327
Tokugawa Yoshikumi 徳川慶恕, 318
Tokugawa Yoshimune 徳川義宗, eighth shogun, 5, 52, 58, 148, 155, 530
 see also Kyōhō reforms
tokumidon'ya 十組問屋 (merchant syndicate), 150
tokusambutsu 特産物 (regional specialties), 546
Tokutomi Roka 徳富蘆花, 778-9
Tokutomi Sohō (Iichirō) 徳富蘇峰(猪一郎), journalist, 39-40, 361, 491, 676, 679, 688, 692, 695-6, 716, 762, 765, 779
Tokyo 東京, 28
Tokyo Imperial University 東京帝国大学, 469-70, 667
Tonghak rebellion 東学党の乱, 763
ton'ya 問屋 (wholesalers and shippers), 507-8, 585, 595-6
Torii Yōzō 鳥居耀蔵, 108n, 239-41, 597
Tosa domain 土佐藩, 19-21, 23-4, 28, 127-8, 138, 158-9, 161-2, 321-2, 325, 327-9, 334, 354-6, 622-3
Tottori domain 鳥取藩, 138
Town and Village Code of 1888, 712-13
towns, 535, 543-4
 see also jōkamachi; shukubamachi
Tōyama Shigeki 遠山茂樹, 44-5
Toyoda Tenkō 豊田天功, 182, 190
tōyō dōtoku seiyō geijutsu 東洋道徳西洋芸術 (Eastern ethics, Western techniques), 681
Toyoda Sakichi 豊田佐吉, and invention of automatic loom, 483
tozama 外様 ("outside vassals"), 18
Tōzenji incident, 288-90
Trans-Siberian Railway and Western colonialism, 760
travel, 64-5
treaty revision, 7, 31, 33
Tsubouchi Shōyō 坪内逍遙, author of

Essence of the Novel, 694
Tsuda Mamichi 津田真道, 453, 676
Tsuda Umeko 津田梅子, 462
Tsuruya Namboku 鶴屋南北, 81, 177
Tsushima domain 対馬藩, 3, 20, 22, 744

uchikowashi 打毀 (smashing, riot), 123, 502
Uchimura Kanzō 内村鑑三, and Christianity, 491-2, 687, 702, 776
udaijin 右大臣 (minister of the right), 641-2
Ueki Emori 植木枝盛, 400, 676
U-in 右院 (Right Chamber), 642, 647, 656
Ukita Kazutami 浮田和民 39-40, 771
Umeda Umpin 梅田雲浜, 318-19
unequal treaties and treaty revision, 463, 466, 473, 480, 487, 650, 688-90, 693, 695, 708, 717, 736-8, 746, 756, 758-9, 764
 see also foreign relations/trade
U.S.-Japan Security treaty (*ampo*), 45
United States of America
 and development of Hokkaidō, 465, 469
 as mediator in Russo-Japanese War, 765
 as mediator in Sino-Japanese War, 765
 see also foreign relations/trade
urbanization, 62-8
Usuki domain 臼杵藩, 137
Utagawa Kuniyoshi 歌川国芳, 145
Utsunomiya domain 宇都宮藩, 137, 153

Verein für Sozialpolitik and Shakai seisaku gakkai, 707
vertical society (*tate shakai*), description of society by Nakane Chie, 499

wakamono gumi (*nakama*) 若者組(仲間) (youth organizations), 80-1, 84
Wakayama (Kii) domain 和歌山(紀伊)藩, 20
Watanabe Kazan 渡辺華山, 16-17, 60-1, 70, 107-10, 129-31, 134, 146, 157, 159, 235-42, 246
Weber, Max, 707
Wei Yüan 魏源, 17, 312
Whitman, Walt, and Japanese mission to U.S., 457-8
Williams, S. Wells, 107, 125, 450

yakunin 役人 (officials), 80
Yamagata Aritomo 山県有朋, Meiji leader, 31, 34, 36, 386, 393, 398, 410, 626, 635-6, 642, 646, 655-6, 667-71, 695,

699, 712, 716, 763–4
Yamaji Aizan 山路愛山, 39–40, 448, 694–5
Yamauchi (Yamanouchi) Yōdō 山内容堂, daimyo of Tosa, 318, 328–9, 332, 342, 356
Yamawaki Tōyō 山脇東洋, and autopsy, 446–7
Yamazaki Ansai 山崎闇斎, 56, 58
Yanagita Kunio 柳田国男, 46
Yasukuni Shrine 靖国神社, 28
Yawata Iron Works 八幡製鉄所, 7, 771
Yi dynasty 李朝, Korea, 745
yōgaku/rangaku 洋学/蘭学 (Western/Dutch learning), 58, 90–3, 180, 182, 231–47, 312, 435–40, 443–5, 447–8, 471
Yokohama 横浜, 22, 304–5
Yokoi Shōnan 横井小楠, 239, 241, 246–53, 337, 444, 457–8
yomihon 読本 (reading books), 68, 70

yonaoshi 世直し (world renewal), 217–18, 221, 226–7, 309
Yoshida Shōin 吉田松陰, loyalist teacher, 171, 182, 193–5, 319, 336, 347, 449–53, 455, 460, 495
Yoshida Tōyō 吉田東洋, 346
Yoshikawa Akimasa 芳川顕正, 684
Yoshimasu Tōdō 吉益東洞, author of *Medical Diagnoses*, 446
Yoshino Sakuzō 吉野作造, 40
Yoshiwara/Shin-Yoshiwara 吉原/新吉原, 143
Yuri Kimimasa 由利公正, 161, 623

zaibatsu 財閥 (financial combines), 31, 773
zaigō gunjinkai 在郷軍人会 (military associations), 714–15
zaikata shōnin 在方商人 (rural merchants), 508, 510, 521
zettaishugi 絶対主義, *see* absolutism